THE GLOBAL WORKPLACE

With the forces of globalization as a backdrop, this casebook develops labor and employment law in the context of the national laws of nine countries important to the global economy – the United States, Canada, Mexico, the U.K., Germany, France, China, Japan, and India. These national jurisdictions are highlighted by considering international labor standards promulgated by the International Labour Organization as well as the rulings and standards that emerge from two very different regional trade arrangements – the labor side accord to NAFTA and the European Union. Across all these different sources of law, this book considers the law of individual employment, collective labor laws dealing with unionization as well as the laws against discrimination, the laws protecting privacy, and the systems used to resolve labor and employment disputes. This is the first set of law school course materials in English covering international and comparative employment and labor law.

Roger Blanpain is a Professor at the University of Tilburg, the Netherlands, and the Katholieke Universiteit Leuven, Belgium, and is the Editor-in-Chief of the International Encyclopedia of Laws.

Susan Bisom-Rapp is Professor of Law and Director of the Center for Law and Social Justice at Thomas Jefferson School of Law.

William R. Corbett is the Frank L. Marist Professor of Law at the Paul M. Hebert Law Center of Louisiana State University.

Hilary K. Josephs is Professor of Law at Syracuse University.

Michael J. Zimmer is Professor of Law at Seton Hall University.

The Global Workplace

INTERNATIONAL AND COMPARATIVE EMPLOYMENT LAW – CASES AND MATERIALS

Roger Blanpain
Katholieke Universiteit Leuven, Belgium

Susan Bisom-Rapp
Thomas Jefferson School of Law

William R. Corbett
Louisiana State University

Hilary K. Josephs
Syracuse University

Michael J. Zimmer
Seton Hall University

CAMBRIDGE
UNIVERSITY PRESS

CAMBRIDGE UNIVERSITY PRESS
Cambridge, New York, Melbourne, Madrid, Cape Town, Singapore, São Paulo

Cambridge University Press
32 Avenue of the Americas, New York, NY 10013-2473, USA

www.cambridge.org
Information on this title: www.cambridge.org/9780521847858

First published 2007

Printed in the United States of America

A catalog record for this publication is available from the British Library.

Library of Congress Cataloging in Publication Data

The Global workplace : international and comparative employment law : cases
and materials / Roger Blanpain . . . [et al.].
      p.   cm.
Includes bibliographical references and index.
ISBN-13: 978-0-521-84785-8 (hardback)
ISBN-10: 0-521-84785-0 (hardback)
1. Labor laws and legislation.   2. Labor laws and legislation, International.
I. Blanpain, R. (Roger), 1932–   II. Title.
K1705.G583   2007
344.01–dc22   2006026907

ISBN   978-0-521-84785-8 hardback

Roger Blanpain
To Lina and our 22 children and grandchildren

Susan Bisom-Rapp
To Charles, Skylar, and Ezra, my parents, Bob and Marilyn,
and my mother-in-law, Jean

William R. Corbett
To Monica, Brock, and my parents, Bill and Sara

Hilary K. Josephs
To Lew and to the memory of my parents, Joseph and Bernice Kromelow

Michael J. Zimmer
To Margaret, Michael, and Lanier

Contents

Acknowledgments   *page* xi

Table of Cases   xiii

Table of Statutes   xxi

Table of Secondary Authorities   xxxiii

1   **The Study of International and Comparative Employment Law** 1
   A. Introduction   1
   B. Thinking Deeply About International and Comparative Employment Law   32
   C. Workplace Law in the International Realm: An Initial Primer   41
   D. The Organization of this Book   51

2   **The International Labour Organization and International Labor Standards** . . . 53
   A. Introduction   53
   B. ILO Standard Setting and Structure   58
   C. ILO Monitoring and Member Nation Compliance   60
   D. The 1998 Declaration on Fundamental Principles and Rights at Work   88

3   **The United States** 92
   A. Introduction   92
   B. Individual Employment Law   93
   C. Unions and Collective Bargaining   110
   D. Wages, Hours, and Benefits   122
   E. Employment Discrimination   124
   F. Privacy   149

4   **Canada** 157
   A. Introduction   157
   B. Individual Employment Law   160
   C. Unions and Collective Bargaining   171
   D. Wages, Hours, and Benefits   185
   E. Antidiscrimination Law   186
   F. Employee Privacy   197
   G. Dispute Resolution Systems   198

5   Mexico   208
    A. Introduction   208
    B. Individual Employment Law   222
    C. Collective Employee Rights   227
    D. Dispute Resolution Systems   233
    E. Antidiscrimination Law   247
    F. Privacy Law   248

6   The Regulatory Approach of the North American Free Trade Agreement   249
    A. Introduction   249
    B. The NAALC's Labor Principles   256
    C. NAALC Structures and Enforcement   258

7   The European Union   276
    A. General Overview   276
    B. The Legislative Process   279
    C. The Social Partners   282
    D. Competence of the EU Regarding Social Policies: In Search of a
       European Social Model (ESM) – A Dream?   283
    E. Individual Employment Law   288
    F. Collective Employment Rights   301
    G. Antidiscrimination Law   315
    H. Privacy   325

8   The United Kingdom   332
    A. Introduction   332
    B. Individual Employment Law: Contracts and Statutes   334
    C. Unions and Collective Bargaining   359
    D. Wages, Hours, and Benefits   367
    E. Employment Discrimination   370
    F. Privacy   392

9   Germany   394
    A. Introduction   394
    B. Individual Employment   398
    C. Unions and Collective Bargaining   404
    D. Antidiscrimination   422
    E. Labor Courts   429
    F. Privacy   430

10 France   432
    A. Introduction   432
    B. Individual Employment   436
    C. Unions and Collective Bargaining   448

D. Wages, Hours, and Benefits   453
E. Employment Discrimination   455
F. Privacy   458

11 **China** 462
A. Introduction   462
B. Socialist Modernization and Liberation of the Productive Forces   471
C. The Labor Law   479
D. Collective Contracts and the Trade Union   509
E. Opening to the Outside: Special Economic Zones and Brain Circulation   518

12 **Japan** 524
A. Introduction to the Social and Historical Context   524
B. The Postwar Employment Scene: Major Developments   526
C. Japanese Transplant Companies in the United States   542

13 **India** 566
A. Introduction to the Historical and Social Context   566
B. Economic Policy and Performance Before and After 1991   568
C. Labor and Trade Unions   576
D. "Equal Opportunities" for the Scheduled Castes, Scheduled Tribes, and
    Other Backward Classes   578
E. Judicial Activism and Public Interest Litigation   580

14 **Pursuing International Labor Standards in U.S. Courts and Through
    Global Codes of Conduct** 590
A. Introduction   590
B. Common Law Actions   591
C. Global Codes of Conduct   601
D. Lawsuits Based on Statutes   607

Index   619

Acknowledgments

Susan Bisom-Rapp is the principal author of Chapters 1, 2, 6, and 14. She expresses gratitude for the skillful assistance and support of James McAllister, who is her research assistant, and Thomas Jefferson School of Law reference librarians Dorothy Hampton and June MacLeod. She also thanks Deans Ken Vandevelde and Rudy Hasl for research grant support and Associate Dean Steve Semeraro for his support more generally. She gratefully acknowledges permission to reproduce Susan Hayter, "The Social Dimension of Globalization: Striking the Balance," *in* CONFRONTING GLOBALIZATION, 55 BULLETIN FOR COMPARATIVE LABOUR RELATIONS 1-10 (Roger Blanpain, ed., 2004), copyright © 2004 by Kluwer Law International, reprinted with permission from Kluwer Law International, www.kluwerlaw.com.

William R. Corbett is the principal author of Chapters 3, 8, and 10. He gratefully acknowledges the research grant support of his school and Chancellor John J. Costonis, the library support of the LSU Law Center's librarians, the secretarial assistance of Kandi Prejean and Karen Taylor, the translation assistance of his colleague Professor Olivier Morteau and his wife Marie Antoinette, and the research assistance of Kimberly LaHaye, LSU Law Center Class of 2006, and Ray Lewis, LSU Law Center Class of 2007.

Hilary K. Josephs is the principal author of Chapters 11, 12, and 13. She expresses gratitude to her research assistants Lin Yanmei, Jack Lin, and Adam Schuster, and to the Syracuse University College of Law library director Thomas French and reference librarians (alphabetical by surname) Alissa DiRubbo, Ted Holynski, Wendy Scott, and Eric Shute. Dean Hannah Arterian and the College of Law were supportive of this project in many ways. She also thanks Juris Publishing, www.jurispub.com, for rescuing her book LABOR LAW IN CHINA from the mergers and acquisitions maelstrom and issuing a second edition. She gratefully acknowledges permission to reproduce selected translations from Kenneth L. Port and Gerald Paul McAlinn, COMPARATIVE LAW: LAW AND THE LEGAL PROCESS IN JAPAN (2d ed. Carolina Academic Press: 2003) and to China Rights Forum for permission to reproduce *The WTO and Chinese Labor Rights: An Interview with Chang Kai by Ma Wei* (2005).

Michael J. Zimmer is the principal author of Chapters 4, 5, and 9. He wants to thank Eileen Denner, one of the world's great reference librarians, and Tina Bae, Seton Hall Class of 2008, who contributed significant research help as did Konjit Gomar, Loyola-Chicago Class of 2007. Finally, thanks to Seton Hall University School of Law, especially Deans Pat Hobbs and Kathleen Boozang, for the continuing support in too many ways to mention.

All of the authors wish to thank John Berger, our editor at Cambridge University Press, and his staff.

The authors welcome questions and comments, as follows: Roger Blanpain (Chapter 7) roger.blanpain@CER-leuven.be; Susan Bisom-Rapp (Chapters 1, 2, 6, and 14) susanb@tjsl.edu; Bill Corbett (Chapters 3, 8, 10) wcorbe1@law.lsu.edu; Hilary Josephs (Chapters 11, 12, and 13) hkjoseph@law.syr.edu; and Mike Zimmer (Chapters 4, 5, and 9) zimmermi@shu.edu.

The materials are current as of October 2006. The learning process for us, as well as our readers, extends into the future.

Table of Cases

A

Abrahamsson v. Fogelqvist, C-407/98 (2000), 320

Adarand Construction v. Pena, 515 U.S. 200, 229 (1995), 128

Agis v. Howard Johnson Co., 355 N.E. 2d 315 (1976), 104

Albertson's, Inc. v. Kirkingburg, 527 U.S. 555, 563, n.10, 144 L. Ed. 2d 518, 119 S. Ct. 2162 (1999), 560, 561, 562

Alexander v. Gardner-Denver Co., 415 U.S. 36 (1974), 206

American Steel Foundries v. Tri-City Central Trades Council, 257 U.S. 184, 114

The Amiable Isabella, 6 Wheat. 1 (1821), 545

Amparo No. 1/96, 242

Amparo No. 53/99, 243

Amparo No. 127/2000, 244

Amparo No. 337/94, 242

Amparo No. 338/95, 242

Amparo No. 1124/2000, 244–245

Atkins v. Virginia, 536 U.S. 304, 317 n.21 (2002), 33

B

Balbuena v. IDR Realty LLC, et al., No. 19, 2006 N.Y. LEXIS 200 (N.Y. Ct. App. Feb. 21, 2006), 272

Balco Employees Union v. Union of India (2001), 570–573, 574

Bammert v. Don's Super Valu, Inc., 646 N.W.2d 365 (Wis. S. Ct. 2002), 93–99, 100, 101, 102, 103, 565

Bandhua Mukti Morcha v. Union of India, 1984 AIR 802, 1984 SCC(3) 161, 581–587

Bank of Augusta v. Earle, 13 Pet. 519 (1839), 550

Bardal v. Globe & Mail Ltd. (1960), 24 D.L.R. (2d) 140 (Ont. H.C.), 163, 164, 166, 168

Barton v. Investec Sec., Ltd., [2003] ICR 1205, 373, 377, 378, 379, 380, 382, 383, 386, 387, 388, 390, 391

Betriebsrat der Firma ADS Anker GmbH v. ADS Anker GmbH, C-349/01 (2004), 301

Bharat Kumar K. Palicha v. State, AIR 1997 Ker. 291, 576

Bienkowski v. American Airlines, Inc., 851 F.2d 1503, 1506–07 (5th Cir. 1988), 142, 143

Bilka-Kaufhouse GmbH. V. Von Hartz, C-170/84 (1986), 316, 317

Bodenheimer v. PPG Indus., Inc., 5 F.3d 955 (5th Cir. 1993), 137

Bormann v. AT&T Communications, Inc., 875 F.2d 399 (2d Cir. 1989), 555–556

Bowers v. Hardwick, 478 U.S. 186, 106 S.Ct. 2841, 92 L.Ed.2d 140 (1986), 151

Bragdon v. Abbott, 524 U.S. 624, 118 S.Ct. 2196, 141 L.Ed.2d 540 (1998), 560

British Aircraft Corporation Ltd. v. Austin [1978] IRLR 332, 347

British Airways v. Starmer, No. EAT/0306/05/SM (July 21, 2005), 372, 373

British Columbia (Public Service Employee Relations Commission) v. BCGSEU, [1999] 3 S.C.R. 3, 187–195, 196, 197

British Home Stores v. Burchell [1980] ICR 303, 358

Brockmeyer v. Dun & Bradstreet, 113 Wis.2d 561, 335 N.W. 2d 834 (1983), 94, 95, 96, 97, 98

Brooks v. NLRB, 348 U.S. 96, 103, 112

Burlington Industries, Inc. v. Ellerth, 524 U.S. 742 (1998), 148

C

Canada (Canadian Human Rights Commission) v. Canadian National Railway ("Action Travail des Femmes"), (1985), 20 D.L.R. 668 (F.C.A.), 85 C.L.L.C. 17, 013 (F.C.A.), rev'd [1987] 1 S.C.R. 1114, 40 D.L.R. (4th) 193, 196

Capital Iron & Steel-Japan Electric Electronics Company v. Chen Jingke–Damages for Breach of Employment Contract, CEILAW, Selected People's Court Cases, Case 115211995036, 507–509

Case C-379/87 Groener v. Minister for Education and the City of Dublin Vocational Educational Committee [1989] ECR 3967, 294

Castaneda v. Partida, 430 U.S. 482, 499, 97 S.Ct. 1272, 1282, 51 L.Ed.2d 498 (1977), 145

Centre for Public Interest Litigation v. Union of India (2003), 574

CGT v. GE Healthcare (Mar. 2, 2006), 437

Chen Weili v. Lai Guofa–Dispute Arising from Contract for Hire, CEILAW, Selected People's Court Cases, Case 113312200012, 477, 499–502

Chinnaiah v. State of Andhra Predesh (2004), 579

Circuit City Stores, Inc. v. Adams, 532 U.S. 105 (2001), 206

City of Yonkers v. Otis Elevator Co., 844 F.2d 42 (2d Cir. 1988), 110

Cleveland Bd. of Educ. v. LaFleur, 414 U.S. 632, 94 S.Ct. 791, 39 L.Ed.2d 52 (1974), 151

C.O.J., 7 December 1995, Case C-449/93, ECR, 1995, 4291, 304

C.O.J., 7 February 1985, H.B.M. Abels v. The Administrative Board of the Bedrijfsvereniging voor de Metaal Industrie en de Electronische Industrie, No. 135/83, ECR, 1985, 519, 308

C.O.J., 7 May 1998, Clean Car Autoservice GesmbH v. Landeshauptmann von Wien, C-350/96, ECR, 1998, 2512, 293

C.O.J., 8 June 1982, Commission v. Italy, No. 91/81, ECR, 1982, 2455, 307

C.O.J., 10 July 1986, No. 235/84, ECR, 1986, 2291, 281

C.O.J., 11 March 1997, Ayse Süzen v. Zehnacker Gebüudereinigung GmbH Krankenhausservice, C-13/95, ECR, 1997, 1259, 312

C.O.J., 12 November 1992, A. Watson Rask and K. Christensen v. ISS Kantineservice A/S, No. C-209/91, ECR, 1992, 5755, 310

C.O.J., 12 October 2004, Wolff & Müller GmbH & Co. KG v José Filipe Pereira Félix, C-60/03, 296, 297

C.O.J., 13 December 1989, S. Grimaldi v. Fonds des Maladies Professionnelles, No. 322/88, ECR, 1989, 4407, 282

C.O.J., 14 July 1974, G. Dona v. M. Mantero, No. 13/76, ECR, 1976, 1333, 293

C.O.J., 15 March 2001, Criminal proceedings against André Mazzoleni and Inter Surveillance Assistance SARL C-165/98, ECR., 2001, 2189, 295, 296, 297

C.O.J., 17 February 1998, L.J. Grant /South West Trains Ltd., C-249/96, ECR, 1998, 621, 280

C.O.J., 19 May 1992, S. Redmond Stichting v. H. Bartol and Others, No. C-29/91

C.O.J., 19 May 1992, S. Redmond Stichting v. H. Bartol and Others, No. C-29/91, op. cit, 310

C.O.J., 19 November 1991, A. Frankovich and D.Others v. Italian Republic, Nos. C-6/90 and C-9/90, ECR, 1991, 5357, 282

C.O.J., 28 March 1979, Regina v. V.A. Saunders, No. 175/78, ECR, 1979, 1129, 293

C.O.J., Bork International A/S, No. 101/87, ECR, 1988, 310

C.O.J., Landeshauptstadt Kiel v. Jaeger, C-151/02, ECR, 2003, 298–299

Commission v. UK, C-382/92 and 383/92, ECR-I-2435, 1994, 305

Committee on Freedom of Association, Complaint against the Government of Canada Concerning the Province of Ontario Presented by the Ontario Federation of Labour (OFL) and the Canada Labour Congress (CLC), Case No. 2182, Report No. 330 (2003), 83–87

Communist Party of India v. Bharat Kumar, AIR 1998 SC 184, 576

Conley v. Gibson, 355 U.S. 41, 45-46, 78 S.Ct. 99, 101-102, 2 L.Ed.2d 80 (1957), 125

Consolidated Rail Corporation v. Darrone, 465 U.S. 624, 634, 104 S. Ct. 1248, 79 L. Ed. 2d 568 (1984), 560

Courtaulds Northern Textiles Ltd. v. Andrew [1979] IRLR 84, 347, 348

Courtaulds Northern Textiles Ltd. v. Andrew [1979] IRLR 84, 344

Coventry v. U.S. Steel Corp., 856 F.2d 514 (3d Cir. 1988), 556

Cuddy Chicks Ltd. v. Ontario (Labour Relations Board), [1991] 2 S.C.R. 5, 203

D

David Taylor & Son, Ltd. v. Barnett, [1953] 1 All E.R. 843 (C.A.), 202

Defrenne v. Societe Anonyme Belge de Navigation Aerienne Sabena, C-43/75 (1976), 316, 317

Desert Palace, Inc. v. Costa, 539 U.S. 90, 123 S.Ct. 2148, 156 L.Ed.2d 84 (2003), 137, 138, 139, 140, 143, 144, 320

Dhaliwal v. Woods Division, 930 F.2d 547 (7th Cir. 1991), 555

Dietemann v. Time, Inc., 449 F.2d 245, 247-48 (9th Cir. 1971), 154

Doe v. Belleville, 119 F.3d 563 (7th Cir. 1997), 146

Doe I v. Unocal Corp., 395 F.3d 932 (9th Cir. 2002), 83, 607–614, 615, 616, 617, 618

Doe I v. Unocal Corp., 395 F.3d 978 (9th Cir. 2003), 616

Doe I v. Wal-Mart Stores, Inc., Complaint, No. BC399737 (Sup. Ct. L. A. Country, 2005)

Doe I v. Wal-Mart Stores, Inc., Motion to Dismiss, No. Cv05-7307 NM (Manx) (CD. C A 2006), 596

Douds v. Local 1250, 173 F.2d 764 (2d Cir. 1949), 114

Douglas/Kwantlen Faculty Assn. v. Douglas College, [1990] 3 S.C.R. 570, 202, 203

Dukes v. Wal-Mart Stores, Inc., 222 F.R.D. 137 (N.D. Cal. 2004), 603

Dunbar v. Pepsi-Cola Gen. Bottlers of Iowa, Inc., 285 F.Supp.2d 1180, 1197-98 (N.D. Iowa 2003), 140

Dunmore v. Ontario (Attorney General), [2001] 3 S.C.R. 1016, 172

Dunnachie v. Kingston Upon Hull City Council, [2004] 3 WLR 310, 355

E

Eastwood v. Magnox Electric, [2004] IRLR 733 (HL), 2004 WL 1476578, 352, 354

EEOC v. Arabian American Oil, Co., 499 U.S. 244 (1991), 607

Egan v. Canada, [1995] 2 S.C.R. 513, 186

Eisenstadt v. Baird, 405 U.S. 438, 92 S.Ct. 1029, 31 L.Ed.2d 349 (1972), 151

Electromation, Inc., 309 N.L.R.B. 990 (1992), enforced, 35 F.3d 1148 (7th Cir. 1994) 116, 419

Espinoza v. Farah Manufacturing Co., 414 U.S. 86, 92 (1973), 545, 553

Estades-Negroni v. Assoc. Corp. of N. Am., 345 F.3d 25, 31 (1st Cir. 2003), 139

F

Farber v. Royal Trust Co., [1997] 1 S.C.R. 846, 162

FDIC v. Philadelphia Gear Corp., 476 U.S. 426, 437-438, 90 L. Ed. 2d 428, 106 S. Ct. 1931 (1986), 560

Federal Constitutional Court, 1 BVR 258/86, November 16, 1993, 425–427

Federal Constitutional Court, 1 BVR 779/85, June 26, 1991, 409–412

Federal Constitutional Court, 10 Inter Labor, L. Reports 29, May 30, 1990, 399

Federal Labor Court, 1 ABR 22/94 November 8, 1994, 417

Federal Labor Court, 1 ABR 85/90, August 20, 1991, 419

Federal Labor Court, 1 AZR 622/93, Mar. 22, 1994, 415

Federal Labor Court, 1 AZR 1016/94, June 26, 1995, 415

Federal Labor Court, 2 AZR 227/92, October 10, 1992, 428

Federal Labor Court, 2 AZR15/00, Feb. 21, 2001, 400

Federal Labor Court, 4 AZ R 30/92, September 23, 1992, 424

Federal Labor Court, 5 AZB 29/96, July 16, 1997, 402

Federal Labor Court, 5 4ZR 598/90, October 9, 1991, 425

Federal Labor Court, GS3/85s, November 7, 1989, 419

Filartiga v. Pena-Irala, 630 F.2d 876 (2d Cir. 1980), 614, 616

First National Maintenance Corp. v. NLRB, 452 U.S. 666 (1981), 313

First Scotrail Ltd. v. Griffin, Appeal No. UKEATS/0027/05RN (Mar. 7, 2006), 358

Forrer v. Sears, Roebuck & Co., 153 N.W. 587 (1967), 222

Forsyth v. Eton College, Case.No. 2702463/03, 357

Fortino v. Quasar Co., 751 F. Supp. 1306 (N.D.Ill. 1990), 552

Fortino v. Quasar Co., 950 F.2d 389 (7th Cir. 1991), 552–556, 565

Froelich v. Werbin, 219 Kan. 461, 548 P.2d 482 (1976), 154

G

Garcia v. Elf Atochem North America, 28 F.3d 446 (5th Cir. 1994), 145

General Dynamics Land Systems, Inc. v. Cline, 540 U.S. 581 (2004), 127

General Motors of Canada Ltd. v. C.A.W.-Canada, 31 C.L.R.B.R. (2d) 161 (1996), 159

Gogay v. Hertfordshire County Council [2000] IRLR 703, 354

Goluszek v. H.P. Smith, 697 F.Supp. 1452 (N.D. Ill.1988), 145

Goodwin v. United Kingdom, 323, 324

Google, Inc. and Kai-Fu Lee v. Microsoft Corp., No. C-05-03095 RMW, 2005 U.S. Dist. LEXIS 40678 (N.D. Ca. Oct. 27, 2005), 598

Gover v. Propertycare Ltd., Appeal No. UKEAT/0458/05/ZT (Nov. 22, 2005), 339

Grano v. Department of Development of Columbus, 637 F.2d 1073, 1081 (C.A.6 1980), 133

Grant v. South-West Trains Ltd., C-249/96 (1998), 324

Grattan Plc v. Kamran Hussain EAT/0802/02/TM, 358

Gratz v. Bollinger, 539 U.S. 244 (2003), 580

Gretencord v. Ford Motor Co., 538 F. Supp. 331 (D. Kan. 1982), 155

Griggs v. Duke Power Co., 401 U.S. 424, 431, (1971), 124

Griswold v. Connecticut, 381 U.S. 479, 486, (1965), 151

Grutter v. Bollinger, 539 U.S. 306 (2003), 580

H

Harper v. Virgin Net, Ltd., [2005] I.C.R. 921, 2004 WL 343845, 340

Harris v. Forklift Systems, Inc., 510 U.S. 17, 21 (1993), 145, 146–147

Hausman v. St. Croix Care Ctr., 214 Wis.2d 655, 571 N.W.2d 393 (1997), 97, 99

Hazen Paper Co. v. Biggins, 507 U.S. 604 (1993), 132, 137, 321

Hellmut Marschall v. Land Nordrhein Westfalen, 319, 320

Hill v. Lockheed-Martin Logistics Mgmt., Inc., 354 F.3d 277 (4th Cir. 2004), 139

Hinks v. Riva Systems Ltd. (unreported) 22 November 1996, 377

Hoffman Plastic Compounds, Inc. v. NLRB, 535 U.S. 137 (2002), 2, 24–26, 27, 272

I

I. v. United Kingdom, 323

ICC v. Parker, 326 U.S. 60, 65 (1945), 560

Iceland Frozen Foods Ltd. v. Jones 1983 ICR 17, 358

Igen Ltd. v. Wong, [2005] ICR 931, 2005 WL 353346, 372, 373, 374–391

ILO International Labour Standards Department, Committee of Experts on the Application of Conventions and Recommendations Individual Observation concerning Convention No. 182, Worst Form of Child Labour, 1999 United States (2003), 32

Indra Sawhney v. Union of India, 80 AIR 1993 S.C. 477, 580

The Industrial Tribunals Extension of Jurisdiction (England and Wales) Order 1994, Statutory Instrument 1994 No. 1623, 334

INS v. National Center for Immigrants' Rights, 502 U.S. 183, 194, and n. 8 (1991), 25

Inter-American Court of Human Rights, Advisory Opinion OC-18/03, Juridical Condition and Rights of the Undocumented Migrants, ¶136 (Sept. 17, 2003), 27

International Labor Organization, Committee on Freedom of Association, Complaints against the Government of the United States Presented by the American Federation of Labor (AFL-CIO) and the Congress of Industrial Organizations and the Confederation of Mexican Workers (CTM), Case No. 2227, Report No. 332, ¶ 613 (2003), 27

International Labor Organization, Committee on Freedom of Association, Complaints against the Government of the United States Presented by the American Federation of Labor and the Congress of Industrial Organizations (AFL-CIO) and the Confederation of Mexican Workers (CTM), Case No. 2227, Report No. 332 (2003), 2

International Ladies' Garment Workers' Union, AFL-CIO v. NLRB, 366 U.S. 731 (1961), 114, 115, 116

Int'l Bhd. of Teamsters v. United States, 431 U.S. 324, 335 n.15 (1977), 129

Irvine v. California, 347 U.S. 128, 129-130 (1954), 564

Isle of Wight Tourist Board v. Coombes [1976] IRLR 413, 348

J

J. I. Case Co. v. NLRB, 321 U.S. 332, 339, 112

Jane Doe I v. Wal-Mart Stores, Inc., Case BC339737 (2006), 591–596, 597, 598, 599, 602

Jeffrey Mfg. Co., 208 N.L.R.B. 78, 83 (1974), 422

Jenkins v. Kingsgate (Clothing Productions) Ltd., C-96/80 (1981), 316, 317

Johnson v. Transportation Agency of Santa Clara County, 480 U.S. 616, 640 (1987), 128

Johnson v. Unisys, [2003] 1 AC 518 (HL), 352, 353, 354

K

Kadic. Karadzic, 70 F.3d 232 (2d Cir. 1995), 615

Kalanke v. Freie Hansestadt Bremen, C-450/93 (1995), 319, 320

Kasky v. Nike, Inc., 45 P.3d 243 (Cal. 2002), 606

K.B. v. National Health Service Pensions Agency and Secretary of State for Health, C-117/01, ECR, 2004, 541 (2004), 322

Kim v. University of Regina (1990), 74 D.L.R. (4th) 120, 201

King v. Great Britain–China Centre [1992] ICR 516, 375, 379

Knight v. American Guard & Alert, Inc., 714 P.2d 788 (Alaska 1986), 152

Kolovrat v. Oregon, 366 U.S. 187 (1961), 547, 548

Kono v. Dentsu, Inc., 1707 Hanrei Jiho 87 (March 24, 2000), 529–532, 533

Kouno v. Company X et al. (1992), 541

Kreil v. Federal Republic of Germany, C-285/98 (2000), 318

L

Labor Union of Pico Korea, Ltd. v. Pico Products, Inc., No. 90-CV-774, 1991 WL 299121 (N.D.N.Y. Dec. 23, 1991), 599

Lanning v. Southeastern Pennsylvania
Transportation Authority, 181 F.3d 478 (3d Cir.
1999), 197
Lanning v. Southeastern Pennsylvania
Transportation Authority, 308 F.3d 286 (3d Cir.
2002), 197
Lavigne v. Ontario Public Service Employees'
Union, [1991] 2 S.C.R. 211, 182
The Law Society v. Bahl [2003] IRLR 640, 382,
386
The Law Society v. Bahl [2004] IRLR 799, 382
Lawrence v. Texas, 539 U.S. 558, 572-77 (2003), 33
Lewen v. Denda, Case C-333/97 (1999), 300
Lewis v. Motorworld Garages Ltd. [1985] IRLR
465, 344
Lewis v. Motorworld Garages Ltd. [1986] ICR
157, 351
L'Exuyer v. Aéroports de Montréal, (2003) 233
F.T.R. 234, 207
Linden Lumber Div., Summer & Co. v. NLRB,
419 U.S. 301 (1974), 117
Linskey v. Heidelberg Eastern, Inc., 470 F.
Supp. 1181 (E.D.N.Y. 1979), 554
*Liu Jianfa v. Shanghai Otis Elevator
Company–Unfair Dismissal, CEILAW,
Selected People's Court Cases, Case
115211996037, 503–506*
Logan v. Commissioners of Customs and Excise
[2004] IRLR 63, 344
London Borough of Waltham Forest v. Omilaju
[2004] EWCA Civ 1493, 350
Louis v. E. Baton Rouge Parish Sch. Bd., 303 F.
Supp.2d 799, 801-04 (M.D.La.2003), 138, 140
Lucent Technologies v. SA ESCOTA, Cour
d'Appel d'Aix-en-Provence, No. 2006-170
3/13/06, 461
*Luedtke v. Nabors Alaska Drilling, Inc., 768 P.2d
1123 (Alaska 1989), 149–155*

M
Machtinger v. HOJ Industries Ltd., [1992] 1
S.C.R. 986, 164, 165, 169
MacNamara v. Korean Air Lines, 863 F.2d 1135
(3d Cir. 1988), 554
Malik v. Bank of Credit & Commerce
International SA [1997] IRLR / [1997] ICR
606, 346, 347, 349, 351
Maria Paz Merino Gómez v. Continental
Industrias del Caucho SA, Case C-342/01
(E.C.J. Mar. 18, 2004), 369
Martin v. Lancehawk Ltd. UKEAT/0525/03/ILB,
389
Mason v. The Governing Body of Ward End
Primary School, Appeal No.
UKEAT/0433/05/ZT (Apr. 12, 2006), 339

Matvia v. Bald Head Island Management, Inc.,
259 F.3d 261 (2001), 148
Maximov v. United States, 373 U.S. 49 (1963), 545
*McDonald v. Santa Fe Trail Transportation Co.,
427 U.S. 273 (1976), 124–126, 127, 553*
McDonnell Douglas Corp. v. Green, 411 U.S. 792
(1973), 125, 126, 131, 133, 136, 137, 138, 140, 143,
144, 391
McKinley v. B.C. Telephone Co., [2001] 2 S.C.R.
161,
McLain v. Boise Cascade Corp., 271 Or. 549, 533
P.2d 343 (1975), 154
McWilliams v. Fairfax County Board of
Supervisors, 72 F.3d 1191 (C.A.4 1996), 146
Medlock v. Ortho Biotech, Inc., 164 F.3d 545, 553
(10th Cir.1999), 138
Mehta v. State of Tamil Nadu, AIR 1997 S.C.
699, 567
*Merckx v. Ford Motor Company Belgium SA,
C-171/94, C-172/94 (1996), 311–312*
Meritor Savings Bank, FSB v. Vinson, 477 U.S.
57, 64 (1986), 145, 146, 147, 541
Metropolis Theatre Co. v. Chicago, 228 U.S. 61
(1913), 572
Mitford v. de LaSala, 666 P.2d 1000 (Alaska 1983),
152
Mooney v. Aramco Serv. Co., 54 F.3d 1207,
1216-17 & n. 11 (5th Cir. 1995), 138, 139, 140
Moore v. British Columbia (1988), 50 D.L.R.
(4th) 29, 203
Moores v. Bude-Stratton Town Council [2000]
IRLR 676, 347
Morey v. Doud, 354 U.S. 457 (1957), 572
Morgan v. South Bend Community School
Corp., 797 F.2d 471 (7th Cir. 1991), 555
Morrow v. Safeway Stores plc [2002] IRLR 9, 345,
346, 349
Murphy v. Bord Telecom Eireann, C-157/86
(1988), 316

N
Nagarajan v. London Regional Transport [2000] 1
AC 501, 382
NAO Submission No. 2001-01, 271, 272
NAO Submission No. 9701, 20
NAO Submission No. 9803, 272
NAO Submission No. 940003, 269
National Westminster Bank Case 782
Roudouhevrei 23 (July 15, 2000), 537–540
Nelson v. Carillion Services Ltd. [2003] ICR
1256, 379
Neocel v. Spaeter, Cass. Soc., Oct. 2, 2001, Bull.
Civ. No. 291, 460
New Brunswick v. O'Leary, [1995] 2 S.C.R. 967,
199, 205, 206

Newport News Shipbuilding & Dry Dock Co. v. EEOC, 462 U.S. 669, 682 (1983), 145

Nicholas v. Allstate Ins. Co., 765 So. 2d 1017 (La. 1992), 103

Nike, Inc. v. Kasky, 123 S.Ct. 2554 (2003), 606

Nissan Motors, Inc. v. Nakamoto (1981), 528

NLRB v. General Motors Corp., 373 U.S. 734 (1963), 246

NLRB v. Gissel Packing Co., 395 U.S. 575 (1969), 174

NLRB v. Mackay Radio & Telegraph Co., 304 U.S. 333 (1938), 119–121, 122

NLRB v. Pennsylvania Greyhound Lines, 303 U.S. 261, 267, 112

North West Thames Regional Health Authority v. Noone [1988] ICR 813, 376

O

O'Connor v. Consolidated Coin, 517 U.S. 308, 313 (1996), 140–141

O.J., 15 June 1988, P. Bork International A/S in liquidation and others v. Foreningen of Arbejdsledere i Danmark, acting on behalf of Birger E. Peterson, and Junckers Industries A/S, No. 101/87, ECR, 1988, 3057 ???, 308

Oncale v. Sundowner Offshore Services, Inc., 83 F.3d 118 (5th Cir. 1996), 145

Oncale v. Sundowner Offshore Services, Inc., 523 U.S. 75 (1998), 144–147, 148

Ontario Public Service Employees Union v. Seneca College of Applied Arts & Technology, Docket C43274, May 4, 2006, 206

Ontario v. Simpson Sears, [1985] 2 S.C.R. 536, 195

P

P v. S, C-13/94 (1996), 324

Palasota v. Haggar Clothing Co., 342 F.3d 569 (5th Cir. 2003), 137, 141, 143

Parry Sound (District) Social Services Administration Board v. Ontario Public Service Employees Union, Local 324, [2003] 2. S.C.R. 157, 195, 207

Pena v. Am. Meat Packing Corp., 362 F.3d 418, 421 (7th Cir. 2004), 107

Phillipe K. v. Cathnet-Science, 458–460, 461

Pilon v. Peugeot Canada Ltd. (1980), 114 D.L.R. (3d) 378 (Ont. H.C.), 161

Pilon v. University of Minnesota, 710 F.2d 466 (8th Cir. 1983), 556

Polkey v. AE Dayton Services Ltd. [1988] AC 344, 339

Pollock v. Williams, 322 U.S. 4 (1944), 611

Post Office v. Roberts [1980] IRLR 347, 347

Prairie Micro-Tech Inc. HL, 176

Price Waterhouse v. Hopkins, 490 U.S. 228, (1989), 137, 138, 139, 140, 143

Prosecutor v. Furundzija, IT-95-17/1 T (Dec. 10, 1998), 612, 613

Prosecutor v. Musema, ICTR-96-13-T (Jan. 27, 2000), 612, 613

Prosecutor v. Tadic, ICTY-94-1, ¶ 688 (May 7, 1997), 612, 613

Public Report of Review of NAO Submission No. 9702, 259–271

Pugh v. Attica, 259 F.3d 619 (7th Cir. 2001), 131

R

R. v. Advance Cutting & Coring, [2001] 3 S.C.R. 209, 183

Rachid v. Jack in the Box, Inc., 376 F.3d 305 (5th Cir. 2004), 135–143, 144

Raytheon Co. v. Hernandez, 540 U.S. 44 (2003), 129–134

Re Ontario Council of Regents for Colleges of Applied Arts & Technology and Ontario Public Service Employees Union (1986), 24 L.A.C. (3d) 144, 203

Reeves v. Sanderson Plumbing Products, Inc., 530 U.S. 133, 143 (2000), 131, 137

Reference Re Public Service Employee Relations Act (Alta.), [1987] 1 S.C.R. 313, 165

Reference re Public Service Relations Act (Alta.) [1987], 87 C.L.L.C. 14, 021 (S.C.C.), 172

Report of the Commission of Inquiry appointed under article 26 of the Constitution of the International Labour Organization to examine the observance by Myanmar of the Forced Labour Convention, 1930 (No. 29), 75–81

Report of the Committee set up to examine the representation made by the Senegal Teachers' Single and Democratic Trade Union (SUDES) under article 24 of the ILO Constitution alleging non-observance by Senegal of the Abolition of Forced Labour Convention, 1957 (No. 105), 70–73

Rhys-Harper v. Relaxion Group plc [2003] ICR 867, 378

Riley v. American Family Mutual Ins. Co., 881 F.2d 368 (7th Cir. 1989), 556

Rishel v. Nationwide Mut. Ins. Co., 297 F.Supp.2d 854, 865 (M.D.N.C.2003), 140

Robinson v. Crompton Parkinson [1978] IRLR 61, 348

Roe v. Wade, 410 U.S. 113 (1973), 151

Roper v. Simmons, 543 U.S. 551 (2005), 33–36, 616

Roquet v. Arthur Andersen LLP, 398 F.3d 585 (7th Cir. 2005), 105–110

Russell v. McKinney Hosp. Venture, 235 F.3d 219, 229 (5th Cir. 2000), 143

RWDSU Local 558 v. Pepsi-Cola Canada
Beverages (West) Ltd., [2002], 208 D.L.R. (4th)
385 (S.C.C.), 184
RWDSU Local 558 v. Pepsi-Cola Canada
Beverages (West) Ltd., [2002] 1 S.C.R. 156, 183
RWDSU Local 580 v. Dolphin Delivery Ltd.,
[1986] 2 S.C.R. 573, 184

S
Sainsbury's Supermarket v. Hitt [2003] IRLR 23,
358
Sandstad v. CB Richard Ellis, Inc., 309 F.3d 893,
897 (5th Cir. 2002), 138
*Saskatchewan Indian Gaming Authority Inc. and
C.A.W.-Canada, (2002) 84 C.L.R.B.R. (2d) 233,*
175–181
Senogles v. Security Benefit Life Ins. Co., 217
Kan. 438, 536 P.2d 1358 (1975), 154
Shamoon v. Chief Constable of the RUC [2003]
IRLR 285, 382
Shioda v. Kochi Broadcasting Company, 268
Rodo Hanrei (January 31, 1977), 534–540
SIMAP v. Conselleria de Sanidady Consumo de
la Generalidad Valenciana, C-303/98 (1998),
299
*Sime v. Imperial College London, Appeal
No.UKEAT/0875/04/CK (April 20, 2005),* 338,
340, 341–350, 351
Sinclair Roche v. Temperly [2004] IRLR 763, 350
Singleton v. Wulff, 428 U.S. 106, 96 S.Ct. 2868,
49 L.Ed.2d 826 (1976), 552
Sirdar v. The Army Board and Secretary of State
for Defence, C-273/97 (1999), 318
Sistok v. Northwestern Tel. Sys., Inc., 189 Mont.
82, 615 P.2d 176, 182 (1980), 154
Slaight Communications Inc. v. Davidson, [1989]
1 S.C.R. 1038, 165
Smith v. City of Jackson, Miss., 351 F.3d 183,
188-190 (5th Cir. 2003), 139
Societe La Louisiane/Societe Les Carlines v.
Daniel Alzas, Cour de Casssation, Arret No.
877-FS-P+B, 3/5/02, 438, 441, 457
Société Nikon France c/ Monsieur O., 439–440,
447–448, 460, 461
Sosa v. Alvarez-Machain, 542 U.S. 692 (2004),
616, 617
Spiess v. C. Itoh & Co., 643 F.2d 353 (5th Cir.
1981), vacated on other grounds, 457 U.S. 1128
(1982), 545, 554
St. Anne Nackawic Pulp & Paper Co. v.
Canadian Paper Workers Union, Local 219
(1982), 142 D.L.R. (3d) 678, 200
St. Anne Nackawic Pulp & Paper Co. v.
Canadian Paper Workers Union, Local 219,
[1986] 1 S.C.R. 704, 200, 201, 203

St. Mary's Honor Center v. Hicks, 509 U.S. 502
(1993), 320
Stanford v. Kentucky, 492 U.S. 361, 109 S.Ct.
2969, 106 L.Ed.2d 306 (1989), 33
Stegall v. Citadel Broad. Co., 350 F.3d 1061,
1066-67 (9th Cir. 2003), 138
Strauch v. Am. College of Surgeons, 301
F.Supp.2d 839, 844 (N.D.Ill.2004), 139
Sumitomo Shoji America Inc. v. Avagliano, 457
U.S. 176 (1982), 544–552, 554, 564
Sumitomo Shoji America Inc. v. Avagliano, 473
F.Supp. 506 (S.D.N.Y. 1979), 544
Sumitomo Shoji America Inc. v. Avagliano, 638
F.2d 552 (2d Cir. 1981), 545, 550
Sure-Tan v. NLRB, 467 U.S. 883 (1984), 25, 26
Surrey County Council v. Henderson, Appeal
No. UKEAT/0326/05/ZT (Nov. 23, 2005),
340
Susie Radin Ltd. v. GMB and others [2004] IRLR
400, 366
Sutton v. United Air Lines, Inc., 527 U.S. 471, 479
(1999), 560, 562, 563

T
Taylor v. Gordon Flesch Co., 793 F.2d 858 (7th
Cir. 1986), 555, 556
Teamsters v. United States, 431 U.S. 324 (1977),
132, 196
Tesco Stores Ltd. v. Pryke, Appeal No.
UKEAT/0576/05/DM (May 10, 2006),
357
Texas Dept. of Community Affairs v. Burdine,
450 U.S. 248, 252, n. 5 (1981), 133
Thomas v. State of Indiana, 910 F.2d 1413 (7th
Cir. 1990), 552
Thompson v. Proviso Township High Sch. Dist.
209, No. 01-C-5743, 2003 WL 21638808
(N.D.Ill. July 10, 2003), 139
Timekeeping Systems, Inc., 323 N.L.R.B. 244
(1997), 118
Tokyo Oxygen Gas Company v. Shimazaki
(1979), 538
Toronto Electric Commissioners v. Snider, [1925]
2 D.L.R. 5, A.C. 396, 1 W.W.R. 785 (U.K.P.C.),
158–159, 171
Toyota Motor Manufacturing, Kentucky, Inc. v.
Williams, 224 F.3d 843 (6th Cir. 2000), 563
Toyota Motor Manufacturing, Kentucky, Inc. v.
Williams, 523 U.S. 970 (2001), 559
*Toyota Motor Manufacturing, Kentucky, Inc. v.
Williams, 534 U.S. 184 (2002)* 543, 556–564, 565
Travelers Cas. & Sur. Co. of Am. v. Baptist Health
Sys., 313 F.3d 295, 297 (5th Cir. 2002), 136
Trop v. Dulles, 356 U.S. 86, 100-101 (1958), 34

U

UEAPME v. Council, T-135/96 (1996), 283

United Kingdom v. Council, Case C-84/94, 1996
E.C.R. 1-5755, 299

United States v. Arthur Andersen, LLP, 374 F.3d
281 (5th Cir. 2004), 106

United Steelworkers of America v. Weber, 443
U.S. 193, 208 (1979), 128

URBSFA v. Bosman, C-415/93, ECR, 1995, 4921,
289–293, 294

V

Voice v. Construction & General Workers'
Union, Local 92, [2004] 1. S.C.R. 609, 206

Vorvis v. Insurance Corporation of British
Columbia, [1989] 1 S.C.R. 1085, 161, 162, 167

Vriend v. Alberta, [1998] 1 S.C.R. 493, 186

W

Wainwright v. Vancouver Shipyards Co. (1987),
38 D.L.R. (4th) 760 (B.C.C.A.), 202

Wal-Mart [1997] O.L.R.B. Rep. Jan./Feb. 141,
174

Wallace v. United Grain Growers Ltd., [1997] 3
S.C.R. 701, 160–168, 169, 170, 171, 198

Wallace v. United Grain Growers Ltd., Manitoba
Court of Queen's Bench (1993), 87 Man. R.,
(2d) 161, 160

Watson v. Michigan Industrial Holdings, Inc., 311
F.3d 765, 108

Weber v. Ontario Hydro, [1995] 2 S.C.R. 928,
199–205, 206, 207

Webster v. Brunel University (6th Cir. 2002), 380,
381

West v. Nabors Drilling USA, Inc., 330 F.3d 379,
383-85 (5th Cir. 2003), 137

Western Excavating (ECC) Ltd. v. Sharp [1978] 1
QB 761, 350

Western Excavating (EEC) Ltd. v. Sharp [1978]
ICR 221, 344

Wickes v. Olympic Airways, 745 F.2d 363 (6th
Cir. 1984), 554

Wilson & National Union of Journalists v. The
United Kingdom, [2002] IRLR 568, 35 Euro.
Ct. H.R. 20 (2002), 361

Woods v. W. M. Car Services (Peterborough) Ltd.
[1981] ICR 666, 344, 347, 351

Workmen of Meenakshi Mills Ltd. v. Meenakshi
Mills Ltd. (1991), 574

Wrightson v. Pizza Hut of America, 99 F.3d 138
(C.A.4 1996), 146

Wygant v. Jackson Bd. Of Educ., 476 U.S. 267
(1986), 128

Wyvill v. United Cos. Life Ins. Co., 212 F.3d 296,
302 (5th Cir. 2000), 142

Y

Ye Shenghua v. Wuhan Transportation
Information Center, 486

Younger v. Harris, 401 U.S. 37 (1971), 552

Table of Statutes

Canada

Alberta Public Service Employee Relations Act, 165

Alberta Public Service Relations Act, 172

British North America Act of 1867, 158

Canada Act, 157

Charter of Rights and Freedoms, 159, 172, 182, 183, 186, 199, 200, 202, 203, 204, 205
  § 1, 159
  § 2, 159
  § 2(d), 172
  § 7, 199
  § 8, 199
  § 15, 186

Colleges Collective Bargaining Act, 86

Constitution, 157

Constitution Act
  § 91, 159
  § 92, 159
  Schedule B, 159

Education Act, 86

Employment Insurance Act, 185

Fire Protection and Prevention Act, 1997, 86

Industrial Disputes Investigation Act of 1907, 159, 171

Labour Code, 204
  § 2, 159

Labour Relations Amendment Act, 1995, 85

Labour Relations Amendment Act, 2000, 84, 85, 86
  § 63, 88
  § 63.1, 84, 85, 86, 87, 88

Ontario, Bill 144, 1st Session, 38th Legislature, 54 Elizabeth II, 2005, 88

Ontario Human Rights Code, 195

Ontario Labour Relations Act, 87
  c. L.2, 199
  c. L.2, § 45(1), 200, 201, 203, 204, 205

Order in Council 1003 (P.C. 1003), 171

Personal Information Protection and Electronic Documents Act (PIPEDA), 197, 198, 207

Police Services Act, 86

Provincial Schools Negotiations Act, 86

Public Service Act, 86

China

Constitution of 1954, 473

Constitution of 1975, 473

Constitution of 1982, 464, 465, 468, 469, 473, 481, 516
  Article 5, 467, 469
  Article 6, 467
  Article 7, 467
  Article 9, 467–468
  Article 10, 468, 519
  Article 11, 468
  Article 31, 519
  Article 42, 469
  Article 48, 470
  Article 57, 480
  Article 62(3), 480
  Article 67(1), 480
  Article 67(2), 480
  Preamble, 465–467, 468, 521

Economic Contract Law, 487

General Principles of Civil Law, 487, 501, 502
  Article 44, 506

Implementing Measures, Article 5, 505

Labor Law, 480, 481, 483, 484, 485, 487, 488–499,
    502, 503, 506, 512, 513, 514, 515, 541
  Article 2, 501
  Article 4, 509
  Article 13, 470
  Article 17, 508
  Article 19, 506
  Article 21, 506
  Article 22, 479
  Article 25, 484
  Article 26(ii), 506, 534
  Article 27, 485
  Article 30, 515
  Article 36, 484
  Article 38, 484
  Article 46, 484
  Article 48, 470, 484
  Article 48–49, 480
  Article 49, 484
  Article 52–57, 503
  Article 56, 516
  Article 70–76, 470, 479
  Article 98, 506
  Article 99, 477, 484
  Article 102, 479, 484
Labor Management Regulations for
    Chinese–Foreign Joint Ventures, Article 2,
    505
Labor Union Law, 513
Law for the Protection of Women's Rights and
    Interests, 484
Law of Civil Procedure, Article 153(1)(i), 502, 505
Law on State Functionaries, 502

Ministry of Labor, Provisional Measures for
    Worker's Compensation in Enterprises,
    Article 14, 499
Ministry of Labor and State Bureau of Personnel
    Records, Regulations Concerning the
    Management of Personnel Files of State
    Enterprise Workers and Staff, 473
1986 Contract Employment Regulations, 482, 483
1992 Women's Protection Law, 471

Provisional Regulations for the Resolution of
    Labor Disputes in Enterprises, 486

Regulations for the Resolution of Labor Disputes
    in Enterprises, 486–487
  Article 2, 485, 508
  Article 39, 485

Trade Union Law, 468–469, 506, 515, 516, 517

European Community/European Union

Amsterdam Treaty, 276, 278, 285, 315, 324, 332
  Article 13, 377

Charter of Fundamental Rights, 284, 435
Community Charter of Fundamental Social
    Rights of Workers, 284
Constitution, 277
Convention for the Protection of Human Rights
    and Fundamental Freedoms, 280, 323, 324,
    392
  Article 8, 440, 441, 459
  Article 11, 290, 361, 362
  Article 12, 323, 324

Declaration of Basic Social Rights of Workers, 282
Directive 75/117/EC (Equal Treatment), 315, 322,
    323, 324, 371, 425
Directive 75/129/EC, 306
Directive 76/207/EC, 316, 317, 318, 319, 423
  Article 1, 317
  Article 1(1), 318
  Article 2, 317
  Article 2(1), 317, 318, 319
  Article 2(2), 318
  Article 2(3), 317, 318
  Article 2(4), 318, 319
Directive 77/187/EC, 281, 307, 311, 312, 359
  Article 1(1), 311, 312
  Article 3(1), 311
  Article 4(1), 312
Directive 79/7/EC, 316
Directive 86/378/EC, 316
Directive 91/533/EC, 398
Directive 92/56/EC, 306, 307
Directive 93/104/EC (Working Time), 297, 298,
    299, 367
  Article 6, 299
  Article 17(2), subparagraph 2.1(c)(i), 299
  Article 18, 368
Directive 94/45/EC (Works Council), 281, 301,
    303, 361, 453
Directive 95/46/EC (Privacy), 325, 326, 328
  Article 1(1), 325
  Article 1(2), 325
  Article 2, 328
  Article 2(a), 326
  Article 2(b), 326
  Article 4, 326
  Article 4(1), 326
  Article 6, 326
  Article 7, 327, 329
  Article 7(a), 328
  Article 8(1), 327
  Article 8(2)(a), 328

Article 25(1), 328
Article 25(2), 328
Article 26, 329
Article 26(1), 329
Article 26(2), 329
Directive 95/46/EC (Privacy Protection), 392
Directive 96/34/EC (Parental Leave), 300, 369,
    370
Directive 96/71/EC, Article 5, 296
Directive 96/97/EC, 316
Directive 97/74/EC (Works Council), 361
Directive 97/80/EC (Burden of Proof), 143, 316,
    317, 372, 373, 376, 377, 378, 382, 391
    Article 1, 376
    Article 2(1), 382
    Article 4(1), 317, 372, 376, 377, 382
    Article 4(2), 376, 377
Directive 97/81/EC, 300
Directive 98/50/EC, 307, 359
Directive 98/52/EC, 376–377
Directive 98/59/EC (Collective Redundancies),
    307, 364
    Article 2,
    Article 2(1), 305
    Article 2(2), 305
    Article 2(3), 304
    Article 2(4), 305
    Article 3(1), 304
    Article 3(2), 305
Directive 99/70/EC (Fixed-Term Work), 300,
    337
Directive 2000/43/EC (Race), 316, 321, 377, 428
    Article 1, 321
    Article 2(1), 383
    Article 8, 377
    Article 8(1), 377
    Article 8(2), 377
Directive 2000/78/EC (Equal Treatment
    Framework), 316, 321, 324, 370, 377, 428, 458
    Article 2, 321
    Article 2(1), 383
    Article 5, 321
    Article 6, 321
    Article 10, 377
    Article 10(1), 377
    Article 10(2), 377
Directive 2001/14/EC (Employee Information
    and Consultation), 364
Directive 2001/23/EC (Transfer of Undertakings),
    307, 308, 313, 314, 364
Directive 2002/14/EC, 302
Directive 2002/58/EC (Privacy and Electronic
    Communications), 392
Directive 2002/73/EC, 316, 428
    Article 1(2), 317

Directive 2003/88/EC, 297, 298

EC Treaty, 46, 279, 280, 281, 284, 285, 290, 292,
    294, 295, 306, 316, 377
    Article 2, 277, 290, 315
    Article 3(2), 315
    Article 3C, 288
    Article 6, 284
    Article 6(2), 280
    Article 10, 428
    Article 12, 293
    Article 13, 315
    Article 17, 294
    Article 39, 288, 289, 290, 291, 292, 293
    Article 39–42, 278
    Article 39(2), 292, 293
    Article 39(3)(c), 293
    Article 49, 295, 296
    Article 50, 295
    Article 94, 307–308
    Article 94–96, 278
    Article 119, 315
    Article 130–145, 278
    Article 136, 284
    Article 137(1), 299
    Article 137(3), 285
    Article 137(6), 285, 297, 300, 301
    Article 138(1), 301
    Article 139, 280
    Article 139(1), 301
    Article 141, 315, 316, 317, 322, 323, 324
    Article 148, 278
    Article 149–150, 278–279
    Article 158–162, 279
    Article 213(2), 279
    Article 226, 428
    Article 226–227, 279
    Article 228, 282
    Article 230–231, 279
    Article 249, 282
    Article 249(2), 280
    Article 249(3), 280–281
    Article 250(1), 279
    Article 254(1), 280
    Article F(2), 290

Maastricht Treaty, 276, 285
    Social Protocol, 332

Nice Treaty, 46, 286

Regulation No. 1612/68, 15 October 1968, 288

Single European Act, 290
Social Charter of 1996, 279, 362, 376

France

Civil Code of 1804, 216, 433
   Article 9, 440, 441, 458, 459
   Article 1108, 436
   Article 1134, 446, 447
Code of Civil Procedure
   Article 9, 440, 441, 459
   Article 700, 459
Constitution of 1946, 434
   Preamble, 448
Constitution of 1958, 432, 448, 451
   Section 34, 432

Data Protection Act, 325
Decree No. 2004-1381 of Dec. 21, 2004, 453

First Job Contract, 433, 434, 444, 445,
   446

Labor Code, 435, 439, 453
   Article L. 120-2, 440, 441, 459
   Article L. 121-1, 437
   Article L. 121-9, 447
   Article L. 122-4, 437
   Article L. 122-6, 438
   Article L. 122-12, 444
   Article L. 122-14, 438
   Article L. 122-14-1, 438
   Article L. 122-39-1, 437
   Article L. 122-49-122-54, 457
   Article L. 133-2, 449
   Article L. 135-3, 446
   Article L. 223, 454
   Article L. 321-1, 441
   Article L. 321-4-1, 443
   Article L. 431-1, 452
   Article L. 431-2, 452
   Article L. 521-1, 451
   Article L. 521-2, 451
Law No. 70-643 of July 17, 1970, 458
Law No. 2001-1066 of Nov. 16, 2001, 456
Law No. 2002-73 of Jan. 17, 2002, 442, 453, 457
Law No. 2003-591 of July 2, 2003, 436
Law No. 2003-721 of Aug. 1, 2003, 447, 454
Law No. 2004-22 of Mar. 15, 2004, 457
Law No. 2004-391 of May 4, 2004, 449
Law No. 2005-32 of Jan. 18, 2005, 441, 442, 443,
   454, 457
Law on Equal Pay Between Men and Women,
   434, 444, 456

Penal Code, Article 222-33-2, 457

Social Modernization Law of 2002, 442, 443

Germany

Act on Collective Agreements, § 12a, 402
Act on Court Procedure in Labor Matters,
   428–429

Civil Code of 1896, 396, 398, 399, 464
   § 242, 400
   § 611a, 423, 426
   § 611a(1), 424, 426, 427
   § 612(3), 423, 424
   § 612a, 423
   § 623, 399
   § 626, 399, 423
Codetermination Extension Statute of 1952,
   420
Codetermination Statute of 1976, 397, 420, 421
Collective Bargaining Agreements Law of 1969,
   396, 405
Company Pension Plan Act of 1974, 404
Constitution (Basic Law), 394, 395, 396, 410, 411,
   413, 422, 426, 430
   Article 2(1), 430
   Article 3, 422
   Article 3(1), 399
   Article 3.1, 423
   Article 3(2), 425, 426, 427
   Article 3(3), 425, 426
   Article 3.3, 423
   Article 9, 406
   Article 9(1), 408, 410
   Article 9(3), 395, 396, 406, 408, 409, 410, 411,
   412
   Article 12(1), 395
   Article 14, 406
   Article 20(3), 411

Employees Protection Act of 1974, 423

Federal Data Protection Act, 430

Industrial Relations Act of 1952, 416

Labor Courts Act of 1953, 428
Labor Courts Act of 1957, 429
Law on Modernization of the Law of Obligations,
   398

Maternity Leave Statute of 1968, 428
Montan Codetermination Statute of 1951, 420

Severely Disabled Persons Act, 424
Social Law Code, Ninth Book, § 81.2, 424

Termination Protection Statute of 1969, 399, 400,
   401, 429

Unfair Dismissal Act of 1969, 398
Unification Treaty of 1990
    Article 8, 395
    Article 30, 395

Wages Act, § 1, 425
Works Construction Act
    § 75, 423
    § 77(3), 419
    § 87(1)(1), 418
    § 87(1)(2), 419
Works Council Statute of 1952, 397, 420
Works Council Statute of 1972, 396

India

Bonded Labour System (Abolition) Act, 1976,
    582, 584
    § 13, 584

Companies Act, 1956, 570
Constitution, 63, 566, 578, 579, 582, 583
    Article 14, 578
    Article 15, 578, 580
    Article 16, 578
    Article 17, 578, 579
    Article 23, 582
    Article 32, 580, 582, 583
    Article 46, 578
    Article 226, 580, 583
    Directive Principles of State Policy, 583
    Fundamental Rights, 583
    Preamble, 583
Contract Labour (Regulation and Abolition) Act,
    1970, 573, 583

Defense of India Rules, 573

Employment of Manual Scavengers and
    Construction of Dry Latrines (Prohibition)
    Act, 1993, 62, 63

Industrial Disputes Act, 1947, 573, 574, 588
    Chapter V-B, 573
Inter-State Migrant Workmen Act, 583
Inter-State Migrant Workmen Rules, 583

Maternity Benefit Act, 1961, 586
Maternity Benefit (Mines and Circus) Rules,
    1963, 586
Mines Act, 1950, § 20, 585
Mines Act, 1952
    § 19, 583–584
    § 21, 585–586
Mines Creche Rules, 1966, 586

Mines Rules, 1955
    Rule 30-32, 584
    Rule 33-36, 585
    Rule 40-45A, 586
    Rule 45, 586
Mines Vocational Training Rules, 1966, 586

Protection of Civil Rights Act, 579

Untouchability (Offenses) Act, 1955, 579

International Labour Organization

Constitution, 53, 55, 83
    Annex I(a), 11
    Article 19, 58
    Article 22, 60, 61, 64, 81
    Article 24, 70, 72
    Article 26, 74, 75, 82
    Article 29, 75
    Article 33, 81
Convention No. 29, Forced Labour, 72, 75, 76,
    80, 81, 82, 89
    Article 1, paragraph 1, 80
    Article 1(1), 76
    Article 2, paragraph 1, 72
    Article 2, paragraph 2, 79
    Article 2, paragraph 2(d), 79
    Article 2, paragraph 2(e), 79
    Article 2(1), 76, 79, 80
    Article 2(2), 76
    Article 25, 76, 80, 81
Convention No. 81, Labor Inspection, 61
Convention No. 87, Freedom of Association and
    Protection of the Right to Organize, 56, 65,
    74, 83, 84, 85, 86, 88, 89, 117, 122, 171, 220,
    236, 243, 244, 262, 514, 516, 526, 577
    Article 2, 88
    Article 8(2), 88
    Article 11, 88
Convention No. 97, Migration for Employment
    Convention (Revised), 23
Convention No. 98, Right to Organise and
    Collective Bargaining, 56, 74, 83, 84, 85, 89,
    117, 122, 171, 220, 262, 514, 516, 526, 577
Convention No. 100, Equal Remuneration, 90,
    247, 516
Convention No. 105, Abolition of Forced Labour,
    70, 71, 73, 89, 90
    Article 1(b), 72
Convention No. 111, Discrimination–
    Employment and Occupation, 63, 64, 69,
    90, 127, 247, 516
    Article 1, 62
    Article 1, paragraph 1, 63
    Article 1, paragraph 1(a), 62, 63

Convention No. 111, Discrimination–
    Employment and Occupation (*cont.*)
  Article 2, 62
  Article 3(d), 62
Convention No. 122, Employment Policy, 61
Convention No. 129, Labor Inspection in
    Agriculture, 61
Convention No. 138, Minimum Age, 28, 29, 89,
    516
Convention No. 143, Migrant Workers
    (Supplementary Provisions), 23
Convention No. 144, Tripartite Consultation
    (International Labor Standards), 61, 65, 66,
    67, 68
  Article 2, 65
  Article 5, 65–66
Convention No. 151, Labour Relations (Public
    Service), 84, 85
Convention No. 154, Collective Bargaining, 84,
    85
Convention No. 158, Termination of
    Employment, 101, 110, 439
Convention No. 182, Worst Forms of Child
    Labour, 28, 29, 30, 31, 89, 90, 275, 516
  Article 3(d), 30
Convention No. 185, Seafarers' Identity
    Documents, 66, 68

Declaration of Philadelphia, 53, 54–55, 83,
    220
  Article III, 55
  Article V, 55
Declaration on Fundamental Principles and
    Rights at Work, 2, 28, 43, 48, 55, 58, 68,
    88–89, 90, 91, 117, 273, 516, 577

Recommendation No. 119, 357
Recommendation No. 166, 439
Recommendation No. 190, Worst Forms of Child
    Labour, 30

Tripartite Declaration of Principles concerning
    Multinational Enterprises and Social Policy,
    590

Japan

Civil Code, 528, 536
  Article 1, 533
  Article 1–2, 528
  Article 1(3), 533
  Article 626, 533
  Article 627, 533
  Article 709, 541
  Article 715, 529, 531, 532, 542
  Article 722–2, 532

Constitution of 1947, 525, 528
  Article 14, 528
  Article 25, 525–526
  Article 27, 526
  Article 28, 526
  Article 90, 528

Equal Employment Opportunity Law, 528, 529,
    542
  Article 21(1), 542

Labor Relations Adjustment Law, 526
Labor Standards Law of 1947, 509, 526, 532, 533,
    536
  Article 18-2, 536
  Article 20, 533
  Article 36, 530

Meiji Constitution of 1889, 518, 525

Protection of Workers Safety and Health Law,
    Article 65-3, 532

Trade Union Law, 526

Mexico

Constitution of 1917, 211, 212, 217, 220, 221, 222,
    225, 239, 241, 243, 244, 245, 262, 264, 270
  Article 2-28, 241
  Article 4, 18
  Article 5, 18, 225, 241, 244, 245
  Article 9, 241, 244, 245
  Article 14, 234, 241
  Article 16, 241, 248
  Article 19, 264
  Article 27, 217
  Article 103, 240–241
  Article 123, 217, 218, 219, 227, 243
  Article 123, paragraph II, 223
  Article 123, paragraph III, 223
  Article 123, paragraph VI, 218
  Article 123, paragraph XIX, 232
  Article 123, paragraph XVI, 218, 242, 244, 245
  Article 123, paragraph XVII, 218, 231, 232
  Article 123, paragraph XVIII, 218, 231
  Article 123, paragraph XXII, 218, 219
  Article 123, paragraph XXIX, 218, 224
  Article 123, paragraph XXVII, 218
  Article 123, paragraph XXXI, 228
  Article 123, Part A, 218, 220, 264
  Article 123, Part B, 220, 242
  Article 123, Part B, paragraph VII, 247
  Article 123, Part B, paragraph X, 242, 243, 245
  Article 133, 220, 243, 245

Constitution of 1824, 216, 221
Constitution of 1857, 216

Federal Labor Law, 19, 220, 221, 222, 224, 225, 227,
    228, 229, 230, 235, 239, 244, 245, 247, 248, 264,
    266, 270
  Article 2, 220
  Article 3, 18, 220, 247
  Article 4, 232
  Article 5, 223, 245
  Article 6, 220
  Article 8, 220
  Article 10, 220
  Article 25, 223
  Article 35, 222
  Article 42, 243
  Article 46, 222
  Article 47, 222, 223, 264,
    265
  Article 48, 235
  Article 56, 223, 247
  Article 75, 244
  Article 99, 223
  Article 117, 224
  Article 133, 18, 264, 265
  Article 136–138, 224
  Article 162, 224
  Article 164, 18
  Article 164–280, 224
  Article 170, 19
  Article 174, 223
  Article 182, 230
  Article 356, 228, 236
  Article 357, 227
  Article 357–359, 264
  Article 358, 227
  Article 360, 264, 266, 267
  Article 364, 236
  Article 365, 236
  Article 366, 236
  Article 368, 267
  Article 374, 267
  Article 387, 229, 264, 267
  Article 388, 229, 264
  Article 389, 264
  Article 391, 230
  Article 395, 227, 244, 265
  Article 396, 230
  Article 399, 229, 268
  Article 404, 230
  Article 413, 244
  Article 427, 224
  Article 427–439, 230
  Article 434, 224
  Article 440, 231
  Article 443, 231
  Article 449, 232
  Article 450, 231, 239
  Article 451, 231
  Article 459, 231, 239
  Article 472–522, 224
  Article 527, 264, 266
  Article 604–624, 264
  Article 625–675, 264
  Article 652, 219, 237
  Article 685, 234
  Article 784, 234
  Article 870–891, 264
  Article 890, 268
  Article 892–899, 264
  Article 920–938, 239
  Article 931, 264, 266
  Article 931(IV), 266
  Title III, 222
Federal Law of Workers in the Service of the
    State, 220
  Article 1, 242
Federal Law to Prevent and Eliminate
    Discrimination, 247
  Article 4, 247
Federal Regulation on Workplace Safety,
    Hygiene, and Environment of April 21, 1997,
    224–225

Law of Industrial Property, 225

Social Security Law, Articles 50 et seq.,
    224

Miscellaneous

Corpus Juris Civilis, 216

OECD Guidelines for Multinational
    Corporations, 590, 604

Soviet Constitution of 1977, 464

Twelve Tablets of Rome, 216

Versailles Treaty, 11, 53

WTO, Singapore Ministerial Declaration, 48,
    49, 90

Myanmar

Penal Code, 78, 80, 81

Towns Act (1907), 76, 77, 79, 80, 82

Village Act (1908), 76, 77, 79, 80, 82

North American Free Trade Agreement

North American Agreement on Labor
    Cooperation (NAALC), 17, 20, 21, 41, 44, 51,
    172, 221, 249, 250, 253, 256, 257, 258, 259, 263,
    270, 272, 273, 274, 275, 590
  Annex 1, 256, 263
  Annex 39, 259
  Article 1, 250, 265
  Article 2, 250
  Article 3, 251, 265, 270
  Article 3(1), 253, 262, 263
  Article 4, 251
  Article 5, 251
  Article 5(1), 270
  Article 5(2)(b), 270
  Article 5(4), 270
  Article 6, 252
  Article 7, 252
  Article 11, 258
  Article 22, 270, 271
  Article 42, 252, 253
  Article 43, 253
  Article 49, 253, 257, 275
  Article 50, 256
North American Free Trade Agreement
    (NAFTA), 15, 17, 20, 44, 175, 210, 214, 215, 221,
    240, 247, 249, 253, 254, 255, 258, 259, 271, 273,
    275, 288, 294

United Kingdom

Births and Deaths Registration Act, 323

Data Protection Act 1998, 325, 392, 393
  § 51, 392
Disability Discrimination Act 1995, 356, 371, 374,
    375
  § 17A(1C), 375, 377
Disability Discrimination Act 1995 (Amendment)
    Regulations 2003, 375

Employment Act 2002, 334, 335, 337, 338, 339,
    358, 369, 370
  § 30, 338
Employment Equality (Age) Regulations of 2006,
    371
Employment Equality (Religion or Belief)
    Regulations 2003, 371, 372
  Reg. 29, 374
Employment Equality (Sex Discrimination)
    Regulations 2005, 371
Employment Equality (Sexual Orientation)
    Regulations 2003, 371
  Reg. 2(1), 371
  Reg. 29, 374

Employment Practices Code, 392, 393
Employment Relations Act 1999, 332, 361
  § 57A, 370
Employment Relations Act 2004, 361, 362, 363
  § 26(3), 362
Employment Rights Act 1996, 338, 339, 340, 352
  § 8, 367
  § 80 F, 370
  § 86, 337
  § 86(1)(a), 340
  § 92, 337, 338
  § 94, 356
  § 97, 340
  § 98, 356, 357
  § 98(1)(b)(2), 357
  § 98(2), 357
  § 98(2)(c), 358
  § 98(4), 355, 357, 358
  § 98(4)(a), 339
  § 98A, 338
  § 98A(2), 339
  § 108, 356
  § 139, 359
  § 155, 359
  § 162, 359
  § 210–219, 336
English Declaration of Rights of 1689, 34
Environmental Information Regulations 2004,
    392
Equal Pay Act 1970, 356, 370, 371, 372
Equal Pay Act (Questions and Replies) Order
    2003, 371
Equality Bill 2005, 372

Fixed-term Employees (Prevention of Less
    Favourable Treatment) Regulations 2002,
    337
Fixed-Term Employees Treatment Regulations
    2002, 371
Flexible Working (Eligibility, Complaints and
    Remedies) Regulations 2002, 370
Flexible Working (Procedural Requirements)
    Regulations 2002, 370
Freedom of Information Act 2000,
    392

Health and Safety at Work Act 1974,
    356
Human Rights Act 2001, 392
  Article 8, 392

Industrial Relations Act 1971, 360
Industrial Tribunals Extension of Jurisdiction
    (England and Wales) Order 1994, Statutory
    Instrument 1994 No. 1623, 334

Information and Consultation of Employees
    (ICE) Regulations 2004, 364, 367

Maternity and Parental Leave (Amendment)
    Regulations 2002, 369
Maternity and Parental Leave Regulations, 369
Matrimonial Causes Act 1973, 323

National Minimum Wage Act 1998, 367
National Minimum Wage Regulations 1999, 367

Part-Time Workers Treatment Regulations 2000,
    371
Paternity and Adoption Leave Regulations 2002,
    369, 370
Privacy and Electronic Communications
    Regulations 2003, 392
Protection from Harassment Act 1997, 351–352

Race Relations Act 1965, 370
Race Relations Act 1968, 370
Race Relations Act 1976, 356, 370, 371, 374, 375,
    380
  § 1(1)(a), 382
  § 4, 380
  § 32(1), 384
  § 54A, 375, 377
  § 65(2)(b), 376
Race Relations Act 1976 (Amendment)
    Regulations 2003, 375

Sex Discrimination Act 1975, 356, 371, 374, 375
  § 1(1)(a), 381–382
  § 1(2)(a), 373
  § 1(2)(b), 373
  § 1(2)(b)(i), 373
  § 1(2)(b)(iii), 373
  § 5(3), 373, 389
  § 41, 377, 390
  § 42, 377, 390
  § 56A(10), 378, 391
  § 63A, 374, 377, 379, 390
  § 63A(2), 390
  § 74(2), 377, 391
  § 74(2)(b), 377, 391
Sex Discrimination Act 1986, 371
Sex Discrimination (Indirect Discrimination and
    Burden of Proof) Regulations 2001, 374

Trade Disputes Act 1906, 362
Trade Union Act of 1984, 363
Trade Union and Labour Relations
    (Consolidation) Act 1992, 361, 363, 364, 367
  § 178, 362
  § 188, 364

§§ 188–189, 364
§ 188(7), 366
§ 189, 365, 366
§ 236, 363
§ 259, 361
Transfer of Undertakings (Protection of
    Employment) Regulations 1981, 359
  § 4, 359
  § 6, 359
Transfer of Undertakings (Protection of
    Employment) Regulations 2006, 359, 366,
    367
  § 14, 366

Work and Families Bill, 370
Working Time Regulations 1998, 356, 367, 368,
    369

United Nations

Convention on the Elimination of All Forms of
    Discrimination Against Women, 247, 470,
    528
Convention on the Rights of the Child, 28
    Article 37, 34, 35

Global Compact, 604

International Convention on the Protection of
    the Rights of All Migrant Workers and
    Members of Their Families, 22–23
International Covenant on Civil and Political
    Rights (ICCPR), 35, 42, 220, 514
International Covenant on Economic, Social and
    Cultural Rights (ICESCR), 42, 514

Sub-commission on the Promotion and
    Protection of Human Rights, Norms on the
    Responsibilities of Transnational
    Corporations and Other Business
    Enterprises with Regard to Human Rights,
    604–605

Universal Declaration of Human Rights, 42, 514,
    611

United States

Age Discrimination in Employment Act of 1967,
    126, 129, 132, 135, 136, 137, 138, 139, 140, 143,
    552, 607
  29 USC § 623(a)(1), 137
  29 USC § 623(f)(1), 139, 140
Alaska Constitution, Article I, § 22, 149, 151, 152
Alien Tort Claims Act, 83, 607, 610, 611, 612, 613,
    614, 615, 616, 617, 618

Alien Tort Statute Reform Act, 2005 S. 1874, 617, 618
Americans with Disabilities Act of 1990, 92, 126, 129, 130, 131, 132, 133, 134, 556, 557, 558, 559, 560, 561, 562, 563, 565, 607
  § 12101, 562
  § 12101(a)(1), 562
  § 12102(2), 131, 560, 562
  § 12102(2)(A), 556, 558, 560, 561
  § 12102(2)(B)-(C), 131, 558
  §§ 12111–12117, 563
  § 12111(2), 559
  § 12111(8), 559, 560
  § 12112(a), 129
  § 12112(b), 133
  § 12112(b)(5)(A), 556, 559
  §§ 12141–12150, 563
  §§ 12161–12165, 563
  §§ 12181–12189, 563
  § 12201(a), 560
Austria–Friendship, Commerce and Consular Rights Treaty, 551

Belgium–Commerce and Navigation Treaty, 550
Bipartisan Trade Promotion Authority Act of 2002 (BTPAA), 275

California Business and Professions Code, 596
California Constitution, Article I, § 1, 151
Canada–United States Free Trade Agreement (CUFTA), 254
Central America–Dominican Republic Free Trade Agreement (CAFTA-DR), 45, 274
  Article 16, 274
  Article 16.2, 274, 275
  Article 16.2(1)(a), 274
  Article 16.2(1)(b), 275
  Article 16.8, 274
China–Commerce Treaty, 550
China–Friendship, Commerce and Navigation Treaty, 550
Civil Rights Act of 1964, Title VII, 92, 95, 124, 125, 126, 127, 129, 138, 139, 140, 143, 144, 145, 146, 147, 196, 199, 206, 370, 455, 544, 545, 552, 553, 554, 555, 556, 565, 607
  § 703(a)(1), 124, 144, 145
Civil Rights Act of 1991, 92, 143
Clayton Anti-Trust Act of 1914, 15 U.S.C. § 17 (2005), 11
Consolidated Omnibus Budget Reconciliation Act (COBRA), 123, 124, 444
Constitution, 216, 217
  Article II, § 2, 35
  Article III, 618

Article IV, 297
Commerce Clause, 10
Eighth Amendment, 33, 34
First Amendment, 606
Fourteenth Amendment, 33
Thirteenth Amendment, 611

Economic Espionage Act of 1996, 479
18 U.S.C. § 1512(b)(2), 106
El Salvador–Friendship, Commerce and Consular Rights Treaty, 551
Employee Free Choice Act, S. 842 & H.R. 1696, 109th Cong., 1st Sess. (Apr. 19, 2005), 117
Employee Polygraph Protection Act, 155
Employee Retirement Income Security Act, 123, 124
Employment Act of 1946, 56
Equal Pay Act of 1963, 370
  29 USC § 206(d)(1), 316
Estonia–Friendship, Commerce and Consular Rights Treaty, 551

Fair Labor Standards Act, 92, 118, 123, 453
Family and Medical Leave Act of 1993, 92, 123, 300, 558, 559
Federal Rules of Civil Procedure
  Rule 12(b)(6), 544
  Rule 56(c), 136
Finland–Friendship, Commerce and Consular Rights Treaty, 551
Foreign Sovereign Immunities Act, 610
42 Fed. Reg. 22676, 22685 (1977), 561
42 USC § 1981, 124, 126, 127, 544
42 USC § 2000e-2(k), 134
42 USC § 2000e-5(f)(1), 544
45 CFR § 84.3(j)(2)(i), 560
45 CFR § 84.3(j)(2)(ii), 561
France–Amity and Commerce Treaty, 550
Full Employment Act of 1945, 55

Generalized System of Preferences (GSP), 43, 44
  19 USC §2462(b)(2)(G), 43
  19 USC §2467(4)(A-E), 44
Germany–Commerce Treaty, 550
Germany–Friendship, Commerce and Consular Rights Treaty, 551
Germany–Friendship, Commerce and Navigation Treaty, 550
  Article VIII(1), 545, 546
Great Britain–Amity, Commerce and Navigation Treaty, 550
Greece–Friendship, Commerce and Navigation Treaty, 550
  Article XII(4), 545, 546

Hawaii Constitution, Article I, § 6, 151
Honduras–Friendship, Commerce and Consular
    Rights Treaty, 551
H.R. Res. 568, 108th Cong., 2nd Sess. (Mar. 17,
    2004), 33
Humphrey–Hawkins Bill of 1976, 56
Hungary–Friendship, Commerce and Consular
    Rights Treaty, 551

Immigration Reform and Control Act of 1986
    (IRCA), 24, 25
  § 1324a(a)(1), 25
  § 1324a(h)(3), 25
  §§ 1324c(a)(1)–(3), 25
Israel–Friendship, Commerce and Navigation
    Treaty, 550
  Article VIII(1), 545
Italy–Commerce and Navigation Treaty, 550
Italy–Friendship, Commerce and Navigation
    Treaty, 550

Japan–Commerce and Navigation Treaty,
    551
  Article VII, 551
Japan–Friendship, Commerce and Navigation
    Treaty, 545, 546, 547, 548, 550, 551,
    553
  Article VII(1), 546, 547
  Article VII(4), 547
  Article VIII(1), 544, 545, 546, 547, 548, 551, 553,
    564
  Article XVI(2), 546, 547
  Article XXII, 546
  Article XXII(1), 549
  Article XXII(2), 549
  Article XXII(3), 546, 547, 551
Jordan–Agreement on the Establishment of a
    Free Trade Area, 273, 274
Judiciary Act of 1789, 614

Kentucky Civil Rights Act, 558, 559
Kentucky Workers' Compensation Act, 557

Labor Management Reporting and Disclosure
    Act, 228
Latvia–Friendship, Commerce and Consular
    Rights Treaty, 551
Liberia–Friendship, Commerce and Navigation
    Treaty, 551

Montana Constitution, Article II, § 10, 151
Montana Wrongful Discharge from
    Employment Act of 1987, Mont. Code Ann.
    §§ 39-2-901 to 39-2-914, 99

National Labor Relations Act, 10, 24, 25, 26, 27,
    28, 92, 93, 110, 113, 114, 115, 116, 117, 118, 171,
    226, 232
  § 2(3), 120
  § 7, 112, 114, 118, 121
  § 8, 120
  § 8(1), 120
  § 8(3), 120
  § 8(a)(1), 111, 112
  § 8(a)(2), 111, 112, 113, 115, 116, 419, 420
  § 8(a)(3), 24, 246, 422
  § 8(a)(3) (29 USC § 158(a)(3)), 24
  § 8(a)(5), 113
  § 8(b)(1)(A), 111, 112
  § 8(d), 182, 240
  § 9(a), 112
  § 10(c), 182
  § 13, 120, 232
Netherlands–Friendship, Commerce and
    Navigation Treaty, 550
Netherlands–Commerce and Navigation Treaty,
    550
19 USC § 3803(b)(2), 275
Norway–Friendship, Commerce and Consular
    Rights Treaty, 551

Occupational Safety and Health Act, 123,
    124
Omnibus Crime Control and Safe Streets Act of
    1968, 155
Omnibus Trade and Competitiveness Act
    (OCRA), 275
110 Cong. Rec. 2578 (1964), 125
110 Cong. Rec. 7213 (1964), 125
110 Cong. Rec. 8912 (1964), 125
110 Cong. Rec. 13088 (1964), 129

Pakistan–Friendship, Commerce and Navigation
    Treaty, 550
Poland–Friendship, Commerce and Consular
    Rights Treaty, 551

Rehabilitation Act of 1973, 560
  29 USC § 706(8)(B), 560
  29 USC § 794, 560
  29 USC §790 et seq., 560

Senate Committee on Foreign Relations,
    International Covenant on Civil and
    Political Rights, S. Exec. Rep. No. 102-23,
    (1992), 35
Siam–Friendship, Commerce and Navigation
    Treaty, 551
Spain–Commerce Treaty, 550

Sweden and Norway–Commerce and Friendship
        Treaty, 550

Trade Act of 2002, Pub. L. No. 107-210, 116 Stat.
        933 (codified in sections of 19 U.S.C.), 275
20 CFR § 639.9(b)(1), 107, 108
20 CFR § 639.9(b)(2), 107
28 USC § 1292(b), 545
29 CFR §§ 1630.2(g)–(j), 560
29 CFR § 1630.2(j), 561
29 CFR §§ 1630.2(j)(2)(i)–(iii), 561
29 CFR §§ 1630.2(j)(2)(ii)–(iii), 562
29 CFR § 1630.2(j)(3), 563

29 USC § 157, 114
2001 HR 2782, 605

Wiretapping Act, 155
Wisconsin Fair Employment Act, 95
Wisconsin Stat. § 346.63, 96
Wisconsin Stat. § 765.001(2), 96
Wisconsin Stat. § 946.10, 98
Wisconsin Stat. § 946.10(1), 98
Worker Adjustment and Retraining Notification
        Act (WARN), 105, 107, 108, 109, 110,
        307
    29 USC § 2102(b)(2)(A), 105, 108

Table of Secondary Authorities

Articles and Papers

Acuff, J.L., Note: The Race to the Bottom: The United States' Influence on Mexican Labor Law Enforcement, 5 San Diego Int'l L. J. 387 (2004), 217

Adams, R.J., Choice or Voice? Rethinking American Labor Policy in Light of the International Human Rights Consensus, 5 Emp. Rts. & Emp. Pol'y J. 521 (2001), 87

Agarwal, R.K., The Barefoot Lawyers: Prosecuting Child Labour in the Supreme Court of India, 21 Ariz. J. Int'l & Comp. Law 663 (2004), 588

Aizawa, M., An International Perspective: A Proposal to Combine Disparate Approaches to the Maternal Wall, 7 Empl. Rts & Employ. Pol'y J. 495 (2003), 528–529

Alexander, R., FAT Obtains First Secret Ballot Election: International Observers Report on Experience, www.ueinternational.org/Mexico_info/mlna_articles.php?id=88, 239

Alston, P., 'Core Labour Standards' and the Transformation of the International Labour Rights Regime, 15 Eur. J. Int'l L. 457 (2004), 44, 90

Anderson, K., The Limits of Pragmatism in American Foreign Policy: Unsolicited Advice to the Bush Administration on Relations with International Non-Governmental Organizations, 2 Chi. J. Int'l L. 371 (2001), 20

Andrias, K.E., Gender, Work, and the NAFTA Labor Side Agreement, 37 U.S.F. L. Rev. 521 (2003), 21

Araki, T., Corporate Governance Reforms, Labor Law Developments, and the Future of Japan's Practice-Dependent Stakeholder Model (2005), http://www.jil.go.jp/english/documents/JLR05_araki.pdf, 506, 527, 536, 537

Archibold, R.C., Immigrants Take to U.S. Streets in Show of Strength, The New York Times, May 2, 2006, 28

Arthurs, H.W., Globalization of the Mind: Canadian Elites and the Restructuring of Legal Fields, 12 Canadian J. Law & Soc'y 219 (1998), 255

Arthurs, H.W., Reinventing Labor Law for the Global Economy: The Benjamin Aaron Lecture, 22 Berkeley J. Emp. & Lab. L. 271 (2001), 11

Atleson, J., The Voyage of the Neptune Jade: The Perils and Promises of Transnational Labor Solidarity, 52 Buff. L. Rev. 85 (2004), 11, 15, 362, 363

Austen, I., Wal-Mart To Close Store In Canada With a Union, N.Y. Times, Feb. 10, 2005, 517

Austin, R., Employer Abuse, Worker Resistance, and the Tort of Intentional Infliction of Emotional Distress, 41 Stan. L. Rev. 1 (1988), 104

Bagenstos, S.R., The Structural Turn and the Limits of Antidiscrimination Law, 94 Cal. L. Rev. 1 (2006), 135

Bai, M., The New Boss, N.Y. Times Magazine, Jan. 30, 2005, 15

Barbaro, M., Maryland Sets a Health Cost for Wal-Mart, N.Y. Times, Jan. 13, 2006, 600

Barboza, D., The New Power Brokers, N.Y. Times, July 19, 2005, 521

Barboza, D., Wal-Mart Bows To Trade Unions At Stores in China, N.Y. Times, Nov. 25, 2004, 517

Barboza, D. & Barbaro M., Judge Gives Wal-Mart Reprieve on Benefits, N.Y. Times, July 20, 599

Barcelo, R., Seeking Suitable Options for Importing Data from the European Union, 36 Int'l Law. 985 (Fall, 2002),

Barnard, C. & Deakin, S., 'Negative' and 'Positive' Harmonization of Labor Law in the

European Union, 8 Colum. J. Eur. L. 389 (2002), 45, 46

Barnard, C., Deakin, S. & Hobbs, R., Opting Out of the 48-Hour Week: Employer Necessity or Individual Choice? An Empirical Study of the Operation of Article 18(1)(B) of the Working Time Directive in the UK, 32 Indus. L.J. 223 (2003), 368

Befort, S.F. & Cornett, V.E., Beyond the Rhetoric of the NAFTA Treaty Debate: A Comparative Analysis of Labor and Employment Law in Mexico and the United States, 17 Comp. Lab. L. 269 (1996), 217

Befort, S.F., The Labor and Employment Law Decisions of the Supreme Court's 2003–04 Term, 20 Lab. Law. 177 (2004), 596–597

Benoit, B. & Milne, R., Germany's Best Kept Secret: How Its Exporters Are Beating the World, Financial Times, May 19, 2006, 395, 397, 398, 401

Berkowitz, D., Pistor, K. & Richard, J.-F., The Transplant Effect, 51 Am.J. Comp. L. 163 (2003), 518

Bernstein, A., Treating Sexual Harassment With Respect, 111 Harv. L. Rev. 446 (1997), 148

Bernstein, N., Invisible to Most, Women Line Up for Day Labor, N.Y. Times, Aug. 15, 2005, 580

Bhagwati, J. & Alvarez, J.E., Afterword: The Question of Linkage, 96 Am. J. Int'l L. 126 (2002), 49

Bird, R.C., Rethinking Wrongful Discharge: A Continuum Approach, 73 U. Cinn. L. Rev. 517 (2004), 100

Bisom-Rapp, S., An Ounce of Prevention is a Poor Substitute for a Pound of Cure: Confronting the Developing Jurisprudence of Education and Prevention in Employment Discrimination Law, 22 Berkeley J. Emp. & Lab. L. 1 (2001), 148

Bisom-Rapp, S., Discerning Form from Substance: Understanding Employer Litigation Prevention Strategies, 3 Employee Rts. & Employment Pol'y J. 1 (1999), 50

Bisom-Rapp, S., Exceeding Our Boundaries: Transnational Employment Law Practice and the Export of American Lawyering Styles to the Global Worksite, 25 Comp. Lab. L. & Pol'y J. 257 (2004), 2, 39, 455

Blackett, A., Global Governance, Legal Pluralism and the Decentered State: A Labor Law Critique of Codes of Corporate Conduct, 8 Ind. J. Global Legal Stud. 401 (2001), 605

Blackett, A., Toward Social Regionalism in the Americas, 23 Comp. Lab. L. & Pol'y J. 901 (2002), 47

Bogg, A.L., Employment Relations Act 2004: Another False Dawn for Collectivism?, 34 Indus. L.J. 72 (2005), 362

Bognanno, M.F., Keane, M.P. & Yang, D., The Influence of Wages and Industrial Relations Environments on the Production Location Decisions of U.S. Multinational Corporations, 58 Indus. & Lab. Rel. Rev. 171 (2005), 10

Bortin, M. & Smith, C.S., Hundreds of Thousands Protest Against Labor Law in France, www.nytimes.com/2006/03/28/intenational/europe/28cnd-france.html, 444

Bowers, J.W. & Lewis, J., Non-Economic Damage in Unfair Dismissal Cases: What's Left After Dunnachie? 34 Indus. L.J. 83 (2005), 354, 355

Bowers, J.W., Section 8(a)(2) and Participative Management: An Argument for Judicial and Legislative Change in a Modern Workplace, 26 Val. L. Rev. 525 (1992), 116

Brandeis, L. & Warren, S., The Right to Privacy, 4 Harv.L.Rev. 193 (1890), 150, 151

Brewster, C.R., Restoring Childhood: Saving the World's Children from Toiling in Textile Sweatshops, 16 J.L. & Com 191 (1997), 29

British Trade Unions, The Economist (June 8, 2006), 360

Broder, J.M., Immigrants and the Economics of Hard Work, N.Y. Times, April 2, 2006, 23, 24

Brodie, D., Protecting Dignity in the Workplace: The Vitality of Mutual Trust and Confidence, 33 Indus. L.J. 349 (2004), 352, 355

Brooke, J., Factory Jobs Move Overseas As Japan's Troubles Deepen, N.Y. Times, Aug. 31, 2001, 527

Browne, M.N., et al, Universal Moral Principles and the Law: The Failure of One-Size-Fits-All Child Labor Laws, 27 Hous. J. Int'l L. 1 (2004), 31

Brudney, J.J., Neutrality Agreements and Card Check Recognition: Prospects for Changing Paradigms, 90 Iowa L. Rev. 819 (2005), 117

Brudney, J.J., Reflections on Group Action and the Law of the Workplace, 74 Tex L. Rev. 1563 (1996), 118

Bruns, M.M., Worker Representation at the Enterprise Level in France, 15 Comp. Lab. L. J. 15 (1993), 449, 453

Cameron, C.D.R., Borderline Decisions: Hoffman Plastic Compounds, The New Bracero Program, and the Supreme Court's Role in Making Federal Labor Policy, 51 UCLA L. Rev. 1 (2003), 27

Campbell, M., A new minister, a dysfunctional work force, The Globe and Mail, March 4, 2004, 88

Cardonsky, L.B., Towards a Meaningful Right to Privacy in the United Kingdom, 20 B.U. Int'l L.J. 393 (2002), 392

Carniero, Carpal Tunnel Syndrome: The Cause Dictates the Treatment, 66 Cleveland Clinic J. Medicine 159 (1999), 562

Carr, M. & Chen, M., Globalization, Social Exclusion and Gender, 143 Int'l Lab. Rev. 129 (2004), 13

Carrington, W.J. and Detragiache, E., How Extensive Is the Brain Drain?, 36 Fin. & Dev. 46 (1999), 520–521

Case, K.L., An Overview of Fifteen Years of United States-Japanese Economic Relations, 16 Ariz. J. Int'l & Comp. L. 11 (1999), 542

Chang, L.T., Company Town: In Chinese Factory, Rhythms of Trade Replace Rural Life, Wall St. J., Dec. 31, 2004, 517

Chen, M.A., Rethinking the Informal Economy, Research Paper No. 2005/10, World Institute for Development Economic Research, U.N. University, p. 6, www.wider.unu.edu/ publications/rps/rps2005/rp2005-10.pdf, 210

Chirac OKs Youth Employment Plan: Charter Tighten Rules on Internships, Daily Lab. Rep. (BNA) No. 81 (Apr. 27, 2006), 434

Cho, S., Linkage of Free Trade and Social Regulation: Moving beyond the Entropic Dilemma, 5 Chi. J. Int'l L. 625 (2005), 49

Choudhry, S., Globalization in Search of Justification: Toward a Theory of Comparative Constitutional Interpretation, 74 Ind. L.J. 819 (1999), 37

Choudhury, B., Beyond the Alien Tort Claims Act: Alternative Approaches to Attributing Liability to Corporations for Extraterritorial Abuses, 26 Nw. J. Int'l L. & Bus. 43 (2005), 604, 605

Chuan Sun, The European Union Privacy Directive and Its Impact on the U.S. Privacy Protection Policy: A Year 2003 Perspective, 2 Nw. J. Tech. & Intell. Prop. 99 (Fall, 2003), 328

Clarke, S., Lee, C.-H. and Qi Li, Collective Consultation and Industrial Relations in China, 42 Brit. J. Indus. Rel. 235 (2004), 517

Cleveland, S.H., Norm Internationalization and U.S. Economic Sanctions, 26 Yale J. Int'l L. 1 (2001), 43

Coles, P., Wanted! Teachers, Education Today Newsletter (UNESCO), January-March 2005, 74

Collingsworth, T., The Key Human Rights Challenge: Developing Enforcement Mechanisms, 15 Harv. Hum. Rts. J. 183 (2002), 615, 618

Collins, E.C., International Employment Law, 39 Int'l Law. 449 (2005), 450

Collins, E.C., Mokros, R.B. & Simmons, J., Labor and Employment Developments From Around the World, 37 Int'l Lawyer 329 (2003), 446, 453

Collins, R.K.L. & Skover, D.M., The Landmark Free-Speech Case That Wasn't: The Nike v. Kasky Story, 54 Case W. Res. L. Rev. 965 (2004), 604, 606

Compa, L.A. and Vogt, J.S., Labor Rights in the Generalized System of Preferences: A 20-Year Review, 22 Comp. Lab. L. & Pol'y J. 199 (2001), 44

Compa, L.A., NAFTA's Labor Side Accord: A Three Year Accounting, 3 NAFTA L. & Bus. Rev. Americas 6 (1997), 250

Compa, L.A., Pursuing International Labour Rights in U.S. Courts: New Uses for Old Tools, 57 Indus. Rel. (Can.) 48 (2002), 591, 598, 607

Compa, L.A., The ILO Core Standard's Declaration: Changing the Climate for Changing the Law, Perspectives on Work, June 2003, 10–11

Cooney, S., A Broader Role for the Commonwealth in Eradicating Foreign Sweatshops?, 28 Melb. U. L. Rev. 290 (2004), 87

Corbett, W.R., The Need for a Revitalized Common Law of the Workplace, 69 Brook. L. Rev. 91 (2003), 39

Córdova, E., Some Reflections on the Overproduction of International Labour Standards, 14 Comp. Lab. L.J. 138 (1993), 60

Correales, R.I., Did Hoffman Plastic Compounds, Inc. Produce Disposable Workers? 14 Berkeley La Raza L.J. 103 (2003), 27

Craig, J.D.R., Privacy in the Workplace and the Impact of European Convention Incorporation on United Kingdom Labour Law, 19 Comp. Lab. L. & Pol'y J. 373 (1998), 392

Crook, J.R., Tentative Settlement of ATCA Human Rights Suits Against Unocal, 99 Am. J. Int'l L. 497 (2005), 617

Cunniah, D., The ICTWU and Its Policies within the ILO Workers' Group, 55 Bull. Comp. Lab. Rel. (2004), 15

Dannin, E.J., Consummating Market-Based Labor Law Reform in New Zealand: Context and Reconfiguration, 14 B.U. Int'l L.J. 267 (1996), 87

D'Avolio, M., Child Labor and Cultural
Relativism: From 19th Century America to 21st
Century Nepal, 16 Pace Int'l L. Rev. 109
(2004), 29

Dassbach, C.H.A., Where is North American
Automobile Production Headed?: Low-Wage
Lean Production, http://www.sociology.org/
content/vol001.001/dassbach.html (1994), 543

DeStefano, Nordstrom, & Uierkant, Long-term
Symptom Outcomes of Carpal Tunnel
Syndrome and its Treatment, 22A J. Hand
Surgery 200 (1997), 562

Dickerson, C.M., Transnational Codes of
Conduct through Dialogue: Leveling the
Playing Field for Developing-Country
Workers, 53 Fla. L. Rev. 611 (2001), 606

Dobbin, F., Do the Social Sciences Shape
Corporate Anti-Discrimination Practice?: The
United States and France, 23 Comp. Lab. L. &
Pol'y J. 829 (2002), 435, 455

Dowling, D.C., Jr., The Multi-National's
Manifesto on Sweatshops, Trade/Labor
Linkage, and Codes of Conduct, 8 Tulsa J.
Comp.& Int'l L. 27 (2000), 590

Dowling, D.C., Jr., The Practice of International
Labor and Employment Law: Escort your
Labor/Employment Clients into the Global
Millennium, 17 Lab. Law 1 (2001), 1, 50

Dube, A. & Jacobs, K., Hidden Cost of Wal-Mart
Jobs: Use of Safety Net Programs by Wal-Mart
Workers in California, University of California,
Berkeley Center for Labor Research and
Education, 2004, 600

Dube, A. & Wertheim, S., Wal-Mart and Job
Quality – What Do We Know, and Should We
Care? (unpublished paper, October 16, 2005),
600

Duruigbo, E., The Economic Cost of Alien Tort
Litigation, 14 Minn. J. Global Trade 1 (2004),
614, 617

Eberle, E.J., Human Dignity, Privacy, and
Personality in German and American
Constitutional Law, 1997 Utah L. Rev. 963, 542

Edelman, L.B. & Suchman, M., When the
"Haves" Hold Court: Speculations on the
Organizational Internalization of Law, 33 Law
& Soc'y Rev. 941 (1999), 50

Ehrenreich, R., Dignity and Discrimination:
Toward a Pluralistic Understanding of the
Workplace, 88 Geo. L.J. 1 (1999), 148

Epstein, R.A., In Defense of the Contract At
Will, 51 U. Chi. L. Rev. 947 (1984), 101

Estlund, C.L., How Wrong Are Employees
About Their Rights, and Why Does It Matter?,
77 N.Y.U.L. Rev. 6 (2002), 102, 105

Estlund, C.L., Rebuilding the Law of the
Workplace in an Era of Self-Regulation, 105
Colum. L. Rev. 319 (2005), 50, 606

Estlund, C.L., The Ossification of American
Labor Law, 102 Colum. L. Rev. 1527 (2002), 27

EU backs free movement principle, BBC News,
May 2, 2006, available at: http://news.bbc.co.
uk/2/hi/europe/4966434.stm, 46

EU Has Strict Curbs on Employee Monitoring
Compared to Weak Rules in the Untied States,
Daily Lab. Rep. (BNA) No. 49 (March 14,
2006), 458

European Commission Justice and Home Affairs,
The Status of Implementation of Directive
95/46, http://ec.europa.eu/justice_home/fsj/
privacy/law/implementation_en.htm, 325

Fahlbeck, R., Comparative Law – Quo Vadis?, 25
Comp. Lab. L. & Pol'y J. 7 (2003), 39

Fairris, D. and Levine, E., Declining Union
Density in Mexico, 1984–2000, Monthly Labor
Review, Sept. 2004, p. 10, 209

Fairris, D., Unions and Wage Inequality in
Mexico, 56 Indus. & Lab. Rel. Rev. 481 (2003),
233

Filartiga, D., American Courts, Global Justice,
The N.Y. Times, March 30, 2004, 614

Final Decision in the Huawei Trade Secrets
Case, A Sensation in the Country's IT World,
http:www.itxian.com/get/index_btxw/rig_btxw/
103712739.htm, Aug. 10, 2005, 479

Finder, S., The Supreme People's Court of the
People's Republic of China, 7 J. Chinese L.
145 (1993), 480

Fisher, B.D. & Lenglart, F., Employee
Reductions in Force: A Comparative Study of
French and U.S. Legal Protections for
Employees Downsized Out of Their Jobs: A
Suggested Alternative to Workforce
Reductions, 26 Loy. L.A. Int'l & Comp. L. Rev.
181 (2003), 443, 444

Fleishman, J., German Businesses Not Immune
to Scandal, Los Angeles Times, August 24,
2005, 422

Foote, D.H., Judicial Creation of Norms in
Japanese Labor Law: Activism in the Service
of – Stability?, 43 UCLA L. Rev. 635 (1996), 533

Forero, J., As China Gallops, Mexico Sees
Factory Jobs Slip Away, N.Y. Times,
September 3, 2003, A3, 219

France Enacts Equal Pay Law, Plans Greater
Maternity Leave Protection, Daily Lab. Rep.
(BNA) No. 39 (Feb. 28, 2006), 456

France Looks to Create New Body to Promote
Workplace Equality, Daily Lab. Rep. (BNA)
No. 196 (Oct. 12, 2004), 456

France Should Consider Union Reforms in Light of Low Membership, Study Says, Daily Lab. Rep. (BNA) No. 87 (May 5, 2006), 450

France's Highest Court Says Firms Can Fire Workers Found Guilty of Sexual Harassment, Daily Lab. Rep. (BNA) No. 57 (Mar. 25, 2002), 441

Freeman, A.D., Legitimizing Racial Discrimination Through Anti-Discrimination Law: A Critical Review of Supreme Court Doctrine, 62 Minn. L. Rev. 1049 (1978), 128

French, H.W., China Luring Foreign Scholars To Make Its Universities Great, N.Y. Times, Oct. 28, 2005, 522

French Appeals Court Finds Employer Is Liable for Employee Internet Activity, Daily Lab. Rep. (BNA) No. 68 (Apr. 10, 2006), 461

French Code of Conduct for Blogs Includes Standards for Employees, Daily Lab. Rep. (BNA) No. 217 (Nov. 10, 2005), 460

French Court Fines GE Subsidiary for Providing English-Only Documents, Daily Lab. Rep. (BNA) No. 45 (Mar. 8, 2006), 437

French Court Invalidates Provision Restricting Employer's Firing of Workers, Daily Lab Rep. (BNA) No. 27 (Feb. 8, 2002), 443

French Data Protection Commission Issues GPS Employee Monitoring Guidelines, Daily Lab. Rep. (BNA) No. 62 (Apr. 1, 2005), 460

French Supreme Court E-Mail Ruling Bars Employers From Reading Personal Files, Daily Lab. Rep. (BNA) No. 193 (Oct. 9, 2001), 440, 441

Friedman, G.S. & Whitman, J.Q., The European Transformation of Harassment Law: Discrimination Versus Dignity, 9 Colum. J. Eur. L. 241 (2003), 542

Gang, I.N., Sen, K. & Myeong-Su Yun, Caste, Ethnicity and Poverty in Rural India (Nov. 2002), available at http://www.ssrn.com, 579

Garcia, R.J., Ghost Workers in an Interconnected World: Going Beyond the Dichotomies of Domestic Immigration and Labor Laws, 36 Univ. of Mich. J. L. Reform 737 (2003), 26–27

Garg, A., Note, A Child Labor Social Clause: Analysis and Proposal for Action, 31 N.Y.U. J. Int'l L. & Pol. 473 (1999), 29

George, B.C., et al., U.S. Multinational Employers: Navigating Through the "Safe Harbor" Principles to Comply with the EU Data Privacy Directive, 38 Am. Bus. L.J. 735 (2001), 328

Gergen, M.P., A Grudging Defense of the Role of the Collateral Torts in Wrongful Termination Litigation, 74 Tex. L. Rev. 1693 (1996), 103

Ginsburg, R.B. & Merritt, D.J., Affirmative Action: An International Human Rights Dialogue, 21 Cardozo L. Rev. 253 (1999), 33

Global Perspectives on Workplace Harassment Law: Proceedings of the 2004 Annual Meeting, Association of American Law Schools Section on Labor Relations and Employment Law, 8 Employee Rts. & Emp. Pol'y J. 151 (2004), 456

Gordon, M.W., Of Aspirations and Operations: The Governance of Multinational Enterprises by Third World Nations, 16 U. Miami Inter-Am. L. Rev. 301 (1984), 221, 222

Gould, W.B. IV, Recognition Laws: The U.S. Experience and Its Relevance to the U.K., 20 Comp. Lab. L. & Pol'y J. 11 (1998), 360

Graubart, J., "Politicizing" a New Breed of "Legalized" Transnational Political Opportunity Structures: Labor Activists Uses of NAFTA's Citizen-Petition Mechanism, 26 Berkeley J. Emp. & Lab. L. 97 (2005), 249, 271, 272

Green, T.K., Work Culture and Discrimination, 93 Cal. L. Rev. 623 (2005), 135

Greenhouse, S. & Barbaro, M., An Ugly Side of Free Trade: Sweatshops in Jordan, N.Y. Times, May 3, 2006, 273

Greenhouse, S., 4 Major Unions Plan To Boycott A.F.L.-CIO Events, N.Y. Times, July 25, 2005, 509–510

Greenhouse, S. Among Janitors, Labor Violations Go With the Job, N.Y. Times, July 13, 2005, 517, 580

Greenhouse, S., Rights Group Condemns Meatpackers On Job Safety, N.Y. Times, Jan. 26, 2005, 580

Greenhouse, S., Splintered, but Unbowed, Unions Claim a Relevancy, N.Y. Times, July 30, 2005, 510

Grossman, J.L., The Culture of Compliance: The Final Triumph of Form Over Substance in Sexual Harassment Law, 26 Harv. Women's L.J. 3 (2003), 148

Guerrero, M.I.S., The Development of Moral Harassment (Or Mobbing) Law in Sweden and France as a Step Towards EU Legislation, 27 B.C. Int'l & Comp. L. Rev. 477 (2004), 457

Gunter, B.G. & van der Hoeven, R., The Social Dimensions of Globalization: A Review of the Literature (ILO working paper No. 24, 2004), www.ilo.org/public/english/bureau/integration/globaliz/publicat.htm, 4

Guzman, A.T., Global Governance and the WTO, 45 Harv. Int'l L.J. 303 (2004), 49

Guzman, A.T., Trade, Labor, Legitimacy, 91 Cal. L. Rev. 885 (2003), 48

Hagen, K.A., Fundamentals of Labor Issues and NAFTA, 27 U.C. Davis L. Rev. 917 (1994), 256

Hakim, D., A U.A.W. Chief Awaits a G.M. Showdown, N.Y. Times, June 23, 2005, 509

Hall, M., Assessing the Information and Consultation of Employees Regulations, 34 Indus. L.J. 103 (2005), 364, 367

Haskovec, J., Student Note, A Beast of Burden? The New EU Burden-Of-Proof Arrangement in Cases of Employment Discrimination Compared to U.S. Law, 14 Transnat'l L. & Contemp. Probs. 1069 (2005), 391

Hayashi, H., Sexual Harassment in the Workplace and Equal Employment Legislation, 69 St. John's L. Rev. 37 (1995), 541, 542

Hayter, S., The Social Dimension of Globalization: Striking the Balance, 55 Bull. Comp. Lab. Rel. 1 (2004), 7–8

Hiatt, J.P., Policy Issues Concerning the Contingent Workforce, 52 Wash. & Lee L. Rev. 739 (1995), 13

Hindman, H.D., Global Child Labor: What We Know, What We Need to Know, in Proceedings, 53rd Annual Meeting of the Industrial Relations Research Ass'n (2001), 31

Ho, L., Catherine Powell & Leti Volpp, (Dis)Assembling Rights of Women Workers Along the Global Assembly Line: Human Rights and the Garment Industry, 31 Harv. C.R.-C.L. L. Rev. 383 (1996), 16

Hoagland, J., Protests Demonstrate Need to Deal With Pressures of Globalization (syndicated column Apr. 3, 2006), 446

Hornung-Draus, R., "Between e-economy, Euro and enlargement. Where are employer organisations in Europe heading?", June 2001, www.iira2001.org, 287

Howse, R., Back to Court After Shrimp/Turtle? Almost but not Quite Yet: India's Short Lived Challenge to Labor and Environmental Exceptions in the European Union's Generalized System of Preferences, 18 Am. U. Int'l L. Rev. 1333 (2003), 517

Huang Yasheng & Khanna, T., Can India overtake China's economic development?, For. Pol'y (July 1, 2003), 518, 519, 575

Hyde, A., Sheed, F. & Uva, M.D., After Smyrna: Rights and Powers of Unions That Represent Less Than a Majority, 45 Rutgers L. Rev. 637 (1993), 115

Hymowitz, C., Chinese Women Bosses Say Long Hours Don't Hurt Their Kids, http://www.careerjournal.com, May 18, 2005, 471, 529

ILAB Head Questioned over Bureau's Future under Proposed Deep Cuts in New Budget, BNA Workplace Law Report, April 8, 2005, 69

India Steps Back On Privatization of 13 Companies, Wall St. J., Aug. 17, 2005, 575

International Labor Rights Fund Press Release, Human Rights Watchdog and Civil Rights Firm Sue Nestle, ADM, Cargill, for Using Forced Child Labor, July 14, 2005, available at http://www.laborrights.org/press/ChildLabor/cocoa/cocoa_pressrel_071405.htm, 615

Iwata, E., How Barbie is making business a little better, USA Today, Mar. 27, 2006, 591

Jackson, V.C., Narratives of Federalism: Of Continuities and Comparative Constitutional Experience, 51 Duke L.J. 223 (2001), 36

Jackson, V.C., The Court Has Learned from the Rest of the World Before, Legal Affairs, July/Aug 2004, available at http://www.legalaffairs.org/issues/July-August-2004/feature_jackson_julaug04.html, 33

Jarsulic, M., Protecting Workers from Wrongful Discharge: Montana's Experience With Tort and Statutory Regimes, 3 Employee Rts. & Emp. Pol'y J. 105 (1999), 100

Jeffery, M., The Free Movement of Persons within the European Union: Moving from Employment Rights to Fundamental Rights?, 23 Comp. Lab. L. & Pol'y J. 211 (2001), 45

Jiang Jingjing, Wal-Mart's China inventory to hit US 18b this year, China Daily, November, 29 2004, 600

Josephs, H.K., Labor Law in a "Socialist Market Economy": The Case of China, 33 Colum. J. Transnat'l L. 559 (1995), 481

Josephs, H.K., Legal Institutions and Their "Proper" Place in Economic Development: India and China Compared (Dec. 27, 2004; revision of paper presented at the Center for the Advanced Study of India, The University of Pennsylvania, June 13–14, 2004), 573

Josephs, H.K., The Multinational Corporation, Integrated International Production, and the United States Antidumping Laws, 5 Tul. J. Int'l & Comp. L. 51 (1997), 542

Josephs, H.K., The Upright and the Low-Down: An Examination of Official Corruption in the United States and the People's Republic of

China, 27 Syracuse J. Int'l L. & Com. 269 (2000), 469

Josephs, H.K., Upstairs, Trade Law; Downstairs, Labor Law, 33 Geo. Wash. Int'l L. Rev. 849 (2001), 4, 517

Joyce, A., Calif. Jury Backs Wal-Mart Workers, Washington Post, Dec. 23, 2005, 603

Kahn-Freund, O., On Uses and Misuses of Comparative Law, 37 Mod. L. Rev. 1 (1974), 37

Chan, Kam Wing & Li Zhang, The Hukou System and Rural-Urban Migration in China: Processes and Changes, 160 China Q. 818 (1999), 472

Keller, P., Legislation in the People's Republic of China, 23 U.B.C. L. Rev. 653 (1989), 480

Keller, P., Sources of Order in Chinese Law, 42 Am. J. Comp. L. 711 (1994), 480

Khan, J., Chinese Girls' Toil Bring Pain, Not Riches, N.Y. Times, Oct. 2, 2003, 479

Killion, M.U., Post-WTO China: Quest for Human Right Safeguards in Sexual Harassment Against Working Women, 12 Tul. J. Int'l & Comp. L. 201 (2004), 471

Kilpatrick, C., Has New Labour Reconfigured Employment Legislation?, 32 Indus. L.J. 135 (2003), 333

Kochan, D.J., No Longer Little Known But Now a Door Ajar: An Overview of the Evolving and Dangerous Role of the Alien Tort Statute in Human Rights and International Law Jurisprudence, 8 Chap. L. Rev. 103 (2005), 618

Kolben, K., The New Politics of Linkage: India's Opposition to the Workers' Rights Clause, 13 Ind. J. Global Legal Stud. 1 (2006), 517, 576

Kovács, E., The Right to Strike in the European Social Charter, 26 Comp. Lab. L. & Pol'y J. 445 (2005), 362

Krawiec, K.D., Cosmetic Compliance and the Failure of Negotiated Governance, 81 Wash. U. L.Q 487 (2003), 148

Krieger, L.H., Civil Rights Perestroika: Intergroup Relations After Affirmative Action, 86 Cal. L. Rev. 1251 (1998), 128

Krieger, L.H., The Burdens of Equality: Burdens of Proof and Presumptions in Indian and American Civil Rights Law, 47 Am. J. Comp. L. 89 (1999), 579

Krieger, L.H., The Content of Our Categories: A Cognitive Bias Approach to Discrimination and Equal Employment Opportunity, 47 Stan. L. Rev. 1161 (1995), 134

Krueger, A.B., Economic Scene, N.Y. Times, Dec. 11, 2003, 519

Kumar, C.R., Corruption and Human Rights: Promoting Transparency in Governance and the Fundamental Right to Corrupt-Free Service in India, 17 Colum. J. Asian L. 31 (2003), 566

Kuziemko, I. & Rapp, G., India's Wayward Children: Do Affirmative Action Laws Designed to Compensate India's Historically Disadvantaged Castes Explain Low Foreign Direct Investment by the Indian Diaspora?, 10 Minn. J. Global Trade 323 (2001), 576

LaBotz, D. & Alexander, R., The Escalating Struggles Over Mexico's Labor Law, www. nacla.org/art_display_printable.php?art=2566, 216

Landler, M., Rumblings of a German Revival, N.Y. Times, January 17, 2006, 395

Langille, B.A., Core Labour Rights – The True Story (Reply to Alston), 16 Eur. J. Int'l L. 407 (2005), 64, 90, 91

Langille, B.A., Eight Ways to Think About International Labour Standards, 31 J. World Trade 27 (1997), 10

Larkin, J., India's Talent Pool Drying Up, Wall St. J., Jan. 4, 2006, 575

Larsen, J.L., Importing Constitutional Norms from a "Wider Civilization": Lawrence and the Rehnquist Court's Use of Foreign and International Law in Domestic Constitutional Interpretation, 65 Ohio St. L.J. 1283 (2004), 36

Lawrence, C.R. III, The Id, the Ego, and Equal Protection: Reckoning with Unconscious Racism, 39 Stan. L. Rev. 317 (1987), 134

Lee, S., British Tribunal Weighs Reporter's Case, seattlepi.nwsource.com/tv/1401AP_Britain_Reporter_ABC.html, 358

Lee, T.R., Global Employment Claims: Emerging International Labor and Employment Issues, 730 PLI/Lit 681 (2005), 605

Leiman, L., Should the Brain Drain Be Plugged? A Behavioral Economics Approach, 39 Tex. Int'l L. J. 675 (2004), 520, 522

Lester, G., Careers and Contingency, 51 Stan. L. Rev. 73 (1998), 12, 13

Lewis, K.R., Well-paid U.S. workers struggle to compete on a global scale, The Post-Standard, July 24, 2005, 522

Li, K., How to Protect Trade Secrets, China Bus. Rev., May 1, 2005, 479

Lifsher, M., Unocal Settles Human rights Lawsuit Over Alleged Abuses at Myanmar Pipeline, Los Angeles Times, March 22, 2005, 83

Lin, C.X., A Quiet Revolution: An Overview of China's Judicial Reform, 4 Asian-Pacific L. & Pol'y J. 180 (2003), 469

Liu, Yuzhen, Gender Patterns and Women's Experience in the IT Industry in China, 5 Perspectives 20 (2004), http:www.oycf.org/Perspectives/26_0930004/Sep04_Issue.pdf, 471, 528

Lobel, O., The Renew Deal: The Fall of Regulation and the Rise of Governance in Contemporary Legal Thought, 89 Minn. L. Rev. 342 (2004), 135

Long, A.B., "If the Train Should Jump the Track . . .": Divergent Interpretations of State and Federal Employment Discrimination Statutes, 40 Ga. L. Rev. 469 (2006), 127

Luce, E. & Merchant, K., From India's forgotten fields, a call for economic reform to lift the poor, Financial Times (London), May 18, 2004, 569

Lyall, S., Britain to Restrict Workers From Bulgaria and Romania, N.Y. Times, Oct. 25, 2006,

Lyon, B., When More "Security" Equals Less Workplace Safety: Reconsidering U.S. Laws that Disadvantage Unauthorized Workers, 6 U. Pa. J. Lab. & Emp. L. 571 (2004), 23

Machin, S. & Wood, S., Human Resource Management as a Substitute for Trade Unions in British Workplaces, Indus. & Lab. Rel. Rev. 201 (2005), 360

Mackenzie, J., German Strikes Put Merkel's Coalition Under Strain, Reuters, March 13, 2006, 394–395

Macklem, P., Labour Law Beyond Borders, 5 J. Int'l Econ. L. 605 (2002), 8

Madrick, J., Economic Scene, N.Y. Times, Mar. 18, 2004, 523

Madrick, J., Wal-Mart may be the new model of productivity, but it isn't always wowing workers, N.Y. Times, September 2, 2004, 12

Malkin, E., Fox's Party Is Said to Trail In a Key State, N.Y. Times, July 4, 2005, 212

Manjoo, F., United's ESOP Fable: Did Employee Stock Ownership Drive the Airline into Bankruptcy?, http://dir.salon.com/story/tech/feature/2002/12/12/esop/index2.html, 422

Manley, T.J. & Lauredo, L., International Labor Standards in Free Trade Agreements of the Americas, 18 Emory Int'l L. Rev. 85 (2004), 273, 275

Maurer-Fazio, M., Rawski, T.G. and Wei Zhang, Inequality In the Rewards for Holding Up Half the Sky: Gender Wage Gaps in China's Urban Labour Market, 1988–94, 41 China J. 55 (1999), 471

McGinley, A.C.,! Viva la evolucion!: Recognizing Unconscious Motive in Title VII, 9 Cornell J. L. & Pub. Pol'y 446 (2000), 134–135

McGuinness, M.J., The Politics of Labor Regulation in North America: A Reconsideration of Labor Law Enforcement in Mexico, 21 U. Pa. J. Int'l Econ. L. 1 (2000), 225

Medina, M.I., In Search of Quality Childcare: Closing the Immigration Gate to Childcare Workers, 8 Geo. Immigr. L. J. 161 (1994), 17

Merchant, T.D., Note, Recognizing ILO Rights to Organize and Bargain Collectively: Grease in China's Transition to a Socialist Market Economy, 36 Case W. Res. J. Int'l L. 223 (2004), 510

Mexican Labor News & Analysis, No. 5, May, 2005, www.ueinternational.org/Mexico_info/mla_articles.php?id=87, 221

Michigan Law Battling Identity Theft Shields Social Security Numbers in the Workplace, Daily L. Rep. (BNA) No. 129 (July 7, 2005), 155

Milberg, W., The Changing Structure of International Trade Linked to Global Production Systems: What are the Policy Implications? (ILO working paper No. 33, 2004), www.ilo.org/public/english/bureau/integration/globaliz/publicat.htm, 4

Miller, R.L., The Quiet Revolution: Japanese Women Working Around the Law, 26 Harvard Women's L.J. 163 (2003), 528, 537

Moldof, S.B., The Application of U.S. Labor Laws to Activities and Employees Outside the United States, 17 Lab. Law. 417 (2002), 590

Morris, C.J., A Tale of Two Statutes: Discrimination for Union Activity under the NLRA and RLA, 2 Employee Rts. & Employment Pol'y J. 317 (1998), 115

Morriss, A.P., Exploding Myths: An Empirical and Economic Reassessment of the Rise of Employment At-Will, 59 Mo. L. Rev. 679 (1994), 100

Muchlinski, P.T., Globalisation and Legal Research, 37 Int'l Law. 221 (2003), 3

Nagel, J., Mexico's President Fox Signs New Anti-Discrimination Law, 112 Daily Lab. Rep. (BNA)(June 11, 2003), 248

Naturally gifted, The Economist, May 20, 2006, 569

Navia, P. & Rios-Figueroa, J., The Constitutional Mosaic of Latin America, 38 Comparative Political Studies 189 (2005), 241

Neumark, D., Junfu Zhang & Ciccarella, S., The Effects of Wal-Mart on Local Labor Markets (unpublished paper, November 2005), 601

Norris, F., In France, An Economic Bullet Goes Unbitten, www.nytimes.com/2006/04/11/business/worldbusiness/11euro.html, 444, 445

Note, Subsidiary Assertion of Foreign Parent Corporation Rights Under Commercial Treaties to Hire Employees "Of Their Choice," 86 Colum. L. Rev. 139 (1986), 554

Number of Strikes Dip to Record Low in United Kingdom, Statistics Office Says, Daily Lab. Rep. (BNA) No. 107 (June 4, 2004), 363

Ontiveros, M.L., A Vision of Global Capitalism that Puts Women and People of Color at the Center, 3 J. Small & Emerging Bus. L. 27 (1999), 17

Ouellette, Nerve Compression Syndromes of the Upper Extremity in Women, 17 Journal of Musculoskeletal Medicine 536 (2000), 562

Overdorf, J., Commies vs. Capitalists, Newsweek, Nov. 22, 2004, 577

Pape, E. & Dickey, C., Rising Barriers, Newsweek, Int'l ed., March 25, 2006, 434

Pearce, G. & Platten, N. Orchestrating Transatlantic Approaches to Personal Data Protection: A European Perspective, 22 Fordham Int'l L.J 2024 (1999), 325, 328, 329, 330

Peel, Q., Europe's guaranteed gridlock, Financial Times, July 9, 2001, 286

Peerenboom, R., Out of the Pan and Into the Fire: Well-Intentioned But Misguided Recommendations to Eliminate All Forms of Administrative Detention in China, 98 Nw. U. L. Rev. 991 (2004), 469–470

Pencavel, J., The Appropriate Design of Collective Bargaining Systems: Learning from the Experience of Britain, Australia, and New Zealand, 20 Comp. Lab. L. & Pol'y J. 447 (1999), 360

Peters, N., The United Kingdom Recalibrates the U.S. National Labor Relations Act: Possible Lessons for the United States?, 25 Comp. Lab. L. & Pol'y J. 227 (2004), 361, 363, 364

Phan, P.N., Enriching the Land or the Political Elite? Lessons from China on Democratization of the Urban Renewal Process, 14 Pac. Rim L. & Pol'y 607 (2005), 519

Polivka, A.E., Contingent and Alternative Work Arrangements, Defined, 119 Monthly Lab. Rev. 3 (Oct. 1996), 12

Posner, R., The Court Should Never View a Foreign Legal Decision as a Precedent in Any Way, Legal Affairs, July/Aug 2004, available at http://www.legalaffairs.org/issues/July-August-2004/feature_posner_julaug04.html, 37

Postrel, V., Economic Scene: Research Changes Ideas About Children and Work, N.Y. Times, July 14, 2005, 567

Press, E., Human Rights – The Next Step, The Nation, Dec. 25, 2000, 42

Preston, J., Rules Collide with Reality in the Immigration Debate, www.nytimes.com/2006/05/29/us/29broken.html.4, 208, 209

Prime Minister Blair Announces Hike in United Kingdom's Minimum Wage, Daily Lab. Rep. (BNA) No. 41 (March 3, 2005), 367

Prior, E.J., Constitutional Fairness or Fraud on the Constitution? Compensatory Discrimination in India, 28 Case W. Res. J. Int'l L. 63 (1996), 579, 580

Prosser, Privacy, 48 Calif.L.Rev. 383 (1960), 151

Qin, J.Y., "WTO-Plus" Obligations and Their Implications for the World Trade Organization Legal System, 37 J. World Trade 483 (2003), 472, 477

Qin, J.Y., WTO Regulation of Subsidies to State-Owned Enterprises (SOEs): A Critical Appraisal of the China Accession Protocol, 7 J. Int'l Econ. L. 863 (2004), 478

Quayle, D., Perspective: United States International Competitiveness and Trade Policies for the 1980s, 5 Nw. J. Int'l L. & Bus. 1, 10 (1983), 542

Rai, S., India Abandons Plan to Sell Stakes in State-Owned Companies, N.Y. Times, Aug. 17, 2005, 575

Rai, S., Outsourcers Struggling to Keep Workers in the Fold, N.Y. Times, Nov. 12, 2005, 575

Raja, A.V. & Xavier, F. Economic Efficiency of Public Interest Litigation (PIL): Lessons from India (conference paper, 2005), available at http://www.ssrn.com, 588

The Real Great Leap Forward, The Economist, Oct. 2, 2004, 472

Reber, E.A.S., Buraku Mondai in Japan: Historical and Modern Perspectives and Directions for the Future, 12 Harv. Hum. Rts. J. 297 (1999), 525

Rehder, J. & Collins, E.C., The Legal Transfer of Employment Related Data to Outside the European Union, 39 Int'l Law. 129 (Spring, 2005), 327, 328, 329, 330

Returnee: What is Your Foreign Diploma Worth?, http://www.people.com.cn, Feb. 5, 2005, 522

Ritualo, A.R., Castro, C.L. & Gormly, S.,
Measuring Child Labor: Implications for
Policy and Program Design, 24 Comp. Lab. L.
& Pol'y J. 401 (2003), 28

Rivchin, Y., Building Power Among Low-Wage
Immigrant Workers: Some Legal
Considerations for Organizing Structures and
Strategies, 28 N.Y. U. Rev. L. & Soc. Change
397 (2004), 28

Rohter, L. & Bumiller, E., Protesters Riot as Bush
Attends 34-Nation Talks, N.Y. Times, Nov. 5,
2005, 275

Rosencranz, A. & Louk, D., Doe v. Unocal:
Holding Corporations Liable for Human
Rights Abuses on Their Watch, 8 Chap. L.
Rev. 135 (2005), 615–616, 617

Rothstein, L.E., Privacy or Dignity?: Electronic
Monitoring in the Workplace, 19 N.Y.L. Sch. J.
Int'l & Comp. L. 379 (2000), 458

Royle, T., Worker Representation Under Threat?
The McDonald's Corporation and the
Effectiveness of Statutory Works Councils in
Seven European Countries, 22 Comparative
Lab. L. & Pol'y J. 395 (2001), 453

Russell, J.B., Implied Contracts and Creating a
Corporate Tort, One Way State and Local
Governments Are Starting to Fight Plant
Closings, 90 W. Va. L. Rev. 1249 (1988), 110

Saguy, A.C., Employment Discrimination or
Sexual Violence? Defining Sexual Harassment
in American and French Law, 34 Law & Soc'y
Rev. 1091 (2000), 456

Santoni, G.J., The Employment Act of 1946:
Some History Notes, Federal Reserve Bank of
St. Louis, Nov. 1986, available at:
http://research.stlouisfed.org/publications/
review/86/11/Employment_Nov1986.pdf, 56

Saxenian, A., Bangalore: The Silicon Valley of
Asia?, http://www.sims.berkeley.edu/anno/
papers/bangalore_svasia.htm, 575

Scalia, E., Ending Our Anti-Union Federal
Employment Policy, 24 Harv. J.L. Pub. Polc'y
489 (2001), 93

Schlossberg, S.I., United States' Participation in
the ILO: Redefining the Role, 11 Comp. Lab.
L.J. 48 (1989), 57

Schultz, V., The Sanitized Workplace, 112 Yale
L.J. 2061 (2003), 148

Schurer, W., India, China, and North Korea: A
New Understanding, 29 Fletcher F. World Aff.
145 (2005), 569

Schurtman, M., Los "Jonkeados" and the
NAALC: The Autotrim/Customtrim Case and
its Implications for Submissions Under the

NAFTA Labor Side Agreement, 22 Ariz. J. Int'l
& Comp. L. 291 (2005), 258, 272

Schwab, S.J., Life-Cycle Justice: Accommodating
Just Cause and Employment At Will, 92 Mich.
L. Rev. 8 (1993), 527

Schwartz, J.M., Democracy Against the Free
Market: The Enron Crisis and the Politics of
Global Deregulation, 35 Conn. L. Rev. 1097
(2003), 433, 445

Sciolino, Elaine, Chirac Will Rescind Labor
Law That Caused Wide French Riots,
www.nytimes.com/2006/04/11/world/europe/
11france.html, 445

Seifert, A. & Funken-Hötzel, E., Wrongful
Dismissals in the Federal Republic of
Germany, 25 Comp. Lab. L. & Pol'y J. 487
(2004), 400

Selbmann, F., The Drafting of a Law against
Discrimination on the Grounds of Racial or
Ethnic Origin in Germany, European
Centre for Minority Issues, Issue 3/2002,
423–424

Shamir, R., Between Self-Regulation and the
Alien Tort Claims Act: On the Contested
Concept of Corporate Social Responsibility, 38
Law & Soc'y Rev. 635 (2004), 618

Sidhu, R., Child Laborers: The World's Potential
Future Labor Resource Exploited and
Depleted, 15 Hastings Women's L.J. 111 (2004),
32

Slaughter, A.-M. & Bosco, D.L., Alternative
Justice: Facilitated by Little-Known 18th-
Century Law, Tribunals, May 2001, available at
http://crimesofwar.org/tribun-mag/mag_relate_
alternative.html, 615

Smith, A.M., Making Itself at Home:
Understanding Foreign Law in Domestic
Jurisprudence: The Indian Case (2005), 24
Berkeley J. Int'l L. 218 (2006), 589

Smith, C.S., Four Ways to Fire a Frenchman,
www.nytimes.com/2006/03/26/weekinreview/
26smith.html, 443, 445

Smith, J.F., Confronting Differences in the
United States and Mexican Legal Systems in
the Era of NAFTA, 1 U.S.-Mex. L.J. 85 (1993),
211, 212, 216, 217, 218, 241

Smith, L. & Mattar, M., Creating International
Consensus on Combating Trafficking in
Persons: U.S. Policy, The Role of the UN, and
Global Responses and Challenges, 28-WTR
Fletcher F. World Aff. 155 (2004), 29

Smith, P.R., Contingent Workers: Lesson 5, 5
Emp. Rts. & Emp. Pol'y J. 661 (2001), 12

Smith, P.R., Organizing the Unorganizable:
Private Paid Household Workers and

Approaches to Employee Representation, 79 N.C. L. Rev. 45 (2000), 28

Solberg, S.G., After Immigration Protests, Goal is Still Elusive, The New York Times, May 3, 2006, 28

Sono, K. & Fujioka, Y., The Role of the Abuse of Right Doctrine in Japan, 35 La. L. Rev. 1037 (1975), 533

Sridharan, P., Representations of Disadvantage: Evolving Definitions of Disadvantage in India's Reservation Policy and United States' Affirmative Action Policy, 6 Asian L.J. 99 (1999), 580

Stern, N.S., The Challenge of Parental Leave Reforms for French and American Women: A Call for a Revised Feminist-Socialist Theory, 28 Vt. L. Rev. 321 (2004), 455

Sternlight, J.R., In Search of the Best Procedure for Enforcing Employment Discrimination Laws: A Comparative Analysis, 78 Tul. L. Rev. 1401 (2004), 39

Stiglitz, J.E., The Broken Promise of NAFTA, The New York Times, January 6, 2004, 254

Stinnett, N., Note: Defining Away Religious Freedom in Europe: How Four Democracies Get Away With Discriminating Against Minority Religions, 28 B.C. Int'l & Comp. L. Rev. 429 (2005), 457

Stone, K.V.W., The New Psychological Contract: Implications of the Changing Workplace for Labor and Employment Law, 48 UCLA L. Rev. 519 (2001), 1

Stone, K.V.W., To the Yukon and Beyond: Local Laborers in a Global Labor Market, 3 J. Small & Emerging Bus. L. 93 (1999), 8, 249, 250

Struck, D., Canada Looks for Spot in the Big Picture, The Washington Post, Dec. 29, 2004, 255

Students, Unions Stage Protests Over France's New Labor Law Contracts, Daily Lab. Rep. (BNA) No. 53 (March 20, 2006), 434, 444

Sturm, S., Second Generation Employment Discrimination: A Structural Approach, 101 Colum. L. Rev. 458 (2001), 135

Suda, Y., Monitoring E-Mail of Employees in the Private Sector: A Comparison Between Western Europe and the United States, 4 Wash. U. Global Stud. L. Rev. 209 (2005), 458, 460

Sugeno, K., The Birth of the Labor Tribunal System in Japan: A Synthesis of Labor Law Reform and Judicial Reform, 25 Comp. Lab. L. & Pol'y J. 519 (2004), 536, 540

Suh, R.W.-P. & Bales, R., German and European Employment Discrimination Policy, 9 Oregon Rev. of Int'l L. (forthcoming), 423, 424, 428

Summers, C.W., A Summary Evaluation of the Taft-Hartley Act, 11 Indus. & Lab. Rel. Rev. 405 (1958), 226

Summers, C.W., Comparative Labor Law in America: Its Foibles, Functions, and Future, 25 Comp. Lab. L. & Pol'y J. 115 (2003), 38

Summers, C.W., The Battle in Seattle: Free Trade, Labor Rights, and Societal Values, 22 U. Pa. J. Int'l Econ. L. 61 (2001), 48, 91

Summers, C.W., Unions Without Majority-A Black Hole, 66 Chi-Kent L. Rev. 531 (1990), 115

Symposium, Backlash Against the ADA: Interdisciplinary Perspectives and Implications for Social Justice Strategies, 21 Berkeley J. Emp. & Lab. L. 1 (2000), 134

Symposium on Workplace Bullying, 8 Employee Rights & Employment Pol'y J. 235 (2004), 105

Tanaka, H., Equal Employment in Contemporary Japan: A Structural Approach to Equal Employment and the Equal Employment Opportunity Law, PS: Political Science & Politics, eSymposium (Jan. 2004), 529

Tanner, R., Trapped in the Debt Zone, The Post-Standard, Sept. 4, 2005, 523

Taylor, W.C., These Workers Act Like Owners (Because They Are), www.nytimes.com/2006/05/21/business/yourmoney/21mgmt.html, 421–422

Ten Years of NAFTA: Free Trade on Trial, The Economist, Dec. 30, 2003, available at http://www.economist.com, 255

Tezuka, K., Issue of Foreign Labor in Japan, Sept. 27, 2004, http://www.fpcj.jp/e/mres/briefingreport/bfr_11.html, 525

The Tiger in Ffront: A Survey of India and China, The Economist, March 5, 2005, 569

Gong,Ting, Corruption and reform in China: An analysis of unintended consequences, 19 Crime, L. & Soc. Change 311 (1993), 470

Trebilcock, M.J. & Howse, R., Trade Policy and Labor Standards, 14 Minn. J. Global Trade 261 (2005), 257, 274–275, 605

Triplett, M.R., SOX Compliance, Corporate Codes of Conduct Create Challenges for Advising Firms Abroad, Daily Labor Report, Mar. 20, 2006, 605

Trnavci, G., The Meaning and Scope of the Law of Nations in the Context of the Alien Tort Claims Act and International Law, 26 U. Pa. J. Int'l Econ. L. 193 (2005), 614

Trubek, D.M., Mosher, J. & Rothstein, J.S., Transnationalism in the Regulation of Employment Relations: International Regimes and Transnational Advocacy Networks, 25 Law & Soc. Inquiry 1187 (2000), 11

Tucker, E., "Great Expectations" Defeated?: The Trajectory of Collective Bargaining Regimes in Canada and the United States Post-NAFTA, 26 Comp. Labor Law & Pol'y J 97 (2004), 157, 159, 172, 173, 175, 183

Tushnet, M., The Possibilities of Comparative Constitutional Law, 108 Yale L.J. 1225 (1999), 36–37

Ubber, T., Agenda 2010: Reform of German Labour Law: Impact on Hiring and Firing Staff, 5 German L.J. No.2 (Feb. 2004), 395, 399, 400

UK Retains Right to Working Time Opt-Out, http://www.workplacelaw.net/display.php?resource_id=7149, 368

UK Union Objects to Wearbale Devices, Says Technology Is Used to Track Workers, Daily Lab. Rep. (BNA) No. 115 (June 16, 2005), 393

United Kingdom Proposes Regulations to Implement EU Age Discrimination Directive, Daily Lab. Rep. (BNA) No. 48 (Mar. 13, 2006), 371

United States Receives Low Marks in Global Economic Security Survey, Daily Lab. Rep. (BNA) No. 171 (Sept. 3, 2004), 333

Unrest Flares as Students Press Villepin to Rescind Jobs Legislation, Int'l Herald Tribune, March 14, 2006, 434

Vargas, J.A., Privacy Rights under Mexican Law: Emergence and Legal Configuration of a Panoply of New Rights, 27 Hous. J. Int'l L. 73 (2004), 248

Vigneau, C., Labor Law Between Changes and Continuity, 25 Comp. Lab. L. & Pol'y J. 129 (2003), 432, 433, 434, 446, 451, 461

Visser, J., Union Membership in 24 Countries, 129 Monthly Lab. Rev. 38 (Jan. 2006), 360

Wagatsuma, H. & Rosett, A., The Implications of Apology: Law and Culture in Japan and the United States, 20 Law & Soc'y Rev. 461 (1986), 534

Walker, H., Jr., Modern Treaties of Friendship, Commerce and Navigation, 42 Minn. L. Rev. 805 (1958), 550

Walker, H., Jr., Provisions on Companies in United States Commercial Treaties, 50 Am. J. Int'l L. 373 (1956), 546, 547, 550

Walker, H., Jr., Treaties for the Encouragement and Protection of Foreign Investment: Present United States Practice, 50 Am. J. Comp. L. 229 (1956), 546

Walsh, T.J., Hoffman Plastic Compounds, Inc. v. N.L.R.B.: How the Supreme Court Eroded Labor Law and Workers Rights in the Name of Immigration Policy, 21 Law & Ineq. 313 (2003), 27

Weiss, M., The Future of Comparative Labor Law as an Academic Discipline and as a Practical Tool, 25 Comp. Lab. L. & Pol'y J. 169 (2003), 39

Weiss, M., The Interface Between Constitution and Labor Law in Germany, 26 Comp. Labor & Pol'y J. 181 (2005), 396, 406, 409, 430, 431

Weiss, M.S., Two Steps Forward, One Step Back – or Vice Versa: Labor Rights Under Free Trade Agreements from NAFTA, Through Jordan, Via Chile, to Latin America, and Beyond, 37 U.S.F. L. Rev. 689 (2003), 44, 249, 253, 257, 258, 259, 273, 275

Weldon, K., Note, Piercing the Silence or Lulling You to Sleep: The Sounds of Child Labor, 7-SPG Widener L. Symp. J. 227 (2001), 31

West, M.S., Preventing Sexual Harassment: The Federal Courts' Wake-Up Call for Women, 68 Brook. L. Rev. 457 (2002), 148

Whitman, J.Q., Enforcing Civility and Respect: Three Societies, 109 Yale L.J. 1279 (2000), 105, 542

Willborn, S.L., Onward and Upward: The Next Twenty-Five Years of Comparative Labor Law Scholarship, 25 Comp. Lab. L. & Pol'y J. 183 (2003), 52

Williams, N., Pre-Hire Pregnancy Screening in Mexico's Maquiladoras: Is it Discrimination, 12 Duke J. of Gender L. & Pol'y 131 (2004), 247

Wing, A.K. & Smith, M.N., Critical Race Feminism Lifts the Veil?: Muslim Women, France, and the Headscarf Ban, 39 U.C. Davis. L. Rev. 743 (2006), 457

Wishnie, M.J., Emerging Issues for Undocumented Workers, 6 U. Pa. J. Lab. & Emp. L. 497 (2004), 26

Wisskirchen, G., Jordan, C. & Bissels, A., Cross-Border Ethics Codes: The Case of Wal-Mart in Germany, www.abanet.org/labor/2005, 418, 431

Womack, J.P., Why Toyota Won, Wall St. J., Feb. 13, 2006, 543

Wonacott, P., Wallets Crack Open in India, Wall St. J., Jan. 3, 2006, 575–576

Wonnell, C.T., The Contractual Disempowerment of Employees, 46 Stan. L. Rev. 87 (1993), 101

Woo, M.Y.K., Biology and Equality: Challenge for Feminism in the Socialist and the Liberal State, 42 Emory L.J. 143 (1993), 470, 471

Woods, G.P., In Aging Japan, Young Slackers Stir Up Concerns, Wall St. J., Dec. 29, 2005, 540

The WTO and Chinese Labor Rights, 3 China Rights Forum 39 (2005), 510

Yamada, D.C., Crafting a Legislative Response to Workplace Bullying, 8 Employee Rts. & Emp. Pol'y J. 475 (2004), 352, 457

Yamakawa, R., Labor Law Reform in Japan: A Response to Recent Socio-Economic Changes, 49 Am. J. Comp. L. 627 (2001), 506, 527

Yamakawa, R., We've Only Just Begun: The Law of Sexual Harassment in Japan, 22 Hastings Int'l & Comp. L. Rev. 523 (1999), 541

Chen, Yanyuan and Darimont, B., Occupational accident insurance reform and legislation in China, 58 Int'l Soc.Sec.Rev.85 (2005), 503

Yerkey, G.G., Jordan Vows to Curb Abuse of Workers, as Required Under Free Trade Pact With U.S., International Trade Reporter, June 22, 2006, 274

Young, D.E., Working Across Borders: Global Restructuring and Women's Work, 2001 Utah L. Rev. 1, 17

Zeng, D.Z., China's Employment Challenges and Strategies after the WTO Accession (World Bank Policy Research Working Paper 3522, Feb. 2005), http://www.ssrn.com, 471

Zhao Shukai, Criminality and the Policing of Migrant Workers, 43 China J. 101 (2000), 479

Zhu Jian'gang, Not Against the State, Just Protecting the Residents' Interests: A Residents' Movement in a Shanghai Neighborhood, 5 Perspectives 25 (2004), 477

Zimmer, M.J., The New Discrimination Law: Price Waterhouse Is Dead, Whither McDonnell Douglas?, 53 Emory L.J. 1887 (2004), 144

Zwanziger, B., Collective Labor Law in a Changing Environment: Aspects of the German Experience, 26 Comp. Lab. L. & Pol'y J. 303 (2005), 405

Books & Book Chapters

Alston, P., Labor Rights Provisions in U.S. Trade Law: "Aggressive Unilateralism?", in Human Rights, Labor Rights, and International Trade (Compa, L.A. & Diamond, S.F., eds., 1996), 44

Anderman, S., Termination of Employment: Whose Property Rights, in The Future of Labour Law (Barnard, C., et al. eds. 2004), 355, 357

Arthurs, H.W., Private Ordering and Workers' Rights in the Global Economy: Corporate Codes of Conduct as a Regime of Labour Market Regulation, in Labour Law in an Era of Globalization (Conaghan, J., Fischl, R.M. & Klare, K., eds., 2002), 602, 605

Arthurs, H.W., The Collective Labour Law of a Global Economy, in Labour Law and Industrial Relations at the Turn of the Century (Engels, C. & Weiss, M., eds., 1998), 9, 50

Austin, G., Working A Democratic Constitution: A History of the Indian Experience (1999), 566, 569

Avalos, F.A., The Mexican Legal System (2d ed. 2000), 217

Baily, Harris & Jones, Civil Liberties: Cases and Materials (Butterworths 1985), 392

Bamber, G.J. & Lansbury, R.D., An Introduction to International and Comparative Employment Relations, in International & Comparative Employment Relations (3rd ed., Bamber. G.J. & Lansbury, R.D., eds., 2003), 14

Bamber, G.J. & Sheldon, P., Collective Bargaining in Comparative Labour Law, 450, 451

Bamber, G.J., Lansbury, R.D. & Wailes, N., International and Comparative Employment Relations: Globalisation and the Developed Market Economies (4th ed. 2004), 157, 172, 183, 184, 395

Baxi, U., Taking Suffering Seriously: Social Action Litigation in the Supreme Court of India, in Tiruchelvam, N. & Coomaraswamy, R., The role of the judiciary in plural societies (1987), 581

Beer, L.W. and Itoh, H., The Constitutional Case Law of Japan, 1970 through 1990 (1996), 528

Beiner, T.M., Gender Myths v. Working Realities: Using Social Science to Reformulate Sexual Harassment Law (New York University Press, 2005), 148

Bhagwati, J., In Defense of Globalization (2004), 9, 21, 31

Black's Law Dictionary (7th ed.1999), 611

Blanpain, R. & Colucci, M., The Globalization of Labour Standards: The Soft Law Track (2004), 4

Blanpain, R., Comparativism in Labour Law and Industrial Relations, in Comparative Labour Law and Industrial Relations in Industrialized Market Economies (Blanpain, R., ed., 2004), 38, 40

Blanpain, R., European Labour Law, 10th and revised ed., Kluwer Law International (2006), 276, 294

Blanpain, R., The European Union and Employment Law, in Comparative Labour Law and Industrial Relations in Industrialized Market Economies (8th ed., Blanpain, R., ed., 2004), 45, 46, 47

Blau, F.D., Ferber, M.A. & Winkler, A.E., The Economics of Women, Men and Work (4th ed. 2002), 12

Burgess, K., Mexican Labor at a Crossroads, in Mexico's Politics and Society in Transition (2003), 213, 214, 215

Carter, D. D., England, G., Etherington, B. & Trudeau, G., Labour Law in Canada (5th ed. 2002), 158, 169, 171, 172, 173, 175, 185, 186, 198, 207

Carter, S.L., Reflections of an Affirmative Action Baby (Basic Books, 1991), 128

Chan, A., Trade Unions, Conditions of Labor, and the State, in Der Chinesische Arbeitsmarket: Strukturen, Probleme, Perspectiven (Hebel. J. & Schucher, G., eds., 1999), 506

Chen, J., Chinese Law: Towards an Understanding of Chinese Law, Its Nature and Development (1999), 462, 463, 464, 465, 468, 472, 480

Clarke, O., Bamber, G.J. & Lansbury, R.D., Conclusions: Towards a synthesis of international and comparative experience in employment relations, in International & Comparative Employment Relations (3rd ed., Bamber, G.J. & Lansbury, R.D., eds., 2003), 57

Cleveland, S.H., Why International Labor Standards?, in International Labor Standards: Globalization, Trade, and Public Policy (Flanagan, R.J. & Gould, W.B. IV, eds., 2003), 42, 47, 49, 91, 250

Commission for Labor Cooperation, Labor Relations Law in North America (2000), 159, 181, 182, 183, 184, 198, 219, 221, 224, 227, 228, 229, 230, 231, 232, 234, 238, 241

Compa, L.A., Blood, Sweat and Fear: Workers' Rights in U.S. Meat and Poultry Plants (Human Rights Watch, 2005), http://hrw.org/reports/2005/usa0105/usa0105.pdf, 11

Compa, L.A., Justice for All: In Mexico (2003), 214, 215, 235, 237, 238, 247

Compa, L.A., Justice for All: The Struggle for Worker Rights in Mexico: A Report by the Solidarity Center (Solidarity Center 2003), available at: http://www.solidaritycenter.org/document.cfm?documentID=346, 272, 273

Compa, L.A., Unfair Advantage: Workers' Freedom of Association in the United States under International Human Rights Standards (Human Rights Watch, 2000), 115, 122, 509

Compa, L.A., Workers' Freedom of Association in the United States: The Gap between Ideals and Practice, in Workers Rights as Human Rights (Gross, J.A., ed., Cornell University Press, 2003), 117

Confucius, Analects, 463, 464

Cornelius, W.A. & Tsuda, T., Controlling Immigration: The Limits of Government Intervention, in Controlling Immigration: A Global Perspective (Cornelius, W.A., et al., eds., 2004), 23–24

Creighton, B., The Future of Labour Law: Is There a Role for International Labour Standards?, in The Future of Labour Law (Barnard, C., Deakin, S. & Morris, G.S, eds., 2004), 56, 60

Darby, T.J., Extraterritorial Application of U.S. Laws, in International Labor and Employment Laws (2d ed., Keller. W.L. & Darby, T.J., eds., 2003), 607

Davies, P. and Freedland, M. Kahn-Freund's Labour and the Law (3rd ed. 1983), 165

de Buen Unna, C., Mexican Trade Unionism in a Time of Transition, in Labour Law in an Era of Globalization (Conaghan, J., Fischl, R.M. & Klare, K., eds., 2002), 11

de la Cueva, M., El Nuevo Derecho Mexicano del Trabajo, Vol. I (10th ed. 1985), 234

de la Garza Toledo, E., Free Trade and Labor Relations in México, in International Labor Standards: Globalization, Trade, and Public Policy (Flanagan, R.J. & Gould, W.B. IV, eds., 2003), 254

Deale, F.E., The Pico Case: Testing International Labor Rights in U.S. Courts, in Human Rights, Labor Rights, and International Trade (Compa, L.A. & Diamond, S.F., eds., 1996), 599

Despax, M. & Rojot, J., France, in International Encyclopaedia for Labour Law and Industrial Relations (Blanpain, R., ed., Kluwer Law Int'l 1987), 432, 434, 436, 437, 439, 441, 444

Dias, M., Strategy for Effective Disposal of Cases: Role of Conciliation, in Prevention and Settlement of Disputes in India (Sivananthiran, A. & Ratnam, C.S.V., eds. 2003), available at http://www.ilo.org/public/english/region/asro/newdelhi/download/prevnton.pdf, 588–589

Discrimination: The Limits of Law (Hepple & Szyszczak eds. 1992), 370

Dobbs, D.B., The Law of Torts (West, 2000), 32

Dower, J.W., Embracing Defeat: Japan in the Wake of World War II (1999), 525, 526, 528

Duggan, M., Wrongful Discharge and Breach of Contract: Law, Practice & Precedents § 7.3 (Emis Prof. Pub. 2003), 338, 351

Dull, J.L., The Evolution of Government in China, in Heritage of China: Contemporary Perspectives on Chinese Civilization (Ropp, P.S., ed., 1990), 463

Ebrey, P., Women, Marriage, and the Family, in Heritage of Chinese: Contemporary Perspectives on Chinese Civilization (Ropp, P.S., ed., 1990), 470

Fairbank, J.K. & Goldman, M., China A New History (1999), 463, 468, 470, 472, 477, 478

Fairbank, J.K., Reischauer, E.O. & Craig, A.M., East Asia: Tradition & Transformation (rev. ed. 1989), 518, 524, 525, 542

Fields, G.S., International Labor Standards and Decent Work: Perspectives from the Developing World, in International Labor Standards: Globalization, Trade, and Public Policy (Flanagan, R.J. & Gould, W.B. IV, eds., 2003), 58

Fineman, M.A., The Autonomy Myth: A Theory of Dependency (The New Press, 2004), 33, 128

Frankel, F.R., India's Political Economy 1947–2004 (2d ed. 2004), 568, 575, 576

Fredman, S., The Ideology of New Labour Law, in The Future of Labour Law (Barnard, C. et al. eds. 2004), 333, 363

Frundt, H.J., Four Models of Cross-Border Maquila Organizing, in Unions in a Globalized Environment (Nissen, B., ed., 2002), 15

Galanter, M., Competing Equalities: Law and the Backward Classes in India (1984), 567, 578, 579, 580

Ghai, Y., Hong Kong's New Constitutional Order (2d ed. 1999), 469

Gilbert, D.G., Burkett. B.W. & McCaskill, M.K., Canadian Labour and Employment Law for the U.S. Practitioner (2000), 159, 168, 169, 174, 183, 187, 197, 198

Glenn, H.P., Legal Traditions of the World (2000), 462, 463

Global Insight, The Economic Impact of Wal-Mart, 2005, 600

Gong Shuji ed., The Practice of Labor Optimization (Science Press ed. 1987), 474

Gonzalez Casanova, P., Democracy in Mexico (1965), 241

Gorman, R.A. & Finkin, M.W., Basic Text on Labor Law: Unionization & Collective Bargaining (2d ed. 2004), 232, 240

Gould, W.B. IV, Labor Law for a Global Economy: The Uneasy Case for International Labor Standards, in International Labor Standards: Globalization, Trade, and Public Policy (Flanagan, R.J. & Gould, W.B. IV, eds., 2003), 42

Gross, J.A., A Long Overdue Beginning: The Promotion and Protection of Workers' Rights as Human Rights, in Workers' Rights as Human Rights (Gross, J.A., ed., 2003), 42, 118

Haley, J.O., Authority Without Power: Law and the Japanese Paradox (1991), 524

Hanami, T., Labor Relations in Japan Today (1979), 527

Hardgrave, R.L. & Kochanek, S.A., India: Government and Politics in a Developing Nation (6th ed. 2000), 567, 569, 576, 579

Hardin, P., in International Labor and Employment Laws (1st ed., Keller, W.L., ed., BNA Books 1997), 92

Hare, D. and Shukai Zhao, Labor Migration as a Rural Development Strategy: A View from Migration Origin, in West, L.A. and Yaohui Zhao, Rural Labor Flows in China (2000), 519–520

Harvey, Industrial Relations and Employment Law, 351

Hathaway, D., Allies Across the Border: Mexico's "Authentic Labor Front" and Global Solidarity (2000), 213, 214

Heenan, R.L. et al., NAFTA/NAALC, in International Labor and Employment Laws (2d ed., Keller, W.L. & Darby, T.J., eds., 2003), 249, 256, 258, 259, 271, 272

Hepple, B., Coussey, M. & Choudhury, T., Equality: A New Framework (Report of the Independent Review of the Enforcement of UK Anti-Discrimination Legislation) (Hart 2000), 370–371, 372

Hepple, B., Introduction, in Social and Labour Rights in a Global Context (Hepple, B., ed., 2002), 9

Hepple, B., Labour Laws and Global Trade (2005), 11, 47, 49, 50, 51, 53, 56, 57, 58, 60, 61, 68, 70, 75, 82, 83, 89, 91, 117, 249, 253, 256, 259, 275, 435, 591, 597, 603, 607

Herrera, F. & Melgoza, J., Recent Evolution of Labor Union Affiliation and Labor Regulation in Mexico, in State of Working in Mexico, 2003 (de la Garza, E. & Salas, C., ed. 2003), 209, 210

Honig, E., Sisters and Strangers: Women in the Shanghai Cotton Mills 1919–1949 (1986), 517

International Encyclopaedia for Labour Law and Industrial Relations (Blanpain, ed.), 449

International Labor & Employment Laws (Keller, W.L. & Darby, T.J., eds., 2d ed. 2003), 15, 159, 169, 171, 173, 175, 182, 185, 186, 206, 207, 214, 222, 223, 225, 228, 229, 231, 234, 247–248, 334, 357, 364, 367, 368, 396, 397, 398, 399, 401, 403, 404, 405, 406, 407, 413, 414, 415, 417, 418, 421, 424, 429, 430, 436, 437, 438, 439, 441, 442, 443, 447, 449, 452, 454, 458

Ishida, M., Death and Suicide from Overwork: The Japanese Workplace and Labour Law, in Labour Law in an Era of Globalization (Conaghan, J., Fischl. R.M. & Klare, K., eds., 2002), 533

Iwasawa, Y., International Law, Human Rights, and Japanese Law (1998), 525, 528

Josephs, H.K., Labor Law in China: Choice and Responsibility (1990), 10, 519

Josephs, H.K., Labor Law in China (2d ed. 2003), 473, 476, 477, 478, 479, 486, 488, 499, 507, 514

Jusawalla, M. & Taylor, R.D., ed., Information Technology Parks of the Asia Pacific (2003), 519

Kaufman, B.E., The Global Evolution of Industrial Relations: Events, Ideas and the IIRA (2004), 14, 15

Kenner, J., The European Union, in International Labor and Employment Laws (2d ed., Keller, W.L. & Darby, T.J., eds., 2003), 45, 46

Knight, J. and Song, L., Towards a Labour Market in China (2005), 478, 479, 480, 527

Kraamwinkel, M., The Imagined European Community: Are Housewives European Citizens?, in Labour Law in an Era of Globalization (Conaghan, J., Fischl, R.M. & Klare, K., eds., 2002), 45

Krause & Sekiguchi, Japan and the World Economy, in Asia's New Giant: How the Japanese Economy Works (Patrick, H. & Rosovsky, H., eds. 1976), 544

Labour Market Trends (June 2000), 363

Langille, B.A., Global Competition and Canadian Labor Law Reform: Rhetoric and Reality, in Global Competition and the American Employment Landscape: As We Enter the 21st Century (Estreicher, S., ed., 2000), 10

Langille, B.A., Seeking Post-Seattle Clarity, in Labour Law in an Era of Globalization (Conaghan, J., Fischl, R.M. & Klare, K., eds., 2002), 5

Leary, V.A., "Form Follows Function": Formulations of International Labor Standards – Treaties, Codes, Soft Law, Trade Agreements, in International Labor Standards: Globalization, Trade, and Public Policy (Flanagan, R.J. & Gould, W.B. IV, eds., 2003), 49, 68, 69, 91

Locke, R., Kochan, T. & Piore, M., Employment Relations in a Changing World Economy (1995), 416

Maddison, A., Chinese Economic Performance in the Long Run (1998), 464, 472, 525

Malik, P.L., Industrial Law (18th ed. 2003)., 588

Markovits, I., Imperfect Justice: An East-West German Diary (1995), 394

Martin, A. & Ross, G., The Brave New World of European Labor: European Trade Unions at the Millennium (1999), 407

McCann, M.W., Rights At Work: Pay Equity Reform and the Politics of Legal Mobilization (1994), 477

Milhaupt, C.J., Ramseyer, J.M. & Young, M.K., Japanese Law in Context: Readings in Society, the Economy, and Politics (2001), 533, 538, 541

Moorhead, T.B., U.S. Labor Law Serves Us Well, in Workers' Rights as Human Rights (Gross, J.A., ed., Cornell University Press, 2003), 69, 115, 122

Morris, C.J., The Blue Eagle at Work: Reclaiming Democratic Rights in the American Workplace (Cornell University Press, 2005), 55, 115

Murphy, E.E., Jr., The World Trade Organization, in International Labor and Employment Laws (2d ed., Keller, W.L. & Darby, T.J., eds., 2003), 48

Nakane, C., Japanese Society (1970), 527

Naughton, B., Growing out of the plan: Chinese economic reform, 1978–93 (1995), 478

New Oxford American Dictionary, 182

North, D.C., Institutions, Institutional Change and Economic Performance (1990), 518

Nussbaum, M.C. & Sen, A., The Quality of Life (Nussbaum, M.C. & Sen, A., eds. 1993), 42

O'Higgins, N., The challenge of youth unemployment (1997), http://www.ilo.org/public/english/employment/strat/publ/etp7.htm, 540

O'Rourke, K., Enabling Transnational Union Activity, in Global Competition and the American Employment Landscape: As We

Enter the 21st Century (Estreicher, S., ed., 2000), 14

Oxford English Dictionary (2d ed. 1989), 561

Parker, M., Transplanted to the U.S.A., http://multinationalmonitor.org/hyper/issues/1990/01/parker.html(1990), 543

Polaski, S., Jobs, Wages, and Household Income, in NAFTA's Promise and Reality: Lessons from Mexico for the Hemisphere (Carnegie Endowment for International Peace, 2003), 254

Port, K.L. & McAlinn, G.P., Comparative Law: Law and the Legal Process in Japan (2d ed. 2003), 525, 527, 529, 534, 536, 537

Posner, M. & Nolan, J., Can Codes of Conduct Play a Role in Promoting Workers' Rights?, in International Labor Standards: Globalization, Trade, and Public Policy (Flanagan, R.J. & Gould, W.B. IV, eds., 2003), 50, 602, 603, 604

Potter, E.E., A Pragmatic Assessment from the Employers' Perspective, in Workers' Rights as Human Rights (Gross, J.A., ed., 2003), 68, 81, 82, 83

Potter, E.E., The International Labor Organization, in International Labor and Employment Laws (2d ed., Keller, W.L. & Darby, T.J., eds., 2003), 53, 58, 59, 60, 61, 65, 70

Reid, N., The Geography of Japanese Direct Investment in the United States: The State of Knowledge and an Agenda for Future Research (2002), http://www.iar.ubc.ca/centres/cjr/reid.pdf, 542, 543

Restatement of Torts, 151

Restatement (Second) of Conflicts of Laws, 598

Restatement (Second) of Torts, 151, 154

Rittich, K., Feminization and Contingency: Regulating the Stakes of Work for Women, in Labour Law in an Era of Globalization, (Conaghan, J., Fischl, R.M. & Klare, K., eds., 2002), 16

Roberts, K.D., Chinese Labor Migration: Insights from Mexican Undocumented Migration to the United States, in West, L.A. & Yaohui Zhao, Rural Labor Flows in China (2000), 478, 520, 589

Rojot, J., Security of Employment and Employability, in Comparative Labour Law and Industrial Relations in Industrialized Market Economies (Blanpain & Engels eds., Kluwer Law Int'l, 2001), 434

Rothstein, M.A., Craver, C.B., Schroeder, E.P. & Shoben, E.W., Employment Law §§ 9.9–9.13 (3d ed. Thomson-West 2005), 103

Sack & Poskanzer, Contract Clauses, 3rd ed. (Toronto: Lancaster House, 1996), 181

Saguy, A.C., What is Sexual Harassment? From Capitol Hill to the Sorbonne (2003), 39, 456

Sathe, S.P., Judicial Activism in India: Transgressing Borders and Enforcing Limits (2002), 588

Saxenian, A., Silicon Valley's New Entrepreneurs (1999), 521

Schwartz, B., Los Poderes del Gobierno: Comentario Sobre La Constitucion de los Estados Unidos (1966), 241

Sen, A., Capability and Well-Being, in The Quality of Life (Nussbaum, M. C. & Sen, A., eds., 1993), 473, 567

Sen, A., Development As Freedom (1999),

Shaw, M.N., International Law (5th ed., 2003), 41

Shen Tan, The Relationship between Foreign Enterprises, Local Governments, and Women Migrant Workers in the Pearl River Delta, in West, L.A. & Yaohui Zhao, Rural Labor Flows in China (2000), 506–507

Shenoy, P.D., Effective Labour Court Administration: Trends and Issues, in Prevention and Settlement of Disputes in India (Sivananthiran, A. & Ratnam, C.S.V., eds., 2003), 589

Shourie, A., Courts and their Judgments (2001), 588

Spence, J., Western Perceptions of China from the Late Sixteenth Century to the Present, in Heritage of China: Contemporary Perspectives on Chinese Civilization (Ropp, P.S., ed., 1990), 464

Stiglitz, J.E., Globalization and its Discontents (2003), 5

Sugeno, K. & Kanowitz, L. (trans.), Japanese Employment and Labor Law (2d ed. 2002), 509, 526, 527, 528, 533, 541

Swepston, L., Closing the Gap between International Law and U.S. Labor Law, in Workers' Rights as Human Rights (Gross, J.A., ed., 2003), 43, 69

Sweptson, L., International Labour Law, in Comparative Labour Law and Industrial Relations in Industrialized Market Economies (Blanpain, R., ed., 8th ed., 2004), 43, 53, 59, 60, 70, 75, 81, 83

Swinton, K., "Contract Law and the Employment Relationship: The Proper Forum for Reform," in Studies in Contract Law (Reiter, B.J. & Swan, J., eds., 1980), 165

Tanaka, H., The Japanese Legal System (1976), 525, 536

Torriente, Mexican & U.S. Labor Law & Practice (1997), 220, 221, 223, 224, 229, 234, 235, 241, 242

Tsunoda, Y., Sexual Harassment in Japan, in Directions in Sexual Harassment Law (MacKinnon, C.A. & Siegel, R.B., eds., 2004), 541

Tu Wei-ming, The Confucian Tradition, in Heritage of China: Contemporary Perspectives on Chinese Civilization (Ropp, P.S., ed., 1990), 462

Turner, K., Sage Kings and Laws, in Heritage of Chinese: Contemporary Perspectives on Chinese Civilization (Ropp, P.S., ed., 1990), 463

Twining, W., Globalisation and Legal Theory (2000), 5

Upham, F.K., Law and Social Change in Postwar Japan (1987), 525, 528

van Scheltrnazaal, A., Strikes in an International Perspective, 1979–2000 (2005), www.iisg.nl/research/strikes-intro.php, 240

Walder, Andrew G., Communist Neo-Traditionalism: Work and Authority in Chinese Industry (1986), 472, 476, 506

Webster's Third New International Dictionary (1976), 561

Wedderburn, Common Law, Labour Law, Global Law, in Social and Labour Rights in a Global Context (Hepple, B., ed., 2002), 10, 87

Weiss, M. & Schmidt, M., Labour Law & Industrial Relations in Germany (3rd ed. 2000), 394, 396, 399, 400, 407, 413, 414, 415, 418, 420, 421, 428, 429, 430

Weiss, M., Labor Law, in Introduction to German Law (Reimann, M. & Zekoll, J., ed. 2005), 399, 400, 401, 402, 403, 405, 406, 408, 413, 416, 417, 418, 421

West, L.A. & Yaohui Zhao, Rural Labor Flows in China (2000), 478

Wichterich, C., The Globalized Woman: Reports from a Future of Inequality (2000), 16

Williams, L.A., Beyond Labour Law's Parochialism: A Re-envisioning of the Discourse of Redistribution, in Labour Law in an Era of Globalization (Conaghan, J., Fischl, R.M. & Klare, K., eds., Oxford University Press, 2002), 255

Windmuller, J.P., Pursey, S.K. & Baker, J., The International Trade Union Movement, in Comparative Labour Law and Industrial Relations in Industrialized Market Economies (8th ed., Blanpain, R., ed. 2004), 57

Wirth, L., Breaking through the Glass Ceiling: Women in Management (ILO, 2004), http://www.ilo.org/public/english/support/publ/textww.htm#b8457, 16

Yozell, E., The Castro Alfaro Case: Convenience and Justice – Lessons for Lawyers in Transcultural Litigation, in Human Rights, Labor Rights, and International Trade (Compa, L.A. & Diamond, S.F., eds., 1996), 597

Zamora, S., Cossio-Diaz, J.R., Pereznieto-Castro, L. & Xopa, J.R., Mexican Law (2004), 208, 212, 216, 218, 219, 227, 231, 235, 246

Reports

Article 29-Data Protection Working Party Opinion 8/2001 On the Processing of Personal Data in the Employment Context, Sept. 13, 2001, available at http://ec.europa.eu/justice_home/fsj/privacy/docs/wpdocs/2001/wp48en.pdf, 326, 327

China Statistical Yearbook 2003, http://210.72.32.36/tjsj/ndsj/yearbook2003_c.pdf, 478

China Statistical Yearbook 2004 (Table 23-5), 488

Executive Office of the President of the United States, Major Savings and Reforms in the President's 2007 Budget, Feb. 2006, http://www.whitehouse.gov/omb/budget/fy2007/pdf/savings.pdf/, 70

Foreign Labor Trends-Mexico 2002, www.dol.gov/ILAB/media/reports/flt/mexico-2002.htm, 209, 223, 224

Human Rights Watch, Fingers to the Bone: United States Failure to Protect Child Farmworkers (June 2000), http://www.hrw.org/reports/2000/frmwrkr/index.htm, 32

ICFTU, behind the brand names: Working conditions and labor rights in export processing zones (2004), http://www.icftu.org, 506, 519, 520

ILO, Committee on Employment and Social Policy, Employment and social policy in respect of export processing zones (EPZs) (March 2003), http://www.ilo.org, 519

ILO, General Report of the Committee of Experts on the Application of Conventions and Recommendations, 2005, 64, 65

ILO, Global Employment Trends for Women 2004 (2004), http://www.ilo.org/public/english/employment/strat/download/getyen.pdf, 16

ILO, Global Report, Your Voice at Work, 91

ILO, Report of the Director-General (1999), 57

ILO, Women and Men in the Informal Economy: A Statistical Picture (2002), 209

ILO-FIFA Programme, http://www.fifa.com/en/fairplay/humanitariansection/0,1422,5,00.html, 604

Inside the Workplace: First Findings From the 2004 Workplace Employment Relations Survey (WERS 2004), http://www.routledge.com/textbooks/0415378133/pdf/insideWP.pdf., 360

International Federation of Human Rights, Mexico: The North American Free Trade Agreement: Effects on Human Rights, no. 448/2, April, 2006, 208

Int'l Labour Office, Int'l Programme on the Elimination of Child Labour, Every Child Counts: New Global Estimates on Child Labour (ILO, 2002), 28

Int'l Labour Office, Int'l Programme on the Elimination of Child Labour, IPEC Action Against Child Labour: Highlights 2004 (ILO 2005), 29

Int'l Labour Office, Report of the Director-General, The End of Child Labour: Within Reach (ILO, 2006), 29

Joint ILO/UNESCO Committee of Experts on the Application of Recommendations Concerning Teaching Personnel – Report 30 (2003), 74

Joint ILO/UNESCO Committee of Experts on the Application of the Recommendation Concerning the Status of Teachers – Report, Annex 2(2)(D) (2000), 74

Joint ILO/UNESCO Committee of Experts on the Application of the Recommendation Concerning the Status of Teachers – Report, Part 6, D. (1997), 73

Mexican Labour Law, Review of Public Communication CAN 2003-1, www.hrsdc/gc/ca/en/lp/spila/ialc/pcnaalc/12mexican_law.shtml, 220, 223, 225, 229, 234, 235, 236, 238

Ministry of Labour and Employment, Seventh Report to the Standing Committee on Labour (Fourteenth Lok Sabha)(Dec. 2005), http://164.100.24.208/ls/CommitteeR/Labour&Wel/7rep.pdf, 588

NAFTA: A Decade of Strengthening a Dynamic Relationship, Joint Report from the offices of the Canadian Minister of International Trade, the Mexican Secretary of the Economy, and the U.S. Trade Representative (2003), 254–255

OECD, Employment Outlook (2005), 395

OECD, International Trade and Core Labour Standards (2000), http://www.oecd.org/dataoecd/2/36/1917944.pdf, 9, 10

OECD, Trade, Employment and Labour Standards: A Study of Core Workers' Rights and International Trade (1996), 9

Privacy International, PHR2004 – Country Reports – Federal Republic of Germany, http://www.privacyinternational.org/article.shtml?cmd[347]=x-347-83513, 325

Privacy International, PHR2004 – Country Reports – French Republic, http://www.privacyinternational.org/article.shtml?cmd[347]=x-347-83516, 326

Privacy International, PHR2004 – Country Reports – United Kingdom of Great Britain, http://www.privacyinternational.org/article.shtml?cmd[347]=x-347-83802, 325

Review of Annual Reports under the Follow-up to the ILO Declaration on Fundamental Principles and Rights at Work, Part II (International Labor Office, 2000), 118

SEC Commission Staff Working Document (2006), http://ec.europa.eu/justice_home/fsj/privacy/docs/modelcontracts/sec_2006_95_en.pdf, 329

Second National Labour Commission Report (2002), Table 4.2 (Share of GDP at Factor Cost by Economic Activity), http://www.labour.nic.in/lcomm2/nlc_report.html, 566, 568, 576, 577, 588

State Council, Notice to the Ministry of Public Security Approving Its Views on Resolution of Serious Problems in the Household Registration System, July 22, 1998, 473

UN Conf. on Trade & Dev., Development and Globalization 2004: Facts and Figures, http://globstat.unctad.org/html/index.html, 4, 6

UN Dept. of Econ. and Social Affairs, Population Div., International Migration Report 2002, 21

UN Development Programme (2004), Human Development Indicators, http://hdr.undp.org/

statistics/data/indicators.cfm?x=23,
   24&y=1&z=1, 567
UN Global Compact: Advancing Corporate
   Citizenship (Global Compact Office, June
   2005), 604
US Dept. of Commerce, Safe Harbor, http://www.
   export.gov/safeHarbor/index.html, 331
US Dept. of Commerce, Survey of Current
   Business (May 1981), 546
US Dept. of Labor, A Chartbook of International
   Labor Comparisons: The Americas, Asia,
   Europe, January 2006, http://www.dol.gov/asp/
   media/reports/chartbook/index.htm, 40,
   41
US Dept. of Labor, Bureau of International
   Labor Affairs, North American Agreement on
   Labor Cooperation: A Guide, Oct. 2005,
   http://www.dol.gov/ilab, 258
US Dept. of Labor, Bureau of International
   Labor Affairs, Public Submissions, April 2006,
   www.dol.gov/ilab/programs/nao/status.htm,
   259
US Dept. of Labor, Bureau of International
   Labor Affairs, Status of Submissions on the
   North American Agreement on Labor
   Cooperation (NAALC), http://www.dol.gov/
   ilab/programs/nao/status.htm#iib6, 272
US Dept. of Labor, Bureau of Labor Statistics,
   Press Release, Jan. 20, 2006, http://www.bls.
   gov/news.release/union2.nr0.htm,
   14
US Dept. of State, Country Reports on Human
   Rights Practices – 2004, China,
   http://www.state.gov, 471, 503
US Dept. of State, Country Reports on Human
   Rights Practices – Mexico 2004, www.stategov/
   g/drl/rls/hrrpt/2004/41767.htm, 219, 238,
   240
US Government Accountability Office, Trade
   Adjustment Assistance: Most Workers in Five
   Layoffs Received Services, but Better Outreach
   Needed on New Benefits, January 2006,
   http://www.gao.gov/new.items/d0643.pdf,
   255–256
US Senate Committee on Labor and Human
   Resources, Statement by Senator Strom
   Thurmond, Examination of the Relationship
   Between the United States and the
   International Labor Organization, 99th Cong.
   1st Sess., Vol. 1 (1985), 68

US Senate Subcommittee on Foreign Relations,
   Hearing on Treaties of Friendship, Commerce
   and Navigation Between the United States and
   Colombia, Israel, Ethiopia, Italy, Denmark
   and Greece, 82d Cong., 2d Sess. (1952), 551
US Senate Subcommittee on Foreign Relations,
   Hearing on Treaties of Friendship, Commerce
   and Navigation with Israel, Ethiopia, Italy,
   Denmark, Greece, Finland, Germany, and
   Japan, 83d Cong., 1st Sess. (1953), 550
US Trade Representative Rob Portman,
   Statement Regarding Entry Into Force of the
   U.S. – Central America – Dominican
   Republic Free Trade Agreement (CAFTA-DR)
   for El Salvador, Office of the United States
   Trade Representative, February 24, 2006, 274

Wall-Mart Stores, Inc., Standards for Suppliers
   (2005), 600
White Paper on the Labour Economy 2004:
   Summary, http://www.mhlw.go.jp/english/wp/
   l_economy/2004, 533
Working Document on the Surveillance of
   Electronic Communications in the Workplace
   (29 May 2002), http://ec.europa.eu/
   employment_social/labour_law/docs/
   dataprothendrixstudyreport_en.pdf, 392
Working Party on the Social Dimension of
   Globalization, A Stronger Social Dimension of
   Globalization: Follow-Up to the November
   Meeting of the Working Party (ILO Report,
   2005), 49
World Bank, World Development Indicators 2004
   (2004), http://www.worldbank.org/data/
   wdi2004/index.htm, 5, 6
World Bank, World Development Indicators
   2005, www.devdata.worldbank.org, 208
World Comm'n on the Social Dimension of
   Globalization, A Fair Globalization: Creating
   Opportunities for All 25 (2004), http://www.
   commissiononglobalization.org/homelinks/
   AFairGlobalization.pdf, 6, 7, 13, 21
World Comm'n on the Social Dimension of
   Globalization, Facts and Figures (2002), 6
World Labour Report 1997–98 (ILO
   Publications, 1997), 14
WTO, Trade and Labour Standards: Subject of
   Intense Debate, http://www.wto.org/english/
   thewto_e/minist_e/min99_e/english/about_e/
   18lab_e.htm, 49

1 The Study of International and Comparative Employment Law

> [C]oming out of nowhere, international labor law has grabbed the attention of globalizing multinationals, the international labor movement, activists, newspapers, governments, and non-governmental diplomatic organizations (NGOs) the world over. In the process, international employment law morphed from an arcane backwater into a tinderbox that (quite literally) ignites violence in the world's streets. Today, it is little wonder that the outlook is indeed rosy for international employment law practitioners.
>
> Donald C. Dowling, Jr., *The Practice of International Labor and Employment Law: Escort your Labor/Employment Clients into the Global Millennium,* 17 LAB. LAW. 1, 3 (2001).

A. INTRODUCTION

Imagine that you are an employment lawyer whose firm represents transnational corporations. Your client, a U.S. manufacturer of medical devices, plans to issue stock options to its executives. In return for the options, the client wants executives located in twenty-two national jurisdictions to sign covenants not to compete that will prevent them from working for the client's competitors for a certain period of time after their departure from the company.

Think about the ways in which this assignment is challenging. Noncompete agreements are devices increasingly used domestically by U.S. employers to prevent former employees from using the human capital they develop on the job on behalf of a competitor. In the United States, employers sometimes enforce these agreements by filing suit seeking to enjoin the postemployment activities of former employees. *See* Katherine V. W. Stone, *The New Psychological Contract: Implications of the Changing Workplace for Labor and Employment Law,* 48 UCLA L. REV. 519, 576-92 (2001). Yet some countries do not permit restrictive covenants. And of those that do, some restrict their use. Germany, for example, prohibits the agreements from running longer than two years, and requires the former employee be paid an amount equal to at least one-half of his or her last salary. *See* Chapter 9 on German employment law. In Canada, restrictive covenants are considered prima facie unenforceable. Only a limited range of employer interests are held to justify them. *See* Chapter 4 on Canadian employment law.

Your project is challenging, however, not simply because there are national differences in substantive law that must if possible be harmonized to meet the client's needs. There are also logistical and cultural barriers to be surmounted. How will you determine the content of the law in other countries? If, like most employment lawyers, you are not licensed to practice in another national jurisdiction, who will advise your client and draft enforceable agreements? Unless your firm employs lawyers who are licensed to practice abroad, you will need to contact foreign law firms. Will lawyers in countries, where the use of restrictive covenants is prohibited or more limited than in the United States, balk at developing a strategy to achieve the client's goals? How might the foreign executives asked to sign the agreements react?

Although in general labor and employment law practice is a local endeavor, interest in the transnational aspects of workplace law has grown as lawyers increasingly encounter issues implicating the laws of other countries. In Western Europe, legal practitioners have grown accustomed to working on employment matters that span national borders. Practice is beginning to change in the United States as well. The example here is not a law professor's hypothetical. It was a project given to a large U.S. labor and employment law firm. *See* Susan Bisom-Rapp, *Exceeding Our Boundaries: Transnational Employment Law Practice and the Export of American Lawyering Styles to the Global Worksite*, 25 Comp. Lab. L. & Pol'y J. 257, 333-34 (2004) (hereinafter Bisom-Rapp, *Exceeding Our Boundaries*).

Moreover, workers' representatives share this interest, which extends to the possible uses of international law. In 2002 the American Federation of Labor and Congress of Industrial Organizations (AFL-CIO) filed a complaint against the United States with the International Labour Organization (ILO), a specialized agency of the United Nations (UN). The complaint challenged the U.S. Supreme Court's decision in *Hoffman Plastic* as violating U.S. obligations under the ILO's 1998 Declaration on Fundamental Principles and Rights at Work. In *Hoffman*, the Court held that back pay may not be awarded to undocumented workers illegally discharged for union activity. Hoffman Plastic Compounds, Inc. v. N.L.R.B., 535 U.S. 137 (2002). The ILO's Committee on Freedom of Association (CFA) found that eliminating the back pay remedy leaves the government with insufficient tools for ensuring that undocumented workers are protected against antiunion discrimination. What might the AFL-CIO hope to accomplish with this victory for organized labor? The CFA's powers are limited to making recommendations and requesting follow-up reports when it finds a complaint meritorious. *See* International Labour Organization, Committee on Freedom of Association, Complaints against the Government of the United States Presented by the American Federation of Labor and Congress of Industrial Organizations (AFL-CIO) and the Confederation of Mexican Workers (CTM), Case No. 2227, Report No. 332 (2003).

Changes in the economy and methods of production, trade liberalization, and improvements in technology and communication affect the workplace and the efficacy of the legal systems that were designed to regulate it. In order to represent a broad range of clients, and when necessary collaborate with lawyers from other countries, advocates for employers and employees alike benefit from a familiarity with labor and employment laws outside their borders. Acquaintance with international and foreign national law also promotes reflection on the effectiveness of regulatory systems back home, and can produce important insights about one's own workplace laws, an especially helpful exercise for policy makers.

This book surveys the legal scene by taking both an international and a comparative approach. It reviews materials and discusses the mechanisms for attempting to achieve global labor standards, matters that transcend national boundaries, and that we refer to as "international." The book also considers and compares the laws and legal environments of several important national jurisdictions, an exercise in comparative workplace law. As you read through these materials, keep in mind some fundamental questions. Why do governments regulate the labor market? How do different nations conceptualize and attempt to secure core labor rights for workers? How is the success of those regulatory efforts to be measured? What is the best way to achieve humane working conditions for all employees?

To set the stage for considering these questions, this chapter first turns to the phenomenon known as globalization and its implications for labor and employment law and its practitioners. Having laid out the problem – globalization and its effects – we advance to a discussion of international and comparative law as possible tools for meeting its challenges. The chapter concludes with a brief primer on workplace law in the international realm.

Before beginning, a word about terminology is in order. In this book, as in American legal parlance more generally, the term "labor law" refers to the legal regulation of collective bargaining and labor relations, including laws structuring the relationship between unions and employers, and also that between unions and employees. "Employment law," as used in this text, is defined more expansively than is typical in the United States, covering not only labor law but also legal regulation considered more individual in orientation, including laws prohibiting discrimination, the regulation of wages and hours, the safeguarding of pensions, and the individual contractual terms of employment. A term synonymous with employment law in this book is "workplace law," an umbrella term encompassing both labor and individual employment law.

1. Globalization

Globalization is a buzzword often bandied about but less frequently defined. Professor Peter Thomas Muchlinski has identified five ways in which the term is used. The first is a geographical approach, which sees rapid communications and ease of travel as the basis for a new global order. Technological advances in this view facilitate geographic alterations of economic activity away from national economies toward, for example, the transnational production and distribution chains developed by transnational corporations (TNCs). A second definition centers on interpreting economic data, which show growing cross-border economic integration evidenced by increases in international trade, foreign direct investment (FDI), and cross-border financial flows. Muchlinski's third approach, the business management approach, focuses on the rise and activities of global corporations, which are viewed as the vehicles for worldwide integration of trade and production. The sociological approach, a fourth conception of globalization, places the emphasis on the effects of global cultural exchange, and examines phenomena such as worldwide consumption patterns, globalization backlash in the form of nationalism, and the development of multiculturalism. Finally, the political science approach is characterized by discussions about the displacement by supranational structures of the nation-state as the primary site of political governance. Peter Thomas Muchlinski, *Globalisation and Legal Research*, 37 INT'L LAW. 221 (2003).

There is overlap between these globalization categories, and debate surrounding both category content and the effects of the phenomena the categories describe. In light of its close connection to employment matters, it seems reasonable first to examine the globalization of business management, looking particularly at TNCs.

a. *The Globalization of Business Management*

The UN defines a TNC as an enterprise controlling the assets of another entity outside its home economy, usually by owning at least 10 percent of the foreign enterprise.
Most such corporations situate their headquarters within the United States, the European
Union, or Japan. Of the top fifty nonfinancial TNCs, eleven are headquartered in the
United States, Germany and France each claim eight, the United Kingdom is home
to seven, and Japan is the base for four. Overall, there are sixty-four thousand TNCs
involved in international production. These entities operate through 866,000 foreign
affiliates. More than half the foreign affiliates are located in developing countries, with
the greatest concentrations in Asia, Latin America, and the Caribbean. U.N. CONF. ON
TRADE & DEV., DEVELOPMENT AND GLOBALIZATION 2004: FACTS AND FIGURES 40, 44,
http://globstat.unctad.org/html/index.html (hereinafter DEVELOPMENT AND GLOBALIZA-
TION 2004).

As a result of a wave of mergers and acquisitions over the last fifteen years, these
mega-corporations have increased their share of economic activity along with their
power and influence. Today TNCs generate over two-thirds of world trade. Bernhard
G. Gunter & Rolph van der Hoeven, *The Social Dimensions of Globalization: A
Review of the Literature* 18 (ILO working paper No. 24, 2004), www.ilo.org/public/
english/bureau/integration/globaliz/publicat.htm. TNCs also employ tremendous numbers of people worldwide. In the early 1980s, only nineteen million employees worked for
foreign affiliates. In 2002, foreign affiliates of TNCs employed fifty-three million people.
DEVELOPMENT AND GLOBALIZATION 2004, at 44. Although this increase is significant, one
should note that the numbers nevertheless represent a small percentage of the total global
workforce.

To demonstrate how the presence of foreign affiliates affects national industries, Professor Roger Blanpain and researcher Michele Colucci recently recounted the penetration of such interests in Belgium's technology industry:

> [T]he Americans have a very important piece of the cake. 25% of employment in the
> technological enterprises is in US hands. France is good for 13%, Germany and the
> Netherlands each for 11%. Japan employs 3.3% of the workforce.
>
> ROGER BLANPAIN & MICHELE COLUCCI, THE GLOBALIZATION OF LABOUR STANDARDS:
> THE SOFT LAW TRACK 3 (2004).

As grateful as they may be for the creation of jobs, worker insecurity or a sense of a
national "loss of control" may well accompany this state of affairs. Blanpain and Colucci
observe that "decision-making power regarding many jobs in Belgium lies with far away
headquarters." *Id.*

The numbers detailed here hint at a massive global trend: the rise over the last
ten years of global production chains or international production sharing. Production
under these systems is carved up and outsourced, sometimes to foreign affiliates but
also to contractors and subcontractors located outside the producer's home territory.
William Milberg, *The Changing Structure of International Trade Linked to Global Production Systems: What are the Policy Implications?* (ILO working paper No. 33, 2004),
www.ilo.org/public/english/bureau/integration/globaliz/publicat.htm; Hilary K. Josephs,
Upstairs, Trade Law; Downstairs, Labor Law, 33 GEO.WASH. INT'L L. REV. 849, 860
(2001). The industries in which global production predominates include high technology,

labor-intensive consumer goods, and even the service sector, as exemplified by foreign call centers and financial services offices.

b. *Global Economic Integration*

The growth of TNCs and new methods of production are both symptoms of and catalysts for global economic integration, a phenomenon associated with the creation and consolidation of a unified world economy. WILLIAM TWINING, GLOBALISATION AND LEGAL THEORY 4 (2000). The concept of a unified global economy implies much more than greater trade between nations. As Professor Brian Langille notes:

> To get to the real phenomenon of globalization. . . . we must shift from a world in which not only goods, but services, ideas, money, markets, and production are truly global and mobile by virtue of advances in communication and transportation technologies. We must move from the model of *shallow* economic integration to a model of *deep* economic integration in which advancements in transportation and technology enable capital to see the whole world as its stage.

> Brian A. Langille, *Seeking Post-Seattle Clarity, in* LABOUR LAW IN AN ERA OF GLOBALIZATION 137, 143 (Joanne Conaghan, Richard Michael Fischl & Karl Klare, eds., 2002).

Law and policy play a great role in global economic integration. Deep connections between national economies could not be made in the absence of a hospitable legal and policy environment. Indeed, *neoliberalism*, an economic and political movement championing free markets that was embraced by most governments around the globe in the 1980s and 1990s, greatly facilitated significant "removal of government interference in financial markets, capital markets, and barriers to trade. . . . " JOSEPH E. STIGLITZ, GLOBALIZATION AND ITS DISCONTENTS 59 (2003). During this period, public policy analysis became dominated by pro-market economic theory that promised deregulation would provide worldwide opportunity for growth and development. The magnitude of global economic integration that took place in the wake of this movement can be appreciated by considering increases in trade, foreign direct investment, and large cross-border financial flows. Twenty years into the process, we are now positioned to evaluate the contentions of proponents of neoliberal strategy.

For example, the claim underpinning free trade, a linchpin of neoliberalism, is that the total economic pie for the world as a whole is larger with free trade than without. Potentially, all people could be better off in a world without trade barriers. Think of the advantages we gain from free trade as consumers. The blue jeans or consumer electronics we buy are less expensive when they are produced in a global free market than if each country created its own market for these products. With free trade, a huge purchaser of consumer goods, such as Wal-Mart, can search the globe for the lowest cost blue jeans or DVD players, thereby driving down the retail price for these items.

But does an opening of markets lead to a larger economic pie? Spurred by international, regional and national liberalization policies encouraging free markets, world trade has expanded significantly over the last twenty years. In 2002, 54 percent of the world's output was globally traded, an increase from 31 percent in 1980. THE WORLD BANK GROUP, WORLD DEVELOPMENT INDICATORS 2004 303 (2004) (hereinafter World Development Indicators 2004), http://www.worldbank.org/data/wdi2004/index.htm. From 1980 to 2000, the value of worldwide manufacturing exports tripled. WORLD COMM'N ON THE SOCIAL DIMENSION OF GLOBALIZATION, FACTS AND FIGURES (2002) (hereinafter FACTS AND FIGURES). Merchandise exports from all the world's countries totaled U.S.$6.4 trillion in 2002. Service exports in 2002 were valued at U.S.$1.6 trillion. DEVELOPMENT AND GLOBALIZATION 2004, at 48.

Despite this impressive economic activity, the expansion in trade is unevenly distributed. Two-thirds of the merchandise exports in 2002 and close to three-fourths of the service exports were from the affluent nations of the developed world. *Id.* Moreover, an uneven growth pattern is also evident within the developing world. For example, although developing countries increased their share of manufacturing exports from 23 percent in 1970 to 38 percent in 1997, most of the growth is due to the performance of just thirteen economies. Although some East Asian and Latin American economies saw a significant increase in exports, most developing nations did not. DEVELOPMENT AND GLOBALIZATION 2004, at 50. Notwithstanding the implementation of trade liberalization programs, over the last two decades most of what the UN terms Least Developed Countries (LDCs) sustained a proportional decline in their share of global markets. WORLD COMM'N ON THE SOC. DIMENSION OF GLOBALIZATION, A FAIR GLOBALIZATION: CREATING OPPORTUNITIES FOR ALL 25 (2004), http://www.commissiononglobalization. org/homelinks/AFairGlobalization.pdf (hereinafter A Fair Globalization).

Another sign and catalyst of global economic integration is foreign direct investment (FDI), which, with the exception of brief declines in the early 1980s and early 1990s, has grown steadily for the last thirty years. FDI occurs when an individual or business entity from one national economy obtains an interest in and influence over an enterprise in another national economy. That the foreign investor maintains significant control over management of the entity invested in is a notable aspect of FDI. Cross-border-mergers and acquisitions make up a portion of global FDI. DEVELOPMENT AND GLOBALIZATION 2004, at 32. Much of this investment is tied to the globalization of manufacturing production processes and services. A Fair Globalization, at 33.

Like trade, FDI has been enabled by liberalization measures adopted at the international, regional, and national levels. One is hard-pressed to identify countries that do not wish to lure foreign investment. From 1991 to 2002, 95 percent of the amendments made to FDI laws by 165 countries made it easier for FDI to occur. DEVELOPMENT AND GLOBALIZATION 2004, at 36. Despite an improving legal environment for FDI overall, three-quarters of the foreign investment takes place in wealthy developed countries. Most of the FDI in the developing countries touches just ten nations, including China, Brazil, Mexico, Singapore, and Argentina. In 2000, the percentage of FDI inflows in African nations was less than 1 percent. FACTS AND FIGURES, at 1.

There has been a recent dropoff in FDI. Global FDI, which was valued at U.S.$202 billion in 1990, peaked in 2000 at U.S.$1.5 trillion. In 2002, it had dropped to U.S.$631 billion. World Development Indicators 2004, at 304. Reasons cited for the drop include weak economic growth, falling stock markets, a decrease in cross-border mergers and acquisitions, and the completion of privatization in a number of countries. DEVELOPMENT AND GLOBALIZATION 2004, at 32. Whether the dropoff will persist is unclear. Nonetheless, FDI remains a major indicator of the extent to which various national economies are integrated.

In addition to FDI, other forms of private financial flows are associated with growing international economic integration. These resources include foreign investments in national equity markets, foreign bank lending, bonds and trade-related lending by foreign private creditors, and short-term speculative foreign investment into currency markets. A Fair Globalization, at 29.

Beginning in the late 1980s, the trend toward greater liberalization of financial markets made possible significant capital mobility, and greatly increased the influence of private banks, hedge funds, equity funds, and rating agencies over the economies of developing nations. Id. at 34. These flows are volatile and subject to speculation; the rapid outflow of such resources can wreak havoc on an emerging economy, leaving unemployment and poverty in its wake. Moreover, like FDI and trade, cross-border financial flows reach only a few emerging market economies; most developing nations and the LDCs are largely left out of the private global financial system. Id. at 35.

Some of the data referenced above appeared in a 2004 report issued by the ILO's World Commission on the Social Dimension on Globalization. The Commission was established to review in addition to economic growth, changes in employment, income distribution, and poverty reduction over the roughly twenty-year period in which neoliberal economic policy came to dominate public policy and law reform. The following excerpt, by Susan Hayter, summarizes the Commission's findings.

SUSAN HAYTER, THE SOCIAL DIMENSION OF GLOBALIZATION: STRIKING THE BALANCE

55 Bull. Comp. Lab. Rel. 1–10 © 2004 by Kluwer Law International, reprinted with permission from Kluwer Law International, www.kluwer.com

A startling feature of the global economy is that since 1990, aggregate global GDP [gross domestic product] growth has in fact been slower than previous decades. A few points about the trends behind this picture of aggregate global GDP growth deserve mentioning:

First, this growth has been uneven across countries. Industrialized countries with a strong initial economic base, abundance of capital, skill and technological know-how were well placed to benefit from globalization. Importantly, countries, with large populations such as China and India experienced significant improvements in economic growth. However, few developing countries were able to benefit from the fruits of global economic integration and some suffered negative growth.

Second, the income gap between the richest and poorest countries has significantly increased.

Third, as evidenced by the Asian financial crisis, countries with remarkable past records of economic growth can suffer dramatic reversals and heavy social costs. . . .

Moving beyond economic performance. . . . [a]gain there were significant benefits for some countries and many people. Increased trade and FDI flows did lead to economic growth in some countries and new jobs in certain sectors, even good quality jobs in, for example, the overseas affiliates of multinationals. However, as the Commission's report notes, it is not possible to make broad generalizations about the impact of FDI and trade on employment and incomes.

A growing body of evidence shows that the impact has been mixed. For example, a set of recent ILO studies on the impact of trade on employment and wages in the manufacturing sector show that in the three Asian economies studied, trade growth had favourable impacts on employment and wages in manufacturing. By contrast, in Latin American countries such as Brazil and Mexico, employment levels have either fallen, or there has been no significant impact on employment. Real wages of unskilled workers declined and the wage differential between skilled and unskilled workers increased significantly. . . . .

The picture on income inequality has been mixed. While it increased in some countries in both the industrialized and developing world, the extent to which globalization is to blame for this remains an open question and there is significant debate among economists. However, what is startling is the increase in the concentration of wealth and growing share of gross income that goes to the top 1 percent of income earners in countries such as the United States, the United Kingdom and Canada. These high earnings are typically linked to compensation paid by MNEs [multinational enterprises] and so the increased concentration in wealth can most likely be attributed to globalization.

Notes

1. What are the implications of the report's conclusions for national, regional and international policy making? Should governments of the world "stay the course" and hope that globalization's rising tide will raise all boats? What are the dangers associated with maintaining the status quo?

2. How can a developing nation that has not shared in the fruits of globalization get more of its benefits? Must it engage in a "race to the bottom" by lowering its labor standards in order to gain economic growth? Should it instead invest in infrastructures such as education and health services, to produce the kind of workers TNCs are looking for? Must it forego taxing foreign direct investment in order to attract it?

---

c. Globalization and Legal Regulation

That globalization produces economic effects is beyond dispute. What about globalization's impact on labor and employment law? One of the most common observations on this subject is that globalization makes it harder for nation-states to regulate their labor markets through protective laws. Professor Katherine Van Wezel Stone describes the phenomenon this way:

> [G]lobalization encourages regulatory competition. Regulatory competition occurs when nations compete for business by using lower labor standards. Regulatory competition leads nonlabor groups to oppose labor regulation on the ground that business flight hurts them. Thus, regulatory competition could trigger a downward spiral: nations compete with each other for lower labor standards, while labor loses its historic allies at the domestic level, rendering labor powerless to resist.
>
> Katherine Van Wezel Stone, *To the Yukon and Beyond: Local Laborers in a Global Labor Market* 3 J. SMALL & EMERGING BUS. L. 93, 96 (1999).

Professor Stone's analysis implies that there is tension between a country's desire to attract foreign direct investment (or retain domestic investment) and its ability to maintain laws guaranteeing just relations at work. Is this so? Logically, the threat of capital flight might in theory affect the state's willingness to protect its workers. Patrick Macklem, *Labour Law Beyond Borders* 5 J. INT'L ECON. L. 605 (2002). To achieve business friendly environments, countries could fail to revise outdated labor and employment laws or adopt laws antithetical to workers' interests. Bob Hepple, *Introduction, in* SOCIAL AND LABOUR RIGHTS IN A GLOBAL CONTEXT 14 (Bob Hepple, ed., 2002). As Professor Harry Arthurs puts it: "The least that can be said is that few, if any, national governments in the industrialized west have concluded that the strengthening of collective labour laws is the best strategy for enhancing their global competitiveness." Harry W. Arthurs, *The Collective Labour Law of a Global Economy, in* LABOUR LAW AND INDUSTRIAL RELATIONS AT THE TURN OF THE CENTURY, 143, 154 (Chris Engels & Manfred Weiss, eds., 1998) (hereinafter Arthurs, *Collective Labour Law*).

One outspoken advocate of globalization and free trade takes issue with this description of how and why countries adopt or make changes in workplace legislation. Professor Jagdish Bhagwati denies that regulatory competition was a causal factor in the movement toward deregulation that began in the United States in the 1980s. Instead, politicians' use of competitive disadvantage rhetoric to justify deregulation was merely a case of political expediency:

> [I]f you wished to deregulate for reasons that had nothing to do with international competition (e.g., if cost-benefit analysis implied there was too much regulation, or if there was an ideological preference for deregulation), the smart thing nonetheless was to say that you were suffering from competition from rivals elsewhere who were less regulated.
>
> JAGDISH BHAGWATI, IN DEFENSE OF GLOBALIZATION 128 (2004) (hereinafter Bhagwati, IN DEFENSE OF GLOBALIZATION).

Bhagwati argues that there has been no "race to the bottom" in the United States because the economic pressures from globalization are not significant enough to reverse the gains in labor standards made and continually defended by unions, the Democratic Party, and pro-regulatory groups in general. In fact, he maintains that the pressure runs in the other direction toward a "race to the top." Organized labor in developed countries, fearing the undermining of labor standards at home, agitates for raising labor standards in poor countries. *Id.* at 131. Professor Bhagwati is correct that there are such campaigns aimed at developing nations by unions and other nongovernmental organizations (NGOs). How might developing nations react to demands that they give up their comparative advantage in lower labor costs?

The empirical evidence on whether countries do or can attract and retain investment by downgrading or failing to enforce labor and employment law is controversial and mixed. The Organisation for Economic Cooperation and Development (OECD), an intergovernmental policy forum for discussion and research on globalization, in 1996 produced a groundbreaking study on trade, labor standards, and employment. ORGANISATION FOR ECONOMIC CO-OPERATION AND DEVELOPMENT, TRADE, EMPLOYMENT AND LABOUR STANDARDS: A STUDY OF CORE WORKERS' RIGHTS AND INTERNATIONAL TRADE (1996). Both that study and a subsequent policy brief found that in general, "countries where core labour standards are not respected continue to receive a very small share of global investment flows." ORGANISATION FOR ECONOMONIC CO-OPERATION AND DEVELOPMENT, INTERNATIONAL TRADE AND CORE LABOUR STANDARDS 3 (2000), http://www.oecd.org/dataoecd/2/36/1917944.pdf. An exception to that conclusion is the case of China. *Id.* Moreover, research indicates that some non-OECD countries create export-processing zones (EPZs) that are exempt from national workplace law in the hope of luring investment from developed countries. *Id.* Working conditions in some EPZs are notoriously oppressive. HILARY K. JOSEPHS, LABOR LAW IN CHINA 111 (2d ed. 2003).

There is some evidence that U.S. TNCs' production location decisions are in fact influenced in part by industrial relations environments and wage rates, factors that are distinct from but related to workplace law. One recent study found that U.S. TNCs prefer to locate in countries with decentralized bargaining and few restrictions on layoffs. U.S. TNCs also prefer to locate in low-wage countries. Mario F. Bognanno, Michael P. Keane & Donghoon Yang, *The Influence of Wages and Industrial Relations Environments on the Production Location Decisions of U.S. Multinational Corporations*, 58 INDUS. & LAB. REL. REV. 171 (2005). As noted, it is clear that many low-wage countries are not able to attract FDI. What other factors might determine TNCs' location decisions?

Professor Brian Langille observes that whether TNCs are actually lured to countries that actively downgrade or undermine their employment laws is really beside the point. Empirical evidence aside, international competitiveness is an important part of political debates about labor law reform. In Canada, for example, labor law reform efforts in Ontario in the 1990s were driven by discussions of the need to attract foreign investment. Brain A. Langille, *Global Competition and Canadian Labor Law Reform: Rhetoric and Reality*, in GLOBAL COMPETITION AND THE AMERICAN EMPLOYMENT LANDSCAPE: AS WE ENTER THE 21ST CENTURY 621–43 (Samuel Estreicher, ed., 2000). Unlike Professor Bhagwati, who sees such rhetoric as relatively inconsequential, Langille argues that "it is not actual divestment or investment which is the real key; it is the credible threat of such actions" that can drive policy discussion and outcome. Brian A. Langille, *Eight Ways to Think About International Labour Standards*, 31 J. WORLD TRADE 27, 43 (1997).

Thus far our discussion begs an important question: Why *do* nation states regulate the employment relation? Many scholars and policy makers fret about the effectiveness of legal regulation in the face of globalization. Such concern makes little sense, however, if the market produces optimal outcomes. With these points in mind, it makes sense to pause and consider why governments adopt labor and employment laws.

The answer to this foundational question may vary depending on the national jurisdiction one considers. Most continental European policy makers would no doubt find sufficient justification for regulation in the inherent inequality between employers and employees. Lord Wedderburn, *Common Law, Labour Law, Global Law*, in SOCIAL AND LABOUR RIGHTS IN A GLOBAL CONTEXT 27 (Bob Hepple, ed., 2002). Some Anglo-Saxon commentators, by contrast, would find unequal power relations as a necessary but insufficient rationale for placing limitations on the employment relation. *Id.* The adherents of this school would in addition require demonstration of economic market failures or vastly skewed distributive outcomes before formal law could be brought to bear on the workplace. *Id.*

A look at employment regulation in the United States serves as an example of the latter approach. U.S. law historically did not recognize the potential for abuse in employment relationships. The 1935 Wagner Act, organized labor's Magna Carta, takes a step toward acknowledging workplace reality by referencing the disparity in bargaining power between employers and employees. Rather than base the statute on a conception of social justice, however, Congress tied its observations on inequality to economic concerns. Moved by the very real and practical need to ensure the constitutionality of the legislation, Congress passed the Wagner Act by invoking the Commerce Clause of the U.S. Constitution, and referencing the goal of reducing strikes and industrial unrest. Lance Compa, *The ILO*

Core Standard's Declaration: Changing the Climate for Changing the Law, PERSPECTIVES ON WORK 24–26, June 2003.

Sir Bob Hepple's description of the role of labor law combines economics and morality. While acknowledging the economic function of workplace law – it redistributes benefits and risks between employers and workers, affects the efficiency of the firm, and provides incentives and disincentives for skill acquisition and productivity increases – the law also has a moral dimension. BOB HEPPLE, LABOUR LAWS AND GLOBAL TRADE 13 (2005) (hereinafter Hepple, Labour Laws). This latter aspect of labor market regulation is grounded in the notion of human dignity and the idea that labor is "not a commodity or article of commerce." Treaty of Peace, June 28, 1919, Part XIII, §2, art. 427, 225 Consol. T.S. 188, 385; CONST. OF THE INT'L LABOUR ORG., annex I(a); Clayton Anti-Trust Act of 1914, 15 U.S.C. §17 (2005). In this sense, workplace laws seek to affect the physical and psychological well-being of workers as human beings. Hepple, Labour Laws, at 13.

Yet agreeing that inequality, morality or market failures provide some justification for labor market regulation, and even proceeding to regulate – to put labor and employment laws on the books – is not the end of the matter. For laws on the books may paint an inaccurate picture of what life is really like for a nation's workers. In some developing countries, for example, the gap between legal doctrine and actual enforcement is wide indeed. Carlos de Buen Unna, *Mexican Trade Unionism in a Time of Transition*, *in* LABOUR LAW IN AN ERA OF GLOBALIZATION 401, 409 (Joanne Conaghan, Richard Michael Fischl & Karl Klare, eds., 2002). The same may true for developed countries. LANCE COMPA, BLOOD, SWEAT AND FEAR: WORKERS' RIGHTS IN U.S. MEAT AND POULTRY PLANTS (Human Rights Watch, 2005), http:// hrw.org/reports/2005/usa0105/usa0105.pdf. Additionally, favorable law on the books is not necessarily a precondition for meaningful collective action on the part of workers. However, its absence, as Professor James Atleson has noted, may greatly complicate efforts aimed at promoting transnational labor solidarity. James Atleson, *The Voyage of the Neptune Jade: The Perils and Promises of Transnational Labor Solidarity*, 52 BUFFALO L. REV. 85, 87 (2004) (hereinafter Atleson, Voyage of the Neptune Jade).

All this is to say that thinking about the effects of globalization on legal regulation is a complicated endeavor. Capital mobility and the preferences of many governments for creating business friendly legal environments present compelling challenges to labor, the one factor of production that generally is not mobile. Harry Arthurs, *Reinventing Labor Law for the Global Economy: The Benjamin Aaron Lecture*, 22 BERKELEY J. EMP. & LAB. L. 271, 281-5 (2001). Because protecting vulnerable workers is a more complex endeavor than ever before, it is necessary for workers' advocates – unions and other NGOs, social movements and pro-regulatory groups – to be conversant with all the tools – legal and otherwise – at their disposal. David M. Trubek, Jim Mosher & Jeffrey S. Rothstein, *Transnationalism in the Regulation of Employment Relations: International Regimes and Transnational Advocacy Networks*, 25 LAW & SOC. INQUIRY 1187, 1194 (2000).

d. *Globalization and Workplace Trends*

Globalization is associated with a number of workplace trends that are detrimental to worker welfare. These trends include: increases in nonstandard work; the diminished power of unions; the feminization of labor; the use of migrants as cheap sources of labor; and the problem of child labor. As you read through the following chapters, these developments can be used as lenses through which to assess the effectiveness of the different legal regimes.

i. Nonstandard work. Studies indicate that industrialized countries in the last several decades are experiencing an increase in nonstandard work. Francine D. Blau, Marianne A. Ferber & Anne E. Winkler, The Economics of Women, Men and Work 283 (4th ed. 2002) (hereinafter Blau, Women, Men and Work). Nonstandard work, sometimes called contingent work, is characterized by impermanence; it may be limited in duration, hours available, or job security. Workers occupying these jobs work without "an explicit or implicit contract for long-term employment." Anne E. Polivka, *Contingent and Alternative Work Arrangements, Defined*, 119 Monthly Lab. Rev. 3, 7 (Oct. 1996). Although definitions vary, forms of nonstandard work typically include temporary work, seasonal agricultural work, part-time employment, self-employment, and labor accomplished in the informal economy such as day labor and other forms of "off-the-books" employment. Such workers generally lack the attachment to the labor force of the traditional, full-time employee who works for a single employer. Peggy R. Smith, *Contingent Workers: Lesson 5*, 5 Emp. Rts. & Emp. Pol'y J. 661, 662 (2001).

Most troubling for critics of the trend is that nonstandard workers frequently do without benefits and protections like sick pay, holidays, pensions, and, in the United States, health insurance. As Professor Gillian Lester notes:

> [C]ontingent workers may fail to meet the legal definition of a covered "employee" under both statutory and private rules. Moreover, even those contingent workers who qualify as employees may be denied benefits or protections under any number of bright-line "gatekeeper" tests. Unemployment insurance (UI), for example, is available only to workers who have worked some minimum number of hours, earned some minimum level of income from wages, or both, over a particular period; these factors may exclude contingent workers at a disproportionate rate.

> Gillian Lester, *Careers and Contingency*, 51 Stan. L. Rev. 73, 75-6 (1998) (hereinafter *Lester, Careers and Contingency*).

Nonetheless, the limited responsibilities employers owe contingent workers no doubt motivate them to cultivate these nonstandard relationships. *Id.* Wal-Mart's economic success, for example, is tied in part to its practice of hiring temporary and part-time workers. Jeff Madrick, *Wal-Mart May be the New Model of Productivity, But It Isn't Always Wowing Workers*, N.Y. Times, Sept. 2, 2004, at C 2. *See* Chapter 14, for details on Wal-Mart.

Neoclassical economic accounts of nonstandard work emphasize the demand and supply factors driving the phenomenon and, in general, recommend against state regulatory intervention. On the demand side, these accounts focus on the cost savings that employers can realize in the face of fluctuating need for labor, and the use of contingent work by employers as an efficient screening device for the permanent workforce. With respect to supply, neoclassical explanations emphasize the voluntary nature of such work arrangements. Caregivers with family responsibilities, young people pursuing schooling, and workers transitioning from full-time employment to retirement may seek and value the flexibility inherent in contingent work. Blau, Men, Women and Work, at 288.

Labor market segmentation theory, by contrast, highlights the exploitive, involuntary character of work in a secondary labor market bereft of the benefits and protections, and lacking the opportunity for training and advancement available to employees in the primary labor market. Emphasizing the need for decent work and increased regulation, those subscribing to this descriptive account note that many of the worst jobs in the secondary labor market track racial, gender and ethnic lines. Jonathan P. Hiatt, *Policy Issues Concerning the Contingent Workforce*, 52 WASH. & LEE L. REV. 739, 744 (1995).

Both neoclassical and labor segmentation explanations contain accurate descriptions of reality for at least some contingent work relationships. In light of this, how should policy makers determine whether additional regulation is warranted? Professor Lester suggests narrowing the category of nonstandard workers who merit further protection to those who are underemployed; in other words, reform proposals should be geared to assist those whose skills are underutilized. Employers required to provide these individuals with increased compensation might "receive sufficient returns . . . to render the change efficient." Lester, *Careers and Contingency*, at 124-5. Can solutions grounded in economic efficiency adequately address charges of worker exploitation and oppression?

Nonstandard work is not only a feature of industrialized economies; it is the predominant form of employment in many developing countries as well. Such forms of work predate the modern era of globalization, yet competitive markets and global production systems certainly benefit from them. Take the development of export processing zones (EPZs), for example. Many developing nations in Asia and Latin America created these districts holding out tax breaks, the absence of unions, and cheap labor to lure TNCs, especially producers in the garment, footwear and electronics industries. These efforts produced many jobs; one estimate indicates that by 1995, twenty-seven million jobs had been created in EPZs. Today EPZs employ fifty million workers. A Fair Globalization, at 111. Many of the jobs, however, are typified by low pay, poor working conditions, and few if any benefits. The same is true of the jobs created by global production chains, which utilize an array of transnational subcontracting arrangements in order to hold down the price of a final product or service. Marilyn Carr & Martha Chen, *Globalization, Social Exclusion and Gender*, 143 INT'L LAB. REV. 129, 135-6 (2004).

Although nonstandard work arrangements are found in both industrial and developing countries, the policy implications for the latter are different than those for the developed world. In the developed world, where high employment and, at least outside the United States, a robust welfare state are the expectations, the discussions about contingent work often reference unemployment and exclusion from the social safety net. Most developing countries, however, have not experienced high employment in a primary labor market, nor has there been a social safety net to catch those who are displaced from it. Moreover, those concerned with developing economies that have benefited from globalization by the creation of jobs – such as jobs located in EPZs or as part of global production chains – are more likely to talk about improving the conditions associated with those jobs than they are to try to shift the jobs to the formal sector. *Id.*

ii. The declining power of trade unions. Unions have developed on a national basis. As will be seen, the nature of unions and of the effects of unionization varies country to country, even among neighboring nations such as the United Kingdom, France, and Germany. Additionally, union density and strength may vary within a country. For example, unions traditionally have fared poorly in large sections of the southern United States. Today, the predominant trend affecting the labor movement is a worldwide decline in unionization.

In the United States, union density has been falling for decades. In 2005, a mere 12.5 percent of U.S. workers were union members, down from 20.1 percent in 1983. Although respectable in the public sector, organized labor's share of the private sector is negligible. In 2005, only 7.8 percent of the private sector workforce belonged to unions. These percentages, however, must be kept in perspective. There are 15.7 million union members in the United States. U.S.DEPT OF LABOR BUREAU OF LABOR STATISTICS PRESS RELEASE, Jan. 20, 2006, http://www.bls.gov/news.release/union2.nro.htm.

A similar global trend was described in the ILO's WORLD LABOUR REPORT 1997–98. The report noted that of ninety-two countries sampled in 1995, only fourteen had a union density rate of more than 50 percent. More than half the sample – forty-eight countries – had unionization rates of less than 20 percent. WORLD LABOUR REPORT 1997–98 (ILO Publications, 1997). Again, percentages only tell part of the story. Although the numbers are disputed, by one estimate there are presently over 150 million union members worldwide. Another estimate pegs global union membership at fifty million. In either case, many more employees, although not members of unions, are covered by collective agreements. BRUCE E. KAUFMAN, THE GLOBAL EVOLUTION OF INDUSTRIAL RELATIONS: EVENTS, IDEAS AND THE IIRA (2004) (hereinafter Kaufman, Global Evolution of Industrial Relations).

Although conditions vary by country and region, most commentators believe globalization has weakened unions' influence, especially in industrialized nations. Capitol mobility places traditionally unionized blue collar industries in competition with lower cost producers abroad, and has resulted in the loss of unionized jobs. How can a union respond to an employer's demand during collective bargaining to meet $6 per hour labor costs outside the United States when the existing labor cost is $25 per hour? Can the union's members agree to such wage cuts?

Shifts in employment toward nonstandard work pose particular challenges for organized labor. Contingent workers are traditionally thought to be difficult to organize because they lack attachment to the labor market and work at its periphery in the worst jobs. Additionally, new human resources techniques emphasizing employee flexibility, promoting deference to managerial goals, and discouraging union affiliation undercut workers' impetus to unionize. Although not all these changes are attributable to globalization, they tend to be accentuated by the practices of TNCs. Greg J. Bamber & Russell D. Lansbury, *An Introduction to International and Comparative Employment Relations, in* INTERNATIONAL & COMPARATIVE EMPLOYMENT RELATIONS 313 (3rd ed. 2003).

Notwithstanding apparently gloomy prospects, organized labor is attempting to meet the challenges of globalization. The primary locus for high level cross-border collaboration is the International Confederation of Free Trade Unions (ICFTU). Founded in 1949, the ICTWU in May 2006 boasts 236 affiliated organizations from 154 countries, which represent 155 million workers. It provides a forum for national union centers or confederations – each an umbrella organization with national union members – to work on issues of common interest, to share information, and to present a united voice on fundamental human and labor union rights. Katherine O'Rourke, *Enabling Transnational Union Activity, in* GLOBAL COMPETITION AND THE AMERICAN EMPLOYMENT LANDSCAPE: AS WE ENTER THE 21ST CENTURY 1201, 1204–05 (Samuel Estreicher, ed., 2000).

A number of international organizations rely on the ICFTU to represent the international labor movement. It plays a major role in the Workers' Group of the ILO's Governing

Body, is the official representative of organized labor at the United Nations, and represents workers' interests in its contacts with the International Monetary Fund (IMF), the World Bank, and the World Trade Organization (WTO). Jonathan P. Hiatt, Deborah Greenfield & Stacey Heath, *Union Participation in International Labor Affairs, in* INTERNATIONAL LABOR AND EMPLOYMENT LAWS 43-7 (2d ed., William L. Keller & Timothy J. Darby, eds., 2003) (hereinafter Keller & Darby, International Labor and Employment Laws). Despite its size and potential clout, even representatives from the ICTWU sometimes sound besieged. Not long ago, Dan Cunniah, at the time director of the ICFTU's Geneva Office, complained that there were forces in the ILO who seek to weaken international labor standards setting and oversight, and even labor's role within that international organization. Dan Cunniah, *The ICTWU and Its Policies within the ILO Workers' Group*, 55 BULL. COMP. LAB. REL. (2004).

Although the international labor movement surely benefits from the official status granted the ICTWU by international organizations, none of those organizations is empowered to deal with the day-to-day problems of workers or to pass judgment on individual employers. Realizing that they are severely disadvantaged in their dealings with TNCs, national unions are exploring new ways of building and strengthening a multinational labor movement. Some industry-specific international confederations of unions, such as the International Metalworkers Federation, have attempted coordinated bargaining across national borders. Atleson, Voyage of the Neptune Jade, at 107 (2004). The North American Free Trade Agreement (NAFTA) has inspired U.S. and Mexican unions to engage in cooperative organizing efforts on both sides of the border. Henry J. Frundt, *Four Models of Cross-Border Maquila Organizing, in* UNIONS IN A GLOBALIZED ENVIRONMENT, 45-61 (Bruce Nissen, ed., 2002).

There also have been sympathetic shows of transnational solidarity. In 1997, for example, dockworkers in the United States, Canada, and Japan refused to unload cargo thought to have been loaded by an employer that had terminated over three hundred longshoremen in Liverpool, England. Atleson, *Voyage of the Neptune Jade*, at 110–15. Andy Stern, president of the Service Employees International Union, the largest and fastest growing union in the United States, has been meeting with union leaders from Europe, Australia, and China to discuss the formation of a new global federation. Matt Bai, *The New Boss*, THE NEW YORK TIMES MAGAZINE, Jan. 30, 2005, at 38, 45.

Whether such efforts will flower into a truly transnational labor movement that will be an effective counterweight to TNCs defies prediction. As Professor Bruce Kaufman observes:

> In the here and now, however, the facts are plain to see – unions are declining, despite much effort at union renewal, and significant new sources of growth are not on the horizon. Thus organized labour may be able to hold its own in some countries, but overall union density is likely to continue to diminish across the world – absent some unforeseen economic or social shock that causes widespread Depression-era job insecurity and deprivation, major war-time disruption and economic controls, and/or a major liberalization of labour law to promote more unionism.
>
> Kaufman, Global Evolution of Industrial Relations, at 627-8.

In other words, something more than union leaders' best efforts or even ordinary employer overreaching may be needed to catalyze global worker solidarity.

iii. Globalization and Gender. One of the most striking changes in the world of work over the last several decades is the significant increase in the numbers of women engaged in paid labor. In 2003, 40 percent of the world's 2.8 billion workers were female, an increase of almost two hundred million women over the last decade. Economic parity, however, continues to elude women as a group. Women make up a majority of the world's working poor – 60 percent. They have higher rates of unemployment than men. Women earn less than men for the same type of work, even in occupations traditionally held by women. They are less likely than men to be employed in regular wage and salaried jobs. INTERNATIONAL LABOR ORGANIZATION, GLOBAL EMPLOYMENT TRENDS FOR WOMEN 2004 (2004), http://www.ilo.org/public/english/employment/strat/download/getyen.pdf. Even those women most advantaged typically fare worse than their male counterparts. The rate of progress for women in managerial and professional jobs varies by country but is in general slow and uneven. LINDA WIRTH, BREAKING THROUGH THE GLASS CEILING: WOMEN IN MANAGEMENT (ILO, 2004), http://www.ilo.org/public/english/support/publ/textww. htm#b8457.

Social and cultural factors play a large role in the disadvantage experienced by women who work for pay. In many developing countries, deep-rooted gender inequalities greatly constrain women's options. Across the globe, family matters continue to be the responsibility of women, and countless occupations are segregated by gender. As a result, many women occupy poorly paid, unstable jobs and are among the most vulnerable workers in the new economy. These are workers whose paid labor may fall outside formal state regulation, and who in addition shoulder the burdens of unpaid household work, including care of children and elderly relatives. Professor Kerry Rittich notes that the feminization of labor underscores the need for regulation designed to meet the new realities of the labor market. Ironically, however, neoliberal economic principles counsel against attempts to obtain protection through legislative or collective means. Kerry Rittich, *Feminization and Contingency: Regulating the Stakes of Work for Women, in* LABOUR LAW IN AN ERA OF GLOBALIZATION, 117-22 (Joanne Conaghan, Richard Michael Fischl & Karl Klare, eds., 2002).

Although women as a whole experience disadvantage in the formal and informal economies, there are great differences among female workers. Women privileged by race, class, and ethnicity lead lives that bear scant resemblance, for example, to those whose labor is central to the global garment and electronics industries. Women of color, especially those who are immigrants, occupy a disproportionate share of "the most degraded positions on the economic ladder." Laura Ho, Catherine Powell & Leti Volpp, *(Dis)Assembling Rights of Women Workers Along the Global Assembly Line: Human Rights and the Garment Industry*, 31 HARV. C.R.-C.L.L. REV. 383, 384–5 (1996). Those working in the "typically female industries" – processing textiles, producing toys, electronic goods, and pharmaceuticals – certainly have gained jobs but also "appalling working conditions, few rights, meager pay and no social security of sustainable livelihood." CHRISTA WICHTERICH, THE GLOBALIZED WOMAN: REPORTS FROM A FUTURE OF INEQUALITY 2 (2000).

It is a relatively simple matter for Westerners to argue for better working conditions for women who labor in factories in distant EPZs or even in sweatshops in the developed world. What happens when oppressive conditions hit closer to home? Professor Donna Young, in words bound to cause discomfort, tackles the issue of professional middle-class women hiring immigrant women to perform household domestic work, work that frequently falls outside the protections of formal labor and employment law:

> Employers of domestic workers – who by virtue of their citizenship, class, and/or race are able to exploit global economic forces that drive women from their homes in search of remunerative jobs in other countries – plainly benefit from the law's unequal treatment of domestic workers. Many of the employers are women. This fact has spurred a reevaluation of the assumptions of feminist jurisprudence that patriarchy is the root of gender oppression in which women are subordinate to men, and in which legal institutions sustain women's subordination.

> Donna E. Young, *Working Across Borders: Global Restructuring and Women's Work*, 2001 UTAH L. REV. 1, 52.

When a woman lawyer hires a Central American immigrant as a nanny to care for her children, is the lawyer perpetuating the subordinate status of her employee? Professor M. Isabel Medina notes the "irony in the fact that the candidacies of the first two women ever to be nominated for the position of United States Attorney General failed, in essence, because the two . . . were working mothers" who had hired undocumented workers to care for their children. M. Isabel Medina, *In Search of Quality Childcare: Closing the Immigration Gate to Childcare Workers*, 8 GEO. IMMIGR. L. J. 161 (1994). President Clinton's nominations began as a celebration of Zoë Baird's and Kimba Wood's accomplishments but degenerated quickly into a reminder of the barriers to equality faced by professional women under a system unresponsive to their needs, the needs of their children, and those of undocumented childcare workers as well. *Id.*

Professor Maria Ontiveros has called for "a vision of global capitalism that puts [women and people of color] at the center." Maria L. Ontiveros, *A Vision of Global Capitalism that Puts Women and People of Color at the Center*, 3 J. SMALL & EMERGING BUS. L. 27 (1999). One way to begin is to consider the conditions under which women in the global production system labor, and the legal mechanisms that exist for redressing their grievances.

PUBLIC REPORT OF REVIEW OF NAO SUBMISSION NO. 9701

U.S. National Administrative Office
Bureau of International Labor Affairs
U.S. Department of Labor

January 12, 1998

I. INTRODUCTION

The U.S. National Administrative office (NAO) was established under the North American Agreement on Labor Cooperation (NAALC). The NAALC, the labor supplemental agreement to the North American Free Trade Agreement (NAFTA), provides for the review of submissions concerning labor law matters arising in Canada or Mexico by the U.S. NAO. . . .

II. SUMMARY OF SUBMISSION 9701

U.S. NAO Submission No. 9701 was filed on May 16, 1996 by Human Rights Watch (HRW), the International Labor Rights Fund (ILRF), and the National Association of Democratic Lawyers (Asociación Nacional de Abogados Democráticos, hereinafter ANAD) of Mexico. The submission raises issues of discrimination against women job applicants and women workers in Mexico's export processing (maquiladora) sector. The submitters allege that maquiladora employers regularly require female job applicants to verify their pregnancy status as a condition of employment and deny employment to pregnant women. Additionally, the submitters allege that some maquiladora employers discharge pregnant employees or deliberately mistreat them in order to provoke their resignation.

Mexican law guarantees financial and medical support to pregnant workers and their families through the social security system. However, when workers have not been employed for a sufficient period (30 weeks) to qualify for social security benefits, employers are required to provide maternity benefits to pregnant workers, including six weeks of paid leave before and after delivery. Thus, the alleged basis for the discrimination is economic.

The submitters assert that such discrimination is widely countenanced by Mexican government officials charged with enforcing Mexico's labor laws, and may even be condoned as part of a wider effort to curb population growth. They assert that these actions are in violation of Mexican domestic law which prohibits gender discrimination and provides special protection for pregnant workers. . . .

VI. ANALYSIS

MEXICAN LAW AND PRACTICE

Gender discrimination is clearly prohibited in Mexico's Constitution and in its Federal Labor Law [FLL]. Article 4 of the Mexican Constitution states "Man and woman are equal before the law. . . . " Article 5 guarantees that individuals shall not be prevented from pursuing the work of their choice. Article 4 further provides that all persons have the right to determine the spacing of their children. Article 3 of the FLL states that "[t]here shall not be established distinctions among workers for motives of race, sex, age, religious creed, political doctrine, or social position." Article 133 states that employers may not "[r]efuse to accept workers for reason of age or sex. . . . " Article 164 states that "[w]omen enjoy the same rights and have the same obligations as men." . . .

Pre-Employment . . .

In support of their position that pregnancy screening is widespread, the submitters point to responses from companies identified in the original *HRW Report* of August, 1996. In letters to HRW and the U.S. NAO, four of the companies acknowledged that they have engaged in the practice of screening female job applicants for pregnancy. . . . In a letter appended to the HRW Report, one of these companies additionally stated that the practice is used to avoid the possibility that pregnant women may seek employment only to obtain maternity benefits that the Social Security system does not provide. . . .

The submitters' position is further supported by the testimony of women workers at the public hearing conducted. . . . Women testified that they were required to fill out medical questionnaires that went beyond simply ascertaining whether they were pregnant. These included questions on their last menstruation, sexual activity, birth control methods, and the number of children they had. They testified that they were interviewed on these same matters and required to produce urine samples which, they were told, were for the purpose of determining pregnancy. They told of being hired for training periods and being required to sign documents agreeing to their dismissal if they became pregnant during that period. They testified as to warnings they received that they would be dismissed if they became pregnant and told of being compelled to resign after it was learned by their employer that they were pregnant. . . .

The Mexican Government has provided information that pregnancy screening is not widely practiced, and that to the extent that it is, it is legal in Mexico. . . . The Mexican NAO also stated that, in the absence of an employment relationship, the FLL provides for no legal process for bringing forth cases of employment discrimination.

However, the *Alliance for Equality* discusses the practice of pre-employment pregnancy screening. This document states that discrimination in hiring and in dismissal for reason of pregnancy occurs "frequently." The *Alliance for Equality* is a five-year policy guideline prepared by the Secretariat of the Government of Mexico, a cabinet level government agency. In that document, the government discusses both discrimination in hiring due to pregnancy and dismissal from employment for reason of pregnancy. The government proposes to establish "mechanisms to ensure the respect for the rights of women workers and their access to the welfare and social security systems, on an equal footing with men, in compliance with Federal Labor Law, in order to avoid discrimination for reason of sex, age, civil status and pregnancy. . . . "

[T]he Mexican Government indicates that it is conducting programs of consciousness awareness among women workers and has sought to obtain the voluntary cooperation of the maquiladora employers to cease the practice of pre-employment pregnancy screening. Evidently, the government finds these practices to be inappropriate, even if they may be technically legal under Mexican law.

Moreover, the Human Rights Commission for the Federal District offers a markedly different interpretation to that of the Mexican NAO on the legality of pre-employment pregnancy screening. The Commission found (1) that the federal agencies it investigated did, in fact, conduct pregnancy screening and, (2) this practice violated Mexico's Constitution. . . .

Post-Hire
Mexico's laws are clear on the matter of post-hire dismissal or reprisal on the basis of gender, pregnancy, or for any reason not provided by law. Mexico's Constitution and labor law guarantee the right of all citizens to employment and the FLL provides specific causes and procedures by which the employment relationship can be terminated. Essentially, the employment relationship imposes contractual obligations that are enforceable by the labor authorities and by the courts. Pregnancy is not listed as a justified cause for dismissal from employment and, therefore, dismissal for reason of pregnancy is prohibited under the FLL. Actions taken against pregnant workers to coerce them into resigning violate maternity protection clauses under Article 170 of the FLL. Finally, the FLL makes no provision for probationary labor contracts under which a worker could be dismissed without cause. . . .

Despite information that women have been able to win their cases in the CABs [the conciliation and arbitration boards charged to investigate and adjudicate labor disputes] against post-hire dismissal for reason of pregnancy, the submitters assert that women workers lack confidence in the CABs for the enforcement of their rights against dismissal for reason of pregnancy. . . . Working women's perceptions of the CABs may be reinforced by the lack of awareness of their rights and their economic circumstances, which mitigates against challenging authority. Women with little formal education and limited economic means may lack the wherewithal to pursue legal remedies. Further, fear exists, whether real or perceived, of the blacklisting of workers who cause trouble. Moreover, a number of the women approached their union and were advised that there was nothing that the union could do in their defense. Indeed, the need for a program of orientation and information for women workers is recognized by the Mexican Government in its *Alliance for Equality* program.

The *Alliance for Equality* addresses dismissal for reason of pregnancy and indicates that the government is preparing steps to bring about compliance with the law. The existence of the document and the action plan included indicates that the Government of Mexico is aware of this problem and intends to address it. . . .

Notes

1. Consider the submitters in the case. Human Rights Watch is an international NGO that conducts research, publishes reports and books, consults with international organizations, and agitates for the amelioration of human rights abuses around the globe. It is headquartered in New York. The International Labor Rights Fund is an international NGO dedicated to protecting workers rights and creating fair global labor standards. Its headquarters are in Washington, DC. The National Association of Democratic Lawyers of Mexico is a national group of independent lawyers that provides representation in cases involving labor and indigenous rights. Professor Kenneth Anderson criticizes international NGOs as undemocratic institutions using international law to achieve results that have been rejected at the domestic level. They are not elected and yet assume the mantel of representing civil society and its interests. This, argues Anderson, is a tremendous threat to democracy and to national sovereignty. Kenneth Anderson, *The Limits of Pragmatism in American Foreign Policy: Unsolicited Advice to the Bush Administration on Relations with International Non-Governmental Organizations*, 2 CHI. J. INT'L L. 371 (2001). Is Anderson's criticism a fair one regarding NAO Submission NO. 9701?

2. The submission was filed with the U.S. NAO under procedures provided for in the NAALC, the labor side agreement to NAFTA. Details of the NAALC will be provided in Chapter 6, but it suffices to say that both the procedures and remedies for cases involving discrimination are limited. Kate Andrias describes the outcome of the case:

    The report criticized the practice of pressuring pregnant women to quit their jobs, but stopped short of condemning the practice of pre-hire pregnancy testing. The NAO recommended ministerial consultations "for the purpose of ascertaining the extent of protections against pregnancy-based gender discrimination afforded by Mexico's laws and their effective enforcement by the appropriate institutions." As a result of the consultations, several conferences were held – in Mexico and the United States – to address issues related to women's rights at work.

Kate E. Andrias, *Gender, Work, and the NAFTA Labor Side Agreement*, 37 U.S.F. L. REV. 521, 555 (2003).

Andrias notes that despite the insistence of the Mexican government throughout most of the NAALC proceedings that preemployment pregnancy screening was legal under domestic law, Mexican authorities ultimately succumbed to political pressure, changing their interpretation of their own laws. At a conference that was part of the ministerial agreement in the case, Mexican officials stated that the practice violates domestic standards. *Id.* at n. 147. How would you describe what the submitters achieved by filing a NAALC submission?

3. Are you sympathetic to the economic concerns that motivate employers to undertake pregnancy screening? Can one characterize the women as acting opportunistically?

4. Is Mexican law to blame in this case? By placing on employers an obligation the state itself was unwilling and perhaps unable to undertake – providing social security benefits to a class of pregnant workers – the government increased the cost of hiring women workers along with the risk that employers would attempt to externalize that cost. The submitters allege that Mexican authorities were generally unresponsive to complaints about lack of employer compliance with the law. Is their indifference to the women's claims traceable to the fact that many factory workers in the Mexican maquila sector come from different parts of the country or from Central America? Why would a country pass a law that it cannot and will not ultimately enforce? Professor Jagdish Bhagwati explains that "the generosity of these provisions in the face of acutely limited resources is simply meant to produce a good feeling – the legislators mean well, but beyond that, alas. . . . " Bhagwati, In Defense of Globalization, at 174. Is Bhagwati's account of legislative process in the developing world plausible?

---

iv. Globalization and Migrant Workers. Although there are several international conventions designed to protect migrant workers, there is no multilateral framework that structures the movement of people across national borders. Rather, immigration law, and in particular workplace law that can be invoked and enforced by immigrant workers, is by and large national law. This regulatory scheme does little to discourage migration, which continues to accelerate. In 2000, an estimated 175 million people were living outside the country in which they were born. INTERNATIONAL MIGRATION REPORT 2002, DEPT. OF ECON. AND SOC. AFFAIRS, POPULATION DIV., U.N. Doc. ST/ESA/SER.A/220 (2002). The World Commission on the Social Dimensions of Globalization estimates that worldwide there are fifteen to thirty million irregular immigrants – people who lack legal permission to be present and/or to work in the country where they are located. A Fair Globalization, at 96. Given, as noted later, that an estimated eleven million undocumented persons reside in the United States alone, the worldwide estimates appear low.

THE INTERNATIONAL CONVENTION ON THE PROTECTION OF THE RIGHTS OF ALL MIGRANT WORKERS AND MEMBERS OF THEIR FAMILIES

G.A. Res. 45/158, annex 45 U.N. GAOR Supp. (No. 49A) at 261, U.N. Doc. A/45/49 (1990), *entered into force* July 1, 2003

Preamble

The States Parties to the present Convention. . . .

Have agreed as follows:

Article 1

1. The present Convention is applicable . . . to all migrant workers and members of their families without distinction of any kind such as sex, race, colour, language, religion or conviction, political or other opinion, national, ethnic or social origin, nationality, age, economic position, property, marital status, birth or other status. . . .

Article 2

For the purposes of the present Convention:

1. The term "migrant worker" refers to a person who is to be engaged, is engaged or has been engaged in a remunerated activity in a State of which he or she is not a national. . . .

Article 25

1. Migrant workers shall enjoy treatment not less favorable than that which applies to nationals of the State of employment in respect of remuneration and:

   a. Other conditions of work, that is to say, overtime, hours of work, weekly rest, holidays with pay, safety, health, termination of the employment relationship and any other conditions of work which, according to national law and practice, are covered by these terms;

   b. Other terms of employment, that is to say, minimum age of employment, restriction on home work and any other matters which, according to national law and practice, are considered a term of employment;

2. It shall not be lawful to derogate in private contracts of employment from the principle of equality of treatment referred to in paragraph 1 of the present article.

3. States Parties shall take all appropriate measures to ensure that migrant workers are not deprived of any rights derived from this principle by reason of any irregularity in their stay or employment. In particular, employers shall not be relieved of any legal or contractual obligations, nor shall their obligations be limited in any manner by reason of such irregularity.

Article 26

1. States Parties recognize the right of migrant workers and members of their families:

   a. To take part in meetings and activities of trade unions and of any other associations established in accordance with law, with a view to protecting their economic, social, cultural and other interests, subject only to the rules of the organization concerned;

 b. To join freely any trade union and any such association as aforesaid, subject only to the rules of the organization concerned;

 c. To seek the aid and assistance of any trade union and of any such association as aforesaid.

2. No restrictions may be placed on the exercise of these rights other than those that are prescribed by law and which are necessary in a democratic society in the interests of national security, public order (ordre public) or the protection of the rights and freedoms of others.

Notes

1. As of September 2006, only thirty-four countries had become parties to the International Convention on the Protection of the Rights of All Migrant Workers and Members of their Families. Not one of the thirty-four is a developed nation. Do the excerpts from the Convention above shed light on why so-called receiving nations are reluctant to embrace it? What rights, if any, are parties bound to extend to undocumented workers?

2. The Convention is notable not only for extending workplace equal treatment rights to all migrant workers but also for providing protections to their families. These protections include the right to freedom of religion and expression, privacy, property, urgent medical care, access to education and where possible other state-supported programs, and freedom from arbitrary arrest or detention. Countries that become parties also pledge to take steps to end illegal recruitment and trafficking of migrant workers and to discourage the employment of the undocumented.

3. From its beginning, the ILO has worked for the protection of migrant workers and their families. The ILO's two major conventions on the subject are the Migration for Employment Convention (Revised) (No. 97) of 1949 and the Migrant Workers (Supplementary Provisions) Convention (No. 143) of 1975. Convention No. 97 requires ratifying states to ensure migrants legally within their borders are afforded treatment no less favorable than nationals regarding a range of workplace conditions without discrimination on the basis of nationality, race, religion, or sex. Convention No. 143 contains provisions pertaining to migrations in abusive conditions and sections regarding equality of opportunity and treatment. As of October 2006, the conventions have been ratified by forty-five and nineteen countries, respectively. The ILO has 179 member states. The United States has ratified neither convention.

4. The United States is thought to have about eleven million undocumented persons residing within its borders. A majority of these individuals are employed. One estimate places the number of unauthorized workers in the United States at 7.2 million, about 4.9 percent of the nation's labor force. These employees are highly concentrated in low-wage industries including agriculture, food processing, garment manufacturing, construction, foodservice, hotels and landscaping. John M. Broder, *Immigrants and the Economics of Hard Work*, N.Y. TIMES, April 2, 2006, Week in Review, at 3 (hereinafter Broder, *Economics of Hard Work*); *see also* Beth Lyon, *When More "Security" Equals Less Workplace Safety: Reconsidering U.S. Laws that Disadvantage Unauthorized Workers*, 6 U. PA. J. LAB. & EMP. L. 571, 583-5 (2004). Undocumented workers represent 10 percent of the low-wage workers in the United States, and in agriculture are thought to comprise between 50 to 60 percent of the workforce. Wayne A. Cornelius & Takeyuki Tsuda,

Controlling Immigration: The Limits of Government Intervention, in CONTROL-
LING IMMIGRATION: A GLOBAL PERSPECTIVE 1, 20 (Wayne A. Cornelius et al., eds.,
2004).

5. In terms of origin, 78 percent of undocumented persons in the United States
come from Latin America, 56 percent of those are from Mexico. Whether undocumented workers produce wage effects injurious to other workers is a matter of
some debate. A study by Professor George J. Borjas, who teaches economics and
social policy at Harvard's Kennedy School of Government, concluded that from
1980 to 2000 the inflow of undocumented migrants caused an "average annual
wage loss for all American male workers . . . [of] $1200, or 4 percent, and nearly
twice that, in percentage terms, for those without a high school diploma." Broder,
Economics of Hard Work, at 3. Wage depression, Borjas found, fell disproportionately on African-Americans and Hispanic-Americans. *Id.* Does the U.S. economy
depend on undocumented workers to perform jobs that Americans refuse to do?
If the wages and working conditions for those jobs were better, might those jobs
be more appealing to American workers? Would working conditions in the lowest
paid jobs improve by providing undocumented workers with legal status?

HOFFMAN PLASTIC COMPOUNDS V. N.L.R.B.

535 U.S. 137 (2002)

Chief Justice REHNQUIST delivered the opinion of the Court, in which Justice O'CONNOR,
Justice SCALIA, Justice KENNEDY, and Justice THOMAS joined. . . .

The National Labor Relations Board (Board) awarded backpay to an undocumented alien
who has never been legally authorized to work in the United States. We hold that such relief
is foreclosed by federal immigration policy, as expressed by Congress in the Immigration
Reform and Control Act of 1986 (IRCA).

Petitioner Hoffman Plastic Compounds, Inc. (petitioner or Hoffman), custom-formulates
chemical compounds for businesses that manufacture pharmaceutical, construction, and
household products. In May 1988, petitioner hired Jose Castro to operate various blending
machines that "mix and cook" the particular formulas per customer order. Before being hired
for this position, Castro presented documents that appeared to verify his authorization to
work in the United States. In December 1988, the United Rubber, Cork, Linoleum, and
Plastic Workers of America, AFL-CIO, began a union-organizing campaign at petitioner's
production plant. Castro and several other employees supported the organizing campaign
and distributed authorization cards to co-workers. In January 1989, Hoffman laid off Castro
and other employees engaged in these organizing activities.

Three years later, in January 1992, respondent Board found that Hoffman unlawfully selected
four employees, including Castro, for layoff "in order to rid itself of known union supporters"
in violation of §8(a)(3) of the National Labor Relations Act (NLRA).[1] To remedy this violation,
the Board ordered that Hoffman (1) cease and desist from further violations of the NLRA, (2)

---

[1] Section 8(a)(3) of the NLRA prohibits discrimination "in regard to hire or tenure of employment or any
term or condition of employment to encourage or discourage membership in any labor organization." 49
Stat. 452, as added, 61 Stat. 140, 29 U.S.C. §158(a)(3).

post a detailed notice to its employees regarding the remedial order, and (3) offer reinstatement and backpay to the four affected employees. . . .

In June 1993, the parties proceeded to a compliance hearing before an Administrative Law Judge (ALJ) to determine the amount of backpay owed to each discriminatee. On the final day of the hearing, Castro testified that he was born in Mexico and that he had never been legally admitted to, or authorized to work in, the United States. He admitted gaining employment with Hoffman only after tendering a birth certificate belonging to a friend who was born in Texas. He also admitted that he used this birth certificate to fraudulently obtain a California driver's license and a Social Security card, and to fraudulently obtain employment following his layoff by Hoffman. . . . Based on this testimony, the ALJ found the Board precluded from awarding Castro backpay or reinstatement as such relief would be contrary to Sure-Tan v. NLRB, 467 U.S. 883 (1984), and in conflict with IRCA, which makes it unlawful for employers knowingly to hire undocumented workers or for employees to use fraudulent documents to establish employment eligibility.

[The Board reversed with respect to backpay, concluding that the best way to further IRCA's policies is to treat undocumented workers in the same manner as other employees. The Court of Appeals denied Hoffman's petition for review and the Supreme Court granted certiorari.]

This case exemplifies the principle that the Board's discretion to select and fashion remedies for violations of the NLRA, though generally broad, is not unlimited. . . . Since the Board's inception, we have consistently set aside awards of reinstatement or backpay to employees found guilty of serious illegal conduct in connection with their employment. . . .

. . . As we have previously noted, IRCA "forcefully" made combating the employment of illegal aliens central to "[t]he policy of immigration law." INS v. National Center for Immigrants' Rights, 502 U.S. 183, 194, and n. 8 (1991). It did so by establishing an extensive "employment verification system," §1324 a(a)(1), designed to deny employment to aliens who (a) are not lawfully present in the United States, or (b) are not lawfully authorized to work in the United States, §1324a(h)(3). This verification system is critical to the IRCA regime. To enforce it, IRCA mandates that employers verify the identity and eligibility of all new hires by examining specified documents before they begin work. If an alien applicant is unable to present the required documentation, the unauthorized alien cannot be hired.

Similarly, if an employer unknowingly hires an unauthorized alien, or if the alien becomes unauthorized while employed, the employer is compelled to discharge the worker upon discovery of the worker's undocumented status. Employers who violate IRCA are punished by civil fines, and may be subject to criminal prosecution. IRCA also makes it a crime for an unauthorized alien to subvert the employer verification system by tendering fraudulent documents. It thus prohibits aliens from using or attempting to use "any forged, counterfeit, altered, or falsely made document" or "any document lawfully issued to or with respect to a person other than the possessor" for purposes of obtaining employment in the United States. §§1324c(a)(1)–(3). Aliens who use or attempt to use such documents are subject to fines and criminal prosecution. There is no dispute that Castro's use of false documents to obtain employment with Hoffman violated these provisions. . . .

We therefore conclude that allowing the Board to award backpay to illegal aliens would unduly trench upon explicit statutory prohibitions critical to federal immigration policy, as expressed in IRCA. It would encourage the successful evasion of apprehension by immigration authorities, condone prior violations of the immigration laws, and encourage future violations. However broad the Board's discretion to fashion remedies when dealing only with the NLRA, it is not so unbounded as to authorize this sort of an award.

Lack of authority to award backpay does not mean that the employer gets off scot-free. The Board here has already imposed other significant sanctions against Hoffman – sanctions Hoffman does not challenge. . . .

Justice BREYER, with whom Justice STEVENS, Justice SOUTER, and Justice GINSBURG join, dissenting.

[T]he general purpose of the immigration statute's employment prohibition is to diminish the attractive force of employment, which like a "magnet" pulls illegal immigrants toward the United States. To permit the Board to award backpay could not significantly increase the strength of this magnetic force, for so speculative a future possibility could not realistically influence an individual's decision to migrate illegally.

To *deny* the Board the power to award backpay, however, might very well increase the strength of this magnetic force. That denial lowers the cost to the employer of an initial labor law violation (provided, of course, that the only victims are illegal aliens). It thereby increases the employer's incentive to find and to hire illegal-alien employees. Were the Board forbidden to assess backpay against a *knowing* employer – a circumstance not before us today – this perverse economic incentive, which runs directly contrary to the immigration statute's basic objective, would be obvious and serious. But even if limited to cases where the employer did not know of the employee's status, the incentive may prove significant – for, as the Board has told us, the Court's rule offers employers immunity in borderline cases, thereby encouraging them to take risks, *i.e.*, to hire with a wink and a nod those potentially unlawful aliens whose unlawful employment (given the Court's views) ultimately will lower the costs of labor law violations.. . . .

_____

Notes

1. After *Hoffman Plastic*, does an employer who fires an undocumented worker for union activity violate U.S. labor law? The answer is clearly yes. *Hoffman Plastic* is a case about permissible legal remedies not statutory coverage. The Supreme Court's decision in *Sure-Tan, Inc. v.N.L.R.B.*, cited in the *Hoffman Plastic* opinion, held that undocumented workers are employees under the National Labor Relations Act. *See Sure-Tan, Inc. v. N.L.R.B.*, 467 U.S. 883, 892–4 (1984).

2. Many state courts in the United States have held their workplace laws apply to undocumented workers. As a practical matter, however, those courts only approve reinstatement orders for the wrongfully discharged that are conditioned on the employee obtaining work authorization within a reasonable period of time. Michael J. Wishnie, *Emerging Issues for Undocumented Workers*, 6 U. PA. J. LAB. & EMP. L. 497, 505 (2004). Moreover, although *Hoffman Plastic* precludes, at least under the NLRA, awarding back pay for work not performed, wage and hour laws "continue to require payment of minimum wages and overtime premiums for work that was performed, regardless of the immigration status of the employee." *Id.* at 509. Does *Hoffman Plastic* affect the availability of punitive and compensatory damages under federal antidiscrimination law? Do its remedial strictures apply to cases where the employer *knowingly* hires and illegally fires an undocumented worker?

3. Professor Ruben Garcia argues that *Hoffman Plastic* represents "a failure to see immigration as a labor issue and vice versa." Ruben J. Garcia, *Ghost Workers in an Interconnected World: Going Beyond the Dichotomies of Domestic Immigration*

and Labor Laws, 36 U<small>NIV.</small> of M<small>ICH.</small> J. L. R<small>EFORM</small> 737, 740 (2003). Rather than harmonize the two policy goals at stake, the majority pitted immigration control against the right to organize and determined that the former trumped the latter, leaving perhaps the most vulnerable group of workers in the United States without meaningful legal protection. *Id.* Other commentators are similarly critical of the decision. *See e.g.* Cynthia L. Estlund, *The Ossification of American Labor Law*, 102 C<small>OLUM.</small> L. R<small>EV.</small> 1527, 1564 (2002); Christopher David Ruiz Cameron, *Borderline Decisions: Hoffman Plastic Compounds, The New Bracero Program, and the Supreme Court's Role in Making Federal Labor Policy*, 51 UCLA L. R<small>EV.</small> 1 (2003); Robert I. Correales, *Did Hoffman Plastic Compounds, Inc. Produce Disposable Workers?* 14 B<small>ERKELEY</small> L<small>A</small> R<small>AZA</small> L. J. 103 (2003); Thomas J. Walsh, Hoffman Plastic Compounds, Inc. v. N.L.R.B.: *How the Supreme Court Eroded Labor Law and Workers Rights in the Name of Immigration Policy*, 21 L<small>AW</small> & I<small>NEQ.</small> 313 (2003).

4. As noted earlier, pursuant to an AFL-CIO complaint filed against the United States, the ILO's Committee on Freedom of Association found that *Hoffman Plastic* leaves the NLRB with insufficient remedies to ensure that undocumented workers are protected against antiunion discrimination. The CFA concluded its report with the following recommendation:

> The Committee invites the Government to explore all possible solutions, including amending the legislation to bring it into conformity with freedom of association principles, in full consultation with the social partners concerned, with the aim of ensuring effective protection for all workers against acts of anti-union discrimination in the wake of the Hoffman decision. The Government is requested to keep the Committee informed of the measures taken in this regard.

> International Labour Organization, Committee on Freedom of Association, Complaints against the Government of the United States Presented by the American Federation of Labor and Congress of Industrial Organizations (AFL-CIO) and the Confederation of Mexican Workers (CTM), Case No. 2227, Report No. 332, ¶ 613 (2003).

The Inter-American Court of Human Rights (IACHR) issued an advisory opinion in September 2003 in response to a case filed by the Mexican government, the latter having reacted with concern to the *Hoffman* decision. The advisory opinion held that despite their irregular status, undocumented workers are entitled to the same labor rights as all workers, including back pay. This principle is of special importance given that undocumented workers are frequently afforded unfavorable conditions compared to other workers. Inter-American Court of Human Rights, Advisory Opinion OC-18/03, Juridical Condition and Rights of the Undocumented Migrants, ¶136 (Sept. 17, 2003). Neither the ILO nor the IACHR opinion is binding on the United States.

5. *Hoffman Plastic* aside, many undocumented workers labor in industries and occupations that are excluded from coverage under the NLRA. Notable among these are domestic workers and farm workers. Statutorily excluded workers may still organize and engage in collective activities but lack the legal protections of federal law when they do so. Nonetheless, groups of such workers have had some successes in organizing for better working conditions, in some cases taking advantage of their

exclusion from the NLRA by engaging in boycott activities that would be illegal if they were covered by the statute. Julie Yates Rivchin, *Building Power Among Low-Wage Immigrant Workers: Some Legal Considerations for Organizing Structures and Strategies*, 28 N.Y.U. Rev. L. & Soc. Change 397, 418–24 (2004); Peggie R. Smith, *Organizing the Unorganizable: Private Paid Household Workers and Approaches to Employee Representation*, 79 N.C.L. Rev. 45 (2000).

6. A formative immigrant rights movement is taking root in the United States. Beginning in March 2006, civil rights protests have been held by immigrants and their supporters in a number of major American cities, including New York, Chicago, and Los Angeles. Sheryl Gay Stolberg, *After Immigration Protests, Goal is Still Elusive*, N.Y. Times, May 3, 2006, at A1. On May 1, 2006, hundreds of thousands "skipped work, school and shopping . . . and marched in dozens of cities coast to coast" in support of a boycott aimed at demonstrating the economic clout of documented and undocumented immigrants. Randal C. Archibold, *Immigrants Take to U.S. Streets in Show of Strength*, N.Y. Times, May 2, 2006, at A1. The protesters also hope to influence Congress by undermining support for a bill in the House of Representatives "making it a felony for an illegal immigrant to be in the country. . . . " *Id.*

---

v. Globalization and Child Labor. The issue of child labor is one of global dimensions, in which clear definitions are needed to measure the extent of the problem and flexible approaches are required to fashion effective, country-specific, contextual solutions. *See* Amy R. Ritualo, Charita L. Castro, and Sarah Gormly, *Measuring Child Labor: Implications for Policy and Program Design*, 24 Comp. Lab. L. & Pol'y J. 401 (2003). As an initial matter, both the UN Convention on the Rights of the Child and the ILO's Worst Forms of Child Labour Convention (No. 182) define a child as an individual less than eighteen years old. Children under five, however, are generally thought to be too young to work or to begin school. Thus, for measurement purposes, the ILO, for example, has focused on statistical compilation for the group of children ages five to seventeen years of age. Int'l Labour Office, Int'l Programme on the Elimination of Child Labour, Every Child Counts: New Global Estimates on Child Labour 23–4 (ILO, 2002) (hereinafter Every Child Counts).

A key challenge, both for measurement and regulatory activity, is determining how to draw the line between permissible work and child labor, the latter being targeted for elimination under the ILO's Fundamental Principles and Rights at Work, its Minimum Age Convention (No. 138), the Worst Forms of Child Labour Convention (No. 182), and the conventions' supplementary but nonbinding Recommendations. Some forms of economic activity engaged in by children are regarded by many as positive, while child labor, it is hoped, will someday cease to exist. Additionally, all child labor is not equal in its detrimental effect, creating the necessity of identifying the worst forms of child labor, "which require urgent action for elimination." Every Child Counts, at 25.

While work is ongoing to establish an internationally recognized definition of child labor, the ILO's International Programme on the Elimination of Child Labour (IPEC) has produced startling estimates on the extent of the global child labor problem, and, much more recently, in a new ILO report, very heartening news about its decline. For the purpose of its seminal 2002 report, IPEC defined child labor through a process of exclusion and then addition. More specifically, and based in part on the Minimum Age Convention (No. 138), child labor consists of all economic activity engaged in by children under the age of fifteen, excluding those under five years old, and excluding those between twelve and fourteen years of age who spend fewer than fourteen hours a week working, unless their activities are hazardous. Added to those numbers are fifteen- to seventeen-year-olds engaged in the worst forms of child labor. Using that definition, IPEC estimated in 2002 that approximately 246 million children were engaged in child labor. Of those, 171 million worked in hazardous situations, and 8.4 million in the unconditional worst forms of child labor. INT'L LABOUR OFFICE, INT'L PROGRAMME ON THE ELIMINATION OF CHILD LABOUR, IPEC ACTION AGAINST CHILD LABOUR: HIGHLIGHTS 2004 13 (ILO 2005) (hereinafter IPEC Action).

The new report, released in May 2006, describes an 11 percent worldwide drop in child labor. Today, child laborers number 218 million, 126 million of whom work under hazardous conditions. The percentage drop in that latter category over a four-year period was 26 percent. INT'L LABOUR OFFICE, REPORT OF THE DIRECTOR-GENERAL, THE END OF CHILD LABOUR: WITHIN REACH xi (ILO, 2006) (hereinafter The End of Child Labour). As encouraging as these numbers are, the eventual elimination of child labor will depend on a sustained global commitment to eradication of this tragic phenomenon.

Child labor is ubiquitous in the developing world, although the problem varies by global region. In Sub-Saharan Africa, for example, over forty-nine million children work. *Id.* at 8. Children are used in armed conflict, work in mining, engage in hazardous agricultural work, and are the victims of trafficking and sexual exploitation. Reports of children sold into bonded labor and slavery have been made in some areas. IPEC Action, at 29. Drought, civil war, and the HIV/AIDS epidemic exacerbate the problem by destabilizing and increasing the vulnerability of African families. *Id.* at 58. *See also* Linda Smith & Mohamed Mattar, *Creating International Consensus on Combating Trafficking in Persons: U.S. Policy, The Role of the UN, and Global Responses and Challenges*, 28-WTR FLETCHER F. WORLD AFF. 155, 158–9 (2004).

Asia and the Pacific region are home to the highest number of child laborers. An estimated 122.3 million children, ages five to fourteen, are economically active. The End of Child Labour, at 8. Many of the worst forms of child labor exist in the region. Tolerance of child labor coupled with political instability in some countries makes addressing the problem a particular challenge. IPEC Action, at 31.

Poverty and limited access to public schooling are among the most important factors affecting the supply of children as workers. On the demand side, children provide a cheap, easily exploitable source of labor. Domestic political indifference, lack of regulatory expertise and apparatuses, and cultural attitudes perpetuate the practice. Michele D'Avolio, *Child Labor and Cultural Relativism: From 19th Century America to 21st Century Nepal*, 16 PACE INT'L L. REV, 109, 136–9 (2004); Angli Garg, *A Child Labor Social Clause: Analysis and Proposal for Action*, 31 N.Y.U.J. INT'L L. & POL. 473, 478–84 (1999); Claudia R. Brewster, *Restoring Childhood: Saving the World's Children from Toiling in Textile Sweatshops*, 16 J.L. & COM 191, 194–7 (1997).

As a practical matter, it is vitally important to address and eradicate child labor in its most egregious form. The ILO's Worst Forms of Child Labour Convention (No. 182), as of October 2006 ratified by 162 countries including the United States, defines the range of activities that urgently require prohibition and elimination.

CONVENTION CONCERNING THE PROHIBITION AND IMMEDIATE ACTION FOR
THE ELIMINATION OF THE WORST FORMS OF CHILD LABOUR (ILO NO. 182)

38 I.L.M. 1207 (1999), *entered into force* Nov. 19, 2000.

Article 3

For the purposes of the Convention, the term *worst forms of child labour* comprises:

(a) all forms of slavery or practices similar to slavery, such as the sale and trafficking of children, debt bondage and serfdom and forced or compulsory labour, including forced or compulsory recruitment of children for use in armed conflict;

(b) the use, procuring or offering of a child for prostitution, for the production of pornography or for pornographic performances;

(c) the use, procuring or offering of a child for illicit activities, in particular for the production and trafficking of drugs as defined in the relevant international treaties;

(d) work which, by its nature or the circumstances in which it is carried out, is likely to harm the health, safety or morals of children.

Notes

1. Of the definitions above, Article 3(d) is the subsection most open to varying interpretations. The Convention leaves it to Member States to determine the types of work that fall under Article 3(d), in consultation employer and labor organizations, and in consideration of international standards. Particular attention is to be paid to the ILO's non-binding Worst Forms of Child Labour Recommendation, which provides that:

   > In determining the types of work referred to under Article 3(d) of the Convention, and in identifying where they exist, consideration should be given, inter alia, to:
   >
   > (a) work which exposes children to physical, psychological or sexual abuse;
   >
   > (b) work underground, under water, at dangerous heights or in confined spaces;
   >
   > (c) work with dangerous machinery, equipment and tools, or which involves the manual handling or transport of heavy loads;
   >
   > (d) work in an unhealthy environment which may, for example, expose children to hazardous substances, agents or processes, or to temperatures, noise levels, or vibrations damaging to their health;
   >
   > (e) work under particularly difficult conditions such as work for long hours or during the night or work where the child is unreasonably confined to the premises of employer.
   >
   > ILO Recommendation Concerning the Prohibition and Immediate Elimination of the Worst Forms of Child Labour Recommendation (No. 190), p 3, June 17, 1999, 38 I.L.M. 1211 (1999).

2. Jagdish Bhagwati describes the child labor problem as "long-standing and historically inherited" and posits that globalization is neither a cause nor an exacerbating

factor. Indeed, to the extent that globalization results in poverty reduction, he argues that it accelerates a reduction in child labor. Bhagwati, In Defense of Globalization, at 68. Bhagwati counsels against the use of international pressure to eliminate the practice except in the case of global trafficking of children, which he agrees calls for "corrective action." *Id.* Developing nations have in general made similar arguments. Calls for the World Trade Organization, the international organization that develops and enforces rules for conducting international trade, to become a forum for addressing issues such as child labor are strongly resisted by the developing world. Such trade-labor linkage is seen by developing countries as veiled protectionism by industrialized nations, a way to deprive them of their comparative advantage in cheap labor, and an encroachment on their national sovereignty. Kristin Weldon, *Piercing the Silence or Lulling You to Sleep: The Sounds of Child Labor*, 7-SPG Widener L. Symp. J. 227, 239-40 (2001).

3. Professor Hugh Hindman portrays pervasive child labor as a scourge of economically underdeveloped nations, arguing that industrialization is initially the cause of the problem and somewhat later, its eradication. Hugh D. Hindman, *Global Child Labor: What We Know, What We Need to Know, in* Proceedings, 53rd Annual Meeting of the Industrial Relations Research Ass'n 14, 15 (2001). Using the United States as an instructive model, Hindman notes:

> In early phases of industrialization [in the U.S.], factors such as habit, custom and tradition, uneven technological advancement, and lack of alternatives (especially schools) virtually ensured that children would be put to work. In later stages of industrialization, factors such as the emergence of a reform movement, continued technological advancement, and growing availability of alternatives (especially schools) operated to curb child labor.
>
> *Id.* at 15.

Hindman believes that the United States has eradicated child labor in mining, manufacturing, and commercial retail. He notes that the United States is still vulnerable to the problem in the street trades, in sweatshops, and most glaringly, in agriculture. *Id.* at 20.

4. Are there lessons for the rest of the world to be drawn from U.S. experience? Discussing the example of India, Professor M. Neil Browne and his colleagues caution that the U.S. style approach of adopting a legislative response to child labor may not work in the developing world. An outright ban on child labor can result "in children being pushed into worse forms of labor for even lower pay." M. Neil Browne, et al., *Universal Moral Principles and the Law: The Failure of One-Size-Fits-All Child Labor Laws*, 27 Hous. J. Int'l L. 1, 35 (2004). These commentators argue that a "one-size-fits-all" moral regulatory structure . . . constitutes an abdication of responsible policy-making." *Id.* at 6. Instead, they advocate crafting context-specific solutions by carefully considering national, economic, cultural, and historical factors.

5. Child labor has not been entirely eliminated in the developed world. For example, the NGO Human Rights Watch charges that the United States has failed to comply with the ILO's Worst Forms of Child Labor Convention (No. 182) because of the number of children working – often for extremely long hours – in the agricultural sector, the fact that some operate dangerous machinery, and that many are exposed to pesticides. Both the existing legislation covering child agricultural work and its

enforcement apparatus are accused of being ineffective. The NGO estimates that there are between three hundred thousand to eight hundred thousand child farm workers in the United States. The majority of these children are Latino. HUMAN RIGHTS WATCH, FINGERS TO THE BONE: UNITED STATES FAILURE TO PROTECT CHILD FARMWORKERS (June 2000), at http://www.hrw.org/reports/2000/frmwrkr/index. htm; *see also* Rupneet Sidhu, *Child Laborers: The World's Potential Future Labor Resource Exploited and Depleted*, 15 HASTINGS WOMEN'S L.J. 111, 125–30 (2004).

6. In 2003, the ILO Committee of Experts on the Application of Conventions and Recommendations (CEACR) published an Individual Observation on the subject of child labor in the U.S. Responding to allegations of the International Confederation of Free Trade Unions that U.S. labor standards on child labor contain insufficient employer penalties and are inadequately enforced, the CEACR observed that U.S. law exempts the agricultural sector from restrictions on the number of hours worked by children. It also cited U.S. government reports noting that children in agriculture employment are legally allowed to work at younger ages, for longer periods of time, and in more hazardous occupations than children in other industries. The CEACR expressed the hope that the United States will amend relevant legislation and regulations to correct these deficiencies. ILO International Labour Standards Department, Committee of Experts on the Application of Conventions and Recommendations Individual Observation Concerning Convention No. 182, Worst Form of Child Labour, 1999 United States (2003).

B. THINKING DEEPLY ABOUT INTERNATIONAL AND COMPARATIVE EMPLOYMENT LAW

The text, up to this point, has proceeded as if studying international and comparative employment law is a straightforward and uncontroversial undertaking. That there is a casebook on the subject certainly implies that there is value in the exercise. For example, possible solutions to the workplace problems described above may be discovered by exploring labor market regulation in different countries, and at the supra- and international level. Yet the use of foreign law by public policy makers, especially those in the judicial branch, has recently generated considerable debate in the United States. Moreover, those interested in looking at law outside their national jurisdiction should begin by acknowledging the complexity of the undertaking, and remaining mindful of the possible uses and abuses of the comparative enterprise. To that end, this section will focus on the American dispute over the propriety of using international and foreign national law in judicial opinions, offer some cautionary and enthusiastic exhortations about comparative labor and employment law study, and provide some comparative employment data.

1. The U.S. Debate over Judges' Use of Foreign Law

As most students discover early in their law school careers, American law traces its roots to English law. English common law not only governed the American colonies, after Independence through so-called reception statutes it became the basis for state common law. DAN B. DOBBS, THE LAW OF TORTS 262 (West, 2000). Professor Vicki Jackson notes that the country's founders had a healthy interest in both the laws of other countries and in international law, which was at that time referred to as the "law of nations." Indeed, a few of the Supreme Court's early constitutional decisions referenced international practices and foreign national law. Vicki Jackson, *The Court Has Learned from the Rest of the World Before*, LEGAL AFFAIRS, July/Aug 2004, available at http://www.legalaffairs.org/issues/July-August-2004/feature_jackson_julaug04.html.

Nonetheless, and unlike some other countries whose courts frequently cite judicial decisions from other national jurisdictions, the jurisprudence of the United States can be characterized as relatively isolationist. American judges rarely venture beyond U.S. borders in crafting their opinions. MARTHA ALBERTSON FINEMAN, THE AUTONOMY MYTH: A THEORY OF DEPENDENCY 284 (2004). Writing in 1999, U.S. Supreme Court Justice Ruth Bader Ginsburg remarked favorably upon foreign courts that acknowledge American law, and bemoaned the fact that "[t]he same readiness to look beyond one's own shores has not marked the decisions of the court on which I serve." Ruth Bader Ginsburg & Deborah Jones Merritt, *Affirmative Action: An International Human Rights Dialogue*, 21 CARDOZO L. REV. 253, 282 (1999).

More recently, several notable decisions of the Supreme Court indicate that Justice Ginsburg and her more internationally minded colleagues may be reversing the trend that prompted her comments in 1999. In 2002, the Court referenced the disapproval of the world community to buttress its decision that execution of the mentally retarded is constitutionally impermissible. Atkins v. Virginia, 536 U.S. 304, 317 n.21 (2002). More controversial was the Court's decision the next year, which used foreign law to support its conclusion that a Texas statute criminalizing consensual homosexual conduct violated the Due Process Clause of the Fourteenth Amendment. Lawrence v. Texas, 539 U.S. 558, 572–77 (2003). The majority's reference to international and foreign national law was described by Justice Scalia in dissent as "meaningless" and "[d]angerous dicta." *Id.* at 598. A group of incensed U.S. congressional representatives thereafter sponsored a bill "[e]xpressing the sense of the House of Representatives that judicial determinations regarding the meaning of the laws of the United States should not be based on judgments, laws, or pronouncements of foreign institutions" unless those sources "inform an understanding of the original meaning of the laws of the United States." H.R. Res. 568, 108th Cong., 2nd Sess. (Mar. 17, 2004).

ROPER V. SIMMONS

543 U.S. 551 (2005)

Justice KENNEDY delivered the opinion of the Court, in which Justice STEVENS, Justice SOUTER, Justice GINSBURG, and Justice BREYER joined.

This case requires us to address, for the second time in a decade and a half, whether it is permissible under the Eighth and Fourteenth Amendments to the Constitution of the United States to execute a juvenile offender who was older than 15 but younger than 18 when he committed a capital crime. In *Stanford v. Kentucky*, 492 U.S. 361, 109 S.Ct. 2969, 106 L.Ed.2d 306 (1989), a divided Court rejected the proposition that the Constitution bars capital punishment for juvenile offenders in this age group. We reconsider the question. . . .

II

The Eighth Amendment provides: "Excessive bail shall not be required, nor excessive fines imposed, nor cruel and unusual punishments inflicted." The provision is applicable to the States through the Fourteenth Amendment. . . .

The prohibition against "cruel and unusual punishments," like other expansive language in the Constitution, must be interpreted according to its text, by considering history, tradition, and precedent, and with due regard for its purpose and function in the constitutional design. To implement this framework we have established the propriety and affirmed the necessity of referring to "the evolving standards of decency that mark the progress of a maturing society" to determine which punishments are so disproportionate as to be cruel and unusual. *Trop v. Dulles*, 356 U.S. 86, 100–101, 78 S.Ct. 590, 2 L.Ed.2d 630 (1958) (plurality opinion). . . .

[The Court reviewed objective indicia of U.S. practice and concluded that there exists a national consensus rejecting the juvenile death penalty. It also elaborated on the differences between juveniles and adults to demonstrate that juvenile offenders cannot reliably be classified among the most deserving of execution.]

IV

Our determination that the death penalty is disproportionate punishment for offenders under 18 finds confirmation in the stark reality that the United States is the only country in the world that continues to give official sanction to the juvenile death penalty. This reality does not become controlling, for the task of interpreting the Eighth Amendment remains our responsibility. Yet at least from the time of the Court's decision in *Trop*, the Court has referred to the laws of other countries and to international authorities as instructive for its interpretation of the Eighth Amendment's prohibition of "cruel and unusual punishments." . . . .

As respondent and a number of *amici* emphasize, Article 37 of the United Nations Convention on the Rights of the Child, which every country in the world has ratified save for the United States and Somalia, contains an express prohibition on capital punishment for crimes committed by juveniles under 18. United Nations Convention on the Rights of the Child, Art. 37, Nov. 20, 1989, 1577 U.N.T.S. 3, 28 I.L.M. 1448, 1468–1470 (entered into force Sept. 2, 1990). . . . No ratifying country has entered a reservation to the provision prohibiting the execution of juvenile offenders. Parallel prohibitions are contained in other significant international covenants. . . .

Respondent and his *amici* have submitted, and petitioner does not contest, that only seven countries other than the United States have executed juvenile offenders since 1990: Iran, Pakistan, Saudi Arabia, Yemen, Nigeria, the Democratic Republic of Congo, and China. Since then each of these countries has either abolished capital punishment for juveniles or made public disavowal of the practice. . . . In sum, it is fair to say that the United States now stands alone in a world that has turned its face against the juvenile death penalty.

Though the international covenants prohibiting the juvenile death penalty are of more recent date, it is instructive to note that the United Kingdom abolished the juvenile death penalty before these covenants came into being. The United Kingdom's experience bears particular relevance here in light of the historic ties between our countries and in light of the Eighth Amendment's own origins. The Amendment was modeled on a parallel provision in the English Declaration of Rights of 1689. . . . As of now, the United Kingdom has abolished the death penalty in its entirety; but, decades before it took this step, it recognized the disproportionate nature of the juvenile death penalty; and it abolished that penalty as a separate matter. . . .

It is proper that we acknowledge the overwhelming weight of international opinion against the juvenile death penalty, resting in large part on the understanding that the instability and emotional imbalance of young people may often be a factor in the crime. . . . The opinion of the world community, while not controlling our outcome, does provide respected and significant confirmation for our own conclusions. . . .

Justice SCALIA, with whom Chief Justice REHNQUIST and Justice THOMAS join, dissenting.

III

Though the views of our own citizens are essentially irrelevant to the Court's decision today, the views of other countries and the so-called international community take center stage.

The Court begins by noting that "Article 37 of the United Nations Convention on the Rights of the Child, [1577 U.N.T.S. 3, 28 I.L.M. 1448, 1468–1470, entered into force Sept. 2, 1990], which every country in the world has ratified *save for the United States* and Somalia, contains an express prohibition on capital punishment for crimes committed by juveniles under 18." *Ante*, at 1199 (emphasis added). The Court also discusses the International Covenant on Civil and Political Rights (ICCPR), December 19, 1966, 999 U.N.T.S. 175, *ante*, at 1194, 1199, which the Senate ratified only subject to a reservation that reads:

> The United States reserves the right, subject to its Constitutional restraints, to impose capital punishment on any person (other than a pregnant woman) duly convicted under existing or future laws permitting the imposition of capital punishment, including such punishment for crime committed by persons below eighteen years of age.

> Senate Committee on Foreign Relations, International Covenant on Civil and Political Rights, S. Exec. Rep. No. 102–23, (1992).

Unless the Court has added to its arsenal the power to join and ratify treaties on behalf of the United States, I cannot see how this evidence favors, rather than refutes, its position. That the Senate and the President – those actors our Constitution empowers to enter into treaties, see Art. II, §2 – have declined to join and ratify treaties prohibiting execution of under-18 offenders can only suggest that *our country* has either not reached a national consensus on the question, or has reached a consensus contrary to what the Court announces. That the reservation to the ICCPR was made in 1992 does not suggest otherwise, since the reservation still remains in place today. . . .

More fundamentally, however, the basic premise of the Court's argument – that American law should conform to the laws of the rest of the world – ought to be rejected out of hand. In fact the Court itself does not believe it. In many significant respects the laws of most other countries differ from our law – including not only such explicit provisions of our Constitution as the right to jury trial and grand jury indictment, but even many interpretations of the Constitution prescribed by this Court itself. . . .

The Court's special reliance on the laws of the United Kingdom is perhaps the most indefensible part of its opinion. It is of course true that we share a common history with the United Kingdom, and that we often consult English sources when asked to discern the meaning of a constitutional text written against the backdrop of 18th-century English law and legal thought. . . . [T]he Court undertakes the majestic task of determining (and thereby prescribing) *our* Nation's *current* standards of decency. It is beyond comprehension why we should look, for that purpose, to a country that has developed, in the centuries since the Revolutionary War – and with increasing speed since the United Kingdom's recent submission to the jurisprudence of European courts dominated by continental jurists – a legal, political, and social culture quite different from our own. If we took the Court's directive seriously, we would also consider relaxing our double jeopardy prohibition, since the British Law

Commission recently published a report that would significantly extend the rights of the prosecution to appeal cases where an acquittal was the result of a judge's ruling that was legally incorrect. . . . We would also curtail our right to jury trial in criminal cases since, despite the jury system's deep roots in our shared common law, England now permits all but the most serious offenders to be tried by magistrates without a jury. . . .

The Court should either profess its willingness to reconsider all these matters in light of the views of foreigners, or else it should cease putting forth foreigners' views as part of the *reasoned basis* of its decisions. To invoke alien law when it agrees with one's own thinking, and ignore it otherwise, is not reasoned decisionmaking, but sophistry. . . .

_____

Notes

1. To what end and for what purpose does the majority in *Roper v. Simmons* use international and British law? Foreign law in this case has no value as precedent; it is not controlling in the sense of binding the Court. Justice Kennedy professes only to be looking at such authority for confirmation of the Court's conclusion that the juvenile death penalty is unconstitutional. Is he not also using foreign law to illustrate that society's evolving standards of decency reject the execution of those who commit crimes when they are under the age of eighteen? Can one argue that the majority uses foreign law to help inform an understanding of what actions constitute cruel and unusual punishment under the U.S. Constitution?

2. Professor Joan Larsen describes three ways in which the Supreme Court uses foreign authority. The first she labels "expository" use, which occurs when the Court contrasts foreign law with U.S. law in order to better explain the latter. By explaining what U.S. law is not, one gets a better sense of what it is. Larsen calls a second type of use "empirical." Here the Court looks to foreign law and experience to examine the possible consequences or effect of the United States adopting a similar legal approach. The final use Larsen dubs "substantive." Substantive use of foreign authority "seek[s] foreign and international guidance in defining the content of the domestic constitutional rule." Joan L. Larsen, *Importing Constitutional Norms from a "Wider Civilization": Lawrence and the Rehnquist Court's Use of Foreign and International Law in Domestic Constitutional Interpretation*, 65 Ohio St. L. J. 1283, 1291 (2004).

3. What benefits may flow from judges considering foreign law? Professor Vicki Jackson notes:

   > [U]nderstanding comparative constitutional law can be helpful in discerning the meaning of terms or provisions that have transnational meaning; can illuminate the particularities of one's own constitutional experience to better enable constitution interpreters to constitute and reconstitute the constitutional narrative; and can shed light on the functional consequences or rationality of different rules.
   >
   > Vicki C. Jackson, *Narratives of Federalism: Of Continuities and Comparative Constitutional Experience*, 51 Duke L. J. 223, 259 (2001).

   She also notes, with greater hesitation, that "transnational constitutional discourse may strengthen . . . the quality of decisions. . . . " *Id.* In other words, access to a broader range of ideas, may improve the written judicial decision as an "intellectual product." *Id.* at 260. *See also* Mark Tushnet, *The Possibilities of Comparative*

Constitutional Law, 108 YALE L. J. 1225 (1999); Sujit Choudhry, *Globalization in Search of Justification: Toward a Theory of Comparative Constitutional Interpretation*, 74 IND. L.J. 819 (1999).

4. Judge Richard Posner worries that consulting foreign law for its persuasive reasoning opens up "promiscuous opportunities" for citing opinions produced by judicial systems that are far different from our own. He argues that to truly understand and know how much weight to give a foreign decision, one must comprehend the "complex socio-historico-politico-institutional background" that gave birth to it, knowledge that those on the U.S. bench simply do not have. Judge Posner further notes that jurists from other countries lack democratic legitimacy in the United States, and thus their decisions should not affect the functioning of our legal system. Finally, citing foreign decisions, says Judge Posner, is just a form of judicial "fig-leafing." Judges should state their own views rather than hiding behind those of jurists from other countries. Richard Posner, The Court Should Never View a Foreign Legal Decision as a Precedent in Any Way, LEGAL AFFAIRS, July/Aug 2004, available at http://www.legalaffairs.org/issues/July-August-2004/feature_posner_julaug04.html.

5. If a judge's citation to Shakespeare, a folk tale, or popular music is considered within the bounds of proper opinion writing, should reference to foreign authorities be any different? In a world of increasing global connections – financial, legal, technological, cultural – is an isolationist approach to legal interpretation justifiable? The release by the ILO of a new CD ROM facilitates the international trend by making available with indexes a comprehensive collection of judicial decisions that rely on international law principles. USE OF INTERNATIONAL LABOUR LAW IN DOMESTIC COURTS: SUMMARIES OF DOMESTIC COURT DECISIONS USING INTERNATIONAL LAW (ILO 2006) (on CD ROM).

---

2. The Risks and Benefits of the Comparative Enterprise

There are a number of reasons for studying international and comparative employment law apart from encouraging the citation of such materials in judicial opinions. One should undertake such a study, however, with a sense of humility. The critics of the judicial trend are correct that comparing and contrasting different legal systems is a complex and somewhat perilous endeavor. What they neglect to mention, however, is that it is also a rewarding one. As we proceed to consider the risks and benefits of the enterprise, Sir Otto Kahn-Freund's famous caveat on comparative study is well worth keeping in mind:

> [The use of the comparative method] requires a knowledge not only of the foreign law, but also of its social, and above all its political context.
>
> Otto Kahn-Freund, *On Uses and Misuses of Comparative Law*, 37
> MOD. L. REV. 1, 27 (1974).

In other words, there is a great risk of misunderstanding the employment laws of another country by relying solely on law on the books. If one hopes to explain why things operate the way they do, law cannot be viewed apart from the society that creates, molds, and ignores or makes use of it.

The classical mode of comparative study is the functional approach. Professor Roger Blanpain explains that similarly named institutions – labor courts, works councils, union delegations – perform different roles and tasks in different countries. Thus, the comparison is between the functions institutions perform rather than the institutions themselves. For example, one might focus on a broad principle such as worker participation in company management, and then identify the various ways and the degree to which workers or their representatives affect employer decisions on investment. Different institutional arrangements may well be used in different national jurisdictions for this purpose. Roger Blanpain, *Comparativism in Labour Law and Industrial Relations*, in COMPARATIVE LABOUR LAW AND INDUSTRIAL RELATIONS IN INDUSTRIALIZED MARKET ECONOMIES 3, 12-13 (Roger Blanpain, ed., 2004) (hereinafter Blanpain, Comparativism).

Using the example of job security, Professor Blanpain notes that there are different models for promoting this principle. Some countries may utilize lifetime employment to secure it. Other nations may legally require just cause before termination or a notice period before discharge. Still others may compel the employer to seek permission for termination of the employment relationship from a government official. *Id*. at 14. Again, one cannot state often enough the need to use of a wide variety of sources to determine how these models work in practice. Wherever possible, this book uses a wide range of primary and secondary materials to contextualize the legal systems it profiles.

Professor Blanpain also warns of the traps that language and terminology can present. He begins with the word "eventually," which in French is "éventuellement." These seemingly identical words have opposite meanings. In French, the word means "possibly," whereas in English it means "ultimately." Turning to labor law terminology, Professor Blanpain contrasts the English word "arbitration" with the French word "arbitrage." Although the word in either language "usually means a binding decision by an impartial umpire, [it] signifies in Luxemburg a recommendation by a government conciliator to the conflicting parties." *Id*. at 16–17.

Another pitfall is continually using one's own system as a referent, an easy trap to fall into if one is a scholar working alone. Professor Clyde Summers likens a single author writing in the field of comparative labor law to an academic tourist, bound to view the terrain through a parochial lens and in a superficial way. The problem, he notes is that some features of another legal system "may be so counter-intuitive that their existence and significance may be overlooked." Clyde Summers, *Comparative Labor Law in America: Its Foibles, Functions, and Future*, 25 COMP. LAB. L. & POL'Y J. 115, 117 (2003). For example, in Italy a strike may consist of the legally protected actions of a single worker, a situation that is impossible in the United States. *Id*. This warning to academics, which the authors of this book take to heart, applies equally to students. The point of the comparative enterprise is to expand one's boundaries. To accomplish this, one must let go of the familiar and the "idea that our own system should be a model for others." Blanpain, Comparativism, at 17.

A number of benefits flow from intellectual border-crossing. First, it provides an excellent opportunity for gaining insight into one's own national system. As Professor Blanpain notes:

> [W]hen studying other systems one often experiences a (cultural) shock in discovering that a similar problem is resolved in another country in a completely different way, such that one cannot help but initiate the analysis and evaluation of one's own system again, but now from another angle, from an enriched point of view, from a new insight.
>
> Blanpain, Comparativism, at 4.

Indeed, Professor Manfred Weiss declares that a comparative perspective "is the only way to really identify the uniqueness of one's own system," and suggests that studying other legal systems is of profound importance to the law students. Manfred Weiss, *The Future of Comparative Labor Law as an Academic Discipline and as a Practical Tool*, 25 COMP. LAB. L. & POL'Y J. 169, 178 (2003).

Second, acquiring an outsider's view of one's own system of labor market regulation may catalyze questions about the assumptions that underlie it. The American employment at-will rule, which allows employers to terminate employees for good reason, bad reason or no reason at all, takes on a different complexion when one is informed that the United States is unique among industrialized nations in basing its foundational workplace rule on a notion of unfettered employer power and prerogative. William R. Corbett, *The Need for a Revitalized Common Law of the Workplace*, 69 BROOK. L. REV. 91, 126-7 (2003). Rejection of the rule is not necessarily a foregone conclusion. Nevertheless, understanding how significantly the U.S. approach differs from other countries prompts many students to carefully evaluate a principle they might otherwise uncritically accept as inevitable.

Third, comparative study may enliven the mind of the policy maker or advocate looking for better ways to accomplish goals that individual's country shares with other nations. Rheinhold Fahlbeck, *Comparative Law – Quo Vadis?*, 25 COMP. LAB. L. & POL'Y J. 7, 11 (2003). Professor Susan Bisom-Rapp argues that equal employment opportunity is a fertile subject for the exchange of ideas not only about what law should be but how it should work in practice. Bisom-Rapp, *Exceeding Our Boundaries*, at 310–20. While Professor Bisom-Rapp focused mainly on the possibility that American ideas about employment discrimination law compliance might influence the thinking of lawyers elsewhere, Professor Jean Sternlight, in a recent study, compared the civil rights enforcement mechanisms in Australia, the United Kingdom, and the United States, with an eye to improving how we do things in America. Jean R. Sternlight, *In Search of the Best Procedure for Enforcing Employment Discrimination Laws: A Comparative Analysis*, 78 TUL. L. REV. 1401 (2004).

Of course, some types of workplace law are not easily transplantable, especially the rules that structure employees' collective rights. Moreover, adopting a solution that has proven effective in another jurisdiction does not mean that the device will operate exactly the way it did in its place of birth. Instead, one expects transplanted ideas and techniques to have the characteristics of hybrids. They adapt to and take on the cultural, political and institutional environments they encounter in their new homes and they are shaped by domestic power relations. Sociologist Abigail Saguy's fascinating study of how sexual harassment is defined and experienced differently in the United States and France is a good example of this phenomenon. Whereas the norms against sexual harassment were imported from the United States, French activists, legislators and employers have transformed them. In the United States, sexual harassment is understood as a form of employment discrimination, and employers feel responsible for eradicating it because it is bad for business. In France, sexual harassment is conceptualized as a crime, a form of interpersonal violence. French employers, who due to French culture and law bear little risk of liability, view sexual harassment as a personal problem that the state should solve. ABIGAIL C. SAGUY, WHAT IS SEXUAL HARASSMENT? FROM CAPITAL HILL TO THE SORBONNE (2003).

A fourth benefit of comparative study relates to practical matters. At least rudimentary knowledge of labor market regulation in some key national jurisdictions and on the international scene is necessary for those who work for TNCs as legal advisors. The globalization of business practices and economies makes it more likely that management lawyers will encounter issues implicating the laws of other countries. Likewise, those who represent the workers employed by TNCs, namely international trade unions, are very interested in keeping up with developments outside their home borders. Blanpain, Comparativism, at 6. To these ends, this book seeks to promote basic cultural literacy so that practitioners can effectively represent a diverse client pool. It is a survey of the field intended to introduce students to the global lay of the land to assist them, once they are lawyers, in working cooperatively and successfully with advocates in other countries.

Finally, comparative employment law study contributes to the lofty goal of helping promote the realization of international labor standards. Learning about the work of the ILO, which bases its conventions and recommendations on surveys of national law, examining how a member country has sought to implement a particular E.U. workplace directive, or reviewing a TNC's voluntary code of conduct that uses fundamental labor rights as its touchstone, requires one to think about the minimum standards that all workers are entitled to as human beings. Globalization greatly complicates the project of protecting vulnerable workers. Conceptualizing worker rights in fundamental terms is an important step toward ensuring that globalization advances rather than undercuts social justice.

3. Some Comparative Employment Data

Reviewing comparative employment data renders differences between national jurisdictions readily apparent. For this purpose, a recent study by the U.S. Department of Labor is instructive. A CHARTBOOK OF INTERNATIONAL LABOR COMPARISONS: THE AMERICAS, ASIA, EUROPE, U.S. DEPARTMENT OF LABOR, January 2006, available at: http://www.dol.gov/asp/media/reports/chartbook/index.htm. Take the standard of living in the signatory countries of the North American Free Trade Agreement, for example. Data on Gross Domestic Product (GDP) per capita converted to U.S. dollars using Purchasing Power Parities (PPPs) provides a comparative measure of the living standards of the people in different countries. By this measure, people in the United States appear to fare quite well. In thousands of dollars, the U.S. GDP per capita was 39.9. At 31.9, Canada, its northern neighbor, shows a GDP per capita that is 80 percent of that of the United States. Compare that to Mexico, which at 9.8 has a GDP per capita equal to 25 percent of the U.S. level. How about three key national jurisdictions in the E.U.? The United Kingdom evidences a GDP per capita that is comparable to Canada, 31.5. France and Germany come in a little lower at 29.6 and 28.4, respectively. Japan's GDP is comparable at 29.8 *Id.* at 2.

The size of the labor force among national jurisdictions also varies considerably. The U.S. labor force numbers 147.4 million. Canada, a relatively small industrialized nation, has 17 million in its labor force. Mexico comes in at 42.6 million. Of the three E.U. countries featured in this book, Germany has the largest labor force with 39.8 million. The United Kingdom is next with 29.7 million, followed by France at 26.9 million. Japan's labor force in comparison to the European countries is sizeable, numbering 65.8 million. *Id.* at 6.

Differences in hours worked also make for interesting comparisons. In 2004, North Americans worked many more hours annually as compared to their European counterparts. U.S. workers worked 1,824 hours annually in 2004. Canadians worked 1,751 hours annually in that same year, and Mexican workers logged 1,848 hours annually. Workers in the United Kingdom, in contrast, worked 1,669 hours annually in 2004. Germans worked

1,443 hours, and French workers spent 1,441 hours working. In Japan in 2004, workers logged 1,789 hours annually. *Id.* at 13.

Finally, as one might expect, unemployment rates vary between countries. In 2004, the unemployment rate in the United States was 5.5 percent. Canada's unemployment rate that year was 6.4 percent. Mexico's unemployment rate, which the Department of Labor considers understated, was 3 percent. Unemployment in the United Kingdom was 4.8 percent in 2004, the same rate as in Japan. France and Germany, however, had much higher rates of unemployment, 9.8 and 9.9 percent, respectively. *Id.* at 14.

C. WORKPLACE LAW IN THE INTERNATIONAL REALM: AN INITIAL PRIMER

U.S. labor and employment lawyers are just beginning to familiarize themselves with labor and employment law in the international realm. This is not because international workplace law is a new legal development; rather, it is because until recently, it was not viewed as a tool that could be used by American advocates and policy makers. As noted earlier, labor and employment law practitioners' interest in things international has in the last decade begun to grow. The globalization of business, communications, the economy, and culture create both a climate and increased opportunities to consider workplace law beyond our borders. For the purpose of this book, we consider as "international" various methods and mechanisms for achieving global labor standards, matters that transcend national boundaries.

1. Public International Workplace Law

For starters, it helps to think about international workplace law as falling into two categories: public and private. The former encompasses the human rights of workers, and necessitates identifying which labor rights should be considered universally guaranteed. An overlapping component of public international workplace law is the so-called international labor code comprised of the ILO's conventions and recommendations. Public international workplace law, under our expansive definition, also includes trade and regional agreements between sovereign states that contain provisos on labor issues and reference core labor standards, agreements that are often referred to as bilateral, multilateral, or supranational rather than international. Examples of such instruments include the North American Free Trade Agreement's side agreement on labor cooperation and the labor-themed provisions of the treaties, protocols, and directives structuring the European Union. Finally, the as yet unsuccessful effort to convince the World Trade Organization to adopt a social clause that links trade privileges to the maintenance of global labor standards can arguably be considered if not a form of public international workplace law, at least an aspirational topic within its ambit.

a. *Human Rights Law and the International Labor Code*

In its modern form, human rights law dates to the immediate aftermath of World War II. A field of international law articulated in response to the atrocities perpetrated during that war, it exists to protect groups and individuals from violations of their internationally guaranteed rights. MALCOLM N. SHAW, INTERNATIONAL LAW 252 (5th ed., 2003). Human rights fall into two general categories: civil and political rights; and economic, social and cultural rights. The United States has given primacy to the first category, which includes the right to life, liberty, the prohibition of torture, the right to a fair trial, privacy, and property, and freedom of speech, religion, and assembly. Traditionally, these rights are viewed as "negative" in that they require nothing from the state but restraint. James A. Gross, *A Long Overdue Beginning: The Promotion and Protection of Workers' Rights as Human Rights, in* WORKERS' RIGHTS AS HUMAN RIGHTS 1, 3–4 (James A. Gross, ed., 2003).

Economic, social and cultural rights, such as the right to work, just and favorable conditions of work, social security, an adequate standard of living, medical care, and education have not been readily embraced as human rights in the United States. These rights are sometimes conceptualized as "positive" in that they require the state to take action for their realization. *Id.*

Are there links between the two categories? Professors Martha Nussbaum and Amartya Sen have argued that civil and political rights cannot be exercised in the absence of some requisite level of economic security. They pioneered the "capabilities" approach to human welfare, which obligates the state to make available to its citizens the material preconditions necessary for them to be capable of living life with human dignity. Amartya Sen, *Capability and Well-Being, in* THE QUALITY OF LIFE 30 (Martha C. Nussbaum & Amartya Sen, eds., 1993); Martha C. Nussbaum, *Capabilities and Human Rights*, 66 FORDHAM L. REV. 273 (1997). The capabilities approach makes clear the interrelationship between economic entitlements and more traditionally accepted human rights. For example, Nussbaum has noted that for the right to bodily integrity to be meaningful, a woman in an abusive marriage will need access to the economic resources that make leaving her spouse a possibility. Eyal Press, *Human Rights – The Next Step*, THE NATION, Dec. 25, 2000, at 13 (quoting Martha Nussbaum).

Many of the major human rights instruments – the Universal Declaration of Human Rights; the International Covenant on Economic, Social and Cultural Rights (ICESCR); the International Covenant on Civil and Political Rights (ICCPR) – detail rights that implicate the workplace. All three of the instruments mentioned, for example, identify freedom of association, an essential aspect of workplace collective activity, as a fundamental right. William B. Gould IV, *Labor Law for a Global Economy: The Uneasy Case for International Labor Standards, in* INTERNATIONAL LABOR STANDARDS: GLOBALIZATION, TRADE, AND PUBLIC POLICY 81, 87 (Robert J. Flanagan & William B. Gould IV, eds., 2003). The ICESCR, which unlike the ICCPR has not been ratified by the United States, contains a catalog of important rights for workers including the right to work, just and favorable workplace conditions, an adequate standard of living, equal pay, a safe and healthy work environment, reasonable limits on working hours, and sufficient rest and leisure. For its part, the ICCPR prohibits discrimination, slavery, servitude, and forced labor and also protects the right to form and join trade unions. Sarah H. Cleveland, *Why International Labor Standards?, in* INTERNATIONAL LABOR STANDARDS: GLOBALIZATION, TRADE, AND PUBLIC POLICY 129, 137–8 (Robert J. Flanagan & William B. Gould IV, eds., 2003) (hereinafter Cleveland, Why International Labor Standards?).

The ILO, a specialized agency of the United Nations charged with examining and elaborating international labor standards, has played a major role in facilitating the process of identifying which workers' rights are to be considered human rights. Over the last decade, the ILO has formalized four categories of rights considered to be fundamental, and achieved near universal adoption of its 1998 Declaration on Fundamental Principles and Rights at Work. ILO DECLARATION ON FUNDAMENTAL PRINCIPLES AND RIGHTS AT WORK, June 18, 1998, 37 I.L.M. 1233 (1998). As Lee Swepston has noted, the Declaration is essentially a pledge by ILO members to respect, promote, and realize the following rights and principles:

1. Freedom of association and the effective recognition of the right to collective bargaining;
2. The elimination of all forms of forced or compulsory labor;
3. The effective abolition of child labor; and
4. The elimination of discrimination in respect of employment and occupation.

Lee Swepston, *Closing the Gap between International Law and U.S. Labor Law, in* WORKERS' RIGHTS AS HUMAN RIGHTS 53, 59 (James A. Gross, ed., 2003).

Apart from the Declaration, the ILO, which at present has 179 member states, has as of October 2006 produced a body of 187 conventions, which after ratification bind member states as treaties, and 198 recommendations, which are advisory in nature. The conventions and recommendations cover a broad range of workplace subjects in addition to those covered in the Declaration including: employment, wages, conditions of work, occupational safety and health, various forms of social insurance (known outside the United States as "social security"), industrial relations, women workers, older workers, migrant workers, and labor standards administration. Lee Swepston, *International Labour Law, in* COMPARATIVE LABOUR LAW AND INDUSTRIAL RELATIONS IN INDUSTRIALIZED MARKET ECONOMIES 141, 152–8 (Roger Blanpain, ed., 8th ed., 2004). Chapter 2, devoted specifically to the ILO, will provide further details about these instruments, the structure of this specialized UN agency, and its supervisory machinery.

b. *Labor Provisions in Trade-Related Instruments*

Our expansive definition of public international workplace law also has a trade agreement component. More specifically, bilateral, multilateral, and supranational agreements between sovereign states often contain provisions on labor and employment law that seek to promote core labor standards. Indeed, the United States has been a world leader in its advocacy of linking labor standards to various trade-related instruments, an approach dating back over a century to 1890, when Congress prohibited the import of goods made by convict labor. Sarah H. Cleveland, *Norm Internationalization and U.S. Economic Sanctions*, 26 YALE J. INT'L L. 1, 31 (2001).

The modern era of trade-labor linkage in the United States arguably dates to the early 1980s, and the largely successful effort to pass the 1984 labor rights amendment to the Generalized System of Preferences (GSP). The GSP, which was last reauthorized in 2002 and runs through 2006, provides developing countries with tariff preferences in the form of duty free entry, giving their products greater access to the U.S. market than those from developed countries. Its labor rights clause, signed into law by President Ronald Reagan in 1984, ties GSP status to whether a country is "taking steps to afford internationally recognized labor rights." 19 U.S.C.A. §2462(b)(2)(G). These rights are defined as: the right of association; the right to organize and bargain collectively; the prohibition on the use of forced or compulsory labor; a minimum age for employing child labor; and minimum acceptable employment conditions covering wages, hours of work, and occupational safety and health. *Id.* §2467(4)(A-E).

Notably, the provision contains no reference to the ILO. Moreover, to avoid a presidential veto of the amendment, its sponsors compromised, agreeing to cut from the enumerated list in the original draft the prohibition of discrimination, and providing the administration with maximum discretion in the decision of whether to apply economic sanctions to those running afoul of the labor rights provision. Nevertheless, the U.S. Trade Representative's subsequent regulations and guidelines for filing challenges to a country's GSP status augmented the labor proviso, providing a way for workers' advocates to investigate and publicize labor abuses in other countries. Even more importantly, the labor amendment created a legal and policy template for linking trade with labor rights. More than a half dozen labor rights amendments to unilaterally applied trade statutes were thereafter passed by Congress. Lance Compa & Jeffrey S. Vogt, *Labor Rights in the Generalized System of Preferences: A 20-Year Review*, 22 COMP. LAB. L. & POL'Y J. 199, 202-6 (2001).

Opponents of the GSP's labor rights provision criticize it for its unilateralism. Professor Philip Alston, for example, considers several aspects of the approach to be highly questionable:

> These include: the use of the rhetoric but not the substance of "international standards"; the application to other countries of standards that have not been accepted by those countries and that are not generally considered to be part of customary international law; the invocation of international instruments that the United States itself has not ratified; and the neglect of existing and potential international mechanisms for achieving comparable objectives.
>
> Philip Alston, *Labor Rights Provisions in U.S. Trade Law: "Aggressive Unilateralism?," in* HUMAN RIGHTS, LABOR RIGHTS, AND INTERNATIONAL TRADE 71, 71-2 (Lance A. Compa & Stephen F. Diamond, eds., 1996).

Writing more recently, Alston notes that under the GSP program the labor practices of some forty-two countries have been scrutinized *not* against international standards but against U.S. standards "invoking the mantel of internationalism." Philip Alston, *'Core Labour Standards' and the Transformation of the International Labour Rights Regime*, 15 EUR. J. INT'L L. 457, 498 (2004).

While acknowledging the flaws in the GSP program, Lance Compa and Jeffrey Vogt argue that it has on balance produced positive results, including inspiring the crafting of labor rights provisions in bilateral, multilateral, and regional trade agreements. Compa & Vogt, at 200. Beginning with NAFTA's labor side agreement, the practice of addressing labor rights in the context of trade agreements has become standard in the U.S. Marley S. Weiss, *Two Steps Forward, One Step Back – Or Vice Versa: Labor Rights under Free Trade Agreements from NAFTA, Through Jordan, via Chile, to Latin America, and Beyond*, 37 U.S.F.L. REV. 689 (2003). Over time, the American approach has evolved into one that anticipates inclusion of a labor rights chapter in all U.S. trade agreements. These chapters reference some fundamental workplace rights, provide an oversight mechanism for the chapter's provisions, and require each of the signatories to observe their own domestic labor and employment law regimes. Chapter 6 on the North American Free Trade Agreement will cover in depth the labor rights provisions of that agreement and its American progeny, including the free trade agreement concluded with

Jordan and the recent Central America – Dominican Republic Free Trade Agreement (CAFTA-DR).

The United States is, of course, not alone in explicitly promoting the observance of labor rights through trade accords and related instruments. Perhaps the most interesting, of such efforts is that of the European Union, a free trading bloc and unique supranational organization with executive, legislative and judicial functions comprised of twenty-five member states, and scheduled to grow by two in January 2007. The E.U.'s ambitions are nothing less than achieving "superpower status while maintaining . . . high levels of employment and social welfare protection and strong trade unions" partnered with employers' organizations. Jeff Kenner, *The European Union, in* INTERNATIONAL LABOR AND EMPLOYMENT LAWS 1-1, 1-2 (2d ed., William L. Keller & Timothy J. Darby, eds., 2003) (hereinafter Kenner, The European Union). However, as you will see in the following chapters, the labor and employment laws of the member states are incredibly varied. As Professor Roger Blanpain notes:

> Diversity is the general rule and this will stay so. In other words, there is no European system of employment law or industrial relations. The systems are mainly national and will remain so for a long time to come.

> Roger Blanpain, *The European Union and Employment Law, in* COMPARATIVE LABOUR LAW AND INDUSTRIAL RELATIONS IN INDUSTRIALIZED MARKET ECONOMIES 165, 166 (8th ed., Roger Blanpain, ed., 2004) (hereinafter Blainpain, The European Union).

That labor market regulation continues to be a national affair does not mean that the E.U. abstains entirely from legislating on or providing judicial review of some workplace matters. The E.U.'s labor and employment law output, however, must be understood in terms of the policies the trading bloc pursues. First and foremost, the E.U. is a free trading region that seeks to curtail the anticompetitive impulses of its member states. Professors Catherine Barnard and Simon Deakin note that from its earliest days in the 1950s, the European Community (E.C.) left most of the details of labor and employment law and welfare state expenditures to its individual members, reasoning that the market and political pressure would generate both effective standards and a convergence of wages and incomes. Catherine Barnard & Simon Deakin, *'Negative' and 'Positive' Harmonization of Labor Law in the European Union*, 8 COLUM. J. EUR. L. 389 (2002) (hereinafter Barnard & Deakin, Harmonization). Simultaneously, the members anticipated the need to cede sovereignty, giving sweeping power to the Community in order to promote economic integration. To that end, the power to "harmonize" national legislation to support the common market is the province of the supranational entity.

The free movement of goods, capital, workers, and services across the members' national borders is guaranteed in the E.U. *Id.* In particular, the free movement of workers, allowing them to relocate to any member country in order to engage in economic activity, is considered a fundamental right and a key component of E.U. citizenship. Margriet Kraamwinkel, *The Imagined European Community: Are Housewives European Citizens?, in* LABOUR LAW IN AN ERA OF GLOBALIZATION 321, 324 (Joanne Conaghan, Richard Michael Fischl & Karl Klare, eds., 2002); Mark Jeffery, *The Free Movement of Persons within the European Union: Moving from Employment Rights to Fundamental Rights?*, 23 COMP. LAB. L. & POL'Y J. 211 (2001). Somewhat surprisingly, out of 370 million people, there are only 5.5 million E.U. nationals resident in another member state. Blanpain, The European Union, at 173. This may be a testament to the continuing power of language differences and the resiliency of national identity.

Interestingly, the E.U., which in May 2004 grew from fifteen to twenty-five countries, does not apply free movement principles across the entire trading bloc. Eight of the new members are subject to a transitional period, during which they may face movement restrictions and impose reciprocal controls on the fifteen members who made up the E.U. before their accession. As of May 2006, seven of the old E.U. countries – Ireland, Sweden, the United Kingdom, Finland, Greece, Portugal, and Spain – had lifted all movement restrictions on new member states' workers. The remaining eight preaccession members continue to maintain some restrictions on access to their labor markets. *EU backs free movement principle*, BBC News, May 2, 2006, available at: http://news.bbc.co.uk/2/hi/europe/4966434.stm. Britain will impose movement restrictions on workers from Bulgaria and Romania after those two countries join the E.U. in January 2007. Sarah Lyall, *Britain to Restrict Workers from Bulgaria and Romania*, N.Y. Times, Oct. 25, 2006, at A6.

Active supranational involvement in social policy issues – and for our purposes workplace issues – dates from the 1970s, when the member states began to realize that the market alone would fail to produce optimal distributional outcomes. Barnard & Deakin, Harmonization, at 402. In deference to national social policy autonomy, workplace-related legislative activity has rarely taken the form of legally binding regulations that are directly applicable to the citizens of member states. Rather, it has more typically takes the form of directives, which although legally binding, are general statements that require member country action for implementation. Each member state must decide on a form and method to realize a given directive at the national level by a specific date. This approach seeks to place a brake on a potential race to the bottom between the member states while "preserving space for experimentation on the state level." *Id.* at 413.

Directives exist in a number of fields including: sex discrimination; race discrimination; disability and age discrimination; health and safety law; collective redundancies (known as layoffs in the United States); insolvency; transfers of undertakings; immigrant workers; working time; part-time work; fixed-term work; data privacy; European works councils; and employee information and consultation. Yet there are some workplace topics that the Community is prohibited from legislating on: pay; the right of association; the right to strike; and the right to impose lockouts. Blanpain, The European Union, at 167.

Moreover, the E.U.'s recent approach to employment matters, set forth in the Treaty of Nice in 2000, is to encourage innovation at the national level. As Professor Jeff Kenner reports:

> Coordination, rather than legislative harmonization, is the Community's chosen tool for advancing its objectives under the Employment Title [of the E.C. Treaty]. Rather than use the blunt instrument of legislation, the Community acts as an enabler of change on the ground. This is consistent with the Community's guiding principle of "subsidiarity," whereby decisions are taken at the level closest to the citizen, and the Community acts only where it can "add value" to achieve its objectives more effectively. . . . [T]his has meant that legislation has been a last resort rather than a first reflex.
>
> Kenner, The European Union, at 1–12.

The resulting Open Method of Co-ordination (OMC) seeks to operate through intergovernmental rather than supranational methods. E.U. national governments exchange information on best practices, make periodic reports, set benchmarks and targets, and provide surveillance of one another's labor and employment regimes and market outcomes. Hepple, Labour Laws, at 225. To operationalize the OMC, the European Council, which when dealing with workplace matters is comprised of labor ministers from the member states, coordinates the employment policies of the members by annually publishing employment guidelines. Each member state submits a national action plan describing the steps that have been taken to implement the guidelines. The Council reviews these reports and is empowered to make recommendations to member states if necessary. No formal sanctions may be taken against a member state that fails to consider the guidelines. *Id.* at 226. Although some praise this approach as enlightened and innovative, Professor Blanpain is concerned that the E.U.'s ability to manage the challenges of globalization and its inevitable dislocations through "socially inspired corrections" has been handicapped due to national self-interest. Blanpain, The European Union, at 188. Chapter 7 on the European Union will cover these matters in much greater detail.

Those interested in other approaches to supranational regulation of workplace matters might examine other regional agreements. Professor Adelle Blackett, for example, describes the nascent efforts of the Caribbean Common Market (CARICOM) nations to harmonize their labor and employment laws through the drafting of model laws on a few subjects like termination of employment, trade union recognition, occupational safety and health, and equal opportunity and treatment. Adelle Blackett, *Toward Social Regionalism in the Americas*, 23 Comp. Lab. L. & Pol'y J. 901, 940-1 (2002). She likewise argues that there are lessons to be learned from the Southern Common Market (MERCOSUR) – created in 1991 by Argentina, Brazil, Paraguay, and Uruguay. MERCOSUR's executive body, the Common Market Group (GMC), has reporting to it a tripartite working subgroup, Subgroup No. 10 on Labour, Employment, and Social Security matters, whose members, representatives from government, workers and employers, conduct policy research on the social dimensions of economic integration. In addition to preparing studies on the costs and benefits of labor law harmonization, Subgroup No. 10 observes labor inspections in the member countries. *Id.* at 948-50.

c. *The World Trade Organization and Labor Rights*

The World Trade Organization (WTO), the successor to the entity that evolved from 1948 General Agreement on Tariffs and Trade (GATT), is the multilateral forum that promulgates the rules governing international commerce. Its first day of existence was January 1, 1995. As of December 2005, the WTO boasted 149 members, which are governments that act on behalf of separate customs territories. Successive rounds of negotiation between members lead to treaties on goods, services and intellectual property that seek to free trade from unnecessary constraints. The WTO has a dispute settlement system, the ability to authorize economic sanctions for trade rule noncompliance, and a surveillance mechanism to assess the trade policies of its members. Its central principle is that of nondiscrimination; in other words, with few exceptions, such as establishing free trade agreements and creating targeted programs for developing nations, states should treat their trading partners equally.

An effort to convince the WTO to address labor rights as a serious trade consideration began over a decade ago. In 1996 the issue was the subject of extensive discussion at the First WTO Ministerial Conference in Singapore. A proposal for a social clause or other device linking core labor standards compliance to the WTO trade enforcement regime was soundly rejected. Cleveland, Why International Labor Standards?, at 148–9. Despite or perhaps because of U.S. support for WTO involvement, the conference ended with a Ministerial Declaration that pronounced labor issues beyond the competence of the organization:

> We renew our commitment to the observance of internationally recognized core labor standards. The International Labor Organization (ILO) is the competent body to set and deal with these standards, and we affirm our support for its work in promoting them.
>
> MINISTERIAL CONFERENCE OF THE WORLD TRADE ORGANIZATION, SINGAPORE MINISTERIAL DECLARATION, adopted Dec. 13, 1996, 36 I.L.M. 218 (1997).

The Declaration, voicing the concerns of developing nations, condemned using labor standards for protectionist purposes, and noted that the comparative advantage of low-wage developing countries must not be questioned. *Id.*

In late November 1999, the issue of trade-labor linkage erupted on the streets of Seattle, when representatives from 135 nations in the WTO, there to discuss the agenda for upcoming negotiations, were met by thirty thousand to forty thousand protesters. Among the protesters' grievances was that the WTO's trade-promoting rules do not give consideration to labor rights or human rights. Clyde Summers, *The Battle in Seattle: Free Trade, Labor Rights, and Societal Values*, 22 U. PA. J. INT'L ECON. L. 61 (2001) (hereinafter Summers, Battle in Seattle). During the ministerial, the US sought to reinvigorate the issue. President Bill Clinton, addressing the representatives, plugged his administration's relatively modest proposal that the WTO create a working group on trade and labor that would study the issue and prepare a report for the trade ministers. He subsequently made "an unplanned statement to a newspaper" that the WTO should eventually utilize trade sanctions to promote core labor rights around the globe. *Id.* at 62. The E.U. similarly proposed the creation of a standing working forum on labor issues to be jointly organized by the WTO and ILO. Both proposals were met with decisive opposition from the developing world. Ewell E. Murphy, Jr., *The World Trade Organization, in* INTERNATIONAL LABOR AND EMPLOYMENT LAWS 45-1, 3-4 (2d ed., William L. Keller & Timothy J. Darby, eds., 2003).

Supporters of using trade sanctions to promote core labor standards note that the members of the WTO are also members of the ILO. As such, they are already bound by the ILO's Declaration on Fundamental Principles and Rights at Work. Yet although subject to the Declaration, many states ignore their obligations, and the ILO lacks an effective mechanism for inducing state compliance. Andrew T. Guzman, *Trade, Labor, Legitimacy*, 91 CAL. L. REV. 885, 886-7 (2003) (hereinafter Guzman, Legitimacy). Moreover, core labor standards are minimal. They do not encompass a key ingredient of developing states' comparative advantage: wages. Thus, adopting a trade sanctions approach to enforcing fundamental labor rights should not appreciably increase the labor costs of poor nations. Summers, Battle in Seattle, at 66–8.

Those who oppose linking the WTO's enforcement mechanism to the observance of core labor standards argue that trade liberalization increases the welfare of all states. Economic growth produced by freer international trade is the best way to promote improved labor conditions, especially in poor countries. In contrast, targeting poor nations for labor-based sanctions would harm poor workers, undermine the comparative advantage of the developing world, and open the door to the protectionist actions of developed nations unjustifiably seeking to protect their jobs at home. Guzman, Legitimacy, at 886. As to the argument that the ILO's approach to enforcing labor standards lacks teeth, the opponents of linkage note the advantage of soft law shaming. In Professor Jagdish Bhagwati's famous words: " . . . God gave us not just teeth but also a tongue. A good tongue-lashing today, with the ubiquity of CNN and civil society groups, can be very effective." Jagdish Bhagwati & José E. Alvarez, *Afterword: The Question of Linkage*, 96 Am. J. Int'l L. 126, 131 (2002).

WTO antipathy to trade-labor linkage continues to the present time, and was once again expressed by the Doha Ministerial Conference in November 2001, which reaffirmed the Singapore Ministerial Declaration, noting that international labor issues are the jurisdiction of the ILO. Cleveland, Why International Labor Standards?, at 149. An attempt to revive the labor linkage issue at the 2003 Cancun Ministerial Conference also failed. Hepple, Labour Laws, at 130. Rather than embrace labor rights as a central trade-related concern, the WTO advocates collaboration with the ILO, including participation by the organization in meetings of ILO bodies, and informal cooperation between the secretariats of the two international entities. WTO, Trade and Labour Standards: Subject of Intense Debate, available at http://www.wto.org/english/thewto_e/minist_e/min99_e/english/about_e/18lab_e.htm.

Despite the firm and unchanging position of the WTO, the debate over trade and labor rights rages on, at least in academic circles. Given the current political reality, most importantly that developing nations within the WTO have officially "delinked" labor from trade in Ministerial Declarations, Professor Sungjoon Cho argues that "a calm, modest yet incrementally effective approach to linkage, using soft law and cooperative networking" seems the only pragmatic alternative. Sungjoon Cho, *Linkage of Free Trade and Social Regulation: Moving beyond the Entropic Dilemma*, 5 Chi. J. Int'l L. 625, 668-9 (2005). Professor Andrew Guzman, by contrast, recommends expanding the WTO's competence beyond trade by establishing separate departments in the organization dealing with discrete subjects such as labor and the environment. Andrew T. Guzman, *Global Governance and the WTO*, 45 Harv. Int'l L.J. 303, 328–37 (2004).

Ironically, the WTO's refusal to become entangled with the labor standards issue has boosted the role and the confidence of the ILO. Cleveland, Why International Labor Standards, at 152. That organization has undertaken several new initiatives, including establishing a World Commission on the Social Dimension of Globalization, and engaging in collaborative efforts with the World Bank and other development banks. Virginia A. Leary, *"Form Follows Function": Formulations of International Labor Standards – Treaties, Codes, Soft Law, Trade Agreements*, in International Labor Standards: Globalization, Trade, and Public Policy 179, 185 (Robert J. Flanagan & William B. Gould IV, eds., 2003). The ILO's Working Party on the Social Dimension of Globalization has recommended a policy coherence initiative, which involves strengthening the contacts between the ILO and other multilateral organizations like the WTO. To further the goal of developing policies that balance economic, social, and developmental concerns, the ILO's Working Party held two informal technical consultations in May and November 2004 with staff in attendance from organizations including the WTO, the World Bank, and the International Monetary Fund. Working Party on the Social Dimension of Globalization, A Stronger Social Dimension of Globalization: Follow-Up to the November Meeting of the Working Party (ILO Report, 2005).

2. Private International Workplace Law

Private international workplace law is perhaps best understood by using as a theoretical touchstone a conception of law advocated by legal pluralists. Legal pluralism views law as generated by both state and nonstate sources, and is especially concerned with the exam-ination of nonstate legal systems and their relation to government. TNCs are arguably the most active nonstate, law-generating actors. Thus their actions, as creators of regimes of private ordering – webs of rules that affect employees collectively and individually – are especially worthy of attention. Arthurs, *Collective Labour Law*, at 156-61.

Students of the American workplace are familiar with the proliferation of employers' internal rules and structures. Encouraged and assisted by human resource professionals and management lawyers, many U.S. corporations boast nonunion employee grievance procedures, mandatory predispute arbitration agreements, corporate codes of conduct, and detailed employee handbooks. Susan Bisom-Rapp, *Discerning Form from Substance: Understanding Employer Litigation Prevention Strategies*, 3 EMPLOYEE RTS. & EMPLOY-MENT POL'Y J. 1, 9 (1999); Lauren B. Edelman & Mark Suchman, *When the "Haves" Hold Court: Speculations on the Organizational Internalization of Law*, 33 LAW & SOC'Y REV. 941 (1999). Indeed, Professor Cynthia Estlund characterizes self-regulation of the workplace as a "movement." Cynthia Estlund, *Rebuilding the Law of the Workplace in an Era of Self-Regulation*, 105 COLUM. L. REV. 319 (2005). This trend, she notes, carries with it potential promise and pitfalls. If coordinated with state-made law, outside monitoring, and employee participation, self-regulatory structures and practices may be innovative enforcement mechanisms. But without some form of independent oversight and in the absence of employee voice, internal regulation can undermine basic workplace rights and standards. *Id.* at 321.

Self-regulation is ubiquitous on the international scene too, driven by the actions of TNCs. Among the most interesting and controversial forms of self-regulation are volun-tarily adopted, global codes of conduct that seek to promote international labor rights and standards. Michael Posner & Justine Nolan, *Can Codes of Conduct Play a Role in Promoting Workers' Rights?*, *in* INTERNATIONAL LABOR STANDARDS: GLOBALIZATION, TRADE, AND PUBLIC POLICY 207, 208–211 (Robert J. Flanagan & William B. Gould IV, eds., 2003). Sir Bob Hepple dates the upsurge in the adoption of these mechanisms to the late 1980s. TNCs embracing conduct codes seek to avoid negative publicity, real-ize the benefits of good employment practices, and strengthen the power of senior managers over outside contractors. Hepple, Labour Laws, at 71. The diverse types of voluntary codes, their potential effects, efforts to connect internal codes to public inter-national law, and the arguments of their supporters and detractors are the subject of Chapter 14.

TNCs also engage in private employment law rule-making by entering into individual employment contracts with their employees. This type of rule-making can be considered international to the extent that a TNC incorporates by contract standards that will apply across borders, wherever the TNC does business. It is also, however, simultaneously comparative, in that the contractual terms must conform to the particular requirements of specific national jurisdictions. Many countries require individual employment contracts, and specify the subjects that must be included within. Additionally, expatriate agreements, covering executives temporarily stationed abroad, are common devices that structure and define the nature of the posting. Donald C. Dowling, Jr., *The Practice of International Labor and Employment Law: Escort Your Labor/Employment Clients into the Global Millennium*, 17 LAB. LAW 1, 17 (2001).

Finally, on the collective front, five sectoral federations of the International Confed-eration of Free Trade Unions (ICFTU) have negotiated over thirty framework collective agreements with TNCs, which seek to commit the employer to observing the ILO's core labor standards. The vast majority of the TNCs that have agreed to such agreements are European. Unions or workers representatives take part in monitoring the agreements. Hepple, Labour Laws, at 76-7. Is it likely that U.S.-based TNCs will be amenable to negotiating such devices?

D. THE ORGANIZATION OF THIS BOOK

Making sense of a field as complex as international and comparative employment law is quite a challenge. As you work through the book, we suggest you consider the four themes mentioned at the start of this chapter, questions that are often eclipsed in basic employment and labor law courses. Why do governments promulgate labor and employment laws? How do different countries conceptualize and attempt to secure fundamental labor rights for their workers? How do we determine whether those efforts are successful? Assuming we can agree on a definition, how might we best secure decent working conditions for all? In addition, as noted earlier, globalization has made it more difficult for states to regulate their labor markets. What other mechanisms exist to fill the regulatory gap?

This book will begin the process of answering these questions in the international realm with a thorough treatment of the International Labour Organization in Chapter 2. The ILO's work in setting international labor standards provides an important lens through which to view all the other legal regimes that attempt to regulate the workplace. Having set the stage, the book then proceeds by reviewing labor and employment law in three important regions: North America; Europe; and Asia. It concludes with a look at attempts by TNCs at self-regulation.

After reviewing the ILO materials, we turn to workplace law in North America. First, the book covers the distinguishing features of the labor and employment law regimes of the three North American nations. Workplace law in the United States is the subject of Chapter 3. Canadian law is covered in Chapter 4. Labor market regulation in Mexico is reviewed in Chapter 5. Next, Chapter 6 takes up the details of and the debates surrounding the North American Agreement on Labor Cooperation (the NAALC), NAFTA's labor side agreement, under which the three signatory countries pledge to enforce their own workplace laws.

The European Union and three of the major member countries comprise the subject matter of the next set of chapters. Chapter 7 describes the unique, multifaceted efforts of the European Union to influence labor market regulation and promote innovation in its member countries. The United Kingdom's regulatory regime is the subject of Chapter 8. Chapter 9 reviews the labor and employment laws of Germany. This section concludes with Chapter 10, which covers workplace law in France.

Attention then turns to Asia, and three countries whose economies have a significant impact on the global scene. Chapter 11 covers workplace law in China. Chapter 12 takes up the subject of Japan. Finally, the Asian section ends with a look at India.

Chapter 14, the book's concluding chapter, considers corporate self-regulation and the enforcement of international labor rights in U.S. courts. The world's largest TNCs are entities with economic power that dwarfs that of many sovereign nations. Are these private entities poised to become law givers that promulgate the rules that govern their own conduct? And how do state, civil society's, and workers' interests figure into self-regulatory regimes? Are there mechanisms for enforcing the rights of workers abroad in the courtrooms of the United States?

Writing recently, Professor Steven Willborn predicted "a bright future for research on comparative labor law and policy." Steven L. Willborn, *Onward and Upward: The Next Twenty-Five Years of Comparative Labor Law Scholarship*, 25 Comp. Lab. L. & Pol'y J. 183, 195 (2003). He noted that the trends, in terms of increased scholarly interest in the subject, are favorable, and that the tools, especially the expansive access to foreign law provided by the internet, have never been better. *Id.* This book, then, comes at an important moment. Changes to the workplace brought about by increasing global economic competition create the need for a resource that can help students navigate labor market regulation beyond our borders. The aim of this book is to play that role.

2 The International Labour Organization and International Labor Standards

A. INTRODUCTION

That inferior labor conditions in one country can supply it with a trade advantage over its competitors is not an idea of recent vintage. Likewise, pleas for universal labor standards on humanitarian and economic grounds were first made over 150 years ago. Edward E. Potter, *The International Labor Organization, in* INTERNATIONAL LABOR AND EMPLOYMENT LAWS 40-1 (2d ed., William L. Keller & Timothy J. Darby, eds., 2003) (hereinafter Potter, The ILO). Despite some insipient efforts, however, scant progress was made toward establishing global labor standards until 1919. In that year, in the aftermath of World War I, the International Labour Organization (ILO) was established by the Treaty of Versailles as an autonomous body within the ill-fated League of Nations. BOB HEPPLE, LABOUR LAWS AND GLOBAL TRADE 29-30 (2005) (hereinafter Hepple, Labour Laws). The ILO survived the disintegration of League, becoming in 1946 a specialized, tripartite agency of the United Nations, with member nations sending delegations comprised of representatives from government, organized labor and employers. As of October 2006, it had 179 member countries.

Animating the formation of the new organization in 1919 were the goals of promoting fair trade and ensuring worker protection from exploitation. The ILO was also founded on the principle that advancing social justice is a key element to establishing lasting peace. To those ends, the ILO's role is to promulgate international standards for implementation by its member nations, mainly by adopting, as will be described later, conventions and recommendations. Lee Sweptson, *International Labour Law, in* COMPARATIVE LABOUR LAW AND INDUSTRIAL RELATIONS IN INDUSTRIALIZED MARKET ECONOMIES 141, 142 (8th ed., 2004) (hereinafter Sweptson, International Labour Law).

Guiding the work of the agency at its inception were nine principles of special importance set forth in Article 427 of the Treaty of Versailles. The list included a statement that labor should not be regarded as a commodity or article of commerce, recognition of employees' freedom of association, endorsement of the eight-hour workday or forty-eight-hour workweek standard, and an admonition that men and women should receive equal pay for work of equal value. Potter, The ILO, at 40-3–40-4. These guiding principles were refined and updated by the 1944 Declaration of Philadelphia, which was annexed to the ILO Constitution.

DECLARATION CONCERNING THE AIMS AND PURPOSES OF THE INTERNATIONAL
LABOUR ORGANIZATION (DECLARATION OF PHILADELPHIA)

ILO Constitution, *as amended* Oct. 9, 1946, Annex, 62 *Stat.* 3485, 15 U.N.T.S. 35

I

The Conference reaffirms the fundamental principles on which the Organization is based and, in particular, that-

- (a) labour is not a commodity;
- (b) freedom of expression and of association are essential to sustained progress;
- (c) poverty anywhere constitutes a danger to prosperity everywhere;
- (d) the war against want requires to be carried on with unrelenting vigor within each nation, and by continuous and concerted international effort in which the representatives of workers and employers, enjoying equal status with those of governments, join with them in free discussion and democratic decision with a view to the promotion of the common welfare.

II

Believing that experience has fully demonstrated the truth of the statement in the Constitution of the International Labour Organization that lasting peace can be established only if it is based on social justice, the Conference affirms that-

- (a) all human beings, irrespective of race, creed or sex, have the right to pursue both their material well-being and their spiritual development in conditions of freedom and dignity, of economic security and equal opportunity;
- (b) the attainment of the conditions in which this shall be possible must constitute the central aim of national and international policy;
- (c) all national and international policies and measures, in particular those of an economic and financial character, should be judged in this light and accepted only in so far as they may be held to promote and not to hinder the achievement of this fundamental objective;
- (d) it is a responsibility of the International Labour Organization to examine and consider all international economic and financial policies and measures in the light of this fundamental objective; . . .

III

The Conference recognizes the solemn obligation of the International Labour Organization to further among the nations of the world programmes which will achieve:

- (a) full employment and the raising of standards of living;
- (b) the employment of workers in the occupations in which they can have the satisfaction of giving the fullest measure of their skill and attainments and make their greatest contribution to the common well-being;
- (c) the provision, as a means to the attainment of this end and under adequate guarantees for all concerned, of facilities for training and the transfer of labour, including migration for employment and settlement;

- (d) policies in regard to wages and earnings, hours and other conditions of work calculated to ensure a just share of the fruits of progress to all, and a minimum living wage to all employed and in need of such protection;
- (e) the effective recognition of the right of collective bargaining, the cooperation of management and labour in the continuous improvement of productive efficiency, and the collaboration of workers and employers in the preparation and application of social and economic measures;
- (f) the extension of social security measures to provide a basic income to all in need of such protection and comprehensive medical care;
- (g) adequate protection for the life and health of workers in all occupations;
- (h) provision for child welfare and maternity protection;
- (i) the provision of adequate nutrition, housing and facilities for recreation and culture;
- (j) the assurance of equality of educational and vocational opportunity. . . .

Notes

1. Do the principles listed in the 1944 Declaration continue to be relevant? Think of the laws and public policies of a country you are familiar with. How do they measure up against the aspirations of the Declaration of Philadelphia?

2. What kind of instrument is the Declaration? It is not considered a treaty. It is an annex to the ILO Constitution. Do its text and placement give guidance on the Declaration's affect on member countries? Article V of the Declaration states "that the principles set forth in this Declaration are fully applicable to all peoples everywhere. . . . " ILO Constitution, Annex, Art. V. Professor Charles Morris argues that ILO membership commits the member states to an affirmative obligation to further the Declaration's objectives, a conclusion he believes was later confirmed by the 1998 ILO Declaration on Fundamental Principles and Rights at Work. CHARLES J. MORRIS, THE BLUE EAGLE AT WORK 142 (2005).

3. As noted in Chapter 1, human rights are traditionally conceptualized as falling into two categories: (1) civil and political rights; and (2) economic, social, and cultural rights. Does the Philadelphia Declaration contain references to both types of rights? How would you describe the 1944 Declaration's treatment of the relationship between civil and economic rights?

4. An interesting feature of the Declaration of Philadelphia is Article III's objective of furthering national programs of full employment. One such ultimately unsuccessful national effort was the Full Employment Act of 1945, which sought to create in the United States an entitlement to full-time employment and a corresponding obligation on the part of the federal government to maintain conditions to make the entitlement a reality. Its sponsors, influenced by writings of economist John Maynard Keynes, believed that business cycles of boom and bust were inevitable, could be catastrophically socially disruptive, and were capable of stabilization through a method known as "compensatory finance." As described by economist G. J. Santoni:

> Section 3 [of the Act] laid out a formula for the federal government to follow in pursuing this goal. The formula required the President of the United States to submit a national budget to Congress at the beginning of each regular session. The

budget was to contain a forecast of both the level of output necessary to generate full employment over the next year and the level of output that was likely to result if government did not intervene. If the projected level of output was less than the level necessary for full employment, the President was required to recommend legislation that would produce a big enough deficit in the federal government's budget to raise output to the full employment level. If the relationship between the two output forecasts were reversed, the President was required to recommend legislation that would result in a budget surplus big enough to reduce output to the full employment level.

G. J. Santoni, *The Employment Act of 1946: Some History Notes*, Federal Reserve Bank of St. Louis, Nov. 1986, 5, 9, available at: http://research. stlouisfed.org/publications/review/86/11/Employment_Nov1986.pdf.

The bill was attacked as un-American and socialistic. Subsequent amendments eliminated the right to full employment, the federal government's obligation to create conditions conducive to full employment, and the requirement of budgeting through compensatory finance. *Id.* at 11. The bill passed as the Employment Act of 1946. *Id.* at 12. The Humphrey/Hawkins Bill of 1976, an attempted revival of the central aspects of the 1945 bill, fared no better than its predecessor. *Id.* at 15.

The ILO in the Post-War Period

Human rights concerns received little attention by the ILO in the period between 1919 and 1939. Breen Creighton, *The Future of Labour Law: Is There a Role for International Labour Standards?, in* THE FUTURE OF LABOUR LAW 253, 254 (Catherine Barnard, Simon Deakin & Gillian S. Morris, eds., 2004) (hereinafter Creighton, Future of Labour Law). Instead, the conventions adopted were generally more technical and prescriptive in orientation. For example, among the early conventions adopted were the Hours of Work Convention, which mandated adherence to the eight-hour workday/forty-eight-hour workweek standard, and conventions restricting night work for women and young persons. Human rights concerns came to the fore in the period after 1945, beginning with the adoption of the freedom of association Conventions 87 and 98 in 1948 and 1949, respectively. *Id.* at 254-55.

Sir Bob Hepple identifies decolonization and the Cold War as the two main challenges confronting the ILO in the period following World War II. The former more than tripled the ILO's membership in a little over 50 years, taking it "[f]rom an elite of 52 mainly western industrial states in 1946" to its present composition of 179 member nations, many of which are poor, developing countries. Hepple notes:

> This mass admission of developing countries had profound repercussions. Their main preoccupation was with technical co-operation, such as assistance with the drafting of labour codes, which would help them to claim compliance with international standards although the reality was often much different.

Hepple, Labour Laws, at 34.

The developing nations also put increased pressure on the agency for flexibility in standard setting, and emphasized political issues like the activities of multinational corporations and states whose policies they deemed objectionable, such as the apartheid regime of South Africa and Israel. *Id.*

The Cold War, in turn, hampered the ILO's functioning due to strife between Western and Communist nations. Western countries argued that the ILO's principle of tripartism, which requires member countries to staff their delegations not only with government functionaries but also with independent workers' and employers' representatives, was threatened by the Soviet Union and its allies. Those countries, after all, had governments that neither permitted independent labor organizations nor private employment. *Id.* When ILO committees ruled that practices of the Communist countries, such as the "trade union monopoly, . . . and rules concerning 'social parasitism,'" violated the ILO's conventions on freedom of association and forced labor, the Communist bloc countries leveled charges of Western bias at the ILO's supervisory machinery and sought to change it. *Id.*

During the Cold War, the United States, which waited to join the ILO until 1934, grew increasingly disenchanted with the organization. From the U.S. perspective, the agency had become too politicized. The United States took particular issue with the ILO's denunciations of South Africa and Israel, the ILO's criticism of the United States for its involvement in Vietnam, its approval of observer status for the Palestine Liberation Organization, and its perceived willingness to disregard the Soviet Union's record on human rights violations. In 1977, the United States withdrew from the ILO, citing, *inter alia*, these issues but vowing to return when its concerns were effectively addressed. As a country that contributed 25 percent of the ILO's budget, the U.S. withdrawal represented a means of applying political and economic pressure to the agency. By 1980, the United States sensed enough movement on some of its concerns to rejoin the ILO. Stephen I. Schlossberg, *United States' Participation in the ILO: Redefining the Role*, 11 COMP. LAB. L. J. 48, 68-71 (1989).

In 1984 the ILO, acting on a complaint of the International Confederation of Free Trade Unions (ICTWU), reported on Poland's dissolution of the free trade union Solidarność as a violation of freedom of association. This watershed event "sent shockwaves not just through the Soviet-dominated countries of Central and Eastern Europe but throughout the world." John P. Windmuller, Stephen K. Pursey & Jim Baker, *The International Trade Union Movement*, in COMPARATIVE LABOUR LAW AND INDUSTRIAL RELATIONS IN INDUSTRIALIZED MARKET ECONOMIES 75, 97 (8th ed., Roger Blanpain, 2004). The ILO's contribution in safeguarding union rights in Poland during this period, and striking a blow against the concept of Communist Party control over organized labor, is widely acknowledged. Oliver Clarke, Greg J. Bamber & Russell D. Lansbury, *Conclusions: Towards a Synthesis of International and Comparative Experience in Employment Relations*, in INTERNATIONAL & COMPARATIVE EMPLOYMENT RELATIONS 294, 318 (3rd ed., Greg J. Bamber & Russell D. Lansbury, eds., 2003). In the end, the collapse of the Soviet Union and the overthrow of Communism in Eastern Europe saw an end to that particular brand of ideological warfare within the ILO.

Today, the ILO's focus is on addressing the policy challenges posed by globalization. Since 1999, the ILO has described its primary goal as that of securing "decent work" for all people. The four strategic objectives encompassed within the decent work program are: (1) promoting rights at work; (2) creating actual employment opportunities of acceptable quality; (3) obtaining and enhancing social protection for the risk of job loss; and (4) promoting social dialogue, the modern term for tripartism, as a mechanism to resolve conflicts, obtain equity, and create and implement policy. JUAN SOMAVIA, REPORT OF THE DIRECTOR-GENERAL (ILO 1999). Professor Gary Fields notes that the ILO's new agenda "shifts the focus of the ILO to workplace outcomes: once core labor standards are satisfied, attention shifts to how much work there is, how remunerative and secure" it is, and the conditions under which it is carried out. Gary S. Fields, *International Labor Standards and Decent Work: Perspectives from the Developing World, in* INTERNATIONAL LABOR STANDARDS: GLOBALIZATION, TRADE, AND PUBLIC POLICY 61, 67 (Robert J. Flanagan & William B. Gould IV, eds., 2003). A major initiative to review, revise, and integrate the existing conventions is also underway. HEPPLE, LABOUR LAWS, at 63.

In addition to those recent initiatives, the ILO is engaged in promoting the 1998 Declaration on Fundamental Principles and Rights at Work, the pledge by ILO member nations that they will adhere to four core labor rights – freedom of association and collective bargaining; the elimination of forced or compulsory labor; the abolition of child labor; and the elimination of discrimination. *Id.* at 57-62. The potential of the 1998 Declaration to enhance the ILO's ability to affect real change for workers around the globe is addressed in the final section of this chapter. Before taking up that subject, however, one must first understand how the ILO has traditionally carried out its work.

B. ILO STANDARD SETTING AND STRUCTURE

Since its creation, the ILO has primarily set international labor standards by adopting conventions and recommendations, both of which may be thought of as forms of ILO "legislation." ILO legislation, however, differs from laws passed by national legislatures. At the time of ILO adoption, neither a convention nor a recommendation is binding on the member countries.

Nonetheless, while a national government need not accept the ILO's conventions, it is required to submit them for consideration to the competent authorities – generally its own legislature – within eighteen months, and is subject to two reporting obligations. Hepple, Labour Laws, at 30. Article 19 of the ILO Constitution requires member countries to report on the steps they take to bring to the attention of the competent authorities the existence of new, unratified conventions. An additional reporting requirement under Article 19 requires member states, on request, to detail their law and practice regarding a convention's subject, and to explain why ratification has been prevented or delayed. The member country responses to this provision are analyzed in a general survey of the convention topic. *Id.* at 48.

Once ratified by a member state without reservations, a convention is considered a multilateral treaty containing international obligations. Recommendations, in contrast, are designed to provide guidance only, need not be ratified by ILO member governments, and do not constrain their actions. Potter, The ILO, at 40-5. This latter form of ILO legislation often supplements a particular convention, providing additional details to assist member countries in fashioning national policy.

Conventions and recommendations must be approved by two-thirds of the delegates attending the ILO's annual International Labour Conference (ILC), which functions as the quasi-legislative branch of the agency. The unique tripartite structure requires each member nation to send to the annual conference in June a four-person delegation comprised of two government officials, one representative of employers' interests, and one representative of organized labor, although many countries also send additional individuals as advisers.

A delegation's employer and worker representatives must be nominated with the agreement of the most representative organizations for those constituencies in its home country.

The U.S. delegation includes a representative from the U.S. Council for International Business (USCIB), an organization comprised of over three hundred multinational corporations, law firms, and business associations, and a delegate from the American Federation of Labor and Congress of Industrial Organizations (AFL-CIO), the voluntary federation of fifty-three national and international unions. ILC voting is by secret ballot, with delegates casting ballots individually. Thus, there is no need for the employer or worker representatives to vote in tandem with their government's representatives.

Setting the agenda for future ILCs, establishing the program and budget for the ILC to adopt, reviewing the status of various ILO projects, and electing the ILO Director-General are the tasks of the Governing Body (GB), which operates as the agency's board of directors or executive council. It, too, is tripartite in composition. Half of its fifty-six members are drawn from government, and there are fourteen employers' representatives and fourteen individuals representing workers. Ten of the government seats are reserved for representatives of ten countries deemed to be of "chief industrial importance," including the United States. Other members are elected every three years by the ILC, the government representatives on a geographically distributed basis, and the others by their respective constituencies. Sweptson, International Labour Law, at 143. The GB meets three times a year.

The site of the ILO's overall activities is the agency's permanent secretariat, the International Labor Office (the "Office"), which is headquartered in Geneva, Switzerland. Almost two thousand ILO employees work out of the Geneva headquarters, and in the ILO's forty field offices. Missions throughout the world are also undertaken by the up to six hundred ILO experts staffing the agency's technical cooperation program. A Director-General, elected to a five-year term, is the head of the Office. The Office is also the headquarters of the ILO's substantial research, documentation and publication activities. Potter, The ILO, at 40-7.

All three main ILO bodies – the ILC, the GB, and the Office – play a role in setting international labor standards. Promulgation and adoption of a convention or recommendation is typically a two-year process. The process begins with the Office, which prepares a paper each year detailing possible subjects for action at future ILCs. In light of the paper, the GB may decide to place a particular subject on the agenda of an ILC to be held in two years' time. The Office then produces during the first year a global law and practice report and a questionnaire on the issue. Answers to the questionnaire, provided by the member nations and employer and labor groups, are the basis for draft conclusions and a report on the subject for discussion at a first ILC. At the ILC, a tripartite technical drafting committee amends the draft conclusions, conducts discussions and prepares a new report with conclusions that is submitted to the conference for approval. Once the report is approved, the ILC places the matter on the agenda for the next conference.

The report that emerges from discussions at the first conference is used by the Office to prepare a draft of the proposed instrument – a convention or a recommendation. The draft instrument is sent for comments by member governments, workers and employers. These comments are used to prepare a final report and draft convention or recommendation, which is sent to member governments in advance of the ILC, and will be discussed, possibly amended, and ultimately voted upon at the second conference. Id. at 40-9–40-10. Once adopted by the ILC, a convention enters into force when two member countries ratify it.

As of October 2006, the ILO had adopted 187 conventions and 198 recommendations. The subjects covered by this international labor code include: (1) freedom of association and the right to organize; (2) the abolition of forced labor; (3) protection from discrimination in employment; (4) child labor; (5) general employment matters; (6) conditions of work; (7) occupational safety and health; (8) the employment of women; (9) older workers; (10) migrant workers; (11) seafarers; and (12) labor administration, including inspection and the compilation of statistics. Sweptson, International Labour Law, at 149-58.

Although the depth and breadth of the ILO's corpus juris is impressive, some commentators query whether there are too many standards of questionable quality and relevance. Creighton, Future of Labour Law, at 257-9; Efren Córdova, *Some Reflections on the Overproduction of International Labour Standards*, 14 Comp. Lab. L.J. 138 (1993). Also of concern are the uneven ratification rates among conventions and countries. Some conventions have high levels of ratification while the vast majority receives little attention. Potter, The ILO, at 40-15. Moreover, although by September 2006 there were 7,421 ratifications of the 187 conventions, member states vary considerably in their receptivity to ratification. Unlike most of its industrial counterparts, for example, the United States has ratified only fourteen conventions, two of which are no longer in force. The U.S. ratification rate is one of the lowest in the world.

The ILO's initiative to revise and integrate its conventions acknowledges and responds to criticism that the proliferation of ILO labor standards has proven counterproductive for the agency. The ILO's Working Party on Policy Regarding the Revision of Standards recently issued recommendations that prompted the GB to conclude that "only 71 conventions and 73 recommendations are up to date, 24 conventions and 15 recommendations have to be revised, and 54 conventions and 67 recommendations are outdated." Hepple, Labour Laws, at 63.

Over time, the ILO has engaged in less standard setting through the adoption of conventions. Sir Bob Hepple notes that in the ILO's first two decades, a little over three conventions were adopted each year. In contrast, from 1997 to 2004, only five conventions were adopted – none in 1998, 2002, and 2004. *Id*. at 35.

C. ILO MONITORING AND MEMBER NATION COMPLIANCE

International labor standards are enforced by the ILO in two main ways: through the examination of reports and through the consideration of complaints. As noted earlier, conventions do not bind the member states unless they are ratified. Once ratified, however, the member country must maintain its national law and practice in conformity with the convention, which is considered a treaty. In some countries, ratification makes the convention part of national law, enforceable at the national level. Most ILO conventions are not drafted as self-executing, however, and instead require supplementary enacting legislation to be passed by the member country's legislature to bring about a direct national effect. Sweptson, International Labour Law, at 159.

Article 22 of the ILO Constitution sets forth the obligations of all member states that ratify conventions:

> Each of the Members agrees to make an annual report to the International Labour Office on the measures which it has taken to give effect to the provisions of Conventions to which it is a party. These reports shall be made in such form and shall contain such particulars as the Governing Body may request.

ILO Constitution, Article 22.

Although the express wording of Article 22 refers to an annual report, in practice the intervals in which the reports on various conventions are due are longer. Typically, reports are requested at two- or five-year intervals. Hepple, Labour Laws, at 48. Eight fundamental conventions that are the touchstones of the Declaration on Fundamental Principles and Rights at Work generally require reporting every two years. So too do four so-called "priority conventions" covering labor inspection (No. 81), employment policy (No. 122), labor inspection in agriculture (No. 129), and tripartite consultation at the national level (No. 144). Reports on all other ratified conventions are due every five years. Potter, The ILO, at 40-16–40-17.

1. Committee of Experts on the Application of Conventions and Recommendations

Article 22 reports are reviewed by the ILO's Committee of Experts on the Application of Conventions and Recommendations (CEACR), a body of at present twenty distinguished individuals, including judges, academics and lawyers, who meet once a year in December. Approximately two thousand reports are reviewed annually. The CEACR also reviews submissions from employer and workers' groups, and may examine national law, court decisions, collective bargaining agreements, and other relevant texts. Potter, The ILO, at 40-18. A country deemed to fall short of full compliance with a ratified convention may receive from the CEACR a "direct request" soliciting additional or clarifying information on points of concern. Another mechanism by which the CEACR makes known its initial conclusions about convention non-compliance is by issuing "observations" in its annual report to the Conference Committee on the Application of Standards, a tripartite committee of the ILC that meets each June during the annual conference. The observations are also sent to the countries whose actions prompt them.

CEACR: INDIVIDUAL OBSERVATION CONCERNING CONVENTION NO. 111, DISCRIMINATION (EMPLOYMENT AND OCCUPATION), 1958

India (ratification: 1960) Published: 2005

Discrimination on the basis of social origin

1. In its 2002 observation, the Committee had referred to a communication from the [International Confederation of Free Trade Unions] ICFTU dated 2 September 2002 and to the Government's reply, which had been received during the Committee's session, on 3 December 2002. The Committee notes that an additional reply was received on 19 December 2002.

2. The communication of the ICFTU referred to the practice of manual scavenging, i.e. the removal of human and animal excreta from public and private latrines and open sewers. Manual scavenging is performed almost exclusively by Dalits (also known as untouchables) and according to government statistics, an estimated 1 million Dalits in India are manual scavengers. Women clean public latrines daily, removing the excrement with brooms and small tin plates and piling it into baskets which are carried on the head to faraway locations. Manual scavengers may also be engaged in underground sewage work, or in cleaning faeces from the railway systems, or in the disposal of dead animals. They work for state municipalities or for private employers. They are exposed to the most virulent forms of viral and bacterial

infections, including tuberculosis. They may be paid as little as 12 rupees (US$ 0.30) a day, for unlimited hours. Sometimes, they do not receive their pay.

3. According to the ICFTU, the allocation of labour on the basis of caste is a fundamental part of the caste system. Within the caste system, Dalits, who are considered "polluted" from birth, are assigned, through threats and coercion, tasks and occupations which are deemed ritually polluting by other caste communities, such as scavenging. Refusal to perform such tasks can lead to physical abuse, social boycott and exclusion from any other form of employment. This practice is described as clearly discrimination on the basis of social origin, as defined in Article 1 of the Convention.

4. The ICFTU alleges that, although legislation was enacted in 1993 to prohibit the employment of manual scavengers and the construction of dry latrines and funds exist for the construction of flush latrines and the rehabilitation of scavengers under a government national scheme, the employment of Dalits as manual scavengers continues throughout India. . . .

5. The ICFTU submits that the Government of India has failed to fulfil [*sic*] its obligation under Article 2 of the Convention to pursue a policy to eliminate discrimination in employment, and its obligation under Article 3(d) to implement this policy in respect of employment under the direct control of a national authority. . . .

6. In its reply dated 2 December 2002, the Government states that the eradication of manual scavenging is a matter of priority concern for the Government of India. It recognizes that manual scavenging still exists in certain pockets, due mainly to unchanged societal structures and mores. In order to resolve the problem of dry latrines, the Government has enacted a central legislation – the Employment of Manual Scavengers and Construction of Dry Latrines (Prohibition) Act, 1993, which came into force in 1997 – and it has made every effort to implement the Act in full earnest. . . .

[The observation notes that the Government referenced two programs aimed at converting dry latrines into low-cost flush latrines, and providing alternative employment to "liberated scavengers." Under the programs, over 437,000 scavengers have been liberated and over 154,000 trained for alternative occupations.]

10. The Committee notes that in the practice of manual scavenging, persons belonging to a certain social group called the Dalits, are usually engaged on account of their social origin. This constitutes discrimination, as defined in Article 1, paragraph 1(a), of the Convention.

11. The Committee takes note of the Government's statement that the eradication of manual scavenging in the country is a matter of priority concern for the Government. It notes that the Employment of Manual Scavengers and Construction of Dry Latrines (Prohibition) Act, 1993, punishes the employment of persons for manually carrying human excreta and the construction or maintenance of dry latrines with imprisonment and/or a fine, and that a number of schemes have existed for a number of years for the construction of flush latrines and the liberation and rehabilitation of manual scavengers.

12. The Committee notes with concern that despite those measures, manual scavenging continues to be used in large parts of the country and large numbers of men and women have still to perform degrading tasks by reason of social origin and economic circumstances in inhuman conditions, in contravention of the Convention. The Committee expresses the hope that the Government will step up its efforts to ensure the prompt elimination of this

practice and the access of the persons involved to other, more decent, jobs. In particular, the Committee requests the Government:

- to take measures to ensure that the state, local and railway authorities apply and enforce the prohibitions contained in the Employment of Manual Scavengers and Construction of Dry Latrines (Prohibition) Act, 1993, and that the penalties provided for their violation are effectively imposed (please provide indications on the number of prosecutions engaged and the number and nature of penalties imposed);
- to evaluate the effectiveness of the existing schemes for the construction of flush latrines and the rehabilitation of manual scavengers, taking into account the reports and recommendations of the competent organs including the National Commission for Safai Karamcharis [the official name for manual scavengers] and the National Commission on Scheduled Castes and Tribes; and
- to launch and/or expand public awareness programmes for the population and educational and training programmes for the authorities involved, in order to promote the changes in mentalities and social habits which are necessary to bring about the elimination of manual scavenging.

The Government is requested to provide information on the concrete measures taken with regard to these matters. . . .

Notes

1. The CEACR specifically references Article 1, paragraph 1(a) of C. 111, the Discrimination (Employment and Occupation) Convention, which, true to its name, prohibits employment discrimination. Article 1, paragraph 1 of the Convention provides:

   1. For the purpose of this Convention the term *discrimination* includes
      a. any distinction, exclusion or preference made on the basis of race, colour sex, religion, political opinion, national extraction or social origin, which has the effect of nullifying or impairing equality of opportunity or treatment in employment or occupation;
      b. such other distinction, exclusion or preference which has the effect of nullifying or impairing equality of opportunity or treatment in employment or occupation as may be determined by the Member concerned after consultation with representative employers' and workers' organisations, where such exist, and with other appropriate bodies.

   Discrimination (Employment and Occupation) Convention, June 25, 1958, ILOLEX C111, http://www.ilo.org/ilolex/english/convdisp1.htm.

   Paragraph 10 of the 2005 observation notes that the Dalits are a social group engaged in the occupation of manual scavenging because of their social origin. The Committee also concludes that the plight of the Dalits in this case constitutes discrimination on the basis of social origin in violation of the Convention. Is the objection of the CEACR to the relegation of a particular social group to this occupation or to the inhuman nature of the work itself?

2. In 1950, the concept of untouchability was abolished by the Constitution of India. What factors explain the persistence of a despised caste and the assignment of its members to the worst jobs in the Indian economy? For information about the social

and legal status of the Dalits, *see* Chapter 13, Section IV ("Equal Opportunities" for the Scheduled Castes, Scheduled Tribes & Other Backward Classes).

3. In its 2005 observation concerning India's noncompliance with Convention No. 111, the CEACR provided that nation with a list of steps it wants India to take to increase the pace at which manual scavenging is eliminated. The CEACR also expects to receive from India an update on the measures taken to address this exploitive and discriminatory occupation. Making a request, however, does not guarantee that the committee will receive the information. Indeed, in a part of the observation not reproduced here, the CEACR noted that its 2002 observation on sex discrimination in India had included a request that the government provide statistical data on the educational gap between Indian boys and girls, statistics on female labor force participation, and information on the status of the National Policy for the Empowerment of Women, the body that monitors programs aimed at the economic empowerment of women. Instead of supplying the requested data, the Indian government responded that the information will be supplied "as and when it becomes available." CEACR: INDIVIDUAL OBSERVATION CONCERNING CONVENTION NO. 111, DISCRIMINATION (EMPLOYMENT AND OCCUPATION), 1958 India (ratification: 1960) Published 2005.

4. The CEACR's 2006 observation concerning India's noncompliance with Convention No. 111 regarding the Dalits notes that "the Government's [2005] report contains very little new information on this matter and no replies to the specific requests made by the Committee." CEACR: INDIVIDUAL OBSERVATION CONCERNING CONVENTION NO. 111, DISCRIMINATION (EMPLOYMENT AND OCCUPATION), 1958 India (ratification: 1960) Published 2005.

5. Monitoring through reporting may seem an odd enforcement mechanism to those used to quasi-judicial or judicial proceedings involving the possibility of concrete sanctions. The ILO's reporting procedures, in contrast, rely on moral suasion and public shaming. Professor Brian Langille characterizes the ILO supervisory mechanism as "a decidedly soft law system." Brian A. Langille, *Core Labour Rights – The True Story (Reply to Alston)*, 16 EUR. J. INT'L L. 407, 413 (2005). Yet although the enforcement techniques lack "teeth" in the sense of providing for monetary sanctions, one must remember that ratified conventions are binding legal instruments. They thus may be distinguished from purely voluntary tools, such as some international declarations, guidelines or corporate codes of conduct.

6. The number of Article 22 reports received from member states is substantially less than the number requested by the CEACR. For example, the CEACR requested that a total of 2,569 Article 22 reports be submitted to it by September 1, 2004. It received 1,645 reports or only 64.03 percent of the reports requested. GENERAL REPORT OF THE COMMITTEE OF EXPERTS ON THE APPLICATION OF CONVENTIONS AND RECOMMENDATIONS, 2005, at ¶16. Moreover, the majority of the reports received are submitted late. "[B]y 1 September 2004, the proportion of reports received was only 25.65 per cent." *Id.* at ¶24. Lateness in submitting reports hampers the functioning of the supervisory process, making it impossible to consider some cases, which then must be deferred for examination prior to the next year's meeting of the ILC.

7. Since 1964, the CEACR has compiled a list of cases in which member countries exhibit progress in bringing their laws and practice into compliance with ratified conventions after receiving committee comments. The 2005 report notes

that progress was made in fifty-three cases in thirty-five countries. The total list of such cases from 1964 to 2004 numbers 2,429. GENERAL REPORT OF THE COMMITTEE OF EXPERTS ON THE APPLICATION OF CONVENTIONS AND RECOMMENDATIONS, 2005, at ¶¶38–9.

---

2. Conference Committee on the Application of Standards

After reviewing the annual CEACR report, the Conference Committee on the Application of Standards (CCAS), the tripartite committee of the ILC that meets during the annual conference, typically considers about twenty-five of the most serious cases detailed. The CCAS then conducts detailed discussions with the governments involved in those cases, and adopts conclusions in its annual report to the ILC. Potter, The ILO, at 40-18–40-19.

Many of the cases involve factual circumstances that are shocking. For example, the 2005 CCAS report provides a synopsis of the discussion involving Columbia's violation of Convention No. 87, Freedom of Association and Protection of the Right to Organize. At the start of the discussion, a government representative from Columbia addressed the progress his country had made in reducing violence directed against labor union leaders:

> . . . In the specific case of labour union leaders, whereas in 2002, unfortunately 205 had been murdered, in 2004 the number of murdered trade unionists had been 89, representing a reduction of 56.58 per cent. . . .

> According to the report of the National Prosecutor's Office for the period 2002–04 on cases currently under investigation for offences of homicide, in which the victim was associated with a labour union, there had been 36 preventive detentions, 21 charges, four sentences and 131 investigations, which amounted to significant progress in comparison with ten years ago.

> Report of the Conference Committee on the Application of Standards, Provisional Record 22, Part II, Ninety-Third Session, Geneva, 2005, Convention 87, Freedom of Association and Protection of the Right to Organise, 1948 Columbia (ratification: 1976).

Despite this progress, the CCAS condemned in the strongest terms all such acts of violence, and concluded that "organizations of workers and employers could exercise their activities in a free and meaningful manner only in a climate that was free from violence. . . . " *Id.* The Columbian government was exhorted to redouble its efforts to put an end to a situation that obviously presented a great obstacle to the realization of the rights guaranteed by Convention No. 87. Finally, the CCAS decided that a high level tripartite visit to Columbia by ILO representatives was necessary. *Id.*

Conditions affecting Columbian trade unionists clearly fit within the category of the CCAS's most serious cases. Some of the other cases categorized as serious may strike students of international labor law as surprising and very revealing. The CCAS's consideration in 2005 of the possible noncompliance of the United States with Convention No. 144, Tripartite Consultation (International Labor Standards) is such a case. *See* TRIPARTITE CONSULTATION (INTERNATIONAL LABOUR STANDARDS) CONVENTION, JUNE 26, 1976, ILOLEX C144, http://www.ilo.org/ilolex/english/convdisp1.htm.

Article 2 of Convention No. 144 requires ratifying countries to "operate [national level] procedures which ensure effective consultations . . . between representatives of the government, of employers and of workers" on ILO-related activities. *Id.* Article 5 of the

Convention requires that "consultation . . . shall be undertaken at least once a year." *Id.* The AFL-CIO, in comments attached to a U.S. government report for the period from 2001–2004, alleged that under the Bush Administration the tripartite consultation process had ground to a halt. In an individual observation, the CEACR requested the U.S. government to provide information in its next report on the steps it has taken to ensure effective consultation and to resolve the issues raised by the AFL-CIO. Interestingly, the CCAS selected this case as one of the twenty-five most serious cases to come before it in 2005.

REPORT OF THE CONFERENCE COMMITTEE ON THE APPLICATION OF STANDARDS, CONVENTION NO. 144, TRIPARTITE CONSULTATION (INTERNATIONAL LABOUR STANDARDS), 1976

United States (ratification: 1988); Published 2005

A [U.S.] Government representative stated that the United States took its obligations under ratified Conventions very seriously. . . .

She recalled that tripartite arrangements had been established in 1975 when the United States was contemplating withdrawal from the ILO. There had been tripartite consultation at the highest level on the decision to withdraw and, during the period of withdrawal, on whether and when to return. The mechanism was a Cabinet Level Committee that included the President of the AFL-CIO and a representative from the United States Chamber of Commerce. Upon rejoining the ILO in February 1980, the United States formalized the Cabinet Level Committee as a federal advisory committee called the President's Committee on the ILO. . . .

The President's Committee was the pinnacle of the tripartite mechanism and provided for consultation at the highest level. More continual consultation occurred through a staff-level consultative group and in the Tripartite Advisory Panel on International Labour Standards (TAPILS) that was created specifically to examine the legal feasibility of ratifying selected ILO Conventions. One of the first conventions that TAPILS had examined was Convention No. 144. . . . The framework for tripartite consultations had not changed since.

The [U.S. government representative] pointed out that this was the first time that the Committee of Experts had expressed any concern at all about United States application of the Convention. The question, she noted, was whether tripartite consultations in the United States were effective. [The U.S. government representative described the Convention as a flexible promotional instrument that requires consultations but does not specify that they must take the form of a meeting.]

Turning to the factual issues of the case, [the U.S. government representative] stated that there had indeed not been a meeting of the President's Committee since May 2000. In fact, since the United States ratified Convention No. 144 in 1988, the President's Committee had met on only six occasions. This was because the President's Committee only met when warranted by ILO-related issues that required a decision at the highest level. . . . As a consequence, most ILO consultations were held less formally.

The observation also indicated that the TAPILS did not meet during the reporting period. [The U.S. government representative] announced that the Panel had met last month [May 2005] to begin reviewing Convention No. 185 on Seafarers' Identity Documents. . . .

With regard to the Committee of Experts' observation that for the first time since 1991, the Government had not convened a full meeting of the consultative group in preparation of the 2004 ILO Conference, [the U.S. government representative] pointed out that the Department of Labor had in fact scheduled its usual full pre-Conference briefing but learned subsequently that a significant portion of the delegation, particularly from the AFL-CIO, could not attend. Consequently, the meeting had to be rescheduled at a time that could include the AFL-CIO, closer to the opening of the Conference, with more limited attendance. . . . This year, the Government had again hosted a full tripartite meeting in preparation of the 2005 ILO Conference.

The [CCAS] Worker members recalled that Convention No. 144 set forth the obligation for ratifying States to establish, in accordance with national practice, effective tripartite consultations with respect to the matters concerning the activities of the ILO. To contravene these provisions or to interpret this instrument in a restrictive manner imperiled the credibility of trade unions as well as the efficiency of ILO standards. . . . For the past three years, the Government had not convoked the President's Committee or the Tripartite Advisory Panel on International Labour Standards (TAPILS), the bodies intended to implement Convention No. 144. . . . The observation of the Committee of Experts had established that the Government had clearly ceased to be active in the tripartite process and had taken no action toward further ratifications of ILO standards. . . .

The Worker member of India stated that this case was a clear violation of Convention No. 144. For the first time since 1991, the United States Government had not convened a full consultative group in 2004 in preparation for the Conference. . . . This lack of this preparation was a violation of democratic norms and was unbecoming for a country which never failed to project itself as the champion of democracy. . . .

The Government member of Cuba stated. . . . [i]t was clear that greater attention should be focused on Governments that only ratified a small number of Conventions. . . .

The Worker member of Pakistan stated that the United States, in its role as the leader of the developed world and as one of the states of chief industrial importance in the Governing Body, should play an exemplary role not only in the ratification of ILO Conventions but in their implementation in letter and spirit. . . . He concluded by noting that the United States often pressed for the ratification and implementation of fundamental Conventions in other countries. In the light of this, the United States should take the lead in ratifying and implementing such Conventions itself. . . .

The Committee noted the statement made by the [U.S.] Government representative and the discussion that followed. The Committee noted that, in accordance with the Convention and the comments made by the Committee of Experts in its observation, the Government and the social partners should establish procedures to ensure effective consultations. . . .

The Committee requested the Government to take all the appropriate measures to promote tripartite dialogue on international labour standards. The Committee hoped that the Government would provide information in its next report on the progress made to guarantee the holding in practice of tripartite consultations in a manner that was satisfactory for all the parties concerned.

———————

Notes

1. Why did the CCAS select the U.S. tripartite consultation case for review in 2005 as one of the most serious cases? Although Convention No. 144 is considered a "priority convention," perhaps the situation was addressable in a less public forum. The CEACR did produce an individual observation that was forwarded to the U.S. government. What more is gained by characterizing the case as among the most serious?

2. As noted earlier, the U.S. government convened the Tripartite Advisory Panel on International Labor Standards (TAPILS) in May 2005 to begin reviewing Convention No. 185 on Seafarers' Identity Documents, and also held a tripartite meeting of the full consultative group to prepare for the 2005 ILC. Is this evidence that the ILO's enforcement mechanism works?

3. Interestingly, whereas the United States, at fourteen conventions, has one of the world's lowest ILO ratification rates, it is considered to be a high compliance nation; in other words, the CEACR has not often issued individual observations based on the U.S. government's actions regarding its ratified conventions. Hepple, Labour Laws, at 42. In contrast, United Kingdom, France, Italy, Spain, Netherlands, Norway and Finland all have ratified eighty or more conventions but are considered low compliance member states. *Id.* at 40.

4. An obvious subtext in the case is the perceived hypocrisy of the United States in refusing to ratify most of the ILO's conventions, yet using the ILO's eight fundamental conventions, which act as references to the 1998 Declaration on Fundamental Principles and Rights at Work, as a touchstone for judging the labor standards of its trading partners, especially in the context of negotiating free trade agreements. Is there a different way to interpret U.S. actions in this respect?

5. The U.S. reluctance to ratify ILO conventions has been attributed to a number of factors. First, during the ILO's early decades the U.S. labor movement's approach to securing worker rights centered mainly on voluntarily negotiating collective bargaining agreements. Excessive government involvement was seen as antithetical to workers' interests. Virginia A. Leary, *"Form Follows Function": Formulations of International Labor Standards – Treaties, Codes, Soft Law, Trade Agreements, in* International Labor Standards: Globalization, Trade, and Public Policy 179, 181 (Robert J. Flanagan & William B. Gould IV, eds., 2003) (hereinafter, Leary, Form Follows Function).

6. Next, some U.S. policy makers and business people believe that extensive ratification of ILO conventions would "usurp the jurisdiction of Congress to establish a National labor policy, and the jurisdiction of the individual States to regulate labor matters traditionally within their authority." Statement by Senator Strom Thurmond, Examination of the Relationship Between the United States and the International Labor Organization," Hearing Before the Senate Committee on Labor and Human Resources, 99th Cong. 1st Sess., Vol. 1, Page 5 (1985). Those espousing this view are especially concerned about ratifying conventions that would require changes in domestic labor and employment law. Edward E. Potter, *A Pragmatic Assessment from the Employers' Perspective, in* Workers' Rights as Human Rights 118, 134 (James A. Gross, ed., 2003). Is this a valid concern? U.S. policy, even under presidential administrations favorably disposed toward the ILO, has been

to consider ripe for ratification only those conventions that are clearly non-self-executing, and thus not directly enforceable as U.S. law in U.S. courts. Moreover, the conventions considered candidates for U.S. ratification are those that TAPILS concludes require no change in existing U.S. law.

7. Some tie the reticence of the United States to its unique system of labor market regulation, which tends to emphasize individual over collective rights, and is far more flexible and less protective of employee job security as compared with other industrialized nations. Lee Swepston, *Closing the Gap between International Law and U.S. Labor Law, in* WORKERS' RIGHTS AS HUMAN RIGHTS 53, 55 (James A. Gross, ed., 2003). The ILO's conventions are seen as in harmony with European approaches to labor and employment law, and out of step with those in the United States. Thomas B. Moorhead, *U.S. Labor Law Serves Us Well, in* WORKERS' RIGHTS AS HUMAN RIGHTS 136, 138 (James A. Gross, ed., 2003).

8. Others ascribe the low U.S. ratification rate to American "lack of interest and knowledge of international organizations," and a preference for unilateralism. Leary, Form Follows Function, at 181-2.

9. Even where U.S. law is clearly in compliance with an important fundamental convention, there has been little political will for ratification. As noted by the U.S. government representative in the U.S. tripartite consultation case:

> With regard to Convention No. 111 [Discrimination (Employment and Occupation)], progress had been slow. On the basis of a finding by TAPILS that United States law and practice were in full conformity with its provisions, Convention No. 111 had been forwarded by the President in May 1998 to the United States Senate with a request for advice and consent to ratification. Since then, Convention No. 111 had consistently been on a list of treaties that the Executive Branch considered to deserve priority attention. The Senate, however, while apparently not disinclined to consider the Convention, had given precedence to treaties having a direct bearing on national security.
>
> REPORT OF THE CONFERENCE COMMITTEE ON THE APPLICATION OF STANDARDS, CONVENTION NO. 144, TRIPARTITE CONSULTATION (INTERNATIONAL LABOUR STANDARDS), 1976, United States (ratification: 1988); Published 2005.

For his part, the U.S. CCAS worker member complained that ratification of Convention No. 111 was not a priority of the Bush Administration, and that he would like to see the administration actively lobbying the Senate to move on the matter. *Id.*

10. The Bureau of International Labor Affairs (ILAB) carries out the U.S. Department of Labor's international responsibilities. ILAB is the U.S. government's "primary point of contact with the ILO," and its activities include preparing U.S. government reports for submission to the international organization. REPORT OF THE CONFERENCE COMMITTEE ON THE APPLICATION OF STANDARDS, 2005 CONVENTION NO. 144: TRIPARTITE CONSULTATION (International Labour Standards), 1976 UNITED STATES (ratification: 1988). In March 2005, the Bush Administration proposed an 87 percent cut in funds for ILAB, which received U.S.$93 million in fiscal year 2005. The proposed budget for ILAB for fiscal year 2006 was U.S.$12.4 million. *ILAB Head Questioned over Bureau's Future under Proposed Deep Cuts in New Budget,* BNA WORKPLACE LAW REPORT, April 8, 2005. Congress instead

cut ILAB's funding to U.S.$73 million. In February 2006, the Bush Administration once again sought cuts to ILAB's budget, proposing that ILAB receive U.S.$12 million for fiscal year 2007, a cut of U.S.$61 million from the previous year's funding level. MAJOR SAVINGS AND REFORMS IN THE PRESIDENT'S 2007 BUDGET, EXECUTIVE OFFICE OF THE PRESIDENT OF THE UNITED STATES, FEB. 2006, at 82, 112, available at: http://www.whitehouse.gov/omb/budget/fy2007/pdf/savings.pdf/.

11. What are the costs to U.S. global influence of its policy and practice on ILO convention ratification? Would pursuing a more aggressive ratification policy jeopardize U.S. interests?

---

3. Adversarial Procedures

The ILO supervisory mechanism also has two forms of adversarial procedures. One involves the filing of representations. The other provides for the filing of complaints.

a. *Filing representations under Article 24*

Article 24 of the ILO Constitution allows workers' or employers' organizations to file representations to the GB that a particular member country is not effectively observing a convention it has ratified. Swepston, International Labour Law, at 161. If the representation is found receivable, the GB establishes a three-person tripartite committee to investigate the merits of the case, and make recommendations. The committee prepares a report for the GB, and the GB invites the member nation at issue to attend a meeting at which the case is discussed. Alternatives available to the GB in deciding how to dispense with the case include: (1) adopt the report and refer the case to the regular supervisory process; (2) publish the report in order to increase the pressure for the non-conforming country to comply; or (3) refer the case to a Commission of Inquiry, a mechanism that will be described below. Potter, The ILO, at 40-21. The representations procedure has only been invoked on about seventy occasions, fifty-eight of these in the period from 1994 to 2003. Hepple, Labour Laws, at 49.

REPORT OF THE COMMITTEE SET UP TO EXAMINE THE REPRESENTATION MADE BY THE SENEGAL TEACHERS' SINGLE AND DEMOCRATIC TRADE UNION (SUDES) UNDER ARTICLE 24 OF THE ILO CONSTITUTION ALLEGING NON-OBSERVANCE BY SENEGAL OF THE ABOLITION OF FORCED LABOUR CONVENTION, 1957 (NO. 105)

Published: 1997

Decision

The Governing Body adopted the report of the tripartite committee. Procedure closed.

A. Introduction

1. By letter of 28 August 1995, the Senegal Teachers' Single and Democratic Trade Union (SUDES), referring to article 24 of the Constitution of the International Labour Organization, made a representation alleging the non-observance by Senegal of the. . . . Abolition of Forced Labour Convention, 1957 (No. 105). . . .

B. Examination of the Representation . . .

9. The SUDES alleges failure by the Government of Senegal to observe the Abolition of Forced Labour Convention, 1957 (No. 105), by virtue of its recruitment through a press advertisement. . . . of "1,200 education volunteers".

10. As regards the facts, the SUDES alleges that the Government's press advertisement. . . . specifies that it is aimed at young people who have at least the equivalent of the BFEM diploma and have "no short-term employment prospects". The purpose of this recruitment is among other things to "reopen over 500 classes that have been closed because no teacher is available" and "to halt the decline" in the school enrol[l]ment rate, but also "to combat unemployment and underemployment among young people". The advertisement explains the Government's strategy in this area by stating that "given the constraints facing the State", the Government is seeking to "launch a movement of young education volunteers" and, for the next four years, "to recruit 1,200 education volunteers for elementary classes each year, especially for children in Senegal's most backward areas". These young people, according to the advertisement, will "find work which makes good use of their intellectual, moral and physical potential", will "learn the profession of teacher", and will "receive a monthly scholarship of 50,000 CFA francs and free housing on the spot in backward areas". . . .

13. As regards observation of the Abolition of Forced Labour Convention, 1957 (No. 105), the SUDES emphasizes that, under the terms of Article 1(b) of the Convention, any Member of the ILO which ratifies the Convention undertakes to suppress and not to make use of any form of forced or compulsory labour "as a method of mobilizing and using labour for purposes of economic development". According to the SUDES, this provision has not been observed by the Government of Senegal which specifies in its "advertisement" for "education volunteers" that it wishes to "mobilize" the potential for commitment of young people who have "no short-term employment prospects" in a "movement" which would contribute to the development of the country. According to the SUDES, the population groups targeted by the recruitment drive (unemployed graduates, young people without employment prospects) clearly show that economic constraints, the need to find work at all costs are the real "motivation" for these "volunteers". For them, there is no possibility of choice. Under such circumstances, using the term "volunteer" is inappropriate, since those recruited are forced by economic constraints to accept the offer. . . .

II. Observations and Comments by the Government . . .

17. . . . . . [T]he Government observes that the country is facing severe economic difficulties at a time when it is required to face up to the challenge of providing education for all by the year 2000, in accordance with the commitments accepted at Jomtien. Those commitments of 1990, taken as a whole, confront it and other governments of developing countries with very difficult choices and necessitate alternative solutions other than tried and tested conventional models. . . .

[The Government responded to SUDES's charges of political bias in the selection process by describing at length the system by which candidates were hired. It also noted that of the 32,595 candidates, 1,200 were selected.]

24. As regards observance of the Abolition of Forced Labour Convention, 1957 (No. 105), the Government states that the provisions of the Convention have not been infringed. There is no question of forced labour, still less of compulsory labour. The education volunteers are

able to await developments. If they find other employment, they are released at their own request. If, on the other hand, they decide to pursue a career in teaching, they can continue with their training for four years and complete their voluntary work before being recruited by the public sector or local collectives. . . .

Conclusions . . .

27. Definition of forced or compulsory labour. The SUDES alleges non-observance by the Government of Senegal of Article 1(b) of the Abolition of Forced Labour Convention, 1957 (No. 105), which has been ratified by Senegal. Pursuant to that provision, the Government has undertaken not to make use of any form of forced or compulsory labour as a method of mobilizing and using labour for purposes of economic development. The Convention does not define the concept of forced or compulsory labour. According to the established practice of the ILO's supervisory bodies the definition of the concept of forced labour contained in Article 2, paragraph 1, of the Forced Labour Convention, 1930 (No. 29) is generally valid and can thus also be used to determine what constitutes "forced or compulsory labour" within the meaning of the 1957 Convention, namely "all work or service which is exacted from any person under the menace of any penalty and for which the said person has not offered himself voluntarily". It was noted during the examination of the draft 1930 Convention by the International Labour Conference that the penalty in question did not necessarily have to take the form of a penal sanction, but could also take the form of the loss of any rights or privileges. . . .

28. Economic constraints. The concept of forced or compulsory labour implies that the worker has not offered himself voluntarily for the work or service in question. In the case which is the subject of the present representation, the workers concerned responded to a public appeal directed at volunteers with certain qualifications. Of 32,595 candidates who came forward, 1,200 were selected. Without contesting the voluntary nature of the offer of service by the candidates responding to the appeal, the SUDES claims that the candidates were not free. . . . The Committee notes that the concept of economic constraint was at the heart of the conclusions drawn by ILO bodies concerning previous representations alleging non-observance of the Forced Labour Convention, 1930 (No. 29). It thus appears appropriate to identify the criteria on which those conclusions were based.

29. Precedents. The Committee set up by the Governing Body to examine the representation presented in 1983 by the National Trade Union Co-ordinating Council of Chile (CNS) under article 24 of the Constitution alleging non-observance by Chile of Convention . . .
29 . . . examined the bearing of official employment programmes, namely, the "Minimum Employment Programme" (PEM) and the "Employment Programme for Heads of Household" (POJH), on the observance of the Forced Labour Convention, 1930 (No. 29). The Committee concluded that persons enrolled in these programmes "cannot be considered to enjoy freely chosen employment". In particular, the Committee took the view that "work carried out by many persons, paid for with excessively low wages and not offering the protection of the labour and social security legislation, can give rise to doubts concerning its voluntary nature, particularly when it involves not a temporary or emergency solution but a situation that tends to last. . . .

30. Criteria regarding constraint by the Government. If the case submitted to the Committee for examination has certain similarities with those mentioned above (absence of better alternatives for the candidates, the hope of finding stable employment), there are a number of important differences that were taken into account by previous Committees, in particular

the level of remuneration and benefits and the number of persons affected. In a case where an objective situation of economic constraint exists but has not been created by the Government, then only if the Government exploits that situation by offering an excessively low level of remuneration could it to some extent become answerable for a situation that it did not create. Moreover, it might be held responsible for organizing or exacerbating economic constraints if the number of people hired by the Government at excessively low rates of pay and the quantity of work done by such employees had a knock-on effect on the situation of other people, causing them to lose their normal jobs and face identical economic constraints.

31. This has not happened in the present case. Rather than "a large number of persons paid at excessively low rates", 1,200 people were selected from more than 30,000 candidates for the period beginning 1995, and their remuneration, according to the Government, is above that of student teachers in teacher training schools having broadly similar functions . . . In short, the Committee considers that economic constraints may in practice be such as to be conducive to forced labour. However, in the present case the Government could not be held responsible for having created or exacerbated economic constraints, nor for having exploited them by offering people who had no other options, employment on terms that would not normally be acceptable.

32. Conclusion. In the light of the above, the Committee concludes that the representation alleging non-observance by Senegal of the Abolition of Forced Labour Convention, 1957 (No. 105) is unfounded.

—————————

Notes

1. Why do you think the union brought a representation against the Senegalese government? One major concern, articulated subsequently by the union in an allegation before a joint ILO/United Nations Educational, Scientific and Cultural Organization (UNESCO) committee, is the potential for the Education Volunteers Program to undermine the status and working conditions of the teaching profession. The volunteers initially received a monthly stipend worth just a little over the Senegalese minimum wage, representing less than half of the monthly salary of a regular starting teacher. Moreover, the volunteers, who perform work identical to regular teachers, could be required to teach double-shift classes without additional compensation that would be due were they employed as regular teachers. Additionally, the collective rights and interests of education professionals are implicated by the program. By decree, the volunteers were prohibited from the right to freedom of association and to organize into trade unions. SUDES also complained that the government failed to consult with teachers' unions in the development of the program. The government contested this last point. JOINT ILO/UNESCO COMMITTEE OF EXPERTS ON THE APPLICATION OF THE RECOMMENDATION CONCERNING THE STATUS OF TEACHERS – REPORT, PART 6, D., 1997.

2. The Joint ILO/UNESCO Committee of Experts, which promotes and monitors UNESCO's two recommendations on the status of teachers and of higher education teaching personnel, expressed concern in 1997 "that any extensive or permanent use of volunteers or contract teachers could undermine the status of professional teachers." *Id.* at Part 7. The committee also noted that volunteers who work as teachers should have the same associational rights as regular teachers. *Id.* at Part 7.

3. Following up on the matter in 2000, the Joint ILO/UNESCO Committee of Experts
    noted the following:

    > The Joint Committee is most concerned with the evidence presented by both
    > the Government and SUDES that the volunteers policy has become anchored
    > as a permanent feature in the long-term educational development programme of
    > Senegal. The suggestion by SUDES that all prospective teachers will henceforth
    > pass through the voluntary programme is particularly disturbing. . . . The Joint
    > Committee. . . . again calls on the Government's attention to paragraph 141 of
    > the ILO/UNESCO Recommendation, 1966, which emphasizes that measures to
    > deal with teacher shortages should be exceptional and not endanger teachers'
    > professional standards.
    >
    > JOINT ILO/UNESCO COMMITTEE OF EXPERTS ON THE APPLICATION OF THE
    > RECOMMENDATION CONCERNING THE STATUS OF TEACHERS – REPORT,
    > ANNEX 2(2)(D) (2000).

    Was the initial SUDES representation before the ILO's GB premature? Should
    SUDES have based the representation on a different ILO convention? Senegal
    ratified Convention No. 87 (Freedom of Association and the Right to Organize)
    in 1960 and Convention No. 98 (Right to Organize and Collective Bargaining) in
    1961.

4. For its part, the Senegalese government was in an exceptionally tight spot. Structural
    adjustment curbs on hiring public sector employees, accepted as a condition for
    international loans, constrain the creation of a sufficient pool of teachers to meet its
    goal of universal primary education. The latter, in conjunction with a lack of public
    financial resources, prompted the creation of the volunteers program, which sought
    to create a corps of low paid paraprofessionals. Today, with some improvements in
    pay and the creation of a career path to contract status, and even the possibility
    of regular civil service employment, so-called volunteers make up a significant
    percentage of the primary school teaching force. Peter Coles, *Wanted! Teachers*,
    EDUCATION TODAY NEWSLETTER (UNESCO), January–March 2005, at 4–7.

5. Despite the government's reliance on the volunteer program, SUDES reported in
    2000 to the Joint ILO/UNESCO Committee of Experts that "the policy had so far
    failed to bring Senegal into the group of African countries with an average school
    attendance rate of 75 percent." Joint ILO/UNESCO Committee of Experts on the
    Application of the Recommendation Concerning the Status of Teachers – Report,
    Annex 2(2)(D) (2000). No further communication from the government or the
    union was received in 2003, the date of the last Joint ILO/UNESCO report. Joint
    ILO/UNESCO Committee of Experts on the Application of Recommendations
    concerning Teaching Personnel – Report 30 (2003). The next report is due out in
    2006.

    ---

b. *Complaints filed under Article 26*

A second adversarial mechanism involves the filing of complaints under Article 26 of
the ILO Constitution. The complaint procedure is reserved for serious cases of member
nation noncompliance with ratified conventions. Complaints may be filed against a
member nation by another member country that is a party to the treaty at issue. The GB

may also initiate the process on its own motion or after receiving a complaint from any ILC delegate. In some cases, the GB will establish a Commission of Inquiry to investigate and report on the case. In others, the case is forwarded to the Committee on Freedom of Association, which will be described later. In still other cases, the ILO has settled the matter. Swepston, International Labour Law, at 160.

The complaint process, unlike the process administered by the CEACR, can result in a legally binding determination that a member state is in breach of its treaty obligations. Commission of Inquiry findings become binding when the member country agrees to accept them, or declines to appeal the matter to the International Court of Justice, which it is permitted to do under Article 29 of the ILO Constitution, but which no member nation has done to date. Hepple, Labour Laws, at 50.

REPORT OF THE COMMISSION OF INQUIRY APPOINTED UNDER ARTICLE 26 OF THE CONSTITUTION OF THE INTERNATIONAL LABOUR ORGANIZATION TO EXAMINE THE OBSERVANCE BY MYANMAR OF THE FORCED LABOUR CONVENTION, 1930 (NO. 29)

Published: 1998

1. By a letter dated 20 June 1996 addressed to the Director-General of the ILO, 25 Workers' delegates to the 83rd Session of the International Labour Conference (June 1996) presented a complaint under article 26 of the Constitution against the Government of Myanmar for non-observance of the Forced Labour Convention, 1930 (No. 29), which it ratified on 4 March 1955 and which came into force for Myanmar on 4 March 1956. . . .

Part III . . . Summary of the Complaint and the Government's Observations

100. In their complaint and supplementary evidence, the complainants referred to earlier findings by ILO supervisory bodies concerning non-compliance with the forced labour Convention by Myanmar. The complainants alleged that, far from acting to end the practice of forced labour, the Government of Myanmar was still engaged actively in its promotion, so that it was today an endemic abuse. . . .

110. Before responding to the complainants' allegations, the Government described its initiatives for the emergence of a peaceful, modern and developed nation, its political, economic and social objectives, and the benefits which the local population and the nation as a whole draw from the building of infrastructures throughout the country, in particular the building of new railroads, but also motor roads, irrigation facilities, schools, hospitals, market places, parks and new towns through the collective efforts of the State, the people and the members of the Myanmar armed forces (Tatmadaw). . . .

[The Government asserted that all labor utilized as porters by the military, and for major public and private construction projects, was voluntary and compensated. It further noted that all relevant national laws had been reviewed and redrafted.]

120. In conclusion, the Government indicated that the Myanmar authorities were aware of the criticisms made by some Worker delegates relating to the use of labour in Myanmar for national development projects. A considerable portion of the criticisms were unfortunately based on biased and specious allegations made by expatriates living outside Myanmar who wished to denigrate the Myanmar authorities for their own ends. . . .

Part IV Examination of the Case by the Commission

B. Requirements of the Forced Labour Convention, 1930 (No. 29)

205. The basic obligation undertaken by a State which ratifies the Forced Labour Convention, 1930, is "to suppress the use of forced or compulsory labour in all its forms within the shortest possible period". [Article 1(1)] This obligation to suppress the use of forced or compulsory labour, as defined in the Convention, includes for the State both an obligation to abstain and an obligation to act. In the first place, the State must neither exact forced or compulsory labour nor tolerate its exaction, and it must repeal any laws and statutory or administrative instruments that provide or allow for the exaction of forced or compulsory labour, so that any such exaction, be it by private persons or public servants, is found illegal in national law. Secondly, the State must ensure that "the illegal exaction of forced or compulsory labour shall be punishable as a penal offen[s]e" and "that the penalties imposed by law are really adequate and are strictly enforced". [Article 25] . . .

206. The Convention defines "forced or compulsory labour" as "all work or service which is exacted from any person under the menace of any penalty and for which the said person has not offered himself voluntarily". [Article 2(1)] As noted by the Committee of Experts on the Application of Conventions and Recommendations, it was made clear during the consideration of the draft instrument by the Conference that the penalty here in question need not be in the form of penal sanctions, but might take the form also of a loss of rights or privileges. . . .

[The Commission noted that Article 2(2) of the Convention specifically exempts from the definition of forced or compulsory labor, certain types of service including: compulsory military service of a purely military character; normal civic obligations like jury service; some types of prison labor; service required in emergencies; and minor communal service.]

Legislation of Myanmar relevant to the case

237. After having stated for many years that the provisions of the Village Act (1908) and the Towns Act (1907) which empower headmen and rural policemen to impose compulsory labour on residents of the labouring class had become obsolete and were no longer applied, the Government indicated in October 1993 that "the use of voluntary labour, alleged compulsory or forced labour, is made only for the urgent necessity in accordance with the following provisions: (a) section 8(1)(g)(n) and (o) of the Village Act (1908); (b) section 9(b) of the Towns Act".

238. The relevant provisions of section 8(1) of the Village Act (1908) were submitted by the Government in October 1993 in the following wording:

Every headman shall be bound to perform the following public duties, namely:

   (g)   to collect and furnish, upon receipt of payment for the same at such rates as the Deputy Commissioner may fix, guides, messengers, porters, supplies of food, carriage and means of transport for any troops or police posted in or near or marching through the village-tract or for any servant of the Government travelling on duty: provided that no headman shall requisition for personal service any resident of such village-tract who is not of the labouring class and accustomed to do such work as may be required;

(n) generally to assist all officers of the Government in the execution of their public duties; and

(o) generally to adopt such measures and do such acts as the exigency of the village may require.

Section 7(1)(m) of the Towns Act (1907) corresponds to section 8(1)(n) of the Village Act (1908) and is also preceded by a proviso "that no headman shall requisition for personal service any resident of such ward who is not of the labouring class and accustomed to do such work as may be required".

239. Under Section 11 of the Village Act:

Every person residing in the village-tract shall be bound to perform the following public duties, namely:

(. . .)(d) on the requisition of the headman or of a rural policeman, to assist him in the execution of his duties prescribed in sections 7 and 8 of the Act and the rules made under the Act. . . .

Under section 12 of the same Act:

If any person residing in a village-tract refuses or neglects to perform public duties imposed upon him by this Act or by any rule thereunder, he shall, in the absence of reasonable excuse, the burden of proving which shall lie upon him, be liable:

(i) by order of the headman, to fine . . . ; or
(ii) by order of the village committee, on the case being referred to it by the headman, to fine . . . , or to confinement for a term not exceeding 48 hours in such place as the Deputy Commissioner may appoint in this behalf, or to both; or
(iii) on conviction by a Magistrate, to fine . . . , or to imprisonment for a term not exceeding one month, or to both. . . .

[Similar provisions to those above are found in section 9 of the Towns Act (1907)]

245. . . . [The Government's] concern about "causing misery and sufferings to the local population" and the non-remuneration of labour obtained "from the local populace in carrying out national development projects, such as construction of roads, bridges and railways as well as the building of dams and embankments. . . . " was expressed in an Order dated 2 June 1995 by the Chairman of the State Law and Order Restoration Council (SLORC) to State/Division Law and Order Restoration Councils on the subject of "Prohibiting unpaid labour contributions in national development projects". While marked "secret", this Order has according to the Government "the full legal force and effect in Administrative Law". The Order makes no reference to the Village Act or the Towns Act. It notes in paragraph 1 that "it has been learnt that in obtaining labour from the local populace in carrying out national development projects, such as construction of roads, bridges and railways as well as building of dams and embankments, the practice is that they have to contribute labour without compensation". While observing (in paragraph 3) that "causing misery and sufferings to the people in rural areas due to the so-called forced and unpaid labour is very much uncalled for", the Order does not put into question the requisition of labour for national development projects but stresses (in paragraph 2) that "it is imperative that in obtaining the necessary labour from the local people, they must be paid their due share. . . . "

258. Under section 374 of the [Myanmar] Penal Code: Whoever unlawfully compels any person to labour against the will of that person shall be punished with imprisonment of either description for a term which may extend to one year, or with fine, or with both.

Findings of the Commission concerning the facts

274. Information provided to the Commission indicated that the Myanmar authorities, including the local and regional administration, the military and various militias, forced the population of Myanmar to carry out a wide range of tasks. Labour was exacted from men, women and children, some of a very young age. Workers were not paid or compensated in any way for providing their labour, other than in exceptional circumstances, and were commonly subjected to various forms of verbal and physical abuse including rape, torture and killing. The vast majority of the information covered the period since 1988, the year in which the State Law and Order Restoration Council (SLORC) came to power. While the information indicated that the use of forced labour for all the purposes discussed was prevalent since at least 1988, the use of forced labour on infrastructure-related work appeared to have been much less common before 1992. . . .

275. The information provided indicated that Myanmar's military and various militias made systematic and widespread use of civilians to provide logistical support. This most commonly involved the use of porters to carry a range of supplies and equipment. In comparison to other forms of compulsory labour, the treatment of porters, especially during military offensives, was particularly brutal; such porters were also likely to be exposed to danger in combat situations.

276. In addition to providing porters for the military, villagers across the country, and to a lesser extent urban residents, were required to construct and repair military camps and provide general workers for these facilities on a permanent basis. A number of villagers had to be on permanent stand-by at camps to act as messengers. Villagers also had to provide the necessary materials for the construction and repair of these facilities. . . .

277. The information also disclosed a variety of other tasks that people throughout Myanmar were requisitioned to carry out in support of the military, such as acting as guides, sentries and minesweepers. It appeared that such people were also used as human shields, in that they would be sent ahead of troops to draw enemy fire, trip booby-traps, or as hostages to prevent attacks against columns or army camps. . . .

278. The question of forced recruitment into the Tatmadaw and various militia forces was also brought to the attention of the Commission. In some cases recruits appeared to be arbitrarily requisitioned, without any reference to compulsory military service legislation, and included minors. . . .

280. The information revealed that over the last ten years the Government of Myanmar had implemented a large number of national and local infrastructure projects, in particular the construction and improvement of various roads and railways and associated infrastructure such as bridges. These projects appeared to be constructed in large part with the use of forced labour, sometimes involving hundreds of thousands of workers.

281. Similarly, it appeared that forced labour was used by the Government in relation to a range of other infrastructure projects and public works such as dams, irrigation works and airports.

282. Urban residents in particular were required to work, usually one day per week, on the cleaning and maintenance of urban areas. This was organized by the ward authorities, but was often supervised by the military. . . .

284. It appeared that persons exacting forced labour in Myanmar were not subject to legal sanction, and were therefore enjoying full impunity. Several witnesses who had undertaken general research and investigation informed the Commission that there had been, to their knowledge, no cases of persons being punished for forcing others to provide their labour, or for committing abuses against those so forced.

285. The numbers of people in Myanmar affected by forced labour appeared to be vast. In 1995, Human Rights Watch/Asia estimated that since 1992 at least two million people had been forced to work without pay on the construction of roads, railways and bridges. . . .

292. The information before the Commission was that the penalties for failing to comply with forced labour demands were harsh. Punishments included detention at the army camp, often in leg-stocks or in a pit in the ground, commonly accompanied by beatings and other forms of torture, as well as deprivation of food, water, medical attention and other basic rights. Women were subject to rape and other forms of sexual abuse at such times. . . .

National laws and statutory or administrative standard-setting instruments, considered in the light of the Convention

470. The Commission notes that section 11(d), read together with section 8(1)(g), (n) and (o) of the Village Act, as well as section 9(b) of the Towns Act provide for the exaction of work or services from any person residing in a village tract or in a town ward, that is, work or services for which the said person has not offered himself or herself voluntarily, and that failure to comply with a requisition made under section 11(d) of the Village Act or section 9(b) of the Towns Act is punishable with penal sanctions under section 12 of the Village Act or section 9A of the Towns Act. Thus, these Acts provide for the exaction of "forced or compulsory labour" within the definition of Article 2(1) of the Convention. . . .

471. The Commission notes that the provisions of the Village Act and the Towns Act under which residents may be required to perform forced or compulsory labour on a general or individual requisition of the headman are "widely worded", as was also noted in Executive Orders made under the Village Act; indeed, residents are to assist the headman in the execution of his public duties, which in turn include the duty to supply guides, messengers, porters, etc., to any troops or police posted near or marching through a village tract and generally to assist all officers of the Government in the execution of their public duties. Thus, the labour and services that may be exacted under the Village Act and the Towns Act are as indefinite as the needs of the Government; they are limited neither to emergencies nor to minor communal services as defined in Article 2, paragraph 2(d) and (e), of the Convention, and more generally do not come under any of the exceptions listed in Article 2, paragraph 2. . . .

473. Section 8(1)(g) of the Village Act provides for payments to headmen for the collection and supply of guides, messengers, porters, etc., but nowhere in the Village Act or Towns Act is provision made for any payment to residents called up for labour or services. The (secret) order dated 2 June 1995 on "Prohibiting unpaid labour contributions in national development projects" stresses that "in obtaining the necessary labour from the local people, they must be paid their full share". . . . [T]he mere payment of wages for labour obtained through the

call-up of local residents does not remove such labour from the scope of the definition of forced or compulsory labour in Article 2(1) of the Convention. Payment does not change the character of labour exacted compulsorily or by force; it merely becomes paid compulsory or forced labour. . . .

475. More importantly, evidence before the Commission on actual practice . . . shows the continued call-up of local people for labour and services (without any compensation) . . .

478. Section 374 of the Penal Code. . . . complies with the first requirement of Article 25 of the Convention, namely that "The illegal exaction of forced or compulsory labour shall be punishable as a penal offence". Whether the penalties under section 374, which may range from a fine to imprisonment of up to one year or both, do comply with the second requirement of Article 25 of the Convention, namely that they "are really adequate", could only be appreciated if they were "strictly enforced", as Article 25 of the Convention furthermore requires. In the absence of any indication that section 374 of the Penal Code was ever applied, the Commission is bound to point out that penalties under that provision, as well as under Article 25 of the Convention, are to be imposed for the exaction of forced or compulsory labour that is found illegal. Thus, only a requisition of labour and services that is not covered by the very wide provisions of the Village Act or the Towns Act could, in theory, be punished at the present stage under section 374 of the Penal Code, while forced labour imposed in violation of the Convention but in conformity with the Village Act or the Towns Act might not be punishable at the national level. . . .

Part V Conclusions and Recommendations . . .

536. In conclusion, the obligation under Article 1, paragraph 1, of the Convention to suppress the use of forced or compulsory labour is violated in Myanmar in national law, in particular by the Village Act and the Towns Act, as well as in actual practice in a widespread and systematic manner, with total disregard for the human dignity, safety and health and basic needs of the people of Myanmar.

537. Concurrently, the Government violates its obligation under Article 25 of the Convention to ensure that the penalties imposed by law for the illegal exaction of forced or compulsory labour are both really adequate and strictly enforced. While section 374 of the Penal Code provides for the punishment of those unlawfully compelling any person to labour against the will of that person, that provision does not appear to be ever applied in practice, even where the methods used for rounding up people do not follow the provisions of the Village Act or the Towns Act, which are in any event never referred to in practice. . . .

539. In view of the Government's flagrant and persistent failure to comply with the Convention, the Commission urges the Government to take the necessary steps to ensure:

(a) that the relevant legislative texts, in particular the Village Act and the Towns Act, be brought into line with the Forced Labour Convention, 1930 (No. 29) as already requested by the Committee of Experts on the Application of Conventions and Recommendations and promised by the Government for over 30 years, and again announced in the Government's observations on the complaint. This should be done without further delay and completed at the very latest by 1 May 1999;

(b) that in actual practice, no more forced or compulsory labour be imposed by the authorities, in particular the military. . . .

(c) that the penalties which may be imposed under section 374 of the Penal Code for the exaction of forced or compulsory labour be strictly enforced, in conformity with Article 25 of the Convention. This requires thorough investigation, prosecution and adequate punishment of those found guilty. . . .

540. The recommendations made by the Commission require action to be taken by the Government of Myanmar without delay. The task of the Commission of Inquiry is completed by the signature of its report, but it is desirable that the International Labour Organization should be kept informed of the progress made in giving effect to the recommendations of the Commission. The Commission therefore recommends that the Government of Myanmar should indicate regularly in its reports under article 22 of the Constitution of the International Labour Organization concerning the measures taken by it to give effect to the provisions of the Forced Labour Convention, 1930 (No. 29), the action taken during the period under review to give effect to the recommendations contained in the present report. . . .

Notes

1. The establishment of a Commission of Inquiry is a rare event reserved for cases involving the most serious, persistent violations of the ILO's conventions. Indeed, since 1919, the GB has appointed less than a dozen Commissions of Inquiry. Commissions, which consist of three eminent jurists or scholars, play both investigatory and adjudicatory roles. To those ends, they establish their own procedures, take testimony, request and review documentation, and, if permitted by the country in question, may make site visits to ascertain conditions first hand. Sweptson, International Labour Law, at 160. The report prepared by a Commission of Inquiry is a manifestation of its adjudicatory function, stating the factual findings, legal conclusions and recommendations in the case. The member country in question is given three months to either accept the report or indicate that it will appeal to the International Court of Justice, the latter, which, as noted earlier, is a step that has never been taken by any country. Potter, The ILO, at 40-22.

2. A country that refuses to carry out the recommendations of a Commission of Inquiry is subject to Article 33 of the ILO Constitution, which provides:

   > In the event of any Member failing to carry out within the time specified the recommendations, if any, contained in the report of the Commission of Inquiry, or in the decision of the International Court of Justice, as the case may be, the Governing Body may recommend to the [International Labor] Conference such action as it may deem wise and expedient to secure compliance therewith.
   >
   > ILO Constitution, Article 33.

   This constitutional provision lay dormant until the Myanmar case.

3. In June 1999, almost one year after the Commission of Inquiry in the Myanmar case issued its recommendations, the ILC passed a resolution that: condemned the state's refusal to institute the Commission's recommendations; prohibited any ILO technical assistance other than that necessary to implement the recommendations; and banned Myanmar from attending most ILO meetings. Potter, The ILO, at 40-23. The following year, in June 2000, the ILC adopted a resolution proposed by the GB invoking Article 33. Among other things, the resolution asked ILO members and international organizations to review and take appropriate measures regarding

their relationships with Myanmar to avoid abetting the practice of forced labor. Hepple, Labour Laws, at 51. Encompassed within such a reexamination was the possibility that trade sanctions might be imposed on Myanmar by the member states. Potter, The ILO, at 40-24.

4.   Since then, the Myanmar government has agreed to the appointment of an ILO liaison officer in Myanmar, and allowed an ILO very High Level Team to travel to the country to assess the progress being made to eliminate the use of forced labor. A 2005 CCAS report on Myanmar, however, noted that the extent of the use of forced labor in most areas of Myanmar has not been significantly reduced. Moreover, neither the Village Act nor the Towns Act, which authorize the use of forced labor, has been repealed. The ILO liaison officer has not been permitted to travel freely throughout the country, and the very High Level Team was not met by high level government officials, and cut short its mission. The CSAS noted that it was particularly alarmed at the government's stated intention to prosecute those accused of falsely lodging complaints of forced labor, and also at the apparent intimidation of complainants seeking contact with the ILO liaison officer. CONFERENCE COMMITTEE ON THE APPLICATION OF STANDARDS, SPECIAL SITTING TO EXAMINE DEVELOPMENTS CONCERNING THE QUESTION OF THE OBSERVANCE BY THE GOVERNMENT OF MYANMAR OF THE FORCED LABOUR CONVENTION, 1930 (No. 29) (2005).

5.   At its November 2005 session, the ILO's GB discussed developments in Myanmar and concluded that its "overwhelming reaction was one of profound concern at the continued lack of any meaningful progress in the situation." Especially troubling was:

> [T]he determination expressed by Myanmar authorities to prosecute individuals involved in lodging "false allegations" represent[ing] a further deterioration in the situation which seriously undermined any prospect of progress, and was in direct contradiction with the conclusions adopted at the International Labour Conference in 2005.
>
> Conclusions on document GB.295/7: Developments concerning the question of the observance by the Government Myanmar of the Forced Labour Convention, 1930 (No. 29) (2006).

The subject was an agenda item of the 95th Session of the International Labour Conference, which took place May–June 2006. Id.

6.   The ILO's procedures for enforcing international labor standards are directed at member states rather than at private employers. Yet private employers may directly or indirectly bear responsibility for abysmal working conditions. In the Myanmar case, for example, there was evidence in the form of secondary statements that forced labor was used for helipad construction and ground clearance work for the Yadana gas pipeline project, a joint venture of French oil company Total, American-owned oil giant Unocal, and the Myanmar Oil and Gas Enterprise, a state-owned company established by the Myanmar military. The Commission of Inquiry, which had requested and been denied access to the country by the Myanmar government, could make no finding on the matter. REPORT OF THE COMMISSION OF INQUIRY APPOINTED UNDER ARTICLE 26 OF THE CONSTITUTION OF THE INTERNATIONAL LABOUR ORGANIZATION TO EXAMINE THE OBSERVANCE BY MYANMAR OF THE FORCED LABOUR CONVENTION, 1930 (No. 29) at ¶452.

7. Human rights activists found another device for addressing the alleged atrocities committed in connection with the Yadana gas pipeline project. In the fall of 1996, two suits were filed in U.S. federal court by Myanmar villagers who suffered abuses at the hands of the Myanmar military related to the project. The suits were brought against Myanmar, Total and Unocal, and based largely on the U.S. Alien Tort Claims Act ("ATCA"), 28 USC §1350, a controversial two-hundred-year-old statute that lay dormant until 1980. The ATCA confers on the U.S. federal district courts "original jurisdiction of any civil action by an alien for a tort only, committed in violation of the law of nations." *Id.* Ultimately, the claims against the Myanmar Military and Myanmar Oil were dismissed because those entities were entitled to sovereign immunity. The claims against Total were dismissed for lack of personal jurisdiction. Doe I. v. Unocal Corp., 395 F.3d 932, 943 (9th Cir. 2002). The case against Unocal, however, wound its way through federal and California state court, and was ultimately settled in March 2005. Although the settlement amount is confidential, the parties announced that the money will be used to compensate and protect the villagers, and develop programs in the pipeline region to improve healthcare, living conditions, and education. Marc Lifsher, *Unocal Settles Human Rights Lawsuit Over Alleged Abuses at Myanmar Pipeline*, Los Angeles Times, March 22, 2005. Chapter 14 includes an excerpt of the *Unocal* case and discusses in greater detail use of the Alien Tort Claims Act as a mechanism for enforcing international labor right is U.S. courts.

---

c. *The Committee on Freedom of Association*

A special body was created by the ILO in 1950 to examine complaints brought by governments, workers' organizations or employers' organizations that an ILO member nation's law or practice violates principles of freedom of association. The Committee on Freedom of Association (CFA) is a tripartite body composed of nine members of the GB, and presided over by an independent chair. It draws its authority from the ILO Constitution, along with the Declaration of Philadelphia, both of which embody, *inter alia*, freedom of association as a fundamental principle that all ILO members agree to observe. Thus, ratification of the freedom of association conventions, Conventions Nos. 87 and 98, is not a prerequisite to bringing a complaint against a member country before the CFA. Sweptson, International Labour Law, at 161.

The CFA generally decides cases on the basis of documentary evidence. It usually reaches decisions by consensus. Hepple, Labour Laws, at 52. The CFA meets three times annually, and has reviewed over 2000 cases. Potter, The ILO, at 40-27.

COMMITTEE ON FREEDOM OF ASSOCIATION, COMPLAINT AGAINST THE
GOVERNMENT OF CANADA CONCERNING THE PROVINCE OF ONTARIO
PRESENTED BY THE ONTARIO FEDERATION OF LABOUR (OFL) AND THE CANADA
LABOUR CONGRESS (CLC)

Case No. 2182, Report no. 330 (2003)

Introduction

Allegations: The complainants allege that some provisions of the Ontario Labour Relations Act encourage the decertification of workers' organizations by requiring employers to post and distribute in the workplace documents setting out the process to terminate trade union bargaining rights. . . .

308. Canada has ratified the Freedom of Association and Protection of the Right to Organise Convention, 1948 (No. 87). It has not ratified the Right to Organise and Collective Bargaining Convention, 1949 (No. 98), the Labour Relations (Public Service) Convention, 1978 (No. 151), nor the Collective Bargaining Convention, 1981, (No. 154).

Background

A. The Complainants' Allegations

309. The Ontario Federation of Labour (OFL), affiliated to the Canadian Labour Congress, is made up of 650,000 workers in more than 1,500 affiliated local unions. This complaint concerns some provisions of the Labour Relations Amendment Act, 2000 (Bill No. 139) which, according to the OFL, infringe guarantees of freedom of association and, in particular, ILO Conventions Nos. 87, 98 and 151. These provisions encourage the decertification of workers' organizations by requiring employers to post and distribute in the workplace documents prepared by the Minister of Labour, setting out the process to terminate trade union bargaining rights.

310. Bill No. 139 passed third reading and received royal assent in December 2000. These provisions are now contained in section 63.1 of the Labour Relations Act (the LRA), which provides:

63.1(1) Within one year after the day the Labour Relations Amendment Act, 2000, receives royal assent, the Minister shall cause to be prepared and published a document describing the process for making an application for a declaration that the trade union no longer represents the employees in a bargaining unit. . . .

63.1(3) The document shall explain who may make an application, when an application may be made and the procedure, as set out in this Act and in any rules made by the chair of the Board. . . . that the Board follows in dealing with an application.

63.1(4) An employer with respect to whom a trade union has been certified as a bargaining agent. . . . shall use reasonable efforts:

  (a) to post and keep posted a copy of a document published under this section in a con-spicuous place in every workplace of the employer at which employees represented by the trade union perform work;
  (b) to post and keep posted with that copy a notice that any employee represented by the trade union may request a copy of the document from the employer;
  (c) once in each calendar year, to provide a copy of the document to all employees of the employer who are represented by the trade union; and
  (d) upon the request of an employee . . . to provide a copy of the document to him or her, even though the employer has previously provided or will subsequently provide the employee with a copy of the document.

63.1(5) An employer shall not be found to be in violation of this Act as a result of doing anything set out in subsection (4).

311. In accordance with these provisions, the Minister of Labour prepared and published a document describing the process for decertification in December 2001. A copy of the poster

and brochure were mailed that same month to all employers who had registered a collective bargaining relationship with the Ministry of Labour.

312. The complainants allege that section 63.1 of the LRA contravenes Convention No. 87, ratified by Canada, and is entirely inconsistent with the Government's obligations under international law to encourage, promote and protect the right of employees to bargain collectively. This provision constitutes a powerful message by the State of its opposition to the unionization of employees and a clear interference with that right. By virtue of freedom of association principles, all workers have the right to establish and join organizations of their own choosing; governments must take measures to encourage and promote the full development and utilization of machinery for voluntary negotiation between unions and employers, and must allow trade unions to operate in full freedom.

313. The complainants submit that this provision constitutes a significant interference with the rights of employees to join and participate in the activities of trade unions. Rather than meeting its obligations at international law to encourage the process of collective bargaining, the Government of Ontario clearly intends to weaken trade unions and to encourage individuals not to exercise their right to organize or to engage in collective bargaining. Rather than encouraging the exercise of the right to collective bargaining the Government has chosen in a discriminatory and one-sided manner to promote the decertification of existing trade unions by conducting a campaign which can only be seen as designed to encourage interference with the exercise of trade union freedoms. . . .

315. The legislation in question is noteworthy in that it advises employees only of their rights to decertify under the Labour Relations Act. It does not mention any of the rights that are intended to protect freedom of association including the right to engage in certification and in lawful activities of trade unions and to be free from discrimination or anti-union reprisal, all matters which are covered by the LRA. . . .

316. In addition, the Government has not chosen to require that similar posters or brochures be distributed in non-union workplaces advising employees of their rights to unionize, thus making it plain that the intention of the legislative provisions is not to inform employees about relevant labour relations laws in an even-handed fashion but is rather to interfere with the right of employees who have chosen to unionize. . . .

B. The Government's Reply

318. In its communication of 3 October 2002, the Government of Ontario submits that the obligation made to employers in unionized workplaces to post a decertification information poster under Bill No. 139 does not violate ILO Conventions Nos. 87, 98, 151 and 154.

319. The Labour Relations Amendment Act, 2000 (Bill No. 139), which received royal assent on 21 December 2000, among other things, amended the Labour Relations Act, 1995 (LRA) to require within one year the publication of a document describing the process for making an application for a declaration that a trade union no longer represents the employees in a bargaining unit. . . .

320. The document sets out neutral factual information about union decertification. It explains who may make an application, when an application may be made and the procedure as set out in the Act and in the rules of the Ontario Labour Relations Board (OLRB). Every unionized employer is required to use reasonable efforts to post a copy of the document in the workplace,

provide a copy of the document to every unionized employee once per calendar year and provide a copy to unionized employees who request it. Compliance with these reasonable efforts requirements by an employer will not constitute an unfair labour practice under the Act.

321. Generally, the statutory reasonable efforts to post and distribute apply to employers with a collective bargaining relationship governed by the LRA. These requirements do not apply to employers who have no unionized employees or employers whose unionized employees are governed under other statutes, for example, firefighters covered by the Fire Protection and Prevention Act, 1997; police and related employees covered by the Police Services Act or the Public Service Act; employees of a college covered by the Colleges Collective Bargaining Act; or teachers covered by the Education Act and the Provincial Schools Negotiations Act. . . .

323. The Government of Ontario submits that these provisions support workplace democracy and the individual right of workers freely to decide whether they wish to be represented by a union and continue with union representation. Certification information is made available to employees by unions during an organization drive but, until now, there had been little information available to employees about decertification. Unions did not provide it and employers were generally prohibited from doing so. The purpose of the decertification poster is simply to inform employees of their rights under the LRA, which they may otherwise not be aware of, by providing neutral, factual information. . . .

Conclusions

C. The Committee's Conclusions

328. The Committee notes that this case concerns section 63.1 of the Labour Relations Act of Ontario (the "LRA") which provides that employers in unionized settings must post and circulate information, prepared by the Ministry of Labour, on rules and procedures for trade union decertification. . . .

329. The Committee recalls that measures should be taken to guarantee freedom of association, which includes the effective recognition of collective bargaining. This necessarily implies the taking of positive steps, conducive to achieving freedom of association and the collective regulation of employment terms and conditions.

330. The Committee considers that the provisions challenged in the present case cannot promote and encourage freedom of association. Quite the contrary, the poster and accompanying notice, being information prepared by the Ministry of Labour and posted in unionized workplaces with the Ministry's formal endorsement may be considered, at best, as a message by the Government that a decertification application would be entertained favourably and, at worst, as an incitement to apply for decertification, thus contravening Convention No. 87 ratified by Canada.

331. The Government's argument that the object of this provision is to provide neutral and factual information might have been more convincing had the amending legislation introduced parallel provisions, with the official endorsement of the Labour Ministry, to inform workers in all non-unionized workplaces . . . of their right to organize and the procedures to do so, and of the various existing legal guarantees to ensure the free exercise of that right, e.g. protection against trade union discrimination (before and during certification), protection against employer interference, etc. . . .

333. The Committee considers that section 63.1 of the LRA does not encourage the promotion of freedom of association, is not conducive to harmonious labour relations and may rather ultimately prove counterproductive by creating a recurring climate of confrontation over certification issues. The Committee considers that it would be actually advantageous for the Government to avoid this type of provision and therefore requests it to repeal section 63.1 of the LRA and to keep it informed of developments in this respect.

Recommendations

The Committee's recommendation

334. In the light of its foregoing conclusions, the Committee invites the Governing Body to approve the following recommendation:

The Committee requests the Government of Ontario to repeal section 63.1 of the Labour Relations Act and to keep it informed of developments in this respect.

Notes

1. What message do the posters required under the Ontario Labour Relations Act send to unionized employees? What was the provincial government trying to achieve by requiring decertification information to be posted in unionized workplaces?

2. The government in its reply stated that it was intent on safeguarding the individual worker's right to choose to be part of a union or not. This emphasis on individual choice rather than collective workplace voice is not unique to Canadian law. Indeed, it can be found in aspects of British, American, Australian, and New Zealander law as well. Focusing on U.S. labor policy, Professor Roy Adams argues that in order to meet international human rights standards, a nation's laws must do more than guarantee an employee's choice to engage in collective bargaining. Rather, "states must ensure that all employees have in place an independent collective voice through which their employment interests may be represented." Roy J. Adams, *Choice or Voice? Rethinking American Labor Policy in Light of the International Human Rights Consensus*, 5 EMP. RTS. & EMP. POL'Y J. 521, 522 (2001). Similarly, Lord Wedderburn recently took to task British labor law for an "obsession with individualism," evidenced by the dominance of individual employment contracts over collective bargaining agreements. Lord Wedderburn, *Common Law, Labour Law, Global Law*, in SOCIAL AND LABOUR RIGHTS IN A GLOBAL CONTEXT 19, 35-37 (Bob Hepple, ed., 2002). For information on the Australian and New Zealander approaches, *see* Sean Cooney, *A Broader Role for the Commonwealth in Eradicating Foreign Sweatshops?*, 28 MELB. U. L. REV. 290, 339 (2004); Ellen J. Dannin, *Consummating Market-Based Labor Law Reform in New Zealand: Context and Reconfiguration*, 14 B.U. INT'L L.J. 267 (1996).

3. The CFA notes that it is incumbent upon the government to "tak[e] . . . positive steps, conducive to achieving freedom of association and the collective regulation of employment terms and conditions." Committee on Freedom of Association, Complaint against the Government of Canada concerning the Province of Ontario presented by the Ontario Federation of Labour (OFL) and the Canada Labour Congress (CLC), Case No. 2182, Report No. 330, at ¶329. Does this imply that

public policy must favor unionization? Article 2 of Convention No. 87 states that "[w]orkers . . . shall have the right to establish and . . . join organisations of their own choosing. . . . " Article 8(2) provides that "[t]he law of the land shall not be such as to impair, nor shall it be so applied as to impair, the guarantees provided for in this Convention." Article 11 constitutes a pledge by ratifying members "to take all necessary and appropriate measures to ensure that workers . . . may exercise freely their right to organise." Can these three provisions be read as imposing an affirmative duty to promote collective bargaining?

4. Bill 144, An Act to amend certain statutes relating to labor relations, received royal assent and came into force in Ontario, Canada, on June 13, 2005. Sections 4 and 5 of the bill repeal subsection 63 and 63.1 of the Ontario Labour Relations Act, which formerly required the preparation and posting in unionized workplaces of documents on the procedures for obtaining union decertification. Bill 144, 1st Session, 38th Legislature, Ontario, 54 Elizabeth II, 2005. Does the Ontario legislature's repeal of a provision found by the CFA to contravene Convention No. 87 constitute evidence that the ILO machinery was effective in this case? Bill 144 was introduced by Ontario's reigning Liberal Party, which came to power in 2003 promising to restore fairness and balance to labor relations, a balance it maintained had been upset by the actions of the pro-labor New Democratic Party and pro-business Progressive Conservative Party during the 1990s. Murray Campbell, *A New Minister, a Dysfunctional Work Force*, THE GLOBE AND MAIL, March 4, 2004, at A11.

D. THE 1998 DECLARATION ON FUNDAMENTAL PRINCIPLES AND RIGHTS AT WORK

As noted in Chapter 1, the ILO in 1998 formalized four categories of rights considered to be fundamental when the ILC adopted the Declaration on Fundamental Principles and Rights at Work. In doing so, the organization helped define a set of workers' rights that are to be considered human rights.

ILO DECLARATION ON FUNDAMENTAL PRINCIPLES AND RIGHTS AT WORK

Adopted June 18, 1998, 37 I.L.M. 1233 (1998)

Whereas the ILO was founded in the conviction that social justice is essential to universal and lasting peace;

Whereas economic growth is essential but not sufficient to ensure equity, social progress and the eradication of poverty, confirming the need for the ILO to promote strong social policies, justice and democratic institutions; . . . .

Whereas, in seeking to maintain the link between social progress and economic growth, the guarantee of fundamental principles and rights at work is of particular significance in that it enables the persons concerned to claim freely and on the basis of equality of opportunity their fair share of the wealth which they have helped to generate, and to achieve fully their human potential;

Whereas the ILO is the constitutionally mandated international organization and the competent body to set and deal with international labour standards, and enjoys universal support and acknowledgement in promoting fundamental rights at work as the expression of its constitutional principles;

Whereas it is urgent, in a situation of growing economic interdependence, to reaffirm the immutable nature of the fundamental principles and rights embodied in the Constitution of the Organization and to promote their universal application;

The International Labour Conference,

1. Recalls:

   (a) that in freely joining the ILO, all Members have endorsed the principles and rights set out in its Constitution and in the Declaration of Philadelphia, and have undertaken to work towards attaining the overall objectives of the Organization to the best of their resources and fully in line with their specific circumstances;

   (b) that these principles and rights have been expressed and developed in the form of specific rights and obligations in Conventions recognized as fundamental both inside and outside the Organization.

2. Declares that all Members, even if they have not ratified the Conventions in question, have an obligation arising from the very fact of membership in the Organization, to respect, to promote and to realize, in good faith and in accordance with the Constitution, the principles concerning the fundamental rights which are the subject of those Conventions, namely:

   (a) freedom of association and the effective recognition of the right to collective bargaining;
   (b) the elimination of all forms of forced or compulsory labour;
   (c) the effective abolition of child labour; and
   (d) the elimination of discrimination in respect of employment and occupation. . . .

4. Decides that, to give full effect to this Declaration, a promotional follow-up, which is meaningful and effective, shall be implemented in accordance with the measures specified in the annex hereto, which shall be considered as an integral part of this Declaration.

5. Stresses that labour standards should not be used for protectionist trade purposes, and that nothing in this Declaration and its follow-up shall be invoked or otherwise used for such purposes; in addition, the comparative advantage of any country should in no way be called into question by this Declaration and its follow-up.

Notes

   1. Before the adoption of the Declaration, the GB identified seven conventions considered to be fundamental; an eighth was adopted in 1999. Hepple, Labour Laws, at 57. Two of the fundamental conventions fall under each of the Declaration's four fundamental rights categories. Convention 87 (Freedom of Association and Protection of the Right to Organize) and Convention 98 (Right to Organize and Collective Bargaining) support the first category, freedom of association and collective bargaining. Convention 29 (Forced Labor) and Convention 105 (Abolition of Forced Labor) are the references for the second, the elimination of forced or compulsory labor. The child labor category is tied to Convention 138 (Minimum Age) and Convention 182 (Worst Forms of Child Labor). Finally, the antidiscrimination

obligation references Convention 100 (Equal Remuneration) and Convention 111 (Discrimination – Employment and Occupation). These eight fundamental conventions are instruments that do not bind member states until they are ratified by them.

2. Situating the Declaration's adoption historically, Professor Brian Langille notes:

> [T]he modern international consensus on the core labour rights took shape in the 1990s as a result of the international community's endorsement of the idea in a number of fora –. . . . from the ILO's point of view most critically at the WTO [World Trade Organization] Singapore Ministerial of 1996. The context of that meeting was very much the large public debate about a [WTO] 'social clause. . . . ' precisely to get some real teeth into the international labour standards regime. . . . [I]n its over-energetic efforts to expel the labour issue from its agenda and deliberations, the WTO membership and the Singapore Declaration. . . . used some very strong language to propel the issue back into the ILO's court by reasserting its views on the importance of the core rights dimension of globalization and the leading role of the ILO in managing that issue.
>
> Brian A. Langille, *Core Labour Rights – The True Story (Reply to Alston)*, 16 EUR. J. INT'L L. 409, 420-21 (2005) (hereinafter Langille, The True Story).

To its credit, argues Langille, the ILO seized the opportunity, realized that there was a need to be met, and created the Declaration to meet it. *Id*. at 421. For more information on the WTO Singapore Ministerial of 1996, including the opposition of developing nations to the adoption of a WTO "social clause," *see* Chapter 1, Section C(1)(c) (The World Trade Organization and Labor Rights).

3. That member states may pledge fealty to the Declaration without ratifying the fundamental conventions raises the question of the relationship between the Declaration's core labor standards and the instruments used as their touchstones. Professor Philip Alston argues that whereas some linkage between the Declaration and the fundamental conventions is obviously contemplated, the content of the conventions cannot simply be read into the Declaration. Nonratifying states would never have supported the adoption of the Declaration if it were seen as a back door way of binding them to the conventions. Philip Alston, *'Core Labour Standards' and the Transformation of the International Labour Rights Regime*, 15 EUR. J. INT'L L. 457, 490-5 (2004) (hereinafter Alston, Core Labour Standards).

4. One possibility, which concerns Alston, is that the Declaration is nothing more than an aspirational policy statement that allows member states to escape the detailed prescriptions of legally binding conventions and yet claim adherence more generally to ILO standards. Alston, Core Labour Standards, at 490-5. Does this theory explain the enthusiasm of the United States for the Declaration even though it has ratified only two of the fundamental conventions? The two fundamental conventions ratified by the U.S. are Convention 105 on forced labor and Convention 182 on the worst forms of child labor. As a point of comparison, by October 2006, 123 states had ratified all eight of the fundamental conventions.

5. Another point of controversy regarding the Declaration regards those standards considered fundamental by some commentators but which were not enumerated as part of the ILO's core. By designating some standards as central, has the ILO thereby minimized the importance of other equally vital employment concerns?

Professor Sarah Cleveland, for example, argues that providing subsistence wages, protection from ultrahazardous workplace conditions, and protection for migrant workers should be considered core labor standards. Sarah H. Cleveland, *Why International Labor Standards?, in* INTERNATIONAL LABOR STANDARDS: GLOBALIZATION, TRADE, AND PUBLIC POLICY 129, 156-9 (Robert J. Flanagan & William B. Gould IV, eds., 2003). In addition to safe workplace conditions, Professor Clyde Summers notes the widely accepted status of the rights to limits on working hours, periods of rest, and protection from abusive treatment. Clyde Summers, *The Battle in Seattle: Free Trade, Labor Rights, and Societal Values*, 22 U. PA. J. INT'L ECON. L. 61, 68 (2001).

6. Clearly, the Declaration, which is not a convention or a recommendation, is an interesting and important new ILO initiative. Whether it represents a trend away from legally binding conventions in favor of "softer" soft law tools such as declarations and voluntary codes of conduct is as yet unclear. Professor Virginia Leary nonetheless finds notable both the ILO's characterization of The Declaration as a "solemn commitment" by member states, and the instrument's follow-up procedure, which requires nonratifying states to submit reports on their progress toward achieving core labor standards. The latter has resulted in the publication of reports such as the ILO's annual Global Report, Your Voice at Work, containing valuable data about the practices of states that choose not to ratify some of the fundamental conventions. Leary, Form Follows Function, at 186.

7. Professor Langille sees the Declaration as a step toward solving the crisis that threatened to reduce the ILO to irrelevance. The ILO's traditional approach of promulgating detailed standards, embodied in conventions that either had low ratification rates or were ratified and then observed by many countries in the breach, is clearly untenable if the agency hopes to affect change on the ground. Langille, The True Story, at 425-6. Instead, by stating in general terms the fundamental principles that all nations must observe, and then working to help member states achieve them, the ILO can positively promote conditions of social justice that are a precondition for a nation's economic success. *Id.* at 434. Moreover, by promoting respect for core rights, conditions are created for the advancement of other noncore concerns such as minimum wages, maximum hours, and health and safety. *Id.* at 435.

8. Sir Bob Hepple describes the chief effect of the Declaration's adoption as boosting the number of ratifications of the eight fundamental conventions. HEPPLE, LABOUR LAWS, at 60. As noted above, by October, 2006, for example, 123 countries had ratified all eight fundamental conventions. Nonetheless, one central theme of this casebook is that law on the books cannot be considered a substitute for an examination of law in practice. There is no guarantee that countries that ratify fundamental conventions actually implement them.

3   The United States

At the end of the twentieth century, the body of the law of employment in the United States has evolved to a scarcely rational patchwork. It is comprehensible as a whole, if at all, only when viewed through the lens of its history.

Patrick Hardin in I International Labor and Employment Laws, 23-2 (William L. Keller ed. BNA Books 1997).

A. INTRODUCTION

As Professor Hardin suggests in the quote above, the labor and employment law of the United States is not a cohesive set of laws. Instead, it has developed over time with different underlying principles prompting the development of the law at different times. Broadly, the periods of U.S. law may be divided into the organized labor/collective bargaining period from the 1930s to the early 1960s, and the individual employment rights period from the early 1960s to the present. The one prominent exception to these divisions is the Fair Labor Standards Act, an individual employment rights law (imposing a minimum wage and overtime pay and restricting child labor) enacted in 1938. Although the FLSA was not based on the organized labor/collective bargaining model, it was viewed as supporting the collective bargaining model, and the legislation was supported by organized labor.

In the 1930s, the paradigm of organized labor and collective bargaining and collective action prompted Congress to pass the Wagner Act (or National Labor Relations Act), which protected the rights of employees to join unions and engage in collective bargaining with their employers. Organized labor and collective bargaining reached its pinnacle in the 1950s and thereafter began a gradual decline that accelerated in the 1980s.

The 1960s marked a shift from laws based on collective action to development of individual employment rights law at both the federal and state levels. One type of individual employment rights law is antidiscrimination law. The 1960s through the early 1990s was a period in which antidiscrimination laws proliferated, beginning with Title VII of the Civil Rights Act of 1964 and culminating with the enactment of the Americans with Disabilities Act of 1990 and the Civil Rights Act of 1991. Other individual employment laws included labor standards legislation, such as the Family and Medical Leave Act of 1993. In addition to federal individual employment rights legislation, state legislatures passed laws, and state courts developed contract and tort theories to address employment disputes. Beginning around 2000, a theme of individual privacy in the workplace became a prominent concern in U.S. employment law. For example, many states passed laws regulating use of genetic information in employment and insurance decisions.

The historical division between the period of organized labor/collective bargaining and the period of individual employment rights laws has led to a dichotomy in terminology that does not exist in much of the rest of the world. When U.S. lawyers use the term "labor law," they usually are referring to organized labor, unions, and collective bargaining. When they use the term "employment law," they usually mean individual employment rights laws. *See* Eugene Scalia, *Ending Our Anti-Union Federal Employment Policy*, 24 HARV. J.L. PUB. POLC'Y 489, 489 (2001) (Practitioners speak of "labor" and "employment" law as two distinct fields, with "labor" law encompassing labor-management relations – unionization, strikes, collective bargaining, and the law under the National Labor Relations Act ("NLRA") – and "employment" law encompassing everything else: discrimination, wage and hour regulation, occupational health and safety, wrongful termination, etc.). U.S. law schools even further divide the major areas of labor and employment law into (1) labor law, (2) employment discrimination, and (3) employment law. Although employment antidiscrimination law is a subset of individual employment rights law, it is a large subset with distinctive features.

Another feature of U.S. labor and employment law that is different from the law of many other nations is the interrelationship of health insurance and retirement plans and employment law. Lacking a national health insurance system and having very little social safety net other than that provided by employers as a job benefit, the United States' employment law includes regulations on health insurance and pension and retirement plans provided by employers.

As a whole, U.S. labor and employment law does not seem to have any cohesive structure or consistent underlying principles. Instead, as Professor Hardin suggests in the opening quote, the law has developed over time and in reaction to specific problems that garner sufficient attention to prompt action at particular times.

B. INDIVIDUAL EMPLOYMENT LAW

1. Contracts and Torts

It is worth noting that the categories set forth in this chapter overlap. Section C regarding unions, organized labor and the National Labor Relations Act is the only part dealing with rights of employees exercised through collective action; everything else is individual employment rights law. This section, and sections D (wages, hours and benefits), E (employment discrimination), and F (privacy) all deal with types of individual employment rights law. Thus, this chapter demonstrates the emphasis in U.S. labor law on individual employment rights law as the principal method of regulating the workplace.

BAMMERT V. DON'S SUPER VALU, INC.

646 N.W.2d 365 (Wis. S.Ct. 2002)

DIANE S. SYKES, J.

This is an action for wrongful discharge, and it presents a single question of first-impression: can the public policy exception to the employment-at-will doctrine be invoked when an at-will employee is fired in retaliation for the actions of his or her non-employee spouse? We answer this question no.

Karen Bammert worked at Don's Super Valu, Inc. in Menomonie. Her husband is a Menomonie police officer. Don's is owned by Don Williams, whose wife, Nona, was arrested for drunk driving. Bammert's husband assisted in the arrest by administering a breathalyzer test. Shortly thereafter, Bammert was fired, allegedly in retaliation for her husband's participation in the arrest of her boss's wife. She sued for wrongful discharge, invoking the public policy exception to the employment-at-will doctrine. The circuit court dismissed for failure to state a claim, and the court of appeals affirmed. We accepted review.

The public policy exception to the employment-at-will doctrine is a narrow exception that allows at-will employees to sue for wrongful discharge if they are fired for fulfilling, or refusing to violate, a fundamental, well-defined public policy or an affirmative legal obligation established by existing law. It has never been extended to terminations in retaliation for conduct outside the employment relationship; neither has it been applied to terminations in retaliation for the conduct of someone other than the terminated employee. To allow it here would therefore expand the exception beyond its present boundaries in two significant and unprecedented ways, with no logical limiting principles.

Accordingly, we decline to recognize a cause of action for wrongful discharge under the public policy exception to the employment-at-will doctrine for terminations in retaliation for the conduct of a non-employee spouse. The allegations in this case, if true, make Karen Bammert's termination reprehensible, but not actionable.

I

. . . Karen Bammert was employed at Don's Super Valu, Inc. in Menomonie for approximately 26 years. Her husband is a Menomonie police sergeant. Don's is owned by Don Williams, whose wife, Nona, was arrested for drunk driving on June 7, 1997. Bammert's husband participated in the drunk driving field investigation by administering a portable breathalyzer test to Nona Williams, which she failed.

On August 28, 1997, Bammert was fired by Don's in retaliation for her husband's participation in Nona Williams' drunk driving arrest. At the time of her termination, she was an assistant manager at the supermarket.

Bammert sued for wrongful discharge. Don's moved to dismiss, and the Dunn County Circuit Court, the Honorable Eric J. Wahl, dismissed the complaint for failure to state a claim, concluding that the employment-at-will doctrine's public policy exception, announced by this court in *Brockmeyer v. Dun & Bradstreet*, . . . , did not apply. The court of appeals affirmed. We accepted review and now affirm.

II

. . . Bammert was an at-will employee. In general, at-will employees are terminable at will, for any reason, without cause and with no judicial remedy. Whether Bammert has an actionable claim for wrongful discharge turns on the question of whether the public policy exception to the employment-at-will doctrine can be extended to a retaliatory discharge based upon the conduct of a non-employee spouse.

The starting point for any wrongful discharge case is *Brockmeyer*. There, we adopted a public policy exception to the long-standing employment-at-will doctrine which allows an at-will employee to sue for wrongful discharge "when the discharge is contrary to a fundamental and well-defined public policy as evidenced by existing law." *Brockmeyer*, 113 Wis.2d at 573, 335 N.W. 2d 834. *Brockmeyer* noted that ordinarily, an employer may discharge an at-will employee "'for good cause, for no cause, or even for cause morally wrong, without being thereby guilty of legal wrong.'"[3] *Id.* at 567, 335 N.W. 2d 834 (footnote omitted).

The court in *Brockmeyer* specifically declined to engraft a broad implied duty of good faith onto the at-will employment relationship. . . . "Imposing a good faith duty to terminate would unduly restrict an employer's discretion in managing the work force" and "'subject each discharge to judicial incursions into the amorphous concept of bad faith.'" *Id.* Instead, the court concluded that "in the interests of employees, employers and the public, a narrow public policy exception" was justified, applicable only where the discharge "clearly contravenes the public welfare and gravely violates paramount requirements of public interest."[4] *Id.* at 572-73, 335 N.W. 2d 834.

In adopting the exception, the court recognized that "public policy" is too broad a concept to be sufficient as a legal standard for evaluating discharge claims, and therefore articulated several guidelines:

> The public policy must be evidenced by a constitutional or statutory provision. An employee cannot be fired for refusing to violate the constitution or a statute. Employers will be held liable for those terminations that effectuate an unlawful end.
>
> We intend to recognize an existing limited public policy exception. An employer may not require an employee to violate a constitutional or statutory provision with impunity. If an employee refuses to act in an unlawful manner, the employer would be violating public policy by terminating the employee for such behavior. To say that the employer could be prosecuted for criminal involvement as a result of the activities would be little solace for the discharged employee.
>
> Courts should proceed cautiously when making public policy determinations. No employer should be subject to suit merely because a discharged employee's conduct was praiseworthy or because the public may have derived some benefit from it.

Id. at 573-74, 335 N.W. 2d at 834.

Accordingly, to state a claim for wrongful discharge under *Brockmeyer*, a plaintiff must identify a constitutional, statutory, or administrative provision that clearly articulates a fundamental and well-defined public policy. . . . Not every statutory, constitutional, or administrative provision invariably sets forth a clear public policy mandate. . . . The determination of whether a public policy is sufficiently fundamental and well-defined is made by reference to the content of the provision. . . . If a plaintiff identifies a public policy sufficient to trigger the exception, and further demonstrates that the termination violated that public policy, the burden shifts to the employer to show just cause for the termination. . . .

Our cases since *Brockmeyer* have cautioned against interpreting the public policy exception too broadly. The employment-at-will doctrine is a "stable fixture" of our common law, and has been since 1871. . . . It is central to the free market economy and "serves the interests of

---

[3] There are various statutory exceptions to the employment-at-will doctrine. *See* For instance, Title VII of the Civil Rights Act of 1964 and the Wisconsin Fair Employment Act each prohibit employers from discharging an employee on the basis of race, color, religion, sex, or national origin. Other statutes make it unlawful for employers to terminate workers because of participation in union activities, jury service, military service, or testifying at an occupational, safety, and health proceeding.

[4] *Brockmeyer* also held that the cause of action for wrongful discharge pursuant to the public policy exception sounds in contract, not tort: "The contract action is essentially predicated on the breach of an implied provision that an employer will not discharge an employee for refusing to perform an act that violates a clear mandate of public policy." *Brockmeyer v. Dun & Bradstreet*, 113 Wis.2d 561, 575-76, 335 N.W. 2d 834 (1983).

employees as well as employers" by maximizing the freedom of both. . . . The "antidote" to the potential for unfairness in employment-at-will "is an employment contract.". . . .

The prevailing general rule is that an at-will employee has no legal remedy for "an employer's unjustified decision to terminate the employment relationship." . . . The employment-at-will doctrine thus inhibits judicial "second-guessing" of discharge decisions – even those that are unfair, unfortunate, or harsh. . . .

Substantive expansions of the public policy exception since *Brockmeyer* have been few and limited in nature . . . (public policy exception applies where employee is fired for fulfilling an affirmative legal or public policy duty even though there was no command from the employer to violate public policy); . . . (public policy can be embodied in an administrative rule, even though *Brockmeyer* had referred only to the constitution and statutes); . . . (a discharge can violate public policy if it violates the spirit, if not the letter, of a statute).

More often than not, the cases have emphasized the limited scope of the exception. *See, e.g., [case]* (warning that a broad interpretation of the public policy exception would "interject government agencies and the courts into traditional employment relations in a manner inconsistent with employment-at-will"); [case] (suggesting that an expansion of the exception would open a "Pandora's Box for employment litigation"); . . . [case] (stressing the importance of summary judgment as a means of screening out cases that seek to expand the exception beyond its traditionally narrow scope).

Bammert's claim must be evaluated against this backdrop. She has identified two public policies as being implicated here: Wis. Stat. §346.63, which prohibits the operation of a motor vehicle while under the influence of an intoxicant; and Wis. Stat. §765.001(2), which describes the intent of the Family Code as including the promotion of the institution of marriage, for the preservation of the family, society, the state, morality, and indeed, all civilization.

We would be hard-pressed to say that these are not fundamental, well-established public policies. Clearly, both statutes reflect compelling public interests – one requiring the diligent pursuit and punishment of drunk drivers and the other requiring the vigorous promotion of the institution of marriage. But on the assumed facts of this case, that conclusion doesn't get us very far.

Bammert was not fired for *her* participation in the enforcement of the laws against drunk driving; she was fired for *her husband's* participation in the enforcement of those laws. Discharges for conduct outside of the employment relationship by someone other than the discharged employee are not actionable under present law. The public policy generally favoring the stability of marriage, while unquestionably strong, provides an insufficient basis upon which to enlarge what was meant to be, and has always been, an extremely narrow exception to employment-at-will.

Bammert advocates an expansion of the public policy exception far beyond that contemplated by our case law, and she cites no authority for it. Up to now, where the exception has been applied, the public policy at issue has always been vindicated by the employee himself or herself, within the context of the employment relationship. . . .

In contrast, Bammert's claim identifies a public policy completely unrelated to her employment, being enforced by someone else, who is employed elsewhere. That the "someone else" is her husband makes her discharge obviously retaliatory, and reminds us of the sometimes harsh reality of employment-at-will, but it does not provide acceptable grounds for expansion of the public policy exception beyond its present boundaries.

The public policy exception is rooted in the principle that "[a]n employer may not require *an employee* to violate a constitutional or statutory provision with impunity. If an employee refuses to act in an unlawful manner, the employer would be violating public policy by terminating the employee for such behavior." *Brockmeyer*, 113 Wis.2d at 573, 335 N.W. 2d 834 (emphasis added).

In *Hausman*, the most recent case to entertain any expansion of the public policy exception, we held that "[w]here the law imposes an affirmative obligation upon an employee . . . and the employee fulfills that obligation," termination for that reason violates public policy. *Hausman*, 214 Wis.2d at 669, 571 N.W. 2d 393. Thus, as it currently stands, the public policy exception applies to discharges in retaliation for the fulfillment of "an affirmative obligation" which the law places "upon an employee." Extending it to discharges for fulfillment of an affirmative obligation which the law places on *a relative* of an employee would go too far, and have no logical stopping point.

. . .

Public policy comes in many variations, is implicated in many contexts, and is carried out by many people, both publicly and privately. Once expanded in the manner argued here, the public policy exception would no longer be subject to any discernable limiting principles. It would arguably apply to retaliatory discharges based upon the conduct of *any* non-employee relative, for the fulfillment of or refusal to violate public policy in a wide variety of ways and in a manner completely unconnected to the employment relationship.

The public policy exception cannot be stretched that far and still be recognizable under *Brockmeyer's* limited formulation. Accordingly, we decline to recognize a cause of action for wrongful discharge under the public policy exception to the at-will employment doctrine for terminations in retaliation for the conduct of a non-employee spouse.

Of course, a natural sense of outrage over the facts alleged in this case brings on a desire to see the law provide a remedy, but it does not. Sergeant Bammert was doing his duty, for the benefit of the public, but *Brockmeyer* made it clear that the public policy exception does not apply where the "conduct [precipitating the discharge] was praiseworthy or because the public may have derived some benefit from it." *Brockmeyer*, 113 Wis.2d at 573-74, 335 N.W. 2d 834. To expand the public policy exception to fit this case would invite future applications to retaliatory discharges based upon the conduct of any close relative, conduct which is wholly unconnected to the employment relationship. This clearly would be inconsistent with *Brockmeyer's* intention that the public policy exception remain narrow in scope. The case was properly dismissed for failure to state a claim, and we affirm.

The decision of the court of appeals is affirmed.

WILLIAM A. BABLITCH, J. (dissenting).

Karen Bammert's (Bammert) 26 years of employment at Don's Super Valu ended by her being fired. Bammert was not fired for showing up late to work or treating customers poorly. In fact, she was not fired for any job-related reason at all.

She was fired for her husband's actions.

Her husband made no mistake either. He was a police officer. He fulfilled his obligation to society by assisting in the drunk driving arrest of Nona Williams. Nona is the spouse of Bammert's employer.

Retaliation for Bammert's husband's actions as a police officer was the reason Bammert was fired. In my view, this is unacceptable. There is a strong public policy in vigorous enforcement of the law. Society is not served by police officers being influenced in how they do their job because of the potential consequences of a retaliatory firing. Furthermore, extending the employment at-will doctrine to protect police officers is consistent with past precedent. Unfortunately, the majority opinion does not agree. The result is that an individual will be able to influence a police officer in the form of a retaliatory firing. For these reasons, I respectfully dissent.

Bammert was an at-will employee of Don's Super Valu. The general rule regarding employment relationships in Wisconsin is the at-will doctrine. The doctrine generally allows an employer to "discharge an employee 'for good cause, for no cause, or even for a cause morally wrong, without being thereby guilty of legal wrong.'" *Brockmeyer v. Dun & Bradstreet*, 113 Wis.2d 561, 567, 335 N.W. 2d 834 (1983) (footnote omitted). However, Wisconsin law does allow narrow exceptions to the at-will employment doctrine for public policy reasons. The public policy exception allows the firing of employees to recover if the firing violates a well-established and important public policy. . . . The exception that I propose is a narrow one, and certainly is a well-established, important public policy – retaliatory firing in response to a police officer's lawful actions in his or her capacity as a police officer is actionable.

The exception I propose is narrow in that it covers only a police officer acting lawfully in his or her capacity as an officer. This exception will not open the floodgates to litigation, as there are very few instances when a firing could fit into this exception. And when it does, it should.

The public policy in the case at hand is well-established and of utmost importance. Police officers have to be able to do their jobs without being influenced by the possibility of a retaliatory firing. A police officer must be able to arrest a drunk driver without his or her spouse being fired because of the arrest. Public policy dictates the vigorous enforcement of the law no matter who is on the receiving end of the enforcement. Without an exception to the at-will doctrine for retaliatory firings against police officers acting lawfully in their capacity, this public policy will be undermined.

Although there is little doubt that influencing, intimidating, or bribing a police officer is against public policy, *Brockmeyer* dictates that public policy must be shown by a constitutional or statutory provision. *Id.* at 573, 335 N.W. 2d 834. Wisconsin Stat. §946.10(1) (1997–98) states:

> 946.10 Bribery of public officers and employes. Whoever does either of the following is guilty of a Class D felony:
>
> (1) Whoever, with intent to influence the conduct of any public officer or public employe in relation to any matter which by law is pending or might come before the officer or employe in the officer's or employe's capacity as such officer or employe or with intent to induce the officer or employe to do or omit to do any act in violation of the officer's or employe's lawful duty transfers or promises to the officer or employe or on the officer's or employe's behalf any property or any personal advantage which the officer or employe is not authorized to receive; . . . .

As Wis. Stat. §946.10 (1997–98) clearly points out, as a society we do not allow a person to bribe, intimidate, or otherwise illegally influence police officers about any pending matter or any matter that "might come before the officer". In turn, there is no reason to allow an employer to bribe, intimidate or otherwise influence a police officer in this regard. There is no reason to give an employer a get-out-of-jail free card that is not afforded to the rest of society, simply because the employer has some retaliatory influence over a police officer. There should not be one standard of the law for employers and one standard for everyone else.

There is no legitimate reason to protect the conduct of this employer. In a normal circumstance, this employer could not reach the person that the employer wishes to retaliate against. In this circumstance, the employee is married to one of the officers participating in the arrest, which allows the employer to therefore reach this officer. Normally, the officer would be protected from the disgruntled arrestee, but in this case, the arrestee can reach the officer. As stated previously, we do not allow retaliation against a police officer for performing his or her duty, but in this circumstance the employer has a way around the protection of the officer. In my opinion, this loophole that allows an employer to retaliate against a police officer must be put in line with the rest of our laws, and the loophole that provides a retaliatory tool for the employer must be closed, thereby protecting police officers.

Furthermore, society owes its police officers a duty not to put them in the no-win position that Bammert's husband was placed in. On the one hand, he was sworn to uphold the laws of Wisconsin. On the other hand, if he keeps his oath and upholds the laws of our state, he is put in the position that the person that he assists in arresting could retaliate against him. The majority gives Bammert's husband a choice: either do your job and assist in the arrest of the drunk driver or protect your family by looking the other way. I want to eliminate this no-win situation by giving police officers the tools to do their job without the fear of retaliation. We owe such officers, like Bammert's husband, that much.

Moreover, the exception that I propose is consistent with past precedent. This court has recognized that compliance with an affirmative legal duty requiring action comports with a well-defined public policy, and the rationale of the public policy exception to the employment at-will doctrine. *See Hausman v. St. Croix Care Ctr.*, 214 Wis.2d 655, 571 N.W. 2d 393 (1997). In *Hausman*, we gave employees that fulfilled their legal duty protection from retaliatory firing. The idea behind the exception is simply that we want people to fulfill their legal duties. In *Hausman*, it took the form of reporting abuse in a nursing home. We do not want people to be afraid to report nursing home abuse because they are afraid to be fired; therefore, we protect them. In the present case, we do not want a police officer to not enforce the law because the officer is afraid of a retaliatory firing. We should protect the officer, not subject him to retaliatory firing.

I recognize the reluctance to [contract] the at-will doctrine, and I too appreciate the importance of keeping with the policy of the well-defined narrow policy exception rule. We have a well-defined, extremely important policy, and we should carve out a very narrow exception that is consistent with past precedent. Therefore, I respectfully dissent.

Notes

1. The *Bammert* case articulates the presumption of employment at will that exists in 49 of 50 states.[1] Employment at will, although often called a doctrine, is essentially

[1] Montana is the only state that has generally abrogated employment at will through legislation. That state enacted the Montana Wrongful Discharge from Employment Act of 1987, MONT. CODE ANN. §§39-2-901 to 39-2-914. Although the law provides that terminations can only be for "good cause," there is a significant

an evidentiary presumption that, absent evidence to the contrary, an employment relationship or contract does not include a good or just cause employment security provision, and the employment relationship is not for any specified duration. Thus, employment at will is a default rule: If employers and employees do not agree otherwise, employers can terminate employees at any time and for any reason.

Employment at will is not a matter of federal law. Each of the forty-nine states adhering to this presumption/default rule has done it by case law, statute, or both. Most states have stated their adherence to employment at will in only case law. There is much debate in legal scholarship about the history and origins of employment at will. *See generally* Andrew P. Morriss, *Exploding Myths: An Empirical and Economic Rassessment of the Rise of Employment At-Will*, 59 Mo. L. Rev. 679 (1994); Robert C. Bird, *Rethinking Wrongful Discharge: A Continuum Approach*, 73 U. Cinn. L. Rev. 517 (2004). In addition to the legal scholarship in the United States regarding the history of employment at will, there is much writing proposing the general abrogation of the doctrine. There was pervasive speculation in the 1970s and 1980s that employment at will would be changed in many states, if not nationally. *See* Bird, *supra*, at 522. During that period, state courts throughout the United States fashioned contract and tort recoveries for terminations, including contracts based on handbooks and manuals, promissory estoppel, breach of the covenant of good faith and fair dealing, and wrongful discharge in violation of public policy. In the last fifteen years or so, however, the incursions on employment at will have abated, and the principle is now stronger in many states that it has been since the 1960s. The *Bammert* opinion, *supra*, is an example of a supreme court decision rejecting expansion of the theory of wrongful discharge in violation of public policy and extolling the virtues of the employment-at-will doctrine.

2. The court in *Bammert* states several rationales for adhering to employment at will. First, it is old and firmly established. Second, "[i]t is central to the free market economy" and "serves the interests of employees as well as employers by maximizing the freedom of both." Third, if employees do not like the possibly harsh consequences of employment at will, they can contract out of it with their employer. Each of these reasons should be scrutinized.

First, most courts in the United States are quite deferential to the employment-at-will doctrine and are reluctant to fashion remedies for terminations when there is not an express employment contract that varies employment at will. Because employment at will was established by court decision in most jurisdictions and is not enacted as legislation, this reluctance may seem somewhat unusual.

Second, the idea that employment at will is crucial to a free market economy is a strong belief among many in the United States. This may seem unusual in light of the fact that most other nations with developed labor laws, and most with free

---

exception; the law applies only to employees who have completed an employer's probationary period (six months if the employer does not establish a different specific period). The law was supported by businesses and their insurers, and it includes limitations on remedies available in lawsuits by employees. All things considered, the law has not clearly been beneficial to employees. *See generally* Marc Jarsulic, *Protecting Workers from Wrongful Discharge: Montana's Experience With Tort and Statutory Regimes*, 3 Employee Rts. & Emp. Pol'y J. 105 (1999).

market economies, do not recognize employment at will. Indeed, among nations with industrialized market economies, the United States is a maverick in subscribing to employment at will. As you study the labor law of other nations in this text, you will find that they do not adhere to employment at will. The International Labour Organization's Termination of Employment Convention (C158, 1982) provides that "[t]he employment of a worker shall not be terminated unless there is a valid reason for such termination connected with the capacity or conduct of the worker or based on the operational requirements of the undertaking, establishment or service." Still, although most nations' labor laws do not permit termination without a job-related reason, only thirty-four nations have ratified that ILO convention. For discussion of the ILO, its members, and the conventions and other documents, see Chapter 2, *supra*.

Third, the idea that if employees wanted an employment relationship other than at will, they would negotiate for a contract so providing seems to misapprehend the balance of bargaining power between most employers and most applicants for a job. Given that most employment relationships in the United States are at will, what is the likely reaction of an employer considering an applicant for a job who requests a definite duration or good-cause protection in the employment contract? Associated with this idea is the belief that employment at will serves the interests of employees as well as those of employers because it "maximize[es] the freedom of both." That is, employers can terminate employees at any time without giving a reason, and employees can quit at any time without giving a reason. Do employees want such freedom? Would employers, who are favored by the default rule, be willing to negotiate with applicants about modifications of employment at will? Professor Christopher Wonnell posits that there is another reason (in addition to the employment at will rule favoring them) that employers are unlikely to negotiate with applicants for definite terms or good cause protection: U.S. law generally does not provide an effective remedy when employees who have other than at-will contracts breach them. With the prospect of no redress if employees breach and the danger of employees recovering if the employer breaches, employers see no reason to negotiate about altering employment at will. *See* Christopher T. Wonnell, *The Contractual Disempowerment of Employees*, 46 STAN. L. REV. 87 (1993).

The *Bammert* court also suggests a fourth rationale why courts adhere closely to employment at will: it obviates courts' second-guessing of employers' termination decisions. Most employment lawsuits in the United States go to state or federal trial courts with general subject matter jurisdiction; the United States does not have specialized labor courts. This fact may help explain why the courts are uncomfortable about their expertise in reevaluating employers' termination decisions. *See* Morriss, *supra*.

One of the best-known defenses of employment at will in the academic literature is by Richard A. Epstein, *In Defense of the Contract At Will*, 51 U. CHI. L. REV. 947 (1984). In that article, Professor Epstein argues that employment at will is a fair rule because it promotes freedom of contract, which promotes both individual autonomy and efficient operation of labor markets. He further argues that employment at will is the efficient default rule because it is the dominant and preferred arrangement. Professor Epstein enumerates the following reasons why employment at will generally benefits both employers and employees:

> Monitoring behavior – both sides will monitor the benefits and detriments in the relationship because they have the freedom to end it with no need for litigation and little cost.
>
> Reputational Losses – although employees do not have legal protections against terminations for bad reasons, they have the informal protection in the form of negative reputations that employers develop.
>
> Risk Diversification and Imperfect Information – neither side is locked into an employment contract if better options or opportunities arise.
>
> Administrative Costs – It is cheap to administer.
>
> Bilateral Monopoly and Inequality of Bargaining Power – There is not much inequality of bargaining power between employers and employees.

How do you react to the above arguments of Professor Epstein in defense of employment at will?

3. Do you think that most applicants for jobs and employees understand that they can be dismissed from their jobs for any reason? The answer seems to be "no." *See, e.g.,* Cynthia L. Estlund, *How Wrong Are Employees About Their Rights, and Why Does It Matter?*, 77 N.Y.U.L. Rev. 6 (2002).

4. Suppose you are interviewing with a law firm for a position as an associate. You know that you are one of many law students that the firm is interviewing. The attorneys conducting the interview have not mentioned a specified duration for the employment relationship, so it occurs to you that you would be an employee at will. Would you like to have a contract with a specified duration, perhaps three years? Would you bring up the topic in the interview?

    There are types of jobs in the United States in which employment at will is not the default rule. Consider, for example, civil service jobs and teaching positions with tenure.

5. A general and popular statement of employment at will is that an employer may terminate an employee "for a good reason, a bad reason, or no reason at all." Because it is a dubious proposition that anyone ever does anything for no reason at all, this statement is intended to demonstrate the fact that under employment at will, employers are not required to give or defend reasons for terminations. As the *Bammert* court states, employment at will is not unfettered even in the United States. There are various "bad" reasons that have been carved out of employment at will and declared illegal. The largest group of such reasons is discrimination based on certain characteristics, such as race, sex, religion, national origin, age, and disability. U.S. employment antidiscrimination law is a large body of law that will be examined in section E, *infra*.

6. Many U.S. books discuss the contract and tort "erosions" of employment at will. Courts in the United States often speak of an employment-at-will relationship as being something other than an employment contract. Of course, employment at will in fact is an employment contract, but the contract lacks both a good-cause requirement for termination and a definite duration of employment. At-will contracts also generally do not provide for procedures, such as a right to a hearing, before termination. On the contract side, courts in all states recognize that, because

employment at will is a default rule, employers and employees may vary the terms of the employment contract. In most cases in which an employee sues an employer for termination in breach of an employment contract, the pivotal question is what evidence exists that the parties agreed to terms that vary at-will employment. Because many states tenaciously adhere to employment at will, courts in those states tend to be reluctant to find sufficient evidence of an agreement that varies employment at will.

Torts theories that may apply to a termination include the relatively new tort of wrongful discharge in violation of public policy and intentional infliction of emotional distress. Wrongful discharge, which has been recognized by many states for only about twenty to thirty years, is a tort that applies to employment alone. Intentional infliction of emotional distress, in contrast, is a tort of general application (not restricted to employment scenarios). Wrongful discharge is discussed in the *Bammert* case, *supra*. Although the court in *Bammert* characterized wrongful discharge in violation of public policy as a breach of contract claim, most states consider it to be a tort claim. As the case explains, the claim is a very narrow exception to employment at will, and not all bad or abusive discharges satisfy the requirements of the tort; indeed, most do not. There are generally four types of cases that might come within the tort: (1) refusal to participate in illegal activity; (2) performance of a public obligation; (3) exercise of a statutory right; and (4) reporting illegal activity ("whistleblowing"). Mark A. Rothstein, Charles B. Craver, Elinor P. Schroeder & Elaine W. Shoben, Employment Law §§9.9–9.13 (3d ed. Thomson-West 2005). Some states recognize one or more of the foregoing types of cases under wrongful discharge in violation of public policy, but not all. Few employee discharges satisfy the requirements for wrongful discharge in violation of public policy. Courts often say that the tort is recognized not to redress the wrong and harm done to the employee by the employer, but to protect the public from the harm that would result if the employer were permitted to subvert the public policy. Moreover, state courts are sometimes restrictive in their view of where public policy may be found. As the court discusses in *Bammert*, courts are most likely to accept public policy announced in a state statute or state constitution. Courts may reject invitations to announce public policy themselves, or to find a public policy in sources such as city ordinances or federal laws.

Intentional infliction of emotional distress ("IIED"), often referred to as the tort of outrage, has been recognized by various states since the 1960s. IIED does not apply to any specific factual scenario. To prevail, a plaintiff must establish: (1) a voluntary act by the defendant; (2) outrageous conduct (so egregious that it should not be tolerated by a civilized society); (3) intent or recklessness on the part of the defendant; (4) severe and debilitating emotional distress of the plaintiff; and (5) causation (emotional distress caused by the outrageous conduct). A very small percentage of plaintiffs suing under this tort theory in the employment context prevail. *See generally* Mark P. Gergen, *A Grudging Defense of the Role of the Collateral Torts in Wrongful Termination Litigation*, 74 Tex. L. Rev. 1693 (1996). Courts are concerned that permitting recovery for IIED when it is based on a termination will undermine the employment-at-will doctrine. *See, e.g., Nicholas v. Allstate Ins. Co.*, 765 So. 2d 1017 (La. 1992). Closely tied to this idea is the courts' stated belief that part of employers' prerogatives is supervising and disciplining employees, and both of those may fairly and reasonably involve the imposition of some degree of emotional distress.

Professor Regina Austin discusses the wide latitude accorded employers in the exercise of their prerogative in her article, *Employer Abuse, Worker Resistance, and the Tort of Intentional Infliction of Emotional Distress*, 41 STAN. L. REV. 1, 8-10 (1988):

> The courts accord employers wide latitude in directing their employees' activities in ways that cause them emotional distress. The courts leave little doubt as to who is in charge of the workplace. The employer is free to ignore any interest workers may have in performing particular tasks, using particular skills, or doing a job at a particular level of proficiency or ease. Thus, work assignments are "managerial decisions . . . that do not qualify as intentional infliction of severe mental distress." Similarly, while imposition of an inordinate work load may "create an environment which is oppressive to function within . . . it is not the type of action to arouse resentment, by the average member of the community. . . . "
>
> The courts recognize that emotional disturbance is an inherent aspect of being reprimanded, demoted, or discharged. But they allow the victim no cause of action if the emotional harm is an unintended or incidental result of an exercise of legitimate workplace authority, civilly undertaken. The courts are particularly wary of attempts to use Section 46 to evade the rules sanctioning the summary discharge of at-will employees. Assertions to the effect that "if the firing of . . . plaintiff was done in an outrageous manner, then every firing that occurs would be considered outrageous," are quite common.
>
> Liability does not always follow; even when the supervisor is rude or insensitive in carrying out a personnel action. For example, a salesman complained that his supervisor cursed him, took over sales presentations, and otherwise embarrassed him in the presence of customers and fellow workers. The court condoned the behavior; the supervisor's "intentions, much as any supervisor's in a similar situation, were pretty clearly to motivate a recalcitrant employee." In another case, the head of an employer's legal department cursed, hollered at, and fired a secretary for taking the initiative in contacting a person whose qualifications suggested that she might fulfill a personnel need and passing the pertinent information on to another lawyer in the office. Although the supervisor's conduct was "not above reproach," the court would not characterize it as "so extreme and outrageous as to be tortious."

Some plaintiffs have prevailed on IIED claims in the context of terminations when the terminations have been carried out in a remarkably humiliating fashion. Consider, for example, *Agis v. Howard Johnson Co.*, 355 N.E. 2d 315 (Mass. 1976), in which the manager of a restaurant, attempting to get employees to reveal who was stealing, announced that, until he discovered the identity of the thief, he would fire employees in alphabetical order, and then he fired an employee whose name began with "A." The terminated employee's claim survived a motion to dismiss. The tension between the idea that employers can terminate employees for "bad" reasons and cases in which employees recover for terminations under the theory of IIED might be summarized by saying that employees do not have a right not to be terminated, but courts sometimes recognize a right to be terminated with a modicum of respect, permitting the employee to maintain a sense of dignity.

Not all IIED cases based on workplace occurrences involve terminations. The type of workplace IIED case that has been most successful has been sexual harassment in the workplace. Although sexual harassment is also actionable under federal and state employment discrimination law, discussed *infra*, plaintiffs usually will include a claim of IIED. The application and success of IIED claims based on sexual harassment also supports the idea that IIED is a tort that courts sometimes use to redress affronts to a person's dignity and to enforce a requirement of a minimal level of respect among persons.

There has been considerable discussion in the United States in recent years of "bullying" in the workplace. Bullying is general abusive conduct or harassment, not necessarily based on race, sex, or some other characteristic protected by employment discrimination laws. *See generally, Symposium on Workplace Bullying*, 8 EMPLOYEE RIGHTS & EMPLOYMENT POL'Y J. 235 (2004). The United States, in contrast to some other nations, does not have a law that expressly protects personal dignity or requires that people treat others with civility and respect. *See, generally*, James Q. Whitman, *Enforcing Civility and Respect: Three Societies*, 109 YALE L.J. 1279 (2000). Accordingly, incivility and disrespect in the workplace, to the extent addressed at all by law, are addressed via employment discrimination law and the torts of IIED and invasion of privacy. *See* section F *infra* for discussion of invasion of privacy.

7. In view of the large body of employment antidiscrimination law in the United States, which prohibits dismissals because of race, color, sex, religion, national origin, age, and disability (at the federal level, and some other protected characteristics at the state level) and the tort erosions of employment at will discussed in note 6, *supra*, do employers in the United States actually benefit from the employment-at-will doctrine? Professor Estlund discusses data indicating that many employers size their workforces and otherwise behave as though the law required good cause for dismissal. *See* Estlund, *supra*, at 11-13. Professor Estlund says that employers "misapprehend . . . the incidence and probable cost of employment litigation." *Id.* at 12.

---

2. Statutory Requirements for Mass Layoffs and Closures

ROQUET V. ARTHUR ANDERSEN LLP

398 F.3d 585 (7th Cir. 2005)

TERENCE T. EVANS, Circuit Judge.

This case involves the Worker Adjustment and Retraining Notification Act, 29 U.S.C. §§2101–2109, better known by its shortened name, the WARN Act. The Act became law in 1989, and its purpose is to soften the economic blow suffered by workers who unexpectedly face plant closings or mass layoffs. Among other things, the Act requires that companies subject to its reach (generally large employers) give employees 60 days notice in advance of any mass layoffs or plant closings. The notice gives affected workers a little time to adjust to a job loss, find new employment, or, if necessary, obtain retraining.

Our case, however, is not your typical WARN Act fare as it involves hot-button topics like "Enron," "document shredding," and "indictment." And it concerns an exception to the WARN Act's notification requirement: the Act's 60-day-notice obligation is eliminated, or reduced to a shorter term, if a mass layoff or plant closing is "caused by business circumstances that were not reasonably foreseeable as of the time that notice would have been required." *Id.* §2102(b)(2)(A). The defendant here, the giant accounting and consulting firm Arthur Andersen LLP, convinced the district court that its failure to comply with the Act was excused by the exception we just quoted. The plaintiffs, a purported class of former Andersen employees, are here challenging that decision on appeal.

First, a little background. As of early 2002, Andersen had over 27,000 employees in 80 locations throughout the country. In addition to providing direct accounting and consulting services for clients, Andersen performed administrative support services for approximately 80 international practice firms that used the Andersen name. One of the firm's major clients was the Enron Corporation, the infamous Houston, Texas, energy marketer that fell like a house of cards in 2001 when it came to light that the company had grossly misstated its earnings. Andersen was at the center of Hurricane Enron – it audited the company's publicly filed financial statements and provided internal counseling. *See United States v. Arthur Andersen, LLP*, 374 F.3d 281 (5th Cir. 2004).

In November of 2001, Andersen received bad news in the form of a subpoena from the SEC requesting Enron-related documents. During the course of its investigation, the SEC discovered that Andersen employees destroyed thousands of relevant documents in the 6 weeks leading up to its receipt of the subpoena. Over the next few months, the media began to speculate about Andersen's continuing viability. Stories also circulated that Andersen's employees were concerned about layoffs and that some of the company's clients were contemplating defection.

During this time, Andersen worked hard to try to resolve its Enron-related ills with the SEC and the Department of Justice (DOJ). As of February 22, 2002, Andersen had not suffered a significant loss of business nor was it giving any thought to a mass layoff. That day, Andersen's lawyers met with lawyers from the DOJ. The next day, counsel briefed Andersen's management team, and a participating manager e-mailed the following update to employees:

> At our meeting on Saturday, February 23, the current status of the investigation into document destruction was presented by the outside lawyers from Davis Polk. They are moving forward as quickly as possible to bring this matter to a conclusion as it relates to the Firm with the Department of Justice. Our desired timetable is to be in a position at the end of February to have the desired conclusion and an agreement in principle with the DOJ, so that we can finalize our disciplinary actions and prepare an internal announcement followed closely by a public announcement of the resolution of this investigation.

Discussions continued over the next few days.

On March 1, the DOJ delivered dire news – it was going to seek an indictment of the company. Andersen tried to convince the DOJ to change its mind, but to no avail. On March 7, an Andersen managing partner, Terry Hatchett, sent an e-mail informing employees that the firm was "presently engaged in discussions with the Department of Justice regarding the parties' respective views" and that "[n]o final conclusions have been reached." That very day, however, the DOJ filed a sealed indictment charging the firm with obstructing the SEC investigation by destroying and withholding documents (18 U.S.C. §1512(b)(2)). On March 13, Andersen's lawyers asked the DOJ to defer prosecution of the company and focus instead on culpable individual employees. The DOJ refused to budge, and on March 14 the indictment was unsealed.

To the surprise of no one, news of the indictment triggered massive client defection. From March 15 to the 31st, Andersen lost $300 million in business. During this time period, the practice group on West Monroe Street in Chicago alone lost $57 million, roughly 14 percent of its fees. To put the gravity of these losses in perspective, the firm had lost only $5 million, or 1 percent, in the 10 weeks preceding the indictment. On March 28, Andersen announced that it was eliminating support services for its international network, which would result in additional revenue loss.

In light of these setbacks, and with additional hemorrhaging expected, Andersen decided to lay off thousands of employees. On April 8, management at West Monroe gave notices of termination to 560 employees, including . . . the named plaintiffs in this suit. . . .

[Plaintiffs] filed a class-action complaint in federal district court alleging that Andersen violated the WARN Act by failing to give 60 days notice to its workers before laying them off. They sought back pay and lost benefits. In August of 2002, the court certified a class consisting of workers from the two Chicago sites and the St. Charles facility. Both sides eventually moved for summary judgment on the issue of whether Andersen's workforce reduction qualified as a "mass layoff" under the Act. The court concluded that it did and granted the plaintiffs' motion.

The parties then moved for summary judgment on the question of whether Andersen was exempt from liability under the WARN Act's "unforeseen business circumstances" exception. The district court concluded that the need for layoffs was not reasonably foreseeable 60 days before the decision was made and entered summary judgment in favor of Andersen. The plaintiffs appeal that decision. . . .

In evaluating this appeal, we note that the Department of Labor has provided some guidance regarding when the "unforeseen business circumstances" exception applies. In doing so, however, the agency eschewed *per se* rules and instead encouraged a case-by-case examination of the facts. *See Pena v. Am. Meat Packing Corp.*, 362 F.3d 418, 421 (7th Cir. 2004). A business circumstance may be reasonably unforeseeable if it was caused by some sudden, dramatic, and unexpected action, or by conditions outside the employer's control. 20 C.F.R. §639.9(b)(1). When determining whether a mass layoff was caused by unforeseeable business circumstances, courts evaluate whether a similarly situated employer exercising reasonable judgment could have foreseen the circumstances that caused the layoff. *Id.* §639.9(b)(2). Thus, a company will not be liable if, when confronted with potentially devastating occurrences, it reacts the same way that other reasonable employers within its own market would react. . . .

The parties dispute whether Andersen established either element of the exception – causation and foreseeability. . . . The district court concluded that the need for mass layoffs was caused by the public announcement of the indictment on March 14. We agree. Up until then, Andersen suffered no marked loss of business despite a spate of negative publicity. It is clear that economic hemorrhaging really did not begin until word of the indictment got out. The plaintiffs contend that Andersen's felonious misconduct caused the layoffs, not the indictment. But, while it is true that the illegal acts of some Andersen employees were the root cause of the firm's ultimate downfall, not until the indictment became public did it feel the pain. Had the DOJ indicted only individual Andersen employees instead of the firm as a whole, or targeted only the Houston office, the layoffs here may never have occurred.

The heart of the dispute in this case centers on foreseeability. In determining whether a crippling business circumstance is foreseeable, we must bear in mind that "it is the 'probability of occurrence' that makes a business circumstance "reasonably foreseeable,"' 'rather than the 'mere possibility of such a circumstance." . . . The layoffs began on April 23, which means that Andersen was required to notify employees 60 days earlier, or February 22. The plaintiffs argue that the indictment was reasonably foreseeable on that date because "the DOJ disclosed to Andersen that an indictment was highly probable." But the record does not support this position. The plaintiffs point to Andersen's meeting with the DOJ on February 22 and its subsequent efforts to fight off an indictment. The February 23 e-mail summarizing that meeting, however, makes no mention of the firm being indicted. And Andersen's subsequent negotiations with the government do not mean that it knew an indictment was likely. Possible? Certainly. But probable? No. . . . Indeed, as of February 22 it was not a foregone conclusion that Andersen would be indicted as a company – in the past, the government typically went after culpable individuals, not companies as a whole. By all accounts, this was an unusual move by the DOJ. There is evidence in the record suggesting that Andersen could have reasonably foreseen the indictment by March 1 – the date it was told by the DOJ that it was being indicted. But hope still remained that the dreaded act could be stalled if not avoided.

We believe that a reasonable company in Andersen's position would have reacted as it did. Confronted with the possibility of an indictment that threatened its very survival, the firm continued to negotiate with the government until the very end and turned to layoffs only after the indictment became public. The plaintiffs argue that Andersen should have notified employees of layoffs on February 22. We do not agree. At that point, Andersen had not yet lost business or been indicted. Indeed, in our view, a mass layoff at that point would have been a poor business decision. What if the government decided not to indict the firm as a whole, or waited 6 months to make the decision? The only reason for providing notice so early would be to ward off potential WARN Act liability. But, as the Sixth Circuit explained in *Watson*, the WARN Act is not intended to deter companies from fighting to stay afloat:

> WARN was not intended to force financially fragile, yet economically viable, employers to provide WARN notice and close its doors when there is a *possibility* that the business may fail at some undetermined time in the future. Such a reading of the Act would force many employers to lay off their employees prematurely, harming precisely those individuals WARN attempts to protect. A company that is struggling to survive financially may be able to continue on for years and it was not Congress's intent to force such a company to close its doors to comply with WARN's notice requirement.

311 F.3d at 765

These same concerns were at play here. Thus, Andersen's failure to notify employees earlier than it did was not unreasonable.

The plaintiffs argue that the layoffs were foreseeable as a matter of law under 20 C.F.R. §639.9(b)(1) because the indictment was not sudden, dramatic, and unexpected nor outside the employer's control. In their view, Andersen was long aware of its misconduct, and punishment for that misconduct was inherently foreseeable. But the indictment was certainly sudden and dramatic in that Andersen did not know if it would be indicted as a firm. Nor did Andersen really know when the indictment would be returned until the act occurred. Again, the WARN Act deals in reasonable probabilities, not possibilities. Moreover, an employer does not have to be caught completely off guard by a dire business circumstance for it to be "sudden, dramatic, or unexpected." Case law reveals that WARN Act defendants need not show that the circumstances which caused a plant closing or mass layoff arose from out of the blue to qualify for the exception. . . .

. . .

The lead time in the notice Andersen ended up giving varied from employee to employee. Our two named plaintiffs, for example, got 2 . . . and 5 . . . weeks notice before they were out of work. Given the situation here, and the "business circumstances" exception in §2102(b)(2)(A), Andersen, although deserving of no roses for the acts of some of its agents in the Enron mess, did not violate the WARN Act by giving the notice as it did on April 8.

We also reject the notion that the timing of the notice was under Andersen's control. The plaintiffs are confusing Andersen's responsibility and culpability for its misbehavior with its "control" over the indictment within the meaning of the regulation. Stated simply, Andersen could not indict itself. Andersen was not like a company that secretly plotted for a long time to move its operation to Mexico and closed up shop without any notice to its employees. . . .

. . .

The judgment of the district court is AFFIRMED.

WOOD, Circuit Judge, dissenting.

No one could dispute the majority's observation that the layoffs involved in this case were high-profile. The pages of the country's newspapers in 2001 and 2002 were filled for weeks, if not months, with the unfolding Enron story and the role that Enron's advisors, including Arthur Andersen, played in that saga. Nonetheless, the Worker Adjustment and Retraining Notification Act, 29 U.S.C. §§2101–2109, (the WARN Act) applies to all cases, not just to those that are dull enough to stay below the press's radar screen. The majority finds here that Andersen was entitled to take advantage of the unforeseen circumstances exception to the obligation to notify affected workers 60 days prior to a mass layoff or plant closing. In so holding, it either finds that notice was impossible right up to April 8, 2002, when the employees finally received the bad news, or it finds that the statute as a matter of law takes an all-or-nothing approach – if 60 days' notice is impossible, then no notice at all is required. Neither one of those possibilities is correct, in my opinion; the first fails as a matter of fact, and the second as a matter of law. I would find that notice was possible, and thus required, no later than March 1, 2002, and I would remand for further proceedings on that basis. . . .

. . .

The facts simply cannot bear the interpretation that the necessity for mass layoffs was not reasonably foreseeable prior to April 8. Thus, if this is the true rationale of the majority's opinion, I cannot subscribe to it. It is also possible, though by no means necessary, to read the majority's opinion as holding that if the need for the layoffs was not reasonably foreseeable at the 60-day mark (February 22), then no notice at all was required by the statute. In [another case] this court left open the question whether a sufficient unforeseen circumstance occurring within the 60-day window excuses an employer from providing any notice at all, or if instead it merely reduces the amount of notice required. . . .

In my view, we should reach that question in the case before us. Taking into account the language and purpose of the WARN Act, we should hold that the 60-day period is merely reduced, not eliminated, when the necessity for a mass layoff or plant closing becomes apparent within that time period. Indeed, immediately after describing the unforeseen circumstances exception, the statute reads: "An employer relying on this subsection shall give as much notice as is practicable and at that time shall give a brief statement of the basis for reducing the notification period." . . .

The crucial date under the WARN Act is not the date when the company *knows* that a mass layoff is imminent, nor is it the date when the company finally gets around to identifying the exact employees affected by the mass layoff. The Act states plainly that the trigger date is the date when a mass layoff is "reasonably foreseeable." As soon as it is probable that a mass layoff will occur, the employer must provide notice as soon as is practicable. Here, Andersen knew of the indictment on March 1, yet it waited over five weeks before providing any notice to its employees.

. . .

The majority worries that giving the required WARN Act notice might exacerbate problems for a floundering company. While this may be true, the fact is that Congress weighed the interests of companies and workers in the statute, and it drew the 60-day line we have. Companies can protect themselves to a certain degree in the wording of the notices they give. As I stated above, the company need not be able to identify each affected employee by name; a general notice, alerting the employees as a group to the possibility of a layoff, is what the statute requires. Finally, at least on the present facts, Andersen's troubles were not exactly a state secret. There was nothing left to hide after March 14, when the indictment hit the front pages of the country's newspapers. By March 1, it was reasonably foreseeable to the firm that it would need to reduce its staff drastically.

For these reasons, I would reverse and remand for further proceedings. I respectfully dissent.

Notes

1. There are relatively few U.S. cases dealing with the WARN Act, and it probably is one of the least-known of U.S. employment laws. Collective redundancy is a major issue that is the subject of extensive regulation in many other nations. The ILO's Convention 158 on Termination of Employment applies to collective redundancies as well as individual terminations.
2. The United States has one other piece of federal legislation that applies to closures. The NLRA, discussed *infra*, requires employers to bargain with unions representing employees about the effects that a closure will have, such as order of layoff, but it does not require employers to bargain about whether they will close the entire business.
3. The WARN Act requires that notice be given to local governments that will be affected by a mass layoff or closure. Not only will such an employment action have an adverse economic effect on a local economy, but many local governments give tax breaks and other incentives to businesses to induce them to locate there. Should the local governmental bodies be able to seek remedies when businesses that have accepted such incentives close? *See City of Yonkers v. Otis Elevator Co.*, 844 F.2d 42 (2d Cir. 1988) (denying recovery); J. Bradley Russell, *Implied Contracts and Creating a Corporate Tort, One Way State and Local Governments Are Starting to Fight Plant Closings*, 90 W. VA. L. REV. 1249 (1988).
4. There is no U.S. law requiring employers to pay indemnities to employees who lose their jobs in mass layoffs or closures. Compare this with the labor law of other nations.
5. With the WARN Act, as with many other areas of U.S. labor and employment law, many states also have laws that regulate the topic regulated by the federal law. Why have laws at both the federal and state levels? Compare this with the laws of the European Union and the member nations.

C. UNIONS AND COLLECTIVE BARGAINING

INTERNATIONAL LADIES' GARMENT WORKERS' UNION V. N.L.R.B.

(Bernhard-Altmann) 366 U.S. 731 (1961)

Mr. Justice CLARK delivered the opinion of the Court.

We are asked to decide in this case whether it was an unfair labor practice for both an employer and a union to enter into an agreement under which the employer recognized the union as exclusive bargaining representative of certain of his employees, although in fact only a minority of those employees had authorized the union to represent their interests. The Board found that by extending such recognition, even though done in the good-faith belief that the union had the consent of a majority of employees in the appropriate bargaining unit, the employer interfered with the organizational rights of his employees in violation of § 8(a)(1) of the National Labor Relations Act and that such recognition also constituted unlawful support to a labor organization in violation of §8(a)(2).[2] In addition, the Board found that the union violated §8(b)(1)(A),[3] by its acceptance of exclusive bargaining authority at a time when in fact it did not have the support of a majority of the employees, and this in spite of its bona fide belief that it did. Accordingly, the Board ordered the unfair labor practices discontinued and directed the holding of a representation election. . . . We agree with the Board and the Court of Appeals that such extension and acceptance of recognition constitute unfair labor practices, and that the remedy provided was appropriate.

In October 1956 the petitioner union initiated an organizational campaign at Bernhard-Altmann Texas Corporation's knitwear manufacturing plant in San Antonio, Texas. No other labor organization was similarly engaged at that time. During the course of that campaign, on July 29, 1957, certain of the company's Topping Department employees went on strike in protest against a wage reduction. That dispute was in no way related to the union campaign, however, and the organizational efforts were continued during the strike. Some of the striking employees had signed authorization cards solicited by the union during its drive, and, while the strike was in progress, the union entered upon a course of negotiations with the employer. As a result of those negotiations, held in New York City where the home offices of both were located, on August 30, 1957, the employer and union signed a "memorandum of understanding." In that memorandum the company recognized the union as exclusive bargaining representative of "all production and shipping employees." The union representative asserted that the union's comparison of the employee authorization cards in its possession with the number of eligible employees representatives of the company furnished it indicated that the union had in fact secured such cards from a majority of employees in the unit. Neither employer nor union made any effort at that time to check the cards in the union's possession against the employee roll, or otherwise, to ascertain with any degree of certainty that the union's assertion, later found by the Board to be erroneous,[4] was founded on fact rather than upon good-faith assumption. The agreement, containing no union security provisions, called for the ending of the strike and for certain improved wages and conditions of employment. It also provided that a 'formal agreement containing these terms' would "be promptly drafted . . . and signed by both parties within the next two weeks."

---

[2] Section 8(a)(1) and (2), insofar as pertinent, provides:

It shall be an unfair labor practice for an employer –
(1) to interfere with, restrain, or coerce employees in the exercise of the rights guaranteed in section 7;
(2) to dominate or interfere with the formation or administration of any labor organization or contribute financial or other support to it . . . 61 Stat. 140, 29 U.S.C. §158(a)(1, 2), 29 U.S.C.A. § 158(a)(1, 2).

[3] Section 8(b)(1)(A) provides in pertinent part:

It shall be an unfair labor practice for a labor organization or its agents –
(1) to restrain or coerce (A) employees in the exercise of the rights guaranteed in section 7 ***. 61 Stat. 141, 29 U.S.C. § 158(b)(1)(A), 29 U.S.C.A. § 158(b)(1).

[4] The Board found that as of August 30 the union in fact had authority to represent either 70 employees out of a relevant total of 280, or 158 out of 368, depending upon the criteria used in determining employee eligibility. "Accordingly, the Union could not, under any circumstances, have represented a majority of the employees involved on August 30, 1957. . . ."

Thereafter, on October 10, 1957, a formal collective bargaining agreement, embodying the terms of the August 30 memorandum, was signed by the parties. The bargaining unit description set out in the formal contract, although more specific, conformed to that contained in the prior memorandum. It is not disputed that as of execution of the formal contract the union in fact represented a clear majority of employees in the appropriate unit.

At the outset, we reject as without relevance to our decision the fact that, as of the execution date of the formal agreement on October 10, petitioner represented a majority of the employees. As the Court of Appeals indicated, the recognition of the minority union on August 30, 1957, was "a fait accompli depriving the majority of the employees of their guaranteed right to choose their own representative." . . . It is, therefore, of no consequence that petitioner may have acquired by October 10 the necessary majority if, during the interim, it was acting unlawfully. Indeed, such acquisition of majority status itself might indicate that the recognition secured by the August 30 agreement afforded petitioner a deceptive cloak of authority with which to persuasively elicit additional employee support.

Nor does this case directly involve a strike. The strike which occurred was in protest against a wage reduction and had nothing to do with petitioner's quest for recognition. Likewise, no question of picketing is presented. Lastly, the violation which the Board found was the grant by the employer of exclusive representation status to a minority union, as distinguished from an employer's bargaining with a minority union for its members only. Therefore, the exclusive representation provision is the vice in the agreement, and discussion of "collective bargaining," as distinguished from "exclusive recognition," is pointless. Moreover, the insistence that we hold the agreement valid and enforceable as to those employees who consented to it must be rejected. On the facts shown, the agreement must fail in its entirety. It was obtained under the erroneous claim of majority representation. Perhaps the employer would not have entered into it if he had known the facts. Quite apart from other conceivable situations, the unlawful genesis of this agreement precludes its partial validity.

In their selection of a bargaining representative, §9(a) of the Wagner Act guarantees employees freedom of choice and majority rule. *J. I. Case Co. v. National Labor Relations Board*, 321 U.S. 332, 339, 64 S.Ct. 576, 581, 88 L.Ed. 762. In short, as we said in *Brooks v. National Labor Relations Board*, 348 U.S. 96, 103, 75 S.Ct. 176, 181, 99 L.Ed. 125, the Act placed "a nonconsenting minority under the bargaining responsibility of an agency selected by a majority of the workers." Here, however, the reverse has been shown to be the case. Bernhard-Altmann granted exclusive bargaining status to an agency selected by a minority of its employees, thereby impressing that agent upon the nonconsenting majority. There could be no clearer abridgment of §7 of the Act, assuring employees the right "to bargain collectively through representatives of their own choosing" or "to refrain from" such activity. It follows, without need of further demonstration, that the employer activity found present here violated §8(a)(1) of the Act which prohibits employer interference with, and restraint of, employee exercise of §7 rights. Section 8(a)(2) of the Act makes it an unfair labor practice for an employer to "contribute . . . support'" to a labor organization. The law has long been settled that a grant of exclusive recognition to a minority union constitutes unlawful support in violation of that section, because the union so favored is given "a marked advantage over any other in securing the adherence of employees," *National Labor Relations Board v. Pennsylvania Greyhound Lines*, 303 U.S. 261, 267, 58 S.Ct. 571, 574, 82 L.Ed. 831. In the Taft-Hartley Law, Congress added §8(b)(1)(A) to the Wagner Act, prohibiting, as the Court of Appeals held, "unions from invading the rights of employees under §7 in a fashion comparable to the activities of employers prohibited under §8(a)(1)." . . . It was the intent of Congress to impose upon unions the same restrictions which the Wagner Act imposed on employers with respect to violations of employee rights.

The petitioner, while taking no issue with the fact of its minority status on the critical date, maintains that both Bernhard-Altmann's and its own good-faith beliefs in petitioner's majority status are a complete defense. To countenance such an excuse would place in permissibly careless employer and union hands the power to completely frustrate employee realization of the premise of the Act – that its prohibitions will go far to assure freedom of choice and majority rule in employee selection of representatives. We find nothing in the statutory language prescribing scienter as an element of the unfair labor practices are involved. The act made unlawful by §8(a)(2) is employer support of a minority union. Here that support is an accomplished fact. More need not be shown, for, even if mistakenly, the employees' rights have been invaded. It follows that prohibited conduct cannot be excused by a showing of good faith.

This conclusion, while giving the employee only the protection assured him by the Act, places no particular hardship on the employer or the union. It merely requires that recognition be withheld until the Board-conducted election results in majority selection of a representative. The Board's order here, as we might infer from the employer's failure to resist its enforcement, would apparently result in similarly slight hardship upon it. We do not share petitioner's apprehension that holding such conduct unlawful will somehow induce a breakdown, or seriously impede the progress of collective bargaining. If an employer takes reasonable steps to verify union claims, themselves advanced only after careful estimate – precisely what Bernhard-Altmann and petitioner failed to do here – he can readily ascertain their validity and obviate a Board election. We fail to see any onerous burden involved in requiring responsible negotiators to be careful, by cross-checking, for example, well-analyzed employer records with union listings or authorization cards. Individual and collective employee rights may not be trampled upon merely because it is inconvenient to avoid doing so. Moreover, no penalty is attached to the violation. Assuming that an employer in good faith accepts or rejects a union claim of majority status, the validity of his decision may be tested in an unfair labor practice proceeding.[13] If he is found to have erred in extending or withholding recognition, he is subject only to a remedial order requiring him to conform his conduct to the norms set out in the Act, as was the case here. No further penalty results. We believe the Board's remedial order is the proper one in such cases. . . .

Affirmed.

Mr. Justice DOUGLAS, with whom Mr. Justice BLACK concurs, dissenting in part.

I agree that, under the statutory scheme, a minority union does not have the standing to bargain for all employees. That principle of representative government extends only to the majority. But where there is no majority union, I see no reason why the minority union should be disabled from bargaining for the minority of the members who have joined it. Yet the order of the Board, now approved, enjoins petitioner union from acting as the exclusive bargaining representative "of any of the employees," and it enjoins the employer from recognizing the union as the representative of "any of its employees."

---

[13] Section 8(a)(5) makes it an unfair labor practice for an employer "to refuse to bargain collectively with the representatives of his employees***." 61 Stat. 141, 29 U.S.C. s 158(a)(5), 29 U.S.C.A. s 158(a)(5).

. . . But when a minority union seeks only to represent its own, what provision of the Act deprives it of its right to represent them, where a majority have not selected another union to represent them?

Judge Learned Hand in *Douds v. Local 1250*, 2 Cir., 173 F.2d 764, 770, 9 A.L.R. 2d 685, stated that "the right to bargain collectively and the right to strike and induce others to do so, are derived from the common-law; it is only in so far as something in the Act forbids their exercise that their exercise becomes unlawful." In that case a minority union was recognized as having standing in a grievance proceeding outside the collective bargaining agreement, even where a majority had chosen another union. *See American Steel Foundries v. Tri-City Central Trades Council*, 257 U.S. 184, 42 S.Ct. 72, 66 L.Ed. 189.

Honoring a minority union – where no majority union exists or even where the activities of the minority union do not collide with a bargaining agreement – is being respectful of history. Long before the Wagner Act, employers and employees had the right to discuss their problems. In the early days the unions were representatives of a minority of workers. The aim – at least the hope – of the legislation was that majority unions would emerge and provide stabilizing influences. Yet I have found nothing in the history of the successive measures, starting with the Wagner Act, that indicates any purpose on the part of Congress to deny a minority union the right to bargain for its members when a majority have not in fact chosen a bargaining representative.

Notes

1. The current National Labor Relations Act ("NLRA") was passed in original form as the Wagner Act in 1935 and has been amended several times. Section 7, the "heart" of the Act, protects the rights of employees to "self-organization, to form, join, or assist labor organizations, to bargain collectively through representatives of their own choosing, and to engage in other concerted activities for the purpose of collective bargaining or other mutual aid or protection" and the rights of employees to refrain from engaging in any of those activities. 29 U.S.C. §157. Unlike individual employment rights law, the NLRA protects the right of employees to act collectively, using their (and their collective bargaining representative's) power to obtain from the employer whatever terms and conditions they can in a collective bargaining agreement. Thus, the NLRA does not mandate that employers provide specific minimum terms, but only protects the right of employees to collectively pursue what they can obtain. The model of labor-management relations established by the NLRA has been described by many as an adversarial model.

    The NLRA is administered by the National Labor Relations Board ("NLRB"), a federal agency, which has regional offices in major cities. The NLRB consists of five members, one designated as chairman, appointed by the President. The NRLB meets in Washington, D.C. By custom, three members of the NLRB are members of the U.S. president's political party, and two are members of the opposition party. The NRLB has jurisdiction over two types of cases under the NLRA: (1) representation cases – conducting elections in which employees in an appropriate bargaining unit vote on whether they wish to be represented by a union in collective bargaining; and (2) charge cases – deciding unfair labor practice charges. Both functions are performed first at the level of the regional offices by regional directors (representation cases) and administrative law judges (charge cases).

Decisions of the regional offices may be appealed to the NLRB. Decisions of the NLRB on unfair labor practices may be appealed to the federal courts of appeal, but representation cases cannot be appealed to the federal courts.

2. The most common unfair labor practice under the NLRA is employers discharging or taking other adverse employment action against employees who support unions or engage in union activity. A typical scenario involves a union beginning to organize a bargaining unit of employees at a business, an employee voices her support for the union, and she is fired. A 2000 report by Human Rights Watch found that over twenty thousand illegal firings of or reprisals against union supporters occur every year in the United States. The report concluded that U.S. labor law is insufficiently protective of the international human rights of American workers to freely associate and bargain collectively. Lance Compa, UNFAIR ADVANTAGE: WORKERS' FREEDOM OF ASSOCIATION IN THE UNITED STATES UNDER INTERNATIONAL HUMAN RIGHTS STANDARDS 8 (Human Rights Watch, 2000) (hereinafter UNFAIR ADVANTAGE); *See also* Charles J. Morris, *A Tale of Two Statutes: Discrimination for Union Activity Under the NLRA and RLA*, 2 EMPLOYEE RTS. & EMPLOYMENT POL'Y J. 317 (1998); *but cf.*, Thomas B. Moorhead, U.S. *Labor Law Serves Us Well*, in WORKERS' RIGHTS AS HUMAN RIGHTS 135, 137–8 (James A. Gross ed., Cornell University Press, 2003) (criticizing the Human Rights Watch report discussed earlier).

3. Under the NLRA, unions typically have sought to become the collective bargaining representative of "appropriate bargaining units" of employees at a single location of a business. Thus, a union might represent a bargaining unit of clerks and cashiers at a local department store. Multilocation bargaining units, in which a union represents a bargaining unit consisting of certain job classifications at multiple locations of the same business, are permissible under certain circumstances. Also, employers can voluntarily band together in multiemployer bargaining units to bargain with a union that represents bargaining units at each business. Still, the predominant model in the United States is for a union to represent one or more bargaining units at a particular site of a particular employer. Compare this with industry- and sector-wide bargaining that occurs in other countries.

The *Bernhard-Altmann* case, *supra*, articulates the U.S. Supreme Court's interpretation of the NLRA as permitting employers to recognize and bargain with a union only when the union has the support of a majority of the employees in an appropriate bargaining unit. As the case states, it is an unfair labor practice under the NLRA for an employer to recognize and bargain with a union that has not achieved majority status, and it is an unfair labor practice for a union to accept such recognition. The dissent in the case did not interpret the NLRA as requiring that a union have majority status before it could bargain for the employees supporting it. Although *Bernhard-Altmann* represents the current state of the law, there has been considerable scholarship in recent years arguing for interpretation of the NLRA as permitting minority representation. *See, e.g.*, CHARLES J. MORRIS, THE BLUE EAGLE AT WORK: RECLAIMING DEMOCRATIC RIGHTS IN THE AMERICAN WORKPLACE (Cornell University Press, 2005); Clyde Summers, *Unions Without Majority – A Black Hole*, 66 CHI-KENT L. REV. 531 (1990); Alan Hyde, Frank Sheed & Mary Deery Uva, *After Smyrna: Rights and Powers of Unions That Represent Less Than a Majority*, 45 RUTGERS L. REV. 637 (1993).

Section 8(a)(2) of the NLRA, implicated in *Bernhard-Altmann*, has been a particularly contentious provision. It is implicated not just when an employer recognizes a union that does not have majority support in a bargaining unit, but also when an employer creates a labor organization for its employees, or dominates or assists a labor organization. At the time of passage of the NLRA, Congress was concerned with sham company unions – unions formed by employers and offered by the company to employees as a means of avoiding organization by a truly independent union. Company unions, as creations of the employer, did not represent the best interests of the employees. Thus, two scenarios, in addition to the nonmajority union in *Bernhard-Altmann* are employers' creation of "labor organizations" and employers' assisting unions in organizing their employees. Although it may seem unlikely that an employer would assist an independent union in organizing its employees, this sometimes happens when an employer, fearing one union, finds a union that it would prefer (perhaps one more amenable to terms the employer would prefer to have in a collective bargaining agreement). The issue of employers assisting or dominating labor organizations has generated considerable controversy because the Supreme Court and the NLRB have broadly interpreted what may be considered a "labor organization." Thus, even employee committees created by employers to generate discussion between labor and management on various issues and perhaps develop solutions to workplace problems may be considered labor organizations. A decision of the NLRB at the center of the tempest is *Electromation, Inc.*, 309 N.L.R.B. 990 (1992), *enf'd*, 35 F.3d 1148 (7th Cir. 1994). In *Electromation*, an employer which had no union representing bargaining units of employees created five "action committees" to discuss various issues, including attendance bonuses, pay progression, absenteeism, and so on. A union began organizing a proposed bargaining unit and filed an unfair labor practice charge, alleging a violation of §8(a)(2). The NLRB held that the committees did constitute labor organizations, and they were dominated by the employer. Some have argued that the prevailing interpretation of §8(a)(2) pushes the adversarial model of labor-management relations too far, so far that U.S. businesses, unable to work with employee committees, will find it increasingly difficult to compete in global markets. *See, e.g.*, John W. Bowers, *Section 8(a)(2) and Participative Management: An Argument for Judicial and Legislative Change in a Modern Workplace*, 26 VAL. U. L. REV. 525 (1992).

4. As the previous notes have suggested, one way that a union becomes the collective bargaining representative of a bargaining unit of employees is for the union to file a petition for election with a regional office of the NLRB. In order to file a petition, the union must demonstrate that it has the support of at least 30 percent of the proposed bargaining unit, usually accomplished by presentation of authorization cards signed by employees. After a period of time during which the union and the employer campaign, the NLRB regional office administers a secret ballot election, in which the union must receive the vote of a majority of employees voting. This is not the only way in which a union can become the collective bargaining representative of the employees. An employer may voluntarily recognize a union that has majority support in a bargaining unit. In *Bernhard-Altmann, supra*, the employer voluntarily recognized the union, which, unfortunately, did not have majority support. Usually, voluntary recognition occurs when a union presents authorization cards signed by employees in a bargaining unit, and the employer does not wish to go to the time, expense, and workplace tension of an election that it is likely to lose. Unions can also call a strike in support of their demand for recognition, with the work stoppage

bringing economic pressure on the employer to recognize the union without a secret ballot election. Because employers have been able to undermine and defeat union organizing efforts in many instances in the time between the filing of an election petition and the holding of the election, many unions now try to force employers to recognize them without an election. Under current NLRA law, an employer that is presented with a demand for recognition, no matter how much support the union has, may decline to recognize the union voluntarily and instead wait for an election to be held. *Linden Lumber v. NLRB*, 419 U.S. 301 (1974). There have been recent proposals in the U.S. Congress to change the state of the law, and require employers that are presented with evidence that a union has majority support in an appropriate bargaining unit to recognize the union. *See* Employee Free Choice Act, S. 842 & H.R. 1696, 109th Cong., 1st Sess. (Apr. 19, 2005); *see also* James J. Brudney, *Neutrality Agreements and Card Check Recognition: Prospects for Changing Paradigms*, 90 Iowa L. Rev. 819 (2005).

5. As noted in Chapter 2, the United States has one of the world's lowest ILO convention ratification rates, having ratified only fourteen conventions. Sir Bob Hepple classifies the United States as a high compliance nation because the ILO's Committee of Experts on the Application of Conventions and Recommendations (CEACR) has not often issued individual observations based on the U.S. government's actions vis-à-vis its ratified conventions. Bob Hepple, Labour Laws and Global Trade 42 (Hart Publishing 2005). Nevertheless, some commentators see U.S. labor law, both in substance and practice, as at odds with the fundamental principles of freedom of association and the right to collective bargaining. Among the violations alleged are: (1) allowing rampant discrimination against union supporters to flourish; (2) permitting employers to campaign vigorously against unions; (3) allowing employers to compel employees to attend antiunion themed ("captive audience") meetings; (4) countenancing long delays in NLRB and court proceedings; (5) providing remedies that are insufficient to deter employer wrongdoing; and (6) excluding millions of workers, including agricultural and domestic workers, independent contractors and contingent workers, and low-level supervisors and managers, from protection of organizing and bargaining rights. Lance Compa, *Workers' Freedom of Association in the United States: The Gap between Ideals and Practice*, in Workers Rights as Human Rights 23, 32-48 (James A. Gross, ed., Cornell University Press, 2003).

6. Although the United States has not ratified ILO Conventions 87 and 98, the fundamental freedom of association conventions, it did approve the 1998 Declaration on Fundamental Principles and Rights at Work, which designates freedom of association and the effective recognition of the right to collective bargaining as fundamental rights. Professor James Gross describes both a telling U.S. recognition of legal shortfalls and an interesting ILO response to a report filed by the United States in 1999:

> The United States government, in a 1999 report to the ILO assessing its labor law in relation to ILO conventions that it had not signed, asserted that it "has an elaborate system of substantive law and procedures to assure the enforcement of that law [and] is committed to the fundamental principle of freedom of association and effective recognition of the right to collective bargaining." The United States admitted in understated language, however, "that there are aspects of this system that fail to fully protect the rights to organize and bargain collectively of all employees in all circumstances." The report expressed "concern" about that

and said it was "important to re-examine any system of labor laws from time to time to assure that the system continues to protect these fundamental rights." An ILO Committee of Expert Advisors included this U.S. report in a group of reports it termed "striking for their open recognition of difficulties still to be overcome or situations they deemed relevant to achieving full respect in the principles and rights in the Declaration."

James A. Gross, *A Long Overdue Beginning*, in Workers' Rights as Human Rights, 1, 6 (James A. Gross, ed., Cornell University Press, 2003) (quoting Review of Annual Reports under the Follow-up to the ILO Declaration on Fundamental Principles and Rights at Work, Part II 144-58 (International Labor Office, 2000)).

What economic, sociological or political factors might inspire review and reform of U.S. labor law?

7. Many view the NLRA and the law thereunder to be an anachronism that has little relevance to current U.S. labor and employment law and probably less relevance to the future. Union density in the U.S. private sector workforce is now below 9 percent, and below 15 percent in the combined private and public sectors. Many have predicted that the decline will continue unless something occurs that stems the decline, and it is difficult to identify anything on the horizon – whether legal, political, or economic — that could do that. In addition to the small percentage of employees represented by unions, the fact that collective bargaining occurs at the "plant" level rather than at larger levels, such as industry-wide, diminishes the influence of organized labor in the United States.

Unions and organized labor are the engines envisioned by the NLRA. The U.S. Congress has moved, however, from the NLRA model of collective action to a model of individual employment rights legislation. *See, e.g.*, James J. Brudney, *Reflections on Group Action and the Law of the Workplace*, 74 Tex. L. Rev. 1563, 1571 (1996) ("At some point during this legislative barrage, it became clear that Congress viewed government regulation founded on individual employment rights, rather than collective bargaining between private parties, as the primary mechanism for ordering employment relations and redistributing economic resources."). Although the first individual employment rights legislation, the Fair Labor Standards Act, was intended to support collective bargaining, the enactment of numerous individual rights laws since 1963 arguably has diminished the need for unions as collective bargaining representatives. An increasing number of the terms and conditions for which unions bargain are regulated by federal law. Still, organized labor has been at the vanguard supporting passage of the individual rights laws.

Although the NLRA is usually thought of as applying only to employees represented by unions, that is not the case. Under Section 7, employees engaged in concerted activity for mutual aid or protection are protected by the NLRA from adverse action by employers. Thus, an employee who, for example, sends an e-mail message to co-employees protesting a proposed new vacation and holiday plan and is terminated for sending the message, may prevail on an unfair labor practice charge alleging that he was discriminated against because of his protected activity. *See Timekeeping Systems, Inc.*, 323 N.L.R.B. 244 (1997). Still, cases involving NLRA protections of nonunion employees represent a small percentage of the work of the NLRB.

N.L.R.B. V. MACKAY RADIO & TELEGRAPH CO.

304 U.S. 333 (1938)

Mr. Justice ROBERTS, delivered the opinion of the Court.

. . .

The respondent, a California corporation, is engaged in the transmission and receipt of telegraph, radio, cable, and other messages between points in California and points in other states and foreign countries. It maintains an office in San Francisco for the transaction of its business wherein it employs upwards of sixty supervisors, operators and clerks, many of whom are members of Local No. 3 of the American Radio Telegraphists Association, a national labor organization; the membership of the local comprising "point-to-point" or land operators employed by respondent at San Francisco. Affiliated with the national organization also were locals whose members are exclusively marine operators who work upon ocean-going vessels. The respondent, at its San Francisco office, dealt with committees of Local No. 3; and its parent company, whose headquarters were in New York, dealt with representatives of the national organization. Demand was made by the latter for the execution of agreements respecting terms and conditions of employment of marine and point-to-point operators. On several occasions when representatives of the union conferred with officers of the respondent and its parent company the latter requested postponement of discussion of the proposed agreements and the union acceded to the requests. In September, 1935, the union pressed for immediate execution of agreements and took the position that no contract would be concluded by the one class of operators unless an agreement were simultaneously made with the other. Local No. 3 sent a representative to New York to be in touch with the negotiations and he kept its officers advised as to what there occurred. The local adopted a resolution to the effect that if satisfactory terms were not obtained by September 23 a strike of the San Francisco point-to-point operators should be called. The national officers determined on a general strike in view of the unsatisfactory state of the negotiations. This fact was communicated to Local No. 3 by its representative in New York and the local officers called out the employees of the San Francisco office. At midnight Friday, October 4, 1935, all the men there employed went on strike. The respondent, in order to maintain service, brought employees from its Los Angeles office and others from the New York and Chicago offices of the parent company to fill the strikers' places.

Although none of the San Francisco strikers returned to work Saturday, Sunday, or Monday, the strike proved unsuccessful in other parts of the country and, by Monday evening, October 7th, a number of the men became convinced that it would fail and that they had better return to work before their places were filled with new employees. One of them telephoned the respondent's traffic supervisor Monday evening to inquire whether the men might return. He was told that the respondent would take them back and it was arranged that the official should meet the employees at a downtown hotel and make a statement to them.

. . .

. . . Five strikers who were prominent in the activities of the union and in connection with the strike, whose names appeared upon the list of eleven, reported at the office at various times between Tuesday and Thursday. Each of them was told that he would have to fill out an application for employment; that the roll of employees was complete, and that his application would be considered in connection with any vacancy that might thereafter occur.

These men not having been reinstated in the course of three weeks, the secretary of Local No. 3 presented a charge to the National Labor Relations Board that the respondent had violated section 8(1) and (3) of the National Labor Relations Act. Thereupon the Board filed a complaint charging that the respondent had discharged and was refusing to employ the five men who had not been reinstated to their positions for the reason that they had joined and assisted the labor organization known as Local No. 3 and had engaged in concerted activities with other employees of the respondent for the purpose of collective bargaining and other mutual aid and protection; that by such discharge respondent had interfered with, restrained, and coerced the employees in the exercise of their rights guaranteed by section 7 of the National Labor Relations Act and so had been guilty of an unfair labor practice within the meaning of section 8(1) of the act. The complaint further alleged that the discharge of these men was a discrimination in respect of their hire and tenure of employment and a discouragement of membership in Local No. 3, and thus an unfair labor practice within the meaning of section 8(3) of the act.

. . .

. . . The strikers remained employees under section 2(3) of the act, 29 U.S.C.A. § 152(3), which provides: "'The term 'employee' shall include . . . any individual whose work has ceased as a consequence of, or in connection with, any current labor dispute or because of any unfair labor practice, and who has not obtained any other regular and substantially equivalent employment . . . " Within this definition the strikers remained employees for the purpose of the act and were protected against the unfair labor practices denounced by it.

. . . Nor was it an unfair labor practice to replace the striking employees with others in an effort to carry on the business. Although section 13 of the act, 29 U.S.C.A. s 163, provides, "Nothing in this Act (chapter) shall be construed so as to interfere with or impede or diminish in any way the right to strike," it does not follow that an employer, guilty of no act denounced by the statute, has lost the right to protect and continue his business by supplying places left vacant by strikers. And he is not bound to discharge those hired to fill the places of strikers, upon the election of the latter to resume their employment, in order to create places for them. The assurance by respondent to those who accepted employment during the strike that if they so desired their places might be permanent was not an unfair labor practice, nor was it such to reinstate only so many of the strikers as there were vacant places to be filled. But the claim put forward is that the unfair labor practice indulged by the respondent was discrimination in reinstating striking employees by keeping out certain of them for the sole reason that they had been active in the union. As we have said, the strikers retained, under the act, the status of employees. Any such discrimination in putting them back to work is, therefore, prohibiting by section 8.

. . . The Board's findings as to discrimination are supported by evidence. We shall not attempt a discussion of the conflicting claims as to the proper conclusions to be drawn from the testimony. There was evidence, which the Board credited, that several of the five men in question were told that their union activities made them undesirable to their employer; and that some of them did not return to work with the great body of the men at 6 o'clock on Tuesday morning because they understood they would not be allowed to go to work until the superior officials had passed upon their applications. When they did apply at times between Tuesday morning and Thursday they were each told that the quota was full and that their applications could not be granted in any event until a vacancy occurred. This was on the ground that five of the eleven new men remained at work in San Francisco. On the other hand, six of the eleven strikers listed for separate treatment who reported for work early Tuesday morning, or within the next day or so, were permitted to go back to work and were not compelled to await the approval of their applications. It appears that all of the men who had been on strike signed applications for re-employment shortly after their resumption of work. The Board found, and we cannot say that its finding is unsupported, that, in taking back six of the eleven men and excluding five who were active union men, the respondent's officials discriminated against the latter on account of their union activities and that the excuse given that they did not apply until after the quota was full was an afterthought and not the true reason for the discrimination against them.

As we have said, the respondent was not bound to displace men hired to take the strikers' places in order to provide positions for them. It might have refused reinstatement on the grounds of skill or ability, but the Board found that it did not do so. It might have resorted to any one of a number of methods of determining which of its striking employees would have to wait because five men had taken permanent positions during the strike, but it is found that the preparation and use of the list, and the action taken by respondent, was with the purpose to discriminate against those most active in the union.

Notes

1. The right to strike is among the rights protected by Section 7 of the NLRA. Striking, the withholding of labor, is the principal economic weapon that unions and the employees they represent have to attempt to force employers to accede to their demands in collective bargaining. Bereft of the right to strike, unions and employees would have little to use to force employers to give more than they wish to give. It often is not necessary for unions to call strikes; if they can make credible threats of striking, employers sometimes will move in their bargaining positions.

2. In *Mackay Radio*, the U.S. Supreme Court announced, in dicta, that employers have the right to hire permanent replacements for economic strikers. Permanent means that the employer will not terminate the replacements and give the jobs back to the strikers at the end of the strike. The *Mackay Radio* rule is a significant restriction on the right to strike. There are two types of strikes: (1) unfair labor practice strikes, which are caused at least in part by employees' decision to protest unfair labor practices committed by their employer; and (2) economic strikes, which are caused by employees' decision to pressure an employer to accept the bargaining demands of the union and employees it represents. The *Mackay Radio* right of employers to hire permanent replacements for strikers applies only to economic strikes. Employers in the last two decades or so increasingly have announced to striking employees that they were preparing to hire permanent replacements for strikers who did not return to work. Although unions often counter that the strike is an unfair labor practice strike and the employer has no right to hire permanent replacements, the determination of type of strike is not made until much later when an unfair labor practice charge is filed and a hearing is held. Thus, striking employees must decide to abandon the strike or risk their jobs on a subsequent determination of the type of strike. The threat of hiring permanent replacements has ended many strikes. The strike is declining as a viable economic weapon. There have been very few major strikes in recent years compared with the 1950s.

3. Professor Lance Compa notes that while the ILO's fundamental freedom of association conventions, Conventions 87 and 98, do not expressly refer to the right to strike, that subject has been extensively reviewed by the ILO's Committee on Freedom of Association (CFA) and other supervisory bodies. Compa argues that ILO jurisprudence makes clear that the right to strike "is an essential element of freedom of association." UNFAIR ADVANTAGE, *supra*, at 191. Moreover, this right should only be restricted in rare cases, involving for example, national crises, or essential public services. *Id*. at 192. Does the *MacKay Radio* doctrine run afoul of these principles? The ILO's CFA noted the following in a report on a complaint brought against the United States by the AFL-CIO:

> The right to strike is one of the essential means through which workers and their organisations may promote and defend their economic and social interests. The Committee considers that this basic right is not really guaranteed when a worker who exercises it legally runs the risk of seeing his or her job taken up permanently by another worker just as legally. The Committee considers that, if a strike is otherwise legal, the use of labour drawn from outside the undertaking to replace strikers for an indeterminate period entails a risk of derogation from the right to strike which may affect the free exercise of trade union rights.
>
> INTERNATIONAL LABOR ORGANIZATION, COMMITTEE ON FREEDOM OF ASSOCIATION, COMPLAINT AGAINST THE GOVERNMENT OF THE UNITED STATES PRESENTED BY THE AMERICAN FEDERATION OF LABOR AND CONGRESS OF INDUSTRIAL ORGANIZATIONS (AFL-CIO), para. 92, Report No. 278, Case No. 1543 (1991).

    How would you interpret the CFA's conclusion? The United States has not ratified Conventions 87 and 98. However, the United States did, subsequent to the report excerpted here, enthusiastically embrace the ILO's Declaration on Fundamental Principles and Rights at Work, which designates freedom of association and the effective recognition of the right to collective bargaining as fundamental rights. Should U.S. policy makers take seriously the report of the CFA and consider abandoning the *MacKay Radio* doctrine?

4. Thomas B. Moorhead argues that U.S. labor law strikes the proper balance "between workers and management." Moorhead, *supra*, at 136. International labor standards are sometimes at variance with U.S. labor law, he notes, because "European labor law is the usual frame of reference. . . . " *Id*. at 137. If labor rights such as freedom of association are conceptualized as human rights, can one sensibly describe them as having a continental European bias?

D. WAGES, HOURS, AND BENEFITS

In many nations' labor law regimes, wages, hours, and benefits are determined principally through collective bargaining. Although collective bargaining and collective agreements can set these terms and conditions of employment in the United States, this is not the main method in the United States; as discussed in Section C, *supra*, the percentage of the U.S. workforce represented by unions is small, and the typical arrangement in the United States is representation and bargaining for individual sites ("plant-level" bargaining). Thus, to the extent that terms and conditions of employment are regulated at all, for most employees the regulation is in the form of federal and state individual employment rights law.

Among the federal laws implicated are the following (with terms and conditions regulated): (1) the Fair Labor Standards Act ("FLSA") (minimum wage, overtime compensation, and child labor); (2) the Family and Medical Leave Act ("FMLA") (leave for certain purposes); (3) the Employee Retirement Income Security Act ("ERISA") (pension and welfare plans); (4) the Occupational Safety and Health Act ("OSH Act") (conditions in workplaces that pose health and safety risks); and (5) the Consolidated Omnibus Budget Reconciliation Act ("COBRA") (extension of employer-provided health insurance coverage for a period of time beyond separation from employment).

The states, with considerable pressure and incentive from the federal government, passed laws to regulate workers' compensation benefits for work-related accidents and illnesses and laws to regulate unemployment insurance benefits. Many states also have passed wage payment laws that apply to aspects of wages beyond minimum wage and overtime compensation, such as how often employees must be paid. Some state and local governments also have passed laws or ordinances establishing a minimum wage that is higher than the federal minimum wage.

Because of the diversity of terms and conditions of employment covered by federal and state laws, it is difficult to offer many generalizations or statements regarding basic under-girding principles. To return to a point made in the introduction to this chapter, however, because the United States has a more limited government-administered "social safety net" than many other nations, many of the protections, such as health insurance coverage and retirement funds, are provided to employees by employers as part of the terms and conditions of employment. This requires regulation of these in the employment context.

1. Administration and Enforcement

As is the case with other parts of U.S. individual employment rights law, the state and federal district courts are the main fora for lawsuits enforcing the rights. However, as with the federal employment discrimination laws, there is a federal agency charged with enforcement of the laws. The FLSA and the FMLA are administered by the U.S. Department of Labor, Wage and Hour Division. Employees who believe they are aggrieved may file claims with the Wage and Hour Division, or they may instead go directly to the courts and file lawsuits. Moreover, if aggrieved parties file with the Wage and Hour Division, the agency may choose to file a lawsuit in court. The OSH Act is administered by a federal agency known as the Occupational Health and Safety Administration (OSHA). Different from the FLSA and FMLA, aggrieved employees may not sue in court under the OSH Act. OSHA investigates workplaces, issues citations, and imposes penalties. Employers may seek review of OSHA penalties in the federal courts of appeal.

2. Substantive Rights

FLSA: Under the FLSA, the minimum wage is $5.15 per hour, employees are entitled to one and one-half times their regular rate of pay for hours over forty, and child labor is prohibited below the age of fourteen and restricted up to age seventeen.

FMLA: The FMLA provides that covered employees may take up to twelve weeks of unpaid leave (employers may choose, but are not required by the law, to provide some paid leave) for certain delineated family and medical purposes, such as birth of a child, adoption, and serious medical condition of employee and specified relatives.

ERISA: Imposes minimum requirements and fiduciary duties with respect to pension and welfare plans, including some health insurance.

OSH Act: Provides for general duty, promulgation of standards, inspection, and enforcement regarding workplace safety.

COBRA: Provides for employer to offer extension for a specified period of employer-provided health insurance to departing employee if employee continues to pay premiums.

E. EMPLOYMENT DISCRIMINATION

1. Introduction

McDONALD V. SANTA FE TRAIL TRANSPORTATION CO.

427 U.S. 273 (1976)

Mr. Justice MARSHALL delivered the opinion of the Court.

. . . On September 26, 1970, petitioners, both white, and Charles Jackson, a Negro employee of Santa Fe, were jointly and severally charged with misappropriating 60 one-gallon cans of antifreeze which was part of a shipment Santa Fe was carrying for one of its customers. Six days later, petitioners were fired by Santa Fe, while Jackson was retained. A grievance was promptly filed with Local 988, pursuant to the collective-bargaining agreement between the two respondents, but grievance proceedings secured no relief. The following April, complaints were filed with the Equal Employment Opportunity Commission (EEOC) charging that Santa Fe had discriminated against both petitioners on the basis of their race in firing them, and that Local 988 had discriminated against McDonald on the basis of his race in failing properly to represent his interests in the grievance proceedings, all in violation of Title VII of the Civil Rights Act of 1964. Agency process proved equally unavailing for petitioners, however, and the EEOC notified them in July 1971 of their right under the Act to initiate a civil action in district court within 30 days. This suit followed, petitioners joining their §1981 claim to their Title VII allegations.

II

Title VII of the Civil Rights Act of 1964 prohibits the discharge of "any individual" because of "such individual's race," s 703(a)(1), 42 U.S.C. §2000e-2(a)(1). Its terms are not limited to discrimination against members of any particular race. Thus although we were not there confronted with racial discrimination against whites, we described the Act in *Griggs v. Duke Power Co.*, 401 U.S. 424, 431, 91 S.Ct. 849, 853, 28 L.Ed.2d 158 (1971), as prohibiting "(d)iscriminatory preference for *any* (racial) group, *minority* or *majority*" (emphasis added). Similarly the EEOC, whose interpretations are entitled to great deference, . . . has interpreted Title VII to proscribe racial discrimination in private employment against whites on the same terms as racial discrimination against nonwhites, holding that to proceed otherwise would "constitute a derogation of the Commission's Congressional mandate to eliminate all practices which operate to disadvantage the employment opportunities of any group protected by Title VII, including Caucasians." . . .

This conclusion is in accord with uncontradicted legislative history to the effect that Title VII was intended to "cover white men and white women and all Americans," 110 Cong.Rec. 2578 (1964) (remarks of Rep. Celler), and create an "obligation not to discriminate against whites," Id., at 7218 (memorandum of Sen. Clark). See also Id., at 7213 (memorandum of Sens. Clark and Case); Id., at 8912 (remarks of Sen. Williams). We therefore hold today that Title VII prohibits racial discrimination against the white petitioners in this case upon the same standards as would be applicable were they Negroes and Jackson white.

. . .

Respondents contend that, even though generally applicable to white persons, Title VII affords petitioners no protection in this case, because their dismissal was based upon their commission of a serious criminal offense against their employer. We think this argument is foreclosed by our decision in *McDonnell Douglas Corp. v. Green*, 411 U.S. 792, 93 S.Ct. 1817, 36 L.Ed.2d 668 (1973).

In *McDonnell Douglas*, a laid-off employee took part in an illegal "stall-in" designed to block traffic into his former employer's plant, and was arrested, convicted, and fined for obstructing traffic. At a later date, the former employee applied for an open position with the company, for which he was apparently otherwise qualified, but the employer turned down the application, assertedly because of the former employee's illegal activities against it. Charging that he was denied re-employment because he was a Negro, a claim the company denied, the former employee sued under Title VII. Reviewing the case on certiorari, we concluded that the rejected employee had adequately stated a claim under Title VII. See *id.*, 411 U.S. at 801, 93 S.Ct. at 1823. Although agreeing with the employer that "(n)othing in Title VII compels an employer to absolve and rehire one who has engaged in such deliberate, unlawful activity against it," *id.*, 411 U.S. at 803, 93 S.Ct. at 1825, we also recognized:

> (T)he inquiry must not end here. While Title VII does not, without more, compel rehiring of (the former employee), neither does it permit (the employer) to use (the former employee's) conduct as a pretext for the sort of discrimination prohibited by (the Act). On remand, (the former employee) must . . . be afforded a fair opportunity to show that (the employer's) stated reason for (the former employee's) rejection was in fact pretext. Especially relevant to such a showing would be evidence that white employees involved in acts against (the employer) of comparable seriousness to the 'stall-in' were nevertheless retained or rehired. (The employer) may justifiably refuse to rehire one who was engaged in unlawful, disruptive acts against it, but only if this criterion is applied alike to members of all races.

Id., 411 U.S. at 804, 93 S.Ct. at 1825.

We find this case indistinguishable from *McDonnell Douglas*. Fairly read, the complaint asserted that petitioners were discharged for their alleged participation in a misappropriation of cargo entrusted to Santa Fe, but that a fellow employee, likewise implicated, was not so disciplined, and that the reason for the discrepancy in discipline was that the favored employee is Negro while petitioners are white. See *Conley v. Gibson*, 355 U.S. 41, 45-46, 78 S.Ct. 99, 101-102, 2 L.Ed.2d 80 (1957). While Santa Fe may decide that participation in a theft of cargo may render an employee unqualified for employment, this criterion must be "applied, alike to members of all races," and Title VII is violated if, as petitioners alleged, it was not.

We cannot accept respondents' argument that the principles of *McDonnell Douglas* are inapplicable where the discharge was based, as petitioners' complaint admitted, on participation in serious misconduct or crime directed against the employer. The Act prohibits all racial discrimination in employment, without exception for any group of particular employees, and while crime or other misconduct may be a legitimate basis for discharge, it is hardly one for racial discrimination. Indeed, the Title VII plaintiff in *McDonnell Douglas* had been convicted for a nontrivial offense against his former employer. It may be that theft of property entrusted to an employer for carriage is a more compelling basis for discharge than obstruction of an employer's traffic arteries, but this does not diminish the illogic in retaining guilty employees of one color while discharging those of another color.

. . .

Thus, we conclude that the District Court erred in dismissing both petitioners' Title VII claims against Santa Fe, and petitioner McDonald's Title VII claim against Local 988.

III

Title 42 U.S.C. § 1981 provides in pertinent part: "All persons within the jurisdiction of the United States shall have the same right in every State and Territory to make and enforce contracts . . . as is enjoyed by white citizens. . . . " We have previously held, where discrimination against Negroes was in question, that §1981 affords a federal remedy against discrimination in private employment on the basis of race, and respondents do not contend otherwise. . . . The question here is whether § 1981 prohibits racial discrimination in private employment against whites as well as nonwhites

. . .

This cumulative evidence of congressional intent makes clear, we think, that the 1866 statute, designed to protect the "same right . . . to make and enforce contracts" of "citizens of every race and color" was not understood or intended to be reduced by Representative Wilson's amendment, or any other provision, to the protection solely of nonwhites. Rather, the Act was meant, by its broad terms, to proscribe discrimination in the making or enforcement of contracts against, or in favor of, any race. Unlikely as it might have appeared in 1866 that white citizens would encounter stubstantial racial discrimination of the sort proscribed under the Act, the statutory structure and legislative history persuade us that the 39th Congress was intent upon establishing in the federal law a broader principle than would have been necessary simply to meet the particular and immediate plight of the newly freed Negro slaves. And while the statutory language has been somewhat streamlined in re-enactment and codification, there is no indication that §1981 is intended to provide any less than the Congress enacted in 1866 regarding racial discrimination against white persons. . . . Thus, we conclude that the District Court erred in dismissing petitioners' claims under §1981 on the ground that the protections of that provision are unavailable to white persons.

The judgment of the Court of Appeals for the Fifth Circuit is reversed, and the case is remanded for further proceedings consistent with this opinion.

So ordered.

_____

Notes

1. Federal employment antidiscrimination law in the United States prohibits adverse employment actions because of race, color, sex, religion, and national origin (Title VII of the Civil Rights Act of 1964), age (the Age Discrimination in Employment Act of 1967), and disabilities (the Americans with Disabilities Act of 1990).

Section 1981 (42 U.S.C. §1981), a post–Civil War Reconstruction era statute, has been applied in the employment context to prohibit discrimination based on race.

Most states also have employment antidiscrimination statues that protect the same characteristics as federal law, and some cover other characteristics, such as sexual orientation and marital status. *See, e.g.*, Alex B. Long, *"If the Train Should Jump the Track . . . ": Divergent Interpretations of State and Federal Employment Discrimination Statutes*, 40 GA. L. REV. 469 (2006).

Employment discrimination law is the area of labor and employment law in which the United States was the innovator and developer of the theories that European and other nations copied. As the European Union legislates expansively in this area, see *infra* Chapter 7, however, the United States may not continue to be the innovator in this area of law.

2. *McDonald, supra*, makes the point that, although Title VII was enacted principally to eliminate discrimination against those who historically had been discriminated against in employment in the U.S. (*e.g.*, African Americans, women, religious minorities), the statute also prohibits discrimination based on race, sex, and so on, against groups that historically were not victims of employment discrimination (*e.g.*, Caucasians, men). Employment discrimination claims by traditionally favored groups, such as Caucasians and men, have come to be referred to as "reverse discrimination" claims. These claims have raised some controversial issues, such as do the same principles of law and proof apply to reverse discrimination claims as apply to traditional discrimination claims. For example, should a white man be able to proceed with his case by satisfying the light burden of the prima facie case established for African Americans and women?

A related point is that a monolithic set of principles and rules may not apply well to all of employment discrimination law. There is a tendency in U.S. court decisions to try to apply a uniform set of principles to all discrimination cases. However, this does not work well. For example, although *McDonald, supra*, makes clear that reverse discrimination claims are actionable under Title VII, the U.S. Supreme Court held that younger employees cannot sue for age discrimination under the ADEA when older employees are treated better. *See General Dynamics Land Systems, Inc. v. Cline*, 540 U.S. 581 (2004).

3. As noted in Chapter 2, although the United States has determined that its existing antidiscrimination laws are in compliance with ILO Convention No. 111 (Discrimination (Employment and Occupation)), there is little political will for ratification of that fundamental convention. Why would the United States, which has been a leader in the development of employment discrimination law, be disinclined to ratify that international instrument?

4. U.S. case law recognizes that employers can engage in voluntary affirmative action in some circumstances; for example, employers that have very substantial underrepresentations of African Americans or women in a segment of their workforce or their workforce generally, may try to address that underrepresentation through employment decisions. However, the case law sets certain criteria for valid affirmative action plans. Affirmative action is a divisive issue in the United States, and the courts have set rigorous standards for permissible programs. For example, government employers must justify affirmative action under Constitutional standards. Race-based distinctions trigger strict scrutiny review, and "are constitutional only if they are narrowly tailored measures that further compelling governmental

interests." *Adarand Construction v. Pena*, 515 U.S. 200, 228 (1995). Satisfying that demanding standard requires a finding that a public employer engaged in past or present discriminatory acts. Societal discrimination alone is an impermissible basis upon which to base a public employer's voluntary remedial measures. *Wygant v. Jackson Bd. Of Educ.*, 476 U.S. 267 (1986).

The standards for voluntary affirmative action programs embraced by private employers are somewhat less onerous. The purpose of private employer plans must be to eliminate a "conspicuous imbalance in job categories traditionally segregated by race and sex." *Johnson v. Transportation Agency of Santa Clara County*, 480 U.S. 616, 640 (1987). Further, the plan must not unnecessarily trammel or burden the rights of majority employees.*United Steelworkers of America v. Weber*, 443 U.S. 193, 208 (1979). Finally, the plan must be a temporary measure aimed at eliminating racial or gender imbalance rather than maintaining a particular demographic balance among the employer's workforce. *Id.* at 208.

5. Political battles over affirmative action in the United States reveal differing perspectives on both the nature of discrimination and equality. American scholar Alan David Freeman, in a seminal article, argues that resentment over affirmative action is fueled by the orientation of U.S. civil rights law, which he terms the perpetrator perspective. Rather than view discrimination as a broad societal phenomenon requiring a comprehensive strategy for correction, this view blames bias on specific, ill-intentioned bad actors. Discrimination so conceptualized lulls majority group members into complacency over conditions for which they feel no responsibility. Attempting to correct those conditions through affirmative action creates majority group resentment. Alan David Freeman, *Legitimizing Racial Discrimination Through AntiDiscrimination Law: A Critical Review of Supreme Court Doctrine*, 62 Minn. L. Rev. 1049 (1978).

6. Professor Stephen Carter, in an equally seminal work, shifts the perspective to the beneficiaries of affirmative action, noting that the programs can stigmatize their recipients as unqualified. He worries not only about the perceptions of majority group members but also the psychological impact of receiving a race-based preference on recipients. Stephen L. Carter, Reflections of an Affirmative Action Baby (Basic Books, 1991). Professor Linda Hamilton Krieger acknowledges that affirmative action can, in some contexts, heighten inter-group tension. Insights from social cognition and identity theory, however, convince her that affirmative action remains an indispensable tool for confronting discrimination, a subtle, pernicious and often unconscious problem. Linda Hamilton Krieger, *Civil Rights Perestroika: Intergroup Relations After Affirmative Action*, 86 Cal. L. Rev. 1251, 1331-32 (1998).

7. Commenting on affirmative action and other remedial programs, Professor Martha Fineman notes that the American commitment to formal equality – treating everyone alike – ignores the fact that groups are not equally endowed or situated. She argues that the unfairness associated with existing social and economic arrangements warrants a substantive approach to equality that is concerned more with outcomes than with neutrality. Martha Albertson Fineman, The Autonomy Myth: A Theory of Dependency 274, 276 (The New Press, 2004). Some other nations refer to affirmative action as positive discrimination and take a substantive approach to increasing the representation of traditionally disadvantaged groups. *See* Chapter 13 for India's approach to affirmative action.

2. Theories of Discrimination

a. *Disparate Treatment and Disparate Impact*

There are two principal theories of discrimination, which are recognized under Title VII, the ADEA, and the ADA: disparate treatment and disparate impact. In the most often-quoted explanation of these two theories and the differences between them, the U.S. Supreme Court stated as follows:

> "Disparate treatment" such as is alleged in the present case is the most easily understood type of discrimination. The employer simply treats some people less favorably than others because of their race, color, religion, sex, or national origin. Proof of discriminatory motive is critical, although it can in some situations be inferred from the mere fact of differences in treatment. . . . Undoubtedly, disparate treatment was the most obvious evil Congress had in mind when it enacted Title VII. See, e. g., 110 Cong.Rec. 13088 (1964) (remarks of Sen. Humphrey) ("What the bill does . . . is simply to make it an illegal practice to use race as a factor in denying employment. It provides that men and women shall be employed on the basis of their qualifications, not as Catholic citizens, not as Protestant citizens, not as Jewish citizens, not as colored citizens, but as citizens of the United States").
>
> Claims of disparate treatment may be distinguished from claims that stress "disparate impact." The latter involve employment practices that are facially neutral in their treatment of different groups but that in fact fall more harshly on one group than another and cannot be justified by business necessity. . . . . . . Proof of discriminatory motive, we have held, is not required under a disparate-impact theory. . . . . . . Either theory may, of course, be applied to a particular set of facts.
>
> *Int'l Bhd. of Teamsters v. United States*, 431 U.S. 324, 335 n.15 (1977).

Although the distinction between the two can be clearly stated, it is sometimes more difficult in application. In the case below, the Supreme Court explains how an appellate court analyzed a case under the wrong theory.

RAYTHEON COMPANY V. HERNANDEZ.

540 U.S. 44 (2003)

Justice THOMAS delivered the opinion of the Court.

The Americans with Disabilities Act of 1990 (ADA), 104 Stat. 327, as amended, 42 U.S.C. §12101 *et seq.*, makes it unlawful for an employer, with respect to hiring, to "discriminate against a qualified individual with a disability because of the disability of such individual." §12112(a). We are asked to decide in this case whether the ADA confers preferential rehire rights on disabled employees lawfully terminated for violating workplace conduct rules. The United States Court of Appeals for the Ninth Circuit held that an employer's unwritten policy not to rehire employees who left the company for violating personal conduct rules contravenes the ADA, at least as applied to employees who were lawfully forced to resign for illegal drug use but have since been rehabilitated. Because the Ninth Circuit improperly applied a disparate-impact analysis in a disparate-treatment case in order to reach this holding, we vacate its judgment and remand the case for further proceedings consistent with this opinion. We do not, however, reach the question on which we granted certiorari.

Respondent, Joel Hernandez, worked for Hughes Missile Systems for 25 years. On July 11, 1991, respondent's appearance and behavior at work suggested that he might be under the influence of drugs or alcohol. Pursuant to company policy, respondent took a drug test, which came back positive for cocaine. Respondent subsequently admitted that he had been up late drinking beer and using cocaine the night before the test. Because respondent's behavior violated petitioner's workplace conduct rules, respondent was forced to resign. Respondent's "Employee Separation Summary" indicated as the reason for separation: "discharge for personal conduct (quit in lieu of discharge)." App. 12a.

More than two years later, on January 24, 1994, respondent applied to be rehired by petitioner. Respondent stated on his application that he had previously been employed by petitioner. He also attached two reference letters to the application, one from his pastor, stating that respondent was a "faithful and active member" of the church, and the other from an Alcoholics Anonymous counselor, stating that respondent attends Alcoholics Anonymous meetings regularly and is in recovery. Id., at 13a-15a.

Joanne Bockmiller, an employee in the company's Labor Relations Department, reviewed respondent's application. Bockmiller testified in her deposition that since respondent's application disclosed his prior employment with the company, she pulled his personnel file and reviewed his employee separation summary. She then rejected respondent's application. Bockmiller insisted that the company had a policy against rehiring employees who were terminated for workplace misconduct. Id., at 62a. Thus, when she reviewed the employment separation summary and found that respondent had been discharged for violating workplace conduct rules, she rejected respondent's application. She testified, in particular, that she did not know that respondent was a former drug addict when she made the employment decision and did not see anything that would constitute a "record of" addiction. Id., at 63a-64a.

Respondent subsequently filed a charge with the Equal Employment Opportunity Commission (EEOC). Respondent's charge of discrimination indicated that petitioner did not give him a reason for his nonselection, but that respondent believed he had been discriminated against in violation of the ADA.

Petitioner responded to the charge by submitting a letter to the EEOC, in which George M. Medina, Sr., Manager of Diversity Development, wrote:

> The ADA specifically exempts from protection individuals currently engaging in the illegal use of drugs when the covered entity acts on the basis of that use. Contrary to Complainant's unfounded allegation, his non-selection for rehire is not based on any legitimate disability. Rather, Complainant's application was rejected based on his demonstrated drug use while previously employed and the complete lack of evidence indicating successful drug rehabilitation.
>
> The Company maintains it's [sic] right to deny re-employment to employees terminated for violation of Company rules and regulations. . . . Complainant has provided no evidence to alter the Company's position that Complainant's conduct while employed by [petitioner] makes him ineligible for rehire.
>
> Id., at 19a-20a.

This response, together with evidence that the letters submitted with respondent's employment application may have alerted Bockmiller to the reason for respondent's prior termination, led the EEOC to conclude that petitioner may have "rejected [respondent's] application based on his record of past alcohol and drug use." Id., at 94a (EEOC Determination Letter, Nov. 20, 1997). The EEOC thus found that there was "reasonable cause to believe that [respondent] was denied hire to the position of Product Test Specialist because of his disability." *Id.*, at 95a. The EEOC issued a right-to-sue letter, and respondent subsequently filed this action alleging a violation of the ADA.

Respondent proceeded through discovery on the theory that the company rejected his application because of his record of drug addiction and/or because he was regarded as being a drug addict. See 42 U.S.C. §§12102(2)(B)-(C).[2] In response to petitioner's motion for summary judgment, respondent for the first time argued in the alternative that if the company really did apply a neutral no-rehire policy in his case, petitioner still violated the ADA because such a policy has a disparate impact. The District Court granted petitioner's motion for summary judgment with respect to respondent's disparate-treatment claim. However, the District Court refused to consider respondent's disparate-impact claim because respondent had failed to plead or raise the theory in a timely manner.

The Court of Appeals agreed with the District Court that respondent had failed timely to raise his disparate-impact claim. . . . In addressing respondent's disparate-treatment claim, the Court of Appeals proceeded under the familiar burden-shifting approach first adopted by this Court in *McDonnell Douglas Corp. v. Green*, 411 U.S. 792, 93 S.Ct. 1817, 36 L.Ed.2d 668 (1973).[3] First, the Ninth Circuit found that with respect to respondent's prima facie case of discrimination, there were genuine issues of material fact regarding whether respondent was qualified for the position for which he sought to be rehired, and whether the reason for petitioner's refusal to rehire him was his past record of drug addiction.[4] 298 F.3d at 1034–1035. The Court of Appeals thus held that with respect to respondent's prima facie case of discrimination, respondent had proffered sufficient evidence to preclude a grant of summary judgment. *Id.*, at 1035. Because petitioner does not challenge this aspect of the Ninth Circuit's decision, we do not address it here.

The Court of Appeals then moved to the next step of *McDonnell Douglas*, where the burden shifts to the defendant to provide a legitimate, nondiscriminatory reason for its employment action. . . . Here, petitioner contends that Bockmiller applied the neutral policy against

---

[2] The ADA defines the term "disability" as:

  (A) a physical or mental impairment that substantially limits one or more of the major life activities of such individual;

  (B) a record of such an impairment; or

  (C) being regarded as having such an impairment.

  42 U.S.C. §12102(2)

[3] The Court in *McDonnell Douglas* set forth a burden-shifting scheme for discriminatory-treatment cases. Under *McDonnell Douglas* a plaintiff must first establish a prima facie case of discrimination. The burden then shifts to the employer to articulate a legitimate, nondiscriminatory reason for its employment action. . . . If the employer meets this burden, the presumption of intentional discrimination disappears, but the plaintiff can still prove disparate treatment by, for instance, offering evidence demonstrating that the employer's explanation is pretextual. *See Reeves v. Sanderson Plumbing Products*, Inc., 530 U.S. 133, 143, 120 S.Ct. 2097, 147 L.Ed.2d 105 (2000). The Courts of Appeals have consistently utilized this burden-shifting approach when reviewing motions for summary judgment in disparate-treatment cases. . . .

[4] The Court of Appeals noted that "it is possible that a drug *user* may not be 'disabled' under the ADA if his drug use does not rise to the level of an addiction which substantially limits one or more of his major life activities." . . . The parties do not dispute that respondent was "disabled" at the time he quit in lieu of discharge and thus a record of the disability exists. We therefore need not decide in this case whether respondent's employment record constitutes a "record of addiction," which triggers the protections of the ADA. The parties are also not disputing in this Court whether respondent was qualified for the position for which he applied.

rehiring employees previously terminated for violating workplace conduct rules and that this neutral company policy constituted a legitimate and nondiscriminatory reason for its decision not to rehire respondent. The Court of Appeals, although admitting that petitioner's no-rehire rule was lawful on its face, held the policy to be unlawful "as applied to former drug addicts whose only work-related offense was testing positive because of their addiction." . . . The Court of Appeals concluded that petitioner's application of a neutral no-rehire policy was not a legitimate, nondiscriminatory reason for rejecting respondent's application:

> "Maintaining a blanket policy against rehire of *all* former employees who violated company policy not only screens out persons with a record of addiction who have been successfully rehabilitated, but may well result, as [petitioner] contends it did here, in the staff member who makes the employment decision remaining unaware of the 'disability' and thus of the fact that she is committing an unlawful act. Additionally, we hold that a policy that serves to bar the reemployment of a drug addict despite his successful rehabilitation violates the ADA." . . .

In other words, while ostensibly evaluating whether petitioner had proffered a legitimate, nondiscriminatory reason for failing to rehire respondent sufficient to rebut respondent's prima facie showing of disparate treatment, the Court of Appeals held that a neutral no-rehire policy could never suffice in a case where the employee was terminated for illegal drug use, because such a policy has a disparate impact on recovering drug addicts. In so holding, the Court of Appeals erred by conflating the analytical framework for disparate-impact and disparate-treatment claims. Had the Court of Appeals correctly applied the disparate-treatment framework, it would have been obliged to conclude that a neutral no-rehire policy is, by definition, a legitimate, nondiscriminatory reason under the ADA.[5] And thus the only remaining question would be whether respondent could produce sufficient evidence from which a jury could conclude that "petitioner's stated reason for respondent's rejection was in fact pretext."

II

This Court has consistently recognized a distinction between claims of discrimination based on disparate treatment and claims of discrimination based on disparate impact. The Court has said that "'[d]isparate treatment' is the most easily understood type of discrimination. The employer simply treats some people less favorably than others because of their race, color, religion, sex, or [other protected characteristic]." *Teamsters v. United States*, 431 U.S. 324, 335, n. 15, 97 S.Ct. 1843, 52 L.Ed.2d 396 (1977). *See also Hazen Paper Co. v. Biggins*, 507 U.S. 604, 609, 113 S.Ct. 1701, 123 L.Ed.2d 338 (1993) (discussing disparate-treatment claims in the context of the Age Discrimination in Employment Act of 1967). Liability in a disparate-treatment case "depends on whether the protected trait actually motivated the employer's decision." . . . By contrast, disparate-impact claims "involve employment practices that are facially neutral in their treatment of different groups but that in fact fall more harshly on one group than another and cannot be justified by business necessity." *Teamsters, supra*, at 335-336, n. 15, 97 S.Ct. 1843.

---

[5] This would not, of course, resolve the dispute over whether petitioner did in fact apply such a policy in this case. Indeed, the Court of Appeals expressed some confusion on this point, as the court first held that respondent "raise[d] a genuine issue of material fact as to whether he was denied re-employment because of his past record of drug addiction," *id.*, at 1034, but then later stated that there was "no question that [petitioner] applied this [no-rehire] policy in rejecting [respondent's] application," *id.*, at 1036, n. 17.

Under a disparate-impact theory of discrimination, "a facially neutral employment practice may be deemed [illegally discriminatory] without evidence of the employer's subjective intent to discriminate that is required in a 'disparate-treatment' case." . . .

Both disparate-treatment and disparate-impact claims are cognizable under the ADA. *See* 42 U.S.C. §12112(b) (defining "discriminate" to include "utilizing standards, criteria, or methods of administration that have the effect of discrimination on the basis of disability" and "using qualification standards, employment tests or other selection criteria that screen out or tend to screen out an individual with a disability"). Because "the factual issues, and therefore the character of the evidence presented, differ when the plaintiff claims that a facially neutral employment policy has a discriminatory impact on protected classes," *Texas Dept. of Community Affairs v. Burdine*, 450 U.S. 248, 252, n. 5, 101 S.Ct. 1089, 67 L.Ed.2d 207 (1981), courts must be careful to distinguish between these theories. Here, respondent did not timely pursue a disparate-impact claim. Rather, the District Court concluded, and the Court of Appeals agreed, that respondent's case was limited to a disparate-treatment theory, that the company refused to rehire respondent because it regarded respondent as being disabled and/or because of respondent's record of a disability.

Petitioner's proffer of its neutral no-rehire policy plainly satisfied its obligation under *McDonnell Douglas* to provide a legitimate, nondiscriminatory reason for refusing to rehire respondent. Thus, the only relevant question before the Court of Appeals, after petitioner presented a neutral explanation for its decision not to rehire respondent, was whether there was sufficient evidence from which a jury could conclude that petitioner did make its employment decision based on respondent's status as disabled despite petitioner's proffered explanation. Instead, the Court of Appeals concluded that, as a matter of law, a neutral no-rehire policy was not a legitimate, nondiscriminatory reason sufficient to defeat a prima facie case of discrimination. The Court of Appeals did not even attempt, in the remainder of its opinion, to treat this claim as one involving only disparate treatment. Instead, the Court of Appeals observed that petitioner's policy "screens out persons with a record of addiction," and further noted that the company had not raised a business necessity defense, 298 F.3d, at 1036-1037, and n. 19, factors that pertain to disparate-impact claims but not disparate-treatment claims. *See, e.g., Grano v. Department of Development of Columbus*, 637 F.2d 1073, 1081 (C.A. 6 1980) ("In a disparate impact situation the issue is whether a neutral selection device screens out disproportionate numbers of [the protected class]").[7] By improperly focusing on these factors, the Court of Appeals ignored the fact that petitioner's no-rehire policy is a quintessential legitimate, nondiscriminatory reason for refusing to rehire an employee who was terminated for violating workplace conduct rules. If petitioner did indeed apply a neutral, generally applicable no-rehire policy in rejecting respondent's application, petitioner's decision not to rehire respondent can, in no way, be said to have been motivated by respondent's disability.

---

[7] Indeed, despite the fact that the Nation's antidiscrimination laws are undoubtedly aimed at "the problem of inaccurate and stigmatizing stereotypes," *ibid.*, the Court of Appeals held that the unfortunate result of petitioner's application of its neutral policy was that Bockmiller may have made the employment decision in this case "remaining unaware of [respondent's] 'disability.'" The Court of Appeals did not explain, however, how it could be said that Bockmiller was motivated to reject respondent's application because of his disability if Bockmiller was entirely unaware that such a disability existed. If Bockmiller were truly unaware that such a disability existed, it would be impossible for her hiring decision to have been based, even in part, on respondent's disability. And, if no part of the hiring decision turned on respondent's status as disabled, he cannot, *ipso facto*, have been subject to disparate treatment.

The Court of Appeals rejected petitioner's legitimate, nondiscriminatory reason for refusing to rehire respondent because it "serves to bar the re-employment of a drug addict despite his successful rehabilitation." . . . We hold that such an analysis is inapplicable to a disparate-treatment claim. Once respondent had made a prima facie showing of discrimination, the next question for the Court of Appeals was whether petitioner offered a legitimate, nondiscriminatory reason for its actions so as to demonstrate that its actions were not motivated by respondent's disability. To the extent that the Court of Appeals strayed from this task by considering not only discriminatory intent but also discriminatory impact, we vacate its judgment and remand the case for further proceedings consistent with this opinion.

It is so ordered.

_____

Notes

1. The plaintiff in the *Raytheon* case might have had a stronger claim under the disparate impact theory, arguing that a facially neutral practice had a disproportionate impact on people with his disability.

    In a disparate impact case, the structure of the analysis is as follows: (1) plaintiff's burden of persuasion on the prima facie case; (2) defendant employer's burden of persuasion on the defense of business necessity and job relatedness; and (3) plaintiff's burden of persuasion on a less discriminatory and effective alternative employment practice. *See* 42 U.S.C. §2000e-2(k).

2. The Americans with Disabilities Act (ADA), under which the plaintiff in *Raytheon* sued, was passed in 1990. To be covered by the ADA, a person must be a "qualified individual with a disability." Qualified means able to perform the essential functions of the job either with or without a reasonable accommodation. There are three ways in which a person may be disabled: one must have an impairment that substantially limits a major life activity, have a record of such an impairment, or be regarded as having such an impairment. In short, plaintiffs often lose cases under the ADA because they cannot satisfy the coverage requirements. In the federal courts of appeals, defendants have won over 90 percent of the ADA cases that have come before those courts since the passage of the Act. *See generally, Symposium, Backlash Against the ADA: Interdisciplinary Perspectives and Implications for Social Justice Strategies*, 21 BERKELEY J. EMP. & LAB. L. 1 (2000).

3. In disparate treatment cases, U.S. employment discrimination law focuses on intent or motive. The question is whether the employer was motivated by race or sex or other protected characteristic to take the adverse employment action against the claimant. The focus on motivation raises a host of problems: *e.g.*, (1) Whose motivation is relevant or dispositive? (decisions often are not made by a single person); (2) To what extent must the protected characteristic motivate the employment decision?; (3) How does a plaintiff prove the motivation of the employer? Commentators also note that a focus on motive makes it difficult to use disparate treatment theory to address unconscious bias. Charles R. Lawrence III, *The Id, the Ego, and Equal Protection: Reckoning with Unconscious Racism*, 39 STAN. L. REV. 317 (1987); Linda Hamilton Krieger, *The Content of Our Categories: A Cognitive Bias Approach to Discrimination and Equal Employment Opportunity*, 47 STAN. L. REV. 1161 (1995); Ann C. McGinley, *¡Viva la evolucion!: Recognizing Unconscious*

Motive in Title VII, 9 CORNELL J. L. & PUB. POL'Y 446 (2000). Other complex forms of disadvantage, such as organizational culture and patterns of workplace interaction that over time exclude women and people of color fit uneasily within the existing legal framework. Samuel R. Bagenstos, *The Structural Turn and the Limits of Antidiscrimination Law*, 94 CAL. L. REV. 1 (2006); Tristin K. Green, *Work Culture and Discrimination*, 93 CAL. L. REV. 623 (2005); Susan Sturm, *Second Generation Employment Discrimination: A Structural Approach*, 101 COLUM. L. REV. 458 (2001). Professor Orly Lobel suggests a strategy for combating subtle, more structural forms of discrimination. She recommends that antidiscrimination law's traditional top-down approach to legal regulation be supplemented by government-initiated, flexible, non-coercive equal employment strategies utilizing the principles of corporate self-governance. Orly Lobel, *The Renew Deal: The Fall of Regulation and the Rise of Governance in Contemporary Legal Thought*, 89 MINN. L. REV. 342, 419–23 (2004).

---

b. *Proving Discriminatory Intent*

RACHID, V. JACK IN THE BOX, INC.

376 F.3d 305 (5th Cir. 2004)

EDITH BROWN CLEMENT, Circuit Judge:

Ahmed P. Rachid ("Rachid") filed an age discrimination claim under the Age Discrimination in Employment Act ("ADEA"), 29 U.S.C. §§621-34, alleging that he was terminated from his managerial position at Jack In The Box, Inc. ("JIB"). Because Rachid established a prima facie case and because issues of material fact concerning JIB's proffered reason for terminating Rachid are disputed, summary judgment was improper and this case is REVERSED and REMANDED.

I. FACTS AND PROCEEDINGS

Rachid was employed by JIB from October 1995 to February 2001. Patrick Powers ("Powers") became Rachid's supervisor in September 1999. Rachid managed two restaurants, and shared managerial duties at one of the restaurants with Khalil Haidar ("Haidar"). Powers repeatedly criticized Rachid, and, according to both Rachid and Haidar, made disparaging comments about Rachid's age. Rachid, who was 52 years old, reported these comments to JIB's human resources department, and even requested a transfer because he feared that Powers sought to fire him because of his age. A transfer was never approved and Rachid was fired, according to JIB, for failing to follow policies related to recording employee time. The parties sharply join issue over whether Rachid violated company policy. On June 15, 2000, Powers sent the following email to managers of JIB restaurants:

> Each week I down load [sic] the "punch changes" at each store for the prior week. I am concerned about the increased number of "punch changes" that are related to BREAKS. Let me make clear if anyone alters an employee's hours to save labor, THEY [sic] ARE BREAKING THE LAW! This is the type of offense that I have no ability to help an individual. Employees must punch out for breaks on there [sic] own, M[anagers-In-Charge] need to

verify that each employee punched out at the clock. If an employee fails to punch out at the clock they [sic] are to be written up on a P108 [disciplinary form]. NO MANAGER IS TO GO BACK AND DO A PUNCH CHANGE WITHOUT A SIGNED P108 FOR PROOF! The P108 needs to be kept in the employee file. If the employee contests their [sic] hours and there are punch changes without a P108 for back-up documentation, the manager is putting their [sic] job at risk. It becomes a case of "he said/she said" and the manager has no proof that they [sic] didn't "illegally alter" the time clock. The P108 is the only protection you have against this kind of allegation.

Remember: "very few people have ever been fired for missing a number, but all that get caught reporting a false number will always be fired!" I cannot help you out of this kind of problem.

The parties disputed whether this email sent by Powers represents JIB's company policy.[1]

One of JIB's human resources employees, Kellie Teal-Guess ("Teal-Guess"), investigated several "punch changes" entered for employees at restaurants that Rachid managed. Though Rachid disputes whether this investigation revealed any time-card alterations made by Rachid,[2] he concedes in his deposition that he occasionally changed time-cards when employees took breaks, and that he did not fill out P108 forms for all of those changes. Without further investigation, Powers terminated Rachid immediately upon learning that he had altered time-cards without completing P108 forms. Rachid's replacement was 47 years old.

Rachid filed an EEOC charge complaining of age discrimination under the ADEA, acquired a Right to Sue letter, and filed suit. The district court granted summary judgment in favor of JIB and dismissed Rachid's claim. Rachid timely appeals.

II. STANDARD OF REVIEW

This Court reviews a grant of summary judgment de novo, and applies the same standard as the district court. *Travelers Cas. & Sur. Co. of Am. v. Baptist Health Sys.*, 313 F.3d 295, 297 (5th Cir. 2002). District courts properly grant summary judgment if, viewing the facts in the light most favorable to the nonmovant, the movant shows that there is no genuine issue of material fact and that the movant is entitled to judgment as a matter of law. Fed. R. Civ. P. 56(c).

III. DISCUSSION

A. Proper Legal Standard for an ADEA Claim.

It appears that the district court applied the *McDonnell Douglas* approach in analyzing Rachid's claim. *See McDonnell Douglas Corp. v. Green*, 411 U.S. 792, 93 S.Ct. 1817, 36 L.Ed.2d 668 (1973). The district court's opinion states that Rachid did not establish a prima facie case, and later notes that "nothing in the record suggests that J[IB]'s basis for terminating Rachid was a pretext." The term "pretext" strongly suggests that the district court engaged in a *McDonnell*

---

[1] JIB's Employee Handbook directs employees in the following manner: "To make sure there is agreement on what hours you worked, your Manager will post an Hours Report at the end of each pay period for employees to check. If you don't agree with your hours on the report, let your Manager know immediately."

[2] Three of those employees reported alterations in their time-cards. Apparently, none of the employees alleged that Rachid himself (as opposed to another manager) altered his time-card during the period under investigation by Teal-Guess. Teal-Guess informed Powers that certain employees in restaurants where Rachid was a manager had improper deletions of time. Teal-Guess noted that it was Powers's responsibility to determine whether Rachid (or another manager) had made the improper changes.

Douglas burden shifting analysis.[3] *See McDonnell Douglas*, 411 U.S. at 804-05, 93 S.Ct. 1817. It is disputed, however, whether this is the proper legal framework.

(1) Age Discrimination under the ADEA pre- Desert Palace.[4]

Under the ADEA, "[i]t shall be unlawful for an employer . . . to discharge any individual or otherwise discriminate against any individual with respect to his compensation, terms, conditions, or privileges of employment, because of such individual's age." 29 U.S.C. §623(a)(1). "When a plaintiff alleges disparate treatment, liability depends on whether the protected trait (under the ADEA, age) actually motivated the employer's decision." *Reeves v. Sanderson Plumbing Prods., Inc.*, 530 U.S. 133, 141, 120 S.Ct. 2097, 147 L.Ed.2d 105 (2000) (citing *Hazen Paper Co. v. Biggins*, 507 U.S. 604, 610, 113 S.Ct. 1701, 123 L.Ed.2d 338 (1993)). To demonstrate age discrimination a "plaintiff must show that '(1) he was discharged; (2) he was qualified for the position; (3) he was within the protected class at the time of discharge; and (4) he was either i) replaced by someone outside the protected class, ii) replaced by someone younger, or iii) otherwise discharged because of his age.'" *Palasota v. Haggar Clothing Co.*, 342 F.3d 569, 576 (5th Cir. 2003) (quoting *Bodenheimer v. PPG Indus., Inc.*, 5 F.3d 955, 957 (5th Cir. 1993)). That is, regardless of how much younger his replacement is, a plaintiff in the protected class may still establish a prima facie case by producing evidence that he was "discharged because of his age." *Palasota*, 342 F.3d at 576 (quotations omitted).

A plaintiff can demonstrate age discrimination in two ways, either through:

> direct evidence or by an indirect or inferential method of proof. Discrimination can be shown indirectly by following the "pretext" method of proof set out in *McDonnell Douglas Corp. v. Green*, 411 U.S. 792, 93 S.Ct. 1817, 36 L.Ed.2d 668 (1973). . . .
>
> If, however, plaintiff produces direct evidence of discrimination, the *McDonnell Douglas* test is "inapplicable." The *Price Waterhouse [v. Hopkins*, 490 U.S. 228, 109 S.Ct. 1775, 104 L.Ed.2d 268 (1989)], mixed-motives theory of discrimination comes into play where direct evidence of discrimination is presented, but the employer asserts that the same adverse employment decision would have been made regardless of discrimination. Although *Price Waterhouse* can be characterized as a method to prove discrimination, the mixed-motives theory is probably best viewed as a defense for an employer. *See Price Waterhouse*, 490 U.S. at 246, 109 S.Ct. 1775 ("[T]he employer's burden is most appropriately deemed an affirmative defense: the plaintiff must persuade the factfinder on one point, and the employer, if it wishes to prevail, must persuade it on another.").
>
> Unlike *McDonnell Douglas*, which simply involves a shifting of the burden of *production*, *Price Waterhouse* involves a shift of the burden of *persuasion* to the defendant. In other words, under *Price Waterhouse*, once a plaintiff presents direct evidence of discrimination, the burden of proof shifts to the employer to show that the same adverse employment decision would have been made regardless of discriminatory animus. If the employer fails to carry this burden, plaintiff prevails
>
> In summary, *Price Waterhouse* and *McDonnell Douglas* are alternative methodologies for proving discrimination.

> *Mooney v. Aramco Serv. Co.*, 54 F.3d 1207, 1216-17 & n. 11 (5th Cir. 1995) (quotations and citations omitted).

---

[3] Under the *McDonnell Douglas* burden shifting approach: the plaintiff must establish a prima facie case of discrimination; if the plaintiff meets that burden, the defendant must produce a legitimate, non-discriminatory reason for its decision to terminate the plaintiff; if the defendant meets its burden of production, the plaintiff then has the opportunity to demonstrate that the defendant's proffered reason for termination is merely pretextual. *West v. Nabors Drilling USA, Inc.*, 330 F.3d 379, 383–85 (5th Cir.2003).

[4] *Desert Palace, Inc. v. Costa*, 539 U.S. 90, 123 S.Ct. 2148, 156 L.Ed.2d 84 (2003).

One district court in this Circuit recently described the mixed-motives analysis. "A mixed-motives case arises when an employment decision is based on a mixture of legitimate and illegitimate motives. . . . If the employee proves the unlawful reason was a motivating factor, the employer must demonstrate that it would have taken the same action in the absence of the impermissible motivating factor." *Louis v. E. Baton Rouge Parish Sch. Bd.*, 303 F.Supp.2d 799, 801-04 (M.D.La.2003); *see also Medlock v. Ortho Biotech, Inc.*, 164 F.3d 545, 553 (10th Cir.1999) (noting that a mixed-motives analysis applies "where the evidence is sufficient to allow a trier to find both forbidden and permissible motives.") (quotations and citations omitted). Whereas under the pretext prong of the *McDonnell Douglas* analysis, the plaintiff aims to prove that discriminatory motive was the determinative basis for his termination, under the mixed-motives framework the plaintiff can recover by demonstrating that the protected characteristic (under the ADEA, age) was a motivating factor in the employment decision. *See id.; Mooney*, 54 F.3d at 1216-17.

The parties contest whether *Desert Palace, Inc. v. Costa*, 539 U.S. 90, 123 S.Ct. 2148, 156 L.Ed.2d 84 (2003), alters the analysis by allowing a plaintiff to proceed with a mixed-motives approach in a case where there is not direct evidence[6] of discrimination.

(2) Mixed-motives Analysis is Available for ADEA Claims.

Rachid argues that this case should be analyzed under the mixed-motives analysis described in *Price Waterhouse* and, more recently, in *Desert Palace, Inc. v. Costa*, 539 U.S. 90, 123 S.Ct. 2148, 156 L.Ed.2d 84 (2003). JIB maintains that the mixed-motives analysis is relevant only where there is *direct* evidence of discrimination, and that because there is no direct evidence here, the *McDonnell Douglas* approach governs.

In *Desert Palace*, the Supreme Court unanimously held that in the context of Title VII, as amended by Congress in 1991, "direct evidence of discrimination is not required in mixed-motive[s] cases" 123 S.Ct. at 2155. *See also Stegall v. Citadel Broad. Co.*, 350 F.3d 1061, 1066-67 (9th Cir.2003) (applying *Desert Palace* at the summary judgment stage to Title VII and state law discrimination claims, and analyzing the plaintiff's case under both the mixed-motives and the pretext theories). As the district court in *Louis* observed, "[b]ecause the direct evidence requirement has been removed from mixed-motive[s] cases, it is now harder to draw a distinction between *McDonnell Douglas* and mixed-motive[s] cases." *Louis*, 303 F.Supp.2d at 803–04. This Court has not yet addressed whether *Desert Palace* alters the *Price Waterhouse* and *McDonnell Douglas* analyses.

We must first decide whether the mixed-motives analysis discussed in *Desert Palace* in the context of a Title VII claim is equally applicable in the ADEA context. "[T]he starting point for our analysis is the statutory text." *Desert Palace*, 123 S.Ct. at 2153. The ADEA states that "[i]t shall be unlawful for an employer . . . to discharge any individual or otherwise discriminate against any individual with respect to his compensation, terms, conditions, or privileges of employment, *because of* such individual's age." 29 U.S.C. §623(a) (emphasis added). Title VII similarly prohibits discrimination "because of" a protected characteristic. 42 U.S.C. §2000e-2(a) (West 2004); *see also Smith v. City of Jackson, Miss.*, 351 F.3d 183, 188-190 (5th

---

[6] "Direct evidence is evidence that, if believed, proves the fact of discriminatory animus without inference or presumption." *Sandstad v. CB Richard Ellis, Inc.*, 309 F.3d 893, 897 (5th Cir.2002). Although some of the evidence in the case *sub judice* might qualify as direct evidence, Rachid does *not* argue that there was direct evidence of discrimination.

Cir. 2003) (discussing the similarities and differences of Title VII and the ADEA and noting that the "core sections [of the two statutes] overlap[] almost identically. . . . This is
no coincidence; the prohibitions of the ADEA were derived in *haec verba* from Title VII.")
(citations and quotations omitted). In *Desert Palace* the Supreme Court applied the mixed-
motives analysis because, "[o]n its face, [Title VII] does not mention, much less require, that
a plaintiff make a heightened showing through direct evidence." *Desert Palace*, 123 S.Ct. at
2153.

Given that the language of the relevant provision of the ADEA is similarly silent as to the
heightened direct evidence standard,[8] and the presence of heightened pleading requirements
in other statutes, we hold that direct evidence of discrimination is not necessary to receive
a mixed-motives analysis for an ADEA claim.[10] *Accord Estades-Negroni v. Assoc. Corp. of
N. Am.*, 345 F.3d 25, 31 (1st Cir.2003) (holding that after *Desert Palace* the mixed-motives
analysis applies in ADEA cases even without direct evidence of discrimination); *Strauch v.
Am. College of Surgeons*, 301 F.Supp.2d 839, 844 (N.D.Ill. 2004) ("Given the similarities in text
and purpose between Title VII and ADEA, as well as the consistent trend of transferring the
various proof methods and their accompanying rules from one statute to the other, this Court
considers it likely that whatever doctrinal changes emerge as a result of *Desert Palace* in the
Title VII context will be found equally applicable in the ADEA arena."); *Thompson v. Proviso
Township High Sch. Dist. 209*, No. 01-C-5743, 2003 WL 21638808, at *8 (N.D. Ill. July 10,
2003).

This Court's recent holding in *Smith v. City of Jackson, Miss.*, 351 F.3d 183 (5th Cir. 2003),
cert. granted, 541 U.S. 958, 124 S.Ct. 1724, 158 L.Ed.2d 398 (2004) (No. 03-1160), is not to
the contrary. In *Smith* this Court held that "the ADEA was not intended to remedy age-
disparate effects that arise from the application of employment plans or practices that are
not based on age." 351 F.3d at 187. We based our holding that disparate impact claims are
not cognizable under the ADEA on "the ADEA's express exception permitting employer
conduct based on 'reasonable factors other than age' – an exception absent from Title VII" *Id.*
at 187-88 (quoting 29 U.S.C. §623(f)(1)). Section 623(f)(1) provides that it is not unlawful to
make employment decisions "based on reasonable factors other than age" 29 U.S.C. §623(f)(1)
(emphasis added). Unlike a disparate impact claim, which may stem from neutral employment

[8] In response to *Price Waterhouse v. Hopkins*, 490 U.S. 228, 241, 109 S.Ct. 1775, 104 L.Ed.2d 268 (1989), Title VII
was amended in 1991 specifically "to eliminate the employer's ability to escape liability in Title VII mixed-
motive[s] cases by proving that it would have made the same decision in the absence of the discriminatory
motivation." *Hill v. Lockheed Martin Logistics Mgmt., Inc.*, 354 F.3d 277, 284 (4th Cir.2004); *see* 42 U.S.C.
§2000e-2(m) (providing that "an unlawful employment practice is established when the complaining party
demonstrates that [a prohibited characteristic] was a motivating factor for any employment practice, even
though other factors also motivated the practice"). The ADEA was not similarly amended, and Title VII's
amendment was noted by the Supreme Court in *Desert Palace*. *See Desert Palace*, 123 S.Ct. at 2151. One
circuit court assumed in dictum, without so holding, that this difference in statutory text is significant. *See
Hill v. Lockheed Martin Logistics Mgmt., Inc.*, 354 F.3d 277, 284–85 n. 2 (4th Cir.2004) (assuming in dictum,
without deciding, that *Desert Palace* does not apply to ADEA claims, given the absence from that statute
of an explicit mixed-motives provision like the one found in Title VII). Unlike Title VII which explicitly
permits mixed-motives cases, the ADEA neither countenances nor prohibits the mixed-motives analysis.
Because we base our holding on the absence of a heightened direct evidence requirement in the ADEA,
we do not find the statute's silence on the mixed-motives analysis to be dispositive.

[10] This Court's holding in *Mooney*, 54 F.3d at 1216–17, that direct evidence is required for a mixed-motives
analysis has been overruled by the Supreme Court's interpretation of pleading requirements in *Desert
Palace*.

practices, Rachid's claim contains an allegation that the employment action was based-at least in part-on unlawful animus. Because the discrimination in Rachid's case allegedly occurred because of age, §623(f)(1)'s safe-harbor for decisions based on factors "other than age" is inapposite.[11]

Our holding today that the mixed-motives analysis used in Title VII cases post-*Desert Palace* is equally applicable in ADEA represents a merging of the *McDonnell Douglas* and *Price Waterhouse* approaches. Under this integrated approach, called, for simplicity, the modified *McDonnell Douglas* approach: the plaintiff must still demonstrate a prima facie case of discrimination; the defendant then must articulate a legitimate, non-discriminatory reason for its decision to terminate the plaintiff; and, if the defendant meets its burden of production, "the plaintiff must then offer sufficient evidence to create a genuine issue of material fact 'either (1) that the defendant's reason is not true, but is instead a pretext for discrimination (pretext alternative); or (2) that the defendant's reason, while true, is only one of the reasons for its conduct, and another "motivating factor" is the plaintiff's protected characteristic (mixed-motive[s] alternative).'" *Rishel v. Nationwide Mut. Ins. Co.*, 297 F. Supp.2d 854, 865 (M.D.N.C. 2003) (noting that courts need "only modify the final stage of the *McDonnell Douglas* scheme to accommodate *Desert Palace*, by framing the final stage 'in terms of whether the plaintiff can meet his or her "ultimate burden" to prove intentional discrimination, rather than in terms of whether the plaintiff can prove "pretext"'") (citing and quoting *Dunbar v. Pepsi-Cola Gen. Bottlers of Iowa, Inc.*, 285 F. Supp.2d 1180, 1197-98 (N.D. Iowa 2003)). If a plaintiff demonstrates that age was a motivating factor in the employment decision, it then falls to the defendant to prove "that the same adverse employment decision would have been made regardless of discriminatory animus. If the employer fails to carry this burden, plaintiff prevails." *Mooney*, 54 F.3d at 1217. *Accord Louis*, 303 F.Supp.2d at 801-04 (noting that to defeat a mixed-motives claim once a plaintiff shows that the prohibited characteristic was a motivating factor, the defendant must demonstrate that "it would have taken the same action in the absence of the impermissible motivating factor.").

B. Rachid's Claim.

We now turn to whether Rachid's claim survives summary judgment under the modified *McDonnell Douglas* approach detailed above.

(1) Rachid Established a prima facie case.

JIB essentially concedes that Rachid satisfies the first three factors necessary for a prima facie case. Rachid argues that he demonstrated the fourth factor by showing that: (1) his replacement was five years younger; (2) he long suspected that Powers was going to fire him because of his age and he voiced these concerns to human resources; and (3) Powers made ageist comments to and about Rachid.

The parties spend considerable effort contesting whether an age difference of five years is "significant" or "substantial" under *O'Connor v. Consolidated Coin*, 517 U.S. 308, 313, 116

---

[11] We are focused here on the statutory text concerning "differentiation based on reasonable factors other than age." *See* 29 U.S.C. §623(f)(1). This analysis, of course, does not affect the interpretation of §623(f)(1)'s previous phrase which provides that an employment action based on age is not unlawful "where age is a bona fide occupational qualification reasonably necessary to the normal operation of the particular business." *See id.*

S.Ct. 1307, 134 L.Ed.2d 433 (1996) (holding that merely being replaced by someone outside the protected class is not sufficient to establish a prima facie case; rather, an employee demonstrates an inference of age discrimination when he is replaced by an employee "significantly" younger). While this is a close question, we need not reach it because Rachid's other evidence easily establishes a prima facie case.

Evidence in the record demonstrates that Powers repeatedly made ageist comments to and about Rachid. In his deposition Rachid notes that, prior to his termination, he reported to human resources that Powers was harassing him about his age. Haidar testified that Powers suggested that Rachid's absence from a meeting was due to the fact that "he's probably in bed or he's sleeping by [now] because of his age. . . . " Such evidence of discrimination easily establishes a prime facie case that Rachid was "discharged because of his age." *See Palasota*, 342 F.3d at 576 (quotations omitted).

(2) Material Issues of Fact are Disputed, Making Summary Judgment Inappropriate.
JIB argues that it had a non-discriminatory reason for firing Rachid-i.e., Rachid's failure to follow company policy regarding altering subordinates' time-sheets without documentation. JIB notes that "since 1999, the Company has terminated at least 11 other employees [including some of whom were substantially younger than Rachid] in the same region for violating the Company's time[-]sheet policy."

While violating a non-discriminatory company policy is adequate grounds for termination, two fact issues remain: (1) Rachid claims that Powers's email did not reflect JIB's company policy; and (2) he claims that, based on his understanding of the policy, he did not violate the policy. Rachid also argues that JIB's assertion that other employees were terminated for violating the policy is inapposite here because none of those employees were fired by Powers, nor were any of those employees fired for violating the specific time-card policy stated in Powers's email.

(a) Company policy concerning time-card alterations is unclear.
Rachid claims that "Company Policy said nothing about the Manager signing a P108 Discipline Slip." Though JIB argues that a company policy was violated, it cites to nothing other than Powers's email. Rachid notes that the Employee Handbook only requires that if an employee "do[esn't] agree with [his] hours on the [report at the end of each pay period, he must let his] Manager know immediately."

JIB's argument that other employees were fired for violating a time-card policy does not resolve this issue. JIB issued separation notices to employees discharged for "employees' hours deletions," but none of those notices references failure to complete P108 forms. Additionally, all of those notices assume that employee hours were unlawfully deleted. In the instant case, Rachid claims that he only made lawful deletions (i.e., deletions when employees failed to punch out for breaks). The basis of Rachid's termination by Powers seems to have had less to do with whether the deletions were accurate than with whether Rachid had completed P108 forms when he made the deletions.[13] The fact that some employees were terminated for "employees' hours deletions" does suggest that JIB had a policy on this matter, but it does not address the contours of that policy.

---

[13] Powers fired Rachid immediately after Rachid admitted to making some alterations without completing P108 forms. Powers did not make any investigation to determine whether those deletions were accurate.

Furthermore, the other employees were terminated by other managers, mitigating the relevance of their terminations to the question of whether Powers unlawfully discriminated against Rachid. "This court and others have held that testimony from former employees who had different supervisors than the plaintiff, who worked in different parts of the employer's company, or whose terminations were removed in time from the plaintiff's termination cannot be probative of whether age was a determinative factor in the plaintiff's discharge." *Wyvill v. United Cos. Life Ins. Co.*, 212 F.3d 296, 302 (5th Cir. 2000). JIB does not appear to have produced *any* evidence that other managers were fired by Powers (or by anyone else) merely for failing to complete P108 forms in situations where: (1) those managers altered employee hours; and (2) the employees did not-as required by the Employee Handbook-contest the alterations. Therefore, a genuine issue of material fact exists whether Powers's email describes JIB's company policy.

(b) It is uncertain whether Rachid violated the policy stated in Powers's email.
Powers's email states:

If an employee fails to punch out at the clock they [sic] are to be written up on a P108 [disciplinary form]. NO MANAGER IS TO GO BACK AND DO A PUNCH CHANGE WITHOUT A SIGNED P108 FOR PROOF! The P108 needs to be kept in the employee file. If the employee contests their [sic] hours and there are punch changes without a P108 for back-up documentation, the manager is putting their [sic] job at risk.

Rachid argues that his and Haidar's understanding of Powers's email "was that, if the 'employee contests their [sic] hours' after the Manager made the change, the Manager was to write a P108 form." Haidar testified that he did not think a P108 form was necessary unless an employee disputed changes made to the time-card. According to Rachid's and Haidar's interpretation, a P108 was necessary only if, after an employee was notified of an alteration to his hours, he were still to contest it. Therefore, according to Rachid, he never violated the directive as stated in Powers's email. Of course, whether Rachid violated JIB's policy is a question of fact.

Even if JIB did have a policy (which seems likely), and even if that policy required P108 forms to be filled out in certain circumstances (which is uncertain), a factual question remains as to whether Rachid violated that policy by only completing P108s when an employee contested the alteration.

(c) Summary judgment was improper.
Because issues of material fact are disputed, summary judgment in favor of JIB was unwarranted. This Court's decision in *Bienkowski v. American Airlines* informs the analysis of whether summary judgment was appropriate at this stage. *See Bienkowski v. American Airlines, Inc.*, 851 F.2d 1503, 1506-07 (5th Cir.1988). In *Bienkowski*, this Court faced a similar situation: the parties contested the quality of plaintiff's performance, and the plaintiff alleged that his supervisors made ageist comments. *Id.* Bienkowski alleged that his managers commented that he look "'sharp' if he was [sic] going to look for another job [and] commented on his inability or willingness to 'adapt' to new systems in the department." *Id.* at 1507 n. 4. This Court reversed the district court's grant of summary judgment in favor of the defendant, noting:

Unlike the district court, we are unwilling to assume that indirect comments about his age and adaptability are not possibly probative of an unlawful discriminatory intent, given the parties' sharp disagreements over the operative facts of [plaintiff]'s performance. Moreover, live testimony will assist the necessary credibility choices in this case more effectively than printed affidavits.

Id. at 1507.

Comments to look "sharp" and comments concerning an employee's willingness to "adapt" to new systems are rather nebulous, but they allowed Bienkowski to avoid summary judgment. The alleged ageist comments in the instant case are substantially more egregious. Similarly, in *Palasota*, this Court, in reversing a district court's grant of a judgment as a matter of law, explained, "[a]ge-related remarks 'are appropriately taken into account when analyzing the evidence . . . ,' even where the comment is not in the direct context of the termination and even if uttered by one other than the formal decision maker, provided that the individual is in a position to influence the decision." 342 F.3d at 578 (quoting *Russell v. McKinney Hosp. Venture*, 235 F.3d 219, 229 (5th Cir. 2000)).

In the case *sub judice*, Rachid presents far more evidence of age discrimination than was presented in *Bienkowski*. Rachid testified that Powers made numerous ageist comments-including one situation where Powers allegedly said: "[A]nd don't forget it, [Rachid], you're too old, too"-and Haidar supported Rachid's assertions that Powers continually made such comments. Rachid even spoke with human resources prior to his termination to express his fear that Powers would try to fire him because of his age. Despite JIB's focus on Teal-Guess's investigation and company policy, it was Powers who terminated Rachid, and it was Powers who repeatedly made ageist comments to and about Rachid. Such comments preclude summary judgment because a rational finder of fact could conclude that age played a role in Powers's decision to terminate Rachid.

IV. CONCLUSION

For the forgoing reasons we hold that: *Desert Palace* modifies the *McDonnell Douglas* analysis in ADEA cases such that a plaintiff can proceed on a mixed-motives theory even without direct evidence of discrimination; Rachid established a prima facie case of discrimination; and disputed issues of material fact remain concerning JIB's proffered reason for terminating Rachid and concerning whether age was a factor in that decision. Therefore, the district court's summary judgment is REVERSED, and this case is REMANDED for further proceedings not inconsistent with this opinion.

Notes

1. You may get a sense from the opinion in *Rachid* that most of the U.S. Supreme Court's decisions regarding disparate treatment discrimination have been about the proof structure or analytical scheme used to evaluate claims. That is an accurate description of Supreme Court jurisprudence in this area.
2. You will see an analysis similar to the *McDonnell Douglas* or pretext proof structure under the European Union's Burden of Proof Directive. *See* Chapter 7.
3. As the court discusses in *Rachid*, before the Supreme Court's decision in *Desert Palace, Inc. v. Costa*, disparate treatment cases based on direct evidence were analyzed pursuant to the mixed-motives analysis first articulated in the Supreme Court decision *Price Waterhouse v. Hopkins* and later revised in the Civil Rights Act of 1991 (at least for Title VII cases), whereas disparate treatment cases based on circumstantial evidence were analyzed under the *McDonnell Douglas* or pretext proof

structure. Because the Supreme Court rejected direct/circumstantial evidence as a dividing line in *Desert Palace*, federal courts now are left without guidance on which proof structure applies to a particular disparate treatment case. The Fifth Circuit in *Rachid* resolves this issue by merging the two into a modified *McDonnell Douglas* analysis. Other courts of appeals have not followed this approach. *See, generally,* Michael J. Zimmer, *The New Discrimination Law: Price Waterhouse Is Dead, Whither McDonnell Douglas?*, 53 EMORY L.J. 1887 (2004).

---

c. Harassment and Other Theories of Discrimination

In addition to disparate treatment and disparate impact, other theories of discrimination are harassment based on a protected characteristic and failure to make a reasonable accommodation necessitated by a protected characteristic. Harassment is a recognized theory under all of the characteristics protected by federal employment discrimination law. Most of the principles governing the theory of harassment have developed in the context of sexual harassment, in which the largest number of cases have been litigated. Failure to make a reasonable accommodation is recognized only for religious practices and disability. Harassment is discussed in the *Oncale* case below.

ONCALE V. SUNDOWNER OFFSHORE SERVICES, INC.

523 U.S. 75 (1998)

Justice SCALIA delivered the opinion of the Court.

This case presents the question whether workplace harassment can violate Title VII's prohibition against "discriminat[ion] because of sex," 42 U.S.C. §2000e-2(a)(1), when the harasser and the harassed employee are of the same sex.

I

The District Court having granted summary judgment for respondents, we must assume the facts to be as alleged by petitioner Joseph Oncale. The precise details are irrelevant to the legal point we must decide, and in the interest of both brevity and dignity we shall describe them only generally. In late October 1991, Oncale was working for respondent Sundowner Offshore Services, Inc., on a Chevron U.S.A., Inc., oil platform in the Gulf of Mexico. He was employed as a roustabout on an eight-man crew which included respondents John Lyons, Danny Pippen, and Brandon Johnson. Lyons, the crane operator, and Pippen, the driller, had supervisory authority, App. 41, 77, 43. On several occasions, Oncale was forcibly subjected to sex-related, humiliating actions against him by Lyons, Pippen, and Johnson in the presence of the rest of the crew. Pippen and Lyons also physically assaulted Oncale in a sexual manner, and Lyons threatened him with rape.

Oncale's complaints to supervisory personnel produced no remedial action; in fact, the company's Safety Compliance Clerk, Valent Hohen, told Oncale that Lyons and Pippen "picked [on] him all the time too," and called him a name suggesting homosexuality. *Id.*, at 77. Oncale eventually quit-asking that his pink slip reflect that he "voluntarily left due to sexual harassment and verbal abuse." *Id.*, at 79. When asked at his deposition why he left

Sundowner, Oncale stated: "I felt that if I didn't leave my job, that I would be raped or forced to have sex." *Id.*, at 71.

Oncale filed a complaint against Sundowner in the United States District Court for the Eastern District of Louisiana, alleging that he was discriminated against in his employment because of his sex. Relying on the Fifth Circuit's decision in *Garcia v. Elf Atochem North America*, 28 F.3d 446, 451-452 (1994), the District Court held that "Mr. Oncale, a male, has no cause of action under Title VII for harassment by male co-workers." App. 106. On appeal, a panel of the Fifth Circuit concluded that *Garcia* was binding Circuit precedent, and affirmed. . . . We granted certiorari.

II

Title VII of the Civil Rights Act of 1964 provides, in relevant part, that "[i]t shall be an unlawful employment practice for an employer . . . to discriminate against any individual with respect to his compensation, terms, conditions, or privileges of employment, because of such individual's race, color, religion, sex, or national origin." 78 Stat. 255, as amended, 42 U.S.C. §2000e-2(a)(1). We have held that this not only covers "terms" and "conditions" in the narrow contractual sense, but "evinces a congressional intent to strike at the entire spectrum of disparate treatment of men and women in employment." *Meritor Savings Bank, FSB v. Vinson*, 477 U.S. 57, 64, 106 S.Ct. 2399, 2404, 91 L.Ed.2d 49 (1986) (citations and internal quotation marks omitted). "When the workplace is permeated with discriminatory intimidation, ridicule, and insult that is sufficiently severe or pervasive to alter the conditions of the victim's employment and create an abusive working environment, Title VII is violated." *Harris v. Forklift Systems, Inc.*, 510 U.S. 17, 21, 114 S.Ct. 367, 370, 126 L.Ed.2d 295 (1993) (citations and internal quotation marks omitted).

Title VII's prohibition of discrimination "because of . . . sex" protects men as well as women, *Newport News Shipbuilding & Dry Dock Co. v. EEOC*, 462 U.S. 669, 682, 103 S.Ct. 2622, 2630, 77 L.Ed.2d 89 (1983), and in the related context of racial discrimination in the workplace we have rejected any conclusive presumption that an employer will not discriminate against members of his own race. "Because of the many facets of human motivation, it would be unwise to presume as a matter of law that human beings of one definable group will not discriminate against other members of their group." *Castaneda v. Partida*, 430 U.S. 482, 499, 97 S.Ct. 1272, 1282, 51 L.Ed.2d 498 (1977) . . . , a male employee claimed that his employer discriminated against him because of his sex when it preferred a female employee for promotion. Although we ultimately rejected the claim on other grounds, we did not consider it significant that the supervisor who made that decision was also a man. *See id.*, at 624-625, 107 S.Ct., at 1447-1448. If our precedents leave any doubt on the question, we hold today that nothing in Title VII necessarily bars a claim of discrimination "because of . . . sex" merely because the plaintiff and the defendant (or the person charged with acting on behalf of the defendant) are of the same sex.

Courts have had little trouble with that principle in cases like *Johnson*, where an employee claims to have been passed over for a job or promotion. But when the issue arises in the context of a "hostile environment" sexual harassment claim, the state and federal courts have taken a bewildering variety of stances. Some, like the Fifth Circuit in this case, have held that same-sex sexual harassment claims are never cognizable under Title VII. *See also, e.g., Goluszek v. H.P. Smith*, 697 F.Supp. 1452 (N.D. Ill. 1988). Other decisions say that such claims are actionable only if the plaintiff can prove that the harasser is homosexual (and thus presumably motivated by sexual desire). Compare *McWilliams v. Fairfax County Board of Supervisors*, 72 F.3d 1191 (C.A. 4 1996), with *Wrightson v. Pizza Hut of America*, 99 F.3d 138 (C.A. 4 1996). Still others suggest that workplace harassment that is sexual in content is always actionable, regardless of the harasser's sex, sexual orientation, or motivations. *See Doe v. Belleville*, 119 F.3d 563 (C.A. 7 1997).

We see no justification in the statutory language or our precedents for a categorical rule excluding same-sex harassment claims from the coverage of Title VII. As some courts have observed, male-on-male sexual harassment in the workplace was assuredly not the principal evil Congress was concerned with when it enacted Title VII. But statutory prohibitions often go beyond the principal evil to cover reasonably comparable evils, and it is ultimately the provisions of our laws rather than the principal concerns of our legislators by which we are governed. Title VII prohibits "discriminat[ion] because of sex" in the "terms" or "conditions" of employment. Our holding that this includes sexual harassment must extend to sexual harassment of any kind that meets the statutory requirements.

Respondents and their *amici* contend that recognizing liability for same-sex harassment will transform Title VII into a general civility code for the American workplace. But that risk is no greater for same-sex than for opposite-sex harassment, and is adequately met by careful attention to the requirements of the statute. Title VII does not prohibit all verbal or physical harassment in the workplace; it is directed only at "*discriminat[ion]* because of sex." We have never held that workplace harassment, even harassment between men and women, is automatically discrimination because of sex merely because the words used have sexual content or connotations. "The critical issue, Title VII's text indicates, is whether members of one sex are exposed to disadvantageous terms or conditions of employment to which members of the other sex are not exposed." *Harris, supra*, at 25, 114 S.Ct., at 372 (Ginsburg, J., concurring).

Courts and juries have found the inference of discrimination easy to draw in most male-female sexual harassment situations, because the challenged conduct typically involves explicit or implicit proposals of sexual activity; it is reasonable to assume those proposals would not have been made to someone of the same sex. The same chain of inference would be available to a plaintiff alleging same-sex harassment, if there were credible evidence that the harasser was homosexual. But harassing conduct need not be motivated by sexual desire to support an inference of discrimination on the basis of sex. A trier of fact might reasonably find such discrimination, for example, if a female victim is harassed in such sex-specific and derogatory terms by another woman as to make it clear that the harasser is motivated by general hostility to the presence of women in the workplace. A same-sex harassment plaintiff may also, of course, offer direct comparative evidence about how the alleged harasser treated members of both sexes in a mixed-sex workplace. Whatever evidentiary route the plaintiff chooses to follow, he or she must always prove that the conduct at issue was not merely tinged with offensive sexual connotations, but actually constituted "*discrimina[tion]* because of sex."

And there is another requirement that prevents Title VII from expanding into a general civility code: As we emphasized in *Meritor* and *Harris*, the statute does not reach genuine but innocuous differences in the ways men and women routinely interact with members of the same sex and of the opposite sex. The prohibition of harassment on the basis of sex requires neither asexuality nor androgyny in the workplace; it forbids only behavior so objectively offensive as to alter the "conditions" of the victim's employment. "Conduct that is not severe or pervasive enough to create an objectively hostile or abusive work environment-an environment that a reasonable person would find hostile or abusive-is beyond Title VII's purview." *Harris,*

510 U.S., at 21, 114 S.Ct., at 370, citing *Meritor*, 477 U.S., at 67, 106 S.Ct., at 2405-2406. We have always regarded that requirement as crucial, and as sufficient to ensure that courts and juries do not mistake ordinary socializing in the workplace-such as male-on-male horseplay or intersexual flirtation-for discriminatory "conditions of employment."

We have emphasized, moreover, that the objective severity of harassment should be judged from the perspective of a reasonable person in the plaintiff's position, considering "all the circumstances." *Harris, supra*, at 23, 114 S.Ct., at 371. In same-sex (as in all) harassment cases, that inquiry requires careful consideration of the social context in which particular behavior occurs and is experienced by its target. A professional football player's working environment is not severely or pervasively abusive, for example, if the coach smacks him on the buttocks as he heads onto the field-even if the same behavior would reasonably be experienced as abusive by the coach's secretary (male or female) back at the office. The real social impact of workplace behavior often depends on a constellation of surrounding circumstances, expectations, and relationships which are not fully captured by a simple recitation of the words used or the physical acts performed. Common sense, and an appropriate sensitivity to social context, will enable courts and juries to distinguish between simple teasing or roughhousing among members of the same sex, and conduct which a reasonable person in the plaintiff's position would find severely hostile or abusive.

III

Because we conclude that sex discrimination consisting of same-sex sexual harassment is actionable under Title VII, the judgment of the Court of Appeals for the Fifth Circuit is reversed, and the case is remanded for further proceedings consistent with this opinion.
It is so ordered.

Justice THOMAS, concurring.

I concur because the Court stresses that in every sexual harassment case, the plaintiff must plead and ultimately prove Title VII's statutory requirement that there be discrimination "because of sex."

Notes

1. The *Oncale* decision explores what it means for harassment to be "because of sex." Why is this a more difficult issue when the alleged harassment is perpetrated by a person who is of the same sex as the alleged victim? The issue of proof of discrimination requiring proof of different treatment and identifying a similarly situated comparator to make this proof is a recurring theme in employment discrimination law. You will see this issue again in the chapter on the United Kingdom, Chapter 8 *infra*.

2. Sexual harassment claims fall into two general categories. Cases involving tangible employment actions taken against an employee who refuses to submit to a supervisor's sexual demands are commonly referred to as *quid pro quo* cases. Where a tangible employment action, such as a termination or demotion, is not involved, the harassment case is litigated using the hostile environment theory. The latter theory requires a plaintiff to establish: (1) subjectively unwelcome conduct; (2) based on sex or gender; (3) severe or pervasive enough to alter employment conditions and create an environment a reasonable person would consider hostile; and (4) a basis

for imputing employer liability. *See Matvia v. Bald Head Island Management, Inc.,* 259 F.3d 261 (2001). *Oncale* is a hostile environment case.

3. In cases involving harassment by a supervisor, where a tangible employment action is taken against the harassed employee, the basis for holding the employer liable is that the action itself is an official act of the employer. *Burlington Industries, Inc. v. Ellerth,* 524 U.S. 742 (1998). Hostile environment cases involving supervisors in which no tangible employment action is taken against the victim, however, permit the employer to raise an affirmative defense comprised of two elements to be proven by the employer: "(a) that the employer exercised reasonable care to prevent and correct promptly any sexually harassing behavior, and (b) that the plaintiff employee unreasonably failed to take advantage of any preventive or corrective opportunities provided by the employer or to avoid harm otherwise." *Id.* at 765.

4. Sexual harassment law has had a profound effect in American workplaces. The vast majority of U.S. employers have adopted anti-harassment policies and specialized sexual harassment grievance procedures. Some have embraced zero tolerance policies that prohibit any sexualized commentary and punish severely any policy violations. Workplace "no dating" policies are not uncommon. Professor Vicki Schultz argues that employers' emphasis on purging the workplace of sexuality has harmed both men and women workers alike, and eclipsed a pressing need for women to achieve economic parity with men. Vicki Schultz, *The Sanitized Workplace,* 112 YALE L.J. 2061 (2003).

5. The *Ellerth* affirmative defense described above in note 3 also has its critics. The prevention portion of the first prong, in many cases, is easily satisfied by promulgating and disseminating a harassment policy and grievance procedure. Courts seem unconcerned about whether these common structures actually function effectively. Joanna L. Grossman, *The Culture of Compliance: The Final Triumph of Form Over Substance in Sexual Harassment Law,* 26 HARV. WOMEN'S L.J. 3 (2003); Martha S. West, *Preventing Sexual Harassment: The Federal Courts' Wake-Up Call for Women,* 68 BROOK. L. REV. 457 (2002). Courts are also relatively unforgiving of plaintiffs who fail to make use of available grievance procedures, even in cases where fear of retaliation appears reasonable. THERESA M. BEINER, GENDER MYTHS V. WORKING REALITIES: USING SOCIAL SCIENCE TO REFORMULATE SEXUAL HARASSMENT LAW (New York University Press, 2005).

6. Many U.S. employers also provide their employees with sexual harassment training. The courts tend to look favorably upon such efforts – training is relevant to the issue of whether punitive damages are warranted – even though little is known about how, when and if such programs actually work. Susan Bisom-Rapp, *An Ounce of Prevention is a Poor Substitute for a Pound of Cure: Confronting the Developing Jurisprudence of Education and Prevention in Employment Discrimination Law,* 22 BERKELEY J. EMP. & LAB. L. 1 (2001); Kimberly D. Krawiec, *Cosmetic Compliance and the Failure of Negotiated Governance,* 81 WASH. U. L.Q 487 (2003).

7. How important are civility, dignity, and respect in U.S. labor law, and how are they manifested in the law? Consider this in the context of terminations, discrimination and harassment, and invasions of privacy, discussed *infra. See* Anita Bernstein, *Treating Sexual Harassment With Respect,* 111 HARV. L. REV. 446 (1997); Rosa Ehrenreich, *Dignity and Discrimination: Toward a Pluralistic Understanding of Workplace Harassment,* 88 GEO. L.J. 1 (1999).

F. PRIVACY

LUEDTKE V. NABORS ALASKA DRILLING, INC.,

768 P. 2d 1123 (Alaska Sup. Ct.,1989).

COMPTON, Justice.

This case addresses one aspect of drug testing by employers. A private employer, Nabors Alaska Drilling, Inc. (Nabors), established a drug testing program for its employees. Two Nabors employees, Clarence Luedtke and Paul Luedtke, both of whom worked on drilling rigs on the North Slope, refused to submit to urinalysis screening for drug use as required by Nabors. As a result they were fired by Nabors. The Luedtkes challenge their discharge on the following grounds:

1. Nabors' drug testing program violates the Luedtkes' right to privacy guaranteed by article I, section 22 of the Alaska Constitution;

2. Nabors' demands violate the covenant of good faith and fair dealing implicit in all employment contracts;

3. Nabors' urinalysis requirement violates the public interest in personal privacy, giving the Luedtkes a cause of action for wrongful discharge; and

4. Nabors' actions give rise to a cause of action under the common law tort of invasion of privacy.

Nabors argues that the Luedtkes were "at will" employees whose employment relationship could be terminated at any time for any reason. Alternatively, even if termination had to be based on "just cause," such cause existed because the Luedtkes violated established company policy relating to employee safety by refusing to take the scheduled tests.

This case raises issues of first impression in Alaska law including: whether the constitutional right of privacy applies to private parties; some parameters of the tort of wrongful discharge; and the extent to which certain employee drug testing by private employers can be controlled by courts.

I. FACTUAL AND PROCEDURAL BACKGROUND

The Luedtkes' cases proceeded separately to judgment. Because they raised common legal issues, on Nabors' motion they were consolidated on appeal.

A. Paul's Case.

1. *Factual Background.*

Paul began working for Nabors, which operates drilling rigs on Alaska's North Slope, in February 1978. He began as a temporary employee, replacing a permanent employee on vacation for two weeks. During his two weeks of temporary work, a permanent position opened up on the rig on which he was working and he was hired to fill it. Paul began as a "floorman" and was eventually promoted to "driller." A driller oversees the work of an entire drilling crew.

Paul started work with Nabors as a union member, initially being hired from the union hall. During his tenure, however, Nabors "broke" the union. Paul continued to work without a union contract. Paul had no written contract with Nabors at the time of his discharge.

During his employment with Nabors, Paul was accused twice of violating the company's drug and alcohol policies. Once he was suspended for 90 days for taking alcohol to the North Slope. The other incident involved a search of the rig on which Paul worked. Aided by dogs trained to sniff out marijuana, the searchers found traces of marijuana on Paul's suitcase. Paul was allowed to continue working on the rig only after assuring his supervisors he did not use marijuana.

In October 1982, Paul scheduled a two-week vacation. Because his normal work schedule was two weeks of work on the North Slope followed by a week off, a two-week vacation amounted to 28 consecutive days away from work. Just prior to his vacation, Paul was instructed to arrange for a physical examination in Anchorage. He arranged for it to take place on October 19, during his vacation. It was at this examination that Nabors first tested Paul's urine for signs of drug use. The purpose of the physical, as understood by Paul, was to enable him to work on offshore rigs should Nabors receive such contracts. Although Paul was told it would be a comprehensive physical he had no idea that a urinalysis screening test for drug use would be performed. He did voluntarily give a urine sample but assumed it would be tested only for "blood sugar, any kind of kidney failure [and] problems with bleeding." Nabors' policy of testing for drug use was not announced until November 1, 1982, almost two weeks after Paul's examination.

In early November 1982, Paul contacted Nabors regarding his flight to the North Slope to return to work. He was told at that time to report to the Nabors office in Anchorage. On November 5, Paul reported to the office where a Nabors representative informed him that he was suspended for "the use of alcohol or other illicit substances." No other information was forthcoming from Nabors until November 16 when Paul received a letter informing him that his urine had tested positive for cannabinoids. The letter informed him that he would be required to pass two subsequent urinalysis tests, one on November 30 and the other on December 30, before he would be allowed to return to work. In response Paul hand delivered a letter drafted by his attorney to the Manager of Employee Relations for Nabors, explaining why he felt the testing and suspension were unfair. Paul did not take the urinalysis test on November 30 as requested by Nabors. On December 14, Nabors sent Paul a letter informing him he was discharged for refusing to take the November 30 test.

· · ·

II. DISCUSSION

A. The Right to Privacy.

The right to privacy is a recent creation of American law. The inception of this right is generally credited to a law review article published in 1890 by Louis Brandeis and his law partner, Samuel Warren. Brandeis & Warren, *The Right to Privacy*, 4 Harv.L.Rev. 193 (1890). Brandeis and Warren observed that in a modern world with increasing population density and advancing technology, the number and types of matters theretofore easily concealed from public purview were rapidly decreasing. They wrote:

> Recent inventions and business methods call attention to the next step which must be taken for the protection of the person, and for securing to the individual what Judge Cooley calls the right "to be let alone." Instantaneous photographs and newspaper

enterprise have invaded the sacred precincts of private and domestic life; and numerous mechanical devices threaten to make good the prediction that "what is whispered in the closet shall be proclaimed from the housetops.

Id. at 195 (footnotes omitted).

Discussing the few precedential cases in tort law in which courts had afforded remedies for the publication of private letters or unauthorized photographs, Brandeis and Warren drew a common thread they called "privacy." They defined this right as the principle of "inviolate personality." *Id.* at 205.

While the legal grounds of this right were somewhat tenuous in the 1890's, American jurists found the logic of Brandeis and Warren's arguments compelling. The reporters of the first Restatement of Torts included a tort entitled "Interference with Privacy." By 1960, Professor Prosser could write that "the right of privacy, in one form or another, is declared to exist by the overwhelming majority of the American courts." Prosser, *Privacy*, 48 Calif.L.Rev. 383, 386 (1960). He cited cases in which private parties had been held liable in tort for eavesdropping on private conversations by means of wiretapping and microphones, or for peering into the windows of homes. *Id.* at 390. In addition, while Brandeis and Warren were mainly concerned with the publication of private facts, Professor Prosser identified four different manifestations of the right to privacy: intrusion upon the plaintiff's seclusion; public disclosure of embarrassing private facts; publicity which places the plaintiff in a false light; and appropriation, for the defendant's pecuniary advantage, of the plaintiff's name or likeness. *Id.* at 389. Professor Prosser's categories form the framework of the expanded tort of invasion of privacy found in the Restatement (Second) of Torts.

Eventually the right to privacy attained sufficient recognition to be incorporated in several state constitutions. *See* Alaska Const. art. I, §22 (adopted 1972); Cal. Const. art. I, §1 (adopted 1972); Haw. Const. art. 1, §6 (adopted 1978); Mont. Const. art. II, §10 (adopted 1972).

Interpreting the Constitution of the United States, the United States Supreme Court in 1965 held that a Connecticut statute banning the use of birth control devices by married couples was "repulsive to the notions of privacy surrounding the marriage relationship." *Griswold v. Connecticut*, 381 U.S. 479, 486, 85 S.Ct. 1678, 1682, 14 L.Ed.2d 510, 516 (1965). The Supreme Court wrote that "specific guarantees in the Bill of Rights have penumbras, formed by emanations from those guarantees that help give them life and substance. Various guarantees create zones of privacy." 381 U.S. at 484, 85 S.Ct. at 1681, 14 L.Ed.2d at 514 (citations omitted). Justice Goldberg's concurrence suggested that the right of marital privacy was fundamental to the concept of liberty. *See* 381 U.S. at 486, 85 S.Ct. at 1682, 14 L.Ed.2d at 516 (Goldberg, J., concurring). Since *Griswold* the Supreme Court has found the federal constitutional right of privacy to apply to a number of other situations. *See Cleveland Bd. of Educ. v. La Fleur*, 414 U.S. 632, 640, 94 S.Ct. 791, 796, 39 L.Ed.2d 52, 60 (1974) (maternity leave regulations struck down for "penaliz[ing] the pregnant teacher for deciding to bear a child."); *Roe v. Wade*, 410 U.S. 113, 93 S.Ct. 705, 35 L.Ed.2d 147 (1973) (right of privacy broad enough to encompass a woman's decision whether or not to terminate her pregnancy); *Eisenstadt v. Baird*, 405 U.S. 438, 92 S.Ct. 1029, 31 L.Ed.2d 349 (1972) (regulation which made contraceptives less available to unmarried than married couples invalidated). *But see Bowers v. Hardwick*, 478 U.S. 186, 106 S.Ct. 2841, 92 L.Ed.2d 140 (1986) (due process clause of Fourteenth Amendment does not confer any fundamental right on homosexuals to engage in acts of consensual sodomy).

Thus, the concept of privacy has become pervasive in modern legal thought. But a clear definition of this right, so fundamental to ordered liberty, has eluded both courts and legal scholars. It is the fundamental nature of the concept that leads to such great difficulty in application. . . .

. . .

In this case the plaintiffs seek to fit their cases within at least one of four legal frameworks in which the right to privacy has found expression: constitutional law, contract law, tort law, and the emerging mixture of theories known as the public policy exception to the at-will doctrine of employment law.

B. The Right to Privacy Under the Alaska Constitution.

The Alaska Constitution was amended in 1972 to add the following section:

> *Right of Privacy.* The right of the people to privacy is recognized and shall not be infringed. The legislature shall implement this section.

Alaska Const. art. I, §22. We observe initially that this provision, powerful as a constitutional statement of citizens' rights, contains no guidelines for its application. Nor does it appear that the legislature has exercised its power to apply the provision; the parties did not bring to our attention any statutes which "implement this section."

The Luedtkes argue that this court has never clearly answered the question of whether article I, section 22 applies only to state action or whether it also governs private action. The Luedtkes urge this court to hold that section 22 governs private action.

. . .

The parties in the case at bar have failed to produce evidence that Alaska's constitutional right to privacy was intended to operate as a bar to private action, here Nabors' drug testing program. Absent a history demonstrating that the amendment was intended to proscribe private action, or a proscription of private action in the language of the amendment itself, we decline to extend the constitutional right to privacy to the actions of private parties.

C. Wrongful Termination.

In *Mitford v. de LaSala*, 666 P.2d 1000, 1007 (Alaska 1983), this court held that at-will employment contracts in Alaska contain an implied covenant of good faith and fair dealing. In *Knight v. American Guard & Alert, Inc.*, 714 P.2d 788 (Alaska 1986), we acknowledged that violation of a public policy could constitute a breach of that implied covenant. We wrote:

> The [plaintiff's] claim, concerning alleged termination in violation of public policy, is in accord with a theory of recovery accepted in many states. We have never rejected the public policy theory. Indeed, it seems that the public policy approach is largely encompassed within the implied covenant of good faith and fair dealing which we accepted in *Mitford*.

Knight, 714 P.2d at 792 (citations omitted). We conclude that there is a public policy supporting the protection of employee privacy. Violation of that policy by an employer may rise to the level of a breach of the implied covenant of good faith and fair dealing. However, the competing public concern for employee safety present in the case at bar leads us to hold that Nabors' actions did not breach the implied covenant.

1. *The Luedtkes Were At-Will Employees.*

First, we address the Luedtkes' arguments that they were not at-will employees, but rather that they could be fired only for good cause. The key difference between these two types of employment is whether the employment contract is for a determinable length of time. Employees hired on an at-will basis can be fired for any reason that does not violate the implied covenant of good faith and fair dealing. However, employees hired for a specific term may not be discharged before the expiration of the term except for good cause. Neither of the Luedtkes had any formal agreements for a specified term, so any such term, if it existed, must be implied . . .

. . .

2. *There Is a Public Policy Supporting Employee Privacy.*

The next question we address is whether a public policy exists protecting an employee's right to withhold certain "private" information from his employer. We believe such a policy does exist, and is evidenced in the common law, statutes and constitution of this state.

. . .

. . . [T]he citizens' right to be protected against unwarranted intrusions into their private lives has been recognized in the law of Alaska. The constitution protects against governmental intrusion, statutes protect against employer intrusion, and the common law protects against intrusions by other private persons. As a result, there is sufficient evidence to support the conclusion that there exists a public policy protecting spheres of employee conduct into which employers may not intrude. The question then becomes whether employer monitoring of employee drug use outside the work place is such a prohibited intrusion.

3. *The Public Policy Supporting Employee Privacy Must Be Balanced Against the Public Policy Supporting Health and Safety.*

Since the recent advent of inexpensive urine tests for illicit drugs, most litigation regarding the use of these tests in the employment context has concerned government employees. The testing has been challenged under the proscriptions of federal fourth amendment search and seizure law. This body of law regulates only governmental activity, and as a result is of limited value to the case at bar, which involves private activity. However, the reasoning of the federal courts regarding the intrusiveness of urine testing can illuminate this court's consideration of the extent to which personal privacy is violated by these tests. . . .

The . . . analysis is analogous to the analysis that should be followed in cases construing the public policy exception to the at-will employment doctrine. That is, there is a sphere of activity in every person's life that is closed to scrutiny by others. The boundaries of that sphere are determined by balancing a person's right to privacy against other public policies, such as "the health, safety, rights and privileges of others." . . .

The Luedtkes claim that whether or not they use marijuana is information within that protected sphere into which their employer, Nabors, may not intrude. We disagree. As we have previously observed, marijuana can impair a person's ability to function normally. . . .

We also observe that work on an oil rig can be very dangerous. We have determined numerous cases involving serious injury or death resulting from accidents on oil drilling rigs. In addition, in Paul's case the trial court expressly considered the dangers of work on oil rigs. . . .

Where the public policy supporting the Luedtkes privacy in off-duty activities conflicts with the public policy supporting the protection of the health and safety of other workers, and even the Luedtkes themselves, the health and safety concerns are paramount. As a result, Nabors is justified in determining whether the Luedtkes are possibly impaired on the job by drug usage off the job.

We observe, however, that the employer's prerogative does have limitations.

First, the drug test must be conducted at a time reasonably contemporaneous with the employee's work time. The employer's interest is in monitoring drug use that may directly affect employee performance. The employer's interest is not in the broader police function of discovering and controlling the use of illicit drugs in general society. In the context of this case, Nabors could have tested the Luedtkes immediately prior to their departure for the North Slope, or immediately upon their return from the North Slope when the test could be reasonably certain of detecting drugs consumed there. Further, given Nabors' need to control the oil rig community, Nabors could have tested the Luedtkes at any time they were on the North Slope.

Second, an employee must receive notice of the adoption of a drug testing program. By requiring a test, an employer introduces an additional term of employment. An employee should have notice of the additional term so that he may contest it, refuse to accept it and quit, seek to negotiate its conditions, or prepare for the test so that he will not fail it and thereby suffer sanctions.

. . .

D. Common Law Right to Privacy Claims.

We recognize that "[t]he [common law] right to be free from harassment and constant intrusion into one's daily affairs is enjoyed by all persons. . . . As previously discussed, that law is delineated in the Restatement (Second) of Torts §652B, entitled Intrusion upon Seclusion. That section provides: "One who intentionally intrudes . . . upon the solitude or seclusion of another or his private affairs or concerns, is subject to liability . . . if the intrusion would be highly offensive to a reasonable person."

It is true, as the Luedtkes contend, that publication of the facts obtained is not necessary. Instead, the liability is for the offensive intrusion. *See Dietemann v. Time, Inc.*, 449 F.2d 245, 247–48 (9th Cir.1971). However, courts have construed "offensive intrusion" to require either an unreasonable manner of intrusion, or intrusion for an unwarranted purpose. *See Sistok v. Northwestern Tel. Sys., Inc.*, 189 Mont. 82, 615 P.2d 176, 182 (1980) (surreptitious recording of telephone conversations may be unreasonable); *Froelich v. Werbin*, 219 Kan. 461, 548 P.2d 482, 485 (1976) (hair sample taken from hospital trash not invasion of privacy); *Senogles v. Security Benefit Life Ins. Co.*, 217 Kan. 438, 536 P.2d 1358, 1362-63 (1975) (transmission of plaintiff's medical records to life insurance company justified); *McLain v. Boise Cascade Corp.*, 271 Or. 549, 533 P.2d 343, 345-46 (1975) (surveillance of workers' compensation claimant by filming his activities outside his home does not give rise to invasion of privacy claim). Paul has failed to show either that the manner or reason for testing his urine was unreasonable. During his physical, he voluntarily gave a urine sample for the purpose of testing. Therefore, he cannot complain that urine testing is "highly offensive." *Compare Dietemann*, 449 F.2d at 246 (plaintiff did not know he was being filmed) *with Sistok*, 615 P.2d at 178 (recording of conversation was unknown to plaintiff). Paul can only complain about the purpose of the urine test, that is, to detect drug usage. However, we have held, *supra*, that Nabors was entitled to test its employees for drug usage. As a result, the intrusion was not unwarranted. Paul complains additionally that he was not aware his urine would be tested for drug usage. In this regard we observe that Paul was not aware of any of the tests being performed on his urine sample. Nor did he know the ramifications of those tests. But he did know that whatever the results were they would be reported to Nabors. Therefore, his complaint about a particular test is without merit. We conclude that for these reasons Paul could not maintain an action for invasion of privacy with regard to the urinalysis conducted October 19.

As to the urinalyses Paul and Clarence refused to take, we hold that no cause of action for invasion of privacy arises where the intrusion is prevented from taking place. *See Gretencord v. Ford Motor Co.*, 538 F.Supp. 331, 333 (D.Kan. 1982) (no intrusion took place where employee refused to allow security guards to search vehicle.).

. . .

IV. CONCLUSION

For the reasons expressed above, the decision of the trial court in the case of *Paul M. Luedtke v. Nabors Alaska Drilling, Inc.* is AFFIRMED in part and REVERSED in part. The case is REMANDED to the trial court to determine whether Nabors breached the implied covenant of good faith and fair dealing in regard to Paul's suspension. The attorney's fee award must also be reconsidered by the trial court, consistent with this disposition.

For the reasons expressed above, the decision of the trial court in the case of *Clarence G. Luedtke v. Nabors Alaska Drilling, Inc.* is AFFIRMED.

Notes

1. The *Luedtke* case demonstrates the diffuse law in the United States on workplace privacy. Public (governmental) employees may sue for violations of rights of privacy found in the federal or state constitutions. However, the case law interpreting the federal constitution and most state constitutions requires state action, thus excluding claims against private (nongovernmental) employers.
2. Consider the claims brought by the Luedtkes. Their claims are principally common law tort claims.
3. Privacy is a very broad topic, which can include, for example, the following: video and audio surveillance; computer, e-mail, and Internet monitoring; drug testing; psychological testing; controlling nonworking time and activities; administering lie detector tests; and probing into personal and confidential information.
4. There are federal laws on privacy issues. For example, the Employee Polygraph Protection Act so severely circumscribes employers' use of lie detector tests and information obtained from their administration that employers are well advised not to give or rely on polygraphs and other lie detectors. See, for example, the so-called federal Wiretapping Act of the Omnibus Crime Control and Safe Streets Act of 1968, which restricts the interception of telephone calls and other communications, but it is limited in its application, and it has significant exceptions.
5. There are numerous state statutes that involve privacy issues. For example, New York, Colorado, and some other states have laws that prohibit employers from taking adverse actions against employees for engaging in lawful off-duty activities. Michigan passed a law in 2005 that requires employers to guarantee the confidentiality of employees' social security numbers. *See Michigan Law Battling Identity Theft Shields Social Security Numbers in the Workplace*, DAILY L. REP. (BNA) No. 129, at C-1 (July 7, 2005).
6. Surveys in the United States indicate that many employers engage in monitoring of employees' computers, e-mails, and Internet usage. Employers are concerned

principally with potential liability (such as if an employee sends a defamatory e-mail) and employees' disclosure of trade secrets and other confidential information. There is little law, either case law or statutes, in the United States prohibiting or regulating such electronic monitoring. In contrast, the European Union and some other nations do regulate electronic monitoring. What problems does this pose for U.S.-based employers with worksites in nations that regulate electronic monitoring?

———————————

4 Canada

A. INTRODUCTION

By agreeing to form the Dominion of Canada, the provinces of Ontario, Quebec, Nova Scotia, and New Brunswick created the nation of Canada on July 1, 1867, even though it remained tied to England. Over time the Confederation expanded so that it now is made up of ten provinces, each with its own legislature, and three northern territories administered by the federal government. In terms of landmass, Canada is the second largest country in the world but it has a population of only about thirty million. The francophone population comprises about 24 percent of the population but is concentrated in Quebec, which was the original French colonial settlement. In the balance of the country, United Kingdom ancestries predominate, although there has been much immigration from elsewhere. Indigenous peoples live in some concentration in the three northern territories. A member of the G8 and the OECD, Canada has the seventh largest economy in the developed world. While importing 25 percent of its GNP, Canada exports about 33 percent (whereas the United States exports only about 8 percent of its gross national product and the OECD average is about 23 percent). The United States accounts for about 75 percent of the exports from Canada. From 1985 to 2002, trade between the two countries has more than doubled. Eric Tucker, *"Great Expectations" Defeated?: The Trajectory of Collective Bargaining Regimes in Canada and the United States Post-NAFTA*, 26 Comp. Labor Law & Pol'y J 97 (2004) (hereafter, *Great Expectations*. See also, Gregg J. Bamber, Russell D. Lansbury & Nick Wailes, International and Comparative Employment Relations: Globalisation and the Developed Market Economies (4th ed. 2004) (hereinafter International & Comparative Employment Relations) 94. As of April 15, 2006, unemployment was at 6.4 percent, near a thirty-year low; http://www.statcan.ca/english/freepub/71-001-XIE/2006004/bfront1.htm.

Until 1982, Canada remained a colony of the United Kingdom, although in the modern era the United Kingdom ruled Canada in name only. With the passage in 1982 by the British House of Commons of the Canada Act, the present Constitution of Canada

Thanks to Roy L. Heenan and Audrey Best-Bouchard of the Heenan Blaikie firm in Montreal for their help with this chapter.

came into effect though most Canadians view the original British North American Act of 1867 as the nation's original Constitution. Although independent of the United Kingdom, Canada still accepts the monarchy, with the queen appointing the Canadian Governor General, on the advice of the Canadian Prime Minister. The Governor General performs the ceremonial functions the Queen performs for the United Kingdom. The government is a parliamentary system, both at the national and provincial levels.

At the national level, the locus of governmental power is in the House of Commons, made up of 301 seats for representatives from electoral districts across the country. The prime minister is the leader of the political party that holds a majority of seats in the House of Commons or of the lead party in a coalition if no one party holds a majority. The prime minister picks the cabinet ministers from among members of the House of Commons. There is a Senate, but it exercises little real influence over legislation. The political structure of the provinces is similar to the federal one, with an elected legislature. The leader of the party that forms the government is the premier, who appoints the cabinet ministers.

The Liberal and Conservative parties dominated the federal parliamentary process, with the Liberal Party generally forming the government. The 1993 election decimated the Conservatives nationally and the New Democratic Party with which the Canadian Labour Congress is affiliated also lost much of its support in Parliament. Since 1993, new regional parties, the Bloc Quebecois, and in the west the very conservative Canadian Alliance, have made their presence felt at the national level. Thus, there has been a splintering of support so that the government in power tends to be a coalition. *Id.* at 93. Since World War II, three major national political crises turned on government attempts to limit spending to reduce inflation by imposing wage controls that interfered with free collective bargaining by union and management. Donald D. Carter, Geoffrey England, Brian Etherington & Gilles Trudeau, Labour Law in Canada (5th ed. 2002) (hereinafter Labour Law in Canada) at 34.

The Supreme Court of Canada, consisting of nine Justices including the Chief Justice of Canada, is the court of final appeal for the entire country. Although selected by the prime minister, there is no confirmation process but it is the product of extensive consultation; it has not been politicized. The Court hears cases for which it grants a leave to appeal. Each province has its own court system, with discretionary appeals ultimately going from the highest provincial court to the Supreme Court of Canada. "Thus, the Supreme Court of Canada has the final word in all common or civil law controversies, in the interpretation of all federal and provincial statutes, and in the adjudication of constitutional disputes." *Id.* at 37.

The legal background of Canada includes the English-based common law as well as the French-based civil law. Because of the distinct French and English cultures that exist, strong regional and even separatist drives continue to be a challenge for the national unity of Canada. *Id.* at 31.

Unlike England but like the United States, Canada is a federal system. But federalism operates much differently in Canada than in the United States. While early collective bargaining legislation was adopted by the federal government, in 1925 the United Kingdom Privy Council, which was the highest court of appeals for Canada at the time, decided a case, Toronto Electric Commissioners v. Snider, [1925] 2 D.L.R. 5, A.C. 396,

1 W.W.R. 785 (U.K.P.C.), that established the priority of provincial, rather than federal, jurisdiction over most labor and employment matters. In striking down the federal Industrial Disputes Investigation Act, the Privy Council decided that, in absence of a national emergency or an industry of national importance, the federal government lacked jurisdiction to regulate the employment relationship. Section 91 of the Constitution Act grants exclusive powers to the federal parliament, whereas Section 92 does the same for the provinces. Section 2 of the Canadian Labour Code sets forth the limited areas of exclusive federal regulation of employment including navigation and shipping, railways, canals and telegraphs, air transportation, radio broadcasting, bands and "work . . . declared by Parliament to be for the general advantage of Canada. . . . " Industries analogous to those listed, for example, interprovincial trucking, television, telecommunications and nuclear energy, are all within exclusive federal jurisdiction. All other industries continue to be regulated exclusively by the provinces or the territorial governments because employment, as the Privy Council declared in *Toronto Electric*, involves "property and civil rights." About 10 percent of the nation's workforce is covered by federal legislation, with the other 90 percent within the jurisdiction of the provinces. COMMISSION FOR LABOR COOPERATION, LABOR RELATIONS LAW IN NORTH AMERICA 33 (2000)(hereinafter NORTH AMERICA LABOR LAW). "Because labor law in Canada is provincial rather than national, it has been more sensitive to sub-national swings in political strength and labor law reform has been more volatile. Conservative governments have taken steps to 'Americanize' labor laws . . . but NPD and most Liberal governments have resisted that pressure and, indeed, have often pass legislation that moderately strengthened the private sector collective bargaining regime." *Great Expectations*, at 149.

The Canadian Charter of Rights and Freedoms, which is Schedule B to the Constitution Act, serves as the basis for well developed individual rights. The Charter binds all levels of government but does not apply to private parties. Section 2 of the Charter provides that, "Everyone has the following fundamental freedoms: (a) freedom of conscience and religion; (b) freedom of thought, belief, opinion and expression, including freedom of the press and other media of communication; (c) freedom of peaceful assembly; and (d) freedom of association." Section 1, however, provides a basis for limiting the guaranteed freedoms. "The *Canadian Charter of Rights and Freedoms* guarantees the rights and freedoms set out in it subject only to such reasonable limits prescribed by law as can be demonstrably justified in a free and democratic society." See generally, I. INTERNATIONAL LABOR & EMPLOYMENT LAWS (William L. Keller & Timothy J. Darby eds., 2d ed. 2003) (hereinafter INTERNATIONAL LABOR & EMPLOYMENT LAW) and DOUGLAS G. GILBERT, BRIAN W. BURKETT & MOIRA K. MCCASKILL, CANADIAN LABOUR AND EMPLOYMENT LAW FOR THE U.S. PRACTITIONER (2000) (hereinafter CANADIAN LABOR & EMPLOYMENT LAW). There is, however, no constitutional right to strike. In *General Motors of Canada Ltd. V. C.A.W. – Canada*, 31 C.L.R.B.R. (2d) 161 (1996), the Ontario labor board said. "There is no fundamental or constitutionally protected 'right to strike' in Canada. On the contrary, in a series of cases over the last few years, the Courts have consistently affirmed that elected legislatures have considerable latitude to regulate or prohibit industrial conflict – in effect balancing completing claims in the economic area so as to accommodate the commercial and community interest in industrial peace."

B. INDIVIDUAL EMPLOYMENT LAW

WALLACE *v.* UNITED GRAIN GROWERS LTD.

[1997] 3 S.C.R. 701

IACOBUCCI J

1. Facts

In 1972, Public Press, a wholly owned subsidiary of the respondent, United Grain Growers Ltd. ("UGG"), decided to update its operations and seek a larger volume of commercial printing work. Don Logan was the marketing manager of the company's publishing and printing divisions at that time. For Logan, the key to achieving this increase in volume was to hire someone with an existing record of sales on a specialized piece of equipment known as a "Web" press.

In April 1972, the appellant, Jack Wallace, met Logan to discuss the possibility of employment. Wallace had the type of experience that Logan sought, having worked approximately 25 years for a competitor that used the "Web" press. Wallace had become concerned over the unfair manner in which he and others were being treated by their employer. However, he expressed some reservation about jeopardizing his secure position at the company. Wallace explained to Logan that as he was 45 years of age, if he were to leave his current employer he would require a guarantee of job security. He also sought several assurances from Logan regarding fair treatment and remuneration. He received such assurances and was told by Logan that if he performed as expected, he could continue to work for Public Press until retirement.

Wallace commenced employment with Public Press in June of 1972. He enjoyed great success at the company and was the top salesperson for each of the years he spent in its employ.

On August 22, 1986, Wallace was summarily discharged by Public Press's sales manager Leonard Domerecki. Domerecki offered no explanation for his actions. In the days before the dismissal both Domerecki and UGG's general manager had complimented Wallace on his work.

By letter of August 29, 1986, Domerecki advised Wallace that the main reason for his termination was his inability to perform his duties satisfactorily. Wallace's statement of claim alleging wrongful dismissal was issued on October 23, 1986. In its statement of defence, the respondent alleged that Wallace had been dismissed for cause. This allegation was maintained for over two years and was only withdrawn when the trial commenced on December 12, 1988.

At the time of his dismissal Wallace was almost 59 years old. He had been employed by Public Press for 14 years. The termination of his employment and the allegations of cause created emotional difficulties for Wallace and he was forced to seek psychiatric help. His attempts to find similar employment were largely unsuccessful [and he was forced into bankruptcy].

3. Judicial History

C. *Manitoba Court of Queen's Bench* (1993), 87 Man. R. (2d) 161

The appellant contended that he had negotiated a fixed-term contract with UGG that guaranteed him security of tenure until retirement, subject only to termination for just cause.

Lockwood J. rejected that argument. In his view, the making of a fixed-term contract would occur rarely, if at all. He described such a contract as being special in nature so as to require very explicit terms. He concluded that the evidence about the meeting between Logan and Wallace prior to Wallace's being hired was not sufficient to merit a finding that the parties had entered a fixed-term contract. Further, he found that in any event, such a contract would be inconsistent with UGG's employment policy and that any change in company policy would require the endorsement of the personnel manager, the general manager or the president of UGG. A change in the company's employment policy was neither sought nor granted.

In determining the appropriate period of reasonable notice, Lockwood J. took into account a number of factors including the appellant's length of service, his age, the nature of his employment, the history of the employment relationship, his qualifications, and the availability of similar employment. In addition he noted the difficulty that Wallace was experiencing in finding alternate employment. He attributed that difficulty in large measure to the evidence of word having circulated in the trade that Wallace "must have done something reprehensible" to have been dismissed by UGG. Lockwood J. concluded:

> Taking the above factors into account, and particularly the fact that the peremptory dismissal and the subsequent actions of the [respondent] made other employment in [Wallace's] field virtually unavailable, I conclude that an award at the top of the scale in such cases is warranted. I, therefore, fix 24 months as the period of reasonable notice.

In addition to his claim for wages in lieu of notice, Wallace sought damages for mental distress and made claims in both contract and tort. The claim in contract included damages for mental distress, loss of reputation and prestige and punitive damages. Citing *Vorvis v. Insurance Corporation of British Columbia*, [1989] 1 S.C.R. 1085, Lockwood J. determined that Wallace's entitlement to an award under this head of damages turned on whether UGG's conduct constituted a separate actionable wrong. He noted that although there was no fixed-term contract, Wallace had been given a guarantee of security provided he gave UGG no cause to dismiss him. Relying on *Pilon v. Peugeot Canada Ltd.* (1980), 114 D.L.R. (3d) 378 (Ont. H.C.), Lockwood J. concluded that it must have been in the contemplation of UGG that if Wallace was dismissed without cause or warning, he would probably suffer mental distress. This was an implied term of the contract and therefore the dismissal constituted a separate actionable wrong worthy of compensation.

Regarding the claim in tort, the appellant sought damages for negligence including punitive damages or, alternatively, aggravated damages for wilful or negligent infliction of harassment and oppression. Lockwood J. began his analysis by reviewing the evidence concerning mental distress and found that although Wallace's assignment into personal bankruptcy must have caused him an increasing degree of stress, the dismissal itself constituted the "major component" in his depression. Turning to the part of the claim concerning wilful or negligent infliction of harassment, he accepted the evidence of Domerecki that it was UGG's intention to "play hardball" with Wallace, that UGG did not have any reason to dismiss him and that the reason given in Domerecki's letter of August 29, 1986 was not true. He also noted the late withdrawal of the allegations of cause. Lockwood J. held that the behaviour of the respondent ought to lead to compensation for mental distress by way of aggravated damages.

In light of the circumstances and having found that the defendant was liable for aggravated damages resulting from mental distress in both tort and contract, Lockwood J. fixed the award at $15,000.

With respect to the appellant's claim for punitive damages, Lockwood J. relied on the decision in *Vorvis*, and concluded that conduct warranting an award of such damages would have to be of a "harsh, vindictive, reprehensible and malicious nature". In his view, the conduct complained of in this case was not sufficient to constitute an actionable wrong, nor was it of such an extreme nature as to merit condemnation by an award of such damages in either tort or contract. . . .

4. Issues . . .

B. Fixed-Term Contract

The appellant submitted that the courts below erred in rejecting his claim that he had a fixed-term contract for employment until retirement. The learned trial judge exhaustively reviewed all of the circumstances surrounding Wallace's hiring and concluded that there was insufficient evidence to support this claim. The Court of Appeal accepted the facts as they were found by the trial judge and agreed with his conclusion. In light of these concurrent findings of fact, I see no palpable error or other reason to interfere with the conclusion of the courts below.

C. Damages for Mental Distress

Relying upon the principles enunciated in *Vorvis, supra*, the Court of Appeal held that any award of damages beyond compensation for breach of contract for failure to give reasonable notice of termination "must be founded on a separately actionable course of conduct. . . . " The Court of Appeal also noted that this requirement necessarily negates the trial judge's reliance on concepts of foreseeability and matters in the contemplation of the parties. An employment contract is not one in which peace of mind is the very matter contracted for and so, absent an independently actionable wrong, the foreseeability of mental distress or the fact that the parties contemplated its occurrence is of no consequence, subject to what I say on employer conduct below.

The Court of Appeal concluded that there was insufficient evidence to support a finding that the actions of UGG constituted a separate actionable wrong either in tort or in contract. I agree with these findings and see no reason to disturb them. . . .

D. Bad Faith Discharge

The appellant urged this Court to find that he could sue UGG either in contract or in tort for "bad faith discharge". With respect to the action in contract, he submitted that the Court should imply into the employment contract a term that the employee would not be fired except for cause or legitimate business reasons. I cannot accede to this submission. The law has long recognized the mutual right of both employers and employees to terminate an employment contract at any time provided there are no express provisions to the contrary. In *Farber v. Royal Trust Co.*, [1997] 1 S.C.R. 846, Gonthier J., speaking for the Court, summarized the general contractual principles applicable to contracts of employment as follows:

> In the context of an indeterminate employment contract, one party can resiliate [abandon] the contract unilaterally. The resiliation is considered a dismissal if it originates with the employer and a resignation if it originates with the employee. If an

employer dismisses an employee without cause, the employer must give the employee reasonable notice that the contract is about to be terminated or compensation in lieu thereof.

A requirement of "good faith" reasons for dismissal would, in effect, contravene these principles and deprive employers of the ability to determine the composition of their workforce. In the context of the accepted theories on the employment relationship, such a law would, in my opinion, be overly intrusive and inconsistent with established principles of employment law, and more appropriately, should be left to legislative enactment rather than judicial pronouncement.

I must also reject the appellant's claim that he can sue in tort for breach of a good faith and fair dealing obligation with regard to dismissals. The Court of Appeal noted the absence of persuasive authority on this point and concluded that such a tort has not yet been recognized by Canadian courts. I agree with these findings. To create such a tort in this case would therefore constitute a radical shift in the law, again a step better left to be taken by the legislatures. For these reasons I conclude that the appellant is unable to sue in either tort or contract for "bad faith discharge."

E. Punitive Damages

Punitive damages are an exception to the general rule that damages are meant to compensate the plaintiff. The purpose of such an award is the punishment of the defendant. The appellant argued that the trial judge and the Court of Appeal erred in refusing to award punitive damages. I do not agree. . . . Lockwood J. found that UGG did not engage in sufficiently "harsh, vindictive, reprehensible and malicious" conduct to merit condemnation by such an award. He also noted the absence of an actionable wrong. The Court of Appeal concurred. Again, there is no reason to interfere with these findings. Consequently, I agree with the courts below that there is no foundation for an award of punitive damages.

F. Reasonable Notice

The Court of Appeal upheld the trial judge's findings of fact and agreed that in the circumstances of this case damages for failure to give notice ought to be at the high end of the scale. However, the court found the trial judge's award of 24 months' salary in lieu of notice to be excessive and reflective of an element of aggravated damages having crept into his determination. It overturned his award and substituted the equivalent of 15 months' salary. For the reasons which follow, I would restore the trial judge's award of damages in the amount of 24 months' salary in lieu of notice.

In determining what constitutes reasonable notice of termination, the courts have generally applied the principles articulated by McRuer C. J. H. C. in *Bardal v. Globe & Mail Ltd.* (1960), 24 D.L.R. (2d) 140 (Ont. H.C.):

> There can be no catalogue laid down as to what is reasonable notice in particular classes of cases. The reasonableness of the notice must be decided with reference to each particular case, having regard to the character of the employment, the length of service of the servant, the age of the servant and the availability of similar employment, having regard to the experience, training and qualifications of the servant.

This Court adopted the foregoing list of factors in *Machtinger v. HOJ Industries Ltd.*, [1992] 1 S.C.R. 986, at p. 998. Applying these factors in the instant case, I concur with the trial judge's finding that in light of the appellant's advanced age, his 14-year tenure as the company's top salesman and his limited prospects for re-employment, a lengthy period of notice is warranted. I note, however, that *Bardal* does not state, nor has it been interpreted to imply, that the factors it enumerated were exhaustive. Canadian courts have added several additional factors to the *Bardal* list. The application of these factors to the assessment of a dismissed employee's notice period will depend upon the particular circumstances of the case.

One such factor that has often been considered is whether the dismissed employee had been induced to leave previous secure employment. According to one authority, many courts have sought to compensate the reliance and expectation interests of terminated employees by increasing the period of reasonable notice where the employer has induced the employee to "quit a secure, well-paying job . . . on the strength of promises of career advancement and greater responsibility, security and compensation with the new organization" (I. Christie et al.). . . .

In my opinion, such inducements are properly included among the considerations which tend to lengthen the amount of notice required. I concur with the comments of Christie et al., and recognize that there is a need to safeguard the employee's reliance and expectation interests in inducement situations. I note, however, that not all inducements will carry equal weight when determining the appropriate period of notice. The significance of the inducement in question will vary with the circumstances of the particular case and its effect, if any, on the notice period is a matter best left to the discretion of the trial judge.

In the instant case, the trial judge found that UGG went to great lengths to relieve Wallace's fears about jeopardizing his existing secure employment and to entice him into joining their company. [T]he trial judge stated:

> The [respondent] wanted a man with the skills of the [appellant] and to get him was prepared to accommodate his demands. . . . I have found that there was no fixed-term contract. However, there was, in the assurance given to him, a *guarantee of security*, provided he gave the [respondent] no cause to dismiss him. [Emphasis added.]

In addition to the promise that he could continue to work for the company until retirement, UGG also offered several assurances with respect to fair treatment. Further, despite the fact that the company only had salary arrangements with their existing employees, they assured Wallace that they would implement a commission basis for him. Although the trial judge did not make specific reference to the inducement factor in his analysis of reasonable notice, I believe that, in the circumstances of this case, these inducements, in particular the guarantee of job security, are factors which support his decision to award damages at the high end of the scale.

The appellant urged this Court to recognize the ability of a dismissed employee to sue in contract or alternatively in tort for "bad faith discharge". Although I have rejected both as avenues for recovery, by no means do I condone the behaviour of employers who subject employees to callous and insensitive treatment in their dismissal, showing no regard for their welfare. Rather, I believe that such bad faith conduct in the manner of dismissal is another factor that is properly compensated for by an addition to the notice period.

[Several earlier decisions] preclude extending the notice period to account for manner of dismissal. Generally speaking, these cases have found that claims relating to the manner in which the discharge took place are not properly considered in an action for damages for breach of contract. Rather, it is said, damages are limited to injuries that flow from the breach itself, which in the employment context is the failure to give reasonable notice. The manner of dismissal was found not to affect these damages.

Although these decisions are grounded in general principles of contract law, I believe, with respect, that they have all failed to take into account the unique characteristics of the particular type of contract with which they were concerned, namely, a contract of employment. Similarly, there was not an appropriate recognition of the special relationship which these contracts govern. In my view, both are relevant considerations.

The contract of employment has many characteristics that set it apart from the ordinary commercial contract. As K. Swinton noted in "Contract Law and the Employment Relationship: The Proper Forum for Reform", in B. J. Reiter and J. Swan, eds., *Studies in Contract Law* (1980), 357, 363:

> . . . the terms of the employment contract rarely result from an exercise of free bargaining power in the way that the paradigm commercial exchange between two traders does. Individual employees on the whole lack both the bargaining power and the information necessary to achieve more favourable contract provisions than those offered by the employer, particularly with regard to tenure.

This power imbalance is not limited to the employment contract itself. Rather, it informs virtually all facets of the employment relationship. In *Slaight Communications Inc. v. Davidson*, [1989] 1 S.C.R. 1038, Dickson C. J., writing for the majority of the Court, had occasion to comment on the nature of this relationship. At pp. 1051–52 he quoted with approval from P. Davies and M. Freedland, *Kahn-Freund's Labour and the Law* (3rd ed. 1983):

> [T]he relation between an employer and an isolated employee or worker is typically a relation between a bearer of power and one who is not a bearer of power. In its inception it is an act of submission, in its operation it is a condition of subordination. . . .

This unequal balance of power led the majority of the Court in *Slaight Communications, supra,* to describe employees as a vulnerable group in society. The vulnerability of employees is underscored by the level of importance which our society attaches to employment. As Dickson C. J. noted in *Reference Re Public Service Employee Relations Act (Alta.)*, [1987] 1 S.C.R. 313, 368:

> Work is one of the most fundamental aspects in a person's life, providing the individual with a means of financial support and, as importantly, a contributory role in society. A person's employment is an essential component of his or her sense of identity, self-worth and emotional well-being.

Thus, for most people, work is one of the defining features of their lives. Accordingly, any change in a person's employment status is bound to have far-reaching repercussions. In "Aggravated Damages and the Employment Contract", Schai noted that, "[w]hen this change is involuntary, the extent of our 'personal dislocation' is even greater."

The point at which the employment relationship ruptures is the time when the employee is most vulnerable and hence, most in need of protection. In recognition of this need, the law ought to encourage conduct that minimizes the damage and dislocation (both economic and personal) that result from dismissal. In *Machtinger*, it was noted that the manner in which employment can be terminated is equally important to an individual's identity as the work itself. By way of expanding upon this statement, I note that the loss of one's job is always a traumatic event. However, when termination is accompanied by acts of bad faith in the manner of discharge, the results can be especially devastating. In my opinion, to ensure that employees receive adequate protection, employers ought to be held to an obligation of good faith and fair dealing in the manner of dismissal, the breach of which will be compensated for by adding to the length of the notice period.

The obligation of good faith and fair dealing is incapable of precise definition. However, at a minimum, I believe that in the course of dismissal employers ought to be candid, reasonable, honest and forthright with their employees and should refrain from engaging in conduct that is unfair or is in bad faith by being, for example, untruthful, misleading or unduly insensitive. . . . I note that, depending upon the circumstances of the individual case, not all acts of bad faith or unfair dealing will be equally injurious and thus, the amount by which the notice period is extended will vary. Furthermore, I do not intend to advocate anything akin to an automatic claim for damages under this heading in every case of dismissal. In each case, the trial judge must examine the nature of the bad faith conduct and its impact in the circumstances.

The Court of Appeal in the instant case recognized the relevance of manner of dismissal in the determination of the appropriate period of reasonable notice. However, the court found that this factor could only be considered "where it impacts on the future employment prospects of the dismissed employee". With respect, I believe that this is an overly restrictive view. In my opinion, the law must recognize a more expansive list of injuries which may flow from unfair treatment or bad faith in the manner of dismissal.

It has long been accepted that a dismissed employee is not entitled to compensation for injuries flowing from the fact of the dismissal itself. Thus, although the loss of a job is very often the cause of injured feelings and emotional upset, the law does not recognize these as compensable losses. However, where an employee can establish that an employer engaged in bad faith conduct or unfair dealing in the course of dismissal, injuries such as humiliation, embarrassment and damage to one's sense of self-worth and self-esteem might all be worthy of compensation depending upon the circumstances of the case. In these situations, compensation does not flow from the fact of dismissal itself, but rather from the manner in which the dismissal was effected by the employer. . . .

In the case before this Court, the trial judge documented several examples of bad faith conduct on the part of UGG. He noted the abrupt manner in which Wallace was dismissed despite having received compliments on his work from his superiors only days before. He found that UGG made a conscious decision to "play hardball" with Wallace and maintained unfounded allegations of cause until the day the trial began. Further, as a result of UGG's persistence in maintaining these allegations, "[w]ord got around, and it was rumoured in the trade that he had been involved in some wrongdoing". Finally, he found that the dismissal and subsequent events were largely responsible for causing Wallace's depression. Having considered the *Bardal* list of factors, he stated:

> Taking [these] factors into account, and particularly the fact that the peremptory dismissal and the subsequent actions of the defendant made other employment in his field virtually unavailable, I conclude that an award at the top of the scale in such cases is warranted.

I agree with the trial judge's conclusion that the actions of UGG seriously diminished Wallace's prospects of finding similar employment. In light of this fact, and the other circumstances of this case, I am not persuaded that the trial judge erred in awarding the equivalent of 24 months' salary in lieu of notice. It may be that such an award is at the high end of the scale; however, taking into account all of the relevant factors, this award is not unreasonable and accordingly, I can see no reason to interfere. Therefore, for the reasons above, I would restore the order of the trial judge with respect to the appropriate period of reasonable notice and allow the appeal on this ground. . . .

McLACHLIN J. (dissenting in part, joined by LA FOREST and L'HEUREUX-DUBE) – I have read the reasons of Justice Iacobucci. While I agree with much of his reasons, my view of the law leads me to differ both in method and in result.

As to method, I differ from Iacobucci J. in two respects. First, I am of the view that an award of damages for wrongful dismissal should be confined to factors relevant to the prospect of finding replacement employment. It follows that the notice period upon which such damages are based should only be increased for manner of dismissal if this impacts on the employee's prospects of re-employment. Secondly, I am of the view the law has evolved to permit recognition of an implied duty of good faith in termination of the employment.

These differences lead me to a different result than my colleague. I would uphold the trial judge's award of damages for wrongful dismissal based on a 24-month notice period. I would also uphold the trial judge's award of $15,000 for mental distress on the basis of breach of the contractual obligation of good faith in dismissing an employee.

The action for wrongful dismissal is based on an implied obligation in the employment contract to give reasonable notice of an intention to terminate the relationship (or pay in lieu thereof) in the absence of just cause for dismissal. If an employer fails to provide reasonable notice of termination, the employee can bring an action for breach of the implied term. A "wrongful dismissal" action is not concerned with the wrongness or rightness of the dismissal itself. Far from making dismissal a wrong, the law entitles both employer and employee to terminate the employment relationship without cause. A wrong arises only if the employer breaches the contract by failing to give the dismissed employee reasonable notice of termination. The remedy for this breach of contract is an award of damages based on the period of notice which should have been given. The length of the notice period is based on the time reasonably required to find similar employment. The damages represent what the employee would have earned in this period. These damages place the employee in the position that he or she would have been in had the contract been performed – the proper measure of damages for breach of contract. . . .

My colleague, Iacobucci J., holds that the manner of dismissal may be considered generally in defining the notice period for wrongful dismissal. An alternative view is that the manner of dismissal should only be considered in defining the notice period where the manner of dismissal impacts on the difficulty of finding replacement employment, and that absent this connection, damages for the manner of termination must be based on some other cause of action.

I prefer the second approach for the following reasons. First, this solution seems to me more consistent with the nature of the action for wrongful dismissal. Second, this approach, unlike the alternative, honours the principle that damages must be grounded in a cause of action. Third, this approach seems to me more consistent with the authorities, notably *Vorvis v. Insurance Corporation of British Columbia*, [1989] 1 S.C.R. 1085, *per* McIntyre J. Fourth, this approach will better aid certainty and predictability in the law governing damages for termination of employment. Finally, there are other equally effective ways to remedy wrongs related to the manner of dismissal which do not affect the prospect of finding replacement work. . . .

Notes

1. Why was Wallace's claim for an express, oral contract for employment until retirement rejected? Given the fact that, in recruiting Wallace, the employer gave him "a guarantee of security" unless he gave them cause to fire him, why was that not sufficient to support a finding of an express employment contract? What more would be necessary to find that such a contract existed? Assuming that Don Logan, the marketing manager of the publishing division, had authority to hire, aren't his promises binding on the employer? If Logan had actual or apparent authority to hire Wallace, is it relevant that the employer had an employment policy in place that was inconsistent with a fixed term contract? Is the Court stretching to push every employment termination case out of treatment as an express agreement for job security into a case of an implied breach of a duty to provide reasonable notice?

2. What is Canada's default rule for employers terminating employees? "At common law in Canada, an employee can be dismissed summarily only for cause. All other terminations must be on 'reasonable' notice, unless there is an express term of the contract to the contrary." CANADIAN LABOR & EMPLOYMENT LAW, at 136. How does that rule differ from the United States' at-will rule?

3. On what basis is the reasonable notice requirement imposed on the discretion of the parties to terminate the employment relationship? Does implying a term as a matter of law into the contract actually reflect the intent the parties would have if, at the time of hiring, they were asked what notice should be given? The reasonable notice requirement softens the at-will rule by giving the employee income during the notice period and a continuing job, if the payment for the notice period is not made in lieu of continuing employment. One "rule" of practical significance in employment is that it is easier to get a new job when you are employed than if you are unemployed. Should an employee who has received a termination notice try to continue working during the notice period or is it better to take the money and leave?

4. If the rationale for the reasonable notice rule is to give the employee a chance to find suitable replacement employment, what impact does the manner of discharge have on that? Do you find the majority or dissent's position more convincing on this point?

5. Why does the majority refuse to accept a bad faith discharge claim? How close to establishing a "for cause" standard for discharge is the dissent's view that a cause of action for breach of the duty of good faith and fair dealing applies to the manner of discharge? Wouldn't the basic reason for the decision to discharge be put to the test in deciding the manner of discharge? The less justified the decision to discharge, the easier it is to find the manner of the discharge to be in bad faith.

6. What factors did the *Wallace* court say go into deciding what is reasonable notice? The *Bardal* factors include "the character of the employment, the length of service of the servant, the age of the servant and the availability of similar employment, having regard to the experience, training and qualifications of the servant." The *Wallace* majority adds whether the employee had been "induced to leave previous

secure employment" and the manner in which the employer treated the employee in discharging her. Until recently, somewhat longer periods were found reasonable for higher status, managerial and professional jobs. More recently, courts have found that the nonmanagerial nature of the work should not reduce the notice period. INTERNATIONAL LABOR & EMPLOYMENT LAW, at 21-9. Given the impact of globalization on blue collar employment, should the notice period for manufacturing workers be increased to take account of the difficulty they have in finding new jobs? Or is the impact of globalization now increasing for the white collar workers?

7. How should an employer decide what length of time that is reasonable notice. *See* Appendix F, CANADIAN LABOUR & EMPLOYMENT LAW for description of court decisions by length of reasonable notice period found to apply. To some extent, the notice period that is reasonable has been a moving target. "In the 1960s the courts astonished the legal community by making awards of 12 months' notice, thereby demolishing the pre-existing 'unofficial' ceiling of 6 months. By the 1990s, awards of 24 months' duration has become commonplace. Today, some courts have awarded as much as 30 months' reasonable notice." LABOUR LAW IN CANADA, at 181. How should an employee who has been given a notice of termination respond?

8. Every jurisdiction in Canada has established, as part of its basic statutory labor standards, notice periods necessary to be given before employment can be terminated. Why doesn't the court limit the recovery to those periods instead of the case-by-case approach it takes?

9. Do the uncertainties of the reasonable notice rule as developed in *Wallace* give employers an incentive to reach express, written employment agreements? The parties can agree to a period of notice in order to terminate the agreement that will withstand judicial oversight as long as it provides the minimum period provided by the applicable provincial or federal statute. Or would the express agreement have to also comport with the common law notice standards as described in *Wallace*? *Machtinger v. HOJ Industries, Ltd*, [1992] 1 S.C.R. 896 (individual employment contract limiting notice period trumps common law reasonable notice requirement but not statutory notice periods).

10. Until the eve of trial, the United Grain Growers asserted that Wallace had been discharged for cause. The employer's duty to give reasonable notice does not apply if it can show that it has good cause for terminating the employee. Good cause has been found in situations where the employee has a conflict of interest, has excessive or unauthorized absences, theft, sabotage, fighting on the job, insubordination, intoxication or drug use in the workplace, incompetence or negligent performance of the work and some off-duty conduct, *e.g.*, some crimes that are incompatible with continued employment. *See* INTERNATIONAL LABOR & EMPLOYMENT LAWS, at 21-13.

In *McKinley v. B. C. Telephone Co.*, [2001] 2 S.C.R. 161, the Court addressed a split in authority as to whether employee dishonesty is per se good cause or whether a balancing test applied. The case involved an employee who was on extended medical leave because of hypertension. The employee wanted to be transferred to a less stressful position but the employer terminated him when he refused to return to his prior job. In defense of his wrongful discharge claim, the employer originally argued the doctrine of contract frustration – because of McKinley's illness, the contract was frustrated and could be terminated. But, in discovery, the employer learned that McKinley's cardiologist had told him he could return to his prior job if he took a prescription "beta blocker" to control his blood pressure. McKinley had never told the employer of this and instead had insisted his doctors thought he should be transferred to a different job. The Court adopted the following test of how employee dishonesty should be treated in a wrongful discharge case:

> 48. I am of the view that whether an employer is justified in dismissing an employee on the grounds of dishonesty is a question that requires an assessment of the context of the alleged misconduct. More specifically, the test is whether the employee's dishonesty gave rise to a breakdown in the employment relationship. This test can be expressed in different ways. One could say, for example, that just cause for dismissal exists where the dishonesty violates an essential condition of the employment contract, breaches the faith inherent to the work relationship, or is fundamentally or directly inconsistent with the employee's obligations to his or her employer.

> 49 In accordance with this test, a trial judge must instruct the jury to determine: (1) whether the evidence established the employee's deceitful conduct on a balance of probabilities; and (2) if so, whether the nature and degree of the dishonesty warranted dismissal. In my view, the second branch of this test does not blend questions of fact and law. Rather, assessing the seriousness of the misconduct requires the facts established at trial to be carefully considered and balanced. As such, it is a factual inquiry for the jury to undertake.

The Court affirmed a jury finding for the employee based on an instruction that the dishonesty, if any, constituted a breakdown in the employment relationship. Because the employer had not proven good cause, the jury determined that a reasonable notice period would be twenty-two months, and then added four more months following *Wallace* because of the manner in which he was terminated.

11. The *McKinley* Court also addressed the role of aggravated and punitive damages in wrongful discharge cases. Aggravated "damages could be awarded where: (1) an employer's conduct was 'independently actionable', (2) it amounted to a wrong that was separate from the breach of contract for failure to give reasonable notice of termination, and (3) it arises from the dismissal itself, rather than the employer's conduct before or after the dismissal." The judge, finding some evidence of willful or malicious conduct by the employer, instructed the jury on aggravated damages. The jury found for the employee, awarding him C$100,000 in aggravated damages. The Court reversed finding "a fair reading of the evidence does not, in my view, suggest that the respondents acted with an intention to harm the appellant either by deliberately inflicting mental distress or by acting in a discriminatory manner." The fact that the employer tried, but failed, to find an alternative position for McKinley undermined the possibility of finding that the employer committed a wrong separate from the failure to give reasonable notice. Was the "hard ball" treatment of the employee in *Wallace* sufficient to justify aggravated damages? Why did the Court in *Wallace* find insufficient evidence to support a finding that the employer's actions constituted an actionable wrong separate from his reasonable notice claims?

12. The *McKinley* Court also distinguished aggravated and punitive damages. "While aggravated damages aim to compensate for intangible injury, punitive damages are penal and exemplary in nature, and may be awarded only where the conduct

giving rise to the complaint is found to merit punishment." In upholding the trial judge's denial of an instruction on punitive damages, the *Wallace* Court said that the employer's behavior "was not sufficiently harsh, vindictive, reprehensible, malicious or extreme in nature to warrant punishment." What is the difference between aggravated and punitive damages?

13. In Quebec, wrongful dismissal claims involve granting the dismissed employees "*dommage moraux* such as mental distress, humiliation, anxiety and damage to reputation" by the way in which the employer terminated the employee. LABOUR LAW IN CANADA, at 198.

14. Employees have duties under the law applicable to individual employment. "Under both the Canadian common law and civil law systems, all employees owe a duty of loyalty, good faith, and honesty to their employers. . . . Once employment has ended, the employee's duty generally is limited to not making use of confidential information from the former employer." *See* INTERNATIONAL LABOR & EMPLOYMENT LAW, at 21-16.

15. Covenants not to compete are permissible if the employer proves their reasonableness and necessity. Reasonableness "is determined not only as between the parties, but also in light of the public interest in employees' ability to move freely from one employer to another." *Id.* at 21-18.

C. UNIONS AND COLLECTIVE BARGAINING

At common law, the activity of the early-nineteenth-century apprentice and journeyman's associations were criminal as illegal conspiracies in restraint of trade. Even in Quebec which is based on the French civil law tradition, the common law of crimes applied to criminalize union activities. In the 1870s, a number of statutes were adopted decriminalizing union and their activities such as strikes and peaceful picketing. The Industrial Disputes Investigation Act of 1907, struck down as unconstitutional in *Toronto Electric*, contained a number of features that still characterize Canadian labor law. First, the Act was the source for the tradition of having labor law enforced by tripartite boards made up of labor, employer and neutral representatives. The second was that strikes and lockouts could be delayed pending such a board's investigation and public report.

During the 1930s, many of the provinces adopted legislation loosely based on the United State's Wagner Act. These laws were inadequate because they failed to require employers to bargain collectively. In response, workers engaged in massive strikes. "In 1943 the crisis reached its peak as the steel industry was shut down by a nation-wide walkout and one out of every three workers was on strike." LABOUR LAW IN CANADA, at 53. That year the federal government acting pursuant to its emergency powers issued Order in Council 1003 (P.C. 1003), which was modeled on U.S. labor law. P.C. 1003 contained several features that differed from U.S. law, most significantly the arbitration of grievances was mandatory and strikes and lockouts were forbidden during the term of a collective bargaining agreement. After the emergency ended in 1948, the provinces adopted labor legislation that is based on the U.S. model but that retains some of the distinctive features of earlier Canadian labor law. INTERNATIONAL LABOR & EMPLOYMENT LAW, at 21-19–22.

Canada has ratified ILO Convention 87, protecting the freedom of association but it has not ratified Convention 98, which goes further to protect that right. Between 1954 and

2005, 91 complaints have been filed against Canada for violating freedom of association rights, "giving it the dubious distinction of having the most of all G-7 countries." *Great Expectations*, at 129. "The ILO Committee on Freedom of Association has repeatedly noted with regret that various Canadian governments are violating workers' freedom of association and requested that the offending legislation be repealed. These finding and requests have been ignored." *Id.* Only two complaints have been filed against Canada pursuant to the labor side agreement of NAFTA. One complaint was withdrawn and the second was not accepted by the American NAO. *Id.* at 129-130.

The largest confederation of unions is the Canadian Labour Congress (CLC), made up of unions representing about two-thirds of all union members. The second largest confederation, the Confédérération des Syndicats Nationaux (CSN),is geographically centered in Quebec and it has about 10 percent of all union members. Other, smaller confederations and some independent unions represent the rest. LABOUR LAW IN CANADA, at 206. At an earlier time, more of the unions were "international," that is, unions that operated in the United States and Canada. Although still true, there is more focus on Canadian unions especially since the Canadian Auto Workers split from the international United Auto Workers in 1985. "International unions made up 29.9 per cent of total union membership in 1998, a significant decline from levels of . . . 44.7 per cent in 1981." *Id.* at 203.

Like the union movement in the United States, unions in Canada have generally accepted capitalism and tended to focus on representing workers of employers as a first priority with political activism secondary. In the 1960s, however, many unions affiliated with the New Democratic Party (NDP), which had some success particularly at the provincial level for a period of time. LABOUR LAW IN CANADA, at 57. "A variety of union philosophies are represented. Most of the old craft groups still espouse US-style apolitical 'business unionism.' A larger number of unions see themselves as fulfilling a broader role, and actively support the NPD and various social causes. A few groups, principally in Quebec, are highly politicized and occasionally criticize the prevailing economic system from a socialist perspective. But rhetoric aside, the major function of all unions is collective bargaining." INTERNATIONAL & COMPARATIVE EMPLOYMENT RELATIONS, at 99.

"Since the 1980s, union membership in Canada has experienced a gradual but slow decline. In 1998, 32.5 per cent of non-agricultural paid workers were unionized, down from 37.9 per cent in 1984." LABOUR LAW IN CANADA, at 54. "Union density in the private sector has dropped below twenty percent in Canada and nine percent in the United States, while public sector union density is about seventy-five percent in Canada and thirty-seven percent in the United States." *Great Expectations*, at 109.

With the complete independence of Canada in 1982 and, importantly, the adoption of the Canadian Charter of Rights and Freedoms, labor law was to some extent constitutionalized. Section 2(d) of the Charter provides that "everyone has the . . . freedom of association." In *Reference re Public Service Relations Act (Alta.)* [1987], 87 C.L.L.C. 14,021 (S.C.C.), the Supreme Court defined that as "the freedom to work for the establishment of an association, to belong to an association, to maintain it, and to participate in its lawful activity without penalty or reprisal." This includes the right to form, join and maintain a union. In *Dunmore v. Ontario (Attorney General)*, [2001] 3 S.C.R. 1016, the Court considered an attack on Ontario's collective bargaining statute that deprived agricultural workers of access to a statutory collective bargaining scheme but also left them unprotected from employer retaliation for engaging in organizing activity. Finding the law violated the collective aspect of the freedom of association rights of these workers, it found that the Charter required the government of Ontario to protect agricultural workers against employer retaliation and to provide the workers' association the right to make representations to their employer. See, *Great Expectations*, at 130-132.

All jurisdictions protect the rights of workers against discrimination because of unionism. A presumption of dismissal for union activity is relatively easy to establish by showing, for example, that the employee active in the union who was dismissed for poor work had never been previously criticized, or that only union activists were discharged for grounds of redundancy. With such a presumption, the burden of persuasion shifts to the employer to prove that union activities played no part in the decision it made. Labour Law in Canada, at 237.

1. Union Recognition

Generally following tradition of union organizing in the United States, Canadian unions essentially focus on organizing the workers of an employer one bargaining unit at a time. To be treated as a union, the labor board makes sure there is an arms length relationship between the union and any employer, the union has a purpose of engaging in collective bargaining, and that it does not discriminate in its membership. LABOUR LAW IN CANADA, at 257–260. The legal steps in the organization process are: (1) The union files its petition for certification to be certified as the collective bargaining representative with the appropriate labor board along with evidence of support among the targeted group of workers, typically signed union authorization cards. (2) The employer receives and posts the certification procedure. (3) The board verifies the evidence of union membership. (4) The board official gathers evidence on the issue of the appropriateness of the unit of workers the union requests to represent. (5) Employees not wishing to be represented by the union may file a petition to this effect with the labor board. These petitions are perused carefully to make sure that the employer has played no part in them. *Id.* at 264.

Not all jurisdictions, however, follow exactly the same approach. Five provinces follow the U.S. model by having the union file with the labor board a "showing of interest" – in the United States it is 30 percent, among these provinces it varies 40 to 45 percent – of signed authorization cards of workers in the bargaining unit that the union is targeting for organization. With that showing of interest, the board quickly holds an election, which determines representation status. In contrast, federal law and the law of the other provinces allow their labor relations boards to certify unions without holding an election if the union has signed membership cards from at least a majority of the workers in the unit. Only if the petitioning union has a sufficient showing of interest but does not have authorization cards signed by a majority of the workers does the board hold an election. INTERNATIONAL LABOR & EMPLOYMENT LAWS, at 21-26–28. The issue of card-count certifications has been an important issue politically among many of the different provinces, with provincial law bouncing one way and then the next as a result of changes in the provincial governments. See, *Great Expectations*, at 120–123.

Notes

1. What is the effect of certifying a union based on a card showing? In the United States, an employer, even with actual knowledge of a union majority, can reject a union request for recognition to force the union to file an election petition with the N.L.R.B. How should a Canadian union in a province that allowed a union to

be recognized without an election go about organizing a workplace? With a secret organizational campaign and the possibility of recognition without an election, does that mean the employer can be effectively denied any practical access to present its case about unionization before it can be ordered to recognize and bargain with the union?

2. On one hand, quiet organization plus recognition based on a card majority without an election would reduce the number of unfair labor practice charges that typically grow out of election campaigns, if the experience of the United States would be replicated in Canada. In the United States, election campaigns are rife with claims of discriminatory treatment of union supporters, threats to the jobs of workers and other conduct that can undermine employee support for a union. On the other hand, it does limit the chance employees have to hear their employer's side of the story on unionization. Should the United States adopt the approach taken by those Canadian jurisdictions that certify unions without an election if the union can demonstrate that a majority of the workers have signed union authorization cards?

3. Even in those jurisdictions requiring an election to determine union status, the election is held very quickly. In Ontario, for example, an "instant election" is held within five to seven days from the union's filing the petition for certification. Issues regarding the appropriateness of the unit the union wants to represent and the eligibility of voters are not decided until after the election has been held. Would you support moving to an "instant election" approach in the United States where presently the procedures that must be satisfied before an election, including hearings and a decision over the appropriateness of the bargaining unit the union requests, take place before an election is ordered? How would such an approach affect the dynamics of a union organization campaign?

4. In jurisdictions, such as Ontario, where certification is generally by election, there is authority for the labor board to order certification of a union as a bargaining representative as a remedy based on employer election misconduct where no other remedy, including another election, would be sufficient to counter the effects of the employer's conduct. *See Wal-Mart* [1997] O.L.R.B. Rep. Jan./Feb. 141. There is a similar rule in the United States that a union, that at one point had a majority had it destroyed irreparably by employer unfair labor practices, may be entitled to a bargaining order as a remedy for the employer's unfair labor practices. *NLRB v. Gissel Packing Co.*, 395 U.S. 575 (1969). If a union cannot win an election, how can it be expected to bargain successfully, even if the employer is ordered to recognize and bargain with it?

5. As of the date the union applies for certification, all Canadian jurisdictions impose a freeze on existing terms of employment until the application is dismissed or until a notice to bargain is given pursuant to the certification of the union. Basically, a "business as usual" standard applies so that an employer may be obliged to implement scheduled wage increases or benefit improvements. CANADIAN LABOUR & EMPLOYMENT LAW, at 48–49.

2. Collective Bargaining

With certain exceptions for some nationwide industries such as airlines and broadcasting that bargain on a national basis, "the bargaining unit encompasses the employees at a single plant or other installation of the employer, [so] this means that collective bargaining agreements are normally concluded at the plant level." INTERNATIONAL LABOR & EMPLOYMENT LAW at 21–31. In contrast, in France and Germany, bargaining tends to occur between a union and an association of employers one step removed from the employers that are members of the association. In that way, a collective bargaining agreement can have broad coverage in a particular type of business. As is true under French and German law, Quebec provides for the extension of collective bargaining agreements by government decree to employers and employees not party to a collective agreement. This decree procedure has, however, gone out of favor in recent years. LABOUR LAW IN CANADA, at 137–138.

There are signs that unions have had reduced effectiveness since Canada and the United States signed a free trade agreement and later set up NAFTA. "[T]he union-nonunion wage differential is estimated to have shrunk from approximately 25% in the late 1970s to 8% in 1997. Major private sector wage settlements have decreased from an average of 4.8% between 1982 and 1988 to an average of 2.6% between 1989 and 2001. There has also been a breakdown of the linkage between productivity gains and wage increases. For example, between 1992 and 2002, productivity in manufacturing increased nearly 18% while real hourly wages increased just 3.3%." *Great Expectations*, at 127.

As in the United States, twin principles of "majoritarianism" and "exclusivity" apply: Once having been selected by a majority of workers in a unit, the union is the exclusive bargaining representative of all the workers in the unit, even those who have not joined the union. The employer can bargain only with the union and no other entity, or the unit members themselves. *Id.* at 286–288.

Once a union is certified, then there is another freeze on the employer's ability to change terms of employment beyond the business as usual standard. The nature of the duty to bargain is similar to that imposed on the parties to collective bargaining in the United States. There is, however, one difference in the situation where a union is bargaining for a first contract with an employer after certification. Under federal law as well as the law of seven provinces, there is a first contract arbitration procedure in which the labor board will impose a collective bargaining agreement if the parties fail to reach agreement. This "interest" arbitration is not available under private sector labor law in the United States.

SASKATCHEWAN INDIAN GAMING AUTHORITY INC. AND C.A.W. – CANADA

(2002) 84 C.L.R.B.R. (2d) 233

[After two unsuccessful bargaining sessions and twelve meetings with a conciliation officer of the Saskatchewan Labour Relations Board, the union asked for and received first contract arbitration.]

Is it appropriate for the Board to assist the parties in the conclusion of the first collective agreement?

41. In the reasons for decision issued by the Board on January 25, 2001, the Board summarized its approach to providing assistance in the conclusion of a first collective agreement as follows at p. 53:

"[25] Our Board interpreted s. 26.5 of the Act as permitting Board intervention in a first collective agreement setting when negotiations have broken down. The Board stressed that "the overall purpose of the provision is to intervene, where the situation warrants it, in an attempt to preserve the collective bargaining relationship, and the ability of the trade union to continue to represent employees."

42. The reasons that may lead to the breakdown of collective bargaining are varied. In the Prairie Micro-Tech Inc. case, the Board identified the following factors that may result in Board intervention:

"A review of the jurisprudence shows that the problem which most often gives rise to the use of first contract arbitration is the obduracy or illegal conduct of an employer who is determined to thwart or ignore the trade union. Other problems may also threaten to destroy the relationship, such as, for example, the emergence of an insoluble industrial dispute, or roadblocks created by the incompetence or inexperience of negotiators on either side."

43. Again, in the Board reiterated its overall approach to first collective agreement assistance as follows:

"6. [Section] 26.5 of the Act adopts a "mediation/breakdown" model of intervention in first collective agreement negotiations, as opposed to a "bad faith/extraordinary" remedy model. The Board stressed the need to reinforce the collective bargaining system through its intervention under s. 26.5, rather than replace that system."

44. Unlike the Ontario counterpart, our s. 26.5 does not require the Board to determine the reasons why the process of collective bargaining has been unsuccessful. . . .

48. The tenor of this Board's approach is very similar to the approach set out by the Ontario Labour Relations Board in that we try to discern if the applicant has engaged in a serious and concerted effort to achieve a collective agreement with the respondent. If there is any suggestion that the applicant is withholding offers for the purpose of maintaining some wiggle room on an application for first collective agreement assistance, the Board will be reluctant to provide assistance under s. 26.5. The Board agent's intervention is an effective means of determining if the parties are serious about arriving at a collective agreement, or whether they are going through the motions of bargaining while holding back potential settlement offers in the hopes of achieving more from the Board. The "narcotic effect" that may occur if access to the first collective agreement provisions is granted too readily can be counteracted by the intervention of an experienced conciliator in the form of a Board agent who can provide the Board with an assessment of the genuineness of the collective bargaining efforts.

49. Unlike the Ontario board, however, we are not required by our statute to determine the reason why collective bargaining has not been successful. We are not required to assess blame for the failure of the collective bargaining process and can focus instead on assessing the efforts of both parties to conclude the first collective agreement. Obviously, in cases where one party does not engage in the process in a fair and thorough manner, the Board will note how the behaviour contributed to the breakdown of the process. Overall, however, the Board is not required to determine who or what is responsible for the breakdown in the process of collective bargaining so long as the parties have engaged in serious and genuine collective bargaining.

50. In the present case, there are a number of factors which lead the Board to the conclusion that first collective agreement assistance should be provided to the parties. The parties have engaged in extensive and protracted negotiations. They voluntarily accessed the services of a conciliation officer from Saskatchewan Labour prior to seeking first contract assistance

from the Board. The Board agent noted that "during all meetings the parties worked towards resolving the outstanding issues in an effort to reach a collective bargaining agreement". There is no doubt in the Board's mind that the union, in particular, made substantial efforts in order to achieve a first collective agreement. We are most concerned with the union's efforts to ensure that it has not accessed the first collective agreement provisions prematurely.

51. Second, the issues that are outstanding are complex and difficult. The parties have not referred simple issues to the Board. Among the more contentious issues is the interplay of affirmative action and seniority provisions. These are difficult issues to resolve even in mature bargaining relationships.

52. Third, the bargaining has been atypical because of the First Nations' context. In addition, the employer is not a typical private sector employer – the employer is more akin to a public sector employer. It is responsible for implementing policies in support of economic development for First Nations' people in Saskatchewan and its mandate is broader than simply making profits through its business operations. It is also involved in a highly regulated [casino] industry. These factors make collective bargaining unusually complex.

53. Fourth, the union made significant moves in collective bargaining, and in particular, during the last bargaining session. It concluded that it had come to the end of its ability to compromise while maintaining a position that would be acceptable to members of the bargaining unit. The employer does not share this view and insists that there is still room to move. This "room", however, has not been communicated to the union or the Board. Despite the number of meetings, there have been insignificant negotiations on the wage issue due in large part to the employer's insistence on a merit pay system. While the employer moved off the merit pay proposal in the last sessions of bargaining, this movement came rather late in the process. The union was largely left to bargain with itself on the wage issue. The employer was represented in bargaining by experienced labour relations personnel who would understand the likelihood of any union accepting a merit pay system in a collective agreement. We find that the union's assessment that collective bargaining is at an impasse is accurate and that little would be gained by requiring the parties to return to the bargaining table.

54. Overall, for the reasons stated above, we find that, despite their concerted efforts, collective bargaining has broken down between the parties. They are unlikely to a reach collective agreement if left to their own devices. Section 26.5 is designed to overcome the type of difficulties that prevent the achievement of a first collective agreement. In our view, it is appropriate for the Board to assist the parties to conclude a first collective agreement.

Collective Agreement Provisions

55. The principles applied by the Board in determining which collective agreement provision it should implement when settling a first collective agreement were also set out in the Board's reasons for decision of September 18, 2001, supra, where the Board concluded at p. 102 CLRBR, p. 712 Sask. LRBR:

> 19. If the Board decides to intervene in the matter, the manner in which the Board that is asks the parties to address the outstanding issues is by indicating to the Board why the party does not accept the Board agent's recommendations. For instance, on the question of wages, a party may argue that the wages proposed by the Board agent exceed the wage package provided for similar employees under different collective agreements. . . .

56. We will address the collective bargaining issues in the order of their appearance in the proposed collective agreement.

Article 3.02 – Union Security

57. The parties agreed to a basic union security provision in art. 3.02. Originally, the union sought a provision that would require the employer to deduct union dues and forward them to the union without written authorization from employees.

58. The employer objected to such a provision and relied on s. 32 of the Act to support its assertion that the employer can only deduct union dues when it has an authorization signed by the employees.

59. The union countered by requesting that the employer provide it with the names, addresses and telephone numbers of all employees in order that it could obtain the employee's authorization for dues deduction. . . .

61. The Board agent proposed that the agreed-upon art. 3.02 be amended by adding the sentence: "Upon the request of the union, the company shall provide the current names and addresses of all bargaining unit employees." . . .

63. . . . . We would amend the proposed art. 3.02 to read as follows:

> 3.02 Upon the written request of the employee and during the life of this agreement, the Employer will deduct from the earnings of each employee covered by this Agreement, Union initiation fees and dues prescribed by the Constitution and Bylaws of the Union. At the end of each calendar month and prior to the tenth (10th) day of the following month, the Employer shall remit by cheque to the financial secretary of the Local Union, the total of the deductions made. The Employer shall provide the names, addresses and telephone numbers of all its employees who are covered by the terms of this agreement to the Union.

Article 4 – Management Rights

64. The Board agent did not refer to art. 4 in his report. The employer took the position that the management rights clause was outstanding. The employer proposed the following management rights clause:

> 4.01 The Union acknowledges it is the exclusive function and right of the Employer to operate and manage its business in all respects, including without limiting the generality of the foregoing, the right to plan, direct and control the Employer's operation, to contract out work, the right to decide on the number of employees, the mode, method, equipment to carry out the work, the right to make and alter from time to time rules and regulations to be observed by the employees (such rules not to be inconsistent with the specific provisions of this agreement), the power and right to maintain and improve the efficiency of the operations; to hire, classify, transfer, promote, demote, lay off, assign work, and duties, jobs, shifts or employees, to suspend, discipline or discharge employees for just cause, recognizing that just cause for immediate discharge (at the discretion of the Employer and subject to EAP programs) shall include loss or suspension of gaming license, use of alcohol, unlawful drugs or chemical substances during working hours, intoxication on the job, actual or attempted conversion of property of the Employer, any supplier, other employees or any other person at the Casino or conviction of an offense under the Criminal Code involving honesty and subject to the rules below,

other criminal convictions. However, the Employer's right to discipline and discharge shall not be limited to the above and can include other unacceptable conduct as provided in the Employer's rules and regulations. . . .

65. The union's last proposal was as follows:

> 4.01 The Union acknowledges it is the exclusive function and right of the Employer to operate and manage its business in all respects that are not specifically abridged or modified by this Agreement. Management shall exercise its rights in a manner that is fair and consistent with the terms of this Agreement.

66. In justifying its position, the employer referred to the need for security in the casino operation and for trustworthy and honest employees. The employer also referred the Board to three collective agreements negotiated between different unions and employers in the hotel industry that adopt management rights clauses similar to the clauses proposed by the employer. The employer is attempting to avoid having an arbitrator substitute different penalties in place of discharge for certain workplace disciplinary events.

67. We would agree that trustworthiness and honesty are essential characteristics required of casino employees. On the other hand, the employer's proposed management rights clause seriously reduces employees' access to the grievance and arbitration provisions by removing arbitrator discretion over penalty in many serious disciplinary grievances. Access to the grievance and arbitration process is generally considered one of the main benefits of unionization.

68. Legislative policy contained in the Act supports the significance of the grievance and arbitration systems as key rights to be gained when employees form a trade union. Section 26.2 [new S.S. 1994, c. 47, s. 15] provides access to the arbitration process to employees during the period from date of certification until a collective agreement is reached and permits employees who have been discharged or suspended during this pre-agreement period to have their termination or suspension reviewed by an arbitrator on a standard of just cause. Section 25(3) of the Act allows such an arbitrator to substitute "such other penalty for the discharge or discipline as the arbitrator or arbitration board seems just and reasonable in the circumstances".

69. While it may be possible for certain employers to achieve collective agreements that contain a specific penalty for the infraction that is the subject-matter of the arbitration (as is contemplated in part in s. 25(3)), a clause of this nature is uncommon. Generally, it would not be achieved at a bargaining table and, in light of the legislative policy granting ready access to arbitration during the pre-collective agreement period, we find the employer's proposal to be unreasonable.

70. The union's proposed management rights clause is more in keeping with the usual management rights provision achieved in collective agreements. We note that it is similar to the management rights clause contained in the collective agreement between Saskatchewan Gaming Corporation and Public Service Alliance of Canada for Casino Regina (June 1, 2000 to May 31, 2003). [The Board adopts the union's proposal.]

Article 9 – Bulletining and Filling of Positions. . . .

87. The employer opposed the Board agent's recommendations [for a Joint Union Management Employment Equity Committee (JUMEEC) to develop a plan providing a 50% target

for First Nation employment using seniority to select applicants as long as the applicant was qualified]. It argued that one of its key mandates is to provide employment opportunities for First Nations' people as part of the overall strategy of the FSIN and the Government of Saskatchewan to alleviate high unemployment for First Nations' people. The employer noted that the Saskatchewan Human Rights Commission had authorized affirmative action for First Nations' people to the extent of 80% of hiring, promotion and training opportunities in each department. The employer argued that seniority-based hiring is an obstacle to achieving workplace equity for First Nations' employees and it ought to be set aside in the agreement to the extent of the exemption granted by the Saskatchewan Human Rights Commission.

88. The employer also opposed the recommendations of the Board agent because they diluted the exemption already granted from 80% to 50%. In addition, the employer noted that art. 9.03(a) in the Board agent's proposals established a "senior, if qualified" provision on seniority, whereas the parties had previously been working with a skill and ability clause with seniority being the deciding factor if skill and ability are relatively equal.

89. The employer noted that the Board agent's recommendation was drawn from the agreement between Casino Regina and the Public Service Alliance of Canada. It noted that Casino Regina did not have an affirmative action plan in place prior to the signing of the collective agreement, whereas this employer does have an affirmative action plan in place that is approved by the Saskatchewan Human Rights Commission. The employer viewed the purpose of the JUMEEC in the Casino Regina agreement was to develop the affirmative action plan. . . .

91. The main differences between the employer's proposals and the Board agent's proposals relate to the level of First Nations' hiring in each classification; the type of seniority clause; and the role of the union in developing and monitoring the affirmative action program. In the employer's proposal, the level of First Nations' hiring is set at 80% of each classification; the role of seniority is more restricted [as a tie-breaker among equally qualified applicants]; and the union does not play a role in the development or monitoring of the affirmative action program.

92. In the Board agent's report, the level of First Nations' hiring is set at 50%; the role of seniority for the remaining positions is stronger; and the union has a role through the JUMEEC in developing and monitoring the affirmative action program.

93. We will address each of these three areas. First, in relation to the level of First Nations' hiring, we are of the view that the 80% level ought to be used. The employer's principal mandate is to provide employment and training opportunities to First Nations' persons. To achieve this goal, the employer has obtained a human rights exemption permitting it to extend this preference to 80% of each classification. In our view, it is proper to reflect this commitment in the collective agreement as the goal of any employment equity plan even if it is possible to conclude that the target could be reached without an express inclusion of it in the employment equity provisions.

94. Second, in relation to the role of seniority for positions that are filled outside the affirmative action program, the parties have agreed through collective bargaining to accept a competitive clause – that is, one that examines the qualifications, skill, ability and seniority of the applicants and selects the most senior only in the event that qualifications, skill and ability are relatively equal. The parties both approached the application of the seniority principle

from the competitive approach, as opposed to the senior, if qualified, approach proposed by the Board agent. We will adopt the approach agreed to in principle by the parties.

95. Finally, we view the role of the union in the affirmative action development and monitoring to be key to its overall success. Through the JUMEEC, the parties can develop different training and recruitment programs to assist First Nations' employees to obtain and retain employment at the casino. The union is kept informed as a partner in the process of the success of the program and can assist in identifying barriers and training needs. The union is also afforded an opportunity to keep its membership informed of promotional and training opportunities available for First Nations' employees. The type of clause proposed by the Board agent has been used in Casino Regina and is similar to employment equity clauses set out in Sack and Poskanzer, Contract Clauses, 3rd ed. (Toronto: Lancaster House, 1996). . . .

Article 39 – Wages

97. As we indicated above, the parties did not engage in serious or protracted bargaining on the wage issue. It is difficult for the Board to apply the replication theory in circumstances where the parties have not engaged in constructive bargaining on an issue. The Board is left guessing to a great extent on where the parties would have ended up if bargaining had been successful. There are few clues in the history of bargaining to lead us to a logical answer given the lack of meaningful bargaining on this issue. In the circumstances, we prefer to look instead to other agreements in the industry that were achieved through collective bargaining. They provide a picture of what other unions and employers have achieved through collective bargaining in environments that are similar to the ones facing the parties to this application.

98. In this case, the Board agent recommended wage scales taken from the Casino Regina collective agreement. The Board agrees with this recommendation. Casino Regina is a directly comparable employer to the employer in terms of the type of industry and type of positions. Casino Regina is also a relatively new employer. Although the employer opposes the imposition of the Casino Regina rates of pay, there are no factors which lead us to conclude that the rates are unreasonable or unfair to the employer, or the employees, in question. . . .

[The employer representative of the tripartite panel dissented.]

Notes

1. What is "interest" arbitration? Most arbitration agreements deal with "rights" issues, i.e., claims that a contract has been breached thereby breaching the claimant's rights under it. How is interest arbitration different?

2. What is the rationale for making interest arbitration available to first contract parties? Is the reason the inexperience of the parties in bargaining or the need to break the momentum of the preexisting system? Or, is the reason for first contract arbitration the likelihood that employers want to avoid reaching an agreement for fear that would establish the union as permanent? "The underlying rationale of first-contract arbitration is the facilitation of collective bargaining." NORTH AMERICA LABOR LAW, 57. If so, does the existing law imposing liability for a breach of the duty of good faith bargaining, which is a feature of both United States and Canadian labor

law, fail to work adequately to remedy cases where the employer is opposed to agreement? In the United States, §10(c) of the N.L.R.A. gives the National Labor Relations Board authority to grant affirmative relief. But §8(d) has been interpreted to deprive the Board of power to compel a party to agree to any substantive term of a collective bargaining agreement. INTERNATIONAL LABOR & EMPLOYMENT LAW, at 23c–57.

3. Should interest arbitration be available for all collective bargaining relationships, whether or not it is the first contracting situation? In the United States, some states and the federal government provide interest arbitration in lieu of the right to strike for their employees. The workers at the casino here had the right to strike and the employer had the right to lockout. Aren't those rights sufficient to create incentives for the parties to reach agreement rather than face the economic consequences of strikes and lockouts?

4. What triggers a right to go to arbitration to establish the first collective bargaining agreement? The New Oxford American Dictionary defines "impasse" as "a situation in which no progress is possible, esp. because of disagreement; a deadlock." Does the availability of interest arbitration influence whether an impasse occurs? The board tries to avoid the "narcotic effect" of the easy availability of arbitration. Is it successful? There were two bargaining sessions followed by twelve meeting with a labor board conciliation officer. Is that enough to make it clear that an impasse exists?

5. In deciding what the terms of the collective bargaining agreement should be, the labor board here looked at the final bargaining positions of the parties but then imposed a contract of its own design, term by term. Would interest arbitration work better if the arbitrator was limited to choosing the complete final offer of one party or the other but without the authority to modify either final offer? Would the so-called baseball salary arbitration system used in Major League Baseball in the United States work as a better incentive to get the parties to compromise during their collective bargaining and, therefore, be more likely to reach agreement without resort to arbitration? In other words, would bargaining work better if each party had a strong incentive to continue to compromise its positions to appear more reasonable than the opposing party should the case eventually go to arbitration? Would the board be able to make the choice as to which side's last, best offer to adopt as the collective bargaining agreement?

6. Did the labor board here give the union less than it could have as to the collection of union dues? Most Canadian jurisdictions require that, "at the request of the union, the employer deduct and remit to the union the amount of regular union dues from the wages of each worker who is a member of a bargaining unit that it represents, whether or not the worker is a union member." NORTH AMERICA LABOR LAW, at 44. In *Lavigne v. Ontario Public Service Employees' Union*, [1991] 2. S.C.R. 211, the Supreme Court of Canada unanimously rejected the argument of Lavigne that his freedom of association rights were violated because he was required to pay union dues because he was covered by a collective bargaining agreement but was not a member of the union. He objected to political contributions the union was making, including to a nuclear disarmament campaign. Three of the seven justices concluded that freedom of association does not include freedom from compelled association. Three found that, although the Charter of Rights and Freedoms did include freedom to associate, it did not include the freedom *not* to associate, Union

dues fell within a class of required association that is a necessary and inevitable part of membership in a democratic community. The seventh justice ruled that requiring an individual to pay dues to a union which later spends a portion on political causes does not associate that individual with the ideas and values of the union. More recently, a majority of the Court found that a mandatory membership provision in a Quebec construction industry collective bargaining agreement did not violate the negative freedom of association but a majority for the first time recognized such a negative freedom. *R. v. Advance Cutting & Coring*, [2001] 3 S.C.R. 209. *See Great Expectations*, at 209. In the United States, bargaining unit members, who are not members of the union that represents, may be required to pay a representation fee but the union must reduce the fee by that portion of dues expended for purposes other than collective bargaining and contract enforcement. *Id.* at 46.

7. "All Canadian jurisdictions require that certain clauses be included in all collective agreements. Legally mandatory collective agreement clauses generally include: clauses forbidding strikes and lockouts during the term of the agreement, clauses providing for access to binding arbitration of all differences relating to the interpretation, application of alleged violation of the collective agreement, and a minimum collective agreement duration of one year." NORTH AMERICA LABOR LAW, at 56.

8. "Human rights statutes in every province but Alberta expressly permit the use of affirmative action programs to ameliorate conditions of disadvantage experienced by members of the protected groups." CANADIAN LABOR & EMPLOYMENT LAW, at 239. Does the plan approved by the labor board trammel upon the rights of the employees in the unit who were not First Nation people?

---

3. Strikes and Lockouts

There is a history of significant strike activity in Canada. "From 1986 to 1995 Canada's strike rate was about 2.5 times higher than the average of the 24 nations of the OECD. . . . Historically, strike levels have moved in cycles. There was a wave of unrest early in the 20th century, another around World War I, a third beginning in the late 1930s and a fourth in the 1970s. The latest wave abated in 1983, and most measures of disputes have fallen sharply since then." INTERNATIONAL & COMPARATIVE EMPLOYMENT RELATIONS, at 106. "[T]he average number of strikes per year has declined sharply from 693 between 1982 and 1988 and 409 between 1989 and 2001." "Great Expectations," at 127. Canadian labor laws define the right to strike broadly, typically including "concerted refusals to work, cessations or slowdowns of work and other concerted activities designed to restrict or limit output." NORTH AMERICA LABOR LAW, at 65.

In contrast, the right of employees to strike in the United States does not include partial or intermittent strikes or slowdowns. But strikes during the term of a collective bargaining agreement are prohibited in Canada as is striking to gain union recognition. Neither is prohibited by U.S. law. In *RWDSU, Local 558 v. Pepsi-Cola Canada Beverages (West) Ltd.*, [2002] 1 S.C.R. 156, the Supreme Court, for the first time, found that, because of the Charter of Rights and Freedoms, secondary picketing is legal at common law unless the picketing involves conduct that is independently tortius or criminal. See, *Great Expectations*, at 133.

Before a strike may occur, all jurisdictions require a secret ballot strike vote, usually by all the workers represented in the bargaining unit, whether or not they are union members. Most jurisdictions authorize the labor board or labor minister to have the employer's last contract offer be put to a vote by union members either before or after a strike starts. Employers in five provinces can apply to the board for such a vote. Further, all jurisdictions require notice plus attempted conciliation and possibly mediation by the labor board before a legal strike can be initiated. "There are two models: a tripartite board may be appointed and given authority to report publicly on a dispute; alternatively, single mediators function without the power to issue a report." More than half of all agreements reached have involved some type of third-party intervention, with the single mediation model now most common. INTERNATIONAL & COMPARATIVE EMPLOYMENT RELATIONS, at 106.

Peaceful primary picketing is lawful and, as a means of free expression, is granted a measure of constitutional protection. *RWDSU Local 580 v. Dolphin Delivery Ltd.*, [1986] 2. S.C.R. 573. Common law actions, such as trespass and wrongful interference with economic relations, can be brought in court to restrict picketing. Courts had generally held that secondary picketing, directed at a neutral third party to the primary labor dispute for the purpose of persuading customers not to purchase products of the primary employer or do business with it, was not legal. NORTH AMERICA LABOR LAW, at 70–71. Recently, however, the Canadian Supreme Court overturned the preexisting distinction between primary and secondary picketing. In *RWDSU Local 558 v. Pepsi-Cola Canada Beverages (West) Ltd.*, [2002], 208 D.L.R. (4th) 385 (S.C.C.), Pepsi employees went out on strike and in doing so posted pickets at retail outlets selling Pepsi, and at a hotel where replacement workers were staying. The Court found a link between freedom of expression associated with picketing and the need for the workers to counter the imbalance of economic power favoring employers. "Free expression in the labour context thus plays a significant role in redressing or alleviating this imbalance." Because of the right to elicit the support of the general public, an absolute ban on secondary picketing was too restrictive. Instead, only picketing that breaches the criminal law or a specific tort such as trespass, nuisance, intimidation, defamation, or misrepresentation is prohibited. "[T]he difficult and potentially arbitrary distinction between primary and secondary picketing is effectively abandoned on a wrongful action approach to picketing. Secondary picketing has been . . . location defined. . . . A conduct approach based on tortuous and criminal acts does not depend on location. All picketing is allowed, whether 'primary' or 'secondary,' unless it involves tortuous or criminal conduct." *Id.*

The permanent replacement of strikers is not permitted in Canada. The statutes of some provinces prohibit permanent replacement or guarantee strikers their jobs. In other provinces and the federal sector, the labor boards have found that permanently replacing strikers is a reprisal against them for striking and is prohibited. Quebec prohibits even the hiring of temporary replacements for strikers. Generally, the use of temporary replacements for the purpose of destroying the union's representative status is prohibited. NORTH AMERICA LABOR LAW, at 71–72.

As in the United States, the employer has a corresponding right to lockout workers to pressure the union to accept its proposed collective bargaining agreement but it is not available as a justification for closing down a place of business for any other reason. Like strikes, lockouts are lawful only after the process of negotiation, conciliation, and mediation has been followed. "The two rights, to strike and to lock out, are, in fact, always acquired at the same time." INTERNATIONAL LABOR & EMPLOYMENT LAW, at 21–39. The restrictions on replacement workers apply during lockouts. Lockouts, however, are relatively infrequent in Canada.

D. WAGES, HOURS, AND BENEFITS

The federal government as to employment within its jurisdiction and all the provinces establish minimum wages, with the range from C$5.90 to C$8.00 per hour. The different jurisdictions all regulate the length of the workday, the workweek and work on a day of rest. The federal jurisdiction and British Columbia, Manitoba, and Saskatchewan, limit work to eight hours per day and forty hours per week, with some other provinces restricting work to forty-hour weeks, while others provide forty-eight-hour work weeks. Work over the maximums must be paid overtime, typically time and a half. Two provinces have adopted laws that to some extent protect part-time workers. Saskatchewan requires employers to provide pro rata benefits to part-time workers and Quebec imposes an equal pay requirement. LABOUR LAW IN CANADA, at 236. All jurisdictions provide for eight or nine paid public holidays per year. All jurisdictions require a minimum of two weeks paid vacation, with the pay set at 2 percent of the employee's annual pay per week of vacation. Most provide for three weeks' vacation after a certain amount of seniority with the employer. How do these provisions compare with the law in the United States? Should paid vacations be legally mandated or left to the labor market to establish?

Unemployment insurance is administered by the federal government, with benefits equal to 55 percent of the worker's average weekly earnings up to a maximum of C$413. The Canada Pension Plan (CPP) is a universal pension plan administered by the federal government, except for Quebec that administers its own parallel program. Like Social Security in the United States, the CPP provides a minimum pension and is not intended to replace private pension plans or personal savings. The CPP is financed out of contributions by employees and their employers. As in the United States, Canadian law provides for private pension and retirement plans through a variety of vehicles. Individuals can take advantage of tax-sheltered "registered retirement savings plans" (RRSP) and every Canadian jurisdiction has pension benefits legislation, comparable to the ERISA provisions in the United States.

All jurisdictions provide for pregnancy and parental leave that are coordinated with the federal Employment Insurance Act. Generally, the laws do not require that employees be paid for these leaves beyond the seventeen-week period covered by the unemployment insurance benefits. The law allows claimants to "stack" unemployment, maternity, paternity, and sickness benefits for a maximum period of sixty-five weeks.

In addition to occupational health and safety standards set by each province, the Canadian provinces have adopted statutory "no fault" insurances schemes to compensate workers who suffer occupational injury and illness. Each province administers its workers' compensation system by a workers' compensation board.

Although the federal government contributes substantial financial support to health care and sets minimum health care standards, health care is a matter of provincial jurisdiction. All the provinces provide universal access to basic medical care including physical treatments other than cosmetic surgery, hospitalization, laboratory and other diagnostic tests, and drugs and medications administered in hospitals. Four provinces require employers to pay a health care payroll tax set as a percent of total payroll per year. The other provinces fund health care through general tax revenues. Extended health care plans are provided by employers to cover medical expenses beyond the basic medical care covered by the government plans.

Ontario and the federal jurisdiction require the payment of severance pay as an additional payment to employees upon termination. In Ontario, the trigger for payment is the termination of large numbers of employees – fifty or more within six months – or a comparatively large payroll – C$2.5 million per annum. The payment is equal to one week's pay for each year of employment up to a maximum of twenty-six weeks. The federal trigger is if the employee terminated is not retiring on a full pension and has at least twelve months continuous service. Payments under the federal scheme "are meager." LABOUR LAW IN CANADA, at 188.

E. ANTIDISCRIMINATION LAW

All Canadian jurisdictions "prohibit discrimination on grounds of race, color, national or ethnic origin, place of origin, age sex, marital status, physical disability, religion or creed, and mental disability." International LABOR & EMPLOYMENT LAW, at 21-59. Pregnancy discrimination is either expressly prohibited or found to be discrimination because of sex. Some jurisdictions go further and prohibit discrimination on such grounds as political beliefs, criminal convictions, alcohol and drug addiction, family and civil status. Effective in 2004, Quebec legislation prohibits psychological harassment in the workplace.

In 1986, Quebec added an express prohibition against sexual orientation discrimination. In 1997, the federal statute added sexual orientation as a prohibited ground of discrimination. All other provinces, but for Alberta, have now added this ground to their statutes. *Id.*

The Canadian Charter of Rights and Freedoms has played an important part in the development of employment discrimination law. Section 15 sets forth the Equality Rights provision:

> 15. (1) Every individual is equal before and under the law and has the right to the equal protection and equal benefit of the law without discrimination and, in particular, without discrimination based on race, national or ethnic origin, colour, religion, sex, age or mental or physical disability.
> (2) Subsection (1) does not preclude any law, program or activity that has as its object the amelioration of conditions of disadvantaged individual or groups including those that are disadvantaged because of race, national or ethnic origin, colour, religion, sex, age or mental or physical disability.

Although the Charter applies directly only to government action and not to private employers, it has been used to challenge human rights statutes as being "under-inclusive." In *Egan v. Canada*, [1995] 2 S.C.R. 513, the Supreme Court held that the Canadian Charter must be read to include sexual orientation since the problem of sexual orientation discrimination was analogous to the grounds that the Charter dealt with. In *Vriend v. Alberta*, [1998] 1 S.C.R. 493, the Court ruled that the Alberta human rights statute must be read to prohibit discrimination on the ground of sexual orientation, even though the Alberta legislature had expressly declined to include it. The use of this "under-inclusion" theory has the effect of reading Charter rights into the human rights statutes thereby making them applicable to private employment.

If a human rights statute provides protection on the ground of the discrimination that an individual alleges, then "no private cause of action exists and the plaintiff is barred from bringing a case before the courts." The proper venue is the appropriate human rights board or, if the employee is covered by a collective bargaining agreement, arbitration under that agreement. CANADIAN LABOUR & EMPLOYMENT LAW, at 147.

BRITISH COLUMBIA (PUBLIC SERVICE EMPLOYEE RELATIONS COMMISSION) V. BCGSEU [B. C. FIREFIGHTERS]

[1999] 3 S.C.R. 3

THE JUDGMENT OF THE COURT was delivered by MCLACHLIN J . . .

II. Facts

4. Ms. Meiorin was employed for three years by the British Columbia Ministry of Forests as a member of a three-person Initial Attack Forest Firefighting Crew in the Golden Forest District. The crew's job was to attack and suppress forest fires while they were small and could be contained. Ms. Meiorin's supervisors found her work to be satisfactory.

5. Ms. Meiorin was not asked to take a physical fitness test until 1994, when she was required to pass the Government's "Bona Fide Occupational Fitness Tests and Standards for B.C. Forest Service Wildland Firefighters" (the "Tests"). The Tests required that the forest firefighters weigh less than 200 lbs. (with their equipment) and complete a shuttle run, an upright rowing exercise, and a pump carrying/hose dragging exercise within stipulated times. The running test was designed to test the forest firefighters' aerobic fitness and was based on the view that forest firefighters must have a minimum "VO2 max" of 50 ml.kg-1.min-1 (the "aerobic standard"). "VO2 max" measures "maximal oxygen uptake", or the rate at which the body can take in oxygen, transport it to the muscles, and use it to produce energy.

6. The Tests were developed in response to a 1991 Coroner's Inquest Report that recommended that only physically fit employees be assigned as front-line forest firefighters for safety reasons. The Government commissioned a team of researchers from the University of Victoria to undertake a review of its existing fitness standards with a view to protecting the safety of firefighters while meeting human rights norms. The researchers developed the Tests by identifying the essential components of forest firefighting, measuring the physiological demands of those components, selecting fitness tests to measure those demands and, finally, assessing the validity of those tests.

7. The researchers studied various sample groups. The specific tasks performed by forest firefighters were identified by reviewing amalgamated data collected by the British Columbia Forest Service. The physiological demands of those tasks were then measured by observing test subjects as they performed them in the field. One simulation involved 18 firefighters, another involved 10 firefighters, but it is unclear from the researchers' report whether the subjects at this stage were male or female. The researchers asked a pilot group of 10 university student volunteers (6 females and 4 males) to perform a series of proposed fitness tests and field exercises. After refining the preferred tests, the researchers observed them being performed by a larger sample group composed of 31 forest firefighter trainees and 15 university student volunteers (31 males and 15 females), and correlated their results with the group's performance in the field. Having concluded that the preferred tests were accurate predictors of actual forest

firefighting performance – including the running test designed to gauge whether the subject met the aerobic standard – the researchers presented their report to the Government in 1992.

8. A follow-up study in 1994 of 77 male forest firefighters and 2 female forest firefighters used the same methodology. However, the researchers this time recommended that the Government initiate another study to examine the impact of the Tests on women. There is no evidence before us that the Government has yet responded to this recommendation.

9. Two aspects of the researchers' methodology are critical to this case. First, it was primarily descriptive, based on measuring the average performance levels of the test subjects and converting this data into minimum performance standards. Second, it did not seem to distinguish between the male and female test subjects.

10. After four attempts, Ms. Meiorin failed to meet the aerobic standard, running the distance in 11 minutes and 49.4 seconds instead of the required 11 minutes. As a result, she was laid off. Her union subsequently brought a grievance on her behalf. The arbitrator designated to hear the grievance was required to determine whether she had been improperly dismissed.

11. Evidence accepted by the arbitrator demonstrated that, owing to physiological differences, most women have lower aerobic capacity than most men. Even with training, most women cannot increase their aerobic capacity to the level required by the aerobic standard, although training can allow most men to meet it. The arbitrator also heard evidence that 65 percent to 70 percent of male applicants pass the Tests on their initial attempts, while only 35 percent of female applicants have similar success. Of the 800 to 900 Initial Attack Crew members employed by the Government in 1995, only 100 to 150 were female.

12. There was no credible evidence showing that the prescribed aerobic capacity was necessary for either men or women to perform the work of a forest firefighter satisfactorily. On the contrary, Ms. Meiorin had in the past performed her work well, without apparent risk to herself, her colleagues or the public.

III. The Rulings

13. The arbitrator found that Ms. Meiorin had established a *prima facie* case of adverse effect discrimination by showing that the aerobic standard has a disproportionately negative effect on women as a group. He further found that the Government had presented no credible evidence that Ms. Meiorin's inability to meet the aerobic standard meant that she constituted a safety risk to herself, her colleagues, or the public, and hence had not discharged its burden of showing that it had accommodated Ms. Meiorin to the point of undue hardship. He ordered that she be reinstated to her former position and compensated for her lost wages and benefits.

14. The Court of Appeal did not distinguish between direct and adverse effect discrimination. It held that so long as the standard is *necessary* to the safe and efficient performance of the work and is applied through individualized testing, there is no discrimination. The Court of Appeal (mistakenly) read the arbitrator's reasons as finding that the aerobic standard was necessary to the safe and efficient performance of the work. Since Ms. Meiorin had been individually tested against this standard, it allowed the appeal and dismissed her claim. The Court of Appeal commented that to permit Ms. Meiorin to succeed would create "reverse

discrimination", i.e., to set a lower standard for women than for men would discriminate against those men who failed to meet the men's standard but were nevertheless capable of meeting the women's standard. . . .

VI. Analysis

17. As a preliminary matter, I must sort out a characterization issue. The Court of Appeal seems to have understood the arbitrator as having held that the ability to meet the aerobic standard is necessary to the safe and efficient performance of the work of an Initial Attack Crew member. With respect, I cannot agree with this reading of the arbitrator's reasons.

18. The arbitrator held that the standard was one of the appropriate measurements available to the Government and that there is generally a reasonable relationship between aerobic fitness and the ability to perform the job of an Initial Attack Crew member. This falls short, however, of an affirmative finding that the ability to meet the aerobic standard chosen by the Government is necessary to the safe and efficient performance of the job. To the contrary, that inference is belied by the arbitrator's conclusion that, despite her failure to meet the aerobic standard, Ms. Meiorin did not pose a serious safety risk to herself, her colleagues, or the general public. I therefore proceed on the view that the arbitrator did not find that an applicant's ability to meet the aerobic standard is necessary to his or her ability to perform the tasks of an Initial Attack Crew member safely and efficiently. This leaves us to face squarely the issue of whether the aerobic standard is unjustifiably discriminatory within the meaning of the Code.

A. The Test

1. *The Conventional Approach*

19. The conventional approach to applying human rights legislation in the workplace requires the tribunal to decide at the outset into which of two categories the case falls: (1) "direct discrimination", where the standard is discriminatory on its face, or (2) "adverse effect discrimination", where the facially neutral standard discriminates in effect. If a *prima facie* case of either form of discrimination is established, the burden shifts to the employer to justify it.

20. In the case of direct discrimination, the employer may establish that the standard is a BFOR [Bona Fide Occupational Reason] by showing: (1) that the standard was imposed honestly and in good faith and was not designed to undermine the objectives of the human rights legislation (the subjective element); and (2) that the standard is reasonably necessary to the safe and efficient performance of the work and does not place an unreasonable burden on those to whom it applies (the objective element). It is difficult for an employer to justify a standard as a BFOR where individual testing of the capabilities of the employee or applicant is a reasonable alternative.

21. If these criteria are established, the standard is justified as a BFOR. If they are not, the standard itself is struck down.

22. A different analysis applies to adverse effect discrimination. The BFOR defence does not apply. *Prima facie* discrimination established, the employer need only show: (1) that there

is a rational connection between the job and the particular standard, and (2) that it cannot further accommodate the claimant without incurring undue hardship. If the employer cannot discharge this burden, then it has failed to establish a defence to the charge of discrimination. In such a case, the claimant succeeds, but the standard itself always remains intact.

23. The arbitrator considered the aerobic standard to be a neutral standard that adversely affected Ms. Meiorin. The Court of Appeal, on the other hand, did not distinguish between direct and adverse effect discrimination, simply holding that it is not discriminatory to test individuals against a standard demonstrated to be necessary to the safe and efficient performance of the work. Approaching the case purely on the conventional bifurcated approach, the better view would seem to be that the standard is neutral on its face, leading one to the adverse effect discrimination analysis. On the conventional analysis, I agree with the arbitrator that a case of *prima facie* adverse effect discrimination was made out and that, on the record before him and before this Court, the Government failed to discharge its burden of showing that it had accommodated Ms. Meiorin to the point of undue hardship.

24. However, the divergent approaches taken by the arbitrator and the Court of Appeal suggest a more profound difficulty with the conventional test itself. The parties to this appeal have accordingly invited this Court to adopt a new model of analysis that avoids the threshold distinction between direct discrimination and adverse effect discrimination and integrates the concept of accommodation within the BFOR defence.

2. *Why is a New Approach Required? . . .*

27. The distinction between a standard that is discriminatory on its face and a neutral standard that is discriminatory in its effect is difficult to justify, simply because there are few cases that can be so neatly characterized. For example, a rule requiring all workers to appear at work on Fridays or face dismissal may plausibly be characterized as either directly *discriminatory* (because it means that no workers whose religious beliefs preclude working on Fridays may be employed there) or as a neutral rule that merely has an *adverse effect* on a few individuals (those same workers whose religious beliefs prevent them from working on Fridays). On the same reasoning, it could plausibly be argued that forcing employees to take a mandatory pregnancy test before commencing employment is a neutral rule because it is facially applied to all members of a workforce and its special effects on women are only incidental.

29. Not only is the distinction between direct and indirect discrimination malleable, it is also unrealistic: a modern employer with a discriminatory intention would rarely frame the rule in directly discriminatory terms when the same effect – or an even broader effect – could be easily realized by couching it in neutral language. The bifurcated analysis gives employers with a discriminatory intention and the forethought to draft the rule in neutral language an undeserved cloak of legitimacy.

30. The malleability of the initial classification under the conventional approach would not matter so much if both routes led to the same result. But, as indicated above, the potential remedies may differ. If an employer cannot justify a directly discriminatory standard as a BFOR, it will be struck down in its entirety. However, if the rule is characterized as a neutral one that adversely affects a certain individual, the employer need only show that there is a rational connection between the standard and the performance of the job and that it cannot further

accommodate the claimant without experiencing undue hardship. The general standard, however, remains in effect. These very different results flow directly from the stream into which the initial inquiry shunts. . . .

32. From a narrowly utilitarian perspective, it could be argued that it is sometimes appropriate to leave an ostensibly neutral standard in place if its adverse effects are felt by only one or, at most, a few individuals. This seems to have been the original rationale of this Court's adverse effect discrimination jurisprudence. . . .

33. To the extent that the bifurcated analysis relies on a comparison between the relative demographic representation of various groups, it is arguably unhelpful. First, the argument that an apparently neutral standard should be permitted to stand because its discriminatory effect is limited to members of a minority group and does not adversely affect the majority of employees is difficult to defend. The standard itself is discriminatory precisely because it treats some individuals differently from others, on the basis of a prohibited ground. . . .

36. At this point, which exists where women [who are a majority nevertheless] constitute the adversely affected group, the adverse effect analysis may serve to entrench the male norm as the "mainstream" into which women must integrate. Concerns about economic efficiency and safety, shorn of their utilitarian cloaks, may well operate to discriminate against women in a way that is direct in every way except that contemplated by the legal nomenclature. . . .

41. Although the practical result of the conventional analysis may be that individual claimants are accommodated and the particular discriminatory effect they experience may be alleviated, the larger import of the analysis cannot be ignored. It bars courts and tribunals from assessing the legitimacy of the standard itself. Referring to the distinction that the conventional analysis draws between the accepted neutral standard and the duty to accommodate those who are adversely affected by it, Day and Brodsky write:

> The difficulty with this paradigm is that it does not challenge the imbalances of power, or the discourses of dominance, such as racism, ablebodyism and sexism, which result in a society being designed well for some and not for others. It allows those who consider themselves "normal" to continue to construct institutions and relations in their image, as long as others, when they challenge this construction are "accommodated".

Accommodation, conceived this way, appears to be rooted in the formal model of equality. As a formula, different treatment for "different" people is merely the flip side of like treatment for likes. Accommodation does not go to the heart of the equality question, to the goal of transformation, to an examination of the way institutions and relations must be changed in order to make them available, accessible, meaningful and rewarding for the many diverse groups of which our society is composed. Accommodation seems to mean that we do not change procedures or services, we simply "accommodate" those who do not quite fit. We make some concessions to those who are "different", rather than abandoning the idea of "normal" and working for genuine inclusiveness. . . .

42. This case, where Ms. Meiorin seeks to keep her position in a male-dominated occupation, is a good example of how the conventional analysis shields systemic discrimination from scrutiny. This analysis prevents the Court from rigorously assessing a standard which, in the course of regulating entry to a male-dominated occupation, adversely affects women as a

group. Although the Government may have a duty to accommodate an individual claimant, the practical result of the conventional analysis is that the complex web of seemingly neutral, systemic barriers to traditionally male-dominated occupations remains beyond the direct reach of the law. The right to be free from discrimination is reduced to a question of whether the "mainstream" can afford to confer proper treatment on those adversely affected, within the confines of its existing formal standard. If it cannot, the edifice of systemic discrimination receives the law's approval. This cannot be right. . . .

4. Elements of a Unified Approach

54. Having considered the various alternatives, I propose the following three-step test for determining whether a *prima facie* discriminatory standard is a BFOR. An employer may justify the impugned standard by establishing on the balance of probabilities:

(1)   that the employer adopted the standard for a purpose rationally connected to the performance of the job;

(2)   that the employer adopted the particular standard in an honest and good faith belief that it was necessary to the fulfilment of that legitimate work-related purpose; and

(3)   that the standard is reasonably necessary to the accomplishment of that legitimate work-related purpose. To show that the standard is reasonably necessary, it must be demonstrated that it is impossible to accommodate individual employees sharing the characteristics of the claimant without imposing undue hardship upon the employer. . . .

B. Application of the Reformed Approach to the Case on Appeal

3. Introduction

69. Ms. Meiorin has discharged the burden of establishing that, *prima facie*, the aerobic standard discriminates against her as a woman. The arbitrator held that, because of their generally lower aerobic capacity, most women are adversely affected by the high aerobic standard. While the Government's expert witness testified that most women can achieve the aerobic standard with training, the arbitrator rejected this evidence as "anecdotal" and "not supported by scientific data". This Court has not been presented with any reason to revisit this characterization. Ms. Meiorin has therefore demonstrated that the aerobic standard is *prima facie* discriminatory, and has brought herself within s. 13(1) of the Code.

70. Ms. Meiorin having established a *prima facie* case of discrimination, the burden shifts to the Government to demonstrate that the aerobic standard is a BFOR. For the reasons below, I conclude that the Government has failed to discharge this burden and therefore cannot rely on the defence provided by s. 13(4) of the Code.

4. Steps One and Two

71. The first two elements of the proposed BFOR analysis, that is (1) that the employer adopted the standard for a purpose rationally connected to the performance of the job; and (2) that the employer adopted the particular standard in an honest and good faith belief that it was necessary to the fulfilment of that legitimate work-related purpose, have been fulfilled. The Government's general purpose in imposing the aerobic standard is not disputed. It is to enable the Government to identify those employees or applicants who are able to perform the job of a forest firefighter safely and efficiently. It is also clear that there is a rational connection between this general characteristic and the performance of the particularly strenuous tasks expected of a forest firefighter. All indications are that the Government acted honestly and

in a good faith belief that adopting the particular standard was necessary to the identification of those persons able to perform the job safely and efficiently. It did not intend to discriminate against Ms. Meiorin. To the contrary, one of the reasons the Government retained the researchers from the University of Victoria was that it sought to identify non-discriminatory standards.

5. *Step Three*

72. Under the third element of the unified approach, the employer must establish that the standard is reasonably necessary to the accomplishment of that legitimate work-related purpose. To show that the standard is reasonably necessary, it must be demonstrated that it is impossible to accommodate individual employees sharing the characteristics of the claimant without imposing undue hardship upon the employer. In the case on appeal, the contentious issue is whether the Government has demonstrated that this particular aerobic standard is reasonably necessary in order to identify those persons who are able to perform the tasks of a forest firefighter safely and efficiently. As noted, the burden is on the government to demonstrate that, in the course of accomplishing this purpose, it cannot accommodate individual or group differences without experiencing undue hardship.

73. The Government adopted the laudable course of retaining experts to devise a non-discriminatory test. However, because of significant problems with the way the researchers proceeded, passing the resulting aerobic standard has not been shown to be reasonably necessary to the safe and efficient performance of the work of a forest firefighter. The Government has not established that it would experience undue hardship if a different standard were used.

74. The procedures adopted by the researchers are problematic on two levels. First, their approach seems to have been primarily a descriptive one: test subjects were observed completing the tasks, the aerobic capacity of the test subjects was ascertained, and that capacity was established as the minimum standard required of every forest firefighter. However, merely describing the characteristics of a test subject does not necessarily allow one to identify the standard *minimally* necessary for the safe and efficient performance of the task. Second, these primarily descriptive studies failed to distinguish the female test subjects from the male test subjects, who constituted the vast majority of the sample groups. The record before this Court therefore does not permit us to say whether men and women require the same minimum level of aerobic capacity to perform safely and efficiently the tasks expected of a forest firefighter.

75. While the researchers' goal was admirable, their aerobic standard was developed through a process that failed to address the possibility that it may discriminate unnecessarily on one or more prohibited grounds, particularly sex. . . .

76. The expert who testified before the arbitrator on behalf of the Government defended the original researchers' decision not to analyse separately the aerobic performance of the male and female, experienced and inexperienced, test subjects as an attempt to reflect the actual conditions of firefighting. This misses the point. The polymorphous group's average aerobic performance is irrelevant to the question of whether the aerobic standard constitutes a minimum threshold that cannot be altered without causing undue hardship to the employer. Rather, the goal should have been to measure whether members of all groups require the same minimum aerobic capacity to perform the job safely and efficiently and, if not, to reflect that disparity in the employment qualifications. There is no evidence before us that any action was taken to further this goal before the aerobic standard was adopted.

77. Neither is there any evidence that the Government embarked upon a study of the discriminatory effects of the aerobic standard when the issue was raised by Ms. Meiorin. In fact, the expert reports filed by the Government in these proceedings content themselves with asserting that the aerobic standard set in 1992 and 1994 is a minimum standard that women can meet with appropriate training. No studies were conducted to substantiate the latter assertion and the arbitrator rejected it as unsupported by the evidence.

78. Assuming that the Government had properly addressed the question in a procedural sense, its response – that it would experience undue hardship if it had to accommodate Ms. Meiorin – is deficient from a substantive perspective. The Government has presented no evidence as to the cost of accommodation. Its primary argument is that, because the aerobic standard is necessary for the safety of the individual firefighter, the other members of the crew, and the public at large, it would experience undue hardship if compelled to deviate from that standard in any way.

79. Referring to the Government's arguments on this point, the arbitrator noted that, "other than anecdotal or 'impressionistic' evidence concerning the magnitude of risk involved in accommodating the adverse-effect discrimination suffered by the grievor, the employer has presented no cogent evidence. . . . to support its position that it cannot accommodate Ms. Meiorin because of safety risks". The arbitrator held that the evidence fell short of establishing that Ms. Meiorin posed a serious safety risk to herself, her colleagues, or the general public. Accordingly, he held that the Government had failed to accommodate her to the point of undue hardship. This Court has not been presented with any reason to interfere with his conclusion on this point, and I decline to do so. The Government did not discharge its burden of showing that the purpose for which it introduced the aerobic standard would be compromised to the point of undue hardship if a different standard were used.

80. This leaves the evidence of the Assistant Director of Protection Programs for the British Columbia Ministry of Forests, who testified that accommodating Ms. Meiorin would undermine the morale of the Initial Attack Crews. Again, this proposition is not supported by evidence. But even if it were, the attitudes of those who seek to maintain a discriminatory practice cannot be reconciled with the Code. These attitudes cannot therefore be determinative of whether the employer has accommodated the claimant to the point of undue hardship. Although serious consideration must of course be taken of the "objection of employees based on well-grounded concerns that their rights will be affected", discrimination on the basis of a prohibited ground cannot be justified by arguing that abandoning such a practice would threaten the morale of the workforce. If it were possible to perform the tasks of a forest firefighter safely and efficiently without meeting the prescribed aerobic standard (and the Government has not established the contrary), I can see no right of other firefighters that would be affected by allowing Ms. Meiorin to continue performing her job.

81. The Court of Appeal suggested that accommodating women by permitting them to meet a lower aerobic standard than men would constitute "reverse discrimination". I respectfully disagree. As this Court has repeatedly held, the essence of equality is to be treated according to one's own merit, capabilities and circumstances. True equality requires that differences be accommodated. A different aerobic standard capable of identifying women who could perform the job safely and efficiently therefore does not necessarily imply discrimination against men. "Reverse" discrimination would only result if, for example, an aerobic standard

representing a minimum threshold for *all* forest firefighters was held to be inapplicable to men simply because they were men.

VII. Conclusion

83. I conclude that Ms. Meiorin has established that the aerobic standard is *prima facie* discriminatory, and the Government has not shown that it is reasonably necessary to the accomplishment of the Government's general purpose, which is to identify those forest firefighters who are able to work safely and efficiently. Because it has therefore not been established that the aerobic standard is a BFOR, the Government cannot avail itself of the defence in s. 13(4) of the Code and is bound by the prohibition of such a discriminatory standard in s. 13(1)(b). The Code accordingly prevents the Government from relying on the aerobic standard as the basis for Ms. Meiorin's dismissal. As this case arose as a grievance before a labour arbitrator, rather than as a claim before the Human Rights Tribunal or its predecessor, relief of a more general nature cannot be claimed. . . .

Notes

1. This case was initially heard and decided by an arbitrator, pursuant to the collective bargaining agreement that covered Ms. Meiorin. In *Parry Sound (District) Social Services Administration Board v. Ontario Public Service Employees Union, Local 324*, [2003] 2. S.C.R. 157, a probationary employee was discharged shortly after returning from maternity leave. The arbitrator hearing her grievance under the collective bargaining agreement upheld the grievance as family status discrimination. The Supreme Court confirmed the arbitrator's award by finding that, even where a collective agreement did not restrict the employer's right to discharge a probationary employee, the Ontario Human Rights Code was implicit in the collective bargaining agreement and protected her from dismissal for taking maternity leave. The substantive rights and obligations of human rights legislation are incorporated into every collective bargaining agreement and every written or implied contract of employment. Those rights set a floor beneath which an employment contract cannot fall.

2. Canadian antidiscrimination law does not include an intent to discriminate element. Thus in *Ontario v. Simpson Sears*, [1985] 2 S.C.R. 536, commonly referred to as the *O'Malley* case, O'Malley had worked for a large retailer. After converting to the Seventh-Day Adventist Church, she was no longer able to work Saturdays, her day of Sabbath. As a result, the employer switched her to part-time status, which resulted in a lost of some benefits. The reason for the switch was that Saturday was the store's busiest day and the employer wanted all its full-time employees available to work. The Court rejected an intent to discriminate element because it would put "a virtually insuperable barrier" in the way of plaintiffs. *Id.* at 549. The employer was liable therefore even though it had no intent to discriminate and stayed on friendly terms with the employee throughout, including notifying her of every opening as it occurred and not scheduling her for any Saturday work.

3. Before this decision, the conventional description of the two approaches in Canadian law was "(1) 'direct discrimination', where the standard is discriminatory on

its face, or (2) 'adverse effect discrimination', where the facially neutral standard discriminates in effect." An example of direct discrimination would be an advertisement limiting a job to men. Indirect discrimination might be established when an employer uses height and weight standards to screen job applicants.

4.   What Canadian law defines as direct discrimination would be one variant of systemic disparate treatment discrimination under Title VII in the United States, which applies to formal policies that discriminate. The other variant of systemic disparate treatment law uses statistical evidence to prove the existence of a pattern or practice of intentional discrimination. Both lead to a finding of intent to discriminate, which is an element of both types of disparate treatment discrimination under U.S. law. Under Title VII, however, there is another systemic theory, called disparate impact discrimination, where the plaintiff proves an employment practice has an adverse impact on groups protected by Title VII and the employer fails to prove it is justified by business necessity. Disparate impact theory applies even in the absence of proof of the employer's intent to discriminate. How did Canadian and U.S. law differ before *B.C. Firefighters?* Under Title VII, liability under both systemic theories would lead to a remedy that would prohibit the continued use of the challenged practices. How did remedies work in Canada before *B.C. Firefighters?*

5.   In *Canada (Canadian Human Rights Commission) v. Canadian National Railway ("Action Travail des Femmes")*, (1985), 20 D.L.R. 668 (F.C.A.), 85 C.L.L.C. 17,013 (F.C.A.), rev'd [1987] 1 S.C.R. 1114, 40 D.L.R. (4th) 193, the massive underrepresentation of women in unskilled blue-collar jobs on the railroad was found to be proof of pervasive systemic discrimination, even in absence of proof of specific discriminatory incidents. The use of statistical evidence to prove discrimination was similar to pattern or practice proof of systemic disparate treatment using Title VII of the Civil Rights Act in the United States. See *Teamsters v. United States*, 431 U.S. 324 (1977).

6.   What changes does the *B.C. Firefighters* Court make to the preexisting law? What does a claimant need to show to establish a prima facie case of discrimination? What does the employer need to prove to establish a defense? Did the employer establish that there was a rational connection between the challenged standard and the job and was there an honest and good faith belief that the standard was necessary? If both those elements were satisfied, did the employer show that the standard was reasonably necessary to the accomplishment of that legitimate work-related purpose? Isn't running necessary to the job and so finding out the running ability of firefighters reasonably necessary? Would the case be different if the plaintiff was simply an applicant and not someone who had been a successful firefighter for three years? What role does the duty to accommodate play in the new defense announced in *B.C. Firefighters?* Isn't it a separate fourth element of the defense, rather than simply an aspect of the third element of objective reasonable necessity?

7.   What if the employer showed it was impossible to accommodate many applicants, even though it could accommodate this particular employee? The Court found that the validation study was only "descriptive". What more would the employer have to show to justify the running test? Would it have to show that anyone running slower than the time set by the test could not perform the firefighters' job? Why might differential validation of the test for men and women be useful to determine reasonable necessity?

8. In *Lanning v. Southeastern Pennsylvania Transportation Authority*, 181 F.3d 478 (3d Cir. 1999), plaintiffs challenged a running test for a transit police officers job – the candidate would have to run 1.5 miles within twelve minutes – by relying on a systemic disparate impact theory. Only 12 percent of women applicants passed the test as compared to 60 percent of male applicants. Initially the Court of Appeals reversed the lower court's finding that the test was justified by business necessity because the test cutoff was not shown to "reflect the minimum aerobic capacity necessary to perform successfully the job of SEPTA transit police officer." After remand and retrial on the issue of what the minimum qualification standard was for the transit police job, the Court affirmed a finding that the running test did establish the minimum. "[I]ndividuals who passed the run test had a success rate on the job standards from 70% to 90%. The success rate of the individual who failed the run test ranged from 5% to 20%." Further, there was evidence that, with training, most women could pass the running test. 308 F.3d 286, 290 (3d Cir. 2002). Would a showing that most women could satisfy the standard with training have been a successful defense under the approach adopted in *B.C. Firefighters*?

9. How would an employer go about figuring out if accommodation is possible? Must it show that it searched for alternative approaches but none met its needs? Can a single standard ever be imposed on all the individuals if some could do the job without meeting that standard?

F. EMPLOYEE PRIVACY

The law of privacy as applied to the employment relationship is developing on both the common law and statutory fronts in Canada. As far as the common law, "employees do not have a reasonable expectation of privacy in the e-mail messages they send at work or in the work they perform on their employer's computer network or, alternatively, that an employer's interest in preventing inappropriate comments or unauthorized activity over its computer communications system may outweigh any privacy interest an employee may have." Canadian Labour & Employment Law – 2004 Cum. Supp, at 191. But "employers many not be justified in dismissing an employee solely on the basis of a single offensive e-mail message." *Id.* at 192. Furthermore, the employer must have clear rules governing the use of its computer system, including a warning that unauthorized use could lead to discipline and discharge. *Id.*

Before 2000, only Quebec had privacy legislation governing the private sector. In 2000, the federal government enacted the Personal Information Protection and Electronic Documents Act (PIPEDA), which among other things governs the employer's collection use, and disclosure of personal information. By its terms, the federal law appears to apply as of 2004 to all employers, even those otherwise governed by provincial law, unless the province had adopted privacy laws substantially similar to the federal law. That application, of course, may well lead to a constitutional challenge on federalism grounds. In the event, in addition to Quebec, British Columbia and Alberta have now enacted privacy laws that are substantially similar to the federal PIPEDA law.

Under PIPEDA, "personal information" is defined as information about an identifiable individual other than name, title, business address, or business telephone number of an employee. It does, however, include "an employee's home address, home telephone number, age, sex, salary, marital status, race, ethnic origin, religion, information concerning the behaviour of the person at work, information regarding the evaluation of an employee's work, and information contained in a medical report." CANADIAN LABOUR & EMPLOYMENT LAW, at 267.

The key employer obligation is to refrain from collecting, using, or disclosing personal information without the individual's consent. The employer must identify the purposes for collecting the information and limit the personal information to information a reasonable person would consider appropriate to the identified purpose or purposes. Information must not then be used or disclosed for any other purpose unless the individual consents. Personal information may only be retained as long as necessary to fulfill the identified purpose and it must be accurate, complete, and up to date. Individuals must be given access to the information the employer has collected about them.

PIPEDA is enforced by the Privacy Commissioner of Canada (PCC) through a complaint procedure. Thus, the PCC found a violation when an employer refused to provide access to the personnel file requested by a former employee Information regarding compensation paid the employee and the costs relating to his workplace safety claim had to be disclosed. But the employer was not required to disclose other information in the file. PIPED Act Case Summary #147 (7 April 3003), online: http://www.privcom.gc.ca/cf-dc/2003/cf-dc˙030407˙2˙e.asp. In the context of workplace surveillance by video cameras, the PCC has found that the employer did not show that problems of theft and vandalism justified the installation of the cameras at the workplace and the fact of "being watched" had a negative psychological impact on the workers. PIPED Act Case Summary #114 (23 January 2003), online: http://www.privcom.gc.ca/cf-dc/2003/cf-dc_030123_e.asp.

G. DISPUTE RESOLUTION SYSTEMS

Common law courts in Canada have jurisdiction to hear individual employment cases such as *Wallace*, which involved a wrongful dismissal action. Human rights complaints are heard and decided by human rights boards, with their decisions being effectively self-enforcing, though they are subject to limited judicial review. Matters arising out of the labor law statutes of the different jurisdiction are decided by the labor boards established in the labor law statutes. In the federal jurisdiction and some provinces, the tribunal is tripartite with the presiding officer a neutral and equal numbers of union and management representatives. Some provinces, however, have boards made up only of neutral members. LABOUR LAW IN CANADA, at 69.

The Canadian labor boards accept complaints and have officers who investigate and attempt to settle them. But if no settlement is reached, the parties each represent themselves in a single set of hearings before the board and the board then issues a final decision, including the remedy, if any, it finds appropriate. NORTH AMERICA LABOR LAW, at 80–81.The board files its decision with the appropriate court but there is no judicial review since the orders of the board are essentially self-enforcing. CANADIAN LABOUR LAW, at 31. All disputes arising out of the collective bargaining relationship, including torts, contracts and human rights complaints, are to be decided by arbitration, which is mandated in all collective bargaining agreements.

The National Labor Relations Board procedures in the United States contemplate individuals, unions or employers filing unfair labor practice charges with the Board, followed by the General Counsel of the Board exercising discretion whether or not to issue unfair labor practice complaints based on that charge and then litigating the case before an administrative law judge, with the final agency decision made by the National Labor Relations Board, subject to enforcement by the appropriate federal Circuit Court of Appeals. In the United States, torts, contracts and statutory claims (such as claims of discrimination under Title VII of the Civil Rights Act) can be brought in the appropriate federal or state courts unless the individual employee has agreed to arbitrate such disputes. Arbitration agreements for most employees are enforceable, even as to statutory claims, and the awards that result are subject to only the narrowest judicial review.

WEBER V. ONTARIO HYDRO

[1995] 2. S.C.R. 928

McLachlin J. – When may parties who have agreed to settle their differences by arbitration under a collective agreement sue in tort? That is the issue raised by this appeal and its companion case, *New Brunswick v. O'Leary*, [1995] 2 S.C.R. 967.

Mr. Weber was employed by Ontario Hydro. As a result of back problems, he took an extended leave of absence. Hydro paid him the sick benefits stipulated by the collective agreement. As time passed, Hydro began to suspect that Mr. Weber was malingering. It hired private investigators to investigate its concerns. The investigators came on Mr. Weber's property. Pretending they were someone else, they gained entry to his home. As a result of the information it obtained, Hydro suspended Mr. Weber for abusing his sick leave benefits.

Mr. Weber responded by taking the matter to his union, which filed grievances against Hydro on August 28, 1989. One of the grievances alleged that Hydro's hiring of the private investigators violated the terms of the collective agreement. Among other things, the union asked the arbitrator to require Hydro to give an undertaking to discontinue using private security firms to monitor health absences, and to pay Mr. Weber and his family damages for mental anguish and suffering arising out of the surveillance. The arbitration commenced on March 8, 1990, and was subsequently settled.

In the meantime, on December 27, 1989, Mr. Weber commenced a court action based on tort and breach of his *Charter* rights, claiming damages for the surveillance. The torts alleged were trespass, nuisance, deceit, and invasion of privacy. Weber's claims under the *Canadian Charter of Rights and Freedoms* were for breaches of his rights under ss. 7 and 8. Hydro applied for an order dismissing Mr. Weber's court action. The motions judge dismissed it on the grounds that the dispute arose out of the collective agreement depriving the court of jurisdiction, and was moreover a private matter to which the *Charter* did not apply. The Court of Appeal agreed, except with respect to the *Charter* claims, which it allowed to stand. Mr. Weber appeals to this Court, asking that his action be reinstated in its entirety. Hydro cross-appeals the decision to allow the *Charter* claims to stand.

I agree with the Court of Appeal that the tort action cannot stand. I would go further, however, and hold that the action for *Charter* claims is also precluded by the Ontario *Labour Relations Act*, R.S.O. 1990, c. L.2, and the terms of the collective agreement.

Legislation

Labour Relations Act, R.S.O. 1990, c. L.2

45. – (1) Every collective agreement shall provide for the final and binding settlement by arbitration, without stoppage of work, of all differences between the parties arising from the interpretation, application, administration or alleged violation of the agreement, including any question as to whether a matter is arbitrable. . . . .

Analysis

1. When is the Courts' Jurisdiction over Civil Actions Ousted by s. 45(1) of the Labour Relations Act?

The cases reveal three different views on the effect of final and binding arbitration clauses in labour legislation. I shall deal with each in turn.

The Concurrent Model. The appellant Weber's first argument is that the claims in his action do not fall within s. 45(1) because they are based on the common law and the *Charter*, not on the collective agreement. This view of the law contemplates concurrent regimes of arbitration and court actions. Where an action is recognized by the common law or by statute, it may proceed, notwithstanding that it arises in the employment context. Although based on the same facts, the court proceedings are considered independent because the *issues* are different. This view finds its ultimate expression in the proposition that "no collective agreement can deprive a Court of its jurisdiction in tort". . . .

The jurisprudential difficulty [with this view] arises from this Court's decision in *St. Anne Nackawic Pulp & Paper Co. v. Canadian Paper Workers Union, Local 219*, [1986] 1 S.C.R. 704. As the Court of Appeal below noted, both the holding and the philosophy underlying *St. Anne Nackawic* support the proposition that mandatory arbitration clauses in labour statutes deprive the courts of concurrent jurisdiction. In *St. Anne Nackawic*, the employer, after obtaining an interim injunction against the striking union, sued the union in tort for damages caused by its illegal strike. The employer had argued that where the claim could be characterized as arising solely under the common law, and did not depend for its validity on the collective agreement, the mandatory arbitration clause of the legislation did not apply – the same argument which Weber makes on this appeal. . . .

The New Brunswick Court of Appeal in *St. Anne Nackawic* also rejected the concurrency approach (1982), 142 D.L.R. (3d) 678. La Forest J. A. (as he then was) wrote that simply framing the action in terms of the tort of conspiracy would not be sufficient to take the action outside the realm of the collective agreement.

Underlying both the Court of Appeal and Supreme Court of Canada decisions in *St. Anne Nackawic* is the insistence that the analysis of whether a matter falls within the exclusive arbitration clause must proceed on the basis of the facts surrounding the dispute between the parties, not on the basis of the legal issues which may be framed. The issue is not whether the *action*, defined legally, is independent of the collective agreement, but rather whether the *dispute* is one "arising under [the] collective agreement". Where the dispute, regardless of how it may be characterized legally, arises under the collective agreement, then the jurisdiction to resolve it lies exclusively with the labour tribunal and the courts cannot try it. . . .

This brings me to the second reason why the concurrency argument cannot succeed – the wording of the statute. Section 45(1) of the Ontario *Labour Relations Act*, like the provision under consideration in *St. Anne Nackawic*, refers to "all *differences* between the parties arising from the interpretation, application, administration or alleged violation of the agreement" (emphasis added). The Ontario statute makes arbitration the only available remedy for such differences. The word "differences" denotes the dispute between the parties, not the legal actions which one may be entitled to bring against the other. The object of the provision – and what is thus excluded from the courts – is all proceedings arising from the difference between the parties, however those proceedings may be framed. Where the dispute falls within the terms of the Act, there is no room for concurrent proceedings.

The final difficulty with the concurrent actions model is that it undercuts the purpose of the regime of exclusive arbitration which lies at the heart of all Canadian labour statutes. It is important that disputes be resolved quickly and economically, with a minimum of disruption to the parties and the economy. To permit concurrent court actions whenever it can be said that the cause of action stands independent of the collective agreement undermines this goal, as this Court noted in *St. Anne Nackawic*. . . .

The Model of Overlapping Jurisdiction. An alternative model may be described by the metaphor of overlapping spheres. On this approach, notwithstanding that the facts of the dispute arise out of the collective agreement, a court action may be brought if it raises issues which go beyond the traditional subject matter of labour law. Following this line of reasoning, the appellant contends that the issues of trespass, nuisance, deceit and the unreasonable interference with and invasion of privacy pleaded in his action go beyond the parameters of the collective agreement, and that consequently the court action should be permitted to proceed.

This approach was adopted by the Saskatchewan Court of Appeal in *Kim v. University of Regina* (1990), 74 D.L.R. (4th) 120, at p. 124, in ruling that an action which raised issues beyond those raised in the arbitration grievance could proceed. Cameron J. A., speaking for the court, stated: ". . . . it will be seen that while the two proceedings overlap, especially as to matters of fact going to Dr. Kim's early retirement under the collective bargaining agreement and how that came about, the two are not co-extensive. The action raises issues quite beyond the capacity of the arbitration board to deal with."

While more attractive than the full concurrency model, the overlapping spheres model also presents difficulties. In so far as it is based on characterizing a cause of action which lies outside the arbitrator's power or expertise, it violates the injunction of the Act and *St. Anne Nackawic* that one must look not to the legal characterization of the wrong, but to the facts giving rise to the dispute. It would also leave it open to innovative pleaders to evade the legislative prohibition on parallel court actions by raising new and imaginative causes of action. . . . This would undermine the legislative purposes underlying such provisions and the intention of the parties to the agreement. This approach, like the concurrency model, fails to meet the test of the statute, the jurisprudence and policy.

The Exclusive Jurisdiction Model. The final alternative is to accept that if the difference between the parties arises from the collective agreement, the claimant must proceed by arbitration and the courts have no power to entertain an action in respect of that dispute. There is no overlapping jurisdiction.

On this approach, the task of the judge or arbitrator determining the appropriate forum for the proceedings centres on whether the dispute or difference between the parties arises out of the collective agreement. Two elements must be considered: the dispute and the ambit of the collective agreement.

In considering the dispute, the decision-maker must attempt to define its "essential character." The fact that the parties are employer and employee may not be determinative. Similarly, the place of the conduct giving rise to the dispute may not be conclusive; matters arising from the collective agreement may occur off the workplace and conversely, not everything that happens on the workplace may arise from the collective agreement. Sometimes the time when the claim originated may be important, as in *Wainwright v. Vancouver Shipyards Co.* (1987), 38 D.L.R. (4th) 760 (B.C.C.A.), where it was held that the court had jurisdiction over contracts pre-dating the collective agreement. In the majority of cases the nature of the dispute will be clear; either it had to do with the collective agreement or it did not. Some cases, however, may be less than obvious. The question in each case is whether the dispute, in its essential character, arises from the interpretation, application, administration or violation of the collective agreement.

Because the nature of the dispute and the ambit of the collective agreement will vary from case to case, it is impossible to categorize the classes of case that will fall within the exclusive jurisdiction of the arbitrator. However, a review of decisions over the past few years reveals the following claims among those over which the courts have been found to lack jurisdiction: wrongful dismissal; bad faith on the part of the union; conspiracy and constructive dismissal; and damage to reputation.

This approach does not preclude all actions in the courts between employer and employee. Only disputes which expressly or inferentially arise out of the collective agreement are foreclosed to the courts: Additionally, the courts possess residual jurisdiction based on their special powers.

Against this approach, the appellant Weber argues that jurisdiction over torts and *Charter* claims should not be conferred on arbitrators because they lack expertise on the legal questions such claims raise. The answer to this concern is that arbitrators are subject to judicial review. Within the parameters of that review, their errors may be corrected by the courts. The procedural inconvenience of an occasional application for judicial review is outweighed by the advantages of having a single tribunal deciding all issues arising from the dispute in the first instance. This does not mean that the arbitrator will consider separate "cases" of tort, contract or *Charter*. Rather, in dealing with the dispute under the collective agreement and fashioning an appropriate remedy, the arbitrator will have regard to whether the breach of the collective agreement also constitutes a breach of a common law duty, or of the *Charter*.

The appellant Weber also argues that arbitrators may lack the legal power to consider the issues before them. This concern is answered by the power and duty of arbitrators to apply the law of the land to the disputes before them. To this end, arbitrators may refer to both the common law and statutes. As Denning L. J. put it, "[t]here is not one law for arbitrators and another for the court, but one law for all": *David Taylor & Son, Ltd. v. Barnett*, [1953] 1 All E.R. 843 (C.A.), at p. 847. This also applies to the *Charter*: *Douglas/Kwantlen Faculty Assn. v. Douglas College*, [1990] 3 S.C.R. 570, at p. 597.

It might occur that a remedy is required which the arbitrator is not empowered to grant. In such a case, the courts of inherent jurisdiction in each province may take jurisdiction. This Court in *St. Anne Nackawic* confirmed that the New Brunswick Act did not oust the residual inherent jurisdiction of the superior courts to grant injunctions in labour matters. Similarly, the Court of Appeal of British Columbia in *Moore v. British Columbia* (1988), 50 D.L.R. (4th) 29, at p. 38, accepted that the court's residual jurisdiction to grant a declaration was not ousted by the British Columbia labour legislation, although it declined to exercise that jurisdiction on the ground that the powers of the arbitrator were sufficient to remedy the wrong and that deference was owed to the labour tribunal. What must be avoided, to use the language of Estey J. in *St. Anne Nackawic*, is a "real deprivation of ultimate remedy".

To summarize, the exclusive jurisdiction model gives full credit to the language of s. 45(1) of the *Labour Relations Act*. It accords with this Court's approach in *St. Anne Nackawic*. It satisfies the concern that the dispute resolution process which the various labour statutes of this country have established should not be duplicated and undermined by concurrent actions. It conforms to a pattern of growing judicial deference for the arbitration and grievance process and correlative restrictions on the rights of parties to proceed with parallel or overlapping litigation in the courts.

The appellant Weber submits that the arbitrator cannot deal with his *Charter* claims. The Court of Appeal shared his concern, voicing uncertainty about whether *Charter* claims raise unique policy considerations which are best left to the superior courts of inherent jurisdiction.

In so far as this argument turns on policy considerations, it is answered by the comments of the majority of this Court in *Douglas/Kwantlen Faculty Assn. v. Douglas College*. That case, like this, involved a grievance before a labour arbitrator. In that case, as in this, *Charter* issues were raised. It was argued, *inter alia*, that a labour arbitration was not the appropriate place to argue *Charter* issues. After a thorough review of the advantages and disadvantages of having such issues decided before labour tribunals, La Forest J. concluded that while the informal processes of such tribunals might not be entirely suited to dealing with constitutional issues, clear advantages to the practice exist. Citizens are permitted to assert their *Charter* rights in a prompt, inexpensive, informal way. The parties are not required to duplicate submissions on the case in two different fora, for determination of two different legal issues. A specialized tribunal can quickly sift the facts and compile a record for the reviewing court. And the specialized competence of the tribunal may provide assistance to the reviewing court. *Douglas/Kwantlen Faculty Assn. v. Douglas College* also answers the concern of the Court of Appeal below that the *Charter* takes the issue out of the labour context and puts it in the state context. While the *Charter* issue may raise broad policy concerns, it is nonetheless a component of the labour dispute, and hence within the jurisdiction of the labour arbitrator. The existence of broad policy concerns with respect to a given issue cannot preclude the labour arbitrator from deciding all facets of the labour dispute.

This brings us to the question of whether a labour arbitrator in this case has the power to grant *Charter* remedies. The remedies claimed are damages and a declaration. The power and duty of arbitrators to apply the law extends to the *Charter*, an essential part of the law of Canada: *Douglas/Kwantlen Faculty Assn. v. Douglas College, supra*; *Cuddy Chicks Ltd. v. Ontario (Labour Relations Board)*, [1991] 2 S.C.R. 5; *Re Ontario Council of Regents for Colleges of Applied Arts & Technology and Ontario Public Service Employees Union* (1986), 24 L.A.C. (3d) 144. In applying the law of the land to the disputes before them, be it the common law, statute law or the *Charter*, arbitrators may grant such remedies as the Legislature or Parliament has empowered them to grant in the circumstances. For example, a labour arbitrator can consider the *Charter*, find laws inoperative for conflict with it, and go on to grant remedies in the exercise of his powers under the *Labour Code*. If an arbitrator can find a law violative of the *Charter*, it would seem he or she can determine whether conduct in the administration of the collective agreement violates the *Charter* and likewise grant remedies.

Summary of the Law

I conclude that mandatory arbitration clauses such as s. 45(1) of the Ontario *Labour Relations Act* generally confer exclusive jurisdiction on labour tribunals to deal with all disputes between the parties arising from the collective agreement. The question in each case is whether the dispute, viewed with an eye to its essential character, arises from the collective agreement. This extends to *Charter* remedies, provided that the legislation empowers the arbitrator to hear the dispute and grant the remedies claimed. The exclusive jurisdiction of the arbitrator is subject to the residual discretionary power of courts of inherent jurisdiction to grant remedies not possessed by the statutory tribunal. Against this background, I turn to the facts in the case at bar.

Application of the Law to the Dispute in this Case

On the interpretation outlined above, the question is whether the conduct giving rise to the dispute between the parties arises either expressly or inferentially out of the collective agreement between them.

The appellant contends that the dispute in this case falls outside the collective agreement. The act of hiring private investigators who used deception to enter his family home and report on him does not, he contends, relate to the interpretation, application or administration of the collective agreement. It is not in its essential character a labour matter; it is rather a matter of the common law and the constitutional rights of himself and his family. It follows, he submits, that the arbitrator does not have jurisdiction over the claims and that the courts may entertain them.

Hydro, on the other hand, argues that the essential character of the dispute places it firmly within the scope of the collective agreement. It points out that the conduct complained of arose in response to a claim for sick benefits provided for in the collective agreement, and argues that the manner in which the employer monitors entitlement to those benefits is part of the administration of the agreement.

Isolated from the collective agreement, the conduct complained of in this case might well be argued to fall outside the normal scope of employer-employee relations. However, placed in the context of that agreement, the picture changes. The provisions of the agreement are broad, and expressly purport to regulate the conduct at the heart of this dispute.

Article 2.2 of the collective agreement extends the grievance procedure to "[a]ny allegation that an employee has been subjected to unfair treatment or any dispute arising out of the content of this Agreement . . . ". The dispute in this case arose out of the content of the Agreement. Item 13.0 of Part A of the Agreement provides that the "benefits of the Ontario Hydro Sick Leave Plan . . . shall be considered as part of this Agreement". It further provides that the provisions of the plan "are not an automatic right of an employee and the administration of this plan and all decisions regarding the appropriateness or degree of its application shall be vested solely in Ontario Hydro". This language brings the medical plan and Hydro's decisions concerning it expressly within the purview of the collective agreement. Under the plan, Hydro had the right to decide what benefits the employee would receive, subject to the employee's right to grieve the decision. In the course of making such a decision, Hydro is alleged to have acted improperly. That allegation would appear to fall within the phrase "unfair treatment or any dispute arising out of the content of [the] Agreement" within Article 2.2.

I conclude that the wide language of Article 2.2 of the Agreement, combined with item 13.0, covers the conduct alleged against Hydro. Hydro's alleged actions were directly related to a process which is expressly subject to the grievance procedure. While aspects of the alleged conduct may arguably have extended beyond what the parties contemplated, this does not alter the essential character of the conduct. In short, the difference between the parties relates to the "administration. . . . of the agreement" within s. 45(1) of the *Labour Relations Act*.

The case at bar may be compared with *Gendron*. In that case, the fact that the collective agreement imposed a duty of fair representation on the union was held by this Court to oust recourse to the courts for unfair representation. In this case, the fact that the collective agreement covers all unfair treatment regarding matters within its ambit may similarly be said to oust recourse to the courts for complaints of unfair treatment, which is the essence of the appellant's statement of claim. The arbitrator has exclusive jurisdiction to consider the dispute between the parties, provided that the dispute falls under the collective agreement under the test enunciated above. That the facts may be capable of being characterized as a tort or a constitutional breach may be taken into account by the tribunal, which must apply the law as it stands. Having heard the claim, the tribunal awards such relief as it may properly do, having regard to the powers which the Legislature has conferred upon it.

The final question is whether the arbitrator has power to decide the *Charter* claims. The arbitrator has jurisdiction over the parties and the dispute. The arbitrator is further empowered by the Act to award the *Charter* remedies claimed – damages and a declaration. . . .

It follows from these conclusions that the arbitrator in the case at bar has exclusive jurisdiction over all aspects of the dispute. The Court of Appeal correctly struck out the action in tort. It should also, with respect, have struck out the *Charter* claims. In view of the foregoing conclusions, it is unnecessary to consider whether Ontario Hydro is bound by the *Charter*.

Notes

1. Arbitrators need not be trained in the law. Are they, as a group, sufficiently expert to decide legal questions arising from Charter, statutory and tort claims? How will the law in these areas be developed if all cases arising out of collective bargaining agreements are subject to arbitration rather than decision by the courts?

2. In the companion case, *New Brunswick v. O'Leary*, [1995] 2. S.C.R. 967, an employer's claim for damages against an employee for negligence in driving a vehicle while working was found to be subject to resolution pursuant to the collective bargaining agreement covering the employee and could not be tried in court.

3. Judicial review of arbitration awards is available but only on limited grounds. "The courts will set aside an award that is vitiated by bias, fraud, a breach of natural

justice [due process], or by arbitrator or board exceeding its jurisdiction." INTERNA-
TIONAL LABOR & EMPLOYMENT LAW, at 21–45. In *Voice v. Construction & General
Workers' Union, Local 92*, [2004] 1. S.C.R. 609, the union and employer had a hiring
hall agreement by which the union sent a member to work on the employer's construction project. The employer refused to put the member to work and the union
grieved the matter. The arbitrator found that the collective bargaining agreement's
provision for the union to dispatch workers that limited the employer's discretion to
"name hire" employees constituted an express restriction of the employer's broad
right to "hire and select workers." Applying a standard of correctness, the reviewing
court found that the arbitrator had exceeded her jurisdiction by finding an express
restriction on the right of management to select employees that in effect amended
the agreement. The Canadian Supreme Court reversed. Indicating that a "pragmatic and functional approach" to setting the standard of review was necessary
to decide which of three standards applied – "patent unreasonableness, reasonableness [or] correctness." Applying four contextual factors – "(1) the presence or
absence of a privative clause [that the arbitrator's decision was final and binding
without review] or statutory right of appeal; (2) the expertise of the tribunal relative to that of the reviewing court on the issue in question; (3) the purposes of the
legislation and the provision in particular; and (4) the nature of the question – law,
fact or mixed law and fact," the Court said a standard of reasonableness applied in
the case at hand and under that standard the award should be affirmed. In *Ontario
Public Service Employees Union v. Seneca College of Applied Arts & Technology*,
Docket C43274, May 4, 2006, the Ontario Court of Appeals applied the four contextual factors to find that the patently unreasonable test applied. Applying that
test, the Court upheld an arbitration board decision that it did not have jurisdiction to award aggravated and punitive damages when it found that an employee's
termination violated the collective bargaining agreement.

4. All Canadian jurisdictions require that all collective bargaining agreements provide
   for grievance arbitration. In the United States, most collective bargaining agreements include arbitration provisions but they are not legally mandated. Does the
   fact that arbitration is mandated by law justify the Court in *Weber* and *O'Leary*
   requiring that all of these different types of claims be submitted to arbitration and
   thereby removed from the jurisdiction of the courts?

5. In the United States, judicial deference to an arbitration provision in a collective bargaining agreement is not required for statutory claims of individuals such as
   discrimination claims under Title VII of the Civil Rights Act. *Alexander v. Gardner-
   Denver Co.*, 415 U.S. 36 (1974). But in *Circuit City Stores, Inc. v. Adams*, 532 U.S.
   105 (2001), the Court found that arbitration agreements imposed by employers as
   a condition of employment on individual employees did operate to remove court
   jurisdiction to hear an employee's claim that the employer violated an antidiscrimination statute. Thus, in Canada, tort and statutory claims by employees covered by
   a collective bargaining agreement go to arbitration but in the United States they do
   not. Does the fact that arbitration is imposed by statute in all collective bargaining
   agreements justify the difference in outcome?

6. Who are the parties to the collective bargaining agreement and therefore any arbitration proceeding brought pursuant to the arbitration provision in the contract?
   In *Weber*, the arbitration proceeding arising out of Weber's grievance was settled.

Do you think Weber was completely satisfied with that settlement reached by the union and his employer?

7. "[L]egislation in all Canadian jurisdictions imposes on unions a duty to represent all members of the bargaining unit fairly and in good faith. The union's duty of fair representation is not limited to union members but extends, as well, to nonmembers who are part of the bargaining unit." INTERNATIONAL LABOR & EMPLOYMENT LAW, at 21–47. By settling Weber's grievance presumably without his approval, has the union satisfied its duty of fair representation to him? In handling grievances, "where a union's treatment of a grievance has been perfunctory, a breach of the duty will be established. The test is an objective one. It requires the union to put its mind to the grievances. Mistakes, if honestly made, even if due to human shortcomings such as laxness, will not make the union's conduct arbitrary. The union must give an opportunity to the employee to present her/his case. . . . " LABOUR LAW IN CANADA, at 231. Duty of fair representation cases are heard by labor boards. *Id.*

8. In *Parry Sound (District) Social Services Administration Board v. Ontario Public Service Employees Union, Local 324*, [2003] 2. S.C.R. 157, the Court found that arbitrators acting pursuant to a collective bargaining agreement were required to consider human rights statutory claims. In *L'Exuyer v. Aéroports de Montréal*, (2003) 233 F.T.R. 234, the Federal Court applied *Weber* to federal Personal Information Protection and Electronic Documents Act claims.

---

5 Mexico

A. INTRODUCTION

The United Mexican States, the third country in North America, is considerably different in many important ways from the United States and Canada. Unlike the United States and Canada, the initial European explorers, who were from Spain rather than England, France, and the Netherlands, found a large indigenous population made up of Aztec, Mayan, and Olmec cultures. Those differences, along with others, have resulted in a contemporary society that is quite distinct from the two other North American countries. Mexico's population in 2005 was over 105 million, with a per capita gross national income, in U.S. dollars, of $6,613. Some 11.6 million people born in Mexico live in the United States, with about six million Mexican immigrants in the United States not documented. In 2005, about five hundred thousand unskilled workers crossed the border illegally, with only two receiving permanent visas. Julia Preston, *Rules Collide with Reality in the Immigration Debate*, www.nytimes.com/2006/05/29/us/29broken.html.4 (hereinafter Preston, *Rules Collide with Reality*). By comparison, the gross national income per capita for Canada's population of over thirty-one million is almost four times as large at $24,470. In the United States, the population is over 290 million people with a per capita gross national income of $37,870. *See* World Bank, World Development Indicators 2005, www.devdata.worldbank.org.

In 2001, the total number of people engaged in economic activity outside the home was about forty million, with three times as many men as women. Although the official unemployment rate is low, usually reported as less than 3 percent, that is an artificial figure because workers in the informal economy are counted as employed, even if they earn only one peso a day. Stephen Zamora, Jose Ramon Cossio-Diaz, Leonel Pereznieto-Castro, Jose Roldan Xopa, Mexican Law 430 (2004) (hereinafter Mexican Law). Over 62 percent of workers are without benefits. *See*, Mexico: The North American Free Trade Agreement: Effects on Human Rights, International Federation of Human Rights, no. 448/2, April, 2006, p. 13 (hereinafter, Mexico: NAFTA Effects on Human Rights). The minimum daily wage in 2001 was $3.84 and the average daily earnings for laborers was $11.75, for mechanics $24.49 and for commercial assistants $34.41. Over 40 percent of the population was beneath the poverty level, which was

Our thanks to Carlos de Buen Unna, of the firm of Bufete de Buen, Mexico City, Jorge G. De Presno Arizpe, of Thacher, Proffitt & Wood, also of Mexico City, Professor Stephen Zamora, University of Houston law school, and Justice José Ramón Cossío of the Mexican Supreme Court, for their help with this chapter.

about the average earnings of a laborer. See, Foreign Labor Trends – Mexico 2002, www.dol.gov/ILAB/media/reports/flt/mexico-2002.htm. Of the forty million workers, about 64 percent, or twenty-four million, are engaged in informal employment, which is defined to include wage and self-employment "that is not recognized, regulated, or protected by existing legal or regulatory frameworks and non-remunerative work undertaken in an income-producing enterprise." That informal work is done in informal enterprises, outside of enterprises and in agricultural production. INTERNATIONAL LABOUR ORGANIZATION, WOMEN AND MEN IN THE INFORMAL ECONOMY: A STATISTICAL PICTURE 12, 36 (2002). It includes over 1,286,000 street vendors, with 185,000 in Mexico City alone. *Id.* at 51–52. Earnings for domestic workers and those working in micro-establishments, including self-employment, earn less than half the average for all workers. About 32 percent of Gross Domestic Product is produced by workers in the informal economy. About 25 percent of workers in the United States participate in the informal economy, with many working part time or in temporary jobs. *Id.* at 26.

Unions have lost members since 1984. "For the 'formal' sector labor force as a whole, union density declined from just over 30 percent in 1984 to just under 20 percent in 2000." David Fairris and Edward Levine, *Declining Union Density in Mexico, 1984–2000,* MONTHLY LABOR REVIEW, Sept. 2004, p. 10, 11. Whereas 40 percent of all workers are supposedly represented by unions, about 90 percent of them are represented by protectionist or "ghost" unions that employers deal with to forestall real unionism. Fernando Herrera & Javier Melgoza, *Recent Evolution of Labor Union Affiliation and Labor Regulation in Mexico,* in STATE OF WORKING IN MEXICO, 2003, p. 2 (Enrique de la Garza, Carlos Salas, ed. 2003) (hereinafter, STATE OF WORKING IN MEXICO). Union density along the border with the United States, the locus of much of the maquiladora industries, is lower than in the interior. Although also experiencing a decline in union membership, teachers had the highest union density – still 65 percent in 2000 – whereas the commercial and construction sectors had the lowest density, reduced to 2 percent and 3 percent, respectively by 2000. *Id.,* at 12. Private sector union density overall, however, is about twice as high in Mexico as it is in the United States.

Despite the vast economic differences between the United States and Canada compared with Mexico, Mexico still is ranked among the "upper middle income" countries by the World Bank. It joined what is now the World Trade Organization in 1986. Furthermore, since 1994 Mexico has been one of thirty member countries of the Organization for Economic Co-operation and Development, an organization including most of the major economic powers.

Notes

1. Given the stark economic differences between life in the United States and Mexico, is it any wonder that so many Mexicans come to the United States? Mexico has the same number of visa positions for unskilled workers as Botswana or Nepal. Preston, *Rules Collide with Reality.*

2. If you are an informal worker, does that mean you are completely at the mercy of the market? What can a country do to incorporate informal workers into the formal economy? Unless it can effectively formalize most employment, can a nation set meaningful labor standards for its workers? Do high labor standards imposed on the formal economy create a barrier to entry for workers in the informal economy

by increasing the costs for employers to hire employees? Does that worsen the lot of workers in the informal economy?

There are a number of views about the informal economy and workers in that economy. Martha Alter Chen, Rethinking the Informal Economy, Research Paper No. 2005/10, World Institute for Development Economic Research, U. N. University, p. 6, www.wider.unu.edu/publications/rps/rps2005/rp2005-10.pdf, describes some of the perspectives:

> [S]ome poor households and individuals engage in survival activities that have – or seem to have – very few links to the formal economy and the formal regulatory environment; some microentrepreneurs choose to avoid taxes and regulations; while other units and workers are subordinated to larger firms. And, clearly, most informal enterprises (and, it should be added, informal wage workers) contribute to economic growth; the working poor in the informal economy need basic infrastructure and social services; some microentrepreneurs and own account operators face excessive government regulations; while other microentrepreneurs and own account operators (as well as informal wage workers) are subordinated to capitalist interests.

A broad view of the informal economy focuses on the nature of employment as well as the characteristics of enterprises. "Under this new definition, informal economy is seen as comprised of all forms of 'informal employment' – that is, employment without formal contracts (i.e., covered by labour legislation), worker benefits or social protection – both inside and outside informal enterprises." *Id.* at 7. Using this broad definition, microentrepreneurs who employ others are at the top of a hierarchy, with higher income and are made up predominantly of men, while predominantly female homeworkers are at the bottom. *Id.* at 10. Chen proposes that social policy take all of these dimensions into account. Therefore, identified overregulation of microentrepreneurs should be reduced but also rights to benefits and a social safety net should be extended to informal workers. *Id.* at 23–25.

To date, no consistent methodology of collecting data about the extent of informal employment has been implemented. But it is estimated that "informal employment comprises one-half to three-quarters of non-agricultural employment in developing countries: specifically, 48 percent in North Africa; 51 percent in Latin America; 65 per cent in Asia; and 72 per cent in sub-Saharan Africa." *Id.* at 13. If employment in agriculture is added, the estimates are higher: "from 83 per cent of *non-agricultural* employment to 93 per cent of *total* employment in India; from 55 to 62 per cent in Mexico; and from 28 to 34 per cent in South Africa." *Id.* Developed countries tend to use the term "non-standard" work, "which refers to all work that is not regular, stable and protected" and includes "self-employment, part-time work and temporary work." *Id.* at 14. In both developed and developing countries, women are typically more represented in the informal workforce than they are in the formal economy. *Id.* at 13–14.

3. One of the consequences of the free trade provisions of NAFTA is that the Mexican agricultural sector suddenly faced competition from corn and other agricultural products exported from the United States. This undermined the indigenous "white corn" economy in much of rural Mexico, driving agricultural workers into the cities and beyond. *See* STATE OF WORKING IN MEXICO.

1. Primer on Mexican History

By 1521, the land inhabited by the indigenous cultures was invaded and conquered by Spanish Conquistadores under Hernán Cortés. The colonial period lasted until 1821. New Spain ("Nueva España"), as it was called, stretched from Costa Rica in the south to include much of what today is the southwestern United States. Europeans and their white descendants dominated the politics and economy of colonial Mexico. The war for independence from Spain began in 1810 but was not successful until 1821.

> New Spain (colonial Mexico) was not well prepared either for self-government or democracy at the time of its independence in 1821 after centuries of highly centralized Spanish colonial administration. Moreover, the Mexican Creole (Spanish born in Latin America) population was bitterly divided over the continuing domination of the church, army, and large landowners. Also, the population was markedly heterogeneous because of the large native population that was not acculturated to European or democratic values. In the century preceding the Mexican Constitutional Convention of 1917, Mexico was dominated by *caudillismo* (charismatic political and military chieftains) and political chaos. Porfirio Diaz assumed the presidency in 1876, bringing political stability to Mexico until 1910. He united the conservative factions (clergy, army, landowners, rural chieftains) and foreign interests. However, the constituencies of Father Miquel Hidalgo y Castillo, General Jose Maria Morelos, and the liberals, who had fought for a century for religious toleration and for an end to the domination of the army, rural bosses, and foreign interests, [in the 1821 war of independence] were not to be denied. The simmering social tensions exploded in the revolution of 1910 [which ultimately resulted in the 1917 Constitution].
>
> James F. Smith, Confronting *Differences in the United States and Mexican Legal Systems in the Era of NAFTA*, 1 U.S.-Mex. L. J. 85, 92 (1993)(hereinafter Smith).

A new period of instability broke out after Diaz resigned and fled to France in face of a revolution demanding reforms including a one-term presidency. Presidents Madero and Carranza, as well as revolutionary leaders Emiliano Zapata and Pancho Villa were all assassinated. A national federation of unions, the Confederación Regional Obrera Mexicana (CROM), supported the revolution but, after the assassination of President Álvaro Obregón in 1928, the government withdrew its support from CROM and union leaders began to defect.

In 1929, the Partido Naciónal Mexicano (PNM) was formed by General Plutarco Elías Calles, who was serving as president. The PNM, which was the forerunner of what ultimately became the Partido Revolucionario Institucional (PRI), was the institution that began to consolidate power by persuading the revolutionary generals to dissolve their personal armies in order to create the Mexican Army. That brought a real end to the Mexican Revolution and set the stage for the emergence of modern Mexico.

During this period, Vicente Lombardo Toledano, a Marxist with close ties to the Soviet Union, left CROM and, with Fidel Velázquez, formed the Conderación General de Obreros y Compesinos de Mexico (CGOCM), which became the most important union confederation in Mexico.

President Lázaro Cárdenas del Rio, a charismatic leftist, came to power in 1934 and transformed Mexico by removing the army from power and by uniting the other elements of society. Cárdenas nationalized the oil and electricity industries, started land reform and the distribution of free textbooks to children. He called on unions for support to resist a threatened coup by former president Calles and to oppose an employers' lockout of workers in Monterrey. Cárdenas transformed the PNM into the Partido Revolucionario Mexicano, another predecessor to PRI, by turning it into what has been referred to as a three-legged stool – workers, rural peasants, and the masses – that governed Mexico as a one-party state until recently. This has also been called a "corporatist" political system in which various social groups – the legs of the stool or, more respectfully, the pillars of the ruling party – are organized into official constituencies that on one hand use their status to influence government policy while on the other hand are supported by government patronage and co-opted from opposition to the prevailing government and its policies. "The term corporatism refers to a system of government in which the society is organized into industrial, social, and professional organizations that serve in theory as instruments of political representation, but which in fact may operate to control the activities of persons who come within their jurisdiction. . . . The 'labour pillar' of this support was central to the PRI's control of society, and became a means both of distributing benefits to groups and individuals and of controlling dissent." Mexican Law, at 417. These corporatist unions essentially bargained with the government, rather than with employers, while employers also bargained with the government. With the adoption of neoliberal policies, the government no longer is as active a player in the private economy so the establishment unions have lost much of their effectiveness.

Until the 2000 presidential elections, power in Mexico was centralized in the presidency and the PRI party. Although there had been movement away from this monocentric system for some time, the defining moment of a move toward a more polycentric Mexico came in 2000. The election of Vicente Fox, the candidate of the conservative or neoliberal PAN party, left the government divided, with no party holding a majority in control of Congress. For the first time in modern Mexican history, the president faced effective opposition to his policy initiatives. During the era of complete PRI control, the president, while limited to one six-year term, held all the important elements of power. The president initiated legislation and had the power to spend money without the authorization of Congress. He had only a limited duty to report the expenditures after the fact. The Constitution still gives the president the power to appoint unilaterally the most important officials in the government, until 1994 even the attorney general. Although other top-level officials need Senate approval, the president may remove most officials without approval. Until the 2000 election, the president's most important power was in his capacity as leader of the PRI, to decide who would be the next president by picking PRI's candidate. "[By selecting the PRI candidates, t]he president also determines who will be governors, municipal presidents, senators, and the majority of the *deputados* [members of Congress]." Smith, at 98–101. At the present time, no political party has a majority in either chamber of the legislature. The Senate now has sixty PRI members, forty-six in PAN, sixteen in PRD a left of center party, and five Green Party members. The Chamber of Deputies has 223 PRI members, 154 from PAN, 96 from PRD and 17 from the Green Party. This means that PAN President Fox has not gained easy acceptance of his legislative initiatives, although PAN and PRI have joined forces to pass legislation upon occasion. *Id.*

As of October 2003, ten of the thirty-one state governors were members of PAN. Since 2004, PRI has been more successful in state gubernatorial elections, including winning the governorship for the states of Mexico and Nyarit in the summer of 2005. Elisabeth Malkin, *Fox's Party Is Said to Trail In a Key State*, N.Y. TIMES, Monday, July 4, 2005, A6, col.6. This all shows that the power incident of picking candidates from a party to stand for office has been much reduced by the fact that the outcome of the elections is no longer certain.

As part of consolidating power through a single political party, Cárdenas called on the unions to form a unified federation. As a result, the CGOCM transformed itself into the Confederatión de Trabajadores de México (CTM) and was founded in 1936. The CTM became the "labor sector" of the party and thus became effectively part of the government. With that status, the CTM gained many benefits. But Cárdenas took steps to ensure that the CTM did not become the only union organization in the country. For example, he prohibited the CTM from representing federal employees in the civil service or farm workers. Thus, other unions and confederations of unions continued to exist, despite the advantages that the CTM had as part of the government. Many of these unions were affiliated with the government, but without the full official status and state sponsorship enjoyed by the CTM. Most of these unions were members of the Congress of Labor (CT). More recently unions that are independent of any political party or of the government have emerged. *See* DALE HATHAWAY, ALLIES ACROSS THE BORDER: MEXICO'S "AUTHENTIC LABOR FRONT" AND GLOBAL SOLIDARITY 47 (2000) (hereinafter HATHAWAY) for a description of the Frente Auténtico del Trabajo (FAT), an independent union that was formed in 1960. In 1997, a number of unions, including FAT joined together to form a new labor federation, the Unidos Naciónal Trabajo (UNT). More recently, FAT and UNT have been joining forces with social organizations beyond the labor movement in order to try to exercise influence in the social and political arena no longer dominated by PRI.

Toledano stepped down as general secretary of the CTM in 1941 and was replaced by Velázquez, who stayed in power until his death in 1997. Given the ability of the CTM to get is members out to vote for PRI candidates in political elections, the CTM, under Velázquez's direction, was a powerful force in the political and economic life of Mexico. "The CTM played a critical role in sustaining the PRI's long hold on the Mexican political system. . . . Because politicians are constitutionally prohibited from serving more than one term in Mexico, the PRI had to choose a new presidential candidate every six years (*sexenio*). Rather than leaving this critical decision in the hands of party factions, the outgoing president personally selected his own successor in a veiled process known as the dedazo (fingering). . . . The CTM, and particularly Fidel Velázquez, took the lead in circling the wagons around the president's nominee." Katrina Burgess, *Mexican Labor at a Crossroads*, in MEXICO'S POLITICS AND SOCIETY IN TRANSITION 78–79 (2003) (hereinafter Burgess). With the help of the government, the CTM expanded its power and influence by eliminating independent union leaders in many industries.

After World War II, anticommunism was used to push some leftist union leaders out of office. New union leaders, referred to as "charros" or "cowboys" after the leader of the railroad workers' union who was fond of dressing in classic cowboy attire, kept the CTM tied closely to the government, even though the CTM never held a monopoly on labor organizing. Over time the leaders of the CTM came to be called "dinosaurs" because of their resistance to change and support of more repressive measures by the government, even against the interests of the workers. Just as in much of the rest of the world, the 1960s were tumultuous during which the CTM was a stalwart of the establishment.

Until 1982, the economic policy of the PRI governments was based on what is called the "import substitution industrialization" model of economic development. This strategy emphasizes the growth of domestic industries, many of them state-owned, using protection from imports through tariffs as well as non-tariff measures to block foreign competition. With many ups and downs, the import substitution model resulted in steady growth and rising incomes for Mexican workers in the formal economy. From "1951 until 1976, the Mexican economy grew at an average rate of 6.5%, which was 3% faster than population growth." HATHAWAY, at 36. That era was known as the "Mexican miracle" because, by 1964, an unskilled worker in the formal economy earning the minimum wage could support a family of five, including sending his children to school. *Id.* Although most workers in the formal economy were able to escape poverty, most of the population worked in the informal economy and were mired in rural and urban poverty. *See* LANCE COMPA, JUSTICE FOR ALL: IN MEXICO 5 (2003) (hereinafter COMPA). The discovery of new oil fields in 1977 allowed economic progress to continue until 1982, but, as is true in many oil-producing countries, the economic benefits of the oil business did not reach the majority of the population. In 1982, the world price of oil collapsed and interest rates soared. Outgoing President Lopez Portillo nationalized the banks to attempt to stop wealthy Mexicans from sending their money abroad but that did not halt the crisis. Incoming President Miguel de la Madrid turned to the United States and the International Monetary Fund for debt relief. "With Ronald Reagan in the White House, this meant that Mexico could no longer even pretend to put obstacles in the way of global business. To obtain needed financing, Mexico had to implement the structural adjustment program recommended by the IMF. The restructuring of 1982 was followed by Mexico's entry into the General Agreement on Trade and Tariffs (GATT) in 1986." HATHAWAY, at 37. GATT subsequently became the World Trade Organization (WTO) and Mexico signed the NAFTA free trade agreement with Canada and the United States in 1994.

Accepting the debt relief offered by the International Monetary Fund meant turning away from import substitution policies and turning toward free trade, open foreign investment and participation in a globalized economy. Domestically, President Madrid made the transition to neoliberal economic policy by beginning a tradition, which lasted until the 2000 election of President Vicente Fox, of getting the agreement of the important economic groups – peasants, workers, and employers – to agree to wage and price controls that were then implemented throughout society, including in collective bargaining agreements. These compacts, called "pactos de concertación social" or "pactos," substituted the agreement of the major economic sectors for legislative or other direct governmental action to control and regulate the economy. They transferred minimum-wage setting from the tripartite national commission authorized by law to do it to the economic cabinet of the government. Furthermore, the pactos reversed the traditional pattern whereby wage increases negotiated in collective contracts set the pace for minimum-wage adjustments and instead set caps for wages negotiated in collective contracts. Burgess, at 82–83. The last of the nine pactos was agreed to by President Zedillo in 1998. INTERNATIONAL LABOR & EMPLOYMENT LAWS, at 22-45-47.

Critics claim that the adoption of neoliberal, free-market economic policies include as an integral part government support to prevent the emergence of unions independent of the government and the ruling party. That resulted in the continued support of the CTM. In March 2003, an experienced labor lawyer and advisor to the conservative PAN party, gave an interview in which he described how government officials and official union leaders are in a tight alliance to establish and maintain these official unions in order to control workers while meeting employers' demands for low wages and effective labor standards: "Potential investors sit down with people from the governor's economic development office. If it's a major company or a large factory coming in, the governor himself comes to the meeting. The governor tells the company, 'This is the union you will have, and this union will make sure you don't have any labor troubles." COMPA, at 16.

The model of single party governance that had made the PRI so powerful also came under attack. In 1987, Cuauhtémoc Cárdenas, son of former President Lazáro Cardenas who set in place the fundamental corporatist policies, formed the Democratic Current within the PRI. After a call by Velázquez that he be expelled for challenging the established PRI leadership, Cárdenas left the party and formed the Partido de la Revolución (PRD) and ran for President in the 1988 election. While the government announced that the PRI candidate, Carlos Salinas de Gotari, had won, most felt that the election had been stolen from Cárdenas. Though Salinas took office, this began the weakening of the grip of the PRI on Mexican politics. HATHAWAY, at 44. President Salinas and his successor, President Ernesto Zedillo Ponce de Leon, continued to dismantle the nationalist economic policies of the import substitution model by privatizing state-owned industries, which were bastions of CTM strength. Two weeks after the inauguration of Zedillo, "the Mexican peso crashed and the economy when into a deep recession. During 1995, economic output declined more than 6 percent, nearly 1 million workers lost their jobs in the formal sector, and real manufacturing wages contracted by 13.5 percent." Burgess, at 93. Zedillo's response was to reimpose economic austerity and further accelerate structural reforms in order to satisfy the terms set by the United States for an emergency bailout package. *Id.*

In this era of turning toward economic policies that were open to foreign investment and free trade and away from import substitution policies, Velázquez, the general secretary of the CTM, supported the government's actions even though the burden of the IMF structural adjustment program fell most heavily on the workers. Their wages, in real terms, dropped nearly 70% from their highs before 1982. Velázquez, for example, supported NAFTA. Ultimately, the support the CTM gave the government came at a cost of support among the workers. Gradually, the power of the CTM to control its members' votes in political elections weakened and so its political power also declined. Until his death in 1997, Velázquez continued to support the PRI in an effort to maintain influence and power but the contradiction between what the government was doing and what was good for the workers led to a weakened CTM. Its leadership came to be characterized as "dinosaurs." Velazquez was replaced by Leonardo Alcaine, who died of old age in 2005 and was replaced by 78 year old Joaquin Gamboa Pascoe.

Starting in 1995, the CTM began to lose unions and their leaders. "In August 1997, more than 300 delegates from 132 unions claiming to represent more than 1 million workers agreed to create the National Union of Workers (UNT). . . . The UNT's central objectives were (1) to challenge the economic policies imposed through elite pacts, and (2) to free labor organizations from the corporatist practices associated with the PRI." Burgess, at 95. More recently, the UNT has joined with several other confederations, including some of the former CROC unions, to form the National Front for Unity and Union Autonomy (FNUAS), while another new confederation, the Mexican Union Alliance (ASM) has been organized by the rest of the CROC unions.

There have been a number of recent moves towards greater organization among the independent unions and by these unions with other social reform organizations. In protest of labor "reform" legislation proposed by President Fox to further his neoliberal agenda, "hundreds of thousands of workers throughout Mexico . . . walked off the job on August 31, 2004, some for just an hour and some for the day, to protest the government's free trade policies. Thousands more joined in protest demonstrations and marches; the largest of them was procession of hundreds of thousands through Mexico City." Dan LaBotz & Robin Alexander, The Escalating Struggles Over Mexico's Labor Law p. 4, www. nacla.org/art_display_printable.php?art=2566.

Notes

1. In both Canada and the United States, the main focus of unions is on the employees of particular employers, though there has always been a political dimension to their activities. In Mexico, establishment unions historically have focused on politics, not on the particular workplace. Why do you think these differences happened?
2. Now that the PRI party no longer holds all the power but there is developing what might be called a polycentric system of government, politics and the economy, how can the establishment unions make themselves relevant? Is the only real alternative to start over? Or is it too early to tell what these recent developments portend for the future of unionism in Mexico?

2. The Mexican Constitution and Federal Labor Law

The Mexican legal system has its historical roots both in sixteenth-century Spanish law and pre-Columbian indigenous law. Unlike the common law basis of the legal system in most of the United States and Canada, the Mexican legal system is essentially part of the European civil law tradition[1] based on the enactment of codes. "A code in a civil law country is like a constitution in that it presents a broad statement of general principles with specific detail where necessary. . . . The French Napoleonic Code of 1804 targeted the judiciary as a privileged, aristocratic, and even reactionary force that must be relegated to the role of applying, not interpreting legislative norms. Mexico has inherited this tradition, which requires judges to apply the appropriate code provisions, to reason deductively from the principles reflected in them (or a more general one), or, where necessary, to consult doctrinal writing [rather than case law] to arrive at the proper result." Smith, at 88. Thus, during the nineteenth century, Mexico, having no specialized labor legislation, applied the general principles of the Civil Code to labor contracts. MEXICAN LAW, at 415. Because of the reliance on the civil law, the study of Mexican labor and employment law foreshadows our subsequent study of European systems. *See* Chapters 9 and 10.

Despite its quite different legal tradition, the first Mexican Constitution, adopted in 1824, was greatly influenced by the U.S. Constitution. The Constitution of 1857 followed the structure of the original constitution. The Mexican Revolution against Diaz began in 1910 and, during a period of continuing war, religious and political tumult, the present

---

[1] Mexico's private law system, including torts, property, commerce, and inheritance, traces its origin to the Roman civil law, which dates from the Twelve Tablets of Rome in 450 BC. Its milestones include the Corpus Juris Civilis of the Emperor Justinian in the sixth century, its revival in Italian universities in the twelfth century, and its reemergence in the form of modern civil codes in nation-states in Europe and Latin America in the nineteenth century. It is the oldest, most widely used, and most influential legal system in the world. Spanish law, which evolved from the Roman civil law, governed the viceroyalty of Mexico as well as the rest of what is now Latin America for three centuries.
Smith, at 87–88.

Constitution was promulgated in 1917 while Venustiano Carranza was president. It, too, followed the structure of its predecessors as well as the U.S. Constitution. FRANCISCO A. AVALOS, THE MEXICAN LEGAL SYSTEM 1–3 (2d ed. 2000) (hereinafter AVALOS). The Constitution provides for a "federal, democratic, representative Republic composed of free and sovereign States," with all public power derived from the people. Similar to the structure of the U.S. Constitution, Mexico's Constitution has "the basic political structure of a republican and federal national government with three branches: an executive (popularly elected), a legislature (bicameral), and a judiciary (lifetime appointments for the Supreme Court), as well as separate state governments and a bill of rights." Smith, at 91–92. Mexico consists of thirty-one states plus a Federal District in which the national capital, Mexico City, is located.

Although the Constitution provides a federal system, labor and employment law is federal, whereas the administration and enforcement of that federal law is split between the national and state governments. Thus, the federalism of Mexico is quite different from the U.S. or Canadian models. In the United States, the national government has broad authority over labor and employment because of the broad authority given Congress to regulate interstate commerce. Although some work may fall beyond the reach of the commerce clause, the states, given their residual general police powers, have the authority to regulate labor and employment as long as that regulation does not conflict with applicable federal laws and policies. In contrast, the Canadian federal system has left most labor and employment regulation beyond certain national industries such as the railroads and airlines to the provinces rather than the national government. With essentially very similar Constitutional structures, why are the actual operation of the United States and Mexican federal systems so different?

Before the Mexican Revolution, Mexico followed a laissez-faire model of labor relations much like that in the United States. "The typical day for an individual working in Mexico before 1910 consisted of backbreaking work performed with no safety or health regulations for long hours with miniscule amounts of compensation." Jenna L. Acuff, *The Race to the Bottom: The United States' Influence on Mexican Labor Law Enforcement*, 5 SAN DIEGO INT'L L. J. 387, 390 (2004). The participation of Mexico's working and peasant classes in the 1910 Revolution helped redirect the future path of labor relations and labor law. Unlike the U.S. Constitution, which protects individuals against governmental interference with their rights, a so-called negative rights system, the 1917 Constitution reflected that new path by being the first constitution in the world to include positive social guarantees to protect workers and the economically weak. "The Mexican Constitutional Convention, unlike the Philadelphia Convention over a century earlier, addressed economic and social goals and rights, equating social justice with – if not elevating it over – individual liberty." Smith, at -94. Article 27 was written with the intent of breaking up land, water, and other natural resource monopolies held by the Church and a group of no more than one thousand privileged families. AVALOS, p. 5; Stephen F. Befort & Virginia E. Cornett, *Beyond the Rhetoric of the NAFTA Treaty Debate: A Comparative Analysis of Labor and Employment Law in Mexico and the United States*, 17 COMP. LAB. L. 269, 272 (1996).

Article 123 provides a broad, positive right to work: "Every person has the right to dignified and socially useful work. To achieve this, the creation of jobs and the social organization will be promoted conforming to law." While provisions such as Article 123 have been characterized by Mexican constitutional scholars as a "project to be accomplished, a statement of revolutionary ideals that is nominal," Smith, at 94, this positive right to work, even as an aspiration, is in contrast with the negative rights recognized for workers in the United States, such as the right against race or sex discrimination.[2] Is a negative rights system preferable to a positive rights model if many of those positive rights are really only aspirational and cannot be legally enforced?

The opening clause to Part A of Article 123 dealing with private employment – "Among workers, day laborers, employees, domestic workers, artisans, and of a general matter, all contracts of work" – makes clear the Constitution applies to all workers of whatever type of work performed. The basic provision is followed by 31 paragraphs elaborating workers' rights. In contrast to the at-will rule in the United States, paragraph XXII sets forth a basic good cause protection of workers against discharge: "The employer who dismisses a worker without just cause . . . is obligated, at the option of the worker, to rehire him or her, or pay compensation in the amount of three month's wages or salary." Paragraph XXVII restricts contracts between workers and their employers that amounts to a "waiver of any right of the worker that is in the laws of protection and aid for workers."

Further, while phrased in terms of a minimum, paragraph VI requires what might be called a "living wage" to be paid to all workers: "Minimum wages and salaries must be sufficient to satisfy the normal needs of a head of family; in material, social and cultural areas; and to provide the obligatory education to their children." Although the minimum wage was set to provide a living wage during the period called the "Mexican miracle" – the 1950s through the 1970s – the minimum wage since then has been near the poverty level. A number of provisions set labor standards in terms of hours worked per day, a day of rest per week, and double time for overtime. Public workers are guaranteed vacations. Provision is made for workers compensation as well as a guarantee of a safe workplace. Providing equal pay-for-equal work "without taking into account sex or nationality" is required and pregnant women are given special rights including paid leave before and after the birth of the child.

Paragraph XVI recognizes the right of workers and employers to organize: "Workers as well as business owners will have the right to come together with each other in defense of their respective interests; forming unions, professional associations, et cetera." The rights of workers to strike and of employers to shut down are protected by paragraphs XVII and XVIII: "The laws will recognize the right of workers to strike, and employers to stop work. Strikes are legal when they have their object to bring about balance between the different factors of production, reconciling the rights of the worker with those of capital. . . . Strikes will be considered illegal only when the majority of the strikers have committed violent acts against persons or property, or in case of war, when they affect establishments and services on which the government depends."

Paragraph XXIX envisions a broadly applicable social security system: "The Law of Social Security is to the public benefit, and it will include insurance or disability, old age, life, involuntary unemployment, of illnesses and accidents, day care, and any other thing

---

[2] "[T]he labour protections included in the Constitution have proven impossible to enforce consistently, for economic and political reasons. Like certain other provisions of the Mexican constitution, the 'guarantees' written into Article 123 – the right to work, limitations on the work day, the right to a minimum wage – have served as targets or aspirations, rather than as enforceable rights." MEXICAN LAW, at 416.

directed to the protection and well-being of laborers, farm workers, non-salaried persons, and other social sectors and their families." Even beyond these mandated social benefits, the Constitution requires a system of profit sharing and the provision by the employer of housing for employees.

Drawing from European models, Article 123 contemplates that special labor tribunals, called *juntas de conciliation y arbitraje* (CAB), that are not part of the judiciary will administer Mexican labor and employment law. These CABs have exclusive jurisdiction over labor disputes, whether individual or collective. Thus, paragraph XX provides: "The differences or conflicts between capital or labor will be subject to the decision of a Board of Conciliation and Arbitration, formed by an equal number of representatives of the workers and the employers, and one of the government." A federal board hears disputes arising from those industries and businesses that are listed as being subject to exclusive federal control. Each state utilizes similar boards to apply federal labor law to employers and their workers not within federal administrative control. Thus, many of the export industries of Mexico, especially the maquiladoras,[3] are subject to state Conciliation and Arbitration Boards since the nature of the business is not within the list of federal industries. In November 2004, the maquila sector employed about 1.14 million people. "[T]here were 2,809 active maquiladora plants in the country as of September [2004], a dramatic drop from the 3901 reported in 2003. By December [2004], the maquiladora sector appeared to be experiencing a rebound. Compensation packages in the maquiladora sector still were lower than in the traditional manufacturing sector." State Department Human Rights Report, at 18. One explanation for the drop in maquila employment was that manufacturing jobs were being moved to China because of its lower labor costs. *As China Gallops, Mexico Sees Factory Jobs Slip Away*, N.Y. TIMES, September 3, 2003, A3.

All of the CABs, whether federal or state, are tripartite, with one member appointed by the government, one elected by the management sector and the other by the labor sector. The term of office is six years. The elections are in annual assemblies of their respective organizations. COMMISSION FOR LABOR COOPERATION, LABOR RELATIONS LAW IN NORTH AMERICA, 145–46 (2000) (hereinafter NORTH AMERICA LABOR LAW). Article 652 of the Federal Labor Law provides that "duly registered unions and unaffiliated workers rendering services to an employer are entitled to appoint delegates to the conventions. Notice is given of an open convention to elect representatives [to a CAB] and the convention goes forward whatever the number of worker delegates present from a particular industrial sector may be. Representatives are elected by a majority of the votes cast." Review of Public Communication CAN 2003-1, www.hes.dc/gc/en/lp/spila/lalc/PCNAALC/12/Mexican_law.sjml 22 (hereinafter Mexican Labour Law).

There is only one federal CAB located in Mexico City but the Federal Labor Department has established sixty-five special boards with specific venues, with at least one federal special board in each state At the state level, there is usually one CAB in every city with

---

[3] Mexico established its Border Industrialization Program during the mid-1960s to absorb the unemployed along the Mexican United States border after the United States terminated the "bracero" – migrant Mexican worker – program. Initially, components were allowed to be imported duty-free for processing or assembly within a twenty-kilometer strip along the border as the resulting production was exported. Later, maquiladoras were authorized to be established anywhere in Mexico except Mexico City, Guadalajara, and Monterrey. Most of the questions about how well Mexican labor law works arises in maquiladora industries.

a population of more than one hundred thousand people. Some cities, such as Ciudad Juarez, have five state CABs located in it. Anna L. Torriente, Mexican & U.S. Labor Law & Practice (1997), 191 (hereinafter Torriente). There are over one hundred CABs that enforce the Federal Labor Law within their respective jurisdictions.

During the period after the adoption of the 1917 Constitution and before 1931, state and municipal law regulated labor and employment in Mexico. North America Labor Law, at 102). Those laws were pre-empted by the federal labor law. The Constitution's labor provisions were first codified into statutory law for Part A of Constitutional Article 123 – covering the private sector – when the Federal Labor Law (*Ley Federal de Trajajo*) took effect in 1931.[4] As amended, that law is still in effect and it continues to confirm the broadly pro-employee policies established in the Constitution. For example, Article 2 of the Federal Labor Law provides that "Labor norms shall insure balance and social justice in the relations between workers and employers." Foreshadowing the 1944 Philadelphia Declaration of the International Labor Organization, Article 3 defines work at a broad humanistic level: "Work is a social right and obligation. It is not a commodity; it is to be respected for the freedom and dignity of the person performing it and must be performed under conditions that insure the life, health and decent standard of living for the worker and his family." "Worker" is also defined very broadly in Article 8: "A worker is any physical person who personally performs a subordinate work for another individual or legal person." And Article 10 defines the term "employer" quite broadly: "An employer is any individual or legal person using the services of one or more workers." Given these broad definitions, the federal labor law applies without regard to the size of the employer or the nature of the work performed. Any individual working for another is protected by Mexico's Federal Labor Law. Thus, household workers, skilled professionals, and employees of large or small corporations are all covered by its terms. How does that compare with the consequences of the federal system in the United States or in Canada?

The Mexican Constitution applies directly to private actors and so it creates many directly enforceable rights, including some labor and employment rights. In addition to the Constitution and federal statutory labor law, Mexico also makes treaties it has ratified "self-executing." That means they become an integral part of domestic law and enforceable by individuals so long as they do not contravene the Constitution. Thus, Article 6 of the Federal Labor Law provides that "treaties concluded and approved under Article 133 of the Constitution shall apply to labor relations insofar as they are to the workers' advantage." *Id.*, at 103. With a much higher ratification rate than the United States, Mexico is the signatory to a number of important International Labor Organization Conventions, including Convention 87, the Freedom of Association and Protection of the Right to Organize, which protects workers' freedom of association as well as the International Covenant on Civil and Political Rights and the American Convention on Human Rights, both of which guaranteed workers the right to establish and join organizations of their own choosing. *See*, Mexican Labour Law. By contrast, Canada has ratified Convention 87 but treaties under Canadian law are not self-executing and has not incorporated the Convention into Canadian domestic law by separate legislation. The U.S. has not ratified Convention 87; none of the three North American countries has ratified Convention 98, the Right to Organize and Collective Bargaining Convention.

---

[4] The Federal Law of Workers in the Service of the State, adopted in 1963, is the equivalent law covering public employees protected by Part B of Article 123 of the Constitution.

NORTH AMERICA LABOR LAW, at 103. *See* Chapter 2 for the role of international labor law, including the ILO.

The last general amendments to the Federal Labor Law occurred in 1970, with some added procedural modifications made in 1980. Calls from various sectors for reform began in 1989 and have continued, so far to no avail, until the present. Originally the push for reform came from employers and their organizations urging that greater flexibility be given to employers as well as leveling the legal playing field that they claim unfairly favors employees. Since the adoption of NAFTA, another push for reform has come from the workers' side seeking greater opportunities for the development of a union movement independent of the government and of PRI. *See*, TORRIENTE, at 236–244.

In December 2002, the government of President Vicente Fox introduced a proposed to the legislature the so-called Abascal Project, named for Labor Secretary Carlos Abascal, to "reform" the Federal Labor Law. Before joining the government, Abascal was the director of the largest confederation of employers, Confederación Patronal de la República Mexicana (COPARMEX). The Abascal Project produced a huge protest by reformers and representatives of unions that are independent of the Mexican government and PRI. On May 30, 2005, the very introduction of the reform package was challenged as a violation of the labor side accord of NAFTA on the ground that: "The proposed changes would make it virtually impossible for most workers to exercise their rights to strike, bargain collectively, or join a union of their choosing.". *See* U.S. NAO Public Submission US 2005-01, p. 5, www.dol.gov/ilab/media/reports/nao/submissions/Sub2005-01.htm. As of late May 2005, the Abascal Proposal was on the backburner, *See* Mexican Labor News & Analysis, No. 5, May, 2005, www.ueinternational.org/Mexico_info/mla_articles.php?id=87. After consideration of the NAO submission, the U.S. OTAI determined that a review would not further the objectives of the NAALC and, on February 21, 2006, declined to accept it for review An alternative reform bill, introduced in the Mexican Congress in April 2003 by supporters of independent unions, is also languishing.

Notes

1. Given the use of the United States Constitution as a model for the 1824 Mexican Constitution, why has the political and economic history of the two countries since then been so different? Is this situation a good example of the risks of transplanting law which seems successful in one nation or one legal regime to another since essentially similar laws may have quite different effects in different countries? Law in action may not be the same in two countries even if the two attempt to converge their laws on the books.

2. Some provisions of the Constitution and the federal labor law, such as the positive right to work, have not been implemented. While such provisions are clearly aspirations of the drafters, what use is there for putting them in a Constitution if there is no mechanism for their effectuation? How can you tell what is aspirational and what is enforceable public code? Michael W. Gordon, *Of Aspirations and Operations: The Governance of Multinational Enterprises by Third World Nations*, 16 U. MIAMI INTER-AM. L. REV. 301, 332–34 (1984), differentiates such aspirational provisions of laws from what he calls the operational codes that are actually enforced. He calls these operational codes "drawer regulations" that, although not secret, are not widely disseminated in the public either. "They are kept in a ministry official's

drawer, removed on one occasion, and left in the drawer on another." Id at 333–34. The practice of law in such a situation may involve finding out informally what the drawer regulations really require rather than what the public code provides.

3. In sum, Mexican law sets high labor standards based on its Constitution, statutory law and ratified treaties. Why would Mexico adopt such standards, given the challenges it faces because of poverty and underemployment of such a large percentage of economically active people engaged only in the informal economy? Would Mexico be better able to address the problems of informal economy employment if it had less protective labor laws?

B. INDIVIDUAL EMPLOYMENT LAW

Title III of the Federal Labor Law applies to individual employment. A contract of employment is presumed to exist by the fact that a worker performs work for an employer, with a presumption that the relationship will be permanent – "of indefinite duration" – unless it is for a specified piece of work or for a specified duration. *See* Article 35. In contrast, note that, in the heyday of the at-will rule in the United States, a promise of a permanent job was assumed to be at-will. *See* Forrer v. Sears, Roebuck & Co., 153 N. W. 587 (1967) ("Generally speaking, a contract for permanent employment, for life employment, or for other terms purporting permanent employment, where the employee furnishes no consideration additional to the services incident to the employment, amounts to an indefinite general hiring terminable at the will of either party, and a discharge without cause does not constitute a beach of such contract justifying recovery of damages").

Following from the presumption that employment contracts are permanent, workers are protected by a just cause standard for dismissal. I INTERNATIONAL LABOR & EMPLOYMENT LAWS 22–15 (William L. Keller & Timothy J. Darby eds. 2d ed. 2003) (hereafter INTERNATIONAL LABOR & EMPLOYMENT LAWS). Article 46 provides: "The labor relationship may be canceled at any time by a worker or an employer having sufficient justification, without thereby incurring liability." The common law courts adopted the presumption of at-will employment while Mexico in its Constitution and its Federal Labor Law adopted the presumption of permanence.

Although it might be argued that the language of Article 46 does not actually mandate a just cause standard, Article 47 supports a presumption of good cause by listing fifteen reasons that "constitute sufficient grounds for the employer's terminating the labor relationship without liability." The reasons are similar to the numerous bases for just cause that have been developed by arbitrators deciding discipline and discharge cases under collective bargaining agreements in the United States. The list includes what in the United States is called "resume fraud," dishonest or violent behavior against the employer, his family or co-workers, sabotage of the workplace, negligence, carelessness threatening the safety of the workplace, immoral acts in the workplace, disclosing trade secrets, more than three unexcused absences in a 30-day period, insubordination, failure to use preventive measures to avoid accidents or illness, reporting to work under the influence of alcohol or drugs, and incarceration. *Id.* at 22–16. Statutes in civil law systems, such as the Mexican Federal Labor Law, tend to attempt to explicate the law at a more specific level than many statutes in common law countries. One purpose for doing that is to reduce the range of discretion left to judges to the selection of the appropriate statutory rule followed by deciding whether as a matter of fact the rule has been violated. Such an approach tends to produce a rigid body of law and so there typically is at least one open-ended category to allow for new situations that arise that were not contemplated when the statute was enacted. The fifteenth reason in Article 47 is such a catch-all because it allows employers to act based on "grounds similar to those laid down in the preceding items, if they are of equal gravity and entail similar consequences as far as the work is concerned." Does this catch-all give too much discretion to the decision maker? Even more difficult than proving facts supporting a finding that the employee's conduct fit into one of these pigeon holes of good cause, employers may not dismiss workers with at least 20 years seniority unless the cause is shown to be "egregious or recurrent." *Id*. at 22–17.

The employment contract is terminated by the death of the worker, by mutual agreement or if the employer deceived the worker about the conditions of the job, the employer engages in violence or other ill-treatment of the worker or his family, the employer reduces or does not pay the worker's wages, damages the worker's tools, or endangers the worker's health or safety. *See* TORRIENTE, at 91.

Individual employment contracts must be in writing. *Id*. at 57 and *id*. at Appendix D, pp. 269–275, for sample written employment contracts. Article 25 requires the contract to contain important terms and conditions of employment including the name, age, nationality, sex, marital status and address of the worker and the employer, whether the job is for a specific task or time, the service the employee will provide, the place of work, working hours, wages, the date and place where wages will be paid, occupational training the worker is to receive, and "other working conditions such as rest days, vacation leave and other conditions agreed to by the employer and employee." Article 5 prohibits some contractual terms including provisions for excessively long work day, for wages that are not remunerative, and agreements that the place the wages will be paid will be an inn, café, bar or store, and for a waiver of workers compensation claims or damage claims for wrongful discharge. The failure to have a written employment contract is imputed to the employer, not the employee.

Article 56 provides that the standards set by statute operate as a floor, not a ceiling, for wages, hours and conditions of employment. The minimum daily wage is set for three separate geographic regions by a National Commission for Minimum Salaries, which has representatives of the state, employers and unions. *Id*. at 64. In 2002, the minimum daily wages were $4.65, $4.42, and $4.23, respectively. Foreign Labor Trends – Mexico 2002, p. 12. Article 99 establishes the workers' right to the payment of wages which right cannot be waived. An employee can also seek a higher wage before the Conciliation and Arbitration Board by showing that the wage paid is inadequate and not valued properly. The workweek of forty-eight hours is spread over six days from Monday through Saturday, with a 25 percent bonus for Sunday work. The workday is eight hours for the day shift, seven for the night and seven and a half for the swing shift. The normal forty-eight-hour workweek can be scheduled over 6, 5½, or 5 days. MEXICAN LABOUR LAW, at 11. Overtime is limited to three hours a day and is at double pay. Triple pay is required for overtime over nine hours per week.

Children under age fourteen are prohibited from working, with those between fourteen and sixteen limited to six hours per day with no work after 10:00 PM, no overtime or Sunday work. *See* paragraphs II and III of Constitution Article 123(A) and Federal Labor Law Article 174. The applicable Conciliation and Arbitration Board must approve work for minors between ages fourteen and sixteen if the minor has not completed compulsory education. Despite these rules restricting the employment of young people, it is reported millions of children work regularly in the informal economy. *See* Foreign Labor Trends – Mexico 2002, p. 11.

There are seven official paid holidays per year. Six days of paid vacation accrue after one year of work, with paid vacation increasing until it is capped at twenty-six days after thirty-five years of work. There is a vacation bonus of 25 percent of the average daily wage. *See*, TORRIENTE at 62–64. An annual year-end bonus of at least fifteen days wages must be paid by December 20.

About seventeen million workers are enrolled in the national social security system that provide "full medical care . . . , cash sickness benefits, a very modest old age pension . . . long-term disability insurance, survivors benefits, funeral grants, and maternity benefits leave of 6 weeks before and 6 weeks after childbirth." Foreign Labor Trends – Mexico 2002, p. 9. The twenty-three million or more workers in the informal economy lack the protection afforded by enrollment in the social security system. Although experience rated, employer contributions to fund the social security system generally equal about 21 percent of each employee's salary. *Id*. If an employee has at least fifteen years' seniority with an employer when the employment relationship is terminated even for cause, the worker is entitled to a severance payment of twelve days' pay for each year of seniority. See Article 162. There is, however, not a system of public unemployment insurance. Finally, Article 117 provides that all workers, employed for 60 days or more, are entitled to share in the profits of the enterprise. Every 10 years, a tripartite national commission establishes the percentage, currently 10 percent, and workers can petition the Department of the Treasury to have it review the amount of profit the employer has submitted as the basis for profit sharing. The employer, but not the workers, may appeal the determination of the Treasury Department to the Conciliation and Arbitration Board. In the United States, the law does not require any paid holidays, vacation or profit sharing. But there is in the United States a system of public unemployment insurance. Does the absence of unemployment compensation undercut the protections that Mexican labor law does provide workers? If an employee is fired, can the absence of unemployment benefits mean that she may be forced to accept minimal severance payments rather than initiate an action challenging her discharge?

Articles 427 and 434 of the Federal Labor Law require CAB permission for an employer to suspend or terminate employment in situations that in the U.S. would be called a layoff or plant shut down. As part of that, the law requires that seniority be used to layoff or reduce the hours of work of employees. NORTH AMERICA LABOR LAW, at 128.

Article 123(A) paragraph XXIX of Constitution and the Federal Labor Law require that every employer provide housing for its workers. That is done through employer contributions of 5 percent of the workers' salaries to a national agency that operates a national financing systems to enable workers to obtain low cost credit to acquire or improve their housing. The agency, *Instituto Nacional de la Vivienda para los Trabajadores* (INFONAVIT), is administered by a tripartite committee composed of representatives of the labor force, employers and the government. *Id*. at 81, citing Federal Labor Law Articles 136–138.

Through its Social Security Law, Articles 50 *et seq*, Mexico implements the Constitutional requirement that employers provide a system of workers compensation for occupational injury and disease. *Id*. at 83. The requirement of the Federal Labor Law for workplace safety, Articles 164- 280, 472–522, is carried out pursuant to the Federal

Regulation on Workplace Safety, Hygiene, and Environment of April 21, 1997. Mexico has also ratified several ILO conventions dealing with occupational safety issues. Mexican Labour Law, at 13–14. Workplace safety and health standards are enforced by the federal Secretary of Labor and Social Welfare. From 1997 through the end of 2001, the labor department conducted over twenty-three thousand safety inspections. Although there have been many criticisms of the enforcement of workplace safety standards in Mexico, there is also some evidence that the system of workplace inspections is at least as effective as similar enforcement regimes in the United States. *See* Michael Joseph McGuinness, *The Politics of Labor Regulation in North America: A Reconsideration of Labor Law Enforcement in Mexico*, 21 U. PA. J. INT'L ECON. L. 1 (2000). In sum, "every employee is covered by an individual and permanent employment contract based on the minimum work conditions stipulated in the Constitution and the [Federal Labor Law], whether or not the contract is written and whether or not the employee is also covered by a collective agreement." Mexican Labour Law, at 2.

Because Article 5 of the Mexican Constitution expressly protects the right of its citizens to work – "The State cannot permit the execution of any contract, covenant, or agreement having for its object the restriction, loss or irrevocable sacrifice of the liberty of man, whether for work, education, or religious vows – there is a widely accepted view that covenants not to compete extending beyond the period of the employment relationship are not enforceable. INTERNATIONAL LABOR & EMPLOYMENT LAWS, at 22–25. There is, however, some thought that a contract independent of the employment contract between an enterprise and its former worker, including separate consideration might be enforceable since it gives an incentive not to compete against the former employer. Similarly, a separate, postemployment "Confidentiality Agreement" that prohibits the disclosure of trade secrets by a former employee may be enforceable under the Law of Industrial Property. *Id.* at 22–27.

In sum, all workers in Mexico are theoretically protected by the Constitution and the Federal Labor Law. All have a right to a written employment contract and to be provided a broad array of protections that include a minimum wage and extend to profit sharing and to support for decent housing. The social protection net includes wage, hour, maternity protection as well as workers compensation for workplace injuries and a right to a safe place to work. It does not include unemployment benefits. Although theoretically applying to everyone who works for another, the majority of Mexican workers are in the informal economy that leaves them without the protections to which they are theoretically entitled.

Notes

1. Given that the common law is created by the judiciary while civil law relies on statutes passed by the legislature, might a court creating law under the common law be less confident, or less capable, of making the kind of policy judgments that a legislature might be expected to make? Or, is the difference between Mexican and United States law based on the differences of the cultures, economies and expectations about the law between the two cultures?

   Within the United States, there is an example of a jurisdiction that has civil law tradition, sources, and methodology as well as common law. Louisiana is a mixed jurisdiction, having a Civil Code and courts that decide cases in ways similar to courts in common law states. Louisiana courts sometimes state that they are not as free as courts in common law jurisdictions to make or extend law because of the civil law basis, tradition, and methodology. Louisiana courts also say that they do not recognize *stare decisis*, reasoning that one court decision need not be followed, as it is merely a court decision, and not an act of the legislature. Instead, Louisiana courts recognize a civil law principle of *jurisprudence constante*, meaning that a series of cases decided the same way are persuasive authority. *Doerr v. Mobil Oil Corp.*, 774 So. 2d 119, 128 (La. 2000).

Nonetheless, Louisiana law has a strong common law component. In the employment context for example, Louisiana recognizes employment at will, and the state supreme court has said that the doctrine is articulated in Civil Coder Article 2747. When employment at will was first articulated in a state supreme court opinion, however, the opinion cited a compilation of common law court decisions rather than the civil code article. *Pitcher v. United Oil & Gas Syndicate*, 139 So. 760 (La. 1932). Many years later, the court would cite the civil code article as the basis for employment at will. Scholarship has called into question whether Civil Code Article 2747 historically had much to do with a general employment at will doctrine. *See Reconsidering the Louisiana Doctrine of Employment at Will: On the Misinterpretation of Article 2747 and the Civilian Case for Requiring "Good Faith" in Termination of Employment*, 69 TULANE L. REV. 1513 (1995).

2. One justification of the Mexican Revolution was that the judiciary was far too inclined to support the injustice of the status quo. Was this judicial conservatism a product of Mexican culture or is it inherent in judges or in the judicial function? Historically, the common law courts were hostile to employee rights, even to the extent of criminalizing unions and their activities.

3. Except for Montana, Puerto Rico, and the U.S. Virgin Islands, where legislatures have modified the at-will rule, the common law courts of the United States continue to maintain the at-will rule. In part based on the enactment during the Great Depression of the Wagner Act protecting unionization, noted labor law scholar Clyde Summers once said that in enacting legislation Congress did "not move by small steps but rather by sporadic leaps." Clyde W. Summers, *A Summary Evaluation of the Taft-Hartley Act*, 11 INDUS. & LAB. REL. REV. 405 (1958). Would it take the equivalent of a revolution similar in impact to the Depression for the United States to adopt a just cause standard of job protection?

4. As a policy matter, what are the competing values at stake in deciding which rule – at-will or just cause – is better? Canada takes a middle road that employers must give employees reasonable notice of termination unless the employment relationship is terminated for just cause. Is that the best rule, taking into account the interests of employees as well as of employers? Is the at-will presumption most consistent with economic efficiency?

5. When so many terms and conditions of employment are required by law, why should the law also require that individual employment contracts be written? Won't the written contracts for most workers simply mirror the statutory requirements? In the United States only the exceptional employee – the Katie Couric – has an individualized written employment contract but for the recent imposition by employers on employees of agreements to arbitrate disputes arising out of their jobs and agreements not to compete.

6. With so much of the workforce not involved in the formal economy, can a society actually establish labor standards that are effective? Since almost all workers are theoretically covered by the Federal Labor Law, they are, as a matter of law but not of fact, within the formal economy. "[P]articularly in industries that rely on unskilled or semi-skilled labour (of which there has traditionally been a surplus in Mexico) the pressure on workers to earn a subsistence wage causes many businesses and the workers themselves, to ignore labour protections." MEXICAN LAW, at 420–421. What would it take actually to incorporate more of the actual work force into the formal economy so that most workers would be subject to the safety net the legal structure provides? Why don't individual workers take the initiative to make sure their employers accord them their rights as members of the formal economy? Would government enforcement agents have to go house-to-house, to find household workers and make sure their employers have enrolled them in the social security system and otherwise accord them their rights under the Federal Labor Law? What alternative approaches might work? Why have some of those measures not been taken?

7. Would it be a reasonable trade-off for Mexico to reduce the level of protection provided workers in the formal economy, say, to align those protections with the rather minimal protection provided workers in the United States, if the protections that were provided could be extended to the same percentage of workers as in the United States? Are the comparatively extensive labor standards provided to workers in the formal economy in Mexico a reason that wages are comparatively lower than in the rest of North America? In other words, is there a tradeoff between labor standards and wages?

C. COLLECTIVE EMPLOYEE RIGHTS

Article 123 of the Constitution first recognized the right of workers to organize unions as well as the right of employers to form their own associations and confederations. Article 357 of the Federal Labor Law allows unions to be established without prior governmental authorization and Article 358 provides that, "Nobody shall be obliged to join or abstain from joining a trade union." Article 395, however, allows an "exclusion clause," an agreement, that in the United States would be called an illegal "closed shop" agreement, between a union and an employer requiring that to be hired and to keep their jobs workers must be union members: "A collective contract may stipulate that the employer shall admit to his employment only persons who are members of the trade union which is a party to the contract. . . . It may also be established that the employer shall dismiss members who withdraw or who are expunged from the contracting union." In the United States, collective bargaining agreements may lawfully provide for "union shops" but employers cannot discharge an employee who ceases to be a union member as long as the employee continues to pay the union fees equivalent to the cost of their representation. NORTH AMERICAN LABOR LAW, at 176. In Canada, the majority of labor laws require that the employer deduct and remit to the union the amount of regular union dues whether or not the employee is a member of the union. *Id.* at 44.

A minimum of twenty workers in active employment by an employer is required to form a union.[5] "Workers whose jobs are legally classified as 'confidential,' such as managers, general supervisors or workers in a position of trust, are legally prevented from joining other workers' union and in practice rarely form unions." NORTH AMERICAN LABOR LAW, at 109. Before a union can take any action as a union, however, it must register with the Secretary of Labor (*Secretaría de Trabajo y Previsión Social*) in those industries in which the federal government has administrative jurisdiction[6] or with the appropriate Conciliation and Arbitration Board in cases where the state has jurisdiction. In addition to showing the 20 members, registration involves the submission of the by-laws, the names and addresses of the members and their employers, minutes of the general meeting organizing the union, and minutes of the general meeting at which the Board of Directors was elected. INTERNATIONAL LABOR & EMPLOYMENT LAWS, at 22–34.

The government has sixty days to issue the registration and, by law at least, may only deny registration on three narrow grounds – (1) the objective of the union is not the study, advancement, and defense of workers' interests; (2) it does not have at least twenty members in active employment, or (3) it failed to submit all the mandated documents in their required form. Generally, the CAB verifies that a registering union has twenty workers in active employment by checking employer payroll records. "There is controversy in Mexico over whether CABs have any discretion to deny union registration on grounds not specifically set out in Article 356. Some CABs have refused registration on the basis that a registered union already exists in the workplace or the workers seeking to register a new union, and some authorities maintain that this approach complies with Mexican labor law. Other experts disagree." NORTH AMERICAN LABOR LAW, at 113. Look to Section D. 2, *infra*, for a discussion of the legality of the CABs interference with independent unions through its authority to register unions.

In contrast, in the United States and Canada, unions do not need to register with the government to act as a union. *Id.* at 41, 174. In the United States, federal labor law protects the right of two or more employees to form a union. *Id.* Once, however, a union begins to represent workers for purposes of collective bargaining, then unions have an obligation to meet reporting requirements imposed by the Labor Management Reporting and Disclosure Act as well as to operate in conformity with the union members bill of rights. *Id.* at 178. In Canada, unions generally are required to file with the labor minister or board a copy of the union's constitution, names and addresses of its officers and, in most jurisdictions, a copy of all collective bargaining agreements to which they are a party. *Id.* at 47.

Once a Mexican union is registered, it becomes a legal person. Beyond prohibiting unions from intervening in religious activities or engaging in for-profit activities, Federal Labor Law does not contemplate governmental regulation that interferes with trade union autonomy, although union members may bring claims before the CAB against the union for its failure to adhere to its constitution and bylaws. In addition to acting within the

---

[5] The twenty workers in active employment must be in a single enterprise, if the union is an enterprise union. Craft, industrial, and general unions are not limited to single employers.

[6] Article 123 paragraph XXXI lists the following industries within the jurisdiction of federal labor officials: Textiles, electrical, cinematography, rubber, sugar, mining, foundries and steel mills, energy, petrochemicals, cement, limestone, automotive, chemical, pulp and paper, vegetable oils, packaged food, brewing, railroads, lumber, glass, tobacco, banks, and credit unions. In addition, certain other enterprises with federal government participation are also within the exclusive competence of the federal labor authorities.

mandate of its bylaws, a union, once registered, can begin to act vis-à-vis the employers on behalf of its members. By having twenty members employed by an employer, the union has a right to bargain with that employer, with the employer having a duty to reach an agreement. TORRIENTE, at 149. A union that signs a collective agreement is viewed as holding "title" to the agreement and to the relationship with the employer. MEXICAN LABOUR LAW, at 7. The union does not have to win an election nor otherwise show it has the support of a majority of the employer's workers in order to represent the worker and to require an employer to agree to a collective agreement. North American Labor Law, at 120. If the employer fails to negotiate or to reach agreement, the workers may exercise their right to strike. Article 387 provides: "An employer who employs workers who are members of a trade union shall be bound to conclude a collective contract with such trade union upon request. If the employer refuses to sign the contract, the workers may exercise the right to strike. . . . "

This obligation to bargain to agreement is in contrast to the law in the United States and Canada where an employer only has a duty to bargain with a union if it represents a majority of the workers in an appropriate bargaining unit and is barred from bargaining with a minority union. In the United States, an employer may voluntarily recognize a majority union, but it can also refuse to recognize a union that has made a demand for recognition pending a final election establishing majority status in an election held by the National Labor Relations Board. NORTH AMERICAN LABOR LAW, at 181. Once a union has been certified, the employer has a duty to bargain in good faith with the union but there is no obligation to reach an agreement or even to make any concessions in collective bargaining. *Id*. at 187–88. Mexican labor law is also more protective of the right to bargain than Canadian law where, in some jurisdictions, the employer has the duty to bargain upon the union establishing its majority status by means of signed authorization cards without the need for an election to establish majority status. *Id*. at 51.

If only one union represents workers of a particular employer, its contract covers all the employees of that employer. Article 388 establishes rules for determining how collective bargaining works when more than one union represents workers of a particular employer. Craft unions are entitled to their own collective bargaining agreement unless the craft unions agree to join forces. If a workplace includes both craft union members and the members of other unions, the craft union contract shall prevail if its membership is greater than the membership of industrial or enterprise unions working for the employer. If the craft union does not have a majority of all the workers, then the craft contract applies to its members with the other workers covered by the contract of the other union. As between two industrial or enterprise unions, the collective contract "shall be made with the union having the greatest number of members employed in the enterprise."

Agreements are not limited in duration and can be indefinite. But, without regard to the length of the contract, Articles 399 and 399 BIS require in effect a wage reopener once a year and a right to reopen the general agreement every two years. Collective agreements must be in writing, with one original copy filed with the appropriate Conciliation and Arbitration Board. INTERNATIONAL LABOR & EMPLOYMENT LAW, at 22–37. The CAB reviews the legality of collective contracts to determine their "legality and to ensure that they do not diminish workers' minimum rights under the FLL." NORTH AMERICA LABOR LAW, at 127. For example, no-strike clauses are unconstitutional under Mexican law and so the CAB will not accept a labor contract that includes a no-strike clause. Upon the completion of review by the CAB, the contract is treated as a judicial order of the CAB itself and is enforceable without having to go to a court. No provision of the Federal Labor Law requires workers to ratify a collective contract or even to receive a copy of one. As will be discussed later, this absence of transparency is a basis for abuse.

Although U.S. labor law distinguishes between "mandatory" and "permissive" subjects of bargaining, neither Canadian nor Mexican law makes this distinction. Article 391, however, provides that every collective contract must include the names and addresses of the parties, the enterprises or establishments covered by it, its duration, the hours of work, rest days and vacation, wage rates, training the employer will provide, rules for mandatory joint worker-employer joint committees required by the Federal Labor Law,[7] and any other agreements of the parties. North America Labor Law, at 124.

According to Article 396, the collective agreement applies to all the workers of the enterprise or the establishment, even if they are not members of the union that is party to the contract. A collective agreement takes precedence over an individual employment contract. North American Labor Law, at 104. Although workers in positions of trust may be excluded from the coverage of the collective agreement, these workers cannot be subjected to less favorable working conditions than those similarly situated who are covered by the agreement. *See* Article 182. The union or the workers may seek to enforce the rights provided them in collective agreements in CAB actions. This contrasts with the use of voluntary grievance arbitration of rights arising out of collective bargaining agreements in both the U.S. and Canada. North America Labor Law, at 129.

Article 427 through 439 of the Federal Labor Law set forth the rules by which employers may suspend or terminate collective labor relations in case of economic necessity. Suspension is somewhat analogous to a temporary layoff under U.S. or Canadian law and termination is analogous to permanent layoff or plant closure. In addition to overproduction justifying a suspension, work may be suspended or terminated because of "force majeure," the inability to pay either temporarily or permanently, the lack of raw materials for production or the result of insolvency or bankruptcy proceedings. The suspension or termination is subject to prior CAB approval. "Suspension or reduction of the work hours of particular workers takes place in reverse seniority order. In approving a suspension, the CAB awards compensation to the workers in question of up to one month's salary. Workers whose employment is terminated are entitled to receive at least three months' pay plus a seniority allowance." North American Labor Law, at 128.

In addition to collective agreements applying to single employers or single establishments of one employer (*contrato colectivo de trabajo*), Mexican labor law also contemplates broader coverage through what are called law-contracts (*contrato-ley*). The law-contract is similar to the provisions for sector wide collective agreements under some European laws, including Germany and France. See Chapters 9 and 10, *infra*. Article 404 defines a collective agreement that covers more than one employer as "an agreement executed by one or several workers' unions and several employer, or one or several employers' associations, for the purpose of establishing the conditions according to which work in a particular industrial activity should be rendered, and which is declared binding in one or more [states], in one or several economic regions covering one or more such entities, or

---

[7] The committees required by law include those that determine profit sharing, create seniority rules, formulate company disciplinary policies and health and safety committees.

throughout the national territory." The law-contract extends negotiated contracts to all the employers and employees in the specific branch of industry. "In other words, the *contrato ley* is a kind of 'super collective bargaining agreement' that covers worker conditions in an entire industry, and usually encompasses many labour unions and companies." MEXICAN LAW, at 426. To execute a law-contract, the labor unions representing at least two-thirds of the unionized workers in an industrial area in a given region must request one from the federal labor ministry or applicable state Conciliation and Arbitration Board. If the government agency approves the request, then the law-contract must be approved by the unions representing two-thirds of the unionized workers in the sector for which the request is made and by employers who employ a majority of those workers. International Labor & Employment Laws, at 22–41. Originally, the law-contract "served an important corporativist function for the PRI, since it facilitated the consolidation of labour into a highly structured apparatus that was controlled from the top." MEXICAN LAW, at 426. At present, however, few workers are covered by law-contracts. There are law-contracts in four different textile sectors as well as sugar, rubber, and radio and television sectors. *Id.* at 22–40. In 1997, law-contracts involved only a small segment of Mexican employment with forty-seven unions representing a little over ninety thousand workers. NORTH AMERICA LABOR LAW, at 126.

The right to strike is protected by Article 123 paragraph XVII of the Constitution. Paragraph XVIII further provides:

> Strikes are legal when they have their object to bring about balance between the different factors of production, reconciling the rights of the worker with those of capital. In public services, it is obligatory for workers to give notice to the Board of Conciliation and Arbitration ten days before the date set for suspension of work. Strikes will be considered illegal only when the majority of the strikers have committed violent acts against persons or property, or in case of war, when they affect establishments and services on which the government depends.

Article 440 of the Federal Labor Law defines a strike: "The term 'strike' means the temporary suspension of work brought about by a combination of workers." Article 443 limits the definition of a strike to "the mere act of suspending work." Thus, work slowdowns or other tactics that stop short of the complete suspension of work are not protected strikes. Although the Mexican view is consistent with the U.S. view of protected strikes, Canadian labor law includes slowdowns and other concerted activities designed to limit output within the definition of activities protected as a strike. NORTH AMERICA LABOR LAW, at 133. Article 450 lists the legitimate objectives of a strike. Those objectives include a very broad category of obtaining "equilibrium between the different factors of production, harmonizing the rights of labor and capital." Within that broad statement, other objectives include forcing the employer to agree to enter into a collective labor contract, to demand the revision of an agreement when it expires, to demand that the employer comply with a labor contract, to demand observance of the statutory provisions respecting profit sharing, and to demand revision of contractual wages at the time of the annual wage reopener. Article 451 provides that work will not be suspended unless it is for an object described in Article 450 and that "the suspension is carried out by the majority of the workers of the enterprise or establishment." Article 459 provides that a "strike shall be non-existent for all legal purposes" if it does not satisfy the requirements of Articles 450 and 451. As will be seen in the next section, the CABs have authority to determine the legality of strikes.

The limits on the right to strike in Mexico in some ways exceed those imposed by the National Labor Relations Act in the United States. In the United States, section 13 of the N.L.R.A. makes it clear that strikes to achieve a collective bargaining agreement are essentially legal unless the union attempts to expand the impact of the strike beyond the primary employer to neutral, secondary employers far removed from the strike. *See generally*, Robert A. Gorman & Matthew W. Finkin, Basic Text on Labor Law: Unionization & Collective Bargaining (2d ed. 2004). Nevertheless, in some ways, the right to strike is broader in Mexico than in the United States. Thus, strikes are permitted to protest employer breaches of the collective agreement. In the United States, the courts will imply a no-strike commitment to the extent a collective bargaining agreement provides for arbitration. With most collective bargaining agreements providing for arbitration, most strikes during the term of a collective bargaining agreement can be enjoined as a breach of the union's commitment to arbitrate the underlying dispute.

In the United States, an employer whose employees go on strike to achieve a new collective bargaining agreement – so-called economic strikers – may attempt to continue in operation, even by hiring temporary or permanent replacements for the strikers. In contrast, in Mexico a company that is struck must cease all operations except for those necessary to protect equipment and raw materials.[8] Article 4 of the Federal Labor Law prohibits the use of strike replacements. Although the union must assume responsibility for the preservation of equipment and raw materials, including providing workers for that purpose, the CABs are required by Article 449 of the Federal Labor Law to enforce the workers' right to strike.

Article 123 paragraph XVII provides recognizes the right of employers to engage in a "paro," that is to stop work. The employer right to stop work, however, must be distinguished from the concept in U.S. and Canadian labor law of a lockout. In the United States and Canada, a lockout is an economic weapon available to employers to attempt to force employees to accept the employer's bargaining proposals. Thus, a lockout is the employers' equivalent to the employees' right to strike. In contrast, under Mexican law, "paro" has nothing to do with collective bargaining. Employers are not allowed to lock out workers to force them to agree to their bargaining proposals. Instead, "paro" refers to the employer's right to decide to layoff or furlough workers because of economic necessity. Thus, paragraph XIX states that a "lockout shall be lawful only when a production surplus makes it necessary to suspend work to maintain prices at a level with costs, and with prior approval of the Conciliation and Arbitration Board." North America Labor Law, at 131 n.10.

A recent study shows the effect of unions on wage inequality in Mexico. Rising wage inequality is a recent international phenomenon observed in both developed and developing countries. In Mexico, "unions were a strongly equalizing force affecting the dispersion of wages in 1984, but were only half as effective at reducing wage inequality in 1996. Not only did the unionized percentage of the labor force fall considerably over the period, unions also lost some of their ability to reduce the wage dispersion among the workers they continued to represent. Had unions the same structural power they possessed in 1984, the rise in wage inequality in the formal sector of the labor market between those

---

[8] When a strike is initiated, the union posts the workplace with red and black flags as a signal to all that a strike is in progress. Absent special circumstances, the employer must shut down operations but the union must assign sufficient workers to make sure the employer's workplace remains safe.

years would have been reduced by roughly 11%." Fairris, *Unions and Wage Inequality in Mexico*, 56 INDUS. & LAB. REL. REV. 481 (2003).

In sum, Mexican workers have a right to form and to organize unions. To become recognized and thus be able to bargain with an employer, the union must have at least twenty members in active employment with an employer. With that and appropriate legal documentation, the union must register with the Secretary of Labor or the appropriate state CAB. Once recognized as registered by the Secretary or the CAB, the union is empowered to act as a union, including bargaining with the employer. The employer not only has a duty to bargain with the union but it also has the duty to reach an agreement. Once an agreement is reached, the labor contract must be filed with and reviewed by the CAB for its legality. A collective bargaining agreement not only covers union members but all the employees of the employer other than top management and confidential employees. As will be seen in the next section, unions, subject to regulation by the appropriate CAB, have the right to engage in strikes. Employers may not lock out workers and must shut down operations when a strike has been called by a union representing its workers. As is true throughout the world, union density is declining in Mexico.

Notes

1. Should unions be required to register with a government agency before undertaking the representation of workers? What are the pluses and minuses of a registration system?

2. Should employers have a duty to reach an agreement with a union that represents its workers? What happens if the parties fail to agree? In the United States, such an impasse may mean no agreement may ever be reached. Alternatively, the union has the power to call a strike to force an agreement and the employer has the power to lock-out the workers to that same end. Is this resolution by the "market" the preferable system? In Canada, at least in the first contract situation, some jurisdictions provide for interest arbitration, that is, a procedure by which a government agency imposes an agreement if the parties fail to reach one on their own accord. Would that give too much power to the government to interfere in the freedom of the parties to bargain collectively? In absence of sanctions for, or remedies of, the breach of the duty in Mexican law to reach an agreement, does it matter how the law is phrased?

D. DISPUTE RESOLUTION SYSTEMS

The Mexican system of Conciliation and Arbitration Boards operates as the forum to resolve all employment disputes, including individual employment as well as collective bargaining types of disputes. The procedures differ, depending on whether the case involves an individual employee's claim or raises collective issues. Although the decisions of the CABs are final, the Mexican Constitution does provide a procedure – "Amparo" suits – to challenge the constitutionality of actions by governmental bodies, including CABs.

1. Individual Employment Cases

Employers deciding to discharge a worker for cause – dismissal for cause is called a "rescission" – must act within one month of the event giving cause for the action and must notify the worker in writing of that cause for dismissal. The worker then has two months following the dismissal to seek redress before the appropriate Conciliation and Arbitration Board. Some free legal assistance is available to pursue the claim. NORTH AMERICA LABOR LAW, at 106. "A worker who has been dismissed unjustifiably has the right, at his or her option, either to demand reinstatement as a remedy or to claim indemnification equal to three months' salary, in addition to pay for back wages, plus 20 days' pay for every complete year of service, and any accrued salary and bonuses."[9] INTERNATIONAL LABOR & EMPLOYMENT LAWS 22–17. Although given the option to seek reinstatement, almost all workers accept severance pay in lieu of their claim for reinstatement. In two reported studies, only 1 out of 229 workers who won their claims for unjustified discharge opted for reinstatement with the rest taking back pay plus severance pay. NORTH AMERICA LABOR LAW, at 106–107.

Historically, the federal and local Conciliation and Arbitration Boards were "courts of equity in the service of justice, whose function [was] to defend labor against management." TORRIENTE, at 180, quoting MARIO DE LA CUEVA, EL NUEVO DERECHO MEXICANO DEL TRABAJO, VOL. I, p. 383 (10th ed. 1985). This predisposition to aid the worker can be seen in Article 784 of the Federal Labor Law that lists issues, including "cause of rescission of the labor relationship," on which the employer has the burden of proof. "Thus, a discharged Mexican worker does not have to show that antiunion [or other impermissible] motivation was a factor in the dismissal; the burden always rests with the employer to prove that the reason for the discharge falls within the statutory definition of just cause for discharge." MEXICAN LABOUR LAW, at 9. It further provides that the CAB "shall exempt the worker from the duty of evidence when other methods may be used to arrive at the knowledge of the facts and for that purpose shall require the employer to exhibit the documents which, in accordance with the laws, he is legally obligated to keep in the enterprise, under the admonition that if he does not present them, the facts alleged by the worker shall be presumed conclusive."

Cases raising claims by individual workers, which frequently address issues of discharge but can claim a violation of any other individual right including rights based on collective agreements, start with an informal attempt to conciliate the dispute. As in collective bargaining arbitration in the United States, unjustified dismissal cases frequently turn on questions of absenteeism, dishonesty, disobedience, drunkenness and a lack of personal discipline. Torriente, at 195. Workers are entitled to free public legal assistance for claims brought before CABs. Informal conciliation is attempted even before formal proceedings are started. Many claims are resolved at that stage. Once a formal claim is filed, (*see* TORRIENTE, Appendices H & I for sample complaint and answer), there is an official mediation stage, followed by formal proceeding that begin with the receipt of the formal pleadings, and then by the presentation of evidence. Article 14 of the Constitution provides a general guarantee of due process of law and Article 685 of the Federal Labor Law provides

---

[9] Note that severance pay for a justified discharge is calculated as twelve days' pay for every year of service. The greater remedy provided if the discharge is not justified gives workers some incentive to challenge a discharge rather than just accept severance pay when they are terminated.

key aspects of that guarantee by requiring the proceedings be "open to the public; free of charge (that is no filing fees or other procedural costs); immediate, in the sense that the members of the tribunal must be in personal contact with the parties; expeditious; and predominantly oral and short. Proceedings must also be 'conducted with a maximum economy, concentration and simplicity.'" MEXICAN LABOUR LAW, at 21.When all the evidence is heard, the parties submit written arguments to the CAB, which are reviewed along with the entire record. Each "party submits a draft award which includes a summary of the main points of each of the previous stages." MEXICAN LAW, at 433. Once an award has been approved by majority vote of the CAB, it is final and is provided to the parties. Torriente, at 186–189. For a description of recent attempts to improve the efficiency of some of the CABs, *see* TORRIENTE, at 199–204. The decisions of the CABs are final and binding. *See*, Section D. 3, *infra*, for a discussion of the nature of judicial review of CAB decisions by way of so-called "amparo" suits.

Many of the criticisms of how the Conciliation and Arbitration Boards treat individual cases come from the employer side. The claim is that the law and the procedures followed by the CABs are too pro-worker. Putting a burden of proof on the employer to prove a negative while presuming the accuracy of the claimant's assertions does not, the employers' claim, give them a fair chance to establish legal justifications for their actions. *See*, TORRIENTE, at 204–206. Worker's individual claims of antiunion discrimination under Article 48 may, however, raise issues of the integrity of the CAB where the union representative of the CAB is associated with a registered union while the worker claims that she was discriminated against because of her association with an independent union seeking to replace the incumbent registered union. "[t]he employers often fire the organizing leaders [of independent unions] and force them to take a small severance payment so they have money to live on. They could challenge their firings at the state labor board, but these tripartite bodies have seats for governor's political party, the state employers' federation, and the official union federation. Procedures there are a black hole of delays and runarounds, so fired workers usually have no choice but to take their severance pay and look for another job." COMPA, at 16 (quoting an unidentified but moderate labor lawyer who advised PAN). Some reform proposals have suggested abandoning the CAB system in favor of court jurisdiction while others suggest that the CABs be incorporated into the judicial branch of government.

In sum, all workers in Mexico are protected by the Federal Labor Law. While the law requires a written employment contract, the law establishes a broad set of workers rights and benefits, including essentially a for cause standard for discharge. With a right to free public legal assistance and many procedural presumptions in the favor of workers, the CABs provide a free and open forum for workers to assert their rights under individual employment contracts and under the provisions of the Federal Labor Law.

Notes

1. How does the CAB system compare with court, agency or arbitral proceedings in the United States? How would a CAB system work in the United States? How do they compare with the Canadian approach? What is the better system?
2. How do CABs differ from the private arbitration system that is common in collective bargaining agreements in the United States and Canada? How do they differ from

the increasingly common system of private arbitration of individual employment disputes in the United States? Which system is better?

3. Should the same dispute resolution system apply to all kinds of employment disputes, regardless of the nature of the claim? CABs are specialized entities, devoted to the resolution of all labor and employment disputes. But, given the broad range of the issues that can be raised, should an even more specialized system be established instead? Looking at it the other way, would courts of general jurisdiction be better able to put labor and employment disputes into the larger context of dispute resolution generally?

4. Should judicial review of decisions of dispute resolution institutions, such as CABs, be generally available? While the law that governs private employment is federal, its enforcement by CABs at the state level, without any system of central review, means that there is a high risk that the law will not be applied uniformly across the nation.

2. Collective Employment Cases

The government takes an active role in the regulation of unions and in their exercise of the right to strike. This section will first discuss the issues associated with the registration of new unions and then will describe the issues concerning the regulation of the right to strike.

a. *The union registration process*

As described above, the registration process of unions necessary to give them legal status to act as a union, the "registro," appears to be administrative or ministerial. It is mostly a matter of paperwork since registration may only be denied if the union's objectives are not consistent with those required of a union by Article 356, the union does not have the required 20 members in active employment with an employer, a requirement of Article 364[14], or the documents listed in Article 365 are not submitted. Article 366 also provides that "the competent authorities shall not refuse registration." Making registration purely administrative is consistent with ILO Convention 87 and the interpretation of it by the Freedom of Association Committee of the Governing Body of the ILO that has emphasized "that a discretionary approval process for registration of unions is inconsistent with the freedom of association protections of Convention 87, and that the precise legal requirements for registration should be clearly defined. MEXICAN LABOUR LAW, at 5.

There has been some dispute whether the CABs should be able to peruse the documents with a "fine tooth comb" and then reject a registration petition if any technical errors are discovered or whether the CABs ought to give the union an opportunity to correct any technical deficiencies in the documents. *Id.* at 6.

---

[14] If the union is an enterprise union, that is, that all its members work for one company, then all 20 members must work for that employer. If, however, the union is an industrial union representing members working for a number of different employers in the same industry, then the 20 members can be employed by a number of different employers. Finally, professional or craft unions – *sindicatos gremials* – focus on workers in a single profession, such as pilots or actors. So, professional unions must have 20 members working in that profession.

For industries governed by the federal labor authorities, the federal Secretary of Labor exercises the registration function but where state administration applies the state CABs register unions. A long-standing criticism of some of the CABs is that they sometimes use discretion to deny registration to independent unions in order to stifle their development and to support the establishment unions. Most of the claims have recently arisen in the maquila industries that are not under federal administration but are within the jurisdiction of state CABs.

Mexico's labor boards that grant registration and the authority to bargain contracts are tripartite bodies with government, business, and labor representatives. The tripartite arrangement is part of Mexico's long-standing corporatist system that maintained tight government control over many aspects of civil society. The tripartite boards favor official, pro-government, pro-employer unions against independent organizations chosen by workers. COMPA, at 13. The mechanism by which the favored establishment unions control the labor representatives on CABs is that those unions are organized to know when and where the convention will be held to select the union members of the CAB, as provided by Article 652 of the Federal Labor Law, and so they will be able to control those elections. While unaffiliated workers are entitled to attend the conventions, the chances that they would do so in an organized way to contest the power of the established unions is slight. The employer representatives on the tripartite panels obviously reflect the interests of the employers that select them. Finally, the public representatives are appointed by the state governors and so they will likely reflect the interests of the established unions.

Notes

1. The makeup of CABs, with representative of the government, employers and workers, may well bring hands-on expertise to the decisions being made. Canadian labor boards are in general tripartite bodies as well. But, in Mexico, the corporatist tradition put the selection power of all the members effectively in the hands of the government and the PRI party that controlled the government. If you think a system like a CAB system would work well, how should its members be appointed? Should all members, regardless of how they are appointed, be trained in the law?

2. Can tripartite panels ever work as fair dispute resolution fora? Tripartite tribunals work without excessive criticism in Canada and in some European countries. What makes the Mexican system subject to criticism? Assuming some of the charges against them are true, what changes would have to be made in the Mexican CABs to ensure that they were neutral decision makers?

3. Given that Mexico appears to be moving from a monocentric system, typified by the "corporatist" system linking the government, employers and employees to the control of the PRI party, to a more polycentric system, will the problems of CABs solve themselves?

b. "Ghost" unions and "protection" contracts

In addition to claims that the CABs manipulate the union registration process to the disadvantage of independent unions, a second criticism is that the CABs use the claim by employers that their workers are represented by nonexistent unions to block the registration of independent unions that do actually represent them.[10] The scenario is this: The employer, in a strategic action to forestall dealing with an independent union, signs a collective agreement – a "protective contract" – with a union – a "ghost" – that really does not represent any of its workers. For the advantage of having this contract, the company pays a monthly sum to the union in return for labor peace. COMPA, at 15.

The union then files the contract, what in the United States would be called a "sweetheart contract," with the appropriate CAB. As long as the contract does not include illegal terms, the CAB will accept it and will treat that union as having title to the collective agreement and to the collective bargaining relationship with the employer. The labor contract, however, will not be made available to the public and is not required to be given to the incumbent workers. "A union that holds title to a collective agreement has the exclusive right to administer, enforce, and renegotiate its terms. Moreover, a collective contract must be extended to cover all workers in a given enterprise, whether or not they are members of that union." MEXICAN LABOUR LAW, at 7.

If an independent union then organizes the twenty members from among the employees of the employer and files for registration with the CAB, the CAB will use the existence of the existing contract as a bar to the registration of the independent union. The U.S. Department of State's Country Reports on Human Rights Practices – Mexico 2004, pp. 18–19, www.stategov/g/drl/rls/hrrpt/2004/41767.htm (hereinafter State Department Human Rights Report), describes the situation this way. "Protection contracts, to which the workforce was not privy, sometimes were used in the maquila sector and elsewhere to discourage the development of authentic unions. These contracts were collective bargaining agreements negotiated and signed by management and a representative of a so-called labor organization, sometimes even prior to the hiring of a single worker." There have been estimates that an exceedingly high number – up to 90 percent – of collective agreements on file with CABs are protection contracts. COMPA, at 14.

When a collective contract applying to an employer is on file with a CAB and another union tries to register to represent those same workers, the CAB is supposed to determine which union represents a majority of the workers. This is the only stage where majority status of a union as representative of the employees of an employer is relevant. Although not necessary, the CAB can determine that majority status by holding a vote (*recuento*). The law, however, has not required that the election be secret. The process the CABs have used is that the workers are required to come forth and, before representatives of the employer, the incumbent as well as the challenging union and a CAB official, declare which union they want to represent them. NORTH AMERICA LABOR LAW, at 120–121. This disclosure of the union they favor exposes the worker to the risk of retaliation and intimidation. The first secret ballot election ever ordered by a CAB was recently held in an effort by an independent union of adult education workers to represent adult education workers in high schools and universities throughout the state of Guanajuato: "On May 30–31, a team of nine international observers participated in

---

[10] Employers respond that the law allows only unions to strike and that it takes too much time for the CABs to determine that a strike is unlawful. That leaves employers vulnerable to blackmail strikes. Entering into "protection" contracts with "ghost unions" makes it easier for the employer to fend off unions trying to blackmail them.

the first secret ballot election ever ordered by a labor board in Mexico. The decision by Lic. Libia Gómez Padilla, the president of the Junta Local de Conciliación y Arbitraje in León, Guanajuato, to hold an election by secret ballot was unprecedented and a major step forward. . . . Sadly, the independent union, SITESABES, lost the election." Robin Alexander, FAT Obtains First Secret Ballot Election: International Observers Report on Experience, www.ueinternational.org/Mexico_info/mlna_articles.php?id=88.

Notes

1. Should all worker elections be by secret ballot? What reasons might there be to justify the open declaration system used in Mexico?
2. How do you think bargaining works if the union in fact has as members only a small percentage of all of the employees of the employer?
3. Given the problem of "ghost" unions and "protection" contracts, should Mexico change its labor laws to require that all unions claiming "title" to a collective bargaining relationship demonstrate that a majority of workers of the employer in fact support the union? Should Mexico adopt a system closer to the United States or Canadian systems? If it did, would labor relations in fact come to more closely resemble the way the United States and Canadian systems work?

c. The Regulation of Strikes

The third area where the CABs have an active role in the operation and success of unions, particularly independent unions, is in the regulation of strikes. As indicated above, the Constitution and the Federal Labor Law recognize a broad right to strike, but it is limited to actions by unions, not the workers themselves A union desiring to initiate a strike must, pursuant to Articles 920 to 938, file a petition in advance of the strike with the CAB but addressed to the employer expressing the reason for the strike and indicating when it will begin. This strike notice is called the *emplazamiento de huelga*. The CAB then holds a hearing to seek a settlement by way of conciliation. If the parties do not reach an agreement, the CAB resolves the dispute by issuing a decision (*laudo*), which determines the legality of the strike. If the strike is declared not to be legal or not justified, it must be suspended by the union leaders. If another union has title to an existing collective bargaining contract with the employer, then the CAB will act to determine if the union petitioning to initiate a strike has majority support. This may involve a *recuento*, typically requiring workers to express their choice out loud in front of the CAB representative and representatives of the employer and the competing unions.

There are several grounds for finding a strike to be illegal. In addition to the union failing to follow the required notice procedures, a strike may be declared "non-existent" pursuant to Article 459 if it has not carried out for the legitimate purposes listed in Article 450 or that it is not supported by a majority of the employer's workers. A strike can be declared illicit if violence is perpetrated by a majority of the strikers against persons or property. Workers involved in a legally nonexistent strike are considered to have terminated their employment.

Given the practical restrictions on the right to strike, they have been relatively rare in recent years. "Although few strikes actually occur, informal stoppages were fairly common, but uncounted in statistics, and seldom last long enough to be recognized or ruled out of order. The law permits public sector strikes, but form public strikes were rare. Informal ones were more frequent. There were 23 strikes during [2004]. According to the Secretariat of Labor and Social Welfare, in the 4 years that the Fox administration has been in officer there were 147 strikes nationwide." State Department Human Rights Report, at 18. In 2006, however, there have been several very notable strikes. In Oaxaca, the teachers went on strike for a better contract but that dispute has escalated into a full blown challenge to the government of the state and continues to disrupt normal life for the city. Also, after the miners' union were successful in using strikes to their advantage, union advocates claim that the Minister of Labor replaced the union leadership in order to protect the mining industry. Challengers to that action have undertaken strike activity as a form of protest.

In the United States, section 8(d) establishes required procedures before a collective bargaining agreement can be terminated, which procedures include notice to the other party and the Federal Mediation and Conciliation Service and a proscription of a strike or lockout for sixty days. Only by declaring a national emergency by the President, are there any further controls on economic strikes. GORMAN & FINKIN, at 495–501.

In sum, the administration of collective labor law by the federal Secretary of Labor, but especially some of the state CABs, has been criticized for acting beyond their authorized scope of authority in order to maintain the position of unions affiliated with the government and to inhibit the right of workers to organize independent unions. Chapter 5 deals with the labor side agreements to NAFTA and, in doing so, it will revisit some of these issues that have arisen in cases dealing with the NAFTA commitments of Mexico. The next section will look at the role of the Mexican judiciary in labor and employment law.

Notes

1. Why are there so few strikes in Mexico in recent times? On a worldwide basis, the incidence and severity of strikes over collective bargaining issues has declined since the 1970s. Annie van Scheltrnazaal, Strikes in an International Perspective, 1979–2000 (2005), www.iisg.nl/research/strikes-intro.php. One argument is that strikes are increasingly ineffective because globalization has weakened the power of the workers and strengthened that of employers. If that is true, should the rights of workers be somehow augmented in order to reestablish greater equilibrium between the parties to collective bargaining? How might that be done? Should the United States follow the example of Mexico and ban employer lockouts?
2. Is the intervention of the CAB in determining the legality of a strike useful? Do you think that this involvement might allow for mediation to be effective??

3. Judicial Review and "Amparo" Suits

Decisions of CABs are final and binding and are not subject to judicial review. Nevertheless, there is available in Mexico a special judicial procedure, called a *judicious de amparo*, that provides judicial review in the form of a separate lawsuit. Literally translated "amparo" means "shelter." An innovation in legal jurisprudence in Article 103 of the Mexican

Constitution and now followed in some manner by all other Latin American constitutions, the amparo is a lawsuit, brought in federal court, to protect individuals from infringement of their rights under the Constitution. It can lead to Supreme Court jurisdiction if it raises a constitutional question and is one of three bases for seeking judicial review on constitutionality grounds provided in the Mexican Constitution. Patricio Navia & Julio Rios-Figueroa, *The Constitutional Mosaic of Latin America*, 38 COMPARATIVE POLITICAL STUDIES 189 (2005). "It can be used to protect individual's constitutional rights, to challenge unconstitutional law (amparo against law), [11] to resolve conflicts stemming from administrative acts and decisions (amparo administrative) and to review judicial decisions (amparo casacion)." Smith, at 89 n.23.

Articles 2 to 28 of the Mexican Constitution set forth the basic thrust of civil rights that form the basis of amparo actions. In the context of labor cases, Article 5 recognizes the right to work, Article 9 protects the right of association, Article 14 requires procedural due process, and Article 16 provides that decisions of public authorities directly affecting individuals must be specifically authorized by law, are the most important bases for bringing an amparo action. An action to review a final CAB decision, called a "direct" amparo,[12] is "filed with the CAB, requesting that it temporarily suspend the application of the decision in question and that the case file be sent to the Collegiate Circuit Tribunal for review. Where the action challenges the constitutionality of a law or regulation, the Collegiate Circuit Tribunal will send the file to the Mexican Supreme Court for hearing and decision. In general, decision of the Collegiate Circuit Tribunal in direct amparo cases are final and may not be appealed." NORTH AMERICA LABOR LAW, at 154–155.

An amparo decision generally affects only the parties to the action. The law held to be unconstitutional nevertheless remains on the books and is valid since a single amparo decision does not create binding precedent; *id* at 155. "The Mexican Supreme Court and the federal appeals courts (Collegiate Circuit Courts) create binding precedent, referred to as *jurisprudencia firme*, only when they issue five consecutive consistent decisions on the same point." North America Labor Law, at 101.[13] There is, however, an increasing tendency for lower courts to accept as persuasive authority the decisions of higher courts. TORRIENTE, at 172.

Historically, the Mexican Supreme Court has been criticized as lacking independence from the President, *see* PABLO GONZALEZ CASANOVA, DEMOCRACY IN MEXICO, 21–24 (1965) ("there is no doubt that the Supreme Court of Justice is endowed with power; yet it does generally follow the policy of the Executive").[14] In 1994, President Zedillo promulgated amendments to the Mexican Constitution with the object of strengthening the federal

---

[11] The Mexican Supreme Court is the only court with jurisdiction to hear constitutional claims.

[12] An "indirect" amparo action seeks the review of an interlocutory or procedural ruling which the petitioner claims will cause irreparable harm. North America Labor Law, at 155.

[13] This restriction on the precedental effect of Supreme Court decisions is consistent with the underpinnings of the civil law system whereby the legislature is authorized to enact all the law while courts are limited to enforcement of it. Grafting the doctrine of judicial review initiated in the U.S. common law system onto the civil law structure results in a more limited nature of that judicial review. The development of separate constitutional courts in European civil law systems is largely a phenomenon arising in the 1920s and after. Patricio Navia & Julio Rios-Figueroa, *The Constitutional Mosaic of Latin America*, 38 COMPARATIVE POLITICAL STUDIES 189 (2005).

[14] This criticism is contested; *see* BERNARD SCHWARTZ, LOS PODERES DEL GOBIERNO: COMENTARIO SOBRE LA CONSTITUCION DE LOS ESTADOS UNIDOS (1966).

court system and enhancing its independence. The amendments removed all of the then sitting Supreme Court justices, reducing their number from twenty-six to eleven and fixing their terms at fifteen years. As amended, the President now nominates three candidates for each Supreme Court vacancy, with Senate confirmation by two-thirds majority. If the Senate fails to confirm a candidate, the President then can appoint one of those three. TORRIENTE, at 35–39.

Beginning in 1996, the Mexican Supreme Court rendered a series of six decisions finding that various legal restrictions implicating workers' rights violated the constitution. In those decisions, it appears that the Court has adopted a more aggressive role that is consistent with a more independent judiciary. The first five of these decisions all dealt with various aspects of public employment at the federal and the state level. The first decision, *Amparo No. 1/96*, the federal labor law applicable to public sector employees that was under attack, Article 1 of Federal Law of Workers in the Service of the State (*Ley Federal Para Los Trabajadores al Sercicio del Estado*, LFTSE), precluded the existence of more than one federation of government sector unions. The Court found that this law was unconstitutional since it violated the constitutional right of workers to form and join labor organizations. The effect of this decision was to now treat public sector employees the same as private sector employees are treated under Section A of Article 123. Up to the time of this decision, the *Federación de Sindicatos de Tragajadores al Servicio del Estado* (FSTSE), a confederation of unions that was among the unions established by the government, had a monopoly on union membership since it was the sole federation available to unions representing workers subject to Section B of Article 123 dealing with public sector employees. Following the decision, FSTSE lost fifty-two of its eighty-two members. TORRIENTE, at 171.

The next two cases, decided on the same day in 1996, both raised the same issue: whether there could be more than one union representing the workers in a particular governmental body or agency. Under the applicable laws, once one union was given title to a collective bargaining agreement and relationship, no other union could ever represent those same workers. The law of the state of Jalisco explicitly prohibited more than one union from representing workers in a single agency. In Oaxaca, the state law did not explicitly require one-union-per-workplace but the applicable CAB found that implicitly that was the rule since the rest of the statute was cast in terms of a single union. In *Amparo No. 337/94*, an independent union claiming to represent members of the academic staff at the University of Guadalajara, in Jalisco, filed a petition with the applicable CAB to register as a union. The CAB denied the union's petition to register as an official workers' union since the board's records indicated that another union had earlier been registered to represent the University's academic staff. In *Amparo No. 338/95*, a group of state employees in Oaxaca formed a union and its attempt to register with the CAB was also denied because there was an incumbent union.

In the Guadalajara case, the Supreme Court, sitting en banc, decided that the federal Constitution's Article 123 (A)(XVI), governing private employees, and (B)(X), covering public employees, created freedom of association by recognizing the right of each worker to organize individually. Based on the rights of each individual worker, the Court recognized the collective right of all those individuals to organize once a union acquires its own legal status through registration. The laws of the states must recognize those rights. Because the Jalisco state law provided that there can be no more than one union in each governmental agency, that law violated the federal constitutional rights of public workers. Given the federal Supremacy Clause in Article 133 of the Mexican Constitution, the federal right of free association superseded the Jalisco state law.

In the Oaxaco case, the Supreme Court applied in full the reasoning in the Guadalajara decision. Article 123 of the Constitution protects the right to organize and that any act impairing that right conflicts with the Constitution. Furthermore, the Court relied on ILO Convention 87, dealing with the freedom of association, which becomes law in Mexican when ratified,, reinforces the right to associate that applies to these state workers in choosing to organize a new union even though there is an incumbent union that is registered with the CAB. Therefore, pursuant to the Supremacy Clause, the Oaxaca CAB violated the freedom of assembly rights of those workers who joined the union that was denied registration because another union already was registered. In essence, the Court found in both cases that a union could not establish perpetual monopoly control over representation of workers at a particular government agency just by being the first to register as the representative. The workers' constitutional right of freedom of association must allow them to organize new unions that must be given the chance to replace the incumbent union.

The next decision, *Amparo No. 53/99*, extended the application of the Guadalajara and Oaxaco decisions involving state public sector employees to the federal employment sector:

> Constitutional Article 123 establishes the right of Union membership in the broadest sense, starting from the personal right of each worker to unionize and acknowledging a collective right, once the Labor Union is incorporated and exists as a legal entity. Such freedom shall be understood in three main aspects: 1. A positive aspect consisting of the workers' power to join an established Labor Union or to create a new one; 2. A negative aspect that implies the possibility of not joining a specific Labor union *and* not joining any Labor Union; and 3. The freedom to leave or quit being a member of the association. Now, the judicial order for a single Labor Union of bureaucrats by department, established in Article 42 [of the federal act governing federal public employees], violates the social guarantee of free unionization for workers as provided in Article 123, Section B, Paragraph X from the General Constitution of the Republic, since providing for single union membership restricts the workers' freedom of association to defend their interests.

Although these decisions are not binding precedent, they do suggest that the Mexican Supreme Court has decided to put some real bite into the right of freedom of association that is found in the Constitution. As a result, public workers for state and federal agencies now have the opportunity to organize unions and register them pursuant to the procedures presently available in the private sector. That means that the CAB has the obligation to decide whether the incumbent registered union in fact represents a majority of the workers in a particular employment unit, including the use of a vote to determine that question. To force a recalcitrant CAB to undertake the determination of majority status may, however, require the challenging union to undertake an amparo suit since these decisions are not binding precedent under the Mexican system's approach. So far, the question of the constitutionality of the open voting procedures used by CABs to determine majority status has not been established. Presumably, the freedom of association argument advanced in these cases would also support a challenge in an amparo suit to methods of determining majority status that would expose workers to intimidation.

In *Amparo No. 127/2000*, the challenge was to Article 75 of the federal law governing public employees that prohibited union leaders from standing for reelection for offices in the union. Based on the constitutional freedom of association and ILO Convention 87, the Court struck down Article 75.

> [W]orkers are entitled to create the organizations they deem appropriate, to become members of one of such organizations, in accordance with their bylaws, based on which they can freely choose their representatives, establish the terms such representatives shall hold their positions, organizer their administration, activities and action plans. . . . Therefore, as Article 75 of the Federal Act Governing Workers in the Employment of the State stipulates that 'Any act of reelection within the union is forbidden,' we conclude that such prohibition violates the abovementioned right of union membership because it intervenes in the life and internal organization of unions, infringing on the Unions' right to freely choose there representatives and to work effectively and independently in their members interests. The Supreme Court recognizes that the reelection of union leaders which the challenged article prohibits is a liberating right. However, if it is wrongly exercised, it may lead to the creation of powerful sectors within the union and, consequently, his may also lead to problems. However, such deplorable and unwanted results cannot be avoided by limiting the right of union membership granted by the Constitution, but can be prevented by workers exercising their rights in a responsible, democratic and conscious manner.

In these decisions dealing with the freedom of association of public workers to form their own unions, even in the face of a different established union, and to select their own leaders for these new unions. While none of these decisions are binding precedent, they are influential. The next step was to extend these free association rights to the private sector.

AMPARO NO. 1124/2000

MEXICO SUPREME COURT

SECOND CHAMBER

April 17, 2001

[Article 395 of the Federal Labor Law as to collective bargaining agreements and Article 413 as to law-contracts provides that *cláusulas de exclusion* – provisions for closed shops that justify the employer in discharging an employee who ceases to be a member of the union holding title to the labor contract – are legal. This Amparo challenged the constitutionality of these provisions by relying on the right of workers to freedom of association. What follows is the complete, officially published text of the decision.]

EXCLUSION BY SEPARATION CLAUSE. ARTICLES 395 AND 413 OF THE FEDERAL LABOR ACT WHICH AUTHORIZE, RESPECTIVELY, THE INCORPORATION OF SUCH CLAUSE IN COLLECTIVE BARGAINING AGREEMENTS AND IN OFFICIAL LABOR AGREEMENTS EXPRESSLY VIOLATE ARTICLES 5, 9, AND 123, SECTION A, PARAGRAPH XVI, OF THE FEDERAL CONSTITUTION

The abovementioned Articles of the Federal Labor Act authorize the incorporation of the exclusion by separation [closed shop] clause in collective bargaining agreements and law-contracts, therefore allowing the employer, who shall bear no responsibility whatsoever, to dismiss any person specified by the Labor Union administrating the agreement on the grounds that such person left the Labor Union. Such Articles violate the provisions of Article 5 of the Political Constitution of the United Mexican States in that such article only authorizes the dismissal of a worker from his legal job through a court resolution, when a third parties' rights are affected, or through a government resolution, passed in accordance with the legal terms, when society's rights are violated, both cases being significantly different than dismissal due to the enforcement of the exclusion by separation clause. In addition, they also violate Articles 9 and 123, Section A, Paragraph XVI of the Constitution itself, as indicated by the Plenary Session of the Federal Supreme Court of Justice in case law precedents P./J. 28/95 and P./J. 43/99, with the titles:

"CHAMBERS OF COMMERCE AND INDUSTRY, COMPULSORY MEMBERSHIP. ARTICLE 5 OF THE ACT BEING DISCUSSED VIOLATES FREEDOM OF ASSOCIATION ESTABLISHED BY ARTICLE 9 OF THE CONSTITUTION." and "SINGLE UNIONIZATION [MEMBERSHIP]. THE LAWS OR REGULATIONS THAT SEEK TO VIOLATE THE FREEDOM OF UNION MEMBERSHIP ESTABLISHED IN CONSTITUTIONAL ARTICLE 123, SECTION B, PARAGRAPH X.",

since the provisions of such Articles of the Federal Labor Act violate the principles of freedom of association and of union membership. Such is the case because it is contradictory, and therefore legally unacceptable, that the Federal Constitution establishes such rights, according to which, in accordance with the interpretation of such precedents, a person is free to belong to an association or Labor Union, or to leave these entities, and in the abovementioned Articles of the secondary act [the Federal Labor Act], being dismissed from a job is considered a consequence of exercising the right to leave. Finally, the fact that a person can be dismissed from his job for exercising a constitutionally declared right, according to the provisions of a secondary act which allows for the introduction of such concept in collective bargaining agreements, is reprehensible in accordance with the principle of constitutional supremacy set forth in Article 133 of the Constitution.

Notes

1. Article 5 of the Constitution includes a number of different rights. Most pertinent to the exclusion clause issue are the following two paragraphs: "The State cannot permit the execution of any contract, covenant, or agreement having for its object the restriction, loss or irrevocable sacrifice of the liberty of man, whether for work, education, or religious vows." Furthermore, a "labor contract shall be binding only to render the services agreed on for the time set by law and may never exceed one year to the detriment of the worker, and in no case may it embrace the waiver, loss, or restriction of any civil or political right." Assuming a collective agreement between the union and the employer is a labor contract, the constitutional right of workers covered by the agreement implicated in these exclusion clauses must be found elsewhere in the Constitution. Article 9 provides in pertinent part that "The right to assemble or associate peaceably for any lawful purpose cannot be restricted. . . . " Are the earlier decisions of the Court that are based in the freedom of association of workers sufficient to support the Court's conclusion here? Most of those cases involve unions asserting the rights of workers in order to advance the union's own interests. Here, presumably, the adversely affected worker has a direct interest in the outcome in opposition to the interests of the union holding title to

the collective bargaining relationship with the employer. Under Mexican law does it matter whether the workers are in the public or the private sector for them to assert their right to assemble?

2. How does the published opinion of the Mexican Supreme Court differ from opinions issued by the United States or Canadian Supreme Courts?

> [T]he Mexican Supreme Court does not compose lengthy judicial opinions in the style of US Courts. Rather, Supreme Court judgments (*sentencias*) consist of lengthy transcripts of arguments considered by the Court. While copies of these judgments are kept on file at the Supreme Court offices in Mexico City, they are not easily available for consultation by lawyers. The Court's "opinions" (*tesis* and *jurisprudencia obligatoria*) that are published in the official supreme Court Reporter, the *Seminario Judicial de la Federacion*, and which are available at the web page of the Supreme Court [www.scjn.gob.mx], are actually highly reduced summaries, or "squibs", of the Court's final judgment; the summaries do not repeat the facts of the case before the Court, and are often so generally drafted by clerks of the Court that they provide little insight into the precise way in which a rule was applied.

MEXICAN LAW, at 193. One explanation for this procedure is that the Court has too many cases to be able to publish more useful opinions. "[T]he Court is called upon to act as a court of first instance in hundreds of cases annually (930 in 1995 and 674 in 1996); in contrast, the US Supreme Court acts as a court of first instance in only eleven or twelve cases per year. The Mexican Supreme Court is called on to issue opinions in thousands of cases each year, compared with the eighty or ninety opinions of the US Supreme Court that are published each year." *Id.* at 192–93. If the Court continues to act independently, as it seems to be doing in the labor area, will that publication policy change? If you were practicing law in Mexico, how would you go about interpreting decisions of the Mexican Supreme Court?

3. Why would the framers of the Mexican Constitution be reluctant to provide that an amparo decision is precedent, in what in the United States would be called *stare decisis?* Does the absence of precedential effect make the Mexican courts more or less likely to engage in what in the United States is called "judicial activism?"

4. A proviso to section 8(a)(3) of the National Labor Relations Act, by its terms, would appear to allow employers and unions to agree to a provision that makes continuing union membership a condition of employment. In *NLRB v. General Motors Corp.*, 373 U.S. 734 (1963), the Supreme Court construed the proviso as protecting an employee from discharge if she pays union dues even if she does not continue membership in the union. "It is permissible to condition employment upon membership, but membership, insofar as it has significance to employment rights, may in turn be conditioned only upon payment of fees and dues. 'Membership' as a condition of employment is whittled down to its financial core." Is the reason for this narrow interpretation of the union shop proviso a reflection of the significance of the right of association of workers?

5. How does the system of judicial review of CAB decisions by way of amparo suits differ from the way decisions of the National Labor Relations Board are reviewed in the United States? How about decisions by arbitrators in grievance arbitration pursuant to collective bargaining agreements?

E. ANTIDISCRIMINATION LAW

Article 123, Section B, Article VII of the Mexican Constitution establishes an equal pay standard: "Equal wages shall be paid for equal work, regardless of sex or nationality." Furthermore, Article 3 of the Federal Labor Law, as part of its general humanistic definition of work, prohibits discrimination: "No distinction shall be established among the workers by reason of race, sex, age, religious creed, political doctrine or social condition." Also, Article 56 of the Federal Labor Law restates the prohibition on discrimination: "In no event shall working conditions be inferior to those established by [the Federal Labor Law] and they shall be commensurate to the importance of the services and equal for equal work. No distinction may be established by reason of race, nationality, sex, age, religious creed or political doctrine, except for the distinctions expressly set forth in this law." INTERNATIONAL LABOR & EMPLOYMENT LAWS, at 22–61.

The violation of these provisions of the Federal Labor Law leads to the same remedies – reinstatement or statutory severance pay – that are available in unjust discharge cases. *Id.* There are claims that discrimination based on pregnancy is common, especially among the maquila industries. Workers claim that the employers are trying to avoid providing the mandated benefits for pregnant women and women with newborn children where the employer must pay because the social security benefits have yet to vest. *See* Chapter 6 dealing with the issue pursuant to NAFTA. If you represented a worker discharged because she became pregnant, would you bring a basic unjust dismissal claim or would you charge the employer with discrimination because of sex? What factors would you consider in making that decision? What effect might the adoption in the United States of a general good cause for discharge standard have on antidiscrimination law there? Would there be more discrimination claims brought in Mexico if the good cause standard were abrogated?

In 2003, President Fox signed a new antidiscrimination statute that had been passed unanimously by the Mexican Congress. Entitled the Federal Law to Prevent and Eliminate Discrimination, Article 4 of this new law defines discrimination as "any distinction, exclusion or restriction which, on account of national or ethnic origin, sex, age, disability, social or economic condition, health conditions, pregnancy, language, religion, opinions, sexual preference, marital status or any other, effectively impedes or undermines the recognition or exercise of rights, or which limits equality of opportunities." Although the law does not provide civil liability against discriminators, it does require federal authorities to use all their powers to end discrimination within their own agencies. It also requires the authorities to adhere to international conventions ratified by Mexico, including ILO Conventions No. 100 and 111 and the U. N. Convention on the Elimination of All Forms of Discrimination Against Women. A new National Council for the Prevention of Discrimination is to oversee the implementation of this new law. Compa, at 26–27. *See,* Natara Williams, *Pre-Hire Pregnancy Screening in Mexico's* Maquiladoras: *Is it Discrimination,* 12 DUKE J. OF GENDER L. & POL'Y 131 (2004).

Labor lawyers, however, were quoted after the enactment of the new law to the effect that it would not have much effect: "[T]he new law is not expected to have a significant impact on labor markets in Mexico, because discrimination is already prohibited under Mexico's Labor Law and international agreements to which the country is signatory, and even so, discrimination is widespread," particularly against pregnant women, older workers, infirm workers, and homosexuals. INTERNATIONAL LABOR & EMPLOYMENT LAW, at 22–62 n. 162, quoting, John Nagel, *Mexico's President Fox Signs New Anti-Discrimination Law*, 112 DAILY LAB. REP. (BNA) A-4 (June 11, 2003). If the existing laws and remedies have not been effective to end discrimination, what should the new Council do to improve the efficacy of the new law?

F. PRIVACY LAW

The Mexican Constitution, in Article 16, recognizes at least one sense of the right of privacy: "One's person, family, home, papers, or possessions may not be perturbed, except by virtue of a written order by the competent authority that justifies the motive for the legal proceeding." The whole provision, however, appears to be aimed at setting restrictions on search and seizure and does not appear aimed at broader issues of privacy, including those that arise in the employment setting. There is no "comprehensive data protection law in Mexico regulating employers' collection, use, maintenance, transmittal or disposition of their employees' personal data or specifying employees' rights in relation to such data." INTERNATIONAL LABOR & EMPLOYMENT LAW, at 22–23. There are, however, several statutes that do protect privacy in some limited settings, such as the privacy of the mail, protecting data the government gets by way of the issuance of national identity cards, and protecting consumer information in electronic commerce settings. *Id.* at n.43. *See* generally, Jorge A. Vargas, *Privacy Rights under Mexican Law: Emergence and Legal Configuration of a Panoply of New Rights*, 27 HOUS. J. INT'L L. 73, 116, 120 (2004) ("[T]he Federal Labor Act was not intended to protect the privacy rights of workers in the Republic of Mexico . . . In sum, whether a company currently conducts monitoring or surveillance activities to intercept the employees' voice and electronic communications through the use of computer, fax, and telephone equipment is not a matter regulated under Mexican law. . . . ").

6 The Regulatory Approach of the North American Free Trade Agreement

A. INTRODUCTION

When the North American Free Trade Agreement (NAFTA) entered into force on January 1, 1994, it created the world's largest free trade zone. Roy L. Heenan et al., *NAFTA/NAALC*, *in* INTERNATIONAL LABOR AND EMPLOYMENT LAWS 20-1 (2d ed., William L. Keller & Timothy J. Darby, eds., 2003) (hereinafter Heenan *NAFTA/NAALC*). NAFTA also was, by virtue of its labor side agreement, the first trade agreement significantly linking labor rights and trade. BOB HEPPLE, LABOUR LAWS AND GLOBAL TRADE 107 (2005) (hereinafter Hepple, Labour Laws). Indeed, the North American Agreement on Labor Cooperation (NAALC) has provided a template, with some important variations, for systems of cross-border workplace law monitoring in all of the United States' subsequently negotiated free trade agreements. Marley S. Weiss, *Two Steps Forward, One Step Back – or Vice Versa: Labor Rights Under Free Trade Agreements from NAFTA, Through Jordan, Via Chile, to Latin America, and Beyond*, 37 U.S.F. L. REV. 689, 689-90 (2003) (hereinafter Weiss, *Two Steps*).

Despite its subsequent effect, the NAALC at the time of its drafting was an afterthought. Weiss, Two Steps, at 701. NAFTA, at its 1992 signing by U.S. President George H. W. Bush, Mexican President Carlos Salinas de Gortari, and Canadian Prime Minister Brian Mulroney, lacked detailed labor and environmental chapters. That omission provoked considerable public discussion, and was a major issue in the 1992 U.S. presidential campaign. Heenan, *NAFTA/NAALC*, at 20-2, 20-7. In response to the concerns of the American labor and environmental movements, Bill Clinton, while campaigning for president, promised to support NAFTA only if the parties entered into side agreements on labor and environmental issues. Weiss, *Two Steps*, at 703.

After he became president but before NAFTA was submitted for congressional approval, President Clinton negotiated NAFTA's labor side accord, the NAALC. Katherine Van Wezel Stone, *To the Yukon and Beyond: Local Laborers in a Global Labor Market*, 3 J. SMALL & EMERGING BUS. L. 93, 111-2 (1999) (hereinafter Stone, *To the Yukon*). An agreement on environmental issues was also concluded. Jonathan Graubart, *"Politicizing" a New Breed of "Legalized" Transnational Political Opportunity Structures: Labor Activists Uses of NAFTA's Citizen-Petition Mechanism*, 26 BERKELEY J. EMP. & LAB. L. 97, 106-7 (2005) (hereinafter Graubert, *New Breed*). Mexico and Canada, however, balked at the idea that American conceptions of labor standards might be foisted upon them. Thus, the NAALC's signature organizing principle evidences the trading partners' overriding concern for national sovereignty. Rather than provide for international labor standards, the parties agree to enforce their own domestic labor and employment laws. Stone, *To the Yukon*, at 111-2 (1999). These domestic laws, however, include "international labor standards that members have embraced by treaty," including conventions of the International Labor Organization (ILO). Sarah H. Cleveland, *Why International Labor Standards?*, in INTERNATIONAL LABOR STANDARDS: GLOBALIZATION, TRADE, AND PUBLIC POLICY 129, 132 (Robert J. Flanagan & William B. Gould IV, eds., 2003) (hereinafter Cleveland, *Why International Labor Standards*).

The NAALC sets forth no new or universal standards, does not envision harmonization of the laws of the three signatories, and creates no supranational tribunal equipped to rule on employment disputes between workers and their employers. Lance Compa, *NAFTA's Labor Side Accord: A Three Year Accounting*, 3 NAFTA L. & BUS. REV. AMERICAS 6 (1997). Although the NAALC does establish a transnational agency to oversee the agreement, this entity has no authority over the labor standards in the member countries. Stone, *To the Yukon*, at 112.

NORTH AMERICAN AGREEMENT ON LABOR COOPERATION BETWEEN THE GOVERNMENT OF CANADA, THE GOVERNMENT OF THE UNITED MEXICAN STATES, AND THE GOVERNMENT OF THE UNITED STATES OF AMERICA,

Sept. 13, 1993, U.S.-Can.-Mex., 32 I.L.M. 1499 (1993).

PART ONE   OBJECTIVES

Article 1: Objectives

The objectives of this Agreement are to:
    a. improve working conditions and living standards in each Party's territory;
    b. promote, to the maximum extent possible, the labor principles set out in Annex 1;
    c. encourage cooperation to promote innovation and rising levels of productivity and quality;
    d. encourage publication and exchange of information, data development and coordination, and joint studies to enhance mutually beneficial understanding of the laws and institutions governing labor in each Party's territory;
    e. pursue cooperative labor-related activities on the basis of mutual benefit;
    f. promote compliance with, and effective enforcement by each Party of, its labor law; and
    g. foster transparency in the administration of labor law.

PART TWO   OBLIGATIONS

Article 2: Levels of Protection

Affirming full respect for each Party's constitution, and recognizing the right of each Party to establish its own domestic labor standards, and to adopt or modify accordingly its labor laws and regulations, each Party shall ensure that its labor laws and regulations provide for high labor standards, consistent with high quality and productivity workplaces, and shall continue to strive to improve those standards in that light.

Article 3: Government Enforcement Action

1. Each Party shall promote compliance with and effectively enforce its labor law through appropriate government action, subject to Article 42, such as:

   a.   appointing and training inspectors;
   b.   monitoring compliance and investigating suspected violations, including through on-site inspections;
   c.   seeking assurances of voluntary compliance;
   d.   requiring record keeping and reporting;
   e.   encouraging the establishment of worker-management committees to address labor regulation of the workplace;
   f.   providing or encouraging mediation, conciliation and arbitration services; or
   g.   initiating, in a timely manner, proceedings to seek appropriate sanctions or remedies for violations of its labor law.

2. Each Party shall ensure that its competent authorities give due consideration in accordance with its law to any request by an employer, employee or their representatives, or other interested person, for an investigation of an alleged violation of the Party's labor law.

Article 4: Private Action

1. Each Party shall ensure that persons with a legally recognized interest under its law in a particular matter have appropriate access to administrative, quasi-judicial, judicial or labor tribunals for the enforcement of the Party's labor law.

2. Each Party's law shall ensure that such persons may have recourse to, as appropriate, procedures by which rights arising under:

   a.   its labor law, including in respect of occupational safety and health, employment standards, industrial relations and migrant workers, and
   b.   collective agreements, can be enforced.

Article 5: Procedural Guarantees

1. Each Party shall ensure that its administrative, quasi-judicial, judicial and labor tribunal proceedings for the enforcement of its labor law are fair, equitable and transparent and, to this end, each Party shall provide that:

   a.   such proceedings comply with due process of law;
   b.   any hearings in such proceedings are open to the public, except where the administration of justice otherwise requires;
   c.   the parties to such proceedings are entitled to support or defend their respective positions and to present information or evidence; and
   d.   such proceedings are not unnecessarily complicated and do not entail unreasonable charges or time limits or unwarranted delays.

2. Each Party shall provide that final decisions on the merits of the case in such proceedings are:

   a.   in writing and preferably state the reasons on which the decisions are based;
   b.   made available without undue delay to the parties to the proceedings and, consistent with its law, to the public; and

    c. based on information or evidence in respect of which the parties were offered the opportunity to be heard.

3. Each Party shall provide, as appropriate, that parties to such proceedings have the right, in accordance with its law, to seek review and, where warranted, correction of final decisions issued in such proceedings.

4. Each Party shall ensure that tribunals that conduct or review such proceedings are impartial and independent and do not have any substantial interest in the outcome of the matter.

5. Each Party shall provide that the parties to administrative, quasi-judicial, judicial or labor tribunal proceedings may seek remedies to ensure the enforcement of their labor rights. Such remedies may include, as appropriate, orders, compliance agreements, fines, penalties, imprisonment, injunctions or emergency workplace closures.

6. Each Party may, as appropriate, adopt or maintain labor defense offices to represent or advise workers or their organizations.

7. Nothing in this Article shall be construed to require a Party to establish, or to prevent a Party from establishing, a judicial system for the enforcement of its labor law distinct from its system for the enforcement of laws in general.

8. For greater certainty, decisions by each Party's administrative, quasi-judicial, judicial or labor tribunals, or pending decisions, as well as related proceedings shall not be subject to revision or reopened under the provisions of this Agreement.

Article 6: Publication

1. Each Party shall ensure that its laws, regulations, procedures and administrative rulings of general application respecting any matter covered by this Agreement are promptly published or otherwise made available in such a manner as to enable interested persons and Parties to become acquainted with them.

2. When so established by its law, each Party shall:

    a. publish in advance any such measure that it proposes to adopt; and
    b. provide interested persons a reasonable opportunity to comment on such proposed measures.

Article 7: Public Information and Awareness

Each Party shall promote public awareness of its labor law, including by:

    a. ensuring that public information is available related to its labor law and enforcement and compliance procedures; and
    b. promoting public education regarding its labor law. . . .

PART SIX   GENERAL PROVISIONS

Article 42: Enforcement Principle

Nothing in this Agreement shall be construed to empower a Party's authorities to undertake labor law enforcement activities in the territory of another Party.

Article 43: Private Rights

No Party may provide for a right of action under its domestic law against any other Party on the ground that another Party has acted in a manner inconsistent with this Agreement. . . .

Article 49: Definitions

1. For purposes of this Agreement:

A Party has not failed to **"effectively enforce its occupational safety and health, child labor or minimum wage technical labor standards"** or comply with Article 3(1) in a particular case where the action or inaction by agencies or officials of that Party:

    a. reflects a reasonable exercise of the agency's or the official's discretion with respect to investigatory, prosecutorial, regulatory or compliance matters; or

    b. results from *bona fide* decisions to allocate resources to enforcement in respect of other labor matters determined to have higher priorities. . . .

Notes

1. The NAFTA signatories undertake six obligations: (1) the parties must establish and maintain high labor standards; (2) they must promote compliance with, and effectively enforce their respective laws through appropriate government action; (3) private parties must be assured access to enforcement procedures; (4) procedural due process must be guaranteed; (5) the domestic systems must be transparent in that each party must publish or make available its laws, regulations, procedures, and rulings; and (6) public awareness of the law must be promoted. Hepple, Labour Laws, at 112-3.

2. Note that each country's Article 3 obligations are subject to Articles 42 and 49. In what way do Articles 42 and 49 weaken what appear to be fairly strong obligations?

3. Which provisions of the NAALC safeguard the sovereignty of the trading partners' domestic labor policy, legislation, and enforcement activities? In addition to quoting specific language in the agreement, Professor Marley Weiss notes:

> The emphasis on safeguarding sovereignty underlies the failure to provide . . . for a permanent judicial or arbitral tribunal, for any tri-national prosecutorial arm to investigate and pursue claimed violations, for any firm method of enforcing and remedying violations apart from diplomacy, and for a reasonably proportional remedy to assist [victims] . . . of their country's violations of its NAALC obligations.
>
> Weiss, *Two Steps*, at 706.

Nonetheless, Professor Weiss highlights a major innovation of the labor side agreement: "the NAALC transposes domestic law into the tri-lateral agreement, rendering it an international obligation." *Id*. at 707.

4. NAFTA's supporters argued that trade liberalization among the three signatories would fuel economic growth that benefited Mexican, Canadian, and U.S. businesses and workers. The agreement's critics in the United States feared massive job loss to the country's southern neighbor. As this note and those that follow reveal, however, commentators remain divided on NAFTA's effects. According to one commentator, neither the prediction of significant U.S. job loss nor great Mexican

economic growth has come to pass. On the occasion of NAFTA's tenth anniversary, Professor Joseph Stiglitz, chief economist of the World Bank from 1997–2000, remarked that "[t]he first six years of NAFTA saw unemployment in the United States fall to new lows." Joseph E. Stiglitz, *The Broken Promise of NAFTA*, N.Y. Times, Jan. 6, 2004, at A27. Yet although Mexico saw some benefits from the agreement in its early days, those benefits have tapered off, whereas economic growth in Mexico over the ten-year period has been bleak. *Id.*

5. Reviewing Mexico's experience under NAFTA, Professor Enrique de la Garza Toledo notes:

> In general, the opening of markets, particularly in the wake of NAFTA, had important economic effects for Mexico. . . . Foreign investment inflows and manufacturing exports grew, but labor conditions (including worktime, wages and work qualifications) generally did not improve.
>
> Enrique de la Garza Toledo, *Free Trade and Labor Relations in México*, in International Labor Standards: Globalization, Trade, and Public Policy 227, 233 (Robert J. Flanagan & William B. Gould IV, eds., 2003).

Although employment in the export-oriented maquilas grew, it decreased in other manufacturing branches. Professor de la Garza thus concludes that "[t]he global effect [of NAFTA] on the [Mexican] economy as a whole has nevertheless been small" because it has reached only a few export specialized branches of the manufacturing sector. Id. at 235.

6. A similar assessment to that of Professor de la Garza is provided by Sandra Polaski in a report from the Carnegie Endowment for International Peace:

> NAFTA has produced a disappointingly small net gain in jobs in Mexico. Data limitations preclude an exact tally, but it is clear that jobs created in export manufacturing have barely kept pace with jobs lost in agriculture due to imports. . . . About 30 percent of the jobs that were created in maquiladoras (export assembly plants) in the 1990s have since disappeared. Many of these operations were relocated to lower-wage countries in Asia, particularly China.
>
> Sandra Polaski, Jobs, Wages, and Household Income, in NAFTA's Promise and Reality: Lessons from Mexico for the Hemisphere 11, 12 (Carnegie Endowment for International Peace, 2003).

Polaski notes that due in large part to the peso crisis of 1994–1995, "[r]eal wages for most Mexicans today are lower than when NAFTA took effect." *Id.*

7. Polaski also finds that NAFTA has had little effect on U.S. jobs and wages. *Id.* As for effects in Canada, Polaski notes that the Canada-United States Free Trade Agreement (CUFTA), which went into effect in 1989, caused "substantial net job losses in Canada's traded sectors." *Id.* After five years, however, those losses subsided and by 1999 employment in Canadian manufacturing had recovered. *Id.* Neither CUFTA nor NAFTA seem to have negatively impacted Canadian wages. *Id.* at 13.

8. A much more optimistic assessment of NAFTA's economic impact was provided by a joint report from the offices of the Canadian Minister of International Trade, the Mexican Secretary of the Economy, and the U.S. Trade Representative. Citing increases in trade between the signatories, the report notes that between 1993 and 2002 trade among the parties more than doubled, reaching US $621 billion. NAFTA: A Decade of Strengthening a Dynamic Relationship, Joint Report from the

offices of the Canadian Minister of International Trade, the Mexican Secretary of the Economy, and the U.S. Trade Representative 2 (2003). During that period, U.S. exports to Canada and Mexico grew from US $147.7 billion to US $260.2 billion. *Id*. Mexican exports to the U.S. grew by 234 percent and to Canada by almost 203 percent. *Id*. And "Canada's exports to its NAFTA partners increased by 87 percent." *Id*.

9. Professor Harry Arthurs sounds a concern that was voiced by some Canadians when NAFTA was being negotiated:

> For many Canadians, globalization, regional integration within NAFTA, and [North American] continentalism are all more or less synonymous; all imply closer integration of Canada into the economic structures, idiosyncratic ideology and powerful culture of American capitalism.
>
> H. W. Arthurs, *Globalization of the Mind: Canadian Elites and the Restructuring of Legal Fields*, 12 Canadian J. Law & Soc'y 219, 225 (1998).

Although he acknowledges that Canada has in some ways benefited from globalization, Professor Arthurs worries about the increasing domination of Canadian subsidiaries by American TNCs. This "'hollowing out' of corporate Canada" may result in the country's marginalization, and affect all aspects of Canadian society, including its ability to sustain a vibrant welfare state. *Id*. at 233.

10. One business oriented think-tank, the C.D. Howe Institute, maintains that "hollowing out" concerns are misplaced. A study by the institute found that "foreigners control about 20 percent of Canadian corporations – about the same proportion as 15 years ago." Doug Struck, *Canada Looks for Spot in the Big Picture*, Wash. Post, Dec. 29, 2004, at E01. The study, which fails to address some of the subtleties of Professor Arthurs' argument, including the psychic impact on Canadians of their tremendous dependence on trade with the United States, nevertheless concludes that hollowing out "is largely a myth." *Id*. Although Canada experienced some fiscal retrenchment during the 1990s, one commentator notes that despite this and "NAFTA, [Canada's] social-welfare model stands intact, and in sharp contrast with that of the United States." *Ten Years of NAFTA: Free Trade on Trial*, The Economist, Dec. 30, 2003, available at http://www.economist.com.

11. Concerns about trade-related job loss prompted the U.S. Congress in 1993 to create the NAFTA-Transitional Adjustment Assistance Program, which provides extra weeks of unemployment insurance benefits to retrain U.S. workers dislocated by increased imports of the trading partners' goods or capital flight to Mexico or Canada. Lucy A. Williams, *Beyond Labour Law's Parochialism: A Re-envisioning of the Discourse of Redistribution, in* Labour Law in an Era of Globalization 93,111 (Joanne Conaghan, Richard Michael Fischl & Karl Klare, eds., 2002). A recent U.S. Government Accountability Office study of the country's overall trade adjustment assistance (TAA) program, of which the NAFTA program is a part, found that few workers who lose jobs as a result of increased trade avail themselves of new wage insurance and health benefits made available by a 2002 reform of TAA. Significant numbers of displaced workers use the program's One-Stop Career Centers, although a much smaller number actually receive training for new jobs. Trade Adjustment Assistance: Most Workers in Five Layoffs Received Services,

BUT BETTER OUTREACH NEEDED ON NEW BENEFITS, US Government Accountability Office, January 2006, available at http://www.gao.gov/new.items/d0643.pdf.

B. THE NAALC'S LABOR PRINCIPLES

Although the NAALC refrains from establishing universal labor standards, it does, in
Annex 1, list eleven guiding principles. Critics of the agreement note that the principles
do not reference International Labor Organization (ILO) conventions on those topics as
a floor below which the trading partners may not fall. Moreover, the principles are less
"specific and sometimes lower than ILO obligations." Hepple, Labour Laws, at 114.

Also curious is the placement of the principles in an annex rather than, for example,
at start of the agreement. Heenan, NAFTA/NAALC, at 20-12. Dr. Katherine Hagen, who
served for six years with the ILO as deputy director-general for external relations and
executive director for social dialogue, posits that the principles were "deliberately kept
separate" so that it was clear that the domestic labor law of the signatories, rather than
the principles themselves, sets the minimum standards that must be met by the parties.
Katherine A. Hagen, *Fundamentals of Labor Issues and NAFTA*, 27 U.C. DAVIS L. REV.
917, 925 (1994). Nonetheless, Article 50 specifies that all the NAALC's annexes are integral
to the agreement.

ANNEX 1   LABOR PRINCIPLES

The following are guiding principles that the Parties are committed to promote, subject to
each Party's domestic law, but do not establish common minimum standards for their domestic
law. They indicate broad areas of concern where the Parties have developed, each in its own
way, laws, regulations, procedures and practices that protect the rights and interests of their
respective workforces.

1. **Freedom of association and protection of the right to organize**
   The right of workers exercised freely and without impediment to establish and join organizations of their own choosing to further and defend their interests.

2. **The right to bargain collectively**
   The protection of the right of organized workers to freely engage in collective bargaining
   on matters concerning the terms and conditions of employment.

3. **The right to strike**
   The protection of the right of workers to strike in order to defend their collective interests.

4. **Prohibition of forced labor**
   The prohibition and suppression of all forms of forced or compulsory labor, except for types
   of compulsory work generally considered acceptable by the Parties, such as compulsory
   military service, certain civic obligations, prison labor not for private purposes and work
   exacted in cases of emergency.

5. **Labor protections for children and young persons**
   The establishment of restrictions on the employment of children and young persons that
   may vary taking into consideration relevant factors likely to jeopardize the full physical,

mental and moral development of young persons, including schooling and safety requirements.

6. Minimum employment standards

The establishment of minimum employment standards, such as minimum wages and overtime pay, for wage earners, including those not covered by collective agreements.

7. Elimination of employment discrimination

Elimination of employment discrimination on such grounds as race, religion, age, sex or other grounds, subject to certain reasonable exceptions, such as, where applicable, *bona fide* occupational requirements or qualifications and established practices or rules governing retirement ages, and special measures of protection or assistance for particular groups designed to take into account the effects of discrimination.

8. Equal pay for women and men

Equal wages for women and men by applying the principle of equal pay for equal work in the same establishment.

9. Prevention of occupational injuries and illnesses

Prescribing and implementing standards to minimize the causes of occupational injuries and illnesses.

10. Compensation in cases of occupational injuries and illnesses

The establishment of a system providing benefits and compensation to workers or their dependents in cases of occupational injuries, accidents or fatalities arising out of, linked with or occurring in the course of employment.

11. Protection of migrant workers

Providing migrant workers in a Party's territory with the same legal protection as the Party's nationals in respect of working conditions.

Notes

1. Article 49, the section of the NAALC that sets forth statutory definitions, defines "labor law" as the laws and regulations directly related to the eleven principles.
2. As described more fully later, the NAALC's enforcement mechanism provides for three levels of review. The guiding principle at stake determines the level or levels of review available. As Professor Marley Weiss notes:

   > . . . [O]nly eight of the eleven labor law principles may be the subject of higher level procedures, excluding the three pertaining to union organizing, bargaining, and the right to strike. Only three of the eleven labor law subject areas may reach the final stage of the dispute resolution process, where fines or trade sanctions are available.

   Weiss, *Two Steps*, at 710.

   To date, no submission has been taken beyond the first step. Michael J. Trebilcock & Robert Howse, *Trade Policy & Labor Standards*, 14 MINN. J. GLOBAL TRADE 261, 298 (2005) (hereinafter Trebilcock & Howse, *Trade Policy*).

C. NAALC STRUCTURES AND ENFORCEMENT

The Commission for Labor Cooperation (CLC) is the trinational body charged with overseeing the NAALC. In turn, the CLC is comprised of a Ministerial Council, which is the governing body of the CLC, and a Secretariat with a small staff, charged with assisting the Council and preparing reports and studies. Heenan, NAFTA/NAALC, at 20-16. Professor Marley Weiss argues that the Council is not a true tri-national body because it is made up of the labor ministers of the signatories, each of whom owes allegiance to his or her respective country. In contrast, the undivided loyalties of the Secretariat's management and staff are to the tri-national organization. Weiss, *Two Steps*, at 705.

Linked to the CLC are the National Administrative Offices (NAOs) in Canada, Mexico, and the United States. The NAOs, which are domestic entities, organize cooperative activities, such as conferences, seminars, discussions and training sessions on a range of employment-related topics listed in the NAALC's Article 11. Article 11's lengthy topic listing includes: occupational safety and health; child labor; migrant workers; human resource development; labor statistics; work benefits; social programs for workers; labor-management relations and collective bargaining; employment standards; equality of men and women in the workplace; and the provision of technical assistance for the development of labor standards. At least as valuable as promoting cooperative activities, however, is the NAOs' role as contact point for the receipt, investigation and review of public submissions – complaints filed by non-state actors alleging that a signatory nation has failed to enforce or comply with its own labor law. Monica Schurtman, *Los "Jonkeados" and the NAALC: The Autotrim/Customtrim Case and its Implications for Submissions Under the NAFTA Labor Side Agreement*, 22 ARIZ. J. INT'L & COMP. L. 291, 301 (2005) (hereinafter Schurtman, *Los Jonkeados*).

Any person or organization in a signatory country may file a submission so long as the filing is not with the NAO of the country in which the dispute arises. Because the allegations assert a signatory's noncompliance with its obligations under the NAALC, this requirement ensures impartiality in the disposition of the complaint. Each NAO has established its own procedures for processing and accepting or rejecting submissions. In the U.S., the NAO, recently renamed the Office of Trade Agreement Implementation (OTAI), requires at a minimum a submission allege: "(1) that the government that is the subject of the complaint demonstrates a pattern of non-enforcement of its own labor laws; (2) conduct that has caused specific harm to the submitter or other persons; and (3) that relief has been sought under the domestic laws of the government in question." *Id*. at 302.

If the NAO accepts the submission, it begins an investigation, which may involve consultations with the Canadian and Mexican NAOs, and interviews with "the submitter, companies, [and] private consultants." U.S. DEPARTMENT OF LABOR, BUREAU OF INTERNATIONAL LABOR AFFAIRS, NORTH AMERICAN AGREEMENT ON LABOR COOPERATION: A GUIDE, Oct. 2005, available at http://www.dol.gov/ilab. The U.S. NAO also presumes that a hearing will be held unless there is a reason why that mechanism would not be an appropriate one for gathering evidence. Id. Upon completing the investigation, the NAO issues a public report, and may recommend ministerial consultations, which are meetings involving the cabinet-level ministers or secretaries. Schurtman, Los Jonkeados, at 303. Ministerial consultations are in theory available when the allegations relate to any of the eleven guiding principles. Consultations seek to resolve the submission through consensus.

Where ministerial consultations fail to resolve a matter, a NAFTA signatory may request the appointment of an Evaluation Committee of Experts (ECE), the second step of the NAALC enforcement process, so long as the case does not relate to the first three of the guiding principles: freedom of association and protection of the right to organize; the right to bargain collectively; and the right to strike. Moreover, the matter at issue must be both "trade related" and "covered by mutually recognized labor laws." Sir Bob Hepple provides an example of the how the latter concept limits potential second step claims, noting that "since the US does not have a law like that of Mexico on profit-sharing with employe[es] of 10 percent of the firm's profits, it could not request an ECE to evaluate the enforcement of Mexican laws on this subject." Hepple, Labour Laws, at 110-11. The ECE, after reviewing the evidence, must prepare a preliminary report for the Ministerial Council. Time is provided for the signatories involved to respond to that document. After their response, the ECE forwards to the Ministerial Council a final report, which may recommend further ministerial consultations. Heenan, NAFTA/NAALC, at 20-26, 20-27.

The NAALC's third stage, dispute resolution, is only open to matters involving three of the guiding principles: prevention of occupational injuries and illnesses; child labor; and minimum employment standards. This phase, which must be initiated by a NAFTA signatory, has quite a few steps, including: ministerial consultations; the convening of an arbitral panel; further negotiations; resubmission to the arbitral panel; and the possible award of a monetary enforcement assessment. Weiss, *Two Steps*, at 732. This assessment is not paid to the victims of the signatory's NAFTA violation. Rather, it is paid into a fund to enhance labor law enforcement in the country in question. NAALC, Annex 39. A country refusing to pay is subject to trade sanctions, unless that country is Canada, in which case the "penalty becomes domestically enforceable as a judgment in the Canadian courts." *Id.* at 733.

As of July 2006, 34 submissions were filed under the NAALC; 21 were lodged with the U.S. NAO, eight were filed with Mexico's NAO, and five submissions were made to the Canadian NAO. U.S. Department of Labor, Bureau of International Affairs, Public Submissions, July 2006, available at www.dol.gov/ilab/programs/nao/status.htm. Not one case has gone beyond the first phase of the NAALC's enforcement mechanism.

PUBLIC REPORT OF REVIEW OF NAO SUBMISSION NO. 9702 (Han Young)

U.S. National Administrative Office
Bureau of International Labor Affairs
U.S. Department of Labor

April 28, 1998

I. INTRODUCTION

The U.S. National Administrative Office (NAO) was established pursuant to the North American Agreement on Labor Cooperation (NAALC). The NAALC, the labor supplemental agreement to the North American Free Trade Agreement (NAFTA), provides for the review of submissions concerning labor law matters arising in Canada or Mexico by the U.S. NAO. . . .

Submission No. 9702 was filed on October 30, 1997, by the Support Committee for Maquiladora Workers (SCM), the International Labor Rights Fund (ILRF), the National Association of Democratic Lawyers (*Asociacin Nacional de Abogados Democraticos, hereinafter*

ANAD) of Mexico, and the Union of Metal, Steel, Iron, and Allied Workers (*Sindicato de Trabajadores de la Industria Metalica, Acero, Hierro, Conexos y Similares*, hereinafter STIMAHCS) of Mexico. It was accepted for review by the NAO on November 17, 1997 . . .

Submission No. 9702 raises issues of freedom of association . . . at a truck chassis welding/assembly facility in Tijuana, Baja California, Mexico, owned by Han Young de Mexico, S.A. de C.V. (hereinafter Han Young). Han Young assembles chassis for Hyundai Precision America, a subsidiary of Hyundai Corporation of Korea. . . .

II. SUMMARY OF SUBMISSION 9702

A. Case Summary

According to the submitters, beginning in April 1997, workers at the Han Young maquiladora plant in Tijuana, Baja California, Mexico, began to organize an independent union. The submitters state that the workers wanted a union to address issues of safety and health, job classifications and wage scales, low wages, annual bonuses, profit sharing, lack of dining facilities, and the lack of a company doctor in the plant. Among the cited health and safety concerns of the workers was the frequent occurrence of injuries such as burns and broken bones. They also expressed concern about respiratory illnesses, hearing loss, and loss of vision. According to the submitters, the workers believed that these problems were caused by the lack of compliance with government regulations and failure to follow safety practices such as local exhaust ventilation, periodic hazard identification and control, exposure monitoring, medical surveillance, health and safety training and other hazard control measures. The submitters also asserted that the company failed to provide adequate personal protective equipment such as safety shoes, safety glasses, chemical-resistant gloves, respirators and face shields.

The workers elected a union executive committee on May 31, 1997, and presented a petition listing demands to the plant management. After the election of the executive committee, Han Young management arranged for the workers to meet with a representative of a union that was already present at the plant and had previously entered into a collective bargaining agreement with the company. This local union (*Union de Trabajadores de Oficios Varios "Jose, Maria Larroque"*) was affiliated with the Revolutionary Confederation of Workers and Peasants (*Confederacion Revolucionaria de Obreros y Campesinos – CROC*). The CROC is affiliated with the Labor Congress (*Congreso del Trabajo – CT*) which groups together union organizations aligned with Mexico's dominant political party, the Institutional Revolutionary Party (*Partido Revolucionario Institucional – PRI*). The submitters maintain that the union had never before met with the workers at the plant and that workers had not seen a copy of the collective bargaining agreement, which had purportedly been signed between the company and the CROC union.

The workers struck for a day on June 2 and, following what appeared to be positive discussions with company management, returned to work the following day. On July 15, 1997, the workers temporarily suspended their efforts to organize an independent union and elected to affiliate with the already registered STIMAHCS. Though STIMAHCS already possessed registration, it had, at that time, no membership in the maquiladoras and is not affiliated to the CT. The submitters indicated that STIMAHCS is considered to be more responsive to the interest of workers, compared to the unions affiliated to the major confederations. . . .

In mid-July the company hired a new director of human resources and began, according to the submitters, a campaign of harassment, intimidation and reprisals against the supporters of

STIMAHCS. Allegedly, several union supporters were fired and one was physically attacked by the plant manager. The dismissed workers filed petitions for reinstatement with the local Conciliation and Arbitration Board (CAB). The submitters maintain that the company attempted to persuade the fired workers to drop their petitions for reinstatement in return for severance payments, which they refused to do. They also maintain that the company attempted to persuade the workers to remain affiliated to the CROC.

On August 6, 1997, STIMAHCS filed for collective bargaining representation *(titularidad)* with the local CAB, in effect, challenging the CROC union for exclusive bargaining rights at the plant. During the first week of September, according to the submitters, twenty new workers were brought in by the company, allegedly to dilute support for STIMAHCS, and representatives from the Confederation of Mexican Workers *(Confederacion de Trabajadores Mexicanos – CTM)*, which is also affiliated to the CT, arrived at the plant to meet with the workers. . . .

A hearing to verify the credentials of the contending parties, hear challenges, and set a date for a representation election, was scheduled to be held on September 3, 1997, by the CAB. According to the CAB, this hearing was postponed to September 25 because of a clerical error. . . . At the September 25 meeting, the CAB heard arguments, reviewed the credentials of the parties, and set the representation election date for October 6, 1997, despite efforts by the CROC union to further postpone the proceedings. At this hearing, the CAB overruled objections by the CROC union that STIMAHCS lacked the appropriate certification to represent the Han Young workers in Baja California.

As the date of the election approached, the submitters claim that management continued its campaign of intimidation against STIMAHCS supporters and threatened workers with the loss of their jobs if that union won the election. . . .

On October 6, 1997, the representation election took place as scheduled at the offices of the CAB. According to the submitters, fourteen international observers, including representatives from U.S. unions and non-governmental organizations (NGOs) were present. The submitters allege that the company transported a group of thirty-five workers, including supervisory personnel and new hires, to the voting site, where they were allowed to cast their ballots. According to the submitters, none of these people were eligible to vote but STIMAHCS representatives and supporters were prevented from checking the credentials of voters, whereas the credentials of STIMAHCS supporters were carefully scrutinized. Following the balloting, it was announced that STIMAHCS had won the election by a vote of 54–34 over the CROC. . . .

According to the submitters, in the days following the vote, the company dismissed another four workers who were supporters of STIMAHCS and the general manager announced that the company intended to bring in fifty replacement workers from Veracruz and fire all of the union supporters. The submitters maintain that a total of twelve workers were fired by the company for their support of STIMAHCS.

At a CAB hearing on October 16, both STIMAHCS and the CROC challenged a number of the ballots cast at the representation election. The CAB then announced that it had concluded its proceedings in this case and would certify the result of the election after reviewing the evidence. However, on November 10, the CAB issued a ruling that nullified the election results on the grounds that STIMAHCS had failed to adequately substantiate that it had the support of the majority of the workers at the plant and that it lacked the proper registration to represent the workers at Han Young. Union representation remained with the CROC union. STIMAHCS filed an appeal against this decision with a Federal Appeals Court. Additionally, four workers went on a hunger strike in protest.

Following considerable publicity on the case, the Mexican Federal Government intervened and mediated an agreement among the parties. The agreement called for a new representation election, to be conducted under the supervision of state and Federal authorities. The parties agreed to abide by the outcome of this election, suspend all legal action they had undertaken, and desist from further conflict within Han Young. Pursuant to the agreement, registration would be granted to an independent union named the Union of Industrial and Commercial Workers "October 6" (*Sindicato de Trabajadores de la Industria y del Comercio "6 de Octubre"*). The workers intended for this independent union to eventually supplant STIMAHCS as their collective bargaining representative. Additionally, all of the workers who were dismissed were to be offered reinstatement to their jobs.

The second representation election at Han Young took place on December 16, 1997. An affiliate of the CTM took part in this three-way election. The election was won again by STIMAHCS, by a vote of 30 for STIMAHCS, 26 for the CTM affiliate, and two for the CROC union. The hunger strikers ended their fast. On January 12, 1998, STIMAHCS was recognized by the CAB as the collective bargaining representative at the plant and "October 6" was granted registration. All but one of the workers accepted reinstatement to their jobs. . . .

STIMAHCS requested negotiations with Han Young began in mid-March. The submitters assert that these negotiations have not progressed, however, and that the CROC and CTM continue to be active in the plant and continue to harass and intimidate workers with the cooperation of plant management in their joint effort to keep other unions out of the workplace. Further, the submitters assert that the reinstated workers have been subjected to reprisals by the company through denying them wage increases granted to other workers and other forms of harassment and that eleven workers have been fired in retaliation for union activities. Finally, the submitters allege that the company has hired additional workers as part of an effort to defeat STIMAHCS in a new representation election and that the CTM, in alliance with the CROC, has filed a petition for a new union election. The CAB has scheduled a hearing for May 21, 1998, at which a date for a new representation election will be set. The submitters assert that the outcome of this next election is in doubt given the recent efforts against the union by the company.

B. Issues

The submitters argue that Mexico is in violation of NAALC Article 3(1) in failing to enforce its labor laws through appropriate actions. In failing to enforce its labor laws, the submitters argue that Mexico is also in violation of the country's Constitution, which protects freedom of association, ILO Convention 87 on freedom of association, which Mexico has ratified, and ILO Convention 98 on the right to organize and bargain collectively, which Mexico has not ratified. . . .

III. NAO REVIEW

In conducting its review, the NAO sought and obtained information from the submitters, the employer, the Mexican NAO, and the Hyundai Corporation. . . .

B. Information from the Mexican NAO

The U.S. NAO addressed questions to the Mexican NAO on the submission and Mexican law and its implementation in letters dated October 1, 1997 (prior to the receipt of the submission), February 10, and February 25, 1997. The U.S. and Mexican NAOs also engaged in a number of other consultations as the case developed.

[The Mexican NAO provided information on relevant Mexican labor law and reported it "received assurances from the Baja California labor authorities that the law had been complied with. . . . "]

C. Information from Han Young . . .

Mr. Ho Young Lee, President of Han Young, responded by letter dated February 12, 1998, to a written inquiry from the NAO on the issues raised in the submission. In his letter Mr. Lee stated that Han Young pays wages in excess of the minimum wage; the company provides adequate safety and health equipment; the company has been inspected regularly by the safety and health authorities; the company did not take sides in the jurisdictional dispute between the two unions; that workers who were dismissed were dismissed for cause; that he thought it unfair that workers hired after the petition for a representation election were not allowed to vote; and that Han Young had not received formal written notification designating the collective bargaining representative at the plant. . . .

D. Public Hearing

The NAO conducted a public hearing on Submission No. 9702 in San Diego, California, on February 18, 1998. Notice of the hearing was published in the Federal Register on January 14, 1998.
Twenty-seven employees of Han Young testified as to their experiences in the union organizing effort and on health and safety conditions in the plant. Seven additional witnesses provided information on events at Han Young, Mexican labor law, and health and safety issues.

The General Manager of Han Young spoke on behalf of his company and counsel for Han Young testified on behalf of the company and on Mexican labor law as it applied to the case.

Mr. Eric Myers of the USWA [United Steel Workers of America] read a prepared statement on behalf of George Becker, International President of the USWA. . . .

IV. NAALC OBLIGATIONS AND MEXICAN LABOR LAW

A. NAALC Obligations

Part One of the NAALC lists the objectives to which the Parties commit themselves, including the promotion, to the maximum extent possible, of the labor principles set out in Annex 1. The first principle is freedom of association and protection of the right to organize, which protects "the right of workers exercised freely and without impediment to establish and join organizations of their own choosing to further and defend their interests."

Part Two of the NAALC sets out the obligations of the Parties. Article 3 (1) commits the Parties to effectively enforce their labor law through appropriate government action. . . .

B. Relevant Mexican Law on Freedom of Association

Freedom of association is protected by Mexico's Constitution. Article 19 states that "[t]he right to association or to hold meetings for any legal purpose cannot be curbed." Article 123(A) provides the framework for regulating labor matters in the private sector and protects workers from dismissal or reprisal by employers for union activities.

Mexican labor law in the private sector is codified as the Federal Labor Law*(Ley Federal del Trabajo)* (hereinafter FLL). Relevant to the freedom of association issues raised in the instant submission are Articles 47 (dismissal), 133 (employer prohibited practices), 357–359 (right to organize), 360 (types of union organization), 387 (obligation to bargain collectively), 388 and 389 (union representation), 527 (industries under Federal jurisdiction), 870–891 (proceedings before the CABs), 892–899 (jurisdictional disputes), and 931 (representation elections).

C. Relevant Law on Labor Tribunals and Labor Tribunal Proceedings

FLL Articles 604–624 establish the CABs as the primary authorities responsible for the adjudication of individual and collective labor-management disputes, union representation and jurisdictional disputes, and other disputes deriving from the employment relationship. Federal CABs have authority over industries specifically identified in the FLL, while local CABs, operating under the authority of the states, have jurisdiction over all other industries. All CABs, however, enforce the same national law – the FLL. In the case of Han Young, jurisdiction was exercised by the local CAB for the city of Tijuana in the state of Baja California.

FLL Articles 625 through 675 govern the composition of the CABs. Each CAB consists of one representative from the government, who is the President, and one representative each from management and labor. . . . In practice, the largest and most representative labor organizations within the area of jurisdiction of the CAB are those represented on the CABs. These unions are the large and established labor organizations, such as the CTM, CROM, and CROC, aligned with the dominant political party, the PRI. . . . Two important instruments of regulation and oversight by the government are union registration and the determination of union representation rights. . . . At the local level, jurisdiction over both of these important functions of collective labor relations is exercised by the local CABs under state jurisdiction.

1. *Union Registration*
In Mexico, registration by the administrative authorities grants unions the means by which they conduct their affairs. Without registration, a union cannot hold or dispose of property, represent itself or its members, or otherwise conduct business. Before a union can contest a representation election, it must be registered. . . .

2. *Union Representation*
The CABs also award representation rights to unions within a workplace or within an industry, as appropriate, in accordance with FLL Articles 388, 389, 892–899, and 931. The representation election (*recuento*) is one method used for determining the union representation preference of the workers in cases where two or more unions contest representation within the same workplace. Only registered unions may compete in a representation election. A union granted representation by the CAB has exclusive bargaining rights for all workers in the bargaining

unit, or the workplace, as the case may be. FLL Article 395 provides that an "exclusion" clause may be included in the collective bargaining agreement. This clause obliges a company to hire only members of the union and may require the company to dismiss from employment any worker who has been expelled from the union. Most collective bargaining agreements in effect in Mexico have this clause. . . .

V. ANALYSIS

A. Freedom of Association

Article 1 of the NAALC commits the Parties to promote the labor principle of freedom of association and protection of the right to organize while Article 3 obliges the Parties to enforce their labor laws. The instant submission raises two issues related to the enforcement of laws on freedom of association, namely (1) enforcement by Mexico of its laws protecting workers from employer retaliation and interference in the exercise of their rights; and (2) enforcement by Mexico of its laws on union representation and jurisdiction.

Employer efforts to coerce or otherwise persuade workers to affiliate or not affiliate to a union are prohibited by FLL Article 133. There is information that strongly suggests the management of Han Young favored representation first by the CROC union and later the CTM union, and attempted to influence workers on their choice through threats, intimidation, and dismissal. According to the submitters, Han Young organized a meeting between the workers and the CROC union shortly after the workers began their organizing effort. The submitters assert that Han Young offered a cash payment equal to $2000 to one of the worker leaders to stop his union activities. The submitters also provided information that Han Young offered cash payments of about $125 to each worker who would vote for the CTM during the second representation election. There is also information that Han Young threatened to fire all of the supporters of STIMAHCS and replace them if STIMAHCS won the representation election and otherwise expressed its opposition to STIMAHCS. The submitters assert that a total of twelve supporters of STIMAHCS were fired for supporting STIMAHCS.

Dismissal without just cause is prohibited by FLL Article 47. The submitters assert that twelve workers, many of them STIMAHCS union activists or supporters, were dismissed after the organizing drive began and labor-management tensions increased, especially following the one-day strike in June. They assert that the dismissals were in retaliation for the organizing effort and intended to intimidate other workers. Management claims that these workers were dismissed for reasons unrelated to their organizing activities and that instead the dismissals were based on poor work performance or for violations of employer policies.

The NAO finds that the timing of these events raises serious questions about management's motives. All of these employees have been rehired to date, following negotiations and a settlement that was facilitated by both State and Federal Government officials. However, these same employees reported that management continues to single them out and treat them unfavorably as compared to employees who are not affiliated to or did not support STIMAHCS.

Mexican law provides that a representation election may be used to determine the majority preference when two or more unions contest for representation in the same workplace. A representation election took place on October 6. There is considerable testimonial evidence that the election was plagued with irregularities including changing the election date with little notice, threats to the workers supporting STIMAHCS, and the ability of persons without proper credentials to enter the voting premises and cast ballots.

FLL Article 931(IV) provides that workers recruited after the date of the petition for union representation may not participate in the election. Neither may "employees of trust" (*trabajadores de confianza*). STIMAHCS filed for representation on August 8, 1997, and workers hired by Han Young after that date should not have been permitted to vote. The submitters assert, and workers testified, that ineligible workers were brought in by management in support of the CROC union, and were allowed, by CAB officials, to take part in the voting, despite the objections of STIMAHCS representatives. In addition to the testimony of the workers, it was reported by the print media that international observers present at the election recounted similar irregularities with the election process.

Despite considerable irregularities designed to influence the workers and the voting process, STIMAHCS won a convincing victory in the election. However, the CAB nullified the vote, ruling that STIMAHCS failed to demonstrate that it had the support of a majority of the workers in the workplace. The CAB stated that the representation election only showed the sympathies of the workers toward STIMAHCS during a given moment in time and was insufficient to prove that STIMAHCS had majority support. The CAB cited decisions by appeals courts and the Supreme Court dated 1969, 1971, 1972, 1973, and 1974 in support of this position. The CAB did not specify how a union was expected to demonstrate that it had majority support.

The CAB also ruled that STIMAHCS was registered before the Registrar of Associations of the Secretariat of Labor and Social Welfare as a national industrial union in the metallurgical sector, rather than the automotive sector, and could not, therefore, represent Han Young automobile workers in the state of Baja California. The CAB cited FLL Article 360 in support of this argument.

Contrary to the reasoning by the CAB that the election results were an insufficient basis for determining the bargaining representative, the Mexican NAO had previously informed the U.S. NAO that the Supreme Court of Mexico had, in 1979, ruled that the representation election (*recuento*) was the most effective way of determining the union preference of the majority of workers in a workplace. However, in a letter dated March 27, 1998, the Mexican NAO cited a 1993 Supreme Court decision that stated that the representation election is not a sufficient basis to determine representation rights as, in accordance with FLL Article 931, only those workers physically present at the representation election are entitled to vote. According to this decision, the majority of the votes cast for a contesting union must correspond to a majority of the workers in the workplace, less workers who are ineligible to vote, such as recent hires and management employees. . . .

In the absence of a representation election, the only alternative approach available to the workers of Han Young, according to the FLL and from information provided by the Mexican NAO, would have been for the workers to (1) disaffiliate from the CROC union; (2) seek affiliation to STIMAHCS; and (3) petition the CAB for collective bargaining representation. By following this procedure, however, the workers would be vulnerable to dismissal from employment should the CROC invoke the exclusion clause. Such dismissals would be legal and without prejudice to the company. Under this scenario, the workers would face a limited choice of risking dismissal from employment or remaining with the CROC union.

In nullifying the October 6 election results, the CAB also decided that STIMAHCS lacked the proper registration to represent workers at Han Young. The CAB's decision, reversing its earlier recognition of STIMAHCS as a registered union for the purpose of the representation election, seems inexplicable. Mexican labor law requires that a union or union organization be registered before the appropriate authorities, be they of the Federal Government or the state government. FLL Article 527 places a number of industries, including the metal and steel industry, under the jurisdiction of the Federal Government. Once registration is granted, the registered organization is authorized to represent itself and its members before state and Federal authorities. STIMAHCS was registered with the Federal Government and, according to the express language of FLL Articles 368 and 374, should have been recognized as a registered union before the Baja California CAB. Moreover, in arguing that the representation election, in itself, was not sufficient to determine the majority union, the CAB did not explain on what basis it chose to return represension to the CROC, which received fewer votes than STIMAHCS.

FLL Article 360 identifies the different kinds of unions that can be established. These are craft, company, industrial, and national industrial unions, and unions that include various crafts. There does not appear to be a legal delineation of industrial jurisdiction among different industrial unions. As a truck chassis welding operation, Han Young could presumably be classified under either the automobile or metalworking industries.

Moreover, the CAB verified STIMAHCS' credentials at the hearing held on September 25 before allowing the representation vote, rejecting at that time a challenge put forward by the CROC union that STIMAHCS lacked the legal authority to represent maquiladora workers in the state of Baja California. The decision of the CAB overturning the election result made no mention of this earlier decision which allowed the vote to take place and offered no explanation for the reversal.

On December 16, 1997, a second election took place, in part because the Federal Government and the State Government of Baja California intervened and negotiated a settlement between the parties. The terms of the settlement included the second representation election between STIMAHCS and the CROC union and an agreement by both unions to abide by the results of the election. The settlement also called for an end to all legal proceedings, including withdrawal of the NAO petition, by the two unions and an end to the inter-union conflict at the plant. The CAB agreed to grant registration to an independent union called the Industrial and Commercial Workers Union "October 6" (*Sindicato de Trabajadores de la Industria y del Comercio "6 de Octubre"*). It was the apparent intention of the workers for this union to eventually supplant STIMAHCS as the collective bargaining representative at the plant. Following the second representation victory by STIMAHCS, "October 6" was granted registration, and the appropriate certificate was issued on January 12, 1998.

FLL Article 387 requires an employer to enter into a collective bargaining agreement with the union in the establishment. If more than one union exists in the workplace, the employer must negotiate with the union that has representation rights (*titularidad*). Pablo Kang, Han Young Human Resources Director, testified at the February 18 hearing that he had not received official notice of the election results, and that in any event he believed that STIMAHCS enjoyed the support of only about 20 percent of the workers within the plant. When asked how he had arrived at this figure, he replied that he had calculated the number from watching protesters outside the factory gate on one occasion. Though FLL Article 890 requires the CAB to immediately notify the parties of its decisions, the employer was not officially notified of the results of the representation election until March 2, 1998, although the outcome had been common knowledge. FLL Article 399 requires that bargaining begin at least sixty days prior to the expiration of the agreement that is in effect. The current collective bargaining agreement in effect at Han Young is scheduled to expire on May 22, 1998, and negotiations should have begun, therefore, on or about March 22, 1998. Until then, the employer was under no legal obligation to negotiate the terms of a new agreement unless the union initiated negotiations. STIMAHCS made such a request in mid-March. According to the submitters, however, Han Young rejected the union's demands and the negotiations have not progressed.

The submitters have informed the NAO that problems continue at the Han Young plant, that the company has hired twenty-seven new workers, and intends to hire additional workers, even if only for a limited period of time, so as to allow for a new union election which will ensure that STIMAHCS is voted out. If, in fact the company was attempting to influence a future election, it could do so by hiring additional workers. Mexican labor law makes no provision for a grace period during which challenges for union representation rights may not take place. At last report, a CTM union has filed for a new representation election and the CAB has scheduled a May 21, 1998, hearing to set a date. This will be the third representation election held since October 6, 1997.

As of the date of this report, the workers at Han Young have obtained recognition of their independent union, obtained representation rights for STIMAHCS in their workplace, and gained reinstatement of the workers who were dismissed for union organizing activities. The workers also testified, however, that STIMAHCS affiliated workers continue to be harassed and denied benefits available to workers not affiliated to STIMAHCS and that eleven workers have been subjected to retaliatory discharge for their union activities.

The irregularities that the Tijuana CAB permitted to take place during the first representation election, its reasoning in not recognizing STIMAHCS as the bargaining representative, and its delay in formally notifying Han Young of the results of the December 16 representation election, raise questions about its enforcement of those provisions of Mexico's FLL that govern procedures for determining union representation. These actions also raise questions about the impartiality of the CAB, particularly with regard to its duty to enforce the provisions of the FLL protecting workers from employer retaliation for the exercise of their freedom of association rights, and from employer interference in the establishment of a union. . . . .

C. Initiatives by the Government of Mexico

Previous consultations have shown that the Mexican Government recognizes problems involving the effective implementation by the CABs of its labor laws on freedom of association and is making efforts to address them. Two initiatives of note have been undertaken by the Government of Mexico to address problems of labor administration and to improve the system for adjudicating disputes. These are the *New Labor Culture* and the *Program for Employment, Training and the Defense of Labor Rights: 1995–2000*.

1. New Labor Culture

The NAO reported on the New Labor Culture *(Nueva Cultura Laboral)* in its Follow-up Report on NAO Submission No. 940003. The New Labor Culture resulted from efforts by the Government of Mexico to improve labor-management cooperation, competitiveness, and productivity. Following tripartite negotiations among labor, management, and government representatives, a document entitled Principles of the New Labor Culture *(Principios de la Nueva Cultura Laboral)*, was signed on August 13, 1996.

The Principles of the New Labor Culture does not have the effect of law, but rather is a statement of objectives and principles. It calls upon both labor and management to respect each other's rights and honor respective obligations. The document addresses two matters of labor law which were subjects of Submission No. 940003 and the subsequent ministerial consultations: (1) union democracy; and (2) union registration, including the lack of impartiality in the decisions of the labor tribunals. Under the Principles of the New Labor Culture, unions pledge to conduct their business in accordance with the law, to observe the principle of freedom of association, and to conduct their elections in a climate of harmony, respect and democracy. Further, both unions and management call on the government to strengthen the system of labor tribunals by assigning career judges, as opposed to the current practice of assigning members of the executive branch, as the government representatives to these bodies. The document calls for the labor authorities to discharge their responsibilities in strict conformance with the law, and in the case of adjudicating jurisdictional matters, to do so quickly, completely, with justice, and impartially.

2. Program for Employment, Training and the Defense of Labor Rights: 1995–2000

The Program for Employment, Training and the Defense of Labor Rights: 1995–2000 *(Program de Empleo, Capacitación y Defensa de los Derechos Laborales: 1995–2000)* (hereinafter the Program) is a five-year policy and planning document adopted by the Secretariat of Labor and Social Welfare in 1995 and published in 1996. The Program is comprehensive and deals with employment, education, training, productivity, health and safety, and workers' rights and labor justice. . . . . .

In the Program, the Government sets forth guidelines for action, which include:

1. the establishment of an actuarial control system for the issuance of notifications and summons;
2. improving and expediting procedures for the presentation of evidence and determining its admissibility;
3. holding periodic and obligatory meetings of the boards, so they can adopt uniform criteria in the granting of awards, in accordance with the Law;
4. improvement in the professional level of the staff of the Federal CABs through the establishment of a judicial career track to deal with the increased complexity of the matters submitted to the Boards;
5. modernization of the systems for recruiting and selecting both legal and administrative personnel, in order to improve staff and retain highly qualified personnel, including the selection of personnel based on their employment history as well as the results of competitive examinations.

The NAO has observed that the Government of Mexico has begun to implement some of these programs. A registry of all officially registered unions has been prepared and is available on the website of the Secretariat of Labor and Social Welfare. Several new Federal CABs have been established, including one in Tijuana. These measures are directed toward achieving a consistent and uniform application of the law by the CABs. If fully implemented, these steps, among others, would significantly reduce the possibility of a selective application of the law and charges of bias and manipulation of the process. . . .

It is evident that the Federal Government of Mexico is aware of the problems associated with some of the state CABs and has initiated efforts to achieve improved compliance with the law by the appropriate authorities. Unfortunately, it is further evident from the instant submission that in spite of serious efforts on the part of Mexican Federal labor authorities, independent unions continue to experience difficulty gaining the authority and ability to exist and function as provided for under the Mexican Constitution and the FLLj

The NAO makes the following findings:

1. Mexico's Constitution and Federal laws protect the freedom of association of workers to organize and join the unions of their choice. . . .

3. Provisions of the Federal Labor Law on representation elections in determining the majority union are unclear. The U.S. NAO has received conflicting information on this matter. The actions of the Tijuana CAB, including the delay in informing the parties of its decisions in the case, the rationale of its decision not to certify the first representation election, and irregularities in the conduct of the first representation election, appear inconsistent with Mexico's obligations under Articles 5(1), 5(2)(b) and 5(4) of the NAALC.

4. The placement, by the Tijuana CAB, of obstacles to the ability of workers to exercise their right to freedom of association, through the application of inconsistent and imprecise criteria and standards for union registration and for determining union representation, is not consistent with Mexico's obligation to effectively enforce its labor laws on freedom of association in accordance with Article 3 of the NAALC. . . .

Given the above, ministerial level consultations on the implementation of the various recommendations emanating from the Government of Mexico, such as the *Principles of the New Labor Culture and the Program for Employment: 1995–2000*, would further the objectives of the NAALC. Consultations should discuss any strategies being considered by the Government of Mexico to address these issues and in particular those strategies designed to address problems such as those with the Tijuana CAB in Baja California, as well as other measures to ensure that workers' freedom of association and right to bargain collectively are protected.

VII. Recommendation

Accordingly, the NAO recommends ministerial consultations on these matters pursuant to Article 22 of the NAALC.

Irasema Garza
Secretary
U.S. National Administrative Office

April 28, 1998

Based on the foregoing report, I accept the NAO's recommendation to request ministerial consultations under Article 22 of the NAALC on the issues concerning union registration and representation raised in Submission No. 9702.

Alexis M. Herman
Secretary of Labor

_____

Notes

1. The United States and Mexico formally agreed to ministerial consultations on the Han Young submission on May 18, 2000. The agreement, which additionally covered another submission known as the Echlin case, provided for a government-to-government session, and also a public seminar on Mexican CABs, which was held in June of 2000 in Tijuana, Mexico. Heenan, NAFTA/NAALC, at 20-57. Professor Jonathan Graubart reports on the latter meeting and its aftermath:

   > [The public meeting] ended in a disaster when a group of local independent union organizers at Han Young were physically beaten by members of the audience as they protested the forum's failure to specifically address their experiences. Ominously, those doing the beatings belonged to a longtime PRI-allied labor federation, the Revolutionary Confederation of Workers and Campesinos (CROC) that had switched local allegiances to PAN, the party governing the state. A second public meeting held in March, 2002, also provoked great frustration. Mexico's Secretary of Labor switched the location from Mexico City to Monterrey one day before the meeting.

   > Graubart, *New Breed*, at 137.

2. Whereas a majority of the NAFTA submissions involve claims that Mexico is failing to enforce its labor laws, submissions have been filed against both the United States and Canada. Submission No. 2001-01 to the Mexican NAO, for example, took issue with the United States' failure to enforce occupational safety and health, and workers' compensation laws in New York State. Among the specific complaints were that: (1) New York's administrative law judges issued arbitrary workers' compensation decisions; (2) the state's workers' compensation system did not make provision for translators for non-English speakers; (3) migrant workers were deprived of compensation due to their status as migrants; and (4) abuse of the workers' compensation system by employers and insurance companies led to payment delays and undercut workplace health and safety. Heenan, NAFTA/NAALC, at 20-88. The Mexican NAO issued two public reports of review, and technical consultations took place between the U.S. and Mexican NAOs. In its November 2004 report, the Mexican NAO recommended ministerial consultations. Public Report of Review, Mexico NAO Submission No. 2001-1, November 19, 2004. The Mexican Secretary of Labor made a formal request for ministerial consultations on December 7, 2004. The U.S. Department of Labor (DOL) webpage providing information on the current status of NAO submissions notes:

   > On the basis of initiatives undertaken by New York State authorities and related to the issues raised in the submission, DOL has recommended that consultations

on remaining issues or concerns be undertaken at the Council Designee or NAO level.

U.S. Dept. of Labor, Bureau of International Labor Affairs, Status of Submissions on the North American Agreement on Labor Cooperation (NAALC), available at: http://www.dol.gov/ilab/programs/nao/status.htm#iib6.

3. Interestingly, the New York Court of Appeals, that state's highest court, recently held that the U.S. Supreme Court's decision in *Hoffman Plastic*, excerpted in Chapter 1, did not preclude an undocumented worker injured at his worksite as a result of his employer's violation of state occupational health and safety laws from recovering lost wages. Balbuena v. IDR Realty LLC, et al., No. 19, 2006 N.Y. LEXIS 200 (N.Y. Ct. App. Feb. 21, 2006). Could Submission No. 2001–01 have had an indirect effect on the case?

4. Submission No. 9803, filed with the U.S. NAO, challenged the sufficiency of Quebec law in protecting freedom of association and the right to organize and bargain collectively. The submitters argued that a McDonald's franchise manipulated Quebec law in a case allegedly involving anti-union motivation in a plant closing after a labor union filed a petition to become the bargaining representative of a McDonald's restaurant's employees. Although the U.S. NAO accepted the submission, no public hearing was held and the submitters eventually withdrew the submission. Heenan, NAFTA/NAALC, at 20-74.

5. Many commentators argue that the NAALC has failed to live up to its promise. Professor Monica Schurtman, for example, highlights as a chief weakness the failure of the signatories to allow meaningful nonstate actor participation after the NAO issues its public report during the first stage of the enforcement procedure. Schurtman, Los Jonkeados, at 385-6. Professor Lance Compa chalks up the agreement's shortcomings to timidity on the part of the signatories. The governments, he notes, would rather "maintain diplomatic niceties" than address and resolve systemic violations of workers' rights. LANCE COMPA, JUSTICE FOR ALL: THE STRUGGLE FOR WORKER RIGHTS IN MEXICO: A REPORT BY THE SOLIDARITY CENTER 41 (Solidarity Center 2003), available at: http://www.solidaritycenter.org/document.cfm?documentID=346 (hereinafter Compa, Justice for All).

6. Professor Jonathan Graubart argues that disillusionment with NAALC also must be understood in light of changes in political context. He sees the Clinton-appointed NAO as supportive of the petition process, whereas the more recent Bush administration defers to the Mexican government and business interests. The other significant political change, he notes, is the rise to power of the pro-business administration of Mexican President Vicente Fox, who was elected in 2000, and appears more interested "in promoting 'flexibilization'" than forwarding a pro-worker agenda. Graubart, *New Breed*, at 139.

7. What changes, if any, should be made to increase the effectiveness of the NAALC? Professor Compa, in the 2003 Solidarity Center report cited above, recommends, among other things, the following: (1) eliminate the system of dividing the guiding principles into three categories, and allow all violations to be subject to the entire enforcement procedure; (2) require public hearings and participation in all enforcement procedure proceedings; (3) provide that an "adverse inference be

made" against any private party that refuses to participate; (4) strengthen the Secretariat's role by requiring the release of its reports; (5) provide adequate funding for the Secretariat, for ECEs and for arbitral panels; (6) create a private right of action allowing legal actions to be brought against employers in any NAFTA country; and (7) make parent or partner companies liable for violations of subsidiaries or joint ventures. Compa, Justice for All, at 33-4.

8. Experience with and criticism of the NAALC has guided the crafting of subsequent U.S. free trade agreements. For example, the 2000 bilateral trade agreement between the U.S. and Jordan contains a provision binding the signatories to enforce their respective domestic labor laws. However, unlike the NAALC, the labor provisions of the U.S.-Jordan agreement reside within the agreement itself. Moreover, in contrast to the NAALC, the agreement contains what Professor Marley Weiss has termed an "'anti-relaxation' commitment" that requires the parties to refrain from downgrading their labor laws in order to attract trade or investment. Weiss, *Two Steps*, at 713-4. Commentators Thomas B. Manley and Luis Lauredo, the latter the former U.S. Ambassador to the Organization of American States, identify as the most important innovation of the agreement the parties' undertaking to incorporate international labor standards into their domestic labor and employment law regimes. Thomas J. Manley & Ambassador Luis Lauredo, *International Labor Standards in Free Trade Agreements of the Americas*, 18 EMORY INT'L L. REV. 85, 105-6 (2004) (hereinafter Manley & Lauredo, *Free Trade Agreements*). Article 6(1) of the agreement specifically recognizes and reaffirms the parties "obligations as members of the ILO and their commitments under the ILO Declaration on Fundamental Principles and Rights at Work and its Follow-up." Agreement on the Establishment of a Free Trade Area, Oct. 24, 2000, U.S.-Jordan, 41 I.L.M. 63, art. 6(1), at 70.

9. Despite improvements over the NAALC, the Jordan agreement is criticized for, among other things, covering fewer substantive areas of labor law. As Marley Weiss notes:

> Of the NAALC's eleven areas of fundamental labor rights, the U.S.-Jordan FTA's . . . list entirely omits (1) elimination of employment discrimination on grounds such as race, religion, age, and sex; (2) equal pay for men and women; and (3) protection of migrant workers. It fails to expressly include the right to strike . . .
>
> Weiss, *Two Steps*, at 715.

Those studying labor rights provisions in trade agreements will notice variation in the labor rights enumerated in different agreements.

10. Advances in the labor rights provisions of the U.S.-Jordan FTA did not prevent horrendous workplace conditions from flourishing in Jordan's Qualified Industrialized Zones (QIZs), which house factories that produce garments for American retailers such as Wal-Mart and Target. The National Labor Committee, an advocacy group based in New York, recently produced a report detailing substandard working conditions in more than twenty-five of Jordan's over one hundred garment factories. Steven Greenhouse & Michael Barbaro, *An Ugly Side of Free Trade: Sweatshops in Jordan*, N.Y. TIMES, May 3, 2006, at C1. Yet a little over a month after the report became public, Jordan's trade minister "promised tough and immediate action"

by his government against employers responsible for exploitive conditions. Commentators posit that Jordan's speedy response was in part calculated to prevent the United States from imposing trade sanctions under the U.S.-Jordan FTA. Gary G. Yerkey, *Jordan Vows to Curb Abuse of Workers, as Required Under Free Trade Pact With U.S.*, INTERNATIONAL TRADE REPORTER, June 22, 2006, at 962. Actions taken by the Jordanian government include: compilation by the Ministry of Labor of a report on conditions in the QIZs; meetings with representatives of the 114 companies operating in the QIZs; meetings with U.S. officials; and development of a plan to freeze the entry of guest workers into Jordan until the problems are resolved. *Id.*

11. In August 2004, the U.S. signed the Central America – Dominican Republic Free Trade Agreement (CAFTA-DR). In addition to the United States and the Dominican Republic, a Caribbean island nation, the signatories to the agreement are Costa Rica, El Salvador, Guatemala, Honduras, and Nicaragua. Implementing legislation passed Congress in June and July 2005, and was signed by President George W. Bush in August 2005. Statement of USTR Rob Portman Regarding Entry Into Force of the U.S. – Central America – Dominican Republic Free Trade Agreement (CAFTA-DR) for El Salvador, Office of the United States Trade Representative, February 24, 2006, available at http://www.ustr.gov/Document_Library/Press_Releases/2006/February/Statement_of_USTR_Rob_Portman_Regarding_Entry_Into_Force_of_the_US_-_Central_America_-_Dominican_Republic_Free_Trade_Agreement_printer.html.

12. CAFTA-DR's labor provisions reside within the agreement in Chapter 16. Article 16.8 defines "labor laws" as "a Party's statutes or regulations. . . . that are directly related to the following internationally recognized labor rights":

   (a) the right of association;
   (b) the right to organize and bargain collectively;
   (c) a prohibition on the use of any form of forced or compulsory labor;
   (d) a minimum age for the employment of children and the prohibition and elimination of the worst forms of child labor; and
   (e) acceptable conditions of work with respect to minimum wages, hours of work, and occupational safety and health.

   Dominican Republic – Central America – United States Free Trade Agreement, art 16.8, available at: http://www.ustr.gov/Trade_Agreements/Bilateral/CAFTA/CAFTA-DR_Final_Texts/Section_Index.html. Compare this listing with the NAALC's eleven labor principles. Have any important subjects been omitted in CAFTA-DR's labor chapter?

13. CAFTA-DR's Article 16.2 notes that a "Party shall not fail to effectively enforce its labor laws, through a sustained or recurring course of action or inaction, in a matter affecting trade between the parties. . . . " *Id.* at Art. 16.2 (1)(a). Could it be that to establish a violation of the agreement one needs to demonstrate both a systemic disregard of domestic labor law and the impact of that regulatory indifference on trade? Referring to similar language in the U.S.-Jordan agreement, Professors Michael Trebilcock and Robert Howse note "[t]he rather odd language . . . appears to be some sort of qualifier, suggesting that labor obligations only apply in sectors or situations where there is actual trade between [the parties]." Trebilcock &

Howse, *Trade Policy*, at 299. CAFTA-DR's Article 16.2 also provides that a party is in compliance with the agreement "where a course of action or inaction reflects a reasonable exercise of . . . discretion, or results from a *bona fide* decision regarding the allocation of resources." CAFTA-DR, Article 16.2 (1)(b). If interpreted broadly, could this exception clause undo the obligation the parties have undertaken to enforce their respective labor laws? Keep in mind that Article 49 of the NAALC contains similar text.

14. The U.S. Omnibus Trade and Competitiveness Act (OTCA) was amended in 1988 to provide for Congressional "fast track" approval of trade agreements. So long as several negotiating objectives were met, Congress was bound to vote either up or down on a trade agreement. Amendment to the agreement was not possible and congressional debate limited. NAFTA and the NAALC were negotiated and approved in this fashion. Fast track authority, however, expired in 1994. Hepple, Labour Laws, at 115.

15. The current version of fast track authority, known as trade promotion authority, is contained in the Bipartisan Trade Promotion Authority Act of 2002 (BTPAA), which provides a series of objectives that must be met on labor and other matters. Trade Act of 2002, Pub. L. No. 107-210, 116 Stat. 933 (codified in sections of 19 U.S.C.). As Sir Bob Hepple notes, "[f]ast track treatment is conditional upon the FTA 'making progress in meeting the applicable objectives.'" Hepple, Labour Laws, at 115 (quoting 19 USC §3803 (b)(2)). The criteria for trade promotion authority include: (1) incorporating the labor rights clause into the body of the agreement; (2) embodying an obligation to enforce domestic labor laws; (3) requiring the parties to "strive to ensure" that domestic law complies with international standards; (4) containing a labor law antirelaxation commitment that guards against a so-called race to the bottom; (5) promoting ratification of the ILO's Convention No. 182, the Worst Forms of Child Labor, and (6) maintaining parity in enforcement procedures and remedies between labor and other rights and obligations in the agreement. Weiss, *Two Steps*, at 719. These objectives influence the shape of the labor provisions in U.S. trade agreements.

16. The criteria in the BTPAA also bind U.S. negotiators attempting to negotiate an agreement on the Free Trade Area of the Americas ("FTAA"), a proposed thirty-four-country hemispheric agreement that would cover "a market of 700 million people, fourteen percent of the planet, and thirty-one percent of the world's wealth." Manley & Lauredo, Free Trade Agreements, at 96. Negotiation of the agreement, which was slated for creation by 2005, has been difficult and controversial. Brazil, in particular, which leads the South American Mercosur customs union, remains ambivalent about the agreement and is opposed to including extensive labor and environmental provisions. Manley & Lauredo, supra, at 100-01. Popular sentiment in a number of Latin American countries is staunchly resistant to the agreement. Mass protests were triggered by the November 2005 Summit of the Americas, a two-day meeting of the leaders of the thirty-four countries that would be parties to the agreement. The summit was held in Mar del Plata Argentina. Larry Rohter & Elisabeth Bumiller, *Protesters Riot as Bush Attends 34-Nation Talks*, N.Y. TIMES, Nov. 5, 2005, at A1.

7 The European Union

A. GENERAL OVERVIEW[1,2]

1. EU: Growing Number of Member States

Since its beginning, what has become the European Union has been expanding geographically but also conceptually from what was strictly a regional international organization of limited scope made up of independent nations toward something that has some aspects of sovereignty that in some senses makes it a government independent of its Member States. The Treaty of Amsterdam of 1997 marks that change with the language describing the EU as "an ever closer union among the peoples of Europe, where decisions are taken as closely as possible to the citizen." That replaces the language – "Union with a federal goal" – used only five years earlier in the Maastricht Treaty. That movement toward

---

[1] See: BLANPAIN R., EUROPEAN LABOUR LAW, 10th and revised ed., Kluwer Law International, (2006) and the selected bibliography and cases it contains.

[2] Web Sites: The Institutions of the European Union

Committee of the Regions
website: *http://www.cor.eu.int/*
Council of the European Union
website: *http://ue.eu.int/en/summ.htm*
Court of Auditors
website: *http://www.eca.eu.int/*
Court of Justice
website: *http://curia.eu.int/en/index.htm*
Economic and Social Committee
website: *http://www.ces.eu.int/*
European Agency for Safety and Health at Work
website: *http://europe.osha.eu.int/*
European Central Bank (ECB)
website: *http://www.ecb.int/*
European Commission
website: *http://europa.eu.int/comm/index en. htm*
Directorate-General competent for employment and social policy:
http://www.europa.eu.int/comm/dg05/index en.htm
European Parliament
website: *http://europarl.eu.int/*

European Council
website: *http://ue.eu.int/en/info/eurocouncil/*
European Foundation for the Improvement of Living and Working Conditions
website: *http://www.eurofound.ie/*
European Investment Bank
website: *http://eib.eu.int*
European Training Foundation
website: *http://www.etf.eu.int/*
The European Centre for the Development of Vocational Training (CEDEFOP)
website: *http://www.cedefop.gr/*
Ombudsman
website: *http://www.euro-ombudsman.eu.int/*
European Social Partners ETUC (European Trade Union Confederation)
website: *http://www.etuc.org/*
CEEP (European Centre of Enterprises with Public Participation and of Enterprises of General Economic Interest)
website: *http://www.ceep.org/ceep.htm*
UNICE (Union of Industrial and Employers' Confederations of Europe)
website: *http://www.unice.org/unice/*

further union is now on pause because by referenda the French and Dutch people voted against the ratification of the proposed EU Constitution, which was designed to simplify the Treaties underlying the EU. Although eleven states had ratified the Constitution by the time of the vote in France and the Netherlands, the rejection by the two in 2005 has resulted in the establishment of a "period of reflection" about the future. That period was recently extended until mid-2007.

The European Union has, since its beginning in 1957, been engaged in an ongoing process of geographic enlargement. The first six founding members were: Belgium, France, Germany, Italy, Luxemburg and the Netherlands. The EU then had five enlargements: (1973) Denmark, Ireland, and the United Kingdom; (1981) Greece; (1986) Portugal and Spain; (1995) Austria, Finland, and Sweden; (2004), Cyprus, the Czech Republic, Estonia, Hungary, Latvia, Lithuania, Malta, Poland, the Slovak Republic, and Slovenia. With ten new members joining in 2004, there are now twenty-five Member States in the EU. Bulagaria and Romania will join in 2007. Other countries, including states that emerged from the breakup of Yugoslavia as well as Turkey, are seeking membership.

2. Population

The population of the twenty-five EU countries now stands at more than 454 million. Twelve Member States are in the European Monetary Union, which uses the EURO as a common currency. The ten new member states represent almost 16 percent of the total population (74.2 million). This compares with over 300 million for the United States, 126 million for Japan, 1.1 billion for India, and 1.3 billion for China. When Bulgaria and Romania join in 2007, the population of the EU will be close to five hundred million inhabitants. Turkey is presently negotiating to join; it has a population of some seventy million.

3. Objectives: A Common Market, High Level of Employment

The Union has the following four objectives, with the first the most significant for the purposes of this course:

- to promote **economic and social progress and a high level of employment** which is balanced and sustainable, in particular through the creation of an area without internal frontiers, through the strengthening of economic and social cohesion and through the establishment of an economic and monetary union, ultimately including a single currency;
- to assert its identity on the international scene, in particular through the implementation of a **common foreign and security policy** including the eventual framing of a common defence policy, which might in time lead to a common defence;
- to strengthen the protection of the rights and interests of the nationals of its Member States through the **introduction of a citizenship of the Union;**
- to develop a **close cooperation on justice and home affairs** (Article 2 Treaty European Union).

4. Employment

In 2004, 63.6 percent of the working-age population (fifteen to sixty-four years of age) held a job or were engaged other business activity in the EU-25, compared to 63.1 percent one year before. The figures reveal a significant increase in female employment rate, from 55.1 percent in 2003 to 56.1 percent in 2004, whereas the male employment rate stayed unchanged at 71.1 percent.

5. The Institutions and their Competences

The European Communities have a number of common institutions of which the most important are the European Parliament (EP), the Council, the Commission, and the European Court of Justice (ECJ).

a. *The European Parliament*

As the only EU institution directly elected by the citizens of the Member States, the European Parliament's legislative role is slowly expanding. The Treaty of Amsterdam (1997) strengthened the role of the EP through a complex co-decision procedure together with the Council. That role has been extended to quite a number of areas, for example, regarding incentive measures concerning employment, the application of the principle of equal opportunities and equal treatment of men and women in matters of employment and occupation. More than 60 percent of all legislative proposals enacted by the Council of Ministers must proceed through the co-decision process with the Parliament.

Although not empowered to act generally as the principal legislative body of the EU, the EP does have the power to approve the EU budget. It may, acting on the majority of its members and two-thirds of the votes cast, reject the draft budget and ask for the submission of a new draft. The EP also has the power to take a vote of no confidence in the Commission.

Except where otherwise provided in the Treaty, the EP acts by an absolute majority of votes.

b. *The Council*

The Council of the European Communities is undoubtedly the most important European institution because the Council, not the European Parliament, is the principal European legislator.

The Council consists of representatives sent by the national governments of each of the Member States. Which member attends at a given Council meeting depends on the meeting's agenda. If, for example, the Social Council meets, the cabinet members competent for these affairs, for example, the Ministers of Employment of each of the Member States, will attend. The Social Council is one of the so-called sectoral or specialised councils. If general points are on the agenda, the Ministers of Foreign Affairs will meet in the General Council. The European Council is the Council of Heads of Governments and Prime Ministers. The fact that its members are actually leaders of the national governments of the Member States is an important feature that maintains the EU as a supranational organization of nations and not itself a government.

The most important tasks of the Council relating to labor law include the organisation of the free movement for workers (Articles 39–42 EC Treaty); the approximation of labor laws (Articles 94–96 EC Treaty); the elaboration of a social policy (Articles 130–45 EC Treaty); the implementation of decisions regarding the Social Fund (Article 148 EC Treaty); the development of quality education and vocational training (Articles 149–50

EC Treaty); the promotion of a stronger economic and social cohesion (Articles 158–62); and the implementation of the Social Charter (1989).

If action by the Community should prove necessary in order to attain one of the objectives of the Community and the Treaty does not provide the necessary powers, the Council can, acting unanimously on a proposal from the Commission and after consultation with the EP, take appropriate measures.

The Council acts by absolute majority, qualified majority or unanimity of the Member States. Absolute majority is the general rule – Article 250(1) of the EC Treaty provides: "unless otherwise provided in this Treaty, the Council shall act by a majority of its members." In practice, however, this general rule is the exception because a qualified majority is necessary for the enactment of most employment-related legislation. The qualified majority system is complicated because each Member State receives a number of votes, weighted by population, so that a proposal needs 232 of the 321 total votes in order to be enacted. Given that it is the Member States that vote, the decisive legislative action of the EU is by the action of Member States through representatives from each of the national governments that are EU members.

c. *The Commission*

The Commission is, in contrast to the Council that is tied to the governments of the Member States, European *par excellence*. In conformity with Article 213(2) of the EC Treaty "the members must, in the general interest of the Communities, be completely independent in the performance of their duties." They may neither seek nor take instructions from any government or from any other body. Each Member State has the obligation not to influence the members of the Commission. The Commission is, however, as already indicated, accountable to and can be dismissed collectively by the EP.

The Commission enjoys the right of initiative regarding European legislation. Without it initiating a proposal, nothing can happen. Although the Council lacks initiative as to legislation, which resides in the Commission, the Council is the body that enacts the EU legislation.

d. *The European Court of Justice*

The Court, made up of fifteen judges, "ensures that in the interpretation and application of this Treaty the law is observed." The Court is competent to judge whether Member States live up to their duties under the Treaties (Articles 226–27 EC Treaty) and to review the legality of the acts of the Council and of the Commission (Articles 230–31 EC Treaty). The Court is also empowered to decide preliminary rulings concerning the interpretation of Community law when requested to do so by courts or judges of the national courts of all the Member States.

B. THE LEGISLATIVE PROCESS

1. Community Law

Community law distinguishes primary law, on the one hand, and secondary law, on the other. Primary law consists of the legal norms that are contained in the Treaties and accessory documents such as the protocols and accession treaties. Secondary law concerns the legal norms that derive from the primary law and that are contained in the decisions taken by the European institutions pursuant to the powers that the Treaties have conferred on them.

Also part of Community law are the norms that are made by some of the subjects of the Communities themselves if done pursuant to the EC Treaty. Collective agreements are one example of norms that can be concluded to implement of Article 139 of the EC Treaty: "Should management and labour so desire, the dialogue between them at Community level may lead to contractual relations, including agreements."

The general principles common to the laws of the Member States are also part of Community law. These are principles relating to equal treatment, respect for acquired rights, and the like. It is also through this channel that fundamental human rights prevail in Community law.

In this, context Article 6 (2) of the EU Treaty is of the greatest importance. It reads:

> The Union shall respect fundamental rights, as guaranteed by the European Convention for the Protection of Human Rights and Fundamental Freedoms signed in Rome on 4 November 1950 and as they result from the constitutional traditions common to the Member States, as general principles of Community law.

Although respect for fundamental rights that form an integral part of those general principles of law is a condition of the legality of Community Acts, those rights cannot in themselves have the effect of extending the scope of the Treaty provisions beyond the competences of the Community.[3]

2. Secondary Law

In order to enact secondary law, the Council and the Commission can, in accordance with the provisions of the Treaties, take five kinds of measures. Three of them are legally binding, namely the regulation, the directive, and the decision. Recommendations and opinions are not legally binding.

a. *Regulations*

A regulation "shall have general application. It shall be binding in its entirety and directly applicable in all Member States" (Article 249(2) EC Treaty). A regulation is clearly a generally binding norm, like an Act of Parliament. It is immediately and directly binding without any specific action required of the national authorities. A regulation is also directly binding on behalf of citizens, who may invoke it before judges in their national courts. Consequently, regulations supersede national law. National law that is contrary to regulations is null and void and may not be applied. Regulations are published in the Official Journal and enter into force on the date specified or, in the absence thereof, on the twentieth day following their publication (Article 254(1) TEC).

b. *Directives*

A directive is binding upon each Member State to which it is addressed as to the result to be achieved but leaves to the national authorities the choice of form and method (Article

---

[3] C.O.J., 17 February 1998, *L.J. Grant/South West Trains Ltd*, C-249/96, ECR, 1998, 621.

249(3) EC Treaty). A directive is thus, in comparison to a regulation, a much more flexible measure, which leaves it up to the national authorities to translate it into national law in the most appropriate way. Only the result counts.

Compliance can be obtained by an act of the legislature of the Member States, but other ways are also possible. Thus, in some Member States, collective bargaining agreements between unions and employers can be rendered obligatory by a governmental decree and may cover the private sector of the economy as a whole. The extension of collective agreements is possible in quite a number of Member States, including Belgium, France, Germany, and the Netherlands. In Belgium, EU Directive No. 77/187 of 14 February 1977, regarding the transfer of enterprises, was subject to a nationwide collective agreement, No. 32*bis*, which was concluded by the National Labour Council in June 1985 and extended by Royal Decree. According to Belgian law, this means that the normative part of the collective agreement becomes legally binding for all private employers and their employees and was a part of imperative law, which can be enforced through the criminal laws.

In a case arising in Italy, the European Court of Justice decreed that, although it is true that the Member States may leave the implementation of the social policy objectives pursued by a Directive in the first instance to management and labor, this possibility does not discharge them from the obligation of ensuring that all workers in the Community are afforded the full protection provided for in the Directive. The Member State must guarantee that all cases where effective protection is not ensured by other means it is nevertheless provided. Thus, Member States must take additional measures to transpose a Directive when collective agreements only cover specific economic sectors and, because of their contractual nature, create obligations only between members of the trade union in question and employers or undertakings bound by the agreements.[4]

The directive on European Works Councils of 22 September 1994 was partly transposed into the national laws of Belgium and Norway by way of collective agreement. Whether this fundamentally transnational directive could be transposed by way of a collective agreement, in lieu of an Act of Parliament by each Member State, is a matter for discussion.

In fact, directives are published in the Official Journal. The directive indicates the date by which Member States must implement the measures necessary to comply with its provisions. The Member States must inform the Commission that they have done so. If a Member State does not comply in due time, the Commission may bring the matter before the Court. The Court can declare by judgment that, by failing to adopt within the prescribed time period the measures necessary to comply with a directive, a Member State has not fulfilled its obligations under the Treaty. If the Court of Justice finds that a Member State has failed to fulfill an obligation under the EC Treaty, the state is required to take the necessary measures to comply with the judgment of the Court of Justice. If the Commission considers that the Member State concerned has not taken such measures, it shall, after giving that State the opportunity to submit its observations, issue a reasoned opinion specifying the points on which the Member State concerned has not complied with the judgment of the Court of Justice. If the Member State concerned fails to take the necessary measures to comply with the Court's judgment within the time limit laid down by the Commission, the latter may bring the case before the Court of

---

[4] C.O.J., 10 July 1986, No. 235/84, ECR, 1986, 2291.

Justice. In so doing it shall specify the amount of the lump sum or penalty payment to be paid by the Member State concerned, which it considers appropriate in the circumstances. If the Court of Justice finds that the Member State concerned has not complied with its judgment it may impose a lump sum or penalty payment on it (Article 228 EC Treaty).

Directives that contain clear obligations have a direct, binding effect and can be invoked by a citizen against a Member State that does not sufficiently comply by adopting the measures necessary to transpose it into national law. In this situation, a citizen may invoke a directive before a national judge. The Court decided in a landmark judgment that in case of failure by a Member State to transpose a directive, *in casu* relating to the protection of employees in the event of the insolvency of the employer, "interested parties may not assert those rights against the State in proceedings before the national court in the absence of implementing measures adopted within the prescribed period". A Member State is, however, obliged to make good the damage suffered by individuals as a result of the failure to implement the directive.[5]

c. *Decisions*

Like a regulation, a decision is binding in its entirety upon those to whom it is addressed (Article 249 EC Treaty). Decisions can be addressed to natural persons or to legal persons. A decision is not a general norm but is directed to certain specific persons. Decisions, which are addressed to Member States, can have a binding effect on the individual, who can invoke the decision before a judge. Decisions are notified to those to whom they are addressed and take effect on such notification. Some decisions are also published in the Official Journal, although this is not legally obligatory.

d. *Recommendations and Opinions*

Opinions and recommendations have no binding force (Article 249 EC Treaty). Likewise, resolutions and solemn declarations, like that of the Basic Social Rights of Workers, adopted in 1989 in Strasbourg by eleven Member States, are not legally binding. They only contain political commitments. However, because recommendations cannot be regarded as having no legal effect at all, the national courts are bound to take them into consideration in order to decide disputes submitted to them, in particular when they cast light on the interpretation of national measures adopted in order to implement them or when they are designed to supplement binding Community decisions.[6]

C. THE SOCIAL PARTNERS

1. The Employers' Organisations

At the European level, various employers' organisations are active. In addition to UNICE (Union of Industrial and Employers' Confederations of Europe), which has as members

---

[5] C.O.J., 19 November 1991, A. *Francovich and D. Others* v. *Italian Republic*, Nos. C-6/90 and C-9/90; ECR, 1991, 5357.
[6] C.O.J., 13 December 1989, S. *Grimaldi* v. *Fonds des Maladies Professionnelles*, No. 322/88, ECR, 1989, 4407.

thirty-nine central federations of industry from thirty-three countries and groups of national confederations of employers' organizations, for example, the British CBI or the French MEDEF, there are specific organizations for agriculture, namely COPA (*Comité des Organisations Agricoles*), and for enterprises that are active in the public sector, namely CEEP (*Centre Européen des Entreprises Publiques*).

A serious question about the representativeness of those three employers' organizations had been raised by a group, the European Association of Craft, Small and Medium-Sized Enterprises (UEAPME). Although it had been initially consulted by the Commission and had asked to participate in the negotiations for the development of the Parental Leave Directive, the "big three" refused to allow UEAPME to join the negotiations. The European Court of Justice rejected a challenge to the directive based on the failure to allow UEAPME a seat at the negotiations in *UEAPME v. Council*, T-135/96 (1996). UEAPME claimed its member organizations represented eleven million businesses, employing over fifty million people and further that SMEs employ more than 70 percent of the working population in Europe and have been the main generator of new employment in the EU. The basis for rejecting the challenge was that UNICE did include in its membership some small and medium-sized enterprises and so was representative of the full range of the employers. Following the decision of the Court, the presidents of UNICE and UEAPME agreed to strengthen their collaboration by signing a cooperation agreement, with UNICE pledging to consult UEAPME before taking any positions in the dialogue among the social partners. Furthermore, in 2001, UEAPME and the European Trade Union Confederation signed a joint declaration supporting the social dialogue.

2. The Trade Unions

The most important European trade union is the European Trade Union Confederation (ETUC). It has its headquarters in Brussels near most European institutions, which it tries to influence to the utmost. In the same building, one finds the International Confederation of Free Trade Unions (ICFTU), with which the ETUC, whose group is also affiliated to the World Confederation of Labour (WCL), has close ties. The ETUC was created in 1973 and presently represents some sixty million members, who belong to seventy-four national trade unions from thirty-four countries.

The ETUC is a united, yet pluralist, organization that determines its policies through the deliberations of its Congress and its Executive Committee. The Congress meets once every four years.

D. COMPETENCE OF THE EU REGARDING SOCIAL POLICIES: IN SEARCH OF A EUROPEAN SOCIAL MODEL (ESM) – A DREAM?

Europeans do boast about a European Social Model, which they claim is superior to the U.S. social model of free market economics with comparatively few regulatory controls on employment and a minimal social security net. The claimed European Social Model is characterized by fundamental social rights, solidarity, involvement of the social partners and workers' participation, whereas individualism, profit seeking, and shareholder value dominate the American model.

An ESM seems to be taken for granted. What do we mean when we claim the existence of an ESM? What is "the" ESM? Is there one model or are there more models? Is the ESM a dream, a wish or a reality or both? Three elements make up an ESM:

1. *Model.* A model is a way of doing things, of organizing, of how a given problem is solved. In order to have a model, you need a *vision* of what you want, what values, goals and objectives you want to realize. You also need *competence*: The power to make the necessary decisions, so you can organise, solve problems, lay down rules, legislation, create institutions, control the outcome, judge its effectiveness, and the like. You need *material* power (*ratione materiae*) as well as *formal* power (the way how to reach decisions). Finally, *actors* are needed: Those who will implement the vision, utilizing the available power.

2. *Social* What is meant by "social"? Is "social" given a broad or a narrow interpretation? In a *material* sense, social would include the relations involving work and employment and thus would embrace employers, employees, and civil servants, voluntary work included. Social also includes social security in the broadest sense, not only for workers but also for those who do not work. It includes housing, education, and so on, as laid down by the formulation of fundamental social rights that were adopted in Nice (December 2000). Social also implies a *democratic* Europe. Social in the *formal* sense, refers to the actors, the State, but especially to the social partners and NGOs, as well as employers, employees, works councils, shop stewards, committees of hygiene, and the like.

3. *Europe* as an element, relates to its geographical dimension and as a level of decision making in relation to other levels. Do we mean the EU, the European Economic Association, the Council of Europe, or an even wider Europe? Do we also mean an ESM that would be common to various Member States or common to the regions within the EU?

Summarizing, the question is whether the EU has a vision, competence, and power as well as involvement of social actors of such scope and nature that one can speak of one ore more European Social Models?

1. Vision

There are certainly clear European social vision, ambition, and goals. These are, among others, laid down in Article 136 TEC, which include promotion of employment; improved living and working conditions; harmonization while improvement is being maintained; proper social protection; dialogue between management and labor; the development of human resources with a view to lasting employment; and combating social exclusion. This all sounds great; the social sky seems the limit.

There are also fundamental social rights formulated in the Treaty, for example, equality and free movement of labor. These rights are also promulgated in the Community Charter of Fundamental Social Rights of Workers (1989) and in the Charter of Fundamental Rights of the European Union (7 December 2000). These Charters are, however, only political declarations, although some of the rights they contain may be made legally binding, according to Article 6 of the TEU, be it only vertically (to be respected by the European institutions and the Member States, when drafting or implementing legislation) and not horizontally between, for example, private employers and their employees.

In 2000, the European Council adopted the Lisbon Strategy to deal with the low productivity and stagnation of economic growth in the EU and to do that through the formulation of various policy initiatives to be taken by each EU Member State but to be coordinated by the EU. The strategic objectives set out by the Lisbon strategy were to be attained by 2010. It broadly aims at making "the EU the world's most dynamic and competitive economy" by the 2010 deadline. This is to be achieved by transforming Europe into the world's largest knowledge-based economy. By November 2004, the European Council acknowledged that progress in implementation had been disappointing and that efforts should be redoubled, with particular emphasis on developing Europe as the "knowledge society," strengthening the internal market of the EU, improving the business climate, especially for start-up businesses, and strengthening the labor market by developing further lifelong learning and "active ageing."

The "social vision," however, comes in second place as far as objectives of the EU are concerned. In first place, both legally and politically, is the European Monetary Union with its goal of noninflationary growth. Following the Maastricht and Amsterdam treaties, the objective of a noninflationary economy is the primary objective of the EC, at least within the twelve members of the European Monetary Union. The European Central Bank guards against inflation by setting interest rates. In the face of the threat of inflation, the interest rate is to be increased, which means businesses, particularly small and medium-sized enterprises that are dependent on borrowed money, have to reduce or cease their activities. That contributes to higher unemployment. Member States participating in the EMU are required to commit to low inflation controls on public expenses to keep deficits under control. This means there is less money for infrastructure, education, culture, research, and social policies, including health and pensions. Furthermore, in the larger framework of the global economy, shareholders' value is accorded primary place. With the interest of shareholders, being the only goal companies are required to pursue, the interests of employees and consumers take on only a secondary significance. To maximize shareholders' value, companies must constantly rationalize, right size, and get labor costs down, because if not, the shares will go down or someone will take the company over.

So, the social vision of Europe is at best a secondary priority, because it is in the grip of the EMU and shareholders' value and is not bolstered by enforceable fundamental social rights that are horizontally binding.

2. Competence

Does the EU have sufficient competence to develop a full-fledged European social policy? In answering this question, one needs to recall that the EU has only the competences that are transferred by the Member States to the EU and that these competences have to be exercised in the way indicated in the Treaty.

On this point, the ESM is extremely weak. Indeed, important social "core" issues are *excluded* from the EU competence including setting wages and salaries, the right of association, the right to strike and the right to impose lockouts (Art. 137, 6 TEC). For other important matters, *unanimity* in the Council is needed. Those issues include social security and social protection of workers; job security; representation; and collective defence of interests, including co-determination (Art. 137, 3 TEC). *Unanimity* between twenty-five Member States seems almost impossible.

The following issues can be decided by qualified majority voting of the Council: health and safety, working conditions, information and consultation, equal treatment, integration, and excluded persons.

The Treaty of Nice made *qualified majority voting* even more difficult to reach. There is no doubt that "the absurdly complex voting system, enshrined in the Treaty of Nice threatens democracy, efficiency and enlargement."[7] On top of weighted votes, two more requirements were added in Nice for a positive decision: a simple majority of Member States and at least 62 percent of the EU population. The weighted votes are the worst cause of eventual decision-making paralysis. Nice gives the bigger Member States more votes to compensate for the accession of many smaller states. The qualified threshold for passage rises to 74 percent of the votes. The twelve smallest states can form a blocking minority and so can three of the biggest states.

Thus, the competence to undertake a true European Social Model is almost non-existent. Furthermore, this will be a permanent feature, as the Treaty can only be changed by way of unanimity, which will, as far as social policies are concerned, likely prove to be impossible.

Obviously, there are other ways of convergence in the social field, like the so-called enhanced co-ordination strategy enunciated at Lisbon, as shown in the case of the employment guidelines, which lead to National Action Plans and to peer pressure for Member States to conform to the guidelines. This strategy, which is important, could be used in other fields. But this does not take away that the EU is incompetent to enact binding measures on core issues such as a European minimum wage, to make binding a collective wage agreement at EU level; that regarding core issues such as social security, job security, collective bargaining, and others, for which unanimity is required, binding European measures are absolutely unlikely.

The conclusion is clear: the EU lacks the essential competences, which are needed to organise and establish a full-fledged ESM. Even worse is the fact that the political will is lacking to integrate socially further and that, the more countries become member of the EU, the more difficult it will be to muster such a political will.

3. The Actors

The main actors, engaged in elaborating social policies are the institutions of the EU and the EU Social Partners. At the EU level, there is increased reliance on the advice and consultation with the social partners in various tripartite dealings.

Central in this stands the *European social dialogue*, at intersectoral and sectoral levels, which leads to agreements, eventually rendered binding by way of European directive or to voluntary guidelines, codes of conduct, and the like. This social dialogue constitutes an essential feature in the establishment of an ESM. But, again, there are fundamental flaws. First, "European competence" is lacking. The social partners can obviously dialogue and conclude agreements at whatever level and on whatever issue they want. One has to say, however, that there is a lot of "contact" between the social partners but not so much "contract." In fact, there are few agreements at the European level. Moreover, agreements can only get an official sanction and be made legally binding according to the competence rules of the EU, where qualified majority or unanimity in the Council is required. Thus, for example, agreements on pay cannot be rendered legally binding.

---

[7] Peel Q.? *Europe's guaranteed gridlock*, F.T., July 9, 2001.

Second, there are marked weaknesses in the social dialogue process. The power relationship between the social partners at European level is almost nonexistent. Indeed, the trade unions have no "market power" at the EU level. They have only political clout in the sense that, if no agreement is reached, the European Commission can initiate legislation. Although there is talk of bargaining under the sword of Damocles, even this seems to be a thing of the past, as the European Commission has recently indicated that if the partners cannot agree the Commission will not initiate legislation on the topic.

Moreover, the trade unions as well as the EU employers associations have become more and more internally divided about the merits of bargaining at European level. For example, Scandinavian and German unions, which are comparatively strong at their national levels, are less and less willing to pass their power to the ETUC and want to do their own bargaining at the national level. On the employer side, UNICE now wants to conclude only *voluntary* agreements, such as in the cases of telework (2002) and stress-related work (2004).

Underlying it all is the fact that the social partners have no grip on the globalized economy: they paddle in empty air. Because of the consequences of the new information economy, globalization, and the changing nature of the work force, unions have lost members. That both reduces their representativeness and their mandate to act at the European level.[8] The fact is that the majority of workers are not represented at the EU level.

To this has to be added that many trade unions show a consistent democratic deficit. Except for the United Kingdom, rank-and-file members do not vote for the leadership of their trade unions. Self-appointed minorities control the trade union organisations, which first think about their own power and only in the second place the interests of the members. Trade unions need to become more democratic institutions.

There is no doubt that the role of the European Parliament has to be fortified, especially in the areas covered by the social dialogue, where agreements are extended by way of a directive.

To this should be added that there remains a problem with the notion of social partners as the UEAPME (SME's organization) case demonstrates. At present, only the ETUC, UNICE, and CEEP are considered to be *the* social partners, which constitute the club of negotiators. This has to be corrected. It is evident that all the national organizations of employers and workers, which are recognized as representative at national level, should be fully involved.

There is also the fact that the collective agreements concluded at European level reveal a doubtful craftsmanship, so that there is, as the directives regarding European Works Councils, the Societas Europaea (European-wide corporations) amply demonstrate, no real impact on managerial decision making. Most important, the question of when employees have to be informed in case of significant restructurings remains open. Thus, a lot needs to be improved in order to strengthen the social dialogue at the EU level. But the political will is lacking and market forces are not moving in the direction of more employee input. Social partners are involved, but have less and less impact on "real decision making."

Summarizing, there is no doubt that the EU has made a major contribution on a number of important social issues like equal treatment, free movement of labor, health

[8] For the employers' associations, see Hornung-Draus, R., *Between e-economy, Euro and enlargement: Where are employer organisations in Europe heading?* June 2001, *www.iira2001.org.*

and safety, and restructuring, but, by and large, one cannot say that there is a ESM. The greatest flaws are the lack of competence and the fact that there is no political will to increase the EU social competences.

The consequence of the lack of an ESM is that there is not really a European Labor Law System; instead, there are various national systems. Labor law in Europe remains mainly a national affair and this is going to stay so. These national systems diverge considerably. Of course, there are some common fundamental principles between the Member States, for example, trade union freedom, the right to collective bargaining, equal treatment, no child labor, and no forced labor, but these are universal values, embodied in the ILO standards, even in the absence of the existence of the EU.

Various national systems can be discerned, for example, corporatists systems versus shareholders values systems and the like. It is evident that the British and the German systems, to give one example, are oceans apart from each other. Divergence between Member States seems to be growing.

The overall conclusion is that there is no ESM, neither at European nor at national levels. For those, who believe in and hope for an ESM, the answer is clear: continue to push for more European competence and for more social democracy, involvement of the EP, and more binding fundamental social rights.

The road seems long, the path steep and narrow. Miracles are called for. Sometimes dreams come through.

E. INDIVIDUAL EMPLOYMENT LAW

1. Free Movement of Workers

The free movement of persons in general and for workers in particular is one of the cornerstones of the EC. Pursuant to Article 3 of the EC Treaty, the activities of the Community include: "an internal market characterised by the abolition, as between Member States, of obstacles to the free movement of goods, persons, services and capital" (the so-called four fundamental freedoms). Freedom of movement is a fundamental right of workers and their families but it is limited to the purpose of performing economic activity. "Mobility of labour is looked upon as one of the means by which the worker is guaranteed the possibility of improving his living and working conditions and promoting his social advancement, while helping to satisfy the requirements of the economies of the Member States." Regulation No. 1612/68, 15 October 1969.

This important dimension of EU law must be contrasted with the other regional international organization studied in this book, the labor side accord to NAFTA. With claims of a crisis in North America, particularly in the United States over illegal migration from Mexico, it is important to emphasize the unifying effect the free movement of workers has had in the development of the EU. Article 39 establishes the free movement principle:

Article 39 (ex Article 48)

1. Freedom of movement for workers shall be secured within the Community.
2. Such freedom of movement shall entail the abolition of any discrimination based on nationality between workers of the Member States as regards employment, remuneration and other conditions of work and employment.

3. It shall entail the right, subject to limitations justified on grounds of public policy, public security or public health:

    (a) to accept offers of employment actually made;

    (b) to move freely within the territory of Member States for this purpose;

    (c) to stay in a Member State for the purpose of employment in accordance with the provisions governing the employment of nationals of that State laid down by law, regulation or administrative action;

    (d) to remain in the territory of a Member State after having been employed in that State, subject to conditions which shall be embodied in implementing regulations to be drawn up by the Commission.

4. The provisions of this Article shall not apply to employment in the public service.

URBSFA V. BOSMAN

Case C-415/93, ECR, 1995, 4921

[Mr. Bosman, a professional footballer of Belgian nationality, was employed from 1988 by RC Liège, a Belgian first division soccer club, under a contract expiring on 30 June 1990, which assured him an average monthly salary of BEF 120,000,[9] including bonuses. On 21 April 1990, RC Liège offered Mr. Bosman a new contract for one season, reducing his pay to BEF 30,000, the minimum permitted by the URBSFA (Belgian Soccer Federation) federal rules. URBSFA is a member of UEFA – the Union des Associations Europeennes de Football as well as FIFA, the Federation Internationale de Football Association. Mr. Bosman refused to sign and was put on the transfer list. The compensation fee allegedly for training was set, in accordance with the said rules, at BEF 11,743,000.

Since no club showed an interest in a compulsory transfer, Mr. Bosman contracted US Dunkerque, a club in the French second division. On 27 July 1990, a contract was concluded between RC Liège and US Dunkerque for the temporary transfer of Mr. Bosman for one year, against payment by US Dunkerque to RC Liège of a compensation fee of BEF 1,200,000 payable on receipt by the Fédération Française de Football (FFF) of the transfer certificate issued by URBSFA. UEFA and FIFA rules required that the former club is entitled to receive from the new club compensation for training and development and that the former club must issue an international clearance certificate.

However, RC Liège did not ask URBSFA to send the said certificate to FFF. As a result, neither contract took effect. On 31 July 1990, RC Liège suspended Mr. Bosman, thereby preventing him from playing for the entire season.]

Interpretation of Article 39 of the Treaty with Regard to the Transfer Rules

The first question before the Court of Justice was to ascertain whether Article 39 precludes the application of rules laid down by sporting associations, under which a professional footballer who is a national of one Member State may not, on the expiry of his contract with a club, be employed by a club of another Member State unless the latter club has paid to the former a transfer, training or development fee.

[9] 1 US $ = 38 Belgian Francs. Today, 1 Euro = 40, 3399 BEF.

Application of Article 39 to Rules Laid Down by Sporting Associations

It is to be remembered that, having regard to the objectives of the Community, sport is subject to Community law only in so far as it constitutes an economic activity within the meaning of Article 2 of the Treaty. This applies to the activities of professional or semi-professional footballers, where they are in gainful employment or provide a remunerated service. It is not necessary, for the purposes of the application of the Community provisions on freedom of movement for workers, for the employer to be an undertaking; all that is required is the existence of, or the intention to create, an employment relationship.

Furthermore, application of Article 39 is not precluded by the fact that the transfer rules govern the business relationships between clubs rather than the employment relationships between clubs and players. The fact that the employing clubs must pay fees on recruiting a player from another club affects the players' opportunities for finding employment and the terms under which such employment is offered.

As regards the difficulty of severing the economic aspects from the sporting aspects of football, the Court has held that the provisions of Community law concerning freedom of movement of persons do not preclude rules or practices justified on non-economic grounds which relate to the particular nature and context of certain matches. It stressed, however, that such a restriction on the scope of the provisions in question must remain limited to its proper objective. It cannot, therefore, be relied upon to exclude the whole of a sporting activity from the scope of the Treaty.

The argument based on points of alleged similarity between a sport and culture cannot be accepted, since the question relates to the scope of the freedom of movement of workers, which is a fundamental freedom in the Community system.

As regards the arguments based on the principle of freedom of association, it must be recognised that this principle, enshrined in Article 11 of the European Convention for the Protection of Human Rights and Fundamental Freedoms and resulting from the constitutional traditions common to the Member States, is one of the fundamental rights which, as the Court has consistently held and as is reaffirmed in the preamble to the Single European Act and in Article 6(2) of the Treaty on European Union, are protected in the Community legal order.

However, the rules laid down by sporting associations to which the national court refers cannot be seen as necessary to ensure enjoyment of that freedom by those associations, by the clubs or by their players, nor can they be seen as an inevitable result thereof.

Finally, the principle of subsidiarity, as interpreted to the effect that intervention by public authorities, and particularly Community authorities, in the area in question must be confined to what is strictly necessary, cannot lead to a situation in which the freedom of private associations to adopt sporting rules restricts the exercise of rights conferred on individuals by the Treaty.

Existence of An Obstacle to Freedom of Movement for Workers

It is true that the transfer rules in issue apply also to transfers of players between clubs belonging to different national associations within the same Member State and that similar rules govern transfers between clubs belonging to the same national association. However, those rules are likely to restrict the freedom of movement of players who wish to pursue their activity in another Member State by preventing or deterring them from leaving the clubs to which they belong even after the expiry of their contracts of employment with those clubs.

Since they provide that a professional footballer may not pursue his activity with a new club established in another Member State unless it has paid his former club a transfer fee agreed upon between the two clubs or determined in accordance with the regulations of the sporting associations, the said rules constitute an obstacle to the freedom of movement for workers.

Consequently, the transfer rules constitute an obstacle to freedom of movement for workers prohibited in principle by Article 39 of the Treaty. It could only be otherwise if those rules pursued a legitimate aim compatible with the Treaty and were justified by pressing reasons of public interest. But even if that were so, application of those rules would still have to be such as to ensure achievement of the aim in question and not go beyond what is necessary for that purpose.

Existence of Justifications

First, it was argued that the transfer rules are justified by the need to maintain a financial and competitive balance between clubs and to support the search for talent and the training of young players. In view of the considerable social importance of sporting activities and in particular football in the Community, the aims of maintaining a balance between clubs by preserving a certain degree of equality and uncertainty as to results and of encouraging the recruitment and training of young players must be accepted as legitimate.

As regards the first of those aims, Mr. Bosman has rightly pointed out that the application of the transfer rules is not an adequate means of maintaining a financial and competitive balance in the world of football. Those rules neither preclude the richest clubs from securing the services of the best players nor prevent the availability of financial resources from being a decisive factor in competitive sport, thus considerably altering the balance between clubs.

As regards the second aim, it must be accepted that the prospect of receiving transfer, development or training fees is indeed likely to encourage football clubs to seek new talent and train young players. However, because it is impossible to predict the sporting future of young players with any certainty and because only a limited number of such players go on to play professionally, those fees are by nature contingent and uncertain and are in any event unrelated to the actual cost borne by clubs of training both future professional players and those who will never play professionally. The prospect of receiving such fees cannot, therefore, be either a decisive factor in encouraging recruitment and training of young players or an adequate means of financing such activities, particularly in the case of smaller clubs.

It has also been argued that the transfer rules are necessary to safeguard the worldwide organisation of football. However, the present proceedings concern application of those rules within the Community and not the relations between the national associations of the Member States and those of non-member countries.

Interpretation of Article 39 of the Treaty with Regard to the Nationality Clauses

By its second question, the national court seeks in substance to ascertain whether Article 39 of the Treaty precludes the application of rules laid down by sporting associations, under which, in matches in competitions which they organise, football clubs may field only a limited number of professional players who are nationals of other Member States.

Existence of an Obstacle to Freedom of Movement for Workers

Article 39(2) expressly provides that freedom of movement for workers entails the abolition of any discrimination based on nationality between workers of the Member States as regards employment, remuneration and conditions of work and employment. That principle precludes the application of clauses contained in the regulations of sporting associations which restrict the right of nationals of other Member States to take part, as professional players, in football matches.

Existence of Justifications

It was argued that the nationality clauses are justified on non-economic grounds, concerning only the sport as such. Here, the nationality clauses do not concern specific matches between teams representing their countries but apply to all official matches between clubs and thus to the essence of the activity of professional players.

In those circumstances, the nationality clauses cannot be deemed to be in accordance with Article 39, otherwise it would be deprived of its practical effect and the fundamental right of free access to employment which the Treaty confers individually on each worker in the Community would be rendered nugatory. None of the arguments submitted detracts from that conclusion.

The Temporal Effects of this Judgment

In the present case, the specific features of the rules laid down by the sporting associations for transfers of players between clubs of different Member States, together with the fact that the same or similar rules applied to transfers both between clubs belonging to the same national association and between clubs belonging to different national associations within the same Member State, may have caused uncertainty as to whether those rules were compatible with Community law.

In such circumstances, overriding considerations of legal certainty militate against calling in question legal situations whose effects have already been exhausted. An exception must, however, be made in favour of persons who may have taken timely steps to safeguard their rights.

These arguments caused the Court to decide that:

1. Article 39 precludes the application of rules laid down by sporting associations, under which a professional footballer who is a national of one Member State may not, on the expiry of his contract with a club, be employed by a club of another Member State unless the latter club has paid to the former club a transfer, training or development fee.

2. Article 39 precludes the application of rules laid down by sporting associations under which, in matches in competitions which they organise, football clubs may field only a limited number of professional players who are nationals of other Member States.

3. The direct effect of Article 39 cannot be relied upon in support of claims relating to a fee in respect of transfer, training or development which has already been paid on, or is still payable under an obligation which arose before, the date of this judgment, except by those who have brought court proceedings or raised an equivalent claim under the applicable national law before that date.

Notes

1. Article 39 concerning the free movement of workers has a direct effect on the laws of the Member States and confers rights on individuals that national courts must protect.[10] Article 39, however, does not aim to restrict the power of the Member States to lay down restrictions within their own territory on the freedom of movement of all persons subject to their jurisdiction in the implementation of domestic criminal law.[11] Does *Bosman* suggest that the dichotomy between national rules and the EU-based freedom of movement inevitably conflict if any transnational aspect is raised?

2. In order to be truly effective, the right of workers to be engaged and employed without discrimination necessarily entails as a corollary the employer's entitlement to engage them in accordance with the rules governing freedom of movement for workers. Thus, the rule of equal treatment can be relied upon as well by a worker as by an employer.[12] In *Bosman*, would the US Dunkerque team have been able to bring this action if Bosman had not done so?

3. Freedom of movement entails the abolition of any discrimination based on nationality between workers of the Member States as regards employment, remuneration and other conditions of work and employment (Article 39(2), EC Treaty); it also implies the right to stay in a Member State for the purpose of employment in accordance with the provisions governing the employment of nationals (Article 39(3)(c)). These provisions regarding equal treatment are a specification of the more general principle of equality, which is laid down in Article 12 of the EC Treaty and following which provide that "within the scope of application of this Treaty, and without prejudice to any special provisions contained therein, any discrimination on grounds of nationality shall be prohibited."[13]

4. National provisions or practices, where they limit application for an offer of employment, or the right of foreign nationals to take up and pursue employment or subject these to conditions not applicable in respect of their own nationals, are null and void. The rules regarding equality of treatment forbid not only overt discrimination by reason of nationality but also all covert forms of discrimination that, by the application of other criteria of differentiation, lead to the same result. Thus, a Member State may require that full-time teachers possess sufficient ability to work in the official language of that country. The Court, however, has ruled that the principle

[10] C.O.J., 14 July 1974, *G. Dona v. M. Mantero*, No. 13/76, ECR, 1976, 1333.
[11] C.O.J., 28 March 1979, *Regina v. V.A. Saunders*, No. 175/78, ECR, 1979, 1129.
[12] C.O.J., 7 May 1998, Clean Car Autoservice GesmbH v. Landeshauptmann von Wien, C-350/96, ECR, 1998, 2512.
[13] The Council, acting in accordance with the procedure referred to in Article 251c, may adopt rules designed to prohibit such discrimination (Article 12 TEC).

of non-discrimination precludes any requirement that the linguistic knowledge in question must have been acquired within that national territory (*see* Case C-379/87 *Groener v. Minister for Education and the City of Dublin Vocational Educational Committee* [1989] ECR 3967, paragraph 23).

5. Any clause of a collective agreement or any other collective regulation concerning eligibility for employment, remuneration, and other conditions of work or dismissal is null and void insofar as it lays down or authorizes discriminatory conditions in respect to workers who are nationals of other Member States. The same applies to individual employment contracts (See ROGER BLANPAIN, EUROPEAN LABOUR LAW, (10th ed., 2006).

6. Following *Bosman* and some other cases involving sports, the European Commission and FIFA in 2001 reached an agreement that amends the FIFA regulations on player transfers but did so in a way that in essence undid *Bosman* and the other sports cases protecting professional athletes' right to free movement. "[T]he *Bosman* judgment is dead and buried and the political lobbying waged by the [sports] federations has been more than successful in reintroducing the old system of masters who can sell their servants." *Id* at 329.

7. Special transition rules limiting free movement apply to the new Member States added in 2004. They are designed to cushion any potential impact of large scale worker movements from the new Member States to the prior EU countries. Past EU expansions have included similar transition rules but the experience has been that not that many workers leave the new Member States. In part that is because EU membership has brought with it substantial economic growth in the new Member States.

8. Should the NAFTA countries amend the labor side accord to deal with the movement of workers among the three member countries? If they agreed to the free movement of workers, what would happen?

9. The Treaty creates dual citizenship for citizens of Member States. Article 17 provides:

    1. Citizenship of the Union is hereby established. Every person holding the nationality of a Member State shall be a citizen of the Union. Citizenship of the Union shall complement and not replace national citizenship.
    2. Citizens of the Union shall enjoy the rights conferred by this Treaty and shall be subject to the duties imposed thereby.

    Should EU citizens have free movement throughout the EU without need to be connected to employment?

NOTE ON THE FREE MOVEMENT OF SERVICES AND THE EMPLOYEES OF SERVICE PROVIDERS

The free movement of workers allows residents of one Member State to go to another to find work with an employer located in that second Member State. For the purposes of this Note, the question is what rights the workers of service providers employed by an employer in one Member State have if they get sent to provide those services in a different Member State. The

Treaty, in Articles 49 and 50, deals with the situation of a service provider in one Member State going into another to provide those services. Article 49 provides that "restrictions on freedom to provide services within the Community shall be prohibited in respect of nationals of Member States who are established in a State of the Community other than that of the person for whom the services are provided." Article 50 defines "services" as "activities of an industrial character; activities of a commercial character; or activities of craftsmen; activities of the professions" where they are normally provided for remuneration.

The Member States may, despite the free movement of services, enact regulations applicable to transborder service providers: "Even if there is no harmonisation in the field, the freedom to provide services, as one of the fundamental principles of the Treaty, may be restricted only by rules justified by overriding requirements relating to the public interest and applicable to all persons and undertakings operating in the territory of the State where the service is provided, in so far as that interest is not safeguarded by the rules to which the provider of such a service is subject in the Member State where he is established." Community law does not preclude Member States from extending their legislation, or collective labor agreements entered into by both sides of industry, to any person who is employed, even temporarily, within their territory, no matter in which country the employer is established; nor does Community law prohibit Member States from enforcing those rules by appropriate means.

In the *André Mazzoleni* case,[14] I.S.A, a firm established in Mont-Saint-Martin, France, assigned thirteen of its French workers to serve as security officers at a shopping mall in Belgium. Some were employed full-time in Belgium, while others were employed there for only some of the time and also worked in France. The employer explained that it rotated employees among different assignments so that customers would not identify these workers as security officers. Mazzoleni, an agent of I.S.A., was brought up on criminal charges in Belgium for failing to pay these French workers the minimum wage required by Belgium law for the time they worked in Belgium. Four of the workers claimed civil damages. The Court decided that a Member State was not precluded from imposing its minimum wage standards on transborder workers:

> As regards more specifically national provisions relating to minimum wages, such as those at issue in the main proceedings, it is clear from the case-law of the Court that Community law does not preclude Member States from extending their legislation, or collective labour agreements entered into by both sides of industry, relating to minimum wages, to any person who is employed, even temporarily, within their territory, regardless of the country in which the employer is established. It follows that the provisions of a Member State's legislation or collective labour agreements which guarantee minimum wages may in principle be applied to employers providing services within the territory of that State, regardless of the country in which the employer is established.

> It follows that Community law does not preclude a Member State from requiring an undertaking established in another Member State which provides services in the territory of the first State to pay its workers the minimum remuneration fixed by the national rules of that State.

[14] C.O.J., 15 March 2001, *Criminal proceedings against André Mazzoleni and Inter Surveillance Assistance SARL* C-165/98, ECR., 2001, 2189.

However, there may be circumstances in which the application of such rules would be neither necessary nor proportionate to the objective pursued, namely the protection of the workers concerned.

If such be the circumstances, even if it be accepted that the rules of the host Member State imposing a minimum wage have the legitimate objective of protecting workers, the national authorities of that State must, before applying them to a service provider established in an adjacent region of another Member State, consider whether the application of those rules is necessary and proportionate for the purpose of protecting the workers concerned.

Ensuring that these transborder workers receive the same level of welfare protection as its own workers justifies the imposition of the Belgium minimum wage. But, before imposing that wage, the Belgium officials must determine if doing so involves an administrative burden on the employer disproportionate to the value to the workers of the added pay to reach the Belgium minimum wage.

In the *Wolff & Müller* case,[15] Pereira Félix, a Portuguese national, worked from February to May 2000 in Berlin (Germany) as a bricklayer on a building site by a construction undertaking established in Portugal. The latter carried out concreting and reinforced-concrete work on that building site for Wolff & Müller, the general contractor. Félix sought payment jointly and severally from his employer and from Wolff & Müller of unpaid remuneration amounting to DEM[16] 4,019.23. He claimed that Wolff & Müller, as guarantor, was liable, under German law, for sums in respect of wages not received by him. The Court concluded that Wolf & Muller could be held as a guarantor without violating the right of freedom to provide services.

> Article 5 of Directive 96/71/EC of the European Parliament and of the Council of 16 December 1996 concerning the posting of workers in the framework of the provision of services, interpreted in the light of Article 49 EC, does not preclude, in a case such as that in the main proceedings, a national system whereby, when subcontracting the conduct of building work to another undertaking, a building contractor becomes liable, in the same way as a guarantor who has waived benefit of execution, for the obligation on that undertaking or that undertaking's subcontractors to pay the minimum wage to a worker or to pay contributions to a joint scheme for parties to a collective agreement where the minimum wage means the sum payable to the worker after deduction of tax, social security contributions, payments towards the promotion of employment or other such social insurance payments (net pay), if the safeguarding of workers' pay is not the primary objective of the legislation or is merely a subsidiary objective.

Notes

1. Should the object of the EU rules concerning workers' rights in the context of the provision of services by transborder employers be to provide the best protection, highest pay, etc., to the workers? Thus, in *Mazzoleni*, should Belgium only be able to impose its minimum wage on these cross-border French workers of a French

---

[15] C.O.J., 12 October 2004, *Wolff & Müller GmbH & Co. KG v. José Filipe Pereira Félix*, C-60/03, not yet published.
[16] 1 Deutdsche Mark = 0.5 U.S. $.

employer if that minimum was higher than the French minimum wage? Or should it be to prevent one Member State from discriminating against a service provider located in another Member State when it does business in the first Member State? Article IV of the United States Constitution provides that, "The Citizens of each State shall be entitled to all Privileges and Immunities of Citizens in the several States." This has been interpreted as limiting the ability of states to discriminate against out-of-staters with regard to constitutional rights but especially economic activities.

2. In 2004, the European Commission issued, in order to advance the Lisbon Strategy, a draft Directive on services in the internal market. This proposal is aimed at providing a legal framework to eliminate the obstacles to the freedom of establishment for service providers and the free movement of services between the EU Member States. It covers services provided both to consumers and to businesses. This is an important draft directive, as 70 percent of the jobs are in the service sector and job growth is related to services, especially in the area of personalized jobs.

   In total, the services covered by the proposal account for around 50 percent of all economic activity in the EU. Most controversially, however, the proposal provided for a number of measures aimed at eliminating obstacles to the free movement of services, including the application of a "country of origin" principle, according to which a service provider is subject only to the law of the country in which it is established and Member States may not restrict services from a provider established in another Member State.[17] How would the "country of origin" principle, if adopted, affect cases such as *Mazzoleni* and *Wolff & Müller*? Would the "country of origin" principle induce a race to the bottom by businesses within the EU to establish themselves in the countries with the least protective labor starndards and the lowest minimum wages?

3. On 16 February 2006, the European Parliament enacted the new Services Directive but with substantial amendment, including eliminating the "country of origin" principle (but not adopting a "country of destination" principle) and excluding labor relations from its coverage. The European Commission then redrafted the Directive in line with that which Parliament had adopted. On 30 May 2006, the Council of Ministers announced that this amended Directive had received the necessary support for enactment.

---

2. Working Time

Article 137 of the Treaty provides that the Community is to support and complement the activities of the Member States with a view to improving the working environment to protect workers' health and safety. Directive 2003/88/EC,[18] adopted with a qualified majority, significantly amended and replaced Directive 93/104/EC of 23 November 1993,

---

[17] **Opinion** of the Committee on Employment and Social Affairs for the Committee on the Internal Market and Consumer Protection on the proposal for a directive of the European Parliament and of the Council on services in the internal market (COM(2004)0002 – C50069/2004 – 2004/0001(COD)).

[18] Directive 2003/88/EC of the European Parliament and of the Council of 4 November 2003 concerning certain aspects of the organisation of working time, *O.J.*, L 299, 18 November 2003.

concerning certain aspects of the organization of working time. Basically, the Directive requires a minimum daily rest period of eleven consecutive hours a day, a rest break when the working day is longer than six hours, a minimum rest period of one day a week, a maximum working week of forty-eight hours on average including overtime, a right to four weeks of paid annual leave, and normal hours of work for night workers may not exceed an average of eight hours in any twenty-four-hour period.

LANDESHAUPTSTADT KIEL V. JAEGER

European Court of Justice
C-151/02

[Dr. Jaeger works as a doctor in the surgical department of a hospital. He spends three quarters of his normal working hours on call. Generally, Jaeger carries out six periods of on-call duty each month, offset in part by the grant of free time and in part by the payment of supplementary remuneration.

On-call duty begins at the end of a normal working day and the length of each period is sixteen hours in the week, twenty-five hours on Saturdays (from 08:30 p.m. to 09:30 a.m. on Sunday morning), and twenty-two hours forty-five minutes on Sundays (from 08:30 p.m. to 07:15 a.m. on Monday morning). When Jaeger is on call, he stays at the clinic and is called on to carry out his professional duties as the need arises. He is allocated a room with a bed in the hospital, where he may sleep when his services are not required. The appropriateness of that accommodation is in dispute. However, in the question presented to the European Court of Justice by the German court for a preliminary ruling, it was presumed that the average time during which Jaeger is called on to carry out a professional task does not exceed 49 percent of his total time spent on call.

Directive 93/104/EC provides two definitions that define working time: "1. "working time" means any period during which the worker is working, at the employer's disposal and carrying out his activity or duties, in accordance with national laws and/or practice; 2. "rest period" means any period which is not working time . . . " In contrast, German national law distinguishes between readiness for work ("Arbeitsbereitschaft"), on-call service ("Bereitschaftsdienst") and standby ("Rufbereitschaft"). Only readiness for work is deemed to constitute full working time. Conversely, on-call service and standby are categorized as rest time, save for the part of the service during which professional tasks are actually being performed. Thus, the question was whether the German law failed to be consistent with the Directive.]

The Court ruled as follows.

1. Council Directive 93/104/EC of 23 November 1993 must be interpreted as meaning that on-call duty ('Bereitschaftsdienst') performed by a doctor where he is required to be physically present in the hospital must be regarded as constituting in its totality working time for the purposes of that directive even where the person concerned is permitted to rest at his place of work during the periods when his services are not required with the result that that directive precludes legislation of a Member State which classifies as rest periods an employee's periods of inactivity in the context of such on-call duty.

2. Directive 93/104 must also be interpreted as preclude[ing] legislation of a Member State which, in the case of on-call duty where physical presence in the hospital is required, has the effect of enabling, in an appropriate case by means of a collective agreement or a works

agreement based on a collective agreement, an offset only in respect of periods of on-call duty during which the worker has actually been engaged in professional activities; in order to come within the derogating provisions set out in Article 17(2), subparagraph 2.1(c)(i) of the directive, a reduction in the daily rest period of 11 consecutive hours by a period of on-call duty performed in addition to normal working time is subject to the condition that equivalent compensating rest periods be accorded to the workers concerned at times immediately following the corresponding periods worked; furthermore, in no circumstances may such a reduction in the daily rest period lead to the maximum weekly working time laid down in Article 6 of the directive being exceeded.

Notes

1. Directive 93/104, 1993 O.J. (L 307) 18, was upheld by the Court in *United Kingdom v. Council*, Case C-84/94, 1996 E.C.R. 1-5755, as within the Council's authority of what is now Article 137(1)'s provision for the "improvement in particular of the working environment to protect workers' health and safety." In *SIMAP v. Conselleria de Sanidady Consumo de la Generalidad Valenciana*, C-303/98 (1998), the Court, in a case arising from a reference from the Spanish courts, decided that "working time" meant time doctors on primary care teams were required to be on call at the hospital where they were working. Working time did not include time when the doctors were on call, but were not required to be on the hospital premises. Would it be practical for the hospital to schedule Dr. Jaeger's on-call duty so that he need not be in the hospital? Can an emergency room in a hospital function efficiently if the doctors on-call to work when needed are not close at hand?

2. Note that the problem for the German hospital was not the forty-eight-hour work week but, instead, how the rest period requirement worked. What is the justification for requiring rest periods for workers? In the United States, there is a long tradition that medical residents – in their first posting after graduating from medical schools – are expected to work extremely long and continuous hours. Does that tradition lead to good medical care for the patients? To good medical training for the residents?

3. Is worker fatigue the rationale supporting the forty-eight-hour work week limit? If dealing with the issue of worker fatigue is why rest periods are required, why does the Directive allow the Member States to derogate from the rest period by equivalent compensating rest periods to be scheduled for the workers concerned at times immediately following the corresponding periods worked? Is that consistent with addressing worker fatigue?

4. In reaction to the decisions in *Simap* and *Jaeger*, in September 2004 the European Commission proposed to amend the Directive to overturn their results. In May 2005, the European Parliament adopted far-reaching amendments to the Commission's original proposals recognizing on-call time as working time, in line with the ECJ rulings. In June 2006, the Employment Council under the Austrian Presidency once more sought an acceptable political agreement to break the stalemate, but this proved impossible. The issue now moves onto the agenda of the Finnish Presidency (July-December 2006).

---

3. Additional Individual Rights of Workers

Council Directive 96/34, 1996 O.J. (Ll45) 4, is aimed at facilitating "the reconciliation of parental and professional responsibilities for working parents." Like the Family and Medical Leave Act in the United States, the Directive requires the Member States to provide for leaves of absence for parents but also for workers facing other emergency situations in their families. Women and men workers, individually, have a right to a leave upon the birth or adoption of a child to enable them to take care of that child for at least three months, up until age eight. Member States are given wide discretion in establishing by law, or by management-labor agreement, the conditions for the exercise of the leave. Consistent with Article 137(6), the Directive makes no mention whether the leave is to be paid, but Member States are authorized to provide for "more favorable provisions." In *Lewen v. Denda*, Case C-333/97 (1999), the Court held that an employee who had been on extended parental leave under German law was not entitled to a Christmas bonus that was given as a matter of discretion during her leave. The bonus did not constitute a right "acquired or in the process of being acquired by the worker on the date on which parental leave starts" pursuant to Clause 2(6) of the Framework Agreement. Clause 3 provides for additional leaves of absence where sickness or accident in the family makes "the immediate presence of the worker indispensible."

The EU has adopted an equal treatment requirement for part-time workers. An example of a framework agreement between the social partners, Council Directive 97/81, 1998 O.J. (L 14) 9, requires part-time workers to be treated as well as full-time workers:

> In respect of employment conditions, part-time workers shall not be treated in a less favorable manner than comparable full-time workers solely because they work part time unless different treatment is justified on objective grounds.

Who is a part-time worker is determined by comparison with the hours worked by a "comparable full-time worker." More recently, Council Directive 99/70, 1999 O.J. (L 175) 43, another framework agreement that is the product of dialogue between the social partners, imposes an equal treatment requirement regarding workers on fixed-term (versus a contract of indefinite duration) contract:

> In respect of employment conditions, fixed-term workers shall not be treated in a less favorable manner than comparable permanent workers solely because they have a fixed-term contract or relationship unless different treatment is justified on objective grounds.

The Directive further requires Member States to initiate laws to "prevent abuse arising from the use of successive fixed-term employment contracts."

Notes

1. Employers frequently want to be able to hire part-time workers and workers to do a specific job that has a defined end point in order to be able to save labor costs. Do the Directives dealing with part-time and fixed-term workers remove that economic incentive? If they do, does that mean that employers will hire fewer of these workers? Assuming that is true, who will the employers get to do the work that otherwise would be done by part-timers and workers for a fixed term? Do these Directives cause employers to hire more full-time, permanent workers? Or fewer?

2. To avoid the strictures established in these Directives, will employers hire people off the books? Do these Directives have the unintended consequence of increasing the informal economy?

F. COLLECTIVE EMPLOYMENT RIGHTS

The promotion of a dialogue among the social partners is one of the key elements of EU social policy. Article 138(1)(TEC) provides: "The Commission shall have the task of promoting the consultation of management and labour at Community level and shall take any relevant measure to facilitate their dialogue by ensuring balanced support for the parties." Furthermore, Article 139(1) provides that "should management and labour so desire, the dialogue between them at Community level may lead to contractual relations, including agreements." The social partners, however, are confederations of national employer confederations on one hand and confederation of national confederations of unions on the other. Thus, they are a number of steps removed from actual employers of employees or unions with actual members. Their negotiations are directed more toward setting EU social policy than the notions of collective bargaining that students of U.S. labor law have. Finally, "core" issues are *excluded* from the EU competence including setting wages and salaries, the right of association, the right to strike and the right to impose lockouts (Art. 137, 6 TEC). Therefore, the threat of EU legislation is not available to push the parties toward agreement in these core areas of traditional collective bargaining.

1. European Works Councils

By Directive 94/45/EC, the EU created an obligation for the Member States to provide for Works Councils for "undertakings" that operated across the borders of Member States. A "Community-scale undertaking" means an undertaking with at least 1,000 employees within the Member States and at least 150 employees in each of at least two Member States. The purpose of the directive is to improve the right to information and to consultation of employees in these Community-scale undertakings.

The process for creating a European Works Concil in a Community-scale undertaking starts with a request to initiate negotiations toward creating one, which request can be on the initiative of the representative of the employees or of the central managment of the undertaking. Following that request, a negotiating body is established to set up the EuropeaonWorks Council. If no agreement to do so is achieved within three years of the initial request, then the default rules provide the fundamental requirements that must be met. The central management has the obligation for creating the conditons and means necessary for the setting up of the EWC including "an obligation to supply the employees' representatives with the information essential to the opening of negotiations." *Betriebsrat der Firma ADS Anker GmbH v. ADS Anker GmbH*, C-349/01 (2004).

The EWC may be composed of representatives of employees only, based on the German model, or can include representatives of management, the French model. Allocation of seats ususally takes acount of the numerical size of the employers and its different establishments. The default rules that apply if there is no agreement to create an EWC provide the core standards for the operation of all EWCs, whether created by agreement or required by default of such an agreement. The information and consultation required concerns the Community-scale undertaking (or group of undertakings) as a whole or at least two of its establishment or group undertakings situated in different Member States. The key substantive scope is:

> The European Works Council shall have the right to meet with the central management once a year, to be informed and consulted, on the basis of a report drawn up by the central management, on the progress of the business of the Community-scale undertaking or Community-scale group of undertakings and its prospects. The local management shall be informed accordingly.

> The meeting shall relate in particular to the structure, economic and financial situation, the probable development of the business and of production and sales, the situation and probable trend of employment, investments, and substantial changes concerning organization, introduction of new working methods or production processes, transfers of production, mergers, cut-backs or closures of undertakings, establishments or important parts thereof, and collective redundancies.

There is further a provision for "exceptional circumstances affecting the employees' interests to a considerable extent, particularly in the event of relocations, the closure of establishments or undertakings or collective redundancies." The EWC has a right to be informed and to meet "as soon as possible on the basis of a report drawn up by the central management . . . [but this] meeting shall not affect the prerogatives of the central management."

More than eight hundred transnational companies or groups have established EWCs or similar bodies. This represents about 45 percent of the companies or groups of companies and about 70 percent of the employees potentially concerned. The pace of adoption of new EWC agreements has slackened to an average of forty to fifty per year. http://eurofound.eu.int/areas/participationatwork.ewc/htm. About twenty-two hundred multinational corporations headquartered outside the EU but with operations in it fall within the scope of the EWC directive. http://www.ewcdb.org.

Directive 2002/14/EC (2002) established a more general framework for informing and consulting employees of all undertakings or establishments in the European Community. The Directive provides that Member States may entrust management and labor at the appropriate level of the employer to define freely and at any time through negotiated agreements the practical arrangements for informing and consulting employees concerning matters important to the enterprise but not limited to EU-wide concerns.

Notes

1. What is the purpose underlying the imposition of a duty on employers to inform and consult with a Works Council, or equivalent group about matters concerning employment? Is it so that employees will understand and therefore agree with management about the future path the employer is taking? Is it to provide a voice to workers so that management might take better account of the interests of employees in making management decisions? Do Works Councils make employees stakeholders in their employer in the way that shareholders are presumed to be stakeholders?
2. Should Works Councils be empowered to call strikes if management and the council fail to agree about what management should do in face of the information

provided about the future of the business, including decisions with important implications for employment?

3. Enterprises organized outside the EU that nevertheless have operations within
   it to trigger the obligations under the Works Council Directive are required to
   comply with the Member States' laws implementing the Directive. How should
   a transnational corporation headquartered in a country without any works council requirement comply with the laws requiring a works council? Would such a
   transnational corporation ever have any incentive to extend the operation of the
   EWC to its operations outside the EU? Can it avoid providing information and
   consulting about activities outside the EU if that information relates to issues that
   can have an impact on workers within the EU?

2. Collective Redundancies: Information and Consultation

During the 1970s, called by some the golden years for European labor law, three directives were adopted that were intended to protect the workers against the consolidations
that would be an inevitable consequence of a functioning common market. Discussions in the EU group of experts on labour law from the different Member States
reasoned that there was a larger market with an increase in scale as the EU developed to which the undertakings would have to adapt themselves; this meant restructuring, mergers, takeovers, collective dismissals, and bankruptcies.Indeed, it was said,
the worker should not have to pay the price for the establishment of a common, bigger
market; rather the worker should be protected against the social consequences of this
restructuring.

On the basis of this reasoning, three directives were proposed and, also due to the
then-political composition of the Council, adopted. These directives relate respectively to
collective redundancies (1975), the transfer of undertakings or parts thereof (1977), and
the insolvency of the employer (1980). One will notice, when analyzing these directives,
that the managerial prerogative concerning economic decisions remains intact. There
were at some times proposals regarding collective redundancies to prohibit dismissals,
in conformity with the then prevalent French legislation, but these proposals were not
retained, as will be made clear later. In short, the directives only address the effects of
restructuring.

The Directive on Collective Redundancies, No. 75/129 of 17 February 1975 provides:

SECTION II

Information and consultation

1. Where an employer is contemplating collective redundancies, he shall begin consultations with the workers' representatives in good time with a view to reaching an
   agreement.

2. These consultations shall, at least, cover ways and means of avoiding collective redundancies or reducing the number of workers affected, and of mitigating the consequences by recourse to accompanying social measures aimed, inter alia, at aid for
   redeploying or retraining workers made redundant.

   Member States may provide that the workers' representatives may call on the services
   of experts in accordance with national legislation and/or practice.

3. To enable workers' representatives to make constructive proposals, the employers shall in good time during the course of the consultations:

(a) supply them with all relevant information and

(b) in any event notify them in writing of:

(i) the reasons for the projected redundancies;

(ii) the number of categories of workers to be made redundant;

(iii) the number and categories of workers normally employed;

(iv) the period over which the projected redundancies are to be effected;

(v) the criteria proposed for the selection of the workers to be made redundant in so far as national legislation and/or practice confers the power therefor upon the employer;

(vi) the method for calculating any redundancy payments other than those arising out of national legislation and/or practice.

The employer shall forward to the competent public authority a copy of, at least, the elements of the written communication which are provided for in the first subparagraph, point (b), subpoints (i) to (v).

4. The obligations laid down in paragraphs 1, 2 and 3 shall apply irrespective of whether the decision regarding collective redundancies is being taken by the employer or by an undertaking controlling the employer.

In considering alleged breaches of the information, consultation and notification requirements laid down by this Directive, account shall not be taken of any defence on the part of the employer on the ground that the necessary information has not been provided to the employer by the undertaking which took the decision leading to collective redundancies.

Information concerning the collective redundancies must be given before the decision is taken. The text of Article 2(1) is clear on this point: it concerns an employer who is *contemplating* collective redundancies.

The directive explicitly mentions that the employer has to consult the workers' representatives in good time. The directive only applies when the employer projects collective redundancies. Such a projection is necessary if the employer contemplates dismissals and wants to notify the competent authority (Article 3(1)). "The directive applies only where the employer has in fact contemplated collective redundancies or has drawn up a plan for collective redundancies. It does not apply in the case where, because of the financial state of the undertaking, the employer ought to have contemplated collective redundancies but did not do so."[19]

The purpose of the information is to enable the workers' representatives to make constructive proposals. The employer shall at least notify them of the reasons for the projected redundancies; the number or categories of workers to be made redundant; the number or categories or workers normally employed; the period over which the projected redundancies are to be effected; the criteria proposed for the selection of the workers and the method for calculating any redundancy payment (other than those arising out of national legislation and/or practice). The employer is obliged to forward to the competent authority a copy of the information given to the workers with the exception of the information on the method of calculating redundancy payments (Article 2(3)). The workers' representatives are also entitled to a copy of the information that the employer

---

[19] C.O.J., 7 December 1995, Case C-449/93, *ECR*, 1995, 4291.

must forward to the authorities. The workers' representatives may send any comments they may have to the competent authority (Article 3(2)).

The directive applies irrespective of whether the decision regarding collective redundancies is being taken by the employer or by an undertaking controlling the employer (Article 2(4)). In considering alleged breaches of the information and consultation duties, account shall not be taken of any defense on the part of the employer that the necessary information has not been provided to him by the undertaking that took the decision leading to collective redundancies. The employer is obliged to consult the workers' representatives with a view to reaching an agreement (Article 2(1)). This is a very strong form of consultation, which is very close to collective bargaining. The consultations must cover ways and means of avoiding collective redundancies or reducing the number of workers affected, and of mitigating the consequences (Article 2(2)). The amended Article 2(2) specifies that this includes accompanying social measures aimed, *inter alia*, at aid for redeploying or retraining workers made redundant.

Workers' representatives are those provided for by the laws or the practices of the Member States. Since the judgment of the Court of Justice of 8 June 1994,[20] it is no longer possible that there are no workers' representatives in the case where a Member State would not have an overall system of workers' representation. According to the Court of Justice, "employers face a statutory obligation to inform and consult with employees when they are planning collective redundancies, or if they transfer employees from one business to another. This means that even non-unionised companies will have to establish machinery for consultation even if it does not already exist."

Thus, the European Court of Justice ruled that U.K. rules on the protection of employees' rights in the event of companies changing hands or when collective redundancies take place breached EC law. U.K. law did not provide for the designation of employees' representatives in firms where the employer had refused to recognise trade unions. The Court said the United Kingdom, by creating this safe harbor from the application of the rights established in the Directive, had failed to implement fully binding EC directives. The directives relate, as said, to the safeguarding of employees' rights in the event of the transfer of a business or collective redundancies. Both place a duty on employers to inform and consult representatives of workers affected by a transfer or redundancies.

The United Kingdom argued that employers who did not recognize trade unions were not covered by the obligations in the directives because union recognition in companies was traditionally based on voluntary recognition. The Court did not accept that argument. It said the aim of the directives was to ensure comparable protection for employees' rights in all Member States and to harmonise the costs of such provisions for companies in the EC. To that end, the directives laid down compulsory obligations on employers regarding informing and consulting employees' representatives.

The Court found Member States had no right under the directive to limit the rights of employees to those companies that, under national laws, were obliged to have union representation. Although one of the directives specifically provided for situations in which companies did not have employees' representatives, the Court said this provision should not be read in isolation and that its effect was to allow employees without such representation to be properly informed. The Court said it was not the intention of the Community legislature to allow the different legal systems within the EC to accept a situation in which

---

[20] *Commission v. UK*, C-382/92 and 383/92, ECR-I-2435, 1994.

no employees' representatives were designated since designation was necessary to ensure compliance with the obligations established in the directive.

It made no difference that the directives did not contain specific provisions requiring Member States to designate workers' representatives if there were none. The directives required Member States to take all the measures necessary to ensure employees were informed and consulted through their representatives in the event of either a transfer or collective redundancies. That obligation did not require there to be specific provisions on the designation of employees' representatives.

Two further claims were made by the Commission. The first was that U.K. rules only required the employer to consult with the employees' representatives, to take into consideration what was said, to reply and give reasons if the representations were rejected. The obligation under the directives was to consult representatives with a view to seeking agreement. The United Kingdom conceded that its rules did not provide for this.

The second claim was that the sanctions provided for in the national rules for failure to comply with the obligations to consult and inform were not a sufficient deterrent for employers.

The Court said that where a Community directive did not specifically provide any penalty for an infringement, or where it referred for that purpose to national laws, the obligations of the Member States under the Rome Treaty were to require them to ensure that infringements of EC law were penalized under conditions, both procedural and substantive, which were analogous to those applicable to infringements of national law of a similar nature and importance and that, in any event, made the penalty effective, proportionate, and dissuasive.

Notes

1. Directive No. 75/129 of 17 February 1975 on the approximation of laws of the Member States relating to collective redundancies[21] finds its origin in the *AKZO* case. In 1973 akzo, a Dutch-German multinational enterprise, was engaged in a process of restructuring and wanted to make some five thousand workers redundant. As akzo had a number of subsidiaries in different EU Member States, it could compare the costs of dismissal in those countries and choose to dismiss in that country where the cost was the lowest. When this strategy became apparent, there was an outrage in some European quarters and a demand for a European rule to make such strategies impossible in the future and to lay down a European-wide minimum floor of protection in the case of collective dismissals. This led to a proviso in the Council Resolution of 21 January 1974 concerning a social action program and, consequently, to a directive concerning collective redundancies.

2. Directive No. 92/56 of 24 June 1992 amended the Directive No. 75/129. Several reasons inspired the amendments: other forms of termination of employment contracts on the initiative of the employer should be equated to redundancies, and the provisions of the original directive should be clarified and supplemented as regards the employer's obligations regarding informing and consulting of workers' representatives. The amended directive explicitly stated that it can be left to the social partners to take the appropriate measures by way of collective bargaining agreement

---

[21] O.J. L 48, 22 February 1975.

to implement the amendments (Article 2).[22] Both directives were consolidated for reasons of clarity and rationality by Directive 98/59 EC of 20 July 1998 on the approximation of the laws of the Member States relating to collective redundancies.[23]

3. Directive No. 98/59 is based on Article 94 of the EC Treaty that relates to the approximation of laws, regulations or administrative rules of the Member States that directly affect the establishment or the funding of the common market. A "whereas" clause in the directive reads that "it is important that greater protection should be afforded to workers in the event of collective redundancies while taking into account the need for balanced economic and social development within the Community"; "that despite increasing convergence [one wonders which convergence?] differences are still maintained between the provisions in force in the Member States of the Community concerning the practical arrangements and procedures for such redundancies and the measures designed to alleviate the consequences of redundancy for workers, that these differences can have a direct effect on the functioning of the market." The provisions of the directive are thus intended to serve to establish a common body of rules applicable in all Member States, while leaving it up to the Member States to apply or introduce provisions that are more favorable to workers.[24] The directive provides for the information and consultation of the workers in the case of collective redundancies, as well as for a notification of the competent public authority. At the same time, periods are introduced during which no notice of termination may be given.

4. As was described in Chapter 3, in the United States, the WARN Act – Worker Adjustment and Retraining Notification Act – requires employers with one hundred or more employees to give sixty days' notice to representatives of its employees or its employees as well as local government officials when a large-scale layoff is in the works. Are such notice requirements designed to give the workers and their representatives the chance to convince the employer that such massive retrenchment is not necessary? Are they designed so that the effects of the retrenchment can be minimized or at least rationalized in terms of the interests of the workers? Or does the notice period give opponents a chance to organize to oppose the restructuring?

3. Transfer of enterprises and acquired rights

Directive No. 77/187 relates to the safeguarding of employees' rights in the event of transfers of undertakings, businesses or parts of businesses.[25] The directive of 1977 was amended by Directive 98/50 EC of 29 June 1998[26] "in the light of the impact of the internal market, the legislative tendencies of the Member States with regard to the rescue of undertakings in economic difficulties and the case-law of the Court of Justice".[27] The directive was "in the interests of clarity and rationality codified" by Council Directive 2001/23/EC of 12 March 2001.[28] The new directive is also based on Article 94 of the EC

[22] Directive No. 92/56, O.J. L 245, 26 August 1992.
[23] O.J. L 225/16, 12 August 1998.
[24] C.O.J., 8 June 1982, *Commission* v. *Italy*, No. 91/81, ECR, 1982, 2455.
[25] O.J. L 61, 5 March 1977.
[26] O.J. L 201/88, 17 July 1998.
[27] Considerans 3.
[28] O.J., 22 March 2001.

Treaty concerning the approximation of laws. The objective of the directive is to ensure that the rights of employees are safeguarded in the event of a change of employer by enabling them to remain in employment with the new employer on the terms and conditions agreed at the transfer.[29] The purpose of the directive is therefore to ensure that the restructuring of undertakings within the common market does not adversely affect the workers in the undertakings concerned.[30]

DIRECTIVE 2001/23

CHAPTER I

Scope and definitions

Article 1

1. (a) This Directive shall apply to any transfer of an undertaking, business, or part of an undertaking or business to another employer as a result of a legal transfer or merger.

(b) Subject to subparagraph (a) and the following provisions of this Article, there is a transfer within the meaning of this Directive where there is a transfer of an economic entity which retains its identity, meaning an organised grouping of resources which has the objective of pursuing an economic activity, whether or not that activity is central or ancillary.

(c) This Directive shall apply to public and private undertakings engaged in economic activities whether or not they are operating for gain. An administrative reorganisation of public administrative authorities, or the transfer of administrative functions between public administrative authorities, is not a transfer within the meaning of this Directive.

2. This Directive shall apply where and in so far as the undertaking, business or part of the undertaking or business to be transferred is situated within the territorial scope of the Treaty.

3. This Directive shall not apply to seagoing vessels.

Article 2

1. For the purposes of this Directive:

   (a) "transferor" shall mean any natural or legal person who, by reason of a transfer within the meaning of Article 1(1), ceases to be the employer in respect of the undertaking, business or part of the undertaking or business;
   (b) "transferee" shall mean any natural or legal person who, by reason of a transfer within the meaning of Article 1(1), becomes the employer in respect of the undertaking, business or part of the undertaking or business;
   (c) "representatives of employees" and related expressions shall mean the representatives of the employees provided for by the laws or practices of the Member States;

---

[29] O.J., 15 June 1988, *P. Bork International A/S in liquidation and others v. Foreningen of Arbejdsledere i Danmark, acting on behalf of Birger E. Peterson, and Junckers Industries A/S*, No. 101/87, ECR, 1988, 3057.
[30] C.O.J., 7 February 1985, *H.B.M. Abels v. The Administrative Board of the Bedrijfsvereniging voor de Metaal Industrie en de Electronische Industrie*, No. 135/83, ECR, 1985, 519.

(d) "employee" shall mean any person who, in the Member State concerned, is protected as an employee under national employment law.

2. This Directive shall be without prejudice to national law as regards the definition of contract of employment or employment relationship.

However, Member States shall not exclude from the scope of this Directive contracts of employment or employment relationships solely because:

(a) of the number of working hours performed or to be performed,
(b) they are employment relationships governed by a fixed-duration contract of employment within the meaning of Article 1(1) of Council Directive 91/383/EEC of 25 June 1991 supplementing the measures to encourage improvements in the safety and health at work of workers with a fixed-duration employment relationship or a temporary employment relationship(6), or
(c) they are temporary employment relationships within the meaning of Article 1(2) of Directive 91/383/EEC, and the undertaking, business or part of the undertaking or business transferred is, or is part of, the temporary employment business which is the employer.

CHAPTER II

Safeguarding of employees' rights

Article 3

1. The transferor's rights and obligations arising from a contract of employment or from an employment relationship existing on the date of a transfer shall, by reason of such transfer, be transferred to the transferee.

Member States may provide that, after the date of transfer, the transferor and the transferee shall be jointly and severally liable in respect of obligations which arose before the date of transfer from a contract of employment or an employment relationship existing on the date of the transfer.

2. Member States may adopt appropriate measures to ensure that the transferor notifies the transferee of all the rights and obligations which will be transferred to the transferee under this Article, so far as those rights and obligations are or ought to have been known to the transferor at the time of the transfer. A failure by the transferor to notify the transferee of any such right or obligation shall not affect the transfer of that right or obligation and the rights of any employees against the transferee and/or transferor in respect of that right or obligation.

3. Following the transfer, the transferee shall continue to observe the terms and conditions agreed in any collective agreement on the same terms applicable to the transferor under that agreement, until the date of termination or expiry of the collective agreement or the entry into force or application of another collective agreement.

Member States may limit the period for observing such terms and conditions with the proviso that it shall not be less than one year.

4. (a) Unless Member States provide otherwise, paragraphs 1 and 3 shall not apply in relation to employees' rights to old-age, invalidity or survivors' benefits under supplementary company

or intercompany pension schemes outside the statutory social security schemes in Member States.

(b) Even where they do not provide in accordance with subparagraph (a) that paragraphs 1 and 3 apply in relation to such rights, Member States shall adopt the measures necessary to protect the interests of employees and of persons no longer employed in the transferor's business at the time of the transfer in respect of rights conferring on them immediate or prospective entitlement to old age benefits, including survivors' benefits, under supplementary schemes referred to in subparagraph (a).

Article 4

1. The transfer of the undertaking, business or part of the undertaking or business shall not in itself constitute grounds for dismissal by the transferor or the transferee. This provision shall not stand in the way of dismissals that may take place for economic, technical or organisational reasons entailing changes in the workforce.

Member States may provide that the first subparagraph shall not apply to certain specific categories of employees who are not covered by the laws or practice of the Member States in respect of protection against dismissal.

2. If the contract of employment or the employment relationship is terminated because the transfer involves a substantial change in working conditions to the detriment of the employee, the employer shall be regarded as having been responsible for termination of the contract of employment or of the employment relationship.

. . .

The directive applies provided that the undertaking in question retains its identity, as it does if it is a going concern whose operation is actually continued or resumed by the new employer, with the same or similar activities. In order to determine whether those conditions are met, it is necessary to consider all the circumstances surrounding the transaction in question, including, in particular, whether or not the undertaking's tangible and intangible assets and the majority of its employees are taken over, the degree of similarity between the activities carried on before and after the transfer or the period, if any, for which those activities ceased in connection with the transfer.[31]

It is therefore "necessary to determine, having regard to all the circumstances of the facts surrounding the transaction in question, whether the functions performed are in fact carried out or resumed by the new legal person with the same activities or similar activities, it being understood that activities of a special nature which pursue independent aims may, if necessary, be treated as a business or part of a business within the meaning of the directive".[32]

The directive may thus apply in a situation in which an undertaking entrusts another undertaking by contract with the responsibility for running a service for employees, previously managed directed, for a fee and various benefits the terms of which are determined by agreement between them.[33]

---

[31] C.O.J., *Bork International A/S, op. cit.*
[32] C.O.J., 19 May 1992, S. *Redmond Stichting* v. *H. Bartol and Others*, No. C-29/91, *op. cit.*
[33] C.O.J., 12 November 1992, *A. Watson Rask and K. Christensen* v. *ISS Kantineservice A/S*, No. C-209/91, *ECR*, 1992, 5755.

MERCKX V. FORD MOTOR COMPANY BELGIUM SA

C-171/94, C-172/94 (1996)

[Merckx and Neuhuys were salesmen with Anfo Motors. Anfo Motors sold motor vehicles as a Ford dealer in a number of municipalities in the Brussels conurbation; Ford was Afo's main shareholder. On 8 October 1987, Anfo Motors informed Merckx and Neuhuys that it would discontinue all its activities on 31 December 1987 and that with effect from 1 November 1987 Ford would be working with an independent dealer, Novarobel, in the municipalities covered by the Anfo Motors dealership. It stated that Novarobel would take on fourteen of the sixty-four employees of Anfo Motors, who would retain their duties, seniority, and all other contractual rights. Anfo Motors also sent a letter to its customers in order to inform them of the discontinuance of its activities and to recommend to them the services of the new dealer.

By letter of 27 October 1987, Merckx and Neuhuys refused to accept the proposed transfer, claiming that Anfo Motors could not require them to work for another company, in another place and under different working conditions, without any guarantee as to whether the client base would be retained or a particular turnover achieved.

The question was first, whether Article 1(1) of the directive must be interpreted as applying where an undertaking holding a motor vehicle dealership for a particular territory discontinues its business and the dealership is then transferred to another undertaking that takes on part of its staff and is recommended to customers, without any transfer of assets. Second, having regard to the facts in the main proceedings and in order to provide a helpful response to the national court, it was necessary to establish whether Article 3(1) of the directive precludes an employee of the transferor at the date of transfer of the undertaking from objecting to the transfer of his contract of employment or employment relationship to the transferee.]

It is settled case-law that the decisive criterion for establishing whether there is a transfer for the purposes of the Directive is whether the entity in question retains its economic identity, as indicated inter alia, by the fact that its operation is actually continued or resumed. In order to determine whether that condition is met, it is necessary to consider all the facts characterising the transaction in question, including the type of undertaking or business, whether or not the business' tangible assets, such as buildings and movable property, are transferred, the value of its intangible assets at the time of the transfer, whether or not the majority of its employees is taken over by the new employer, whether or not its customers are transferred and the degree of similarity between the activities carried on before and after the transfer and the period, if any, for which those activities were suspended.

All those factors, taken as a whole, support the view that the transfer of the dealership in the circumstances of the main proceedings is capable of falling within the scope of the Directive. It must be ascertained, however, whether certain factors relied on by Merckx and Neuhuys may rebut that finding. The purpose of an exclusive dealership for the sale of motor vehicles of a particular make in a certain sector remains the same even if it is carried on under a different name, from different premises and with different facilities. It is also irrelevant that the principal place of business is situated in a different area of the same conurbation, provided that the contract territory remains the same.

In that regard, if the Directive's aim of protecting workers is not to be undermined, its application cannot be excluded merely because the transferor discontinues its activities when the transfer is made and is then put into liquidation.

Article 4(1) of the Directive provides that the transfer of an undertaking, business or part of the business does not in itself constitute grounds for dismissal. However, that provision is not to stand in the way of dismissals that may take place for economic, technical or organisational reasons entailing changes in the workforce.

Accordingly, the fact that the majority of the staff was dismissed when the transfer took place is not sufficient to preclude the application of the Directive. It is clear from the case-law that, for the Directive to apply, it is not necessary for there to be a direct contractual relationship between the transferor and the transferee. Consequently, where a motor vehicle dealership concluded with one undertaking is terminated and a new dealership is awarded to another undertaking pursuing the same activities, the transfer of the undertaking is the result of a legal transfer for the purposes of the Directive, as interpreted by the Court.

Thus, Article 1(1) of the Directive of 14 February 1977 must be interpreted as applying where an undertaking holding a motor vehicle dealership for a particular territory discontinues its activities and the dealership is then transferred to another undertaking which takes on part of the staff and is recommended to customers, without any transfer of assets.

Notes

1. In *Süzen* v. *Zehnacker*,[34] the question was raised whether the directive applies to a situation in which a person who had entrusted the cleaning of his premises to a first undertaking terminates his contract with that enterprise and, for the performance of similar work, enters into a new contract with a second undertaking without any concomitant transfer of tangible or intangible business assets from one undertaking to the other. A cleaning lady, Mrs. Süzen, whose job it was to clean a school, had been dismissed with seven other persons after the school had terminated the contract that bound it to their employer, the cleaning company, Zehnacker. Out of the eight persons, seven were reemployed by the new cleaning company Leforth, which had signed the new contract with the school. Mrs. Süzen, who had not been taken on again, argued she was part of the same economic entity that had been moved to the new cleaning company. The Court stated as follows:

    The mere fact that the service provided by the old and the new awardees of a contract is similar does not support the conclusion that an economic entity has been transferred. An entity cannot be reduced to the activity entrusted to it. Its identity also emerges from other factors, such as its work-force, its management staff, the way in which its work is organised, its operating methods or indeed, where appropriate, the operational resources available to it.

    The mere loss of a service contract to a competitor cannot therefore by itself indicate the existence of a transfer within the meaning of the directive. In those circumstances, the service undertaking previously entrusted with the contract does not, on losing a customer, thereby cease fully to exist, and a business or part of a business belonging to it cannot be considered to have been transferred to the new awardee of the contract.

[34] C.O.J., 11 March 1997, *Ayse Süzen* v. *Zehnacker Gebäudereinigung GmbH Krankenhausservice*, C-13/95, ECR, 1997, 1259.

It must also be noted that, although the transfer of assets is one of the criteria to be taken into account by the national court in deciding whether an undertaking has in fact been transferred, the absence of such assets does not necessarily preclude the existence of such a transfer.

The national court, in assessing the facts characterizing the transaction in question, must take into account among other things the type of undertaking or business concerned. It follows that the degree of importance to be attached to each criterion for determining whether or not there has been a transfer within the meaning of the directive will necessarily vary according to the activity carried on, or indeed the production or operating methods employed in the relevant undertaking, business or part of a business. Where in particular an economic entity is able, in certain sectors, to function without any significant tangible or intangible assets, the maintenance of its identity following the transaction affecting it cannot, logically, depend on the transfer of such assets.

Since in certain labour-intensive sectors a group of workers engaged in a joint activity on a permanent basis may constitute an economic entity, it must be recognized that such an entity is capable of maintaining its identity after it has been transferred where the new employer does not merely pursue the activity in question but also takes over a major part, in terms of their numbers and skills, of the employees specially assigned by his predecessor to that task.

In those circumstances, the new employer takes over a body of assets enabling him to carry on the activities or certain activities of the transferor undertaking on a regular basis.

It is for the national court to establish, in the light of the foregoing interpretative guidance, whether a transfer has occurred in this case.

One conclusion is certain. A mere change of subcontractors is in itself not a transfer of an enterprise. The transfer must relate to a stable economic activity. The term entity refers to an organised grouping of persons and assets facilitating the exercise of an economic activity that pursues a specific objective. How can the parties be characterized as "transferors" and "transferees" if there was no contract, indeed, no contact between them? If the new company doing the school cleaning is bound to employ the employees of the prior cleaning contractor to do the work at the school, does that eliminate price competition in the school cleaning business because anyone taking on the school cleaning contract will have to undertake to hire the existing workforce with the existing contract terms when they come into a new school cleaning contract? If, in these labor intensive contracting situations, the only "asset" of the employer transferred is the group of employees who have been doing the work, can the employer simply terminate all the workers to escape the impact of the Directive?

2. In the United States with the at-will presumption for most nonunionized workers, there are no restrictions on the employer's discretion to shut down or transfer its work at the expense of the workers. There is, however, limited protection for workers represented by a union. In *First National Maintenance Corp. v. NLRB*, 452 U.S. 666 (1981), the employer provided cleaning services on a cost plus basis to nursing homes. After the amount above its costs that it received from one nursing home was cut in half, the employer terminated its contract with that nursing home and

discharged all of the employees performing that particular work without notifying or bargaining with the union. The Supreme Court held that the employer had no obligation to bargain the decision to terminate its cleaning contract with the nursing home but it did have the duty to bargain the effects that decision had on its employees at that nursing home.

3. Is the Directive out of date, counterproductive; is it time to fundamentally rethink it? In the very early 1970s, when the directive was being prepared, Professor Blanpain was one of the national experts involved in the preparation of the directive. The directive was the brain child of the then only labor lawyer of the European Commission, Mr. Heinz Karl Schilz, who was a German national. The EU then had nine Member States of which two, namely, Germany and France, had specific national regulations concerning the transfer of enterprises and the acquired rights of the workers. Schilz was of the opinion that the German solution should be made the European one. In those early days, as the common market was becoming a fact and thus expanding in real terms, the idea was that enterprises have to adapt, amalgamate, to merge, absorb each other, take over, to grow, to become bigger in order to be able to successfully operate in the enlarged market of nine countries. The slogan was that workers should not pay the social price for the European economic integration. So, acquired rights of workers were guaranteed in case of transfer. Today, thirty years later, we live in the information society: the bigger companies explode, their work becomes outsourced, subcontracted, externalized. Networking is in. The virtual company is a reality. Today, the slogan is: stick to your core business, outsource the rest. Now we globalize, we externalize to other countries, EU Member States included. Jobs are exported, especially IT jobs to lower-wage countries. So, the nature of the exercise has changed but the directive remains the same. Today, if an enterprise contracts out the accounting or IT to a subcontractor, the latter has to take over all the concerned employees, including those he does not necessarily need. The result is that they get dismissed before or after the transfer.

4. If the outsourcing goes to another EU country are workers and their rights then transferred to the other country? In theory, yes, but, *de facto*, no. Indeed, their employment contracts are broken by the unilateral change of their place of work; they lose their jobs. This is counterproductive.

5. Is the directive really effective in protecting the workers' interests? In the 1970s we were convinced that transfer of acquired rights – you keep your job – was not only a right but also an obligation. The worker was obliged to follow the transfer to the transferee. Then came the *Merckx* case. The ECJ said no, the worker is free to go. There is no forced labor. But if a worker refuses to follow the transfer, what are his rights? Is he resigning and, if so, does he lose all his rights?

6. At the same time, the worth of a company depends more and more on the "brains" of the employees. The transferee wants to have them. So, in case one wants to take over a company, the transferee better make the workers sign that they accept to move to the new employer. Otherwise the new employer might have bought an empty box.

7. With so many elements indicating that it is time to fundamentally rethink the transfer of enterprises directive, less in terms of acquired rights but restated in terms of employability. Perhaps the focus needs to be on helping find the affected

workers another job and making it possible for them to survive economically until they do. Indeed, the best job security is the employment security, namely, the one deriving from his competences.

G. ANTIDISCRIMINATION LAW

EU law against discrimination began with the protection of equal rights for women with Article 119 of the original Treaty. That law has continued to expand in terms of the scope of protection given women but also in terms of adding new protected classes. The Treaty of Amsterdam amended Article 2 of the EC Treaty to include among the tasks of the Community the promotion of "equality between men and women" and amended Article 3(2) by providing that the Community "shall aim to eliminate inequalities, and to promote equality, between men and women." Moreover, the Amsterdam Treaty added Article 13, which reads:

> Without prejudice to the other provisions of this Treaty and within the limits of the powers conferred by it upon the Community, the Council, acting unanimously on a proposal from the Commission and after consulting the European Parliament, may take appropriate action to combat discrimination based on sex, racial or ethnic origin, religion or belief, disability, age or sexual orientation.

Article 141 now provides:

1. Each Member State shall ensure that the principle of equal pay for male and female workers for equal work or work of equal value is applied.
2. For the purpose of this Article, 'pay' means the ordinary basic or minimum wage or salary and any other consideration, whether in cash or in kind, which the worker receives directly or indirectly, in respect of his employment, from his employer.

   Equal pay without discrimination based on sex means:
   (a) that pay for the same work at piece rates shall be calculated on the basis of the same unit of measurement;
   (b) that pay for work at time rates shall be the same for the same job.
3. The Council, acting in accordance with the procedure referred to in Article 251, and after consulting the Economic and Social Committee, shall adopt measures to ensure the application of the principle of equal opportunities and equal treatment of men and women in matters of employment and occupation, including the principle of equal pay for equal work or work of equal value.
4. With a view to ensuring full equality in practice between men and women in working life, the principle of equal treatment shall not prevent any Member State from maintaining or adopting measures providing for specific advantages in order to make it easier for the under-represented sex to pursue a vocational activity or to prevent or compensate for disadvantages in professional careers.

The following directives have been based on that expanding authority and reflect the expansion of EU antidiscrimination law that must be transposed by the Member States so that their naitonal laws conform:

- 1975: relating to the application of equal pay for men and women;[35]

---

[35] 10 February 1975, No. 75/117, O.J. L 45/19, 19 February 1975.

- 1976: relating to the implementation of the principle of equal treatment for men and women as regards access to employment, vocational training and promotion, and working conditions;[36]
- 1978: concerning the progressive implementation of the principle of equal treatment for men and women in matters of social security;[37]
- 1986: on the implementation of the principle of equal treatment for men and women in occupational social security schemes;[38]
- 1997: on the burden of proof in cases of discrimination based on sex;[39]
- 2000: establishing a general framework for equal treatment in employment and occupation;[40]
- 2000: implementing the principle of equal treatment between persons irrespective of racial or ethnic origin.[41]

1. Equal Pay for Work of Equal Value

Given that EU antidiscrimination jurisprudence started with equal pay for equal work for male and female workers, it should be no surprise that there is a large number of decisions dealing with that problem. The earliest case of significance is *Defrenne v. Societe Anonyme Belge de Navigation Aerienne Sabena*, C-43/75 (1976), in which a flight attendant for Sabena Airlines alleged gender discrimination by invoking the right to equal pay for equal work directly under Article 119, what is now Article 141 of the EC Treaty. The Court found that the equal pay for equal work provisions of the Treaty were directly enforceable where a plaintiff demonstrates "direct discrimination," that is, "that men and women receive unequal pay for equal work carried out in the same establishment or service."

In *Murphy v. Bord Telecom Eireann*, C-157/86 (1988), plaintiffs showed their work was of greater value than the work done by more highly paid men. They won: If the principle of equal pay for equal work "forbids workers of one sex engaged in work of equal value to that of workers of the opposite sex engaged in work of equal value to that of workers of the opposite sex to be paid a lower wage than the latter on grounds of sex, it *a fortiori* prohibits such a difference in pay where the lower-paid category of workers is engaged in work of higher value." Article 141 now also includes an expanded definition of the duty of employers. No longer is the duty limited to equal pay for the same work, but now the duty includes the duty of equal pay for work of equal value. In the United States, this has come to be known as "comparable worth" that is not within the scope of the Equal Pay Act of 1963, 29 U.S.C. section 206(d)(1).

In *Jenkins v. Kingsgate (Clothing Productions) Ltd.*, C-96/80 (1981), the Court held that paying part-time workers less than what is paid full-time workers did not constitute per se sex discrimination even when a majority of part-time workers were women. In *Bilka-Kaufhouse GmbH. V. Von Hartz*, C-170/84 (1986), however, the Court shifted the

---

[36] 9 February 1976, No. 76/207, O.J. L 39/40, 14 February 1976, amended by Directive Directive 2002/73/EC of 23 September 2002, O.J., 5 October 2002, L 269.
[37] 19 December 1978, No. 79/7, O.J. L 6/24, 10 February 1979.
[38] 24 July 1986, No. 86/378, O.J. L 45/40, 12 August 1986, amended by Directive 96/97 of 2 December 1996.
[39] 15 December 1997, No. 97/80, O.J. L 14/6, 20 January 1998.
[40] Council Directive 2000/78EC of 27 November 2000, O.J. L 303, 2 December 2000.
[41] Council Directive 2000/43EC of 29 June 2000, O.J. L 180, 19 July 2000.

burden of proof after such a showing was made, so that the employer must show "objectively justified economic grounds" to warrant paying part-time workers less than full-time workers. The employer did not use an explicit gender classification in either *Jenkins* or *Bilka*. The holding in *Bilka*, therefore, recognizes that indirect discrimination, what is called disparate impact discrimination in U.S antidiscrimination parlance, is within the scope of EU antidiscrimination law. The 1997 directive explicitly included indirect discrimination, defining it as occurring "where an apparently neutral provision, criterion or practice disadvantages a substantially higher proportion of the members of one sex unless that provison, criterion or practice is appropriate and necessary and can be justified by objective factors unrelated to sex."

2. Sex Discrimination in Employment

In *Defrenne v. Societe Anonyme Belge de Navigation Aerienne Sabena*, C-43/75 (1976), the Court, however, held that Article 119 applied only to discrimination as to pay, not to her claims that she was forced to retire at age forty while flight stewards were not. Had Belgium implemented the Directive 76/207 by the time of Defrenne's discharge, her forced retirement could have been challenged. Article 1 established the principle of equal treatment in hiring, promotion, working conditions and vocation training. Article 2(1) includes discrimination based on "marital or family status" with the proscription of the Directive. Article 1(2) of Directive 2002/73/EC defines sex discrimination quite broadly:

- direct discrimination: where one person is treated less favourably on grounds of sex than another is, has been or would be treated in a comparable situation,
- indirect discrimination: where an apparently neutral provision, criterion or practice would put persons of one sex at a particular disadvantage compared with persons of the other sex, unless that provision, criterion or practice is objectively justified by a legitimate aim, and the means of achieving that aim are appropriate and necessary,
- harassment: where an unwanted conduct related to the sex of the person occurs with the purpose or effect of violating the dignity of a person, and of creating an intimidating, hostile, degrading, humiliating, or offensive environment,
- sexual harassment: where any form of unwanted verbal, non-verbal or physical conduct of a sexual nature occurs, with the purpose or effect of violating the dignity of the person, in particular when creating an intimidating, hostile, degrading, humiliating or offensive environment.

Article 4(1) of the Directive 97/80/EC shifts the burden of proof in discrimination cases to the defendant once a prima facie case of discrimination has been established: "Member States shall take such measures as are necessary, in accordance with their national judicial systems, to ensure that, when persons who consider themselves wronged because the principle of equal treatment has not been applied to them establish, before a court or other competent authority, facts from which it may be presumed that there has been direct or indirect discrimination, it shall be for the respondent to prove that there has been no breach of the principle of equal treatment."

Article 2 of the 1976 Directive establishes three exceptions, with two for the benefit of women and one for employers. Thus Article 2(3) permits protective treatment "as regards pregnancy and maternity" and 2(4) permits affirmative action, that is, "measures to promote equal opportunity . . . by removing existing inequalities."

Article 2(2) allows Member States to permit discrimination in "occupational activities . . . for which, by reason of their nature or the context in which they are carried out, the sex of the worker constitutes a determining factor." In *Sirdar v. The Army Board and Secretary of State for Defence*, C-273/97 (1999), plaintiff, who had been a chef in the British Army and in a commando regiment of its Royal Artillery, challenged the denial of her application to be a chef for the Royal Marines because the Marines did not admit women. The Court rejected plaintiff's claim finding that the Royal Marine's rule was sheltered by the occupational activities exception in Article 2(2) of the Directive. "[T]he organisation of the Royal Marines differs fundamentally from that of other units in the British armed forces, of which they are the 'point of the arrow head.' They are a small force and are intended to be the first line of attack. It has been established that, within this corps, chefs are indeed also required to serve as front-line commandos." In contrast, in *Kreil v. Federal Republic of Germany*, C-285/98 (2000), the Court found that the provision of German law that limited women to medical and military-music service because women were prohibited from any post involving the use of arms was not within the occupational activities exception in Article 2(2). The occupational activities exception can only apply to specific activities and cannot be used to justify a general rule. "[H]aving regard to the very nature of armed forces, the fact that persons serving in those forces may be called on to use arms cannot in inself justify the exclusion of women from access to military posts." In *Kreil*, the Court also rejected the protection of women rationale of Article 2(3).

KALANKE V. FREIE HANSESTADT BREMEN

C-450/93 (1995)

[The German *Land* (state) of Bremen enacted a regulation governing appointments or promotions to public posts in departments where women were under-represented, with under representation presumed if women do not make up half the staff: "[W]omen who have the same qualifications as men applying for the same post are to be given priority." At the final stage of recruitment to a post of Section Manager in the Bremen Parks Department, two candidates were shortlisted, Mr. Eckhard Kalanke, the plaintiff in the main proceedings, a holder of a diploma in horticulture and landscape gardening, who had worked since 1973 as a horticultural employee in the Parks Department and acted as permanent assistant to the Section Manager, and Ms. Glissmann, holder of a diploma in landscape gardening since 1983 and also employed, since 1975, as a horticultural employee in the Parks Department.

The Court of Justice concluded that the regulation constituted "discrimination on grounds of sex" and then turned to whether it was justified by the affirmative action provision of Article 2(4).]

The purpose of the Directive is, as stated in Article 1(1), to put into effect in the Member States the principle of equal treatment for men and women as regards, inter alia, access to employment, including promotion. Article 2(1) states that the principle of equal treatment means that "there shall be no discrimination whatsoever on grounds of sex either directly or indirectly".

A national rule that, where men and women who are candidates for the same promotion are equally qualified, women are automatically to be given priority in sectors where they are underrepresented, involves discrimination on grounds of sex.

It must, however, be considered whether such a national rule is permissible under Article 2(4), which provides that the Directive "shall be without prejudice to measures to promote equal opportunity for men and women, in particular by removing existing inequalities which affect women's opportunities".

That provision is specifically and exclusively designed to allow measures which, although discriminatory in appearance, are in fact intended to eliminate or reduce actual instances of inequality which may exist in the reality of social life.

It thus permits national measures relating to access to employment, including promotion, which give a specific advantage to women with a view to improving their ability to compete on the labour market and to pursue a career on an equal footing with men.

Nevertheless, as a derogation from an individual right laid down in the Directive, Article 2(4) must be interpreted strictly.

National rules which guarantee women absolute and unconditional priority for appointment or promotion go beyond promoting equal opportunities and overstep the limits of the exception in Article 2(4) of the Directive.

Furthermore, in so far as it seeks equal representation of men and women in all grades and levels within a department, such a system substitutes for equality of opportunity envisaged in Article 2(4) the result which is to be arrived at by providing such opportunity.'

Article 2(1) and (4) of the Directive of 1976 precludes national rules whereby candidates of different sexes shortlisted for promotion are equally qualified, automatically give priority to women in sectors where they are under-represented, under-representation being deemed to exist when women do not make up at least half of the staff in the individual pay brackets in the relevant personnel group or in the function levels provided for in the organisation chart.

Notes

1. In *Hellmut Marschall* v. *Land Nordrhein Westfalen*,[42] the Court qualified *Kalanke*. It stated as follows:

   > A national rule which, in a case where there are fewer women than men at the level of the relevant post in a sector of the public service, and both female and male candidates for the post are equally qualified in terms of their suitability, competence and professional performance requires that priority be given to the promotion of female candidates unless reasons specific to an individual male candidate tilt the balance in his favour is not precluded by Article 2(1) and (4) of the Directive, provided that:

   > > in each individual case the rule provides male candidates who are as equally qualified as the female candidates with a guarantee that the candidatures

---

[42] C.O.J., 11 November 1997, C-409/95, ECR, 1997, 6363.

will be the subject of an objective assessment which will take account of all criteria specific to the individual candidates and will override the priority accorded to female candidates where one or more of those criteria tilts the balance in favour of the male candidate, and such criteria are not such as to discriminate.

In *Abrahamsson v. Fogelqvist*, C-407/98 (2000), Swedish law provided that when filling thirty particular posts at universities, a candidate "belonging to an under-represented sex who possesses sufficient qualifications . . . must be granted preference over a candidate of the opposite sex who would otherwise would have been chosen . . . where it proves necessary to do so in order for a candidate of the under-represented sex to be appointed. Positive discrimination must, however, not be applied where the difference between the candidates' qualifications is so great that such application would give rise to a breach of the requirement of objectivity in making appointments." Finding that this provision would justify appointments of candidate who do "not possess qualifications equal to those of other candidates of the opposite sex," the Court found this inconsistent with the Directive despite the proviso that the differences cannot be so great as to be a breach of objectivity. "The scope and effect of that condition cannot be precisely determined, with the result that the selection of a candidate from among those who are sufficiently qualified is ultimately based on the mere fact of belonging to the under-represented sex, and that this is so even if the merits of the candidate so selected are inferior to those of a candidate of the opposite sex." What is the rule based on *Kalante, Helmut Marschall,* and *Abrahamsson?* Is the first step that affirmative action is not permissible unless it is used as a tiebreaker between two candidates found to be equally qualified? Even if the candidates are equally qualified, when can the employer pick the member of the underrepresented sex?

2. Direct discrimination is similar to the concept of disparate treatment discrimination in U.S. antidiscrimination law. But, unlike disparate treatment theory, direct discrimination focuses on the violation of equal treatment and not on the proof that defendant intended to discriminate, which can frequently be shown by proving a violation of equal treatment under U.S. law. *See,* for example, *Desert Palace, Inc. v. Costa,* 539 U.S. 90 (2003), where plaintiff, a trailblazing woman working in a warehouse, proved that she had been the victim of a continuing series of unequal treatment culminating in her discharge when a fellow employee, with whom she was having an altercation, pushed her causing injury. In contrast to her discharge, her co-worker received a short suspension. This evidence was all relevant to finding the ultimate question of whether the employer acted with an intent to discriminate. *See St. Mary's Honor Center v. Hicks,* 509 U.S. 502 (1993). Although U.S. disparate treatment law is complex, plaintiff can establish a prima facie case by showing evidence sufficient to draw an inference that discrimination was a motivating factor for defendant's act. With that showing, liability is established but the employer can limit plaintiff's remedies by showing that it would have made the same decision even if it had not been motivated by discrimination. *Desert Palace.* Alternatively, plaintiff can avoid the so-called same decision defense if she can present evidence upon which factfinder concludes that the "employee's protected trait actually played a role in [defendant's decision making] process and had a

determinative influence on the outcome." *Hazen Paper Co. v. Biggins,* 507 U.S. 604, 610 (1993).

2. Indirect discrimination is similar to the disparate impact theory of discrimination in U.S. law. Neither indirect discrimination nor disparate impact discrimination includes a state of mind element that the defendant acted with an intent to discriminate. In both, plaintiff needs to show that an employer practice caused an impact on a protected group. That prima facie case then shifts the burden of proof to the defendant to prove, in U.S. law, that the practice was job related and justified by business necessity, or, in EU law, that the practice "is objectively justified by a legitimate aim, and the means of achieving that aim are appropriate and necessary."

3. As is true in the United States, harassment is considered sex discrimination in EU law.

---

3. Other Kinds of Discrimination

In Directive 2000/43/EC, racial and ethic discrimination was prohibited: Article 1 provides, "For the purposes of this Directive, the principle of equal treatment shall mean that there shall be no direct or indirect discrimination based on racial or ethnic origin." Article 2 of Directive 2000/78/EC prohibits discrimination that violates the purposes of Article 1, which provides: "The purpose of this Directive is to lay down a general framework for combating discrimination on the grounds of religion or belief, disability, age or sexual orientation as regards employment and occupation, with a view to putting into effect in the Member States the principle of equal treatment."

While including direct, indirect, and harassment discrimination within its scope of proscription as well as the occupation and positive action defenses, Directive 2000/78/EC adds two new provisions dealing specifically with individuals with disabilities and claims of age discrimination. Article 5 establishes a reasonable accommodation concept for individuals with disabilities:

> In order to guarantee compliance with the principle of equal treatment in relation to persons with disabilities, reasonable accommodation shall be provided. This means that employers shall take appropriate measures, where needed in a particular case, to enable a person with a disability to have access to, participate in, or advance in employment, or to undergo training, unless such measures would impose a disproportionate burden on the employer. This burden shall not be disproportionate when it is sufficiently remedied by measures existing within the framework of the disability policy of the Member State concerned.

Article 6 creates two defenses to age discrimination claims:

1. Notwithstanding Article 2(2), Member States may provide that differences of treatment on grounds of age shall not constitute discrimination, if, within the context of national law, they are objectively and reasonably justified by a legitimate aim, including legitimate employment policy, labour market and vocational training objectives, and if the means of achieving that aim are appropriate and necessary. Such differences of treatment may include, among others:
   a. the setting of special conditions on access to employment and vocational training, employment and occupation, including dismissal and remuneration con-

ditions, for young people, older workers and persons with caring responsibilities in order to promote their vocational integration or ensure their protection;

   b. the fixing of minimum conditions of age, professional experience or seniority in service for access to employment or to certain advantages linked to employment;

   c. the fixing of a maximum age for recruitment which is based on the training requirements of the post in question or the need for a reasonable period of employment before retirement.

2. Notwithstanding Article 2(2), Member States may provide that the fixing for occupational social security schemes of ages for admission or entitlement to retirement or invalidity benefits, including the fixing under those schemes of different ages for employees or groups or categories of employees, and the use, in the context of such schemes, of age criteria in actuarial calculations, does not constitute discrimination on the grounds of age, provided this does not result in discrimination on the grounds of sex.

K.B. V. NATIONAL HEALTH SERVICE PENSIONS AGENCY AND SECRETARY OF STATE FOR HEALTH

C-117/01, ECR., 2004, 541 (2004)

["KB" had worked for the UK National Health Service (NHS) as a nurse for twenty years. During that time, she had contributed to the NHS pension scheme, which provides for a survivor's pension to be payable to the surviving spouse (taken to mean the person to whom the scheme member is married).

KB has shared a relationship for many years with "R," who had undergone female-to-male gender reassignment surgery. KB wished R to have the right to the widower's pension under the NHS scheme that would have been available had she been married to a man. However, U.K. legislation prevented transsexuals from marrying in their acquired sex and deemed void any marriage in which the parties are not male and female. Therefore, contrary to their wishes, KB and R have not been able to marry and R is thus prevented from receiving a survivor's pension.

KB took a case to the U.K. courts, claiming that she was a victim of discrimination on grounds of sex in relation to pay. She argued that the term "widower" must be interpreted as also encompassing the surviving member of a couple, who would have acquired the status of a widower, had his gender not resulted from surgical gender reassignment The U.K. court of appeal referred the case to the Court of Justice, with the issue being whether Article 141 of the EC Treaty or the Equal Treatment Directive, 75/117/EC, would be violated if the UK law were applied.]

Benefits granted under a pension scheme which essentially relates to the employment of the person concerned form part of the pay received by that person and come within the scope of Article 141 EC.

The Court has also recognised that a survivor's pension provided for by such a scheme falls within the scope of Article 141 EC. It has stated in that regard that the fact that such a pension, by definition, is not paid to the employee but to the employee's survivor does not affect that interpretation because, such a benefit being an advantage deriving from the survivor's spouse's membership of the scheme, the pension is vested in the survivor by reason of the employment relationship between the employer and the survivor's spouse and is paid to the survivor by reason of the spouse's work.

So a survivor's pension paid under an occupational pension scheme such as the NHS Pension Scheme constitutes 'pay' within the meaning of Article 141 EC and Directive 75/117.

The decision to restrict certain benefits to married couples while excluding all persons who live together without being married is either a matter for the legislature to decide or a matter for the national courts as to the interpretation of domestic legal rules, and individuals cannot claim that there is discrimination on grounds of sex, prohibited by Community law.

In this instance, such a requirement cannot be regarded per se as discriminatory on grounds of sex and, accordingly, as contrary to Article 141 EC or Directive 75/117, since for the purposes of awarding the survivor's pension it is irrelevant whether the claimant is a man or a woman.

However, in a situation such as that before the national court, there is inequality of treatment which, although it does not directly undermine enjoyment of a right protected by Community law, affects one of the conditions for the grant of that right. As the Advocate General noted in point 74 of his Opinion, the inequality of treatment does not relate to the award of a widower's pension but to a necessary precondition for the grant of such a pension: namely, the capacity to marry.

In the United Kingdom, by comparison with a heterosexual couple where neither partner's identity is the result of gender reassignment surgery and the couple are therefore able to marry and, as the case may be, have the benefit of a survivor's pension which forms part of the pay of one of them, a couple such as K.B. and R. are quite unable to satisfy the marriage requirement, as laid down by the NHS Pension Scheme for the purpose of the award of a survivor's pension.

The fact that it is impossible for them to marry is due to the fact, first, that the Matrimonial Causes Act 1973 deems a marriage void if the parties are not respectively male and female; second, that a person's sex is deemed to be that appearing on his or her birth certificate; and, third, that the Births and Deaths Registration Act does not allow for any alteration of the register of births, except in the case of clerical error or an error of fact.

The European Court of Human Rights has held that the fact that it is impossible for a trans-sexual to marry a person of the sex to which he or she belonged prior to gender reassignment surgery, which arises because, for the purposes of the registers of civil status, they belong to the same sex (United Kingdom legislation not admitting of legal recognition of transsexuals' new identity), was a breach of their right to marry under Article 12 of the ECHR (see Eur. Court H.R. judgments of 11 July 2002 in Goodwin v United Kingdom and I. v United Kingdom, not yet published in the Reports of Judgments and Decisions, §§ 97 to 104 and §§ 77 to 84 respectively).

Legislation, such as that at issue in the main proceedings, which, in breach of the ECHR, prevents a couple such as K.B. and R. from fulfilling the marriage requirement which must be met for one of them to be able to benefit from part of the pay of the other must be regarded as being, in principle, incompatible with the requirements of Article 141 EC.

Since it is for the Member States to determine the conditions under which legal recognition is given to the change of gender of a person in R.'s situation – as the European Court of Human Rights has accepted (Goodwin v United Kingdom, § 103) – it is for the national court to determine whether in a case such as that in the main proceedings a person in K.B.'s situation can rely on Article 141 EC in order to gain recognition of her right to nominate her partner as the beneficiary of a survivor's pension.

It follows from the foregoing that Article 141 EC, in principle, precludes legislation, such as that at issue before the national court, which, in breach of the ECHR, prevents a couple such as K.B. and R. from fulfilling the marriage requirement which must be met for one of them to be able to benefit from part of the pay of the other. It is for the national court to determine whether in a case such as that in the main proceedings a person in K.B.'s situation can rely on Article 141 EC in order to gain recognition of her right to nominate her partner as the beneficiary of a survivor's pension.

Notes

1. Article 12 of the European Convention on Human Rights protects the right to marry. The *Goodwin* case was a decision by the European Court of Human Rights (the judicial institution of the Council of Europe, which has 46 European Member States), in Strasbourg, France, that prohibiting marriage by transsexuals was a violation of Article 12. So far, that Court has not extended the right to marry to same-sex couples based on the language of the Article 12: "Men and women of marriageable age have the right to marry and to found a family, according to the national laws governing the exercise of this right."

2. In *P v. S*, C-13/94 (1996), the Court also relied on the decisions of the European Court of Human Rights to hold that the defendant's termination of the plaintiff because she had had gender reassignment to become a woman violated the 1976 Equal Treatment Directive. But in *Grant v. South-West Trains Ltd.*, C-249/96 (1998), the Court found that the failure of the employer to provide fringe benefits to a woman employee's woman partner did not violate the directive even though the two lesbians had a stable relationship outside of marriage. The Court distinguished *P v. S*:

   > The Court considered that such discrimination was in fact based, essentially if not exclusively, on the sex of the person concerned. That reasoning, which leads to the conclusion that such discrimination is to be prohibited just as is discrimination based on the fact that a person belongs to a particular sex, is limited to the case of a worker's gender reassignment and does not therefore apply to differences of treatment based on a person's sexual orientation.

   The Court also referred to the Treaty of Amsterdam, which in Article 141 empowers the EU to address issues of discrimination because of sexual orientation. Directive 2000/78/EC now does that. Will the European Court of Justice now come out the other way in a case like *Grant?*

H. PRIVACY

The EU is a leader in terms of developing general protections for personal data, including data that are collected and transmitted concerning employees. With the creation of the single internal market within the EU in 1992, the amount of personal data that crossed national borders increased, and accordingly, the need to harmonize the scattered European national data protection laws and develop a uniform high level of protection was realized. "The European approach is based upon the premise that privacy is a human right and data protection is an essential means to protect that right through a coherent and enforceable legal regime." Graham Pearce & Nicholas Platten, *Orchestrating Transatlantic Approaches to Personal Data Protection: A European Perspective*, 22 FORDHAM INT'L L.J 2024, 2025 (1999). Therefore, the EU has taken a high level regulatory approach to protect the fundamental right to privacy with regard to personal data for its citizens by enacting the European Union Privacy Directive by approving in 1995 a Privacy Directive 95/46/EC, 1995 O.J. (L281) 31, *available in two parts at* http://ec.europa.eu/justice_home/fsj/privacy/docs/95-46-ce/dir-1995-46-part1_en.pdf and http://ec.europa.eu/justice_home/fsj/privacy/docs/95-46-ce/dir1995-46-part2_en.pdf. The Directive declares two primary objectives: (1) to protect the fundamental rights and freedoms of natural persons, and in particular their right to privacy with respect to the processing of personal data, and (2) to ensure the free flow of personal data between Member States. Directive, Art. 1(1) & 1(2). While setting the conditions for protection of the data, the Directive has opened the door for the free flow of data between Member States. Arguably, however, its restrictions obstruct the free transfer of data to countries outside of the EU because the Directive demands non-member countries provide "adequate" protection of personal data collected from companies operating in the EU.

All twenty-five member states have enacted new or updated existing regulations to be compliant with the Directive. *See* European Commission Justice and Home Affairs, The Status of Implementation of Directive 95/46, http://ec.europa.eu/justice_home/fsj/privacy/law/implementation_en.htm (last visited 21 June 2006). The United Kingdom was one of the first to transpose the Directive into its national laws by adopting the Data Protection Act in July 1998. The Act, however, has been criticized as being too complicated and not effective in promoting the Directives goals. *See generally* Privacy International, PHR2004 – Country Reports – United Kingdom of Great Britain, http://www.privacyinternational.org/article.shtml?cmd[347]=x-347-83802 (last visited 21 June 2006). On the other end of the spectrum, Germany is known to have one of the strictest standards for privacy protection. Its latest revision of data protection laws was adopted in 2001 to be compliant with the Directive. Regulations for transmitting personal data abroad and processing of sensitive data are among the changes that have taken place to bring the German data protection laws into compliance. *See generally* Privacy International, PHR2004 – Country Reports – Federal Republic of Germany, http://www.privacyinternational.org/article.shtml?cmd[347]=x-347-83513 (last visited 21 June 2006). France was one of the last to adopt revisions to bring its existing Data Protection Act into compliance with the Directive. The revision of France's 1978 Data Protection Act was adopted by the Parliament on 15 July 2004. However, this recently adopted bill has yet to be approved by the French Constitutional Council and may face further modifications to ensure the constitutionality of the bill. *See,* generally, Privacy International, PHR2004 – Country Reports – French Republic, http://www.privacyinternational.org/article.shtml?cmd[347]=x-347-83516 (last visited 21 June 2006).

"Personal data" is defined as "any information relating to an identified or identifiable natural person ('data subject'); an identifiable person is one who can be identified, directly or indirectly, in particular by reference to an identification number or to one or more factors specific to his physical, physiological, mental, economic, cultural or social identity." *Id.* Art. 2(a). In addition, processing of personal data is also defined very broadly to include almost any action taken on data such as collecting, destroying, or filing for storage purposes. *See id.* Art. 2(b). Although the Directive was not directed specifically at employment, it obviously applies to every employer operating in the EU because employers process personal data of employees on a regular basis. Employers are required to comply with the national data protection laws promulgated by the EU State in which they are operating and processing personal data. Directive, Art. 4(1). In addition, employers based outside the EU are responsible for acting in compliance with data protection laws of the EU Member State if any personal data is processed within that state. *Id.* Art. 4 Thus, virtually any type of data that an employer might collect from an employee in the course of recruiting, evaluating employee performance or providing employee benefits will fall within the scope of the Directive.

Because the Directive is extremely important to employers, the Article 29 Working Party – a group of representatives from each Member State established by the Directive pursuant to Article 29 to advise, give opinions and make recommendations on all matters relevant to the implementation and enforcement of the Directive – published an opinion in 2001 on the topic of processing personal data in the employment context to help employers understand the requirements and obligations as they pertain to employee data. *See,* generally, Article 29 - Data Protection Working Party Opinion 8/2001 On the Processing of Personal Data in the Employment Context, Sept. 13, 2001 (5062/01/EN/Final WP 48), available at http://ec.europa.eu/justice_home/fsj/privacy/docs/wpdocs/2001/wp48en.pdf.

The Article 29 Working Party opinion tailored the fundamental data protection principles outlined in Article 6 of the Directive as they should apply in the employment context.

1. **FINALITY:** Data must be collected for a specified, explicit and legitimate purpose and not further processed in a way incompatible with those purposes.
2. **TRANSPARENCY:** As a very minimum, workers need to know which data is the employer collecting about them (directly or from other sources), which are the purposes of processing operations envisaged or carried out with these data presently or in the future. Transparency is also assured by granting the data subject the right to access to his/her personal data and with the data controllers' obligation of notifying supervisory authorities as provided in national law.
3. **LEGITIMACY:** The processing of workers' personal data must be legitimate. Article 7 of the Directive lists the criteria making the processing legitimate.
4. **PROPORTIONALITY:** The personal data must be adequate, relevant and not excessive in relation to the purposes for which they are collected and/or further processed. Assuming that workers have been informed about the processing operation and assuming that such processing activity is legitimate and proportionate, such a processing still needs to be fair with the worker.

5. **ACCURACYY AND RETENTION OF THE DATA:** Employment records must be accurate and, where necessary, kept up to date. The employer must take every reasonable step to ensure that data inaccurate or incomplete, having regard to the purposes for which they were collected or further processed, are erased or rectified.

6. **SECURITY:** The employer must implement appropriate technical and organisational measures at the workplace to guarantee that the personal data of his workers is kept secured. Particular protection should be granted as regards unauthorised disclosure or access.

7. **AWARENESS OF THE STAFF:** Staff in charge or with responsibilities in the processing of personal data of other workers need to know about data protection and receive proper training. Without an adequate training of the staff handling personal data, there could never be appropriate respect for the privacy of workers in the workplace. *Id.* at 3.

The most onerous of these principles for employers to apply is legitimacy because its scope is so open-ended. *See,* generally, Jorg Rehder & Erika C. Collins, *The Legal Transfer of Employment Related Data to Outside the European Union,* 39 INT'L LAW. 129 (Spring, 2005). In order for an employer to process personal data of employees, the employer must establish legitimacy by meeting one of the enumerated criteria in Article 7.[43] In the context of employment the most commonly used grounds for legitimately processing personal data are: necessity for the performance of an employment contract (e.g., payment of salary), necessity for compliance with legal obligations (e.g., compliance with tax laws), necessity for legitimate interests of the employer (e.g., selling the business). *See id.* Another grounds to establish legitimacy is unambiguous employee consent. However, unambiguous consent has been interpreted very narrowly in most EU jurisdictions, and thus an employer will likely face an uphill battle to establish that employee consent was obtained unequivocally. *See id.*

An employer must also be aware that the Directive is mindful of processing "sensitive" data. "Sensitive" data is categorized as data revealing "racial or ethnic origin, political opinions, religious or philosophical beliefs, trade-union membership, and the processing of data concerning health or sex life." Directive, at Art. 8(1). Processing of such information

---

[43] Article 7 provides:

Member States shall provide that personal data may be processed only if:

(a) the data subject has unambiguously given his consent; or

(b) processing is necessary for the performance of a contract to which the data subject is party or in order to take steps at the request of the data subject prior to entering into a contract; or

(c) processing is necessary for compliance with a legal obligation to which the controller is subject; or

(d) processing is necessary in order to protect the vital interests of the data subject; or

(e) processing is necessary for the performance of a task carried out in the public interest or in the exercise of official authority vested in the controller or in a third party to whom the data are disclosed; or

(f) processing is necessary for the purposes of the legitimate interests pursued by the controller or by the third party or parties to whom the data are disclosed, except where such interests are overridden by the interests for fundamental rights and freedoms of the data subject which require protection under Article 1 (1).

is generally prohibited unless it falls within one of the enumerated exceptions.[44] The exceptions are reasonable, but include more qualifications than for the processing of simple "personal data." For example, personal data may be processed by an employer if employee consent is obtained unambiguously, however, for sensitive data consent must be explicit. *See id.* at Art. 7(a) and 8(2)(a).

When the Directive was implemented, there was concern by Member States and non member states over the provisions of Chapter IV: Transfer of Personal Data to Third Countries. In short, the Chapter IV requires every Member State to ensure that non-member countries met "adequate levels of data privacy protection" before transferring any personal data to those counterparts. Directive Art. 25(1). Countries that have different approaches and systems in place to protect personal data that are not as comprehensive as the EU Directive are in essence faced with an ultimatum of conforming with EU regulations or not receiving data from EU countries. The United States has been reluctant to regulate data protection at the government level. Instead, it has relied on markets and technology to determine what level of data protection is demanded by the public on an ad hoc basis. In some respects, the "American approach to privacy protection is driven by business interests, as compared to the E.U.'s rights-based approach." Chuan Sun, *The European Union Privacy Directive and Its Impact on the U.S. Privacy Protection Policy: A Year 2003 Perspective*, 2 Nw. J. Tech. & Intell. Prop. 99, 105 (Fall, 2003). The power struggle between these disparate approaches and efforts to reconcile differences has been the topic of much academic literature regarding the EU Directive. *See, e.g.,* Jorg Rehder & Erika C. Collins, *The Legal Transfer of Employment Related Data to Outside the European Union*, 39 Int'l Law. 129 (Spring, 2005); Chuan Sun, *The European Union Privacy Directive and Its Impact on the U.S. Privacy Protection Policy: A Year 2003 Perspective*, Nw. J. Tech. & Intell. Prop. (2003); Rosa Barcelo, *Seeking Suitable Options for Importing Data from the European Union*, 36 Int'l Law. 985 (Fall, 2002); Barbara Crutchfield George et al., *U.S. Multinational Employers: Navigating Through the "Safe Harbor" Principles to Comply with the EU Data Privacy Directive*, 38 Am. Bus. L.J. 735, 742 (2001); Graham Pearce & Nicholas Platten, *Orchestrating Transatlantic Approaches to Personal Data Protection: A European Perspective*, 22 Fordham Int'l L.J 2024, 2025 (1999).

"The adequacy of the level of protection afforded by a third country shall be assessed in light of all the circumstances surrounding a data transfer operation . . . " Directive Art. 25(2). Thus, although a nonmember country might need to establish a higher level

---

[44] Article 2 provides:

  2. Paragraph 1 shall not apply where:
  (a) the data subject has given his explicit consent to the processing of those data, except where the laws of the Member State provide that the prohibition referred to in paragraph 1 may not be lifted by the data subject's giving his consent; or
  (b) processing is necessary for the purposes of carrying out the obligations and specific rights of the controller in the field of employment law in so far as it is authorized by national law providing for adequate safeguards. . . .
  3. Paragraph 1 shall not apply where processing of the data is required for the purposes of preventive medicine, medical diagnosis, the provision of care or treatment or the management of health-care services, and where those data are processed by a health professional subject under national law or rules established by national competent bodies to the obligation of professional secrecy or by another person also subject to an equivalent obligation of secrecy.

of protection than normal, adequate protection does not require a nonmember country to completely conform to the protections that Member States abide by. A handful of non EU countries have been labelled as affording adequate protection by the EU and enjoy the benefits of personal data transfer with the same fluidity as enjoyed by Member States, for example, Switzerland, Hungary, Canada, Argentina, Guernsey, and the Isle of Man. Rehder & Collins, *supra*. However, many countries are still not considered to provide adequate protection of personal data and are required to negotiate with EU entities independently before receiving data from the EU. The economic impact of prohibiting data transfer can be high, especially for multinational companies that operate in EU Member States as well as countries deemed to provide inadequate protection, as the United States. For example, in the context of human resources data, this means data about employees in the EU cannot be collected in cost-efficient, centralized databases that are maintained outside the EU.

To provide flexibility, Article 26 of the Directive outlines circumstances under which Member States can provide a "transfer or set of transfers of personal data to a third country which does not ensure an adequate level of protection." Directive Art. 26(1). There are express derogations listed in Article 26(1) but for the most part, the scope of these derogations are not favored, are very narrow and, for the most part, are ineffective. *See* Commission Staff Working Document SEC (2006) at 2. Available *at* http://ec.europa.eu/justice_home/fsj/privacy/docs/modelcontracts/sec_2006_95_en.pdf. The express derogations listed under Article 26(1) are the least useful for transferring data out of EU Member States because they are interpreted very narrowly, and not favored as a means of transferring data. Employers may export data to countries that provide inadequate protection if the employee has unambiguously consented or if it is necessary. The unambiguous consent grounds for transfer are strictly interpreted and do not provide a realistic means of data transfer on most occasions. The derogations based on necessity are reminiscent of the legal grounds permitted for processing data outlined in Article 7 above, but in the context of exporting data, necessity is more difficult to show. For example, if an employer in the EU seeks to transfer employee data out of the EU on grounds that it is necessary for the administration of payroll and stock options, the prevailing view is that such transfer is not necessary because it could be performed in the Member State. *See* Pearce & Platten, *supra*.

Various comprehensive schemes have been established under the grant of Article 26(2) that provides that data can be transferred "where the controller [EU entity exporting data] adduces adequate safeguards with respect to the protection of the privacy . . . such safeguards may in particular result from appropriate contractual clauses." Directive Art. 26(2). Some examples of techniques implemented pursuant to this article are standard and ad hoc contractual agreements, Corporate Codes of Conduct, or a Safe Harbor Agreement.

Contractual agreements are commonly used mechanisms for exporting data outside the EU. Standard contractual agreements are a straightforward means for employers in the EU to transfer data out to a subsidiary or separate company located in a non-EU country that does not provide adequate protection of data. Standard contractual agreements are prepared and approved by the European Commission and contain specific terms and conditions that pertain to the transfer of data. These contracts do not permit unrestricted transfer of all information, but require parties to identify what types of data and for what purposes the data will be transferred. Ad hoc contracts need to be negotiated between the exporter and importer and must be approved by the exporting EU country. Contracts are executed between *entities* in the Member States with *entities* in non EU countries; for example, the execution of a standard contract between a company in France to export a specific set of data to a company in the United States does not mean that the U.S. company is approved to receive data from all businesses in all EU member states. An important element of the standard contract is that it expressly authorizes the employee whose data is transferred to bring a cause of action as a third party beneficiary against the exporter for any damages that they may suffer for a breach of the contract by either exporter or importer. Having a damages provision is essential to ensure continued compliant processing of data after the initial transfer across borders is complete. Ad hoc contracts between companies across borders are also acceptable but each contract must be approved by data protection authorities in the relevant Member State, and thus can be more burdensome than the standard contracts.

An important element of the contractual agreement is that it must confer third party beneficiary status on the data subject (employee) whose data is being exported. Third party beneficiary status authorizes the employee to bring a cause of action for any damages if either the exporter or importer breaches the terms of the contract. Providing the employee with this power helps to ensure that contracting parties will abide by the terms of the contract which are written to protect the employee's privacy. *See* Rehder & Collins, *supra*. The contractual agreement will specify the type of liability the importer and exporter will accept (e.g., joint and several liability or indemnification by importer). Regardless of whether a standard or ad hoc contract is used, the contracting parties will decide what type of liability clause to include in the terms. Parties base their liability preference depending on the type and volume of data being transferred, how the importing company will use the data, and the relationship between the exporter and importer (whether they are affiliated companies or distinct). *See id.* Liability clauses are essential to help ensure continued protection for the processing of data after the initial transfer across borders is completed.

An alternative approach, similar to creating ad hoc contracts, is the practice of implementing privacy protection guidelines within a corporation's Codes of Conduct. This option is particularly attractive for multinational corporations with multiple entities because one comprehensive Code of Conduct binding on the whole corporation can establish the freedom to transfer data between numerous entities in different countries. The corporation is allowed to prepare the Code of Conduct and establish favorable terms to be compliant with adequate levels of data protection pursuant to the Directive. The Code must be approved by data protection authorities in the EU before it can be used as legitimate grounds for transferring data across borders. The Commission requires that "Codes of Conduct must be 'binding' on, or 'legally enforceable' against, all entities subject to the Code of Conduct" in order to be an adequate grounds for transfer of personal data. Pearce & Platten, *supra*. Again, this ensures that employee data is protected after the initial transfer and employees who suffer from a violation of privacy will have a remedy for injuries sustained. The use of Codes of Conduct is a relatively new innovation in increasing cross-border data transfers, but it appears to be one that has the brightest future. *See id.*

Another means of exporting data from the EU that is available only to companies in the United States that are regulated by the Federal Trade Commission or the Department of Transportation is the Safe Harbor Agreement. The Safe Harbor Agreement was implemented in July of 2000 as the result of negotiations between the European Commission and the U.S. Department of Commerce to alleviate the burden placed on data transfers caused by the fundamentally different approaches to data protection in the two countries. It is a self-certification process that a U.S. company may voluntarily participate in. The U.S. employer conducts an evaluation of its current data protection policies and agrees to adhere to the Safe Harbor Framework – which in most aspects mirror the Directive. Certification grants the company status as an entity that provides an "adequate" level of protection, and thus permits the company to process information exported from all EU states. *See*, generally, Department of Commerce, Safe Harbor, http://www.export.gov/safeHarbor/index.html.

Safe Harbor certification carries benefits, but there are equally high drawbacks. For example, U.S. companies that are certified are held directly liable for violations of privacy protection to EU data subjects. Under the contract framework, liability is primarily born by the EU exporter, however, for Safe Harbor certified companies, the burden shifts solely to the U.S. company. Barcelo, *supra*.

Since its inception in July 2000, about ten to twenty-five U.S. companies have self-certified per month. *Id.* The relatively slow rate of self-certification can be attributed to a mix of fear of the unknown, reluctance to accept increased liability, as well as reluctance to make information public. The future of Safe Harbor is uncertain since the program has not been as successful as the Department of Commerce and the Commission envisioned it would be. Currently, the number of employers on the Safe Harbor List stands at only about 950 after six years, but several large multinational companies have signed on to the program, including Microsoft in 2001, General Motors in 2003, and Google 2005. *See* http://web.ita.doc.gov/safeharbor/shlist.nsf/webPages/safe+harbor+list.

Notes

1. Large-scale enterprises, whether headquartered within the EU or elsewhere, are likely to have the scale of operations to justify complying with the privacy directive. Does the privacy directive, however, create a barrier for smaller enterprises located outside the EU to enter into business in it?
2. Technology makes it ever easier to obtain and to use data, including personal data. Should there be international standards for data protection? Is the protection of personal data a human rights issue? Should the United States implement more extensive legal regulations of data and other matters that are sometimes grouped under the heading privacy?

8   The United Kingdom

A. INTRODUCTION

The United Kingdom consists of England, Scotland, Wales, and Northern Ireland. For the most part, the labor law of the United Kingdom can be treated as a single system with no major differences among the jurisdictions.

The labor law of the United Kingdom must be considered in the context of the supranational law of the European Union. In 1997, after the election of the Labour Party, the United Kingdom signed the Amsterdam Treaty, subjecting it to directives under the Maastricht Treaty's Social Protocol. It is the obligation of EU members to ensure that their law conforms to the requirements of directives, which are Community law. A member, such as the United Kingdom, can determine that its existing law conforms to Community law, can amend its existing law to come into compliance, or it can pass new laws. The United Kingdom has enacted a number of labor laws intended to bring its law into conformity with EU directives. The most significant law is the Employment Relations Act of 1999. The United Kingdom's membership in the EU and its attendant obligations must be kept in mind as one studies U.K. labor law. Refer to Chapter 7 on the European Union for further discussion of European Community labor law. For a useful table correlating EU employment directives with implementing U.K. legislation, see http://www.dti.gov.uk/employment/employment-legislation/employment-directives/index.html.[1]

The labor law of the U.K. may be characterized as being between the labor law of the United States and the continental European nations in terms of the degree of regulation and the level of protection afforded to workers. However, as the United Kingdom brings its law into compliance with EU directives, it moves closer to the greater regulatory approach of the other European nations and farther from the highly unregulated (or abstentionist) approach of the United States. In comparing the labor law of the United Kingdom with that of other nations, it is interesting to note that a 2004 survey by the International Labour Organization ranked ninety nations on workforce economic security, considering the following factors: income security, labor market security, employment security, workplace security, job security, and collective bargaining/trade union representation. The United Kingdom ranked fifteenth, compared with the United States at twenty-fifth, France

---

[1] This particular link is on the Web site of the Department of Trade and Industry (DTI). http://www.dti.gov.uk/about/index.html. The Web site has a wealth of information under "Employment Matters" and then "Employment Policy and Legislation," including guidance documents for much of the legislation.

seventh, Germany ninth, and Canada tenth. *See United States Receives Low Marks in Global Economic Security Survey*, DAILY LAB. REP. (BNA) No. 171, at A-4 (Sept. 3, 2004).

The politics and labor law of the United Kingdom reveal a struggle and ebbing and flowing among ideologies. Until the Conservative governments of Prime Ministers Margaret Thatcher and John Major, the United Kingdom could be described as having an ideology of collective laissez-faire. *See* Sandra Fredman, *The Ideology of New Labour Law*, in THE FUTURE OF LABOUR LAW 9, 18 (Catherine Barnard et al. eds. 2004). In labor law, the United Kingdom was more abstentionist in its approach than the social democracies of the European mainland, with the government not heavily regulating industrial relations. A shift occurred with the election of the Conservative governments of Thatcher and Major. These governments espoused and implemented neoliberal ideology, which elevated free market competition above all else. *See id* at 8; *see also* Claire Kilpatrick, *Has New Labour Reconfigured Employment Legislation?*, 32 INDUS. L.J. 135, 138 (2003). When the New Labour Party and Prime Minister Blair came to power in 1998, it espoused a "Third Way" between social democracy and neoliberalism. The New Labour White Paper, Fairness at Work, cm 3968, called for setting a course in labor law that effected a balance between fairness and efficiency. Fredman, *supra*, at 20. With the rise of the New Labour government and Blair, the United Kingdom also joined the social law of the EU. The New Labour government has pursued the Third Way approach by enacting a considerable body of labor legislation. Thus, a new ideology, as well as participation in the social law of the EU, has marked a new direction in the labor law of the United Kingdom. Still, commentators have criticized the New Labour government for not breaking more completely with the neoliberal tenets of the Thatcher and Major Conservative governments. *See* Fredman, *supra*; Kilpatrick, *supra*. For example, although the United Kingdom has new law regarding the recognition of unions, there has been no significant bolstering of collective action, specifically a right to strike. Fredman, *supra*, at 32-33. Indeed, the United Kingdom's resistance to some aspects of EU labor law may be seen as not following the tenets of the Third Way as tenaciously as does the EU. *See* Fredman, *supra*, at 26-32. Thus, one may view the current state of labor law of the United Kingdom as infused, at least rhetorically, by Third Way principles, but in various aspects shaped by neoliberal and social democratic tenets. Consequently, there is a tension among ideologies in U.K. labor law that is perhaps more diverse and complex than that in the labor law of, on the one hand, Germany and France, and, on the other, the United States. Although France and Germany may be moving from social democracy toward an EU version of the Third Way and thus have some tension in their labor law, they do not have recent governments that have espoused neoliberalism.[2] The United States is a bastion for neoliberalism in labor law. Keep this tension among ideologies in mind as you consider various aspects of U.K. labor law, such as the opt-out on the forty-eight-hour workweek and the lack of protection of a right to strike.

U.K. labor law is complex in that it consists of statutes, common law, and traditions and practices. For example, much of the collective labor law of the United Kingdom is based on traditions and practices.

---

[2] However, in France social democratic ideology is so strongly embedded that labor law changes inconsistent with that ideology have met strong resistance. Consider, for example, the law enacted and repealed in 2006, in the face of massive demonstrations, that would have removed some traditional job protections for youth employment contracts. *See* France, Chapter 10.

Two salient themes in recent years, reflected in legislation, under the influence of the EU and the Labour Government, have been family-friendly laws and increased protection of privacy rights in the workplace.

B. INDIVIDUAL EMPLOYMENT LAW: CONTRACTS AND STATUTES

One of the most important distinctions in U.K. labor law is between contract rights (and claims) and statutory rights (and claims). *See, e.g.,* I INTERNATIONAL LABOR & EMPLOYMENT LAWS, at 7-17 (William L. Keller & Timothy J. Darby eds., 2d ed. 2003) [hereinafter INTERNATIONAL LABOR]. Generally speaking, contractual claims go to the county court or other civil court, and statutory claims go to the employment tribunal. However, the jurisdiction of the employment tribunal was extended in 1994 to include contract claims of wrongful dismissal, subject to a statutory cap of £25,000. *See* The Industrial Tribunals Extension of Jurisdiction (England and Wales) Order 1994, Statutory Instrument 1994 No. 1623. When an employee has an option of making a claim in an employment tribunal or a court, there are several relevant considerations as summarized on the DTI Web site:

> There are a number of factors that a dismissed employee making a claim for breach of employment contract may wish to bear in mind in deciding which of the two alternatives – employment tribunal or civil court – to use. For example, the employment tribunals provide a generally speedier and more informal means of redress than the civil courts for the resolution of employment disputes, and their procedures have been designed to make it unnecessary for the parties to incur the cost of legal representation. On the other hand, employment tribunal claims for breach of contract must be made within three months of the date on which the employment ended (or, if that is not reasonably practicable, within such further period as the tribunal considers reasonably practicable), whereas civil court claims may be made up to a much longer time limit of six years from the date on which the breach of contract occurred. Another consideration might be that employment tribunal awards for an employer's breach of contract are subject to an upper limit, currently £25,000, whereas civil court awards may reflect the full amount of the damages suffered by the dismissed employee.
>
> http://www.dti.gov.uk/employment/employment-legislation/employment-guidance/page16161.html.

The employment tribunals (first called industrial tribunals) were created by statute in 1964, and they adjudicate most of the labor claims in the United Kingdom. The panels sit throughout the country. Each panel has a tripartite composition: a chairman, who is an experienced barrister or solicitor; a representative from a trade union or consulting organization for employees; and a representative from one of the employer federations. In Northern Ireland, appeals go to the Court of Appeal. In Great Britain, appeals go to the Employment Appeal Tribunal (six in London and one in Edinburgh), and then, with leave, to the courts. The bulk of the cases heard by the employment tribunals are unfair dismissal cases. The employment tribunals can award up to £58,400 (as of February 1, 2006) as a compensatory award in an unfair dismissal case, with the limit on a weeks' pay for purposes of calculating an award of £290 per week. The Employment Act 2002 (effective October 1, 2004) imposes a requirement that employees submit complaints regarding employers' actions to grievance procedures before bringing a complaint to an employment tribunal. Failure by the employee to comply with the statutory grievance procedures results in a reduction of any award. *See infra* Section B(1)(b)(ii)-(iii). The Employment Appeal Tribunal has a useful Web site that includes a judgments database: http://www.employmentappeals.gov.uk/.

1. Contracts and Statutory Requirements for Formation of the Employment Relationship and Dismissal

Employers and workers can agree to the terms they want in an individual employment contract, and terms in collective agreements can be, and often are, incorporated into individual contracts. Additionally the common law recognizes some implied terms in employment contracts. However, the labor law of the U.K. has not left employment contract formation and dismissal solely to individual and/or collective bargaining. Statutes, including notably the Employment Rights Act 1996[3] and the Employment Act 2002, have imposed requirements. As you read this section, keep in mind that there are statutory claims, which usually are adjudicated by the employment tribunals, and there are breach of contract claims, which usually are adjudicated by the courts. However, employment tribunals also have limited jurisdiction over breach of contract claims, including wrongful dismissal claims.

a. *Requirement of a Written Statement of Specified Terms and Conditions*

The Employment Rights Act 1996 (ERA 1996) provides that within two months of beginning work, an employee must be given a single written statement setting forth specified terms and conditions of employment. This written statement does not necessarily compose the whole of the employment contract. Section 1 of the ERA provides as follows:

STATEMENT OF INITIAL EMPLOYMENT PARTICULARS

1. - (1) Where an employee begins employment with an employer, the employer shall give to the employee a written statement of particulars of employment.

(2) The statement may (subject to section 2(4)) be given in instalments and (whether or not given in instalments) shall be given not later than two months after the beginning of the employment.

(3) The statement shall contain particulars of-

(a) the names of the employer and employee,

(b) the date when the employment began, and

(c) the date on which the employee's period of continuous employment began (taking into account any employment with a previous employer which counts towards that period).

(4) The statement shall also contain particulars, as at a specified date not more than seven days before the statement (or the instalment containing them) is given, of-

(a) the scale or rate of remuneration or the method of calculating remuneration,

---

[3] Text of sections of the Employment Rights Act 1996, the Trade Union and Labour Relations (Consolidation) Act 1992, and other statutes in Chapter 8 The United Kingdom is CROWN COPYRIGHT. Crown Copyright material is reproduced with the permission of the Controller of HMSO and the Queen's Printer for Scotland. Official copies of acts are available from Her Majesty's Stationery Office.

(b) the intervals at which remuneration is paid (that is, weekly, monthly or other specified intervals),

(c) any terms and conditions relating to hours of work (including any terms and conditions relating to normal working hours),

(d) any terms and conditions relating to any of the following-

(i) entitlement to holidays, including public holidays, and holiday pay (the particulars given being sufficient to enable the employee's entitlement, including any entitlement to accrued holiday pay on the termination of employment, to be precisely calculated),

(ii) incapacity for work due to sickness or injury, including any provision for sick pay, and

(iii) pensions and pension schemes,

(e) the length of notice which the employee is obliged to give and entitled to receive to terminate his contract of employment,

(f) the title of the job which the employee is employed to do or a brief description of the work for which he is employed,

(g) where the employment is not intended to be permanent, the period for which it is expected to continue or, if it is for a fixed term, the date when it is to end,

(h) either the place of work or, where the employee is required or permitted to work at various places, an indication of that and of the address of the employer,

(j) any collective agreements which directly affect the terms and conditions of the employment including, where the employer is not a party, the persons by whom they were made, and

(k) where the employee is required to work outside the United Kingdom for a period of more than one month-

(i) the period for which he is to work outside the United Kingdom,

(ii) the currency in which remuneration is to be paid while he is working outside the United Kingdom,

(iii) any additional remuneration payable to him, and any benefits to be provided to or in respect of him, by reason of his being required to work outside the United Kingdom, and

(iv) any terms and conditions relating to his return to the United Kingdom.

(5) Subsection (4)(d)(iii) does not apply to an employee of a body or authority if-

(a) the employee's pension rights depend on the terms of a pension scheme established under any provision contained in or having effect under any Act, and

(b) any such provision requires the body or authority to give to a new employee information concerning the employee's pension rights or the determination of questions affecting those rights.

Section 1(3) (b) and (c), *supra*, referring to the "date when the employment began" and "the date on which the employee's period of continuous employment began (taking into account any employment with a previous employer which counts towards that period)" may seem redundant, but the term "continuous employment" is a defined term under ERA 1996 in §§210-219. Continuous employment takes into account, among other matters, periods of leave, periods of absence from work due to military service, periods of absence from work due to participation in a strike, and periods of employment by a predecessor business (in a case of transfer of undertakings).

Employment Act 2002 provides that employers must give employees copies of statutory disciplinary and dismissal procedures and grievance procedures, the requirements of which are discussed further below in Section B(1)(b)(ii)-(iii).

Unless a contract provides otherwise, it is a contract of indefinite duration. There is a four-year limit on fixed-term contracts as provided in the Fixed-term Employees (Prevention of Less Favourable Treatment) Regulations 2002 (which implemented the EU Fixed-Term Work Directive). Probationary periods can be included in contracts, during which the employment contract can be terminated on short notice. Notice and termination will be discussed further later in this chapter.

b. *Dismissal*

i. Notice/PILON. The employment contract, whether or not in writing, can provide for what is required to terminate the contract. In addition to contractual provisions, there are statutory requirements. Section 86 of the Employment Rights Act 1996, as amended, provides for notice of termination.

RIGHTS OF EMPLOYER AND EMPLOYEE TO MINIMUM NOTICE

86. - (1) The notice required to be given by an employer to terminate the contract of employment of a person who has been continuously employed for one month or more-

(a) is not less than one week's notice if his period of continuous employment is less than two years,

(b) is not less than one week's notice for each year of continuous employment if his period of continuous employment is two years or more but less than twelve years, and

(c) is not less than twelve weeks' notice if his period of continuous employment is twelve years or more.

(2) The notice required to be given by an employee who has been continuously employed for one month or more to terminate his contract of employment is not less than one week.

(3) Any provision for shorter notice in any contract of employment with a person who has been continuously employed for one month or more has effect subject to subsections (1) and (2); but this section does not prevent either party from waiving his right to notice on any occasion or from accepting a payment in lieu of notice.

(4) Any contract of employment of a person who has been continuously employed for three months or more which is a contract for a term certain of one month or less shall have effect as if it were for an indefinite period; and, accordingly, subsections (1) and (2) apply to the contract. . . .

(6) This section does not affect any right of either party to a contract of employment to treat the contract as terminable without notice by reason of the conduct of the other party.

Section 92 of ERA 1996, as amended, provides that an employee who has been continuously employed for one year is entitled on request to a written statement regarding reasons for dismissal. The employer must provide the statement within fourteen days of the request. Section 92 also dispenses with the prerequisites of one year of employment and a request by the employee if the dismissal occurs while the employee is pregnant or after childbirth if the dismissal occurs during maternity leave.

Notes

1. A breach that constitutes a repudiation of the contract obviates the need for a notice. For example, in the *Sime* case, *infra*, if the employee was constructively discharged, there would be no requirement of notice by the employee. If an employee engages in gross misconduct that is a repudiatory breach, the employer may dispense with compliance with the notice period. *See* Michael Duggan, Wrongful Discharge and Breach of Contract: Law, Practice & Precedents §7.3 (Emis Prof. Pub. 2003).
2. The parties may include an express provision in an employment contract providing for payment in lieu of notice (PILON).

ii. Dismissal procedures. The Employment Act 2002 provides procedures that must be followed to effect a dismissal. The Act amended the Employment Rights Act 1996, adding a §98A "Procedural Fairness." Schedule 2, Part 1 sets forth the procedures that must be followed for dismissal and discipline. Pursuant to Employment Act 2002 §30, every employment contract requires an employer and an employee to comply with statutory procedures, but an employment contract may provide for procedures that are additional to and not inconsistent with the statutory procedures. Under the "standard procedure," in Schedule 2, Part 1, the employer must state in a written notice to the employee "the alleged conduct or characteristics, or other circumstances" that cause the employer to consider discipline or dismissal, and the written notice must invite the employee to a meeting to discuss the matter. The meeting must precede the employer's action, except when the disciplinary action is a suspension. After the meeting, the employer must notify the employee of its decision and of the right to appeal. If the employee appeals, there must be an additional appeal meeting, after which the employer must notify the employee of its final decision. There is a modified procedure provided for in Schedule 2, Part 1 for discipline or dismissal based on alleged misconduct by the employee. The first meeting between employer and employee is not required under the modified procedure, although the second (appellate) meeting is required if the employee avails herself of the appeal.

The Employment Act 2002 also provides for statutory grievance procedures with which an employee must comply in order to complain about any employment action that an employer takes or contemplates taking. *See* Schedule 2, Part 2.

iii. Failure to comply with dismissal procedures (unfair dismissal). The Employment Act 2002, amending the ERA 1996 by adding §98A, provides that failure to comply with the dismissal and disciplinary procedures which is "wholly or mainly attributable to failure by the employer to comply with its requirements" is an unfair dismissal. Note that this is a statutory claim rather than a breach of contract claim. The remedy for procedural noncompliance is four weeks pay (maximum of £290 per week). Additionally, if the employer is "wholly or mainly" responsible for procedural noncompliance, then the employment tribunal must increase the award by 10 percent and may increase it by as much as, but not more than, 50 percent. Similarly, if the employment tribunal finds that the employee was "wholly or mainly" responsible for the noncompliance, then any award must be reduced by 10 percent and may be reduced by as much as 50 percent.

Before the Employment Act 2002, there was a principle, know as the *Polkey* doctrine or *Polkey* deduction (from *Polkey v A E Dayton Services Ltd* [1988] AC 344 HL), under which an award could be reduced if an employer could show that notwithstanding its failure to comply with procedures, which made the dismissal unfair, the employee would have been dismissed anyway. Tribunals did not have to make all or nothing decisions about whether an employee would have been dismissed if appropriate procedures had been followed; percentage reductions were made in cases in which the employee demonstrated a lost chance of surviving dismissal. *Gover v. Propertycare Ltd.*, Appeal No. UKEAT/0458/05/ZT (Nov. 22, 2005). The *Polkey* doctrine is discussed at length in *Gover. Id.* The Employment Act 2002 included an amendment of the ERA 1996, now §98A(2), that is referred to as the "reversal of *Polkey*":

> Subject to subsection (1), failure by an employer to follow a procedure in relation to the dismissal of an employee shall not be regarded for the purposes of section 98(4)(a) as by itself making the employer's action unreasonable if he shows that he would have decided to dismiss the employee if he had followed the procedure.

The Employment Appeal Tribunal discussed the statutory reversal of *Polkey* and made several important holdings regarding the issue in *Mason v. The Governing Body of Ward End Primary School*, Appeal No. UKEAT/0433/05/ZT (Apr. 12, 2006). The EAT held that §98A(2) does not apply to breaches of the statutory dismissal procedures set forth in the Employment Act 2002. The EAT also held that the statutory reversal does not apply retroactively. Although the EAT held that the statutory section was inapplicable to the case before it, it explained the effect of §98A(2) on an award compared with the effect of *Polkey*:

> It is common ground that if, applying *Polkey*, the Tribunal decided that there was a less than 50/50 chance of the employee being dismissed, the dismissal is unfair and an appropriate award would be made. If there was a 33% chance of dismissal, a compensatory award would be reduced by 33%. A finding under §98A(2) is to be made on the balance of probability. Using traditional *Polkey* language, if it is more likely than not that the employee would be dismissed, it is not now appropriate to award compensation reduced by more than 50%. The consequence of a finding on the balance of probability that he or she would have been dismissed, on a scale of anything from 51% to 100%, is that no compensation is awarded at all since §98A(2) makes the dismissal fair. Indeed, it is now no longer necessary under this reversal of *Polkey* doctrine for a percentage to be fixed.

Id. ¶30.

iv. Wrongful dismissal. Wrongful dismissal is to be distinguished from unfair dismissal. Wrongful dismissal is a breach of contract claim, and unfair dismissal is a statutory claim.

The usual remedy for a successful wrongful dismissal claim is damages that put the employee in the position he would have been in had the contract been performed. For example, if an employer fails to give an employee the required notice of termination, the remedy is the employee's pay for the notice period. Some distinctions between wrongful dismissal and unfair dismissal are illustrated by *Harper v. Virgin Net, Ltd.*, [2005] I.C.R. 921, 2004 WL 343845. In that case, the employee was dismissed without notice, and the employment tribunal awarded her £9,514.04 for the three months' pay she would have received during her contractual notice period. The three-month notice was provided for in her employment contract, although the statutorily required notice under §86(1)(a) is one week. The tribunal also awarded her the full amount she would have received for a statutory unfair dismissal claim, notwithstanding the fact that she was terminated thirty-three days before she completed the one-year period required to be entitled to bring an unfair dismissal claim. The rationale of the tribunal was that, had she been given the notice she was due, she would have completed the one-year period. The Employment Appeal Tribunal reversed the award for unfair dismissal. The EAT reasoned that under §97 of the Employment Rights Act 1996, the effective date of termination includes the statutory notice period of one week. Parliament did not provide that the termination date was extended by a longer contractual notice period. The Court of Appeal agreed with the EAT and dismissed the appeal.

Another judgment of the EAT that is useful in considering the differences and similarities between statutory unfair dismissal claims and breach of contract wrongful dismissal claims is *Surrey County Council v. Henderson*, Appeal No. UKEAT/0326/05/ZT (Nov. 23, 2005). An employee who was under investigation for his business dealings allegedly made threats of violence toward various people. He was dismissed, and after invoking grievance procedures, filed a complaint with the employment tribunal, stating claims for unfair dismissal and wrongful dismissal. On the unfair dismissal claim, the EAT identified the principal issue as whether the employer had reasonable grounds, after conducting a reasonable investigation, for believing the employee had engaged in misconduct. The EAT noted that the wrongful dismissal claim raised a different issue: the factual issue of whether the employee by his actions had engaged in a repudiatory breach of his employment contract. Although the EAT found the unfair dismissal claim to depend on application of the reasonableness standard to the facts and the wrongful dismissal to focus on a factual determination, it remanded both so that the new tribunal hearing the case would not be bound by issue estoppel based on the first tribunal's factual findings.

c. *Implied Term of Mutual Trust and Confidence*

One of the most important implied terms of employment contracts recognized by common law is the obligation of mutual trust and confidence. A common law claim exists for breach of the duty of trust and confidence. This claim is to be distinguished from the statutory claim for unfair dismissal set forth in the Employment Rights Act 1996, which will be discussed below.

Consider the discussion of this obligation in the opinion of the Employment Appeal Tribunal in *Sime v. Imperial College London*, Appeal No.UKEAT/0875/04/CK (April 20, 2005).

SIME V. IMPERIAL COLLEGE LONDON

EMPLOYMENT APPEAL TRIBUNAL 20 APRIL 2005

Transcript of Proceedings

JUDGMENT

SUMMARY

Contract of Employment

The Employment Tribunal found that the Respondent had breached implied term of trust and confidence – but breach not repudiatory. Authorities show that if breach was established, it was necessarily repudiatory. Remit for further findings.

HIS HONOUR JUDGE D SEROTA QC

1. This is an appeal from a decision of the Employment Tribunal at Ashford that was sent to the parties on 27 September 2004 chaired by Miss E G Wallis. The Employment Tribunal dismissed the Claimant's complaint that she had been unfairly dismissed. She had alleged that there had been a constructive dismissal. The Respondent maintained that she had resigned. The Respondent accepts that in one fundamental respect the judgment in this case cannot stand, and the parties agree that the matter must be remitted to the Employment Tribunal; but there remain issues as to whether there should be a rehearing or a remittal for consideration by the same Employment Tribunal and there remain issues about other grounds of appeal.

2. We start by setting out the background as found by the Employment Tribunal. The Claimant worked as an Executive Assistant at Wye College in Ashford. Wye College became part of the Respondent, Imperial College, some time in July 2000. At the relevant time in 2002 and 2003, she was working for Professor Waage, who was the head of the Department of Agricultural Sciences. It needs to be said that relations between Professor Waage and the Claimant were not good. The Employment Tribunal found that this was partly because of Professor Waage's exacting methods of work and difficulties in his communications skills: but there were also problems that had been caused by the Claimant and these should not be minimised. The Employment Tribunal found that in the autumn of 2002 the Claimant's colleagues, a Mrs Jovanovich, the Departmental Administrator, expressed concerns as to whether the Management Team should be minuted and serviced by the Claimant. Mrs Jovanovich voted against the proposal, and explained privately to Professor Waage, together with Mrs King, a student counsellor, another colleague of the Claimant, why she was concerned. Both Mrs Jovanovich and Mrs King were concerned at the Claimant's lack of discretion; and told Professor Waage the Claimant was sitting at lunch with colleagues and asking them what a particular drug was, reading from a note. She told the persons with whom she was having lunch she was interested in this because she had found the prescription in Professor Waage's room. Mrs King also told Professor Waage that the Claimant had forwarded to Mrs King a number of Professor Waage's e-mails, and that Mrs King had asked her to stop doing so. Mrs Jovanovich reported that she had received a report from a Senior Security Officer that when she was introduced to the Claimant, when she joined the Department around 2002

in February, the Claimant had described Professor Waage in uncomplimentary and earthy terms, which we need not repeat. Further, Professor Waage had been approached by an independent consultant who had been working with him on the restructuring of the department. He told Professor Waage that he considered that his position was being undermined by the way the Claimant represented him and his views to other staff. The same consultant told Professor Waage that the Claimant had shared confidential information with other staff. The Claimant at the hearing accepted she had allowed Mrs King to see a list of names on her desk in respect of a proposed redundancy exercise, and also accepted at the hearing that she had mentioned Professor Waage's medication to a colleague at lunchtime. She also accepted that she had referred to Professor Waage in uncomplimentary and robust terms, which again it is unnecessary to mention in this judgment.

3.   Professor Waage's relations with the Claimant were obviously undermined by this conduct on behalf of the Claimant, the gravity of which should not be understated. Professor Waage no longer wished to have the Claimant serve the Management Team Committee. He was considering how the team could be serviced, and how the Claimant's role could be adapted so that another post could service the team while she carried on with other types of work. This is how a note, which we shall come to now, came to be written. Professor Waage prepared this note some time shortly before 27 January. The note, which was before the Employment Tribunal, was a personal note and an *aide memoire* prepared by Professor Waage in which he set out his view of his working relationship with the Claimant. The Employment Tribunal has quoted:

> Difficult relationship, indiscrete (sic) on confidential issues, does not present me well to others, some breaches of my personal affairs.

The Employment Tribunal also quoted other concerns:

> Would like her to leave for reasons of compatibility with me and new office;
> Skills – modern skills, willingness to do more and new things, friendliness;
> Change of job – someone who can work with and support Management team;
> Costs – too highly paid for what she does.

4.   The Claimant was preparing a document for Professor Waage and needed to check some information: he was not in the office. She looked through the papers on his desk to find the information, and found the note which she then proceeded to read. Whether she should have read a private note on Professor Waage's desk is a matter for the consideration of the Employment Tribunal. She left work in distress and it is right to say that she, in fact, never returned to work. She remained off sick suffering with stress for a substantial period of time.

5.   Professor Waage was informed by Mrs Brown (the HR Manager – Life Sciences), who had learned from Mrs Jovanovich how distressed the Claimant was. Professor Waage immediately drafted a note of apology, assisted by Mrs Jovanovich and Mrs Brown. The note was e-mailed to the Claimant shortly after 5.30 pm on 27 January; that was the day that the Claimant had discovered his *aide memoire*. Professor Waage said he was sorry that the Claimant had seen his note, that it was a private note to himself to clarify his thoughts and not intended for anyone else, and he regretted causing her so much upset. He went on to say that having thought of reasons not to continue together, he had then gone on to think about the positive side of their working relationship and ways in which to address his concerns. He reiterated his appreciation of her dedication to the job and her efforts and hoped that he would be able to talk to her

soon and that they would be able to continue to work together. The Employment Tribunal was satisfied that Professor Waage had taken prompt steps to try to remedy the situation.

6. It would be right, I think, to say that from 27 January until 11 November when the Claimant resigned and maintained she was constructively dismissed, there were various discussions, which came to nothing, as to her switching jobs. There was an unsuccessful attempt to mediate. There were references to the Occupational Health Medical Service, and there is no doubt that the Respondent was considering the possibility of a dismissal on the grounds of ill health. Be that as it may, on 11 January the Claimant wrote and said she was left to conclude the College did not intend to remedy the fundamental breach of her contract of employment which arose from the actions of Professor Waage:

> Over the months since this happened I have been led to believe the College would remedy that breach of contract. I have attended many consultation meetings and as recently as 21 October 2003 I was asked whether I would consider a swap and go back to work at Wye. I have always made it quite clear that I am not prepared to accept the breach of contract but I have been prepared throughout to consider anything the College might propose to remedy that breach. It was to discuss such possibilities that I came to the meeting with you on 31 October 2003.

> I must now conclude that the College is not prepared to remedy that original breach of contract. In the circumstances you leave me no alternative but to resign immediately. The College's actions leave me with no choice. I intend to issue proceedings to the Employment Tribunal for constructive unfair dismissal.

. . .

8. At the outset of its Decision in paragraph 4, the Employment Tribunal set out the issues which it considered had been agreed at the start of the hearing as follows:

> The issues agreed at the start of the hearing were as follows:-

> Was the conduct of Professor Waage in writing a note about the Applicant's employment a fundamental breach of contract?

> Was the conduct of the Respondent in investigating the Applicant's complaint about that note a fundamental breach of the contract?

> Was the note made by Professor Waage within a sheaf of papers and not left for the Appellant to read?

> Did the Respondent make reasonable efforts to address to the Applicant's concerns?

> Did the Applicant decline to meet Professor Waage in mediation sessions?

> Was this the reason for mediation being discontinued?

> What was the position with regard to redeployment and protected pay?

> If the actions of Professor Waage and/or the Respondent amounted to a fundamental breach of the Applicant's contract of employment, was that breach the effective cause of the resignation?

> (ix) Was there any delay between the effective cause of resignation and the resignation itself; had the Applicant affirmed the contract?

. . .

9. One issue that has been raised before us was an issue as to whether the Claimant had been treated unfairly in that the Respondent applied the sickness policy to the Claimant without

disclosing the fact that she was in fact being subjected to that policy. It is not referred to in paragraph 4 of the Employment Tribunal's Reasons. The Employment Tribunal in paragraph 4 (ii) had this to say:

> Was the conduct of the Respondent in investigating the Applicant's complaint about that note, [that is Professor Waage's note] a fundamental breach of the contract?

It is suggested, and we think probable, that the Tribunal there took in all allegations of repudiatory breach. Be that as it may, it is not altogether satisfactory, but we will return to see how the Employment Tribunal dealt with this issue later in our Judgment.

10.   It is also important to note that the Employment Tribunal recorded that the parties had agreed there was no real dispute about the facts of the case: it was a matter of interpretation. The Applicant suggested the Respondent had not been trying to remedy the situation but was shepherding her towards dismissal. The Applicant suggested the process followed by the Respondent had not been carried out in good faith and was a sham. The Respondent suggested that it had taken all good reasonable steps to deal with the matter following the Applicant's complaint about the note she had found in Professor Waage's private papers.

11.   The Employment Tribunal went on to consider the facts. We do not think it necessary to refer to them in any more detail but we shall refer to certain of them later when we consider other grounds of appeal. The Employment Tribunal in paragraph 43 directed itself by reference to the well-known decision in *Western Excavating (ECC) Ltd v Sharp* [1978] ICR 221, in which the Court of Appeal had set out the requirements for establishing constructive dismissal. It also correctly pointed out that the burden was on the Claimant to show the breach was the effective cause of the resignation and that she had not affirmed the contract. The Employment Tribunal correctly directed itself that once a Claimant had established a constructive dismissal had taken place the Tribunal had to decide whether the dismissal was fair or unfair. The Employment Tribunal then later in paragraph 46 notes that it is not necessary for an employer to *intend* to terminate the contract of employment. That is clearly correct. "Constructive dismissal", the Tribunal say: "is a statutory matter which has been devised to give employees a remedy for an unfair fundamental breach of the contract of employment". We are not certain that it is correct to regard the concept of constructive dismissal as a statutory matter; nonetheless, that does not seem to us to be relevant to any issue we have to decide. The Employment Tribunal then goes on to say:

> 47.   There was no dispute in this case that the claim related to an alleged fundamental breach of the implied term of mutual trust and confidence. In the case of *Courtaulds Northern Textiles Ltd v Andrew* [1979] IRLR 84 the Employment Appeal Tribunal held that a term is to be implied into all contracts of employment stating that employers will not, without reasonable or proper cause, conduct themselves in a manner calculated or likely to destroy or seriously damage the relationship of trust and confidence between the employer and employee. In the case of *Woods v W M Car Services (Peterborough) Ltd* [1981] ICR 666 the Employment Appeal Tribunal confirmed that it was not necessary for the employee to show that the employer intended any repudiation of the contract. It is the Tribunal's function to look at the employer's conduct as a whole and determine whether it is such that its effect, judged reasonably and sensibly, is such that the employee cannot be expected to put up with it.

> 48.   In the recent case *of Logan v Commissioners of Customs and Excise* [2004] IRLR 63 the Court of Appeal confirmed that, commenting on the case of *Lewis v Motorworld Garages Ltd* [1985] IRLR 465 (a last straw case), "what Lewis requires is a view in

its totality of the whole course of conduct in order to see whether the actions of the employer constitute together a breach of the implied obligation of trust and confidence. The employer's actions must be judged cumulatively."

49. We have therefore looked at the whole course of conduct in this case, from the date that the Applicant discovered the note written by Professor Waage until the date of her resignation."

12. The Employment Tribunal then went on at paragraph 50 to consider the submission by the Claimant that there were two fundamental breaches of contract: the preparation of the note by Professor Waage, and the way in which the Respondent dealt with her complaints. The Employment Tribunal then said this:

50. . . . Dealing first with the note itself, the Tribunal concluded that Professor Waage had not deliberately left the note in papers that were referred to by the Applicant. Although those papers were on his desk and therefore some forethought by Professor Waage might have indicated that the Applicant would have looked through them had she needed some information with regard to addresses, we concluded that the note was not placed deliberately for the Applicant to find it. We therefore considered whether or not it could be said that the actual preparation of the note and placing it within paperwork on the desk could constitute a breach of the implied term of mutual trust and confidence. We had noted that some of the matters raised in that note had already been discussed with the Applicant in August 2002. Some other matters in that note had been accepted by the Applicant at the Tribunal hearing. We concluded that the key point in that note were the words "would like her to leave". We also concluded that we had to consider how Professor Waage had responded once he was aware that the Applicant had found the note. We concluded that the writing of the note and leaving it within papers on his desk was a breach of the implied term of mutual trust and confidence. We could not say however that it was a fundamental breach in all the circumstances. The Tribunal accepts that the content of the note was greatly upsetting for the Applicant, but given the way in which she had described the working relationship with Professor Waage, given that they had discussed some concerns that he raised in August 2002, and given that she accepted at the hearing that she had behaved in ways that might be considered "indiscreet", and given that the note was not passed to her and that Professor Waage had not said these words to her, in contrast with the circumstances in the case of *Morrow v Safeway Stores plc* [2002] IRLR 9, the Tribunal concludes that the preparation of the note itself and the discovery of it by the Applicant did not constitute a fundamental breach of the implied term of trust and confidence in her contract of employment.

51. We therefore consider that it is not necessary for us to consider the other two limbs to be made out in claims of unfair constructive dismissal, namely effective cause of resignation and affirmation.

52. Turning to the other fundamental breach claimed by the Applicant, the conduct of the Respondent in investigating her complaint about Professor Waage, we have concluded on the findings of fact set out above that the Respondent's conduct did not constitute a breach of the Applicant's contract of employment and therefore there was no question of a fundamental breach of the contract.

13. The first three grounds of appeal and, indeed, the principal matter with which we have been concerned, are that whereas on the one hand the Employment Tribunal found that the writing and leaving of the note by Professor Waage was in breach of the duty of implied trust and confidence, it went on to find that that breach was not fundamental. It is accepted by both [Counsel] that the Employment Tribunal fell into error and failed to follow the decision in

Morrow v Safeway Stores plc to which it had been expressly referred. A breach of the implied term of trust and confidence, as we shall refer to it as convenient shorthand, is of necessity repudiatory. If it is not repudiatory, then there is no breach. On the other hand if there is a breach it is of necessity repudiatory. Not every action of an employer that causes an employee to feel that trust and confidence has been undermined, will amount to a breach of the implied term. It is perhaps helpful to remind ourselves how the term was formulated by the House of Lords in the decision of *Malik v Bank of Credit & Commerce International SA* [1997] IRLR / [1997] ICR 606. Lord Nicholls had this to say at page 610:

An implied obligation

Two points can be noted here. First, as a matter of legal analysis, the innocent employee's entitlement to leave at once must derive from the bank being [in] breach of a term of the contract of employment which the employee is entitled to treat as a repudiation by the bank of its contractual obligations. That is the source of his right to step away from the contract forthwith.

In other words, and this is the necessary corollary of the employee's right to leave at once, the bank was under an implied obligation to its employees not to conduct a dishonest or corrupt business. This implied obligation is no more than one particular aspect of the portmanteau, general obligation not to engage in conduct likely to undermine the trust and confidence require if the employment relationship is to continue in the manner the employment contract implicitly envisages. Second, I do not accept the liquidators' submission that the conduct of which complaint is made must be targeted in some way at the employee or a group of employees. No doubt that will often be the position, perhaps usually so. But there is no reason in principle why this must always be so. The trust and confidence required in the employment relationship can be undermined by an employer, or indeed an employee, in many different ways. I can see no justification for the law giving the employee a remedy if the unjustified trust-destroying conduct occurs in some ways but refusing a remedy if it occurs in others. The conduct must, of course, impinge on the relationship in the sense that, looked at objectively, it is likely to destroy or seriously damage the degree of trust and confidence the employee is reasonably entitled to have in his employer. That requires one to look at all the circumstances.

Breach

The objective standard just mentioned provides the answer to the liquidators' submission that unless the employee's confidence is actually undermined there is no breach. A breach occurs when the proscribed conduct takes place: here, operating a dishonest and corrupt business. Proof of a subjective loss of confidence in the employer is not an essential element of the breach, although the time when the employee learns of the misconduct and his response to it may affect his remedy.

. . .

15.   It is clear, therefore, that the Employment Tribunal fell into error, and it is necessary for the appeal to be allowed at least in this regard, as [Counsel] has very properly, and helpfully, conceded; and the matter needs to be remitted to the Employment Tribunal. We shall consider later in this judgment whether it should be remitted to the same tribunal or remitted for a new hearing.

16.   In passing, we should say this, the Employment Tribunal must have regard to the fact that for an act of the employer to amount to a breach of the implied term of trust and confidence, the conduct must be of some gravity because it is something which goes to the root of the

contract and amounts to a repudiatory breach which is capable of being accepted by the Respondent. It must be something which can be seen objectively to be likely to destroy or seriously damage the degree of trust and confidence the employee is reasonably entitled to have in his employer. Looking at the facts as found by the Employment Tribunal, we have some difficulty in seeing, in any event, how someone in Professor Waage's position could be in breach of that duty by holding uncommunicated views about the Claimant. We are equally in some doubt as to how the simple preparation of an *aide memoire* recording those views could, in itself, amount to a breach of the implied term. In any well run organisation it is bound on occasions for it to be necessary for the employer to record confidential and unfavourable views about employees without it being suggested that the mere recording of those views is in itself a breach of the implied duty of trust and confidence. Obviously those considerations change if the report is circulated or left to be seen. It follows, therefore, that Professor Waage's carelessness, if it be that, in leaving the report on his desk where it might be seen by the Claimant, *might* be capable of amounting to a breach of the implied term. That, of course, is something for the Employment Tribunal to consider in the light of this judgment.

17.   We now turn to matters which are more controversial. In paragraph 6.4 of the Claimant's Notice of Appeal, it is submitted that the Employment Tribunal was wrong to take account in deciding whether there had been a repudiatory breach of contract, of the actions of Professor Waage, which we have referred to, when he sent an apology to the Claimant. [Counsel] has pressed upon us that the breach crystallised when the Claimant found the note. We invited her to show us authority for that proposition, and she drew our attention to the passage in *Malik* which we have already referred to, in which Lord Nichols said that the breach occurred when the proscribed conduct took place. We asked [Counsel] what, for example, the position might be if an employee was told by her manager that her salary was going to be stopped, and it was. But before the employee treated this conduct as a repudiatory breach of her contract of employment, the director apologised, and offered recompense. We asked her whether in those circumstances the employee could nevertheless say 'I have been constructively dismissed'. Miss Morgan said that was in fact the case, the employer could not alter the nature of the breach by his subsequent conduct.

18.   We have been referred to a number of authorities; we start with the decision in *Woods v W.M. Car Services (Peterborough) Ltd* [1981] ICR 666. That is a decision of the Employment Appeal Tribunal presided over by Browne-Wilkinson J, as he then was. Browne-Wilkinson J had this to say at page 670 G:

> In our view it is clearly established that there is implied in a contract of employment a term that the employers will not, without reasonable and proper cause, conduct themselves in a manner calculated or likely to destroy or seriously damage the relationship of confidence and trust between employer and employee: *Courtaulds Northern Textiles Ltd. v Andrew* [1979] IRLR 84. To constitute a breach of this implied term it is not necessary to show that the employer intended any repudiation of the contract: the tribunal's function is to look at the employer's conduct as a whole and determine whether it is such that its effect, judged reasonably and sensibly, is such that the employee cannot be expected to put up with it: see *British Aircraft Corporation Ltd. V Austin* [1978] IRLR 332 and *Post Office v Roberts* [1980] IRLR 347. The conduct of the parties has to be looked at as a whole and its cumulative impact assessed: *Post Office v Roberts*.

. . .

20.   We now turn to the decision of the Employment Appeal Tribunal in *Moores v Bude-Stratton Town Council* [2000] IRLR 676. In that case, the President of the Employment Appeal

Tribunal, Lindsay J, had the misfortune to differ from the two lay members with whom he sat. However, the disagreement related to an issue as to whether the employer was vicariously liable for certain conduct, and does not, in fact, as we understand the matter, affect what the President had to say at paragraphs 18 and 19 as follows:

(3) *Verbal abuse*

It cannot be doubted but that even a single incident of verbal abuse may found a claim for constructive and unfair dismissal. Thus in *Isle of Wight Tourist Board v Coombes* [1976] IRLR 413 EAT the director of the Tourist Board, the most senior officer or agent of the Board so far as one can tell from the report of the case, said of and in the presence of his personal secretary, a woman of 58 years of age who had serve the Board for some 15 years, 'She is an intolerable bitch on a Monday morning.' Mrs Coombes indicated there and then that she had 'taken enough', gave oral notice to leave, immediately left and drafted a letter of resignation. She was held to have been constructively dismissed, although Bristow J. giving the judgment of the EAT, mentions the possibility that a timely apology might have ended matters. There had, though, been no apology. In *Courtaulds Northern Textiles Ltd v Anderson* [1979] IRLR 84 EAT an assistant manager had said to an employee 'You can't do the bloody job anyway,' although not believing that to be the case. Again, constructive dismissal was established although, again, it was notable that the management had not sought to 'jolly' the employee (as it was put) out of his intended reaction of giving notice – see paragraph 8 on p.85. In *Robinson v Crompton Parkinson* [1978] IRLR 61 the employee, Mr Robinson, having been falsely and unfairly accused of theft, first gave his employers an opportunity to apologise for their actions. Only after he had failed to receive an apology over the next week (having been, he said, promised it) did he say 'I'm off'. The industrial tribunal had dismissed his claim for unfair dismissal; the EAT allowed the appeal and remitted the matter to a fresh tribunal.

These cases suggest that whilst, as one would expect, even a single incident of verbal abuse, though not coming from the employer himself or itself, can ground a successful claim for constructive dismissal on the basis of its having been destructive of the mutual obligations of trust and confidence between employer and employee, each incident needs to be examined in the light of its surrounding circumstances. They will include whether the verbal abuse was, so to speak, 'authorised' in the sense of coming from some senior person in the employer's organisation and thus seeming to have the authority of the employer behind it and whether a timely retraction or apology was offered by the employer. It will be for the Employment Tribunal, using its good sense and practical experience of the working environment, to adjudge, on the facts of each particular case, whether the verbal abuse in question could fairly be regarded as coming from (or as if from) the employer and whether, if an apology or retraction was promptly offered, the employee was being hypersensitive, too thin-skinned or inflexible, in persisting in a view that trust and confidence had been seriously or irremediably wounded. Where verbal abuse has been persisted in and where the employer, knowing of it or having good reason to suspect it, has taken no steps to curb it, a tribunal is, of course, more likely (and, in the minority view, properly more likely) to treat the verbal abuse as 'authorised' in the sense explained above, more likely to treat any apology as necessary and more likely to treat the harm done as irremediable than would otherwise be the case. How far a given incident could have been reasonably foreseen and, if so foreseen, avoided, will also properly be a factor likely to weigh with a tribunal.

21.   [Counsel] has sought to distinguish what Lindsay J had to say because the principle of which he spoke was confined to such matters as there being verbal abuse: a quick flare up on the shop floor where an apology might be seen as part of the same incident. Also the fact that in that particular case Lindsay J was dissenting. She also drew attention to the fact that the apology in the present case went through the Human Relations Department before being sent to the Claimant. We are not able to accept that what Lindsay J said is confined to cases of verbal abuse and a quick flare-up. It seems to us and, indeed, it is consonant with commonsense and with the principle that in determining if there has been a breach of the implied term all relevant facts and circumstances should be looked at, that an apology *may*, and we stress *may*, have the effect of making it unreasonable for a Claimant to treat the event giving rise to the complaint as being in breach of the implied duty of trust and confidence; certainly, if what might otherwise have been a repudiatory breach of contract has not already been accepted.

22.   We have already referred to the decision in *Malik*, in which Lord Nicholls specifically had said that in determining if there had been a breach of the duty of trust and confidence one had to look at all the circumstances. There are similar passages in the decision in *Morrow v Safeway Stores* and the passage from the judgment of Cox J we have referred to. It is important to remember that a repudiatory breach of a contract does not automatically bring the contract to an end. It enables the innocent party, if he or she so elects, to treat the contract as having been discharged by breach, but until there has been an acceptance the contract remains in being.

. . .

29.   In our opinion, the authorities that we have cited show that even if there has been conduct capable of amounting to a renunciation of a contract, a change in circumstances is relevant to the question of whether there has been a repudiatory breach, certainly of the implied duty of trust and confidence, *as at the date of purported acceptance*. The authorities, in our opinion, show that one should never look at an act said to be a repudiatory breach of contract in a vacuum or in isolation. It is necessary to look at all the relevant circumstances and assess whether there has, in fact, been a breach as at the date of the purported acceptance of the breach. The breach does not end the contract until the repudiatory breach has been accepted by the innocent party. The landscape may have changed. It is always a question for the Employment Tribunal in employment cases to determine whether in fact what might be described as 'post-event facts' lend a different colour to the event that was said to be repudiatory. There is no reason in principle why matters such as a prompt apology are not capable of being taken into account in determining whether at a later date when there is said to be an acceptance of the breach, there has in fact been a breach of the implied term. In appropriate circumstances, it may no longer be reasonable to treat conduct as a breach of the implied term than at an earlier point in time, it may have been reasonable to treat it as such. This is always a matter that will be fact sensitive. There may be circumstances when nothing save waiver or affirmation on the part of the innocent party can render the conduct otherwise than repudiatory. There may be, on the other hand, cases going the other way. This will always be a matter that is fact sensitive for consideration by the Employment Tribunal.

. . .

35.   This now leads us on to the final matter. What should we do? The Claimant says that this matter should be remitted to be heard by a new Employment Tribunal panel. Attention

has been drawn to the recent decision of the President in *Sinclair Roche v Temperly* [2004] IRLR 763, in which the President considered in detail the circumstances in which it would be appropriate for the Employment Appeal Tribunal to remit cases to the Employment Tribunal.

. . .

39.   It seems to us, in the exercise of our discretion, that this being a case where the parties have already gone to substantial expense, we are not satisfied that the passage of time is such that the Employment Tribunal will have lost all recollection; it will be refreshed from the notes of the chairman and members. We note in passing that the President in *Sinclair Roche & Temperley* referred to the decision in that case as being having been delivered only "just over a year ago". We do not consider that the Employment Tribunal will have to make any new finding of primary fact for the reasons we have given in relation to effective care and affirmation.

40.   The Employment Tribunal misdirected itself as to a matter of law, and we have every confidence that the Employment Tribunal will be able to direct itself correctly, and we have every faith, as the President put it, in the professionalism of the Employment Tribunal to deal with this matter. We assume with confidence that it is capable of a professional approach in dealing with the matter on remission.

41.   In those circumstances, we also do not consider that the decision can be categorised as one that was totally or wholly flawed. There had been no complete mishandling: there had simply been a mistaken application of the law as to whether or not a breach of the implied duty of trust and confidence was of necessity repudiatory. In those circumstances we allow the appeal, to the extent to which we set out; and we remit the matter for further consideration by the Employment Tribunal as to whether, or not, having regard to what we have said, it was satisfied that there had been a breach of the implied duty of trust and confidence on the part of the Respondent by Professor Waage having prepared and left the note on his desk. If the Employment Tribunal concludes that there was such a breach it will be necessary for the Tribunal to go on to make findings on the question of effective cause and affirmation. No doubt, the Employment Tribunal will give appropriate directions to the parties. We assume that it will want further written submissions and possibly a further oral hearing: that is a matter for the Employment Tribunal.

42.   It remains for us only to thank [counsel] for their very great assistance and to apologise for the length of this judgment.

––––––––––––––

Notes

1.   The Employment Appeal Tribunal in *Sime* states that if there is a breach of the implied term of mutual trust and confidence, the aggrieved party may treat that as a repudiatory breach of the employment contract. In the case of a breach by the employer, the employee will be regarded as constructively discharged.

   A British court summarized this area of the law as follows, *London Borough of Waltham Forest v Omilaju* [2004] EWCA Civ 1493 in the judgment of Dyson LJ:

   14.   The following basic propositions of law can be derived from the authorities:

   1. The test for constructive dismissal is whether the employer's actions or conduct amounted to a repudiatory breach of the contract of employment: *Western Excavating (ECC) Ltd v Sharp* [1978] 1 QB 761.

2. It is an implied term of any contract of employment that the employer shall not without reasonable and proper cause conduct itself in a manner calculated or likely to destroy or seriously damage the relationship of confidence and trust between employer and employee: see, for example, *Malik v Bank of Credit and Commerce International SA* [1998] AC 20, 34H-35D (Lord Nicholls) and 45C-46E (Lord Steyn). I shall refer to this as "the implied term of trust and confidence".

3. Any breach of the implied term of trust and confidence will amount to a repudiation of the contract see, for example, per *Browne-Wilkinson J in Woods v WM Car Services (Peterborough) Ltd* [1981] ICR 666, 672A. The very essence of the breach of the implied term is that it is calculated or likely to destroy or seriously damage the relationship (emphasis added).

4. The test of whether there has been a breach of the implied term of trust and confidence is objective. As Lord Nicholls said in *Malik* at page 35C, the conduct relied on as constituting the breach must "impinge on the relationship in the sense that, looked at objectively, it is likely to destroy or seriously damage the degree of trust and confidence the employee is reasonably entitled to have in his employer" (emphasis added).

5. A relatively minor act may be sufficient to entitle the employee to resign and leave his employment if it is the last straw in a series of incidents. It is well put at para [480] in Harvey on Industrial Relations and Employment Law:

> Many of the constructive dismissal cases which arise from the undermining of trust and confidence will involve the employee leaving in response to a course of conduct carried on over a period of time. The particular incident which causes the employee to leave may in itself be insufficient to justify his taking that action, but when viewed against a background of such incidents it may be considered sufficient by the courts to warrant their treating the resignation as a constructive dismissal. It may be the 'last straw' which causes the employee to terminate a deteriorating relationship.

15. The last straw principle has been explained in a number of cases, perhaps most clearly in *Lewis v Motorworld Garages Ltd* [1986] ICR 157. Neill LJ said (p 167C) that the repudiatory conduct may consist of a series of acts or incidents, some of them perhaps quite trivial, which cumulatively amount to a repudiatory breach of the implied term of trust and confidence.

2. In *Sime*, the Employment Appeal Tribunal sent the case back to the lower tribunal for reconsideration of whether the employer breached the duty of trust and confidence. Based on the comments of the Appeal Tribunal, what is the likely result on reconsideration?

For a survey of cases regarding breach of the duty of trust and confidence, *see* MICHAEL DUGGAN, WRONGFUL DISMISSAL AND BREACH OF CONTRACT: LAW PRACTICE & PRECEDENTS §§2.1.5–2.1.6 (Emis Professional Pub. 2003).

3. Workplace bullying (or harassment) has been an issue of great importance in the United Kingdom in recent years. The implied duty of trust and confidence is a legal theory on which employees may sue their employer for bullying. The United Kingdom has legislation which defines harassment, declares a breach of the non-harassment obligation a crime and creates a civil remedy. *See* Protection from

Harassment Act 1997; *see also* David C. Yamada, *Crafting a Legislative Response to Workplace Bullying*, 8 EMPLOYEE RTS. & EMP. POL'Y J. 475 (2004) (surveying law of various nations, including the United Kingdom, on bullying).

4. Compare the law of the United Kingdom regarding respect and civility in the workplace with the law of the United States. *See* Chapter 3. Although some states in the United States recognize an implied duty of good faith and fair dealing between the employer and employee, this is not a well-developed theory in the United States, as most courts fear that it would run afoul of the employment-at-will doctrine. Refer to the discussion in Chapter 3 about the U.S. tort of intentional infliction of emotional distress. This tort theory has been applied to employer conduct that is outrageous and exceeds all bounds tolerated by civilized society.

5. The House of Lords addressed a problem of overlap between the duty of mutual trust and confidence and statutory claims for unjust dismissal in *Johnson v. Unisys*, [2003] 1 AC 518 (HL). Claims for unfair dismissal are provided for in the Employment Rights Act 1996. The House of Lords held that an employer's ability to dismiss an employee is not limited by the duty of trust and confidence; thus, an employee cannot base a claim for breach of the implied duty on his dismissal from employment. However, the House of Lords defined the scope of the "*Johnson* exclusion area" narrowly in *Eastwood v. Magnox Electric*, [2004] IRLR 733 (HL), 2004 WL 1476578, explaining that acts leading up to dismissal can constitute a breach. Thus, the employer's conduct during the disciplinary process can breach the implied duty. *See* Douglas Brodie, *Protecting Dignity in the Workplace: The Vitality of Mutual Trust and Confidence*, 33 INDUS. L.J. 349 (2004).

The facts in *Eastwood* were summarized in the opinion as follows:

> In the first case, the claimant employees sought damages for stress-related illness and inability to work alleged to have been caused by a campaign on the part of the defendant employer to demoralise the claimants before dismissing them, in breach of an implied term of their contracts of employment not to so conduct itself as to destroy or seriously damage their mutual trust and confidence and/or breach of duty of care. The judge, on a preliminary issue, gave judgment for the defendant on the ground that the claimants had no real prospect of succeeding on their claim. In the second case, the claimant, having obtained the statutory maximum compensation for unfair dismissal, sought damages for psychiatric injury caused by the defendant employers' suspension of him and failure during the next five months to inform him of allegations made against him or to carry out a proper investigation of those allegations, in breach of the relationship of trust and confidence and breach of duty to provide a safe system of work. The judge struck out the claim on the ground that the principle of entitlement to recover at common law for injury caused by the manner of disciplinary proceedings had no application where dismissal in fact followed and that the claimant's industrial tribunal proceedings had covered the substance of the claim. Differently constituted Courts of Appeal dismissed an appeal by the claimants in the first case and allowed an appeal by the claimant in the second case.

The House of Lords stated as follows in *Eastwood* regarding the boundary between unfair dismissal and breach of the duty of trust and confidence:

The boundary line

27. Identifying the boundary of the '*Johnson* exclusion area', as it has been called, is comparatively straightforward. The statutory code provides remedies for infringement of the statutory right not to be dismissed unfairly. An employee's remedy for unfair dismissal, whether actual or constructive, is the remedy provided by statute. If before his dismissal, whether actual or constructive, an employee has acquired a cause of action at law, for breach of contract or otherwise, that cause of action remains unimpaired by his subsequent unfair dismissal and the statutory rights flowing therefrom. By definition, in law such a cause of action exists independently of the dismissal.

28. In the ordinary course, suspension apart, an employer's failure to act fairly in the steps leading to dismissal does not of itself cause the employee financial loss. The loss arises when the employee is dismissed and it arises by reason of his dismissal. Then the resultant claim for loss falls squarely within the Johnson exclusion area.

29. Exceptionally this is not so. Exceptionally, financial loss may flow directly from the employer's failure to act fairly when taking steps leading to dismissal. Financial loss flowing from suspension is an instance. Another instance is cases such as those now before the House, when an employee suffers financial loss from psychiatric or other illness caused by his pre-dismissal unfair treatment. In such cases the employee has a common law cause of action which precedes, and is independent of, his subsequent dismissal. In respect of his subsequent dismissal he may of course present a claim to an Employment Tribunal. If he brings proceedings both in court and before a tribunal he cannot recover any overlapping heads of loss twice over.

30. If identifying the boundary between the common law rights and remedies and the statutory rights and remedies is comparatively straightforward, the same cannot be said of the practical consequences of this unusual boundary. Particularly in cases concerning financial loss flowing from psychiatric illnesses, some of the practical consequences are far from straightforward or desirable. The first and most obvious drawback is that in such cases the division of remedial jurisdiction between the court and an Employment Tribunal will lead to duplication of proceedings. In practice there will be cases where the Employment Tribunal and the court each traverse much of the same ground in deciding the factual issues before them, with attendant waste of resources and costs.

31. Second, the existence of this boundary line means that in some cases a continuing course of conduct, typically a disciplinary process followed by dismissal, may have to be chopped artificially into separate pieces. In cases of constructive dismissal a distinction will have to be drawn between loss flowing from antecedent breaches of the trust and confidence term and loss flowing from the employee's acceptance of these breaches as a repudiation of the contract. The loss flowing from the impugned conduct taking place before actual or constructive dismissal lies outside the Johnson exclusion area, the loss flowing from the dismissal itself is within that area. In some cases this legalistic distinction may give rise to difficult questions of causation in cases such as those now before the House, where financial loss is claimed as the consequence of psychiatric illness said to have been brought on by the employer's conduct before the employee was dismissed. Judges and tribunals, faced perhaps with conflicting medical evidence, may have to decide whether the fact of dismissal was really the last straw which proved too much for the employee, or whether the onset of the illness occurred even before he was dismissed.

32. The existence of this boundary line produces other strange results. An employer may be better off dismissing an employee than suspending him. A statutory claim for unfair dismissal would be subject to the statutory cap, a common law claim for unfair suspension would not. The decision of the Court of Appeal in *Gogay v Hertfordshire County Council* [2000] IRLR 703 is an example of the latter. Likewise, the decision in Johnson's case means that an employee who is psychologically vulnerable is owed no duty of care in respect of his dismissal although, depending on the circumstances, he may be owed a duty of care in respect of his suspension.

33. It goes without saying that an inter-relation between the common law and statute having these awkward and unfortunate consequences is not satisfactory. The difficulties arise principally because of the cap on the amount of compensatory awards for unfair dismissal. Although the cap was raised substantially in 1998, at times tribunals are still precluded from awarding full compensation for a dismissed employee's financial loss. So, understandably, employees and their legal advisers are seeking to side-step the statutory limit by identifying elements in the events preceding dismissal, but leading up to dismissal, which can be used as pegs on which to hang a common law claim for breach of an employer's implied contractual obligation to act fairly. This situation merits urgent attention by the government and the legislature.

6.   *Eastwood*'s effect on the *Johnson* exclusion has been explained as follows: "The approach adopted in *Eastwood* was to define the exclusion area – where there is no duty or implied term – in narrow terms. Acts leading up to dismissal, including the disciplinary process, are not within the exclusion area since once a cause of action has accrued, it remains unimpaired by the subsequent dismissal." *See* John Bowers & Jeremy Lewis, *Non-Economic Damage in Unfair Dismissal Cases: What's Left After Dunnachie?* 34 INDUS. L.J. 83, 88 (2005). The House of Lords in the excerpt from *Eastwood* above rejected the idea that an employee who complains of conduct by the employer leading up to dismissal has only a statutory unfair dismissal claim. As the House of Lords notes, an employee may, under a set of facts, be able to state claims for both common law breach of the implied obligation and statutory unfair dismissal. Dismissal does not extinguish a claim for breach of the implied obligation of trust and confidence based on predismissal conduct. Then it discussed the problem of potential overlap between the common law claim for breach of the implied obligation of trust and confidence and the statutory claim of unfair dismissal. Drawing a distinction between the two claims is important, although hard, because the common law wrongful dismissal claim comes under the jurisdiction of the courts and is not subject to statutory caps, whereas the statutory unfair dismissal claim is under the jurisdiction of the employment tribunal (as noted earlier in this chapter, the employment tribunal can hear some breach of contract claims also) and is subject to a statutory cap on damages (currently £58,400). Additionally, an employee must have been employed for at least one year to have a statutory claim for unfair dismissal. An award for psychological injury attributable to predismissal breach of the implied obligation and an award for financial loss attributable to unfair dismissal must be separated, and overlap must be avoided. The House of Lords notes that different tribunals may hear the claims and consider much of the same evidence, resulting in a waste of resources. The House of Lords urged a legislative solution to this problem.

7. The House of Lords ruled that noneconomic damages (psychiatric, physical injury, anger, anguish, damage to family life, etc.) cannot be recovered in an unfair dismissal case. *Dunnachie v. Kingston Upon Hull City Council*, [2004] 3 WLR 310. *See* Bowers & Lewis, *supra*. Are *Dunnachie* and *Eastwood*, decided by the same panel of the House of Lords, inconsistent?

> At a simplistic level there appears to be something of a tension between the two decisions. One offers a vigorous defence of the fundamental (yet modern and innovative) term of mutual trust and confidence; the other declines to liberalise the approach to award of damages in unfair dismissal cases. Nevertheless, both decisions serve to highlight, directly or indirectly, the limitations in the range of remedies available to the employee.
>
> Brodie, *supra*, at 354.

Dunnachie also creates an incentive for employees to frame their claim as a breach of contract claim rather than or in addition to an unfair dismissal claim.

Problem: Polly was employed by Widgets, Inc. in London as a clerk. For a period of several months, she complains that her supervisor and other employees under his direction have made her life at work intolerable by means of "bullying" conduct. Eventually she quit. Within a month she was employed at another job. Polly files a claim in court for breach of the obligation of trust and confidence and a claim in the employment tribunal for unfair dismissal. Her employer contends in the court that her breach claim should be dismissed because she can assert only a claim for unfair dismissal, as she contends that the bullying conduct caused her to quit. The employer argues in the employment tribunal that she cannot recover non-economic damages in an unfair dismissal claim. Damages for unfair dismissal will be low because Polly quickly found another job. What result?

8. Professor Steven Anderman argues that the standard applied by the courts for determining whether an employer has breached the implied obligation of mutual trust and confidence is based on common law values favoring employers' property rights; thus, "the cases in which the employer's exercise of control has been found wanting have tended to be extreme cases involving arbitrary, unreasonable and capricious treatment." *See* Steven Anderman, *Termination of Employment: Whose Property Rights?* in THE FUTURE OF LABOUR LAW 101, 109 (Catherine Barnard et al. eds. 2004). Anderman also posits that the emphasis in the common law test on employers' property rights is more or less replicated in the standard applied to unfair dismissal claims under §98(4) of the Employment Rights Act 1996:

> Both leave a wide berth to management discretion. Both require an almost indisputable display of poor judgment by management before finding a job termination unlawful. Both are extremely solicitous of the rights of the employer to dispose of its property as it wills. Both apply a[n] . . . unreasonableness test limiting control to the need to avoid "arbitrary and capricious results."
>
> Anderman, *supra*, at 111.

2. Statute

a. *Unfair Dismissal*

The relationship between contract claims and statutory claims can be complicated. Statutory terms often are incorporated into employment contracts. Moreover, even without express incorporation, breaches of statutes also may amount to breaches of the implied duty of trust and confidence.

There are a number of bases for statutory claims in U.K. law, including the Sex Discrimination Act 1975, the Equal Pay Act 1970, the Race Relations Act 1976, the Disability Discrimination Act 1995, the Health and Safety at Work Act 1974, and the Working Time Regulation 1998. Most of those statutes will be addressed in later sections. This section is restricted to the statutory claim for unjust dismissal that is established in §94 of the Employment Rights Act 1996. Section 98 addresses determinations of fairness.

Under §108 of the ERA 1996, as amended, the qualification period to bring a statutory claim for unfair dismissal is one year of continuous employment at the time of termination.

Section 98 ERA 1996, as amended, provides as follows:

Fairness
General. 98. - (1) In determining for the purposes of this Part whether the dismissal of an employee is fair or unfair, it is for the employer to show-
   (a) the reason (or, if more than one, the principal reason) for the dismissal, and
   (b) that it is either a reason falling within subsection (2) or some other substantial reason of a kind such as to justify the dismissal of an employee holding the position which the employee held.
      (2) A reason falls within this subsection if it-
   (a) relates to the capability or qualifications of the employee for performing work of the kind which he was employed by the employer to do,
   (b) relates to the conduct of the employee,
   (ba) is retirement of the employee,
   (c) is that the employee was redundant, or
   (d) is that the employee could not continue to work in the position which he held without contravention (either on his part or on that of his employer) of a duty or restriction imposed by or under an enactment. . . .
      (3) In subsection (2)(a)-
   (a) "capability", in relation to an employee, means his capability assessed by reference to skill, aptitude, health or any other physical or mental quality, and
   (b) "qualifications", in relation to an employee, means any degree, diploma or other academic, technical or professional qualification relevant to the position which he held.
      (3A) In any case where the employer has fulfilled the requirements of subsection (1) by showing that the reason (or the principal reason) for the dismissal is retirement of the employee, the question whether the dismissal is fair or unfair shall be determined in accordance with section 98ZG.
      (4) In any other case where the employer has fulfilled the requirements of subsection (1), the determination of the question whether the dismissal is fair or unfair (having regard to the reason shown by the employer)-

(a) depends on whether in the circumstances (including the size and administrative resources of the employer's undertaking) the employer acted reasonably or unreasonably in treating it as a sufficient reason for dismissing the employee, and

(b) shall be determined in accordance with equity and the substantial merits of the case.

. . .

Notes

1. The analysis of unfair dismissal claims is a two-step process, based on ILO Recommendation 119. Anderman, *supra*, at 112-113. The first step is to identify the reason for dismissal. Section 98, *supra*, places the burden on the employer to show a fair reason for a dismissal. The second step is to classify the reason for the dismissal. One category of reasons is automatically unfair because they are statutorily prohibited: for example, union-related reason; employee's assertion of a statutory right; health-and-safety-related reason; maternity-related reason; reason related to working time; reason related to making a protected disclosure (whistleblowing); and so on. INTERNATIONAL LABOR, *supra* at 7-26 to 7-27. Dismissals for the reasons in §98(2) are presumptively valid reasons: lack of capability or qualification; improper conduct; redundancy; retaining the person violates a statutory duty or enactment; and some other substantial reason, §98(1)(b). Those reasons are subject to the reasonableness analysis in §98(4). In performing this reasonableness analysis, the tribunal is not to substitute its view for that of the employer, and there is not just one reasonable response but a band of reasonable responses that an employer might adopt. *See Tesco Stores Ltd. v. Pryke*, Appeal No. UKEAT/0576/05/DM (May 10, 2006).

    The reasonableness test applied to unfair dismissal cases has been criticized as emphasizing the property rights and prerogatives of employers to the detriment of the statutory protection of employees against unfair dismissal. *See* Anderman, *supra*. Anderman argues that "insistence upon a wide range of reasonable employer responses test in section 98(4) has thwarted that parliamentary intention [to limit misuse of employer power]." *Id.* at 127.

2. A recent judgment of an employment tribunal on an issue of unfair dismissal attracted considerable media attention. The case involved an art teacher at Eton College who alleged that she was ordered to help Prince Harry with an assignment. The teacher secretly recorded conversations with Prince Harry. An Examination Board looking into allegations of cheating by Prince Harry determined that he did not cheat. The teacher claimed that she was unfairly dismissed based on her public interest disclosure and on grounds of sex discrimination. The employer argued that she was dismissed for lack of capability. The employment tribunal concluded that there was an unfair dismissal in that the college could not support its reason of lack of capability, but it found no unfair dismissal based on grounds of violation of public interest or sex discrimination. *Forsyth v. Eton College*, Case No. 2702463/03 (Employment Tribunal at Reading June 2005). The tribunal found that the department head bullied the teacher and that Eton did not perform an objective assessment of the teacher's capabilities in reaching a decision to dismiss her.

3. Regarding what constitutes an unfair reason, consider the case of the American Broadcasting Corporation's London-based freelance journalist Richard Gizbert whose eleven-year freelance contract with ABC News was terminated in 2004. Gizbert filed a complaint, contending that he was unfairly dismissed because he refused to accept assignments in war zones, particularly Iraq. ABC argued that he was terminated for another reason – he was inessential and the network was making cutbacks. The employment tribunal found that he was "unfairly dismissed for a reason related to health and safety." *See* Suevon Lee, *British Tribunal Weighs Reporter's Case*, seattlepi.nwsource.com/tv/1401AP_Britain_Reporter_ABC.html.

4. What if an employer asserts a fair reason for dismissal, such as misconduct of the employee, which may be factually wrong? The proper analysis of such a case under §98(4) was explained in *British Home Stores v. Burchell* [1980] ICR 303, 304. The EAT explained that analysis in a recent case:

> In a case where an employee is dismissed because the employer believes that he has committed an act of misconduct, the first task for the Employment Tribunal is to decide whether that was a reasonable belief for the employer to hold. That task involves three elements. The first is to ask whether it is satisfied that the belief was genuine. The second is to ask whether it has been shown that that belief was formed on reasonable grounds. The third is to ask whether, at the time the belief was formed, the employer had carried out as much investigation into the matter as was reasonable in all the circumstances of the case. When considering the third question, the tribunal require to bear in mind that there is a range of reasonable responses open to an employer as to the nature and amount of investigation it carries out in any particular case. The foregoing analysis is, of course, drawn from the cases of *Burchell, Sainsbury's Supermarket v Hitt* [2003] IRLR 23 and *Grattan Plc v Kamran Hussain* EAT/0802/02/TM. If those three questions are answered in the affirmative, then the tribunal has to ask itself whether dismissal was within the range of reasonable responses which a reasonable employer could adopt in the circumstances: *Iceland Frozen Foods Ltd v Jones* 1983 ICR 17. It is important that an Employment Tribunal bear in mind that the "range of reasonable responses" test is just that and is not an invitation to substitute its own views as to what would have been the way to proceed for that of the employer. Nor does the fact that an Employment Tribunal can identify something that could have been done by an employer that was not done necessarily give rise to the inference that that employer has failed to act reasonably.

> *First Scotrail Ltd. v. Griffin*, Appeal No. UKEATS/0027/05/RN (Mar. 7, 2006).

b. *Redundancy and Transfers of Undertakings*

Section 98(2)(c) of ERA 1996 provides that redundancy is a fair reason for dismissal. The statutory dismissal and disciplinary procedures established by the Employment Act 2002 apply to redundancy dismissals. Thus, even if an employer could prevail on an unfair dismissal by proving redundancy, the dismissal still might be found unfair if the employer failed to comply with the required procedures.

Redundancy is defined by the ERA 1996:

> 139. - (1) For the purposes of this Act an employee who is dismissed shall be taken to be dismissed by reason of redundancy if the dismissal is wholly or mainly attributable to-
> (a) the fact that his employer has ceased or intends to cease-

(i) to carry on the business for the purposes of which the employee was employed by
him, or

(ii) to carry on that business in the place where the employee was so employed, or

(b) the fact that the requirements of that business-

(i) for employees to carry out work of a particular kind, or

(ii) for employees to carry out work of a particular kind in the place where the employee
was employed by the employer,

have ceased or diminished or are expected to cease or diminish.

. . .

Employees who have worked for at least two years with an employer, ERA §155, have a
right to a redundancy payment, and notice period or payment in lieu of notice (PILON).
The redundancy payment is based largely on years of service, and the formula for calculating it is set out in §162 of ERA 1996, as amended.

The Transfer of Undertakings (Protection of Employment) Regulations 1981 (TUPE
Regulations) implement EU Transfer of Undertakings (Acquired Rights) Directive, 77/187
as amended by 98/50/EC. Summed up at its simplest, the transferee steps into the shoes
of the transferor with respect to all rights, duties, liabilities, etc. for employment contracts.
The employees are retained with the same terms and conditions of employment they had
with the transferor. "[A] relevant transfer shall not operate so as to terminate the contract
of employment of any person employed by the transferor and assigned to the organised
grouping of resources or employees that is subject to the relevant transfer, which would
otherwise be terminated by the transfer, but any such contract shall have effect after the
transfer as if originally made between the person so employed and the transferee." TUPE
Regs 2006 §4. Any trade union recognized by the transferor is deemed to have been
recognized by the transferee. *Id.* §6. "Relevant transfers" include transfer of an economic
entity which retains its identity to a new employer and "service provision changes" in
which a contract service provider takes over a service contract from another contractor.
New TUPE Regulations went into effect in April 2006. The Transfer of Undertakings
(Protection of Employment) Regulations 2006, Statutory Instrument 2006, No. 246. A
useful guidance is at http://www.dti.gov.uk/files/file30031.pdf. The guidance summarizes
the principal changes effected by the new regulations, including the following: a widening
of the scope of the regulations to cover outsourcing, insourcing, or assignment of services
by a client to a new contractor; a new duty on the transferor to supply information about
transferring employees to the transferee employer; provisions making it easier for insolvent
businesses to be transferred; and provisions clarifying the circumstances under which it
is unfair for a transferee to dismiss employees.

C. UNIONS AND COLLECTIVE BARGAINING

1. Unions and Collective Bargaining

Collective bargaining is not regulated by a central law or code, as is the case in continental
European nations. There are several laws that relate to collective bargaining, but much of
collective bargaining developed through practice over a century without legal regulation.
Indeed, after World War II, unions actively fought legal regulation. *See, e.g.*, William B.
Gould IV, *Recognition Laws: The U.S. Experience and Its Relevance to the U.K.*, 20
Comp. Lab. L. & Pol'y J. 11, 11 (1998). The history of collective bargaining in the United

Kingdom thus has been largely of voluntary bargaining. Indeed, Britain has been held up as an example of the role of collective bargaining when the government does not regulate heavily. John Pencavel, *The Appropriate Design of Collective Bargaining Systems: Learning from the Experience of Britain, Australia, and New Zealand*, 20 COMP. LAB. L. & POL'Y J. 447, 461 (1999). However, it has been argued that the more correct view is that the extensive collective bargaining system in place in Britain is the result of indirect government support:

> [B]y encouraging the recognition by employers of labor unions, by discouraging product market competition, and by frustrating the competitive workings of nonunion labor markets, the tone of British legislation has not been neutral or hands-off when it comes to collective bargaining. That is, the ability of unions and employers in unionized markets to raise prices and divide the rents between themselves is constrained by the degree of competition in the product markets and by competition from nonunion labor markets. In practice, the rent-seeking potential of unions and unionized employers has been enhanced by a host of government policies.
>
> *Id.* at 462.

Beginning in the 1970s, however, the government, with victories by the Conservative Party, became more involved in passing laws to regulate statutorily collective bargaining, and the change decreased the strength of the unions. The passage of the Industrial Relations Act of 1971 under Prime Minister Edward Heath started the new regulation of unions and collective bargaining, but the regulation did not hit full stride until the election of Prime Minister Margaret Thatcher's Conservative government in 1979. *See* Gould, *supra*, at 11. During Prime Minister Thatcher's three terms many legislative reforms were enacted to reign in unions. *See* Pencavel, *supra*, at 464-467. The result was a substantial decline in union density:

> The sharp union decline in Britain that dates from 1979 is by now well known. Aggregate union density showed a remarkable stability in the postwar period (at around 40-45% membership), followed by a sharp rise in the 1970s, but then an even sharper fall from the late 1970s onward. Since 1979 aggregate union density has trended downward so that, by the end of the 1990s, less than 30% of workers were members of trade unions.
>
> Stephen Machin & Stephen Wood, *Human Resource Management as a Substitute for Trade Unions in British Workplaces*, 58 INDUS. & LAB. REL. REV. 201, 203 (2005).

The decline in union density in the United Kingdom from 1970 to 2003 was 15.5%. *See* Jelle Visser, *Union Membership in 24 Countries*, 129 MONTHLY LAB. REV. 38, 45 tbl.3. While union density in the private sector decreased, however, density in the public sector has remained relatively stable. *See British Trade Unions*, THE ECONOMIST (June 8, 2006). For detailed data on the decline of collective representation in the U.K., see INSIDE THE WORKPLACE: FIRST FINDINGS FROM THE 2004 WORKPLACE EMPLOYMENT RELATIONS SURVEY (WERS 2004). http://www.routledge.com/textbooks/0415378133/pdf/insideWP.pdf.

The election of Prime Minister Blair's New Labour Party in the late 1990s saw a reversal of that trend, as laws were passed to restore the role of unions and to codify the laws and practices regarding unions and collective bargaining.

It is important to remember that European Union law will play a role now and in the future. Article 11 of the European Convention for the Protection of Human Rights and Fundamental Freedoms protects the right of "freedom of assembly and association;" this includes the right to join a trade union. The United Kingdom's Trade Union and Labour Relations (Consolidation) Act 1992 (TULR(C)A) does not require employers to enter into recognition agreements and to conduct collective bargaining with a union that has majority support. The European Court of Human Rights held that Article 11 does not impose an obligation on states to provide a legal mechanism for requiring employers to enter into collective bargaining with a union: "[T]he Court has consistently held that although collective bargaining may be one of the best ways by which trade unions may be enabled to protect their members' interests, it is not indispensable for the effective enjoyment of trade union freedom. . . . The Court has not yet been prepared to hold that the freedom of a trade union to make its voice heard extends to imposing on an employer an obligation to recognize a trade union." *Wilson & National Union of Journalists v. The United Kingdom,* [2002] IRLR 568, 35 Euro. Ct. H.R. 20 (2002).

Another area in which EC law will affect U.K. law is the European Works Council Directive, Council Directive 94/45/EEC (extended to the United Kingdom by Council Directive 97/74/EC). Although the history of collective bargaining in the United Kingdom has been about trade unions engaged in collective bargaining, the future will include European Works Councils. The directive provides for formation of European Works Councils on request by a specified number of employees in Community-scale undertakings.

There are now two ways in which a union can be recognized by an employer: (1) voluntary recognition by the employer; and (2) statutory recognition. As mentioned earlier, the history of collective bargaining in the United Kingdom has been about voluntary recognition. The Employment Relations Act 1999 provided for the new statutory recognition, and it went into effect in 2000 and can be found in TULR(C)A §259. *See generally* Nancy Peters, *The United Kingdom Recalibrates the U.S. National Labor Relations Act: Possible Lessons for the United States?*, 25 Comp. Lab. L. & Pol'y J. 227 (2004). Both approaches are invoked by a union's making a request for recognition. If the employer refuses to voluntarily recognize a union when a proper request is made supported by a certain level of support by employees, then the Central Arbitration Committee (CAC) may decide whether to declare recognition. The CAC may order recognition or may order that a secret ballot election be held. The law is designed to encourage the parties to go the route of voluntary recognition, and the experience so far has been that a vast majority of employers elect to voluntarily recognize. *See* Peters, *supra*, at 237 (chart showing that of 776 recognition deals between Nov. 2000 and Oct. 2002, 732 of them – 94 percent – were voluntary). Statutory recognition does impose a duty to bargain that does not exist at common law, but the subjects of mandatory bargaining are only pay, hours, and holidays. An employer is required to consult and inform the union.

The Employment Relations Act 2004 followed a government review of how well the 1999 Act was working. One of the principal concerns was interference by employers with employees' decision to vote in the statutory recognition ballot. In the *Wilson* case, *supra*, the European Court of Human Rights held that the United Kingdom's law permitted employers to use financial incentives to induce employees to give up rights, and that this constituted a violation of Article 11 of the Convention for the Protection of Human Rights and Fundamental Freedoms. The ERA 2004 seeks to protect employee free choice in the statutory recognition procedure by protecting employees from coercive tactics by employers (or unions) and by increasing union access to employees during the procedure. The Act creates unfair practices by employers during recognition and derecognition balloting, including threatening employees or offering them financial incentives. The Act also modifies the procedures on balloting for recognition by providing that unions are entitled to provide written communications to employees between the time of the election order and the ballot. The employer must provide to the CAC names and addresses of employees in the bargaining unit. The Act also clarifies issues regarding an appropriate bargaining unit. Regarding strikes, the ERA 2004 extends the "protected period" from eight weeks to twelve weeks, during which a dismissal of a striker is automatically unfair. *See* ERA 2004 §26(3).

The ERA 2004 is critiqued and criticized in Alan L. Bogg, *Employment Relations Act 2004: Another False Dawn for Collectivism?*, 34 INDUS. L.J. 72 (2005). Bogg is critical of the Act for not granting unions face-to-face access to employees after the CAC order that an election be held. He considers the employer's duty to provide information and the entitlement of the union to send written communications as not going far enough in altering the access advantage enjoyed by employers. He also is critical of the unfair practices provisions for a number of reasons. Overall, Bogg fears that the elaborate ballot procedure with the attendant delays, which are exacerbated in cases of unfair practice complaints, will take U.K. law down the road of U.S. law, where delay generally erodes union support. In sum, Bogg concludes that while "there are significant new measures in relation to freedom of association and collective bargaining rights. . . . the reforms do not disclose a collectivist turn in this second phase of New Labour's collective labour law reforms." *Id.* at 72.

Section 178 of TULR(C)A defines a bargaining agreement. Bargaining occurs at various levels – industry, district, company, plant, work group.

Collective agreements, unlike those in the United States, generally are not legally binding agreements. It is presumed that collective agreements, other than those reached in a window period of Dec. 1971 to September 1974, are not legally binding unless they are written and have an express provision stating that they are intended to be legally binding. Still, collective agreements, even though not legally binding, often have terms that are incorporated into individual employment contracts, and they thus become binding.

The legal impediments to conducting a strike is one of the most notable features of U.K. labor law. In fact, the European Committee of Social Rights determined that the restrictions imposed by U.K. law on the right to strike amounted to an infringement of the European Social Charter of 1996. Erika Kovács, *The Right to Strike in the European Social Charter*, 26 COMP. LAB. L. & POL'Y J. 445, 460 (2005).

For most of the twentieth century, there was no statutory law regarding strikes, and the law was the common law of torts and contracts. *See* James Atleson, *The Voyage of the Neptune Jade: The Perils and Promises of Transnational Labor Solidarity*, 52 BUFF. L. REV. 85, 127-28 (2004). Employers sued strike organizers for industrial torts. The most significant legal protection of the right to strike came in the Trade Disputes Act 1906, which provided an immunity for trade unions in most tort actions based on a strike. In the 1980s and 1990s, the Thatcher government passed a number of laws rolling back the immunities and imposing restrictions on strikes. *Id.* A significant restriction was a ban of secondary action and picketing away from one's own worksite. *Id.* The Trade Union Act of 1984 imposed the conducting of a vote on a strike as a prerequisite to obtaining the immunity from tort. Although the New Labour government has rolled back some of the restrictions on strikes, it has been criticized for not repealing more of the restrictions:

> The most striking aspect of the record of New Labour law is what it has not done. There is still no right to strike in domestic law, and New Labour has refused to do anything but tinker with the worst excesses of neoliberal strike laws. Its only substantial offering is the provision of protection against dismissal during the first eight weeks of a lawful strike.
>
> Fredman, *supra*, at 32.

[As mentioned earlier, the eight-week protected period was extended to twelve weeks by ERA 2004.]

Industrial actions, such as strikes, are usually in breach of an individual employee's employment contract, but §236 of the TULR(C)A prohibits courts from ordering strikers to return to work. Moreover, it is an automatically unfair dismissal for an employer to dismiss an employee for participating in a protected industrial action, but this protection lasts for only twelve weeks unless the employer has not taken reasonable steps to resolve the dispute. Industrial actions are protected if they are made immune from civil tort liability under TULR(C)A.

Work stoppages and other industrial actions declined significantly from 1970 to 1998. *See* LABOUR MARKET TRENDS at 260 (June 2000). The decline has continued, reaching a new record low in 2003. The number of working days lost in 2003 was under 500,000, whereas the number in the 1970s was 12.9 million. *See Number of Strikes Dip to Record Low in United Kingdom, Statistics Office Says,* DAILY LAB. REP. (BNA) No. 107, at A-9 (June 4, 2004).

Note

> Many unions in the United States have adopted a strategy of trying to pressure employers to voluntarily recognize the union rather than filing a petition and undergoing a secret ballot election conducted by the National Labor Relations Board. Many leaders in organized labor believe that the statutory scheme with the NLRB-conducted election is a formula for defeat because of the opportunity that it affords employers to campaign against the union during the time period between the filing of the petition and the holding of the election. *See* Chapter 3, *supra.* Nancy Peters argues in an article that the United States might improve upon its union recognition procedures by considering the U.K. approach, which, although providing a statutory recognition scheme, has created strong incentives for employers and unions to pursue voluntary recognition. *See* Peters, *supra.* She cites the following incentives for voluntary recognition: (1) when a union demonstrates majority support, recognition by the CAC is nearly automatic; (2) if a union withdraws an application after filing with the CAC, it is barred from reapplying for three years; (3) a union must request voluntary recognition before filing with CAC, and the Advisory, Conciliation & Arbitration Service (ACAS) may be called in to conduct an informal ballot of the workers; (4) if an employer resists voluntary recognition, it is put to the time and expense and added union access to workers; and

(5) if CAC imposes recognition, a model procedural agreement imposes minimum standards for negotiations. Peters, *supra*, at 242-43. Peters concludes that "the United Kingdom has altered the basic North American recognition model from one where the vast majority of recognition deals result from hostile litigation (as in the United States) to one where only a fraction of such deals arise from legal proceedings." *Id.* at 248. Indeed, one can argue that the U.S. model does not create any incentives for employers to voluntarily recognize unions.

2. Collective Consultation

The U.K. law on collective consultation is to be distinguished from law regulating individual consultation. The law in this area has undergone extensive changes in the last two decades. Under the U.K.'s abstentionist approach to labor law, the government did not regulate employers' providing information to and consulting with employees regarding decisions about the business. *See* Mark Hall, *Assessing the Information and Consultation of Employees Regulations*, 34 INDUS. L.J. 103, 104-05 (2005). The United Kingdom's becoming a part of the EU's social law, however, changed this. The first wave of change involved the amendment of U.K. law to comply with the EC Transfer of Undertakings Directive, 2001/23/EC, and the Collective Redundancies Directive, 98/59/EC. TULR(C)A was amended by 1999 regulations to achieve compliance. The duty of collective consultation applied to situations in which the employer was carrying out multiple redundancies and where there is a transfer of undertaking. INTERNATIONAL LABOR, *supra* at 7-82 to 7-83. The second wave of change involved a more extensive adjustment of U.K. law and occurred as the U.K. endeavored to come into compliance with the Employee Information and Consultation Directive, Directive 2002/14/EC OJ L80/29-34. The United Kingdom's implementing regulations, Information and Consultation of Employees (ICE) Regulations 2004, SI 2004/3426, took effect on April 6, 2005. *See* Hall, *supra*.

Employers also have a duty to provide written notice to the Secretary of State of their intention to carry out multiple redundancies: ninety days' notice for one hundred or more employees and thirty days' notice for twenty to ninety-nine. INTERNATIONAL LABOR, *supra*, at 7-82 to 7-83. The government has proposed minor revisions to the law regarding the employer's duty to notify the government. *See* Revised Legal Framework (March 2006), at http://www.dti.gov.uk/files/file28163.pdf.

a. *Collective Redundancies and Transfers of Undertakings*

In Trade Union and Labour Relations (Consolidation) Act 1992 at §§188 & 189, the duty of the employer to consult representatives in cases of multiple redundancy is described as follows:

188. – (1) An employer proposing to dismiss as redundant an employee of a description in respect of which an independent trade union is recognised by him shall consult representatives of the union about the dismissal in accordance with this section.

(2) The consultation must begin at the earliest opportunity, and in any event –

(a) where the employer is proposing to dismiss as redundant 100 or more employees at one establishment within a period of 90 days or less, at least 90 days before the first of those dismissals takes effect;

(b) where the employer is proposing to dismiss as redundant at least 10 but less than 100 employees at one establishment within a period of 30 days or less, at least 30 days before the first of those dismissals takes effect.

(3) In determining how many employees an employer is proposing to dismiss as redundant no account shall be taken of employees in respect of whose proposed dismissals consultation has already begun.

(4) For the purposes of the consultation the employer shall disclose in writing to the trade union representatives –

(a) the reasons for his proposals,

(b) the numbers and descriptions of employees whom it is proposed to dismiss as redundant,

(c) the total number of employees of any such description employed by the employer at the establishment in question,

(d) the proposed method of selecting the employees who may be dismissed, and

(e) the proposed method of carrying out the dismissals, with due regard to any agreed procedure, including the period over which the dismissals are to take effect.

(5) That information shall be delivered to the trade union representatives, or sent by post to an address notified by them to the employer, or sent by post to the union at the address of its head or main office.

(6) In the course of the consultation the employer shall –

(a) consider any representations made by the trade union representatives, and

(b) reply to those representations and, if he rejects any of those representations, state his reasons.

(7) If in any case there are special circumstances which render it not reasonably practicable for the employer to comply with a requirement of subsection (2), (4) or (6), the employer shall take all such steps towards compliance with that requirement as are reasonably practicable in those circumstances.

(8) This section does not confer any rights on a trade union or an employee except as provided by sections 189 to 192 below.

189. – (1) Where an employer has dismissed as redundant, or is proposing to dismiss as redundant, one or more employees of a description in respect of which an independent trade union is recognised by him, and has not complied with the requirements of section 188, the union may present a complaint to an industrial tribunal on that ground.

(2) If the tribunal finds the complaint well-founded it shall make a declaration to that effect and may also make a protective award.

(3) A protective award is an award in respect of one or more descriptions of employees –

(a) who have been dismissed as redundant, or whom it is proposed to dismiss as redundant, and

(b) in respect of whose dismissal or proposed dismissal the employer has failed to comply with a requirement of section 188,

ordering the employer to pay remuneration for the protected period.

(4) The protected period –

(a) begins with the date on which the first of the dismissals to which the complaint relates takes effect, or the date of the award, whichever is the earlier, and

(b) is of such length as the tribunal determines to be just and equitable in all the circumstances having regard to the seriousness of the employer's default in complying with any requirement of section 188;

but shall not exceed 90 days in a case falling within section 188(2)(a), 30 days in a case falling within section 188(2)(b), or 28 days in any other case.

The Court of Appeal explained in *Susie Radin Ltd v GMB and others* [2004] IRLR 400, that the protective award for a breach of §189 is punitive, not compensatory, and that the fact that the consultation may be futile is not relevant to the award:

> It may at first sight seem surprising to say that the fact that consultation would have been futile is something which an Employment Tribunal should not take into account when assessing the length of time for which a protective award should be made. But the argument that took place has convinced me (1) that there is nothing in the statutory wording which requires such futility to be taken into account and (2) that in a collective claim brought by a union it would be impossible to take such futility into account in a fair and practical way.

Section 188(7) of TULR(C)A provides that if it is not "reasonably practicable" for an employer to comply with the consultation requirements, the employer is required to take all steps toward compliance that are reasonably practicable.

The duty of collective consultation in case of a transfer of undertaking is described in the Transfer of Undertakings (Protection of Employment) "TUPE" Regulations 2006. The compensation for non-compliance can be up to thirteen weeks of actual pay per employee.

The appropriate representatives of the employees are the trade union representatives if the employees are represented. If they are not, then the employer may choose any elected employee representatives or hold an election to choose the representatives. Under TUPE regulations, the election must be, so far as is practicable, a secret ballot election. TUPE Regulations 2006 Reg. 14.

b. *Information and Consultation of Employees (ICE) Regulations*

When fully phased in in April 2008, the regulations will apply to any employer with fifty or more employees. The triggering mechanism to initiate negotiations for an agreement on information and consultation is a request by 10 percent of the employees (minimum of fifteen employees and maximum of twenty-five hundred). When there is a "valid pre-existing agreement" in place, at least 40 percent of the employees must vote to proceed with negotiations for a new agreement. The agreement on information and consultation that is the product of the negotiations must specify the circumstances under which employees will be informed and consulted, either through representatives or directly. If an employer fails to initiate the negotiations after a valid request or if the parties do not negotiate an agreement within six months, the regulations provide default terms. The default terms provide for information and consultation with employee representatives, one for every fifty employees, with a minimum of two and a maximum of twenty-five. The requirements are: (a) information on "the recent and probable development of the undertaking's activities and economic situation"; (b) information and consultation regarding "the situation, structure and probable development of employment within the undertaking and any anticipatory measures envisaged, in particular, where there is a threat to employment within the undertaking"; and (c) information and consultation "with a view to reaching an agreement" on "decisions likely to lead to substantial changes in work organization or in contractual relations," including collective redundancies and transfers of undertakings. Hall, *supra*, at 112. Where employers have a duty to consult representatives on collective redundancies and transfers of undertakings under existing legislation (TULR(C)A or TUPE regulations), discussed *supra*, the ICE regulations do not require additional information and consultation, so long as the representatives are notified that the employer is complying with its information and consultation duties under that legislation. INTERNATIONAL LABOR 2005 CUMULATIVE SUPP., *supra*, at 7-15. The Central Arbitration Committee (CAC) is charged with hearing complaints, and may require compliance and impose penalties up to a maximum of £75,000. The information and consultation representatives may be appointed or elected, but how they are chosen can be negotiated and provided for in the agreement.

The CAC issued its first ruling on an ICE violation in December 2005. *See* http://www.eiro.eurofound.eu.int/2006/02/inbrief/uk0602101n.html. In the case, employees made a request for negotiations to establish an information and consultation agreement. The employer contended that there were valid preexisting agreements, which meant that a vote would be required in which at least 40 percent of employees would have to support negotiations for a new agreement. The CAC determined that one of the existing agreements did not constitute a valid preexisting agreement because it was not sufficiently detailed regarding how the employer gives employees information and seeks their views on the information. Accordingly, the CAC ordered the employer to begin negotiations in response to the employee request.

D. WAGES, HOURS, AND BENEFITS

1. Wages

The United Kingdom had no minimum wage until April 1, 1999. The National Minimum Wage Act 1998 and the National Minimum Wage Regulations 1999 were initiatives of the New Labour Party. The minimum wage, at this writing, was £5.05 per hour for adults and £4.25 per hour for eighteen- to twenty-one-year-old workers. The rates will go up again in October 2006 to £5.35 for adults and £4.45 for eighteen- to twenty-one-year-olds. *Prime Minister Blair Announces Hike in United Kingdom's Minimum Wage*, DAILY LAB. REP. (BNA) No. 41 (March 3, 2005). Complaints for unlawful deductions and other violations are made to the employment tribunal. Aside from the requirement of minimum wage, rates of pay are fixed by contract. Section 8 of the Employment Rights Act 1996 provides employees with a right to a written pay statement every time they are paid. *See* discussion *supra* section B(1)(a).

2. Hours

The Working Time Regulations 1998 (as amended), which implement the Working Time Directive, 93/104/EC, became effective on October 1, 1998. The regulations cover four matters: maximum weekly working time (not more than forty-eight hours for a seven-day period, with an opt-out provision available to workers); rest breaks (not less than eleven consecutive hours in each twenty-four-hour period; not less than twenty-four hours in a seven-day period; and not less than twenty minutes for adults if the working time is more than six hours, or thirty minutes for young workers if working time is more than 4.5 hours); night work (no more than an average of eight hours in a twenty-four-hour period, averaged over seventeen-week period); and annual leave (four weeks' paid annual leave, including statutory and public holidays – this entitlement exists from the worker's first day on the job). The Working Time Regulations met stiff criticism from businesses in the United Kingdom, and they were amended to try to lighten the burden on businesses. Pressure in the other direction came in the form of a warning letter sent by the European Commission. The warning letter, the first step in enforcing a directive, noted three concerns in the U.K. regulations: (1) provisions on obligations of employers to enforce workers' rights to breaks and holidays; (2) measurement of workers' voluntary work time; and (3) exclusion of night-shift overtime from count of normal hours. INTERNATIONAL LABOR, *supra*, at 7-95.

One of the points of contention at the European Commission has been the opt-out provision that the United Kingdom succeeded in getting included in Article 18(1)(b) of the Working Time Directive. Pursuant to that Article, the U.K.'s Working Time Regulations provide that employees can agree to work more than forty-eight hours in a week. The United Kingdom, with the support of other member nations resisted the latest efforts to remove the opt-out provision from the directive. *See Alistair Darling Maintains Britain's Opt Out of EU Working Time Directive*, http://www.dti.gov.uk/pressroom/news/page 29821.html. There is evidence that the Working Time Directive has not had much of an impact on the long hours worked by employees in the United Kingdom, and that fact is partly attributable to the widespread use of the opt-out. *See* Catherine Barnard, Simon Deakin & Richard Hobbs, *Opting Out of the 48-Hour Week: Employer Necessity or Individual Choice? An Empirical Study of the Operation of Article 18(1)(B) of the Working Time Directive in the UK*, 32 INDUS. L.J. 223 (2003).

The United Kingdom's opt-out provision is in the 1998 regulations:

Agreement to exclude the maximum

5. - (1) The limit specified in regulation 4(1) shall not apply in relation to a worker who has agreed with his employer in writing that it should not apply in his case, provided that the employer complies with the requirements of paragraph (4).

(2) An agreement for the purposes of paragraph (1) -

(a) may either relate to a specified period or apply indefinitely; and

(b) subject to any provision in the agreement for a different period of notice, shall be terminable by the worker by giving not less than seven days' notice to his employer in writing.

(3) Where an agreement for the purposes of paragraph (1) makes provision for the termination of the agreement after a period of notice, the notice period provided for shall not exceed three months.

(4) The requirements referred to in paragraph (1) are that the employer -

(a) maintains up-to-date records which -

(i) identify each of the workers whom he employs who has agreed that the limit specified in regulation 4(1) should not apply in his case;

(ii) set out any terms on which the worker agreed that the limit should not apply; and

(iii) specify the number of hours worked by him for the employer during each reference period since the agreement came into effect (excluding any period which ended more than two years before the most recent entry in the records);

(b) permits any inspector appointed by the Health and Safety Executive or any other authority which is responsible under regulation 28 for the enforcement of these Regulations to inspect those records on request; and

(c) provides any such inspector with such information as he may request regarding any case in which a worker has agreed that the limit specified in regulation 4(1) should not apply in his case.

3. Leave

a. Annual Leave: A worker is entitled to four weeks of paid annual leave, including statutory and public holidays. In the original 1998 regulations, the entitlement did not accrue until a worker had been employed continuously for thirteen weeks. This requirement was successfully challenged in the European Court of Justice as being inconsistent with EU law. Accordingly, the 2001 amendment of the regulations deleted the qualifying period.

b. Sick leave and sick pay: Generally a worker is entitled to twenty-eight weeks of Statutory Sick Pay (SSP) in any period of incapacity for work. The SSP rate of pay as of April 2006 is £70.05 per week. When SSP is exhausted, a worker can apply to the Department of Social Security for incapacity benefits, which are paid by the state. Employers may not contract out of SSP, but they may contractually provide for more or better benefits.

c. Maternity leave: The Maternity and Parental Leave, etc. Regulations 1999 implemented the EU Directive on Parental Leave, 96/34/EC. The Maternity and Parental Leave (Amendment) Regulations 2002, Statutory Instrument 2002 No. 2789, amended the regulations, and the Employment Act 2002 has a chapter on rights after maternity leave. Compulsory maternity leave (CML) provides that employers cannot permit a woman entitled to ordinary maternity leave to work during the two weeks after the birth of the child. Ordinary maternity leave (OML) is twenty-six weeks, and notice to the employer is required. Contractual benefits other than wages or salary are preserved during ordinary maternity leave. An employee returning from ordinary maternity leave has the right to return to the job she left. Additional maternity leave (AML) of 26 weeks is available to an employee who has worked for at least twenty-six weeks by the fourteenth week before the expected week of childbirth. Thus, for employees who qualify for OML and AML, they may have up to one year of maternity leave. Statutory maternity pay (SMP) is also provided for if the employee satisfies the qualifications. As of April 2006, for the first six weeks of maternity leave, SMP is 90 percent of average weekly earnings, and for the remaining twenty weeks, it is £108.85 per week or 90 percent of weekly earnings if the 90 percent rate is less than £108.85. See http://www.dwp.gov.uk/advisers/ni117a/smp/. Employers may contract with their employees for maternity benefits more favorable than the statutory benefits.

The European Court of Justice held that employees are entitled to maternity leave in addition to paid annual leave. That is, annual leave is not extinguished by maternity leave. *See Maria Paz Merino Gómez v. Continental Industrias del Caucho SA*, Case C-342/01 (E.C.J. Mar. 18, 2004).

d. Paternity leave: The Employment Act 2002 and the Paternity and Adoption Leave Regulations 2002 provide a right that is new to U.K. law – two weeks of paid paternity leave around the time of birth or placement of a child. The rate of pay is the same as for maternity leave.

e. Parental leave: For workers who have worked for at least a year, they are entitled to take up to thirteen weeks of unpaid leave for the birth or placement of a child. An employee cannot take more than four weeks for any one child during a year.

f. Time Off for Dependents: §57A of the Employment Relations Act 1999 (amending the ERA 1996) implements the EU Parental Leave Directive's time off for dependents. An employee may take off a reasonable amount of time during working hours for reasons related to care for a dependent (including illness, death, assault, arranging care).

g. The Employment Act 2002 and the Paternity and Adoption Leave Regulations 2002 create a right to adoption leave and pay – up to twenty-six weeks of leave with statutory adoption pay and up to twenty-six additional weeks of unpaid leave.

h. Flexible working requests: The Employment Act 2002 and the Flexible Working (Procedural Requirements) Regulations 2002 and the Flexible Working (Eligibility, Complaints and Remedies) Regulations 2002 create a right for parents of young children to request flexible working arrangements. One making a request who suffers detriment for making the request can make a claim in the Employment Tribunal.

As mentioned earlier in this chapter, a theme of the New Labour government has been family-friendly workplace legislation. The Work and Families Bill, presented to the Parliament in its 2005 Session, would amend §80F of the ERA 1996 to provide for increases in maternity, paternity and adoption leave and statutory pay. *See* http://www.publications.parliament.uk/pa/cm200506/cmbills/060/06060.1-4.html; http://www.dti.gov.uk/employment/workandfamilies/page29478.html. The basic paid leave period would increase from twenty-six weeks to fifty-two weeks.

E. EMPLOYMENT DISCRIMINATION

Employment antidiscrimination law began developing later in the United Kingdom than in the United States. It also began with a different emphasis. The Equal Pay Act 1970, focusing on equality of pay for women and men, was the seminal employment discrimination legislation in the United Kingdom. Although the United States passed the Equal Pay Act in 1963, and sex was included as a prohibited ground of discrimination in the Civil Rights Act of 1964, the focus of U.S. employment discrimination law, at least in its early stages, was on race discrimination. Race discrimination did not become a major issue in the United Kingdom until the passage of the Race Relations Act 1976 (replacing the Acts of 1965 and 1968). Regarding the United Kingdom's experience with developing race discrimination law, see DISCRIMINATION: THE LIMITS OF LAW (Hepple & Szyszczak eds. 1992). Although development of race discrimination law in the United Kingdom was behind that in the United States, it was years ahead of that in the continental European nations.

Although development of discrimination law in the United Kingdom has lagged behind the United States, the balance has changed in recent years. The EU has launched into discrimination law forcefully, and with the EC Equal Treatment Framework Directive, 2000/78/EC, which prohibits discrimination on several new grounds, the U.K. law has been changing quickly, and has outstripped U.S. law, at least in characteristics covered, if not in volume of litigation, enforcement, and remedies. It has been said that the second-generation U.K. antidiscrimination laws were influenced by the laws of the United States and Canada, but the third-generation discrimination laws have been influenced by EU law. *See* BOB HEPPLE, MARY COUSSEY & TUFYAL CHOUDHURY, EQUALITY:

A New Framework (Report of the Independent Review of the Enforcement of UK Anti-Discrimination Legislation) (Hart 2000).

The principal U.K. laws are as follows: the Equal Pay Act 1970; Sex Discrimination Act 1975 and Sex Discrimination Act 1986; Race Relations Act 1976; Disability Discrimination Act 1995; Part-Time Workers Treatment Regulations 2000; Fixed-Term Employees Treatment Regulations 2002; Employment Equality (Sexual Orientation) Regulations 2003; Employment Equality (Religion or Belief) Regulations 2003; and Equal Pay Act (Questions and Replies) Order 2003. 2003 Regulations also went into effect in July 2003 for all of the older discrimination laws. Age discrimination law will go into effect in October 2006: the Employment Equality (Age) Regulations of 2006. *See United Kingdom Proposes Regulations to Implement EU Age Discrimination Directive*, Daily Lab. Rep. (BNA) No. 48 (Mar. 13, 2006).

Before recent regulations went into effect, the United Kingdom did not have a statutory definition of sexual harassment. Pursuant to the EU Equal Treatment Directive 2002, the U.K. enacted the Employment Equality (Sex Discrimination) Regulations 2005, Statutory Instrument 2005 No. 2467, which went into force in October 2005. The regulations define sexual harassment:

> Harassment, including sexual harassment
> 4A. – (1) For the purposes of this Act, a person subjects a woman to harassment if –
> (a) on the ground of her sex, he engages in unwanted conduct that has the purpose or effect –
> (i) of violating her dignity, or
>
> (ii) of creating an intimidating, hostile, degrading, humiliating or offensive environment for her,
> (b) he engages in any form of unwanted verbal, non-verbal or physical conduct of a sexual nature that has the purpose or effect –
> (i) of violating her dignity, or
>
> (ii) of creating an intimidating, hostile, degrading, humiliating or offensive environment for her, or
> (c) on the ground of her rejection of or submission to unwanted conduct of a kind mentioned in paragraph (a) or (b), he treats her less favourably than he would treat her had she not rejected, or submitted to, the conduct.

The theories, concepts, and principles in U.K. discrimination law closely parallel those of U.S. discrimination law, although there are, of course, differences. Below is a chart of rough equivalents:

U.K.	U.S.
Direct discrimination	Disparate Treatment
Indirect discrimination	Disparate Impact
Victimisation	Retaliation
Positive discrimination	Reverse discrimination
Genuine occupational qualification	Bona fide occupational qualification
Justification	Business necessity and job relatedness

The Employment Equality (Sexual Orientation) Regulations 2003 define sexual orientation as a sexual orientation towards persons of the same sex, persons of the opposite sex or persons of the same sex and the opposite sex. Reg. 2(1). *See* http://www.opsi.gov.uk/si/si2003/20031661.htm#2. Theories of discrimination based on sexual orientation include direct discrimination, indirect discrimination, victimization, and harassment. The basic theories are being applied as new regulations are implemented. *See, e.g.,* Employment Equality (Religion or Belief) Regulations 2003, Statutory Instrument 2003 No. 1660, available at http://www.opsi.gov.uk/si/si2003/20031660.htm.

Notes

1. Does an employment law regime that prohibits unfair dismissal have as much need of antidiscrimination law? Could it be argued that the United States has greater need of antidiscrimination law because its default rule for dismissals is employment at will? Still, it is important to note that antidiscrimination law covers adverse employment actions other than dismissals.

2. As indicated above, the United Kingdom now has many employment discrimination laws, covering many different grounds, and different commissions charged with enforcing the statutes. The principal problem according to an independent review committee is that there is "too much law," with *at that time*, thirty acts, thirty-eight statutory instruments, eleven codes of practice, and twelve EC directives and recommendations. *See* HEPPLE et al., EQUALITY: A NEW FRAMEWORK, *supra*, at 21. The group recommended passage of a single equality act to replace the various laws. At least one change is coming about. The Equality Bill 2005 includes provisions for a new Commission for Equality and Human Rights (CEHR), which will combine the functions of the Equal Opportunities Commission, the Commission for Racial Equality, and the Disability Rights Commission.

3. One of the differences between the direct discrimination theory of the United Kingdom and the analogous disparate treatment theory of the United States is that proof of discrimination in U.K. direct discrimination cases focuses on the concept of equality in proof of the case – treating like things and people similarly. Although U.S. discrimination law also is based principally on a formal equality theory of discrimination, the proof of discrimination focuses on motivation or intent of the decisionmaker. The focus on proof of unequal treatment in U.K. direct discrimination goes back to the Equal Pay Act. The key to proving discrimination under this theory is for the claimant to find a similarly situated comparator of the other race, sex, etc. and show that the claimant was treated differently. This has led to difficulty of application in some cases and some types of cases in which comparators are difficult to find. The U.K. direct discrimination theory rejects the relevance of motivation or intent. Still, the practical significance of these proof differences can be overstated. U.S. disparate treatment cases have been lost because of a lack of comparators, and U.K. direct discrimination cases have been won despite the absence of an actual comparator. Consider the discussion of hypothetical comparators in the discussion of *British Airways v. Starmer*, No. EAT/0306/05/SM (July 21, 2005), discussed in Note 5, *infra*, and in the principal case *Igen Ltd. v. Wong, infra*.

4. One of the most controversial pieces of EC legislation is the Burden of Proof Directive, Council Directive 97/80/EC. Art 4(1) provides as follows:

    > Member States shall take such measures as are necessary, in accordance with their national judicial systems, to ensure that, when persons who consider themselves wronged because the principle of equal treatment has not been applied to them establish, before a court or other competent authority, facts from which it may be presumed that there has been direct or indirect discrimination, it shall be for

the respondent to prove that there has been no breach of the principle of equal treatment.

The directive was incorporated into U.K. employment discrimination laws. In applying the burden of proof, the employment tribunals and the Employment Appeal Tribunal followed the "*Barton* Guidance," which was set forth *in Barton v. Investec Sec., Ltd.*, [2003] ICR 1205. The *Barton* Guidance is set forth in the principal case, *infra, Igen Ltd. v. Wong*, [2005] I.C.R. 931, 2005 WL 353346, in which the court modified the Guidance.

5. In indirect discrimination cases, a claimant must challenge a "provision, criterion or practice," referred to as a "PCP," that is "to the detriment of a considerably larger proportion of women than of men. Sex Discrimination Act 1975 § S1(2)(b). The language of PCP replaced the prior language "requirement or condition," to conform to the requirements of the EC Burden of Proof Directive.

The Employment Appeals Tribunal addressed issues of what constitutes a PCP and in what pool the disproportionality is measured in *British Airways v. Starmer*, No. EAT/0306/05/SM (July 21, 2005). In that case, a female pilot applied to change from full-time to part-time work. The airline denied her request to convert to 50 percent of full-time work and required instead that she must perform 75 percent of full-time work. The employer argued that there was no PCP on which to base a claim of indirect discrimination; instead, the denial of claimant's application and the requirement of 75 percent of full-time was a "one-off management decision, not applying generally to others." *Id*. Thus, "[t]here was no pool to which it applied, nor anyone by reference to whom the detriment suffered by the Claimant can be compared." *Id*. The Employment Appeal Tribunal held that it was a PCP. The EAT also explained that the comparator pool used to determine disproportionality can be a hypothetical comparator pool:

> In our judgment there is no necessity for the impugned PCP actually to apply, or be applied, to others, as would for example be the case if it were the 2000-hour threshold that was in issue in this case, as it is not. What is required in order to test the question of whether the PCP is discriminatory or not is to extrapolate it to others; i.e. the reference under §(2)(b) is not simply to a "*provision . . . which he applies equally to a man*" but also to one which he "*would apply equally to a man*". The creation of a pool constitutes, in our judgment, a similar test to the approach to a comparator in cases of direct discrimination. §(3) which provides that "*a comparison of the cases of persons of different sex . . . under (1) or (2) . . . must be such that the relevant circumstances in the one case are the same, or not materially different in the other*" applies to indirect discrimination cases under §(2)(b) as it does to direct discrimination cases under §(2)(a). Similarly, in our judgment, whereas the detriment under §(2)(b)(iii) to be assessed is the claimant's own detriment, the detriment to be considered under §(2)(b)(i) is and can be that of the hypothetical comparator pool. Of course it may well be that there will be some one-off provisions, such as (to borrow and adapt an analogy from other European jurisprudence) one of specialised knowledge of the Mongolian language, which may fall at the initial hurdle. But that may be rather because it is impossible to show that it is discriminatory rather than that it is not, at least potentially, a PCP.

Id. ¶18.

Although the comparator pool and the statistical disparity presented problems in this case of a one-off decision, the EAT affirmed the decision of the employment tribunal that the 75 percent requirement "would be to the detriment of a considerably larger proportion of women than men."

The EAT then went on to consider whether the employer could satisfy the burden on justification. The EAT explained that justification "involves a weighing exercise, in which the detriment to the Claimant and, in this case, the hypothetical detriment to others, is put on the scales . . . The test is objective. The decision of the [employer] and its business reasons will be respected, but they must not be uncritically accepted." The employment tribunal concluded that the employer did not justify the PCP on safety grounds, and the EAT affirmed.

IGEN LTD. V. WONG

[2005] EWCA Civ 142

Court of Appeal (Civil Division) 18th February, 2005

On Appeals from Employment Appeal Tribunals

JUDGMENT
Lord Justice Peter Gibson (giving the judgment of the court):

Introduction

1. These are three appeals from the Employment Appeal Tribunal ("the EAT"). The circumstances of each differ widely from those of the others, but they all raise questions on the interpretation and application of the statutory provisions comparatively recently introduced into the Sex Discrimination Act 1975 ("the SDA") and the Race Relations Act 1976 ("the RRA") respectively as to the shifting of the burden of proof in direct discrimination cases under those Acts.

2. A similar statutory provision has recently been introduced into the Disability Discrimination Act 1995 ("the DDA"). Similar provisions are also to be found in Reg. 29 of the Employment Equality (Sexual Orientation) Regulations 2003 and in Reg. 29 of the Employment Equality (Religion or Belief) Regulations 2003.

. . .

4. From the statistics provided to us by Mr. Allen it is apparent that a significant proportion of the Originating Applications presented to an Employment Tribunal ("ET") each year raise discrimination complaints. In just under 20,000 cases (17% of all cases) commenced in 2003-4 the main complaint was of discrimination, and although there are no figures available of how many of those cases concerned allegations of direct, rather than indirect, discrimination, it is likely that the majority would have been cases of alleged direct discrimination.

The Law

5. The new provisions in the Discrimination Acts are the following:
(A) SDA
§63A (inserted by the Sex Discrimination (Indirect Discrimination and Burden of Proof) Regulations 2001) provides:

(1) This section applies to any complaint presented under section 63 to an employment tribunal.

(2) Where, on the hearing of the complaint, the complainant proves facts from which the tribunal could, apart from this section, conclude in the absence of an adequate explanation that the respondent –

(a) has committed an act of discrimination against the complainant which is unlawful by virtue of Part II, or

(b) is by virtue of section 41 or 42 to be treated as having committed such an act of discrimination against the complainant, the tribunal shall uphold the complaint unless the respondent proves that he did not commit, or, as the case may be, is not to be treated as having committed, that act.

(B) RRA

§ 54A (inserted by the Race Relations Act 1976 (Amendment) Regulations 2003) provides:

(1) This section applies where a complaint is presented under section 54 and the complaint is that the respondent:

(a) has committed an act of discrimination, on grounds of race or ethnic or national origins, which is unlawful by virtue of any provision referred to in Section 1 (1B)(a) (e) or (f) or Part IV in its application to those provisions, or

(b) has committed an act of harassment.

(2) Where on the hearing of the complaint, the complainant proves facts from which the tribunal could, apart from this section, conclude in the absence of an adequate explanation that the respondent –

(a) has committed such an act of discrimination or harassment against the complainant, or

(b) is by virtue of section 32 or 33 to be treated as having committed such an act of discrimination or harassment against the complainant, the tribunal shall uphold the complaint unless the respondent proves that he did not commit the act or, as the case may be, is not to be treated as having committed that act.

(c) DDA

§ 17A (1C) (inserted by the Disability Discrimination Act 1995 (Amendment) Regulations 2003) provides:

Where, on the hearing of a complaint under subsection (1) the complainant proves facts from which the tribunal could, apart from this subsection, conclude in the absence of an adequate explanation that the respondent has acted in a way which is unlawful under this Part, the tribunal shall uphold the complaint unless the respondent proves that he did not so act.

6. It has long been recognised that proving discrimination claims may pose great difficulties for claimants. Before the new provisions were inserted into the SDA, the RRA and the DDA respectively, ETs generally followed the guidance given by this court in a case under the RRA, *King v Great Britain -- China Centre [1992] ICR 516*. Neill L.J. (with whom Nourse L.J. and Sir John Megaw agreed) said this (at pp 528–9):

From these several authorities it is possible, I think, to extract the following principles and guidance. (1) It is for the applicant who complains of racial discrimination to make out his or her case. Thus if the applicant does not prove the case on the balance of probabilities he or she will fail. (2) It is important to bear in mind that it is unusual to find direct evidence of racial discrimination. Few employers will be prepared to admit such discrimination even to themselves. In some cases the discrimination will not be ill-intentioned but merely based on an assumption that "he or she would not have fitted in." (3) The outcome of the case will therefore usually depend on what inferences it is proper to draw from the primary facts found by the tribunal. These inferences can include, in appropriate cases, any inferences that it is just and equitable to draw in accordance with section 65(2)(b) of the Act of 1976 from an evasive or equivocal reply to a questionnaire. (4) Though there will be some cases where, for example, the non-selection of the applicant for a post or for promotion is clearly not on racial grounds, a finding of discrimination and a finding of a difference in race will often point to the possibility of racial discrimination. In such circumstances the tribunal will look to the employer for an explanation. If no explanation is then put forward or if the tribunal considers the explanation to be inadequate or unsatisfactory it will be legitimate for the tribunal to infer that the discrimination was on racial grounds. This is not a matter of law but, as May L.J. put it in *North West Thames Regional Health Authority v. Noone* [1988] I.C.R. 813, 822, "almost common sense (5) It is unnecessary and unhelpful to introduce the concept of a shifting evidential burden of proof. At the conclusion of all the evidence the tribunal should make findings as to the primary facts and draw such inferences as they consider proper from those facts. They should then reach a conclusion on the balance of probabilities, bearing in mind both the difficulties which face a person who complains of unlawful discrimination and the fact that it is for the complainant to prove his or her case.

7. That guidance received the express approval of the House of Lords. . . . .

8. European law had in the meantime been moving in the direction now enacted in the new provisions. In a series of cases, ... the European Court of Justice ("the ECJ") ruled that in the field of sex discrimination the burden of proof might be shifted when that was necessary to avoid depriving workers, who appeared to be the victims of discrimination, of any effective means of enforcing the principle of equal pay.

9. That was then followed by the promulgation of the Burden of Proof Directive (Council Directive 97/80/EC). This recited the requirement under para. 16 of the 1989 Social Charter that action should be intensified to ensure the implementation of the principle of equality for men and women (recital (3)). It further recited that plaintiffs could be deprived of any effective means of enforcing the principle of equal treatment before the national courts if the effect of introducing evidence of an apparent discrimination were not to impose upon the respondent the burden of proving that his practice is not in fact discriminating (recital (17)). The aim of the Directive was said in Art. 1 to be "to ensure that the measures taken by the Member States to implement the principle of equal treatment are made more effective, in order to enable all persons who consider themselves wronged because the principle of equal treatment has not been applied to them to have their rights asserted by judicial process after possible recourse to other competent bodies." By Art. 4 (1):

> Member States shall take such measures as are necessary, in accordance with their national judicial systems, to ensure that, when persons who consider themselves wronged because the principle of equal treatment has not been applied to them establish, before a court or other competent authority, facts from which it may be presumed that there has been direct or indirect discrimination, it shall be for the respondent to prove that there has been no breach of the principle of equal treatment.

By Art. 4(2) it was provided that the Directive was not to prevent Member States from introducing rules of evidence more favourable to plaintiffs.

10. The United Kingdom did not originally accede to the Social Charter and so was not bound by the Burden of Proof Directive. However, it did so accede in 1997 and by Council Directive

98/52/EC the Burden of Proof Directive was extended to apply to the United Kingdom. § 63A of the SDA was intended to implement the Burden of Proof Directive.

11. Meanwhile in October 1997 Art. 13 of the Amsterdam Treaty amended the Treaty of Rome by including a power for the Council to legislate against discrimination in relation to a range of grounds. The Council exercised that power twice in 2000.

12. In the Race Directive (Council Directive 2000/43/EC) it was recited (in recital (21)):

> The rules on the burden of proof must be adapted when there is a prima facie case of discrimination and, for the principle of equal treatment to be applied effectively, the burden of proof must shift back to the respondent when evidence of such discrimination is brought.

By Art. 8(1) and (2) Member States were directed in like manner as in Art. 4(1) and (2) of the Burden of Proof Directive. § 54A of the RRA was intended to implement Art. 8.

13. In the Framework Employment Equality Directive (Council Directive 2000/78/EC) recital (31) contained the like provision to recital (21) of the recital (21) of the Race Directive. By Art. 10(1) and (2) Member States were directed in like manner as in Art. 8(1) and (2) of the Race Directive. § 17A (1C) of the DDA was intended to implement Art. 10.

The Barton Guidance

14. Following the insertion of § 63A into the SDA, the EAT (His Honour Judge Ansell presiding) in a sex discrimination case, *Barton v Investec Securities Ltd. [2003] ICR 1205* set out in para. 25 the following guidance in the light of the statutory changes:

> (1) Pursuant to section 63A of the 1975 Act, it is for the applicant who complains of sex discrimination to prove on the balance of probabilities facts from which the tribunal could conclude, in the absence of an adequate explanation, that the employer has committed an act of discrimination against the applicant which is unlawful by virtue of Part 2, or which, by virtue of section 41 or 42 of the 1975 Act, is to be treated as having been committed against the applicant. These are referred to below as "such facts".
> (2) If the applicant does not prove such facts he or she will fail.
> (3) It is important to bear in mind in deciding whether the applicant has proved such facts that it is unusual to find direct evidence of sex discrimination. Few employers would be prepared to admit such discrimination, even to themselves. In some cases the discrimination will not be an intention but merely based on the assumption that "he or she would not have fitted in".
> (4) In deciding whether the applicant has proved such facts, it is important to remember that the outcome at this stage of the analysis by the tribunal will therefore usually depend on what inferences it is proper to draw from the primary facts found by the tribunal.
> (5) It is important to note the word is "could". At this stage the tribunal does not have to reach a definitive determination that such facts would lead it to the conclusion that there was an act of unlawful discrimination. At this stage a tribunal is looking at the primary facts proved by the applicant to see what inferences of secondary fact could be drawn from them.
> (6) These inferences can include, in appropriate cases, any inferences that it is just and equitable to draw in accordance with section 74(2)(b) of the 1975 Act from an evasive or equivocal reply to a questionnaire or any other questions that fall within section 74(2): see *Hinks v Riva Systems Ltd* (unreported) 22 November 1996.

(7) Likewise, the tribunal must decide whether any provision of any relevant code of practice is relevant, and if so take it into account in determining such facts pursuant to section 56A(10) of the 1975 Act. This means that inferences may also be drawn from any failure to comply with any relevant code of practice.

(8) Where the applicant has proved facts from which inferences could be drawn that the employer has treated the applicant less favourably on the grounds of sex, then the burden of proof moves to the employer.

(9) It is then for the employer to prove that he did not commit, or, as the case may be, is not to be treated as having committed, that act.

(10) To discharge that burden it is necessary for the employer to prove, on the balance of probabilities, that the treatment was in no sense whatsoever on the grounds of sex, since "no discrimination whatsoever" is compatible with the Burden of Proof Directive 97/80.

(11) That requires a tribunal to assess not merely whether the employer has proved an explanation for the facts from which such inferences can be drawn, but further that it is adequate to discharge the burden of proof on the balance of probabilities that sex was not any part of the reasons for the treatment in question.

(12) Since the facts necessary to prove an explanation would normally be in the possession of the employer, a tribunal would normally expect cogent evidence to discharge that burden of proof. In particular, the tribunal will need to examine carefully explanations for failure to deal with the questionnaire procedure and/or code of practice.

15. That guidance ("the *Barton* guidance") has been applied many times by ETs and EATs not only in the field of sex discrimination to which its wording is directed but also in relation to race and disability discrimination. It is not in dispute that the Discrimination Acts should be construed consistently with each other so far as possible. The appeals considered by the House of Lords in *Rhys-Harper v Relaxion Group plc [2003] ICR 867* provide a striking example of that notwithstanding differences in the statutory language used.

16. Before us there has been no challenge to the broad outline of the *Barton* guidance, although suggestions have been put to us as to how it might be improved. Some criticisms have been made and suggestions put forward by the EATs in other cases. We shall return to the wording of the guidance later. However it is important to stress at the outset that ETs must obtain their main guidance from the statutory language itself. No error of law is committed by an ET failing to set out the *Barton* guidance or by failing to go through it paragraph by paragraph in its decision.

17. The statutory amendments clearly require the ET to go through a two-stage process if the complaint of the complainant is to be upheld. The first stage requires the complainant to prove facts from which the ET could, apart from the section, conclude in the absence of an adequate explanation that the respondent has committed, or is to be treated as having committed, the unlawful act of discrimination against the complainant. The second stage, which only comes into effect if the complainant has proved those facts, requires the respondent to prove that he did not commit or is not to be treated as having committed the unlawful act, if the complaint is not to be upheld.

18. There was some debate before us as to whether the statutory amendments merely codified the pre-existing law or whether it had made a substantive change to the law. Miss Elizabeth Slade Q.C. (appearing in *Wong v Igen Ltd.* for the employer), in initially arguing for the former, relied on the comment by Simon Brown L.J. in *Nelson v Carillion Services Ltd.* [2003] ICR 1256 at para. 26:

> It seems to me tolerably clear that the effect of section 63A [of the SDA] was to codify rather than alter the pre-existing position established by the case law.

That comment was made obiter in a case relating to alleged indirect discrimination. We think it clear, as Mr. Allen submitted and as Miss Slade accepted, that the amendments did not codify, but altered, the pre-existing position established by the case law relating to direct discrimination. It is plain from the Burden of Proof Directive that Member States were required to take measures to ensure that once the complainant established facts from which it might be presumed that there had been discrimination, the burden of proof shifted to the respondent to prove no breach of the principle of equal treatment. Looking at Neill L.J.'s guidelines in King (set out in para. 6 above), it is plain that paras. (1), (4) and (5) need alteration. It is for the applicant complaining of discrimination only to make out his or her case to satisfy the first stage requirements. If the second stage is reached, and the respondent's explanation is inadequate, it will be not merely legitimate but also necessary for the ET to conclude that the complaint should be upheld. The statutory amendments shift the evidential burden of proof to the respondent if the complainant proves what he or she is required to prove at the first stage.

19. Although we have referred to the two stages in the ET's decision-making process, we do not thereby intend to suggest that ETs should divide hearings into two parts to correspond to those stages. No doubt ETs will generally wish to hear all the evidence, including the respondent's explanation, before deciding whether the requirements at the first stage are satisfied and, if so, whether the respondent has discharged the onus shifted to him.

20. One issue which arose before us was whether the words of the statutory amendment, "in the absence of an adequate explanation", precluded considerations of the respondent's explanation at the first stage. . . .

. . .

22. We agree with [Counsel]. The words "in the absence of an adequate explanation", followed by "could", indicate that the ET is required to make an assumption at the first stage which may be contrary to reality, the plain purpose being to shift the burden of proof at the second stage so that unless the respondent provides an adequate explanation, the complainant will succeed. It would be inconsistent with that assumption to take account of an adequate explanation by the respondent at the first stage. . . . It is of course possible that the facts found relevant to the first stage may also relate to the explanation of the respondent.

23. We accept [Counsel's] suggestion that in view of our conclusion it may be helpful for the *Barton* guidance to include a paragraph stating that the ET must assume no adequate explanation at the first stage. . . .

24. We draw attention to another related point on the language of the statutory amendments, although there was no dispute before us on it. The language points to the complainant having to prove facts, and there is no mention of evidence from the respondent. However, it would be unreal if the ET could not take account of evidence from the respondent if such evidence assisted the ET to conclude that in the absence of an adequate explanation unlawful

discrimination by the respondent on a proscribed ground would have been established. Paras. (6) and (7) of the *Barton* guidance give examples of unsatisfactory conduct by the respondent, in response, for example, to the statutory questionnaire or in breach of a code of practice, being relevant to the drawing of inferences at the first stage, and it cannot matter whether the claimant or the respondent gave that evidence.

25. An important point of construction is raised by the decision of the EAT in *Webster v Brunel University*. We shall come to the particular circumstances of that appeal later, but the short point raised is whether the word "could" in the statutory amendments imports that it is not necessary for the complainant to prove that the respondent in fact committed the act of discrimination complained of so long as the complainant proves that there was an act of less favourable treatment on a prohibited ground and that that act could have been committed by the respondent. As Burton J. put it in para. 34 of the judgment of the EAT:

> It will be for a tribunal to ask itself, having found the facts as to what occurred, whether the treatment, which it, on the balance of probabilities, has established, could have been by the respondent.

26. [Counsel] . . . says that the wording of the statutory amendments is clear: at the first stage the burden is on the claimant merely to establish facts from which it could be inferred or concluded, in the absence of an adequate explanation, that the respondent has committed an act of discrimination against the complainant. He relies on the example given by the EAT of a group of 100 people in a room, 30 of whom are employees of the respondent and one of the 100 present uttered a racially discriminatory word, "Paki", offensive to the Asian complainant, but the complainant is unable to identify which of the 100 people said it. Mr. Troop accepted that in those circumstances the ET might not conclude that the respondent employer had committed the act of discrimination. However, he said that if 70 of the 100 were employees, the ET might conclude that the respondent had committed that act.

27. [Counsel] for the employer submits that such a construction is contrary to the statutory language and to that of the Directive. He points out that the effect of this construction is to place the onus on the respondent to disprove certain facts which go to make up the act of discrimination: the respondent not only needs to provide an explanation for his conduct once he has been shown to have acted in a certain way but needs to prove that he did not even do the act in the first place. He describes such a result as startling. He adverts to the fact that the statutory amendments use the words "apart from this section" when describing what the complainant needs to prove. He points out that, apart from the statutory shift of the burden of proof, the EAT's construction runs contrary to existing case law, it being repeatedly said that it is for the complainant to prove his or her case.

28. With all respect to the EAT, we cannot accept its construction. . . . The language of the statutory amendments seems to us plain. It is for the complainant to prove the facts from which, if the amendments had not been passed, the ET could conclude, in the absence of an adequate explanation, that the respondent committed an unlawful act of discrimination. It does not say that the facts to be proved are those from which the ET could conclude that the respondent "could have committed" such act.

29. The relevant act is, in a race discrimination case such as *Webster*, that (a) in circumstances relevant for the purposes of any provision of the RRA (for example in relation to employment in the circumstances specified in § 4 of the RRA), (b) the alleged discriminator treats another person less favourably and (c) does so on racial grounds. All those facts are facts which the complainant, in our judgment, needs to prove on the balance of probabilities. The EAT said (in para. 34) that it was satisfied that the burden of showing that the discriminatory act was done by an employee of the employer should not remain upon the complainant "once a *prima facie* case has been established". That is a direction that what the EAT in *Webster* called the ingredient even more necessary than less favourable treatment on the ground of sex (no doubt the EAT meant race), viz. that the act was by the respondent, need not be proved on the balance of probabilities, so long as it was shown that the ET could conclude, in the absence of an adequate explanation, that there was a possibility that it was by the respondent. There is nothing in the language of the statutory amendments, in the language of the Directive or in the travaux préparatoires to which we were taken, which supports such a construction. On the contrary: the Directive requires the complainant to establish facts from which it may be presumed that there has been discrimination by the alleged discriminator.

. . .

31. The scheme of the statutory amendments appears to us simple and to make good sense given that a complainant can be expected to know how he or she has been treated by the respondent whereas the respondent can be expected to explain why the complainant has been so treated. Of course there may be cases where the complainant will have difficulty in proving that it was the employer who committed the unlawful act. But that is a difficulty faced by many who feel aggrieved and would wish to obtain redress through the courts or the tribunals. The complainant may have no less difficulty in establishing others of the essential facts, but that does not mean that it is sufficient for the complainant to prove only the possibility rather than the probability of those other facts at the first stage.

32. The EAT has read too much into the word "could" without appreciating that its use is linked to the assumption "in the absence of an adequate explanation". The very word "explanation" seems to us a pointer to the legislative intention that the respondent should explain why he has done what he has been proved by the complainant to have done, rather than to the respondent having to prove the fact that it was not he who did it at all.

33. Finally, if there is any doubt at all as to the correct interpretation, it must surely be resolved by the consideration that, if the EAT is right, a very real injustice may be done to the respondent. Take any case where there is a possibility that the alleged discriminator, through an employee, has done the unlawful act but there is also a possibility that a person who has nothing to do with the respondent did it, and the respondent not only does not know any more than the complainant does but has no means of proving that it was not his employee who committed the act. What is the justice of imposing the burden of proof and hence liability on him rather than the complainant? We would add that it does not appear to us to be a sound basis for deciding whether the requirements of the first stage are satisfied by counting heads, in the example given by the EAT as set out in para. 26 above. Once it is accepted that the mere possibility of an employee having uttered the word "Paki" is sufficient to satisfy the first stage requirements, the burden of proof must shift, whether or not employees outnumber non-employees.

34. We also heard argument on the need for there to be a comparator in the ingredient of less favourable treatment which the complainant must prove for there to be sexual or racial discrimination. However there was no real dispute before us on this point. That a comparison must be made is explicit in the language of the definition of discrimination. In § 1(1)(a) of the

SDA one finds "he treats her less favourably than he treats or would treat a man". In § 1(1)(a) of the RRA one finds "he treats that other less favourably than he treats or would treat other persons". The comparison must be such that the relevant circumstances of the complainant must be the same as or not materially different from those of the comparator. It is trite law that the complainant need not point to an actual comparator. A hypothetical one with the relevant attributes may do. Our attention was drawn to what was said by Elias J., giving the judgment of the EAT in *The Law Society v Bahl* [2003] IRLR 640 at paras. 162 and 163. There it was held that it is not obligatory for ETs formally to construct a hypothetical comparator, though it was pointed out that it might be prudent to do so and that the ET might more readily avoid errors in its reasoning if it did so. Similarly, when Bahl went to appeal, this court ([2004] IRLR 799 at para. 156) said that it was not an error of law for an ET to fail to identify a hypothetical comparator where no actual comparator can be found. However, this court also said that not to identify the characteristics of the comparator might cause the ET not to focus correctly on what Lord Nicholls in *Shamoon v Chief Constable of the RUC [2003] IRLR* 285 at para. 7 called "the less favourable treatment issue" (viz. whether the complainant received less favourable treatment than the appropriate comparator) and "the reason why issue" (viz. whether the less favourable treatment was on the relevant proscribed ground). The importance of a failure to identify a comparator or the characteristics of the comparator may vary from case to case, and may be thought to be of particular relevance to the appeal in *Emokpae v Chamberlin Solicitors.*

35. Finally, we should refer to a dispute on whether para. (10) of the *Barton* guidance requires modification. In *Emokpae* His Honour Judge McMullen Q.C., giving the judgment of the EAT, held that the reference in para. (10) to the words "no discrimination whatsoever", which are taken from the Burden of Proof Directive, was inappropriate because they concerned not the definition of or the ingredients in discrimination but merely the forms of discrimination. Instead Judge McMullen suggested that para. (10) be rewritten to read:

> To discharge that burden it is necessary for the respondent to prove, on the balance of probabilities, that the treatment was not significantly influenced, as defined in *Nagarajan v London Regional Transport* [2000] 1 AC 501, by grounds of sex.

That was a reference to the following passage in Lord Nicholls' judgment in *Nagarajan* at pp. 512, 3:

> Decisions are frequently reached for more than one reason. Discrimination may be on racial grounds even though it is not the sole ground for the decision. A variety of phrases, with different shades of meaning, have been used to explain how the legislation applies in such cases: discrimination requires that racial grounds were a cause, the activating cause, a substantial and effective cause, a substantial reason, an important factor. No one phrase is obviously preferable to all others, although in the application of this legislation legalistic phrases, as well as subtle distinctions, are better avoided so far as possible. If racial grounds or protected acts had a significant influence on the outcome, discrimination is made out.

36. . . . We think it sufficient to say that we see no reason to change the original para. (10). In *Nagarajan*, a race discrimination case, unsurprisingly there does not appear to have been any consideration of the Burden of Proof Directive relating to sex discrimination. That Directive is emphatic in its definition in Art. 2(1) of the principle of equal treatment as meaning that there shall be no discrimination whatsoever based on sex, either directly or indirectly, and in requiring by Art. 4(1) that once the burden shifts for the second stage it is for the respondent to prove that there has been no breach of that principle. In Art. 2(1) of the Framework Employment Equality Directive there is a definition of the principle of equal treatment to similar effect (viz. "there shall be no direct or indirect discrimination whatsoever on any of the [proscribed] grounds"). Only in the definition of the principle of equal treatment in Art. 2(1) of the Race Directive is the word "whatsoever" omitted, but it would be idle to suggest that that omission entails a meaning different from that of the other Directives. The language of the definitions in the French texts of the three Directives is in effect the same.

37. In any event we doubt if Lord Nicholls' wording is in substance different from the "no discrimination whatsoever" formula. A "significant" influence is an influence which is more than trivial. We find it hard to believe that the principle of equal treatment would be breached by the merely trivial. We would therefore support the original para. (10) of the *Barton* guidance and, consistently therewith, a minor change suggested by Mr. Allen to para. (11) so that the latter part reads "it is adequate to discharge the burden of proof on the balance of probabilities that sex was not a ground for the treatment in question".

The Appeals

38. We come now to the circumstances of the . . . appeals.

(1) WONG V IGEN LTD.

39. The applicant, Ms. Kay Wong, was employed by Leeds Careers Guidance ("LCG"), the predecessor in title to the appellant, Igen Ltd, in October 1988 as a Careers Adviser specialising in assisting young people to find work. In 1999 she transferred to a new project, The Learning Gateway, the purpose of which was to work with young disaffected people. Her role was to act as a personal adviser to particular individuals.

40. Ms. Wong complained to an ET about her treatment between September 2001 and June 2002. She alleged that she had been unlawfully discriminated against by LCG and Beverley Parsons, her line manager, Christine McNiven, her senior manager, and Liz Green, the Personnel Manager. Those individuals are all white. Ms. Wong is of Afro-Caribbean racial origins. On 10 July 2002 she applied to the ET, complaining against LCG and the three managers of race discrimination, harassment and victimisation. She said she had been less favourably treated in three ways: (a) she had not been allowed to attend a Personal Adviser diploma course; (b) she had been subjected to an unduly critical Individual Performance Review ("IPR") in April 2002; (c) inappropriate and unfair disciplinary proceedings had been pursued against her because (i) she refused to sign the IPR and to accept the assessment in it or to appeal against it, and (ii) she had complained of having been victimised and harassed but had failed to withdraw or justify her complaint.

41. Her complaint was heard by an ET in Leeds over four days. By a decision sent to the parties on 7 October 2003 the ET dismissed complaints (a) and (b), but upheld complaint (c). Applying the *Barton* guidance, it held that it could infer discrimination against Ms. Parsons, Ms. McNiven and Ms. Green in the absence of an adequate explanation and went on to hold that those individuals had not adequately explained the totality of their actions and had not proved that the treatment of Ms. Wong was in no sense whatsoever on the grounds of her race. The ET also found that LCG was liable under § 32(1) of the RRA for the actions of the individuals.

42. On appeal by LCG, Ms. Parsons, Ms. McNiven and Ms. Green (together "the Appellants") the EAT on 12 May 2004 dismissed the appeal. Permission to appeal to this court was granted by Mummery L.J. on the papers.

43. Before us Miss Slade, appearing with Mr. Richard Leiper for the Appellants, submitted that (i) the ET erred by not specifying the primary facts it relied upon to justify concluding in para. 55 of its decision: "we take the view that it could be open to us to draw an inference of discrimination," and by not setting out the process by which it could draw that conclusion; and (ii) the ET wrongly found that the Appellants had failed to discharge the burden of proof once it had transferred to them.

44. On the first point Miss Slade suggested that the ET failed to take into account the Appellants' adequate explanations and failed to make adequate findings in relation to each of the individual Appellants. She pointed out that the only facts directly linked to race were those found in para. 55 that Miss Wong is from a minority ethnic origin whereas Ms. Parsons, Ms. McNiven and Ms. Green are all white Europeans. Miss Slade described the ET as going too far into the realms of conjecture or speculation from the limited facts found by it and as making too great a leap when it said (in para. 55):

> On the basis of the primary facts found by us it seems to us that it would be open to us to conclude that Ms. Parsons resented her authority being challenged by the applicant, by reason of her ethnic origins, and that Ms. McNiven and Ms. Green closed ranks against the applicant to support Ms. Parsons and to try and compel the applicant to "toe the line".

45. On her second point Miss Slade submitted that the ET may have identified alternative, non-discriminatory reasons had it constructed a hypothetical comparator. She said that its failure to do so raised doubts as to whether the ET had properly considered all potentially relevant explanations when identifying whether or not unlawful discrimination existed. She complained that the ET failed to take into account the unhelpful conduct of Miss Wong and her representative, Mr. Dawes. She contended that the discrimination found must have been subconscious but said that the ET failed to explain how it reached that conclusion. She further pointed to the favourable finding by the ET that Ms. Parsons carried out the IPR in good faith and suggested that the ET failed to consider the inherent unlikelihood of Ms. Parsons being motivated by race on that occasion but not on another.

46. Mr. White, appearing with Mr. Laddie for Ms. Wong, submits that no error of law is disclosed by the ET's decision as upheld by the EAT. He argues that the ET did set out at length the facts found in relation to what the ET considered to be the Appellants' unreasonable conduct including their inability to provide any satisfactory explanation for what the ET plainly regarded as a strikingly unreasonable aspect of its conduct, namely transferring Ms. Wong back to her previous job in advance of a disciplinary hearing and without prior consultation with the employee. He further submits that it is clear from the authorities that unexplained unreasonable conduct is capable of giving rise to an inference of unlawful discrimination. He points out that the ET did record matters such as the intransigence of Ms. Wong in refusing to comply with LCG's established procedures and the uncooperative stance of Mr. Dawes, which formed the basis of the Appellants' explanation of their conduct. He stresses that there is no perversity challenge to the ET's decision.

47. Because of the nature of the challenge to the ET's decisions we shall go in a little more detail through how the ET arrived at its decision. The ET in paras. 1-31 of its Extended Reasons set out what it called the relevant facts. It then referred to the applicable statutory provisions before considering the way Ms. Wong's case was put. It made findings destructive of what we have called (in paras. 40 and 41 above) complaints (a) and (b) before turning to complaint (c) in paras. 40ff. It said:

> 40. Thereafter, we find many of the respondents' actions difficult to understand. It is of course a difficulty to have an employee who does not comply with procedures to the precise letter and it is a difficulty when an employee makes allegations of victimisation, harassment and discrimination against her line manager. It does seem to us however, that the application of some common sense at an early stage would have defused the situation. The respondents, be it Ms. Parsons, Ms. McNiven or Ms. Greene could have taken the applicant's response of 19 April as an appeal and set up an appeal hearing, or could have taken her refusal to confirm that she intended to appeal, as an indication that she did not want to do so. Her actions were capable of either interpretation and as long as the position was made sufficiently clear to her, it would be in the applicant's own hands to correct the position were that to be necessary.
>
> 41. As to the complaint made against her manager, this was potentially a very serious matter. To suggest that a manager had failed properly to appraise her performance because she had spoken out about training procedures was a serious complaint to make. That complaint came to the attention of Ms Greene, who told us that she was a very experienced Personnel Manager. The complaint could, and should have been flushed out. Ms Greene or her assistant, Mr Stokes, could have been sent to sit down with the applicant to make it clear that her complaint was being taken seriously and the applicant could then have been compelled either to withdraw her complaint, if it was baseless, or to provide specific information which would have been required to have launched a proper investigation. By placing the onus upon the applicant, as happened in Ms. Greene's memorandum of 1 May 2002, to embark upon formal procedures or to herself seek out Mr. Stokes simply sowed the seeds of what was to follow.
>
> 42. It was unreasonable of Ms Greene to have attended the meeting on 31 May , without giving the applicant prior warning of her intention to do so. This meeting was also an opportunity for a skilled and sympathetic manager to have listened to the applicant, and to her complaints. She was after all meeting with her senior manager with a view to doing just that. Instead Ms Greene turned the meeting into a confrontational meeting which then revolved around what was coming to be the obsessional demand for the IPR form to be properly completed. All hope that the applicant was going to consider Ms Greene, or those who worked with her, as being an avenue for receiving counselling and support in respect of the alleged harassment, went out of the window when Ms Greene started using the language of lawyers and threatening the applicant with breach of contract and disciplinary proceedings. In our view the applicant was entitled to take the view that Ms Greene was conducting herself as if she was defending someone, namely Ms Parsons, as against her, the complainant. She had reason to believe, in those circumstances, that she was not going to get a fair hearing.
>
> 43. The pressure was then increased on 5 June. She found herself in a formal meeting, where the person against whom she was pursuing a complaint was present, supported by her manager, and she was not permitted representation herself. Once again, Ms

Parsons and Ms NcNiven conducted that meeting in a way which was designed to inflame the situation, not to resolve it. As a consequence she was transferred back to become a Careers Adviser once again. Ms Greene was unable to explain the rationale behind that move. To begin with it was being suggested that the respondents were entitled to do it under the terms of their disciplinary procedure. It is true that in the disciplinary procedure, as set out in the Handbook, relegation or transfer is an option as an alternative to dismissal after a full formal Disciplinary Hearing has taken place. No such disciplinary hearing had, of course, taken place. Ms Greene then suggested that the respondents were contractually entitled to effect this change, as it did not involve an alteration to the applicant's terms and conditions of employment. She then however conceded that with her personnel knowledge and experience it would be highly unusual for such a transfer to be imposed upon an employee without any prior discussion or consultation.

44. The issue of the unsigned IPR Form and the refusal to withdraw or pursue the harassment complaint was then formalised into a disciplinary matter. Thus, the respondents became more and more entrenched and a sensible resolution to what was, in reality, a trivial issue, became more and more remote.

45. The applicant then consulted with Mr Dawes, clearly an experienced trade union officer. At an early stage Ms Green had suggested that the applicant should seek advice either internally or externally and sensibly, she had done just that. That was, as it turned out, the final opportunity that the respondents had to resolve the situation. Skilled and sympathetic managers dealing with a professional trade union official should have been able to achieve a situation where the applicant could have been persuaded to confirm whether she wished to appeal the IPR or not and whether she wished to formally pursue the harassment procedure or not. As the applicant told us, she still had faith, in the Chief Executive, Mr Higginbotham, she did not see him as being tainted in the same was as she viewed Ms Parsons, Ms NcNiven and Ms Greene. There were, in our view, many routes by which Mr Dawes could have assisted the respondents to achieve a solution that was mutually acceptable to the respondents and to the applicant. That was an opportunity that Ms Greene should have seized with both hands.

46. Instead she continued to adopt an inflexible and officious approach. True it is that she was not helped by the applicant or by Mr. Dawes, who refused to disclose precisely what his credentials were. As however the Tribunal put to Ms Greene in the situation in which she had found herself, anybody who had the trust of the applicant and who was able to enter into sensible dialogue could, potentially, have provided a way out of this impasse.

48. The ET then directed itself correctly by stating that unreasonable behaviour was not the same as discriminatory behaviour. It referred to the judgment of the EAT in *Bahl* and to Elias J.'s remarks ([2003] IRLR 640 at para. 100) that where the alleged discriminator acts unreasonably, an ET will want to know why he has acted in that way, and (at para. 101) that the significance of the fact that the treatment is unreasonable is that an ET will more readily in practice reject the explanation given than it would if the treatment were reasonable and that, if the reason is not accepted, it may be open to the ET to infer discrimination.

49. The ET considered (at para. 48) whether it need construct a comparator but found little purpose in doing so. It then turned to the *Barton* guidance and directed itself in a way which has not been criticised. It returned again to complaints (a) and (b) which it rejected. In para. 54 it considered what it called the unreasonable actions of the Appellant and whether that unreasonable conduct in itself took the complainant past the first stage, and again noted

what Elias J. said about the possibility of unexplained unreasonable conduct giving rise to a situation where the ET is entitled to find discrimination. It concluded on the first stage

> 55. At any event we take the view in this case that it could be open to us to draw an inference of discrimination. The applicant is a person from a minority ethnic origin. Her manager, Ms Parsons, her senior manager, Ms NcNiven and the Personnel Manager, Ms Greene are all white European. On the basis of the primary facts found by us it seems to us that it would be open to us to conclude that Ms Parsons resented her authority being challenged by the applicant, by reason of her ethnic origins, and that Ms NcNiven and Ms. Greene closed ranks against the applicant to support Ms Parsons and to try and compel the applicant to "toe the line."
> 56. We make it clear of course that that is not a definitive finding that we make but, it seems to us, that that is a finding which, in the absence of an adequate explanation, we could have arrived at.

50. The ET then directed itself at the second stage by reference to the *Barton* guidance. It examined the Appellants' explanations which, they accepted, explained in part the actions of the Appellants. But they concluded:

> 60. What however the respondents have not explained to us, and indeed in part have not even tried to explain to us, is why they adopted the confrontational and inflexible approach that they did. Ms Greene could give no explanation for the confrontational tone of her memorandum of 31 May when she suggested that the applicant would be in breach of contract. She could give no adequate explanation for why she did not proactively question or investigate the allegation of victimisation and harassment. She could give no explanation for why it was thought appropriate to transfer the applicant in advance of any disciplinary proceeding without any consultation at all. She could not explain why such a confrontational approach was adopted with Mr Dawes, who may well have been able to assist the respondents, given the opportunity. Ms Greene of course was not acting on her own, she was clearly consulting with Ms. Parsons and Ms. McNiven.
> 61. We are therefore driven to the conclusion that the respondents have not adequately explained the totality of their actions and have not therefore proved on the balance of probabilities that the treatment was in no sense whatsoever on the grounds of the applicant's race.

51. We recognise, as Mr. White properly acknowledged, that the ET has reached conclusions on the conduct of the Appellants which other ETs may well not have reached. But it is the tribunal of fact, entitled to use its industrial expertise to guide it in reaching its conclusions, and it has not been suggested that in doing so it was perverse. It has directed itself on the law impeccably. We do not accept Miss Slade's criticisms that it failed to make the necessary findings of primary facts from which inferences could be drawn. It is apparent that it is the finding of unexplained unreasonable conduct from which it has drawn the inferences satisfying the requirements of the first stage. Whilst we would caution ETs against too readily inferring unlawful discrimination on a prohibited ground merely from unreasonable conduct where there is no evidence of other discriminatory behaviour on such ground, we cannot say that the ET was wrong in law to draw that inference, and we repeat that there is no perversity challenge. At the second stage it did consider whether the Appellants had discharged the onus on them by their explanations, but it found those explanations inadequate for the reasons which it gave. It did expressly refer to the conduct of Ms. Wong and Mr. Dawes. The fact that one finding favourable to Ms. Parsons has been made does not preclude another finding unfavourable to her. No error of law has been disclosed.

52. For these reasons, we conclude that this appeal must be dismissed.

(II) EMOKPAE V CHAMBERLIN SOLICITORS

53. The applicant, Ms. Emokpae, is from Nigeria where she obtained legal qualifications. She was employed by the First Respondents, Chamberlin Solicitors, on a part time basis as a legal assistant from 29 November 2002 until summarily dismissed on 3 February 2003. The firm comprised at the material time a principal, Ms. Chamberlin, the Second Respondent, Mr. Emezie, the office manager, and approximately five solicitors and two legal assistants. It was Mr. Emezie who dismissed Ms. Emokpae.

54. She complained that she had been unlawfully discriminated against by Mr. Emezie on the grounds of her sex. The claim was put on the basis that she was dismissed because of rumours about a relationship between her and Mr. Emezie and that such rumours would not have occurred in relation to a male employee.

55. The complaint was heard by an ET sitting at London Central. The ET was faced with sharp conflicts of fact. On balance the ET preferred Ms. Emokpae's version of events and rejected the Respondent's evidence that she was dismissed because of her unsatisfactory performance. In its Extended Reasons promulgated on 21 October 2003 it found that there was a culture of rumour and gossip in the firm and that Ms. Emokpae actively participated in the spreading of gossip. It also found that Mr. Emezie acted towards Ms. Emokpae in a way that might have provoked rumours of a relationship, buying perfume for her, giving her lifts home and having a drink with her at least once. The ET took into account that a firm of solicitors working under a legal franchise, subject to good practice requirements, dismissed an employee with no warning of the charges she was to face, no opportunity to be accompanied and with no note taken of the event. The ET commented that the case was not about whether there was an improper relationship between Mr. Emezie and Ms. Emokpae (it made no findings on that) but about the reason for her dismissal.

56. The ET set out the *Barton* guidance and considered whether Ms. Emokpae had proved the facts required to satisfy the first stage. It said (in para. 13):

> There was sufficient evidence to conclude that the Applicant could have been unlawfully dismissed by the Second Respondent because of rumours about a relationship between her and the Second Respondent. This was less favourable treatment on the ground of sex: such rumours would not have led to her dismissal if she had been male.

57. At the second stage the ET found that the Respondents had failed to discharge the burden of proof, and held that the firm was liable for the actions of Mr. Emezie in the course of his employment as well as finding that he knowingly aided the firm to do an unlawful act.

58. On appeal, the EAT on 15 June 2004 upheld the ET, saying that it had applied the correct legal test to a relatively simple dispute of fact. Mummery L.J., on the papers refused permission to appeal, but on a renewed application he and Dyson L.J. permitted the appeal to go ahead.

. . .

60. [Counsel] submits that the ET, in finding that Ms. Emokpae was dismissed because of rumours about a relationship between her and Mr. Emezie, did not make a finding that she was dismissed on the ground of her sex. He submits that the last sentence in para. 13, which we have cited in para. 56 above, is wholly unreasoned. He prays in aid the reasoning of the EAT, Rimer J. presiding, in *Martin v Lancehawk Ltd.* UKEAT/0525/03/ILB.

61. In that case a married woman employee had an affair with a manager of the employer company. When the affair broke down, she was dismissed. She complained to an ET of unfair dismissal and sex discrimination. She succeeded in the former claim but the ET dismissed the latter. The EAT accepted her submission that the irresistible conclusion from the primary facts found by the ET was that the reason for the dismissal was the breakdown of the affair and accepted that but for her sex there would have been no affair. However, the EAT said that the reason for her dismissal was not because she was a woman. It also rejected a suggestion made on her behalf that the ET should have compared her position with that of a heterosexual male employee as a comparator, as the manager would not have had an affair with such a person. The EAT suggested that the appropriate hypothetical comparator would be a male employee with whom the manager had had a homosexual relationship which had broken down. It saw no reason for assuming that the manager would have dealt with any such male comparator differently. Accordingly the EAT dismissed the appeal.

62. [Counsel] relied on both aspects of the decision in Martin. He says that just as a dismissal because of the breakdown of an affair between the female complainant and a male manager is not a dismissal on the ground of the complainant's sex, so a dismissal because of rumours of a relationship between Ms. Emokpae and Mr. Emezie is not a dismissal on the ground of her sex. He also submits that just as the appropriate comparator in Martin was a male employee with whom the manager had had a homosexual affair, so in the case of Ms. Emokpae the appropriate comparator would be a male employee, with whom it was rumoured that the manager was having a homosexual relationship. He argues that there is no reason to think that such a person would have been treated any differently from Ms. Emokpae.

. . .

64. In our judgment,. . . . Ms. Emokpae unequivocally asserted that she was dismissed because of the rumours. It is not enough that there would have been no rumours but for Ms. Emokpae being a woman. The ET had to be able to infer that the reason in the mind of Mr. Emezie was her sex, but the ET's acceptance of the rumours as the reason for dismissal shows that she was not dismissed on the ground of her sex. Further, the ET would have had to be able to infer that Mr. Emezie would have treated a male employee subject to similar rumours more favourably, that is to say that he would not have dismissed such a man. It is important that the comparator should satisfy the test of s. 5(3) of the SDA so that his circumstances are not materially different from those of Ms. Emokpae. There is simply no explanation of the ET's thinking on this point and no attempt has been made to identify the attributes of the comparator. To say only that the rumours would not have arisen and would not have led to Ms. Emokpae's dismissal if she had been male suggests to us that the ET has failed to focus on the necessary attribute that the comparator must be someone in the like circumstances, viz. rumoured to have had a relationship with Mr. Emezie. The obvious comparator, as in Martin, is a male with whom Mr. Emezie was rumoured to have had a homosexual affair. The ET's conclusion, with all respect to it and the EAT, is fundamentally flawed.

65. For the sake of completion we would add that the suggestion, which we are told was raised on the renewal application for permission in this court, that the comparator might be

Mr. Emezie himself, cannot be sustained. This was plainly not how the ET approached the comparison and in any event Mr. Emezie, who dismissed Ms. Emokpae, could not be the comparator.

66. For these reasons we conclude that, in the light of the finding that the reason for the dismissal was the rumours and not on the ground of Ms. Emokpae's sex, her case fails at the first stage. In truth she is the innocent victim of an unfair dismissal, but, unfortunately for her, because she was employed for such a short period she cannot obtain redress for this from the ET. We would allow this appeal, set aside the order of the EAT and the decision of the ET and dismiss her Originating Application.

. . .

The Revised *Barton* Guidance

76. As this is the first time that the *Barton* guidance has been considered by this court, it may be helpful for us to set it out again in the form in which we approve it. In Webster Burton J. refers to criticisms made of its prolixity. Tempting though it is to rewrite the guidance in a shorter form, we think it better to resist that temptation in view of the fact that in practice the guidance appears to be offering practical help in a way which most ETs and EATs find acceptable. What is set out in the annex to this judgment incorporates the amendments to which we have referred and other minor corrections. We have also omitted references to authorities. For example, the unreported case referred to in para. (6) of the guidance may be difficult for ETs to obtain. We repeat the warning that the guidance is only that and is not a substitute for the statutory language.

Order: Appeal in Igen Ltd v Wong is dismissed; appeal in Chamberlin is allowed, the order of the EAT and the decision of the Employment Tribunal set aside and the originating application of the applicant dismissed;. . . .

Annex

(1) Pursuant to section 63A of the SDA, it is for the claimant who complains of sex discrimination to prove on the balance of probabilities facts from which the tribunal could conclude, in the absence of an adequate explanation, that the respondent has committed an act of discrimination against the claimant which is unlawful by virtue of Part II or which by virtue of § 41 or § 42 of the SDA is to be treated as having been committed against the claimant. These are referred to below as "such facts".

(2) If the claimant does not prove such facts he or she will fail.

(3) It is important to bear in mind in deciding whether the claimant has proved such facts that it is unusual to find direct evidence of sex discrimination. Few employers would be prepared to admit such discrimination, even to themselves. In some cases the discrimination will not be an intention but merely based on the assumption that "he or she would not have fitted in".

(4) In deciding whether the claimant has proved such facts, it is important to remember that the outcome at this stage of the analysis by the tribunal will therefore usually depend on what inferences it is proper to draw from the primary facts found by the tribunal.

(5) It is important to note the word "could" in § 63A(2). At this stage the tribunal does not have to reach a definitive determination that such facts would lead it to the conclusion that

there was an act of unlawful discrimination. At this stage a tribunal is looking at the primary facts before it to see what inferences of secondary fact could be drawn from them.

(6) In considering what inferences or conclusions can be drawn from the primary facts, the tribunal must assume that there is no adequate explanation for those facts.

(7) These inferences can include, in appropriate cases, any inferences that it is just and equitable to draw in accordance with section 74(2)(b) of the SDA from an evasive or equivocal reply to a questionnaire or any other questions that fall within section 74(2) of the SDA.

(8) Likewise, the tribunal must decide whether any provision of any relevant code of practice is relevant and if so, take it into account in determining, such facts pursuant to section 56A(10) of the SDA. This means that inferences may also be drawn from any failure to comply with any relevant code of practice.

(9) Where the claimant has proved facts from which conclusions could be drawn that the respondent has treated the claimant less favourably on the ground of sex, then the burden of proof moves to the respondent.

(10) It is then for the respondent to prove that he did not commit, or as the case may be, is not to be treated as having committed, that act.

(11) To discharge that burden it is necessary for the respondent to prove, on the balance of probabilities, that the treatment was in no sense whatsoever on the grounds of sex, since "no discrimination whatsoever" is compatible with the Burden of Proof Directive.

(12) That requires a tribunal to assess not merely whether the respondent has proved an explanation for the facts from which such inferences can be drawn, but further that it is adequate to discharge the burden of proof on the balance of probabilities that sex was not a ground for the treatment in question.

(13) Since the facts necessary to prove an explanation would normally be in the possession of the respondent, a tribunal would normally expect cogent evidence to discharge that burden of proof. In particular, the tribunal will need to examine carefully explanations for failure to deal with the questionnaire procedure and/or code of practice.

Notes

1. Notice in the beginning of the opinion the citation of statistics demonstrating that a significant part of the employment tribunals' case load is discrimination cases.

2. How does the proof structure developed under the Burden of Proof Directive compare with the proof structure developed in the United States in *McDonnell Douglas Corp. v. Green*, 411 U.S. 792 (1973), to analyze disparate treatment employment discrimination claims? See Chapter 3, *supra*. See Jarrett Haskovec, Student Note, *A Beast of Burden? The New EU Burden-Of-Proof Arrangement in Cases of Employment Discrimination Compared to U.S. Law*, 14 TRANSNAT'L L. & CONTEMP. PROBS. 1069 (2005).

3. What is a hypothetical comparator, and what is its role in the discrimination analysis?

4. What causal relationship does the court require between discrimination and the treatment in question?

5. How did the court modify the *Barton* Guidance?

F. PRIVACY

Privacy protection historically has been one of the least developed areas of the law. It has been described as "piecemeal, incomplete and indirect." BAILY, HARRIS & JONES, CIVIL LIBERTIES: CASES AND MATERIALS 352 (Butterworths 1985). Another commentator wrote that "[i]n the United Kingdom there is currently no single enshrined right to privacy." Lauren B. Cardonsky, *Towards a Meaningful Right to Privacy in the United Kingdom*, 20 B.U. INT'L L.J. 393, 393 (2002). Some people have fit claims for privacy invasions into torts, such as nuisance, trespass, and breach of confidence.

As with other areas of the law, privacy protection is undergoing change in the United Kingdom largely because of the EU influence. The European Convention for the Protection of Human Rights and Fundamental Freedom guarantees a right to privacy. The Human Rights Act 2001 is meant to bring U.K. law into conformity. Article 8 of the HRA provides that courts are "bound to uphold a citizen's right to respect for his private and family life, his home, and his correspondence." What remains to be determined is whether private citizens can base claims against other citizens on these rights. Cardonsky, *supra*, at 403-04. The law is developing in this area, and it will affect labor law. *See* John D.R. Craig, *Privacy in the Workplace and the Impact of European Convention Incorporation on United Kingdom Labour Law*, 19 COMP. LAB. L. & POL'Y J. 373 (1998). Addressing issues of workplace monitoring and surveillance, one commentator explained the dearth of workplace privacy law heretofore as follows: "The true reason for the U.K.'s inaction lies in its abstentionist approach to the regulation of the employment relationship, coupled with its lack of a human rights tradition which could form the basis of judicial or legislative intervention to vindicate privacy interests." Craig, *supra*, at 375.

The European Union has been active in the areas of data protection and privacy. The EU adopted a Directive on Privacy Protection, 95/46/EC, which took effect on October 25, 1998. Treating privacy as a fundamental human right, the directive requires member states to adopt national legislation insuring the protection of privacy. The Data Protection Act 1998 is the relevant U.K. law. The EC Directive on Privacy and Electronic Communications 2002, 2002/58/EC, is incorporated in the United Kingdom by the Privacy and Electronic Communications Regulations 2003. Although not limited to workplace privacy, the directive and regulations already have resulted in significant development in this area. The EU may soon have a directive on privacy in the workplace. *See* Working Document on the Surveillance of Electronic Communications in the Workplace (29 May 2002), 5401/01/EN/Final, available at http://ec.europa.eu/employment_social/labour_law/docs/dataprothendrixstudyreport_en.pdf.

In the United Kingdom, the Information Commissioner's Office (ICO) regulates and enforces the Data Protection Act 1998, the Freedom of Information Act 2000, the Privacy and Electronic Communications (EC Directive) Regulations 2003 and the Environmental Information Regulations 2004. The ICO officially presented the Employment Practices Code on June 14, 2005. *See* http://www.ico.gov.uk/documentUploads/ICO˙EmpPracCode.pdf. The Code has four parts: recruitment and selection; employment records; monitoring at work; and information about workers' health. The Code was issued under §51 of the Data Protection Act. The introduction to the Code says the following about its legal status:

> The basic legal requirement on each employer is to comply with the Act itself. The Code is designed to help. It sets out the Information Commissioner's recommendations as to how the legal requirements of the Act can be met. Employers may have alternative ways of meeting these requirements but if they do nothing they risk breaking the law.

Any enforcement action would be based on a failure to meet the requirements of the Act itself. However, relevant parts of the Code are likely to be cited by the Commissioners in connection with any enforcement action that arises in relation to the processing of personal information in the employment context.

Use of technology for monitoring employees at work is a topic that has garnered much attention during the last decade. Many think that technology has run far ahead of the law protecting privacy. The Code does not prohibit monitoring of employees by employers, but it encourages employers to conduct an "impact assessment" that considers (1) purpose of the monitoring and benefits likely to be realized from it, (2) any likely adverse impact, (3) alternatives to monitoring or different ways it might be carried out, and (4) whether the monitoring is justified. One of the "core principles" of the general approach to monitoring is that "[w]orkers should be aware of the nature, extent and reasons for any monitoring, unless (exceptionally) covert monitoring is justified."

The GMB union recently complained about the use of wearable computer technology used to track orders and merchandise in U.K. warehouses. *See U.K. Union Objects to Wearbale Devices, Says Technology Is Used to Track Workers*, DAILY LAB. REP. (BNA) No. 115 (June 16, 2005). Although the makers of the devices and employers claim that it is used to improve accuracy and productivity in filling orders, the union received complaints from employees who fear that it is used to track employees and monitor how long it takes them to get from one part of a warehouse to another.

9 Germany

A. INTRODUCTION

The German Reich was founded as a constitutional monarchy in 1871. The monarchy survived until the end of World War I. The Weimar Republic was then established and it lasted until the Nazi state was established in 1933. After the end of World War II, Germany was divided into four zones occupied by the United States, the United Kingdom, France, and the Soviet Union. In 1949, the three western zones joined to form the Federal Republic of Germany (FRG) and the Soviet zone formed the communist German Democratic Republic (GDR). With the collapse of the Soviet Union and the Berlin Wall, the country was reunified on October 3, 1990, with the east joining the west. *See generally* INGA MARKOVITS, IMPERFECT JUSTICE: AN EAST-WEST GERMAN DIARY (1995), describing the shift from the Socialist system of justice to the Western system as part of the reunification. MANFRED WEISS & MARLENE SCHMIDT, LABOUR LAW & INDUSTRIAL RELATIONS IN GERMANY 16-17 (3rd ed. 2000) (hereinafter LABOUR LAW IN GERMANY).

The Basic Law (the Constitution) of the FRG (*Grundgesetz*) was adopted in 1949 and it establishes "a democratic, parliamentary, and federal republic." *Id.* at 17. Since the 1990 unification, there are sixteen states (*Lander*) in the federal union governed by the Basic Law. In most areas of labor and employment law, the states have the duty to enforce federal labor law. At the federal level, the Federal Parliament (*Bundestag*) holds primary legislative power, with the second house (*Bundesrat*) voting only on matters in which the states have a special interest. The Federal Chancellor (*Bundeskanzler*) is elected by the parliament, upon the proposal of the President (*Bundesprasident*). The Chancellor chairs the government and has authority to set government policy. *Id.* at 17-18.

After sixteen years of government control by the conservative CDU and CSU coalition, Gerhard Schröder, of the SPD party, came to power in 1998 in a coalition with the Green party. Schröder campaigned as a "third way" candidate somewhat in the mold of President Clinton in the U.S. and Prime Minister Blair in the United Kingdom. In the September 2005 elections, no party gained a majority. That led to the creation of a "grand coalition" between the conservatives (CDU/CSU) and the social democrats (SPD), under the leadership of the CDU leader, Angela Merkel. In the winter of 2006, public sector strikes had put pressure on the coalition because the SPD has historically been engaged with unions, whereas the CDU and CSU are associated with employer interests. James

Thanks to Christopher Jordan of CMS Hasche Sigle of Röln.

Mackenzie, *German Strikes Put Merkel's Coalition Under Strain*, REUTERS, Monday, March 13, 2006.

With a population of about 82.4 million, Germany has the largest population in Europe. There are over 39 million employed and about 3.5 million, or 8.3 percent unemployed as of October 2005. http://www.destatis.de/basis/e/bevoe/bevoetxt.htm. It has the third largest national economy in the world, following the United States and Japan, and it is the world's top exporter of goods. Nine million jobs depend directly on exports, which generate 40 percent of gross domestic product. Bertrand Benoit & Richard Milne, *Germany's Best Kept Secret: How Its Exporters Are Beating the World*, FINANCIAL TIMES, May 19, 2006 (hereinafter *Germany's Best Kept Secret*). The economy has been in the doldrums for a number of years. But recently, the economy may be turning more positive, though employment has not yet begun to improve. Mark Landler, *Rumblings of a German Revival*, NY TIMES, January 17, 2006, C1. But more than half of the unemployed have been looking for a job for more than a year, compared with less than one third overall for OECD countries. EMPLOYMENT OUTLOOK, OECD (2005). There is a huge disparity in unemployment between the former East German states and the west, with the rate exceeding 22 percent in the east and about 5 percent in the west. *Id.* Union density is about 24 percent, having decreased by about 25 percent between 1990 and 2000. GREGG J. BAMBER, RUSSELL D. LANSBURY, & NICK WAILES, INTERNATIONAL AND COMPARATIVE EMPLOYMENT RELATIONS: GLOBALISATION AND THE DEVELOPED MARKET ECONOMIES, Table A. 18, 379 (4th ed.2004) (hereinafter INTERNATIONAL & COMPARATIVE EMPLOYMENT RELATIONS).

In recent years, labor and employment policy have become significant issues in German political life. In 2003, the government announced its "Agenda 2010," which included a number of amendments to the labor laws that were supposed to help the economy grow while reducing unemployment. The program was masterminded by Peter Hartz, then the head of human resources for Volkswagen. Essentially, these amendments returned the law to what it was before the SDP and Greens came to power in 1998. Thomas Ubber, *Agenda 2010: Reform of German Labour Law: Impact on Hiring and Firing Staff*, 5 GERMAN L.J. No.2 (Feb. 2004). That did not help the SDP or the Greens with their political bases and, when implemented, did not produce noticeable improvements in the economy or unemployment. The reputation of these reforms was further damaged when scandals arose that caused Peter Hartz to resign from Volkswagen as well as causing the employee who heads the VW works council to be disgraced. In the 2005 election campaign, the CDU/CSU promised more radical changes, but, now that there is a "grand coalition" government, those changes are less likely to be implemented.

The Constitution recognizes the right to work. Most broadly, Article 9(3) provides that, "The right to form associations to safeguard and improve working and economic conditions shall be guaranteed to every individual and to every occupation and profession." Article 12 (1) provides, "All Germans shall have the right freely to choose their occupation or profession, their place of work, and their place of training. The practice of an occupation or profession may be regulated by or pursuant to a law." According to Article 8 of the Unification Treaty of 1990, that united Germany, provided that all of the law of West Germany was extended and made applicable to the former East Germany. Article 30 of the Treaty, however, promised that the Parliament would as soon as possible codify "the law referring to the individual employment relationship as well as the protective standards referring to working time, work on Sundays and holidays and the specific protection of women." This has yet to happen. LABOUR LAW IN GERMANY, 58–59.

The courts have filled in the gap left by the failure of the legislature to adopt a comprehensive code and have done so on the basis of a broad interpretation of the Constitution that protects fundamental rights. Professor Manfred Weiss, *The Interface Between Constitution and Labor Law in Germany*, 26 COMP. LABOR & POL'Y J. 181, 183-84 (2005) (hereinafter *Constitution & Labor Law*), describes that breadth as follows: "Fundamental rights in Germany do have a double face: they are first of all subjective rights of the individual, but to a great extent also institutional guarantees. . . . [T]he State not only has to provide the institutions as guaranteed by the fundamental rights but has a duty to do everything to provide a framework that makes sure that the fundamental rights are becoming relevant in actual practice." With such a broad view of the fundamental right to work, the Federal Labour Court and, to a certain extent, the Federal Constitutional Court have developed an elaborate law on strikes and lockouts. *Id.* at 184. In short sum, those legal developments have overall been quite protective of employees and their rights.

With respect to the individual employment relationship, the Civil Code of 1896, which did not specifically address employment relationships or employment contracts, nevertheless, is the source for the law that applies to individual employment relationships. The Code has been amended frequently to deal specifically with employment issues. Job security is very strongly protected by these laws. 1 INTERNATIONAL LABOR & EMPLOYMENT LAWS 4-4 (2nd ed. 2003, William L Keller & Timothy J. Darby ed.) (hereinafter INTERNATIONAL LABOR & EMPLOYMENT LAWS). Separate legislation also sets high standards for wages, terms and other conditions of employment.

In addition to Article 9 (3) of the Constitution that is the basis for protection of the right of association, including the right to strike and to lockout, the Collective Bargaining Agreements Law of 1969 (*Tarifvertragsgesetz*) is the main foundation for the right to organize and to bargain collectively. Collective bargaining takes place at the sector and regional levels between unions that are organized to represent workers in particular industries and associations of employers in those industries. Because of differences in the economies of the different regions in the country, collective bargaining occurs at the regional level.

Beyond labor law, German law is structured to protect workers because it makes them stakeholders in their employers. The Works Council Statute of 1972 (BetrVG) provides far broader representation rights for German workers than in most countries by providing for the establishment of works councils at individual places of employment and enterprises. Although originally used in the late nineteenth century as a tactic of management to avoid unionization, works council gained the support of unions and came to be legally required in 1920. Works councils are formally independent of unions, a holdover from the original antiunion motivation for having works councils, but many of the workers elected to serve on them are union members. Works councils and employers can negotiate agreements that govern some workplace issues. Works council agreements in effect mold the general standards of the industry-wide collective bargaining agreement to the needs of specific places of employment. There is, however, no right for works councils to go out on strike. LABOUR LAWS IN GERMANY 188; INTERNATIONAL LABOR & EMPLOYMENT LAW 4-40.

An added institutional role that workers play in the governance of their employers is the provision for codetermination providing for worker representation on the supervisory boards of their employers. Unlike corporate governance in the United States, German corporations have two boards of directors splitting the functions usually served by one board in the United States. The management board runs the company, whereas the supervisory board appoints the members of the management board and decides important questions of the direction of the corporation. INTERNATIONAL LABOR & EMPLOYMENT LAWS 4-68. The source of this system of codetermination goes back to the period just after World War II. Important industries, in mining and steel, feared they would be dismembered because of their complicity with the Nazis. To garner the support of unions to prevent that, these industries offered equal representation on their supervisory boards, which was confirmed by legislation in 1951. The Works Council Statute of 1952 expanded codetermination beyond the mining and steel industries but reduced the level of representation of workers on the supervisory boards – employees pick one-third of the supervisory board – in smaller enterprises with more than five hundred employees. The Codetermination Statute of 1976 applies to most large German corporations with more than two thousand employees with employees selecting five of the eleven supervisory board members.

In sum, Germany has the most extensive structure of employment rights of any country that this book surveys. Individual employment rights give workers very strong job security and collective bargaining agreements cover a broad range of employers and their employees. At the level of the particular workplace, works councils provide added representation of workers in the operation of the business as well as added job security. Three levels of contractual protections can apply – individual employment contracts, works agreements between a works council and an employer, and the collective agreement between the union and the employers' association in the sector or geographic region. And, at corporations with more than five hundred employees, employees have the right to select members of the supervisory boards that have the power to select the management boards that run the corporation on a day-to-day basis.

Notes

1. How can Germany, a high-income country with very protective labor standards, manage to compete so successfully that it is the largest exporter of goods in the world? In addition to being the largest exporting country, "the sales of German companies' foreign subsidiaries now exceed exports." *Germany's Best Kept Secret.* Large German companies make three-quarters of their profits abroad and employ over four million people outside Germany. *Id.* To maintain strong employment in their home countries, is it important for businesses to become transnational enterprises, with operations in many different nations? At some point, will these transnational enterprises lose their identity with any particular country?

2. Another explanation offered for the export strength of Germany is that the recent global economic boom has been based on high levels of capital investment in countries such as China and India. "Because engineering accounts for a bigger share of gross domestic product in Germany than in comparable economies, the country has benefited more from investment-driven global growth. German companies, in other words, have provided the machines and vehicles that faster-growing economies have used to build factories, fleets and infrastructure." *Id.* Does that make the continued strength of the German economy contingent on the developing world's continued expansion of production facilities and infrastructure? If the

economies of these countries reach a plateau, will that mean the German economy will lose its leadership as an exporting country?

3. A third explanation is that collective bargaining has, in recent years, resulted in "wage moderation, longer working hours and the selective offshoring of low-value-added tasks," that have kept unit labor costs steady in Germany when they have risen by almost 6 percent in the EU generally. *Id.* Does the participation of workers' representatives in works councils and on supervisory boards make such moderation more likely than in other countries where workers are not so well represented within the structure of employers?

4. Does the representation of workers in works councils and on employer supervisory boards have the effect of reducing new employment in Germany? "While corporate profits are soaring, unemployment remains high at above 9 percent. Among the low-skilled, long-term joblessness has reached endemic proportions." *Id.*

B. INDIVIDUAL EMPLOYMENT

1. Employment Contracts

Because Germany has yet to enact a full Labor Code, the basic structure of individual employment contracts is based on the Civil Code of 1896. The Law on Modernization of the Law of Obligations, effective 2002, has incorporated into the Civil Code numerous regulations concerning employment that amount to codifications of a number of court decisions involving the rights of employees. There is also other legislation that regulates the individual employment relationship, most significantly the Unfair Dismissal Act of 1969.

Most German employees now have written employment agreements, even though that was not required until 1995 when a new law was enacted to meet the requirements of a EU Directive, 91/533 of Oct. 14, 1991. The agreement contains important information about the job, including the term if the term of employment is limited, compensation including fringes, work hours, vacation, and the periods of notice for termination. Oral agreements are still enforceable.

The Act on Continued Remuneration (*Entgeltfortzahl-ungsgesetz*) provides that the employee's obligation of perform his contract is suspended if the employee is incapable of working because of sickness or because a dependent is severely ill. INTERNATIONAL LABOR & EMPLOYMENT LAWS 4-5. The employee, however, retains the right to be paid during the period even though her performance obligation is suspended. *Id.* at 4-13. Furthermore, employees also have a right to be paid if the employee is prevented from working because of "business reasons" of the employer. The law also empowers courts to find clauses in employment contracts to be invalid because they unreasonably disadvantage employees. The purpose of this law is to balance the one-sided advantage employers have in negotiating contracts with employees. *Id.*

Contracts for a limited duration must be in writing. If there is no writing, then the employment is treated as permanent. Part-time and temporary employment is also regulated, so that there must be reasonable cause shown for the job not being permanent and full time. If there is no objective justification for the agreement, then the agreement may be renewed only up to three times but with the total length not to exceed two years. One provision of the Agenda 2010 that affects part time work is that in the four years after an employer is first established, employment contracts can be limited to up to a total of a four year term without any objective reason required. Thomas Ubber, *Agenda 2010: Reform of German Labour Law: Impact on Hiring and Firing Staff*, 5 GERMAN L. J. No. 2, (Feb. 2004) (hereinafter *Agenda 2010*).

2. Termination Rights

Termination law in Germany is complex. First, section 623 of the Civil Code establishes notice requirements. At one time, separate statutory provisions provided longer and more favorable notice periods for white-collar than for blue-collar workers. In 1990, however, the Federal Constitutional Court applied Article 3(1) of the Constitution providing that "All persons shall be equal before the law" to strike down that different treatment. Federal Constitutional Court (First Senate), May 30, 1990, 10 INTER. LABOR L. REPORTS. 29. A notice of termination must be in writing to be valid, though the notice need not include the specification of reasons. The general rule is that the employer must give four weeks' notice, but the notice period gradually increases until a worker with twenty years of seniority is entitled to seven months' notice. INTERNATIONAL LABOR & EMPLOYMENT LAWS 4-17. Employees are to give four weeks' notice without regard to their length of service. By agreement with the worker, a temporary employee may agree to a shorter notice period. Furthermore, employers with twenty or fewer employees may agree with them to shorter notice periods as long as at least four weeks are provided. Finally, the Civil Code expressly provides for these statutory notice periods to be superseded by collective bargaining agreements to either lengthen or shorten them. *Id.* at 4–18. "Collective agreements may provide for shorter terms, because parties to such agreements are supposedly in the best position to judge what is appropriate at a given moment in a given branch and region." Manfred Weiss, *Labor Law, in* INTRODUCTION TO GERMAN LAW (Mathias Reimann and Joachim Zekoll, ed. 2005), at 330 (hereinafter Weiss, *Labor Law*).

Section 626 of the Civil Code, which applies to every labor contract, provides an exception – extraordinary dismissal – to the requirement that notice be given before employment can be terminated where "there are reasons which in view of all circumstances of the case and in evaluating the interests of both parties make it unacceptable for either of the parties to fulfill the contract until the end of the period of notice." "Cause" for purposes of extraordinary dismissals means "circumstances in which, when taken in light of all of the surrounding facts, and after weighing the interests of all parties, the continued employment of the employee is unreasonable." INTERNATIONAL LABOR & EMPLOYMENT LAWS 4-23. Some of the reasons that the courts have accepted as justifying an extraordinary dismissal include misconduct, such as engaging in criminal activities, and incompetence of the employee but also severe economic circumstances that are not attributable to the behavior of the employee. LABOUR LAW IN GERMANY 104–105. The employer must terminate the employee within two weeks of discovering the extraordinary reason for dismissal and it cannot thereafter change its rationale for the termination.

The Termination Protection Statute of 1969 also protects workers against wrongful termination. After having once raised coverage to employers with ten or more employees and then lowered it back to five, more recently the German government in Agenda 2010 raised coverage back to ten. However, employees of small employers who were protected at the time the amendment went into effect are still covered. Therefore, as of the present time, employees who are not protected by the Termination Protection Statute must rely on their individual contracts of employment for protection against dismissal. The idea of raising coverage is to aid small enterprises to generate new employment because employers will be more willing to hire workers if there is more flexibility for how they deal with them.

Under the Termination Protection Statute, termination can be based on a number of different grounds that have been developed by the labor courts. First are reasons concerning the employee's person that makes the employee unable to fulfill the requirements of the job. "The main example for this category is prolonged or recurring illness." Weiss, *Labor Law*, at 331. But termination is justified only if it is a last resort. Thus, where the employer is large and has alternative ways of coping with problems created by employees being temporarily absent as a result of sickness, the courts are reluctant to uphold dismissal for chronic and long-lasting illness. LABOUR LAW IN GERMANY 106. The issue of the continued effect of illness on the employee's ability to work is more likely within the knowledge of the employee and so the burden of proving that missing work will not continue to be a problem is on the employee. *Id.* at 107.

Second are reasons concerning the employee's behavior, including leaving the workplace without permission, chronic lateness, or other reasons that support the employer's conclusion that the employee fails to meet legitimate expectations. Behavior that would not justify extraordinary dismissal might, nevertheless, be the basis for routine termination since extraordinary dismissal "requires a particularly egregious wrongdoing." Weiss, *Labor Law*, at 331.

The third set of reasons deals with economic reasons that include external economic crises as well as measures taken by the employer, such as the adoption of new technology, that make it impossible for the employer to retain the employee any longer. "The dismissal is justified if the economic situation renders it virtually impossible for the employer to retain the employee." *Id.* The employer bears the burden of proof on this issue. Although "it is for the employer to show why continued employment is economically infeasible, . . . the decision of whether or not to take particular organizational measures that caused the economic exigency is not subject to judicial control." *Id.*

When the employer must choose one or more employees from among a group of employees to be dismissed for economic reasons, the law, until recently, required the employer to take into account the "social aspects" associated with that choice. Before this recent amendment, "the employer had to take into consideration all relevant social aspects that are related to the employment relationship, such as the chances of the dismissed employee on the open market." Achim Seifert & Elke Funken-Hötzel, *Wrongful Dismissals in the Federal Republic of Germany*, 25 COMP. LAB. L. & POL'Y J. 487, 499 (2004). Agenda 2010 replaced the "social aspects" formulation with four criteria. *Id.* at 331. Now the law requires that the employer must justify the choice of employees to be terminated by evaluating four criteria – the number of years of service, age, maintenance obligations, and the disabled status of the workers. In making that analysis, the employer may now exempt from the social aspect analysis certain workers for "legitimate operational interests." Before the enactment of Agenda 2010, employees could be saved from undergoing the social aspect calculus only if their retention could be shown to be vital to the continued existence of the company. Agenda 2010 at 2.

In a case that shows how protective the courts have been toward employees, the Federal Labor Court, 2AZR15/00, Feb 21, 2001, used section 242 of the Civil Code, which imposes a duty of good faith on contracting parties, to in effect extend the obligation to consider the "social aspects" of its decision to lay off workers to small employers that are not covered by the Termination Protection Statute. Plaintiff was one of five employees of an auto paint shop. He challenged the employer's decision to lay him off due to economic reasons. Because he was both the oldest and the most senior employee, he would not have been laid off if the employer had considered the social aspects of its decision had the Termination Protection Act applied. Even though the employer was too small to be covered by that Act, the court decided that "small employers who do not employ more than five employees who fail to consider the social aspects violate the principle of good faith and [the Layoff] is therefore void."

In order to challenge a termination for any reason, the employee must bring suit in the local labor court within three weeks of receiving the notice of termination. The local labor court decides whether or not the termination was effective. If the termination was an extraordinary dismissal, the court may uphold the employer's action and so the employment is treated as having been terminated when notice was received. If the termination was upheld as a routine termination, a decision upholding the employer's action means that the employment continues until the end of the notice period. If the court does not accept the validity of the termination, then, rather than award damages, the court will find that the employment relationship continues and the employee is entitled to continue to receive a salary. The labor court can, however, decide that the payment of a severance amount can end the employment relation if it finds that continuation of the employment relationship would be unreasonable. Where the employee requests severance pay in lieu of reinstatement, the severance payment is typically 50 percent of month's salary per year of employment up to a maximum of twelve months of salary. In determining the length of severance pay awarded, older, more senior workers typically can receive awards for even longer periods. If the employer requests severance pay in lieu of reinstatement, it must prove that the commercial interest of the company would not be well served by reinstatement. INTERNATIONAL LABOR & EMPLOYMENT LAWS 4-24–4-25.

The first level of appeal from the local labor court is to the state labor court. Review is de novo, so new evidence may be introduced. Appeal to the Federal Labor Court is allowed if the state labor court permits it, the decision of the state labor court is inconsistent with a decision of the Federal Constitutional or Labor Court, or if there is not a decision on point from those courts. *Id.*

Notes

1. The general rule is that dismissal "is socially unjustified and therefore unlawful." Weiss, *Labor Law*, at 331. Although this presumption can be overcome by the employer, it is strongly protective of employees. Should the standard of protection be lowered in order to make the decision to hire employees less costly an investment for employers? Considering the costs of providing pay through the notice period as well as the prospect that it would lose any case in which a dismissed employee challenges his termination, will employers decide not to hire employees, at least in Germany? Is the high job security standard one of the reasons that German businesses have done so much hiring in foreign subsidiaries? In 2005, Heraeus, the world's largest precious metal trader, "created 779 jobs worldwide, bringing its workforce to 10,600. Just 30 were in Germany." *Germany's Best Kept Secret.*

2. Employers might attempt to engage people in ways so that these people would not be treated as employees for purposes of all of the labor standard protections.

Although the statutes do not define "employee" for purposes of determining who is covered by labor law, the traditional understanding is that being an employee involves "elements of personal subordination within a private contract setting." Weiss, *Labor Law*, at 326. Traditionally, "personal subordination" meant "all those who acted on orders from their employers, regardless of the remuneration they received." Given that many "highly skilled individuals enjoy so much freedom in deciding how and when they carry out their work," the courts have looked beyond the terms of any written contract and that right to control test to find many of these people to be employees. "The factors employed to reach this conclusion include the following: the enterprise expects the individual on a regular basis to be prepared to accept new work assignments; the individual is not free to refuse assignments; the extent to which the individual is integrated in the organizational structure of the enterprise; the length of time the individual spends in performing work for the enterprise." *Id.* at 327.

3. The German courts have also developed a category – an employee-like relationship – to provide some "labor law protection for those who are self-employed but whose economic situation is close to that of an employee." *Id.* Section 12a of the Act on Collective Agreements defines someone as "employee-like" if they are economically dependent on the employer, even if they might otherwise be found to be self-employed. There are two elements to the determination of economic dependency: "first, they perform their contractual obligations personally and essentially without the support of employees; secondly, they work predominately for one person, or receive on average more than half their income from one person." *Id.* Individuals who work for different enterprises within one group are considered to work for only one person. "Employee-like" persons are not protected against dismissals but their working conditions can be regulated by collective agreements, their disputes with the employing person are within the jurisdiction of labor courts and they are entitled to vacation and holiday benefits provided to regular employees. *Id.* Should economic dependency be the sole test of whether an individual is an employee?

4. In 5AZB 29/96, July 16, 1997, the question was whether plaintiff's case should be heard by the labor court because he was an employee or by the civil court if he were determined to be an independent contractor. The Federal Labor Court (Fifth Senate) found him to be an employee and so it had jurisdiction to hear his case. On the basis of a written contract in which he was characterized as a "marketing partner," plaintiff paid defendant DM 20,000, was trained and then assigned to an exclusive geographic area in which he was to sell defendant's frozen products to households and final users. After he quit, plaintiff sought to recoup his payment as well as the value he had provided defendant by building up the business in his franchise area. The Labor Courts Act provides two bases for jurisdiction – cases involving employees or persons akin to employees. To be found to be an employee, the "description of the legal relationship" in the contract is not determinative. "[W]hether someone who becomes active in a franchise system is an employee or is self-employed depends solely on the question whether he is subject to directions and is dependent or whether he seeks profits in the market place independently and mainly without direction." An employee-like person is independent. Normally "they are not at all or to a lesser degree subject to integration, and also because they are not at all or to a lesser degree integrated in defendant's business organization. In

place of personal dependence, their distinguishing characteristic is that of economic dependence. Moreover, they must because of their social position, be in need of protection like employees." Because of his economic and social dependence and his social need for protection, plaintiff was at least akin to an employee. "He was comparable to an employed traveling salesman."

5. Where a works council exists, the employer has a duty to consult it before any dismissal. The "works council is entitled to receive all information necessary to review the legality of the dismissal." *Id.* at 332. It can agree with the employer, say nothing, or object. Although the works council cannot prevent the employer from dismissing the employer, it can make a declaration of objection, which must be provided to the employee and which may form the outline of any subsequent challenge by the employee to the legality of the dismissal. *Id.* at 333.

6. Employees who successfully contest the legality of their dismissal have a right to reinstatement. "In practice, compensation has over time gradually replaced reinstatement as the primary remedy." *Id.* at 334. Employers now typically offer compensation packages to employees who agree to forego any challenge to their dismissal. That is because a 1985 decision of the Federal Labor Court decided that a worker was assumed to have been wrongly dismissed if she was successful at the local labor court. That gave her an unrestricted right to be reinstated for the duration of the lawsuit and introduced real uncertainty for the employer about the final outcome. *Id.* Furthermore, if the works council responds to the employer's decision to terminate with a declaration of objection, then the employee also "is entitled to stay employed until the end of the lawsuit." *Id.* at 333.

3. Employee Benefits

Going back to the period of Bismarck in the last third of the nineteenth century, one "of the characteristic features of employment relationships in Germany is the principle to integrate all employees in the compulsory social security system." *Id.* at 328. Based on the idea of the solidarity within the workforce as a whole, the social security system "includes health insurance, the statutory pension scheme, insurance in case of work accidents, insurance in case of partial or total incapacity to work and unemployment insurance." *Id.* at 328–29. Other than accident insurance, which is financed only by employer contributions, the costs of the social security system are shared equally by employers and employees, with the employees' share deducted each month from their paychecks. *Id.*

Given the broad application of collective bargaining, the statutory provision that would authorize the implementation of minimum wages is rarely used. An exception is a special statute, enacted in 1996, to impose minimum wages for workers in the construction industry. This statute was adopted in response to a massive influx of foreign construction workers. Hours of work are limited to a normal workday of eight hours followed by a rest period of eleven hours. Employees who are on call for a major portion of their working day are allowed to work more than eight hours a day. An employer must treat part-time workers the same as full-time workers unless there are valid business reasons for a difference. Unless the employer can show a valid business reason, full-time workers have a right to work part-time at employers with more than fifteen employees. INTERNATIONAL LABOR & EMPLOYMENT LAWS at 4–82–86.

Official holidays, which vary from ten to thirteen days per year depending on the region, are paid, with collective bargaining agreements generally providing overtime pay for work on holidays. Although a statute sets a floor of a four-week paid vacation each year, collective bargaining agreements typically provide for longer vacations, with the majority of workers entitled to six weeks per year. Generally, the employer is prohibited from offering employees money in lieu of their vacation. "Vacation money," that is, a bonus in addition to vacation pay, is frequently provided in collective bargaining agreements. *Id.* at 4–86–89.

Unemployment compensation is generous. It is based on employer and employee contributions but, since Agenda 2010 was enacted, the employer is exempted from paying its share for any employee age fifty-five or over. *Id.* at 4–103.

The statutory pension system similar to Social Security in the United States. It involves contributions by both the employer and the employee, with annual income limits. The amount of the pension depends on the amount paid in and the life expectancy of the pensioner, with the amount determined at the time of retirement. There are also a variety of tax advantaged employer-sponsored pension plans as well as private annuities. Employer plans are governed by the Company Pension Plan Act of 1974, which provides that employees' rights to a pension vest if the employee is over age thirty-five when she leaves the company and if the pension plan has been in existence for at least ten years, or the employees has worked for the employer for at least twelve years and the promise of a pension plan has been in effect for at least three years. *Id.* at 4–99–102.

Health insurance is paid for by contributions by employers and employees. Over 90 percent of the population is covered by the mandatory health insurance system. Higher income employees, however, can opt out of the national system and purchase private health insurance. *Id.* at 4–103.

Note

1. The cost of this social security system has become a political issue in Germany as it has in most countries. Although political pressure to maintain the traditional system is strong, there has been some reduction in pension benefits plus some contribution being made by the government from its general tax revenues. What are the advantages of using general governmental funding to supplement contributions by employers and employees to maintain the social security system? Should general revenues be used exclusively to fund the social security system? Are there any advantages to linking social security funding to employment?

C. UNIONS AND COLLECTIVE BARGAINING

1. Collective Bargaining

As in England, the first unions came into existence in the mid-1800s. By 1933, when the Association of German Unions was dissolved by the Nazis, about 40 percent of workers were unionized. After World War II, sixteen separate unions created a new confederation, the Association of German Labor Unions (*Deutscher Gerwerkschaftsbund* or DGB). Each of these unions is industry-wide, or branch-based. Thus, all workers in the metal or metal products industry are represented by the Metal Workers Union, which is the largest member of the DGB. "[T]he union is open to all employees (including those with management functions) in the industry concerned, no matter which trade or occupation they are engaged in." Weiss, *Labor Law*, at 305. In 2001, five large unions merged into the "Ver.di," the world's largest labor union made up of service workers. With Ver.di joining the DGB, it includes the major unions that represent blue- and white-collar workers in the service as well as manufacturing sectors. Thus, the major unions, including those representing public as well as private sector members, are now all members of the DGB. "A characteristic feature of today's union structure in Germany is the fact that different political and ideological wings are amalgamated in one association. This means that within the union movement there is not political and ideological fragmentation." *Id.*

Another characteristic of German unions is that they are centralized, with the national headquarters establishing policies and strategies that are then implemented in all regions. "This high degree of centralization explains why German trade unions espouse macro-perspectives whose focus is not on the individual company but the respective sector of economic activity." *Id.* at 306.

Only about 20 percent of the workers are now union members, which is down from about one-third at the peak of unionism. About 48 percent of employers in western Germany, but only 28 percent in the east, are covered by a bargaining agreement. Thus, in 2001, about 71 percent of the workforce in the west and 56 percent in the east worked for employers covered by collective bargaining. In addition to the difference between the east and the west, there is a profound difference in the types of industry that are covered by collective bargaining and those that are not. Traditional industry, such as the metal or chemistry industry, are highly organized but that is not so for "the service sector, including IT firms, where there is virtually no union membership." Bertram Zwanziger, *Collective Labor Law in a Changing Environment: Aspects of the German Experience*, 26 COMP. LAB. L. & POL'Y J. 303 (2005).

With the DGB as the peak organization on the union side, the equivalent employers' association is the National Association of German Employers Association (*Bundesvereinigung der Deutschen Arbeitgeberverbände*, or BDA). The BDA represent the sociopolitical interests of employers as a group. Although the BDA may make recommendations concerning bargaining strategies, the collective bargaining is done by the individual employers' associations that are its members. Weiss, *Labor Law*, at 307.

The Collective Bargaining Agreements Law of 1969 (TVG) governs the organization of both employer associations and unions. A union must be a voluntary association with an interest of representing the common interests of workers in collective bargaining and it must be "independent of employers, political parties, the government and the church." INTERNATIONAL LABOR & EMPLOYMENT LAWS, 4-41. It must be democratic and have adequate financial and organizational resources to represent its members. Finally, the union must be prepared to pursue industrial action including leading a strike if necessary. But, the union must accept that this struggle must be limited to "peaceful labor struggle" (*friedlicher Arbeitskampf*), including an obligation not to strike during the term of a collective bargaining agreement. *Id.*

In their respective industrial sectors, unions represent all the employees, from apprentices to white-collar workers just below the level of executive management. *Id.* at 4-42. If one worker in one plant is a union member, then the union is to be recognized as the representative of the workers of that company. When more than one union has members working for an employer, the DGB attempts to mediate intraunion disputes. Weiss, *Labor Law*, at 306.

Organized in the different industrial sectors but usually limited to a specific geographic area of the country, employer associations, who conduct much of the collective bargaining, must be independent of the state, political parties, and the church. They must be democratically organized and must also commit to "peaceful labor struggle."

The source of the legal right to collective bargaining is in Article 9 (3) of the Constitution, which provides: "The right to form associations to safeguard and improve working and economic conditions shall be guaranteed to every individual and to every occupation and profession." Although couched in terms of individual rights, the German courts have developed the concept of "collective freedom of association," which is implied from the rights of individuals to organize and which protects the existence and the activities of unions and employers' associations. CONSTITUTION & LABOR LAW, at 184.

The terms in Article 9 (3) – "safeguard and improve working and economic conditions" – establish one pole of what questions are appropriate subjects of bargaining. However, the language in Article 9 must be read in context with other constitutional provisions, particularly the rights to property established in Article 14 of the Constitution, to determine the proper scope of bargaining. "Collective agreements may influence the costs of business decisions by setting standards for remuneration, vacation days, working hours and the like. Collective agreements may also regulate the effects of such decisions, for example by stipulating the consequences in cases of lay-offs. However, basic decisions, such as investments and plant closings, fall outside the bargaining process and are left to management alone." Weiss, *Labor Law*, at 308.

Although it is not always the case, the paradigm is for collective bargaining negotiations to be undertaken at the regional level between the union representing the workers in the particular industry and the regional association of employers in that industry. The regional character of the employer associations reflects differences even within a particular industry that are relevant to the underlying businesses. Collective bargaining agreements (*Tarifverträge*) are of two types. Framework agreements, which govern terms and conditions of employment such as vacation, working hours, termination notice periods, grounds for termination, and so on remain in effect on an ongoing basis until one party gives notice to terminate. Wage and salary agreements include job descriptions and are negotiated for a specific term usually for a year or two. INTERNATIONAL LABOR & EMPLOYMENT LAWS 4-43–4-45. The terms of the collective bargaining agreement define its geographic applicability, the industry covered and the personnel covered. The agreement generally covers only the parties to the agreement. The members of the employers association are bound as are the members of the union. By its terms, the agreement does not cover employees who are not members of the union. Usually, the employer will, nevertheless, apply the terms of the agreement to all employees, even those who are not members of the union. This, of course, creates a "free rider" problem (*Trittbrettfahrer* or "running board riders") because nonunion employees benefit from the effort of the union without having paid it any dues. The Federal Labor Court has held that Article 9 (3) of the Constitution includes a so-called negative freedom of association so that provisions such as "closed shop agreements, shop agency agreements and even agreements which are intended to reserve advantages exclusively for trade union members" are forbidden as interferences with the freedom of association rights of employees who are not union members. Weiss, *Labor Law*, at 304–05.

There is pattern bargaining with a large, strong union in an important region, typically IG Metall and the metal industry employer association for Bader-Württemberg, going first and setting the pattern for wage agreements for the rest of the sectors in the metal industry and then forming the baseline for contracts in other sectors.

In 2002, over fifty-seven thousand collective bargaining agreements were filed with the state labor departments. Thirty-three thousand were regional agreements, whereas about twenty-four thousand were between unions and individual employers. Some employers who are not members of employer associations simply incorporate the terms of a particular agreement and apply them to their employees. There are also two mechanisms providing for the extension of collective agreements to employees and employers not otherwise covered by it. The first is that a state or the federal Labor Department can extend a contract to employers who are not members of an employers association bound to the agreement or to employees who are not members of the union. To extend a contract, the labor department must get the consent of the union and the employers association that bargained the contract. Next, it must also find that at least 50 percent of the employees of a particular employer are within the jurisdictional scope of the agreement and its extension to the nonparty employer or employees is in the public interest. *Id.* at 4-47. The second method of extension was created in 1999 and provides for the extension of collective bargaining agreements in the building and construction industry by governmental decree. A decree can extend a collective agreement even in the absence of the agreement of the parties to the contract as long as as it is binding on at least half of all the employees within its occupational or geographic scope of application. LABOUR LAW IN GERMANY at 159.

One feature of sectoral bargaining is that the collective bargaining agreement can provide the employers covered by the agreement, who are competitors in the marker, the benefit of eliminating the risk of price competition in that market based on lower labor costs paid by some competitors. This works as long as the defined sector reflects a separate market. With increasing globalization and, particularly in Germany, the entry of the former eastern part of the country as well as the rest of Eastern Europe into the market limits the ability of a collective agreement to provide protection from price competition. There is emerging in Germany, a two-tier labor market as a feature of some collective agreements. Some wage agreements now provide "opening" or "hardship" clauses which allow members of employers associations to attempt to negotiate individualized, less costly wage agreements based on the unique difficulties faced by the particular employer.

> Unlike most other dual labor markets, however, the lower portion of the [two tier] labor market is *not* an informal sector, but is *also* regulated by organized labor and management. The objective is to create a less expensive compensation package for weaker firms in order to staunch association avoidance among employers and to absorb a good share of the unemployed back into the labor market without completely abandoning control over wage competition. . . . Ultimately, however, the trend toward incorporating opening clauses . . . far from a temporary or exceptional phenomenon, is gradually producing a managed two-tier labor market. . . .
>
> ANDREW MARTIN & GEORGE ROSS, THE BRAVE NEW WORLD OF EUROPEAN LABOR: EUROPEAN TRADE UNIONS AT THE MILLENIUM 118 (1999).

In absence of such opening clauses, some employers nevertheless attempt to reach agreements with individual employees in their employment contracts that are not consistent with the provisions in the collective bargaining agreement. The long-standing principle established by the Federal Labor Court is that an objective test is used to determine if the conditions established in the individual contract are more favorable than those in the collective agreement. Unless the principle of more favorable conditions is satisfied, the terms of the collective agreement govern. Because of the pressure by employers to increase flexibility in work rules, there is presently a dispute as to whether the objective standard of more favorable conditions should continue to be applied. If, for example, a collective agreement reduced the workweek from forty to thirty-five hours, but the employer offered individual workers higher wages to accept a longer work week, the objective standard would likely not be satisfied. It has been argued that the individual employees should decide which arrangement was more favorable, or that a long-term view of what was best for the survival of the employer should govern. Nevertheless, the courts continue to apply the objective test. Weiss, *Labor Law*, at 309.

Notes

1. As is true in much of the world, the rate of union membership is declining in Germany. In part that is because much of the growth in employment has recently been in service sectors, not manufacturing, and unions have had limited success organizing service sectors of the economy. Does that mean that unionization is a phenomenon of the industrial age and will inevitably recede in the postindustrial era? Why do unions have trouble organizing the service sector of the economy? In order to survive, must unions figure out a way of organizing the presently unorganized?

2. What are the advantages of sectoral bargaining versus bargaining between the union and each individual employer? Although there is some sectoral bargaining in specialized niches in the United States, such as the construction industry, that is the exception. Union membership is lower in the United States than in Germany. Is the absence of sectoral bargaining a reason for that? Should U.S. unions move toward a sectoral approach more generally? The Unite Here union representing hotel workers is trying to synchronize the expiration dates of its collective bargaining agreements across the entire country. The purpose is to increase bargaining leverage against the industry and strengthen pattern bargaining. Should more U.S. unions move toward sectoral bargaining? Under U.S. labor laws, bargaining units are defined workplace by workplace but changing the unit is a permissive subject of bargaining. Would U.S. employers likely veto attempts to move to sectoral bargaining since they have no legal obligation to bargain over the definition of the bargaining unit?

3. What are the disadvantages of sectoral bargaining? Would German unions be stronger if they were more closely connected with the employees of the particular employers with whom it ultimately has collective agreements?

2. Strikes and Lockouts

Although there is no legislation establishing the right to strike or lockout, Article 9(1) of the Constitution establishes a general right of association: "All Germans have the right to form associations and societies." Article 9(3) explicitly extends that right to employment: "The right to form associations to safeguard and improve working and economic conditions is guaranteed to everyone and to all trades and professions." Thus, Article 9(3) underlies not only the right for both workers and employers to organize and to bargain collectively, but also is the basis for the workers' right to strike and the employers' corresponding right to lockout. Professor Weiss puts it this way:

> [I]t is accepted that article 9, paragraph 3, of the Constitution – in spite of its wording – also guarantees a system of free collective bargaining as an institution in which the individual freedom of association can play a relevant role in actual practice. This first step implies the second one: Once it is agreed that a system of free collective bargaining is guaranteed by the Constitution, the philosophy . . . requires that this system has to be shaped in a way that makes sure that it can fulfill the function to provide adequate working conditions. This is only possible if one side cannot dictate the conditions to the other one: the system needs a fair balance of power to give each side an equal chance to reach an adequate compromise. This implies the right to strike: without this right collective bargaining would be nothing but collective begging. And, according to the Federal Labor Court, to a certain extent and under very specific conditions, a right to defensive lockout is needed in order to guarantee this balance of power in all circumstances of industrial action.

CONSTITUTION & LABOR LAW, at 184–185.

BVR 779/85

Federal Constitutional Court
(First Senate)
June 26, 1991

[The Federal Constitutional Court, rejected a constitutional challenge by employers to the rules concerning strikes and lockouts developed over time by the Federal Labor Court. Although not a member of the employers' associations, the complainant was an employer in an industrial sector in which the union was engaging in a strike. The Federal Labor Court found that the employer's use of a lockout exceeded the limits allowed by law.]

There is no legislation establishing the law on industrial conflicts. The Large Senate of the Federal Labor Court dealt with the matter in two seminal judgments. In the decision of 28 January 1955 it held that strikes undertaken with a view to obtaining more favorable working conditions through collective agreement were in principle lawful. The German legal order permitted such conflicts. There was freedom to engage in industrial conflict, freedom to strike and freedom to lockout. Within the framework of the concept of social justification, there was freedom of choice of the means of conflict. Each group was entitled to choose within the limits of lawful conduct the means that were suitable for it, had developed historically and were objectively appropriate. A lockout was the counterpart to a strike by the unions, irrespective of whether it was decided by an employer's organization and carried out by individual employers or whether it was undertaken independently by one or more employers. Both offensive and defensive lockouts had the effect of terminating the collective agreement.

In the second decision of the Large Senate, of 21 April 1971, industrial conflicts were made subject to a requirement of proportionality since both strike and lockout frequently had lasting effects not only for participants in the conflict but also for non-strikers, other third parties and the community. Industrial conflict might only be initiated and pursued as far as the conflict was objectively necessary to attain the lawful object of a resulting peace justified. Both in the case of a strike and in that of a lockout, the principle of proportionality had to be applied. The means of conflict had to remain limited to that which was necessary to attain the lawful objective sought to be achieved. Conflict was therefore lawful only when and as long as it was conducted according to the rules of a fair fight. It was not permissible to seek to destroy the opponent: Rather the aim had to be to reestablish the industrial peace that had been disturbed.

Within the framework of the principle of proportionality, not only strikes by employees but also lockouts by employers were lawful. The law assumed that the employer could have recourse to such measures, even as a first, offensive, step in an industrial conflict. Otherwise it could not be guaranteed that, on the basis of the autonomy of the parties, negotiations and if necessary mutual pressure would lead to the conclusion of a collective agreement and the collective regulation of working conditions. If the union alone was able to dictate the evolution of the conflict by initiating a strike with the employer limited to suffering and enduring it, there would be some risk that the regulation of working conditions would no longer be based on agreements freely arrived at. One party to a collective agreement should not be able from the outset to impose its will on the other, but that as far as possible both were entitled to equal bargaining opportunities. According to the principle of proportionality, measures initiating a conflict, whether by strike or by lockout, only had the effect of suspending, not terminating, the collective agreement.

In two judgments of 10 June 1980, the First Senate of the Federal Labor Court further developed the case law on equality in industrial conflicts and the principle of proportionality. Offensive lockouts were no longer allowed. The permissible extent of defensive lockout was dependent on the extent of the offensive strike. The narrower the scope of a strike that the union called against some employers in the association, the stronger was the need for the employers to be able to extend the conflict to other undertakings in that area. In one of the two judgments, concerning a conflict in the metal industry of Baden-Württemberg, the Court used quotas as a guide: If the strike involved fewer than 25 per cent of the employees in the area, the defensive lockout was not disproportionate if it in turn did not affect more than 25 per cent of these employees.

Article 9, paragraph 3 of the Constitution establishes the right to form associations to safeguard and improve working and economic conditions. That right (*Koalitionsfreiheit*) is distinguished from the general freedom of association (*Vereinigungsfreiheit*) provided for in Article 9, paragraph 1, by the inclusion of the specific purpose of the association. In the past, there were periods when the State violently opposed the establishment of associations to safeguard and improve working and economic conditions. This explains the special constitutional protection, going beyond that of Article 9, paragraph 1.

The right to form associations under Article 9, paragraph 3 of the Constitution applies to everyone and to all trades, occupations and professions. Thus, although historically the right was denied primarily to workers and was fought for by them, the constitutional provision is not conceived as a fundamental right only of workers, but is also applicable to employers. Moreover the constitutional rule is not limited to the freedom of the individual to establish such an association, to join or refuse to join it or to withdraw from it. It protects the association itself as regards its existence, its organization and its activity insofar as this consists of safeguarding and improving working and economic conditions.

An essential purpose of the associations protected by Article 9, paragraph 3 of the Constitution is to provide for the parties to reach collective agreements through bargaining. In this respect the associations are, according to the intent of the Constitution, to be free to act. The Constitution in principle leaves to the associations the choice of means that they consider appropriate for the attainment of this aim. Insofar as the pursuit of the purpose of the association is dependent on the use of a particular means, those means are included in the constitutional protection.

Measures of industrial conflict used to achieve collective agreements are among the means protected. They are included in the freedom of association insofar as they are necessary to guarantee that the parties have autonomy in bargaining. The Federal Labor Court considers a defensive lockout to be a reaction to limited partial strike thereby making it an essential means for the maintenance of effective autonomy in bargaining.

An employer who is not a member but who joins a lockout declared by an employers' organization is exercising its right of association. The alliance with an organization with the capacity to conclude a collective agreement can be an association within the meaning of Article 9, paragraph 3 of the Constitution if it is designed to influence the conclusion of such an agreement in the interest of the non-member. That this was the purpose in the present case is evidenced by the fact that the complainant had included a general provision in its individual employment contracts making the collective agreement concluded by the employers' organization incorporated in those individual contracts.

The ruling of the Federal Labor Court limits the power of the complainant to participate in a defensive lockout, as a reaction to a partial strike by the unions. This is tantamount to a restriction of its freedom of association under Article 9, paragraph 3 of the Constitution. That restriction is, however, not open to attack on the basis of constitutional law.

The Federal Labor Court did not infringe upon the freedom of association of the complainant in its development of the applicable principles even in absence of any legislative authorization. The Federal Labor Court was not prevented from limiting the ability of the complainant to use a lockout on the basis that such limitation was exclusively within the purview of the legislature. The doctrine developed by the Federal Constitutional Court, to the effect that in fundamental normative areas the legislature must make all essential decisions itself (*Wesentlichkeistheorie*), applies to the relationship between the State and the citizen. When touching upon constitutional freedoms, the State is subject to the preferred position of legislation. In many areas the State may act only if expressly empowered to do so by a law adopted by Parliament.

In the present action, what is at issue is the relationship between parties, each with equivalent rights under the Constitution. Admittedly, the Federal Constitutional Court has on several occasions expressed the view that it is "a question for the legislature" to give more detailed form to the freedom association of industrial organizations. However, in the absence of sufficient legislative guidance, the courts must determine the law, by means of recognised methods of deduction, on the basis of general legal principles applicable to the relationship in question. This is the only way in which the courts can fulfill the duty imposed on them by the Constitution to decide objectively all legal disputes brought before them.

The Federal Labour Court also did not transgress Article 20, paragraph 3 of the Constitution [which provides that, "Legislation is subject to the constitutional order, the executive and the judiciary are bound by the law"] because, as the complainant contends, the Court did not have sufficient reason to alter its case law on industrial conflict. Judgments of the highest courts are not the same as legislation and do not create similarly binding law. To deviate from them does not in principle offend against Article 20, paragraph 3. The claim of validity extending beyond the specific cases decided rests solely on the power of the arguments of the parties to convince and on the authority and competence of the court. It is not necessary, therefore, for a court to demonstrate that there have been important changes in circumstances to justify a deviation from earlier case law.

The contested decision also does not, in substance, conflict with Article 9, paragraph 3 of the Constitution. The fundamental right provided is admittedly guaranteed without qualification.

But this does not preclude all limitations that may be justified on the basis of the fundamental rights of third parties or of other rights with constitutional significance. Moreover, the law must give content to the freedom of association as regards the relationship between the bargaining partners, both of whom are protected by the constitutional provision.

The present case does not call for a more precise definition of the limits to the "nucleus" or core of the freedom of association. Certainly, bargaining disputes are included within that nucleus. However, neither the capacity nor the ability of the employer to conduct effectively a legal industrial conflict is called in question by the contested judgment. The limitation to its use of a lockout that is imposed on the complainant does not infringe upon the essential content of its freedom of association; nor does the law unduly encroach upon the constitutional right.

The basic assumption of the Federal Labor Court, that industrial conflict measures serve to establish bargaining parity in collective disputes and must be judged by reference to that purpose, is not subject to objection as a matter of constitutional law. The principle restricts the parties recourse to the use of conflict measures so that those measures do not result in one party's superiority in bargaining. Such a restriction is consonant with Article 9, paragraph 3 of the Constitution. The autonomy of the social partners is designed to compensate for the built-in inferiority of the position of individual workers to achieve employment contracts through collective action. The restrictions, therefore, render possible more or less even-handed bargaining over wages and working conditions. Where industrial conflict results in inequality, the functioning of the system of autonomy is prejudiced.

The arguments advanced by the complainant against the principle of bargaining parity cannot prevail. The capacity of employers to engage effectively in conflict is not called into question by the regulation of industrial conflict for the purpose of preserving equality in bargaining power of the parties to collective agreements. As long as the employers are not prevented from using the means of conflict necessary to establish equipoise, there is no infringement of the freedom of association. That freedom can be so fashioned as to avoid, as far as possible, any superiority of either party in bargaining. Article 9, paragraph 3 of the Constitution thus does not guarantee an unlimited power to have recourse to all conceivable forms of conflict.

Further, the fact that the Federal Labor Court permits recourse to defensive lockouts only as a measure circumscribed by the principle of proportionality is not open to objection. This view is based on the consideration that the workers' side is dependent on conflict measures or the threat of such measures for the establishment of an equally strong bargaining position. Because the Court limits itself to checking the escalation of a conflict through excessive defensive action, it safeguards the autonomy of the parties. Any examination of proportionality starting with offensive lockout measures would inevitably imply judicial control of bargaining objectives.

Notes

1. As will be developed in the next section, the trail court for labor disputes is the labor court of first instance, with appeals going to the *Land* labor courts and with the Federal Labor Court having limited jurisdiction to hear appeals from the *Land* labor courts. The Federal Labor Court is comprised of ten divisions, called "senates." The Federal Labor Court also includes the so-called Large Senate "composed of the Court President, one career judge from each of the senates not chaired by

the Court President, and six lay judges serving in the Federal Labor Court, three from the employer's side and three from the employees' side." Weiss, *Labor Law*, at 303. "If a party believes that the Federal Labor Court's decision violates the Constitution (Basic Law), it may file a complaint of unconstitutionality with the Federal Constitutional Court, which has discretion to accept this matter for a final decision." *Id.*

2. In absence of any legislation, the German courts have developed an extensive jurisprudence concerning strikes and lockouts. Industrial action – strikes by workers and lockouts by employers – can only be undertaken for the purpose of achieving a collective agreement. Thus, such action may legally only be carried out by parties to a collective bargaining relationship. Strikes called by a group of workers without backing by the union – wildcat strikes – are illegal. Once the collective agreement has terminated without a new agreement, short "warning strikes" are permitted. Thus, "in Germany the right to strike is in fact a right of the trade unions and not a right of the individual." GERMAN LABOUR LAW at 166–167.

3. Although picketing is lawful, as are attempts by strikers to convince strikebreakers or others to not cross the picket line, blocking workplace entrances is illegal. The overarching principle is the requirement that all industrial action be proportional to the needs of the situation, that is, a measured response. Thus, industrial action should be a last resort, after all efforts at negotiation have been exhausted.

4. Although sympathy strikes – where union strikes employer B to put pressure on employer A, the employer with whom the union has its real dispute – are illegal, strikes are legal if the union is striking to extend the provisions it is seeking from an employer association to an employer in the same business but that is not a member of the employers' association. In 1AZR 332/90, April 9, 1991, a union was on strike to get a new collective bargaining agreement with an employers association of brick manufacturers in Bavaria. The union also struck an employer engaged in brick making in Bavaria that was not a member of the employers' association. "[A] strike against an employer who is an outsider may be lawful when the union seeks a collective agreement with that employer. Unlike a sympathy strike, which the [court] has declared to be normally illicit, a strike against an outside employer is not merely aimed at support for the primary strike with the employers association. Rather, the union also seeks to ensure that the issues it seeks to incorporate in the collective become working conditions for the employer outside the association as well. Contrary to a sympathy strike, the outside employer can satisfy the union's claims since it has the capacity to agree to a collective agreement either at the level either at the level of the undertaking or by subscribing to the agreement with the employers association." Unless the union ratifies it, a wildcat strike is illegal as is a sympathy strike since that puts pressure on an employer other than the employer that is party to the collective bargaining relationship.

5. As is clear from this decision, the right of employers to lockout workers is the limited by the extent of the strike. "While a lockout is generally a permissible *reaction* to strikes by the unions, it may not be used offensively for the achievement of certain goals. . . ." INTERNATIONAL LABOR & EMPLOYMENT LAW AT 4-51. The Federal Labor Court ties the extent of a permissible lockout to the extent workers are on strike. Thus, if more than half the workers are on strike, the employers may not lockout any employees because the effect of the strike is so broad that the solidarity

of the employers is not implicated. If less than half of the workers are on strike, then the employers may lockout employees up until 50 percent of the workers are no longer working either because they are on strike or because they have been locked out. Since unions must pay strike benefits to strikers as well as its members who are locked out, this 50 percent cap allows the union to determine the maximum number of employees to whom it may owe strike benefits. LABOUR LAW IN GERMANY at 176–177.

6. Does the proscription of offensive lockouts and the proportionality limits on the extent a defensive lockout may be used interfere too substantially with the right of employers to engage in industrial action to achieve their objectives in collective bargaining? Because employers are most likely better off continuing operations under the prior collective agreement, offensive lockouts are mostly useful weapons for employers in cyclical business. Assuming that a hotel has little special business booked for several months but then has a series of business conventions scheduled that will fill all the rooms, and will call for the full use of conference, meeting and eating facilities. That employer might want to pressure the union to agree to a new collective bargaining agreement, and use an offensive lockout to do that, in the period before the convention season while the union may feel that it will have heightened bargaining pressure if it can wait to call a strike as the conventions are about to begin. Should the union have the exclusive power to time the use of economic weaponry to its advantage?

7. The Court found that the complainant that was not a member of the employers association had the right to engage in a defensive lockout, subject to the proportionality rules. But how do employers, within or without, the association figure out how to lockout proportionately? If the members of the employers association have already locked out as many employees as proportionality allows, does that mean the nonmember employers in fact do not have the ability to engage in a lockout? Must the employer joining the fray add its employee compliment to the total number of employees of the now-expanded group in order to calculate whether it can lockout any of its employees while staying within the limits set by the proportionality principle?

8. Applying the principle of proportionality may affect employers more severely than unions. Given that workers who go out on strike lose the right to their wages and given that unions typically have limited funds to provide substitute strike benefits, the union has an incentive to limit the strike to as few places of employment as possible that nevertheless cause the greatest negative effect on the employers. For example, if the union can shut down by strike a key facility that must operate if the rest of an enterprise can continue to operate, then, under German law, the employer can only lock out a proportional number of workers. Because "[a] permissible lockout is perceived as merely the suspension of the mutual obligations (in particular the obligation to pay wages) arising out of the employment relationship," INTERNATIONAL LABOR & EMPLOYMENT LAW at 4-51, the employer will still be liable to pay all the workers beyond those it can lockout who, nevertheless, are unable to work because of the effect of the strike. Should the union be able to limit its liability to striking workers while exposing employers to liability for those workers who are unable to work because of the strike but who are beyond the proportionality limits that the law imposes?

9. "[T]he hiring and retention of replacement workers is not permitted." INTERNA-
    TIONAL LABOR & EMPLOYMENT LAW at 4-51. The German law prohibiting even
    temporary replacement of strikers protects them from the risk of losing their jobs. Is
    this a more reasonable protection of the freedom of association than United States
    law that allows economic strikers to be permanently replaced? Would you go on
    strike if there was much of a risk that the employer would permanently replace
    you?

10. The Federal Labor Court, (First Senate) 1 AZR 1016/94, June 26, 1995, held that
    where the employer sent workers home after a brief strike, before the shift began
    but after notice of another brief strike to take place after the shift, it owed the
    workers pay. The employer had failed to make an unambiguous declaration that it
    was locking out the workers. In contrast, the same court held that the employer did
    not owe wages to employees who were sent home after they engaged in at least one
    of a series of short strikes – a "*Wellenstreik*" or wave of strike action. "The workers
    bear the risk of lost wages when an industrial action in which they participate leads
    to a disturbance making resumption of work impossible or unreasonable." 1 AZR
    364/96, Nov. 12, 1996.

11. In, 1 AZR 622/93, Mar. 22, 1994, the Federal Labor Court (First Senate), held that
    the employer did not have to accept the offer by a nonunion employee to work or
    pay wages after he showed up for work during a strike. This was so even though
    the employer did give work to employees named in an agreement with the union
    to provide emergency services. "The employer is entitled to shut down operations
    during a strike which suspends his obligation to provide work and pay remuneration
    even as to employees ready to work." The employee, however, would be entitled
    to his wages if he was not employed in the unit where the strike was called but was
    nevertheless unable to work because of the strike.

12. The Federal Constitutional Court traces extensively the development of the law
    of strikes and lockouts by the Federal Labor Court. Compare the justification the
    Court gives for its exercise of judicial creativity with the approach common law
    courts take in creating law in common law systems. In a civil law system, shouldn't
    the court tell the parties to disputes over the legality of strikes and legislature to
    "take it to the legislature?" Does the long history of judicial involvement without
    any resulting legislative action justify the courts continued development of jurispru-
    dence in this area? Does the fact that both employers and unions have constitutional
    rights to association justify the courts deciding what the law of industrial conflict
    is? Given the Court's differentiation of this situation from a case where a State was
    a party, would a case involving a strike or lockout in public employment be treated
    differently?

13. The parties to collective bargaining have, in the different economic sectors, cre-
    ated joint dispute resolution boards that are configured somewhat differently in
    the different industries. Although theoretically available during bargaining, these
    joint boards tend to become much more active and involved once industrial action
    is undertaken. GERMAN LABOUR LAW at 165. Furthermore, each German *Lan-
    der* provides for mediation and for voluntary arbitration of collective bargaining
    disputes.

3. Works Councils and Works Agreements

With the general model for collective bargaining having the bargaining and the agreement at the sector level between unions and employers associations in the particular business and geographic region, the institution of works councils provides a mechanism for individualizing the relationship between the employer and the employees at the place of employment. Although there is a long history of various laws dealing with works councils, the 1952 Industrial Relations Regulation Act was enacted by a conservative government with the goal of keeping unions off the shop floor and limiting their influence to sectoral bargaining. The law established the right to a works council for specific workplaces with five or more employees. Works councils are nonunion organs for employee representation, with members of the council selected from among the employees by the entire workforce, not just union members. Despite the antiunion origin of the law, the majority of those workers elected to the works council are union members, and the council and union typically work closely together. RICHARD LOCKE, THOMAS KOCHAN & MICHAEL PIORE, EMPLOYMENT RELATIONS IN A CHANGING WORLD ECONOMY 234 (1995). The works council, however, cannot call a strike and must remain neutral during one, but members of the works council may participate in legal strikes called by the union. Weiss, *Labor Law*, at 314.

Whereas covered employers are required to deal with works councils, it is up to the employees to take action to implement their right to a works council. Any three employees entitled to vote or any union representing employees may call a meeting of employees to propose establishing an election committee to create a works council. The meeting can decide to move to the next step without regard to how many employees attend the meeting. Works council membership is selected by secret ballot for four-year terms, with the number of members determined by the total number of employees. For example, the works council for employers with as few as twenty employees is made up of only one member, whereas the works council membership of an employer with 1,001 to 1,500 employees is set at fifteen. Both unions with members working for the employer and non-union groups may submit slates of candidates for the election. All employees are entitled to vote and to stand for election. Although most larger employers have works councils, many smaller ones have not had them. Because an amendment to the law in 2001 simplifying election procedures, more employees of small and medium-sized enterprises have called for the creation of works councils. Weiss, *Labor Law*, at 310–11. The works council, made up of employees and not including management representatives, meets privately. The employer has no right to attend or to participate.

When an employer has a number of different work places with separate works councils, then a joint works council is created to deal with common issues. Its membership comes from among the members of the separate councils, with each appointing two of its members. "If works councils are established in different establishments of a multi-plant enterprise, they shall form a company works council. The works council of the individual establishments are not subordinate to the company works council. The company works council is only authorized to deal with matters which either cannot be resolved within the individual establishment or which are delegated to it by an individual works council." *Id.*

The members of the works council are protected from retaliation for their work but they are bound to maintain the confidentiality of trade secrets and they are forbidden from undertaking industrial action. INTERNATIONAL LABOR & EMPLOYMENT LAWS, at 4–67–68. Because the works council must not share the information it received from the employer with its constituency of workers, the resulting lack of transparency can be a source of tension and alienation between the works council and the employees. Weiss, *Labor Law*, at 315.

The role of the works council varies, depending on the type of issue involved. On some issues, the works council only has a right to information and to be heard; on some issues the works council has a right of approval and veto; and on others there is a right to codetermination. The right only to information and to be heard arises concerning issues of the employer's observance of laws (such as workplace safety laws) that benefit workers, plans concerning the construction or renovation of production facilities, and information about personnel matters such as anticipated labor needs. As to terminations, the works council has a right to be heard before the termination. In any subsequent proceeding to challenge the termination, the employer can only rely on those grounds that it raised with the works council. If it objects to a dismissal, the works council sends the employer a declaration of objection, which is provided the employee and which typically describes the basis for any challenge the employee might bring to the dismissal. *Id.* at 333.

"A works council has approval and veto rights with respect to hiring, deployment, [and] transfer . . . of employees." INTERNATIONAL LABOR & EMPLOYMENT LAWS, at 4–67–68. For employers with at least 100 employees, the works council is entitled to information concerning general business matters, which is dealt with by a special economic committee. In businesses that normally have more than twenty workers, the employer is obligated to inform the works council before every new hire, redeployment, or transfer. The works council can veto certain measures, such as the hiring of a new employee, if it can identify particular objections (for example, if the job not had been properly posted.). *Id.* at 4–61. Works council vetoes can be appealed by the employer to the labor court.

Codetermination, which means in the context of works councils that the employer may not undertake the activity without prior agreement of the works council, applies to a wide variety of issues dealing with employment rules and benefits. At the broadest, the issue of the deployment of labor in the business is subject to codetermination, as are scheduling daily work hours, temporary reduction of work, increases in overtime, when and where wages are paid, vacation policies, the introduction of new technical control systems that affect employment, workplace safety rules, employee benefits (such as cafeterias) and the overall salary structure. *Id.* at 4–63. Where the employer proposes changes in the business that will have an adverse impact on employees, for example, the relocation or the closing of a plant, the employer and the works council have an obligation to negotiate a works agreement – a social plan – that balances the interests of the employees and the employer. "A social plan means nothing less than a special works agreement to compensate or reduce the disadvantages that employees suffer in the event of a substantial change of the establishment or in cases of insolvency." Weiss, *Labor Law*, at 318. Thus, in a plant relocation situation, a works agreement might provide for commuting expenses for the employees while, if a plant is shutdown, the agreement might involve severance packages. INTERNATIONAL LABOR & EMPLOYMENT LAWS, at 4–64.

In 1 ABR 22/94 November 8, 1994, the Federal Labour Court (First Senate), the employer was concerned about excessive absences by the employees in its veneer department. The head of personnel went to the department and discussed the issue with twenty-seven of the employees. He obtained signed releases from most of them to allow the company to talk to their physicians. The works council sued, claiming it had a right of codetermination because the matter involved a matter "relating to the organization of the establishment and the conduct of employees in the establishment" as set forth in Works Construction Act section 87(1)(1). Without deciding whether dealing with the issue of excessive abuses dealt with job performance rather than with the conduct of employees, the court found this to be subject to co-determination because of the organized way the employer acted as to an entire group and because of the effect that had on the right of privacy of the workers. More recently, Wal-Mart ran afoul of the codetermination requirements when it promulgated a thirty-three-page code of conduct to all its employees in Germany without first presenting it to its works councils. The local and *Lander* labor courts found that this unilateral promulgation violated codetermination. *See* Dr. Gerlind Wisskirchen, Christopher Jordan & Alexander Bissels, Cross-Border Ethics Codes: The Case of Wal-Mart in Germany, http://www.abanet.org/labor/2005.

Employers have an obligation to participate in proceedings with its work council until an agreement is reached. If an employer violates its obligations, the labor courts can provide a remedy including ordering damages for the affected employees, with the union empowered to bring suit. Weiss, *Labor Law*, at 312. In some German states, there is authority for the labor court to issue a temporary restraining order against the employer. Agreements on all these codetermination issues must be reduced to writing. If an impasse is reached, then either party can call for a dispute resolution panel to be established. It is made up equal number of representatives from both sides plus a neutral chairman. If the parties cannot agree to the chair, the labor court names one, typically a career labor judge. *Id.* at 315. The dispute resolution panel issues a resolution that is binding on the parties. Though rare, that resolution is subject to limited review by the labor court. INTERNATIONAL LABOR & EMPLOYMENT LAWS at 4–63. The court may annul, but not rewrite, the decision "only if the arbitration committee exceeded its discretionary powers." Weiss, *Labor Law*, at 315.

The relationship between a collective bargaining agreement and a works agreement is as follows: If a specific matter is "already regulated" by the collective agreement, a works agreement on that matter is void unless it is made pursuant to a so-called "opening" or "hardship" clause in the collective agreement. GERMAN LABOUR LAW at 206–07. Where the issue is one of codetermination in which the works council has a duty to reach a works agreement, "codetermination is only excluded if the provision provided for in the collective agreement is so detailed and specific that no room is left for alternative decisions. If there is any leeway for alternative managerial decisions, the right of the works council to codetermination shall be respected." GERMAN LABOUR LAW at 209. Despite the legal priority of the collective bargaining agreement, "works councils and individual employers frequently ignore the provisions in collective agreements. Confronted with the employer's demand to reduce costs in order to save jobs, works councils increasingly conclude works agreements that ignore minimum standards fixed in collective agreements." Weiss, *Labor Law*, at 319. Unions "rarely dare to challenge these works agreements in court because they would run the risk of losing members as a result." *Id.* As a result of "opening clauses" and greater flexibility in collective bargaining agreements so that they are increasingly more like framework agreements, works councils are becoming increasingly integrated into the structure of collective bargaining. "The collective agreements for a branch of activity now have become very flexible instruments, not only containing opening clauses but also options to be chosen by works agreements." *Id.* at 319–20.

The relationship between individual employment contracts and works agreements turns on which is more advantageous to the employee, that is, the principle of more favorable conditions. In GS3/85s, Federal Labour Court (Large Senate) November 7, 1989, the individual employment contract incorporated by reference the provisions of the works agreement. At that time, the works agreement provided for mandatory retirement six months after the worker turned age sixty-five. Subsequently, the work agreement was negotiated to set the retirement at "the end of the month in which age of 65 is attained." The court concluded that "the determining conflict rule is the principle that the provision which is to the advantage of the worker prevails." In applying the principle, the court found that the reduction of the time within which the employee had to choose whether to quit or to continue working was a disadvantage to the worker even though he was entitled to a pension upon retirement. "Rules on a retirement age are more favorable to the worker the longer he has the choice between work and retirement. Any reduction of the period is a disadvantage."

A collective bargaining agreement trumps an inconsistent works agreement on the same matter unless the matter is one on which the works counsel has the right of code-termination. In 1 ABR 85/90, August 20, 1991, the Federal Labor Court (First Senate) was confronted with the claim by the union that a works agreement dealing with work on Saturdays and Sunday was in conflict with mandatory provisions of a framework collective bargaining agreement. On the one hand, section 77(3) of the Works Constitution Act provides that, "Remuneration and other conditions of employment normally governed by a collective agreement shall not be the subject of works agreements." On the other, section 81(1)(2) provides that, "Where an arrangement is not prescribed by law or collective agreement, works councils shall participate in decisions on . . . the beginning and end of daily working hours, including breaks, and the distribution of working hours among the various days of the week." The works agreement here involved a question on which the works council had a right of codetermination and so the union could not sue the employer to enforce the collective agreement.

Notes

1. Why might employees at smaller employers be less likely to exercise their right to have a works council established? Is it that they perceive less of a need since the "boss" may be close at hand to deal with problems? Or do you think that such proximity breeds fear if the employees undertake something the employer does not want?

2. What are the advantages and disadvantages of leaving to employees the choice to implement a works council? Is the workplace that needs representation the most, the least likely to get it? In the United States, polls indicate that a significant majority of employees would like some sort of representation, be it a union or some other institution. Should the United States make provision for the creation of works councils? Should they be at the choice of the employees or mandatory? Section 8(a)(2) of the National Labor Relations Act prohibits employer domination of unions. In *Electromation, Inc.*, 309 N.L.R.B. 990 (1992), *enforced*, 35 F.3d 1148 (7th Cir. 1994), the employer, in response to opposition by a significant group of employees to a newly promulgated attendance policy, created a number of joint employee-management "Action Committees" to deal with various workplace issues. Finding the Action Committees to be labor organizations that dealt with the

employer about conditions of employment, the NLRB found that their creation and continued existence constituted domination in violation of Section 8(a)(2). In 1996, President Clinton vetoed the so-called TEAM Act that would have amended Section 8(a)(2) by adding a proviso that in situations where the employees were not represented by a union, "that it shall not constitute or be evidence of an unfair labor practice . . . for an employer to establish, assist, maintain, or participate in any organization . . . in which employees . . . participate, to address matters of mutual interest, including, but not limited to, issues of quality, productivity, efficiency, and safety and health, and which does not claim . . . to be the exclusive bargaining representative of the employees. . . . " How would organizations set up under TEAM differ from German works councils?

3. If the United States were to provide for works councils, what effect would their existence have on unions? In Germany, the unions have come to be very involved in them. Would that be true in the United States as well? Or would works councils operate as an alternative to unions? Although employers supported the TEAM amendments to Section 8(a)(2) and unions opposed them, what would their responses be to a proposal to provide for works councils on the German model?

4. As German collective agreements come to be frameworks structuring but not specifying the exact terms and conditions of employment that then are subject to works agreements between the employer and its works council, will the collective agreement eventually be reduced to an agreement setting wages, salary, and total labor costs, but leaving to a works agreement the specifics of how those total labor costs are allocated at individual workplaces. This would give employers the "carrot" of eliminating price competition with other employers covered by the collective agreement without hindering their flexibility in achieving the most efficient means of operating at the workplace level.

4. Workers Representation in Corporate Governance

The final step that makes it clear that employees are treated as stakeholders in their employers is that workers are represented on the supervisory boards of their employers. There are two levels of boards of directors for German corporations. At the highest level, the supervisory board appoints the members of the management board and supervises the activities of that board. The management board is responsible for the day-to-day operation of the company.

Four different statutes set up the corporate structure for different types of entities. The oldest, the Montan Codetermination Statute of 1951, applies to the mining, iron and steel businesses. Supervisory boards have eleven members, with five chosen by shareholders and five by employees, plus a chair. The Codetermination Extension Statute of 1956 extends the Montan law to companies that manage employers covered by the Montan law. The Works Council Statute of 1952 applies to smaller employers with between five hundred and two thousand employees. Employees of employers covered by the Works Council Statute select one-third of the supervisory board under this law.

The more generally applicable statute, the Codetermination Statute of 1976, applies to companies organized in Germany that are stock companies, limited partnerships that issue shares or limited liability and companies that normally employee at least two thousand employees working in Germany. In 1996, 728 companies with an estimated five million employees were covered by this act. GERMAN LABOUR LAW at 216. Under this law, half of the supervisory board is made up of representatives of employees, with the unions represented in the company having two seats while the employees elect the rest of the employee representatives. Employee representatives are predominately members of unions. Only about 3 percent are not. Weiss, *Labor Law*, at 324. The chairman and vice chairman of the supervisory board (as well as the labor director who sits on the management board) are selected by the supervisory board. The chairman and vice chairman must be elected by two-thirds majority of the supervisory board. If that fails, the representatives of the shareholders select the chairman and the representatives of the employees select the vice chairman. INTERNATIONAL LABOR & EMPLOYMENT LAW at 4–69 to 71. The other members of the management board are elected by majority vote of the whole supervisory board. GERMAN LABOUR LAW at 212. The 1976 Codetermination Act was held by the Federal Constitutional Court not to be an unconstitutional intrusion on the right of private property or the right to freedom of association. *Id.* at 218.

The employee and shareholder representatives on the supervisory board have equal status. "Employee and shareholder representatives on the supervisory board are co-equals. The law assigns identical rights and obligations to either group. Employee representatives are privy to any information accessible to members of the supervisory board." Weiss, *Labor Law*, at 324. They share a goal of acting in the "interest of the enterprise" but that interest includes the interest of the employees of the enterprise. Although "interest of the enterprise" was formerly "understood as referring solely to the interests of the capital owners, it is today generally accepted as covering employee interests as well. However, the standard has become so malleable that it is difficult to delineate the permissible scope of the board's activities." *Id.* at 325.

Worker representation on the supervisory board works in tandem with the system of works councils. "In practice, at least some of the employee representatives on the supervisory board belong to the work force of the enterprise and in most cases are also works council members. On the whole, this has strengthened both. . . . " *Id.* at 326. Employee representatives have the right to deal with all issues coming before it, but "employee representatives focus primarily on the social aspects of company policies and less on economic and financial strategies that lead to basic management decisions." *Id.*

A duty of secrecy applies to all members. "Thus, employee representatives are unable to communicate with their constituency, discuss issues with them, listen to their views, and to transmit these views to the supervisory board. . . . The duty of secrecy even prevents employee representatives on the supervisory board from supplying information to the works council." GERMAN LABOUR LAW at 219.

Notes

1. The employee representatives on the supervisory board are not necessarily share-holders in the employer and the other members are not necessarily employees of the employer. Is this the best way to make sure that both the interests of shareholders and employees are taken into account in selecting the management board and setting the overall direction of the employer? In the United States, the closest mechanism to German codetermination is the possibility that employees as a group can become major shareholders of their employers through Employee Stock Option Plans (ESOPs). As shareholders, employees have an incentive to take on the perspective of owners. Some employers are completely owned by their employees through ESOPs. William C. Taylor, These Workers Act Like Owners (Because They

Are), http://www.nytimes.com/2006/05/21/business/yourmoney/21mgmt.html. But any employees who are selected for the corporate board of directors are chosen by the shareholders. Does this mean that in 100 percent employee-owned corporations, employees who sit on the board of directors have a duty to put shareholders' interests ahead of employee interests, even if all the shareholders are employees?

In 1994, when United Airlines was on the brink of bankruptcy, management and some but not all of its unions agreed to adopt an ESOP as a way of giving covered employees stock in the company in lieu of higher wages. The Flight Attendants and non-union employees were not covered and the plan was to last for five years. At first things went well, but in December 2002, the company filed for bankruptcy. That made all the company stock, including that held by employees pursuant to the ESOP plan, essentially worthless. Although United Airlines has become the poster child for why ESOPs are not a good idea, the supporters of ESOPs have a different view: basically, that neither management nor its labor unions were truly committed to transform the culture of the workplace so that employees in fact took ownership. *See* Farhad Manjoo, United's ESOP Fable: Did Employee Stock Ownership Drive the Airline into Bankruptcy?, http://dir.salon.com/story/tech/feature/2002/12/12/esop/index2.html.

2. Should the corporate laws of the United States be amended to provide for employee representation on the board of directors? U.S. corporate law provides only one level of corporate boards. If the United States were to consider providing for management representation of employees, should it also adopt the two-tier approach to corporate governance that Germany uses?

3. The shareholder and employee representatives supposedly have equal status. But, of course, there are likely to be substantial economic differences between members of each group. Does that make the employee representatives vulnerable to manipulation by management? In 2005, the head of VW's works council and member of the VW supervisory board, Klaus Volkert, was forced to step down after reports surfaced that VW's management had bribed union representatives with vacations and prostitutes to get their support for cost-cutting measures. VW's director of human resources, Peter Hartz, was also forced to resign over the scandal. Jeffrey Fleishman, *German Businesses Not Immune to Scandal*, Los Angeles Times, August 24, 2005, p. A13. In the United States, it is a violation of section 8(a)(3) of the N.L.R.A. for the same employee to serve in both union leadership and management positions. *See* Jeffrey Mfg. Co., 208 N.L.R.B. 78, 83 (1974) (employee in supervisory position cannot serve as local union president).

D. ANTIDISCRIMINATION

Antidiscrimination law is set forth in a number of different laws, including the Constitution and a number of statutes, which make somewhat of a patchwork. The German Constitution prohibits employment discrimination because of gender, race, language, homeland, national origin, beliefs, religion, and political views. Article 3 provides:

(1) All persons shall be equal before the law.
(2) Men and women shall have equal rights. The state shall promote the actual implementation of equal rights for women and men and take steps to eliminate disadvantages that now exist.

(3) No person shall be favored or disfavored because of sex, parentage, race, language, homeland and origin, faith, or religious or political opinions. No person shall be disfavored because of disability.

The Constitution does not apply directly to private action. "However, since the judiciary is bound to the rules of the German Constitution, all judges must interpret and apply the national laws in light of the German Constitution. Thus, Articles 3.1 and 3.3 have – according to German constitutional doctrine – 'limited indirect horizontal effect,' i.e. the constitutional anti-discrimination clauses must be applied by civil law judges in the context of interpreting general clauses in civil law." Raphael Won-Pil Suh & Richard Bales, *German and European Employment Discrimination Policy*, 9 OREGON REV. OF INT'L L. (forthcoming) (hereinafter, *German & European Employment Discrimination Policy*).

Several statutes ban some discrimination in some situations. Section 75 of the Works Constitution Act of 1975, the basic law establishing works councils, requires that employers and their works councils treat employees fairly and that "nobody is discriminated against because of his or her religion, nationality, origin, political or trade union activities or opinions, gender, or sexual orientation." *Id.* Limited to workplaces with works councils, section 75 is also limited to current employees and does not protect against discrimination against applicants for jobs. *Id.* In response to the first gender equality directive promulgated by the EU, Directive, 76/207/EEC (1976), Germany in 1980 added section 612a to the Civil Law Code to prohibit sex discrimination. Section 611a, however, allows employers to discriminate if gender is an "indispensable requirement" for the job. This defense is a mixture of what in the United States is the Bona Fide Occupational Qualification defense to intentional disparate treatment and the business necessity defense to disparate treatment discrimination, but read more broadly than either. Thus, an employer can justify its sex discrimination if authentic performance of the job depends on sex, that is, the actor/actress defense aspect of the BFOQ defense. Business necessity can be shown by demonstrating customer preference for service by one gender. This seems broader than the allowed scope of that defense in the United States. *Id.* Section 612(3) of the Civil Law Code requires equal pay for work of equal value:

> In a contract of employment, it is prohibited to use as a criterion the sex of the employee when awarding remuneration that is less than that of an employee of another sex, for the same job or for a similar job. Lower contractual remuneration will not be justified by the fact that particular protective measures must be complied with, taking account of the sex of the employee.

Sexual harassment is prohibited by the Employees Protection Act of 1994, with harassment defined as "any intentional sexually determined behavior which violates the dignity of employees at the workplace" as well as sexually determined touching and sexual remarks. *Id.* The act has been criticized as ineffective, however, because it does not provide for compensation to the harassed employee against her employer. All the act does is provide the harassed employee with the right to stop work without any loss of salary for as long as the employer fails to stop the harassment. *Id.* Civil Law Code section 626 – "A person who willfully causes damage to another in a manner contrary to public policy is bound to compensate the other for the damage" – has been used to remedy intentional discrimination because of sexual orientation. Franck Selbmann, *The Drafting of a Law against Discrimination on the Grounds of Racial or Ethnic Origin in Germany*, EUROPEAN CENTRE FOR MINORITY ISSUES, Issue 3/2002, p, 4.

Section 81.2 of the Ninth Book of the Social Law Code prohibits employment discrimination because of disability. A disabled person is one whose physical functions, mental capacities or psychological health are highly likely to deviate for more than six months from the norm typical for that person's age, and whose participation in the life of society is therefore restricted. Only severely disabled persons are protected against discrimination, which means their degree of disability is at least 50 percent. *Id.* Severely disabled employees have a right to be reasonably accommodated unless the accommodation would impose an undue burden on the employer or if the accommodation conflicts with safety or other civil service laws. The Severely Disabled Persons Act requires that employers with more than twenty employees must make sure that 5 percent of all its jobs are filled with people with disabilities. In lieu of meeting the required level of jobs reserved for the disabled, employers must make a monthly payment for each unfilled job. The termination of a disabled person requires the prior approval of the local social services agency in addition to the normal restraints that apply to all terminations. INTERNATIONAL LABOR & EMPLOYMENT LAWS at 4–93.

The German courts have read these laws against discrimination rather expansively. In 4 AZ R 30/92, September 23, 1992, the Federal Labor Court (Fourth Senate) found a violation of equal pay for men and women. Men and women worked in the warehouse of the defendant. Despite performing substantially the same work, the employer voluntarily paid nearly half the men but only one tenth of the women at a higher pay scale than what was required by the collective bargaining agreement. The fact that men sometimes drove a forklift track to handle heavy merchandise did not justify overturning the finding that the work was substantially equal. Although the state labor court had not made a finding that the employer acted with the intent to discriminate, that did not undermine the finding for the plaintiffs.

> The defendant argues unsuccessfully that there cannot be a violation of section 612, paragraph 3, of the Civil Code without awareness of, if not intent regarding, discrimination on the grounds of sex since no intent was shown here. The *Land* Labor Court failed to make factual findings on this point.
>
> The defendant, however, does not admit that a finding of discrimination on the grounds of sex can be shown to exist by means other than proof of the discriminatory intent of those concerned. Under section 612, paragraph 3, third sentence, read together with section 611 a, paragraph 1, third sentence, such a finding can be arrived at by establishing auxiliary facts that lead to an inference that there was such discrimination. Discrimination must then be assumed unless that inference is refuted by objective reasons for the treatment that are unrelated to sex. This was the approach followed by the *Land* Labor Court in a permissible manner.
>
> The plaintiffs have demonstrated auxiliary facts that lead one to suppose that there was discrimination on the grounds of sex. According to the case law of the European Court [of Justice] (e.g. judgment of 13 May 1986-*Bilka Kaufhaus*), a substantially greater number of members of one sex among those who are disadvantaged serves as an indication of discrimination on the ground of sex. In such case, the court should presume the existence of discrimination unless the employer demonstrates that there were objective reasons unrelated to sex for the difference. In the present case, with a total number of 28 men and women employed in the warehouse, the random distribution of the sexes between wage groups is unlikely to be so uneven.

So-called indirect discrimination can be the basis for a finding of a violation of the equal pay requirement. In 54ZR 598/90, October 9, 1991, plaintiffs challenged the exclusion of sick pay for part-time workers based on the EU directive on equal work, Directive 75/117/EEC, February 10, 1975.

The *Land* Labor Court found that in the Federal Republic 85 percent of all employees in commerce and industry who work ten hours a week or less are women. The disadvantages resulting from section 1 of the Wages Act excluding sick pay for part-time employees derive from the sex or the sex role of the woman. Part-time work for very limited hours continues to be women's work. The traditional allocation of roles among the sexes still generally allots educational and domestic tasks to women. These societal circumstances make it difficult, particularly for married women, to reconcile full-time employment with family burdens. Often the only solution is to work part-time for limited hours; the short daily working time and its flexibility make it possible to harmonize gainful employment and family obligations. The reason for entering into an employment relationship of this kind is made clear by the very fact that this form of employment is used so overwhelmingly by married women. This then means that the high proportion of women among those employed for very limited hours is directly related to the traditional division of roles among the sexes.

This violates the EU Directive unless it is shown that the legal rules in question are justified by objective factors unrelated to discrimination on the ground of sex. This has not been done. The exclusion of workers employed for very limited hours is not justified either on the ground that this group of employees is less integrated into or less attached to the undertaking than other employees. The only difference between the two groups of employees is the length of their working hours.

The appellants argue that the earnings of these women constitute only a second income, since they are inadequate for providing a family with economic security. It is unnecessary in their view, to provide security in case of illness. However, this argument misjudges the actual situation in the labor market. For many workers, part-time employment is their only possible gainful activity. These workers are dependent on such employment for their subsistence and hence are in need of protection in the same manner as full-time employees.

1 BVR 258/86

Federal Constitutional Court
(First Senate)
November 16, 1993

[A professor at a technical college advertised a job opening for a fitter or toolmaker. A woman who had completed training as a fitter applied. She was the only woman applicant. The notice said that all who meet the formal requirements would be interviewed. Instead, the professor interviewed eight of the forty male applicants but not the plaintiff. Two male applicants were selected. When she inquired about the job, she was told, over the phone and in writing, that the job was not suitable for a woman. Plaintiff's complaint was dismissed by the local labor court, which dismissal was affirmed by the *Land* Labor Court. Appeal was taken to the Federal Constitutional Court.]

This complaint is well founded. The contested judgment infringes the fundamental right of the complainant derived from Article 3, paragraph 2 of the Constitution. According to that provision men and women have equal rights. This is designed to preclude discrimination on the basis of sex, which is also prohibited by paragraph 3. However, paragraph 2 establishes the principle that equal rights are applicable to social conditions in a wider sense. Its scope is intended not merely to do away with legal rules that attach advantages or disadvantages to the characteristics of a particular sex, but also to achieve equal rights for the members of the two sexes in the future. Its aim is to equalize their conditions of life.

Section 611a of the Civil Code serves the same objectives. It extends the prohibition of discrimination to private employment relationships and seeks to ensure equal opportunities for women in their occupation, particularly in the establishment of an employment relationship.

The interpretation and application of that provision are matters for the courts having jurisdiction in the field of the dispute; their decisions cannot, in principle, be reviewed by the Constitutional Court. The role of the latter is only to determine whether, in the interpretation and application of ordinary law, these courts have failed to recognize the influence of constitutional rights. This may be so as regards the interpretation and application not only of legal provisions circumscribing constitutional rights but also of those laws enacted to give substance to the constitutional protection. In the case of provisions intended to develop constitutional protection, the relevant constitutional right is violated if a court's interpretation and application fail fundamentally to achieve the protective purpose of the Constitution. At the same time, it is not the role of the Constitutional Court to verify the manner in which the courts provide protection on the basis of ordinary law or to determine whether their interpretation guarantees the best possible protection.

The *Land* Labor Court fundamentally misjudged the protective purpose of Article 3, paragraph 2 of the Constitution in its interpretation and application of Section 611a, paragraph 1, of the Civil Code. As interpreted below, that section would not provide effective protection against discrimination on the ground of sex for a job. Yet a different interpretation, which would make the prohibition of discrimination effective, is possible and readily compatible with the letter and spirit of the provision.

That the *Land* Labor Court did not adequately examine the possibility that there had been discrimination in the procedures leading to the appointment is not compatible with Article 3, paragraph 2 of the Constitution. For instance, it did not consider the question whether the failure of the employer to invite the complainant for an interview, contrary to the original notice of the job opening, could constitute an infringement of section 611a, paragraph 1 of the Civil Code.

That section prohibits discrimination on the ground of sex in actions relating to establishing the employment relationship. If the chances of a female candidate have been diminished because of discriminatory selection procedures, it becomes irrelevant whether sex actually played a demonstrable role in the final decision. Such an interpretation of section 611a, paragraph 1, assures effective protection against discrimination, as sought by Article 3, paragraph 2 of the Constitution. If, in respect of hiring decisions, the consideration of procedural steps prior to the hiring decision were left out of the analysis, the employer could protect against discriminatory measures in those steps from having any legal consequence by giving, ex post facto, objective reasons for its decision. By manipulating its prior procedures, the employer could reduce the chances of candidates whom it regards as less suitable because of that person's sex so that its final decision becomes practically beyond attack.

There is discrimination on the ground of sex within the meaning of Article 3, paragraph 3 of the Constitution whenever an unequal treatment in law is related to sex. It is irrelevant whether there were reasons in addition to sex for the inequality. If compliance with the constitutional prohibition of discrimination is to be required of the employer in decisions regarding hiring – and that is the purpose of Section 611a, paragraph 1 of the Civil Code – the employer must be barred from taking account of the sex of an applicant, to the latter's detriment, in its decision. That is, however, the case whenever, in the combination of all the reasons influencing the decision, the sex of the unsuccessful candidate constitutes a negative and the other sex a positive criterion.

Furthermore, the circumstances which the *Land* Labor Court considered sufficient to rebut the inference of discrimination on the ground of sex are incompatible with Article 3, paragraph 2 of the Constitution. The Court's interpretation in that manner largely prevents the legislative prohibition of discrimination from serving its function of safeguarding constitutional rights.

The court should have demanded that the employer prove a special justification for the belated introduction of new criteria. Otherwise, the employer could exonerate itself in almost every case with the result that the judicial enforcement of the prohibition of discrimination would encounter a practically insurmountable obstacle.

The employer may seek workers with experience doing the particular job or, on the contrary, it can prefer novices whose capacities will be developed on the job. It may prefer older or younger workers. It may attach importance to the ability to work in a team, or rather value work performed individually. A varied curriculum vitae may be a criterion for selection or, conversely, long experience in a particular occupation. It is also within the employer's discretion to call for a specific combination of qualities and to give different weights to particular qualifications.

An interpretation of section 611a, paragraph 1 of the Civil Code, which would give the employer so wide a choice of reasons in answer to the assertion of discrimination, runs counter to the protective purpose of Article 3, paragraph 2 of the Constitution. That purpose can be fulfilled only if it is so interpreted as to require that the employer effectively refute the existence of discrimination. A reason advanced after the fact to explain the preference for an application of someone of the other sex can only be regarded as "objective" in the meaning of the provision if the particular circumstances show that the employer has not merely used that reason as a pretext. Such a circumstance might be the fact that, in the course of the procedure of selection, the tasks of the job and hence the required qualifications have changed. It may also be possible that one applicant appears virtually predestined for the job, but that this was unforeseeable at the time of the call for applications. Only by asserting such circumstances and, as appropriate, proving them, can the employer refute the allegation that the sex of the rejected candidate influenced his decision negatively.

A particularly critical evaluation of criteria advanced ex post facto is appropriate when these criteria typically can rarely not be met by persons of the same sex as the rejected candidate. This is always the situation of the prerequisite of "long experience" when the occupation in question has until recently been mainly exercised by persons of the opposite sex. The occupation of fitter is a traditional male preserve. The German Council for Women states in its submission that, between 1973 and 1985, only just over one per cent of the trainees in that occupation were women. Therefore the number of women who could acquire greater experience as fitters was minimal.

_____

Notes

1. How did plaintiff establish prima facie case of sex discrimination? Were the responses on the phone and in writing that the job was not suitable for women necessary to prove her case? Would showing the failure to interview plaintiff while

interviewing eight men be sufficient to establish a prima facie case? Or was it changing the announced procedure of interviewing all applicants meeting the objective
job requirements when a women applied that made out the case? Would plaintiff's
showing here suffice to establish a prima facie case of sex discrimination in the
United States? Does that depend on whether the lower court made a finding of
fact that the employer did not act with an intent to discriminate? Would disparate
impact theory under U.S. law apply here?

2.   How could the employer carry its burden of proving that there was no discrim-
     ination? What objective explanations for changing the posted procedures would
     suffice?

3.   It is discrimination on the basis of sex to fail to hire an applicant because she is
     pregnant. In 2AZR 227/92, October 10, 1992, the Federal Labor Court (Second
     Senate), plaintiff was recruited to replace a pregnant employee. When asked if she
     was pregnant, she said no, even though at that time she was five months' pregnant.
     When the employer later learned of her pregnancy, it claimed that the employment
     contract was invalid because she lied. She sued and the court found in her favor.
     "A pregnant woman who, in answer to a question before she is hired, untruthfully
     denies she is pregnant, has a right to the job unless the employer is entitled to contest
     the validity of hiring a pregnant person [by showing the applicant is "objectively
     unsuited for the work"]."

4.   The Maternity Leave Statute of 1968 provides for pregnant women to take a paid
     leave six weeks before their due date and for eight weeks after giving birth. Except
     for limited duration employment relationships that expire, women cannot be ter-
     minated during pregnancy. Time on pregnancy leave counts toward entitlement
     to vacation. Child rearing leave is available to mothers for up to three years after
     the birth. The employer is not required to pay wages during the leave, but, for up
     to two years, the social security system pays the mother up to € 300 per month.

5.   In May 2006, the government agreed to implement the most recent EU
     directives on discrimination with the General Equal Treatment Act (*Allgemeines
     Gleichbehand-lungsgesetz* AGG). It adds new prohibitions against employment dis-
     crimination because of ethnic background, philosophy of life (*Weltanschauung*),
     disability, age, sexual orientation, and harassment. In an action brought by
     the EU Commission against Germany under Article 226 of the EC Treaty,
     the European Court of Justice had ruled On April 28, 2005, that Germany
     has breached its obligation to transpose Directive 2000/43/EC into German
     law,   http://ec.europa.eu/employment_social/news/2005/apr/courtruling_en.html.
     The new law uses the definitions of discrimination familiar in German law – direct
     and indirect discrimination – but applies them to these new categories. Harassment
     is defined as any conduct related to the grounds of prohibited discrimination done
     with the purpose or effect of violating the dignity of a person and creating an
     intimidating, hostile, degrading, or offensive environment.

E. LABOR COURTS

The labor courts are the principal means of conflict resolution in both individual and
collective labor disputes. The legal basis for labor courts is the Labor Courts Act of 1953, as
amended in 1979. GERMAN LABOUR LAW at 122. According to the Act on Court Procedure

in Labor Matters, the Federal Labor Court has the sole power to develop labor law. Thus, the labor courts have been a principal source for the development of labor and employment law even though Germany is a civil code jurisdiction. *Id.* at 38.

There are now 123 labor courts of first instance, that is, trial courts, and a total of 19 (*Land*) labor courts for the states that serve as courts of second instance, that is, courts of appeal of questions of fact and law. The Federal Labor Court sits atop the other labor courts and only hears appeals of questions of law. The Federal Constitutional Court is available for appeals of constitutional questions arising from decisions of the Federal Labor Court. Where questions of European Union law are implicated, all of the labor courts can refer the matter to the European Court of Justice for a preliminary ruling on the EU law question.

Labor courts of the first instance are made up of panels of three with a career judge as the chair and two lay judges, one each from the employer and employee sides. *Land* Labor Courts have exclusive jurisdiction for appeals of decisions of the labor courts of the first instance, with panels composed of a career judge and two lay judges. The Federal Labor Court has ten panels, called "Senates," made up of three career judges and two lay judges, with one from the employer and one from the employee side. There is also the so-called Large Senate made up of the Federal Labor Court President, one career judge from each Senate and six lay judges, again split three and three for the employer and the employee side. At every level, the judges all have equal voting authority.

The career judges at the courts of first and second instance are typically appointed by the state Minister of Labour and Social Affairs. The minister, along with the state Minister of Justice, picks from a list prepared by an advisory committee made up of equal representatives of the state's career judges, employers associations and trade unions. Career judges for the Federal Labor Court are appointed by the Federal President based on joint proposals of the Federal Minister of Labour and Social Affairs and an election committee made up of the state labor ministers and of the election committee for federal judges. After an initial three years of service, career judges, who have all studied law and passed two bar exams, receive an appointment until they reach retirement age.

State lay judges are appointed for a four-year term and are selected by the state labor minister from lists submitted by labor and employer groups from their respective jurisdiction. Lay judges for the Federal Labor Court typically are chosen from among experienced state lay judges. Just as career judges, lay judges are to be independent of the group from which they come.

The labor courts play a comprehensive role in settling disputes that arise over employment questions, especially individual employee claims. "Labour courts have exclusive jurisdiction in matters involving civil legal disputes between employer and employee arising from an employment relationship, in questions relating to the existence or nonexistence of an employment contract, as regards obligations remaining after the dissolution of an employment contract, and, in addition, in civil legal disputes involving torts, in so far as these are connected with the employment relationship." *Id.* at 129–130.

The largest share of cases filed with labor courts involve individual employee claims. Employees have three weeks to challenge a termination under the Termination Protection Act. INTERNATIONAL LABOR & EMPLOYMENT LAW at 4–24. Although the general rules of civil court procedure are followed, the 1957 Labor Courts Act modified those procedures to provide simple, timely and inexpensive procedures. Every case starts with a conciliation hearing, held by the chairperson of the panel. Almost one-third of the cases are settled at this stage. If the case does not settle, it goes to trial, with the chair organizing the trial, which typically includes oral testimony of the witnesses. GERMAN LABOUR LAW at 128.

This extensive and exclusive jurisdiction of labor courts extends to all collective bargaining issues. "Labour courts are exclusively competent in all disputes of rights between parties to a collective agreement or between them and third parties, whether it concerns a dispute arising from collective agreements or whether it concerns a dispute about the existence of collective agreements. The same is true for disputes referring to industrial conflicts [such as strikes and lockouts]. The labour courts are not only competent in all matters concerning the works constitution . . . as well as in matters referring to the election procedure for employee representatives on the supervisory board, but also in matters concerning the capacity to conclude collective agreements and collective bargaining jurisdiction of employees' and employers' organizations." GERMAN LABOUR LAW at 222.

A boundary between labor courts and the general civil courts is that, as to corporate law questions, labor courts only deal with issues arising from employee representatives on the supervisory board while the general civil courts enforce German corporate law generally. *Id.* Similarly, civil courts have jurisdiction over commercial disputes involving contracts between individuals and businesses, such as franchise agreements. But the labor courts have jurisdiction over cases brought by employees and employee-like persons against entities with whom they have contracts. *Id.*

Different procedures are followed in collective cases than in individual employee cases. Conciliation is at the option of the chairperson and "it is up to the court itself to ascertain the underlying facts from the petitions of interested parties and to take evidence." *Id.* at 222. Although in the minority in terms of numbers of cases on the dockets of labor courts, collective labor law cases tend to have more significant impact than individual employment cases.

F. PRIVACY

The right to privacy is based on the Constitution and federal statutory law on data protection. The Constitution protects personal data, with the individual in control of its dissemination. Carefully drafted legislation, however, can provide for limited disclosure for specific well-justified bases. This constitutional right is protected by a private cause of action.

The Federal Data Protection Act, which was updated to comply with the EU Directive in May 2001, prohibits the use of personal data by employers unless its use is limited for specific purposes of the employment relationship, such as timekeeping, or the employee gives permission for its use. Even stricter rules apply to particularly sensitive personal data such as race, ethnic origin, political opinions including party membership, religious or philosophical views, union membership, health and sexual matters such as cohabitation. INTERNATIONAL LABOR & EMPLOYMENT LAW at 4–27. The federal statute also limits the permissible transmission of such personal data outside of the employer. Video surveillance in public, but not private, places is also regulated by the federal law. *Id.*

Based on Article 2(1) of the Constitution – "Everyone has the right to the free development of his personality insofar as he does not violate the rights of others or offend against the constitutional order or the moral code" – German courts have developed the right to have one's personality respected. CONSTITUTION & LABOR LAW IN GERMANY at 187. Based on that general right, there has developed the right of self-determination of an individual to her personal data, which restricts employers in their getting information from job applicants. Thus, "the Courts only allow questions that are in the employer's justified and approvable interest [that] need to be answered because of the employment relationship to be established." *Id.* at 188. The applicant need not answer inadmissible questions and can answer such questions with a lie. "Only a false answer to a rightfully asked question can be considered fraudulent misrepresentation with the legal consequence that the employer may contest the contract of employment." *Id.* Thus, the labor courts would protect individual employees from being discharged if the employer tries to rescind the employment contract on the grounds of misrepresentation.

In a case involving Wal-Mart, a *Land* labor court recently found that the implementation of a code of ethics for employees violated the privacy or personality rights of the employees. The personality rights invaded included a requirement that employees whistleblow breaches of the code by other employees and that prohibited private romantic relationships with fellow workers and required disclosure of information about family members' jobs and financial investments. *See* Dr. Gerlind Wisskirchen, Christopher Jordan & Alexander Bissels, Cross-Border Ethics Codes: The Case of Wal-Mart in Germany, http://www.abanet.org/labor/2005.

10 France

At the end of the century during which labor law has developed and at the dawn of a new one, it appears difficult for western European countries to develop optimistic views about the evolution of employment rights and social protection. In this sense, fears about the future are underpinned by a glorified past and a troubled present.

. . .

. . . . Another phenomenon is the ever-invading process of market logic. The market tends to become the only logic by which any exchange of goods is carried out or any service is provided. Under this trend competition law becomes the prominent discipline and any element that could disrupt the functioning of the market is considered harmful. In this approach, which is greatly influenced by neo-liberal ideology, labor law is considered as having a disruptive effect on the market. In France, this conception damages the idea that some services, being of general interest . . . justify restrictions of competition and cannot be organized on pure market logic.

Christophe Vigneau, *Labor Law Between Changes and Continuity*, 25 COMP. LAB. L. & POL'Y J. 129, 129 & 133 (2003).

A. INTRODUCTION

The French Constitution, the basis of the Fifth Republic, was approved by the populace and promulgated in 1958. The Parliament does not have the predominant role in the government that it occupied in the Constitution of the Fourth Republic. In former regimes, the Parliament had the power to determine law. Section 34 of the Constitution lists the areas in which the Parliament can legislate. All subjects not listed in Section 34 come within the executive branch's regulatory power. The president is directly elected by the people of France and is more powerful than under past regimes. The president has the power to dissolve the National Assembly, which is the main chamber of the Parliament. The president also exercises significant power through the appointment of the prime minister. *See generally* Michael Despax & Jacques Rojot, *France* in 6 INTERNATIONAL ENCYCLOPAEDIA FOR LABOUR LAW AND INDUSTRIAL RELATIONS at 17-18 (Roger Blanpain ed., Kluwer Law Int'l 1987) [hereinafter Despax & Rojot].

For help with translations, we thank Professor Olivier Moréteau and his wife Marie Antoinette. Professor Moréteau is the Russell B. Long Eminent Scholars Academic Chair and Director of the Center of Civil Law Studies at the Paul M. Hebert Law Center of Louisiana State University.

French labor law is, in part, a manifestation of the nation's social democratic political ideology. French law provides numerous and substantial benefits and protections to employees. France's comprehensive social security system imposes a substantial obligation on employers to contribute to the social security system. Although both employers and employees pay social security contributions, a significant portion of contributions is made by employers, which equals an additional expense for employers of about 40 percent over employee wages. Contrasting the United States and Western European nations on this issue, one writer observes as follows:

> European unions and social democratic parties are not willing to support a proliferation of low-paid, non-union jobs. Instead, Europe subsidizes the unemployed through substantial transfer payments from the employed to the unemployed. Europe sustains higher living standards for both the employed and the unemployed than does the United States. Undoubtedly, such policies can socially marginalize (if not economically) the unemployed, though public policy places the burden disproportionately on young, first-time job seekers – thus creating a generational queuing to enter lifetime employment. The return benefit for this cost is the maintenance of higher overall living standards (though the discontent of marginalized immigrant youth is the Achilles heel of this "queuing" strategy of unemployment). Obviously, this juggling act cannot continue much longer.
>
> Joseph M. Schwartz, *Democracy Against the Free Market: The Enron Crisis and the Politics of Global Deregulation*, 35 CONN. L. REV. 1097, 1114 (2003).

We will return to efforts in French labor law to address the issues of youth unemployment, and more specifically immigrant youth unemployment, in this chapter in the discussion of the recently repealed First Job Contract.

One hallmark of French labor law is the substantial consultation and participation rights employees are guaranteed in the management of the business. The notion that employees have a right to information and consultation about the management of the business is more predominant in France than in many other European Union countries.

French law governing employment security/termination of employment differs significantly from the law of the United States. In the United States, this relationship is generally governed by "employment at will," meaning that an employer may terminate an employee for good reason, bad reason, or no reason at all. In France, by contrast, employees generally can be terminated for real and serious grounds or "just cause." In addition to the substantive requirement of just cause for termination, French labor law also imposes numerous procedural steps to effectuate a termination and costs in the form of indemnities. But French labor law has not always been so protective of employees, and as discussed further later, under the increasing pressures of globalized competition, it may not remain as protective as it is now.

The highly developed and protective French labor law evolved from inauspicious beginnings. As with most nations, the need for substantial labor regulation came about with industrialization. *See* Vigneau, *supra*, at 130. The French Civil Code of 1804 had only three sections on lease of services and fifty sections on the lease of things. This dearth of law in part reflected the reluctance of liberal doctrine to have the state intervene in labor relationships. Industrialization demonstrated a need for regulation, however, and was the basis for overcoming the reluctance. Moreover, although being employed is of paramount concern to people today, being employed "was nothing to be proud of" two hundred years ago. "It is only in recent times, following profound changes in society and widespread industrialization, that the status of the employee has become an enviable one." J. Rojot, *Security of Employment and Employability*, in COMPARATIVE LABOUR LAW AND INDUSTRIAL RELATIONS IN INDUSTRIALIZED MARKET ECONOMIES 427, 427 (Blanpain & Engels eds., Kluwer Law Int'l, 2001) [hereinafter COMPARATIVE LABOUR LAW]. For almost a century after the French Revolution, the law prohibited collective organization and action. In 1840, Dr. Vuillermè presented a famous report on the miserable condition of workers employed in manufacturing to the Academy of Moral and Political Sciences. The shocking detail of the Vuillermè report, including the treatment of children, was the catalyst for a legal revolution. The development of labor law can be traced through the Second Empire, which in the act of 25 May 1864 made strikes legal by eliminating the crime of conspiracy. Many labor laws, including those protecting unions and establishing collective bargaining as the usual means of establishing terms and conditions of employment, were enacted during the Third Republic between World War I and World War II. After the German occupation and the Vichy government, labor law restarted its development with the Constitution of 1946, the preamble of which guaranteed the individual and collective rights of workers. The act of 11 February 1950 established a guaranteed minimum wage and a new legal framework for collective bargaining. During the Fifth Republic, the pace of labor law reform increased. After the economic crisis of 1972–74 and soaring unemployment levels unseen since the end of World War II, numerous labor laws were enacted, including two revisions of the law regarding dismissals. *See generally* Despax & Rojot, *supra*, at 34-36; *see also* Vigneau, *supra*, at 131.

Recent events in France illustrate the tension between France's popularly embraced job protections and the impetus to reduce employment security in an effort to combat unemployment. Prime Minister Dominique de Villepin, on taking office in June 2005, said that unemployment is "the true evil" and pledged to "mobilize every asset of our economic and industrial policy" in the battle against unemployment. *See* Eric Pape & Christopher Dickey, *Rising Barriers*, NEWSWEEK, Int'l ed., March 25, 2006. The First Job Contract ("*Contrat Premiere Embauche*" or CPE) approaches U.S. employment at will for workers under twenty-six years of age. This change, part of the Law on Equal Pay Between Men and Women, was approved by the Parliament on 23 February 2006. The unemployment rate for the age group is around 25 percent. *See Students, Unions Stage Protests Over France's New Labor Law Contracts*, DAILY LAB. REP. (BNA) No. 53, at A-6 (March 20, 2006). The reaction to this reduction in job protection for a particular group of workers was massive and sometimes violent demonstrations by students and unions. *See Unrest Flares as Students Press Villepin to Rescind Jobs Legislation*, INT'L HERALD TRIBUNE, March 14, 2006. In the face of the demonstrations and strikes, the government yielded and replaced the law creating the First Job Contract with a new law that creates financial incentives for employers to hire young workers who meet educational requirements or live in designated urban areas. *See Chirac OKs Youth Employment Plan: Charter Tighten Rules on Internships*, DAILY LAB. REP. (BNA) No. 81, at A-4 (April 27, 2006). This recent saga will be discussed further below. Notwithstanding the latest resolution, the larger issue will not abate: pressures will continue (and perhaps increase) to reduce job protections in an attempt to address unemployment in the context of the global economy and competition. Because France has perhaps one of the most protective legal regimes on employment security/employment termination, it will be important to watch how this issue develops there.

A large administrative structure is necessary to implement the complex legal institutions and instruments that govern French labor law. Athough it may be more expensive for French employers to provide employees with significantly more benefits than United States employers, the French system is more predictable, which makes the risk of employment litigation far less likely. It has been suggested that the uncertainty regarding judicial interpretation of the law and the accompanying prospect of liability in the United States and the comparative certainty regarding judicial interpretation and the unlikelihood of liability in France is one factor that has led to the development, innovation, and proliferation in employment discrimination law in the United States and the "stagnation" of employment discrimination law in France until the passage of new legislation in 2001. *See* Frank Dobbin, *Do the Social Sciences Shape Corporate Anti-Discrimination Practice? The United States and France*, 23 COMP. LAB. L. & POL'Y J. 829 (2002).

French laws regarding employment are generally compiled in the *Code du Travail*, or the French Labor Code. The process of codification began in 1910. The first Labor Code was promulgated between 1920 and 1927. The current Labor Code dates to 1973, when the Assembly undertook to include in the new Labor Code previously excluded documents. The Labor Code is divided into nine parts: (1) agreements relating to employment; (2) statutory regulation of working conditions, including leaves, safety, and health; (3) placement and development of employment; (4) employee representation and professional groups; (5) labor disputes; (6) applications and controls of labor regulation; (7) special schemes (including mines and energy industry); (8) special regulations applicable to overseas French territories; and (9) French education.

Two international bodies of which France is a member have influenced French labor law. Most importantly, France is a founding member of the European Union (EU), making it subject to EU directives, regulations, and decisions of the European Court of Justice. Because French labor law must conform to EU legislation, the recent evolution of French labor law has been partly a function of the development of EU law. In 2005, France was one of two EU members (the Netherlands being the other) to hold a referendum and reject the treaty establishing the constitution for Europe. The constitution's future is uncertain. Although there would have been no new legal principles in the constitution, it would have included the Charter of Fundamental Rights. France is also a member of the International Labor Organization (ILO). France has ratified 123 out of 185 ILO conventions, giving it one of the highest ratification rates of all nations in the ILO. Although France has ratified a very high percentage of ILO conventions, it also is listed as high on noncompliance. *See* BOB HEPPLE, LABOUR LAWS AND GLOBAL TRADE 40 (Hart Pub. 2005). Thus, as with many other aspects of labor law, France contrasts with the United States, which has ratified very few ILO conventions, but is considered to be in high compliance on the few it has ratified. *Id.* at 41.

Labor disputes involving individual employment contracts are heard in the *Conseils de Prud'hommes*, or Labor Courts. Each Labor Court has four members who are not judges. Two members are appointed by pro-employer organizations while pro-employee groups appoint the other two. These members are usually not attorneys and receive very limited training in employment law. Most of their experience is gained while serving on the Labor Courts because they are appointed to five-year terms. There are two stages in the Labor Courts. In the first stage, parties must appear before a Conciliation Panel composed of representatives from each side. If the dispute is not settled at the first stage, then the dispute is heard in front of the full Labor Court consisting of two representatives from each side. The Labor Courts operate by majority vote and ties or deadlocks are a rarity. When the dispute is below a certain value (set annually by decree), a decision by a labor court is final and may be appealed only to the Cour de Cassation.[1] I Inter-national Labor & Employment Laws, at 3-15 (Keller & Darby eds. 2d ed. 2003) [hereinafter International Labor]. The Cour de Cassation does not retry the case, but may quash the judgment for error. If the dispute is above the amount, then the case may be retried by the Cour d'Appel of the same region as the Labor Court, and the decision of that court may be appealed to the Cour de Cassation on issues of law but not fact. *Id.* at 3-16.

The future of French labor law will be affected by the election of a new president in 2007. President Jacques Chirac has served since 1995.

B. INDIVIDUAL EMPLOYMENT

1. Contract Formation

In France "employment contract" is not a defined term; rather, it is a form of civil contract. Therefore it is governed by Article 1108 of the French Civil Code, which sets forth the requirements for the validity of a contract. Article 1108 provides:

> Four conditions are essential to the validity of an agreement:
> * Consent of the party who binds himself;
> * His capacity to contract;
> * A definite object (*objet certain*) forming the subject matter of the undertaking; and
> * A lawful cause for the obligation.

French courts have articulated a definition of an employment contract: "The contract of employment is the agreement by which a person agrees to put his activity at the disposal of another person under whose subordination he places himself in exchange for payment." *See* Despax & Rojot, *supra*, at 81. Generally, employment contracts may be oral; however, for disfavored employment contracts, such as a contract for a definite term, a temporary contract, or part-time work, a writing is required.

As in the United States and the United Kingdom, a contract for an indefinite period (*Contrat à Duree Indeterminee* or *CDI*) is the favored and the presumed type of employment contract. Therefore, in a typical employment formation situation, the employee is presumed to be employed indefinitely. Employment contracts for a definite period (*Contrat à Duree Determinee or CDD*) can only be formed under limited circumstances according to the French Labor Code. Such circumstances include times of temporary need related to increased business and seasonal workers. Definite term contracts cannot be used for the normal activities of the business. A recent law, Law No. 2003-591 of 2 July 2003, permits the use of definite-term contracts for temporary replacement of a company manager, some partners, or independent professionals. Definite term employment contracts must be in writing, and the definite term must be determined at the time the contract is formed. Furthermore, definite term contracts may only be renewed one time,

---

[1] The Cour de Cassation often is referred to as the French Supreme Court, but this is not correct because France has both courts of the judiciary and administrative courts. Despax & Rojot, *supra*, at 23. The Cour de Cassation is the highest court of the judiciary, and the Conseil d'Etat is the highest of the administrative courts.

but in most cases a contract and its renewal period cannot extend beyond eighteen months (twenty-four months in specific circumstances). INTERNATIONAL LABOR, *supra*, at 3-6.

Employment contracts and other employment documents implicate a requirement about use of the French language. Article L. 121-1 of the Labor Code requires that employment contracts signed in France must be written in French. Employers are required to provide translations to non-French employees, and if there is a conflict between the French version and the translation, only the version in the foreign employee's language can be used against her. An employer may not use against an employee any clause in a contract that violates the article. Additionally, Article L. 122-39-1 provides that all documents including obligations of employees or provisions that employees must know about in order to perform their jobs must be drafted in French. Those documents may be accompanied by translations. In *CGT v. GE Healthcare* (March 2, 2006), the Cour d'Appeal de Versailles ordered a branch of a company based in the United States to comply with Art. 122-39-1 for technical documents the company was distributing in France. *See French Court Fines GE Subsidiary for Providing English-Only Documents*, DAILY LAB. REP. (BNA) No. 45, at A-1 (March 8, 2006). The court of appeal ordered the employer to pay €580,000 to unions and other organizations representing the employees. The case is the first enforcement of the 1994 law involving a labor dispute at a foreign-owned business. *Id.* The court interpreted the article as applying to technical documents relating to products manufactured and present on the French market and those the company will manufacture for the French market, if the documents are necessary for French employees to properly do their work in France. *Id.*

2. Contract Termination

Labor Code Section 122-4 recognizes the right of employers to dismiss employees. However, the act of 13 July 1973 created significant procedural and substantive protections for employees. Employers must have genuine and serious grounds for the termination of an employment contract. However, when a worker is hired for an indefinite duration, the employer and the employee generally agree on a trial period during which the employee may be fired without formalities or any particular reason. The quid pro quo is that the employee can also resign without giving notice during this trial period. The law does not impose a limit on the length of this trial period; however, as a practical matter, the trial period ranges from one to three months, with some extending beyond that customary period if the job is more advanced. The primary reason for the allowance of this trial period is to give the employer an opportunity to evaluate the employee because such an opportunity is not adequately provided for in the hiring process. Once the trial period expires, any dismissal of an employee must be for legitimate reasons – "real and serious cause" (*cause réelle et sérieuse*). The employer bears the burden of proving that the employee was terminated for legitimate reasons. Legitimate reasons for a termination fall under two categories: personal reasons and economic reasons.

If the employee terminates the employment contract, pursuant to Art. L. 122-4 of the Labor Code, there is little legal regulation. Two aspects of resignation merit comment. First, in rare cases, employers sue employees for abusive resignation, such as when the employee times the resignation to cause harm to the employer. *See* Despax & Rojot, *supra*, at 113. Second, the Cour de Cassation has recognized a concept analogous to constructive discharge when an employee resigns but contends that she was forced to resign by conditions imposed by her employer. *See* INTERNATIONAL LABOR, *supra*, at 3-14.

a. *Dismissal For Personal Reasons (Licenciement Pour Motif Personnel)*

i. Procedures. Even if an employer has an acceptable reason for terminating an employee, the employer must comply with procedures imposed by law. First, the employer must request the employee's presence at a conciliatory meeting. Notice of the pending conciliatory meeting must be in writing and state the subject, date, time, and place, of the meeting. It must also inform the employee of the right to representation by a fellow employee or employee representative of the company. Under a recently passed law, the employee must receive this notice at least five business days before the meeting. Ordinance No. 2004-602 of June 24, 2004, Labor Code Art. L. 122-14. *See* INTERNATIONAL LABOR Supp. 2005, *supra*, at 3-3.

The purpose of this meeting is to give the employee an opportunity to hear the allegations of the employer and to respond to such allegations. As a result, if the requirements for the notice letter are not complied with or the notice is insufficient, then the termination process is considered never to have begun. In such a case, if the employer terminates the employee without complying with procedures, the employer would be liable for unlawful dismissal.

At the conciliatory meeting, the employer must explain the allegations and give the employee an opportunity to answer these allegations. However, at this stage, only another member of the company represents the employee, and no attorneys are present on behalf of either the company or the employee.

After the conciliatory meeting and the expiration of no fewer than two business days, the employer may notify the employee of termination or dismissal. Labor Code Art. L. 122-14-1 (Ordinance No. 2004-602 of June 24, 2004). This notice of dismissal must be sent by registered mail or with acknowledgment of receipt and must state the reason for dismissal. If reason for dismissal is not provided, then the dismissal is presumed to be for lack of genuine or serious grounds. Furthermore, the employer must provide information regarding all terminations to the proper French labor authorities.

In addition, an employee is entitled to a notice period that runs from the date of delivery of the notice of dismissal. The length of the notice period depends on the seniority and position held by the employee; however, notice periods generally range from one to three months in duration. During this notice period, the employee is obligated to work and the employer is obligated to compensate the employee for his services. However, the employer can waive the right to the employee's work during this period but must still compensate the employee as if he had worked throughout the notice period. The employee could request not to work during this notice period while waiving the right to compensation; however, this is subject to the employer's discretion. Article L. 122-6 of the Labor Code provides that if an employee is terminated for gross negligence or willful misconduct then no notice period is required. As *Societe La Louisiane*, discussed *infra*, suggests, sexual harassment would be an example of termination based on gross negligence for which a notice period would not be required.

In cases in which an employee with at least two years of service is terminated for personal reasons other than gross negligence or willful misconduct, or for economic reasons, indemnities are legally required to be paid to the employee. These indemnities are set by statutory formula based on seniority or can be set in a collective bargaining agreement. When the dismissal is based on economic reasons, the indemnity is twice what it is for dismissal based on personal reasons. Regardless of whether an employee has provided at least two years of service, an employee is also entitled to an accrued vacation indemnity if the employee has not used all of her vacation for that year. As noted earlier, an employer can waive the right to an employee's services by simply paying the employee what she would have earned during the notice period. This essentially creates another type of voluntary indemnity arrangement – that is, indemnity in lieu of the notice period.

If an employer fails to comply with these dismissal procedures, even when the grounds for dismissal are justified, the employee's damages are usually calculated to be about one month's worth of wages. However, if an employer cannot provide justification for the termination, the damages are calculated according to the actual damage suffered, and these damages tend to be about six months' worth of wages if the employee has been employed for at least two years.

Although French employers have many procedures to comply with when terminating employees, the damages for noncompliance are fairly certain and predictable. In the United States, by contrast, termination of employees is a rather simple process. However, when an employer dismisses an employee in the United States, it is difficult to determine what the employer can be sued for and even more difficult to determine to what liability, if any, the employer may be exposed.

Compare the French law regarding termination of employment with International Labor Organization Convention 158 and Recommendation 166, which are available on the ILO Web site at http://www.ilo.org. How close is French law to the ILO Convention and Recommendation?

ii. Substance. The Labor Code does not specify what constitutes legitimate personal reasons for termination. The French jurisprudence or case law is the best source for determining accepted justifications for dismissing an employee based on personal reasons. The most significant personal reasons accepted by the case law include the following: (1) professional incompetence; (2) insufficient results (including failure to meet quotas or sales targets); (3) professional shortcomings (for example: failure to respect company rules, use of company vehicle for personal use, and staying on vacation beyond authorized leave); (4) loss of confidence in the employee; and (5) sexual harassment. *See* INTERNATIONAL LABOR, *supra*, at 3-10; Despax & Rojot, *supra*, at 122.

Consider the case below, in which the employer terminated the employee for personal reasons.

SOCIÉTÉ NIKON FRANCE C/ MONSIEUR O.
COUR DE CASSATION, chambre sociale, 2 octobre 2001
02/10/2001

Labor Chamber

Appeal reference no.: 99-42942

President: M. Waquet, dean bencher.
Reporter: Mrs. Lemoine-Jeanjean.
Auxiliary to the Attorney General (*avocat général*)

REPUBLIC OF FRANCE

IN THE NAME OF THE FRENCH PEOPLE

[The part of the opinion addressing the noncompete covenant is reproduced below in part B(3)]

Whereas Nikon France has hired Mr. Onof on April 22, 1991 for the position of engineer, responsible for the topographic department;

. . .

Regarding the appeal of Mr. Onof:

With respect to article 8 of the European Convention on the safeguard of human rights and fundamental liberties, article 9 of the Civil Code, article 9 of the new Code of civil procedure and article L. 120-2 of the Labor Code (*code du travail*);

Whereas the employee has the right, even during his working hours and on his place of work, to the respect of his private life; that this implies in particular the secrecy of correspondence, that the employer can not, as a consequence, without violating this fundamental liberty, be informed of the personal messages sent by the employee and received through computer equipment made available for his work and that even if the employer has forbidden the non-professional use of the computer;

Whereas to decide that the dismissal of Mr. Onof was justified by a serious violation, the Court of Appeal has notably ruled that the employee had proceeded to a parallel activity; that it has based its argument to establish this behavior on the content of messages emitted and received by the employee, which the employer had discovered by consulting the computer made available to Mr. Onof by the company which contained a file named "personal";

That by ruling of the sort, the Court of Appeal had violated the above texts;

ON THESE GROUNDS:

QUASHES AND ANNULS, in all its provisions, the judgement rendered on March 22, 1999, among the parties, by the Paris Court of Appeal; and, as a consequence, returns the parties and the cause to their initial condition prior to such judgement and, for justice to be made, remands them to the Paris Court of Appeal, composed differently.

Notes

1. In *Société Nikon France c/ Monsieur O.*, the employee had been using his company computer during working hours to engage in unauthorized freelance activities; thus, the court's reference to the employee's proceeding to a "parallel activity." *See French Supreme Court E-Mail Ruling Bars Employers From Reading Personal Files*, DAILY LAB. REP. (BNA) No. 193, at A-8 (Oct. 9, 2001). This ruling was unexpected, as all the lower courts had upheld the dismissal *Id.* The decision was described by some as "revolutionary" and likely to have a far-reaching impact in employers' revision of their policies regarding electronic surveillance and employees' personal

use of e-mail. *Id.* Did the Cour de Cassation hold that the employer did not have real and serious grounds for terminating the employee?

2. The Cour de Casssation relied upon several French and EU articles protecting privacy: Art. L. 120-2 of the Labor Code (civil rights or personal freedoms of employees); Art. 9 of the French Civil Code (general privacy rights); Art. 9 of the New Code of Civil Procedure (evidence gathering); and Art. 8 of the European Convention on Human Rights (person's right to respect in privacy, family life, home, and correspondence). Secrecy of correspondence or secrecy of letters is a fundamental right in the constitutions of several European nations.

3. As will be discussed more fully later, French labor law has been one of the most protective regimes of privacy rights of employees. In the United States, if an employee is given use of a company computer and put on notice of limitations regarding personal use and fired for violating those limitations, in a lawsuit for invasion of privacy, most courts hold that the employee lacks an expectation of privacy. Apparently, in France the employee's expectation of privacy, at least regarding correspondence, cannot be undermined by limitations that the employer communicates to the employee.

4. The Cour de Cassation has held that sexual harassment is always an offense for which an employee can be terminated. *Societe La Louisiane/Societe Les Carlines v. Daniel Alzas*, Cour de Casssation, Arret No. 877-FS-P + B, 3/5/02, reported in *France's Highest Court Says Firms Can Fire Workers Found Guilty of Sexual Harassment*, DAILY LAB. REP. (BNA) No. 57, at A-8 (Mar. 25, 2002). The decision overturned an appellate court decision that although Alzas had sexually harassed employees under his supervision, this conduct did not constitute an immediate firing offense. What result in other nations: Is a finding that an employee engaged in sexual harassment always an adequate basis for termination?

---

b. *Economic Reasons (Licenciement économique)*

An employer may terminate an employee for economic reasons. Act of 3 January 1975 addressed individual and collective dismissals for economic reasons. Despax & Rojot, *supra*, at 130. Art. L 321-1 of the Labor Code defines dismissal for economic reasons as reasons not related to the behavior of the employee that result from the restructuring of the company in that it affects the employee's position, or from an essential modification of the employment contract resulting from economic difficulties or technological changes. Law No. 2005-32 of 18 January 2005 amended the definition in Art. 321-1, adopting the more restrictive definition of the case law, changing "substantial" modification of the employment contract to "essential" modification. INTERNATIONAL LABOR Supp. 2005, *supra*, at 3-7. The courts have determined that it is proper to terminate an employee for economic reasons when the company:

- Enters bankruptcy or financial concerns require cutbacks in spending;
- Sees turnover drop because a principal client is lost;
- Reorganizes in order to implement new strategies;
- Closes a branch because it is losing money even though the rest of the company is not;

- Eliminates a position; or
- Substantially modifies the employment contract because of economic or technological changes, and the employee refuses the modifications.

INTERNATIONAL LABOR, *supra*, at 3-47 to 3-48.

As with the termination of individual employees for personal reasons, in order for an employer to terminate employees for economic reasons, several procedures govern such reduction in force dismissals. What exact procedures an employer must comply with depends on the number of employees being laid off during a thirty-day period. *See*, INTERNATIONAL LABOR *supra*, at 3-51 to 3-55. The requirements for collective dismissals for economic reasons are detailed; they are discussed in general terms below. An individual or collective dismissal for economic reasons can be completed only after approval by the Department Director of Labor.

One employee: For an individual reduction in force, the employer is required to follow the same procedures required for termination for personal reasons. Additionally, the employer must give notice of the dismissal to labor authorities within eight days of dismissal. The law provides criteria for employers to use in determining order of dismissal for economic reasons, such as seniority, family responsibilities, professional qualifications, etc. Law No. 2005-32 of 18 January 2005 made changes in procedures. For employers with fewer than one thousand employees, the law replaced the requirement of a PARE *anticipé* with a personalized reclassification agreement (*convention de reclassement personalize*), which is a plan to provide counseling, evaluation, and training to enable the employee to obtain reemployment. For employers with more than one thousand employees, an employee dismissed for economic reasons gets a redeployment or reclassification leave of between four and nine months for training and job search. If the employee refuses the leave, then the employee is given a personalized reclassification agreement.

Collective Dismissal of Two to Nine Employees: If the company has more than eleven employees and plans to dismiss from two to nine of them, the procedures described above for individual dismissal are supplemented by consultation with employee representatives, which precedes the meeting with the employee. At the meeting, the employer must give the employee representatives information regarding the dismissals and give them an opportunity to express their opinions about the dismissals.

Collective Dismissals of Ten or More Employees: For an employer that has fifty or more employees that wants to dismiss more than ten of them, two meetings are required with the employee representatives or the enterprise committee[2] before the dismissals can be carried out. The representatives or committee are provided information by the employer about the dismissals and the proposed social plan, and they may express opinions and suggestions, which are included in the minutes that are transmitted to the labor administration. The labor administration is more involved in the review of the dismissals. Pursuant to the *Loi de Modernisation Sociale* (Law No. 2002-73 of 17 January 2002), the employer must submit an employment safeguard plan to the labor administration. The Social Modernization Law of 2002 also restricted the circumstances under which employers could downsize by limiting "economic termination" to three specific causes (serious economic difficulties that could not be addressed in any other way, technological changes

---

[2] Employee representatives and enterprise committees are discussed in part C(5)(a)-(b), *infra*.

that put the future of the company in doubt, and workplace reorganization necessary to guarantee the future of the company). However, the Constitutional Council, France's highest constitutional court, ruled that that part of the law violated the constitutional "freedom to engage in entrepreneurial activities," and thus struck down that part of the law. *See French Court Invalidates Provision Restricting Employer's Firing of Workers,* DAILY LAB REP. (BNA) No. 27, at A-4 (Feb. 8, 2002). "French law, therefore, remains subject to the jurisprudential definition of the legal basis for economic downsizing." *See* Bruce D. Fisher & Francois Lenglart, *Employee Reductions in Force: A Comparative Study of French and U.S. Legal Protections for Employees Downsized Out of Their Jobs: A Suggested Alternative to Workforce Reductions,* LOY. 26 L.A. INT'L & COMP. L. REV. 181, 203 (2003).

Law No. 2005-32 of 18 January 2005 provides that for collective dismissals of more than ten employees, agreements may be negotiated with employee representation committees regarding information and consultation procedures that are different from those in the Labor Code. INTERNATIONAL LABOR Supp. 2005, *supra,* at 3-8.

Plan d'Aide au Retour á l'Emploi (PARE) is a government program that is administered by the French unemployment agency for the purpose of creating incentives for the rapid reemployment of terminated employees. Employers report dismissals to this agency, and the employee has the option to participate in training programs and receive benefits. PARE provides training and allowances to employees who participate. For employers that hire employees who have been unemployed and receiving benefits for more than twelve months, they can receive a subsidy under PARE.

The *Loi de Modernisation Sociale* revised the name and procedures of what was formerly a "social plan" to an "employment safeguard plan." *See* INTERNATIONAL LABOR, *supra,* at 3-52. Such plans are required for companies with fifty or more employees that are dismissing ten or more. This plan differs from the PARE in that it is established by the employer. The contents of the plan are specified by law (Art. L.321-4-1 of the Labor Code). Generally, the plan must address what the employer will do to alleviate the difficulties of dismissed employees and to avoid future collective dismissals. Law No. 2005-32 of 18 January 2005, discussed earlier, permits the negotiation of agreements that establish the conditions and content of an employment safeguard plan, but the agreement may not waive certain requirements: the employer's obligation to seek an employment alternative prior to termination; the termination rules in case of liquidation or receivership; and the consultation rules between employer and employee representation committee. INTERNATIONAL LABOR Supp. 2005, *supra,* at 3-8. The 2005 law also repealed some content requirements of the employment safeguard plan established by the *Loi de Modernisation Sociale.* If the plan is deemed insufficient by a court, the court can cancel the safeguard plan and the dismissals. *See* INTERNATIONAL LABOR, *supra* at 3-53; *see also* Craig S. Smith, *Four Ways to Fire a Frenchman,* http://www.nytimes.com/2006/03/26/weekinreview/26smith.html (quoting French lawyer Joël Grangé for the proposition that if the court does not approve of the employment safeguard plan, it may order reinstatement of dismissed employees).

The indemnities to employees laid off in an economic downsizing are increased by the 2002 law to one-third of a month's salary for those who have worked ten years or more, and one-fifth for those who have worked less than ten years. This doubles the cost over the prior law. *See* Fisher & Lenglart, *supra,* at 203.

Fisher and Lenglart conclude that French workers have far more protections than their U.S. counterparts: (1) worker presence at the board of directors meetings; (2) French companies that fail to give the required notices of downsizing could face criminal sanctions; (3) unemployment benefits in France can last up to five years – ten times longer than U.S. unemployment benefits; and (4) French national health insurance coverage, whereas U.S. employees have only the COBRA extension of health coverage. *Id.* at 208-09.

When there is a merger or acquisition of a company, the employment contract is not disturbed. The new owner of the company is bound by the employment contracts of the previous company just as they are bound by other contracts in other regards. Art. L. 122-12 Labor Code.

c. *The Persistent Problem of Youth Unemployment and the Recent Passage and Revocation of the Contrat Premiere Embauche*

France has been plagued by high unemployment among young people for decades, and the government has endeavored to address the problem in several different ways. For example, in 1977 "pacts for employment" excluded employers' contributions to social security for employees hired below the age of 25. Despax & Rojot, *supra*, at 28. Other measures have included providing state-paid allowances to employers for hiring young employees, and contracts of solidarity by which the state pays compensation to retiring workers if the employer replaces them with young unemployed persons. *Id.*

The riots in France in October–November 2005, marked by burnings of cars and public buildings, have been traced in large part to very high unemployment among young Arab immigrants. *See* Floyd Norris, *In France, An Economic Bullet Goes Unbitten*, http://www.nytimes.com/2006/04/11/business/worldbusiness/11euro.html.

The most recent attempt by the French government to address the problem of an unemployment rate of approximately one quarter of all persons under age twenty-six was the inclusion in the Law on Equal Opportunity of provision for a *Contrat Premiere Embauche* (CPE) or First Employment Contract, which would have permitted employers with twenty or more employees who hire workers under age twenty-six to terminate them for any reason during a two-year probationary period. *See Students, Unions Stage Protests Over France's New Labor Law Contracts*, DAILY LAB. REP. (BNA) No. 53, at A-6 (March 20, 2006). Such employees who were terminated also would have been entitled to lower indemnities than those under standard labor contracts. *Id.* For employees working under the CPE who remained on jobs beyond two years, the CPE automatically would have converted to the standard indefinite term employment contract, *Contrat à Duree Indeterminee* or CDI. *Id.*

Prime Minister Dominique de Villepin forced the CPE through Parliament, using emergency procedures to limit debate. *Id.* The response to the law was massive demonstrations and strikes as young people, students, and unions protested what was viewed as a significant erosion of employment security under French labor law. *See* Meg Bortin & Craig S. Smith, *Hundreds of Thousands Protest Against Labor Law in France*, http://www.nytimes.com/2006/03/28/intenational /europe/28cnd-france.html. In the face of the protests and strikes, the government rescinded the law creating the First Employment Contract and replaced it with a law that creates financial incentives for employers to hire young workers. *See* Elaine Sciolino, *Chirac Will Rescind Labor Law That Caused Wide French Riots*, http://www.nytimes.com/2006/04/11/world/europe/11france.html.

Notes

1. A U.S. journalist, writing about the CPE, described the situation as follows: "The French government wants to make it easy to fire young workers. Easier firing, easier hiring, the logic goes. Who wants to add people to the permanent payroll if it's painful and costly to undo a mistake?" Craig S. Smith, *Four Ways to Fire a Frenchman*, http://www.nytimes.com/2006/03/26/weekinreview/26smith.html. Smith describes the four ways to fire a Frenchman as follows: "prove you can't afford the job"; "prove he did a bad, bad thing"; "pay him to scram"; and "put him in a cupboard and throw away the key." *Id.* Which of these does not match up with the law regarding termination of employment contracts discussed earlier? Smith defines the cupboard approach as "moving them out of the way and leaving them alone in hopes that they eventually quit." *Id.*

2. Is the French experiment with the CPE evidence that in a world of globalized trade and competition, an employment-at-will regime like that of the United States is needed to give employers sufficient flexibility? Consider again the issue of the problem of youth unemployment in France and other Western European nations. Professor Joseph M. Schwartz, in a passage excerpted above in the Introduction to this chapter, explained high youth unemployment as the cost of a system that provides substantial employment security to the employed and refuses to accept low-wage, nonunion jobs. In such a system the unemployed receive benefits and wait their turn for employment in good jobs. He also warned: "the discontent of marginalized immigrant youth is the Achilles heel of this 'queuing strategy' of unemployment). Obviously, this juggling act cannot continue much longer." Schwartz, *supra*, at 1114. The First Employment Contract is the latest effort of the French government to address the plight and unrest of young people, particularly young immigrants, who are unemployed. How long can France continue the "juggling act"?

   One writer, criticizing France's retreat on the First Employment Contract law, explains that Europe must change its rigid labor markets, but to make such unpopular changes, politicians would have to be willing to accept defeat in the next elections, a price that most politicians are unwilling to accept. *See* Floyd Norris, *In France, An Economic Bullet Goes Unbitten*, http://www.nytimes.com/2006/04/11/business/worldbusiness/11euro.html.

   At the other extreme, is the United States, with its creation of low-wage, insecure jobs, engaged in a different juggling act? What is at risk? How likely is change?

3. American journalist Jim Hoagland writes of parallels between the French demonstrations and strikes over the CPE and the demonstrations and debates in the United States regarding illegal immigrant workers. He sees common themes regarding the pressures of globalization and the generational economic conflict involving the young who are starting their careers and their elders who are moving toward retirement. For example, regarding globalization and immigrant workers he writes, "The global connections need to be grasped and articulated if societies are to do a better job of dividing the fruits of the prosperity that globalization brings for some of

their citizens and the burdens of unemployment or low wages that others experience." Regarding the French experiment with the CPE, he writes, "By giving
private employers the right to fire workers under 26 without cause within two years
of being hired, the government effectively denied young workers labor protections
that are deeply entrenched for their elders." Jim Hoagland, *Protests Demonstrate
Need to Deal With Pressures of Globalization* (syndicated column 3 April 2006).

4. Christophe Vigneau writes of the shift in both content and perception of labor
    law in the mid-1970s: "Changes in labor law do not improve work security but
    organize flexibility as part of a policy against unemployment." Vigneau, *supra*, at 132.
    Consider how this change impacts the French labor law regime: "[D]evelopment
    of precarious jobs is also the consequence of the dominated market economy. The
    reaction of the French system has been to regulate and, to some extent, limit the
    use of new forms of working relations." *Id.* How does the French experiment with
    the First Employment Contract relate to these points?

3. Duty of Loyalty and Noncompetition

According to the Civil Code, contracts must be carried out in good faith, French Civil
Code Art. 1134. This article applies to all conventional obligations, including employment
contracts. As will be discussed later, signatories to a collective bargaining agreement must
not do anything that would compromise the loyal execution of the agreement, Labor
Code, Section 135-3. However, a signatory to the collective agreement may call a strike
against an agreement, and this would not constitute an unfair labor practice under French
law.

The law regarding an employee's duty of loyalty to her employer and the law regarding
covenants not to compete have in the last five years or so been moving in the direction
of permitting employees to compete with their employers. The driving force behind
this movement of the law is the desire to make the climate more hospitable to the
establishment of new businesses.

A noncompetition agreement must be expressly provided for in the contract of employment. These are designed to prevent the employees from terminating their employment
because their former employer often assesses a penalty against them. Furthermore, future
employers are reluctant to persuade employees to come to their business in fear that they
will be liable for their interference with a contractual obligation of the employee to her
former employer. Previously, these noncompetition agreements were presumed to be the
law of the parties and upheld by French courts. However, judges have begun to scrutinize
carefully noncompetition agreements because of their limitations on freedom of work
policies and unemployment problems in France. French courts have held noncompete
agreements null and void if they did not satisfy the following conditions: (1) justified by
a legitimate business interest of the company; (2) limited in duration and geographic
scope; (3) based on an employee's specific job; and (4) supported by sufficient consideration in proportion to the employee's salary. *See* Erika C. Collins, R. Bradley Mokros &
John Simmons, *Labor and Employment Developments From Around the World*, 37 INT'L
LAWYER 329, 338 (2003).

The law of France was that an employee that competes with his current employer is
subject to dismissal. However, the competition must be existent and cannot be a mere

rumor. Law No. 2003-721 of 1 August 2003 reformed the duty of loyalty to permit employees to set up their own businesses while still employed. *See* INTERNATIONAL LABOR 2004 Supp., *supra*, at 3-1 to 3-2. New Article L. 121-9 of the Labor Code suspends any exclusivity agreement for one or two years if the employee wishes to take over an existing business or create a new business. At the end of the one or two year suspension, the employee must comply with the noncompetition agreement or resign from the employment.

SOCIÉTÉ NIKON FRANCE C/ MONSIEUR O.
COUR DE CASSATION, chambre sociale, 2 octobre 2001
02/10/2001

Labor Chamber

Appeal reference no.: 99-42942

President: M. Waquet, dean bencher.
Auxiliary to the Attorney General (*avocat général*)

REPUBLIC OF FRANCE
IN THE NAME OF THE FRENCH PEOPLE

Whereas Nikon France has hired Mr. Onof on April 22, 1991 for the position of engineer, responsible for the topographic department; on September 7, 1992, the employee has entered into a confidentiality agreement with Nikon Corporation and Nikon Europe BV forbidding him from revealing some of the confidential information communicated by both these companies; on June 29, 1995, he was dismissed for serious offence, pursuant to the motive, notably, of using equipment for personal purposes which had been made available by the company for professional purposes; he has filed a claim in industrial disputes with respect to the payment of indemnities founded on a dismissal without good and sufficient cause and an amount as a counterpart for the conventional non-competition provision;

Regarding the sole argument of appeal of Nikon France:

With respect to article 1134 of the Civil Code;

Whereas to condemn Nikon France to pay an indemnity provided for in the conventional non-competition provision, the court of appeal has ruled that the non-communication obligation of confidential information was equivalent to forbidding an employee to be hired as surveyor-engineer by a competitor and that the confidentiality agreement should therefore produce the effects of this non-competition provision;

Whereas, however, the confidentiality agreement entered into on September 7, 1992 between the employee and Nikon Corporation and Nikon BV only bound the employee to non-communication of information, which had been communicated to him by both these companies, expressly identified as being confidential and with a nature enabling the development of a specific program; that, contrarily to the non-competition provision provided for at article 28 of the national Collective Agreement applicable to engineers and executives within the metallurgy field applicable to this case, the agreement did not forbid the employee from being hired by a competing company after his departure from the company;

That by ruling as it had done, the Court of Appeal, by giving to the confidentiality agreement the provisions of which were clear and specific, a scope which it did not have, has denatured this agreement and thereby violated the above text;

Notes

1. As the court's ruling in *Société Nikon France c/ Monsieur O.* indicates, noncompetes are strictly construed by French courts. Employers that do not expressly provide for restrictions in the agreements are not likely to be helped by the courts.

2. Do you notice any common themes in (1) the movement of French law regarding the employee duty of loyalty and the courts' treatment of noncompete agreements and (2) the recent French law on youth employment contracts? Consider again the Lisbon Strategy, discussed in Chapter 7 on the European Union, *supra*. The European Council at a meeting in Lisbon in 2000 developed a ten-year strategy "to become the most competitive and dynamic knowledge-based economy in the world, capable of sustainable economic growth with more and better jobs and greater social cohesion." http://ue.eu.int/ueDocs/cms_Data/docs/pressData/en/ec/00100-r1.en0. htm. Part of the strategy states as follows: "The competitiveness and dynamism of businesses are directly dependent on a regulatory climate conducive to investment, innovation, and entrepreneurship. Further efforts are required to lower the costs of doing business and remove unnecessary red tape, both of which are particularly burdensome for SMEs. The European institutions, national governments and regional and local authorities must continue to pay particular attention to the impact and compliance costs of proposed regulations, and should pursue their dialogue with business and citizens with this aim in mind." *Id.* ¶14. At the midway point of the Lisbon Strategy in 2005, the Council decided to relaunch the strategy and refocus on key targets: "making knowledge and innovation the engines of sustainable European growth; making Europe a more attractive area in which to invest and work; and reinforcing the European social model based on the quest for full employment and greater social cohesion." http://europa.eu/generalreport/en/2005/rg38.htm.

C. UNIONS AND COLLECTIVE BARGAINING

1. Generally

The recognition of unions in France dates back to the nineteenth century. The French Constitution guarantees the freedom to form unions and the right to strike. This was stated in the Preamble to the 1946 French Constitution, which is referred to in the 1958 Constitution. The preamble of the Constitution of 27 October 1946 provides "that any person can defend his rights and interests by taking part in the activities of a union and by joining a union of his choice."

However, actual collective bargaining did not become prevalent in France until the 1950s when the requirement of prior government authorization to collective negotiation was abolished. Collective bargaining in France initially began without much law in place;

thus, the development of this area of the law has its roots in custom and practice. Moreover, union representation and collective bargaining occurred at the industry level rather than the enterprise or company level. It was not until 1968 that French lawmakers, in response to a series of devastating strikes, provided for representation and collective bargaining at the company level. *See* Marie Mercat Bruns, *Worker Representation at the Enterprise Level in France*, 15 COMP. LAB. L. J. 15, 16-18 (1993). Further reforms in 1982 strengthened the position of unions as collective bargaining representatives at the enterprise level. *Id.* at 18-20.

Unlike the system of employee representation in the United States, unions are not the sole means of representation in France. Employee representatives and employee representation committees (*comités d'enterprise*) will be discussed further later. These alternative methods of employee representation were developed in the 1930s largely because of the aversion of employers and unions to union representation at the company or enterprise level. *Id.* at 16-17.

If a company employs fewer than fifty employees, employees themselves may negotiate a collective agreement with an employer without any union representation. Unions representing employees have the right to negotiate collective agreements, to set up union sections, and to designate union delegates. INTERNATIONAL LABOR, *supra*, at 3-21. As a practical matter, most unions are created for a specific sector of business or industry; however, negotiations can take place at various levels. For example, negotiation can take place on behalf of employees of a specific plant, specific company, or a specific industry. The freedom to create and join unions has been succinctly stated as follows: "[E]xcluding the exceptional cases, all those having an occupation, whether a profession, trade, or in industry, agriculture, etc., and sharing common occupational interests may establish or join a union." Despax & Rojot, *supra*, at 156. Thus, whereas the United States has a regime of exclusive representation whereby an employee can be represented by only one union, France has a system of pluralism in which unions can represent employees without being elected by a majority of employees in a bargaining unit.

The pluralism of unions also raises some problems, such as which union chooses representatives or delegates for particular purposes. Thus emerged the idea of designating some unions as "representative." There are many "privileges, tasks, and advantages" that accompany the designation of representative. Despax & Rojot, *supra*, at 159. Representativeness can be established at various levels, including multi-occupational, national, regional, local, and plant. *Id.* at 160. There are four criteria in the Labor Code for determining representativeness: number of members, independence in relation to the employer, amount of dues, and age of the union. Section L 133-2. In the private sector, there are no formal procedures for gaining status as representative. Rather, these determinations have been made by the courts. Five associations of unions have been declared by French law as "representative" on a national scale: (1) *Confederation Générale des Travailleurs* (CGT), which is affiliated with the communist party, (2) *Force Ouvrière* (FO); (3) *Confédération Française Démocratique du Travail* (CFDT), affiliate of the Socialist Party; (4) *Confédération Française des Travailleurs Chrétiens* (CFTC); and (5) *Confédération Générale des Cadres* (CGC), for executives. Despax & Rojot, *supra*, at 161.

A law passed in 2004, Law No. 2004-391 of 4 May 2004, made several changes in the law regarding unions and collective bargaining. *See* INTERNATIONAL LABOR Supp. 2005, *supra*, at 3-5. One change effected by the law is that collective bargaining agreements negotiated by representative unions can be opposed by unions with majority support ("right of opposition"). A second major change is that collective bargaining agreements at the company level may diverge from terms in an industry- or sector-level agreement, and may even provide for less favorable terms. *See* http://www.eiro.eurofound. eu.int/2005/07/feature/fr0507104f.html. The changes are summarized as follows:

> 1. The allowance of collective agreements between unions and companies at the company level even if they are less favourable than agreements signed at higher branch levels;
> 2. The allowance of agreements signed between companies without legally recognized unions but with employees empowered by legally recognized unions, even when no employee representative exists;
> 3. The enforcement of agreements signed by unions representing the majority of a company's employees, even though the union is not legally considered a representative union; and
> 4. The allowance of union access to company employees via e-mail communication or through an internet website.

> Erika C. Collins, *International Employment Law*, 39 INT'L LAW. 449, 457 (2005).

For analysis of the effects of the new law, see http://www.eiro.eurofound.eu.int/2005/07/feature/fr0507104f.html. The report concludes that there is a great deal of uncertainty about the new law and that its right of opposition and permission of variance from sector-level collective agreements have not been used much thus far.

A report of a commission in 2006 recommends reform of French law on collective bargaining and employee representation. *See France Should Consider Union Reforms in Light of Low Membership, Study Says*, DAILY LAB. REP. (BNA) No. 87, at A-6 (May 5, 2006). The report notes that France's union density of 8 percent of the overall workforce and 5 percent of the private workforce is among the lowest of industrialized nations. The report also notes the paradox of low union density and the considerable strength of unions in national debates about labor policy, as recently evidenced in the demonstrations over the youth employment contract law. *Id.* One of the principal recommendations of the commission was to reform the law to permit smaller unions to be "proven representative" and to participate in collective bargaining. The report notes the near monopoly on collective bargaining since World War II of the five major union confederations. *Id.*

Most French employers negotiate through the *Mouvement des enterprises de France* (Medef), or the French national employer association.

2. Coverage by Collective Agreements

Roughly 90 percent of French employees are covered by collective agreements. This is one of the highest coverage rates in the world. In contrast, France has one of the lowest union density rates in the world (the percent of employees that are actually members of a union) at around 8 percent or 9 percent, which is lower than the union density rate in the United States. *See* G.J. Bamber & P. Sheldon, *Collective Bargaining* in COMPARATIVE LABOUR LAW, *supra*, at 566, tbl. I. How is this achieved? Citing Spain and France as examples, Bamber and Sheldon explain that "high levels of collective bargaining coverage are more closely correlated with the centralization of collective bargaining than union density." *Id.* at 567. In contrast, the United States has decentralized collective bargaining, and "under predominantly decentralized collective bargaining regimes, collective bargaining coverage levels closely approximate union density levels." *Id.*

In France, an employer may become bound by a collective bargaining agreement in several ways. The most basic way in which an employer may become bound by a collective bargaining agreement is through the signatory agreement, in which the employer signs the agreement at the company or plant level. An employer may also find and adopt an existing agreement that was negotiated at a broader level. Furthermore, employers often form associations with other employers in an effort to have more bargaining power against the unions. If an employer's union or association signs the agreement, the members of that association become bound by the collective bargaining agreement. Finally, the French Labor Ministry can extend by decision certain collective bargaining agreements covering certain industries or geographic areas to all employers of the concerned industry or geographic location. For data and analysis of extension procedures in France and other EU nations, see http://www.eiro.eurofound.eu.int/2002/12/study/tn0212102s.html.

3. Effects of Collective Agreements

In France, minimum standards regarding leave, wages, hours, and maximum workweeks, are set by law. Thus, "[c]ollective agreements have historically been a secondary source of legislation in the French legal system . . . conceived to improve statutory labor standards" Vigneau, *supra*, at 133. Collective agreements can supplement these minimum standards but only to the extent that they provide for more favorable conditions than those provided by law. *See id.* at 133-34 (discussing the "favorability principle."). There are three primary effects that collective agreements have on the individual employment contract. First, they are immediate in that they apply to all employment contracts, even those already existing. Second, they are binding on the employer regarding all employees, regardless of whether they are members of the union. An individual employment contract can vary from the collective agreement only to the extent that it provides more benefits to the employee than the collective agreement. Finally, collective agreements are automatic, meaning that more favorable collective agreement provisions automatically replace less favorable clauses in individual contracts.

There has been a shift in French law in recent years in which collective bargaining agreements have been used not to add benefits and protections to statutorily provided minimum benefits and protections, but instead to provide flexibility by permitting agreement to terms less favorable to employees. Vigneau, *supra*, at 134. For example, collective agreements may provide for working time arrangements that are less favorable to employees than those provided by statute. *Id.* This is part of a new purpose and substance for labor law: "[L]abor legislation no longer aims to consolidate labor rights, but to organize a flexible labor market and reduce unemployment." *Id.*

4. Strikes and Lockouts

The right to strike is provided for in both Article L. 521-1 of the Labor Code and the French Constitution. The right extends to both private and public sector employees, but Article L. 521-2 imposes some restrictions on public sector strikes, *e.g.*, only representative unions can initiate a strike, and notice must be given to the employer prior to the strike.

Unlike in the United States, French employers are prohibited from hiring replacements during strikes. The lockout, the temporary closing of the business by the employer, is allowed in France as a defensive measure taken in reaction to an ongoing strike. If the lockout is done for offensive purposes, French courts consider this illegal activity by the employer. The United States, by contrast, permits both defensive and offensive lockouts.

5. Representation by Entities Other than Unions

French law provides mechanisms for employee representation in addition to representation by unions. There are three ways in which employees may be represented other than through unions: (1) Employee Representatives; (2) Employee Representation Committee; and (3) Health and Safety Committee. INTERNATIONAL LABOR, *supra*, at 3-39. Employees that are representatives or members of the representation committee are elected. The employee representation committee appoints members of the health and safety committee. Members serving on a representation system are afforded more legal protection regarding their termination. The three ways in which French employees may be represented regarding employment, other than by unions, are explored briefly below.

a. *Représentants du personnel (Employee Representatives)*

The main function of employee representatives is to act as an information liaison among the employer, employee, and the French labor administration. If a company has eleven or more but fewer than fifty employees, then this will be the primary link between the employee and employer. The law requires the disclosure by the employer of information to the employee representatives. Furthermore, the employees often bring complaints to employee representatives rather than directly to the employer. Although employee representatives do not have much formal power, for example, they cannot negotiate collective agreements on behalf of the employees, they are a good source of information for both employers and employees.

b. *Comité d'entreprise (Employee Representation Committee) or Works Councils*

Employee representation committees are required by law to be formed in any company that employs fifty or more employees. Art. L 431-1. How many members are on this committee varies depending on the type and size of the company. Unlike German works councils, these committees are not employee-only bodies; the committee is presided over by the head of the enterprise or his representative. Art. L 432-2. An employer must provide information and consult with the committee before implementing mergers, worker transfers, employee dismissals, layoffs and employee training. Furthermore, employee representation committees can send two members to shareholders' meetings. In cases in which a tender offer is made, the prospective purchaser can be requested by the committee to present its plans and proposals to the committee. If this is not done, the bidder may not exercise its votes until this requirement is complied with. Two members of the committee are also allowed to attend board of directors meetings in order to stay informed regarding the financial state of the company.

These committees were never empowered by law to participate in management decisions as are works councils in Germany. *See* Bruns, *supra*, at 20. Rather, their functions are better described as receipt of information, consultation, and recommendation. *Id.*

c. *Comité d'hygiène, de securité des conditions de travail (Health and Safety Committee)*

This committee is organized to ensure that working conditions are safe, clean, and healthy. If the company wants to change anything regarding safety matters or working conditions, the health and safety committee must be consulted.

The size of the company (number of employees) determines the number of employee representatives and the number of members on an employee representation committee.

As a member of the European Union, France is subject to the European Works Council Directive, which requires the establishment of European Works Councils for Community–scale undertakings. The Labor Code was amended to conform with the EU directive.

For an interesting discussion of the McDonald's Corporation's dealings with the French regime of employee representation, see Tony Royle, *Worker Representation Under Threat? The McDonald's Corporation and the Effectiveness of Statutory Works Councils in Seven European Countries*, 22 COMP. LAB. L. & POL'Y J. 395 (2001).

D. WAGES, HOURS, AND BENEFITS

1. Wages

The minimum wage in France is called the *salaire minimum de croissance* (SMIC). French economists characterize the SMIC as both a stimulant to economic growth and an instrument of social justice. The SMIC is evaluated every 1 July. However, if the consumer price index increased by 2 percent or more, the SMIC is automatically adjusted. As of July 2006, the French minimum wage was 8.27 euros. http://www.insee.fr/en/indicateur/smic.html.

2. Hours

On 1 February 2000, new legislation went into effect making the standard workweek thirty-five hours (below which overtime is not owed for hours worked). However, in 2002, legislation was enacted that liberalized this thirty-five-hour workweek by enacting a ceiling of sixteen hundred hours per year and otherwise relaxing the law without modifying the basic thirty-five-hour workweek. Law No. 2002-73 of January 17, 2002. *See* Collins, Mokos, & Simmons, *supra*, at 338. There are certain exceptions for management level employees (*cadres*) as there are under the Fair Labor Standards Act in the United States. Overtime in France is paid on work above thirty-five hours a week, and overtime is tiered. For employers that employ twenty or more, for the first eight hours of overtime an employee makes an additional 25 percent per hour. However, any hours beyond forty-three hours worked in a week is paid an additional 50 percent per hour. For employers with fewer than twenty employees, the first overtime tier for hours thirty-six to thirty-nine is an additional 10 percent. By Decree No. 2004-1381 of December 21, 2004, the total permitted annual hours of overtime was increased from 180 to 220. INTERNATIONAL LABOR Supp. 2005, *supra*, at 3-9. Overtime hours beyond 220 must be approved by labor authorities and addressed in consultation with the enterprise committee. Compensatory time may be given rather than overtime pay if provided for in a collective bargaining agreement or if it is the product of information and consultation with agreement by the employee representatives.

Employers are required to give employees eleven consecutive hours off per working day and a weekly break of at least twenty-four consecutive hours. This weekly break must be provided on Sundays unless it is the type of business that cannot close on Sundays.

Whit Monday, a French national holiday, has been added as a seven-hour workday for which employees do not receive pay (unless they work over seven hours). Salaries collected by the businesses on those days go to a solidarity fund for the disabled and elderly. This is referred to as "solidarity day."

3. Leave

a. Annual leave – Art. L 223 – After one year of employment, every worker gets a minimum of five weeks' paid leave. If an employee takes vacation time, this time may not exceed twenty-four consecutive days, for example, the fifth week cannot be taken with the other four weeks. Between May 1 and October 31, the employee must take twelve consecutive days, which essentially guarantees each employee something similar to a summer vacation. Furthermore, young adults ranging from ages eighteen to twenty-one are entitled to thirty days' annual leave regardless of the time that they have served the company.

b. Maternity leave – An employee must take a minimum of sixteen weeks of maternity leave, ten of which must be taken after birth. Although the employer is not required to provide compensation during maternity leave, many collective agreements provide for compensation during this period. Law No. 2005-32 of January 18, 2005 requires that a mother returning to work after maternity leave must be given a personal interview to adapt her work activity. INTERNATIONAL LABOR Supp. 2005, *supra*, at 3-10.

c. Paternity Leave – In 2001, the French government enacted legislation that provides paternity leave of eleven consecutive days to be taken within four months of the birth of a child. Law No. 2005-32 of January 18, 2005 provides that at least 50 percent of a paternity leave period must be included in calculating length of service and rights to benefits.

d. Parental Leave – French law provides unpaid parental leave to foster the education of children. Parental leave is one year in duration and can be extended until the child is three years of age.

e. Business Creation Leave – Law No. 2003-721 of August 1, 2003 created a new type of leave – business creation leave. Employees who have at least twenty-four months of service with a company may take one year of leave (extendable to a second year) for purposes of taking over an existing business or creating a new business. *See* INTERNATIONAL LABOR 2004 Supp., *supra*, at 3-2.

f. Educational Leave – Up to one year's leave for training or education for qualifying employees, during which the employment contract is suspended, but the time is counted for length of service and benefits. INTERNATIONAL LABOR, 2005 Supp., *supra*, at 3-10 to 3-11.

In an interesting comparison of parental leave in France and the United States, a commentator argues that both systems have deficiencies, characterizing that of France as "subordinating women's employment to their reproductive capacity," and that of the United States as "providing women with equal rights to alienate other women's caregiving labor." Naomi S. Stern, *The Challenges of Parental Leave Reforms for French and American Women: A Call for a Revived Feminist-Socialist Theory*, 28 VT. L. REV. 321, 340-41 (2004).

E. EMPLOYMENT DISCRIMINATION

France, as a member of the EU, has essentially followed the European Union's recent active development of employment discrimination law.

Employment discrimination law in France traces back to the law of 1972, which prohibited hiring and firing based on race and defined race as including religion, ethnicity, and national origin. Frank Dobbin, *Do the Social Sciences Shape Corporate Anti-Discrimination Practice? The United States and France*, 23 COMP. LAB. L. & POL'Y J. 829, 838 (2002). Comparing the earliest employment discrimination law in France with Title VII of the Civil Rights Act of 1964 in the U.S., Professor Dobbin says,

> [T]he core principle – that employers should be color-blind rather than race-conscious – was very much the same. French and American law also took very similar forms in terms of who could bring complaints, who bore the responsibility for discrimination, and what kinds of discrimination were covered. French policy recognized individual claims, but not group claims; it recognized individual perpetrators, but not corporate responsibility; it recognized direct discrimination, but not unintentional and indirect discrimination.
>
> *Id.* at 837.

But French law classified employment discrimination as a crime sanctionable by incarceration and fines, and it did not establish an agency like the Equal Employment Opportunity Commission in the United States. Despite the numerous commonalities at the beginning, the development of the law in each nation was very different. U.S. employment discrimination law proliferated and evolved, whereas French law generated little litigation, and it changed very little. *Id.* Dobbin explains the difference in development in the regimes of the two nations because the state fragmentation and porousness in the United States made it possible for activists and human resource specialists to incorporate social science into employer practices as a preemptive move to avoid liability because employers could not be certain how agencies and courts would interpret the employment discrimination laws. In contrast, in France, such evolution did not occur as a result of centralization and impermeability in the French system: French employers were fairly certain that courts would not adopt expansive definitions of employment discrimination law. *Id.* at 863. *See also* Susan Bisom-Rapp, *Exceeding Our Boundaries: Transnational Employment Law Practice and the Export of American Lawyering Styles to the Global Worksite*, 25 COMP. LAB. L. & POL'Y J. 257 (2004) (discussing how human resource professionals in the United States advised businesses to adopt personnel practices that "bulletproofed" their employment decisions against liability, and arguing that this did not happen to a great extent in other nations).

In 2001, France passed legislation that expanded the definition of discrimination and prohibited discrimination in the employment context against a person based on sexual orientation, physical appearance, family name, or age. Law No. 2001-1066 of November 16, 2001. Under the 2001 law, discrimination is still treated as a crime.

In 2004, legislation was passed, for conformity with the EU's antidiscrimination directives, which created a new High Authority on Discrimination and Equality (*Haute Autorité de Lutte Contre les Discriminations et pour l'Egalité* or HALDE) charged with combating discrimination in employment, housing, provision of service, and in the media. *See France Looks to Create New Body to Promote Workplace Equality*, DAILY LAB. REP. (BNA) No. 196, at A-6 (Oct. 12, 2004).

On 23 February 2006, the French Parliament passed the Law on Equal Pay Between Men and Women (*Loi Relatif à l'Egalité Salariale Entre les Femems et les Hommes*) which is directed at eliminating sex-based pay inequality by 2010. *See France Enacts Equal Pay Law, Plans Greater Maternity Leave Protection*, DAILY LAB. REP. (BNA) No. 39, at A-4 (Feb. 28, 2006). The law also makes several provisions regarding maternity leave: (1) mandatory minimum salary raises for women returning from maternity leave; (2) extension of maternity leave for mothers of premature children; (3) greater pregnancy discrimination protections in termination cases; and (4) child care subsidies when employees are required to undergo training outside normal working hours.

French law's treatment of sexual harassment (*haracèment sexuel*) provides an interesting basis for comparison with the United States and other nations. Abigail Saguy has written extensively in this area. *See, e.g.,* ABIGAIL C. SAGUY, WHAT IS SEXUAL HARASSMENT? FROM CAPITOL HILL TO THE SORBONNE (2003); Abigail C. Saguy, *Employment Discrimination or Sexual Violence? Defining Sexual Harassment in American and French Law*, 34 LAW & SOC'Y REV. 1091 (2000) [hereinafter, Saguy, *Employment Discrimination*]. Professor Saguy depicts the sexual harassment law of the United States and France as an exemplar of law that defies the general convergence theory of law. The convergence theory posits that national differences are becoming less important, law and labor law are converging, and globalization is producing uniformity across national borders. In France, sexual harassment is covered under the Penal Code as a form of sexual violence, along with rape, sexual assault, and exhibitionism. Until an amendment in 2002, the definition of sexual harassment was limited to an abuse of authority by a supervisor; the amendment expanded the definition to include coworker harassment. The penalties are incarceration and a fine, with some modest compensatory damages available in the context of the criminal trial. The party held liable is the individual harasser, not the employer. There also is a labor provision which prohibits retaliation by the employer that is linked to sexual harassment. Saguy concludes that whereas U.S. management views sexual harassment as its problem which it must address, French management does not consider sexual harassment to be a problem that it is obligated to address. *See Global Perspectives on Workplace Harassment Law: Proceedings of the 2004 Annual Meeting, Association of American Law Schools Section on Labor Relations and Employment Law*, 8 EMPLOYEE RTS. & EMP. POL'Y J. 151, 163-64 (2004).

Historically, sexual harassment law in France dates back to the early 1990s, whereas in the United States it dates back to the 1970s. However, Saguy rejects the time lag theory as a sufficient explanation of the difference in the law of the two nations. *See Saguy, Employment Discrimination, supra,* at 1118-19. Instead, she explains the differences as being attributable more to the differences in political, legal, and cultural constraints and resources.

The further development of sexual harassment law in France will be interesting to observe. The Cour de Cassation approved an employee's engaging in sexual harassment as a genuine and serious ground for termination in *Societe La Louisianae/Societe Les Carlines vs. Daniel Alzas*. Sexual harassment is also covered under the law on moral harassment, discussed later.

Note

The convergence school of thought subscribes to the view that labor law throughout the world will become more uniform, whereas the divergence school posits that labor law is part of each nation's history, culture, politics, and society, and thus, the labor law of nations will remain distinctive. Is the employment discrimination law, and more specifically the sexual harassment law, of France, compared with that of the United States a strong argument for the triumph of the divergence school? Or, are the differences better explained by time lag? What will be the effect of the law of the European Union?

Loi de modernization sociale, or the law on social modernization, Law No. 2002-73 of 17 January, 2002, provides a definition of harassment and provides sanctions. Furthermore, this law imposes obligations on companies regarding moral harassment or "mobbing." The law requires employers to protect the physical and mental health of their employees. Articles L. 122-49 through L. 122-54 of the Labor Code and article 222-33-2 of the Penal Code address moral harassment. *See, e.g.,* Maria Isabel S. Guerrero, *The Development of Moral Harassment (Or Mobbing) Law in Sweden and France as a Step Towards EU Legislation*, 27 B.C. INT'L & COMP. L. REV. 477 (2004); David C. Yamada, *Crafting a Legislative Response to Workplace Bullying*, 8 EMPLOYEE RTS. & EMP. POL'Y J. 475 (2004). Although French law lags behind U.S. law in development in employment discrimination and sexual harassment, it arguably is ahead of U.S. law on moral harassment or bullying. *See* Yamada, *supra.* As discussed in the U.S., Chapter 3 in this book, the only employee harassment covered by legislation is harassment based on the characteristics covered by employment discrimination laws – race, color, sex, religion, national origin, age, and disability. As far as general harassment, unrelated to those characteristics, it is left to tort law, specifically the tort theory of intentional infliction of emotional distress, under which plaintiffs rarely win.

On the issue of religious discrimination, French law has been criticized (not specifically in the employment context) for permitting discrimination against religious sects. *See generally* Note, Nathaniel Stinnett, *Defining Away Religious Freedom in Europe: How Four Democracies Get Away With Discriminating Against Minority Religions*, 28 B.C. INT'L & COMP. L. REV. 429 (2005). In 2004, France passed a law that prohibits the wearing of "ostentatious" religious symbols in the public schools. Law No. 2004-22 of Mar. 15, 2004. *See* Adrien Katherine Wing & Monica Nigh Smith, *Critical Race Feminism Lifts the Veil? Muslim Women, France, and the Headscarf Ban*, 39 U.C. DAVIS. L. REV. 743 (2006). Although the law applies to many types of religious symbols, it is widely viewed as being directed at the hijabs (headscarves) worn by Muslim women and girls.

Law No. 2005-32 of January 18, 2005 provides that a foreign national who intends to settle in France for a long term must demonstrate a sufficient understanding of the French language or must agree to acquire such language ability within two years of arrival. International Labor Supp. 2005, *supra*, at 3-15 to 3-16.

The future of French employment discrimination law seems bound to follow the law of the EU, which is quite progressive. *See* EC Equal Treatment Framework Directive, 2000/78/EC.

F. PRIVACY

Article 9 of the Civil Code, Law No. 70-643 of July 17, 1970 provides as follows:

> Everyone has a right to respect for his privacy.
> Judges may, without prejudice to compensation for injury suffered, prescribe all measures, such as sequestration, seizure and others, appropriate to prevent or terminate an attack on privacy; such measures may, in urgent cases, be ordered summarily.

France appears to be a country to watch regarding privacy issues in the workplace. One of the biggest concerns in the workplace today is unauthorized checking and monitoring of computers in the workplace. Although privacy in the workplace has long been a concern for developed nations, the nations of Western Europe tend to recognize stronger privacy rights and to provide greater legal protection of those rights than many other nations. *See* Yohei Suda, *Monitoring E-Mail of Employees in the Private Sector: A Comparison Between Western Europe and the United States*, 4 Wash. U. Global Stud. L. Rev. 209 (2005); *EU Has Strict Curbs on Employee Monitoring Compared to Weak Rules in the United States*, Daily Lab. Rep. (BNA) No. 49, at A-4 (March 14, 2006). Professor Lawrence Rothstein has explained the difference in privacy protection in the U.S. and Europe as follows:

> At least in part, the difference in legal protection stems from a differing conception of what values are being protected. In the U.S. the value of privacy is most frequently mentioned with regard to protection against surveillance; in continental Europe (and countries influenced by continental labor law), the value most frequently mentioned in the electronic surveillance context is human dignity.

> Lawrence E. Rothstein, *Privacy or Dignity?: Electronic Monitoring in the Workplace*, 19 N.Y.L. Sch. J. Int'l & Comp. L. 379, 381 (2000).

Professor Rothstein argues that dignity rather than privacy provides a better basis for developing legal protections for workers against electronic monitoring. What is the difference?

France is at the forefront as far as addressing the modern privacy concerns at work. The Cour de Cassation recently addressed the issue of employers reading employees' e-mail messages.

PHILLIPE K V. CATHNET-SCIENCE

Cour de Cassation
Labor Chamber
Public hearing dated May 17, 2005

Appeal reference no.: 03-40017

President: M. Sargos

REPUBLIC OF FRANCE
IN THE NAME OF THE FRENCH PEOPLE

IN THE NAME OF THE FRENCH PEOPLE

THE COUR DE CASSATION, LABOR CHAMBER, has ruled as follows:

Regarding the sole argument:

With respect to articles 8 of the European convention on safeguard of human rights and fundamental liberties, 9 of the Civil Code, 9 of the new Code of civil procedure and L. 120-2 of the Labor Code;

Whereas, pursuant to a judgement challenged, Mr. X . . . , hired as drafter (*dessinateur*) on October 23, 1995 by Nycomed Amersham Medical Systems named since Cathnet-Science, has been dismissed for serious violation on August 3, 1999 for the motive that pursuant to finding erotic photographs in the drawer of his desk, a research had been performed on his computer which enabled to find a bunch of files, which were totally foreign to his duties and filed in a file named "personal";

Whereas to rule that the dismissal was based on a serious offence, the court of appeal states that in the present case the employer when opening the employee's files, had not done this in the context of systematical control performed during his absence as such a control was neither permitted by the employment agreement, nor by the in-house rules, but had done this pursuant to finding erotic photographs with no link to the activity of Mr. X . . . , which formed exceptional circumstances enabling it to control the content of the computer's hard disk, it being recalled that the access to this hard disk was free, as no personal code had been granted to the employee to stop any person other than its user from opening files;

Whereas, however, that, with the exception of a risk or of a particular event, the employer can not open the files identified by the employee as being personal contained on the computer's hard disk made available to the latter except in the sole presence of the latter or after the latter has been duly called;

That by ruling of the sort, while the opening of the personal files, in the absence of the interested person, had not been justified by any risk or particular event, the court of appeal has violated the above texts.

ON THESE GROUNDS:

QUASHES AND ANNULS, in all its provisions, the judgement rendered on November 6, 2002, among the parties, by the Paris Court of Appeal;

returns, as a consequence, the parties and the cause to their initial condition prior to such judgement and, for justice to be made, remands them before the Versailles Court of Appeal;

Condemns Cathnet-Science, formerly Nycomed Amersham Medical Systems to the costs;

With respect to article 700 of the new Code of civil procedure, rejects the claim of Cathnet-Science, formerly Nycomed Amersham Medical Systems;

Rules that the Attorney General (*Procureur Général*) of the Cour de Cassation shall take care of forwarding this judgement for transcription in the margin or for attachment to the cancelled judgement;

Performed and judged by the Cour de Cassation, Labor chamber, and pronounced by the president in his public hearing of seventeen May two thousand five.

Challenged decision: Paris Court of Appeal (22nd chamber, section A) 2002-11-06

————————

The result in *Phillipe K.* follows from the Cour de Cassation's decision in *Société Nikon France c/ Monsieur O.*, *supra*, in which the employer's termination of an employee based on his personal use of a company computer in violation of express company policies was overturned. Before *Nikon France*, the Cour de Cassation had declared two limitations on private sector employers' monitoring of employees: (1) employers must give advance notice of monitoring; and (2) employers could not monitor employees during off-duty hours. *See Neocel v. Spaeter*, Cass. Soc., Oct. 2, 2001, Bull. Civ. No. 291, discussed in Suda, *supra*, at 253. *Nikon France* expanded the privacy rights of an employee by recognizing privacy rights in activities during working hours. Suda, *supra*, at 255. Yohei Suda describes the innovation of *Nikon France* as follows:

> According to the European and American approaches, including French case law before *Nikon France*, an employer in the private sector may legally monitor the personal e-mail of employees sent during business hours as long as there is advance notice of the monitoring. This means that the interests of an employer prevailed so long as advance notice was given. The court in *Nikon France*, on the other hand, considered complete access to personal messages to be disproportionate. Thus, the decision prohibits an employer from having unlimited access to personal e-mail, unless exceptional circumstances exist, because personal e-mail is protected by the right of secrecy of correspondence, which forms a part of the right to privacy in the workplace during business hours. In this sense, *Nikon France* puts the interests of employee above those of an employer.
>
> Suda, *supra*, at 257.

Furthermore, the Attorney General of the Cour de Cassation in his conclusion opined that a total prohibition on personal use of a company computer during business hours would be unrealistic; thus, employers must tolerate some nonwork use of company computers during working hours. *Id.* at 258.

In March 2005, the French Data Protection Authority published a report regarding employee rights and employer responsibilities on geolocalization systems (GPS). This report recommended that employers notify employees when these systems are being used, identify what information is stored and retained, place limitations on the duration of storing this information, and provide access to this information to employees. *See French Data Protection Commission Issues GPS Employee Monitoring Guidelines*, DAILY LAB. REP. (BNA) No. 62, at A-4 (Apr. 1, 2005).

The Internet Rights Forum (*Forum des Droits surl'Internet*), a body of experts that advises the government on Internet law and regulatory issues, issued guidelines for bloggers. *See French Code of Conduct for Blogs Includes Standards for Employees*, DAILY LAB. REP. (BNA) No. 217, at A-4 (Nov. 10, 2005). The forum recognized that French courts have given employees a range of personal use on company-provided equipment and networks, but it cautioned that employers' interests must be considered, and abuse of freedom of expression by employees can be considered a fault.

Now that the balance has tipped in favor of employees on the privacy issue of employer computer monitoring in France, what problems might employers face? In a recent case, a French appellate court (not the Cour de Cassation) held an employer liable for trademark violation perpetrated on a company computer. *See Lucent Technologies v. SA ESCOTA*, Cour d'Appel d'Aix-en-Provence, No. 2006-170 3/13/06, reported in *French Appeals Court Finds Employer Is Liable for Employee Internet Activity*, DAILY LAB. REP. (BNA) No. 68 (Apr. 10, 2006). Employer Lucent had issued rules on personal use of company computers authorizing employees to make "reasonable use" of company computers and Internet connections for personal use so long as the activity was not during normal working hours and complied with French law. *Id.* The employee downloaded the plaintiff company's logo and created a parody Web site. Lucent argued that it could not be held vicariously liable for acts of its employee beyond his job description and official role in the company. The court reasoned that under Lucent's rules on personal use, the employee was acting within his job description and role in the company.

Notes

1. In view of *Nikon France* and *Cathnet-Science*, on the one hand, and *Lucent Technologies* (although not a decision of the Cour de Cassation), on the other, are employers in France in a quandary? What rules or policies should they issue regarding their computer monitoring and employees' personal use of employer-owned computers and systems?

2. It seems that France has been less innovative and less pro-employee than the United States in the development of employment discrimination law, but more innovative and more pro-employee than the United States in the development of workplace privacy law. How do you explain this? Do you think the development of workplace privacy law in the EU will spur the United States to develop more employee-protective law in that area?

3. Christophe Vigneau suggests that labor law in the age of globalization may be "reduced" to recognition and protection of fundamental human rights, such as privacy. Vigneau, *supra*, at 141. What does this suggest about the future of labor law in France? In the United States? Is the International Labour Organization's emphasis on the Declaration on Fundamental Principles and Rights at Work, see *supra* Chapter 2 on the ILO, a recognition of this scaled down role of labor law?

---

11 China

A. INTRODUCTION

1. Introduction to the Social and Historical Context

If sheer size, populousness, and continuity of influence are the measures of a superpower, China stands virtually unchallenged among the nations of the world. The actual age of a civilization self-identified as Chinese remains unknown and subject to reestimation with every stunning archaeological discovery, but if one were to apply retrospectively the definition of statehood under modern international law, China has been a "state" for more than two thousand years: it has had a defined territory (although ever expanding), a population (although ever growing), a government in control of the population and territory (which became ever more sophisticated in managing a large, densely inhabited space), and the capacity to engage in foreign relations with other states (the nomadic peoples of Inner Asia in ancient times, the global community today).

Given China's long history, in order to understand any aspect of contemporary Chinese law, it is important to recognize the persistence of tradition, in particular the influence of Confucianism. "Indeed, Confucianism is still an integral part of the 'psycho-cultural construct' of the contemporary Chinese intellectual as well as the Chinese peasant; it remains a defining characteristic of the Chinese mentality." Tu Wei-ming, *The Confucian Tradition in* Paul S. Ropp., ed. Heritage of China: Contemporary Perspectives on Chinese Civilization 136 (1990). In the West, we tend to forget that, if one looks closely enough at so-called Western legal systems, the threads of tradition, from Greece to Rome to modern Europe and the Americas, are clearly present. H. Patrick Glenn, Legal Traditions of the World 35, 133 (2000).

In order to justify its own legitimacy, the Communist regime which came to power in 1949 necessarily rejected traditional culture and law as "feudal." Now that the Party has consolidated its control and proved itself by improving living conditions for the vast majority of the population, it is no longer heretical to recognize the ongoing influence of tradition. J. Chen, Chinese Law: Towards an Understanding of Chinese Law, Its Nature and Development 7 (1999).

A common misconception about Chinese legal culture is that, prior to modern times, China did not have "law" as it is understood in the West, or if it did, "law" was viewed in purely negative terms as an instrument of repression. Written law has existed in China for at least four thousand years, and probably much earlier. J. Chen, *supra*, at 6. However, with the establishment of the imperial system in the second century B.C. and the adoption of Confucianism (itself highly syncretic) as state orthodoxy, Chinese legal culture came to be characterized by certain distinct features. It may be argued that these features form a fundamental core of the tradition, "underlying structures" which will persist as long as the tradition itself survives. GLENN, *supra*, at 35.

In the Chinese scheme of things, law evolves naturally as a by-product of social organization and is inextricably intertwined with the practical concerns of government. It is not of divine origin, in contrast to Western traditions such as Judaism and Christianity.

> Moses received his golden tablets on a mountain top, but Confucius reasoned from daily life without the aid of any deity . . . [The rules of propriety] came from the moral character of the universe itself, from this world, not from another world beyond human ken . . . [Legal rules] were but one expression of this morality – models or examples to be followed, or working rules of administration or ritual observance.
>
> JOHN KING FAIRBANK & MERLE GOLDMAN, CHINA A NEW HISTORY 183 (1999).

Hence, law contributes to the preservation of social order and stability, without which the regular rhythms necessary for (what was, and today still is) a primarily agricultural society are threatened.

Since the state occupies the apex of a social pyramid with families at the base, law is merely a supplement to the correct ordering of interpersonal relations within the family.

> There is [true] government, when the prince is prince, and the minister is minister; when the father is father, and the son is son.
>
> ANALECTS XII.11 (Legge trans.)

If the family functions properly, invoking the law will only become necessary in rare situations where conflict occurs despite best efforts to prevent it or deviant behavior does not respond to gentler methods of education and persuasion. As Confucius remarks:

> In hearing litigations, I am like any other body. What is necessary, however, is to cause the people to have no litigations.
>
> ANALECTS XII.13 (Legge trans.)

Thus, Chinese law was "first and foremost a political tool, [and] operated in a vertical direction with its primary concern for state interests." J. CHEN, *supra*, at 15. It was not primarily intended to facilitate economic interaction among autonomous individuals. And it did not provide a basis for asserting "natural rights" against state interference, which, even in the West, is a comparatively recent development. Karen Turner, *Sage Kings and Laws in* ROPP, *supra*, at 104; Jack L. Dull, *The Evolution of Government in China in* ROPP, *supra*, at 55.

This is not to say that, although the Chinese state was authoritarian, hierarchical, and paternalistic, Chinese tradition gave rulers free rein to oppress and exploit the masses. As the benevolent patriarch of all his people, the ruler justified his power only by taking proper care of them. The ruler leads by example, not by the threat of punishment. Although many rulers in fact failed to meet these exacting standards, the ideal remained intact.

> [Ji Kang] asked Confucius about government, saying, What do you say to killing the unprincipled for the good of the principled? Confucius replied, Sir, in carrying on your government, why should you use killing at all? Let your evinced desires be for what is

good, and the people will be good. The relation between superiors and inferiors, is like
that between the wind and the grass. The grass must bend, when the wind blows across it.

ANALECTS XII.19 (Legge trans.)

In its first encounters with the countries of post-Renaissance Europe, eager for trade,
imperial China viewed Europeans with considerable disdain; Europeans in turn regarded
China with awe and respect – a large, well-ordered empire quite capable of providing for its
own material needs and the dominant presence – culturally, militarily, and economically –
in northeast Asia. Jonathan Spence, *Western Perceptions of China from the Late Sixteenth
Century to the Present, in* ROPP, *supra*, at 1. The eighteenth century philosopher Voltaire
praised China's laws, because they did more than punish crime – they rewarded virtue.
Spence, *supra*, at 4. In 1820 China produced about a third of the world's GDP, more than
all of Europe. ANGUS MADDISON, CHINESE ECONOMIC PERFORMANCE IN THE LONG RUN
40 (1998) (Table 2.2a).

However, soon thereafter, following a often repeated historical pattern, China
descended into a period of internal weakness and foreign occupation which lasted a
century. In its search for new sources of vitality, China looked to foreign models for inspi-
ration. To construct a legal system more responsive to the demands of the modern world,
China drew mainly upon continental legal systems, especially the German Civil Code,
directly, and indirectly, through Japan and the former Soviet Union. J. CHEN, *supra*,
at 21-22.

Especially after the founding of the People's Republic of China (PRC) in 1949, Soviet
law served as the primary model. It remains the foreign legal system which has influenced
China the most, although the Soviet Union itself no longer exists. The current system
of labor and employment law, its dominant purpose being the optimal administration of
human resources, is still deeply rooted in the old Soviet system.

Generally speaking, the influence of the common law on the development of the
Chinese legal system has been limited.

> [A]s Roscoe Pound pointed out, materials in common law were too unsystematic, too
> bulky, and too scattered, and its technique was too hard to acquire . . . Romanist
> Continental law was based on the central concept of two authorities, that of the state
> over the citizen and that of the *pater familias* over his dependents. This concept fitted
> well into the traditional Chinese conception of law . . .

> J. CHEN, *supra*, at 22 (footnotes omitted).

During the last quarter century, as China has diversified beyond a Soviet-style command economy, it has drawn in eclectic fashion from a number of modern legal systems
to confront particular problems which the Soviet model did not address – corporate governance, securities markets, intellectual property rights. The process of borrowing, from
its inception, has been intensely practical and purposive: looking for what will best contribute to China's economic development and reemergence as a world power, and not
for internal consistency or elegant structure per se. J. CHEN, *supra*, at 40-43.

2. The Constitutional Framework

China has had four constitutions since 1949: 1954, 1975, 1978, and 1982. All of the PRC's
constitutions were influenced, in greater or lesser part, by Soviet law; the 1982 Constitution
was based on the 1977 Soviet Constitution. These numerous changes in China's basic legal

structure – for the Constitution is referred to as the "mother" law – reflect the tumultuous era of early Communist rule. With the ascension of the pragmatic leader Deng Xiaoping in the late 1970s, and the adoption of a new Constitution shortly thereafter, the legal system entered a period of relative stability. Although the 1982 Constitution has been amended four times (1988, 1993, 1999, and 2004), the revisions are in the nature of fine-tuning the basic vision. "The 1982 Constitution is essentially a Dengist constitution, reflecting Deng Xiaoping's ideas for modernising China, i.e., social stability, economic development and opening to the outside." J. CHEN, *supra*, at 69.

1982 Constitution (as amended)
http://www.oefre.unibe.ch/law/icl/ch00000_.html

Preamble

China is one of the countries with the longest histories in the world. The people of all nationalities in China have jointly created a splendid culture and have a glorious revolutionary tradition.

Feudal China was gradually reduced after 1840 to a semi-colonial and semi-feudal country. The Chinese people waged wave upon wave of heroic struggles for national independence and liberation and for democracy and freedom. Great and earth-shaking historical changes have taken place in China in the 20th century. The Revolution of 1911, led by Dr. Sun Yat-sen, abolished the feudal monarchy and gave birth to the Republic of China. But the Chinese people had yet to fulfill their historical task of overthrowing imperialism and feudalism.

After waging hard, protracted and tortuous struggles, armed and otherwise, the Chinese people of all nationalities led by the Communist Party of China with Chairman Mao Zedong as its leader ultimately, in 1949, overthrew the rule of imperialism, feudalism, and bureaucrat-capitalism, won the great victory of the new democratic revolution and founded the People's Republic of China. Thereupon the Chinese people took state power into their own hands and became masters of the country.

After the founding of the People's Republic, the transition of Chinese society from a new democratic to a socialist society was effected step by step. The socialist transformation of the private ownership of the means of production was completed, the system of exploitation of man by man eliminated and the socialist system established. The people's democratic dictatorship led by the working class and based on the alliance of workers and peasants, which is in essence the dictatorship of the proletariat, has been consolidated and developed. The Chinese people and the Chinese People's Liberation Army have thwarted aggression, sabotage, and armed provocations by imperialists and hegemonists, safeguarded China's national independence and security and strengthened its national defence. Major successes have been achieved in economic development. An independent and fairly comprehensive socialist system of industry has in the main been established. There has been a marked increase in agricultural production. Significant progress has been made in educational, scientific, cultural, and other undertakings, and socialist ideological education has yielded noteworthy results. The living standards of the people have improved considerably.

Both the victory of China's new-democratic revolution and the successes of its socialist cause have been achieved by the Chinese people of all nationalities under the leadership of the Communist Party of China and the guidance of Marxism-Leninism and Mao Zedong Thought, and by upholding truth, correcting errors and overcoming numerous difficulties and hardships. China will stay in the primary stage of socialism for a long period of time. The basic task of the nation is to concentrate its efforts on socialist modernization along the road of Chinese-style socialism. Under the guidance of Marxism-Leninism, Mao Zedong Thought, Deng Xiaoping Theory and the important thought of 'Three Represents', the Chinese people of all nationalities will continue to adhere to the people's democratic dictatorship, follow the socialist road, persist in reform and opening-up, steadily improve socialist institutions, develop a socialist market economy, advance socialist democracy, improve the socialist legal system and work hard and self-reliantly to modernize industry, agriculture, national defense and science and technology step by step, promote the co-ordinated development of the material, political and spiritual civilizations to turn China into a powerful and prosperous socialist country with a high level of culture and democracy.

The exploiting classes as such have been eliminated in our country. However, class struggle will continue to exist within certain limits for a long time to come. The Chinese people must fight against those forces and elements, both at home and abroad, that are hostile to China's socialist system and try to undermine it.

Taiwan is part of the sacred territory of the People's Republic of China. It is the lofty duty of the entire Chinese people, including our compatriots in Taiwan, to accomplish the great task of reunifying the motherland.

In building socialism it is imperative to rely on the workers, peasants and intellectuals and unite with all the forces that can be united. In the long years of revolution and construction, there has been formed under the leadership of the Communist Party of China a broad patriotic united front that is composed of democratic parties and people's organizations and embraces all socialist working people, all builders of socialism, all patriots who support socialism and all patriots who stand for reunification of the motherland. This united front will continue to be consolidated and developed. The Chinese People's Political Consultative Conference is a broadly representative organization of the united front, which has played a significant historical role and will continue to do so in the political and social life of the country, in promoting friendship with the people of other countries and in the struggle for socialist modernization and for the reunification and unity of the country. The system of multi-party cooperation and political consultation led by the Communist Party of China will exist and develop in China for a long time to come.

The People's Republic of China is a unitary multinational state built up jointly by the people of all its nationalities. Socialist relations of equality, unity and mutual assistance have been established among them and will continue to be strengthened. In the struggle to safeguard the unity of the nationalities, it is necessary to combat big-nation chauvinism, mainly Han chauvinism, and also necessary to combat local national chauvinism. The state does its utmost to promote the common prosperity of all nationalities in the country.

China's achievements in revolution and construction are inseparable from support by the people of the world. The future of China is closely linked with that of the whole world. China adheres to an independent foreign policy as well as to the five principles of mutual respect for sovereignty and territorial integrity, mutual nonaggression, non-interference in each other's internal affairs, equality and mutual benefit, and peaceful coexistence in developing diplomatic relations and economic and cultural exchanges with other countries; China consistently opposes imperialism, hegemonism, and colonialism, works to strengthen unity with the people of other countries, supports the oppressed nations and the developing countries in their just struggle to win and preserve national independence and develop their national economies, and strives to safeguard world peace and promote the cause of human progress.

This Constitution affirms the achievements of the struggles of the Chinese people of all nationalities and defines the basic system and basic tasks of the state in legal form; it is the fundamental law of the state and has supreme legal authority. The people of all nationalities, all state organs, the armed forces, all political parties and public organizations and all enterprises and undertakings in the country must take the Constitution as the basic norm of conduct, and they have the duty to uphold the dignity of the Constitution and ensure its implementation.

Article 5 [Socialist Legal System, Rule of Law]

(1) The People's Republic of China practices ruling the country in accordance with the law and building a socialist country of law.
(2) The state upholds the uniformity and dignity of the socialist legal system.
(3) No law or administrative or local rules and regulations shall contravene the Constitution.
(4) All state organs, the armed forces, all political parties and public organizations, and all enterprises and undertakings must abide by the Constitution and the law. All acts in violation of the Constitution and the law must be looked into.
(5) No organization or individual may enjoy the privilege of being above the Constitution and the law.

Article 6 [Socialist Public Ownership]

(1) The basis of the socialist economic system of the People's Republic of China is socialist public ownership of the means of production, namely, ownership by the whole people and collective ownership by the working people. The system of socialist public ownership supersedes the system of exploitation of man by man; it applies the principle of "from each according to his ability, to each according to his work."
(2) During the primary stage of socialism, the State adheres to the basic economic system with the public ownership remaining dominant and diverse sectors of the economy developing side by side, and to the distribution system with the distribution according to work remaining dominant and the coexistence of a variety of modes of distribution.

Article 7 [State Economy]

The State-owned economy, that is, the socialist economy under ownership by the whole people, is the leading force in the national economy. The State ensures the consolidation and growth of the State-owned economy.

Article 9 [Resources]

(1) Mineral resources, waters, forests, mountains, grassland, unreclaimed land, beaches, and other natural resources are owned by the state, that is, by the whole people, with the exception of the forests, mountains, grassland, unreclaimed land, and beaches that are owned by collectives in accordance with the law.

(2) The state ensures the rational use of natural resources and protects rare animals and plants. The appropriation or damage of natural resources by any organization or individual by whatever means is prohibited.

Article 10 [Land Ownership]

(1) Land in the cities is owned by the state.

(2) Land in the rural and suburban areas is owned by collectives except for those portions which belong to the state in accordance with the law; house sites and privately farmed plots of cropland and hilly land are also owned by collectives.

(3) The State may, in the public interest and in accordance with the provisions of law, expropriate or requisition land for its use and shall make compensation for the land expropriated or requisitioned.

(4) No organization or individual may appropriate, buy, sell or otherwise engage in the transfer of land by unlawful means. The right to the use of land may be transferred according to law.

(5) All organizations and individuals who use land must make rational use of the land.

Notes

1. Note, that after calling attention to China's long and glorious past, the Preamble "fast forwards" more than two thousand years to the period of the Opium War of 1839–1842, in which China was defeated by the British and forcibly opened to foreign trade. Britain balanced its importations of tea to the homeland by exporting opium to China from its empire in India. FAIRBANK & GOLDMAN, *supra*, at 198. This shameful period of internal weakness and foreign exploitation was only brought to an end by the founding of the People's Republic of China in 1949. But bitter memory of the past has not disappeared and still characterizes China's determined independence in international relations.

2. In the 1950s, "[t]he socialist transformation of the private ownership of the means of production was completed, the system of exploitation of man by man eliminated and the socialist system established." After this period of often violent intimidation, ownership of land, natural resources, and the means of production was vested in the state. 1982 Constitution art. 9, 10 (art. 10 first constitutional provision to define explicitly ownership of land). J. CHEN, *supra*, at 69 and source cited. The distinction between land ownership in rural areas as opposed to urban areas is of little practical significance. Private ownership and private enterprise were revived by the policies of Deng Xiaoping in the late 1970s as part of a transitional phase to the ultimate goal of socialism. During this interim period (of undetermined duration) China practices a "socialist market economy." (1993 amendments) Art. 11 states that "[i]ndividual, private and other non-public economies that exist *within the limits prescribed by law* are major components of the socialist market economy." (Emphasis supplied.)

3. In stark contrast to the U.S. Constitution, in which political parties are not mentioned at all, the PRC Constitution gives center stage to the role of the Communist Party. Other political parties are permitted a (marginal) existence but yield to the leadership of the Communist Party. The Party dominates all areas of political, economic, and social life. J. CHEN, *supra*, at 81. It is not meaningful to speak of any organization which is independent of Party control. *See infra* discussion of the Trade

Union Law. However, art. 5 of the Constitution does state that "[n]o organization or individual may enjoy the privilege of being above the Constitution and the law." This provision was inserted to control the excesses of political factionalism which prevailed during the Cultural Revolution. Party membership does not provide an automatic shield against the proscriptions of the criminal law, and since Party members occupy virtually all positions of power and influence, they are more likely to be prosecuted for white collar crimes such as bribery and corruption. Hilary K. Josephs, *The Upright and the Low-Down: An Examination of Official Corruption in the United States and the People's Republic of China*, 27 SYRACUSE J. INT'L L. & COM. 269 (2000).

Article 42 [Work]

(1) Citizens of the People's Republic of China have the right as well as the duty to work.

(2) Using various channels, the state creates conditions for employment, strengthens labor protection, improves working conditions, and, on the basis of expanded production, increases remuneration for work and social benefits.

(3) Work is the glorious duty of every able-bodied citizen. All working people in State-owned enterprises and in urban and rural economic collectives should perform their tasks with an attitude consonant with their status as masters of the country. The State promotes socialist labor emulation, and commends and rewards model and advanced workers. The State encourages citizens to take part in voluntary labor.

(4) The state provides necessary vocational training to citizens before they are employed.

Notes

1.   It is typical of constitutions in socialist countries *both* to bestow rights *and* impose duties upon their citizens. Also, *both* civil/political rights *as well as* cultural, economic and social rights are protected. YASH GHAI, HONG KONG'S NEW CONSTITUTIONAL ORDER 125 (2d ed. 1999). By contrast, the U.S. Constitution is in the liberal democratic mold; citizens enjoy various rights against government interference without being subject to any duties towards society.

     [Liberal democratic constitutions are] oriented towards the market, emphasize individual civil, political and property rights and the equality of all citizens under the law as well as the generality of rules and their impartial administration . . .

     GHAI, *supra*, at 83.

     At this writing, there is considerable doubt that rights under the PRC Constitution are directly justiciable, without implementing legislation; until recently, it was assumed definitively that they were not. Chris X. Lin, *A Quiet Revolution: An Overview of China's Judicial Reform*, 4 ASIAN-PACIFIC L. & POL'Y J. 180 (2003). In any event, because of reforms to the labor and employment system since the 1980s, no Chinese court is likely to rule that the state is required to provide jobs to all citizens, in order to effectuate their "right to work." By contrast, lack of gainful employment subjects one to the accusation of "social parasitism" and technically speaking, may provide justification for administrative detention. Randall Peerenboom, *Out of the Pan and Into the Fire: Well-Intentioned But Misguided Recommendations to Eliminate All Forms of Administrative Detention in China*, 98 Nw. U. L. Rev. 991, 1008 (2004) (noting that even liberal democracies have laws that are thinly veiled efforts to deter vagrancy).

2.   Chinese labor law guarantees minimum wages, which are set by local authorities according to local living standards. Labor Law art 48 *infra*. The state does not guarantee universal availability or equitable distribution of fringe benefits, such as health insurance, worker's compensation, retirement pensions, and housing subsidies. Labor Law art. 70-76 (Social Insurance and Benefits) *infra*. These benefits are tied to one's employer and one's status within the establishment; two people performing exactly the same work, even within the same company, may receive very different benefit packages. Ting Gong, *Corruption and Reform in China: An Analysis of Unintended Consequences*, 19 Crime, L. & Soc. Change 311 (1993).

Article 48 [Gender Equality]

(1) Women in the People's Republic of China enjoy equal rights with men in all spheres of life, political, economic, cultural, and social, including family life.
(2) The state protects the rights and interests of women, applies the principle of equal pay for equal work for men and women alike, and trains and selects cadres from among women.

Notes

1.   From a modern perspective, one of the negative legacies of the Confucian heritage was the subordination of women in all areas of social life. Women are hardly even mentioned in the Analects of Confucius. Traditional Chinese society was patriarchal and patrilinear: property belonged to the men of the family; fathers enjoyed legal authority over women and children; and women were considered morally and intellectually inferior to men. Patricia Ebrey, *Women, Marriage, and the Family*, in Ropp, *supra*, at 204. In fact, women exercised a great deal of power behind the scenes, particularly in their role as mothers and mothers-in-law. The Empress Dowager of the last dynasty, the Qing, ruled "from behind the screen" (chuilian tingzheng) for more than forty years until her death in 1908. Fairbank & Goldman, *supra*, at 212-13.

2.   The Chinese Communist Party was very successful in making the emancipation of women one of the cornerstones of its reformist agenda. The Party popularized the saying, "Women hold up half the sky" (fünü neng ding banbian tian). Women from all classes of society flocked to the Communist movement during the 1930s and 1940s. After 1949, women achieved legal equality with men within the family and outside the home, entering the labor force in large numbers. Margaret Y. K. Woo, *Biology and Equality: Challenge for Feminism in the Socialist and the Liberal State*, 42 Emory L.J. 143, 148-49 (1993). In addition to the promise of equality in the constitution, there are numerous laws which are protective of women's rights. Woo, *supra*, at 155. *See, e.g.*, Labor Law art. 13, 58-63, *infra*. China is a party to the Convention on the Elimination of All Forms of Discrimination Against Women ("CEDAW").

3. In spite of formal legal protections, women remain a minority in positions of authority and power, are paid less than men for comparable work, and are limited in their access to higher education. Woo, *supra*, at 151-53; Margaret Maurer-Fazio, Thomas G. Rawski, & Wei Zhang, *Inequality In the Rewards for Holding Up Half the Sky: Gender Wage Gaps in China's Urban Labour Market, 1988-94*, 41 CHINA J. 55 (1999). Gains achieved by women during the period of the command economy have eroded since the 1970s under the influence of market reforms. Because women are still primarily responsible for household duties, as wives and mothers, efficiency-driven businesses prefer male employees. Woo, *supra*, at 151-52; Yuzhen Liu, *Gender Patterns and Women's Experience in the IT Industry in China*, 5 PER-SPECTIVES 20 (2004), http:www.oycf.org/Perspectives/26_0930004/Sep04_Issue.pdf. Women are subject to redundancy dismissal in far greater numbers than men. U.S. Department of State, Country Reports on Human Rights Practices – 2004, China, available at http://www.state.gov. It is common for employers to place advertisements that specify gender (and age) as hiring qualifications.

4. As in other legal systems, laws which are protective of women as a class, such as paid maternity leave, may have the unintended effect of reinforcing discrimination against them. Additional legislation, equally difficult to implement, then becomes necessary to counter unintended consequences or loopholes in existing law. The 1992 Women's Protection Law (Funü quanyi baozhang fa) prohibited dismissal on the basis of marriage, pregnancy, childbirth, or nursing. The 2005 amendments also prohibit reduction in salary for the same reasons. *See* http://npc.people.com.cn/GB/14957/3648641.html.

5. Another of the 2005 amendments to the Women's Protection Law expressly authorizes a civil cause of action for sexual harassment (xing saorao). The law does not define sexual harassment. Although the phenomenon appears to be widespread, few cases have been filed. See M. Ulric Killion, *Post-WTO China: Quest for Human Right Safeguards in Sexual Harassment Against Working Women*, 12 TUL. J. INT'L & COMP. L. 201 (2004).

6. On the positive side, anecdotal evidence suggests that working women in China receive more support from the extended family in caring for their children than in other countries. Carol Hymowitz, Chinese Women Bosses Say Long Hours Don't Hurt Their Kids, http://www.careerjournal.com, May 18, 2005.

B. SOCIALIST MODERNIZATION AND LIBERATION OF THE PRODUCTIVE FORCES

For the last quarter century, China has had one of the world's fastest growing economies. According to official statistics, China's annual growth rate of Gross Domestic Product (GDP) has averaged 9.2 percent. Real per capita GDP (PPP adjusted) increased from $430 international dollars in 1980 to $4,475 international dollars in 2002. China is now the sixth largest trading nation. At the same time, China has been able to dramatically reduce the proportion of the population living in "absolute poverty" (less than $1.00/day by the World Bank standard). Douglas Zhihua Zeng, China's Employment Challenges and Strategies after the WTO Accession (World Bank Policy Research Working Paper 3522, Feb. 2005), http://www.ssrn.com. China is projected to succeed the United States as the world's greatest economic power by the middle of the twenty-first century. *The Real Great Leap Forward*, THE ECONOMIST, Oct. 2, 2004 (available on Lexis).

In the context of China's long history, its ability to progress with great speed once conditions are ripe should come as no surprise. J. CHEN, *supra*, at 40-43. As in the past, China's success is due to skill at maximizing its human resources. Although inports of raw materials and modern technology are indispensable to China's rapid rate of growth, the main factor is the energy and resourcefulness of its people.

> [W]hat distinguishes China from other countries that have so far acceded to the WTO is the sheer size of its economy . . . Given the ample supply of low-cost labour in this populous country and the tremendous energy being released by the further deepening of its economic reforms, the potential for economic growth in China is enormous.
>
> Julia Ya Qin, *"WTO-Plus" Obligations and Their Implications for the World Trade Organization Legal System*, 37 J. WORLD TRADE 483, 510 (2003).

With respect to labor and employment, we will now review the accomplishments and deficiencies of the planned economy, which lasted from the 1950s until the late 1970s, and then perform the same kind of evaluation for the "socialist market economy," which was launched in the late 1970s and has continued until the present day.

1. The Planned Economy

When the PRC was founded in 1949, the country was in shambles after prolonged civil war and occupation by Japan. In 1952, it produced 5.2 percent of world GDP, as compared to 32.4 percent of world GDP in 1820. MADDISON, *supra*, at 40 (Tables 2.1 and 2.2a). The economy was overwhelmingly agricultural; most of the manufacturing sector consisted of self-employed craftsmen. FAIRBANK & GOLDMAN, *supra*, at 357. The United States had supported the Nationalist Party in the 1946–49 civil war and continued to support it as the legitimate government of China after its retreat to Taiwan. Because of U.S. foreign policy, China was largely isolated from contact with developed countries in the West, which might have provided capital and technological know-how for its economic development. In its search for a model of rapid industrialization, a source of economic aid, and a sympathetic political ally, China logically turned to the Soviet Union. FAIRBANK & GOLDMAN, *supra*, at 358-59.

However, China's industrial revolution was largely internally financed by a transfer of resources from rural agriculture to urban industry. The state *created* a new urban industrial class with privileged access to food, jobs, and fringe benefits, while the rural population was expected to be largely self-supporting. *See generally* ANDREW G. WALDER, COMMUNIST NEO-TRADITIONALISM: WORK AND AUTHORITY IN CHINESE INDUSTRY (1986). Even as between major urban areas, strict limitations were imposed on geographic and occupational mobility.

The legal mechanisms for effectuating state control of human resource flows were (1) the household registration system (hukou zhidu), supplemented in 1985 by citizen identification cards; (2) job allocation through unified placement (tong'yi fenpei); and (3) the personnel dossier (dang'an zhidu). Although these restrictions have been modified and relaxed since the 1970s to accommodate a more diversified economy, the basic systems are still in place. Kam Wing Chan & Li Zhang, *The Hukou System and Rural-Urban Migration in China: Processes and Changes*, 160 CHINA Q. 818 (1999).

Although the 1954 Constitution guaranteed citizens' rights of free residential choice and migration, it was effectively superseded by regulations that tied every member of the population to a specific residential location. The constitutional right to freedom of movement was deleted by the 1975 Constitution; it is absent from the 1982 Constitution. A child's household registration was originally based on the mother's place of residence until 1998, when the regulations were amended to allow for a child to obtain status from either parent. *See* State Council, Notice to the Ministry of Public Security Approving Its Views on Resolution of Serious Problems in the Household Registration System [Guowuyuan pizhuan gong'an bu guanyu jiejue dangqian hukou guanli wenti gongzuozhong jige tuchu wenti yijian de tongzhi], CEILAW 112102199802, July 22, 1998. Without household registration in a major city such as Beijing or Shanghai, one did not have access to food staples (in the period when food was rationed), housing, education, and employment. Few avenues for changing to a more desirable household registration existed, admission to an institution of higher education or job transfer at the employer's behest being among them. Marriage to a resident was by itself not sufficient.

Contemporaneously with the establishment of the household registration system, government labor and education bureaus began filling job vacancies through the system of unified placement. HILARY K. JOSEPHS, LABOR LAW IN CHINA 20 (2d ed. 2003). On completion of their education, whether at the secondary or tertiary level, graduates were assigned to jobs. Assignments were made without regard to personal preference or in the case of university graduates, even educational background. Married couples were regularly assigned to jobs in different parts of the country, able to meet for one month personal leave per year. Technically, one could refuse to accept an assignment, but few dared. Disobedience to an official order was unpatriotic, "counterrevolutionary." Furthermore, employment opportunities outside the unified placement system were virtually nil.[1] The state had already nationalized private and foreign enterprise.

Together with the household registration system, job assignment controlled the growth of urban populations and maintained urban living standards. On the positive side, the government thereby prevented the growth of urban slums typical of developing countries. The system of job assignment also fostered the dispersion of trained personnel in a country with highly uneven levels of development. Educated people from the more economically advanced areas of China would not have gone willingly to less developed areas. JOSEPHS, *supra*, at 20-21. The Nobel Prize–winning economist Amartya Sen credits the Maoist policies of land reform, expansion of literacy, and improved health care as laying the necessary foundations for the post-1978 reforms. DEVELOPMENT AS FREEDOM 259-61 (1999).

The third instrument of control was the personnel file, or dossier. The dossier records all job changes, transfers, and disciplinary violations. The individual has no right to even examine its contents, let alone take possession of it. JOSEPHS, *supra*, at 97; Ministry of Labor and State Bureau of Personnel Records [Laodongbu Guojia dang'an ju], Regulations Concerning the Management of Personnel Files of State Enterprise Workers and Staff [Qiye zhigong dang'an guanli gongzuo guiding] (1992), art. 17 (4), 19 (1). During the era of the planned economy, typically, once a person was assigned a job, he spent his entire

---

[1] One limited alternative to job assignment was "substitution," whereby a permanent worker in a state enterprise could designate one of his children to succeed him as a permanent employee in the same enterprise, though not necessarily the same job as that which the parent had held. The substitution system was abolished in 1986. JOSEPHS, *supra*, at 21-25.

working career with that employer and the dossier remained with that employer. In the unusual situation where a person found another job on his own initiative, he could not change jobs without the original employer's consent to release his dossier. The case below illustrates the difficulty of job-switching without the employer's cooperation.

. . .

Background History of a Worker Who Resigned her Position for Another Job Source: Beijing Daily, July 12, 1988, p. 1, col. 1.

For a Worker to Change Jobs it Is Difficult Indeed

To relieve this difficulty, each district and county in Beijing municipality has set up a job market, and the municipal government has promulgated new regulations governing job changes by enterprise workers. So long as the job change is consistent with official policy, workers may now resign their positions to take other jobs.[2]

Who dares to be the first to resign? On April 6 of this year, a woman worker entered the job market of Xicheng District.

Background Item 1: An Ordinary Worker's Aggravations

The woman was named Ji Jingli, 29 years old, nothing spectacular in her past. She was sent down to the countryside after graduating high school in 1976. In 1978 she was assigned to a job in the wholesale dry goods division of the general merchandise company under the jurisdiction of the First Commercial Bureau (later to become the wholesale marketing division of the First Commercial Bureau). She worked in turn as a storekeeper, as a clerk, and as a child-care worker. With her employer's consent, she enrolled in a technical school from March 1984 to July 1985, thereby acquiring training in commercial enterprise management.

After graduating from the technical school, she requested a job transfer, hoping to put her knowledge to practical use. The response of the personnel department was that she should work contentedly in her present position and they would consider how best to employ her. However, until March of this year, Ji Jingli continued as a child-care worker. (During this period, she took a year and a half of maternity leave with her employer's permission. According to the authorities in the personnel department, there had been some preliminary discussion about reassigning her to another job, but because she went on leave, nothing materialized.)

Consequently, Ji Jingli wanted to leave her employer. By chance she found a suitable position at the Rosefinch Arts Palace, which is run by the Beijing Photographic Slide Factory. Within a short period, she and her husband had made no less than thirty visits to various department heads in order to secure her transfer.

But her employer would not release her. The reason was quite simple. Ji Jingli had received a detailed statement of account from the personnel department, demanding payment of the 1276 yuan she had earned in salary and bonus during her attendance at the technical school. The demand made by the personnel department was based on Document 104 (1986), Notice of Transmittal from the General Affairs Office of the Municipal Government, Accompanying

---

[2] According to regulations issued by the Beijing Labor Bureau which applied in Ji Jingli's situation, workers could resign unless they fell into officially certified categories, for example, jobs in industries with labor shortages or jobs which were deemed to be key positions. *See* Gong Shuji ed., The Practice of Labor Optimization [Youhua laodong zuhe shijian] 71-72 (Science Press ed. 1987).

an Investigation and Opinion of the Municipal Labor Bureau on the Payment of Training Fees by Workers Changing Jobs. Ji Jingli was unable to pay this sum of money. Even if she had been able, she would have been unwilling to do so.

On the morning of April 6, she went to the labor market of Xicheng District, carrying a letter of resignation.

The director of the labor market Wang Zhenliang listened to her narrative and then placed a call to her employer. The general affairs department and the personnel department of the company both corroborated her story. (Later they would claim that the demand for training fees was former company policy, no longer in effect. They claimed that the new municipal regulations governing job mobility, though effective January 1,[3] did not reach them until March, and therefore, they had extended application of the old policy for an extra three months.) Just as he was ending the conversation with company officials, Wang Zhenliang added, in a genial tone, that if the company would not release her, she could request a resignation.

Background Item 2: Company Policies Confronted By the Labor Market

There are quite a few people who have experienced the same problems as Ji Jingli. Almost every day at the Xicheng District labor market one would encounter someone whose hopes of changing jobs had been dashed by some arbitrary company policy.

There was an electrician who, through the job market, had found a position which was more conveniently located to his home. Little did he suspect that he would have to pass eleven "checkpoints" to transfer out of his present position. He "struggled through brambles and thorns," only to fail at the tenth checkpoint.

One factory instituted the following rules: a woman worker who wanted to transfer would have to find a man to replace her; a fifth-grade [wage level] worker would have to find an eighth-grade worker to replace him; a man who wanted to transfer would have to take his wife with him.

Seeing that the official policy of rational job mobility was going nowhere, the caseworkers at the job market lost their patience. Wang Zhenliang resolved to promote a policy encouraging unilateral resignations.

When Ji Jingli returned to work at noon on April 6, she was told that the manager wanted to see her.

As soon as they met, he told her that there was a way out of her dilemma. She responded that she would take it at once. He continued by saying that the matter of her resignation had already been discussed and that she should proceed to the personnel department. Ji Jingli was not at all surprised: if the company had reacted in this way, then they would surely let her go. And the whole thing had been accomplished in a few hours!

Background Item 3: Policy and the Ability to Take Advantage of It

Ji Jingli was intelligent and had made a detailed study of the municipal government's regulations on job switching. With her husband's assistance she had even made a photocopy of implementing regulations issued by the municipal labor bureau. On January 4, she had submitted to her employer a formal request for transfer. She was the only one who realized that in so doing, an ordinary worker was using official policy to challenge an employer.

---

[3] Under the new regulations, the old employer may request payment of training fees from the new employer, but the amount is limited to the actual costs of training. *Id.*

According to the regulations, an employer had three months to respond to a request for transfer. In Ji Jingli's case, the time for response expired on April 4. On that day she knocked on the manager's door. He told her that he was busy and would talk to her another time. So, on April 6, she entered the workplace feeling confident.

On April 7 her request for resignation was approved and stamped with the official seal.

On April 8 she changed jobs.

On April 9 she started work as an accountant at the Rosefinch Arts Palace.

The case of Ji Jingli represents a major advance in the role of the job market, as opposed to effecting job changes through the use of personal connections and string-pulling. In the middle of April, the wholesale marketing division was completely cooperative in transferring her dossier through the job market to the Rosefinch Arts Palace.

Notes

1. Ji Jingli was typical of an entire generation of "rusticated youth" who were sent to the countryside during the Cultural Revolution (1966–76), to experience hardship firsthand and to relieve pressure on the urban job market. When she was allowed to return to Beijing, she was assigned a job under the unified placement system.

2. Beginning in the 1980s, the government began to phase out the unified placement system, first for secondary graduates and then for post-secondary graduates. With respect to secondary school graduates, the government faced the practical impossibility of finding enough state sector jobs for all available recruits. WALDER, *supra*, at 56-57. As it was, labor bureaus compelled companies to accept more and more unnecessary hires. Once hired, an employee could not be easily dismissed, even for criminal misconduct. JOSEPHS, *supra*, at 113-14. When policy shifted from achieving full employment at any cost to raising labor productivity, the government sought to relieve enterprises from the consequences of overstaffing. In 1983, the state introduced the contract employment system for new hires.

   > The current system of employment in China, under which the majority are permanent workers, in practice operates as a kind of unconditional system of life tenure. . . . The major aspects of the employment system are inability to dismiss workers once they have been hired; advancement without the corresponding risk of demotion; equality of reward regardless of productivity, technical proficiency, or the nature of the job. . . . The fundamental aims of the contract employment system are to "break the iron rice bowl and the big pot, "[permanent employment] to realize truly the socialist principle of "from each according to his ability, to each according to his work," to stimulate fully people's initiative to serve socialism, and to liberate the productive forces.

   > JOSEPHS, *supra*, at 115-16.

3. Ji Jingli took an opportunity to upgrade her skills, but her employer did not place her in a suitable position when she returned to work. She found a suitable position with another company in Beijing but her employer would not release her. The article does not explore the employer's motives in being obstructionist, other than its demand for reimbursement. It may be that the manager was fearful that other, key (from his point of view) employees would follow her example.

Ultimately Ji was successful in attaining her goal, because of a combination of factors: extraordinary determination to work through the bureaucratic process; backing from her husband; support from the Beijing labor bureau, which was promoting a new policy of occupational mobility for local residents; and knowledge of the applicable law. To effectuate the job change, she did not have to reimburse her employer for the costs of her training. Under current law, Ji Jingli would be employed under contract and free to leave without liability upon expiration of the contract term. If she left without cause before the contract expired, she and her new employer would have been jointly responsible for reimbursing the costs of her training. *See* Labor Law art. 99; Capital Iron & Steel-Japan Electric Electronics Company v. Chen Jingke – Damages for Breach of Employment Contract, *infra*.

4. In the last two decades, the Chinese legal system has become much more transparent, mostly to bolster the legitimacy of the Party, the government and the legal system itself, after the chaos and mob violence of the Cultural Revolution. External pressure exerted on China when it was negotiating its "ticket of admission" to the WTO also played a part. Qin, *supra*, at 491-99. In contrast to a time when few books on law were published and available for purchase, today bookstores have entire sections devoted to legal materials, including "how-to" reference works for lay people. Many government agencies, including the Ministry of Labor and Social Security, maintain free Web sites. However, in order for a lay person to bargain effectively for his rights, consultation with a lawyer is usually necessary. Compare Chen Weili v. Lai Guofa – Dispute Arising from Contract for Hire, *infra* (assistance from legal aid attorney); Zhu Jian'gang, *Not Against the State, Just Protecting the Residents' Interests: A Residents' Movement in a Shanghai Neighborhood*, 5 PERSPECTIVES 25 (2004); MICHAEL W. McCANN, RIGHTS AT WORK: PAY EQUITY REFORM AND THE POLITICS OF LEGAL MOBILIZATION (1994), esp. Chapter Three (Law as a Catalyst). On the development of the legal profession in China, and the limited role of lawyers in employment-related cases, *see* JOSEPHS, LABOR LAW IN CHINA, excerpted later.

---

2. The Socialist Market Economy

With the death of Mao Zedong in 1976, the wing of the Party that favored a pragmatic rather than ideological approach to modernization came to power. The strategy of making economic progress through "revolutionary fervor" alone had been a clear failure. Deng Xiaoping is credited with the saying that "it does not matter whether a cat is black or white so long as it catches mice" (bu guan bai mao hei mao, hui zhuo laoshu jiushi hao mao).

Because the vast majority of the population still lived in rural areas, agriculture was the first sector targeted for reform. The rural collectives were gradually disbanded; peasants began to cultivate land under long-term leases from the government; peasants were allocated "private plots" where they could raise cash crops, fruits and vegetables, and animals; farmers' markets sprang up in urban areas, providing cash income for farmers and improving the variety and quality of food for urban residents; peasants were allowed to leave the farm for temporary employment in commerce, industry, services, and construction. FAIRBANK & GOLDMAN, *supra*, at 410-13.

Factory jobs proliferated in so-called village and township enterprises which clustered in smaller urban communities as well as in state enterprises and foreign-invested companies. *See generally* LORAINE A. WEST & YAOHUI ZHAO, RURAL LABOR FLOWS IN CHINA (2000). The jobs available in state enterprises were those rejected by urban residents as dirty, dangerous, and physically arduous. Despite low wages and harsh working conditions, migrant laborers found the "trade-off" for cash income to be worthwhile. *Compare* Kenneth D. Roberts, *Chinese Labor Migration: Insights from Mexican Undocumented Migration to the United States*, in WEST & ZHAO, *supra*, at 179, 208-09.

Having achieved impressive success in the agricultural sector, the government turned to industrial reform. The shift away from a command economy dedicated to heavy industry towards a more diversified economy stressing light industry and services has been more difficult to accomplish. While the rural population had everything to gain from reform, the urban industrial labor force of over one hundred million had long enjoyed a privileged position. Most were satisfied with the "iron rice bowl," low wages but a panoply of fringe benefits including pensions on retirement or disability, subsidized housing and health care, and education for one's dependents.

To avoid the sort of widespread social unrest that later accompanied large-scale privatization of state enterprises in the Soviet Union, as well as the failed messianic transformations of the Maoist era, China under Deng Xiaoping progressed gradually and in stages. The incremental approach is popularly referred to as "crossing the river by feeling the stones underfoot" (mozhe shitou guohe). FAIRBANK & GOLDMAN, *supra*, at 411-19. State sector hiring was slowed; under the new contract employment system, new hires were not guaranteed lifetime tenure; labor exchanges were set up to match applicants with available vacancies; state workers were offered various incentives to find alternative employment or self-employment in the growing private sector; the state allowed large inflows of foreign investment, particularly in the new Special Economic Zones (SEZs), which in turn created employment opportunities for both the rural population and urban residents with entrepreneurial spirit.

Over time, as anticipated, the share of GDP produced by the state sector shrank dramatically, but the government continued to support loss-making state enterprises and sustain employment levels through infusions of "loans." BARRY NAUGHTON, GROWING OUT OF THE PLAN: CHINESE ECONOMIC REFORM, 1978–93 322-23 (1995). The one-child policy instituted in the late 1970s slowed the growth of the population, but still millions of new entrants to the workforce had to be somehow accommodated every year. By the late 1990s, the state began to force plant closures and mass lay-offs. Between 1999 and 2002, the state sector workforce declined from 85.7 million to 71.6 million. China Statistical Yearbook, http://210.72.32.36/tjsj/ndsj/yearbook2003_c.pdf. By one estimate, in 2002 alone, eleven million jobs were eliminated. Julia Ya Qin, *WTO Regulation of Subsidies to State-Owned Enterprises (SOEs): A Critical Appraisal of the China Accession Protocol*, 7 J. INT'L ECON. L. 863, 873 (2004).

Layoffs hit certain areas of the country, such as the northeastern provinces, with devastating impact. High unemployment and street demonstrations ensued. JOSEPHS, *supra*, at 2. Those most likely to be laid off were women over thirty-five, workers with chronic health problems, middle-aged workers who were too old to retrain but too young for retirement, and those of low educational attainment. JOSEPHS, *supra*, at 2-3; JOHN KNIGHT & LINA SONG, TOWARDS A LABOUR MARKET IN CHINA 121 (2005). Retrenched workers had great difficulty finding alternative employment, and if reemployed, earned wages lower than they had received previously. KNIGHT & SONG, *supra*, at 233. As yet, China does not have in place a fully functioning national welfare system to cushion the blow of unemployment. Labor Law art. 70-76 (Social Insurance and Benefits) *infra*; KNIGHT & SONG, *supra*, at 242-43 (discussing limited availability of income support programs).

In the reform period, the government relaxed, but did not abolish, the instruments of human resource allocation. For those well-educated people with special skills in high demand, changing one's household registration to a desirable destination – such as Shanghai or Beijing – is considerably easier than previously. Others obtain temporary residence permits through their employers, by purchasing an apartment, or starting a business. The unified placement system only applies to a select few, for example, students whose education has been subsidized by an employer. The personnel dossier may be deposited for safekeeping with one's alma mater, a "talent exchange center," a former employer, a government ministry, or the local street committee in one's place of permanent residence. JOSEPHS, *supra*, at 97. Those who work in a city without obtaining local household registration or a residence permit are vulnerable to forced repatriation, but public security authorities tend to leave people alone so long as they are gainfully employed and law-abiding. Zhao Shukai, *Criminality and the Policing of Migrant Workers*, 43 CHINA J. 101 (2000); *cf.* State Department Report, *supra*, sec. 2(d).

With increased occupational and geographic mobility, a new phenomenon has emerged: "job-hopping" (tiao cao) in search of higher pay, better working conditions, and opportunities for quick advancement. In order to stabilize the workforce and recoup their investment in worker recruitment and training, employers resort to a variety of measures, legal and illegal. Impermissible measures include the payment of "deposits" when workers join the company, withholding of wages, and "exit fees" if they quit, even for good cause. Joseph Kahn, *Chinese Girls' Toil Bring Pain, Not Riches*, N.Y. TIMES, Oct. 2, 2003, at A1 (factory demanded "exit fees" from exploited workers). For permissible contractual provisions, such as repayment of training costs, *see* Capital Iron & Steel-Japan Electric Electronics Company v. Chen Jingke – Damages for Breach of Employment Contract, *infra*.

To guard against the theft of trade secrets by employees "in the know", many companies, both foreign and domestic, include confidentiality and non-competition clauses in their employment contracts. Kening Li, How to Protect Trade Secrets, China Bus. Rev., May 1, 2005 (available on Westlaw). Such provisions are expressly authorized by the Labor Law (art. 22, 102). Breach of such agreements may have criminal as well as civil law consequences. In a well-publicized case, Huawei Technologies, a Chinese telecom equipment manufacturer, initiated criminal proceedings against three former employees. Two were sentenced to three years in prison and fined 50,000 yuan; the other was sentenced to two years and fined 30,000 yuan. Their sentences were upheld on appeal in May 2005. Li, *supra*; Final Decision in the Huawei Trade Secrets Case, A Sensation in the Country's IT World [Hongdong quanguo IT jie "Huawei qiemi an" zhongshen panjue], http:www.itxian.com/get/index_btxw/rig_btxw/103712739.htm, Aug. 10, 2005. Compare U.S. law, prosecutions under the Economic Espionage Act of 1996, http://www.cybercrime.gov.eeapub.html.

C. THE LABOR LAW

Under the command economy, China did not have a "labor market" as the term is commonly understood – a mechanism for matching the supply and demand for labor by means of contracts between employers and employees. Rather, China had a "labor system," involving state direction of labor and bureaucratic determination of wages and benefits. The labor system had its advantages, such as the avoidance of open unemployment in urban areas and related social ills. On the negative side, the system was characterized by inefficiency and immobility. KNIGHT & SONG, *supra*, at 13. Once the market reform program achieved a degree of stability and direction, the time was ripe for providing a statutory framework within which it could operate.

1. The Law-Making Process

As a formal matter, the National People's Congress, the Chinese legislature, is the supreme organ of government. PRC Constitution art. 57. Statutes approved by the NPC are second only to the Constitution in authority. The NPC is empowered to enact legislation dealing with "criminal offenses, civil affairs, the state organs, and other matters." Art. 62 (3). Because the NPC only meets once a year, its Standing Committee is empowered to enact "specific" legislation when the NPC is not in session "with the exception of those [basic laws] which should be enacted by the NPC." Art. 67 (2). In practice, the line between the NPC's sphere of authority and that of the Standing Committee has been difficult to ascertain. Perry Keller, *Legislation in the People's Republic of China*, 23 U.B.C. L. REV. 653 (1989); *Sources of Order in Chinese Law*, 42 AM. J. COMP. L. 711 (1994).

Furthermore, as in other modern societies, the source of most legislation is the executive branch of government, the State Council and its constituent ministries. In addition, the State Council issues a multitude of detailed rules and regulations, implementing and interpreting both legislation and administrative regulations of more general scope. It is not incorrect to say that the State Council is, for all practical purposes, the most powerful law-making institution in China. J. CHEN, CHINESE LAW: TOWARDS AN UNDERSTANDING OF CHINESE LAW, ITS NATURE AND DEVELOPMENT 103 (1999).

Of the three branches of government, the judiciary is the least powerful, both on paper and in practice. Officially China does not adhere to the model of separation of powers. The power to interpret the Constitution is vested in the Standing Committee of the NPC. Art. 67 (1). Nonetheless, the Supreme People's Court and the lower courts have emerged as an important and active interpretive authority for the same reasons that courts exercise a crucial function in other societies. Social and technological change race ahead of the law. Even when a rule is put in place, it is impossible to anticipate all its consequences in advance. Courts are the necessary bridge between an abstract rule and the multitude of different factual situations. J. CHEN, *supra*, at 108-110; Susan Finder, *The Supreme People's Court of the People's Republic of China*, 7 J. CHINESE L. 145, 164-67 (1993).

China is a unitary state, not a federal system. National law automatically takes precedence over local law; local governments do not enjoy residual authority vis-à-vis the central government. However, in practice, it is difficult to draw boundaries between national and local jurisdiction. In a country as vast and populous as China, the central government necessarily delegates considerable law-making authority to local governments. For example, pursuant to the Labor Law, minimum wages are determined by local rules. Labor Law art. 48-49, *infra*. The Standing Committee of the NPC and the State Council rarely exercise their power to nullify "conflicting" local regulations. J. CHEN, *supra*, at 119.

2. The 1994 Labor Law

Hilary K. Josephs, *Labor Law in a "Socialist Market Economy"*:
The Case of China, 33 COLUM. J. TRANSNAT'L L. 559 (1995) (excerpts)
[footnotes deleted]

In 1994 China promulgated a Labor Law, the culmination of approximately four decades of
debate and revision. Thus, the very fact of its promulgation is significant. The Law is a summary of basic principles drawn from an extensive body of existing administrative regulations.
It lends an importance to worker rights which they did not have previously and demonstrates
a conscious effort of the Chinese government to bring its system of labor law and industrial relations into closer compliance with international standards. The Law also reflects the
extraordinarily complex nature of the Chinese economic scene, which combines features of
the old command economy with elements of a market-driven system. However, the Law does
not indicate any change in the government's repressive attitude toward independent union
activity, the right of association, and the right to strike and engage in collective bargaining
over terms and conditions of employment.

I. Introduction

In July 1994 the Standing Committee of the National People's Congress promulgated a Labor
Law which became effective on January 1, 1995. The Law was the outcome of an extremely
protracted drafting process, the beginning of which dated back to the 1950s. Its promulgation
occurred at a point well after the resumption of normal legislative activity in the 1970s,
following the end of the Cultural Revolution.

The very fact that the Law was only recently adopted is an indication of how sensitive
and contentious the subject of labor relations is in China. An analysis of the provisions of
the Labor Law reveals a delicate and precarious balance which the government attempts to
maintain between preservation of certain features of the older command economy and the
market-driven forces which have been permitted to develop in the last fifteen years. Other laws
reflect this tension as well: in 1992, the PRC Constitution was amended to state that China
practices a "socialist market economy" (shehui zhuyi shichang jingji), neither the "planned
economy" of the original 1982 text nor, for that matter, a pure "market" economy.

Labor law developments in China, including the promulgation of the new Code, are
therefore representative of the development of the economy and the legal system generally.
They evidence the costs and benefits associated with economic development in a still very
poor country. Because of China's unusually rapid rate of economic growth and increased
participation in the international trading system, understanding of its domestic labor law
developments is of considerable importance to other countries, including our own. Among
the countries which originally had planned economies on the Soviet model, China has been
unique in its ability to make the transition to a mixed economy while still sustaining a high
rate of growth. This phenomenon is well worth investigation even if it is largely due to specific
local factors which cannot readily be imitated by other countries.

The second section of this article is devoted to analysis of labor law developments of the
last decade. To a considerable extent, the analysis focuses on those changes manifest in the
written law. Some evidence is available with respect to implementation of the written law,

but no researcher, Chinese or foreigner, has been able to do a systematic and statistically meaningful study of implementation in any aspect of China's legal system. Therefore, evidence of implementation remains fragmentary and anecdotal. Nonetheless, even the law "on the books" is informative for its reflection of societal values and aspirations, no matter how imperfectly realized.

The third section of this article deals with a phenomenon virtually unknown in China until recent years, the resolution of labor disputes through third party arbitration and litigation. After the socialization of private industry in the 1950s, and until the 1980s, there was no formal mechanism by which a worker could obtain resolution of an employment-related grievance. Most employment-related disputes were resolved on an informal basis between the workshop director and the disaffected worker; even the upper levels of management in the factory rarely became involved. In this respect, China was quite unlike other socialist countries, such as the Soviet Union, which had a formal grievance procedure. However, China adopted a system of formal labor dispute resolution in 1987. The number of disputes handled through this process has grown steadily, and the applicable regulations amended to enlarge its jurisdictional scope. As the administrative bureaucracy has become less responsible for placing workers in jobs (a function taken over in part by market mechanisms), it has found a new mission in the resolution of disputes. To a limited extent, Chinese courts, which rarely accepted jurisdiction of employment cases before 1987, are now becoming involved in this area.

II. Labor Law Developments Under Economic Reform

From 1986 to 1987, the Chinese government issued a series of administrative regulations designed to reform the existing system of bureaucratic allocation of labor. In the previous three decades, people in blue-collar (and white-collar) occupations had been assigned to jobs; labor mobility was severely restricted by law. The 1986 Contract Employment Regulations authorized employers to hire regular employees under fixed-term contracts, instead of having to accept workers assigned to them through bureaucratic allocation. Theoretically, the contract employment system would also benefit workers by allowing them to select their own employment initially or to change employers once a contract expired.

In enacting the new regulations, the central government was not acting solely from altruistic motives (for example, to allow people to find jobs which were better-paying or more personally satisfying). The government sought to reduce the importance of state enterprises to the economy (many of which survived only because of government subsidies), to increase productivity in state enterprises, and ultimately, to diminish the proportion of the labor force employed in the state sector. Actually, those employed in the state sector enjoyed wages and fringe benefits which were disproportionate to their economic productivity.

However, to date, the Chinese government has not fully achieved its goals. China's recent economic success is not related to a comprehensive reform of the state sector; state enterprises continue to act as a drag on the economy. Labor turnover among even contract workers in state enterprises continues to be very low, for good reason from the worker's perspective: employment outside the state sector does not provide the same job security and fringe benefits. Indeed, China's dramatic rate of economic growth in the past decade is attributable to the non-state sector, which employs migrants from the countryside at far lower cost. To borrow a phrase from Marx, the peasant population of China supplies an almost inexhaustible reserve industrial army.

The new Labor Law, and other laws enacted in recent years, reflect the contradictions which persist in this bifurcated economic system. On the one hand, such laws express a commitment to equality for all workers. At the same time, the laws accommodate differential treatment of particular classes of workers. On the one hand, China seeks to improve its international image in the area of labor rights. Yet China adamantly refuses to compromise on certain features of its domestic system of industrial relations, including rigid government control of trade union activities. Western economists continually express doubt that China can continue to move forward on a two-track system, but there is little likelihood that the government will forsake this strategy.

The Labor Law is a code in the manner typical of civil law jurisdictions, a statutory distillation which organizes and systematizes existing (in this case, primarily administrative) law on the subject. It is organized into 13 sections and contains a total of 107 articles. The Law begins with a statement of general principles and then proceeds to address specific subject matter such as contracts, wages, and social insurance. One of the reasons that the Law took so long to complete is that the body of administrative regulations concerning labor was sizable and difficult to encapsulate in code form.

The discussion of the new Labor Law which follows first addresses those aspects of the Law which are protective of worker rights (as generally agreed upon in international human rights instruments). The second part of the discussion of the Law deals with those aspects of the law which may be termed anti-egalitarian or anti-democratic: they perpetuate existing inequalities between sectors of the industrial labor force or prevent the formation of trade unions independent of government and Party control.

By its terms, the Law governs all employment relationships: it covers all forms of business organization, encompasses both blue-collar and white-collar occupations, and applies equally to companies owned by domestic interests and employers which are affiliates of foreign companies. Therefore, a significant achievement of the Law is, at least in principle, to unify various regulatory schemes which differentiated among workers on the basis of the above-mentioned criteria. A positive effect of the Law is to reinforce the authority of government agencies in requiring the standards for those employed in "private" and "foreign" enterprises to meet the same level enjoyed by those employed in state enterprises.

Another salient feature of the Labor Law is the prominence given to the subject of contract employment. An entire section of the Law is devoted to this subject. The provisions of the Law essentially track the 1986 regulations on contract employment (as amended in 1992). They set forth the requirement of a written contract for all employment relationships, specify the basic terms of an employment contract, and describe termination procedures for both parties. Even though the contract employment system still does not apply to most state enterprise workers, who were originally hired under the old system of administrative allocation, the percentage of contract workers in state enterprises has steadily increased, and the Labor Law restates the commitment of the central government to generalize the contract employment system throughout the economy.

The Labor Law squarely addresses the subject of gender discrimination, which has been one of the most controversial effects of economic liberalization. Although women never achieved political and economic parity with men at any time after the establishment of the PRC, the Party did make improvement of the status of women one of its key political objectives. Significantly, after 1949, the workforce participation of women in China was extremely high relative to other countries. However, with the emergence of a socialist market economy and a greater concern with cost-cutting and economic efficiency, there is ample evidence that the position of women in the workforce has deteriorated. At present, women are particularly subject to discriminatory hiring practices, unfair dismissal, demotions, and wage cuts.

The Chinese government has not been unresponsive to evidence of discrimination. For example, it adopted a Law for the Protection of Women's Rights and Interests in 1992. It is beyond the scope of this article to determine whether the status of women would in fact be helped by the elimination of so-called protective legislation or other measures. Suffice it to say, the Labor Law is consistent with official efforts to remedy the problem.

Another feature of the Labor Law which is responsive to well publicized abuses of worker rights is the section which deals with normal working hours, mandatory rest periods, limitations on over-time, and overtime pay. Factories in the Special Economic Zones, employing mainly temporary workers from rural areas, have been notorious for regular and compulsory over time. Article 36 of the Law now provides for a normal work week of forty-four hours [subsequently reduced to forty hours by State Council regulation –Ed.], and article 38 provides for at least one rest day per week.

By providing for a guaranteed minimum wage in articles 48 and 49, the Labor Law fills a major lacuna in the regulatory scheme. The Law states general factors which should be taken into account by local governments in setting minimum wages, for example, the local cost of living for a worker and his dependents as mentioned in article 49. Since local governments are required to report actual minimum wages to the State Council "for the record," the central government has, in effect, the power of oversight and an opportunity to use administrative guidance against those local governments it deems to be violators. Significantly, in article 46, the central government retains the power to control "total wages." This provision presumably applies to state enterprises under the jurisdiction of the central government, and therefore allows the central government to depart from guaranteed minimum wages if necessary to prevent inflation of the state enterprise wage bill.

In a subtle doctrinal shift from prior law, the Labor Law generally emphasizes civil liability for breach of contract as an incentive to compliance with contractual obligations in place of administrative sanctions. This aspect of the Law harmonizes with efforts to endow state enterprises with independent legal personality, rather than view them as operating units of the government. As the legal relationship of state enterprises vis-à-vis the government changes, it is logical that the legal relationship of a state enterprise vis-à-vis its workforce will also change. For example, the Law does not contain a section on rewards and disciplinary measures for workers. In the Law, disciplinary violations are treated as a breach of contract, entitling the employer to terminate the employee (art. 25), rather than as a violation of administrative regulations. The employer may no longer prevent a worker from quitting by refusing permission, but may sue the worker and/or his new employer for damages (art. 99, 102). Further, the section of the Law on legal liability is devoted almost exclusively to breaches by the employer, e.g., for excessive over-time or unsafe working conditions. In a sense, the Law appears to acknowledge that the same inequality of bargaining power between employer and employee which prevails in market economies can also exist in a transitional economy, and therefore the worker requires added legal protection, including the ability to enforce his rights as a private litigant.

In a more conservative vein, the provisions of the Labor Law dealing with layoff and redundancy are consistent with prior law in giving the administrative authorities tight control of the termination process. In this respect, the Law continues to reflect a strong commitment to job security, at least for permanent workers or workers employed under fixed-term contracts or contracts of unlimited duration. An employer can only lay off workers if it is experiencing serious economic difficulties, has solicited the views of the enterprise trade union, and has "submitted a report" to the labor authorities (art. 27). Although the Law technically does not require the labor authorities to give advance approval in cases of economic layoff, an enterprise would probably be most reluctant to act in the face of an objection by the authorities once they have been notified.

Because employers, particularly state enterprises, have long operated as mini-societies, providing workers not only with cash income but also essential fringe benefits like housing and medical care, termination is likely to have catastrophic consequences for the individual. The expectation that an employer will provide welfare benefits is so firmly rooted in China that even the newly established "private" firms are pressured into operating as social caretakers.

III. Resolution of Labor Disputes

The subjugation of individual aspirations to the "collective welfare" under socialism was nowhere better illustrated than by the inability of workers to obtain external review of employment-related problems. Therefore, one measure of democratization in China is certainly the protection afforded individual rights and the ability of individuals to obtain legal redress of grievances, especially when such grievances are intimately connected to the concerns of everyday life.

Since the labor reforms of 1986–87, there has been a conspicuous rise in the number of employment-related disputes being processed by labor arbitration tribunals and the courts. The number of disputes heard by arbitration panels is still infinitesimal as measured against the size of the workforce and the number of civil cases accepted by the courts. Nonetheless, the increase in labor cases is probably related to expanded subject matter jurisdiction, a change which was initiated at the provincial level and then generalized by central government regulations. The original dispute resolution process only covered contract disputes or cases involving the termination of permanent workers in state enterprises. The 1993 amendments to the labor dispute regulations made actionable claims involving wages, fringe benefits, and occupational safety and health, as well as termination (art. 2). The amendments also extended the arbitration process to cover collective and private enterprises (art. 39).

The number of "employment" disputes may be understated because personal service contracts or contracts involving "independent contractors" are governed by the civil law. Thus, a worker who performs services outside the scope of his usual employment, whether for his regular employer or a third party, engages in a civil law, rather than labor law, relationship. The Chinese government has adopted various policies to encourage both skilled workers and professionals to undertake consulting or moonlighting arrangements in order to increase their income. In this respect China has imitated Hungary, another transitional economy struggling to reform the state sector. In a transitional economy, consulting arrangements or service contracts benefit both the worker and the state. The worker retains job security in his permanent job, while increasing his overall income. The state can keep wages in the state sector at a low level, while gaining additional productivity from the worker. In China, an added benefit arising from these arrangements is the diffusion of knowledge and expertise, which are in very short supply.

As previously noted, even after the promulgation of enabling regulations in 1986 and 1987, the number of employment-related cases brought to the formal arbitration process has been relatively small, and the residual number of cases litigated much smaller yet. Case reports published by the Supreme People's Court include few labor cases. Labor cases, that is, cases in which the cause of action is predicated on the labor laws themselves, are now occasionally reported in the Supreme People's Court publication Selected Court Cases, which began appearing in 1992. While it is difficult to generalize based on such a limited sample, one may conclude from reported cases that it is usually an aggrieved employee who resorts to the dispute resolution process and that the courts are more likely to rule in favor of the employee than in favor of the employer. Therefore, it appears that given the opportunity to act, the courts indeed do protect the individual against arbitrary actions by the employer.

A recent decision illustrates the uncertain, but nonetheless challenging, environment in which Chinese courts now function. In the case of Ye Shenghua v. Wuhan Transportation Information Center, the mother of a deceased employee brought suit against the employer in order to collect various health insurance benefits. The employer was officially registered as a "collective" enterprise. Plaintiff's decedent, after earning a master's degree from a university in Shanghai, had arranged for his own employment through an employment agency rather than accept an assignment from the government. Apparently he did not find the job to his liking and asked for a transfer. The defendant refused to process this request. The employee stopped coming to work and the employer stopped paying his salary. Shortly thereafter, the employee became ill and died. The defendant refused to pay his hospital bills, lost wages, funeral expenses, or survivors' benefits. These were all awarded by the court as damages.

This case was decided at a time when the labor dispute resolution process was compulsorily applied to state enterprises, but had not yet been extended to collective enterprises. However, the court relied on language in the regulations in effect at the time to extend their application by analogy. Therefore, this case illustrates the willingness of Chinese courts to fashion a remedy in actual cases even if there is no controlling statute or regulation. Another interesting aspect of this case is that the court overlooked the formal requirement of a writing for an employment contract, but rather focused on the fact that the plaintiff's decedent had worked pursuant to a verbal understanding for a period of months.

Like most employment contract cases which are reported in official journals, the court gave judgment for the employee. The outcome in this case suggests that once employed, an individual will be deemed an employee until such time as the employment relationship is formally terminated (and replaced by a new employment relationship). Even though the plaintiff's decedent had stopped coming to work and was not receiving salary at the time of his last illness, he was still employed by the defendant for the purpose of health insurance benefits. In this respect, the court's decision reflects pre-reform attitudes about the permanence of an employment relationship.

HILARY K. JOSEPHS, LABOR LAW IN CHINA
86-92 (2d ed. 2003) (excerpts) [footnotes deleted]

As part of the scheme of local implementation of the contract employment system during the early and mid-1980s, labor arbitration committees attached to local labor departments were specially established in various places. But details on important questions such as jurisdiction, appointment of arbitrators, and arbitration procedures were not forthcoming until 1987 when the State Council promulgated the Provisional Regulations for the Resolution of Labor Disputes in State Enterprises (the 1987 Labor Dispute Regulations). These regulations were superseded in turn by the 1993 Regulations on Resolution of Enterprise Labor Disputes (the 1993 Labor Dispute Regulations).

The original dispute resolution process only covered contract disputes or cases involving the termination of permanent workers in state enterprises. The 1993 amendments to the labor dispute regulations made actionable claims involving wages, fringe benefits, and occupational safety and health, as well as termination. The amendments also extended the arbitration process to cover collective and private enterprises. With the adoption of the Labor Law in 1994, the dispute resolution process encompassed all employment relationships including those with foreign invested enterprises (FIEs), whether joint ventures or wholly owned subsidiaries of foreign companies.

Parties to an employment dispute are encouraged to resolve the problem through mediation within the workplace. The enterprise mediation committee consists of employee, employer, and trade union representatives. If mediation fails, petitioners must go first to arbitration; the decision of the arbitration panel may be appealed in an ordinary court of law. The labor arbitration panel consists of representatives of the local labor bureau, the trade union, and government economic administration, but the labor bureau plays the dominant role.

The number of "employment" disputes may be understated because personal service contracts or contracts involving "independent contractors" are governed by the civil law. Thus, a worker who performs services outside the scope of his usual employment, whether for his regular employer or a third party, engages in a civil law, rather than labor law, relationship. An important consequence of how a legal relationship is characterized is that a dispute arising out of a "civil" law relationship can be brought directly in court, without first being submitted to arbitration. Also, the body of governing law is different. Civil law disputes are resolved according to the General Principles of Civil Law, rather than the Labor Law or regulations issued by the labor authorities. Courts enjoy greater freedom and flexibility in interpreting civil law rules.

The discussion to follow will generalize from an examination of approximately two hundred labor arbitration decisions and forty court cases.

It is estimated that only a fraction of actual claims reach the labor arbitration committees because of procedural barriers. The statute of limitations for filing a claim is only sixty days from the date the claim "arose." This time limit is much shorter than the statutes of limitation provided for in the General Principles of Civil Law (one or two years) or the Economic Contract Law (four years for international sales of goods or technology import or export contracts). Until the People's Supreme Court issued an interpretive document in 2001, a decision by an arbitration committee to reject a claim as untimely was not reviewable in court.

The 1993 Labor Dispute Regulations expressly authorize the use of counsel. In China, representation in court or arbitral proceedings is not restricted to practicing attorneys. Judging from the labor arbitration cases, the frequency of representation by professional counsel is relatively low, only twenty out of approximately two hundred cases. However, considering the small size of the PRC bar – only about one hundred thousand for a population in excess of one billion – and its uneven dispersion, the modest degree of professional representation is not surprising.

Statistics show that labor arbitration activity tends to be concentrated in the more affluent and urbanized areas of China, such as Beijing, Shanghai, Guangdong, and Jiangsu. Based on available information, one can only surmise that there is a higher percentage of professional representation in the same geographic areas. Claimants would be more likely to bring a case if they could find able counsel to represent them.

There is very little pro bono legal assistance available. At a one-day clinic sponsored by East China University of Politics & Law in Shanghai, almost one thousand people appeared seeking advice on labor-related problems. In a highly unusual case, a legal aid center set up by Beijing University Law School was able to obtain relief for twenty-five women migrant workers at a garment factory. The legal aid center reports that cases involving employment issues, though a small percentage of its total workload, are complex, time-consuming, and have a long litigation cycle. Despite reports that trade unions supply legal assistance to workers, such activity is not reflected in either arbitration or judicial decisions.

Note

1. Since the dispute resolution process was first established, the number of cases has steadily grown. In 2003, over 225,000 new cases were accepted, involving more than 800,000 people. As previously, the vast majority of cases were brought by employees and they prevail in the majority of cases. China Statistical Yearbook 2004 (Table 23-5).

Labor Law
Approved by the Standing Committee of the National People's Congress on July 5, 1994; effective January 1, 1995
CEILAW 111801199401
(from Hilary K. Josephs, Labor Law in China 2d. ed. 2003)

Table of Contents

I. General Provisions (art. 1-9)
II. Promotion of Employment (art. 10-15)
III. Employment Contracts and Collective Contracts (art. 16-35)
IV. Working Hours, Rest Times, and Vacations (art. 36-45)
V. Wages (art. 46-51)
VI. Occupational Safety and Health (art. 52-57)
VII. Special Protection for Women and Underage Workers (art. 58-65)
VIII. Vocational Training (art. 66-69)
IX. Social Insurance and Benefits (art. 70-76)
X. Employment Disputes (art. 77-84)
XI. Supervision and Inspection (art. 85-88)
XII. Legal Liability (art. 89-105)
XIII. Supplementary Provisions (art. 106-107)

I. General Provisions (art. 1-9)

1. In order to protect the lawful rights and interests of employees,[4] adjust employment relationships, establish and support an employment system which is appropriate to a socialist market economy, and promote economic development and social progress, this Law has been enacted pursuant to the Constitution.

2. All enterprises and individual economic organizations (hereinafter "employers") and those who engage in employment relationships with them within the territory of the People's

---

[4] The term "employee" (literally, "laborer" [laodongzhe]) includes both those who engage in manual labor and those who occupy staff and professional positions.

Republic of China shall apply this Law. State organs, service organizations, and social groups, as well as those who engage in employment relationships with them, shall refer to this Law when appropriate.

3. Employees enjoy the rights of equal treatment in employment, choice of occupation, compensation for their work, rest and vacation periods, occupational safety and health, occupational training, social insurance and welfare, and access to employment dispute resolution, as well as any other rights provided by law.

Employees shall complete work obligations, raise their skill levels, follow occupational safety and health regulations, and respect labor discipline and professional ethics.

4. Employers shall establish and improve their system of work rules according to law, so as to protect employee rights and enable employees to complete their work obligations.

5. The State shall utilize various approaches to promote employment, develop occupational education, set labor standards, equalize income distribution, improve social insurance, harmonize employment relationships, and gradually raise employees' standard of living.

6. The State shall promote employee participation in voluntary labor; sponsor labor competitions and suggestions for improvement of working conditions; encourage and protect scientific research, technological progress, and creative innovation; and recognize and reward model laborers and advanced workers.

7. Employees have the right to join and organize trade unions according to law. The trade union represents and supports the lawful rights and interests of employees; it conducts its activities independently and autonomously according to law.

8. In accordance with law, by means of the worker-staff congress, the worker-staff representative congress, or comparable organization, employees participate in democratic management or otherwise protect their lawful rights and interests through egalitarian dialogue with management.

9. The labor administration departments under the State Council are in charge of labor matters for the entire country.

The labor administration departments at the county level and above are in charge of labor matters within their respective jurisdictions.

II. Promotion of Employment (art. 10-15)

10. By promoting economic and social development, the State creates conditions for employment and expands employment opportunities.

The State encourages enterprises, service organizations, and social groups to initiate production and extend operations as permitted by statute and regulation so as to increase employment.

The State supports the efforts of the unemployed to organize their own employment opportunities or to become self-employed.

11. Local government shall utilize various approaches to promote employment, develop various job placement organizations, and provide various services to job-seekers.

12. No one shall suffer discrimination in employment on the basis of nationality, race, gender, or religious belief.

13. Women enjoy the right of equal treatment in employment with men. Unless otherwise provided by laws which prohibit their employment in certain occupations and positions, women shall not be refused employment or subjected to higher standards than men.

14. Protective laws shall apply to the employment of the disabled, minority nationalities, and demobilized servicemen.

15. Employers are forbidden to employ anyone less than sixteen years of age.

In the arts, sports, and other activities for which employment of underage employees is allowed, the employer must follow national regulations, obtain the necessary approvals, and safeguard a child's right to compulsory education.

III. Employment Contracts and Collective Contracts (art. 16-35)

16. The employment contract is the agreement which establishes an employment relationship between the parties and sets forth their respective rights and duties.

To establish an employment relationship the parties shall conclude an employment contract.

17. In concluding or modifying an employment contract, the parties shall observe the principles of equality and voluntariness and shall not violate statutes or administrative regulations.

When the parties conclude an employment contract in accordance with law and it thereby acquires binding force, the parties must perform their respective duties.

18. An employment contract is void if:
    (i) it is contrary to statute or administrative regulation;
    (ii) fraud, duress, or similar means were used to induce agreement.
    A void contract has no legal effect ab initio. If a contract is only partially invalid, and the invalid provisions can be severed from the remainder of the agreement, the remaining provisions shall have legal effect.
    A determination of validity shall be made by a labor arbitration committee or a court.

19. An employment contract shall be executed in writing and shall contain the following provisions:
    (i) duration;
    (ii) job description;
    (iii) occupational safety and health and conditions of work;
    (iv) compensation;
    (v) labor discipline;
    (vi) termination;
    (vii) liability for breach.
    In addition to the above-enumerated mandatory provisions, the parties may agree to additional terms.

20. The duration of the employment contract may be limited, unlimited, or for the performance of a specified task.

When an employee has been continuously employed with the same employer for a period of ten years, and the parties agree to a renewal, the employee is entitled to a contract of unlimited duration.

21. An employment contract may set forth a probationary period, but not to exceed six months.

22. An employment contract may contain provisions affording protection to the employer's trade secrets.

23. An employment contract automatically expires at the end of its term or as otherwise provided in the contract.

24. An employment contract may be terminated by mutual agreement.

25. In any of the following circumstances, the employer may terminate the contract:
(i) the employee proves unqualified for employment during the probationary period;
(ii) the employee commits a serious violation of labor discipline or work rules;
(iii) the employee commits a serious dereliction of duty or engages in self-dealing, causing significant detriment to the employer;
(iv) the employee has been sentenced for a crime, convicted but not sentenced, or exempted from prosecution.

26. In any of the following circumstances the employer may terminate the contract but must give 30 days advance written notice to the employee:
(i) the employee suffers a non work-related illness or injury and after his sick leave is exhausted is neither able to resume his original job nor another work assignment arranged by the employer;
(ii) the employee is still unable to discharge his work responsibilities even after training or reassignment;
(iii) the objective circumstances under which the contract was formed undergo fundamental change and thereby render the contract impossible of performance, and the parties are unable to reach agreement on a modification.

27. If the employer has received official notice of impending bankruptcy and is undergoing reorganization, or has encountered serious production difficulties, and workforce reduction is necessary, the employer must give 30 days advance notice to the trade union or other representative, listen to the views of the union or workforce, and report the matter to the labor administration authorities. Only after following these procedures may the workforce reduction be implemented.
If the employer engages in hiring during the six months following a workforce reduction, the employer shall first hire from among those laid off.

28. If the employer terminates the contract under art. 24, 26 or 27, it shall pay severance to the employee as required by law.

29. In any of the following circumstances, the employer may not terminate the contract under art. 26-27:
(i) the employee has been certified as partially or totally disabled due to work-related illness or injury;
(ii) the employee is on authorized sick leave for non work-related illness or injury;
(iii) the employee is pregnant, on maternity leave, or nursing a child;
(iv) as otherwise provided by statute or administrative regulation.

30. If the employer terminates the contract and the trade union believes this action to be unjustified, the union has the right to express its opinion. If the employer has violated statutes, regulations or the provisions of the contract, the union has the right to seek reconsideration. If the employee applies for arbitration or files suit in court, the trade union shall provide support and assistance according to law.

31. If the employee terminates the contract, he shall give 30 days advance written notice to the employer.

32. In any of the following circumstances, the employee may terminate the contract without advance notice:

(i) during the probationary period;

(ii) the employer uses force, intimidation, or other means violative of the employee's right of personal freedom in the workplace;

(iii) the employer does not pay wages or provide working conditions as stipulated in the contract.

33. The workforce may sign a collective contract with the enterprise which determines such matters such as compensation, working hours, rest times and vacation, occupational safety and health, insurance and fringe benefits. A draft of the collective contract shall be submitted to the worker-staff representative congress or the workforce for discussion and approval.

The trade union shall sign the collective contract as representative of the workforce. If there is no union in the enterprise, the collective contract shall be signed by a representative chosen by the workforce.

34. Upon signature the collective contract shall be submitted to the labor administration authorities. The contract shall automatically become effective if the authorities do not raise any objection within 15 days of receipt.

35. A collective contract executed in accordance with law is binding upon the enterprise and the workforce. To the extent that employment contracts signed by individual employees contain inferior terms, they are superceded by the collective contract with respect to such matters as working conditions and compensation.

IV. Working Hours, Rest Times, and Vacations (art. 36-45)

36. The State mandates an eight hour workday and a 44 hour work week.[5]

37. With respect to workers employed on a piece rate basis, the employer shall apply the standard of art. 36 in setting quotas and compensation.

38. The employer shall assure the employee at least one rest day per week.

39. If an enterprise cannot implement the provisions of art. 36 and 38 because of special production considerations, the enterprise may establish a different schedule with the approval of labor administration authorities.

40. The following are official holidays: New Year's Day, Chinese New Year, International Labor Day, and National Day, as well as other holidays provided by statute or regulation.

41. If production so requires, the employer may extend working hours after consultation with the trade union and the employee, but in general not more than one hour per day. Under special circumstances working hours may be extended as production requires, but under

[5] Reduced to forty hours by State Council [Guowuyuan], Regulations on the Working Hours of Workers and Staff [Guanyu zhigong gongzuo shijian de guiding], CEILAW 112601199502, Mar. 25, 1995.

conditions which protect the employee's health, not more than three hours per day or thirty six hours in a single month.

42. The limits imposed under art. 41 do not apply in the following circumstances:

(i) emergency measures in response to a natural disaster, an accident or other similar event which poses a threat to life, health or property;

(ii) emergency repairs to equipment, transportation, or public facilities to protect production and the public interest;

(iii) other circumstances as provided by statute or regulation.

43. The employer shall not violate the provisions of this law dealing with overtime.

44. Overtime wages shall be paid as follows:

(i) not less than 150 percent of the employee's regular wage;

(ii) not less than double the employee's regular wage if he works on a rest day and compensatory rest time cannot be arranged;

(iii) not less than triple the employee's regular wage if he works on an official holiday.

45. The State mandates annual paid vacation.

An employee is entitled to paid vacation after one full year of service. State Council regulations contained detailed provisions.

V. Wages (art. 46-51)

46. The distribution of wages shall follow the principle of "to each according to his work" and implement equal pay for equal work.

Wage levels shall increase in accordance with economic development. The State exercises macroeconomic control of total wages.

47. The employer shall exercise autonomy in accordance with law in setting the method of wage distribution and wage levels, taking into account the special characteristics of its production and level of economic efficiency.

48. The State mandates a system of minimum wages. Local minimum wage standards shall be established by governments at the provincial level and reported to the State Council for the record.

The employer shall not pay wages which are below the local minimum wage.

49. In setting and adjusting minimum wages, local authorities shall take all of the following factors into consideration:

(i) minimum living expenses for the employee and his dependents;

(ii) average wages across occupations;

(iii) labor productivity;

(iv) labor force participation;

(v) differences in levels of economic development across the country.

50. Wages shall be paid monthly in cash. The employer may not withhold wages or unreasonably delay payment.

51. Wages shall be paid for official holidays, marriage and funeral leave, and time off to participate in social activities as permitted by law.

VI. Occupational Safety and Health (art. 52-57)

52. The employer must establish and perfect a system which protects occupational safety and health, strictly implement rules and standards set by the State, educate the workforce in occupational safety and health, prevent accidents, and reduce hazards in the workplace.

53. Facilities for the protection of occupational safety and health must strictly comply with standards instituted by the State.

   In new construction, repair or expansion projects, occupational safety and health facilities shall be incorporated into the overall plan for design, construction, operation, and utilization.

54. The employer must provide working conditions and supply safety gear as mandated by State regulations. Workers engaged in hazardous occupations shall undergo regular physical examinations.

55. Employees must be trained and certified for the performance of special operations.

56. Employees must follow occupational safety and health procedures and regulations.

   Employees have the right to refuse performance of instructions which are contrary to regulations and which pose a serious risk of harm. Employees have the right to criticize, report, or file charges against conduct which is hazardous to safety or health.

57. The State mandates a system for reporting statistics and taking remedial measures with respect to workplace accidents and occupational diseases. Labor authorities at the county level and above shall cooperate with relevant agencies and with employers to collect statistics on workplace accidents and occupational diseases, report on such matters to higher authorities, and develop remedial measures.

VII. Special Protection for Women and Underage Workers (art. 58-65)

58. The State mandates special labor protection for women and underage workers.
   An underage worker is one who is between the ages of sixteen and eighteen.

59. It is absolutely prohibited for women to engage in mining, labor which is at the Fourth Degree of Labor Intensity, or as otherwise provided by law.

60. During their menstrual periods, women shall not engage in labor at high elevations, low temperatures, or cold water, or other labor which is at the Third Degree of Labor Intensity.

61. Pregnant women shall not engage in labor at the Third Degree of Labor Intensity or labor otherwise prohibited to pregnant women. After the seventh month of pregnancy, women shall not work overtime or be assigned the night shift.

62. Women are entitled to at least 90 days paid maternity leave after giving birth.

63. Women who are nursing a child under one year of age shall not engage in labor at the Third Degree of Labor Intensity or other labor prohibited to nursing mothers, nor work overtime or be assigned the night shift.

64. Underage workers shall not engage in mining, unhealthy or hazardous work, labor at the Fourth Degree of Labor Intensity, or as otherwise prohibited by law.

65. The employer shall arrange for underage workers to have regular physical examinations.

VIII. Vocational Training (art. 66-69)

66. The State uses various channels and selects various methods to develop vocational training, improve employees' vocational skills, raise their proficiency levels, and increase their suitability for employment and working capabilities.

67. Every level of government shall incorporate the expansion of vocational training into its plan for social and economic development. It shall encourage and support enterprises, service organizations, social groups and individuals to undertake vocational training programs as appropriate.

68. Employers shall establish a system of vocational training, fund and utilize training expenses as provided by law, and conduct vocational training programs in a manner which is adapted to enterprise needs and which proceeds according to a definite plan.

   Employees engaged in skilled occupations must receive training before commencing work.

69. The State determines occupational classifications and skills levels for each occupational classification. The State mandates a system of occupational certification. Examination and certification agencies approved by the State are in charge of examination and certification of occupational skills.

IX. Social Insurance and Benefits (art. 70-76)

70. The State develops social insurance institutions, establishes a social insurance system, and sets up social insurance funds, so as to afford employees assistance and compensation for such circumstances as retirement, illness, occupational injury, unemployment, and child bearing.

71. The level of social insurance protection shall comport with levels of social and economic development and the availability of resources.

72. Sources of social insurance funds shall be a function of each type of insurance, with gradual progress towards pooling of insurance funds. Both employers and employees must participate in the social insurance system as required by law and make social insurance contributions.

73. Employees are entitled to the following types of social insurance:
   (i) retirement pensions;
   (ii) benefits for non work related illness or injury;
   (iii) worker's compensation;
   (iv) unemployment compensation;
   (v) maternity benefits.
   In the event of death, an employee's next-of-kin are entitled to benefits according to law.
   Conditions for the receipt of benefits and benefit amounts are determined by statute and regulation.
   Social insurance benefits must be paid in a timely manner and in full.

74. Agencies which administer social insurance funds must collect premiums, manage funds, and disburse payments in accordance with law. They are responsible for maintaining and increasing the value of funds.

   Agencies which are in charge of supervising social insurance funds are responsible for ensuring the collection of premiums, proper management of the funds, and disbursement of payments according to law.

The establishment of, and delegation of authority to, administering agencies and supervisory agencies shall be determined by law.

No organization or individual may appropriate social insurance funds for unauthorized purposes.

75. The State encourages employers to set up supplementary funds for their employees to the extent the employer's resources permit.

The State advocates that individuals open self-insurance savings accounts.

76. The State develops social welfare institutions, constructs public welfare facilities, and creates proper conditions for rest, recuperation, and rehabilitation.

Employers shall promote favorable conditions for social welfare, improve collective welfare, and raise the level of benefits for employees.

X. Employment Disputes (art. 77-84)

77. In the event of an employment related dispute, the parties may request mediation, apply for arbitration, or file suit in court as provided by law, or resolve the dispute through mutual consultation.

Mediation may also be applied in arbitration and litigation proceedings.

78. The process of dispute resolution shall apply the principles of legality, justice, and prompt determination so as to safeguard the lawful rights and interests of the parties.

79. In the event of a dispute, the parties may request mediation from the enterprise mediation committee. If mediation is unsuccessful, the aggrieved party may apply for arbitration from the labor arbitration committee. An aggrieved party may also apply for arbitration directly without attempting mediation. If dissatisfied with the arbitration decision, the aggrieved party may file an action in court.

80. An employer may set up an internal mediation committee. The committee shall consist of representatives from the workforce, management, and the trade union. The trade union representative shall serve as chair.

The parties shall carry out the terms of an agreement produced by mediation.

81. The labor arbitration committee shall consist of representatives from labor administration, the trade union organization at the same level of government, and management. The representative of labor administration shall serve as chair.

82. A party applying for arbitration must submit an application in writing within 60 days of the time the claim arose. Ordinarily, the arbitration decision shall issue within 60 days of receipt. If the parties do not dispute the decision they must comply with its terms.

83. A party who disagrees with the arbitration decision may file suit in court within 15 days of receipt. If a party neither files suit within the allotted time nor carries out the terms of the arbitration decision, the other party may apply to the court for compulsory enforcement.

84. In the case of a dispute arising from the signing of a collective contract, which mutual consultation fails to resolve, labor administration may arrange for conciliation among the relevant departments.

In the case of a dispute arising from performance of a collective contract, the parties may apply for arbitration if consultation fails. A party who disagrees with the arbitration decision may file suit in court within 15 days of receipt.

XI. Supervision and Inspection (art. 85-88)

85. Labor administration at the county level and above exercises supervision and inspection to ensure that employers comply with law. Labor administration has the right to prohibit unlawful conduct and to order corrective measures.

86. Supervisory and inspection personnel have the right to enter the employer's premises to verify compliance, examine pertinent records, and inspect facilities.

As official functionaries, supervisory and inspection personnel must show proper identification, perform their duties in the public interest, and abide by relevant regulations.

87. Every department at the county level or above, within its jurisdictional scope, shall exercise supervision over employers' compliance with labor laws.

88. Trade unions at every level shall support the lawful rights and interests of employees and exercise supervision over employers' compliance with labor laws.

Every organization and individual has the right to report or file charges against unlawful conduct.

XII. Legal Liability (art. 89-105)

89. If an employer's internal rules are in violation of statute or regulation, labor administration authorities shall issue a warning and order corrective measures. If such rules have caused harm to employees, the employer has a duty to compensate them.

90. If an employer extends working hours in violation of law, labor administration authorities shall issue a warning and order corrective measures and may also impose fines.

91. If an employer violates an employee's lawful rights and interests in any one of the following situations, labor administration authorities shall order payment of wages and other compensation as well as economic loss, and may also order payment of damages:
    (i) withholding of wages or unjustified delay in payment of wages;
    (ii) refusal to pay overtime wages;
    (iii) payment of wages below the official minimum wage;
    (iv) failure to pay severance in accordance with law.

92. If an employer does not comply with occupational safety and health requirements or does not supply employees with necessary safety gear or facilities, labor administration authorities or other agencies with jurisdiction shall order corrective measures and may also impose fines. In especially serious cases, authorities may request local government to close down the employer's operations. If an employer does not take proper precautions against potential accidents and a serious accident does occur which causes harm to life or property, criminal responsibility shall be pursued under art. 187 of the Criminal Law.[6]

---

[6] Under the revised Criminal Law, criminal responsibility for industrial accidents is imposed under art. 135.

93. If an employer issues instructions which are contrary to regulations and which pose a risk of harm, and a major accident ensues with serious consequences, those in charge shall bear criminal responsibility.

94. If an employer hires workers under the age of sixteen, labor administration authorities shall order corrective measures and impose fines. In especially egregious cases, the industrial and commercial administration shall cancel the employer's business license.

95. If an employer violates laws protective of women and underage workers, labor administration authorities shall order corrective measures and impose fines. Where the employee has suffered harm, s/he is entitled to damages.

96. In either of the following circumstances, public security may detain those responsible for up to 15 days, impose fines, or give a warning,[7] or if appropriate, pursue a criminal indictment:
   (i) the use of force, intimidation, or other means violative of the employee's right of personal freedom in the workplace;
   (ii) humiliation, corporal punishment, assault, illegal searches, or confinement.

97. If the employer is responsible for the invalidity of an employment contract, and harm is caused to the employee, the employer is liable for damages.

98. If the employer terminates an employment contract in violation of law or intentionally delays in the conclusion of an employment contract, labor administration authorities shall order corrective measures. If the employee has suffered harm, the employer is liable for damages.

99. Where the employer has hired an employee who has not yet terminated a previous employment contract, and economic loss is suffered by the original employer, the employer bears joint liability with the employee.

100. If the employer unjustifiably fails to make social insurance contributions, labor administration authorities shall order payment by a set deadline, and if the payment is not made, penalty interest may be added to the amount due.

101. If an employer unreasonably interferes with the rights of supervisory and inspection personnel, or assaults or retaliates against a complainant, labor administration or other authorities shall impose fines. If appropriate, criminal prosecution may be instituted against those responsible.

102. If an employee violates the provisions for termination of an employment contract or violates the confidentiality provisions of the contract, and the employer thereby suffers economic loss, the employee shall bear liability for damages according to law.

103. If labor administration or other authorities abuse their power, are derelict in performance of their duties, or engage in self-dealing as prohibited by law, they are subject to criminal prosecution. If their conduct does not rise to the level of a crime, they are subject to administrative sanctions.

---

[7] National People's Congress Standing Committee [Quanguo renmin daibiao dahui changweihui], Regulations on Administration of Penalties by Public Security Authorities [Zhonghua renmin gongheguo zhian guanli chufa tiaoli], http://www.mps.gov.cn effective March 1, 2006, art. 40.

104. If State personnel or administrators of social insurance funds appropriate funds for unauthorized purposes, and their conduct rises to the level of a crime, they are subject to criminal prosecution.

105. If existing statutes and regulations have prescribed sanctions for violation of employee rights and interests, they shall have precedence over this Law.

XIII. Supplementary Provisions (art. 106-107)

106. Governments at the provincial level shall promulgate regulations in accordance with this Law and in light of their particular circumstances, and report such regulations to the State Council for the record.

107. This Law shall take effect on January 1, 1995.

---

3. Cases

CHEN WEILI V. LAI GUOFA

Dispute Arising from a Contract for Hire
CEILAW; Selected People's Court Cases; Case 113312200012
From HILARY K. JOSEPHS, LABOR LAW IN CHINA (2d ed. 2003)

Plaintiff: Chen Weili, male, 35 years old, native of Zhongjiang county, Sichuan province, occupation: peasant.

Agent: Fan Jun, attorney with the Jinxiu Law Firm, Deyang municipality, Sichuan province.

Defendant: Lai Guofa, male, 54 years old, a native of Guanghan municipality, Sichuan province, employee of the Lianshan Township supply and marketing cooperative, Guanghan municipality.

Agent: Jiang Peifeng, wife of Lai Guofa.

Agent: Tang Bin, attorney with the Hongfayuan Law Firm, Deyang, Sichuan province.

Plaintiff Chen Weili filed a civil lawsuit in Guanghan Municipality People's Court arising out of a contract for hire with Lai Guofa.

Plaintiff alleged that while he was employed as defendant's helper for the use of a sand trailer, his left lower leg was crushed by a moving truck. He has received official certification of Fifth Degree Disability.[8] Plaintiff requested that defendant be held liable for work-related damages in the amount of 3944.20 yuan for medical expenses, 2800 yuan for hospitalization, 900 yuan for supplementary hospitalization expenses, 2000 yuan for nursing care, a one-time disability consolation payment of 70,560 yuan, a one-time supplementary disability payment of 8960 yuan, a one-time payment of 7840 yuan for supplementary medical expenses, 12,80

---

[8] There are three categories of disability: total, major, and partial. Fifth Degree is considered "major." Ministry of Labor [Laodongbu], Provisional Measures for Worker's Compensation in Enterprises [Guanfabu qiye zhigong gongshang baoxian shixing banfa], CEILAW L35301199607, Aug. 12, 1996, art. 14.

yuan for a wheelchair, and 2000 yuan for attorney's fees and travel expenses, for a total of 111,760.20 yuan [approximately US$13,630], plus court costs.

Defendant argued that because this dispute was employment-related, it should first be heard by a labor arbitration panel. [As more than sixty days had elapsed since the claim arose, plaintiff's request would probably be denied as untimely and his claim would be dismissed. – Ed.] Defendant also argued that plaintiff's injury was the result of his own serious failure to observe safety procedures and therefore plaintiff was at fault for the accident. In addition, defendant had already rendered immediate financial assistance to plaintiff and had paid him 1000 yuan in settlement. Defendant was under no further obligation. After the parties agreed on a settlement, plaintiff had aggravated his own injury, for which defendant was not responsible.

The Guanghan People's Court made the following findings of fact:

In August 1996 plaintiff Chen Weili was hired by defendant Lai Guofa. His primary duties were to help Lai with the use of a trailer for hauling sand, such as changing tires on the truck, securing the triangular coupler which attached the truck to the trailer, and providing safety directions to the driver. The parties orally agreed that Chen would be paid a salary of 300 yuan a month and that Lai would take care of Chen's housing and food expenses. In the evening of October 7, 1996, the rig was being used to haul sand in Chengdu. As the truck was moving in reverse, the upper and lower sections of the coupler were out of alignment. The truck backed up so that the pintle could be properly inserted through the slots in the coupler. Chen Weili jumped onto the coupler to secure the pintle in place, but as the truck was backing up, he lost his balance. His left foot slipped into the coupler and his lower leg was crushed when the coupler swung to one side.

Plaintiff was immediately sent to the No. 1 Hospital of West China Medical University for treatment. While plaintiff was hospitalized, his father, being financially pressed, agreed with Lai Guofa that defendant would pay for all of the expenses of this hospitalization plus a one-time payment of 1000 yuan to cover recuperation, but otherwise would have no liability. According to the settlement agreement, plaintiff was released from the hospital on October 21 with the following diagnosis: open annular avulsion fracture of the left tibia. The agreement 'ated that plaintiff and his family requested his discharge, and that they were instructed to prove the patient's nutrition, change his wound dressings, and return to the hospital for w-up care. As agreed Lai Guofa paid all the expenses of this hospitalization.

er Chen Weili returned home, he continued to recuperate at the Longtai Center Clinic ngjiang county. But family finances did not permit him to remain in the clinic and he arged. The expenses of his stay in the clinic were 2643.20 yuan. Thereafter, Chen ht assistance on numerous occasions from the law office in Lianshan township in ain damages from Lai Guofa, but was unsuccessful. Finally, with the support of ces center in Deyang municipality, he filed suit. On July 23, 1999, following a ation, the Deyang Intermediate People's Court certified that Chen suffered ability.

court further determined that on January 13, 1995 Lai Guofa had entered ith the Lianshan township transportation cooperative that he would buy wn funds in order to join the cooperative. The actual operation of the responsibility. Lai Guofa paid the cooperative for its management ses. The truck involved in the accident (Sichuan license number Guofa bought pursuant to his agreement with the cooperative.

On the truck's license and other registration papers, it was registered in the name of the cooperative.

The Guanghan court decided as follows:

Plaintiff Chen Weili entered into a contract for hire (guyong hetong) with defendant Lai Guofa based on an oral agreement. Plaintiff was to supply labor in exchange for compensation. This contract qualifies in every respect as a valid civil act under the General Principles of Civil Law and is deserving of legal protection. While employed by Lai Guofa, Chen Weili enjoyed the benefits of occupational safety and health law. *See* Supreme People's Court, Reply Concerning Strict Compliance with Occupational Safety and Health Regulations in a Contract for Hire, Oct. 14, 1988.[9] Because Chen Weili was injured while engaged in activities within the scope of his employment, Lai Guofa bears civil liability. Lai Guofa has not proved that Chen Weili caused his own injuries intentionally or as a result of gross negligence. Hence Lai Guofa should bear total responsibility for the consequences.

For the precise measure of damages owing to Chen Weili, the court obtains guidance from the Labor Ministry's Provisional Measures for Worker's Compensation in Enterprises[10] and the normative interpretation of the Implementing Measures by the Labor Office of Sichuan Province.[11] As the losing party, Lai Guofa is also responsible for reimbursing the necessary expenses of the legal aid center which represented Chen Weili in this case. See art. 7 of the Notice Regarding Certain Issues of Legal Aid in Civil Litigation, issued jointly by the Ministry of Justice and the Supreme People's Court.[12] Chen Weili's request for compensatory damages and the costs of this litigation shall be granted.

Art. 2 of the Labor Law[13] provides in pertinent part:

All enterprises and individual economic organizations (hereinafter "employers") and those who engage in employment relationships with them within the territory of the People's Republic of China shall apply this Law.

Art. 1 of the Labor Ministry's Opinion on Certain Issues Regarding Thorough Implementation of the Labor Law[14] provides the following explanation:

The term "individual economic organization" in art. 2 of the Labor Law means an individual business which employs seven workers or less.

Defendant Lai Guofa did not obtain a business license and was not legally authorized to hire employees. He was not able to engage in an "employment relationship" within the meaning of the Labor Law. This case does not involve an "employment relationship." It involves a contract for hire subject to the original jurisdiction of the courts. Prior submission of the case

---

[9] *See* Collection of Normative Interpretations of the Law of the People's Republic of China 1949-1989 [Zhonghua renmin gongheguo falü guifanxing jieshi jicheng] 594 (1990).

[10] *See* note 8.

[11] Document not publicly available.

[12] Supreme People's Court and Ministry of Justice [Zuigao renmin fayuan Sifabu], Notice Regarding Certain Issues of Legal Aid in Civil Litigation [Guanyu minshi falü yuanzhu gongzuo ruogan wenti de lianhe tongzhi], http://www.chinajudge.com/fgzhchh.htm (site visited Oct. 23, 2002).

[13] Translation appears *supra*.

[14] *See* Ministry of Labor [Laodongbu], Opinion on Certain Issues Regarding Thorough Implementation of the Labor Law [Guanyu guanqie zhixing Zhonghua renmin gongheguo laodongfa ruogan wenti de yijian], CEILAW L35901199539, Aug. 4, 1995.

to a labor arbitration panel is not required. Lai Guofa's argument that the case should first be submitted to a labor arbitration panel is simply not tenable.

The agreement which Chen Weili's father made with Lai Guofa did not express Chen's own true intentions and has no legal effect. Lai Guofa's argument that Chen aggravated his injury after termination of the contract is unproven and not credible. Accordingly the Guanghan court ordered Lai Guofa to pay damages to Chen Weili within 10 days of the order's effective date, as follows: 2643.20 yuan for medical expenses previously incurred, 71,442 yuan as consolation for permanent disability, and supplementary medical expenses of 7938 yuan, for a total of 82,023.20 yuan [approximately US$10,000]. The court also ordered Lai to pay legal aid expenses of 2000 yuan within 10 days of the order's effective date. The remainder of Chen's claims were dismissed. Court costs of 150 yuan to Lai Guofa.

Lai Guofa did not accept the judgment and filed an appeal with the Deyang Intermediate People's Court. Lai argued that he had an employment relationship "in fact" with Chen Weili which came within the scope of the Labor Law. By accepting 1000 yuan in settlement, Chen's father acknowledged that the family would bear all further expenses. The parties' obligations under the settlement agreement had been performed, thereby ratifying the agreement. Appellee had no legal grounds for bringing suit.

Chen Weili accepted the decision of the court of first instance.

On appeal the Deyang Intermediate People's Court determined that the legal relationship between the parties was a contract for hire. Because Chen Weili was injured while performing services which inured to the benefit of Lai Guofa, Lai bears civil liability. Since Lai failed to prove that Chen was in any way responsible for his own injuries, the court of first instance was correct in concluding that Lai is liable for the full measure of damages. By failing to properly register as an individual business, Lai cannot assert the applicability of the Labor Law.

Lai's argument regarding the validity of the settlement agreement is also unsupported. Throughout the period in question, Chen Weili had legal capacity to contract. Any abridgement of his civil rights should have been effected by Chen himself or his duly authorized representative. The findings of fact by the court of first instance were clear and its application of the law correct. The decision was proper and procedurally in accordance with law.

Accordingly, on March 15, 2000, pursuant to art. 153(1)(i) of the Law of Civil Procedure, the Deyang court rejected Lai Guofa's appeal. Costs of 150 yuan to Lai Guofa.

Notes

1. The Labor Law, and its dispute resolution process, applies to "employment relationships." It does not apply to civil servants (gongwuyuan), who are subject to a different legal regime. Civil servants do not have a right of appeal to the courts. *See* the Law on State Functionaries [Gongyuanfa], passed by the Standing Committee of the NPC, April 27, 2005. The Labor Law also does not govern "contracts for hire" where the parties are of equal status, that is, contracts involving independent contractors. Such contracts are within the purview of the General Principles of Civil Law. A contractual dispute may be brought directly in court; it does not have to be first submitted to arbitration. An "independent contractor" is distinguished from an "employee" based on the following criteria: (1) whether he determines his own working conditions and supplies his own equipment; (2) whether he is subject to instruction and supervision; (3) whether he retains the profits from his work; (4) whether he is paid wages; (5) whether he is subject to

discipline or dismissal for breach of contract. 4 Selected Supreme People's Court Cases [Renmin fayuan anli xuan] 165 (2003). Where an "independent contractor" is injured or killed while performing his contractual obligations, the other party is liable for damages unless the independent contractor has been negligent, and damages are then reduced to the extent of the contractor's negligence. *Id.* at 161. *See also* Supreme People's Court, Explanation Concerning Certain Problems in the Adjudication of Personal Injury Cases [Guanyu shenli renshen sunhai peichang anjian shiyong falü ruogan wenti de jieshi], art. 10-12, Dec. 29, 2003, http://www.court.gov.cn/lawdata/explain/civlcation/200312300005.htm. Worker's compensation for "employees" is a no-fault scheme.

2. The decision in this case is very much results oriented. Based on the criteria enumerated above, Chen Weili was an "employee," not an "independent contractor." However, under the Labor Law, Chen should have filed a claim within the statutory period specified in the Labor Law. Exceptions to the sixty day statute of limitations are made only for reasons beyond the employee's control or similar justification. *See* Explanation Regarding Certain Legal Problems in the Handling of Labor Disputes art. 3, *supra.* The court of first instance finesses the jurisdictional issue by concluding that, because Lai Guofa was not properly licensed to do business, the Labor Law does not apply.

3. Expansion of the nonstate sector of the economy produces many situations of the kind illustrated by this case, where thinly capitalized private businesses engage in hazardous operations without proper equipment, training, and liability coverage. *Cf.* Labor Law Art. 52-57 (Occupational Safety and Health); 2004 State Department Report, sec. 6(e). Local governments charged with enforcement of occupational safety and health laws are caught between a rock and a hard place: the nonstate sector provides jobs, even if the rate of accidents is very high.

4. There is no indication that Lai Guofa or the township transportation cooperative carried liability insurance. Both may well have been judgment-proof. As of January 1, 2004, all employers are required to insure all their workers against occupational accidents. Yanyuan Cheng and Barbara Darimont, *Occupational Accident Insurance Reform and Legislation in China*, 58 INT'L SOC.SEC.REV. 85 (2005).

LIU JIANFA V. SHANGHAI OTIS ELEVATOR COMPANY

Unfair Dismissal
CEILAW; Selected People's Court Cases;
Case 115211996037

Plaintiff: Liu Jianfa, male, 39 years old, home address: No. 4, Lane 181, Anshun Road, Shanghai.

Defendant: Shanghai Otis Elevator Company Ltd., address: 2 Jinling East Road, Shanghai.

Plaintiff Liu Jianfa was originally employed by the Shanghai branch of China Tianjin Otis Elevator Company ("Tianjin Otis"). He signed an employment contract of unlimited duration with Tianjin Otis on October 21, 1989. On March 26, 1993 Tianjin Otis, Shanghai International Trust & Investment Company, and the Far East Group of Otis Company (U.S.A.) signed a joint venture agreement, to establish Shanghai Otis Elevator Company ("Shanghai Otis"). On June 1, Shanghai Otis was incorporated. On August 28, Shanghai Otis conducted its first board of directors meeting, resolved that the Shanghai branch of Tianjin Otis would cease operations, and announced its decision at the formal opening ceremony. Thereupon the workforce of the Shanghai branch, including plaintiff, was absorbed into the workforce of Shanghai Otis, but Shanghai Otis neither terminated their existing employment contracts nor did it sign new employment contracts with them.

On November 16, Liu Jianfa was appointed manager of the installation department. On February 15, 1994, the management committee of Shanghai Otis removed Liu Jianfa from his position, alleging problems with quality control and engineering management. In the letter informing him of this decision, he was given two options: (1) submit a letter of resignation within four days, in which case he would receive four months' salary and assistance in finding a new job; or (2) otherwise, the company would terminate him forthwith. Liu did not submit a letter of resignation and was terminated. He then filed a complaint with the Shanghai Labor Dispute Arbitration Committee. On January 26, 1995 the Committee decided that Liu Jianfa had been terminated as of February 23, 1994. Liu filed an appeal with the Huangpu District Court on February 9, 1995. In his appeal Liu Jianfa argued that he had only served as manager of the installation department for three months and could not be blamed for several years of ongoing difficulties with quality control. Furthermore, the company had terminated him without consulting with the labor union, a violation of the procedural requirements of the labor law. He requested that his employment relationship with the company be restored.

In response, Shanghai Otis argued that it was not bound by the contract which Liu had signed with Tianjin Otis. It had not signed an employment contract with Liu and thus, according to local regulations, he was employed on a month-to-month basis. In lieu of one month's notice of termination, the company was willing to pay him one month's salary as severance. During his tenure, there had been many problems with quality control and the installation department was in a state of chaos. The image of the company had suffered accordingly. It was unaware of the existence of a labor union. Because of workplace rule violations and for other reasons, the company opposed reinstatement.

The Huangpu District Court found that the Shanghai Foreign Invested Enterprise Trade Union Federation had approved a change of name for the company union on June 26, 1993. The company had not consulted with the union before terminating Liu. After he was terminated, the union had submitted written objection, but the company refused to accept it.

The court determined that all foreign invested enterprises are required to implement the contract employment system. Upon its establishment, Shanghai Otis had accepted all of the employees of the branch company. Even though it had not expressly terminated Liu's previous employment contract or signed a new contract with him, in practice the parties carried out their obligations under the original employment contract. Defendant's denial of an ongoing employment relationship does not comport with reality. In not consulting with the union prior to terminating Liu, Shanghai Otis had acted contrary to fact and law. For these reasons, Liu's request for reinstatement should be granted. On June 19, 1995, pursuant to art. 10 (1) and art. 16 (1)(2) of the 1987 Shanghai Municipal Regulations on Labor Management in Sino-Foreign Joint Ventures, the court ordered that Liu be reinstated and that Shanghai Otis sign an employment contract with him.[15]

---

[15] Art. 10 of the regulations [Shanghaishi zhongwai hezi jingying qiye laodong renshi guanli tiaoli] required a written employment contract. Art. 16 required consultation with the union and one month's advance notice for termination. *See* Shanghai Overseas Investment Manual [Shanghaishi liyong waizi gongzuo shouce] 209-10 (1993). The court made a technical error in not citing to the national regulations (discussed later in the commentary) and the revised local regulations of Dec. 9, 1994. Art. 10 was renumbered as 11, and art. 16 as 17.

Shanghai Otis appealed the district court decision to the Second Intermediate Court. Shanghai Otis argued that it had not signed an employment contract with Liu and was not bound by the terms of his original contract with Tianjin Otis. When it discovered his dereliction of duty, it had the right to terminate the employment relationship. Furthermore, at that time, it was unaware of the existence of a trade union. The company's decision to terminate Liu should be sustained.

Liu argued that the parties had a de facto employment relationship which was an extension of the original contract, that he had not committed any dereliction of duty, and that Shanghai Otis had not sought approval for termination from the company union. The decision of the court of first instance should be affirmed.

Pursuant to art. 153 (1), first clause, of the Civil Procedure Law, the intermediate court decided that the district court was correct in its findings of fact. For the reasons stated in the proceedings below, it upheld the district court's decision and dismissed the appeal on September 27, 1995.

Commentary

The threshold issue in this case is whether plaintiff and defendant actually had an employment relationship, i.e., whether plaintiff was employed by defendant. Defendant argued in the first instance and on appeal that it had not signed a contract with plaintiff and that it was not bound by the contract between the now defunct branch company and plaintiff. In denying that an employment relationship existed, defendant's assertions were plainly in conflict with reality. Pursuant to art. 2 of the Labor Management Regulations for Chinese-Foreign Joint Ventures and art. 5 of the Implementing Measures, joint ventures must practice the contract employment system. The parties must sign an employment contract and thereby establish an employment relationship.

The objective reality in this case is that defendant failed to observe the necessary formalities. However, it is also true that when defendant was established, it absorbed the workforce of the prior entity, but it did not sign new employment contracts with them. The employer changed but the employees did not. Thus, the original employment contracts continued in full force and effect. According to civil law theory, though one party to a contract may undergo a change of corporate form in accordance with law, the rights and obligations of the original contract pass to the successor entity. Therefore, the court of first instance and the appellate court were correct in rejecting defendant's argument.

The next point is that the lawful rights and interests of Chinese-foreign joint ventures operating within the territory of the PRC are protected under art. 2 of the Joint Venture Regulations, but by the same token a joint venture must comply in every respect with relevant laws. This requirement applies likewise to labor management. In its investigation of a case involving termination of an employee, the court must first look into the matter of procedural regularity. In other words, no matter what the employer's reasons or manner of termination, a joint venture must comply with mandated procedures. The employer bears the burden of proving that in making and carrying out its decision it was acting in accordance with its management rights. In this case, the employer did not comply with mandated procedure in two respects.

First, by removing the employee from his position, the employer attempted to coerce him into resigning against his will. Such intimidation is contrary to the concept of voluntary resignation. Secondly, the employer did not give one month's advance notice of termination to the employee and the union. When the union did object, the employer flatly refused to consider its views. The trade union is a mass organization charged with protecting workers' lawful rights and interests. According to the Trade Union Law, it is specially charged with particular responsibilities, including matters involving termination and discipline. When the employer dismisses or disciplines a worker without giving necessary notice to the union, the decision has no legal validity.

The employer's argument that it was "unaware" of the existence of a union at the time it dismissed the employee is absurd. The company union was in existence and officially recognized from the very month that the company was incorporated. To argue otherwise is pure sophistry. Since a finding of procedural regularity is a necessary predicate to an examination of the substantive legality of the employer's decision, the court can void the decision on procedural grounds alone and order that the employee be reinstated. Therefore, the decisions of first and second instance were correct.

Notes

1. Liu Jianfa was employed in the foreign invested sector of the economy, which was nonexistent before 1978. By 2002, thirty million people were employed in special economic zones, set up to attract FDI. ICFTU, behind the brand names: Working Conditions and Labor Rights in Export Processing Zones (2004), http://www.icftu.org.

2. In the prereform period, dismissal of a permanent, state sector employee for incompetence was almost inconceivable. ANDREW G. WALDER, COMMUNIST NEO-TRADITIONALISM: WORK AND AUTHORITY IN CHINESE INDUSTRY 143 (1986). The Labor Law authorizes a probationary period for new hires (art. 21); if a probationary employee is not up to the demands of the job, he can be let go. However, during the term of an employment contract, dismissal is allowed only if the employer has made an effort to retrain or reassign a worker (art. 26).

3. Chinese law recognizes successor liability. General Principles of Civil Law [Minfa Tongze], art. 44. A company cannot retrench its workforce simply by undergoing some form of corporate reorganization. *Compare* Japanese law, Takashi Araki, Corporate Governance Reforms, Labor Law Developments, and the Future of Japan's Practice-Dependent Stakeholder Model sec. 4.3.1 (2005) http://www.jil.go.jp/english/documents/JLR05_araki.pdf; Ryuichi Yamakawa, *Labor Law Reform in Japan: A Response to Recent Socio-Economic Changes*, 49 AM. J. COMP. L. 627, 648-49 (2001). *See also* Chapter 7, "European Labour Law, Transfer of Enterprises and Acquired Rights: The Merckx-Ford Case." The responsibility for observing contract formalities, such as memorialization in writing, is on the employer (art. 19, 98).

4. Foreign invested enterprises are required by law to set up trade unions, although many – if not most – in fact do not. Anita Chan, *Trade Unions, Conditions of Labor, and the State*, in JÜTTA HEBEL & GUNTER SCHUCHER ED., DER CHINESISCHE ARBEITSMARKT: STRUKTUREN, PROBLEME, PERSPECTIVEN 237 (1999). The very absence of powerful, independent unions is a major attraction for foreign investors. Local governments are reluctant to press the issue, grateful that the enterprises are generating employment and tax revenue. Shen Tan, *The Relationship between Foreign Enterprises, Local Governments, and Women Migrant Workers in the Pearl River Delta*, in LORAINE A. WEST & YAOHUI ZHAO, RURAL LABOR FLOWS IN CHINA

292 (2000). Trade unions, whether in foreign enterprises or the state sector, are fairly toothless in protecting worker rights. *See* "Collective Contracts and the Trade Union," *infra*. In this particular case, the labor union did intervene on the plaintiff's behalf, which was an important factor in voiding the dismissal.

5. Chinese law provides for one appeal as of right. In this case, the decision of the court of first instance was upheld both on the law and the facts. The Supreme People's Court hears those few appellate decisions where the court of first instance is a provincial level court. JOSEPHS, *supra*, at 106 n. 24.

CAPITAL IRON & STEEL-JAPAN ELECTRIC ELECTRONICS COMPANY V. CHEN JINGKE

Damages for Breach of Employment Contract
CEILAW; Selected People's Court Cases; Case 115211995036

Defendant/appellant: Chen Jingke, 27 years old, a former employee of Capital Iron & Steel-Japan Electric Electronics Company.

Plaintiff/appellee: Capital Iron & Steel-Japan Electric Electronics Company.

Defendant Chen Jingke was hired by plaintiff Capital Iron & Steel-Japan Electric Electronics Company (hereinafter "Electronics Company") in December 1990. In October 1992 Chen signed two contracts with Electronics Company, an employment contract and a contract for employees going abroad for training. Art. 12 of the employment contract provided that "Employer has the right to recover, in whole or in part, any training expenses incurred on behalf of Employee if Employee resigns or is absent without leave during the term of the contract." Art. 13 provided that "if Employee is absent without leave, he shall compensate Employer's damages in the amount of three months' average wage for the company's workforce; the contract shall automatically expire as of the date of Employee's absence."

Chen Jingke went to Japan for training, from November 1992 until October 1993. Before his departure Chen borrowed 20,000 yen from Electronics Company for travel expenses. In Japan Chen participated in 177 days of training, at a cost of 3,461,273 yen. Upon his return to China, Chen obtained permission to visit his family in Sichuan from Nov. 22, 1993 until Dec. 4, 1993.

Chen did not return to work at the appointed time nor did he request an extension as company rules required. Instead, his father sent a letter requesting additional leave, accompanied by a forged medical excuse recommending six months' recuperation time for Hepatitis B. On Jan. 22, 1994, Electronics Company dispatched someone to call on Chen Jingke at his parents' home in Sichuan, but Chen was not there. On Feb. 2, Electronics Company sent Chen a warning letter, ordering him back to work by Feb. 16 or else he would be disciplined under the Regulations on Rewards and Punishments for Enterprise Workers and Staff.[16] After receiving the letter, Chen did not return to work or reply in any way. He did not return to Beijing until March 10, 1994.

Electronics Company terminated Chen's employment contract for having been absent without leave for two months. In February 1994 Electronics Company filed a complaint with

---

[16] Art. 19 permits "expungement" (chuming) for more than fifteen days of continuous absence or more than thirty days in a given year. Under either measure of unauthorized absence, Chen Jingke met the criterion for expungement.

the Beijing Labor Arbitration Committee, requesting compensation of training expenses, the loan for travel expenses, and economic damages. In April 1994 the committee ordered repayment, as well as 2400 yuan in economic damages.

In May 1994 Chen filed an appeal with the Beijing Intermediate Court, requesting reinstatement and back pay. He disclaimed liability for training expenses, arguing that they had been underwritten by the Japanese government.

Electronics Company argued that Chen had been properly terminated according to the provisions of his employment contract and that it was entitled to the award made by the arbitration committee.

The Beijing Intermediate Court decided that the two contracts which Chen had signed should be enforced since they expressed the true intention of the parties and were consistent with national law. After his authorized leave expired, Chen Jingke did not return to work, submit a valid medical excuse, or obtain an extension. After receiving notification from Electronics Company, Chen still did not return to work and therefore was absent without leave. According to the terms of the contract, it automatically expired as of the time Chen was absent without leave. Chen's request for reinstatement and back pay is unreasonable and unsupportable. It was clearly proven that Electronics Company paid for Chen's training in Japan. Based on the two contracts, Chen is liable for training expenses, the loan for travel expenses, and economic damages. After an unsuccessful attempt at mediation, the court decided to reject Chen's appeal and to rule the employment contract terminated. Within a month of the judgment, Chen was to pay the amounts owed in Chinese currency, at the rate of exchange published by the Bank of China.

Commentary

Under art. 2 of the Regulations for the Resolution of Labor Disputes in Enterprises, "labor disputes" are limited to the following four categories: (1) disputes involving expulsion, expungement, dismissal, resignation, and voluntary absence from work; (2) disputes involving wages, social insurance, fringe benefits, training, and occupational safety and health; (3) disputes arising from employment contracts; and (4) other disputes, as provided by law. This case involves a dispute arising from an employment contract. [The case belongs in the third category, rather than the first, because the employee was dismissed for "breach of contract." – Ed.] In a case of this kind, aside from ascertaining the pertinent facts, special attention should be paid to a determination of the validity of the employment contract which provides justification for worker discipline. Under art. 17 of the Labor Law, a valid employment contract requires (1) that its formation observe the principles of equality, voluntariness, and mutual agreement; and (2) that the contract be in compliance with law. A court may only recognize and uphold a contract which is valid according to the above criteria.

In this case, Chen Jingke did not accept the decision of the labor arbitration committee and furthermore, sued for reinstatement and back pay. Therefore, the key issue in the case is determining whether or not the employment relationship was terminated. Since the two contracts which Chen signed were indeed valid, they are the basis for termination of the employment relationship.

The employment contract provided that "Employer has the right to recover, in whole or in part, any training expenses incurred on behalf of Employee if Employee resigns or is absent without leave during the term of the contract" and that "it shall automatically expire as of the date of Employee's unauthorized absence." After his authorized leave expired, Chen did not obtain an extension nor did he return to work by the date specified in the warning letter. This behavior satisfies the contractual conditions for termination and a claim for damages. Electronics Company's actions are supported both in fact and in law. The decision of the court was correct on every point.

Notes

1. This case illustrates the importance of observing legal formalities. Chen Jingke's employment contract expressly provided for reimbursement of training expenses and also included a liquidated damages clause. *See* discussion of trade secrets protection, *supra*.

2. Given the precise numbers in the case report the employer was able to adduce proof (presumably written) as to the costs of training Chen Jingke.

3. Perhaps because the employer was a Chinese-Japanese joint venture, it had detailed company rules, for example, on leaves of absence. The Chinese partner was an affiliate of one of the country's major steel companies, which should have had its own detailed internal rules. *See* Labor Law art. 4. Furthermore, the Japanese partner would have been accustomed to the requirements of the Japanese Labor Standards Law. This law requires companies which continuously employ ten or more workers to draw up work rules, to solicit the opinion of the company trade union or other worker representative, and to publish the rules. *See* KAZUO SUGENO & LEO KANOWITZ (TRANS.), JAPANESE EMPLOYMENT AND LABOR LAW 110-28 (2002).

4. The total damages awarded in this case was approximately the equivalent of $28,500. This is a gargantuan sum by local standards, which Chen is not likely to repay. However, the employer may have believed that the case would have an in terrorem effect on other employees and would discourage Chen himself from trying to exploit the value of his training in another position.

D. COLLECTIVE CONTRACTS AND THE TRADE UNION

Trade unions the world over are not faring well in the era of globalization. Even in developed countries where, at one time, a significant portion of the work force belonged to unions and enjoyed the protection of collective bargaining agreements, the situation is getting worse. In the United States, for example, with shrinkage of the manufacturing sector, the percentage of the workforce that is unionized has declined from approximately one-third to about a tenth.

> In the United States, millions of workers are excluded from coverage by laws to protect rights of organizing, bargaining, and striking. For workers who are covered by such laws, recourse for labor rights violations is often delayed to a point where it ceases to provide redress. When they are applied, remedies are weak and often ineffective.
>
> Lance Compa, Unfair Advantage: Workers' Freedom of Association in the United States under International Human Rights Standards, http://www.hrw.org.

See also, Danny Hakim, *A U.A.W. Chief Awaits a G.M. Showdown*, N.Y. TIMES, June 23, 2005, at C4 (describing decline of United Auto Workers union). Steven Greenhouse,

4 Major Unions Plan To Boycott A.F.L. – CIO Events, N.Y. TIMES, July 25, 2005, at A1;
Steven Greenhouse, *Splintered, but Unbowed, Unions Claim a Relevancy*, N.Y. TIMES,
July 30, 2005, at C1.

The original arguments made for recognizing trade unions and respecting the collective bargaining process are still valid, that workers, employers and the public at large all benefit from social peace. Toby D. Merchant, *Note, Recognizing ILO Rights to Organize and Bargain Collectively: Grease in China's Transition to a Socialist Market Economy*, 36 CASE W. RES. J. INT'L L. 223 (2004). However, nothing in China's past or present indicates that trade unions will achieve a meaningful role in the near future.

The WTO and Chinese Labor Rights
3 CHINA RIGHTS FORUM 39 (2005)
http://hrichina.org/fs/view/downloadables/pdf/crf/CRF-2005-3_EWE_wto.pdf.
Reprinted with permission.

AN INTERVIEW WITH CHANG KAI BY MA WEI

China's membership in the WTO provides a new opportunity to reexamine the position of China's workers in a world economy, and to address problems that have been growing since China embarked on its reform and opening 20 years ago.

Ma Wei is a reporter with Worker's Daily (Gongren Ribao). Chang Kai, who holds a Ph.D. in Labor Law from Peking University, is director of the China Institute of Industrial Relations and a member of the Labor Law Institute at Peking University Law School.

NEW CHALLENGES TO LABOR UNDER A WORLD ECONOMY

Ma Wei (MW): Countries joining the WTO must meet a minimum condition – implementing a market economy. This was the primary obstacle standing between China and the WTO for some fifteen years. We know that when China joined the organization, it voluntarily followed the WTO's common rules to reform its economic management system, and this caused general concern about how China's economy would be affected. But what effect does membership in the WTO have on a Chinese social structure built on the foundation of a planned economy, especially in terms of labor relations?

Chang Kai (CK): The WTO is the organizational manifestation of economic globalization. It is the embodiment of capitalism carving up the globe, and the free circulation of capital across national boundaries. And of course WTO regulations are the common rules of the capitalist market economy. Today, in the 21st century, the world has formed itself into a common market and capitalism has gained linguistic and disciplinary rights. There is no escaping this fact.

The emergence of the WTO has had an indisputably positive significance in pushing forward the realization of a global "market economy and free trade." However, this push has as its means and end the expansion of capital, and expansion of capital requires the suppression and deprivation of labor. The trend in international development is for the conflict between labor and capital to grow rather than weaken; most glaringly, workers do not enjoy a greater right to speak because of free trade, but rather have become more passive – capital may be able to circulate globally, but workers certainly do not have the freedom to do so. At the same time, unions have found themselves in an increasingly inferior and weakened position in their confrontations with capital.

MW: We can state the following as fact: 1) Transnational capital always moves from areas with high wage levels to areas with low wage levels. 2) Multinational corporations can monopolize the profits from an entire industry. 3) The gap between poverty and wealth is growing, and wealth is increasingly concentrated in the hands of a few. My feeling is that the WTO is more like a multinational corporation or a rich man's club. What impact will the rules of this club have on China's existing labor relations?

CK: It isn't easy to be optimistic. Introducing a market economy inevitably introduces the basic conflict of market economy, that between labor and capital. In fact, this conflict appeared as soon as we set marketization as our reform goal: basic economic reforms from diversified ownership to marketization of the labor force, and on to supply and demand will inevitably change the strength of labor relative to capital. Speaking concretely, the former position of the worker as master of his own affairs was based on the system of public ownership and labor supply. The market economy, however, is based on the pluralization of ownership and supply and demand. The fact that supply in the labor market is greater than demand puts the worker in an even less advantageous position.

Capital seeks to maximize profits, while workers seek to maximize wages: each is rational in its way, but they are mutually contradictory. Who wins out? The position of capital continues to rise; this is a major trend. A detailed analysis of China's ten-plus years of effort to join the WTO shows that labor-capital relations in China were changing at the same time. On the one hand there has been the large-scale influx of international capital into China, while on the other hand important changes have taken place in the structure of China's system of ownership and the establishment of marketization-related regulations, including private property rights, management rights and the regulation and handling of labor relations. All this has accelerated the restructuring of Chinese labor-capital relations while at the same time exacerbating the conflict between them.

With the departure of public ownership, labor relations that in the past were strongly political, bureaucratically controlled and based on a concept of common interest, have become labor relations based on economic advantage, regulated by trends in the market economy and based on a coordination of interests. As problems such as unemployment, distribution, social security, security of employment and health have become increasingly serious, the contradictions and conflicts between labor and capital have intensified daily.

THE GOVERNMENT'S ROLE IN LABOR RIGHTS

MW: You've observed that many enterprises default on wages, and in recent years there has been a shocking incidence of other violations of workers' rights such as excessive working hours, poor working conditions and horrific labor-related accidents. The disconnect between the steady increase in unemployment and inadequate social security is a source of additional concern. In your opinion, is there a way out of these problems?

CK: First of all, the government cannot escape its responsibility. Take unemployment rights, for example. The government has a duty to implement public policy to increase employment and improve the social security system. Or take the problem of defaulting on wages, which tops the list of issues provoking labor disputes. Private enterprises routinely withhold wages, while state-owned enterprises routinely lack the money to pay.

Workers have gone through all kinds of hardships and difficulties to win court cases, but there has been no way to enforce the decisions, and they come away empty-handed.

It would be worth drawing on the Hong Kong government's system of wage guarantees. The government sets aside funds to guarantee unpaid wages, and when a labor dispute results in a decision against an enterprise, workers can go directly to the government for the money. The government then pursues the enterprise, which has nowhere to run.

It used to be popular to say that in the past, under the "iron rice bowl" system before reform and openness, workers became lazy. I think that's a rather superficial way of putting it. In fact is that workers are still paid very little for the huge contribution they've made in laying the economic foundations of socialism, and no one can deny that the cost of reform has hit workers the hardest. Failing to recognize these facts implies that the debts of history and the debts of the present can be written off in one stroke.

MW: In 1995, China tabled its Labor Law, which stipulates basic principles for regulating labor-capital relations, the main safeguard of workers' interests. At present this law is constantly flouted. Do you think it's time to review the compliance and implementation of this law?

CK: It should be said that the implementation of the Labor Law laid the foundation for the present labor law framework centered on market principles. But the law places undue emphasis on principles, exacerbating the influence of systemic reforms and the rule of law environment, and increasing the difficulty of concrete implementation. As a result, labor disputes and infringement of workers rights have run rampant.

The reasons are three-fold: first of all, an employer starts with profit as the goal and hires as few people as possible to reduce costs; second, the reform process has given very little consideration to workers' interests, and much of the cost of reform has been borne by workers; third, in handling labor disputes, especially when policies are involved, workers' compensation tends to be inadequate. For example, in the case of wages in arrears, the enterprise is responsible for paying what it owes, but if it goes bankrupt, no one takes responsibility. Labor issues involve three areas: 1) workers must organize; 2) the government must be impartial and cannot be unduly biased in favor of capital; and 3) enterprises must bear social responsibility rather than taking the short-sighted view of caring only for their own development at the expense of social development and stability.

What is needed now is to stress that the economy and society must develop in tandem; labor and capital must be in balance, and enterprises and workers must each get their due. Our present situation could be much more equitable.

MW: I've noticed in your essays that you frequently refer to international labor standards and that you feel this is an inescapable issue for us at present. Could you apply your views to the Labor Law?

CK: The question of WTO and labor standards or social provisions remains a source of conflict between developed and developing nations. I'm certainly not proposing that we raise our labor standards to match the wages and hours in developed countries. Actually, when the issue is raised internationally that labor standards should be tied to economic and trade regulations, it is mainly referring to basic standards, such as the establishment of labor unions, collective bargaining, opposition to forced labor and child labor, equal pay for equal work. All these are basic labor rights.

We should say that Chinese labor standards and legislation do not diverge greatly from international norms except in reference to freedom of assembly and forced labor. Some standards, such as those for working hours, even exceed international standards. What we need to do is merge these with international standards while maintaining our fundamental principles, because economic legislation must conform to international standards. We shouldn't imagine that we can bring China into conformance with capital, management and distribution norms without conforming to labor law, which is likewise part of economic law.

MW: Can you be more specific?

CK: The right to organize is a basic labor right. The main problem at present is first of all, that the rate of unionization in non-state-owned enterprises is very low, just a few percentage points, and secondly, that there is a high incidence of management control of unions, with unions organized by the employer and relatives of the boss heading up the union. This is more damaging to workers than not setting up a union at all, because neglecting or prohibiting the establishment of a union is a straightforward infringement of workers' rights, but management control of a union actually deprives workers of their rights. The seriousness of the problem is demonstrated by a special provision in the amended Labor Union Law, which states that close relatives of an enterprise's main top manager cannot serve on the enterprise's union committee. Even though this is now stipulated by law, there is still the question of enforcement. If this provision is ignored, it might as well not exist.

In addition, labor standards should be more detailed. For example working hours are an issue, and excessive overtime is a widespread problem; there are many workplace injuries and fatalities, but compensation is inadequate. Labor law enforcement and court judgments need to do more to strengthen the protective dynamic of labor rights. The protection of labor rights has been neglected in the course of developing the economy; if this situation continues following entry into the WTO, I fear the resulting social problems will not be easily resolved.

UNIONS NEED TO CHANGE WITH THE TIMES

MW: A few years ago, there was an incident in which a union head represented the enterprise against workers in a labor arbitration tribunal. While there have been no reports of such cases recently, it's not at all unusual to find the unions unwilling to take a position at odds with management. In recent years the All-China Federation of Trade Unions has been proposing rights protection and actively adapting to new circumstances by transforming its own role, but its bureaucratic style doesn't seem to have changed.

CK: Unions must be involved whenever labor issues are raised. In this respect, the market economy offers unions an opportunity to realize their potential, but also poses them with a huge challenge. The unions have been changing constantly over the past 20 years to adapt to marketization, and they're making progress, but the gap is still quite large.

I think unions should evolve mainly according to legal requirements. The core issue here is that unions represent the interests of workers; unions are their protectors. This point is clearly stipulated in the Labor Law and in the Labor Union Law. This is the legal precondition for the work of the labor unions and their legal foundation, and it is here that we should focus our questions.

A lot of people have the impression that the rights of labor unions are granted by those higher up, but this isn't actually the case. The unions represent the rights of workers, not the interests of a higher-level organization. From representing workers in collective bargaining to signing labor contracts to defending rights through litigation, in all of these activities workers urgently need labor unions.

MW: On the subject of whom unions represent, a lot of people think that since enterprises put up most of the union funds, unions shouldn't confront them.

CK: I think this is faulty logic. Superficially, union funds now come from two sources: 0.5 percent comes from workers' wages, and the enterprise contributes a payment equivalent to 2 percent of total wages. But in theory, this 2 percent is actually the social organization fee that is part of a worker's wages. Although the enterprise contributes the money directly to the union, it's calculated into basic overheads before taxes, not as raw material or technology, but as a labor cost. But it's true that the contribution coming directly from the enterprise breaks the connection between the workers and the union.

As the market economy penetrates further, the need for Chinese workers to unite to defend their own rights and interests will become more urgent, and as the representative of the interests of the majority of workers, the demands on union employees will also become greater. They must become familiar with the workings of labor relations, the labor economy, the Labor Law, and with wage distribution, unemployment insurance and so on. And Chinese labor unions must step up their pace of change to keep up with the developing times.

Translated by a friend of HRIC

This article was posted in Chinese on the Web site of Gongnong Tiendi: http://gongntd. iwebland.com/jinri/jr020630019.htm.

Hilary K. Josephs, Labor Law in China 71-77 (2d ed. 2003) (footnotes omitted)

A. Introduction

Under international human rights law, the two employment-related rights which are most fundamental to the assurance of the rest are the rights of free association and collective bargaining, enshrined in International Labor Organization (ILO) Conventions 87 and 98, respectively. The importance of these rights is further established by respective provisions of international human rights conventions of general application, such as the Universal Declaration of Human Rights, the International Covenant on Economic, Social and Cultural Rights (ICESCR), and the International Covenant on Civil and Political Rights (ICCPR).

China ratified the ICESCR in March 2001 with the following proviso:

> The application of Article 8.1(a) of the Covenant [relating to freedom of association] to the People's Republic of China *shall be consistent* with the *relevant* provisions of the Constitution of the People's Republic of China, the Trade Union Law of the People's Republic of China and the Labor Law of the People's Republic of China. (Emphasis supplied.)

China has signed but not yet ratified the ICCPR, which also protects freedom of association, including the right to form and join trade unions.

Although a member of the United Nations (and a permanent member of the Security Council), as well as a member of the ILO, China does not accept the rights of free association and collective bargaining as these concepts are universally understood. There is but a single official trade union, the All China Federation of Trade Unions (ACFTU), subject to the domination of the Chinese Communist Party. Even as China undergoes economic reform and integrates itself into the global trading system, non-violent efforts to organize trade unions independent of the Party and the state have been methodically and ruthlessly suppressed. At the extreme margin, such efforts are prosecuted as crimes against national security.

It is highly dubious that the rights of free association and collective bargaining will take root in China in the foreseeable future. First, China has no historical experience whereby labor activism provided essential support to political and economic transformation. The Communist revolution was launched from the countryside, not from the cities. Mass industrialization of the economy occurred after the Communist Party established firm political control. The Party created the industrial working class, not the other way around. Those in the Party leadership who advocated a more prominent role for the ACFTU and greater worker autonomy vis-à-vis the Party, such as Li Lisan and Lai Ruoyu, were purged in the 1950's.

Secondly, China has achieved phenomenal economic growth and poverty reduction since the 1970's without making any substantive concessions in the area of international labor rights. The productivity of China's "reserve industrial army," drawn from the rural population, fuels economic growth. Other former command economies are worse off than under communism, including Poland where the labor movement Solidarity was instrumental in bringing down the incumbent regime.

Thirdly, while domestic law expressly protects certain labor rights such as minimum wages, maximum hours, and security against arbitrary dismissal, it does not support the rights of free association and collective bargaining. The written law is carefully crafted to perpetuate the official monopoly of the ACFTU. In its most recent revision, despite years of contact with and pressure from international groups, the Trade Union Law reaffirms that the ACFTU is the unified national labor organization and all subordinate levels operate under its exclusive auspices.

Fourthly, even assuming that the law were amended or creatively interpreted by the courts to support such rights, trade union officials at the grass roots level have operated for half a century in a culture of impotence. It was not unusual for the trade union representative to be a "shadow" position, occupied by the Party secretary or a member of management. Trade union officials often represent management, not workers, in the formal dispute resolution process. This conduct is directly contrary to the mandate imposed on the union under art. 30 of the Labor Law.

As SOEs [state owned enterprises] have retrenched or closed, the ACFTU is losing membership. Like their comrades on the production lines, union cadres have gone unremunerated; hence, a new provision in the Trade Union Law which allows them to sue for unpaid union contributions. A complete institutional transformation would be required to persuade workers that a trade union, any trade union, is legitimate *and* effective in representing their interests.

B. Collective Contracts and Collective Bargaining

In theory, the Labor Law provides an opportunity for workers to obtain the benefits of group solidarity through collective contracts (jiti hetong). The subject matter of a collective contract is the same as that of an individual contract – remuneration, working hours, rest periods and vacation time, occupational safety and health, social insurance and fringe benefits. If a trade union exists within the firm, it represents the workers in the negotiation of a collective contract.

The negotiation of a collective contract does not automatically nullify existing individual contracts but does supercede them to the extent that it establishes higher standards. The revised Trade Union Law now gives the trade union itself standing to sue for enforcement of a collective contract before the labor arbitration committee, whereas previously only the affected workers could do so.

There is evidence that some form of "collective consultation" or collective bargaining takes place in foreign invested enterprises of Western countries, though not in enterprises run by Hong Kong, Macau and Taiwanese investors, who provide the lion's share of foreign direct investment. In May 2001, the ILO's Workers Activities Branch signed a Memorandum of Understanding (MOU) with the ACFTU looking to strengthen the ACFTU's education and training capacity with regard to negotiation and collective bargaining. Significantly, programs conducted pursuant to the MOU emphasize foreign invested companies in the Special Economic Zones, where the presence of overseas Chinese investment is concentrated.

Nonetheless, a collective contract or collective bargaining has no real significance in the absence of a right to take collective action. The right to strike was purposefully omitted in the 1982 PRC Constitution. Art. 56 of the Labor Law justifies workers' refusal to perform dangerous operations or lodge complaints about working conditions which are unsafe or injurious to health. However, these rights are to be distinguished from the right to strike over salary, fringe benefits, and other terms of employment. The trade union is empowered to "consult" with management in the event of a work stoppage or slow down, but with the ultimate objective of restoring "normal" production as soon as possible.

C. Suppression of Independent Union Activity; Complaints Filed in the ILO

When the PRC assumed the "China" seat in the UN in 1971, it also resumed membership in the ILO. However, the PRC did not become active in the ILO until 1983. Over the next fifteen years, China's posture in the ILO evolved from implacable opposition to meddling in its internal affairs to a grudging acceptance of monitoring for compliance with international labor standards.

This was the same period during which the U.S. Congress annually scrutinized China's human rights record in connection with renewal of Most-Favored-Nation status; China began the long process of negotiating its entry into the General Agreements on Tariffs and Trade/World Trade Organization; and China was twice censured in the U.N. Sub-Commission on Human Rights. By June 2002, China's more cooperative attitude was richly rewarded when the ACFTU was elected to a Worker Deputy Member seat in the ILO's Governing Body.

China has declared itself bound by 14 ILO conventions ratified before 1949 (of which three are no longer in force) and nine ratified since 1983. Of those nine, three are considered "fundamental" by the ILO – Convention 100 on Equal Remuneration for Men and Women Workers for Work of Equal Value, Convention 138 on Minimum Age for Admission to Employment, and Convention 182 on the Worst Forms of Child Labor. [In January 2006 China ratified Convention 111, on Discrimination in Employment and Occupation.]

Although China is not party to either of the ILO's two fundamental conventions on freedom of association, Conventions 87 and 98, the Committee on Freedom of Association (CFA) regularly examines complaints against China, on the grounds that they are fundamental obligations arising from the very fact of membership and were affirmed in the 1998 Declaration on Fundamental Principles and Rights at Work.

The CFA has criticized China both on the substance of the Trade Union Law and specific punitive measures taken against individual activists for attempting to exercise international labor rights. Pressure from the CFA is effective in obtaining the release of individuals, but not in changing the written law. The basic principles of freedom of association are simply too "threatening to the survival of the political system."

Notes

1. Organizing an independent trade union is made more difficult by natural cleavages within the work force such as race, gender, ethnic origin, and language. In China, divisions are usually based on different languages and provincial origins. *See* EMILY HONIG, SISTERS AND STRANGERS: WOMEN IN THE SHANGHAI COTTON MILLS 1919–1949 (1986); Leslie T. Chang, *Company Town: In Chinese Factory, Rhythms of Trade Replace Rural Life*, WALL ST. J., Dec. 31, 2004 (available on Westlaw).

2. Wal-Mart, the mass merchandising giant, has expressed "willingness" to allow unionization of its employees in China. This move was taken in response to pressure from the ACFTU. David Barboza, *Wal-Mart Bows To Trade Unions At Stores in China*, N.Y. TIMES, Nov. 25, 2004, at C1; David Lague, *Official Union Set Up in China At Wal-Mart*, N.Y TIMES, July 31, 2006, at C1. Because unions in China function mostly as a tool of management, Wal-Mart's concession is not inconsistent with its general policy of opposing unionization. Ian Austen, *Wal-Mart To Close Store In Canada With a Union*, N.Y. TIMES, Feb. 10, 2005, at C3. *See also,* Steven Greenhouse, *Among Janitors, Labor Violations Go With the Job*, N.Y. TIMES, July 13, 2005, at A1 (in March 2005, Wal-Mart reached an $11 million settlement with the U.S. Justice Department for employing illegal immigrants as janitors in its stores).

3. A study of actual implementation of collective contracts found that there is no significant negotiation, little active participation by union members in framing proposals, and deference by the union to management. Workers still take their problems to their line managers, not their trade union representatives. *See* Simon Clarke, Chang-Hee Lee, & Qi Li, *Collective Consultation and Industrial Relations in China*, 42 BRIT. J. INDUS. REL. 235, 250 (2004).

4. The weakness of the ILO as an enforcer of international employment rights, as distinct from its role as a standard-setter and publicist of abuses, has lent support to the argument that the WTO should become more involved. WTO rules legitimate economic retaliation for breach. If the WTO is active in protecting the interests of corporations, for example, to intellectual property rights, it should also concern itself with worker rights. See Hilary K. Josephs, *Upstairs, Trade Law; Downstairs, Labor Law*, 33 GEO. WASH. INT'L L. REV. 849 (2001); Robert Howse, *Back to Court After Shrimp/Turtle? Almost but not Quite Yet: India's Short Lived Challenge to Labor and Environmental Exceptions in the European Union's Generalized System of Preferences*, 18 AM. U. INT'L L. REV. 1333 (2003). Developing countries with a comparative advantage in low labor costs, such as China and India, are adamantly opposed to WTO involvement. *See* Chapter 1, The World Trade Organization and Labor Rights; Kevin Kolben, *The New Politics of Linkage: India's Opposition to the Workers' Rights Clause*, 13 IND. J. GLOBAL LEGAL STUD. 1 (2006).

E. OPENING TO THE OUTSIDE: SPECIAL ECONOMIC ZONES AND BRAIN CIRCULATION

Whenever a developing country is able to sustain a high rate of economic growth, the question inevitably arises as to whether its "strategy" can be borrowed and imitated with the same results. Some economists argue that "institutions" are the key factor in economic development. DOUGLASS C. NORTH, INSTITUTIONS, INSTITUTIONAL CHANGE AND ECONOMIC PERFORMANCE 3 (1990) (defining institutions as "the rules of the game in a society . . . the humanly devised constraints that shape human interaction").

The "rules of the game" include the legal system. *Id.* at 96-100 (discussing the precedent-based evolution of the common law). Much ink has been spilled as to whether legal systems, or selected features of legal systems, can be successfully transplanted to new and different environments. *See, e.g.,* Daniel Berkowitz, Katharina Pistor, & Jean-François Richard, *The Transplant Effect*, 51 AM. J. COMP. L. 163 (2003) (concluding that transplantation generally fails).

Asian countries bent on economic modernization have long looked to Western countries as models. Japan, the first and still the only Asian country to make a full transition to developed country status, sent students abroad and imported foreign experts to gain knowledge of the West. It adopted the Western-style Meiji Constitution in 1889 and a civil code based largely on the German model in 1896. JOHN K. FAIRBANK, EDWIN O. REISCHAUER, & ALBERT M. CRAIG, EAST ASIA: TRADITION & TRANSFORMATION 525-26 (rev. ed. 1989). China, at various times, studied the example of Western countries, Japan, and the Soviet Union. However, in all these situations, the "borrower" actively sought outside guidance and adapted foreign models to the domestic environment. *Id.* at 534-46 (Japan), 776-77 (China). As the Preamble to the 1982 PRC Constitution states:

> [t]he basic task of the nation is to concentrate its efforts on socialist modernization along the road of *Chinese-style socialism.* (Emphasis supplied.)

Today, China in turn has become a role model to other developing countries. India, the world's second most populous country and the world's largest democracy, views China with a mixture of admiration and envy. Huang Yasheng & Tarun Khanna, *Can India overtake China's economic development?*, FOR. POL'Y (July 1, 2003), at 74 (available on Westlaw). Some India experts postulate that the country's political system and legal system are costly in terms of economic growth. *Id.*

In this chapter, we focus on two aspects of China's reform program that experts generally agree have – on balance – positively contributed to economic growth. The first is the creation of special economic zones for foreign investment. The second is attraction of financial and intellectual capital from the Chinese diaspora. These two phenomena are related and mutually reinforcing. "China has a large and wealthy diaspora that has long been eager to help the motherland, and its money has been warmly received." *Id.*

1. Special economic zones

China's first Special Economic Zones (SEZs) were established in 1979. The first major law governing operations in the SEZs, the Regulations on Special Economic Zones in Guangdong Province, was passed by the Standing Committee of the National People's

Congress in 1980. Art. 31 of the 1982 Constitution codified the practice of establishing "special administrative regions."

The concept of the special economic zone was not original to China. Many countries, developed and developing, create such enclaves for a variety of purposes: to attract foreign investment through incentives such as low land use and labor charges and preferential tax schemes; to expand exports and promotion of foreign exchange earnings; to generate new employment opportunities; and to promote transfer of technology and managerial skills. Alan B. Krueger, *Economic Scene*, N.Y. Times, Dec. 11, 2003, at C2 (discussing use of incentives by American cities). In countries with inadequate public infrastructure, economic zones provide a relatively regular supply of water, electricity, and telecommunications. Hilary K. Josephs, Labor Law in China: Choice and Responsibility 88 (1990); Meheroo Jusawalla & Richard D. Taylor ed., Information Technology Parks of the Asia Pacific (2003); International Confederation of Free Trade Unions, Behind the Brand Names: Working Conditions and Labour Rights in Export Processing Zones (2004), http://www.icftu.org; ILO, Committee on Employment and Social Policy, Employment and Social Policy in respect of Export Processing Zones (EPZs) (March 2003), http://www.ilo.org. In China's case, the Shenzhen and Zhuhai SEZs served another useful purpose, to create economically developed areas adjoining Hong Kong and Macau and thereby facilitate their return to PRC sovereignty, which occurred in 1997 and 1999, respectively.

After 1979, economic zones proliferated throughout China. Because the state effectively owns all land, requisitioning occupied or cultivated land for conversion to industrial parks was straightforward. *See* 1982 Constitution art. 10. Pamela N. Phan, *Enriching the Land or the Political Elite? Lessons from China on Democratization of the Urban Renewal Process*, 14 Pac. Rim L. & Pol'y 607 (2005). In particular, peasants displaced by commercial development were often given little or no compensation. Jian'gang Zhu, *Not Against the State, Just Protecting the Residents' Interests: A Residents' Movement in a Shanghai Neighborhood*, 5 Perspectives 25 (2004). In India, public interest litigation thwarts or stalls redevelopment.

By 2002, China had thirty million employed in over two thousand special economic zones, economic and technological development zones, EPZs, and border zones. ILO Report, *supra*, at 6. Where the original SEZs were set up to attract low-technology manufacturing, in toys, apparel, and consumer electronics, the government policy today emphasizes high level technology and research and development of cutting edge products. Jusawalla & Taylor, *supra*, at 28.

On the positive side, SEZs have been instrumental in China's emergence as the world's "manufacturing floor." Behind the Brand Names, *supra*. However, the SEZ concept has done little to encourage the growth of entrepreneurship domestically. Few products exported to foreign markets are manufactured by indigenous companies. Huang & Khanna, *supra* (hard to find a single domestic Chinese firm which competes globally).

Nor has the SEZ fulfilled its vaunted potential as an "island of excellence," diffusing advanced technology through osmosis to less developed parts of the country. Those with work experience in an SEZ operation do not return home to set up new businesses, as they tend not to acquire managerial and entrepreneurial skills. Migration is a specialized activity and an end in itself, rather than preparation for entry into local nonagricultural activities. Denise Hare & Shukai Zhao, *Labor Migration as a Rural Development Strategy: A View from Migration Origin, in* Loraine A. West & Yaohui Zhao, Rural Labor Flows

IN CHINA 148, 166 (2000). Remittances from migrants to their families are used to improve housing or pay for weddings and dowries. Kenneth D. Roberts, *Chinese Labor Migration: Insights from Mexican Undocumented Migration to the United States, in* WEST & ZHAO, *supra*, at 179, 198-99.

Advocates of worker rights criticize the SEZ, in China and elsewhere, as a vehicle for exploiting low-cost labor.

ICFTU, Behind the Brand Names: Working Conditions and Labour Rights in Export Processing Zones (excerpts; endnotes omitted)

China is now the largest developing country exporter, the world's largest recipient of foreign direct investment (FDI) and the fourth-largest industrial producer behind the US, Japan and Germany. . . . China has emerged in the last 20 years as the world's leading electronics manufacturing location. . . . Huge factory complexes, many funded by Taiwanese capital, produce the components and parts for the global electronics industry.

Chinese success is based in part on low wages. China's wages are a fraction of those of its main competitors. . . . The labour force is based on a massive pool of migrant labour from rural China.

Very long, compulsory overtime and wages below the legal minimum are endemic in Chinese factories. . . . However, Chinese labour authorities do not enforce the law [on rest days, overtime, and minimum wages], partly because of their weak capacity: their staff are under-resourced and lack appropriate training.

Low basic pay and overtime rates are not the only wage problem. Wages are often reduced further by the need to pay back debts to labour agencies who charge a high fee to place workers in jobs. Often factories retain wages so that workers receive them some weeks after they are due [so as to prevent workers from quitting during the high season]. . . .

Factories have harsh penalty systems [for rule infractions, absenteeism, production errors, talking while working]. . . .

The need to deliver quality products on time often means that workers are under great pressure not to make mistakes and to achieve production quotas. . . . Workers live in fear of criticism from supervisors and feel under intense psychological pressure. . . .

[M]any electronics workers operate in a dangerous or unhealthy environment. . . . Some workers are exposed to dangerous chemicals without appropriate protection or training. . . .

All attempts at establishing independent workers' organisations in China are repressed. Organisers are arrested. . . . There is no right to strike in China. . . . Chinese legislation only allows workers to affiliate to the All-China Federation of Trade Unions (ACFTU), which is fully controlled by the Chinese Communist Party (CCP). . . .

---

2. Brain circulation

"Brain drain" is a term commonly used to describe the flow of highly skilled workers from developing to developed countries. The developed countries offer them better opportunities for advanced research, higher remuneration, more educational opportunities for their children, and access to venture capital. Lisa Leiman, *Should the Brain Drain Be Plugged? A Behavioral Economics Approach*, 39 TEX. INT'L L. J. 675 (2004); William J. Carrington and Enrica Detragiache, *How Extensive Is the Brain Drain?*, 36 FIN. & DEV.

46 (1999) (U.S., Australia, Canada, France, and Germany account for 93 per cent of total migratory flows to OECD countries).

In recent years, the complementary phenomenon of "brain circulation" has been recognized. This term refers to the reversal of brain drain, whereby highly skilled workers return to their native countries or commute regularly between bases of operations in the developed world and their native countries. *See* ANNALEE SAXENIAN, SILICON VALLEY'S NEW ENTREPRENEURS (1999) (analyzing how immigrant entrepreneurs have built long-distance economic networks back to their home countries). As China's economy has grown and the standard of living has risen, it has become a desirable destination for "returned students" and other members of the Chinese diaspora. *See* David Barboza, *The New Power Brokers*, N.Y. TIMES, July 19, 2005, at C1 (investment bankers born in China and educated in the United States).

For centuries, Chinese, particularly those from the southern provinces, have emigrated in search of better economic opportunities. The usual destinations were the countries of Southeast Asia, where ethnic Chinese became dominant in trade and commerce. In the nineteenth century, Chinese laborers were brought to the United States to help build the railroads. They advanced into small business ownership, but their limited numbers and discriminatory laws prevented them from achieving the same measure of dominance as in Southeast Asia. The extent to which "overseas Chinese" (huaqiao) have continued to identify with the homeland and its culture, despite generations of residence abroad, varies greatly, from country to country and from person to person, and is not susceptible to easy generalization.

The ethnic Chinese of Hong Kong, Macau, and Taiwan are special situations. Macau was a colony of Portugal from the sixteenth century until reverting to Chinese sovereignty in 1999. Hong Kong became a colony of Great Britain in the mid-nineteenth century, after China's defeat in the Opium Wars, and so remained until 1997 when it reverted to PRC sovereignty.

Taiwan was an outlier within the traditional Chinese empire, populated by Malayo-Polynesian peoples and emigrants from Fujian province, across the Taiwan Straits. Taiwan was ceded to Japan after China's defeat in the Sino-Japanese War of 1894–95. It returned to Chinese sovereignty in 1945 at the end of World War II. In 1949 the Nationalists under Chiang Kai-shek withdrew to Taiwan after their defeat by Communist forces.

More than fifty years later, the status of Taiwan remains one of the most contentious and fascinating issues in international law. The PRC asserts that Taiwan is an integral part of China and reserves the right to use force if Taiwan ever makes a formal declaration of independence. *See* Preamble to the 1982 Constitution:

> Taiwan is part of the sacred territory of the People's Republic of China. It is the lofty duty of the entire Chinese people, including our compatriots in Taiwan, to accomplish the great task of reunifying the motherland.

Meanwhile, Taiwan functions as though it were an independent nation-state and has its own seat in some, although not all, international organizations. For example, both China and Taiwan are members of the WTO, but only China is a member of the UN.

The economies of Hong Kong and Taiwan flourished in the post–World War II period. Together with South Korea and Singapore, they became known as the Four Dragons. They benefitted from their physical and cultural proximity to China in carrying on trade relations without being directly ruled from Beijing. "Native" Taiwanese who had grown up under Japanese colonial rule and could speak the language fluently were able to forge commercial ties with Japanese companies. After the United States and Canada revised their immigration laws in the 1960s to attract the well-educated and business investors, large numbers of Hong Kong Chinese and Taiwanese Chinese emigrated to North America.

A new segment of the Chinese diaspora was added in the 1980s when the PRC sent students abroad and permitted those with relatives in Western countries to emigrate. According to one estimate, seven hundred thousand students went abroad in the period 1978–2003, the vast majority of whom remained abroad, either obtaining permanent residence or foreign citizenship.[17] Splendid accomplishments of returned students [Zhongguo liuxue renyuan huiguo chuangye chengjiu feiran], http://news.xinhuanet.com/overseas/2005-02/25/content2619295.htm.

However, China has instituted preferential policies to encourage ethnic Chinese, whatever their nationality, to do business there. Investors from Hong Kong, Macau, and Taiwan are treated as a separate category from other foreign investors. "Returned students" are eligible for various forms of financial and logistical support from the government. *See* Certain Opinions on the Encouragement of Various Forms of Service by Returned Students [Guanyu guli haiwai liuxuesheng yi duo zhong xingshi wei guo fuwu de ruogan yijian], CEILAW L35401200105, May 14, 2001; Howard W. French, *China Luring Foreign Scholars To Make Its Universities Great*, N.Y. TIMES, Oct. 28, 2005, at A1 (recruitment of top foreign-trained Chinese and Chinese-American specialists, particularly in science and technology).

Not all returnees meet with success in finding satisfactory employment, giving rise to the phenomenon of "unemployed returnees" (haigui haidai). According to media reports, such people face difficulty because they have unrealistic salary demands, seek jobs only in the larger cities, do not have practical work experience, have not acquired fluency in a foreign language, and do not prepare adequately for job interviews. *See* Returnee: What is Your Foreign Diploma Worth? [Haigui: Ni de yangwen ping zhi duoshao qian?], http://www.people.com.cn, Feb. 5, 2005.

Notes

1. Western TNCs, in particular U.S. companies, have long engaged in arbitrage between low labor costs in the developing world and high incomes in their export markets. So-called outsourcing has progressed from the manufacturing sector to the service sector. Katharine Reynolds Lewis, *Well-Paid U.S. Workers Struggle to Compete on a Global Scale*, THE POST-STANDARD, July 24, 2005, at E5. Despite a negative trade balance for more than two decades, the American standard of living is propped up by cheap imports and the purchase of U.S. government securities by exporting nations, which keeps domestic interest rates low. The general public in the United States is aware of the situation, but the political will to change it

---

[17] China does not recognize dual nationality. A PRC citizen who is naturalized in a foreign country automatically loses PRC citizenship. However, if naturalized in a country which does accept dual nationality, such as the United States and Canada, he risks being treated as a PRC citizen if he travels back to China on PRC travel documents. Recognition of dual nationality might encourage more people to return. Leiman, *supra*, at 690.

is lacking. See Jeff Madrick, *Economic Scene*, N.Y. TIMES, Mar. 18, 2004, at C2 (discussing the negative consequences of outsourcing); Robert Tanner, *Trapped in the Debt Zone*, THE POST-STANDARD, Sept. 4, 2005, at E1 (trade imbalance roughly 6.5 percent of GDP, or more than twice what it was in the 1980s); Joseph E. Stiglitz, *How to Fix the Global Economy*, N.Y. TIMES, Oct. 3, 2006, at A27 (blaming global financial imbalances on U.S. trade deficits).

2. Leiman's article discusses the costs of the brain drain to developing countries and measures to counteract it, such as making staying at home more attractive to professionals, allowing dual citizenship, requiring monetary guarantees or restitution for the costs of public education, and taxing the incomes of expatriates. Trying to physically prevent people from emigrating is contrary to international law and impractical. *Id.*

12 Japan

A. INTRODUCTION TO THE SOCIAL AND HISTORICAL CONTEXT

Although one of several countries around the rim of the traditional Chinese empire, Japan was able to develop its own distinctive indigenous culture without being overwhelmed by Chinese influence. Unlike Korea or Vietnam, Japan was physically separated from the Asian continent by over one hundred miles of water. It was never invaded by China. Japanese absorption of Chinese culture – its writing system, Buddhist religion, and Confucian ethics – was slow, gradual, and voluntary. JOHN KING FAIRBANK, EDWIN O. REISCHAUER, & ALBERT M. CRAIG, EAST ASIA: TRADITION & TRANSFORMATION 324 (rev. ed. 1989). *See also* JOHN OWEN HALEY, AUTHORITY WITHOUT POWER: LAW AND THE JAPANESE PARADOX 31 (1991) (law was a small, although still important, element in borrowing from China).

The origins of the Japanese "people" in the islands dates back one hundred thousand to two hundred thousand years, based on archaeological evidence. The Japanese language is a member of the Altaic family, similar to Korean, the languages of north and central Asia, and ultimately, Turkish. Therefore, despite extensive borrowing of vocabulary from Chinese, its distinctiveness has contributed to the maintenance of a separate ethnic identity from China. FAIRBANK ET AL., *supra*, at 326-27.

When Admiral Perry sailed into Yokohama harbor in 1854, to compel Japan to open its doors to foreign trade, the country had been virtually closed to all outside contact for 250 years. The Tokugawa shogunate, or military aristocracy, which had governed Japan since 1600, gradually weakened in the face of social and economic change, but without external pressure from the West, might have continued for some time. *Id.* at 434. In any event, the Tokugawa period came to an end in 1867. The following year a group of young samurai from the more backward areas of the country established a new government, with the young Meiji emperor as its nominal head. *Id.* at 502.

The rapidity of Japan's modernization in the second half of the nineteenth century is a feat that no other Asian country has matched. The leaders of the Meiji Restoration succeeded beyond expectation in making Japan a "wealthy country with a strong military" (fukoku kyouhei). Less than thirty years after the Meiji Restoration, Japan defeated China in the war of 1894–95. Ten years later, Japan defeated Russia, "[t]he event that really won for Japan full status as a world power." *Id.* at 555. In the Paquete Habana case, the U.S. Supreme Court complimented the Empire of Japan as "the last State admitted into the rank of civilized nations." 175 U.S. 677, 700 (1900).

The accomplishments of the Meiji period, and Japan's economic prominence today, may be traced to a number of factors: a strong sense of separate identity; acceptance (however resigned) of a pluralistic international order; a tradition of borrowing from other countries; cultural and linguistic homogeneity;[1] economic and intellectual centralization. FAIRBANK ET AL., *supra*, at 490-91.

The consensus for modernization was easier to develop in an island country the size of Montana with a population of about forty million. *Id.* at 325, 651. By contrast, in the nineteenth century, China's population was approximately ten times larger. ANGUS MADDISON, CHINESE ECONOMIC PERFORMANCE IN THE LONG RUN 40 (1998) (Table 2.1)(1820 figures). Having been the dominant power in North Asia for so long, China was unable to comprehend, let alone respond to the challenge posed by Western nations. *Id.* at 41. Having stood in the shadow of a great power for many centuries, the Japanese were quicker to understand a multipolar international order.

Buoyed by its successes and the ambition to create an "Greater East Asian Co-Prosperity Sphere" equaling the Western colonial empires, Japan embarked on a fifty-year plan of expansion and occupation of Korea, China, and Southeast Asia. By 1941, its competition in the Pacific with the United States erupted into open military conflict. With defeat in World War II, Japan was, for the first time, occupied by a foreign power. The occupation lasted until 1952.

The U.S. administration, known as General Headquarters (GHQ) and headed by General Douglas MacArthur, drafted a new constitution for Japan in 1946, to replace the Meiji Constitution of 1889. Although the Diet, the Japanese legislature, debated the draft and accepted it almost unanimously, the new Constitution has never quite shed the image of having been imposed on a defeated people. HIDEO TANAKA, THE JAPANESE LEGAL SYSTEM 665 (1976); JOHN W. DOWER, EMBRACING DEFEAT: JAPAN IN THE WAKE OF WORLD WAR II 346-47 (1999).

One of the major changes from the Meiji Constitution was the guarantee of human rights. However, in contrast to the U.S. Constitution, the 1947 Japanese Constitution includes socioeconomic rights as well as civil and political rights. Compare the constitutions of China and India.

> Art. 25. All people shall have the right to maintain the minimum standards of wholesome and cultured living.

[1] The dark side to ethnic and cultural homogenity is a long tradition of discrimination against resident aliens, mainly Koreans and Taiwanese brought to Japan during the era of empire. YUJI IWASAWA, INTERNATIONAL LAW, HUMAN RIGHTS, AND JAPANESE LAW 123-204 (1998). Despite a declining birth rate, an aging population, and labor shortages, Japan is highly ambivalent toward "guest workers". Less than 2 percent of the workforce consists of foreign workers. Kazuaki Tezuka, Issue of Foreign Labor in Japan, Sept. 27, 2004, http://www.fpcj.jp/e/mres/briefingreport/bfr_11.html.

Japan also has a small class of outcastes (burakumin) who are "racially, linguistically, and culturally identical to other Japanese" but whose inferior status was based traditionally on occupations degrading or ritually unclean. FRANK K. UPHAM, LAW AND SOCIAL CHANGE IN POSTWAR JAPAN 79 (1987). Discrimination against this group in employment, as well as other areas of life, keeps them out of the mainstream. *Id.* at 123. *See also* Emily A. Su-lan Reber, *Buraku Mondai in Japan: Historical and Modern Perspectives and Directions for the Future*, 12 HARV. HUM. RTS. J. 297 (1999). *Compare* Chapter 13 on the dalits of India.

Yet another group that has been marginalized in Japanese society are the aboriginal Ainu of northern Japan. KENNETH L. PORT & GERALD PAUL McALINN, COMPARATIVE LAW: LAW AND THE LEGAL PROCESS IN JAPAN 895-911 (2d ed. 2003).

2. In all spheres of life, the State shall use its endeavors for the promotion and extension of social welfare and security, and of public health.

Art. 27. All people shall have the right and the obligation to work.
2. Standards for wages, hours, rest and other working conditions shall be fixed by law.
3. Children shall not be exploited.

Art. 28. The right of workers to organize and bargain and act collectively is guaranteed.

http://www.solon.org/Constitutions/Japan/English/english-Constitution.html.

The "right to work" places an affirmative obligation on government to actively intervene in the labor market so as to make jobs available for those seeking employment. The government is also under an obligation to provide support to those who, through no fault of their own, are unable to secure employment. KAZUO SUGENO & LEO KANOWITZ (TRANS.), JAPANESE EMPLOYMENT AND LABOR LAW 16 (2d ed. 2002). Pursuant to this constitutional mandate, the Diet has enacted various laws, including the Labor Standards Law of 1947 (as amended), discussed *infra*. English translation at http://www.jil.go.jp/english/laborinfo/library/documents/ilj_law1.pdf. Article 27 also imposes on the individual an obligation to work. Unemployment compensation is not available to those who are able to work but refuse to do so. *Id.* at 17.

Article 28, which guarantees the right to organize and bargain collectively, is elaborated upon in the Trade Union Law (prohibiting unfair labor practices) and the Labor Relations Adjustment Law (establishing labor commissions to resolve labor disputes). *Id.* at 22, 727. English translation at http://www.jil.go.jp/english/laborinfo/library/documents/ilj_law1.pdf. Japan is a party to both ILO Convention 87, protecting the right of association and the right to organize, and ILO Convention 98, protecting the right to organize and engage in collective bargaining. *Id.* at 21.

In the immediate postwar period, left-wing parties became politically active, and workers quickly asserted their rights to unionize, bargain collectively, and strike. DOWER, *supra*, at 255. These developments led to a "red purge" in 1949–50, when thousands of union members in the public and private sector were fired. Though leftist parties were politically marginalized from that time forward, their agenda – active state intervention in the economy, job security, and distributive equity – was absorbed into national economic policy. *Id.* at 273.

B. THE POSTWAR EMPLOYMENT SCENE: MAJOR DEVELOPMENTS

1. Long-term employment

The postwar period witnessed the establishment of the so-called lifetime or long-term employment relationship (shuushin koyou seido). In this pattern of employment, companies hire from among new school graduates. After a probationary period, the employee becomes a permanent member of the work force and will be retained until retirement age (usually sixty) unless the employee engages in serious misconduct. Increases in salary and promotions are mostly a function of seniority.

Short of bankruptcy or some other extraordinary event, the employer maintains the permanent work force, although it may be necessary to reduce their remuneration, transfer surplus workers to other positions or to affiliated companies, and engage in other job-preserving measures. During the recession that followed the 1973 oil crisis, one large steel firm kept "surplus" employees occupied planting trees on the grounds of the company. TADASHI HANAMI, LABOR RELATIONS IN JAPAN TODAY 31 (1979).

The Japanese economy entered a prolonged recession in the 1990s, resulting in a relatively steep increase in unemployment. Nonetheless, at least some labor experts believe that the long-term employment system survives. Takashi Araki, Corporate Governance Reforms, Labor Law Developments, and the Future of Japan's Practice-Dependent Stakeholder Model, http://www.jil.go.jp/english/documents/JLR05_araki.pdf; Ryuichi Yamakawa, *Labor Law Reform in Japan: A Response to Recent Socio-Economic Changes*, 49 AM. J. COMP. L. 627, 648-49 (2001). See also James Brooke, *Factory Jobs Move Overseas As Japan's Troubles Deepen*, N.Y. TIMES, Aug. 31, 2001, at A1 (Japanese firms avoid mass layoffs; workforce reduction achieved through elimination of jobs in overseas operations, early retirement, attrition, and reduced hiring). Therefore, it may be concluded that the long-term employment system is as fundamental to labor relations in Japan as employment-at-will is in the United States.

The long-term employment system is not universal among Japanese firms, but it is predominant in large and mid-size firms in manufacturing, finance, public utilities, wholesale and retail, and other industries. SUGENO & KANOWITZ, *supra*, at 75. To cushion against fluctuations in labor supply and demand, Japanese companies employ a contingent work force of part-time, temporary, or contract workers, who are paid less than permanent workers and do not have job security. It is estimated that approximately one-fifth of the Japanese work force is so employed. *Id. See also*, Araki, *supra*, at 49 (estimating the contingent workforce at 30 percent).

Thus, as compared with other market economies, Japan has very strong internal labor markets and low rates of job-switching. JOHN KNIGHT & LINA SONG, TOWARDS A LABOUR MARKET IN CHINA 135 and source cited (2005). For the employee, the company is a kind of extended family. Although said to have originated in the twentieth century,[2] the long term employment system fits in quite naturally with attitudes carried over from the feudal period of Japanese history, when lord and vassal were bound to one another for life. CHIE NAKANE, JAPANESE SOCIETY 69-74 (1970).

The relative immobility of labor helps to explain the very high percentage of enterprise unionism in Japan. According to 1997 statistics, 95.6 percent of unions were enterprise-based (including both blue and white collar employees) and 91.2 percent of all unionized workers belong to enterprise unions. Araki, *supra*, at 42.

However, as in other developed countries, the percentage of the workforce that is unionized has steadily declined. In 2003, the unionization rate was 19.2 percent. *Id.* at 46-47; *see also* SUGENO & KANOWITZ, *supra*, at 498-99. Traditionally only permanent workers were members of the enterprise union, so the rise in the number of contingent workers bears an inverse relationship to the unionization rate. Araki, *supra*, at 46. In the past quarter century, strikes and other job actions have been rare. PORT & MCALINN, *supra*, at 554.

2. Occupational tracking

Another prominent characteristic of Japanese employment relations is the segregation of men and women within the workforce. Women are tracked into secretarial positions

---

[2] *Compare* Stewart J. Schwab, *Life-Cycle Justice: Accommodating Just Cause and Employment At Will*, 92 MICH. L. REV. 8, 60 (1993) (career employment in U.S. became common only after World War II).

(ippan shoku), whereas men are tracked into managerial positions (sogo shoku). Women also predominate in the contingent workforce. Robbi Louise Miller, *The Quiet Revolution: Japanese Women Working Around the Law*, 26 HARVARD WOMEN'S L.J. 163 (2003); SUGENO & KANOWITZ, *supra*, at 161-80. *Compare* Yuzhen Liu, *Gender Patterns and Women's Experience in the IT Industry in China*, 5 PERSPECTIVES 20 (2004) http://www.oycf.org/Perspectives/26_093004/Sep04_Issue_pdf (women hold "traditional" jobs as accounting assistants and secretaries; on the technical side, they work on "lower-level" training or technical support).

Japanese law provides various protections against gender discrimination, including art. 14 of the 1947 Constitution,[3] which states in pertinent part:

> All of the people are equal under the law and there shall be no discrimination in political, economic or social relations because of race, creed, *sex*, social status or family origin. (Emphasis supplied.)

Beginning in the 1960s, Japanese women started to litigate against various forms of employment discrimination. For example, the Constitution and corresponding provisions of the Civil Code[4] were invoked to invalidate a company practice requiring women to retire at an earlier age than men. Nissan Motors, Inc. v. Nakamoto (1981), trans. in LAWRENCE W. BEER & HIROSHI ITOH, THE CONSTITUTIONAL CASE LAW OF JAPAN, 1970 THROUGH 1990 179-81 (1996).

When Japan became a party to the Convention Against All Forms of Discrimination Against Women (CEDAW), it adopted an Equal Employment Opportunity Law (EEOL) in 1985. See FRANK K. UPHAM, LAW AND SOCIAL CHANGE IN POSTWAR JAPAN 124-65 (1987); IWASAWA, *supra*, at 213-226. To counter criticisms of its ineffectiveness, the law was amended in 1997. Whereas the 1985 law only obligated employers to "endeavor" (tsutomenakereba naranai) to provide equal treatment in hiring, assignment, and promotion, a low bar which could be met by hiring a few token women, the 1997 amendments "prohibit" discrimination (sabetsu no kinshi).

However, even these amendments were but half-measures. Employers can circumvent the ban on discriminatory job advertisements by simply ignoring inquiries from female applicants. Miller, *supra*, at 206. Sanctions are weak: the Labor Ministry "is able to" (but not required to) make a public announcement that an employer is in violation of the law. *Id.* at 204. Mediation through the Ministry of Labor is available but nonbinding. *Id.* at 196, 202-03, 204.

Given the extremely long hours and frequent internal job transfers which the managerial track demands, only further, major changes in the law *and* social attitudes will allow Japanese women the same opportunities for professional advancement as men. "[A workaholic culture and lack of child care infrastructure] denies the professional aspirations

---

[3] Inclusion of women's rights clauses in the postwar constitution was largely a result of the efforts of Beate Sirota (Gordon), a young woman working in the occupation administration. She had grown up in Japan, acquiring fluency in the language, and later attended Mills College, an all-women's institution in California. DOWER, *supra*, at 365, 380.

[4] Civil Code art. 1-2. This Code shall be construed from the standpoint of the dignity of individuals and the essential equality of the sexes.

  Art. 90. A juristic act which has for its object such matters as are contrary to public policy or good morals is null and void.

of mothers just as it eliminates career women's incentives for entertaining the idea of motherhood." Miller, *supra*, at 208. *See also* Michiko Aizawa, *An International Perspective: A Proposal to Combine Disparate Approaches to the Maternal Wall*, 7 EMPL. RTS & EMPLOY. POL'Y J. 495, 521-22 (2003) (discussing research on discrimination against women who returned to work after taking child care leaves); Hiromi Tanaka, *Equal Employment in Contemporary Japan: A Structural Approach to Equal Employment and the Equal Employment Opportunity Law*, PS: POLITICAL SCIENCE & POLITICS, eSYM-POSIUM (Jan. 2004). By contrast, working mothers in China are more likely to obtain support from the extended family. Carol Hymowitz, Chinese Women Bosses Say Long Hours Don't Hurt Their Kids, http://www.careerjournal.com, May 18, 2005.

3. Wrongful death from overwork

In spite of, or perhaps because of, the grueling pace of the managerial track, Japanese law recognizes the tort of "wrongful death from overwork" (karoshi). The concept extends not only to heart disease or stroke proximately caused by overwork but also depression. In the case of Kono v. Dentsu, Inc., the parents of a twenty-five-year-old advertising executive recovered damages for the exhaustion-induced suicide of their son. Plaintiffs' son was hired in April 1990; in less than eighteen months he was dead.

KONO V. DENTSU INC.

1707 Hanrei Jiho 87 (March 24, 2000)
Supreme Court

KENNETH L. PORT & GERALD PAUL McALINN, COMPARATIVE LAW: LAW AND THE LEGAL PROCESS IN JAPAN 575-79 (2d ed. 2003). Reprinted with permission.

[In this case, the plaintiffs, under the pseudonyms Taro and Hanako Kono, sought damages against the defendant in their capacity as the heirs of their first son, Ichiro Kono. The defendant, Dentsu Inc., is the largest advertising agency in Japan and was the employer of Ichiro. The claim sounded in tort under Article 715 of the Civil Code (the principle of respondeat superior). The District Court and the High Court both found that the Defendant was liable and awarded damages to the parents of Ichiro on the theory that Ichiro's death was the result of overworking. The Defendant appealed to the Supreme Court]

Summary of Judgment:

1. The Appellant-Defendant's appeal is dismissed.
2. Parts of the High Court's decision, where Defendant-Appellant did not prevail are reversed and the case is to be remanded to the High Court for further determination.
3. The cost of this litigation concerning section 1 are to be borne by the defendant.

Facts:

The facts as found by the trial court are as follows:

1. Ichiro Kono was born on November 30, 1966, as the first son of Taro and Hanako Kono, the plaintiffs. He was healthy and was good at playing sports. He had a cheerful, honest and

responsible personality. He was tenacious and tended to carry things out to perfection. From 1990 until 1991, he lived with his parents who both worked.

2. In March of 1990, Ichiro graduated from the Faculty of Law of Meiji Gakuen University. He started working for defendant from April of 1990, along with 178 new employees. He had a physical examination two months before starting working and nothing serious was found other than a skin color disorder.

3. After the new employees completed their training, Ichiro was assigned to the Radio Promotion Division. This division had a total of 13 employees divided into two groups under a single supervisor. Ichiro belonged to the group under the direction of "S" and was assigned to the 7th Tsukiji and 8th Irifune areas [of Tokyo] along with two other employees.

4. In 1990, the Work Rules of the defendant stated that "Holidays are provided two days in a week; working hours are from 9:30 am to 5:30 pm with a lunch break from noon until 1:00 pm." According to the agreement made by the defendant and the Union pursuant to Article 36 of the Labor Standards Law (as amended), overtime work shall not exceed six hours and 30 minutes per day. Specifically, overtime work at the said division from July 1990 to August 1991 in each month was limited. However, the overtime hours of each employee were declared individually in a written document. Employees were to obtain a superior's permission prior to working overtime, but the reality was that employees obtained that permission after the fact. At defendant's company, it seemed a general practice that employees engaged in long overtime work, and many employees were found to declare hours exceeding the agreed number of hours per day, and per month. This issue had been brought to the labor conference held between defendant and the union. Moreover, it was routinely the case that employees declared fewer hours than they actually worked. The defendant recognized such an environment and knew there was a tendency to have burdens on a specific group or an individual. The defendant provided special treatment for employees working from 10:00 pm to 5:00 am, and the company provided five rooms at a hotel for those who engaged in work later than midnight but had to be back at the office at the regular time. However these were not used by new employees, due to the lack of awareness.

5. Ichiro, when assigned to the said division, was in a position called *Hancho-tsuki* (meaning to stick close to his superior), and he worked with S group all day long. The work was mainly to solicit companies to be sponsors for a radio program, and to plan and to implement the advertising promotion campaigns of the customers. His working day is found to be as follows: leave home by 8:00 am, arrive at the office by 9:00 am, run errands which are ritually done by new employees, make contacts and coordinate arrangement with the solicited companies and other sections of defendant's company and the production company, have dinner around 7:00 pm, prepare agenda and/or materials thereafter. He was perceived as being enthusiastic with his work, and he was accepted on friendly terms by his superior and co-workers.

6. Ichiro's declared total number of overtime hours for the months from July 1990 to August 1993 were [962 or an average of over 66 hours a month]. However, those reported hours were definitely fewer than the actual overtime work he worked. During this time, he left the office later than 2:00 am [90] times. He scarcely spent time for meals, naps or private errands, mostly devoting his time to his duties at work.

7. Ichiro increasingly began, around August 1990, arriving home by 1:00 am or 2:00 am. In a written document, "T" [an anonymous Dentsu employee] wrote Ichiro and complimented him on his effort and his attitude toward his duties, as well as the significance of meeting deadlines. On the other hand, Ichiro expressed in a document he submitted to the defendant

in the fall of 1990, the joy he felt when his projects were successfully carried out and that he hid the feeling his work really counted. However, he complained about the overtime work. Ichiro took a physical examination in the fall of 1990 and received the same result as his first physical.

8. By around the end of November 1990, Ichiro was returning home by 4:00 am and 5:00 am. There were days when he did not go back home or when he stayed at the plaintiff's (Taro) office in Minato ward. The plaintiffs began to worry about Ichiro's health due to his fatigue. Plaintiff Taro suggested Ichiro take some paid days off, which Ichiro refused saying that there was no substitute or back up for his position or duty so he would have to bear even more work when he returned. He also assumed from his own experience that a day off would not be permitted by his boss.

9. By around January of 1991, Ichiro started to do about 70% of his duties independently. Written documents prepared by Ichiro then said that he would try to carry out his duties efficiently and within the fixed time. He also commented that his duties tended to be overloaded. His superior's evaluation of Ichiro was good, and a document written by T complimented Ichiro for being hardworking and following instructions.

10. Around May of 1991, T told S that Ichiro often times worked over night, so S told Ichiro to go home and rest then come back early in the morning if his work is not completed. Ichiro's evaluation showed that Ichiro tried hard during this time. Ichiro was entitled to take 10 paid days off in 1990, however, he used only one half of a day.

11. No new employees joined the group until July of 1991. After this period, Ichiro became independent from the group and was assigned to 7th Tsukiji area, partial 3rd Irifune area, and to assist with the 8th Irifune area. After that, more days occurred where Ichiro did not go home, or arrived at home at 6:30 or 7:00 in the morning and then left again by 8:00 am. Plaintiff Hanako was concerned for Ichiro's health and tried to help him by making a nutritious breakfast and other things, and she also gave him a ride to the nearest station. Plaintiff Taro hardly saw Ichiro during that time. The plaintiffs were in an unstable health condition due to Ichiro's circumstances. Ichiro himself was totally exhausted because of the heavy work load and a lack of sleep. He became pale, lethargic and depressed with unfocused eyes. He would doze often. At the same time, S noticed Ichiro's physical deterioration.

12. Except for August 3rd to 5th on which days Ichiro went on a trip, he appeared for work almost everyday from August 1, 1990 through the 23rd including weekends. These two paid days off were the first such he took in 1991. He confessed to S that he lost his self-confidence, that he was not aware of what he was talking about, and that he was suffering from insomnia.

13. On August 23, 1991, Ichiro came home at 6:00 pm and left by 10:00 pm to drive to Nagano where an event would be held from the next day. At this time S noticed that Ichiro's speech and conduct were not right. From the 24th to the 26th, Ichiro performed his duties at the event, and then left the place on the 26th at around 5:00 pm to drive home.

14. Ichiro arrived home on the 27th at 6:00 am and told his brother that he would go to the hospital. He made a phone call to his office saying that he was sick so he would skip work on that day. At 10:00 am, he was found dead in his bathroom.

15. As noted above, Ichiro was totally exhausted, mentally and physically, by July of 1991. It is assumed that he was ill with depression by the beginning of August as a result of this exhaustion. His condition was that of being relieved from just finishing a big project but depression from thinking about having to return to the office and so much overtime work. It is recognized that this depression worsened his condition and caused his death.

Reasoning:

Based on the facts stated above, we consider the High Court's decision affirming the liability of the defendant pursuant to Article 715 of the Civil Code.

. . .

1. It is widely accepted that a heavy amount of fatigue or mental burden resulting from, for example, overtime labor, can damage the physical or mental health of an employee. The Labor Standards Law provides a limitation on working hours. Article 65-3 of Protection of Workers Safety and Health Law provides that employers must exercise care with the health condition of employees and, therefore, employers need to supervise the duties of individual employees. The purpose of this provision is to prevent the kind of harm seen in this case. These things show that an employer owes a duty to its employees not to endanger their health due to fatigue or mental burden resulting from work assigned by the employer. Moreover, those in a supervisory position should use their authority to make sure this purpose is fulfilled.

2. The duties Ichiro performed after being assigned to the Radio Promotion Division were mainly contacting people, meeting, planning and making proposals. His regular working hours were filled with contacts and meetings, therefore he had to do the rest of his duties in the extended hours, and this became the normal attitude and practice in the defendant's company. In making a proposal, Ichiro might have some latitude for his time management. However, he was under the direction or an order to pursue the duty, according to the fact that his superior T and others emphasized the fixed time limit. As a result, the circumstances were hustle and bustle and forced him to work extra hours. At the defendant's company, often times the employees' overtime work was raised as an issue, besides it was recognized that the employees' declared working hours were not the actual hours. Therefore, T and others were aware by March of 1991, at the latest, that Ichiro's reported working hours were definitely shorter than the actual ones that Ichiro stayed all night, and that S noticed Ichiro's bad condition by July. Nevertheless, T and S did not reduce Ichiro's work load other than by advising him to sleep and come to work early in the morning to finish assignments on the premise that duties should be carried out within the deadlines. Unfortunately, this worsened Ichiro's burden therefore Ichiro was physically and mentally exhausted, and this led him to depression by the beginning of August. His depression became aggravated around the 27th, causing Ichiro to impulsively and suddenly commit suicide. The High Court stated: "In addition to the circumstances above and the description of depression noted thereof, there is a proximate cause between Ichiro's duty and the suicide committed due to the depression, and that T and S negligently failed to alleviate Ichiro's duty even though they knew Ichiro engaged in extremely long hours of working and of his ill health." The court found the defendant liable under Article 715 of the Civil Code, and this court reasonably affirms the decision.

> [The portion of the Supreme Court's opinion reversing the High Court's decision regarding the amount of damages is omitted. Basically, the Supreme Court rejected the High Court's decision to reduce the damages by 30 percent under Article 722-2 of the Civil Code. The High Court's reasoning was that Ichiro's personality and inability to control his own time contributed to his depression. The Supreme Court acknowledged that contributory negligence is a valid basis on which to reduce tort damages, even in a case of karoshi, however, the employer has a duty to be aware of the personality traits of its employees. The employer bears the duty to determine the suitable range of duties to be assigned to each employee. Ichiro's personality was not so unusual as to go beyond the normal range.

The Supreme Court also rejected the High Court's argument that the plaintiffs lived with Ichiro and also hear some responsibility for not interceding on his behalf. The Supreme Court stated that even though Ichiro lived with his parents he was an adult and his parents had no effective way to better his working conditions. Thus, the Supreme Court remanded the damages portion of this case to the High Court. Eds.]

Notes

1. *See also* White Paper on the Labour Economy 2004: Summary, at 15 (increase in number of employees applying for industrial accident compensation insurance as a result of stress and physical fatigue) http://www.mhlw.go.jp/english/wp/l_economy/2004.

2. As the *Kono* Case illustrates, Japanese culture imposes great pressure on the individual to conform to the group, to meet the expectations of one's superiors, and to earn the respect of one's colleagues. Such pressure contributes to one of the highest suicide rates in the world, both for males and females: 35.2 and 12.8 per 100,000 (2002 statistics), where the rates for the United States were 17.6 and 4.1, respectively. See http://www.who.int/mental_health/prevention/suicide_rates/en/index.html.

3. The Labor Standards Law authorizes agreements between employers and unions regulating, inter alia, overtime work. The agreement then supersedes specific requirements of the Law. SUGENO & KANOWITZ, *supra*, at 84-85. Although such an agreement was in place in the Kono Case, it was routinely ignored. The union complained to the employer, but no other action was taken. It is typical for overtime rules not to be enforced. *See* Makoto Ishida, *Death and Suicide from Overwork: The Japanese Workplace and Labour Law*, in JOANNE CONAGHAN, RICHARD MICHAEL FISCHL, & KARL KLARE, LABOUR LAW IN AN ERA OF GLOBALIZATION 219, 225 (2002).

4. The *Kono* Case was tried in district court, appealed to the High Court, and again appealed to the Supreme Court. Despite the strong influence of German law generally, Japan does not have separate labor courts for resolution of individual or collective disputes.

4. Wrongful termination and abuse of right

At first glance, Japanese law appears to follow the employment at will doctrine. Art. 20 of the Labor Standards Law allows termination of an employee, with or without cause, by either giving thirty days' notice or paying thirty days' salary in lieu of notice. http://www.jil.go.jp/english/laborinfo/library/documents/llj_law1.pdf. Art. 626 and 627 of the Civil Code also gives employers the right to dismiss workers employed under contracts of definite and indefinite duration, respectively.

However, beginning in the 1970s, the courts developed the doctrine of wrongful termination. Termination of a permanent[5] employee "without just cause" is considered an

---

[5] Temporary staff who are continuously employed under a series of fixed term contracts are treated the same as regular employees for purposes of determining just cause for termination. Sanyo Electric Company v.

"abuse of right" (kaikoken o ranyou suru) under art. 1 of the Civil Code[6] and therefore null and void (mukou). *See generally* Daniel H. Foote, *Judicial Creation of Norms in Japanese Labor Law: Activism in the Service of – Stability?*, 43 UCLA L. REV. 635 (1996).

In one seminal case, *Shioda v. Kochi Broadcasting Company*, excerpted here, a radio announcer was discharged for twice oversleeping and missing the morning broadcast. He subsequently apologized for being negligent, a very significant cultural gesture. *See* Hiroshi Wagatsuma & Arthur Rosett, *The Implications of Apology: Law and Culture in Japan and the United States*, 20 LAW & SOC'Y REV. 461 (1986). The Supreme Court affirmed the lower courts' determination that the employer had committed an abuse of right. PORT & MCALINN, *supra*, at 566-68. Thus, a "minor" infraction of company rules does not justify termination.

Similarly,

[m]ere incompetence would probably *not* satisfy the standard *unless* the company has made *every effort to train the employee or to find a job within the company which the employee could handle*.[7] Employers are expected to carry unproductive employees on the payroll until retirement, out of social duty and sympathy. . . . This enables employees to support themselves and their families and prevents them from becoming unemployable burdens on society.

PORT & MCALINN, *supra*, at 560. (Emphasis supplied.)

SHIODA V. KOCHI BROADCASTING COMPANY

268 Rodo Hanrei (January 31, 1977)
Supreme Court
Translated by Rui Fukazawa

KENNETH L. PORT & GERALD PAUL MCALINN, COMPARATIVE LAW: LAW AND THE LEGAL PROCESS IN JAPAN 566-68 (2d ed. 2003). Reprinted with permission.

[Shioda was an announcer employed by the Kochi Broadcasting Company. When he overslept on two occasions and missed his scheduled news broadcasts, the company dismissed him under the provisions of their Work Rules that allowed for termination when an employee was unfit for duty. Shioda brought suit in the District Court seeking an order confirming his continuing status as an employee, that is, that the dismissal was improper. The District Court found for Shioda and Kochi Broadcasting Company appealed to the High Court, where a de novo trial was held. The High Court also found for Shioda, which led Kochi Broadcasting to appeal to the Supreme Court.]

Ikeda (1990), trans. in CURTIS J. MILHAUPT, J. MARK RAMSEYER, & MICHAEL K. YOUNG, JAPANESE LAW IN CONTEXT: READINGS IN SOCIETY, THE ECONOMY, AND POLITICS 389-91 (2001).

[6] Civil Code art. 1 (3): No abuse of rights shall be committed. *See* Kazuaki Sono & Yasuhiro Fujioka, *The Role of the Abuse of Right Doctrine in Japan*, 35 LA. L. REV. 1037 (1975)(quoting the Japanese Supreme Court as stating "[i]n all cases a right must be exercised in such a fashion that the result of the exercise remains within a scope judged reasonable in the light of the prevailing social conscience").

[7] *Compare* PRC Labor Law art. 26 (ii):

In any of the following circumstances the employer may terminate the contract but must give 30 days advance written notice to the employee: the employee is still unable to discharge his work responsibilities *even after training or reassignment*. (Emphasis supplied.)

SUMMARY OF JUDGMENT

The Appellant [*Kochi Broadcasting*] has appealed a judgment of the Kochi District Court in December 19, 1973, regarding a lawsuit between the two parties. The Appellant seeks a reversal of the lower court judgment. This court rules as follows: The judgment for Appellee [*Shioda*] is affirmed. The costs of the appeal shall be borne by the Appellant.

REASONING

. . .

In this case, according to the facts established, the Appellee was working as an announcer in the editorial and news collection department of the company from 6:00 pm on February 22, 1967, until 10:00 am of the following day. The Appellee was on night duty and manning the fax machine along with a reporter, Tsutomu Kurokawa. However, because the Appellee took a nap and did not wake up until 6:20 am on the 23rd, the 10 minute radio news program scheduled to go on the air at 6:00 am was not broadcast as scheduled (the "First Incident").

On March 7th and 8th of the same year, the Appellee, as in the First Incident, was on night duty with Fukuzo Yamazaki. He again overslept and the 6:00 am news broad cast was about five minutes late (the "Second Incident"). The Appellee failed to report the Second Incident to his employer and when his manager, Mr. Ogura, learned of the incident, around the 14th or 15th of the same month, he asked the Appellee to submit an incident report. The Appellee did so but the incident report contained false information.

The Appellant decided to dismiss the Appellee in the form of an ordinary dismissal even though the conduct of the Appellee could have been considered a reasonable grounds to dismiss him for disciplinary reasons under the Work Rules. The company decided to use the ordinary dismissal grounds taking into consideration the Appellee's future such as the difficulty of finding a new job if he were dismissed for disciplinary reasons.

Article 15 of the Appellant's Work Rules provides, in the case of an ordinary dismissal, that: "When an employee meets any of following conditions, the company can dismiss the employee by giving notice 30 days prior to the date of dismissal. However, when the company deems it necessary to dismiss the employee immediately, the company can do so by paying 30 days of average salary in lieu of notice. This provision governs unless the individual is covered by the dismissal restrictions of the Labor Standards Law: 1. When a mental or physical disability makes the individual unable to perform the job, 2. When a natural disaster or some other unforeseeable cause makes continuing business impossible, or 3. Any other causes of a similar nature." The behavior of the Appellee would constitute grounds for dismissal under number 3 of Article 15 of the Work Rules.

However, even in a situation with grounds for an ordinary dismissal, the employer does not necessarily have the unilateral right to dismiss, especially in a case where the dismissal will be considered an abuse of the right and will therefore be deemed invalid. In this case, the incidents caused by the Appellee caused the Appellant, a company which regards punctuality as an imperative, to lose public credibility. The fact that the Appellee overslept twice and caused the same incident to occur within a two week period shows a lack of responsibility as an announcer. Moreover, when taking into consideration the failure to confess one's fault, immediately after the Second Incident, the Appellee cannot be absolved of responsibility. On the other hand, according to the facts presented at the trial, the incidents in question were brought about when the Appellee overslept, which is an act of negligence, not intentional or malicious conduct. Furthermore, the fax operator who was supposed to get up first and to wake up Appellee at a specified time, failed to do so on both occasions because he also overslept. Therefore, blaming the incidents on the Appellee alone would be too severe.

The Appellee apologized immediately after the First and the Second Incidents. He also made efforts to get to the studio as soon as possible after waking up. In both the First and Second Incidents, the gap in the broadcast was not that long. The company did not take extra precautions for the early morning news broadcast which they should have done.

As for turning in a false report, the Appellee misunderstood the condition of the "open and close" hall door on the first floor and because the Appellee had been feeling distressed for causing two broadcasting incidents within a short period of time, condemning him too harshly for the false report would not be just. The Appellee has no record of broadcasting incidents up until now and his employment reviews have not been notably bad. The fax operator, Yamazaki, was only censured and the company has had no other examples of dismissing an employee for a similar broadcasting incident in the past. Eventually, the Appellee admitted wrongdoing in the Second Incident and expressed his sincere apology. Taking these facts under consideration, a dismissal is somewhat severe and lacks reasonableness, and so it cannot be considered a fit punishment in terms of public opinion.

For these reasons, we affirm the judgment of the original trial court that dismissal in this case is, under the circumstances, an abuse of the right to dismiss. The arguments by counsel for the Appellant take a different position and therefore cannot be adopted by the court.

Through case law interpretation of the Civil Code, the courts developed a four requirements test for "just cause" dismissal (seiri kaiko) for economic reasons: (1) retrenchment of the work force is absolutely necessary; (2) the firm must have made every effort to avoid retrenchment; (3) the selection of those to be retrenched must be rational; (4) the appropriate procedures for termination must be followed. Araki, *supra*, at 35. Dismissal for the economic convenience of the employer, due to temporary business difficulties or to increase profits, does not constitute "just cause."

In 2003 the Labor Standards Law was amended to incorporate the judicial doctrine of "just cause." Art. 18-2 states:

> In cases where a dismissal is not based upon any objectively reasonable grounds, and is not socially acceptable as proper, the dismissal will be null and void as an abuse of right.

Because of opposition from management, the "four requirements" rule was not included in the language of the amendment. Although the government of Prime Minister Koizumi proposed the amendment to accelerate economic retrenchment and corporate restructuring, experts are divided as to whether the amendment will have this effect. "Upgrading" a case law rule to a statutory provision[8] may make retrenchment even more difficult. Araki, *supra*, at 42.

---

[8] Because Japan is a civil law jurisdiction, the legal system regards statutes as "law" and judicial precedents as "practice." Araki, *supra*, at 26. *See also* TANAKA, *supra*, at 143 ("Today, analysis of cases is an indispensable part of legal scholarship. . . . Still there has been much discussion among legal scholars on the nature of judicial precedents, e.g., whether they are sources of law by themselves or are mere expositions of other sources of law").

Most employment disputes are settled out of court, or if suit is filed, judges will pressure the parties to settle. One form of pressure is to simply delay in rendering a decision. PORT & MCALINN, *supra*, at 561. The usual outcome of a settlement is a monetary award, not reinstatement and back pay. A terminated employee may petition the court for provisional disposition (kari shobun), requiring the employer to continue to pay salary and benefits until the case is resolved. *Id.*; TANAKA, *supra*, at 536. To obtain such an order, the claimant must produce prima facie evidence on the merits and the urgency for temporary relief. Kazuo Sugeno, *The Birth of the Labor Tribunal System in Japan: A Synthesis of Labor Law Reform and Judicial Reform*, 25 COMP. LAB. L. & POL'Y J. 519, 520-21 (2004). This strategy was utilized in the National Westminster Bank case, discussed later, where plaintiff continued to receive salary and benefits for two years while a decision on the merits was pending.

The National Westminster Bank case has been criticized, especially by plaintiffs' attorneys, as a revolutionary and disturbing departure from the "four requirements" rule. According to the third, and final, decision of the Tokyo District Court, the so-called four requirements (shi youken) are better characterized as four factors in determining whether a dismissal is abusive or not. If, "after comprehensive consideration of all the facts and circumstances" (gutaiteki na jiyou o sougou kouryo shite okanau), the dismissal is not abusive, then failure to satisfy one criterion is not a fatal defect, leading to nullification of the employer's decision. Araki, *supra*, at 38. After the third decision, the case was settled. *See* Opinion Letter No. 2 on Loser's Liability in Employment Cases, May 30, 2003, http://homepage1.nifty.com.rouben/teigen03/gen030530.htm.

However, if the litigation is viewed in its entirety, the facts cited by the court in successive opinions and the subtlety of its discussion do not seem to lead to the inevitable conclusion that the "four requirements" rule is being discarded. The third decision, issued on January 21, 2000,[9] was the final step in a long process that began more than two years earlier. The first decision on provisional disposition was issued on January 10, 1998,[10] and the second on January 29, 1999.[11] At both stages, the court concluded that the dismissal had been abusive and awarded the plaintiff salary and fringe benefits. It was only at the third stage of the proceedings that defendant prevailed and plaintiff was denied her requested remedy.

Plaintiff had been hired by defendant, the Tokyo branch of a U.K. bank, in 1983. Previously, she had worked for two other banks, one Japanese and one foreign, and had studied in England. The first position she held was on the secretarial track (ippan shoku) as a clerk. Eventually she advanced to the managerial track (kanri shoku) and was appointed assistant manager in the Global Trade Banking Services (GTBS) department.[12] In 1997, defendant decided to reorganize all of its operations in Asia to focus on investment banking and closed the department in which plaintiff was employed. Plaintiff and two other

---

[9] 782 ROUDOU HANREI 23 (July 15, 2000).

[10] 736 ROUDOU HANREI 78 (June 15, 1998).

[11] 782 ROUDOU HANREI 35, Appendix.

[12] Professional women in Japan often prefer to work for foreign companies or to go abroad because of better opportunities for advancement. Miller, *supra*, at 188-89. Japanese men, by contrast, are reluctant to work for foreign companies, even when high salaries are offered, because of the absence of job security. PORT & MCALINN, *supra*, at 557-59.

managers were offered early retirement packages. The package included outplacement assistance.

Plaintiff was the only one who refused to accept. Over the next few months, the enterprise labor union held a series of meetings with upper management. While keeping the option of early retirement open, the bank offered plaintiff another position as a clerk, at a substantially reduced salary. A contract employee now occupied the job, at an even lower salary, but the bank would dismiss that person if plaintiff agreed to take the position. Plaintiff ultimately agreed to accept the position but reserved her right to renegotiate the salary. The bank countered with a proposal to grant her a salary supplement for one year but would not agree to raise her base salary. Finally, after repeated attempts at compromise, the bank cut off negotiations as fruitless and plaintiff was terminated.

In the first decision, the court concluded that the bank had abused its right of dismissal with respect to all four requirements. In response to the defendant's assertion that it was a foreign bank that did not practice the lifetime employment system, the court determined that, aside from the fact that the branch was operating in Japan and therefore subject to Japanese law, its personnel practices were similar enough to that of a domestic company to justify applying the doctrine of abusive dismissal. After all, plaintiff had been employed for fourteen years and had been steadily promoted. The court was particularly troubled by defendant's unwillingness to compromise on the salary issue and its abruptness in cutting off further negotiations. In addition, the plaintiff's personal situation deserved sympathy. She had no source of income outside her job; she was the sole support of herself and her ailing mother; and she had considerable outstanding indebtedness on a home loan.

In the second decision, by a different judge, the court explores the issue of "business necessity" in great depth before concluding that the bank had not made a case for it. The discussion concedes to the employer broad latitude in determining what constitutes "business necessity." The concept is not limited to those situations in which the firm is on the verge of imminent collapse but also situations in which the employer needs to anticipate a future crisis so as to preserve the survival of the firm.[13] Nonetheless, the employer must still demonstrate that a "balance" between business necessity and the means chosen to achieve business objectives is maintained.

Also, this decision departs from the previous one, in its opinion that the bank's hiring practices did *not* closely approximate the lifetime employment system. In some situations it had hired experienced employees – like the plaintiff herself – and promoted people from the secretarial to the managerial track. When business conditions changed and the bank was overstaffed, it would reassign long-term secretarial employees to new duties but did not follow this practice for managers. Although the court awarded plaintiff another year of salary and benefits, its nuanced discussion of business necessity showed a high degree of concern for employer autonomy. The second decision thus provided a segue to a later determination in the employer's favor.

In the third decision, by yet a different judge, the court ruled against plaintiff on all her claims. On the question of business necessity, the bank revealed that all of its Asian branch banks had been losing money for years. The GTBS department where plaintiff

---

[13] *Compare* Tokyo Oxygen Gas Company v. Shimazaki (1979), trans. in MILHAUPT ET AL., *supra*, at 385-88 (decline of division in question not temporary; as a result of structural change in business and low productive efficiency).

had been employed operated at a loss annually from 1992 to 1994. Between 1993 and 1998, the bank's workforce in its finance operations worldwide declined from 91,400 to 64,400. Thus, the decision to close down the GTBS department was part of an overall strategy to restructure the bank's operations in Asia and make them profitable.

Furthermore, although the bank had recruited to a degree from the pool of new graduates, it gradually moved entirely to mid-level recruitment, hiring people with highly specialized skills and work experience. In order to attract and retain specialists, the bank changed its compensation structure to a market priced system. Every position in the bank was reevaluated to reflect market conditions. Within the restructured Tokyo operations, there was no managerial position suitable for someone with plaintiff's background.

The court balances the employer's and employee's interests in the following manner.

> According to the facts as set forth above . . . it may be acknowledged that the decision to close the GTBS department was made as part of a so-called "business restructuring." The purpose of such restructuring was to improve capital efficiency and to strengthen competitiveness, by concentrating limited human and material resources in strategically important business operations and by downsizing or eliminating underperforming business operations. Since business judgment involving business strategy as such is highly professional by itself, decisions made by the corporate decision-making body, like executive management appointed by the shareholders, should generally be respected. During the implementation of the restructuring process, while new demand for human resources with desired skills rises with respect to new business initiatives or business with growth potential, on the other hand, the issue of excess personnel cannot be avoided with respect to operations which are to be downsized or eliminated. Thus, there may not be a match between the existing workforce on the supply side and restructured operations on the demand side. Whether management is currently facing a crisis or not, considering the purpose of restructuring, confronting the problem of excess personnel is inevitable.

> However, on the other hand, an employee who becomes subject to termination as excess personnel and receives a termination notice without having any other options will certainly have difficulty maintaining his/her standard of living until s/he finds another job. Especially given currently stagnant economic conditions and the progressive collapse of the uniquely Japanese lifetime employment system, it is obvious that dismissed employees have considerably more difficulties finding alternative employment. The social infrastructure to support mobility and flexibility of employment is more or less absent. Therefore, companies should try to maintain as many employment relationships as possible by relocating excess personnel to other departments, provided that such relocation is considered reasonable from a business management perspective. Even in cases where a company can be found to have a reasonable basis to dismiss the employee because the employee cannot be relocated to another department, the company should deal in good faith with the retrenched employee by paying utmost consideration to maintaining the employee's standard of living, assisting with the search for alternative employment, and also explaining the reason for termination so as to obtain the employee's understanding of the situation.

> In accordance with the considerations set forth above, the court will decide whether the termination of the employment agreement constitutes an abuse of the employer's right to dismiss the employee. The plaintiff claims that whether termination constitutes an abuse of right should be determined after examining the so-called four elements for dismissal applicable to a business restructuring. However, the so-called four elements

for dismissal only stipulate categories that should be taken into consideration when determining whether the dismissal constitutes an abuse of right. Thus, the so-called four elements cannot be understood as four legal elements which all have to be fulfilled in order to disprove an abuse of right. The judgment whether the termination constitutes an abuse of right has to be determined by examining the entire detailed facts of each case as a whole. Therefore, the court does not adopt the plaintiff's analysis.

It may be inferred from the court's statement of the facts that the severance package offered plaintiff was extremely generous. When the bank transferred her accumulated pension funds to her account in October 1997, the amount was based on a full year's salary, even though she had been terminated as of September 30. Moreover, the bank had agreed to subsidize her job search for an unlimited period.

In terms of procedural regularity, the court noted that defendant had participated in seven consultations with the union over a period exceeding three months. Plaintiff and the union consistently rejected defendant's proposals but did not produce any concrete counterproposals.

The court concluded that defendant's decision to terminate plaintiff was reasonable, that it had demonstrated concern for plaintiff's livelihood and ability to find alternative employment, and that it had been sincere in its efforts to convince plaintiff that retrenchment was absolutely necessary. Thus, although the court contends that the "four requirements" rule should not be applied mechanically, in fact the bank did produce ample evidence that the test had been met.

Notes

1. Plaintiff's age is not given. However, from other facts in the opinions, it may be inferred that she was at least in her forties, but well before regular retirement age. It was not likely that she would find another position with another employer at all comparable to an assistant manager. Would this fact argue for or against her hard bargaining with the bank over the clerk position they offered her?

2. Should the calculation of plaintiff's retirement package have taken into account the fact that she had most probably advanced far higher than if she had been employed at a Japanese bank? Perhaps the bank could argue that it did her a great favor by hiring her and promoting her.

3. Because the case came before the court on a request for provisional disposition, the first court took special note of plaintiff's personal situation. To what extent should an employer be responsible for personal expenses, such as payments on a home mortgage, undertaken by the employee in expectation of continued employment?

4. If plaintiff had accepted the clerk position, the bank would have discharged the contract employee who occupied it. Measures taken by Japanese companies to avoid lay offs – such as reduced hiring or dismissal of temporary employees – are not without negative consequences. Providing job security to the incumbent workforce prejudices younger people looking for entry-level positions. Countries whose laws impede dismissal of permanent workers have higher rates of youth unemployment. Ginny Parker Woods, *In Aging Japan, Young Slackers Stir Up Concerns*, WALL ST. J., Dec. 29, 2005, at A1 (difficulty experienced by young Japanese finding full-time

permanent jobs); Niall O'Higgins, The challenge of youth unemployment sec. 1.3.1 (1997), http://www.ilo.org/public/english/employment/strat/publ/etp7.htm.

5. In this case, litigation might have been a lose-lose situation for both sides. The bank had to reveal confidential information in order to make a case for business necessity. By filing suit instead of accepting the bank's final offer, plaintiff further diminished her chances of finding another job.

6. Because of a steep increase in the number of employment disputes since the early 1990s, the Japanese government has undertaken a variety of new measures, including the establishment of a labor tribunal system. Sugeno, *The Birth of the Labor Tribunal System*, *supra*, at 529-31. Beginning in April 2006, either party to an employment relationship may file a complaint in district court. The court will organize a tribunal composed of one career judge and two experts in labor relations. Although hearings are held informally and are not open to the public, the parties may be represented by counsel. Ordinarily the tribunal will hold no more than three hearings, over a period of three to four months, at the last of which it will propose a settlement. If the parties refuse to compromise, the tribunal will issue a decision. The decision is not binding. Either party may reject it, and the dispute is transformed into a regular civil case. According to Professor Sugeno,

> [T]he new Labor Tribunal System borrows ideas from the European labor court systems, and creates an expeditious court procedure with the participation of expert lay judges. But even though it includes features common to foreign procedures, the System is still uniquely Japanese especially in the respects that it is set up within the ordinary court, closely coordinated with ordinary civil procedure. The three sessions of hearing and an integrated mediation procedure may also be unique aspects.

Compare this system of mediation to that under the PRC Labor Law described in Chapter 11. In the latter, if mediation is unavailing, parties are *required* to submit to arbitration. Only after an arbitration decision has issued, within sixty days of receipt of the complaint, may a party appeal to the regular courts (art. 82-83). If the labor tribunal system had been in place at the time of the National Westminster Bank case, do you think it would have disposed of the controversy between the parties within three months?

5. Gender discrimination and sexual harassment

Japanese law treats sexual harassment as a tort, rather than as a form of employment discrimination. The first case holding that sexual harassment was a tort under art. 709 of the Civil Code, Kouno v. Company X et al., was decided in 1992 by the Fukuoka District Court. Art. 709 provides: A person who violates intentionally or negligently the right of another is bound to make compensation for damage arising therefrom. A body of case law on sexual harassment quickly resulted. *See* Ryuichi Yamakawa, *We've Only Just Begun: The Law of Sexual Harassment in Japan*, 22 Hastings Int'l & Comp. L. Rev. 523 (1999); Sugeno & Kanowitz, *supra*, at 176-77. Some cases have been litigated on breach of contract theory. Yamakawa, *supra*.

The attorneys who represented plaintiff in the so-called Fukuoka sexual harassment case were inspired by developments in U.S. law but had to formulate a cause of action within the conceptual framework of Japanese law.

> Another factor [to spurring litigation] was the arrival in Japan of the idea, articulated in a pamphlet published in the United States, that change be effected through the legal system. That pamphlet, along with the 1986 U.S. Supreme Court decision in *Meritor Savings Bank v. Vinson*, which several Japanese law journals synopsized, inspired me and my colleagues to formulate a plan to correct workplace injustices and effect change by working within existing laws such as the Japanese Civil Code.
>
> Yukiko Tsunoda, *Sexual Harassment in Japan*, in CATHARINE A. MacKINNON & REVA B. SIEGEL (ED.), DIRECTIONS IN SEXUAL HARASSMENT LAW 618, 619 (2004).

In the Fukuoka Case, a female editor sued her employer and her former supervisor for his actions in spreading rumors about her personal life that insinuated that she was promiscuous. The supervisor was motivated by a desire to get plaintiff out of the workplace, not by sexual attraction. In order to resolve the conflict between plaintiff and her supervisor, the employer pressured her to resign. She was paid the equivalent of one month's salary plus bonus. For a summary of the case, *see* Yamakawa, *supra*, at 533-37; Hiroko Hayashi, *Sexual Harassment in the Workplace and Equal Employment Legislation*, 69 ST. JOHN'S L. REV. 37 (1995); *see also*, translation in MILHAUPT ET AL., *supra*, at 421-25.

The court determined that plaintiff had suffered an infringement of her privacy as well as her personal right to work in a conducive environment. The concept of "personal right" (jinkakuken) in Japanese law is derived from German law (Persoenlichkeitsrecht). On the European approach to sexual harassment as a violation of individual dignity, *see* Gabrielle S. Friedman & James Q. Whitman, *The European Transformation of Harassment Law: Discrimination Versus Dignity*, 9 COLUM. J. EUR. L. 241 (2003). *See also* James Whitman, *Enforcing Civility and Respect: Three Societies*, 109 YALE L.J. 1279 (2000); Edward J. Eberle, *Human Dignity, Privacy, and Personality in German and American Constitutional Law*, 1997 UTAH L. REV. 963. Dignity includes one's right to bodily integrity, liberty, honor, life, reputation, and privacy. Hayashi, *supra*, at 50. The court held the employer liable under the doctrine of respondeat superior, art. 715 of the Civil Code. Plaintiff was awarded damages for emotional suffering and attorney's fees. She had not requested economic damages.

When the EEOL was amended in 1997, a new provision art. 21(1) was added to impose a duty of care (hitsuyou na hairyo o shinakereba naranai) on the employer to prevent sexual harassment. Thus, this provision of the EEOL is another illustration of the codification of judicial precedent in Japanese statutory law. See discussion of the doctrine of unjust dismissal, *supra*. However, because the EEOL does not create a private right of action for sexual harassment, further development of the doctrine remains with the courts under the law of tort and contract.

C. JAPANESE TRANSPLANT COMPANIES IN THE UNITED STATES

In the postwar period, the United States became Japan's most important trading partner. The openness of the U.S. market to Japanese manufactured goods was a crucial factor in the postwar recovery. JOHN K. FAIRBANK, EDWIN O. REISCHAUER, & ALBERT M. CRAIG, EAST ASIA: TRADITION & TRANSFORMATION 830 (rev. ed. 1989). However, by the 1980s, the balance of trade in Japan's favor began to climb steeply. Although the United States was not the only country affected by a hunger for Japanese goods – notably automobiles, cameras, electronic equipment, and other high value-added manufactures – the growing trade imbalance sparked a heated debate as to whether Japan's trade advantage was the result of unfair trade practices. *Id.* at 863-64. *See also* Kristin Leigh Case, *An Overview of Fifteen Years of United States-Japanese Economic Relations*, 16 Ariz. J. Int'l & Comp. L. 11 (1999); Sen. Dan Quayle, *Perspective: United States International Competitiveness and Trade Policies for the 1980s*, 5 Nw. J. Int'l L. & Bus. 1, 10 (1983) ("The causes of our long-term decline in productivity growth are deep-seated and complex. They derive from habits and policies that spur domestic consumption at the expense of savings and investment").

Japan responded by investing its trade surpluses in U.S. government securities, real estate, and manufacturing facilities. For the most part, Japanese companies built "greenfields" operations rather than acquire existing U.S. companies. Goods "produced" by U.S. subsidiaries of Japanese corporations were deemed to be of domestic manufacture and therefore not subject to quotas or penalties under the U.S. antidumping and countervailing duties laws applicable to imports. *See* Hilary K. Josephs, *The Multinational Corporation, Integrated International Production, and the United States Antidumping Laws*, 5 Tul. J. Int'l & Comp. L. 51 (1997).

Between 1985 and 1990, the real value of Japanese Direct Investment in the United States ("JDIUS") quadrupled. Neil Reid, The Geography of Japanese Direct Investment in the United States: The State of Knowledge and an Agenda for Future Research 1 (2002) http://www.iar.ubc.ca/centres/cjr/reid.pdf. JDIUS is concentrated in five sectors: transportation equipment, primary metal industries, electronic equipment, industrial machinery, and rubber products. *Id.* However, automotive-related investment dominates. *Id.* at 4.

Japanese automotive assembly plants and automobile component parts makers are mainly located in "Auto Alley" (Illinois, Indiana, Kentucky, Michigan, Ohio, and Tennessee). *Id.* Parts makers located close to assembly plants to facilitate "just in time" delivery of component parts. Under the "just-in-time" approach, suppliers produce components in small batches and deliver them to the main company as needed. This approach economizes on inventory maintenance and also quickly reveals manufacturing defects which can be rectified before the next batch arrives. Carl H.A. Dassbach, Where is North American Automobile Production Headed?: Low-Wage Lean Production 11, http://www.sociology.org/content/vol001.001/dassbach.html (1994).

JDIUS plants implemented the same production strategies as in Japanese plants. In contrast to Fordist assembly line production, Japanese-style "lean production" is based on self-managing teams. *Toyota v. Williams*, 534 U.S. 184, 188-89 (2002). Work roles are assigned to groups of workers who reallocate them internally. Multitasking is essential. Dassbach, *supra*, at 6 and source cited therein. Perhaps most important, lean production allows workers to stop the line in order to solve problems. Labor-management relations are characterized by cooperation and consensus. *Id.* at 7. The results are telling: lean production lowers manufacturing costs and improves quality. *See* James P. Womack, *Why Toyota Won*, Wall St. J., Feb. 13, 2006, at A16.

Lean production has not been without its critics. Japanese transplants tend to locate in areas which are not fertile ground for unions – rural locations and small towns. Reid, *supra*, at 7. The UAW was unsuccessful in organizing a Nissan plant in Tennessee and a Honda plant in Ohio. Joint venture companies with U.S. producers are unionized, but the union tends to be compliant, if not subservient to management. Mike Parker, Transplanted to the U.S.A. 4-5, http://multinationalmonitor.org/hyper/issues/1990/01/parker.html(1990). Transplant companies have low labor costs because they hire younger workers without health problems.

> [W]hen workers grow older or get injured, they are not able to maintain the same pace. These workers are forced out because the management system employed in the transplants does not make lighter jobs available for those with seniority.
>
> *Id.* at 5.

Furthermore, the trickle down benefits and multiplier effects of JDIUS are limited. Transplant companies retain the highly skilled jobs at home, make extensive use of robotics and other technology, and demand massive subsidies from local communities in order to locate production facilities there. *Id.* at 5-6.

As the Japanese presence in the U.S. economy has grown, so too the volume of litigation against Japanese employers. Two of the cases excerpted below are decisions of the U.S. Supreme Court; the other a decision of the Seventh Circuit Court of Appeals. All of them raise questions about the autonomy of the employer vis-à-vis the workforce. As in the National Westminster Bank case, *supra*, the court has to strike a delicate balance between the employer's determination of how best to optimize its business operations and the host country's regulatory system which is protective of weaker members of society.

SUMITOMO SHOJI AMERICA, INC. V. AVAGLIANO

457 U.S. 176 (1982)

CHIEF JUSTICE BURGER delivered the opinion of the Court.

We granted certiorari to decide whether Article VIII (1) of the Friendship, Commerce and Navigation Treaty between the United States and Japan provides a defense to a Title VII employment discrimination suit against an American subsidiary of a Japanese company.

I

Petitioner, Sumitomo Shoji America, Inc. is a New York corporation and a wholly owned subsidiary of Sumitomo Shoji Kabushiki Kaisha, a Japanese general trading company or *sogo shosha*.[14] Respondents are past and present female secretarial employees of Sumitomo.[15]

---

[14] General trading companies have been a unique fixture of the Japanese economy since the Meiji era. These companies each market large numbers of Japanese products, typically those of smaller concerns, and also have a large role in the importation of raw materials and manufactured products to Japan. In addition, the trading companies play a large part in financing Japan's international trade. The largest trading companies – including Sumitomo's parent company – in a typical year account for over 50 percent of Japanese exports and over 60 percent of imports to Japan. See Krause & Sekiguchi, *Japan and the World Economy*, in ASIA'S NEW GIANT: HOW THE JAPANESE ECONOMY WORKS 383, 389-97 (H. Patrick & H. Rosovsky, eds. 1976).

[15] Respondents have also filed a cross-petition in this case. Thus, the past and present secretaries, generally referred to as respondents, are the respondents in No. 80-2070 and the cross-petitioners in No. 81-24. Sumitomo is the petitioner in No. 80-2070 and the cross-respondent in No. 81-24.

All but one of the respondents are United States citizens; that one exception is a Japanese citizen living in the United States. Respondents brought this suit as a class action claiming that Sumitomo's alleged practice of hiring only male Japanese citizens to fill executive, managerial, and sales positions violated both 42 U. S. C. § 1981 and Title VII of the Civil Rights Act of 1964, 78 Stat. 253, as amended, 42 U. S. C. § 2000e *et seq.* (1976 ed. and Supp. IV).[16] Respondents sought both injunctive relief and damages.

Without admitting the alleged discriminatory practice, Sumitomo moved under Rule 12(b)(6) of the Federal Rules of Civil Procedure to dismiss the complaint. Sumitomo's motion was based on two grounds: (1) discrimination on the basis of Japanese citizenship does not violate Title VII or § 1981; and (2) Sumitomo's practices are protected under Article VIII(1) of the Friendship, Commerce and Navigation Treaty between the United States and Japan, Apr. 2, 1953, [1953] 4 U. S. T. 2063, T. I. A. S. No. 2863. The District Court dismissed the § 1981 claim, holding that neither sex discrimination nor national origin discrimination are cognizable under that section. The court refused to dismiss the Title VII claims, however; it held that because Sumitomo is incorporated in the United States it is not covered by Article VIII (1) of the Treaty. The District Court then certified for interlocutory appeal to the Court of Appeals under 28 U. S. C. § 1292(b) the question of whether the terms of the Treaty exempted Sumitomo from the provisions of Title VII.

The Court of Appeals reversed in part. The court first examined the Treaty's language and its history and concluded that the Treaty parties intended Article VIII (1) to cover locally incorporated subsidiaries of foreign companies such as Sumitomo. The court then held that the Treaty language does not insulate Sumitomo's executive employment practices from Title VII scrutiny. The court concluded that under certain conditions, Japanese citizenship could be a bona fide occupational qualification for high-level employment with a Japanese-owned domestic corporation and that Sumitomo's practices might thus fit within a statutory exception to Title VII.[17] The court remanded for further proceedings.[18]

We granted certiorari, and we vacate and remand.

---

[16] Before bringing this suit, respondents each filed timely complaints with the Equal Employment Opportunity Commission. The EEOC issued "right to sue" letters to the respondents on October 27, 1977. This suit was filed on November 21, 1977, well within the statutory ninety-day period allowed for filing suits after receipt of an EEOC notice of right to sue. 42 U. S. C. § 2000e-5(f) (1).

[17] Sumitomo argued in the District Court that discrimination on the basis of national citizenship, as opposed to national origin, was not prohibited by Title VII. The District Court disagreed, however. It relied on *Espinoza v. Farah Manufacturing Co.*, 414 U.S. 86, 92 (1973), in which we noted that "Title VII prohibits discrimination on the basis of citizenship whenever it has the purpose or effect of discriminating on the basis of national origin." Although discussed at length in the briefs, this issue is not properly before the Court and we do not reach it. It was not included in the question certified for interlocutory review by the Court of Appeals under 28 U. S. C. §1292(b), was not decided by the Court of Appeals, and was not set forth or fairly included in the questions presented for review by this Court as required by Rule 21.1(a).

[18] In a nearly identical case, a divided panel of the Court of Appeals for the Fifth Circuit came to somewhat contrary results. *Spiess v. C. Itoh & Co.*, 643 F.2d 353 (1981), cert. pending, No. 81-1496. The Fifth Circuit majority agreed with the Second Circuit decision that a locally incorporated subsidiary of a Japanese corporation is covered by Article VIII(1) of the Treaty, but disagreed with the latter court's decision on the effect of the Treaty on Title VII. The court held that the Treaty provision did protect the subsidiary's practices from Title VII liability. In dissent, Judge Reavley disagreed with the majority's initial conclusion. He would have held that under the plain language of the Treaty, locally incorporated subsidiaries are to be considered domestic corporations and are thus not covered by Article VIII(1).

II

Interpretation of the Friendship, Commerce and Navigation Treaty between Japan and the United States must, of course, begin with the language of the Treaty itself. The clear import of treaty language controls unless "application of the words of the treaty according to their obvious meaning effects a result inconsistent with the intent or expectations of its signatories." *Maximov v. United States*, 373 U.S. 49, 54 (1963). See also *The Amiable Isabella*, 6 Wheat. 1, 72 (1821).

Article VIII(1) of the Treaty provides in pertinent part:

> "*[Companies] of either Party* shall be permitted to engage, within the territories of the other Party, accountants and other technical experts, executive personnel, attorneys, agents and other specialists of their choice." (Emphasis added.)[19]

Clearly Article VIII(1) only applies to companies of one of the Treaty countries operating in the other country. Sumitomo contends that it is a company of Japan, and that Article VIII(1) of the Treaty grants it very broad discretion to fill its executive, managerial, and sales positions exclusively with male Japanese citizens.[20]

---

[19] Similar provisions are contained in the Friendship, Commerce and Navigation Treaties between the United States and other countries. *See, e. g.*, Article XII(4) of the Treaty with Greece, [1954] 5 U. S. T. 1829, 1857, T. I. A. S. No. 3057 (1951); Article VIII(1) of the Treaty with Israel, [1954] 5 U. S. T. 550, 557, T. I. A. S. No. 551 (1951); Article VIII(1) of the Treaty with the Federal Republic of Germany, [1956] 7 U. S. T. 1839, 1848, T. I. A. S. No. 3593 (1954).

These provisions were apparently included at the insistence of the United States; in fact, other countries, including Japan, unsuccessfully fought for their deletion. *See, e.g.*, State Department Airgram No. A-453, dated Jan. 7, 1952, pp. 1, 3, reprinted in App. 130a, 131a, 133a (discussing Japanese objections to Article VIII(1)); Foreign Service Despatch No. 2529, dated Mar. 18, 1954, reprinted in App. 181a, 182a (discussing German objections to Article VIII(1)).

According to Herman Walker, Jr., who at the time of the drafting of the Treaty served as Adviser on Commercial Treaties at the State Department, Article VIII(1) and the comparable provisions of other treaties were intended to avoid the effect of strict percentile limitations on the employment of Americans abroad and "to prevent the imposition of ultranationalistic policies with respect to essential executive and technical personnel." Walker, Provisions on Companies in United States Commercial Treaties, 50 Am. J. Int'l L. 373, 386 (1956); Walker, Treaties for the Encouragement and Protection of Foreign Investment: Present United States Practice, 5 Am. J. Comp. L. 229, 234 (1956). According to the State Department, Mr. Walker was responsible for formulation of the postwar form of the Friendship, Commerce and Navigation Treaty and negotiated several of the treaties for the United States. Department of State Airgram A-105, dated Jan. 9, 1976, reprinted in App. 157a.

See also Foreign Service Despatch No. 2529, *supra*, App. 182a (Purpose of Article VIII(1) of Treaty with Germany "is to preclude the imposition of 'percentile' legislation. It gives freedom of choice as among persons lawfully present in the country and occupationally qualified under the local law").

[20] The issues raised by this contention are clearly of widespread importance. As we noted in n. [19], *supra*, treaty provisions similar to that invoked by Sumitomo are in effect with many other countries. In fact, some treaties contain even more broad language. *See, e.g.*, Article XII(4), Treaty of Friendship, Commerce and Navigation with Greece, [1954] 5 U. S. T., at 1857–1859 ("Nationals and companies of either party shall be permitted to engage, within the territories of the other Party, accountants and other technical experts, executive personnel, attorneys, agents *and other employees of their choice* . . . ") (emphasis added). As of 1979, United States affiliates of foreign corporations employed over 1.6 million workers in this country. Howenstine, *Selected Data on the Operations of U.S. Affiliates of Foreign Companies, 1978 and 1979*, in SURVEY OF CURRENT BUSINESS 35, 36 (U.S. Dept. of Commerce, May 1981).

Article VIII(1) does not define any of its terms; the definitional section of the Treaty is contained in Article XXII. Article XXII(3) provides:

"As used in the present Treaty, the term 'companies' means corporations, partnerships, companies and other associations, whether or not with limited liability and whether or not for pecuniary profit. Companies constituted under the applicable laws and regulations within the territories of either Party *shall be deemed companies thereof* and shall have their juridical status recognized within the territories of the other Party." (Emphasis added.)

Sumitomo is "constituted under the applicable laws and regulations" of New York; based on Article XXII(3), it is a company of the United States, not a company of Japan.[21] As a company of the United States operating in the United States, under the literal language of Article XXII(3) of the Treaty, Sumitomo cannot invoke the rights provided in Article VIII(1), which are available only to companies of Japan operating in the United States and to companies of the United States operating in Japan.

Several other Treaty provisions would make little sense if American subsidiaries were considered companies of Japan. Articles VII(1), VII(4), and XVI(2) contain clauses dealing with companies or enterprises controlled by companies of either party. If those companies or enterprises were themselves companies of the country of their parents, this separate treatment would be unwarranted.

The Governments of Japan and the United States support this interpretation of the Treaty. Both the Ministry of Foreign Affairs of Japan and the United States Department of State agree that a United States corporation, even when wholly owned by a Japanese company, is not a company of Japan under the Treaty and is therefore not covered by Article VIII(1). The Ministry of Foreign Affairs stated its position to the American Embassy in Tokyo with reference to this case:

"The Ministry of Foreign Affairs, as the Office of [the Government of Japan] responsible for the interpretation of the [Friendship, Commerce and Navigation] Treaty, reiterates its view concerning the application of Article 8, Paragraph 1 of the Treaty: For the purpose of the Treaty, companies constituted under the applicable laws . . . of either Party shall be deemed companies thereof and, therefore, a subsidiary of a Japanese company which is incorporated under the laws of New York is not covered by Article 8 Paragraph 1 when it operates in the United States."[22]

---

[21] The clear language of Article VII(1) and Article XXII(3) is consistent with other Treaty provisions. For example, Article XVI(2) accords national treatment to "[articles] produced by nationals and companies of either Party within the territories of the other Party, *or by companies of the latter Party controlled by such nationals and companies. . . .* " (Emphasis added.) This provision obviously envisions that companies of one party may be controlled by companies of the other party. If the nationality of a company were determined by the nationality of its controlling entity as Sumitomo proposes, rather than by the place of its incorporation, this provision would make no sense.

[22] State Department Cable, Tokyo 03300, dated Feb. 26, 1982 (cable from the United States Embassy in Tokyo to the Secretary of State relaying the position of the Ministry of Foreign Affairs of Japan). *See also* Diplomatic Communication from the Embassy of Japan in Washington to the United States Department of State, dated Apr. 21, 1982 ("The Government of Japan reconfirms its view that a subsidiary of a Japanese company which is incorporated under the laws of New York is not itself covered by article 8, paragraph 1 of the Treaty of Friendship, Commerce and Navigation between Japan and the United States (the FCN Treaty) when it operates in the United States").

The United States Department of State also maintains that Article VIII (1) rights do not apply to locally incorporated subsidiaries.[23] Although not conclusive, the meaning attributed to treaty provisions by the Government agencies charged with their negotiation and enforcement is entitled to great weight. *Kolovrat v. Oregon*, 366 U.S. 187, 194 (1961).[24]

The Court of Appeals and Sumitomo dismiss the Atwood letter as incorrect, and point to a letter written by a previous State Department Deputy Legal Adviser as taking the contrary view. Letter of Lee R. Marks, Deputy Legal Adviser, U.S. Department of State, to Abner W. Sibal, General Counsel, Equal Employment Opportunity Commission, dated Oct. 17, 1978, reprinted in App. 94a. However neither of these letters is indicative of the state of mind of the Treaty negotiators; they are merely evidence of the later interpretation of the State Department as the agency of the United States charged with interpreting and enforcing the Treaty. However ambiguous the State Department position may have been previously, it is certainly beyond dispute that the Department now interprets the Treaty in conformity with its plain language, and is of the opinion that Sumitomo is not a company of Japan and is not covered by Article VIII(1). That interpretation, and the identical position of the Government of Japan, is entitled to great weight. *Kolovrat v. Oregon*, 366 U.S. 187 (1961).

Our role is limited to giving effect to the intent of the Treaty parties. When the parties to a treaty both agree as to the meaning of a treaty provision, and that interpretation follows from the clear treaty language, we must, absent extraordinarily strong contrary evidence, defer to that interpretation.[25]

III

Sumitomo maintains that although the literal language of the Treaty supports the contrary interpretation, the intent of Japan and the United States was to cover subsidiaries regardless of their place of incorporation. We disagree.

Contrary to the view of the Court of Appeals and the claims of Sumitomo, adherence to the language of the Treaty would not "overlook the purpose of the Treaty." 638 F.2d, at 556. The Friendship, Commerce and Navigation Treaty between Japan and the United States is but one of a series of similar commercial agreements negotiated after World War II.[26] The

---

[23] Brief for United States as *Amicus Curiae* 8-22; Letter of James R. Atwood, Deputy Legal Adviser, U.S. Department of State, to Lutz Alexander Prager, Assistant General Counsel, Equal Employment Opportunity Commission, dated Sept. 11, 1979, reprinted in App. 307a. ("On further reflection on the scope of application of the first sentence of Paragraph 1 of Article VIII of the U.S.-Japan FCN, we have established to our satisfaction that it was not the intent of the negotiators to cover locally-incorporated subsidiaries, and that therefore U.S. subsidiaries of Japanese corporations cannot avail themselves of this provision of the treaty").

[24] Determining the nationality of a company by its place of incorporation is consistent with prior treaty practice. *See* Walker, 50 AM. J. INT'L L., *supra* n. [19], at 382-383. The place-of-incorporation rule also has the advantage of making determination of nationality a simple matter. On the other hand, application of a control test could certainly make nationality a subject of dispute.

[25] We express no view, of course, as to the interpretation of other Friendship, Commerce and Navigation Treaties, which, although similarly worded, may have different negotiating histories.

[26] See, *e.g.*, Treaties of Friendship, Commerce and Navigation with China, 63 Stat. 1299, T. I. A. S. No. 1871 (1946); Italy, 63 Stat. 2255, T. I. A. S. No. 1965 (1948); Israel, [1954] 5 U. S. T. 550, T. I. A. S. No. 551 (1951); Greece, [1954] 5 U. S. T. 1829, T. I. A. S. No. 3057 (1951); Japan, [1953] 4 U. S. T. 2063, T. I. A. S. No. 2863 (1953); Federal Republic of Germany, [1956] 7 U. S. T. 1839, T. I. A. S. No. 3593 (1954); The Netherlands, [1957] 8 U. S. T. 2043, T. I. A. S. No. 3942 (1956); and Pakistan, [1961] 12 U. S. T. 110, T. I. A. S. No. 4683 (1959). The provisions of several of the treaties are compared in tabular form in Commercial Treaties: Hearing on

primary purpose of the corporation provisions of the Treaties was to give corporations of each signatory legal status in the territory of the other party, and to allow them to conduct business in the other country on a comparable basis with domestic firms. Although the United States negotiated commercial treaties as early as 1778, and thereafter throughout the 19th century and early 20th century,[27] these early commercial treaties were primarily concerned with the trade and shipping rights of individuals. Until the 20th century, international commerce was much more an individual than a corporate affair.[28]

As corporate involvement in international trade expanded in this century, old commercial treaties became outmoded. Because "[corporations] can have no legal existence out of the boundaries of the sovereignty by which [they are] created," *Bank of Augusta v. Earle, 13 Pet. 519, 588 (1839),* it became necessary to negotiate new treaties granting corporations legal status and the right to function abroad. A series of Treaties negotiated before World War II gave corporations legal status and access to foreign courts,[29] but it was not until the postwar Friendship, Commerce and Navigation Treaties that United States corporations gained the right to conduct business in other countries.[30] The purpose of the Treaties was not to give

---

Treaties of Friendship, Commerce and Navigation with Israel, Ethiopia, Italy, Denmark, Greece, Finland, Germany, and Japan, before the Subcommittee of the Senate Committee on Foreign Relations, 83d Cong., 1st Sess., 7-17 (1953).

[27] See, *e.g.,* Treaty of Amity and Commerce with France, 8 Stat. 12, T. S. No. 83 (1778); Treaty of Amity, Commerce and Navigation with Great Britain, 8 Stat. 116, T. S. No. 105 (1794); Treaty of Commerce and Friendship with Sweden and Norway, 8 Stat. 232, T. S. No. 347 (1816); Treaty of Commerce and Navigation with the Netherlands, 8 Stat. 524, T. S. No. 251 (1839); Treaty of Commerce and Navigation with Belgium, 8 Stat. 606, T. S. No. 19 (1845); Treaty of Commerce and Navigation with Italy, 17 Stat. 845, T. S. No. 177 (1871); Treaty of Commerce with Spain, 23 Stat. 750, T. S. No. 337 (1884); Treaty of Commerce with Germany, 31 Stat. 1935, T. S. No. 101 (1900); Treaty of Commerce with China, 33 Stat. 2208, T. S. No. 430 (1903).

[28] See Walker, 50 Am. J. Int'l L., *supra* n.19, at 374-378.

[29] Treaty of Commerce and Navigation with Japan, 37 Stat. 1504, T. S. No. 558 (1911); Treaties of Friendship, Commerce and Consular Rights with Germany, 44 Stat. 2132, T. S. No. 725 (1923); Estonia, 44 Stat. 2379, T. S. No. 736 (1925); Hungary, 44 Stat. 2441, T. S. No. 748 (1925); El Salvador, 46 Stat. 2817, T. S. No. 827 (1926); Honduras, 45 Stat. 2618, T. S. No. 764 (1927); Latvia, 45 Stat. 2641, T. S. No. 765 (1928); Austria, 47 Stat. 1876, T. S. No. 838 (1928); Norway, 47 Stat. 2135, T. S. No. 852 (1928); Poland, 48 Stat. 1507, T. S. No. 862 (1931); Finland, 49 Stat. 2659, T. S. No. 868 (1934); Treaties of Friendship, Commerce and Navigation with Siam, 53 Stat. 1731, T. S. No. 940 (1937); Liberia, 54 Stat. 1739, T. S. No. 956 (1938).

These rights given to corporations by these Treaties were quite limited. For example, Article VII of the 1911 Treaty with Japan provided:

> Limited liability and other companies and associations... already or hereafter to be organized in accordance with the laws of either High Contracting Party and domiciled in the territories of such Party, are authorized, in the territories of the other, to exercise their rights and appear in the courts either as plaintiffs or defendants, subject to the laws of such other Party.
>
> The foregoing stipulation has no bearing upon the question whether a company or association organized in one of the two countries will or will not be permitted to transact its business or industry in the other, this permission remaining always subject to the laws and regulations enacted or established in the respective countries or in any part thereof. 37 Stat. 1506.

A similarly limited provision was contained in the other Treaties.

[30] The significance of this advance was emphasized in the Senate hearings on an early set of postwar Friendship, Commerce and Navigation Treaties:

> Perhaps the most striking advance of the postwar treaties is the cognizance taken of the widespread use of the corporate form of business organization in present-day economic affairs. In the treaties antedating World War II American corporations were specifically assured only small protection against possible discriminatory treatment in foreign countries. In the postwar treaties, however, corporations are accorded essentially the

foreign corporations greater rights than domestic companies, but instead to assure them the right to conduct business on an equal basis without suffering discrimination based on their alienage.

The Treaties accomplished their purpose by granting foreign corporations "national treatment"[31] in most respects and by allowing foreign individuals and companies to form locally incorporated subsidiaries. These local subsidiaries are considered for purposes of the Treaty to be companies of the country in which they are incorporated; they are entitled to the rights, and subject to the responsibilities of other domestic corporations. By treating these subsidiaries as domestic companies, the purpose of the Treaty provisions – to assure that corporations of one Treaty party have the right to conduct business within the territory of the other party without suffering discrimination as an alien entity – is fully met.

Nor can we agree with the Court of Appeals view that literal interpretation of the Treaty would create a "crazy-quilt pattern" in which the rights of branches of Japanese companies operating directly in the United States would be greatly superior to the right of locally incorporated subsidiaries of Japanese companies. 638 F.2d at 556. The Court of Appeals maintained that if such subsidiaries were not considered companies of Japan under the Treaty, they, unlike branch offices of Japanese corporations, would be denied access to the legal system, would be left unprotected against unlawful entry and molestation, and would be unable to dispose of property, obtain patents, engage in importation and exportation, or make payments, remittances, and transfers of funds. *Ibid.* That this is not the case is obvious; the subsidiaries, as companies of the United States, would enjoy all of those rights and more. The only significant advantage branches may have over subsidiaries is that conferred by Article VIII(1).

IV

We are persuaded, as both signatories agree, that under the literal language of Article XXII(3) of the Treaty, Sumitomo is a company of the United States; we discern no reason to depart

same treaty rights as individuals in such vital matters as the right to do business, taxation on a nondiscriminatory basis, the acquisition and enjoyment of real and personal property, and the application of exchange controls. Furthermore, the citizens and corporations of one country are given substantial rights in connection with forming local subsidiaries under the corporation laws of the other country and controlling and managing the affairs of such local companies." Commercial Treaties: Hearing on Treaties of Friendship, Commerce and Navigation Between the United States and Colombia, Israel, Ethiopia, Italy, Denmark and Greece before a Subcommittee of the Senate Committee on Foreign Relations, 82d Cong., 2d Sess., 4-5 (1952) (opening statement of Harold Linder, Deputy Assistant Secretary of State for Economic Affairs).

[31] "National treatment" is defined in Article XXII(1) of the Treaty:

The term 'national treatment' means treatment accorded within the territories of a Party upon terms no less favorable than the treatment accorded therein, in like situations, to nationals, companies, products, vessels or other objects, as the case may be, of such Party.

In short, national treatment of corporations means equal treatment with domestic corporations. It is ordinarily the highest level of protection afforded by commercial treaties. In certain areas treaty parties are unwilling to grant full national treatment; in those areas the parties frequently grant "most-favored-nation treatment," which means treatment no less favorable than that accorded to nationals or companies of any third country. See Article XXII(2) of the Treaty. "The most-favored-nation rule can now, therefore, imply or allow the status of alien disability rather than of favor. In applicable situations nowadays, the first-class treatment tends to be national treatment; that which the citizens of the country enjoy." Walker, Modern Treaties of Friendship, Commerce and Navigation, 42 MINN. L. REV. 805, 811 (1958).

from the plain meaning of the Treaty language. Accordingly, we hold that Sumitomo is not a company of Japan and is thus not covered by Article VIII(1) of the Treaty.[32] The judgment of the Court of Appeals is vacated, and the case is remanded for further proceedings consistent with this opinion.

Vacated and remanded.

FORTINO V. QUASAR COMPANY

950 F.2d 389 (7th Cir.1991)

POSNER, *Circuit Judge.* This suit charges the American subsidiary of a Japanese company with discriminating against its American executives on the basis of their age and national origin, in violation of the Age Discrimination in Employment Act, 29 U.S.C. § 626(b), and Title VII of the Civil Rights Act of 1964, 42 U.S.C. § 2000, respectively. A jury and judge (only the age claim was triable to a jury, since Title VII authorizes only equitable relief) awarded the three plaintiffs – John Fortino, Carl Meyers, and F. William Schulz, all former executives of Quasar Company, an unincorporated division of a U.S. corporation wholly owned by Matsushita Electric Industrial Company, Ltd., of Japan – $2.5 million in damages, to which the judge added almost $400,000 in attorneys' fees and costs.

The most important question is whether a claim of discrimination on the basis of national *origin* is tenable when, as in this case, the discrimination is in favor of foreign citizens employed temporarily in the United States in accordance with a treaty between the U.S. and Japan that entitles companies of each nation to employ executives of their own choice in the other one. The plaintiffs ask us to close our eyes to the treaty because Quasar failed to mention it to the district judge. Ordinarily we will not consider a point that was not raised in the district court, but we can do so, *Singleton v. Wulff,* 428 U.S. 106, 121 (1976), and, for the sake of international comity, amity, and commerce, we should do so when we are asked to consider the bearing of a major treaty with a major power and principal ally of the United States. Comity between the federal government and the states, though a weaker interest because states of the U.S. are only quasi-sovereigns, is an accepted reason for an appellate court to consider issues that would otherwise have been deemed waived because not raised in timely fashion, as held in *Younger v. Harris,* 401 U.S. 37, 40 (1971), and the other cases cited in *Thomas v. State of Indiana,* 910 F.2d 1413, 1415-16 (7th Cir. 1990). This is a stronger case for overlooking waiver – especially since Quasar does not, as we understand its position, argue that the treaty is a defense to Title VII, and hence a ground for appeal, but merely that it is part of the essential

---

[32] We express no view as to whether Japanese citizenship may be a bona fide occupational qualification for certain positions at Sumitomo or as to whether a business necessity defense may be available. There can be little doubt that some positions in a Japanese controlled company doing business in the United States call for great familiarity with not only the language of Japan, but also the culture, customs, and business practices of that country. However, the Court of Appeals found the evidentiary record insufficient to determine whether Japanese citizenship was a bona fide occupational qualification for any of Sumitomo's positions within the reach of Article VIII(1). Nor did it discuss the bona fide occupational qualification exception in relation to respondents' sex discrimination claim or the possibility of a business necessity defense. Whether Sumitomo can support its assertion of a bona fide occupational qualification or a business necessity defense is not before us. See n. [17], *supra.*

We also express no view as to whether Sumitomo may assert any Article VIII(1) rights of its parent.

background for understanding why this case is not within the scope of the statute. The treaty permits discrimination on the basis of citizenship, not of national origin; Title VII forbids discrimination on the basis of national origin, not of citizenship. The treaty is a reminder that the two forms of preference discrimination – citizenship and national origin – must not be run together, since one is permitted by treaty and the other forbidden by statute.

Quasar markets in the United States products made in Japan by Matsushita, which assigns several of its own financial and marketing executives to Quasar on a temporary basis. They are employees of Quasar and are under its day-to-day control but they also retain their status as employees of Matsushita and are designated as "MEI [Matsushita Electric Industrial] personnel" on Quasar's books. Quasar does not evaluate their performance – Matsushita does, and also keeps their personnel records and fixes their salaries and assists with the relocation of their families to the United States during the period of the assignment. These executives enter this country under "E-1" or "E-2" temporary visas, which permit the holder of the visa to work here, provided (so far as applicable to this case, which involves Japanese executives) that the work is executive or supervisory in character, the worker is a Japanese citizen, the company he is working for in the U.S. is at least half owned by Japanese nationals and has substantial trade or investment relations with Japan, and he is doing work authorized by the Treaty of Friendship, Commerce and Navigation between the United States and Japan.

In 1986 there were ten of these Japanese expatriate executives working for Quasar. (The parties call them "expatriates," though in common parlance the word is not applied to a person on merely temporary assignment to another country.) One was named Nishikawa. In 1985 Quasar had lost $20 million, and Nishikawa had been sent by Matsushita to prevent a recurrence of the loss. He was put in charge of Quasar and proceeded to reorganize the company, in the process reducing the work force, including management, by half. The three plaintiffs were among the American executives of non-Japanese origin who were discharged. None of the Japanese expatriate executives was discharged, although it appears that two were rotated back to Japan and replaced by only one new expatriate. Far from being discharged, the expatriates received salary increases; the American executives of Quasar who were not discharged did not. Two out of Quasar's three Japanese-American employees were also discharged, but none of these was an executive.

Article VIII(1) of the treaty authorizes "companies of either Party [i.e., the U.S. and Japan], to engage, within the territories of the other Party . . . executive personnel . . . of their choice." The propriety of Matsushita's assigning its own executives to Quasar is further confirmed by the issuance of E-1 and E-2 visas to the Japanese expatriate executives. Nevertheless the district judge based his conclusion that Quasar had violated Title VII on the better treatment the company gave the Japanese expatriates compared to its American executives in 1986: it discharged none of the former but many of the latter, and it gave raises to all of the former and none of the latter. This was favoritism all right, but discrimination in favor of foreign executives given a special status by virtue of a treaty and its implementing regulations is not equivalent to discrimination on the basis of national origin.

We may assume that just as Title VII protects whites from discrimination in favor of blacks as well as blacks from discrimination in favor of whites, *McDonald v. Santa Fe Trail Transportation Co.*, 427 U.S. 273 (1976), so it protects Americans of non-Japanese origin from discrimination in favor of persons of Japanese origin. Title VII does not, however, forbid discrimination on grounds of citizenship. *Espinoza v. Farah Mfg. Co.*, 414 U.S. 86 (1973). Of course, especially in the case of a homogeneous country like Japan, citizenship and national origin are highly correlated; almost all citizens of Japan were born there. But to use this correlation to infer national-origin discrimination from a treaty-sanctioned preference for Japanese citizens who happen also to be of Japanese national origin would nullify the treaty. This is true whether the correlation is used to prove intentional discrimination, as in this case, or to establish a disparate impact that the employer must justify on nondiscriminatory grounds. The exercise of a treaty right may not be made the basis for inferring a violation of Title VII. By virtue of the treaty, "foreign businesses clearly have the right to choose citizens of their own nation as executives because they are such citizens." *MacNamara v. Korean Air Lines*, 863 F.2d 1135, 1144 (3d Cir. 1988) (emphasis in original). See also *Wickes v. Olympic Airways*, 745 F.2d 363, 368 (6th Cir. 1984). That right would be empty if the subsidiary could be punished for treating its citizen executives differently from American executives on the ground that, since the former were of Japanese national origin and the latter were not, it was discriminating on the basis of national origin. Title VII would be taking back from the Japanese with one hand what the treaty had given them with the other. This collision is avoided by holding national origin and citizenship separate. That was not done here.

But can Quasar, not being a Japanese company in the technical sense in which this term is used in the treaty, rely on the treaty even to the limited extent suggested? *Sumitomo Shoji America, Inc. v. Avagliano*, 457 U.S. 176 (1982), held that an American subsidiary of a foreign parent was not protected by the treaty. But there was no contention that the parent had dictated the subsidiary's discriminatory conduct, and the Court left open the question whether the subsidiary might in such a case assert any of its parent's treaty rights. *Id. at 189 n. 19*. We think it must be allowed to in a case such as this, at least to the extent necessary to prevent the treaty from being set at naught. A judgment that forbids Quasar to give preferential treatment to the expatriate executives that its parent sends would have the same effect on the parent as it would have if it ran directly against the parent: it would prevent Matsushita from sending its own executives to manage Quasar in preference to employing American citizens in these posts. Note, *"Subsidiary Assertion of Foreign Parent Corporation Rights Under Commercial Treaties to Hire Employees 'Of Their Choice,'"* 86 COLUM. L. REV. 139 (1986).

But suppose a Japanese company buys an American company, fires all of its new subsidiary's occidental executives because it is prejudiced against occidentals, and replaces them with Japanese citizens. The question would then arise whether the treaty of friendship in effect confers a blanket immunity from Title VII. On this there are different views. Compare *MacNamara v. Korean Air Lines, supra*, and *Linskey v. Heidelberg Eastern, Inc.*, 470 F. Supp. 1181, 1185-87 (E.D. N.Y. 1979), with *Spiess v. C. Itoh & Co. (America), Inc.*, 643 F.2d 353 (5th Cir. 1981), vacated on other grounds, 457 U.S. 1128 (1982). We need not choose sides in this case, because (setting to one side the question of age discrimination, discussed next) there is no evidence of discrimination here save what is implicit in wanting your own citizens to run your foreign subsidiary. There is no evidence that if John Fortino had had three or for that matter four Japanese grandparents he would not have been fired. No favoritism was shown Quasar's Japanese-American employees, which would have been true national-origin discrimination since they are not citizens of Japan; and whatever his ancestry, Fortino would have had the irremediable disability of not being an executive of Matsushita. That was the real source of the "prejudice" against him, and it is not prejudice based on national origin. It may have had a similar effect to national-origin prejudice (though not identical – for look what happened to Quasar's Japanese-American employees) because of the correlation between citizenship and national origin, but the treaty prevents equating the two forms of discrimination or, what as a practical matter would amount to the same thing, allowing the first to be used to prove the second. If this conclusion seems callous toward the Americans who lost their jobs at Quasar, we remind that the rights granted by the treaty are reciprocal. There are Americans employed abroad by foreign subsidiaries of U.S. companies who, but for the treaty, would lose their jobs to foreign nationals. Indeed, the treaty provision was inserted at the insistence of the United States. Japan was opposed to it. *Sumitomo Shoji America, Inc. v. Avagliano, supra,* 457 U.S. at 181 n. 6.

The Title VII claim must be dismissed, which leaves the age discrimination claim. We agree with the plaintiffs that there was enough evidence of age discrimination to make a jury issue, but we agree with Quasar that there must be a new trial because of trial error. We also agree that plaintiff Fortino's claim is barred altogether by the release that he executed. Let us begin with the release. Fortino executed a release of all pertinent claims against Quasar, including the age discrimination and Title VII claims, in exchange for additional severance benefits. The release is unambiguous, and indeed emphatic and comprehensive to the nth degree, as shown by the following paragraph:

As a material inducement to the Company to enter into this Agreement, I hereby irrevocably and unconditionally release, acquit and forever discharge the Company and each of the Company's predecessors, successors, assigns, agents, directors, officers, employees, attorneys, divisions, subsidiaries, affiliates (and agents, directors, officers, employees, representatives and attorneys of such parent companies, divisions, subsidiaries and affiliates), and all person acting by, through, under or in concert with any of them (collectively "Releasees"), or any of them, from any and all charges, complaints, claims, liabilities, obligations, promises, agreements, controversies, damages, actions, causes of action, suits, rights, demands, costs, losses, debts and expenses (including attorneys' fees and costs actually incurred) of any nature whatsoever, known or unknown, suspected or unsuspected, including but not limited to, rights under federal, state or local laws prohibiting age or other forms of discrimination, claims growing out of any legal restrictions on the Company's right to terminate its employees ("Claim" or "Claims"), which I now have, own or hold, or claim to have, own or hold, or which I at any time heretofore have, owned or held, or claimed to have, own or hold, which I at any time hereinafter may have, own or hold or claim to have, own or hold against each or any of the Releasees.

We cannot imagine a more emphatic release, and nothing in the circumstances of its execution indicates that it should not be given the force that its words convey. Fortino, a business executive of more than twenty years' experience, educated, and earning in excess of $60,000, was not rushed to sign the release, and was told he could consult a lawyer before signing. Fortino testified that he didn't understand a lot of the terms, like "predecessors" and "successors." He should have. Anyway those particular terms are not germane; he is not trying to sue any predecessor or successor to Quasar. Fortino's wife showed the release to a lawyer at her place of work and he advised her, and through her Fortino, to sign the release and take the benefits because it would not stand up in court. Fortino signed, and took. The judge allowed the jury to consider whether Fortino understood the release, and it found he did not. The jury's conclusion went beyond the bounds of reason, and if upheld would make all accords and satisfactions, and perhaps all contracts, unenforceable.

We might as an original matter have supposed that the validity of a release of legal claims would be governed by the ordinary principles of contract law – a release of federal claims either by federal common law, the approach this court took in *Taylor v. Gordon Flesch Co.*, 793 F.2d 858, 862 (7th Cir. 1986), or by state law, as suggested in *Morgan v. South Bend Community*

School Corp., 797 F.2d 471, 474-76 (7th Cir. 1986), and *Dhaliwal v. Woods Division*, 930 F.2d 547, 548-49 (7th Cir. 1991). Then Fortino would lose because he does not argue fraud, unconscionability, duress, or other conventional defenses to the enforcement of a contract. A number of the cases dealing with the validity of releases of federal discrimination claims, however, have sorted the question into the waiver bin rather than the contract bin, and examined circumstances probative of the question whether the plaintiff's waiver of his legal claims was truly voluntary. Examples are *Bormann v. AT&T Communications, Inc.*, 875 F.2d 399, 403 (2d Cir. 1989), and *Coventry v. U.S. Steel Corp.*, 856 F.2d 514, 522-23 (3d Cir. 1988), and from this court *Riley v. American Family Mutual Ins. Co.*, 881 F.2d 368, 374 (7th Cir. 1989), where we suggested that if "a plaintiff is represented by counsel who actively negotiates the release," the plaintiff will be deemed to have made an effective waiver of the claims released, unless fraud or duress or other such "vitiating circumstances" are proved. Here the representation was indirect and the release was not negotiated, but that cannot be the end of the inquiry. Representation and negotiation cannot be the sine qua non of an effective waiver. If criminal defendants can effectively waive assistance of counsel, as of course they can, so can persons asked to release civil claims. And there is no suggestion that Quasar would have refused to negotiate over the terms of the release if requested to do so, which it was not. Even courts that follow a "totality of circumstances" approach, discussed in *id.* at 372, to the question of waiver would be bound to find that Fortino had made an effective release. For of the seven circumstances that these courts have identified, only one favors Fortino ("the role of plaintiff in deciding the terms of the agreement") – and that actually is ambiguous, since for all we know Fortino could have negotiated for better terms had he chosen to do so. He did not, because he thought he could have his cake and eat it. Quasar argues ratification as a back-up to its claim that the release was voluntary. We need not address the argument. If you sign a release knowing what you are giving up but believing on a lawyer's erroneous advice that really you're giving up nothing because the release is unenforceable, you are bound by your decision. *Id.* at 374; *Taylor v. Gordon Flesch Co., supra*, 793 F.2d at 864; *Pilon v. University of Minnesota*, 710 F.2d 466, 468 (8th Cir. 1983). Otherwise no releases, no accords and satisfactions, no contracts, period, would be enforceable against a party who became dissatisfied with the deal he had struck.

Some day we may have to choose among the three approaches that are on the table concerning the law governing settlements of federal antidiscrimination laws: federal common law, state law, waiver doctrine – and the last comes in several varieties. But not today. Under any approach, Fortino must lose. . . .

The judgment is reversed with directions to enter judgment for the defendant on the Title VII claims, to dismiss Fortino, and to conduct a new trial, consistent with this opinion, on Meyers' and Schulz's claims of age discrimination.

REVERSED AND REMANDED, WITH DIRECTIONS.

TOYOTA V. WILLIAMS

534 U.S. 184 (2002)

JUSTICE O'CONNOR delivered the opinion of the Court.

Under the Americans with Disabilities Act of 1990 (ADA or Act), 104 Stat. 328, 42 U.S.C. § 12101 *et seq.* (1994 ed. and Supp. V), a physical impairment that "substantially limits one or more . . . major life activities" is a "disability." 42 U.S.C. § 12102(2) (A) (1994 ed.). Respondent, claiming to be disabled because of her carpal tunnel syndrome and other related impairments, sued petitioner, her former employer, for failing to provide her with a reasonable accommodation as required by the ADA. See § 12112 (b) (5) (A). The District Court granted summary judgment to petitioner, finding that respondent's impairments did not substantially limit any of her major life activities. The Court of Appeals for the Sixth Circuit reversed, finding that the impairments substantially limited respondent in the major life activity of performing manual tasks, and therefore granting partial summary judgment to respondent on the issue of whether she was disabled under the ADA. We conclude that the Court of Appeals did not apply the proper standard in making this determination because it analyzed only a limited class of manual tasks and failed to ask whether respondent's impairments prevented or restricted her from performing tasks that are of central importance to most people's daily lives.

I

Respondent began working at petitioner's automobile manufacturing plant in Georgetown, Kentucky, in August 1990. She was soon placed on an engine fabrication assembly line, where her duties included work with pneumatic tools. Use of these tools eventually caused pain in respondent's hands, wrists, and arms. She sought treatment at petitioner's in-house medical service, where she was diagnosed with bilateral carpal tunnel syndrome and bilateral tendinitis. Respondent consulted a personal physician who placed her on permanent work restrictions that precluded her from lifting more than 20 pounds or from "frequently lifting or carrying of objects weighing up to 10 pounds," engaging in "constant repetitive . . . flexion or extension of [her] wrists or elbows" performing "overhead work," or using "vibratory or pneumatic tools." Brief for Respondent.

In light of these restrictions, for the next two years petitioner assigned respondent to various modified duty jobs. Nonetheless, respondent missed some work for medical leave, and eventually filed a claim under the Kentucky Workers' Compensation Act. Ky. Rev. Stat. Ann. § 342.0011 *et seq.* (1997 and Supp. 2000). The parties settled this claim, and respondent returned to work. She was unsatisfied by petitioner's efforts to accommodate her work restrictions, however, and responded by bringing an action in the United States District Court for the Eastern District of Kentucky alleging that petitioner had violated the ADA by refusing to accommodate her disability. That suit was also settled, and as part of the settlement, respondent returned to work in December 1993.

Upon her return, petitioner placed respondent on a team in Quality Control Inspection Operations (QCIO). QCIO is responsible for four tasks: (1) "assembly paint"; (2) "paint second inspection"; (3) "shell body audit"; and (4) "ED surface repair." App. 19. Respondent was initially placed on a team that performed only the first two of these tasks, and for a couple of years, she rotated on a weekly basis between them. In assembly paint, respondent visually inspected painted cars moving slowly down a conveyor. She scanned for scratches, dents, chips, or any other flaws that may have occurred during the assembly or painting process, at a rate of one car every 54 seconds. When respondent began working in assembly paint, inspection team members were required to open and shut the doors, trunk, and/or hood of each passing car. Sometime during respondent's tenure, however, the position was modified to include only visual inspection with few or no manual tasks. Paint second inspection required team members to use their hands to wipe each painted car with a glove as it moved along a conveyor. *Id.*, at 21-22. The parties agree that respondent was physically capable of performing both of these jobs and that her performance was satisfactory.

During the fall of 1996, petitioner announced that it wanted QCIO employees to be able to rotate through all four of the QCIO processes. Respondent therefore received training for the shell body audit job, in which team members apply a highlight oil to the hood, fender, doors, rear quarter panel, and trunk of passing cars at a rate of approximately one car per minute. The highlight oil has the viscosity of salad oil, and employees spread it on cars with a sponge attached to a block of wood. After they wipe each car with the oil, the employees visually inspect it for flaws. Wiping the cars required respondent to hold her hands and arms up around shoulder height for several hours at a time.

A short while after the shell body audit job was added to respondent's rotations, she began to experience pain in her neck and shoulders. Respondent again sought care at petitioner's in-house medical service, where she was diagnosed with myotendinitis bilateral periscapular, an inflammation of the muscles and tendons around both of her shoulder blades; myotendinitis and myositis bilateral forearms with nerve compression causing median nerve irritation; and thoracic outlet compression, a condition that causes pain in the nerves that lead to the upper extremities. Respondent requested that petitioner accommodate her medical conditions by allowing her to return to doing only her original two jobs in QCIO, which respondent claimed she could still perform without difficulty.

The parties disagree about what happened next. According to respondent, petitioner refused her request and forced her to continue working in the shell body audit job, which caused her even greater physical injury. According to petitioner, respondent simply began missing work on a regular basis. Regardless, it is clear that on December 6, 1996, the last day respondent worked at petitioner's plant, she was placed under a no-work-of-any-kind restriction by her treating physicians. On January 27, 1997, respondent received a letter from petitioner that terminated her employment, citing her poor attendance record.

Respondent filed a charge of disability discrimination with the Equal Employment Opportunity Commission (EEOC). After receiving a right to sue letter, respondent filed suit against petitioner in the United States District Court for the Eastern District of Kentucky. Her complaint alleged that petitioner had violated the ADA and the Kentucky Civil Rights Act, Ky. Rev. Stat. Ann. § 344.010 *et seq.* (1997 and Supp. 2000), by failing to reasonably accommodate her disability and by terminating her employment. Respondent later amended her complaint to also allege a violation of of the Family and Medical Leave Act of 1993 (FMLA), 107 Stat. 6, as amended, 29 U.S.C. § 2601 *et seq.* (1994 ed. and Supp. V).

Respondent based her claim that she was "disabled" under the ADA on the ground that her physical impairments substantially limited her in (1) manual tasks; (2) housework; (3) gardening; (4) playing with her children; (5) lifting; and (6) working, all of which, she argued, constituted major life activities under the Act. Respondent also argued, in the alternative, that she was disabled under the ADA because she had a record of a substantially limiting impairment and because she was regarded as having such an impairment. See 42 U.S.C. § § 12102(2) (B-C) (1994 ed.).

After petitioner filed a motion for summary judgment and respondent filed a motion for partial summary judgment on her disability claims, the District Court granted summary judgment to petitioner. The court found that respondent had not been disabled, as defined by the ADA, at the time of petitioner's alleged refusal to accommodate her, and that she had therefore not been covered by the Act's protections or by the Kentucky Civil Rights Act, which is construed consistently with the ADA. The District Court held that respondent had suffered from a physical impairment, but that the impairment did not qualify as a disability because it had not "substantially limited" any "major life activity," 42 U.S.C. § 12102(2) (A). The court rejected respondent's arguments that gardening, doing housework, and playing with children are major life activities. Although the court agreed that performing manual tasks, lifting, and working are major life activities, it found the evidence insufficient to demonstrate that respondent had been substantially limited in lifting or working. The court found respondent's claim that she was substantially limited in performing manual tasks to be "irretrievably contradicted by [respondent's] continual insistence that she could perform the tasks in assembly [paint] and paint [second] inspection without difficulty." The court also found no evidence that respondent had had a record of a substantially limiting impairment, or that petitioner had regarded her as having such an impairment.

The District Court also rejected respondent's claim that her termination violated the ADA and the Kentucky Civil Rights Act. The court found that even if it assumed that respondent was disabled at the time of her termination, she was not a "qualified individual with a disability," 42 U.S.C. § 12111 (8) (1994 ed.), because, at that time, her physicians had restricted her from performing work of any kind. Finally, the court found that respondent's FMLA claim failed, because she had not presented evidence that she had suffered any damages available under the FMLA.

Respondent appealed all but the gardening, housework, and playing-with-children rulings. The Court of Appeals for the Sixth Circuit reversed the District Court's ruling on whether respondent was disabled at the time she sought an accommodation, but affirmed the District Court's rulings on respondent's FMLA and wrongful termination claims.. The Court of Appeals held that in order for respondent to demonstrate that she was disabled due to a substantial limitation in the ability to perform manual tasks at the time of her accommodation request, she had to "show that her manual disability involved a 'class' of manual activities affecting the ability to perform tasks at work". Respondent satisfied this test, according to the Court of Appeals, because her ailments "prevented her from doing the tasks associated with certain types of manual assembly line jobs, manual product handling jobs and manual building trade jobs (painting, plumbing, roofing, etc.) that require the gripping of tools and repetitive work with hands and arms extended at or above shoulder levels for extended periods of time." In reaching this conclusion, the court disregarded evidence that respondent could "tend to her personal hygiene [and] carry out personal or household chores," finding that such evidence "does not affect a determination that her impairment substantially limited her ability to perform the range of manual tasks associated with an assembly line job," Because the Court of Appeals concluded that respondent had been substantially limited in performing manual tasks and, for that reason, was entitled to partial summary judgment on the issue of whether she was disabled under the Act, it found that it did not need to determine whether respondent had been substantially limited in the major life activities of lifting or working, or whether she had had a "record of" a disability or had been "regarded as" disabled.

We granted certiorari to consider the proper standard for assessing whether an individual is substantially limited in performing manual tasks. We now reverse the Court of Appeals' decision to grant partial summary judgment to respondent on the issue whether she was substantially limited in performing manual tasks at the time she sought an accommodation.

We express no opinion on the working, lifting, or other arguments for disability status that were preserved below but which were not ruled upon by the Court of Appeals.

II

The ADA requires covered entities, including private employers, to provide "reasonable accommodations to the known physical or mental limitations of an otherwise qualified individual with a disability who is an applicant or employee, unless such covered entity can demonstrate that the accommodation would impose an undue hardship." 42 U.S.C. § 12112 (b) (5) (A) (1994 ed.); see also § 12111(2) ("The term 'covered entity' means an employer, employment agency, labor organization, or joint labor-management committee"). The Act defines a "qualified individual with a disability" as "an individual with a disability who, with or without reasonable accommodation, can perform the essential functions of the employment position that such individual holds or desires." § 12111(8). In turn, a "disability" is:

(A) a physical or mental impairment that substantially limits one or more of the major life activities of such individual;

(B) a record of such an impairment; or

(C) being regarded as having such an impairment. § 12102 (2).

There are two potential sources of guidance for interpreting the terms of this definition – the regulations interpreting the Rehabilitation Act of 1973, 87 Stat. 361, as amended, 29 U.S.C. § 706(8)(B) (1988 ed.), and the EEOC regulations interpreting the ADA. Congress drew the ADA's definition of disability almost verbatim from the definition of "handicapped individual" in the Rehabilitation Act, § 706(8)(B), and Congress' repetition of a well-established term generally implies that Congress intended the term to be construed in accordance with pre-existing regulatory interpretations. *Bragdon v. Abbott*, 524 U.S. 624, 631 (1998); *FDIC v. Philadelphia Gear Corp.*, 476 U.S. 426, 437-438 (1986); *ICC v. Parker*, 326 U.S. 60, 65 (1945). As we explained in *Bragdon v. Abbott,*, Congress did more in the ADA than suggest this construction; it adopted a specific statutory provision directing as follows:

"Except as otherwise provided in this chapter, nothing in this chapter shall be construed to apply a lesser standard than the standards applied under title V of the Rehabilitation Act of 1973 (29 U.S.C. 790 *et seq.*) or the regulations issued by Federal agencies pursuant to such title." 42 U.S.C. § 12201 (a) (1994 ed.)

The persuasive authority of the EEOC regulations is less clear. As we have previously noted, see *Sutton v. United Air Lines, Inc.*, 527 U.S. 471, 479, 144 L. Ed. 2d 450, 119 S. Ct. 2139 (1999), no agency has been given authority to issue regulations interpreting the term "disability" in the ADA. Nonetheless, the EEOC has done so. See 29 CFR §§ 1630.2(g)-(j) (2001). Because both parties accept the EEOC regulations as reasonable, we assume without deciding that they are, and we have no occasion to decide what level of deference, if any, they are due.

To qualify as disabled under subsection (A) of the ADA's definition of disability, a claimant must initially prove that he or she has a physical or mental impairment. See 42 U.S.C. § 12102(2) (A). The Rehabilitation Act regulations issued by the Department of Health, Education, and Welfare (HEW) in 1977, which appear without change in the current regulations issued by the Department of Health and Human Services, define "physical impairment," the type of impairment relevant to this case, to mean "any physiological disorder or condition, cosmetic disfigurement, or anatomical loss affecting one or more of the following body systems: neurological; musculoskeletal; special sense organs; respiratory, including speech organs; cardiovascular; reproductive, digestive, genito-urinary; hemic and lymphatic; skin; and endocrine." 45 CFR § 84.3(j) (2)(i) (2001). The HEW regulations are of particular significance because at the time they were issued, HEW was the agency responsible for coordinating the implementation and enforcement of § 504 of the Rehabilitation Act, 29 U.S.C. § 794 (1994 ed. and Supp. V), which prohibits discrimination against individuals with disabilities by recipients of federal financial assistance. *Bragdon v. Abbott* (citing *Consolidated Rail Corporation v. Darrone*, 465 U.S. 624, 634 (1984)).

Merely having an impairment does not make one disabled for purposes of the ADA. Claimants also need to demonstrate that the impairment limits a major life activity. See 42 U.S.C. § 12102(2) (A) (1994 ed.). The HEW Rehabilitation Act regulations provide a list of examples of "major life activities," that includes "walking, seeing, hearing," and, as relevant here, "performing manual tasks." 45 CFR § 84.3(j)(2)(ii) (2001).

To qualify as disabled, a claimant must further show that the limitation on the major life activity is "substantial." 42 U.S.C. § 12102(2) (A). Unlike "physical impairment" and "major life activities," the HEW regulations do not define the term "substantially limits." See Nondiscrimination on the Basis of Handicap in Programs and Activities Receiving or Benefiting from Federal Financial Assistance, 42 Fed. Reg. 22676, 22685 (1977) (stating the Department of Health, Education, and Welfare's position that a definition of "substantially limits" was not possible at that time). The EEOC, therefore, has created its own definition for purposes of the ADA. According to the EEOC regulations, "substantially limited" means "unable to perform a major life activity that the average person in the general population can perform"; or "significantly restricted as to the condition, manner or duration under which an individual can perform a particular major life activity as compared to the condition, manner, or duration under which the average person in the general population can perform that same major life activity." 29 CFR § 1630.2(j) (2001). In determining whether an individual is substantially limited in a major life activity, the regulations instruct that the following factors should be considered: "the nature and severity of the impairment; the duration or expected duration of the impairment; and the permanent or long-term impact, or the expected permanent or long-term impact of or resulting from the impairment." § § 1630.2 (j) (2) (i)-(iii).

III

The question presented by this case is whether the Sixth Circuit properly determined that respondent was disabled under subsection (A) of the ADA's disability definition at the time that she sought an accommodation from petitioner. 42 U.S.C. § 12102 (2) (A). The parties do not dispute that respondent's medical conditions, which include carpal tunnel syndrome, myotendinitis, and thoracic outlet compression, amount to physical impairments. The relevant question, therefore, is whether the Sixth Circuit correctly analyzed whether these impairments substantially limited respondent in the major life activity of performing manual tasks. Answering this requires us to address an issue about which the EEOC regulations are silent: what a plaintiff must demonstrate to establish a substantial limitation in the specific major life activity of performing manual tasks.

Our consideration of this issue is guided first and foremost by the words of the disability definition itself. "Substantially" in the phrase "substantially limits" suggests "considerable" or "to a large degree." See WEBSTER'S THIRD NEW INTERNATIONAL DICTIONARY 2280 (1976) (defining "substantially" as "in a substantial manner" and "substantial" as "considerable in amount, value, or worth" and "being that specified to a large degree or in the main"); see also 17 Oxford English Dictionary 66-67 (2d ed. 1989) ("substantial": "relating to or proceeding from the essence of a thing; essential"; "of ample or considerable amount, quantity, or dimensions"). The word "substantial" thus clearly precludes impairments that interfere in only a minor way with the performance of manual tasks from qualifying as disabilities. *Cf. Albertson's, Inc. v. Kirkingburg,* 527 U.S. at 565 (explaining that a "mere difference" does not amount to a "significant restriction" and therefore does not satisfy the EEOC's interpretation of "substantially limits").

"Major" in the phrase "major life activities" means important. See Webster's, *supra*, at 1363 (defining "major" as "greater in dignity, rank, importance, or interest"). "Major life activities" thus refers to those activities that are of central importance to daily life. In order for performing manual tasks to fit into this category – a category that includes such basic abilities as walking, seeing, and hearing – the manual tasks in question must be central to daily life. If each of the tasks included in the major life activity of performing manual tasks does not independently qualify as a major life activity, then together they must do so.

That these terms need to be interpreted strictly to create a demanding standard for qualifying as disabled is confirmed by the first section of the ADA, which lays out the legislative findings and purposes that motivate the Act. See 42 U.S.C. § 12101. When it enacted the ADA in 1990, Congress found that "some 43,000,000 Americans have one or more physical or mental disabilities." § 12101(a) (1). If Congress intended everyone with a physical impairment that precluded the performance of some isolated, unimportant, or particularly difficult manual task to qualify as disabled, the number of disabled Americans would surely have been much higher. *Cf. Sutton v. United Air Lines, Inc.,* 527 U.S. at 487 (finding that because more than 100 million people need corrective lenses to see properly, "had Congress intended to include all persons with corrected physical limitations among those covered by the Act, it undoubtedly would have cited a much higher number than 43 million disabled persons in the findings").

We therefore hold that to be substantially limited in performing manual tasks, an individual must have an impairment that prevents or severely restricts the individual from doing activities that are of central importance to most people's daily lives. The impairment's impact must also be permanent or long-term. See 29 CFR § § 1630.2(j) (2) (ii)-(iii) (2001).

It is insufficient for individuals attempting to prove disability status under this test to merely submit evidence of a medical diagnosis of an impairment. Instead, the ADA requires those "claiming the Act's protection . . . to prove a disability by offering evidence that the extent of the limitation [caused by their impairment] in terms of their own experience . . . is substantial." *Albertson's, Inc. v. Kirkingburg, supra,* at 567 (holding that monocular vision is not invariably a disability, but must be analyzed on an individual basis, taking into account the individual's ability to compensate for the impairment). That the Act defines "disability" "with respect to an individual," 42 U.S.C. § 12102(2), makes clear that Congress intended the existence of a disability to be determined in such a case-by-case manner. An individualized assessment of the effect of an impairment is particularly necessary when the impairment is one whose symptoms vary widely from person to person. Carpal tunnel syndrome, one of respondent's impairments, is just such a condition. While cases of severe carpal tunnel syndrome are characterized by muscle atrophy and extreme sensory deficits, mild cases generally do not have either of these effects and create only intermittent symptoms of numbness and tingling. Carniero, Carpal Tunnel Syndrome: The Cause Dictates the Treatment, 66 Cleveland

Clinic J. Medicine 159, 161-162 (1999). Studies have further shown that, even without surgical treatment, one quarter of carpal tunnel cases resolve in one month, but that in 22 percent of cases, symptoms last for eight years or longer. See DeStefano, Nordstrom, & Uierkant, Long-term Symptom Outcomes of Carpal Tunnel Syndrome and its Treatment, 22A J. Hand Surgery 200, 204-205 (1997). When pregnancy is the cause of carpal tunnel syndrome, in contrast, the symptoms normally resolve within two weeks of delivery. See Ouellette, Nerve Compression Syndromes of the Upper Extremity in Women, 17 Journal of Musculoskeletal Medicine 536 (2000). Given these large potential differences in the severity and duration of the effects of carpal tunnel syndrome, an individual's carpal tunnel syndrome diagnosis, on its own, does not indicate whether the individual has a disability within the meaning of the ADA.

IV

The Court of Appeals' analysis of respondent's claimed disability suggested that in order to prove a substantial limitation in the major life activity of performing manual tasks, a "plaintiff must show that her manual disability involves a 'class' of manual activities," and that those activities "affect the ability to perform tasks at work." Both of these ideas lack support.

The Court of Appeals relied on our opinion in *Sutton v. United Air Lines, Inc.*, for the idea that a "class" of manual activities must be implicated for an impairment to substantially limit the major life activity of performing manual tasks. But *Sutton* said only that *"when the major life activity under consideration is that of working*, the statutory phrase 'substantially limits' requires . . . that plaintiffs allege that they are unable to work in a broad class of jobs." 527 U.S. 471 at 491 (emphasis added). Because of the conceptual difficulties inherent in the argument that working could be a major life activity, we have been hesitant to hold as much, and we need not decide this difficult question today. In *Sutton*, we noted that even assuming that working is a major life activity, a claimant would be required to show an inability to work in a "broad range of jobs," rather than a specific job. But *Sutton* did not suggest that a class-based analysis should be applied to any major life activity other than working. Nor do the EEOC regulations. In defining "substantially limits," the EEOC regulations only mention the "class" concept in the context of the major life activity of working. 29 CFR § 1630.2(j)(3) (2001) ("With respect to the major life activity of *working*[,] the term *substantially limits* means significantly restricted in the ability to perform either a class of jobs or a broad range of jobs in various classes as compared to the average person having comparable training, skills and abilities"). Nothing in the text of the Act, our previous opinions, or the regulations suggests that a class-based framework should apply outside the context of the major life activity of working.

While the Court of Appeals in this case addressed the different major life activity of performing manual tasks, its analysis circumvented *Sutton* by focusing on respondent's inability to perform manual tasks associated only with her job. This was error. When addressing the major life activity of performing manual tasks, the central inquiry must be whether the claimant is unable to perform the variety of tasks central to most people's daily lives, not whether the claimant is unable to perform the tasks associated with her specific job. Otherwise, *Sutton*'s restriction on claims of disability based on a substantial limitation in working will be rendered meaningless because an inability to perform a specific job always can be recast as an inability to perform a "class" of tasks associated with that specific job.

There is also no support in the Act, our previous opinions, or the regulations for the Court of Appeals' idea that the question of whether an impairment constitutes a disability is to be answered only by analyzing the effect of the impairment in the workplace. Indeed, the fact that the Act's definition of "disability" applies not only to Title I of the Act, 42 U.S.C. §§ 12111-12117 (1994 ed.), which deals with employment, but also to the other portions of the Act, which deal with subjects such as public transportation, §§ 12141-12150, 42 U.S.C. §§ 12161-12165 (1994 ed. and Supp. V), and privately provided public accommodations, §§ 12181-12189, demonstrates that the definition is intended to cover individuals with disabling impairments regardless of whether the individuals have any connection to a workplace.

Even more critically, the manual tasks unique to any particular job are not necessarily important parts of most people's lives. As a result, occupation-specific tasks may have only limited relevance to the manual task inquiry. In this case, "repetitive work with hands and arms extended at or above shoulder levels for extended periods of time," the manual task on which the Court of Appeals relied, is not an important part of most people's daily lives. The court, therefore, should not have considered respondent's inability to do such manual work in her specialized assembly line job as sufficient proof that she was substantially limited in performing manual tasks.

At the same time, the Court of Appeals appears to have disregarded the very type of evidence that it should have focused upon. It treated as irrelevant "the fact that [respondent] can . . . tend to her personal hygiene [and] carry out personal or household chores." Yet household chores, bathing, and brushing one's teeth are among the types of manual tasks of central importance to people's daily lives, and should have been part of the assessment of whether respondent was substantially limited in performing manual tasks.

The District Court noted that at the time respondent sought an accommodation from petitioner, she admitted that she was able to do the manual tasks required by her original two jobs in QCIO. In addition, according to respondent's deposition testimony, even after her condition worsened, she could still brush her teeth, wash her face, bathe, tend her flower garden, fix breakfast, do laundry, and pick up around the house. The record also indicates that her medical conditions caused her to avoid sweeping, to quit dancing, to occasionally seek help dressing, and to reduce how often she plays with her children, gardens, and drives long distances. But these changes in her life did not amount to such severe restrictions in the activities that are of central importance to most people's daily lives that they establish a manual-task disability as a matter of law. On this record, it was therefore inappropriate for the Court of Appeals to grant partial summary judgment to respondent on the issue whether she was substantially limited in performing manual tasks, and its decision to do so must be reversed.

In its brief on the merits, petitioner asks us to reinstate the District Court's grant of summary judgment to petitioner on the manual task issue. In its petition for certiorari, however, petitioner did not seek summary judgment; it argued only that the Court of Appeals' reasons for granting partial summary judgment to respondent were unsound. This Court's Rule 14(1)(a) provides: "Only the questions set out in the petition, or fairly included therein, will be considered by the Court." The question whether petitioner was entitled to summary judgment on the manual task issue is therefore not properly before us. See *Irvine v. California*, 347 U.S. 128, 129-130 (1954).

Accordingly, we reverse the Court of Appeals' judgment granting partial summary judgment to respondent and remand the case for further proceedings consistent with this opinion.

So ordered.

Notes

1. All three cases were unanimous decisions, that is, no dissenting or concurring opinions. In each case, to what extent is that outcome because of the narrow question of law presented? Was Sumitomo wise to pursue an appeal in the face of opposition from both the U.S. and Japanese governments? The U.S. Constitution confers authority over foreign affairs and commerce to the executive and legislative branches. The role of the judiciary is decidedly secondary and deferential. In the words of Chief Justice Burger, "[o]ur role is limited to giving effect to the intent of the Treaty parties."

2. Plaintiffs in *Sumitomo* had alleged that only male Japanese citizens were hired to fill executive, managerial, and sales positions. Assuming that these allegations could be proved, was Sumitomo "simply" replicating in its U.S. operations the employment patterns it practiced in Japan? Would it be convincing to argue that Sumitomo was creating jobs in the United States, even if they were not high-level, highly skilled, well-paying jobs? As U.S.-based TNCs increasingly outsource employment to foreign locations, are foreign-based TNCs operating in the United States being subjected to unequal treatment with respect to job creation?

3. In *Fortino v. Quasar*, defendant did not argue that the FCN treaty provided a defense to Title VII. Did defendant learn from the experience of Sumitomo? Should it have argued that Japanese citizenship was a BFOQ or that it had a business necessity defense? In a footnote, Chief Justice Burger stated:

   > We express no view as to whether Japanese citizenship may be a bona fide occupational qualification for certain positions at Sumitomo or as to whether a business necessity defense may be available.

4. In *Fortino*, plaintiffs were discharged in the wake of a year when the company had lost $20 million. Under U.S. law an employer does not have to be in difficult financial straits to justify dismissal of even long-term employees. *See Bammert v. Don's Super-Valu, Inc.* in the chapter on U.S. law. Japanese law is otherwise, as we have discovered.

5. Fortino signed a release in exchange for additional severance benefits. In enforcing the release, Judge Posner observes:

   > Fortino, a business executive of more than twenty years' experience, educated, and earning in excess of $60,000, was not rushed to sign the release, and was told he could consult a lawyer before signing. . . . Fortino's wife showed the release to a lawyer at her place of work and he advised her, and through her Fortino, to sign the release and take the benefits because it would not stand up in court. Fortino signed, and took. . . . [H]e thought he could have his cake and eat it.

6. In *Toyota v. Williams*, Justice O'Connor does not address the fact that the employer was a Japanese transplant or that it utilized lean production methods. Are these factors relevant? If Williams could not, or would not, perform one or more tasks assigned to her team, then the other members of the team would have to pick up the slack. In effect, they would be performing more work for the same pay. In her recitation of the facts, Justice O'Connor does take note of accommodations made when Williams developed carpal tunnel syndrome and bilateral tendonitis. It appears that Williams had only worked at the plant for about a year before developing physical

problems. Initially, she claimed physical impairments which affected her at home as well as in the workplace. But the record shows that notwithstanding her physical impairments she could still attend to her personal hygiene and perform household chores. Does Justice O'Connor's narrative suggest suspicion that Williams was a "shirker" and not really disabled for purposes of the ADA?

———————

13 India

A. INTRODUCTION TO THE HISTORICAL AND SOCIAL CONTEXT

As the world's second most populous country after China, India is, at the same time, the world's largest democracy. Where China and other developing countries sought economic progress through the imposition of one-party, authoritarian rule, since gaining independence in 1947, modern India has pursued the three strands of a "seamless web:" national unity and integrity, the institutions and spirit of democracy, and socioeconomic revolution to better the material lot of the masses. The framers of India's Constitution were motivated by the belief that these three strands were "mutually dependent and inextricably intertwined," no one strand should be advanced at the expense of another. GRANVILLE AUSTIN, WORKING A DEMOCRATIC CONSTITUTION: A HISTORY OF THE INDIAN EXPERIENCE 6 (1999).

The reality at present is quite far from achievement of these noble goals. National unity is precariously maintained in the face of border conflict with India's neighbors, Pakistan and China, and frequent police actions to quell separatist movements and interreligious conflicts. Political power is centralized in the prime minister, the Cabinet, and the top echelons of the administrative bureaucracy. Prime ministers insulate – and isolate – themselves by relying on an inner circle of loyal advisers. Although more representative of the population at large than at Independence, Parliament occupies a diminished role as the power of the executive branch has grown. The civil service, once the favored destination of the best and the brightest, is widely regarded as impersonal, inflexible, and corrupt. See C. Raj Kumar, *Corruption and Human Rights: Promoting Transparency in Governance and the Fundamental Right to Corrupt-Free Service in India*, 17 COLUM. J. ASIAN L. 31 (2003). The one branch of government which is still held in high respect, at least its upper echelons, is the judiciary. "The Supreme Court's Delphic pronouncements carry almost mythical power in India." Balakrishnan Rajagopal, *The Role of Law in Counter-hegemonic Globalization and Global Legal Pluralism: Lessons from the Narmada Valley Struggle in India*, 18 LEIDEN J. INT'L L. 345, 374 (2005). *See* Judicial Activism and Public Interest Litigation, *infra*.

More than a half century after Independence, approximately 60 percent of the workforce is still engaged in agricultural activities, which account for but 25 percent of Gross Domestic Product (GDP). The manufacturing sector produces about 25 percent of GDP, and services about 50 percent. 2nd National Labour Commission Report (2002), Table 4.2 (Share of GDP at Factor Cost by Economic Activity) http://www.labour.nic.in/lcomm2/nlc_report.html. Furthermore, 34.7 percent of the population lives on less than $1.00 a day and 79.9 percent lives on less than $2.00 a day. United Nations Development Programme (2004), Human Development Indicators, http://hdr.undp.org/statistics/data/indicators.cfm?x=23, 24&y=1&z=1. The comparable figures for China are 16.6 percent and 46.7 percent, respectively. India ranks 127 out of 177 countries on the UNDP's Human Development Index; China ranks 86.

In the view of Indian-born Nobel Prize–winning economist Amartya Sen, widespread poverty abets dysfunctional institutions, and vice versa.

> [The real issues] involve taking note of extensive interconnections between political freedoms and the understanding and fulfillment of economic needs. . . . [P]olitical freedoms can have a major role in providing incentives and information in the solution of acute economic needs. . . . Our conceptualization of economic needs depends crucially on open public debates and discussions, the guaranteeing of which requires insistence on basic political liberty and civil rights.
>
> DEVELOPMENT AS FREEDOM 147–48 (1999).

Compare Chapter 2, The International Labor Organization and International Labor Standards.

Empirical research supports the conclusion that poverty reduction is crucial to resolving one of the most egregious violations of international employment law, that of child labor. Virginia Postrel, *Economic Scene: Research Changes Ideas About Children and Work*, N.Y. TIMES, July 14, 2005, at C2 (as family income rises, children tend to stop working and attend school); *Mehta v. State of Tamil Nadu*, AIR 1997 S.C. 699, para. 9 ("[e]xtreme poverty, lack of opportunity for gainful employment and intermittancy of income and low standards of living are the main reasons for the wide prevalence of child labour [in India]").

In contrast to both China and Japan, which have largely homogeneous cultures, India is extraordinarily diverse. Approximately four-fifths of the population is Hindu, but every major world religion is represented. The biggest religious minority, at about 12 percent, is Muslim, giving India one of the largest Muslim populations of any country. ROBERT L. HARDGRAVE & STANLEY A. KOCHANEK, INDIA: GOVERNMENT AND POLITICS IN A DEVELOPING NATION 15 (6th ed. 2000). The Hindu population is further subdivided into a myriad of castes ("jati"). Although India is often therefore characterized as a "compartmentalized" society, one should resist the notion that it is, or was, fixed and static.

> *Caste as a principle of social order has persisted over millenia.* . . . Political, religious, and economic changes have all affected the caste order. . . . Conquest, migration, emulation, isolation and segregation, occupational specialization, conversion and sectarianism, the incorporation of tribal groups – all led to the addition, fission, and fusion of castes and to changes in their relative standing. . . . *But what endured was a pattern of graded inequality* of corporate groups in which differential access to life chances corresponded in large measure to membership in different communities. (Emphasis supplied.)
>
> MARC GALANTER, COMPETING EQUALITIES: LAW AND THE BACKWARD CLASSES IN INDIA 12–13 (1984).

Another source of India's diversity is that of language. Despite linguistic diversity, China, by contrast, has been unified for millennia by a common written language, and in the twentieth century, by the adoption of Mandarin (putonghua) as the official spoken language. The two major linguistic "families" of India are the Indo-Aryan languages of the North and the Dravidian languages of the South. Each "family" is further subdivided into mutually unintelligible languages. Hindi, an Indo-Aryan language, and English are the two main official languages and the most widely used. But political blocs with separatist tendencies form around various other languages, such as Tamil and Telugu in the south, Punjabi in the north, Marathi in the west, and Bengali in the east.

B. ECONOMIC POLICY AND PERFORMANCE BEFORE AND AFTER 1991

Politically constituted as a democracy, modern India has not pursued a policy of economic growth to the exclusion of other social goals. It rejected both the violent reordering of society which occurred in China as well as the market capitalism of Western countries. Mahatma Gandhi advocated a return to traditional Indian values, uncorrupted by Western materialism, and agricultural villages as the basic units of society.

> The Gandhians' picture of Indian society as it was to be after Independence was at complete odds with the outline of a modern industrial state. Clearly, for Gandhi and his followers, the path ahead was also the road back. . . . In principle, Gandhi's vision of a just economic system was indistinguishable from pure communism. . . . Moreover, Gandhi not only believed that strict limitation of private property and the virtual elimination of the profit motive were basic requirements for a just economic system, he was equally certain that they were crucial to the creation of genuine democracy.
>
> FRANCINE R. FRANKEL, INDIA'S POLITICAL ECONOMY 1947–2004 11–15 (2d ed. 2004).

Aspects of the Gandhian vision still exert a powerful influence on Indian policy makers.

Second Labour Commission Report, http://www.labour.nic.in/lcomm2/2nlc-pdfs/Chap1-2.pdf. (2002). Footnotes and charts have been omitted.

[This Commission, under the aegis of the Ministry of Labour, was appointed in December 1998. The resolution appointing the Commission assigned it two tasks: "(1) to suggest rationalisation of existing laws relating to labour in the organised [i.e., unionized] sector; and (2) to suggest an Umbrella Legislation for ensuring a minimum level of protection to the workers in the unorganised sector."]

2.27 At this point, we should make some reference to the small-scale industries, artisans and craftsmen. The special role that this sector has played in our economy, in achieving our once acclaimed prosperity, has been recognized and hailed from times even before Independence. The products and skills of our artisans and craftsmen once won universal praise for their excellence, quality and uniqueness. They attracted buyers and traders from all over the world. History records how our craftsmen and artisans were persecuted, and how our cottage industries were systematically destroyed to make us dependent on British industries even for essentials for which resources, technical skills and trained workers were available in our country. It is well known that the policy of imperialism and colonialism was to destroy local industry, cart away natural resources where this could be done, exploit immovable resources with profligacy, and convert countries into captive markets. During the struggle for

Independence, and immediately thereafter, there was widespread hope that this process would stop and that small-scale and cottage industries and crafts and artisanry would revive and enter a period of renaissance. Economists as well as national leaders taught the country to look upon "Swadeshi" or the resurrection of indigenous industries as a symbol of Independence and self-reliance, without which there could be, no Independence. It was this conviction that made leaders like Mahatma Gandhi on the one hand, and Jamshedji Tata, Acharya P.C. Ray and others on the other, start movements for the revival of industry, and for building indigenously owned industry. The relation between national Independence and self-reliance and the question whether the goals of national economic policy and the interests of the people of a state can be pursued effectively without retaining the control of economic policy in the hands of those who are answerable to the people, will not lose relevance as long as the concept of the sovereignty of nation-states and their responsibility for the interests and welfare of the people of their territories, retain relevance.

By contrast with Gandhi, Nehru, who served as prime minister during the crucial early period after independence, aspired to build a "strong, centralized, industrialized state" capable of meeting the needs of the impoverished masses and restoring India to a prominent place on the world stage. HARDGRAVE & KOCHANEK, *supra*, at 368. At tremendous, though temporary, cost to political democracy and the rule of law, Indira Gandhi, during her tenure as prime minister in the 1970s, completed important aspects of her father's vision of a government-dominated economy. Entire sectors, including banks, insurance companies, textile mills, iron and steel mills, and wholesale trade in certain agricultural commodities were either nationalized or brought under regulatory control. GRANVILLE AUSTIN, WORKING A DEMOCRATIC CONSTITUTION: A HISTORY OF THE INDIAN EXPERIENCE (1999), Parts II & III. It began the era of the "license raj," when bureaucratic red tape strangled entrepreneurial initiative. The excesses of executive power reached their apex during the Emergency of 1975–77, until Indira Gandhi was voted out of office.

Nonetheless, private business survived, and even benefited from the closing of the economy to foreign competition and investment. India's modern business and industrial conglomerates, such as the House of Birla, the House of Tata, and Reliance Industries are thriving multinational companies. HARDGRAVE & KOCHANEK, *supra*, at 403; Wolfgang Schurer, *India, China, and North Korea: A New Understanding*, 29 FLETCHER F. WORLD AFF. 145, 155 (2005); *Naturally Gifted*, THE ECONOMIST, May 20, 2006 (available on Lexis) (protectionist policies "gave the Indian private banks the space to learn how to grow, and to gain confidence as they went").

By 1991, India's anemic rate of growth, compounded by a balance of payments crisis, produced consensus that a new set of economic policies – tilted towards growth and efficiency – was required to meet the tide of rising expectations and to create employment for an ever-expanding population. Since that time, despite lurches and setbacks, successive governments have relaxed regulatory controls, encouraged foreign investment, and sought greater integration with the world economy. Over the past fifteen years, the economy as a whole has expanded at a much faster rate than previously, with manufacturing and services posting much higher growth rates. Agriculture, where most Indians earn their living, has grown far more slowly. *See The Tiger in Front: A Survey of India and China*, THE ECONOMIST, March 5, 2005; Edward Luce & Khozem Merchant, *From India's Forgotten Fields, A Call for Economic Reform to Lift the Poor*, FINANCIAL TIMES (London), May 18, 2004.

Initially, the judiciary had qualms about "economic liberalization" and disinvestment from the public sector. The *BALCO* case, excerpted and discussed here, is an example of success in gaining judicial approval for privatization of a "sick" government enterprise. Although the original purpose of privatization had been to raise revenue, it eventually came to be seen as an opportunity to revitalize the private sector and to encourage foreign direct investment.

BALCO EMPLOYEES UNION V. UNION OF INDIA

AIR 2002 S.C. 350
http://judis.nic.in/supremecourt/qrydisp.asp?tfnm=18166 (2001)
(excerpts)

KIRPAL, J.

The validity of the decision of the Union of India to disinvest and transfer 51% shares of M/s Bharat Aluminium Company Limited (hereinafter referred to as 'BALCO') is the primary issue in these cases.

BALCO was incorporated in 1965 as a Government of India Undertaking under the Companies Act, 1956. . . . The company is engaged in the manufacture of aluminium and had plants at Korba in the State of Chhattisgarh and Bidhanbag in the State of West Bengal. The Company has integrated aluminium manufacturing plant for the manufacture and sale of aluminium metal including wire rods and semi-fabricated products. . . .

Since 1990–91 successive Central Governments had been planning to disinvest some of the Public Sector Undertakings. In pursuance to the policy of disinvestment by a Resolution dated 23rd August, 1996 the Ministry of Industry (Department of Public Enterprises) Government of India constituted a Public Sector DisInvestment Commission initially for a period of three years. . . .

The Disinvestment Commission in its 2nd Report submitted in April, 1997 advised the Government of India that BALCO needed to be privatised. . . .

The Commission had recommended the appointment of a Financial Advisor to undertake a proper valuation of the company and to conduct the sale process. The Commission had categorized BALCO as a non-core group industry. . . . The Cabinet Committee on Economic Affairs had, in the meantime, in September 1997 granted approval for appointment of a technical and financial advisor, selected through a competitive process, for managing the strategic sale and restructuring of BALCO. Global advertisement was then issued inviting from interested parties Expression of Interest for selection as a Global Advisor. The advertisement was published in four financial papers in India and also in 'The Economist', a renowned financial magazine published abroad. Eight Merchant Banks showed their interest in appointment of the Global Advisor. The lowest bid of M/s Jardine Fleming Securities India Ltd. was accepted and approved by the Cabinet Committee on Disinvestment on 9th March, 1999. The Cabinet Committee on Disinvestment also approved the proposal of strategic sale of 51% equity in respect of BALCO.

The decision of the Government to the aforesaid strategic sale was challenged by the BALCO Employees' Union by filing Writ Petition No. 2249 of 1999 in the High Court of Delhi. This petition was disposed of by the High Court vide its order dated 3rd August, 1999. . . .

When the financial bids were opened, it was found that the bid of Sterlite Industries was the highest. . . . Pursuant to the execution of sale, 51% of the equity was transferred to Sterlite Industries Limited and a cheque for Rs. 551.5 crores [one crore=ten million] was received. It is not necessary to refer to the terms of the agreement in any great detail except to notice a few clauses which pertain to safeguarding the interest of the employees of the company. Clauses H and J of the preamble reads as follows:

> "H. Subject to Clause 7.2 [which contains the Representations, Warranties, and Covenants of Sterlite Industies], the Parties envision that all employees of the Company on the date hereof shall continue in the employment of the Company.

> J. The SP [Strategic Partner, Sterlite Industries] recognises that the Government in relation to its employment policies follows certain principles for the benefit of the members of the Scheduled Caste/Scheduled Tribes, physically handicapped persons and other socially disadvantaged categories of the society. The SP shall use its best efforts to cause the Company to provide adequate job opportunities for such persons. Further, in the event of any reduction in the strength of the employees of the Company, the SP shall use its best efforts to ensure that the physically handicapped persons are retrenched at the end."

[The agreement for sale of BALCO shares further provides]

> (e) Notwithstanding anything to the contrary in this Agreement, [Sterlite Industries] shall not retrench any part of the labour force of the Company for a period of one (1) year from the Closing Date other than any dismissal or termination of employees of the Company from their employment in accordance with the applicable staff regulations and standing orders of the Company or applicable Law; and

> (f) Notwithstanding anything to the contrary in this Agreement, but subject to subclause (e) above, any restructuring of the labour force of the Company shall be implemented in the manner recommended by the Board and in accordance with all applicable laws. . . .

On behalf of the Union of India, the Attorney General submitted that since 1990–91 successive Governments have gone in for disinvestment. Disinvestment had become imperative both in the case of Centre and the States primarily for three reasons. Firstly, despite every effort the rate of returns of governmental enterprises had been woefully low, excluding the sectors in which government have a monopoly and for which they can, therefore, charge any price. The rate of return on central enterprises came to minus 4% while the cost at which the government borrows money is at the rate of 10 to 11%. In the States out of 946 State level enterprises, about 241 were not working at all; about 551 were making losses and 100 were reported not to be submitting their accounts at all. Secondly, neither the Centre nor the States have resources to sustain enterprises that are not able to stand on their own in the new environment of intense competition. Thirdly, despite repeated efforts it was not possible to change the work culture of governmental enterprises. As a result, even the strongest among them have been sinking into increasing difficulties as the environment is more and more competitive and technological change has become faster.

We pointed out in [an earlier case, R.K. Garg v. Union of India] that laws relating to economic activities should be viewed with greater latitude than laws touching civil rights such as freedom of speech, religion, etc. We observed that the legislature should be allowed some play in the joints because it has to deal with complex problems which do not admit of solution through any doctrinaire or strait-jacket formula and this is particularly true in case of legislation dealing with economic matters, where, having regard to the nature of the problems required to be dealt with, greater play in the joints has to be allowed to the legislature. We

quoted with approval the following [sic]admonition given by Frankfurter,J. [dissenting] in
Morey v. Dond [sic] [Morey v. Doud, 354 U.S. 457 (1957)].

> In the utilities, tax and economic regulation cases, there are good reasons for judicial self-
> restraint if not judicial deference to legislative judgement. The legislature after all has the
> affirmative responsibility. The Courts have only the power to destroy, not to reconstruct.
> When these are added to the complexity of economic regulation, the uncertainty, the
> liability to error, the bewildering conflict of the experts, and the number of times the
> judges have been overruled by events self-limitation can be seen to be the path to judicial
> wisdom and institutional prestige and stability.

What we said in that [earlier] case in regard to legislation relating to economic matters
must apply equally in regard to executive action in the field of economic activities, though
the executive decision may not be placed on as high a pedestal as legislative judgement
insofar as judicial deference is concerned. We must not forget that in complex economic
matters every decision is necessarily empiric and it is based on experimentation or what one
may call 'trial' and error method' and, therefore, its validity cannot be tested on any rigid 'a
priori' considerations or on the application of any strait-jacket formula. The Court must while
adjudging the constitutional validity of an executive decision relating to economic matters
grant a certain measure of freedom or 'play in the joints' to the executive. The problem[s] of
government" as pointed out by the Supreme Court of the United States in Metropolis Theatre
Co. v. State [sic] of Chicago [228 U.S. 61 (1913)]

> are practical ones and may justify, if they do not require, rough accommodations, illogi-
> cal, it may be, and unscientific. But even such criticism should not be hastily expressed.
> What is best is not discernible, the wisdom of any choice may be disputed or condemned.
> Mere errors of government are not subject to our judicial review. It is only its palpably
> arbitrary exercises which can be declared void.

. . .

Process of disinvestment is a policy decision involving complex economic factors. The
Courts have consistently refrained from interfering with economic decisions as it has been
recognised that economic expediencies lack adjudicative disposition and unless the economic
decision, based on economic expediencies, is demonstrated to be so violative of constitutional
or legal limits on power or so abhorrent to reason, that the Courts would decline to interfere.
In matters relating to economic issues, the Government has, while taking a decision, right to
"trial and error" as long as both trial and error are bona fide and within limits of authority.
There is no case made out by the petitioner that the decision to disinvest in BALCO is in any
way capricious, arbitrary, illegal or uninformed. Even though the workers may have interest in
the manner in which the Company is conducting its business, inasmuch as its policy decision
may have an impact on the workers' rights, nevertheless it is an incidence of service for an
employee to accept a decision of the employer which has been honestly taken and which is
not contrary to law. . . .

Public interest is the paramount consideration, and if in the public interest the Government
thought it fit to take over a sick company to preserve the productive unit and the jobs of those
employed therein, the government can, in the public interest, with a view to reducing the
continuing drain on its limited resources, or with a view to raising funds for its priority welfare
or developmental projects, or even as a measure of mobilising the funds needed for running
the government, disinvest from the public sector companies.

The aforesaid observations, in our opinion, enunciates the legal position correctly. The policies of the Government ought not to remain static. With the change in economic climate, the wisdom and the manner for the Government to run commercial ventures may require reconsideration. What may have been in the public interest at a point of time may no longer be so. The Government has taken a policy decision that it is in public interest to disinvest in BALCO. An elaborate process has been undergone and majority shares sold. It cannot be said that public funds have been frittered away. In this process, the change in the character of the company cannot be validly impugned. While it was a policy decision to start BALCO as a company owned by the Government, it is as a change of policy that is investment has now taken place. If the initial decision could not be validly challenged on the same parity of reasoning, the decision to disinvest also cannot be impugned without showing that it is against any law or mala fide . . .

We are satisfied that the workers' interests are adequately protected in the process of disinvestment. Apart from the aforesaid undertaking given in the Court, the existing laws adequately protect workers' interest and no decision affecting a huge body of workers can be taken without the prior consent of the State Government. Further more, the service conditions are governed by the certified orders of the company and any change in the conditions thereto can only be made in accordance with law.

Hilary K. Josephs, *Legal Institutions and Their "Proper" Place in Economic Development: India and China Compared*
(Dec. 27, 2004; revision of paper presented at the Center for the Advanced Study of India, The University of Pennsylvania, June 13–14, 2004)
(excerpts; footnotes omitted)

[M]uch of the controversy over labor law reform is concentrated around laws which mainly affect the organized sector, namely, the Industrial Disputes Act, 1947 (hereinafter the "IDA") and the Contract Labour (Regulation and Abolition) Act, 1970 (hereinafter the "CLA"). It is far from clear how legislative reforms would directly improve the lot of the vast unorganized sector [an estimated 92 percent of the workforce].

The IDA, which was based closely on the Defense of India Rules promulgated by the British, provides a framework for settling disputes between employers and employees. The sort of dispute which is most germane to the subject of this paper involves lay-offs and retrenchment, covered by Chapter V-B of the Act. In any industrial establishment employing 100 workers or more, the employer must seek government permission before retrenching the workforce or closing the establishment. Permission has been frequently denied. If permission is granted, the employer is responsible for paying severance to the affected workers.

Government permission is not required (though severance is still due) where ownership of the undertaking is transferred, e.g., through merger or acquisition. In recent years, foreign investors have been allowed to acquire controlling interests in joint ventures, convert joint ventures to wholly owned subsidiaries, and acquire Indian companies. Layoffs often accompany these changes. Any loss of jobs is highly problematic under stagnant labor market conditions.

Moreover, employers with good political connections circumvent the IDA through measures such as lock-outs, manipulation of reporting requirements, and payment of modest statutory penalties. Another ploy to close down an unprofitable factory is to stop paying the electricity bill, which eventuates in a power shut-off.

Decided shortly after the reform period commenced in 1991, the case of *Workmen of Meenakshi Mills Ltd. v. Meenakshi Mills Ltd.* defended the IDA against constitutional attack [on the grounds that the IDA violated an employer's right to carry on his business]. Thus, the *Meenakshi Mills* case is part of a long line of precedent dating back to the immediate post-independence period which favored worker interests over those of employers. Judicial intervention was believed necessary to compensate for a fundamental inequality of bargaining power between workers and management.

The year 2001 has been called a watershed year for the Supreme Court in its support for liberalization. The Ministry of Disinvestment achieved a major victory in *BALCO Employees Union v. Union of India* (hereinafter the "*BALCO* Case"). In a decision of a three judge panel, the Supreme Court of India approved the central government's decision to disinvest and transfer a 51 percent interest in Bharat Aluminium Company Ltd. (*BALCO*) to Sterlite Industries Ltd. The court concluded that the policy of disinvestment was outside the competence of the judiciary under the separation of powers doctrine. It also concluded that the record demonstrated a fair, just, and equitable procedure had been followed in carrying out this disinvestment.

Justice Kirpal's opinion contains a lengthy recitation of the factual background of the case, from which it may be adduced that different facts might have led to a different conclusion. Among the key points were facts that successive governments had pursued a policy of disinvestment for a decade; a special commission was established to make recommendations to the government; the commission determined that BALCO was a non-core group industry; the government was selling a controlling interest, not closing the company altogether; the valuation of the company was conducted in an open and transparent fashion under the supervision of an international investment firm; the winning bid was well in excess of the reserve price; and the interests of the workforce were considered and given protection.

The workforce was involved in the dialogue over disinvestment although it had no legal right to veto any decision. Sterlite agreed not to retrench any part of the workforce for one year and no part of the company would be closed for a minimum period of ten years. Employees were offered the option of voluntary retirement with severance.

Justice Kirpal stated that:

> The *policies* of the Government ought not to remain static. With the change in economic climate, the wisdom and the manner for the Government to run commercial ventures may require reconsideration. What may have been in the *public interest* at a point of time may no longer be so. The Government has taken a *policy* decision that it is in the *public interest* to disinvest in BALCO. An elaborate process has been undergone and majority shares sold. It cannot be said that public funds have been frittered away. (Emphasis supplied.)

However, the Supreme Court is accused of [again] undermining the disinvestment policy through another decision in September 2003. In *Centre for Public Interest Litigation v. Union of India* (hereinafter the "Centre for PIL Case"), the Court ruled that disinvestment in two public sector oil companies, Bharat Petroleum and Hindustan Petroleum, could not occur without parliamentary approval. Since the companies had been nationalized by act of parliament, privatization also required parliamentary clearance. A decision from Canada provided support for this conclusion.

But the Centre for PIL Case presented an entirely different factual situation from BALCO. It should not be interpreted as a repudiation of BALCO. In the later case, the companies to be affected by disinvestment were in a core industry, and profitable. The Petroleum Ministry had strenuously opposed disinvestment. In the words of the decision, "[s]uccess of the [privatization] programme hinges on, among other things, a *basic consensus* among Parliament, Government, and head of state on the scope and broad lines of the programme." (Emphasis supplied.) Such a consensus, even between the Petroleum Ministry and the Ministry of Disinvestment, was obviously lacking.

Notes

1. After the 2004 elections, the coalition government led by the Hindu nationalist Bharatiya Janata Party (BJP) was replaced by a Congress Party led coalition which included communist parties opposed to market-oriented changes. "[P]rivatization slowed to a trickle amid resistance from the communist parties, which have close ties to trade unions in India's large public sector." *India Steps Back On Privatization of 13 Companies*, WALL ST. J., Aug. 17, 2005, at A9; Saritha Rai, *India Abandons Plan to Sell Stakes in State-Owned Companies*, N.Y. TIMES, Aug. 17, 2005, at C6.

2. India's information technology sector has been a major beneficiary of outsourcing: software programming, customer service and back-office operations for multinational companies. *See* AnnaLee Saxenian, Bangalore: The Silicon Valley of Asia?, <http://www.sims.berkeley.edu/~anno/papers/bangalore_svasia.htm> (site visited Nov. 25, 2003). Despite rising pay in the outsourcing industry, there is heavy turnover as firms compete for a limited pool of skilled English speakers. Saritha Rai, *Outsourcers Struggling to Keep Workers in the Fold*, N.Y. TIMES, Nov. 12, 2005, at C13; John Larkin, *India's Talent Pool Drying Up*, WALL ST. J., Jan. 4, 2006, at A9.

3. Prof. Frankel, a longtime observer of the Indian scene, expresses doubts about any economic strategy that aims to "leapfrog" the Industrial Revolution. Creating "islands of excellence" in the IT sector is a costly process for government and it does not produce the much-vaunted "trickle down" effects for agriculture and manufacturing. FRANKEL, *supra*, at 595–625. By contrast, Chinese reformers targeted agriculture first and after dramatic gains in that sector, began creating employment opportunities in manufacturing for peasants whose labor was no longer necessary on the farm. *See* Chapter 11, Socialist Modernization and Liberation of the Productive Forces.

4. Prof. Frankel is also dubious as to whether India can attract foreign investment to the same extent that China has. The BJP-led coalition pursued the contradictory aims of protecting India's industries from foreign competition while trying to attract foreign investment. FRANKEL, *supra*, at 730. Globalization was "another kind of foreign invasion of India, this time in the guise of multi-nationals." *Id.* at 729. Yet China, too, has an ambivalent attitude toward foreigners based on its historical experience. Given a large market, the prosperity of a growing middle class, widespread education in English, its democratic government, and common law legal system, why shouldn't India attract substantial foreign investment? *See* Huang Yasheng & Tarun Khanna, *Can India Overtake China's Economic Development?*, FOR. POL'Y, July 1, 2003, at 74 (available on Westlaw); Peter Wonacott, *Wallets Crack Open in*

India, WALL ST. J., Jan. 3, 2006, at A14 (estimated ninety million people are middle class with household income between $4,500 and $22,000).

5. In sharp contrast to the Chinese diaspora, overseas Indians (Non-Resident Indians, or NRIs) have not invested significantly in the motherland. One source attributes the lack of investment to a "vicious circle of resentment between NRIs and resident Indians." *See* Ilyana Kuziemko & Geoffrey Rapp, *India's Wayward Children: Do Affirmative Action Laws Designed to Compensate India's Historically Disadvantaged Castes Explain Low Foreign Direct Investment by the Indian Diaspora?*, 10 MINN. J. GLOBAL TRADE 323 (2001). NRIs who left in the 1960s were mostly well-educated people who felt cheated of professional advancement by the government's affirmative action policies on behalf of the lower castes. *See* Section D, "Equal Opportunities" for the Scheduled Castes, Scheduled Tribes, and Other Backward Classes. NRIs also had felt frustrated by excessive government regulation of the economy. Resident Indians, for their part, are bitter toward those who received precious higher education at government expense, only to leave for greener pastures. To encourage investment by NRIs, legislation was adopted in 2003 to allow overseas Indians with foreign citizenship to acquire "overseas citizenship" in India. While OCI registration allows such benefits as a multiple entry lifetime visa and ownership of real estate, holders are not permitted to vote or stand for elective office. *See* Ministry of Home Affairs, http://mha.nic.in/oci/oci_main.htm.

C. LABOR AND TRADE UNIONS

As in many other countries, the organized [unionized] sector of the workforce is small, fragmented, and self-interested. Approximately 92 percent of the workforce is unorganized. Second Labour Commission Report, *supra*, at sec. 1.15. Trade unions have shown little interest in the unorganized sector. "Due to [political] party control of trade unions in India . . . unions were used more as instruments of mass mobilization than as representatives of working-class interests." HARDGRAVE & KOCHANEK, *supra*, at 211. Indian trade unions joined the government in opposing any discussion of labor issues in the WTO. Kevin Kolben, *The New Politics of Linkage: India's Opposition to the Workers' Rights Clause*, 13 IND. J. GLOBAL LEGAL STUD. 1, 11-12, 20-21 (2006).

Central government domination of the economy placed a premium on stable growth and production. In 1974, under Indira Gandhi, the central government invoked emergency powers to declare a strike of the railway union illegal. The army was called in; labor leaders were arrested; tens of thousands of workers and union activists were jailed; and after twenty days the strike was called off. FRANKEL, *supra*, at 528–30; HARDGRAVE & KOCHANEK, *supra*, at 212. The two year Bombay textile strike, and other major industrial disputes in the 1980s, ended in defeat for the trade unions. HARDGRAVE & KOCHANEK, *supra*, at 213–14. Strikes ("bandhs") not only alienated the general public, but were also ruled illegal by the courts as violating the fundamental constitutional rights of others and causing national losses. *Bharat Kumar K. Palicha v. State*, AIR 1997 Ker. 291, upheld by the Supreme Court in *Communist Party of India v. Bharat Kumar*, AIR 1998 SC 184.

That a trade union was the plaintiff in the BALCO case illustrates how trade unions can play a defensive role in economic reform, for example, by blocking or retarding privatization of state enterprises. According to a commission of experts, unions have yet to create a positive role for themselves in meeting the needs of the unorganized sector and in responding to the forces of globalization. The Self-Employed Women's Association (SEWA), described later, is a notable exception. There are no labor unions in the fast-growing IT sector. In West Bengal, which has a communist government and a long tradition of trade unionism, strikes are banned in the IT sector. Jason Overdorf, *Commies vs. Capitalists*, NEWSWEEK, Nov. 22, 2004 (available on Lexis).

India is a party to numerous ILO Conventions but, interestingly, *not* Conventions 87 and 98, the core agreements on union organization and collective bargaining. See Chapter 2, Part D (The 1998 Declaration on Fundamental Principles and Rights at Work).

Second Labour Commission Report (excerpts)

2.256 The decade from 1980 also witnessed the growth of independent trade unions in many enterprises in the major industrial centres of India. These unions preferred to stay away from the Central Federations of Trade Unions, and to be on their own. In many cases, they were free from the influences of political parties and were led by individual leaders who engaged in competitive militancy and promised higher gains to the workers in their unions. Notable among these is Self Employed Women's Association (SEWA). The emergence of SEWA led to the induction of pioneering methods that combined struggle and organization, co-operation and self-reliance.

2.258. Thus, one sees an increase in the number of registered unions in the years from 1983 to 1994. But one also sees a reduction in the average membership per union and in the number of unions submitting returns.

2.260 We must also make specific mention of the emergence of the Trade Union SEWA group of organization. This include[s] organizations that have been modelled on the SEWA, Ahmedabad, that have later become branches of the SEWA set up or in some cases, remained local. The SEWA organization in Ahmedabad came into being in 1972, and was established by leading workers of the Trade Union movement in Ahmedabad, like Ms. Elaben Bhatt. With her long experience in Ahmedabad Textile Labour Association (ATLA), and elsewhere, Ms. Ela Bhatt built up a new type of Trade Union or working class organization. It was a membership based organization like Trade Union. But it combined the method of agitation and constructive organization. It did not confine itself to the traditional method of presenting demands and resorting to industrial action in pursuit of them. On the other hand, it took up the work of organizing the women workers, who were engaged in hitherto unorganized sector of employment, combining other constructive activities like marketing, the provision of micro-credit, banking, training, representing the views and interests of workers. Today, the SEWA and its affiliates have a membership of 4,19,891, and 10 offices in six states.

D. "EQUAL OPPORTUNITIES" FOR THE SCHEDULED CASTES, SCHEDULED TRIBES, AND OTHER BACKWARD CLASSES

Indian Constitution (as amended):

Preamble:

We, the people of India, having solemnly resolved to constitute India into a sovereign democratic republic and to secure to all its citizens: Justice, social, economic and political; liberty of thought, belief, faith and worship; equality of status and opportunity; and to promote among them all fraternity assuring the dignity of the individual and the unity of the Nation. . . .

Fundamental Rights

Art. 14: The State shall not deny to any person equality before the law or the equal protection of the laws within the territory of India.

Art. 15 (1): The State shall not discriminate against any citizen on grounds only of religion, race, caste, sex, place of birth or any of them.

Art. 15 (4): Nothing in this article . . . shall prevent the State from making any special provision for the advancement of any socially and educationally backward classes of citizens or for the Scheduled Castes and the Scheduled Tribes.

Art. 16 (1): There shall be equality of opportunity for all citizens in matters relating to employment or appointment to any office under the State.

Art. 16 (4): Nothing in this article shall prevent the State from making any provision for the reservation of appointments or posts in favour of any backward class of citizens which, in the opinion of the State, is not adequately represented in the services under the State.

Art. 17: "Untouchability" is abolished and its practice in any form is forbidden. The enforcement of any disability arising out of "Untouchability" shall be an offence punishable in accordance with law.

Directive Principles of State Policy

Art. 46: The State shall promote with special care the educational and economic interests of the weaker sections of the people, and, in particular, of the Scheduled Castes and the Scheduled Tribes, and shall protect them from social injustice and all forms of exploitation.

––––––––––––

The major traditional caste divisions ("varnas"), ranked hierarchically, were the Brahmins (priests), the Kshatriyas (rulers and warriors), the Vaisyas (merchants and agriculturalists), and Sudras (menials and servants). GALANTER, *supra*, at 10. Outside and below the four varnas were the untouchables, essentially the lowest castes, polluted by their traditional occupations as scavengers and sweepers. *Id.* at 13–16. *See* Chapter 2, ILO Monitoring and Member Nation Compliance, CEACR: Individual Observation concerning Convention No. 111, Discrimination (Employment and Occupation), 1958 India (ratification: 1960), Published 2005.

After Independence, the institution of Untouchability was formally eliminated by the Indian Constitution. . . . Although numerous provisions are implicated in its disestablishment, the most directly applicable is found in Article 17. . . . This provision . . . prohibits the enforcement of civil disabilities not only by the state, but by private actors as well. This Constitutional prohibition was soon reinforced by the Untouchability (Offenses) Act of 1955 [renamed the Protection of Civil Rights Act in 1976].

Linda Hamilton Krieger, *The Burdens of Equality: Burdens of Proof and Presumptions in Indian and American Civil Rights Law*, 47 AM. J. COMP. L. 89, 94 (1999).

Discrimination in various forms, including discrimination in employment, is therefore treated as a criminal offense, punishable by imprisonment, fines, cancellation of licenses, and loss of government funding. *Id.* at 94–95.

Today, the untouchables (or "dalits" as they prefer to be called) account for approximately 20 percent of the Hindu population. Through political mobilization and education, many have been able to improve upon their traditional status. One of the chief architects of the Constitution, Dr. B. R. Ambedkar, was a dalit. GRANVILLE AUSTIN, THE INDIAN CONSTITUTION: CORNERSTONE OF A NATION 337–38 (1966). He tirelessly advocated for "untouchable" causes in the run-up to Independence and afterward. In 1997, K. R. Narayanan became India's first dalit president, after a long and distinguished career in politics and public service. However, especially in rural areas, dalits still occupy inferior status relative to higher castes. They are much more likely to be landless agricultural laborers, poor and illiterate. Ira N. Gang, Kunal Sen & Myeong-Su Yun, Caste, Ethnicity and Poverty in Rural India (Nov. 2002), available at http://www.ssrn.com.

The Indian Constitution sanctions compensatory discrimination – in political representation, education, and government employment – to correct for past injustices. The beneficiaries of compensatory discrimination are divided into three groups: the Scheduled Castes (SC), the Scheduled Tribes (ST), and Other Backward Classes (OBC). An extraordinary complex classification system has been developed to identify beneficiaries, varying from state to state, and even within states. GALANTER, *supra*, at 139. Designation for inclusion as a member of an OBC has been particularly controversial and productive of litigation. GALANTER, *supra*, chapters 5–6.

Compensatory discrimination was not intended to perpetuate differences based on caste or other disadvantaged status. Despite judicial monitoring, legal preferences for dalits and other historically disadvantaged groups are manipulated to give disproportionate advantage to those who belong to a politically influential group. *See* E. J. Prior, *Constitutional Fairness or Fraud on the Constitution? Compensatory Discrimination in India*, 28 CASE W. RES. J. INT'L L. 63 (1996); Chinnaiah v. State of Andhra Pradesh, http://judis.nic.in/supremecourt/qrydisp.asp?tfnm=26583 (2004) (Supreme Court decision disallowing subdivision of Scheduled Castes, where effect is to give preference to one sub-group over others). Compensatory discrimination ignites hostility from those who are of only slightly better socioeconomic status than the protected groups. HARDGRAVE & KOCHANEK, *supra*, at 199–200. Even upper caste students engaged in violent protests against such preferences in 1985 and 1990. *Id.* at 209.

Notes

1. India and the United States have very different policies toward remedying past discrimination. The U.S. Supreme Court has consistently rejected the idea of

quotas for disadvantaged groups in education and employment. *See generally* Priya Sridharan, *Representations of Disadvantage: Evolving Definitions of Disadvantage in India's Reservation Policy and United States' Affirmative Action Policy*, 6 Asian L.J. 99 (1999). By the same token, the Indian Supreme Court has set limits on quotas and disallowed preferences for the "creamy layer," those who have adequate economic means to advance themselves. Prior, *supra*, at 90–95. *Compare* Indra Sawhney v. Union of India, 80 A.I.R. 1993 S.C. 477 *with* Grutter v. Bollinger, 539 U.S. 306 (2003) *and* Gratz v. Bollinger, 539 U.S. 244 (2003).

2. In both countries, there is an unending cycle of litigation about entitlement to remedial measures. Why? Is such litigation one measure of slow but steady progress by disadvantaged groups? Or, does litigation over "higher echelon" benefits, such as access to prestigious universities and executive employment, mask the problems which afflict the vast majority of disadvantaged people, such as poor academic performance, high dropout rates from school, meager opportunities for advancement out of dead-end jobs, and outright unemployment?

3. In all societies, even the most affluent, there are jobs that are dangerous, dirty, physically exhausting, humiliating, and usually poorly paid, such as those involving the handling of corpses, slaughter of animals, and cleaning of waste. In the United States, such jobs tend to be filled by illegal immigrants who are invisible to the rest of society. *See* Steven Greenhouse, *Rights Group Condemns Meatpackers On Job Safety*, N.Y. Times, Jan. 26, 2005, at A13; Steven Greenhouse, *Among Janitors, Labor Violations Go With the Job*, N.Y. Times, July 13, 2005, at A1; Nina Bernstein, *Invisible to Most, Women Line Up for Day Labor*, N.Y. Times, Aug. 15, 2005, at A1. In India and Japan, the solution was social compartmentalization. "Caste groups live not in isolation but in the midst of a set of other groups with which they have fixed and customary relationships – economic, political, social, and religious. . . . Each group has its duties and disabilities; each, even the lowest, has its special prerogatives and privileges." Galanter, *supra*, at 9. Does the fact of inclusion, albeit in a subordinate relationship, ultimately make the elimination of discrimination easier?

E. JUDICIAL ACTIVISM AND PUBLIC INTEREST LITIGATION

Indian Constitution (as amended)

Art. 15 (3): Nothing in this article shall prevent the State from making any special provision for women and children.

Art. 32 (1): The right to move the Supreme Court by appropriate proceedings for the enforcement of the rights conferred by this Part [Fundamental Rights] is guaranteed.

Art. 32 (2): The Supreme Court shall have power to issue directions or orders or writs . . . for the enforcement of any of the rights conferred by this Part [Fundamental Rights].

Art. 226: [E]very High Court shall have power . . . to issue to any person or authority . . . directions, orders, or writs . . . for the enforcement of any of the [Fundamental Rights] and for any other purpose.

Upendra Baxi, *Taking Suffering Seriously: Social Action Litigation in the Supreme Court of India*, in N. TIRUCHELVAM & R. COOMARASWAMY, THE ROLE OF THE JUDICIARY IN PLURAL SOCIETIES 32–33 (1987):

The Supreme Court of India is at long last becoming . . . the Supreme Court for Indians. . . . Now, increasingly, the Court is being identified by justices as well as people as the 'last resort for the oppressed and the bewildered. . . . ' A post-Emergency phenomenon . . . the Court is augmenting its support base and moral authority in the nation at a time when other institutions of governance are facing a legitimation crisis. . . . [B]onded and migrant labourers, unorganized labourers, untouchables and scheduled tribes, landless agricultural labourers . . . women who are bought and sold . . . – these and many other groups – now flock to the Supreme Court seeking justice.

BANDHUA MUKTI MORCHA V. UNION OF INDIA

(The Bonded Labour Case)
1984 AIR 802, 1984 SCC(3) 161
http://judis.nic.in/supremecourt/qrydisp.asp?tfnm=9643
(excerpts)

BHAGWATI, J.

The petitioner is an organisation dedicated to the cause of release of bonded labourers in the country. The system of bonded labour has been prevalent in various parts of the country since long prior to the attainment of political freedom and it constitutes an ugly and shameful feature of our national life. This system based on exploitation by a few socially and economically powerful persons trading on the misery and suffering of large numbers of men and holding them in bondage is a relic of a feudal hierarchical society which hypocritically proclaims the divinity of men but treats large masses of people belonging to the lower rungs of the social ladder or economically impoverished segments of society as dirt and chattel. This system under which one person can be bonded to provide labour to another for years and years until an alleged debt is supposed to be wiped out which never seems to happen during the life time of the bonded labourer, is totally incompatible with the new egalitarian socioeconomic order which we have promised to build and it is not only an affront to basic human dignity but also constitutes gross and revolting violation of constitutional values. The appalling conditions in which bonded labourers live, not as humans but as serfs, recall to the mind the following lines from "Man with the Hoe" which almost seem to have been written with reference to this neglected and forlorn species of Indian humanity: "Bowed by the weight of centuries he leans Upon his hoe and gazes on the ground The emptiness of ages on his face, And on his back the burden of the world." They are non-beings, exiles of civilization, living a life worst than that of animals, for the animals are at least free to roam about as they like and they can plunder or grab food whenever they are hungry but these out castes of society are held in bondage, robbed of their freedom and they are consigned to an existence where they have to live either in hovels or under the open sky and be satisfied with whatever little unwholesome food they can manage to get inadequate though it be to fill their hungry stomachs. Not having any choice, they are driven by poverty and hunger into a life of bondage a dark bottomless pit from which, in a cruel exploitative society, they cannot hope to be rescued.

This pernicious practice of bonded labour existed in many States and obviously with the ushering in of independence it could not be allowed to continue to blight the national life any longer and hence, when we framed our Constitution, we enacted Article 23 of the Constitution which prohibits "traffic in human beings and beggar and other similar forms of forced labour" practised by any one. The system of bonded labour therefore stood prohibited by Article 23 and there could have been no more solemn and effective prohibition than the one enacted in the Constitution in Article 23. But, it appears that though the Constitution was enacted as far back as 26th January, 1950 and many years passed since then, no serious effort was made to give effect to Article 23 and to stamp out the shocking practice of bonded labour. It was only in 1976 that Parliament enacted the Bonded Labour System (Abolition) Act, 1976 providing for the abolition of bonded labour system with a view to preventing the economic and physical exploitation of the weaker sections of the people. But, unfortunately, as subsequent events have shown and that is borne out also by [various reports] that the pernicious practice of bonded labour has not yet been totally eradicated from the national scene and that it continues to disfigure the social and economic life of the country at certain places. There are still a number of bonded labourers in various parts of the country and significantly, as pointed out in the Report of the National Seminar on "Identification and Rehabilitation of Bonded Labour" a large number of them belong to Scheduled Castes and Scheduled Tribes account for the next largest number while the few who are not from Scheduled Castes or Scheduled Tribes are generally landless agricultural labourers. . . . The petitioner made a survey of some of the stone quarries in Faridabad district near the city of Delhi and found that there were a large number of labourers from Maharashtra, Madhya Pradesh, Uttar Pradesh and Rajasthan who were working in these stone quarries under "inhuman and intolerable conditions" and many of whom were bonded labourers.

The petitioner therefore addressed a letter to one of us on 25th February, 1982 pointing out that in the mines of Shri S.L. Sharma, Gurukula Indra Prastha, Post Amar Nagar, Faridabad District, a large number of labourers were languishing under abject conditions of bondage for last about ten years, and the petitioner gave the names of 11 bonded labourers. . . . Almost 99% of the workers are migrant from drought prone areas of Rajasthan, Madhya Pradesh, Andhra Pradesh, Orissa, Maharashtra and Bihar. . . . The petitioner also set out the various provisions of the Constitution and the statutes which were not being implemented or observed in regard to the labourers working in these stone quarries. The petitioner in the end prayed that a writ be issued for proper implementation of these provisions of the Constitution and statutes with a view to ending the misery, suffering and helplessness of "these victims of most inhuman exploitation".

The letter dated 25th February 1982 addressed by the petitioner was treated as a writ petition and by an order dated 26th February 1982 this Court issued notice on the writ petition and appointed two advocates, namely, M/s. Ashok Srivastava and Ashok Panda as commissioners to visit the stone quarries of Shri S.L. Sharma in Godhokhor (Anangpur) and Lakkarpur in Faridabad district and to interview each of the persons whose names were mentioned in the letter of the petitioner as also a cross section of the other workers with a view to finding out whether they are willingly working in these stone quarries and also to inquire about the conditions in which they are working. . . .

We are so much accustomed to the concepts of Anglo-Saxon jurisprudence which require every legal proceeding including a proceeding for a high prerogative writ to be cast in a rigid or definitive mould and insist on observance of certain well settled rules of procedure, that we implicitly assume that the same sophisticated procedural rules must also govern a proceeding under Article 32 and the Supreme Court cannot permit itself to be freed from the shackles of these rules even if that be necessary for enforcement of a fundamental right. It was on the basis of this impression fostered by long association which the Anglo-Saxon system of administration of justice that for a number of years this court had taken the view that it is only a person whose fundamental right is violated who can approach the Supreme Court for relief under Article 32 or in other words, he must have a cause of action for enforcement of his fundamental right. It was only in the year 1981 . . . that this Court for the first time took the view that where a person or class of persons to whom legal injury is caused by reason of violation of a fundamental right is unable to approach the court for judicial redress on account of poverty or disability or socially or economically disadvantaged position, any member of the public acting bona fide can move the court for relief under Article 32 and a fortiorari, also under Article 226, so that the fundamental rights may become meaningful not only for the rich and the well-to-do who have the means to approach the court but also for the large masses of people who are living a life of want and destitution and who are by reason of lack of awareness, assertiveness and resources unable to seek judicial redress. . . . While interpreting Article 32, it must be borne in mind that our approach must be guided not by any verbal or formalistic canons of construction but by the paramount object and purpose for which this Article has been enacted as a Fundamental Right in the Constitution and its interpretation must receive illumination from the trinity of provisions which permeate and energies the entire Constitution namely, the Preamble, the Fundamental Rights and the Directive Principles of State Policy. Clause (1) of Article 32 confers the right to move the Supreme Court for enforcement of any of the fundamental rights, but it does not say as to who shall have this right to move the Supreme Court nor does it say by what proceedings the Supreme Court may be so moved. . . .

But if we want the fundamental rights to become a living reality and the Supreme Court to become a real sentinel on the qui vive, we must free ourselves from the shackles of outdated and outmoded assumptions and bring to bear on the subject fresh outlook and original unconventional thinking. . . .

Even when the thekedar or jamadar [labor contractors] recruits or employs workmen for the stone quarries and stone crushers by sending word through the "old hands," the workmen so recruited or employed would be inter-State migrant workmen, because the "old hands" would be really acting as agents of the thekedar or jamadar for the purpose of recruiting or employing workmen. The Inter-State Migrant Workmen Act being a piece of social welfare legislation intended to effectuate the Directive Principles of State Policy and ensure decent living and working conditions for the workmen when they come from other States and are in a totally strange environment where by reason of their poverty, ignorance and illiteracy, they would be totally unorganised and helpless and would become easy victims of exploitation, it must be given a broad and expansive interpretation so as to prevent the mischief and advance the remedy and therefore, even when the workmen are recruited or employed by the jamadar or thekedar by operating through the "old hands," they must be regarded as inter-State migrant workmen entitled to the benefit of the provisions of the Inter-State Migrant Workmen Act and the Inter-State Migrant Workmen Rules. . . .

The Report of Dr. Patwardhan also points out that it is the children or women of the workmen who are usually engaged in the work of transporting water from distant places like the tube well but they are not paid anything for this work which is being done by them. Neither any mine-lessee or stone crusher owner nor any jamadar or thekedar regards it as his duty to make provision for drinking water for the workmen nor does any officer of the Central Government or of the State Government bother to enforce the provisions of law in regard to supply of drinking water. It is clear that, quite apart from the provisions of the Contract Labour Act and the Inter-State Migrant Workmen Act, there is a specific prescription in section 19 of the Mines Act 1952 and Rules 30 to 32 of the Mines Rules 1955 that the mine-lessees and stone crusher owners shall make effective arrangements for providing and maintaining at suitable points conveniently situated a sufficient supply of cool and wholesome drinking water for all workmen employed in the stone quarries and stone crushers. . . .

We accordingly allow this writ petition and issue the above directions to the Central Government and the State of Haryana and the various authorities mentioned in the preceding paragraphs of this judgment so that these poor unfortunate workmen who lead a miserable existence in small hovels, exposed to the vagaries of weather, drinking foul water, breathing heavily dust-laden polluted air and breaking and blasting stone all their life, may one day be able to realise that freedom is not only the monopoly of a few but belongs to them all and that they are also equally entitled along with others to participate in the fruits of freedom and development. These directions may be summarized as follows:

(1) The Government of Haryana will, without any delay and at any rate within six weeks from today, constitute Vigilance Committee in each sub-division of a district in compliance with the requirements of section 13 of the Bonded Labour System (Abolition) Act 1976 keeping in view the guidelines given by us in this judgment.

(2) The Government of Haryana will instruct the district magistrates to take up the work of identification of bonded labour as one of their top priority tasks and to map out areas of concentration of bonded labour which are mostly to be found in stone quarries and brick kilns and assign task forces for identification and release of bonded labour and periodically hold labour camps in these areas with a view to educating the labourers inter alia with the assistance of the National Labour Institute.

(3) The State Government as also the Vigilance Committees and the district magistrates will take the assistance of non-political social action groups and voluntary agencies for the purpose of ensuring implementation of the provisions of the Bonded Labour System (Abolition) Act, 1976.

(4) The Government of Haryana will draw up within a period of three months from today a scheme or programme for rehabilitation of the freed bonded labourers in the light of the guidelines set out by the Secretary to the Government of India, Ministry of Labour in his letter dated 2nd September 1982 and implement such scheme or programme to the extent found necessary.

(5) The Central Government and the Government of Haryana will take all necessary steps for the purpose of ensuring that minimum wages are paid to the workmen employed in the stone quarries and stone crushers. . . .

(6) If payment of wages is made on truck basis, the Central Government will direct the appropriate officer of the Central Enforcement Machinery or any other appropriate authority or officer to determine the measurement of each truck as to how many cubic ft. of stone it can contain and print or inscribe such measurement on the truck so that appropriate and adequate wage is received by the workmen for the work done by them and they are not cheated out of their legitimate wage.

(7) The Central Government will direct the inspecting officers of the Central Enforcement Machinery or any other appropriate inspecting officers to carry out surprise checks at least once in a week for the purpose of ensuring that the trucks are not loaded beyond their

true measurement capacity and if it is found that the trucks are loaded in excess of the true measurement capacity, the inspecting officers carrying out such checks will immediately bring this fact to the notice of the appropriate authorities and necessary action shall be initiated against the defaulting mine owners and/or thekedars or jamadars.

(8) The Central Government and the Government of Haryana will ensure that payment of wages is made directly to the workmen by the mine lessees and stone crusher owners or at any rate in the presence of a representative of the mine lessees or stone crusher owners and the inspecting officers of the Central Government as also of the Government of Haryana shall carry out periodic checks in order to ensure that the payment of the stipulated wage is made to the workmen.

(9) The Central Board of Workers Education will organise periodic camps near the sites of stone quarries and stone crushers in Faridabad district for the purpose of educating the workmen in the rights and benefits conferred upon them by social welfare and labour laws and the progress made shall be reported to this Court by the Central Board of Workers Education at least once in three months.

(10) The Central Government and the Government of Haryana will immediately take steps for the purpose of ensuring that the stone crusher owners do not continue to foul the air and they adopt either of two devices, namely, keeping a drum of water above the stone crushing machine with arrangement for continuous spraying of water upon it or installation of dust sucking machine. . . .

(11) The Central Government and the Government of Haryana will immediately ensure that the mine lessees and stone crusher owners start supplying pure drinking water to the workmen on a scale of at least 2 litres for every work man by keeping suitable vessels in a shaded place at conveniently accessible points and such vessels shall be kept in clean and hygienic condition and shall be emptied, cleaned and refilled every day and the appropriate authorities of the Central Government and the Government of Haryana will supervise strictly the enforcement of this direction and initiate necessary action if there is any default.

(12) The Central Government and the Government of Haryana will ensure that minimum wage is paid to the women and/or children who look after the vessels in which pure drinking water is kept for the workmen.

(13) The Central Government and the Government of Haryana will immediately direct the mine lessees and stone crusher owners to start obtaining drinking water from any unpolluted source or sources of supply and to transport it by tankers to the work site with sufficient frequency so as to be able to keep the vessels filled up for supply of clean drinking water to the workmen and the Chief Administrator, Faridabad Complex will set up the points from where the mine lessees and stone crusher owners can, if necessary, obtain supply of potable water for being carried by tankers.

(14) The Central Government and the State Government will ensure that conservancy facilities in the shape of latrines and urinals in accordance with the provisions contained in section 20 of the Mines Act, 1950 and Rules 33 to 36 of the Mines Rules 1955 are provided at the latest by 15th February 1984.

(15) The Central Government and the State Government will take steps to immediately ensure that appropriate and adequate medical and first aid facilities as required by section 21 of the

Mines Act 1952 and Rules 40 to 45A of the Mines Rules 1955 are provided to the workmen not later than 31st January 1984.

(16) The Central Government and the Government of Haryana will ensure that every workmen who is required to carry out blasting with explosives is not only trained under the Mines Vocational Training Rules 1966 but also holds first aid qualification and carries a first aid outfit while on duty as required by Rule 45 of the Mines Rules 1955.

(17) The Central Government and the State Government will immediately take steps to ensure that proper and adequate medical treatment is provided by the mine lessees and owners of stone crushers to the workmen employed by them as also to the members of their families free of cost. . . .

(18) The Central Government and the State Government will ensure that the provisions of the Maternity Benefit Act 1961, the Maternity Benefit (Mines and Circus) Rules 1963 and the Mines Creche Rules 1966 where applicable in any particular stone quarry or stone crusher are given effect to by the mine lessees and stone crusher owners.

(19) As soon as any workman employed in a stone quarry or stone crusher receives injury or contracts disease in the course of his employment, the concerned mine lessee or stone crusher owner shall immediately report this fact to the Chief Inspector or Inspecting Officers of the Central Government and/or the State Government and such Inspecting Officers shall immediately provide legal assistance to the workman with a view to enabling him to file a claim for compensation before the appropriate court or authority and they shall also ensure that such claim is pursued vigorously and the amount of compensation awarded to the workman is secured to him.

(20) The Inspecting Officers of the Central Government as also of the State Government will visit each stone quarry or stone crusher at least once in a fortnight and ascertain whether there is any workman who is injured or who is suffering from any disease or illness, and if so, they will immediately take the necessary steps for the purpose of providing medical and legal assistance.

(21) If the Central Government and the Government of Haryana fail to ensure performance of any of the obligations set out in clauses 11, 13, 14 and 15 by the mine lessees and stone crusher owners within the period specified in those respective clauses, such obligation or obligations to the extent to which they are not performed shall be carried out by the Central Government and the Government of Haryana.

PATHAK, J. (concurring)
   I have read the judgments prepared by my brothers Bhagwati and A.N. Sen, and while I agree with the directions proposed by my brother Bhagwati I think it proper, because of the importance of the questions which arise in such matters, to set forth my own views.
   Public interest litigation in its present form constitutes a new chapter in our judicial system. It has acquired a significant degree of importance in the jurisprudence practised by our courts and has evoked a lively, if somewhat controversial, response in legal circles, in the media and among the general public. In the United States, it is the name "given to efforts to provide legal representation to groups and interests that have been unrepresented or under-represented in the legal process. These include not only the poor and the disadvantaged but ordinary citizens who, because they cannot afford lawyers to represent them, have lacked access to courts,

administrative agencies and other legal forums in which basic policy decisions affecting their interests are made". . . . In our own country, this new class of litigation is justified by its protagonists on the basis generally of vast areas in our population of illiteracy and poverty, of social and economic backwardness, and of an insufficient awareness and appreciation of individual and collective rights. These handicaps have denied millions of our countrymen access to justice. Public interest litigation is said to possess the potential of providing such access in the milieu of a new ethos, in which participating sectors in the administration of justice co-operate in the creation of a system which promises legal relief without cumbersome formality and heavy expenditure. In the result, the legal organisation has taken on a radically new dimension and correspondingly new perspectives are opening up before judges and lawyers and State Law agencies in the tasks before them. A crusading zeal is abroad, viewing the present as an opportunity to awaken the political and legal order to the objectives of social justice projected in our constitutional system. New slogans fill the air, and new phrases have entered the legal dictionary, and we hear of the "justicing system" being galvanised into supplying justice to the socioeconomic disadvantaged. These urges are responsible for the birth of new judicial concepts and the expanding horizon of juridical power. They claim to represent an increasing emphasis on social welfare and a progressive humanitarianism.

On the other side, the attempts of the judge and the lawyer are watched with skeptical concern by those who see interference by the courts in public interest litigation as a series of quixotic forays in a world of unyielding and harsh reality, whose success in the face of opposition bolstered by the inertia and apathy of centuries is bound to be limited in impact and brief in duration. They see judicial endeavour frustrated by the immobility of public concern and a traditional resistance to change, and believe that the temporary success gained is doomed to waste away as a mere ripple in the vastness of a giant slow-moving society. Even the optimistic sense danger to the credibility and legitimacy of the existing judicial system, a feeling contributed no doubt by the apprehension that the region into which the judiciary has ventured appears barren, uncharted and unpredictable, with few guiding posts and direction finding principles, and they fear that a traditionally proven legal structure may yield to the anarchy of purely emotional impulse. To the mind trained in the certainty of the law, of defined principles, of binding precedent, and the common law doctrine of Stare decisis the future is fraught with confusion and disorder in the legal world and severe strains in the constitutional system. At the lowest, there is an uneasy doubt about where we are going. . . .

As new areas open before the Court with modern developments in jurisprudence, in a world more sensitive to human rights as well as the impact of technological progress, the Court will become increasingly conscious of its expanding jurisdiction. That is inevitable. But its responsibilities are correspondingly great, and perhaps never greater than now. And we must remember that there is no higher Court to correct our errors, and that we wear the mantle of infallibility only because our decisions are final. That we sit at the apex of the judicial administration and our word, by constitutional mandate, is the law of the land can induce an unusual sense of power. It is a feeling we must guard against by constantly reminding ourselves that every decision must be guided by reason and by judicial principles.

Notes

1. As noted by Upendra Baxi, the phenomenon of social interest litigation (also called public interest litigation, or PIL) was part of the judiciary's effort to rehabilitate itself

after the excesses of executive power during the 1970s. *See also* S. P. SATHE, JUDICIAL ACTIVISM IN INDIA: TRANSGRESSING BORDERS AND ENFORCING LIMITS (2002), especially Chapter 6. Standing was expanded to allow any concerned citizen to file a lawsuit on behalf of the disadvantaged group. At the same time, the Supreme Court is accused of usurping the authority of other branches of government and involving itself in social and economic objectives which it is ill-equipped to achieve. *See* the concurring opinion of Judge Pathak. Indeed, although the Supreme Court set down specific directives for implementing its decision in the Bonded Labour Case and subsequent litigation, many directives have been ignored. ARUN SHOURIE, COURTS AND THEIR JUDGMENTS 51 (2001). *See also* Ranjan K. Agarwal, *The Barefoot Lawyers: Prosecuting Child Labour in the Supreme Court of India*, 21 ARIZ. J. INT'L & COMP. L. 663 (2004) (faulting Supreme Court for failing to close loopholes in protective legislation). Moreover, PIL litigation has stood in the way of much needed infrastructure development, such as the Narmada Dam and urban renewal in Mumbai. Others praise PIL as effective and efficient in addressing issues of mass concern, at least in the environmental context. A. V. Raja & Francis Xavier, Economic Efficiency of Public Interest Litigation (PIL): Lessons from India (conference paper, 2005), *available at* http://www.ssrn.com.

2. Like other common law jurisdictions, such as the United States and the United Kingdom, India has not adopted a comprehensive labor code, although one was drafted in the 1990s. 2d Labour Commission Report, *supra*, sec. 6.12. The law is a complex mixture of statutes (some carried over from colonial times) and case law, both at the central and local state levels. P.L. MALIK, INDUSTRIAL LAW 1–2 (18th ed. 2003).

3. By virtue of their tenuous status, extreme poverty, and social isolation, the bonded laborers were ill-equipped to avail themselves of the regular process for resolving employment disputes. Under the Industrial Disputes Act, 1947, discussed in Josephs, *Legal Institutions*, *supra*, both the Central Government and state governments are authorized to set up labor courts and industrial tribunals for dealing with disputes, both collective and individual, within their respective jurisdictions. Public sector enterprises (PSUs) such as Air India, coal mines in the state of Jharkhand (formerly part of Bihar), banks, and insurance companies come under Central Government jurisdiction. The Central Government has established 22 labour courts cum industrial tribunals (CGITs) as of this writing. Ministry of Labour and Employment, Seventh Report to the Standing Committee on Labour (Fourteenth Lok Sabha)(Dec. 2005), at 20, *available at* http://164.100.24.208/ls/CommitteeR/Labour & Wel/7rep.pdf. Government-sponsored conciliation to promote voluntary settlement of disputes is available but only mandatory if a strike or lockout has occurred or is threatened in a public utility service. Even in situations of "mandatory" conciliation, the parties tend to view this phase as a necessary "going through the motions" prior to adjudication. Unlike most other administrative proceedings in India, decisions of industrial tribunals may be appealed within the general court system, and are routinely reviewed by the High Courts under the procedure for writ petitions. The availability of appellate review undermines the finality of industrial tribunal decisions. Many cases drag on for years, typically with the employer in a better position to wait things out. On the other hand, workers also abuse the process by bringing frivolous claims. *See* M. Dias, *Strategy for Effective*

Disposal of Cases: Role of Conciliation, in Prevention and Settlement of Disputes in India (A. Sivananthiran & C.S. Venkata Ratnam eds. 2003), *available* at http://www.ilo.org/public/english/region/asro/newdelhi/download/prevnton.pdf, at 132–33 ("[labour] courts have been indulgent in favour of the worker even when he engages in criminal activity"). In any event, industrial dispute resolution is hardly the informal, speedy, and inexpensive alternative to civil litigation that was originally planned. *See* P. D. Shenoy, *Effective Labour Court Administration: Trends and Issues*, in Sivananthiran & Ratnam, *supra*, at 10.

4. Bonded labor has consequences for entire families, not just for the men who are employed as quarry workers. Wives and children are tasked with uncompensated chores such as hauling water.

5. "Migrant labor" is supplied to the quarries by labor contractors who use the social networks of the incumbent workforce, a phenomenon common among migrant populations. *See* Kenneth D. Roberts, *Chinese Labor Migration: Insights from Mexican Undocumented Migration to the United States*, in LORAINE A. WEST & YAOHUI ZHAO, RURAL LABOR FLOWS IN CHINA (2000).

6. PIL decisions frequently refer approvingly to the progressive jurisprudence of the United States, the UK, and Canada. *See* Adam M. Smith, *Making Itself at Home: Understanding Foreign Law in Domestic Jurisprudence: The Indian Case*, 24 BERKELEY J. INT'L L. 218 (2006) Note the citations to U.S. Supreme Court decisions in the *BALCO* case. However, in the Bonded Labour Case, the Court distances itself from traditional "Anglo-Saxon jurisprudence," which, obsessed with procedural technicalities, neglects substantive justice.

14 Pursuing International Labor Standards in U.S. Courts and Through Global Codes of Conduct

A. INTRODUCTION

The globalization of business management greatly increases the chances that the actions of American corporations will affect the lives of foreign workers toiling outside U.S. borders. Stephen B. Moldof, *The Application of U.S. Labor Laws to Activities and Employees Outside the United States*, 17 LAB. LAW. 417 (2002). Whether operating a foreign subsidiary or as a virtual corporation that has outsourced to contractors a core function such as production, U.S. transnational corporations (TNCs) clearly derive benefits from foreign labor. Consequently, they are increasingly seen as bearing responsibility for working conditions on foreign soil. Undoubtedly, many of the jobs provided by the international activities of U.S. TNCs are equal or superior to those not connected to the global economy. Donald C. Dowling, Jr., *The Multi-National's Manifesto on Sweatshops, Trade/Labor Linkage, and Codes of Conduct*, 8 TULSA J. COMP. & INT'L L. 27 (2000). Yet well-publicized cases of U.S. corporate connections to foreign workers laboring in sweatshop conditions are a troubling reminder that low cost goods for American consumers are often the product of the hardships of those who produce them.

Many of the devices available for promoting corporate accountability have been discussed in previous chapters of this book. For example, advocates concerned about substandard working conditions might make use of the labor and employment laws in the country where the workers reside. Although this strategy makes sense if the workers are employed in an industrialized country, labor market regulation by developing nations can be problematic. These national jurisdictions, eager for jobs produced by TNC economic activity and simultaneously pressured by countries like the United States to uphold minimum labor standards, often lack the resources, legal culture and infrastructure necessary to ensure that international labor standards are observed within their borders.

Pressure also might be brought to bear against a TNC by filing a submission under the labor provisions of a trade agreement like the North American Agreement on Labor Cooperation (NAALC). See Chapter 6, The Regulatory Approach of the North American Free Trade Agreement. Or one might use the contact procedures of an international organization like the International Labor Organization (ILO) or the thirty-country member Organization for Economic Cooperation and Development (OECD). The former adopted a Tripartite Declaration of Principles concerning Multinational Enterprises and Social Policy in 1977, and the latter has promulgated Guidelines for Multinational Corporations. Both instruments, which provide corporate guidelines that are voluntary and not legally enforceable, were updated in 2000. However, as Professor Lance Compa notes, the soft law measures available through trade agreements and other international mechanisms – meetings, investigations, hearings, reports, and recommendations – can be "frustratingly inconclusive." Lance Compa, *Pursuing International Labour Rights in U.S. Courts: New Uses for Old Tools*, 57 INDUS. REL. (Can.) 48, 49 (2002) (hereinafter Compa, *Labour Rights*).

This chapter considers two additional strategies for securing humane working conditions for workers abroad: filing lawsuits in U.S. courts on behalf of foreign workers; and TNCs adopting and implementing global codes of conduct. Although relatively infrequent, TNCs consider law suits filed by nongovernmental organizations (NGOs) and their attendant publicity very bad for public relations. Many of the claims are based on simple common law principles of tort and contract. Others are based on American state or federal statutes. In either case, the factual allegations are anything but flattering to TNCs.

The second strategy discussed in this chapter is in some respects a response to the first. Over the past two decades, many TNCs have adopted global codes of conduct that aim to promote international labor rights and standards. By doing so, TNCs hope to head off litigation and adverse publicity, promote sound employment practices, and exert control over their foreign contractors. BOB HEPPLE, LABOUR LAWS AND GLOBAL TRADE 71 (2005) (hereinafter HEPPLE, LABOUR LAWS). Codes of conduct exhibit great variation both in terms of the contents of the rights protected, and whether and what kind of a monitoring systems are employed. Edward Iwata, *How Barbie Is Making Business a Little Better*, USA TODAY, Mar. 27, 2006, at 1B-2B. The promise and perils of this international form of self-regulation, and the utility of U.S. litigation as a workers' rights strategy are reviewed here.

B. COMMON LAW ACTIONS

SUPERIOR COURT OF THE STATE OF CALIFORNIA

FOR THE COUNTY OF LOS ANGELES, CENTRAL DISTRICT

[Suit filed September 13, 2005]

JANE DOE I . . . and JOHN DOE I . . . , Individually and on behalf of Wal-Mart workers in Shenzhen, China;	)))
JANE DOE III and JANE DOE IV, Individually and on behalf of Wal-Mart workers in Dhaka, Bangladesh;	) CASE NO.:))
JANE DOE V . . . and JOHN DOE III, Individually and on behalf of Wal-Mart workers in Bogor, Indonesia;	) CLASS ACTION) COMPLAINT FOR) INJUNCTIVE RELIEF AND) DAMAGES
JANE DOE VII, and JANE DOE VIII, Individually and on behalf of Wal-Mart workers in Mastapha, Swaziland;	))))
JANE DOE IX . . . and JOHN DOE IV,	) JURY TRIAL DEMANDED

Individually and on behalf of Wal-Mart   )
workers in Managua and Sebaco, Nicaragua, . . .   )
)
                                  Plaintiffs,   )
v.   )
)
WAL-MART STORES, INC . . .   )
                                  Defendant.   )
)

I. INTRODUCTION AND SUMMARY OF THE ACTION

1. Plaintiffs . . . [referred to in the complaint as the "China Plaintiffs;" the "Bangladesh Plaintiffs;" the "Indonesia Plaintiffs;" the "Swaziland Plaintiffs;" and the "Nicaragua Plaintiffs;"] bring this class action suit on behalf of themselves, as well as all those similarly situated within the designated regions of the aforementioned countries, for injunctive relief and damages.

2. All Plaintiffs . . . bring suit for breach of contract as third party beneficiaries to Defendant Wal-Mart Stores, Inc.'s (hereinafter "Wal-Mart") supply contracts with garment factories located in China, Bangladesh, Indonesia, Swaziland and Nicaragua. The supply contracts require that the foreign suppliers in the identified countries producing goods for Wal-Mart adhere to Wal-Mart's Standards for Suppliers Agreement (hereinafter referred to interchangeably as "Code of Conduct") as a direct condition of supplying merchandise to Wal-Mart. In exchange, Wal-Mart was obligated to ensure supplier compliance with their Code of Conduct, and adequately monitor working conditions in supplier factories. Indeed, Wal-Mart represents to the public at large that it is committed to and, in fact does, strictly undertake such obligations given the well-documented evidence by public reports and its own monitoring audits that serious worker rights violations were notoriously routine in the identified countries.

3. In failing to leverage its economic position and actual control over supplier factories to undertake adequate monitoring, ensure supplier compliance, and/or otherwise terminate its business relationship with non-complying supplier factories, Wal-Mart breached its obligations under its supply contract to the direct detriment of Plaintiffs, as well as similarly situated members of the proposed class. As a result, . . . Plaintiffs were subjected to forced overtime, payments below the legal minimum and overtime wages as established by the laws of supplier countries identified herein, and overall were forced to work in sub-standard sweatshop conditions detrimental to their health and safety and in violation of their basic human rights. Such violations also constitute negligence and unjust enrichment under California state law. . . .

5. Plaintiffs bring their claims against Wal-Mart in the United States because Wal-Mart's Standard for Suppliers Agreement is premised and controlled by U.S. law, Wal-Mart explicitly claims that it monitors and enforces its Code of Conduct from its headquarters in the U.S., and the Standard for Suppliers is routinely advertised in the U.S. as Wal-Mart's Code of Conduct for foreign suppliers. Moreover, as more fully discussed below, the courts of the . . . Plaintiffs' home forums do not provide an adequate, alternative forum due to, *inter alia*, notoriously corrupt judiciaries, lack of independent judicial branches, and lack of effective and enforceable remedies.

6. More importantly, Plaintiffs and their families would be subjected to threats of reprisal, including threats of current and future job loss, and in many cases, threats of physical danger

by the supplier companies and/or their home country governments if they were to fully pursue and enforce these claims in their home countries. Accordingly, Plaintiffs also bring their claims using pseudonyms, in lieu of their true identities, to protect themselves and their families from such harm and retaliation.

II. PARTIES

[Part II of the Complaint provides details on the terms and conditions of employment of the Plaintiffs, alleges that these conditions are illegal and violate Wal-Mart's Code of Conduct, and asserts that the Plaintiffs do not have access to an independent and unbiased judiciary system in which to bring their claims. The paragraphs below on the Bangladesh Plaintiffs are illustrative.]

B. The Bangladesh Plaintiffs

12. Plaintiff Jane Doe III is a Bangladeshi citizen residing in Dhaka, Bangladesh. Approximately between September 2002 through April 2004, she was employed as a helper and junior sewing operator by Western Dresses factory where she was subjected to forced overtime and denied full overtime pay. These violations occurred while Plaintiff Jane Doe III was producing garments for a Wal-Mart work-order issued to Western Dresses. Western Dresses is a factory located in Dhaka, Bangladesh that supplies clothing merchandise to Wal-Mart for sale in the U.S. market on a regular and routine basis. She brings this suit on behalf of herself and all others similarly situated employed by Wal-Mart supplier factories in Dhaka, Bangladesh. . . .

14. The Bangladesh Plaintiffs are unable to bring their claim in Bangladesh due to a well-known record of violent reprisal against workers who complain about labor rights conditions or who attempt to secure their labor rights. Factory owners in Bangladesh routinely employ private security squads, known locally as "Mastans", for this very purpose. These "Mastans" routinely assault, rape and in some cases kill workers who complain even about the most minute labor rights violations or who attempt to form trade unions. Nazma Akther, for example, who was the leader of the national union federation of garment workers, had acid thrown on her and was badly injured as a result. Plaintiffs would be subjected to the same sort of violence if they were to pursue their claims in Bangladesh. Moreover, even assuming that such claims could safely be brought, the Bangladeshi judiciary is notoriously corrupt and could not adequately ensure Plaintiffs a fair trial or provide adequate remedies. . . .

[Part II also describes Defendant Wal-Mart]

G. Defendant Wal-Mart and the Wal-Mart Code of Conduct

35. Defendant Wal-Mart Stores, Inc. is a for-profit corporation with headquarters in Bentonville, Arkansas. Today, it is the world's largest retailer and is engaged in the business of selling discounted merchandise, including garments and toys, both in the U.S. and internationally. Its retail stores are located throughout the United States, including California. Wal-Mart owns and operates over 140 stores and Sam's Clubs in California, where it directly employs over 40,000 workers. In addition, it has four distribution centers and one office facility located in California, and receives massive amounts of shipments by sea and air in California from its suppliers abroad, including from the specific suppliers at issue in this case. Much of Wal-Mart's products enter the stream of commerce from California.

36. Despite its revenue and position as a market leader in the retail industry, Wal-Mart is notoriously known for its consistent failure to protect worker rights in its own stores, as well as in the factories of its overseas suppliers. Since the 1990's, numerous investigations have revealed Wal-Mart's consistent practice of sourcing merchandise from suppliers using sweatshop conditions. Probably the most well known was the 1992 Kathie Lee Gifford controversy. Based on this and other controversies, in 2001 KLD Research & Analytics, Inc., who compile the Domini 400 Social Index, removed Wal-Mart from its index of socially responsible corporations. The company had not done enough to ensure that its domestic and international vendors operate factories that meet basic human rights and labor standards. KLD is not alone in sanctioning Wal-Mart. Investigation after investigation of Wal-Mart's operations and suppliers reveal that Wal-Mart is an unrepentant and recidivist violator of human rights.

37. Precisely because of the notorious worker rights violations in its supplier factories, which there is no question Wal-Mart had knowledge of, Wal-Mart developed in 1992 a Code of Conduct (known formally as the "Standards for Suppliers"). This was a central decision, made by upper management at the company headquarters in Arkansas, and from its inception, was to apply to all suppliers, including those that are the subject of this litigation. The Code of Conduct, which is incorporated into its supply contracts with foreign suppliers, purports to require all suppliers to adhere to applicable laws regarding basic conditions of employment, including: Compensation; Hours of Labor; Forced Labor/Prison Labor; Child Labor; Discrimination/Human Rights; Freedom of Association and Collective Bargaining; and Workplace Environment. There have been various versions of this Code of Conduct produced by Wal-Mart since 1992, but all versions purport to extend these fundamental rights to workers in Wal-Mart suppliers. As part of its public representations, Wal-Mart promises to do business with suppliers who are in compliance with the Code of Conduct.

38. This supply contract and Code of Conduct is uniform and globally-applicable, and is imposed and monitored from Wal-Mart's headquarters in Arkansas. Regional offices, including Bangalore, India, Shenzhen, China, Singapore, and Honduras oversee local production and report directly to Wal-Mart's headquarters in Arkansas. The power to hire and fire staff responsible for monitoring activities is vested in the Central Management office. The regional offices implement the policies and practices of the Wal-Mart headquarters, resulting in a uniform practice and procedure being applied to all Wal-Mart suppliers in Asia, Africa, and Latin America. Among the requirements imposed by the regional offices, at the direction of the headquarters office, is the requirement that Wal-Mart's Code of Conduct be incorporated in all supplier agreements, including those located in China, Bangladesh, Indonesia, Swaziland, and Nicaragua, the countries identified herein.

39. As part of its obligations under the supply contract, and as per its specific promise to the consuming public in the U.S., including California, Wal-Mart promises to monitor supplier factories to ensure compliance with the Code of Conduct. Specifically, the preamble to a 2003 version of the Code of Conduct states that "the conduct of its suppliers can be attributed to Wal-Mart and affect its reputation, . . . and hereby reserves the right to make periodic, unannounced inspections of supplier's facilities to satisfy itself of supplier's compliance with these standards." The 2005 version reinforces that Wal-Mart has the "right of inspection."

40. Paragraph 5 of the 2004 version of the Code of Conduct (FACTORY INSPECTION REQUIREMENTS) requires that "[s]cheduled inspections should typically be conducted a maximum of three times per year to ensure compliance with the standards, terms, and conditions set forth herein. Wal-Mart reserves the right to conduct unannounced factory inspections. . . . In the case of suppliers working through Global Procurement Direct

Imports, audits should be conducted by Wal-Mart's internal auditors." The 2005 version provides a specific "right of inspection" to Wal-Mart.

41. Wal-Mart's monitoring consists of factory investigations by Wal-Mart hired auditors based on a color coded system: factories with low-risk violations are assessed as Green, factories with medium-risk violations are assessed as Yellow, factories with high-risk violations are assessed as Red, and factories with critical violations are Failed. However, significant numbers of factories receive Yellow (medium risk) and Red (high risk) ratings, particularly those in China, but Wal-Mart continues to source from them. Further, other than child labor, there are not clear guidelines on what violations fall under the particular ratings. It also requires two consecutive Red ratings for Wal-Mart to suspend orders, but the company can request purchases again from these same factories once the factory receives a Yellow rating, still medium risk. Thus, Wal-Mart products are being produced by workers in facilities that are known risks. Further, at most, only 8% of all Wal-Mart audits in 2004 are unannounced, and while auditors are supposed to perform off-site worker interviews for each audit, Wal-Mart admits that workers are often coached on the answers to give inspectors.

42. Because Wal-Mart's system limits factory inspections to those conducted by internal Wal-Mart auditors, or relies upon consultants paid for by Wal-Mart, it is far from effective and allows rampant violations to continue. In essence, based on its policy created by central management, Wal Mart's code enforcement is a closed loop: Wal-Mart adopts the code, monitors the code, and reports on whether code compliance has been achieved – in the absence of meaningful transparency and in the absence of any independent, external mechanisms for enforcing the code. . . .

43. The conditions endured by the Plaintiffs in violation of law and the Wal-Mart Code of Conduct are the result of Wal-Mart's central practices of ignoring the requirements of its Code of Conduct, and knowingly imposing price and time requirements on suppliers that necessarily result in sweatshop conditions. Further, Wal-Mart fails to take account of its knowledge of risk and knowingly uses factories that have failed to pass even Wal-Mart's lax system of inspection and monitoring. Knowing of the risks in many of its suppliers, Wal-Mart still fails to exercise adequate supervision of compliance with its Code of Conduct, as well as compliance with local laws and well-established international standards, such as Conventions of the ILO. In contrast, Wal-Mart has an effective system of monitoring and supervision to ensure that all of its suppliers, including those named herein, meet Wal-Mart's standards for price, quality and timely delivery.

44. Wal-Mart acknowledges, and represents to the public, in both its 2002 and 2003 Annual Report on Supplier Standards and/or Factory Certification Report (hereinafter "Supplier Standards Reports") that its "Factory Certification Program" used to implement the Code of Conduct has the "fundamental objective" of "encourag[ing] implementation of necessary changes that will ultimately result in an improved quality of life for the workers who supply our stores with the merchandise our customers demand." In 2005 Wal-Mart began calling its overall monitoring effort the "Ethical Sourcing Program." . . .

47. Plaintiffs, and members of the proposed subclasses, as a matter of economic reality, have been and are dependent upon Wal-Mart for their livelihoods and supplier compliance with the minimum and overtime wage protections within Wal-Mart's Code of Conduct. Based on its vast economic power, Wal-Mart, based on its Code of Conduct, can and does control the working conditions within the supplier factories. It could use its power and position to prevent its producers from profiting from the inhumane treatment of Plaintiffs and members of the proposed subclasses. Instead, Wal-Mart is itself the reason for the inhumane conditions. It uses its vast market power to insist on low unit prices that are possible only if workers are

squeezed to such an extreme degree that they can barely survive the long hours and low wages they are forced to endure. . . .

48. Specifically, Wal-Mart controlled the working conditions imposed upon Plaintiffs by the identified suppliers through its supply contract, as evidence by the following:

(a) Wal-Mart exercised meaningful control over the minimum wage and overtime policies of the identified supplier factories due to its obligation under the supply contract to monitor and audit the working conditions therein;

(b) Wal-Mart exercised meaningful control over the minimum wage and overtime policies of the supplier factories through the power to cancel any and all outstanding orders, refusal or return of any shipment, and the ability to cease a business relationship with the supplier in non-compliance the Code of Conduct;

(c) Wal-Mart exercised meaningful control over the operative details of Plaintiffs' tasks, including the quantity, quality standards, turnaround time, and other operative details of the production process with regards to the production of goods to be exported to Wal-Mart stores;

(d) Wal-Mart personnel and/or its agents supervised the production process by, according to its own obligations under the supply contract, being present at the supplier factories where Plaintiffs worked, and because they review, inspect, oversee, monitor and audit such work, routinely taking random samples from the production line before shipment to ensure quality control; and

(e) Wal-Mart ultimately has control over the working conditions at all of its suppliers because of its notorious policy of requiring the lowest possible prices, which Wal-Mart knows, makes it impossible for suppliers to comply with even the most basic laws where they operate, including wage and hours laws.

49. Wal-Mart operates with specific knowledge that a large [number] of its suppliers operate in violation of law, as well as in violation of Wal-Mart's Code of Conduct and Wal-Mart further knows its monitoring process may be the sole mechanism available to workers in supplier factories to obtain legal compliance. Indeed, in both its 2002 and 2003 Supplier Standards Reports, Wal-Mart admits that "[m]any countries we source from have very good labor laws but, for a variety of reasons, they may not be routinely enforced. In many cases our auditing process is the main law enforcement mechanism for the factories from which we source." . . .

[The Complaint brings causes of action for, *inter alia*: 1) breach of contract for denial of minimum and overtime wages; 2) breach of contract for forced labor; 3) breach of contract for denial of the right to freely associate (on behalf of only the Indonesia, Swaziland and Nicaragua Plaintiffs); 4) negligence and recklessness; 5) negligence per se; 6) negligent hiring and supervision; 7) unjust enrichment; and 8) violation of California's Business and Professions Code (Plaintiff's allege that Wal-Mart's fraudulent, deceptive practices constitute unfair business practices).]

_____

Notes

1. Note that the Wal-Mart case was brought in state rather than in federal court. That the claims are based on California common and statutory law likely influenced the plaintiffs' choice of forum. Some plaintiffs' lawyers may also shy away from filing in federal court due to a perception that federal courts are hostile to labor and employment law claims. Professor Stephen Befort has written at length about what he believes is a conscious policy by the U.S. Supreme Court of diverting labor and employment claims away from the federal court system. Stephen F. Befort, *The*

Labor and Employment Law Decisions of the Supreme Court's 2003–04 Term, 20 LAB. LAW. 177, 215–24 (2004).

2. Wal-Mart reacted to this very novel suit in a manner common to employer defendants by filing a motion to remove the case to federal court. The motion was granted, and the case was removed effective January 11, 2006. Superior Court of California, County of Los Angeles, Case Summary, Case BC339737, filed Sept. 13, 2005, available at http://www.lasuperiorcourt.org/civilCaseSummary/index.asp?CaseType=Civil. Wal-Mart thereafter filed a motion to dismiss on February 13, 2006 in U.S. District Court for the Central District of California. Among Wal-Mart's arguments are that: (1) the issues in the case should be litigated where the alleged wrongs occurred; (2) the foreign plaintiffs are no more than incidental beneficiaries under the supplier agreements; (3) there is no employment relationship between Wal-Mart and the foreign workers; and (4) the plaintiffs' negligence claims fail because Wal-Mart did not owe the foreign plaintiffs a duty of care. Wal-Mart Stores, Inc.'s Notice of Motion and Motion to Dismiss Plaintiffs' First Amended Complaint, Feb. 13, 2006, at i. As this book goes to press, the motion is set to be argued on November 20, 2006.

3. Regardless of the outcome of this particular suit, an important threshold issue in cases with international implications is whether a U.S. court has jurisdiction over the matter. How does the complaint above attempt to establish that California's courts have personal jurisdiction over Wal-Mart? Is paragraph 35 of the complaint persuasive on this point? California is the most populous state in the United Sates and a significant market for Wal-Mart's products.

4. Plaintiffs' lawyers bringing suits on behalf of workers in U.S. courts must anticipate that defendants will raise the defense of *forum non conveniens*. This common law defense asserts that although a U.S. court might have technical jurisdiction over a claim, the inconvenience of litigating in that forum, because, for example, evidence and witnesses are located elsewhere, requires dismissal of the suit. In cases where the workers' home country is a developing nation, however, a U.S. court may be the only forum in which the plaintiffs can seek justice. Emily Yozell, *The Castro Alfaro Case: Convenience and Justice – Lessons for Lawyers in Transcultural Litigation, in* HUMAN RIGHTS, LABOR RIGHTS, AND INTERNATIONAL TRADE 273, 278 (Lance A. Compa & Stephen F. Diamond, eds., 1996). How do the plaintiffs in the complaint against Wal-Mart attempt to head off a *forum non conveniens* defense? Do paragraphs 5, 6, and 14 of the complaint preemptively refute such an argument?

5. A choice of law issue may arise in the Wal-Mart case. In other words, if the suit is not dismissed, what substantive law should the court apply? Should the court apply the contract and tort law of California because that is where the suit was brought (the *lex fori* rule) or the law of the places where the disputed actions occurred or where the alleged contracts were made (the *lex loci* rule)? The European Union, which aspires to the free movement of workers throughout its member countries, has a model for resolving employment conflict of laws problems on a regional scale. HEPPLE, LABOUR LAWS, at 152. In the United States, however, no universally agreed upon choice of law model exists for international labor rights cases because, *inter alia*, so few have been litigated. Although traditionally American courts have favored the *lex loci* rule in cases where the law of more than one U.S. state is at issue, some courts have more recently taken a flexible, policy-oriented approach,

applying the law of the jurisdiction with the "most significant relationship" to the parties concerned. Compa, *Labour Rights*, at 61-2.

6. Are the plaintiffs in *Jane Doe I et al. v. Wal-Mart Stores, Inc.* vulnerable on the choice of law issue? In a part of the complaint not excerpted above, the plaintiffs argued that Wal-Mart is a joint employer of its suppliers' workers. By doing so, are they making the case for applying Arkansas law, as that is where Wal-Mart is headquartered? Indeed, in Wal-Mart's motion to dismiss, the company cites Arkansas contract law to support its argument that the foreign workers are at most incidental beneficiaries of the supplier agreements. Wal-Mart Stores, Inc.'s Notice of Motion and Motion to Dismiss Plaintiffs' First Amended Complaint, Feb. 13, 2006, at 7-8.

7. An interesting choice of law problem was presented in *Google, Inc. and Kai-Fu Lee v. Microsoft Corp.*, No. C-05-03095 RMW, 2005 U.S. Dist. LEXIS 40678 (N.D. Ca. Oct. 27, 2005). In that case, Microsoft sued Lee, a former employee, and Google, Lee's new employer, in Washington state court for breach of the covenant not to compete that was part of Lee's employment agreement at Microsoft. Lee, Microsoft's Vice President for Research and Development, had been hired away from the company by Google to develop the latter's business in China. In a bid to prevent Microsoft from successfully obtaining and enforcing an injunction against them, Google and Lee sought a declaration from a California Superior Court that the covenant not to compete was invalid and unenforceable under California law. *Id.* *1–4. California is both the state where Google is headquartered and where Lee had moved from Washington. *Id.* at *20.

8. Microsoft removed the case to federal district court, and that court, while granting Microsoft's motion to stay the California proceedings until the completion of the Washington state action, nonetheless articulated the Restatement (Second) of Conflict of Laws approach to determining which state's contract law should apply in the case:

> Section 188 [of the Restatement (Second) of Conflict of Laws] requires a court to apply the contract law of the state most intimately connected with the deal:
>
> (1) The rights and duties of the parties with respect to an issue in contract are determined by the local law of the state, which, with respect to that issue, has the most significant relationship to the transaction and the parties under the principles stated in § 6.
>
> (2) In the absence of an effective choice of law by the parties . . . the contacts to be taken into account in applying the principles of § 6 to determine the law applicable to an issue include:
>
> (a) the place of contracting,
>
> (b) the place of negotiation of the contract,
>
> (c) the place of performance,
>
> (d) the location of the subject matter of the contract, and
>
> (e) the domicile, residence, nationality, place of incorporation and place of business of the parties.
>
> Google, Inc. and Kai-Fu Lee v. Microsoft Corp., 2005 U.S. Dist. LEXIS at *18 (quoting Rest. (Second) Confl. Laws § 188(1)–(2) (1971)).

Using the principles listed here, does it appear that the plaintiffs in *Jane Doe I et al. v. Wal-Mart Stores, Inc.* have a colorable argument the California's law should be applied in the case?

9. Note that the manufacturers that employ the foreign plaintiffs are not named as co-defendants. Why do you suppose this is so? Paragraphs 47 and 48 of the complaint describe the plaintiffs as economically dependent on Wal-Mart and assert that Wal-Mart controls the terms and conditions of their employment. As noted earlier, in a portion of the complaint not reproduced in this text, the plaintiffs assert that Wal-Mart acted as a joint employer of the plaintiffs. The need to "pierce the corporate veil" to hold a seemingly unrelated corporation accountable as an employer of foreign workers often arises in international labor rights cases. In the *Pico Products* case, for example, a Korean labor union sued Pico Products, a New York corporation, over the latter's decision to close its then recently-unionized Korean subsidiary. Labor Union of Pico Korea, Ltd. v. Pico Products, Inc., No. 90-CV-774, 1991 WL 299121 (N.D.N.Y. Dec. 23, 1991). The first cause of action attempted to pierce the corporate veil, and hold Pico Products liable for breach of the collective bargaining agreement between the plaintiff union and the Korean subsidiary. New York law required that the union prove *inter alia* that Pico Products was the alter ego of the subsidiary, and that the subsidiary was subject to the complete domination of its parent. *Id.* at *5. The judge in the trial found that while the Korean subsidiary lacked the ability to control all but its daily operations, the evidence was insufficient to pierce the veil insulating Pico Products from liability. Frank E. Deale, *The Pico Case: Testing International Labor Rights in U.S. Courts, in* HUMAN RIGHTS, LABOR RIGHTS, AND INTERNATIONAL TRADE 251, 256–8 (Lance A. Compa & Stephen F. Diamond, eds., 1996) (hereinafter Deale, *The Pico Case*). In terms of piercing the corporate veil, is the *Wal-Mart* suit distinguishable from the situation in *Pico Products*?

10. Representing workers whose cultural backgrounds differ greatly from that of their American counsel is another challenge in international labor rights litigation. In the Pico case cited above, lawyers for the Center for Constitutional Rights, a prominent NGO, were assisted by a facilitator, described as a "member of the legal team who shared the language and culture of the clients and the lawyers." Deale, *The Pico Case*, at 265. Despite the good work of the Korean facilitator, the case outcome turned on cultural differences. Before trial, Pico made a settlement offer that the NGO lawyers and Korean facilitator strongly believed their clients should accept. The settlement would have given the plaintiffs over 75 percent of what they might obtain from a successful trial, and avoided the risk that the plaintiffs' alter ego argument would be rejected by the judge. The clients, however, felt that settlement, even accompanied by a public apology from the company, was tantamount to capitulation, and turned down Pico's offer. The case was tried, and the judge rejected the workers' claims. *Id.* at 267.

11. Wal-Mart is in many ways an irresistible target for workers' advocates. It is the world's largest retailer, employing 1.8 million employees worldwide. The company enjoyed U.S.$312.4 billion in sales during the fiscal year ending in January 2006. *See* Wal-Mart Fact Sheets, http://www.walmartfacts.com/doyouknow/. Wal-Mart's international sales total US$64 billion, 20 percent of its annual sales. Wal-Mart operates in 13 countries around the globe. In 2006, Wal-Mart shut its operations in

     Germany and South Korea. David Barboza & Michael Barbaro, *Wal-Mart is said to be acquiring a chain in China*, N.Y. TIMES, Oct. 17, 2006, at A-1, C-9.

12. Wal-Mart's economic might is extraordinary. For example, in 2003, Wal-Mart purchased products totaling US $15 billion from China. If Wal-Mart were a country, it would be "China's eighth-biggest trading partner, ahead of Russia, Australia and Canada." Jiang Jingjing, Wal-Mart's China inventory to hit US 18b this year, China Daily, November, 29 2004 (quoting Xu Jun, Wal-Mart China's director of external affairs).

13. Wal-Mart's success is attributed to its low-price/high-volume business model, and its aggressive pursuit of supply chain efficiencies. However, evidence also indicates that Wal-Mart pays its U.S. employees 14.5 percent less than other large retailers, and employs a greater percentage of workers who lack health insurance. Arindrajit Dube & Steve Wertheim, Wal-Mart and Job Quality – What Do We Know, and Should We Care? (unpublished paper, October 16, 2005).

14. A study of Wal-Mart workers in California found that these employees' reliance on public assistance programs costs the state U.S.$86 million annually, $32 million of which is comprised of health-related expenses. Family members of California Wal-Mart employees use 40 percent more in public health benefits than the average for families of employees working at large retail establishments. ARINDRAJIT DUBE & KEN JACOBS, UNIVERSITY OF CALIFORNIA, BERKELEY CENTER FOR LABOR RESEARCH AND EDUCATION, HIDDEN COST OF WAL-MART JOBS: USE OF SAFETY NET PROGRAMS BY WAL-MART WORKERS IN CALIFORNIA, 2004. Similar concerns prompted the Maryland legislature to pass a law requiring "employers with 10,000 or more employees in the state [to] spend at least 8 percent of their payrolls on health insurance, or pay the difference into [a] state Medicaid fund." Michael Barbaro, *Maryland Sets a Health Cost for Wal-Mart*, NY TIMES, Jan. 13, 2006, at A1. The measure, which was passed over a gubernatorial veto, was the first such law in the nation. *Id.* A federal district court judge struck down the law in July 2006, holding that it violates the Employment Retirement Income Security Act of 1974 (ERISA). Reed Abelson & Michael Barbaro, *Judge Gives Wal-Mart Reprieve on Benefits*, N.Y.TIMES, July 20, 2006, at C1.

15. Accusations by its critics that Wal-Mart hurts American workers by undercutting the pay and benefits of its competitors, prompted the retailer in October 2005 to host an academic conference on its effects on the U.S. economy. A study presented at the conference, paid for by Wal-Mart, and authored by Global Insight, Inc., an independent economic research firm, concluded that in 2004, Wal-Mart was directly and indirectly responsible for U.S.$263 billion dollars of savings to consumers. That figure translates to a savings of U.S.$2,329 per household. When the inflation rate and small nominal wage increases are accounted for, the net increase in consumer purchasing power in 2004 was U.S.$118 billion dollars or U.S.$1046 per household. GLOBAL INSIGHT, THE ECONOMIC IMPACT OF WAL-MART (2005).

16. A paper presented at the Wal-Mart conference, however, found that the company negatively impacts county employment in the retail sector. More specifically, the authors, who looked at the employment effects of openings of 3,066 Wal-Mart stores in the United States, conclude that countywide retail employment declines by 2–4 percent following the opening of a Wal-Mart store. County payroll measured per person also drops by 5 percent, indicating that a Wal-Mart store adversely

affects take-home pay not simply in the retail industry but across the entire county in which it is located. David Neumark, Junfu Zhang & Stephen Ciccarella, The Effects of Wal-Mart on Local Labor Markets (unpublished paper, November 2005). Do the documented price savings made possible by Wal-Mart offset the negative wage and employment effects revealed by recent studies? Do the savings, which benefit many American working class and rural consumers, excuse the working conditions of the employees of some of Wal-Mart's international suppliers? And, more importantly, should Wal-Mart be held responsible for working conditions in its suppliers' factories?

C. GLOBAL CODES OF CONDUCT

A central focus of the Wal-Mart litigation is whether in allegedly allowing substandard working conditions to flourish in the factories of its suppliers, the company breached the agreements it had with those suppliers, which require them to adhere to Wal-Mart's Code of Conduct. Among the most interesting and controversial forms of corporate self-regulation is the voluntarily adopted global code of conduct, which seeks to govern the worldwide activities of TNCs and, in some cases, those with whom they contract.

Wal-Mart posts its Code of Conduct on its Web site. The Code, dated January 10, 2005 is reproduced here.

WAL-MART STORES, INC. STANDARDS FOR SUPPLIERS

. . . [B]ecause the conduct of Wal-Mart's suppliers can be attributed to Wal-Mart and its reputation, Wal-Mart requires its suppliers, and their subcontractors, to meet the following standards, and reserves the right to make periodic, unannounced inspections of suppliers' facilities and the facilities of suppliers' contractors to ensure suppliers' compliance with these standards:

1. COMPLIANCE WITH APPLICABLE LAWS AND PRACTICE
Suppliers shall comply with all local and national laws and regulations of the jurisdictions in which the suppliers are doing business as well as the practices of their industry. . . .

2. EMPLOYMENT CONDITIONS
. . . [T]he following are specific requirements relating to employment conditions:

Compensation
Suppliers shall fairly compensate their employees by providing wages and benefits that are in compliance with the local and national laws of the jurisdictions in which the suppliers are doing business or which are consistent with the prevailing local standards in the country if the prevailing local standard is higher.

Hours of Labor
Suppliers shall maintain employee work hours in compliance with local standards and applicable laws of the jurisdictions in which the suppliers are doing business. Employees shall not work more than 72 hours per 6 days or work more than a maximum total working hours of 14 hours per calendar day (midnight to midnight). Supplier's factories should be working toward achieving a 60-hour work week. Wal-Mart will not use suppliers who, on a regularly scheduled basis, require employees to work in excess of the statutory requirements without proper compensation as required by applicable law. Employees should be permitted reasonable days off (at least one day off for every seven-day period) and leave privileges.

Forced/Prison Labor
Forced or prison labor will not be tolerated by Wal-Mart. . . .

Child Labor
Wal-Mart will not tolerate the use of child labor. Wal-Mart will not accept products from suppliers or subcontractors who directly or indirectly use child labor. No person shall be employed at an age younger than the legal minimum age for working in any specific country and not less than 14 years, whichever is greater.

Discrimination /Human Rights
. . . Wal-Mart favors suppliers who have a social and political commitment to basic principles of human rights and who do not discriminate against their employees in hiring practices or any other term or condition of work, on the basis of race, color, national origin, gender, sexual orientation, religion, disability, or other similar factors.

Freedom of Association and Collective Bargaining
Suppliers will respect the rights of employees regarding their decision of whether to associate or not to associate with any group, as long as such groups are legal in their own country. Suppliers must not interfere with, obstruct or prevent such legitimate activities.

3. WORKPLACE ENVIRONMENT
Factories producing merchandise to be sold by Wal-Mart shall provide adequate medical facilities and ensure that all production and manufacturing processes are carried out in conditions that have proper and adequate regard for the health and safety of those involved. Wal-Mart will not do business with any supplier that provides an unhealthy or hazardous work environment or which utilizes mental or physical disciplinary practices. . . .

5. FACTORY INSPECTION REQUIREMENTS
Scheduled inspections are conducted a maximum of three times per year or as necessary to ensure compliance with Wal-Mart's communicated standards, terms, and conditions. Wal-Mart reserves the right to conduct unannounced factory inspections. Suppliers are required to fully disclose to Wal-Mart all material facts relating to the production of merchandise including the use of subcontractors.

. . . Any supplier who fails or refuses to comply with these practices is subject to immediate cancellation of any and all outstanding orders, refusal or return of any shipment, and termination of its business relationship with Wal-Mart. . . .

Notes

1. Are voluntary codes of conduct enforceable? That, of course, is the question posed by the *Wal-Mart* suit discussed here. Some commentators assert that the codes are not generally considered legally binding. Michael Posner & Justine Nolan, *Can Codes of Conduct Play a Role in Promoting Workers' Rights?, in* INTERNATIONAL LABOR STANDARDS: GLOBALIZATION, TRADE, AND PUBLIC POLICY 207, 208 (Robert J. Flanagan & William B. Gould IV, eds., 2003) (hereinafter Posner & Nolan, *Codes of Conduct*). Others posit that given the right factual circumstances, some codes may constitute legally binding contracts. Harry Arthurs, *Private Ordering and Workers' Rights in the Global Economy: Corporate Codes of Conduct as a Regime of Labour Market Regulation, in* LABOUR LAW IN AN ERA OF GLOBALIZATION 471, 484 (Joanne Conaghan, Richard Michael Fischl & Karl Klare, eds., 2002) (hereinafter Arthurs, *Private Ordering*).

2. Codes of conduct vary considerably by company and industry, although most attempt to guarantee at least some basic labor rights. One challenge for TNCs is to articulate principles of freedom of association and collective bargaining that enable factories operating in China and Vietnam, countries that severely restrict those rights, to achieve Code of conduct compliance. Posner & Nolan, *Codes of Conduct*, at 208-11. Does Wal-Mart's Code attempt to account for China's legal regime? See Chapter 11 for China's legal approach to unions.

3. TNCs often argue that their overseas activities help to better or "ratchet up" the labor standards of the countries where they do business. This is especially true in the area of compensation. Note how Wal-Mart's Code of Conduct attempts to prevent the compensation paid by suppliers and subcontractors from falling below prevailing standards. Is Wal-Mart attempting to improve labor standards with respect to hours of labor?

4. Ironically, Wal-Mart's own domestic labor practices are controversial and have been subject to suit. For example, Wal-Mart is the focus of the largest class action discrimination lawsuit in the history of the United States. The suit alleges widespread discrimination in promotion and pay against approximately 1.5 million women in the U.S. Dukes v. Wal-Mart Stores, Inc., 222 F.R.D. 137 (N.D. Cal. 2004). Recently, a California jury awarded U.S.$172 million to thousands of Wal-Mart workers claiming that they were illegally denied lunch breaks. Amy Joyce, *Calif. Jury Backs Wal-Mart Workers*, WASHINGTON POST, Dec. 23, 2005, at D01. There are presently about 40 class action wage and hour cases pending against Wal-Mart in the U.S. *Id.* In March 2005, the U.S. Department of Justice and Immigration and Customs Enforcement reached an U.S.$11 million dollar settlement with Wal-Mart for using contractors employing undocumented workers to perform cleaning services at Wal-Mart stores throughout the country. http://www.ice.gov/pi/news/factsheets/worksite031805.htm.

5. Michael Posner and Justine Nolan classify codes of conduct into four categories. First generation codes are those developed by individual TNCs without consultation with industry groups, NGOs, or unions. Monitoring is not always provided for but where it is, compliance review relies on internal systems. In other words, the TNC's own employees staff the compliance function. Critics of this type of code argue that the standards in the devices are often self-referential and imprecise, and that the monitoring systems lack the independence necessary to make them credible and effective. Posner & Nolan, *Codes of Conduct*, at 210.

6. Rather than use their own employees as monitors, some TNCs employ outside consulting firms such as Ernst & Young to conduct compliance reviews. This form of monitoring is criticized as lacking in independence. HEPPLE, LABOUR LAWS, at 74-5. A related issue is the transparency of a TNC's monitoring process. Companies are under increasing pressure to release to the public both the locations of their factories and reports on factory conditions. Posner & Nolan, *Codes of Conduct*, at 215.

7. A second type of code is designed to ameliorate some of the criticisms of the first. This category consists of common standards and reporting mechanisms designed by industry or trade associations. Examples from this group include the 1996 International Federation of Football Associations (FIFA) Code of Labour Practice, which was created to combat child labor in soccer ball production, and the World-Wide Responsible Apparel Production (WRAP) initiative, which was

launched by the American Apparel Manufacturing Association. Although such initiatives may make inroads toward standardizing guidelines and monitoring procedures, they are still criticized for being excessively industry-oriented and for lacking credible oversight. Posner & Nolan, *Codes of Conduct*, at 210. Indeed, to meet such criticisms, over time FIFA greatly enhanced its approach to child labor in conjunction with ILO child labor programs. The ILO-FIFA Programme, http://www.fifa.com/en/fairplay/humanitariansection/0,1422,5,00.html.

8. The third category consists of codes developed by an external party, like an NGO, in consultation with industry and other stakeholders, like labor unions and other NGOs. Monitoring of the codes in this category is external. Compliance is assessed by an independent third party, and transparency is part of the process. Well-known examples of initiatives in this category are the Fair Labor Association (FLA), Social Accountability International (SAI), the Worker Rights Consortium (WRC), and the Ethical Trading Initiative (ETI). The advantage of these efforts is that they attempt to achieve, through multistakeholder dialogue, uniformity in labor standards that is responsive not only to the needs of industry but also to the human rights of workers. Posner & Nolan, *Codes of Conduct*, at 210-1. Nonetheless, these initiatives are not immune from criticism. The FLA, for example, has been called "a corporate front group" and "totally in the pocket of business." Ronald K. L. Collins & David M. Skover, *The Landmark Free-Speech Case That Wasn't: The Nike v. Kasky Story*, 54 CASE W. RES. L. REV. 965, 1021-2 (2004) (quoting activists Kevin Danneher and Jeff Ballinger) (hereinafter Collins & Skover, *Nike v. Kasky Story*).

9. The final category of codes attempts to facilitate government involvement directly or indirectly. Posner & Nolan, *Codes of Conduct*, at 210-1. The OECD Guidelines on Multinational Corporations, mentioned at the start of this chapter, is an example of such an effort. A device addressed to corporations by the thirty-member nations of the OECD and other adhering nations, the Guidelines cover a number of subjects including employment and industrial relations. National Contact Points (NCPs) are responsible for promoting the Guidelines' goals in individual countries, receiving and resolving problems, and reporting annually to the OECD. A weakness of the system, however, is that the Guidelines are non-binding and voluntary in nature. There are no sanctions for failing to abide by the OECD workplace standards. Barnali Choudhury, *Beyond the Alien Tort Claims Act: Alternative Approaches to Attributing Liability to Corporations for Extraterritorial Abuses*, 26 NW. J. INT'L L. & BUS. 43, 64 (2005) (hereinafter Choudhury, *Beyond Alien Torts Claims*).

10. The United Nations' (UN) Global Compact is another example of an effort that falls into Posner's and Nolan's fourth category. The Global Compact, a voluntary initiative, brings together corporations, UN agencies, unions, civil society and governments to advance universal social and environmental principles. Its labor principles include: support of freedom of association and collective bargaining; elimination of forced and compulsory labor; abolition of child labor; and elimination of discrimination in employment and occupation. THE UNITED NATIONS GLOBAL COMPACT: ADVANCING CORPORATE CITIZENSHIP (Prepared by the Global Compact Office, June 2005).

11. A related development is the 2003 adoption by the UN Sub-Commission on the Promotion and Protection of Human Rights of the "Norms on the Responsibilities of Transnational Corporations and Other Business Enterprises with Regard to Human

Rights." Michael J. Trebilcock & Robert Howse, *Trade Policy and Labor Standards*, 14 MINN. J. GLOBAL TRADE 261, 275-6 (2005). This initiative "seeks to provide a universal framework for corporate responsibility, guiding the many uncoordinated existing voluntary initiatives." *Id.* at 275. The Norms set out an implementation mechanism to ensure corporate compliance:

> First, corporations are expected to adopt, disseminate, and implement internal rules of operation in compliance with the Norms and then periodically report on and take other measures to fully implement the Norms. Second, activities of corporations are subject to transparent and independent periodic monitoring and verification by the U.N. and "other international and national mechanisms already in existence or yet to be created" . . . Finally, states are expected to "establish and reinforce the necessary legal and administrative framework" to ensure implementation of the Norms by corporations. Failure to abide by the Norms requires the corporations and business entities to provide reparations to those affected. The Norms indicate that damages should be assessed by national courts and/or international tribunals, but fail to specify which courts or tribunals.

> Choudhury, *Beyond Alien Tort Claims*, at 66.

Is this implementation framework viable? Can many states be expected to facilitate implementation of the Norms?

12. A bill introduced in 2001 by Congresswoman Cynthia McKinney would require U.S. corporations employing more than twenty persons in a foreign country – either directly or indirectly – to adopt a code of conduct governing the working conditions of those employees. H.R. 2782 would additionally provide a private right of action to petition for a government investigation of alleged code violations. Theodora R. Lee, *Global Employment Claims: Emerging International Labor and Employment Issues*, 730 PLI/LIT 681, 705-6 (2005).

13. Are codes of conduct a form of regulation to be applauded? Professor Harry Arthurs argues that, although voluntary codes may appear to reproduce formal legal regulation, codes that are not tied to state sanctions cannot be equated with state law. So long as TNCs are the objects, authors and administrators of their own regulation, they can "conjure it up or make it disappear" whenever they like. Harry Arthurs, *Private Ordering*, at 487. Professor Adelle Blackett assesses codes by juxtaposing them with traditional labor law. She argues that the dual purposes of state labor law are to provide worker protection and worker participation. Self-regulation via codes of conduct may obtain the former but they also increase management's power vis-à-vis the state. As such, codes shift the focus away from and may undermine worker agency and democratic participation. Adelle Blackett, *Global Governance, Legal Pluralism and the Decentered State: A Labor Law Critique of Codes of Corporate Conduct*, 8 IND. J. GLOBAL LEGAL STUD. 401, 418-20 (2001).

14. Global corporate codes of conduct are seen by some European lawyers and corporate leaders as an American phenomenon. Some managers and employees outside U.S. borders view the codes as challenging their own corporate norms, and create the impression that "they are being controlled by the United States." Michael R. Triplett, *SOX Compliance, Corporate Codes of Conduct Create Challenges for Advising Firms Abroad*, DAILY LABOR REPORT, Mar. 20, 2006 (paraphrasing comments of U.K. lawyer Paul A. Callaghan).

15. Professor Cynthia Estlund sees corporate self-regulation as an irreversible trend that might be leveraged to increase employee voice in the United States. The key to reinvigorating employee agency is to develop systems with independent, private, outside monitors that can rely on employees as whistleblowers, informants and watchdogs. Employers might be encouraged to enter into such arrangements, even without direct government intervention, if their employees were provided with private rights of action to obtain redress for corporate wrongdoing. In exchange, employers with effective, monitored systems might be granted partial immunity from ruinous sanctions. Cynthia Estlund, *Rebuilding the Law of the Workplace in an Era of Self-Regulation*, 105 COLUM. L. REV. 319, 324-5 (2005).

16. Professor Claire Moore Dickerson proposes that codes of conduct be responsive to the foreign workers whose lives they attempt to better. Drawing from the legal norm of good faith, she argues that before TNCs make decisions that impact a developing country's workers, those workers should be consulted. This might be accomplished by using an international organization, such as the ILO, as a consultative forum and NGOs to speak for workers by proxy. Clare Moore Dickerson, *Transnational Codes of Conduct through Dialogue: Leveling the Playing Field for Developing-Country Workers*, 53 FLA. L. REV. 611 (2001).

17. The adverse publicity generated by lawsuits, consumer campaigns, and media exposés prompts TNCs not only to adopt codes of conduct but also to launch their own public relations offensives. In the 1990s, sportswear and sports product giant Nike, Inc., a virtual corporation that does none of its own manufacturing, became the target of labor activists concerned about conditions in the company's overseas contractors' factories. Media organizations picked up on the story, and university students, who had long chosen Nike products, began rallying to remove those very same products from their campuses. Nike's response was multifaceted. It adopted a code of conduct, become involved in the Apparel Industry Partnership, President Clinton's task force to explore problems in the industry, helped found the FLA, and embarked on a major publicity campaign to counter the allegations against it. Collins & Skover, *Nike v. Kasky Story*, at 975-6.

18. A TNC's public relations campaign, however, can be turned against it. In Nike's case, a political activist named Mark Kasky sued the company for misleading the public when it denied that its overseas workers are subject to corporal punishment, claimed that its products are made in accordance with foreign labor law, and alleged that workers making its products receive free meals. Collins & Skover, *Nike v. Kasky Story*, at 972. Nike argued that its communications were not subject to state regulation; rather, they were protected speech under the First Amendment. Ultimately, the California Supreme Court found that Nike's communications were commercial speech, for which it could be held liable under state consumer protection laws. Kasky v. Nike, Inc., 45 P.3d 243 (Cal. 2002). The U.S. Supreme Court agreed to review the case but after oral argument issued a surprising per curium opinion dismissing the case as improvidently granted. Nike, Inc. v. Kasky, 123 S. Ct. 2554 (2003). Nike settled with Kasky on September 12, 2003. Part of the settlement included a U.S.$1.5 million payment to the FLA. It is not known whether Nike paid the plaintiff's litigation costs or an award to Kasky himself. The settlement leaves intact the California Supreme Court's ruling against Nike. Collins & Stover, *Nike v. Kasky*, at 1019-20.

D. LAWSUITS BASED ON STATUTES

Although the U.S. Congress has the authority to pass statutes that regulate conduct outside America's borders, U.S. courts interpreting statutes do so in light of a presumption against extraterritorial effect. Timothy J. Darby, *Extraterritorial Application of U.S. Laws*, in INTERNATIONAL LABOR AND EMPLOYMENT LAWS 50-1, 3 (2d ed., William L. Keller & Timothy J. Darby, eds., 2003) (hereinafter Darby, *Extraterritorial Application*). In order for a statute to apply extraterritorially, Congress must clearly express its intent, something it has rarely done. Compa, *Labour Rights*, at 52.

One interesting exception to Congress's usual practice in this regard is the extraterritorial application of U.S. employment discrimination law. The U.S. Supreme Court initially held that Title VII does not apply extraterritorially. E.E.O.C. v. Arabian American Oil, Co., 499 U.S. 244 (1991). Congress, however, reacted to the decision by amending the statute. Title VII, which bans discrimination on the basis of race, color, national origin, religion and sex, now expressly protects U.S. citizens working abroad for an American employer or a foreign corporation controlled by a U.S. employer. Darby, *Extraterritorial Application*, at 50-89. Similarly situated foreign workers may not make claims under Title VII. If they suffer discrimination at the hands of a U.S. TNC while employed outside the U.S., their recourse is to the laws of the country in which the facility is located. Compa, *Labour Rights*, at 53. The Age Discrimination in Employment Act and the Americans with Disabilities Act operate on the same principles. HEPPLE, LABOUR LAWS, at 152.

With the assistance of creative human rights lawyers, foreign workers have filed a number of claims under the Alien Tort Claims Act, 28 U.S.C. §1350. This controversial statute is used as a tool to sue U.S. TNCs in American courts for alleged violations that occur abroad. The case below arises out of conditions in Myanmar, which were also the subject of an ILO Commission of Inquiry Report excerpted in Chapter 2.

DOE I V. UNOCAL, CORP.

395 F.3d 932 (9th Cir. 2002)

PREGERSON, Circuit Judge.

This case involves human rights violations that allegedly occurred in Myanmar, formerly known as Burma. Villagers from the Tenasserim region in Myanmar allege that the Defendants directly or indirectly subjected the villagers to forced labor, murder, rape, and torture when the Defendants constructed a gas pipeline through the Tenasserim region. The villagers base their claims on the Alien Tort Claims Act, 28 U.S.C. § 1350. . . .

The District Court, through dismissal and summary judgment, resolved all of Plaintiffs' federal claims in favor of the Defendants. For the following reasons, we reverse in part and affirm in part the District Court's rulings.

I.

FACTUAL AND PROCEDURAL BACKGROUND

A. *Unocal's Investment in a Natural Gas Project in Myanmar.*

Burma has been ruled by a military government since 1958. In 1988, a new military government, Defendant-Appellee State Law and Order Restoration Council ("the Myanmar Military"), took control and renamed the country Myanmar. The Myanmar Military established a state owned company, Defendant-Appellee Myanmar Oil and Gas Enterprise ("Myanmar Oil"), to produce and sell the nation's oil and gas resources.

In 1992, Myanmar Oil licensed the French oil company Total S.A. ("Total") to produce, transport, and sell natural gas from deposits in the Yadana Field off the coast of Myanmar ("the Project"). Total set up a subsidiary, Total Myanmar Exploration and Production ("Total Myanmar"), for this purpose. The Project consisted of a Gas Production Joint Venture, which would extract the natural gas out of the Yadana Field, and a Gas Transportation Company, which would construct and operate a pipeline to transport the natural gas from the coast of Myanmar through the interior of the country to Thailand.

Also in 1992, Defendant-Appellant Unocal Corporation and its wholly owned subsidiary Defendant-Appellant Union Oil Company of California, collectively referred to below as "Unocal," acquired a 28% interest in the Project from Total. Unocal set up a wholly owned subsidiary, the Unocal Myanmar Offshore Company ("the Unocal Offshore Co."), to hold Unocal's 28% interest in the Gas Production Joint Venture half of the Project. Similarly, Unocal set up another wholly owned subsidiary, the Unocal International Pipeline Corporation ("the Unocal Pipeline Corp."), to hold Unocal's 28% interest in the Gas Transportation Company half of the Project. Myanmar Oil and a Thai government entity, the Petroleum Authority of Thailand Exploration and Production, also acquired interests in the Project. Total Myanmar was appointed Operator of the Gas Production Joint Venture and the Gas Transportation Company. As the Operator, Total Myanmar was responsible, *inter alia*, for "determin[ing] . . . the selection of . . . employees [and] the hours of work and the compensation to be paid to all . . . employees" in connection with the Project.

B. Unocal's Knowledge that the Myanmar Military Was Providing Security and Other Services for the Project.

It is undisputed that the Myanmar Military provided security and other services for the Project, and that Unocal knew about this. The pipeline was to run through Myanmar's rural Tenasserim region. The Myanmar Military increased its presence in the pipeline region to provide security and other services for the Project. A Unocal memorandum documenting Unocal's meetings with Total on March 1 and 2, 1995 reflects Unocal's understanding that "[f]our battalions of 600 men each will protect the [pipeline] corridor" and "[f]ifty soldiers will be assigned to guard each survey team." A former soldier in one of these battalions testified at his deposition that his battalion had been formed in 1996 specifically for this purpose. In addition, the Military built helipads and cleared roads along the proposed pipeline route for the benefit of the Project.

There is also evidence sufficient to raise a genuine issue of material fact whether the Project *hired* the Myanmar Military, through Myanmar Oil, to provide these services, and whether Unocal knew about this. A Production Sharing Contract, entered into by Total Myanmar and Myanmar Oil before Unocal acquired an interest in the Project, provided that "[Myanmar Oil] shall . . . supply[ ] or mak[e] available . . . security protection . . . as may be requested by [Total Myanmar and its assigns]," such as Unocal. Unocal was aware of this agreement. Thus, a May 10, 1995 Unocal "briefing document" states that "[a]ccording to *our contract*, the government of Myanmar is responsible for protecting the pipeline." (Emphasis added.) Similarly, in May 1995, a cable from the U.S. Embassy in Rangoon, Myanmar, reported that Unocal On-Site Representative Joel Robinson ("Unocal Representative Robinson" or "Robinson") "stated forthrightly that *the companies have hired* the Burmese military to provide security for the project." (Emphasis added.)

Unocal disputes that the Project hired the Myanmar Military or, at the least, that Unocal knew about this. For example, Unocal points out that the Production Sharing Contract quoted in the previous paragraph covered only the off-shore Gas Production Joint Venture but not the Gas Transportation Company and the construction of the pipeline which gave rise to the alleged human rights violations. Moreover, Unocal President John Imle ("Unocal President Imle" or "Imle") stated at his deposition that he knew of "no . . . contractual obligation" requiring the Myanmar Military to provide security for the pipeline construction. Likewise, Unocal CEO Roger Beach ("Unocal CEO Beach" or "Beach") stated at his deposition that he also did not know "whether or not Myanmar had a contractual obligation to provide . . . security." Beach further stated that he was not aware of "any support whatsoever of the military[,] . . . either physical or monetary." These assertions by Unocal President Imle and Unocal CEO Beach are called into question by a briefing book which Total prepared for them on the occasion of their April 1996 visit to the Project. The briefing book lists the "numbers of villagers" working as "local helpers hired by battalions," the monthly "amount paid in Kyats" (the currency of Myanmar) to "Project Helpers," and the "amount in Kyats" expended by the Project on "food rations (Army + Villages)."

Furthermore, there is evidence sufficient to raise a genuine issue of material fact whether the Project directed the Myanmar Military in these activities, at least to a degree, and whether Unocal was involved in this. In May 1995, a cable from the U.S. Embassy in Rangoon reported:

> [Unocal Representative] Robinson indicated . . . Total/Unocal uses [aerial photos, precision surveys, and topography maps] to show the [Myanmar] military where they need helipads built and facilities secured. . . .

. . . Moreover, on or about August 29, 1996, Unocal (Singapore) Director of Information Carol Scott ("Unocal Director of Information Scott" or "Scott") discussed with Unocal Media Contact and Spokesperson David Garcia ("Unocal Spokesperson Garcia" or "Garcia") via e-mail how Unocal should publicly address the issue of the alleged movement of villages by the Myanmar Military in connection with the pipeline. Scott cautioned Garcia that "[b]y saying *we* influenced the army not to move a village, you introduce the concept that they would do such a thing; whereas, by saying that no villages have been moved, you skirt the issue of whether it could happen or not." (Emphasis added.) This e-mail is some evidence that Unocal could influence the army not to commit human rights violations, that the army might otherwise commit such violations, and that Unocal knew this.

C. Unocal's Knowledge that the Myanmar Military Was Allegedly Committing Human Rights Violations in Connection with the Project.

Plaintiffs are villagers from Myanmar's Tenasserim region, the rural area through which the Project built the pipeline. Plaintiffs allege that the Myanmar Military forced them, under threat of violence, to work on and serve as porters for the Project. For instance, John Doe IX testified that he was forced to build a helipad near the pipeline site in 1994 that was then used by Unocal and Total officials who visited the pipeline during its planning stages. John Doe VII and John Roe X, described the construction of helipads at Eindayaza and Po Pah Pta, both of which were near the pipeline site, were used to ferry Total/Unocal executives and materials to the construction site, and were constructed using the forced labor of local villagers, including Plaintiffs. John Roes VIII and IX, as well as John Does I, VIII and IX testified that they were forced to work on building roads leading to the pipeline construction area. Finally, John Does V and IX, testified that they were required to serve as "pipeline porters" – workers who performed menial tasks such as such as hauling materials and cleaning the army camps for the soldiers guarding the pipeline construction.

Plaintiffs also allege in furtherance of the forced labor program just described, the Myanmar Military subjected them to acts of murder, rape, and torture. For instance, Jane Doe I testified that after her husband, John Doe I, attempted to escape the forced labor program, he was shot at by soldiers, and in retaliation for his attempted escape, that she and her baby were thrown into a fire, resulting in injuries to her and the death of the child. Other witnesses described the summary execution of villagers who refused to participate in the forced labor program, or who grew too weak to work effectively. Several Plaintiffs testified that rapes occurred as part of the forced labor program. . . .

. . . As detailed below, even before Unocal invested in the Project, Unocal was made aware - by its own consultants and by its partners in the Project - of this record and that the Myanmar Military might also employ forced labor and commit other human rights violations in connection with the Project. And after Unocal invested in the Project, Unocal was made aware - by its own consultants and employees, its partners in the Project, and human rights organizations - of allegations that the Myanmar Military was actually committing such violations in connection with the Project. . . .

. . . [O]n May 10, 1995, Unocal Representative Robinson wrote to Total's Herve Madeo:

> From Unocal's standpoint, probably the most sensitive issue is "what is forced labor" and "how can you identify it." I am sure that you will be thinking about the demarcation between work done by the project and work done "on behalf of" the project. Where the responsibility of the project ends is *very important.*

This statement is some evidence that Unocal knew that the Myanmar Military might use forced labor in connection with the Project. . . .

Later that year, on December 11, 1995, Unocal Consultant John Haseman ("Unocal Consultant Haseman" or "Haseman"), a former military attache at the U.S. Embassy in Rangoon, reported to Unocal that the Myanmar Military was, in fact, using forced labor and committing other human rights violations in connection with the Project. Haseman told Unocal that "Unocal was particularly discredited when a corporate spokesman was quoted as saying that Unocal was satisfied with . . . assurances [by the Myanmar Military] that no human rights abuses were occurring in the area of pipeline construction." . . .

[In earlier proceedings in the *Unocal* case, which formerly consisted of two separate suits that were consolidated for this appeal, the district court dismissed claims against the Myanmar Military and Myanmar Oil on the grounds that these defendants were entitled to immunity pursuant to the Foreign Sovereign Immunities Act, 28 U.S.C. §§ 1330, 1602 et seq. The claims against Total were dismissed for lack of personal jurisdiction.]

II.

ANALYSIS

A. Liability Under the Alien Tort Claims Act.

1. Introduction
The Alien Tort Claims Act confers upon the federal district courts "original jurisdiction of any civil action by an alien for a tort only, committed in violation of the law of nations."

28 U.S.C. § 1350.[12] We have held that the ATCA also provides a cause of action, as long as "plaintiffs . . . allege a violation of 'specific, universal, and obligatory' international norms as part of [their] ATCA claim." [citations omitted] Plaintiffs allege that Unocal's conduct gave rise to ATCA liability for the forced labor, murder, rape, and torture inflicted on them by the Myanmar Military. . . .

One threshold question in *any* ATCA case is whether the alleged tort is a violation of the law of nations. We have recognized that torture, murder, and slavery are *jus cogens* violations and, thus, violations of the law of nations.[14] [citations omitted] Moreover, forced labor is so widely condemned that it has achieved the status of a *jus cogens* violation. *See, e.g.*, Universal Declaration of Human Rights, G.A. Res. 217(A)III (1948) (banning forced labor); [citations omitted] Accordingly, all torts alleged in the present case are *jus cogens* violations and, thereby, violations of the law of nations. . . .

2. *Forced Labor*

a. Forced labor is a modern variant of slavery to which the law of nations attributes individual liability such that state action is not required.

Our case law strongly supports the conclusion that forced labor is a modern variant of slavery. Accordingly, forced labor, like traditional variants of slave trading, is among the "handful of crimes . . . to which the law of nations attributes *individual liability*," such that state action is not required. . . .

Courts have included forced labor in the definition of the term "slavery" in the context of the Thirteenth Amendment. The Supreme Court has said that "[t]he undoubted aim of the Thirteenth Amendment . . . was not merely to end slavery but to maintain a system of *completely free and voluntary labor* throughout the United States." Pollock v. Williams, 322 U.S. 4, 17 (1944) (emphasis added). . . .

b. Unocal may be liable under the ATCA for aiding and abetting the Myanmar Military in subjecting Plaintiffs to forced labor.

Plaintiffs argue that Unocal aided and abetted the Myanmar Military in subjecting them to forced labor. We hold that the standard for aiding and abetting under the ATCA is, as discussed below, knowing practical assistance or encouragement that has a substantial effect on the perpetration of the crime. We further hold that a reasonable factfinder could find that Unocal's conduct met this standard.[20] . . .

We however agree with the District Court that in the present case, we should apply international law as developed in the decisions by international criminal tribunals such as the Nuremberg Military Tribunals for the applicable substantive law. . . .

---

[12] The "law of nations" is "the law of international relations, embracing not only nations but also . . . individuals (such as those who invoke their human rights or commit war crimes)." BLACK'S LAW DICTIONARY 822 (7th ed.1999).

[14] *Jus cogens* norms are norms of international law that are binding on nations even if they do not agree to them. . . .

[20] Plaintiffs also argue that Unocal is liable for the conduct by the Myanmar Military under joint venture, agency, negligence, and recklessness theories. The District Court did not address any of Plaintiffs' alternative theories. Because we reject the District Court's general reasons for holding that Unocal could not be liable under international law, and because we hold that Unocal may be liable under at least one of Plaintiffs' theories, i.e., aiding and abetting in violation of international law, we do not need to address Plaintiffs' other theories, i.e., joint venture, agency, negligence, and recklessness. . . .

In different ATCA cases, different courts have applied international law, the law of the state where the underlying events occurred, or the law of the forum state, respectively. [citation omitted]. Unocal urges us to apply not international law, but the law of the state where the underlying events occurred, i.e., Myanmar. Where, as in the present case, only *jus cogens* violations are alleged- *i.e.*, violations of norms of international law that are binding on nations even if they do not agree to them, . . . it may, however, be preferable to apply international law rather than the law of any particular state, such as the state where the underlying events occurred or the forum state. The reason is that, by definition, the law of any particular state is either identical to the *jus cogens* norms of international law, or it is invalid. Moreover, "reading §1350 as essentially a jurisdictional grant only and then looking to [foreign or] domestic tort law to provide the cause of action mutes the grave *international law* aspect of the tort, reducing it to no more (or less) than a garden-variety municipal tort," [citations omitted]. . . . Significantly, we have already held that the ATCA not only confers jurisdiction but also creates a cause of action. . . .

International human rights law has been developed largely in the context of criminal prosecutions rather than civil proceedings. . . . Accordingly, District Courts are increasingly turning to the decisions by international *criminal* tribunals for instructions regarding the standards of international human rights law under our *civil* ATCA. . . . We find recent decisions by the International Criminal Tribunal for the former Yugoslavia and the International Criminal Tribunal for Rwanda especially helpful for ascertaining the current standard for aiding and abetting under international law as it pertains to the ATCA.

In *Prosecutor v. Furundzija*, IT-95-17/1 T (Dec. 10, 1998), *reprinted in* 38 I.L.M. 317 (1999), the International Tribunal for the former Yugoslavia held that "the *actus reus* of aiding and abetting in international criminal law requires practical assistance, encouragement, or moral support which has a substantial effect on the perpetration of the crime." *Id.* at ¶235. The Tribunal clarified that in order to qualify, "assistance need not constitute an indispensable element, that is, a *conditio sine qua non* for the acts of the principal." *Furundzija* at ¶209; [citations omitted]. Rather, it suffices that "the acts of the accomplice make a significant difference to the commission of the criminal act by the principal." *Furundzija* at ¶233. The acts of the accomplice have the required "[substantial] effect on the commission of the crime" where "the criminal act most probably would not have occurred in the same way [without] someone act[ing] in the role that the [accomplice] in fact assumed." *Prosecutor v. Tadic*, ICTY-94-1, ¶688 (May 7, 1997), *http:// www.un.org/icty/tadic/trials2/judgement/ index.htm.*

Similarly, in *Prosecutor v. Musema*, ICTR-96-13-T (Jan. 27, 2000), *http://www.ictr.org/*, the International Criminal Tribunal for Rwanda described the *actus reus* of aiding and abetting as "all acts of assistance in the form of either physical or moral support" that "substantially contribute to the commission of the crime". *Id.* at ¶126.

As for the *mens rea* of aiding and abetting, the International Criminal Tribunal for the former Yugoslavia held that what is required is actual or constructive (i.e., "reasonabl[e]") "knowledge that [the accomplice's] actions will assist the perpetrator in the commission of the crime." *Furundzija* at ¶245. Thus, "it is not necessary for the accomplice to share the *mens rea* of the perpetrator, in the sense of positive intention to commit the crime." *Id.* In fact, it is not even necessary that the aider and abettor knows the precise crime that the principal intends to commit. *See id.* Rather, if the accused "is aware that one of a number of crimes will probably be committed, and one of those crimes is in fact committed, he has intended to facilitate the commission of that crime, and is guilty as an aider and abettor." *Id.*

Similarly, for the *mens rea* of aiding and abetting, the International Criminal Tribunal for Rwanda required that "the accomplice knew of the assistance he was providing in the commission of the principal offence." *Musema* at ¶180. The accomplice does not have to have had the intent to commit the principal offense. *See id.* at ¶181. It is sufficient that the accomplice "knew or had reason to know" that the principal had the intent to commit the offense. *Id.* at ¶182.

The *Furundzija* standard for aiding and abetting liability under international criminal law can be summarized as knowing practical assistance, encouragement, or moral support which has a substantial effect on the perpetration of the crime. At least with respect to assistance and encouragement, this standard is similar to the standard for aiding and abetting under domestic tort law. . . .

First, a reasonable factfinder could conclude that Unocal's alleged conduct met the *actus reus* requirement of aiding and abetting as we define it today, i.e., practical assistance or encouragement which has a substantial effect on the perpetration of the crime of, in the present case, forced labor.

Unocal's weak protestations notwithstanding, there is little doubt that the record contains substantial evidence creating a material question of fact as to whether forced labor was used in connection with the construction of the pipeline. Numerous witnesses, including a number of Plaintiffs, testified that they were forced to clear the right of way for the pipeline and to build helipads for the project before construction of the pipeline began. . . .

The evidence also supports the conclusion that Unocal gave practical assistance to the Myanmar Military in subjecting Plaintiffs to forced labor. The practical assistance took the form of hiring the Myanmar Military to provide security and build infrastructure along the pipeline route in exchange for money or food. The practical assistance also took the form of using photos, surveys, and maps in daily meetings to show the Myanmar Military where to provide security and build infrastructure.

This assistance, moreover, had a "substantial effect" on the perpetration of forced labor, which "most probably would not have occurred in the same way" without someone hiring the Myanmar Military to provide security, and without someone showing them where to do it. *Tadic* at ¶688. . . .

Second, a reasonable factfinder could also conclude that Unocal's conduct met the *mens rea* requirement of aiding and abetting as we define it today, namely, actual or constructive (i.e., reasonable) knowledge that the accomplice's actions will assist the perpetrator in the commission of the crime. The District Court found that "[t]he evidence does suggest that Unocal knew that forced labor was being utilized and that the Joint Venturers benefitted from the practice." [citation omitted] Moreover, Unocal knew or should reasonably have known that its conduct – including the payments and the instructions where to provide security and build infrastructure – would assist or encourage the Myanmar Military to subject Plaintiffs to forced labor.

Viewing the evidence in the light most favorable to Plaintiffs, we conclude that there are genuine issues of material fact whether Unocal's conduct met the *actus reus* and *mens rea* requirements for liability under the ATCA for aiding and abetting forced labor. Accordingly, we reverse the District Court's grant of Unocal's motion for summary judgment on Plaintiffs' forced labor claims under the ATCA.

[The court thereafter concluded that Unocal may be liable under the ATCA for aiding and abetting the Myanmar Military in subjecting the plaintiffs to murder and rape but that there was insufficient evidence to support the plaintiffs' claims of torture.]

REINHARDT, Circuit Judge, concurring.

I agree with the majority opinion, except for Part II(A), in which the majority discusses the Alien Tort Claims Act. As to that Act, I agree with the majority that material factual disputes exist regarding plaintiffs' claims for forced labor used in connection with the Yadana Pipeline Project. I also agree with the majority that if plaintiffs prove their allegations, Unocal may be held liable under the Act for the use of forced labor as a part of the project. Where I differ from my colleagues is principally with respect to the standard of third-party liability under which Unocal may be held legally responsible for the human rights violations alleged. I do not agree that the question whether Unocal may be held liable in tort for the Myanmar military's alleged human rights violations should be resolved, as the majority holds, by applying a recently-promulgated international criminal law aiding-and-abetting standard that permits imposition of liability for the lending of moral support. In fact, I do not agree that the question of Unocal's tort liability should be decided by applying any international law test at all. Rather, in my view, the ancillary legal question of Unocal's third-party tort liability should be resolved by applying general federal common law tort principles, such as agency, joint venture, or reckless disregard. I also believe that there is no reason to discuss the doctrine of *jus cogens* in this case. Because the underlying conduct alleged constitutes a violation of customary international law, the violation was allegedly committed by a governmental entity, and Unocal's liability, if any, is derivative of that government entity's, *jus cogens* is irrelevant to any issue before us. Assuming the allegations to be true, the fact that the underlying conduct violated customary international law is sufficient to support liability not only on the part of the governmental actor, but also on the part of a third party whose liability is derivative thereof. . . .

Notes

1. The Alien Tort Claims Act (ATCA), 28 U.S.C. §1350, dates back over two hundred years. It was originally enacted by the first U.S. Congress as part of the Judiciary Act of 1789. The exact reasons for its passage are unknown; it is lacking in legislative history. Emeka Duruigbo, *The Economic Cost of Alien Tort Litigation*, 14 MINN. J. GLOBAL TRADE 1, 1-5 (2004) (hereinafter Duruigbo, *Economic Cost*). The statute was used just a few times in the late eighteenth century before entering a nearly two century period of almost complete dormancy. Genc Trnavci, *The Meaning and Scope of the Law of Nations in the Context of the Alien Tort Claims Act and International Law*, 26 U. PA. J. INT'L ECON. L. 193, 195-6 (2005) (hereinafter Trnavci, *Meaning and Scope*).

2. In 1980, in a wrongful death suit conceived by the Center for Constitutional Rights, an NGO, the U.S. Court of Appeals for the Second Circuit resuscitated the statute. The case involved a Paraguayan woman whose brother was kidnapped and tortured to death by a Paraguayan police officer in Paraguay. Filartiga v. Pena-Irala, 630 F.2d 876 (2d Cir. 1980). The court not only accepted the argument that the ATCA confers federal jurisdiction over "any civil action by an alien for a tort only, committed in violation of the law of nations," it additionally held that in interpreting the "law of nations" courts must use modern conceptions of international law rather than the law circa 1789. *Id.* at 880-5. Despite this groundbreaking victory, Dolly Filartiga and her father, also a plaintiff in the case, were never able to collect their $10 million damage award because the defendant Pena-Irala was deported. Dolly Filartiga, *American Courts, Global Justice*, N.Y. TIMES, March 30, 2004, at A21.

3. There are significant obstacles to bringing suit under the ATCA. As noted by Dean Anne-Marie Slaughter and David L. Bosco:

> The *Filartiga* decision, it is important to note, has not made suing on human rights grounds an easy task. In particular, the courts have not allowed Alien Tort claims to trump the legal immunity that is traditionally granted to foreign states and their leaders. In a 1989 decision, the [U.S.] Supreme Court rejected the notion that a plaintiff could bypass the protection of sovereign immunity and sue a foreign government or a sitting foreign leader directly under the Alien Tort statute. . . . Using a similar line of reasoning, federal courts threw out lawsuits against the Saudi Arabian government for torture, and against President Jean-Bertrand Aristide of Haiti for extrajudicial killing. The courts have also ruled that plaintiffs can only sue defendants who venture onto U.S. soil. This requirement immunizes many perpetrators, who know better than to tempt fate by visiting the US.
>
> Anne-Marie Slaughter & David L. Bosco, *Alternative Justice: Facilitated by Little-Known 18th-Century Law*, TRIBUNALS, May 2001, available at http://crimesofwar.org/tribun-mag/mag_relate_alternative.html (last visited Jan. 10, 2006).

Slaughter and Bosco further explain that U.S. courts have only opened "to a very small group of foreign plaintiffs: those victims able to identify and serve process on violators of human rights not protected by sovereign immunity, yet capable of committing a violation of international law." *Id.* Moreover, given the difficulty of collecting judgments against such defendants, they conclude that the main benefit of bringing ATCA suits is for the publicity. *Id.*

4. Until the mid-1990s, the handful of suits that were brought under the ATCA named governments and their officials as defendants. In 1996, the International Labor Rights Fund (ILRF), an NGO, filed a complaint against Unocal, the first effort to hold a corporation liable for human rights violations under the statute. Terry Collingsworth, *The Key Human Rights Challenge: Developing Enforcement Mechanisms*, 15 HARV. HUM. RTS. J. 183, 187 (2002) (hereinafter Collingsworth, *Human Rights*). The ILRF subsequently filed a number of corporate ATCA claims including suits against: Exxon Mobil for incidents in Indonesia; Coca-Cola for the actions of death squads in Colombia; Del Monte Produce for acts committed against union leaders in Guatemala; and DynCorp for deaths and injuries allegedly suffered by Ecuadorian farmers from the spraying of a toxic herbicide on coca plants. *Id.* at 188-95. In July of 2005, the NGO sued Nestle under the ATCA on behalf of a class of children from Mali who were allegedly trafficked from their home country to the Ivory Coast, and forced to work on cocoa farms. International Labor Rights Fund Press Release, Human Rights Watchdog and Civil Rights Firm Sue Nestle, ADM, Cargill, for Using Forced Child Labor, July 14, 2005, available at http://www.laborrights.org/press/ChildLabor/cocoa/cocoa_pressrel_071405.htm.

5. A major issue in *Unocal* was whether a showing of state action was required before the company could be held liable under the ATCA. The Ninth Circuit deemed state action unnecessary under the facts of the case. Citing *Kadic v. Karadzic*, 70 F.3d 232 (2d Cir. 1995), the panel majority held that while ordinarily state action is required for ATCA liability, *jus cogens* violations such as slave trading, genocide, or war crimes do not require state action and "violate the law of nations regardless of whether they are committed under 'color of law.'" Armin Rosencranz & David

Louk, *Doe v. Unocal: Holding Corporations Liable for Human Rights Abuses on Their Watch*, 8 Chap. L. Rev. 135, 141 (2005) (hereinafter Rosencranz & Louk, *Holding Corporations Liable*). From there the majority reasoned that forced labor was a modern variant of slavery for which state action is not required. It then applied the two-pronged aiding and abetting test derived from international law, and found that a reasonable fact finder could conclude that Unocal aided and abetted the Myanmar military in its perpetration of forced labor. *Id.* at 143. Do you understand why Judge Reinhardt, in his concurrence, found it unnecessary to apply international criminal law aiding and abetting standards and equally irrelevant whether or not forced labor is a *jus cogens* violation? Is Judge Reinhardt's approach to corporate liability more or less promising for plaintiffs than that of the majority? Commentators Armin Rosencranz and David Louk argue that Judge Reinhardt's approach, which uses traditional U.S. common law theories of joint liability "created more viable ways for future plaintiffs to pursue corporations. . . . " *Id.* at 149. They also characterize Judge Reinhardt's opinion that the plaintiffs need not prove that the claims were *jus cogens* violations to be "more lenient" than the approach of the panel's majority. *Id.*

6. As noted earlier, the panel majority used international law to ascertain the standard for aiding and abetting. Because the ATCA specifically uses the "law of nations" as its touchstone, is there a stronger rationale for turning to international law in *Unocal* as compared with, for example, *Roper v. Simmons*, excerpted in Chapter 1?

7. The case excerpted here is the decision of a three-judge panel. In February 2003, the Ninth Circuit ordered that the *Unocal* case be reheard en banc. It vacated the panel ruling, which may not be cited as precedent in future cases. Doe I v. Unocal Corp., 395 F.3d 978 (9th Cir. 2003). The case, however, was then withdrawn from submission pending issuance of the U.S. Supreme Court's decision in *Sosa v. Alvarez-Machain*, 542 U.S. 692 (2004).

8. *Sosa*, the Supreme Court's first ruling on the ATCA, was not a case involving a corporate defendant. Nevertheless, the case is instructive. Although *Sosa* does not overrule the *Filartiga* decision, the Court evidenced a very cautious approach to alien tort claims. Trnavci, *Meaning and Scope*, at 244. In *Sosa*, the Court held that the ATCA is a jurisdictional statute that creates no new cause of action. Yet the legislation was not stillborn – it required no further legislative action – because the common law at the time the statute was originally enacted recognized a "modest number of international law violations," which included "violation of safe conducts, infringement of the rights of ambassadors, and piracy." Sosa, 542 U.S. 724. The Court left open the possibility that additional violations might be added to the list but cautioned that "courts should require any claim based on the present-day law of nations to rest on a norm of international character accepted by the civilized world and defined with a specificity comparable to the features" of the paradigmatic offenses in 1789. *Id.* at 725.

9. Footnote 21 in *Sosa* makes an intriguing reference to the corporate ATCA cases:

> [A] possible limitation that we need not apply here is a policy of case-specific deference to the political branches. For example, there are now pending in federal district court several class actions seeking damages from various corporations alleged to have participated in, or abetted, the regime of apartheid that formerly

controlled South Africa. . . . The Government of South Africa has said that these cases interfere with the policy embodied by its Truth and Reconciliation Commission. . . . The United States has agreed. . . . In such cases, there is a strong argument that federal courts should give serious weight to the Executive Branch's view of the case's impact on foreign policy.

Sosa, 542 U.S. at 733, n. 21.

How might advocates for TNCs use the footnote's language in future cases? How might workers' advocates respond?

10. After the *Sosa* decision, the Ninth Circuit asked the parties in the Unocal case to submit briefs discussing the new precedent's impact on the plaintiffs' claims. In December 2004, however, the parties in the Unocal case reached a tentative settlement. John R. Crook, *Tentative Settlement of ATCA Human Rights Suits Against Unocal*, 99 Am. J. Int'l L. 497 (2005). The settlement, for an undisclosed sum, became final in March 2005, and covered not only the federal ATCA suit but also a suit pending in California state court. Rosencranz & Louk, *Holding Corporations Liable*, at 135.

11. Not surprisingly, TNCs are highly critical of the deployment of the ATCA against corporate activities, fearing that litigation will adversely affect international business. Active corporate opposition has been organized by the National Foreign Trade Council, the U.S. Chamber of Commerce, the U.S. Council of International Business, and the International Chamber of Commerce. Duruigbo, *Economic Cost*, at 7-8. For an indication of the litigation activities of these business groups, one may peruse the amicus curiae briefs that they frequently file in corporate ATCA cases. Note that in *Unocal*, the claims against Total, the French oil company, were dismissed for lack of personal jurisdiction. Doe I. v. Unocal Corp., 395 F.3d 932, 943 (9th Cir. 2002). U.S. companies feel disadvantaged vis-à-vis European companies, which may turn a blind eye to human rights abuses without fear of ATCA suits.

12. The Bush Administration has also voiced significant opposition to corporate ATCA suits, taking a position supportive of business interests. Amicus briefs have been filed by the Department of Justice in ATCA cases, and the state Department has opined that such suits would interfere with the war on terrorism. Duruigbo, *Economic Cost*, at 8.

13. On October 17, 2005, Senator Dianne Feinstein, a leading liberal, introduced S. 1874, a bill titled the Alien Tort Statute Reform Act, aimed at amending aspects of the ATCA. Senator Feinstein effectively withdrew the bill eight days later after an outcry from human rights groups. Jim Washer, *Alien Games*, Energy Compass, Nov. 25, 2005. The bill would have greatly narrowed the scope of the ATCA, likely rendering use of the statute against corporations significantly more difficult if not impossible. For example, for ATCA liability to attach to corporate conduct, the bill required plaintiffs to demonstrate direct participation of a corporation in human rights violations. Moreover, actionable violations under the bill were limited to those committed with specific intent. And suits involving the actions of foreign states were prohibited. The bill also narrowed the definition of "slavery" to the status of persons over whom ownership rights are exercised, thus implicitly excluding forced labor from the definition. Finally, Senator Feinstein's bill allowed the President of the United States to terminate any ATCA suit believed to interfere with foreign

relations. S. 1874 Had the ATCA been amended in accordance with S.1874, how would a case like the *Unocal* suit fare?

14. Professor Donald J. Kochan presents four fundamental objections to allowing disputes concerning human rights abuses to be decided in U.S. courts. He argues first that "Article III of the United States Constitution does not give federal judges unlimited authority to fashion federal common law based on international norms." Donald J. Kochan, *No Longer Little Known But Now a Door Ajar: An Overview of the Evolving and Dangerous Role of the Alien Tort Statute in Human Rights and International Law Jurisprudence*, 8 Chap. L. Rev. 103, 130 (2005). Next, he worries that ATCA suits "necessarily make pronouncements regarding the appropriate behavior of foreign countries" and could affect foreign policy and national security. *Id.* His third objection is that courts in ATCA litigation often rely on evidence of customary international law that is not intended to be enforceable law. For example, human rights treaties that the U.S. has not ratified are sometimes referenced in ATCA cases. *Id.* at 131-2. Professor Kochan's last concern is that corporate ATCA litigation will chill investment by TNCs, and thereby stifle "economic development, democracy, and the enhancement of human rights" that follows international corporate activity. *Id.* at 132.

15. Terry Collingsworth, Executive Director of the ILRF, hails the ATCA as an important tool for enforcing human rights norms, and preventing TNCs from profiting from human rights abuses. The ATCA's limitations, however, are substantial. One problem is jurisdictional; ATCA cases can only be brought against those over whom federal jurisdiction can be asserted. Collingsworth, *Human Rights*, at 202. Moreover, there are serious practical problems with such suits. Victims in these cases, frequently poor and lacking ready access to legal representation, are terrified to lodge claims implicating rogue governments. Their reticence, and the fact that the wrongs often occur in remote places, makes evidence gathering very difficult and expensive for attorneys and human rights workers. *Id.* Finally, the wrongs that the ATCA reaches are limited. There is no international consensus on many workplace issues including, "a living wage, minimum health and safety standards, maximum hours, and sexual harassment." *Id.*

16. Professor Ronen Shamir takes a more theoretical view of the ATCA cases. He sees ATCA plaintiffs as actors attempting to define corporate social responsibility as a set of legally binding obligations. TNCs, in contrast, resist these suits as part of a larger strategy that defines corporate social responsibility "as an essentially voluntary and unenforceable issue." Ronen Shamir, *Between Self-Regulation and the Alien Tort Claims Act: On the Contested Concept of Corporate Social Responsibility*, 38 Law & Soc'y Rev. 635, 636 (2004). The outcome of the struggle between these oppositional views of global corporate social responsibility is far from certain, and a long way off.

Index

Abusive resignation
  France, in, 449
Action committees
  US, in, 115–116
    Germany compared, 421–422
Adoption leave
  UK, in, 370
Adverse action for union activity
  US, protection against, 115
Adverse effect discrimination
  Canada, in, 196
Affirmative action
  Canada, indigenous persons in, 183
  EU, exception to gender discrimination for, 318
  US, in (*See* United States)
AFL-CIO. *See* American Federation of Labor-Congress
    of Industrial Organizations (AFL-CIO)
Age discrimination
  EU, defenses to, 321–322
  US, in, 126, 607
Alien Tort Claims Act (ATCA)
  Article 26 complaints compared, 82–83
  Bush Administration (GWB) attitude toward, 617
  corporate defendants, 615, 616–617
  corporate social responsibility and, 618
  forced labor, claims regarding, 82–83
  historical background, 614
  international law, use as standard in actions under,
    616
  judicial review, 616
  limits on use to decide human rights disputes, 618
  Myanmar, claims against, 82–83
  new causes of action not created by, 616
  objections to deciding international human rights
    disputes in US courts, 618
  obstacles to actions under, 615
  overview, 607
  reform attempts, 617–618
  settlements under, 617
  state action requirement, 615–616
  TNC attitude toward, 617
  wrongful death actions under, 614
Alter ego of defendants
  common law actions in US courts, in, 599

American Federation of Labor-Congress of Industrial
    Organizations (AFL-CIO)
  CCAS tripartite consultation requirement,
    complaint regarding, 66
  CFA, actions brought before, 2, 27
  ILO delegation representative from, 59
Amparo suits, 240–246. *See also* Mexico
Amsterdam Treaty
  antidiscrimination law under, 315
  European Parliament under, 278
Antidiscrimination law
  Canada, in, 186–197 (*See also* Canada)
  EU, in, 315–324 (*See also* European Union)
  France, in, 455–458 (*See also* France)
  gender discrimination (*See* Gender
    discrimination)
  Germany, in, 422–428 (*See also* Germany)
  India, in
    caste system, prohibition against discrimination
      based on, 579
    compensatory discrimination to remedy past
      injustices in caste system, 579
  Mexico, in, 248 (*See also* Mexico)
  sexual harassment (*See* Sexual harassment)
  UK, in, 370, 391 (*See also* United Kingdom)
  US, in, 124–148 (*See also* United States)
Apparel Industry Partnership, 606
Appellate review. *See* Judicial review
Arbitration
  Canada
    collective bargaining disputes in, 198
    interest arbitration, 175 (*See also* Canada)
  China, in, 485, 486
  Mexico, dispute resolution systems in individual
    employment law compared, 235–236
Article 24 representations, 70–74
Article 26 complaints, 74–83
  ATCA claims compared, 82–83
  Commissions of Inquiry, 81
  forced labor, regarding, 75–82
  Myanmar, against, 75–82
  private employers, effect on, 82
  procedures, 74–75
ATCA. *See* Alien Tort Claims Act

Bad faith discharge claims
. Canada, in, 168
Bargaining. *See* Collective employee rights
Bargaining units
   Canada, collective employee rights at bargaining
      unit level, 174–175
   United Kingdom, in, 362
   US, in
      multi-location bargaining units, 115
      single-site bargaining units, 115
Belgium
   IT industry, penetration of TNCs into, 4
Benefits. *See* Wages, hours and benefits
Blair, Tony, 333, 361, 394
Bonded labor
   India, in
      consequences of, 589
      public interest litigation and, 588–589
Breach of contract
   China, in, 484
   Japan, sexual harassment as, 541
Bullying in workplace
   France, in, 457
   UK, in, 351–352
   US, employment at will doctrine and, 105
Burden of Proof Directive
   antidiscrimination law and, 372–373
   UK antidiscrimination law and, 372–373
Bureau of International Labor Affairs (ILAB), 69–70
Bush, George H.W., 249
Bush Administration (GWB)
   ATCA, attitude toward, 617
   CCAS tripartite consultation requirement and,
      65–67
   NAALC, attitude toward, 272
Business creation leave
   France, in, 454
Business management, globalization of, 4–5
Business necessity defense
   Canada, in, 197

Canada
   antidiscrimination law, 197
      adverse effect discrimination, 196
      business necessity defense, 197
      Charter of Rights and Freedoms, effect of, 186
      defenses, 196
      direct discrimination, 195–196
      disparate impact discrimination in US compared,
         196
      disparate treatment discrimination in US
         compared, 196
      family status discrimination, 195
      human rights law, effect of, 187
      intent, proof of not necessary, 195
      pregnancy discrimination, 186
      prima facie cases, 196
      protected classes, 186
      reasonable accommodation, 196, 197
      sexual orientation discrimination, 186

      statistical evidence, use of, 196
      UK compared, 370
Bloc Quebecois, 158
Canada Pension Plan, 185
Canadian Alliance, 158
CFA case regarding notice of union decertification
   in, 87–88
Charter of Rights and Freedoms, 159, 172–173, 186
collective employee rights, 185
   affirmative action and indigenous persons, 183
   arbitration of disputes, 198
   bargaining, 174–183
   bargaining unit level, at, 174–175
   exclusivity, 175
   France and Germany compared, 175
   grievance arbitration, 206
   human rights laws and indigenous persons, 183
   majoritarianism, 175
   mandatory clauses, 183
   NAFTA, effect of, 175
   Quebec, in, 175
   strikes (*See* strikes, below)
Conservative Party, 158
Constitution, 157–158
covenants not to compete in, 1
demographics, 157
dispute resolution systems, 207
   arbitration of collective bargaining matters, 198
   expertise of arbitrators, effect of, 205
   grievance arbitration, 206
   human rights boards, 198
   human rights claims included with collective
      bargaining matters, 207
   judicial review, availability of, 198, 205–206
   labor boards, 198
   Mexico compared, 235, 246
   parties, 206–207
   statutory claims included with collective
      bargaining matters, 206
   tort claims included with collective bargaining
      matters, 206
   US compared, 198–199
economic overview, 157
federalism and labor law in, 158–159
freedom of association
   picketing and, 184
   union dues, effect of, 182–183
health care for employees, 185–186
historical background, 157
holidays, 185
hours of work, 185
human rights law and
   antidiscrimination law in, effect on, 187
   arbitration, human rights claims included with
      collective bargaining matters, 207
   human rights boards, dispute resolution in, 198
   indigenous persons, affirmative action, 183
ILO Conventions, level of compliance with, 171–172
individual employment law, 171
   bad faith discharge claims, 168

Canada *(cont.)*
  for cause standard for dismissals, 168, 169–170
  covenants not to compete, 171
  employer duties, 171
  interest arbitration, 175
    extension to all collective bargaining relationships, 182
    first contract parties, rationale for use by, 181–182
    imposition of new contract versus choosing offer of one party, 182
    rights arbitration compared, 181
    triggering events, 182
  labor and trade unions, 185
    authorization card majority, certification based on, 173–174
    business as usual standard during certification process, 174
    certification procedures, 173
    decertification, CFA case regarding notice of, 87–88
    decline of, 172
    discrimination, protection against, 173
    duty of fair representation, 207
    elections, certification without, 173–174
    freedom of association, effect of union dues on, 182–183
    instant elections, 174
    Mexico compared, 228
    NDP, affiliation with, 172
    Ontario, in, 174
    overview, 172
    recognition of, 173–174
    remedy for misconduct, certification as, 174
    showing of interest, 173
    strikes (*See* strikes, below)
  labor history, 171
  legal background, 158
  Liberal Party, 158
  lockouts, 184–185
  minimum wage, 185
  NAALC
    concerns for national sovereignty regarding, 249–250
    Quebec labor laws, submission regarding, 272
  NAFTA
    collective bargaining, effect on, 175
    complaints under, 172
    economic impact of, 254
    hollowing out, concerns regarding, 255
    national sovereignty, concerns regarding, 255
  New Democratic Party (NDP), 158, 172
  occupational safety and health, 185
  overtime, 185
  parental leave, 185
  part-time employees, 185
  pension plans, 185
  picketing
    freedom of association and, 184
    primary picketing, 184
    secondary picketing, 184

  political overview, 157–158
  pregnancy leave, 185
  primary picketing, 184
  privacy law, 198
    common law protections, 197
    federal statutory law, 197–198
    personal information, protection of, 197–198
    provincial statutory law, 197
  Quebec labor laws, NAALC submission regarding, 272
  reasonable notice rule, 168
    basis for imposing rule, 168
    employment contracts, incentive for forming, 169
    factors in determining reasonableness, 168–169
    length of time, 169
    rationale, 168
    statutory periods versus case-by-case approach, 169
  retirement plans, 185
  secondary picketing, 184
  severance pay, 186
  strikes, 183–184
    conciliation, 184
    freedom of association and picketing, 184
    historical background, 183
    mediation, 184
    notice requirement, 184
    primary picketing, 184
    replacement workers, prohibition against, 184
    right to strike, 183
    secondary picketing, 184
    secret ballot votes, 184
    statistical overview, 183
  Supreme Court, 158
  unemployment insurance, 185
  vacations, 185
  wages, hours and benefits, 186
    health care for employees, 185–186
    holidays, 185
    hours of work, 185
    minimum wage, 185
    overtime, 185
    parental leave, 185
    pension plans, 185
    pregnancy leave, 185
    retirement plans, 185
    severance pay, 186
    unemployment insurance, 185
    vacations, 185
    workers' compensation, 185
  workers' compensation, 185
  wrongful discharge claims
    aggravated damages, 170–171
    dishonesty, discharge based on, 170
    punitive damages, 170–171
    Quebec, in, 171
Capital mobility as result of globalization, 7
Cárdenas, Cuauhtémoc, 215
Caribbean Common Market, 47
Carnegie Endowment for International Peace, 254

Caste system
  India, in, 578–580 (*See also* India)
CCAS. *See* Conference Committee on the Application
    of Standards
CEACR. *See* Committee of Experts on the Application
    of Conventions and Recommendations
Center for Constitutional Rights, 599, 614
Central America–Dominican Republic Free Trade
    Agreement (CAFTA–DR)
  enforcement provisions, 274–275
  NAALC, labor provisions compared, 274
  signing of, 274
CFA. *See* Committee on Freedom of Association
Child care in
  China, in, 471
Child labor
  CEACR observation on, 32
  definitions regarding, 28, 30
  differences between nations, effect on remedying, 31
  factors affecting, 29
  globalization and, 28–32
  historical factors independent of globalization, 30–31
  ILO Convention on, 30
  India, child labor and poverty reduction in, 567
  industrialization as cause of, 31
  IPEC and, 28–29
  Mexico, prohibition against, 223–224
  permissible versus impermissible work, 28
  statistical overview, 29
  US agricultural sector, in, 31–32
China
  appellate review, 507
  benefits in, 470
  brain circulation, 520–523
    brain drain and, 520–521, 523
    development of, 521
    Hong Kong and, 521–522
    Macau and, 521
    outsourcing and, 522–523
    preferences for returned students, 522
    Taiwan and, 521–522
    unemployed returnees, problem of, 522
  breach of contract, 484
  case law, 499–509
  CFA, complaints against in, 516–517
  child care in, 471
  civil servants, 502
  codes of conduct in, 603
  collective employee rights, 517
    bargaining, understanding of, 515
    consultation with foreign invested companies, 516
    domestic law not supporting bargaining, 515
    enforcement of collective agreements, 515–516
    lack of history of labor activism and, 515
    lack of real negotiation, 517
    scope of collective agreements, 515–516
    strikes, restrictions on, 516, 520
    WTO membership and, 510–514
  common law, influence of, 464
  Communist Party
    attitudes toward law, 462

  Constitution of 1982, role in, 468–469
    gender discrimination and, 470
    labor and trade unions, domination of, 515
  confidentiality clauses in employment contracts, 479
  Confucianism
    gender discrimination and, 470
    historical role of, 462–464
  Constitution of 1982, 464–471
    benefits under, 470
    Communist Party, role of, 468–469
    foreign exploitation described in, 468
    gender discrimination under, 470
    historical background, 464–465
    right to work under, 469
    rights versus duties under, 469–470
    selected excerpts, 465–468
    socialist market economy under, 468
    US compared, 468–469
    wages under, 470
  consultation with foreign invested companies, 516
  contract employment system
    breach of contract, 484
    Labor Law and, 482, 483
    rise of, 476
  covenants not to compete, 479
  Cultural Revolution, 476
  damages and employment contracts, 509
  dismissal for incompetence, 506
  dispute resolution systems, 485–488
    appellate review, 507
    civil servants, coverage of, 502–503
    geographic concentration, 487
    increasing use of, 485–486, 488
    independent contractors, coverage of, 502–503
    labor arbitration committees, 485, 486
    legal assistance, 487–488
    mediation, 487
    non-state sector, applicability to, 503
    procedural barriers, 487
    right to counsel, 487
    scope of, 485, 486–487
    understatement of number of cases, 485, 487
  economic growth in, 471–472
  employment contracts
    breach of contract, 484
    confidentiality clauses, 479
    covenants not to compete, 479
    damages, 509
    joint ventures, 509
    liquidated damages, 509
  federalism, lack of, 480
  foreign invested companies
    consultation with, 516
    labor and trade unions, establishing, 506–507
    Special Economic Zones, in, 506
  freedom of association
    domestic law not supporting, 515
    economic growth, effect of, 515
    lack of history of labor activism and, 515
    understanding of, 515
  gender discrimination

China *(cont.)*
  child care and, 471
  Communist Party and, 470
  Confucianism and, 470
  Constitution of 1982, under, 470
  current state of, 471
  Labor Law, under, 483–484
  protective legislation, effect of, 471
  sexual harassment, 471
  German, law, influence of, 464
  historical overview, 462–464
  hours of work, 484
  household registration system
    planned economy, in, 473
    socialist market economy, in, 479
  ILO Conventions, ratification of, 516
  incompetence, dismissal for, 506
  increased transparency of legal system, 477
  independent contractors, 502–503
  India, as role model for, 518
  international agreements, ratification of, 514
  Japanese law, influence of, 464, 518
  job-hopping, 479
  joint ventures, 509
  judiciary, 480
  labor and trade unions, 517
    Communist Party domination, 515
    difficulties in organizing, 517
    foreign invested companies establishing, 506–507
    lack of history of labor activism and, 515
    lack of real negotiation, 517
    persecution of individual activists, 517
    restrictions on, 515, 520
    strikes, restrictions on, 516, 520
    unpaid contributions, recovery of, 515
    Wal-Mart, 517
    weakness of, 515
    WTO membership and, 510–514
  labor arbitration committees, 485, 486
  Labor Law, 481–499
    appellate review, 507
    breach of contract under, 484
    civil servants, coverage of, 502
    contract employment system and, 482, 483
    economic contradictions, reflection of, 483
    economic development, relationship with, 481
    gender discrimination under, 483–484
    hours of work under, 484
    independent contractors, coverage of, 502–503
    lateness of adoption, reasons for, 481
    layoffs under, 484–485
    limitations period, 503
    minimum wage under, 484
    non-state sector, applicability to, 503
    organization of, 483
    overtime under, 484
    overview, 481
    promulgation of, 481
    scope of, 483
    selected excerpts, 488–499
  labor system versus labor market, 479–480

  layoffs, 478–479, 484–485
  legal history, 462–464
  liability insurance, 503
  liquidated damages and employment contracts, 509
  mediation, 487
  minimum wage, 484
  mobility of labor, difficulty of, 476–477
  National People's Congress (NPC), 480
  overtime
    Labor Law, under, 484
    Special Economic Zones, in, 520
  personnel dossiers
    planned economy, in, 473–474
    socialist market economy, in, 479
  planned economy, 472–477
    household registration system, 473
    personnel dossiers, 473–474
    post-revolutionary situation, 472
    state creation of urban industrial class, 472
    unified placement system of job allocation, 473
  right to counsel, 487
  right to work in, 469
  sexual harassment, 471
  socialist market economy, 477–479
    agricultural reform, 477–478
    Constitution of 1982, under, 468
    Deng Xiaoping, reforms under, 477, 478
    effects of reforms, 478
    incremental approach to reform, 478
    industrial reform, 478
    job-hopping in, 479
    layoffs and, 478–479
    unemployment and, 478–479
  Soviet law, influence of, 464, 518
  Special Economic Zones, 518–520
    advantages of, 519
    development of, 518–519
    disadvantages of, 519–520
    foreign direct investment in, 520
    foreign invested companies in, 506
    health and safety issues, 520
    labor abuses in, 520
    overtime in, 520
    wages in, 520
  State Council, 480
  strikes, restrictions on, 516, 520
  successor liability, 506
  trade secrets, theft of, 479
  Trade Union Law
    criticism of, 517
    enforcement of collective agreements under, 516
    unpaid contributions, recovery under, 509
  tradition, role of, 462–464
  transfers of undertakings, 506
  unemployment, 478–479
  unified placement system of job allocation
    phasing out of, 476
    planned economy, in, 473
    socialist market economy, in, 479
  unitary state, as, 480

China (*cont.*)
  wages, hours and benefits
    benefits, 470
    hours of work, 484
    minimum wage, 484
    overtime, 484, 520
    wages, 470, 520
  WTO membership, effect of, 510–514
Chirac, Jacques, 436
Choice of forum
  common law actions in US courts, in, 596
Choice of law
  common law actions in US courts, in, 597–598
    Restatement, under, 598–599
Civil servants
  China, in, 502
Clinton, Bill, 249, 394
Clinton Administration
  NAALC
    attitude toward, 272
    negotiation of, 249
Codes of conduct
  Apparel Industry Partnership, 606
  China, in, 603
  collective bargaining and, 603
  commercial speech considerations, 606
  comparison with traditional labor law, 605
  compliance review, 603
  consultation with foreign workers regarding, 606
  electronic monitoring of employees, 603
  enforceability, 602
  Ethical Trading Initiative (ETI), 604
  European attitude toward, 605
  external/NGO codes, 604
  Fair Labor Association (FLA), 604
  FIFA Code of Labour Practice, 603
  first generation codes, 603
  freedom of association, 603
  governmental codes, 604
  industry/trade association codes, 603–604
  Nike, Inc., 606
  OECD Guidelines on Multinational Corporations, 604
  private employment law, as, 50
  public relations campaigns regarding, 606
  reinvigorating employee power through, 606
  Social Accountability International (SAI), 604
  transfer of personal data to third countries and, 330
  UN Global Compact, 604
  UN Subcommission on the Promotion and Protection of Human Rights, Norms on the Responsibilities of Transnational Corporations and Other Business Enterprises with Regard to Human Rights, 604–605
  US, attempts to require in, 605
  Vietnam, in, 603
  Wal-Mart (*See* Wal-Mart)
  Worker Rights Consortium (WRC), 604
  WRAP Initiative, 603
Collective bargaining. *See* Collective employee rights

Collective employee rights
  Canada, in, 185 (*See also* Canada)
  China, in, 517 (*See also* China)
  codes of conduct and, 603
  EU, in, 315 (*See also* European Union)
  France, in, 453 (*See also* France)
  Germany, in, 404–408 (*See also* Germany)
  Japan, under Constitution of 1947, 526
  Mexico, in, 233 (*See also* Mexico)
  strikes (*See* Strikes)
  UK, in, 359–367 (*See also* United Kingdom)
  US, in, 110–122 (*See also* United States)
Collective redundancies
  EU, in, 303–307 (*See also* European Union)
  France, in, 442–443
  Mexico, in, 224
  UK, in
    consultation regarding, 364–366
    Information and Consultation of Employees Regulations (ICE), 366–367
    notice requirement, 364
  US, in, 105–110 (*See also* United States)
Colombia
  CCAS review of violence against trade unionists, 65
Commercial speech considerations regarding codes of conduct, 606
Commission (EU), 279
Committee of Experts on the Application of Conventions and Recommendations (CEACR)
  child labor in US agricultural sector, observation on, 32
  meetings, 61
  members, 61
  observations, 61
  review of reports, 61–65
    lateness of reports, 64
    progress reports, 64–65
    proportion of reports received, 64
    weaknesses of, 64
Committee on Freedom of Association (CFA), 83–88
  AFL-CIO bringing actions before, 2, 27
  Canada, case involving notice of union decertification in, 87–88
  China, complaints against, 516–517
  overview, 83
  tension between individual rights and collective employee rights before, 87
Common law
  China, influence on, 464
Common law actions in US courts, 591–601
  alter ego of defendants, 599
  choice of forum, 596
  choice of law, 597–598
    Restatement, under, 598–599
  covenants not to compete, 598
  forum non conveniens defense, 597
  jurisdictional considerations, 597
  piercing corporate veil of defendants, 599
  removal of cases to federal court, 597
  representation of foreign workers, issues regarding, 599

state court actions, 596
Wal-Mart, vulnerability of, 599–600
Communist Party. *See* China
Company unions
US, in, 115–116
Comparable worth
US, in, 316
Comparative law
domestic law as referent, danger in using, 38
functional approach, 37–38
labor force data, 40
language and terminology, dangers regarding, 38
legal advisors, benefits to, 39–40
limitations on, 39
misunderstanding foreign law by relying solely on
primary law, risk of, 37
new understanding of domestic law as benefit of,
38–39
overview, 32
per capita income data, 40
policy makers and advocates, benefits to, 39
questioning assumptions as benefit of, 39
risks and benefits of, 37–40
substantive law, effect of studying on, 40
unemployment data, 41
US, debate over use of foreign law in, 32–37
criticisms of, 37
historical background, 32–33
isolationist tendency of jurisprudence, 33
recent trends, 33
working hour data, 40–41
Complaints under Article 26 . *See* Article 26 complaints
Concerted activity, protection of
US, in, 118
Conciliation
Canada, strikes in, 184
France, conciliatory meetings in, 438
Germany, in labor courts, 430
Mexico, informal conciliation in, 234–235
Conference Committee on the Application of
Standards (CCAS)
Colombia, review of case involving violence against
trade unionists, 65
US, review of case involving tripartite consultation
requirement, 65–67
Confidentiality clauses in employment contracts
China, in, 479
Confucianism. *See* China
Constructive discharge
France, in, 437–438
UK, in, 350–351
Consultation
China, in, 516
France, in, 433
UK, in (*See* United Kingdom)
Contingent work
globalization, effect of, 12–13
labor market segmentation theory and, 12–13
neoclassical economic theory and, 12
Japan, in, 527
Contract employment system in China. *See* China

Contrat Premiere Embauche (CPE) in France,
444–446. *See also* France
Corporate governance
France, participation of employees in, 433
Germany, worker representation in, 420–422 (*See
also* Germany)
Corporate social responsibility and ATCA claims, 618
Council of the European Communities, 278–279
Court of Justice, 279
Covenants not to compete, 1
Canada, in, 1, 171
China, in, 479
common law actions in US courts and, 598
France, in, 448
Germany, in, 1
Mexico, in, 225
Criminal law
France, employment discrimination classified as
crime in, 455

Damages
Canada, wrongful discharge claims
aggravated damages, 170–171
punitive damages, 170–171
China, employment contracts, 509
liquidated damages, 509
France, noncompliance with procedural
requirements for dismissal of employees, 439
United Kingdom, noneconomic damages for unfair
dismissal, 355
Declaration of Philadelphia
CFA authority under, 83
excerpts, 54–55
full employment as objective of, 55–56
human rights law and, 55
obligations under, 55
relevancy of, 55
Declaration on Fundamental Principles and Rights at
Work, 88–91
aspirational nature of, 90
Conventions deemed fundamental, 89–90
excerpts, 88–89
historical context, 90
ILO promotion of, 58
increased ratification of Conventions, role in, 91
non-core standards, importance of, 90–91
public employment law and, 42–43
relationship with Conventions, 90
relevance of ILO, importance to, 91
Singapore Ministerial Declaration and, 90
trend away from formal Conventions, as, 91
US adoption of, 117, 122
Defensive lockouts
Germany, proportionality limits on, 413–414
Demographics
EU, 277
India, 566–567
Mexico, 208
Deng Xiaoping, 477, 478
Dependent leave
UK, in, 370

Diaz, Porfirio, 211
Direct discrimination
    Canada, in, 195–196
        US compared, 196
    EU, in, 316
        US compared, 320–321
    UK, in, 372
Disability discrimination
    EU, reasonable accommodations, 321
    Germany, in, 424
    US, in, 92, 126, 134, 607
Disparate impact discrimination
    Canada compared, 196
    EU compared, 321
    US, in, 129, 134
Disparate treatment discrimination
    Canada compared, 196
    EU compared, 320–321
    UK compared, 372
    US, in, 129, 134
Dispute resolution systems
    Canada, in, 207 (*See also* Canada)
    China, in, 485–488 (*See also* China)
    Japan, in
        labor tribunal system, 540–541
        lack of, 533
    Mexico, in, 246 (*See also* Mexico)
    NAALC, under, 259
    US, in
        Canada compared, 198–199
        Mexico compared, 235, 246
Doha Ministerial Conference, 49
Domestic workers
    US, in, 16–17
Dual citizenship and free movement of workers in EU,
    294
Duty of fair representation
    Canada, in, 207

EC Treaty
    antidiscrimination law under, 315
    collective employee rights under, 301
    community law under, 280
    Council of the European Communities under,
        278–279
    dual citizenship under, 294
    free movement of workers under, 289
    gender discrimination under, 317
Economic strikes
    US, in, 121
Educational leave
    France, in, 454
Elections
    Canada, in
        labor and trade unions, certification without,
            173–174
        strikes, secret ballot votes, 184
    UK, secret elections for labor and trade unions in,
        361–362
    US, secret ballot elections for labor and trade unions,
        116

Electronic monitoring of employees
    codes of conduct, 603
    France, in, 458, 460, 461
    UK, in, 393
    US, in, 155–156
Employee representation committees
    France, in, 452–453
Employee representatives
    France, in, 452
Employer-dominated unions
    US, in, 115–116
Employers' organizations
    EU, in, 282–283
    France, in, 450
Employment at will doctrine
    US, in, 93–105 (*See also* United States)
Employment contracts
    China, in (*See* China)
    EU, voiding in, 294
    Germany, in, 398–399 (*See also* Germany)
    Mexico, in
        presumption of employment contract, 222
        termination of employment contract, 223
        writing requirement for employment contract, 223,
            226
    private employment law, as, 50
    reasonable notice rule in Canada as incentive for
        forming, 169
Employment safeguard plan
    France, in, 443
England. *See* United Kingdom
Equal pay for work of equal value
    EU, in, 316–317
    France, in, 456
    Germany, in, 424–425
Ethical Trading Initiative (ETI), 604
Ethics codes
    codes of conduct, (*See also* Codes of conduct)
    Germany, in, 431
Ethnic discrimination
    EU, in, 321
European Convention on Human Rights
    right to marry under, 324
European Monetary Union, 285
European Parliament, 278
European Social Model (ESM), 283–288
    actors involved, 286–288
    American model compared, 283
    competence to achieve, 285–286
    divergent national policies as result of failure to
        achieve, 288
    elements of, 284
    employers' organizations, role of, 287
    European Monetary Union and, 285
    European Parliament, role of, 287
    exclusion of core issues, 285
    fundamental rights and, 284
    labor and trade unions, role of, 287
    Lisbon Strategy and, 285, 286
    Nice Treaty and, 286
    social dialogue, 286–287

social vision, 284–285
unanimity requirement, 285
European Union (EU)
age discrimination, defenses, 321–322
antidiscrimination law, 324
age discrimination, defenses, 321–322
Amsterdam Treaty, under, 315
Burden of Proof Directive and, 372–373
direct discrimination, 316, 320–321
directives regarding, 315–316
disability discrimination, reasonable
accommodations, 321
disparate impact discrimination in US compared,
321
disparate treatment discrimination in US
compared, 320–321
EC Treaty, under, 315
equal pay for work of equal value, 316–317
ethnic discrimination, 321
gender discrimination (*See* gender discrimination,
below)
indirect discrimination, 317, 321
racial discrimination, 321
sexual harassment, 321
sexual orientation discrimination, 324
transsexuals, 324
UK compared, 370
Burden of Proof Directive and antidiscrimination
law, 372–373
Centre Européen des Entreprises Publiques
(CEEP), 283
Charter of Fundamental Rights of the European
Union, 284
citizenship in EU as objective of, 277
collective employee rights, 315
collective redundancies (*See* collective
redundancies, below)
EC Treaty, under, 301
European Works Councils (*See* European Works
Councils, below)
exclusion of core issues, 301
free movement of workers, voiding of agreements
conflicting with, 294
overview, 301
strikes, authority of European Works Councils to
call, 302–303
transfer of enterprises (*See* transfer of enterprises,
below)
US compared, 301
collective redundancies, 303–307
consultation requirement, 304, 305
directives regarding, 304, 306–307
information requirement, 304–305
overview, 303
penalties for infringement, 306
US compared, 307
workers' representatives, 305–306
Comité des Organisations Agricoles (COPA), 283
Commission, 279
common foreign and security policy as objective of,
277

Community Charter of Fundamental Social Rights
of Workers, 284
community law, 279–280
Constitution, rejection by France and Netherlands,
276–277
cooperation in justice and home affairs as objective
of, 277
Council of the European Communities, 278–279
Court of Justice, 279
decisions, 282
demographic statistics, 277
direct discrimination, 316, 320–321
directives, 280–282
disability discrimination, reasonable
accommodations, 321
economic and social progress as objective of, 277
employers' Organisations, 282–283
employment statistics, 277–278
equal pay for work of equal value, 316–317
ethnic discrimination, 321
European Association of Craft, Small and
Medium-Sized Enterprises (UEAPME), 283
European Parliament, 278
European Social Model (ESM), 283–288 (*See also*
European Social Model)
European Trade Union Confederation (ETUC), 283
European Works Councils, 301–303
authorization, 301
composition of, 301
creation of, 301
directive relating to, 302, 361, 453
exceptional circumstances provision, 302
purposes of consultation, 302
scope of consultation, 301–302
statistics, 302
strikes, authority to call, 302–303
TNCs and, 303
family leave, 300
free movement of workers, 288–297
collective bargaining agreements, voiding of, 294
corollary obligations of employers, 293
dichotomy between national and EU rules, 293
draft directive regarding, 297
dual citizenship and, 294
EC Treaty, under, 289
employment contracts, voiding of, 294
minimum wage and, 296–297
NAFTA compared, 294
national rules, voiding of, 293–294
nationality-based discrimination and, 293
overview, 288
professional athletes, 294
service sector, in, 294–297
special transition rules for new member states, 294
US Privileges and Immunities Clause compared,
297
gender discrimination, 317–321
affirmative action exception, 318
burden of proof, 317
directives regarding, 317
EC Treaty, under, 317

European Union (EU) *(cont.)*
   equal pay for work of equal value, 316–317
   occupational activities exception, 318
   preferences as, 319–320
   pregnancy and maternity exception, 317–318
   purposes of directives, 318
  high level of employment as objective of, 277
  historical background, 276–277
  indirect discrimination, 317, 321
  individual employment law, 301
   family leave, 300
   free movement of workers (*See* free movement of
    workers, above)
   parental leave, 300
   part-time workers, 300–301
   working time (*See* working time, below)
  International Confederation of Free Trade Unions
   (ICFTU), 283
  labor and trade unions, 283
  layoffs (*See* collective redundancies, above)
  legislative process, 282
   community law, 279–280
   decisions, 282
   directives, 280–282
   opinions, 282
   recommendations, 282
   regulations, 280
   secondary law, 280–282
  member states, 277
  objectives of, 277
  opinions, 282
  parental leave, 300
  part-time workers, 300–301
  personal data protection, 325–326
   codes of conduct and transfer of data to third
    countries, 330
   contractual agreements for transfer of data to third
    countries, 329–330
   human rights law and, 331
   legitimacy of use, 327
   safe harbor agreements and transfer of data to US,
    330–331
   sensitivity of data, 327–328
   transfer of data to third countries, 328–331
  population, 277
  privacy law, 325–331
   Article 29 Working Party opinion, 326–327
   codes of conduct and transfer of personal data to
    third countries, 330
   contractual agreements for transfer of personal
    data to third countries, 329–330
   human rights law and, 331
   legitimacy of use of personal data, 327
   personal data protection, 325–326
   safe harbor agreements and transfer of personal
    data to US, 330–331
   sensitivity of personal data, 327–328
   small companies, burden on, 331
   transfer of personal data to third countries,
    328–331

  public employment law in, 45–46
  racial discrimination, 321
  recommendations, 282
  regulations, 280
  secondary law, 280–282
  service sector, free movement of workers in, 294–297
  sex discrimination (*See* gender discrimination, above)
  sexual harassment, 321
  sexual orientation discrimination, 324
  strikes, authority of European Works Councils to
   call, 302–303
  transfers of undertakings, 307–315
   current relevance of directives, 314
   directives regarding, 308–310
   identity and function of old enterprise, retention
    of, 310
   outsourcing and, 314
   overview, 307–308
   reemployment assistance and, 314–315
   refusal of employees to accept, effect of, 314
   retention of employees by new employer, 314
   termination of contracts and, 312–313
   US compared, 313–314
  transsexual discrimination, 324
  Union of Industrial and Employers' Confederations
   of Europe (UNICE), 282–283
  working time, 297–299
   directive regarding, 297–298, 299
   on-call time for physicians, 299
   rest period requirement, 299
   worker fatigue, 299
  Working Time Directive, opt-out provisions, 368–369
European Works Councils. *See* European Union
Export processing zones (EPZ), 9–10, 13
Extraterritorial application of US statutes
  Age Discrimination in Employment Act, 607
  Americans with Disabilities Act, 607
  Congressional intent requirement, 607
  Title VII, 607

Fair Labor Association (FLA), 604
Family leave
  EU, in, 300
Family status discrimination
  Canada, in, 195
**Fast track authority for negotiating free trade
  agreements in US**
  BTPAA and, 275
  Free Trade Area of the Americas (FTAA), proposal
   for, 275
  OCRA and, 275
FDI. *See* Foreign direct investment
Federalism and labor law
  Canada, in, 158–159
  China, lack of federalism in, 480
  Mexico, in, 216–217
Feinstein, Diane, 617
FIFA Code of Labour Practice, 603
Flexible working time
  UK, in, 370

Foreign direct investment (FDI)
China, in Special Economic Zones, 520
Germany, by, 397–398
globalization and, 6
India, ability to attract, 575–576
Japan, transplant companies in US, 542–543
Forum non conveniens defense
common law actions in US courts, in, 597
Fox, Vicente, 212, 214, 215, 247, 272
Framework agreements
Germany, in, 406
France
abusive resignation, 437
administrative structure of labor law, 435
alternative methods of representation, 452–453
employee representation committees, 452–453
employee representatives, 452
health and safety committees, 453
overview, 449, 452
works councils, 452–453
antidiscrimination law, 458
bullying in workplace, 457
crime, employment discrimination classified as, 455
equal pay for work of equal value, 456
EU directives, conformity with, 456
EU law, in context of, 455, 458
expansion of protections, 455–456
French language requirements and, 457–458
Haute Autorité de Lutte Contre les Discriminations et pour l'Egalité (HALDE), 456
historical development, 455
moral harassment, 457
religious discrimination, 457
sexual harassment, 39, 439, 441, 456–457
US compared, 435, 455, 456–457
bullying in workplace, 457
business creation leave, 454
Civil Code
employment contracts under, 436
privacy law under, 458
collective employee rights, 453
automatic nature of agreements, 451
binding nature of agreements, 451
Canada compared, 175
centralization of bargaining, 450–451
company level, at, 449, 450
flexibility in agreements, 451
historical background, 448–449
immediate nature of agreements, 451
industry level, at, 449, 450
Labor Ministry extending agreements, 451
negotiation, 449
rate of coverage by agreements, 450
recent developments in law, 449–450
recommended reforms, 450
right of opposition, 449–450
signatory agreements, 451
strikes (See strikes, below)

supplementing minimum standards through agreements, 451
collective redundancies, dismissal of employees for, 442
Conciliation Panels, 435
conciliatory meetings, 438
Constitution
labor and trade unions under, 448
overview, 432
strikes under, 448, 451
constructive discharge, 437–438
consultation, 433
Contrat Premiere Embauche (CPE), 444–446
covenants not to compete and, 448
dismissal of employees and, 445
duty of loyalty and, 448
employment at will in US compared, 445
historical background, 444
Lisbon Strategy and, 448
migrant workers in US compared, 445–446
overview, 434
proposal, 444
rescission of, 444–445
response to, 444
shifts in labor law and, 446
corporate governance, participation of employees in, 433
Cour d'Appel, 436
Cour de Cassation, 436
covenants not to compete, 446–448
dismissal of employees, 437–446
abusive resignation, 437
collective redundancies, 442–443
conciliatory meetings, 438
constructive discharge, 437–438
CPE and, 445
damages for noncompliance with procedural requirements, 439
economic reasons, for, 441–444
employment safeguard plan, 443
ILO Conventions and, 439
indemnities, 438–439, 443
individual redundancies, 442
insufficient results, for, 439
loss of confidence, for, 439
notice requirement, 438
personal reasons, for, 438–441
privacy law and, 441
procedural requirements, 438–439
professional incompetence, for, 439
professional shortcomings, for, 439
real and serious cause standard, 433, 437
reemployment assistance, 443
sexual harassment, for, 439, 441
transfers of undertakings, 444
trial period, during, 437
unauthorized freelance activities, for, 440–441
US compared, 439, 444
educational leave, 454
employee representation committees, 452–453

France *(cont.)*
  employee representatives, 452
  employers' associations, 450
  employment contracts
    Civil Code, under, 436
    covenants not to compete, 446–448
    defined, 436
    definite period contracts, 436–437
    dismissal (*See* dismissal of employees, above)
    French language requirements, 437
    indefinite contracts, 436
    loyalty, duty of, 446–448
    writing requirement, 436
  employment safeguard plan, 443
  equal pay for work of equal value, 456
  EU Constitution, rejection of, 276–277
  EU law, labor law in context of, 435
  First Job Contract (*See* Contrat Premiere Embauche
      (CPE), above)
  French language requirements
    antidiscrimination law and, 457–458
    employment contracts, 437
  Haute Autorité de Lutte Contre les Discriminations
      et pour l'Egalité (HALDE), 456
  health and safety committees, 453
  hours of work, 453–454
  ILO Conventions
    dismissal of employees in, 439
    ratification of, 435
  individual employment law, 448
    abusive resignation, 437
    constructive discharge, 437–438
    covenants not to compete, 446–448
    dismissal (*See* dismissal of employees, above)
    employment contracts (*See* employment contracts,
        above)
    loyalty, duty of, 446–448
  individual redundancies, dismissal of employees for,
      442
  labor and trade unions, 453
    alternative methods of representation (*See*
        alternative methods of representation, above)
    company level, at, 449
    Constitution, under, 448
    industry level, at, 449
    negotiation by, 449
    pluralism and, 449
    recent developments in law, 449–450
    recommended reforms, 450
    representatives, designation of, 449
    right of opposition, 449–450
    strikes (*See* strikes, below)
    union density, 450
  Labor Code
    overview, 435
    strikes under, 451
  Labor Courts, 435–436
  labor history, 433–434
  Labor Ministry extending collective bargaining
      agreements, 451

  lockouts, 452
  loyalty, duty of, 446–448
  maternity leave, 454, 456
  minimum wage, 453
  moral harassment, 457
  overtime, 453–454
  parental leave
    overview, 454
    US compared, 455
  Parliament, 432
  paternity leave, 454
  personal data protection, 325
  political overview, 432
  President, 432
  privacy law, 458–461
    blogs and, 460
    Civil Code, under, 458
    dignity and, 458
    dismissal of employees and, 441
    electronic monitoring of employees, 458, 460, 461
    future of labor law and, 461
    GPS, use of, 460
    personal data protection, 325
    trademark violation and, 461
    US compared, 458, 461
  reemployment assistance, 443
  religious discrimination, 457
  sexual harassment in, 39, 439, 441, 456–457
  social democratic ideology and labor law, 433
  strikes
    Constitution, under, 448, 451
    Labor Code, under, 451
    replacement workers, prohibition against, 452
    restrictions on right to strike, 451
  transfers of undertakings, 444
  UK, labor law compared, 333
  US labor law compared, 435
  vacations, 454
  wages, hours and benefits, 455
    business creation leave, 454
    educational leave, 454
    hours of work, 453–454
    maternity leave, 454, 456
    minimum wage, 453
    overtime, 453–454
    parental leave, 454
    paternity leave, 454
    US parental leave compared, 455
    vacations, 454
  Works Council Directive, conformity with, 453
  works councils, 452–453
Free rider problem
  Germany, in, 406
Free trade and globalization, 5
Free Trade Area of the Americas (FTAA)
  proposal for, 275
Freedom of association
  Canada, in
    picketing and, 184
    union dues, effect of, 182–183

China, in (*See* China)
codes of conduct and, 603
Germany, in, 408–409
Mexico, in, 245–246
picketing and, 184
strikes and, 122
union dues, effect of, 182–183
US, in
  low level of ILO Convention ratification, effect of,
    117
  recognition of shortcomings, 117–118

Gandhi, Indira, 569, 576
Gandhi, Mahatma, 568, 569
Gender discrimination
China, in (*See* China)
differential treatment among female workers, 16
EU, in, 317–321 (*See also* European Union)
Germany, in (*See* Germany)
globalization and, 16–21
Japan, in (*See* Japan)
sexual harassment (*See* Sexual harassment)
social and cultural factors, 16
UK, in, 370
unequal status of female workers, 16
US, domestic workers in, 16–17
Generalized System of Preferences (GSP), 43–44
Germany
Agenda 2010, 395
antidiscrimination law, 422–428
  Basic Law (Constitution), under, 422–423
  disability discrimination, 424
  EC directives, harmonization of law with, 428
  equal pay for work of equal value, 423, 424–425
  gender discrimination (*See* gender discrimination,
    below)
  indirect discrimination, 425
  sexual harassment, 423–424
  statutory authority, 423
Basic Law (Constitution)
  adoption, 394
  antidiscrimination law under, 422–423
  collective employee rights under, 406
  freedom of association under, 408–409
  privacy law under, 430
  right to work under, 395
Bundesvereinigung der Deutschen
  Arbeitgeberverbände (BDA), 405
China, influence of German law on, 464
Civil Code of 1896, 396
  employment contracts under, 398
codetermination
  excessive absences, regarding, 417–418
  overview, 396–397
  works councils and, 417
collective employee rights, 404–408
  Basic Law (Constitution), under, 406
  Canada compared, 175
  economic impact of, 398
  extension of contracts, 407

framework agreements, 406
free rider problem, 406
individual employment contracts and, 407–408
joint dispute resolution boards, 415
labor courts, claims in, 430
legal protection of, 396
pattern bargaining, 406–407
picketing, 413
regional negotiation paradigm, 406
sectoral bargaining, 407, 408
strikes (*See* strikes, below)
sympathy strikes, 413
US compared, 408
wage and salary agreements, 406
worker representation in corporate governance
  (*See* worker representation in corporate
  governance, below)
works agreements, relationship with collective
  agreements, 418, 419, 420
works councils (*See* works councils, below)
competitive economy versus protective labor
  standards, 397
conciliation in labor courts, 430
contractual protections for workers, 397
covenants not to compete in, 1
defensive lockouts, proportionality limits on, 413–414
Deutscher Gerwerkschaftsbund (DGB), 404
disability discrimination, 424
economic statistics, 395
employers' associations, 405–406
employment contracts, 398–399
  business reasons, payment of employees when
    work prevented due to, 398
  Civil Code of 1896, under, 398
  collective agreements and, 407–408
  contents of, 398
  duration of, 398–399
  legislation regarding, 398
  suspension of employee obligations under, 398
  voiding of provisions, 398
  works agreements, relationship with, 418–419
employment statistics, 395
equal pay for work of equal value, 424–425
ethics codes, 431
extensive structure of employment rights, 397
extraordinary dismissal, 399
foreign direct investment by, 397–398
gender discrimination
  bona fide occupational qualification defense in
    US compared, 423
  burden of proof, 428
  equal pay for work of equal value, 423, 424–425
  indirect discrimination, 425
  indispensable requirement defense, 423
  pregnancy, based on, 428
  prima facie cases, 427–428
health insurance, 404
historical background, 394
holidays, 403–404
indirect discrimination, 425

Germany *(cont.)*
  individual employment law, 398–404
    employment contracts (*See* employment contracts,
      above)
    labor courts, claims in, 429–430
    termination (*See* termination, below)
  Japan, influence of German law on, 518, 533,
    541–542
  joint dispute resolution boards, 415
  joint works councils, 416
  judicial development of labor law, 396, 413, 415
  labor and trade unions, 404–408
    centralization of, 405
    decline in, 405, 408
    Deutscher Gerwerkschaftsbund (DGB), 404
    free rider problem, 406
    historical background, 404–405
    legal requirements, 405
    representation of workers, 405
    strikes (*See* strikes, below)
    works councils (*See* works councils, below)
  labor courts, 428–430
    appeals regarding termination, 401
    career judges, 429
    challenging termination in, 401
    civil courts compared, 430
    collective bargaining claims in, 430
    conciliation in, 430
    individual employee claims in, 429–430
    labor disputes in, 412–413, 429
    lay judges, 429
    statutory authority, 428–429
    structure of, 429
  labor history, 404–405
  lockouts, 408–415
    defensive lockouts, proportionality limits on,
      413–414
    freedom of association and, 408–409
    judicial development of law regarding, 413, 415
    offensive lockouts prohibited, 413–414
    wages, responsibility to pay during, 415
  maternity leave, 428
  minimum wage, 403
  offensive lockouts prohibited, 413–414
  pension plans, 404
  personal data protection, 325, 430–431
  picketing, 413
  political overview, 394–395
  political structure, 394
  population, 395
  pregnancy, discrimination based on, 428
  privacy law, 430–431
    Basic Law (Constitution), under, 430
    ethics codes, 431
    personal data protection, 325, 430–431
    statutory authority, 430
  reinstatement following termination, 403
  right to work, 406
  sexual harassment, 423–424
  social security system, 403

  strikes, 408–415
    freedom of association and, 408–409
    judicial development of law regarding, 413, 415
    picketing, 413
    replacement workers, prohibition against, 415
    sympathy strikes, 413
    wages, responsibility to pay during, 415
  sympathy strikes, 413
  termination, 399–403
    appeals from labor courts, 401
    behavior of employee, for, 400
    challenges in labor courts, 401
    defining employees for purposes of, 401–402
    economic reasons, for, 400
    employee-like relationships, 402
    extraordinary dismissal, 399
    independent contractors, 402–403
    notice requirement, 399
    presumption of unlawfulness, 401
    prolonged or recurring illness, for, 400
    reinstatement, 403
    small employers, 400–401
    social aspects, consideration of, 400
    works councils, consultation with, 403
    wrongful termination, 399–400
  UK, labor law compared, 333
  unemployment compensation, 404
  Unification Treaty of 1990, 395–396
  vacations, 404
  wages, hours and benefits, 403–404
    cost of benefits, 404
    health insurance, 404
    holidays, 403–404
    lockouts, responsibility to pay wages during, 415
    maternity leave, 428
    minimum wage, 403
    pension plans, 404
    social security, 403
    strikes, responsibility to pay wages during, 415
    unemployment compensation, 404
    vacations, 404
  worker representation in corporate governance,
    420–422
    corporate structure, 420
    economic impact of, 398
    employee stock ownership plans in US compared,
      421–422
    equal status of representatives, 421
    management boards, 420
    manipulation of, 422
    overview, 396–397
    secrecy, duty of, 421
    statutory authority, 420–421
    supervisory boards, 420
    works councils, relationship with, 421
  works agreements, relationship with collective
    agreements, 418, 419, 420
  works councils, 416–420
    action committees in US compared, 419–420
    advantages and disadvantages of, 419–420

codetermination and, 417
collective agreements, relationship with works
    agreements, 418, 419, 420
creation of, 416
economic impact of, 398
employer participation, 418
employment contracts, relationship with works
    agreements, 418–419
historical background, 416
joint works councils, 416
overview, 396
powers and duties of, 417
retaliation against members prohibited, 416–417
small employers, 419
termination, consultation regarding, 403
worker representation in corporate governance,
    relationship with, 421
wrongful termination, 399–400
Ghost unions
    Mexico, in, 237–239
Ginsburg, Ruth Bader, 33
Global economic integration, 5–8
Globalization, 3–32
    business management, of, 4–5
    capital mobility as result of, 7
    child labor and, 28–32 (*See also* Child labor)
    contingent work, effect on, 12–13
        labor market segmentation theory and, 12–13
        neoclassical economic theory and, 12
    defined, 3
    foreign direct investment and, 6
    forms of private financial flow, 6–7
    free trade and, 5
    gender and, 16–21
    global economic integration, 5–8
    ICFTU and, 14–15
    ILO and, 57–58
    ILO World Commission on the Social Dimension of
        Globalization findings on, 7–8
    increase in trade as result of, 5
    labor and trade unions, decline of, 13–15
    legal regulation and, 8–11
    migrant workers and, 21–28 (*See also* Migrant
        workers)
    neoliberalism and, 5
    nonstandard work, effect on, 12–13
        labor market segmentation theory and, 12–13
        neoclassical economic theory and, 12
    OECD study on, 9–10
    protective laws, effect on, 8
    public policy and, 5
    race to the bottom, 9
    race to the top, 9
    regulatory competition as result of, 8, 9
    tension between labor and employment law and
        attracting foreign direct investment, 8
    uneven expansion of trade as result of, 6
Great Britain. *See* United Kingdom
Grievances
    Canada, arbitration in, 206

UK, in, 337, 338
US, sexual harassment, 148

Harassment in workplace
    sexual harassment (*See* Sexual Harassment)
    UK, in, 351–352
    US, in, 144
Health and safety committees
    France, in, 453
Health care for employees
    Canada, in, 185–186
    Germany, in, 404
    US, relationship to labor law, 93
Heath, Edward, 360
Holidays
    Canada, in, 185
    Germany, in, 403–404
    Mexico, in, 224
    UK, in, 369
Hong Kong
    brain circulation in China and, 521–522
Hostile environment sexual harassment
    US, in, 147–148
Hours of work. *See also* Wages, hours and benefits
    Canada, in, 185
    China, in, 484
    France, in, 453–454
    UK, in, 367–368
Housing for workers
    Mexico, in, 224
Household registration system in China. *See* China
Human rights law
    Canada
        antidiscrimination law in, effect on, 187
        arbitration, human rights claims included with
            collective bargaining matters, 207
        human rights boards, dispute resolution in, 198
        indigenous persons, affirmative action, 183
    Declaration of Philadelphia and, 55
    EU, right to marry in, 324
    personal data protection and, 331
    public employment law and, 41–43
Human Rights Watch, 20, 31, 115

ILO. *See* International Labour Organization
ILO Conventions
    administrative procedures in adoption of, 59
    antidiscrimination law and US reluctance to ratify,
        127
    approval at International Labor Conference, 58
    child labor, 30
    China, ratification by, 516
    collective employee rights
        effect of US reluctance to ratify on, 117
        US reluctance to ratify based on historical
            significance of, 68
    discrimination, 63
    France
        dismissal of employees in, 439
        ratification by, 435

ILO Conventions *(cont.)*
  freedom of association, effect of US reluctance to
    ratify on, 117
  fundamental, Conventions deemed, 89–90
  high compliance nation, US deemed, 68, 117
  hypocrisy of US reluctance to ratify, 68
  increased ratification of, role of Declaration in, 91
  India, 577
  individual rights, focus on as reason for US
    reluctance to ratify, 69
  Japan, ratification by, 526
  low political priority in US, 69
  migrant workers, 22–23
  NAALC labor principles, lack of reference in, 256
  number of Conventions, criticisms of, 60
  obligations of ratifying members, 60
  overview, 59–60
  public employment law and, 43
  ratification by member states, 58
  reduction in frequency of, 60
  relationship with Declaration, 90
  revision and integration process, 60
  trend away from formal Conventions, Declaration as,
    91
  unilateralism as reason for US reluctance to ratify, 69
  usurping of national sovereignty as reason for US
    reluctance to ratify, 68–69
Immigrants. *See* Migrant workers
Indemnities
  France, payment to dismissed employees in, 438–439,
    443
  US, payment for plant closings and mass layoffs, 110
Independent contractors
  China, in, 502–503
  Germany, termination in, 402–403
India
  Ahmedabad Textile Labour Association (ATLA), 577
  antidiscrimination law
    caste system, prohibition against discrimination
      based on, 579
    compensatory discrimination to remedy past
      injustices in caste system, 579
  Bharatiya Janata Party (BJP), 575
  bonded labor
    consequences of, 589
    public interest litigation and, 588–589
  caste system, 578–580
    abolition of untouchability, 63–64, 578–579
    brahmins, 578
    compensatory discrimination to remedy past
      injustices, 579
    Constitutional provisions regarding, 578
    contemporary status of dalits, 579
    dalits, 578
    discrimination, prohibition against, 579
    hierarchy of castes, 578
    kshatriyas, 578
    overview, 567
    sudras, 578
    vaisyas, 578

Central Federation of Trade Unions, 577
child labor and poverty reduction, 567
China as role model for, 518
comprehensive labor code, lack of, 588
Congress Party, 575
Constitution
  caste system, provisions regarding, 578
  public interest litigation, provisions regarding, 580
demographics of workforce, 566–567
economic policy and performance, 568–576
  centralization under Indira Gandhi, 569
  decentralization after 1991, 569
  Emergency of 1975–77, 569
  foreign competition, effect of shielding economy
    from, 569
  foreign direct investment, ability to attract, 575–576
  Gandhian vision of society, 568
  industrialization under Nehru, 569
  judicial approval for privatization of businesses,
    569–570
  leapfrogging industrial revolution, 575
  Non Resident Indians, role of, 576
  Second Labour Commission Report and, 568–569
  slowing of privatization, 575
  traditional Indian values and, 568
historical background, 566–568
ILO Conventions and, 577
information technology sector of economy
  islands of excellence, 575
  outsourcing, 575
judicial activism and public interest litigation,
  587–588
labor and trade unions, 576–577
  defensive role of, 577
  Second Labour Commission Report and, 577
  strikes, 576
  weakness of, 576
language diversity, 567–568
litigation regarding remedial measures, 580
manual scavenging in, 64
migrant labor in, 589
outsourcing to, 575
political overview, 566
poverty, effect on institutions, 567
public interest litigation in, 580–589
  Anglo-Saxon jurisprudence, reference to, 589
  bonded labor and, 588–589
  Constitutional provisions regarding, 580
  criticisms of, 588
  judicial activism and, 587–588
  overview, 581
  support for, 588
quotas in, 579–580
religious diversity, 567
Second Labour Commission Report, 568–569, 577
Self-Employed Women's Association (SEWA), 577
social compartmentalization, 580
strikes in, 576
three strands policy, 566
undesirable work, 580

Indirect discrimination
  EU, in, 317, 321
  Germany, in, 425
  UK, in, 373–374
Individual employment law
  Canada, in, 171 (*See also* Canada)
  EU, in, 301 (*See also* European Union)
  France, in, 448 (*See also* France)
  Germany, in, 398–404 (*See also* Germany)
  Mexico, in, 227 (*See also* Mexico)
  UK, in, 334–359 (*See also* United Kingdom)
  US, in, 93–110 (*See also* United States)
Industrialization as cause of child labor, 31
Intentional infliction of emotional distress
  US, in
    breach of duty of mutual trust and confidence in
      UK compared, 352
    overview, 103–104
Inter-American Court of Human Rights (IACHR),
  27
Interest arbitration
  Canada, in, 175 (*See also* Canada)
International Confederation of Free Trade Unions
  (ICFTU), 14–15, 32, 50, 283
International Labour Organization (ILO)
  Cold War and, 57
  Committee of Experts on the Application of
    Conventions and Recommendations (CEACR)
    (*See* Committee of Experts on the Application
    of Conventions and Recommendations
    (CEACR))
  Committee on Freedom of Association (CFA) (*See*
    Committee on Freedom of Association)
  Conference Committee on the Application of
    Standards (CCAS) (*See* Conference Committee
    on the Application of Standards)
  Conventions (*See* ILO Conventions)
  current objectives, 57–58
  Declaration of Philadelphia (*See* Declaration of
    Philadelphia)
  Declaration on Fundamental Principles and Rights
    at Work (*See* Declaration on Fundamental
    Principles and Rights at Work)
  decolonization and, 56
  delegation representatives, 58–59
  enforcement of labor standards, 60–88
    Article 24 representations, 70–74
    Article 26 complaints (*See* Article 26 complaints)
    CCAS review of cases (*See* Conference
      Committee on the Application of Standards)
    CEACR review of reports (*See* Committee of
      Experts on the Application of Conventions and
      Recommendations)
    CFA, complaints before (*See* Committee on
      Freedom of Association)
    overview, 60–61
  globalization and, 57–58
  Governing Body (GB), 59
  historical background, 53
  International Labor Conference (ILC), 58

International Programme on the Elimination of
    Child Labour (IPEC), 28–29
  office, 59
  Solidarnosc, position on, 57
  World Commission on the Social Dimension of
    Globalization, 7–8
  WTO role in enforcing labor standards compared, 49
International Labor Rights Fund, 20, 615
International law
  private employment law, 49–51
    codes of conduct, 50
    ILO core labor standards, voluntary compliance,
      50–51
    individual employment contracts, 50
    international self-regulation by TNCs, 50
    US, self-regulation by TNCs in, 50
  public employment law, 41–49
    Caribbean Common Market, in, 47
    European Union, in, 45–46
    Generalized System of Preferences (GSP) and,
      43–44
    human rights law and, 41–43
    ILO Conventions and, 43
    ILO Declaration on Fundamental Principles and
      Rights at Work, 42–43
    linkage between trade and labor standards, 43–47
    NAALC and, 44
    overview, 41
    Singapore Ministerial Declaration, 47–48
    social policy issues, 46–47
    trade liberalization and, 48–49
    trade-related instruments and, 43–47
    trade sanctions, enforcing labor standards through,
      48
    WTO rules and, 47–49
Isolationist tendency of US jurisprudence, 33

Japan
  antidiscrimination law
    gender discrimination (*See* gender discrimination,
      below)
    sexual harassment (*See* sexual harassment, below)
  China, influence of Japanese law on, 464, 518
  collective employee rights under Constitution of
    1947, 526
  Constitution of 1947
    collective employee rights under, 526
    gender discrimination under, 528
    overview, 525–526
    US compared, 525
  contingent work, long-term employment system and,
    527
  cultural factors in modernization, 525
  dispute resolution systems
    labor tribunal system, 540–541
    lack of, 533
  Equal Employment Opportunity Law, 528, 542
  ethnic and cultural distinctiveness, 524
  gender discrimination
    Constitution of 1947, under, 528

Japan *(cont.)*
  Equal Employment Opportunity Law, 528
  litigation involving, 528
  sexual harassment (*See* sexual harassment, below)
  social attitudes, effect of, 528–529
  transplant companies in US and, 564–565
  weakness of legal protections, 528
German law, influence of, 518, 533, 541–542
historical overview, 524–525
ILO Conventions, ratification of, 526
labor and trade unions
  Constitution of 1947, under, 525–526
  decline in, 527
  enterprise-based unions, 527
  historical overview, 526
Labor Relations Adjustment Law, 526
Labor Standards Law, 533, 536
labor tribunal system, 540–541
long-term employment system, 526–527
  contingent work and, 527
  employment at will doctrine in US compared, 527
  immobility of labor, 527
  maintenance of permanent workforce, 526–527
  overview, 526
  recession, effect of, 527
  transplant companies in US and, 565
  youth unemployment and, 540
Meiji Restoration, 518, 524
occupational tracking, 527–529
  overview, 527–528
  social attitudes, effect of, 528–529
overtime, 533
privacy law and sexual harassment, 541–542
rapidity of modernization, 524, 525
right to work in, 526
sexual harassment, 541–542
  breach of contract, as, 541
  Equal Employment Opportunity Law, under, 542
  privacy law and, 541–542
  removal of employee from workplace as motivation, 541
  tort, as, 541
  US compared, 541
strikes, infrequency of, 527
suicide in, 533
Tokugawa shogunate, demise of, 524
Trade Union Law, 526
transplant companies in US, 565
  ADA actions, 565
  automobile factories, lean production techniques, 543
  foreign direct investment in US, 542–543
  gender discrimination and, 564–565
  long-term employment system and, 565
  releases, enforceability of, 565
  Title VII actions, 565
  trade with US, development of, 542
  treaties, effect of, 564, 565
unemployment in, 527

workers' compensation cases for stress and fatigue, 533
World War II and, 525
wrongful death from overwork, 529
wrongful termination, 533–541
  age, effect of, 540
  employment at will doctrine in US compared, 533
  four requirements test, 536–537
  just cause requirement, 536
  litigation involving, 540
  mere incompetence, for, 534
  minor infractions, for, 534
  National Westminster Bank case, 537–540
  overview, 533
  settlement of cases, 536–537
Joint dispute resolution boards
  Germany, in, 415
Joint ventures
  China, in, 509
Joint works councils
  Germany, in, 416
Jordan–US Free Trade Agreement
  NAALC, effect of, 273
  Qualified Industrial Zones, abuses in, 273–274
Judicial activism
  India, public interest litigation in, 587–588
Judicial review
  ATCA actions, 616
  Canada, labor boards, availability of judicial review, 198, 205–206
  China, in, 507
  Germany, appeals from labor courts, 401
  Mexico
    amparo suits, 240–246 (*See also* Mexico)
    dispute resolution systems in individual employment law, 236
Jurisdiction
  common law actions in US courts, in, 597
  Mexico, CABs, 219
Just case standard for dismissal
  Mexico, in, 222–223

Koizumi, Junichiro, 536

Labor and trade unions
  Canada, in, 185 (*See also* Canada)
  China, in, 517 (*See also* China)
  contingent workers, effect on decline of unions, 14
  EU, in, 283
  France, in, 453 (*See also* France)
  Germany, in, 404–408 (*See also* Germany)
  globalization, decline as result of, 13–15
  human resources techniques, effect on decline of unions, 14
  India, in, 576–577
    defensive role of, 577
    weakness of, 576
  international decline of, 14
  Japan, in, 525
  Mexico, in (*See* Mexico)

migrant workers, remedies for dismissal for union
    activity, 26
multinational labor movement, rise of, 15
strikes (*See* Strikes)
transnational labor solidarity, examples of, 15
UK, in, 359–367 (*See also* United Kingdom)
US, in, 110–122 (*See also* United States)
Labor arbitration committees
    China, in, 485, 486
Labor courts
    Germany, in, 428–430 (*See also* Germany)
Labor force data, 40
Layoffs
    China, in, 478–479, 484–485
    EU, in, 303–307 (*See also* European Union)
    Mexico, in, 224
        CAB, powers and duties of, 224
    UK, in
        consultation regarding, 364–366
        Information and Consultation of Employees
            Regulations (ICE), 366–367
        notice requirement, 364
    US, in, 105–110 (*See also* United States)
Liability insurance
    China, in, 503
Liquidated damages
    China, employment contracts, 509
Lisbon Strategy
    Contrat Premiere Embauche (CPE) in France and,
        448
    European Social Model (ESM) and, 285, 286
Lockouts
    Canada, in, 184–185
    defensive lockouts in Germany, proportionality limits
        on, 413–414
    France, in, 452
    Germany, in, 408–415 (*See also* Germany)
    Mexico, right of employer to stop work, 232
    offensive lockouts in Germany, prohibition against,
        413–414
Long-term employment system
    Japan, in, 526–527 (*See also* Japan)
Loyalty, duty of
    France, in, 446–448

Macau
    brain circulation in China and, 521
Major, John, 333
Mandatory bargaining subjects
    Mexico, in, 230
    UK, in, 361
Mao Zedong, 477
Marriage
    EU, right to marry in, 324
Mass layoffs
    US, in, 105–110 (*See also* United States)
Maternity discrimination
    EU, exception to gender discrimination in, 317–318
Maternity leave
    France, in, 454, 456

Germany, in, 428
UK, in, 369
McKinney, Cynthia, 605
Mediation
    Canada, strikes in, 184
    China, in, 487
Merkel, Angela, 394
Mexico
    agricultural sector, competition in, 210
    amparo suits, 240–246
        Constitutional provisions, 241
        effect of decisions, 241
        lack of independent judiciary, effect of, 241–242
        overview, 240–241
        public sector case law summary, 242–244
        stare decisis and, 246
        US and Canada compared, 246
    antidiscrimination law in, 248
        Constitutional provisions, 247
        Federal Law to Prevent and Eliminate
            Discrimination, 247–248
        good cause standard and, 247
        National Council for the Prevention of
            Discrimination, 247
        pregnancy, based on, 247
        reinstatement as remedy, 247
        remedies, 247
        severance pay as remedy, 247
        statutory provisions, 247
        unjust discharge compared, 247
    collective employee rights, 233
        Constitutional provisions, 227
        dispute resolution systems in (*See* dispute
            resolution systems in, below)
        effect of collective bargaining agreements, 230
        law contracts, 230–231
        mandatory bargaining subjects, 230
        obligation to bargain to agreement, 229, 233
        particulars of collective bargaining agreements,
            229–230
        statutory provisions, 227
        strikes (*See* strikes, below)
        suspension for economic necessity, 230
    Conciliation and Arbitration Boards (CAB)
        child labor, powers and duties regarding, 223–224
        claims against labor unions before, 228
        Constitutional provisions, 219
        dispute resolution, powers and duties regarding,
            233
        enforcement of collective bargaining agreements,
            230
        filing of collective bargaining agreements with, 229
        ghost unions and, 237–239
        individual employment law, powers and duties
            regarding, 234–236
        judicial review (*See* amparo suits, above)
        jurisdiction, 219
        labor union registration, powers and duties
            regarding, 236–237
        law contracts, powers and duties regarding, 231

Mexico *(cont.)*
    layoffs, powers and duties regarding, 224
    membership, 237
    particulars regarding, 219–220
    profit sharing plans, appeals to regarding, 224
    protection contracts and, 237–239
    registration of labor unions, powers and duties
      regarding, 228
    review of collective bargaining agreements by,
      229–230
    strikes, regulation of, 239–240
    suspension of collective employee rights for
      economic necessity, 230
    wages, powers and duties regarding, 223
  Constitution
    amparo suits, provisions regarding, 241
    antidiscrimination law, provisions regarding,
      247
    aspirational provisions of, 221–222
    CABs under, 219
    collective employee rights, provisions regarding,
      227
    high labor standards in, 222
    labor law provisions, 217–219
    overview, 216–217
    US Constitution as model for, 221
  demographic statistics, 208
  dispute resolution systems, 246
    amparo suits *(See* amparo suits, above)
    CAB, powers and duties of, 233
    collective employee rights, 236–240
      ghost unions, 237–239
      labor union registration, 236–237
      polycentric system, in, 237
      protection contracts, 237–239
      strikes, regulation of, 239–240
      tripartite panels, 237
    individual employment law, 234–236
      arbitration compared, 235–236
      criticisms of, 235
      dismissal for cause, 234
      informal conciliation, 234–235
      judicial review, 236
      presumptions in favor of workers, 234
      US and Canada compared, 235
    overview, 233
  economic policies, 213–215
  economic statistics, 208–209
  employment contracts
    presumption of employment contract, 222
    termination of employment contract, 223
    writing requirement for employment contract, 223,
      226
  Federal Labor Law, 220–221
  federalism and labor law in, 216–217
  freedom of association in, 245–246
  ghost unions, 237–239
  historical background, 211–216
  holidays, 224
  housing for workers, 224
  individual employment law, 227

    at-will employment compared, 226
    child labor, prohibition against, 223–224
    common law compared with civil law, 225
    covenants not to compete, 225
    dispute resolution systems in *(See* dispute
      resolution systems, above)
    informal economy, effect of, 227
    judicial conservatism and, 226
    just cause standard for dismissal, 222–223, 226
    layoffs, 224
    presumption of employment contract, 222
    termination of employment contract, 223
    tradeoff between labor standards and wages, 227
    writing requirement for employment contract, 223,
      226
  informal economy in, 209–210, 227
  labor and trade unions
    denial of registration, 228
    ghost unions, 237–239
    legal personhood, 228–229
    majority support, requiring, 239
    membership, 228
    multiple unions, 229
    registration requirement, 228, 233
      dispute resolution systems, 236–237
    strikes *(See* strikes, below)
    US and Canada compared, 228
    wages, effect on, 232–233
  labor history, 211, 213
  law contracts, 230–231
    CAB, powers and duties of, 231
  layoffs, 224
    CAB, powers and duties of, 224
  legal background, 216
  NAALC
    concerns for national sovereignty regarding,
      249–250
    submissions against, 271
  NAFTA, economic impact of, 253–254
  OECD membership, 209
  Partido Acción Naciónal (PAN), 212
  Partido Naciónal Mexicano (PNM), 211
  Partido Revolutionario Institucional (PRI), 211
  political history, 211–213, 215–216
  political nature of labor unions, 216
  privacy law in, 248
  relevance of unions in polycentric system of
    government, 216
  social security, 224
  statutory labor law provisions, 220–221
  stop work, right of employer to, 232
  strikes
    CAB regulation of, 239–240
    declining frequency of, 240
    dispute resolution systems, 239–240
    replacement workers, prohibition against, 232
    restrictions on, 232
    right to strike, 231
  union density in, 209
  unjust discharge, 247
  upper middle income country, as, 209

US, economic differences with, 209
vacations, 224
wages, hours and benefits
  CAB, powers and duties of, 223
  holidays, 224
  housing for workers, 224
  social security, 224
  vacations, 224
  wages, 223
  workers' compensation, 224–225
workers' compensation, 224–225
WTO membership, 209
Migrant workers
developed nations, lack of support for ILO
    Conventions in, 23
economic impact of, 24
families, protection of, 23
globalization and, 21–28
ILO Convention on, 22–23
immigrant rights movement in US, rise of, 28
India, in, 589
NLRA, in industries not covered by, 27–28
remedies for dismissal for union activity, 26
statistical overview, 21
tension between labor law and immigration law,
    26–27
US, in, 23
Minimum wage
Canada, in, 185
China, in, 484
EU, and free movement of workers in, 296–297
France, in, 453
Germany, in, 403
UK, in, 367
Mixed motive cases in antidiscrimination law
US, in, 143
Monitoring of employees. See Electronic monitoring of
    employees
Moral harassment
France, in, 457
Morality and labor and employment law, 11
Mulroney, Brian, 249
Mutual trust and confidence, duty of. See United
    Kingdom
Myanmar
Article 26 complaints against, 75–82
ATCA claims against, 82–83

NAALC. See North American Agreement on Labor
    Cooperation
NAFTA. See North American Free Trade Agreement
Nehru, Jawaharlal, 569
Neoliberalism and globalization, 5
Netherlands
EU Constitution, rejection of, 276–277
Nice Treaty
European Social Model and, 286
Nike, Inc.
codes of conduct, 606
Noncompetition agreements. See Covenants not to
    compete

Nongovernmental organizations (NGO)
codes of conduct, external/NGO codes, 604
criticisms of, 20
Nonstandard work
globalization, effect of, 12–13
  labor market segmentation theory and, 12–13
  neoclassical economic theory and, 12
North American Agreement on Labor Cooperation
    (NAALC)
afterthought to NAFTA, as, 249
Bush Administration (GWB), attitude of, 272
CAFTA–DR, labor provisions compared, 274
Canada
  concerns for national sovereignty regarding,
      249–250
  Quebec labor laws, submission regarding, 272
Clinton Administration
  attitude of, 272
  negotiation by, 249
Commission for Labor Cooperation (CLC), 258
  limitations of, 250
  Ministerial Council, 258
  Secretariat, 258
dispute resolution, 259
enforcement provisions
  dispute resolution, 259
  filing of submissions, 258
  investigation of submissions, 258
Evaluation Committees of Experts (ECE),
    258–259
filing of submissions, 258
harmonization of laws not envisioned by, 250
investigation of submissions, 258
Jordan–US Free Trade Agreement, effect on, 273
labor principles, 256–257
  annex format, 256
  ILO Conventions, lack of reference to, 256
  levels of review, 257
  selected excerpts, 256–257
Mexico
  concerns for national sovereignty regarding,
      249–250
  submissions against, 271
multinational monitoring of workplace laws,
    importance to, 249
National Administrative Offices (NAO), 258
  investigation of submissions, 258
national sovereignty, concerns for, 249–250, 253
New York State labor laws, submission regarding,
    271–272
political context, seen in, 272
public employment law and, 44
Quebec labor laws, submission regarding, 272
recommendations for improving, 272–273
selected excerpts, 250–253
statistics, 259
subsequent free trade agreements, effect on, 273
United States, submission regarding New York State
    labor laws, 271–272
universal standards, lack of, 250
weaknesses of, 272

North American Free Trade Agreement (NAFTA)
  Canada
    collective bargaining in, effect on, 175
    complaints under, 172
    economic impact on, 254
    hollowing out, concerns regarding, 255
    national sovereignty, concerns regarding, 255
  economic impact of, 253–255
  environmental issues, side agreement on, 249
  free movement of workers, EU compared, 294
  labor side agreement (*See* North American
      Agreement on Labor Cooperation)
  linkage of trade and labor rights in, 249
  Mexico, economic impact on, 253–254
  NAALC (*See* North American Agreement on Labor
      Cooperation)
  obligations of signatories, 253
  overview, 249
  US
    economic impact on, 254
    Transitional Adjustment Assistance Program,
        255–256

Occupational safety and health
  Canada, in, 185
Occupational tracking
  Japan, in, 527–529
    overview, 527–528
    social attitudes, effect of, 528–529
Offensive lockouts
  Germany, prohibition against, 413–414
Organization for Economic Cooperation and
      Development (OECD)
  codes of conduct, OECD Guidelines on
      Multinational Corporations, 604
  globalization, study on, 9–10
  Guidelines on Multinational Corporations, 604
  Mexico, membership, 209
Outsourcing
  brain circulation in China and, 522–523
  EU, transfer of enterprises in, 314
  India and, 575
Overtime
  Canada, in, 185
  China, in
    Labor Law, under, 484
    Special Economic Zones, in, 520
  France, in, 453–454
  Japan, in, 533
Overview, 1–3

Parental leave
  Canada, in, 185
  EU, in, 300
  France, in
    overview, 454
    US compared, 455
  UK, in, 370
Part-time employees
  Canada, in, 185
  EU, in, 300–301

Paternity leave
  France, in, 454
  UK, in, 369
Pattern bargaining
  Germany, in, 406–407
Pension plans
  Canada, in, 185
  Germany, in, 404
Per capita income data, 40
Personal data protection
  EU, in, 325–326 (*See also* European Union)
  France, in, 325
  Germany, in, 325, 430–431
  human rights law and, 331
  UK, in, 325
Personnel dossiers in China. *See* China
Picketing
  Canada, in
    freedom of association and, 184
    primary picketing, 184
    secondary picketing, 184
  Germany, in, 413
Piercing corporate veil of defendants
  common law actions in US courts, in, 599
Planned economy in China, 472–477
  See also China
Plant closings
  US, in, 105–110 (*See also* United States)
Poland
  Solidarnosc, ILO position on, 57
Polygraphs
  US, in, 155
Pregnancy discrimination
  Canada, in, 186
  EU, exception to gender discrimination in,
      317–318
  Germany, in, 428
  Mexico, in, 247
Pregnancy leave
  Canada, in, 185
Primary picketing
  Canada, in, 184
Privacy law
  Canada, in, 198 (*See also* Canada)
  EU, in, 325–331 (*See also* European Union)
  France, in, 458–461 (*See also* France)
  Germany, in, 430–431 (*See also* Germany)
  Japan, sexual harassment and, 541–542
  Mexico, in, 248
  UK, in, 392–393 (*See also* United Kingdom)
  US, in, 149–156 (*See also* United States)
Private employment law, 49–51. *See also* International
      law
Protective laws, effect of globalization, 8
Public employment law, 41–49. *See also* International
      law
Public interest litigation
  India, in, 580–589 (*See also* India)
Public policy
  employment at will doctrine in US, exceptions to, 103
  globalization and, 5

Punitive damages
  Canada, wrongful discharge claims, 170–171
Pursuing international labor standards in US courts
  codes of conduct, (*See also* Codes of conduct)
  common law actions, 591–601 (*See also* Common law
    actions in US courts)
  overview, 590–591
  statutory actions, 607–618 (*See also* Statutory actions
    in US courts)

Quid pro quo sexual harassment
  US, in, 147
Quotas
  India, in, 579–580

Racial discrimination
  EU, in, 321
  UK, in, 370
Reasonable accommodation in antidiscrimination
    law
  Canada, in, 196, 197
  US, in, 144
Reasons for regulating labor and employment
  Anglo-Saxon legal tradition, in, 10
  Europe, in, 10
  inequality and, 10
  market failure and, 10
  morality and, 11
  US, in, 10
Recognition of labor and trade unions
  Canada, in, 173–174
  UK, in (*See* United Kingdom)
  US, in
    recognition upon showing of majority support,
      proposals to change law to require, 117
    strikes to force, 116–117
    UK, voluntary recognition in compared, 363–364
    voluntary recognition, 116–117
    voluntary recognition (*See* Voluntary recognition of
      labor and trade unions)
Reemployment assistance
  France, in, 443
Regulatory competition as result of globalization, 8, 9
Reinstatement
  Germany, following termination in, 403
  Mexico, as remedy under antidiscrimination law in,
    247
Religious discrimination
  France, in, 457
Replacement workers
  Canada, prohibition against, 184
  France, prohibition against, 452
  Germany, prohibition against, 415
  Mexico, prohibition against, 232
  US, hiring of, 121
Representations under Article 24, 70–74
Retirement plans
  Canada, in, 185
  US, relationship to labor law, 93
Reverse discrimination
  US, in, 127

Right of opposition
  France, in, 449–450
Right to counsel
  China, in, 487

Salinas de Gortari, Carlos, 249
Same-sex sexual harassment
  US, in, 147
Schröder, Gerhard, 394
Secondary picketing
  Canada, in, 184
Sectoral bargaining
  Germany, in, 407, 408
    US compared, 408
Senegal
  Article 24 representations against, 70–74
Service sector, free movement of EU workers in,
    294–297
Settlements
  ATCA actions, 617
  Japan, wrongful termination cases in, 536–537
Severance pay
  Canada, in, 186
  Mexico, in, 247
Sex discrimination. *See* Gender discrimination
Sexual harassment
  China, in, 471
  EU, in, 321
  France, in, 39, 439, 441, 456–457
  Germany, in, 423–424
  Japan, in, 541–542 (*See also* Japan)
  UK, in, 371
  US, in (*See* United States)
Sexual orientation discrimination
  Canada, in, 186
  EU, in, 324
  UK, in, 371–372
Sick leave
  UK, in, 369
Singapore Ministerial Declaration, 47–48, 49
  Declaration on Fundamental Principles and Rights
    at Work and, 90
Social Accountability International (SAI), 604
Social security
  Germany, in, 403
  Mexico, in, 224
Socialist market economy in China. *See also* China
Soviet Union
  China, influence of Soviet law on, 464, 518
Special Economic Zones in China, 518–520. *See also*
  China
Stare decisis
  Mexico, *amparo* suits in, 246
Statistical evidence
  Canada, use in antidiscrimination law, 196
Statutory actions in US courts, 607–618
  Age Discrimination in Employment Act, 607
  Alien Tort Claims Act (*See* Alien Tort Claims
    Act)
  Americans with Disabilities Act, 607
  Title VII, 607

Strikes
  Canada, in, 183–184 (*See also* Canada)
  China, restrictions in, 516, 520
  European Works Councils, authority to call, 302–303
  France, in (*See* France)
  freedom of association and, 122
  Germany, in, 408–415 (*See also* Germany)
  India, in, 576
  Mexico, in (*See* Mexico)
  replacement workers (*See* Replacement workers)
  US, in (*See* United States)
Successor liability
  China, in, 506
Sympathy strikes
  Germany, in, 413

Taiwan
  brain circulation in China and, 521–522
Thatcher, Margaret, 333, 360, 362
Torts
  Canada, tort claims included with collective
    bargaining matters in dispute resolution systems,
    206
  Japan, sexual harassment as, 541
Trade sanctions, enforcing labor standards through,
    48
Trade secrets
  China, theft of in, 479
Trade unions. *See* Labor and trade unions
Trademarks
  France, privacy law and trademark violation in, 461
Transfers of undertakings
  China, in, 506
  EU, in, 307–315 (*See also* European Union)
  France, in, 444
  UK, in
    consultation regarding, 366
    Information and Consultation of Employees
      Regulations (ICE), 366–367
    statutory requirements, 359
Transnational corporations (TNC)
  ATCA, toward, 617
  Belgian IT industry, penetration into, 4
  codes of conduct (*See* Codes of conduct)
  comparative law study, benefits to legal advisors,
    39–40
  defined, 4
  European Works Councils and, 303
  factors influencing location decisions, 10
  improvement of labor standards in foreign countries,
    603
  labor and employment law, effect on location
    decisions, 10
  statistical overview, 4
Transsexual discrimination
  EU, in, 324

UN Global Compact, 604
UN Subcommission on the Promotion and Protection
  of Human Rights, Norms on the

Responsibilities of Transnational Corporations
  and Other Business Enterprises with Regard to
  Human Rights, 604–605
Unemployment
  China, in, 478–479
  data regarding, 41
  Japan, effect of long-term employment system in,
    527, 540
Unemployment insurance
  Canada, in, 185
  Germany, in, 404
Unfair dismissal
  UK, in, 356–358 (*See also* United Kingdom)
Unfair labor practice strikes
  US, in, 121
Unfair labor practices
  UK, in, 362
  US, in, 114
Unified placement system of job allocation in China.
  See China
Unions. *See* Labor and trade unions
United Kingdom
  adoption leave, 370
  antidiscrimination law, 370, 391
    Burden of Proof Directive and, 372–373
    Canada compared, 370
    causal relationship between discrimination and
      treatment, 391
    complexity of, 372
    direct discrimination, 372
    disparate treatment discrimination in US
      compared, 372
    EU compared, 370
    gender discrimination, 370
    historical overview, 370
    hypothetical comparators, 373–374, 391
    indirect discrimination, 373–374
    proof structure, US compared, 391
    provision, criterion or practice (PCP), 373–374
    racial discrimination, 370
    recent development, 370
    sexual harassment, 371
    sexual orientation discrimination, 371–372
    statutory authority, 371
    unfair dismissal and, 372
    US compared, 370, 371
  bullying in workplace, 351–352
  Central Arbitration Committee (CAC), 361, 367
  collective employee rights, 359–367
    bargaining units, 362
    collective redundancies, consultation regarding,
      364–366
    consultation, 364
    EU law, in context of, 361
    historical background, 359–360
    indirect government support of, 360
    Information and Consultation of Employees
      Regulations (ICE), 366–367
    mandatory bargaining subjects, 361
    nonbinding nature of agreements, 362

United Kingdom *(cont.)*
    transfers of undertakings, consultation regarding, 366
    unfair practices, 362
    voluntary bargaining, 359–360
    Works Council Directive and, 361
  collective redundancies
    consultation regarding, 364–366
    Information and Consultation of Employees Regulations (ICE), 366–367
    notice requirement, 364
  complexity of labor law, 333
  consultation
    Central Arbitration Committee (CAC), 367
    collective employee rights, as, 364
    collective redundancies, regarding, 364–366
    Information and Consultation of Employees Regulations (ICE), 366–367
    transfers of undertakings, regarding, 366
  dependent leave, 370
  direct discrimination, 372
  electronic monitoring of employees, 393
  employment contracts, 335–355
    constructive discharge, 350–351
    continuous employment defined, 336
    disciplinary procedures, 337, 338
    dismissal procedures, 338
    duration of, 337
    employment tribunal, 334–335
    grievance procedures, 337, 338
    implied terms, 335
    mutual trust and confidence, duty of (*See* mutual trust and confidence, duty of, below)
    noncompliance with dismissal or disciplinary procedures, 338–339
    notice of dismissal, 337
    overview, 335
    payment in lieu of notice (PILON), 338
    Polkey doctrine, 339
    reasons for dismissal, statement of, 337–338
    repudiation of contract, 338, 350–351
    statutory employment law compared, 334, 356
    unfair dismissal (*See* unfair dismissal, below)
    written statement required, 335–336
    wrongful dismissal, 339–340
  Employment Equality (Sex Discrimination) Regulations 2005, 371
  Employment Relations Act 1999, 332
  Employment Relations Act 2004, 361–362
  Employment Rights Act 1996
    redundancy defined, 359
    unfair dismissal under, 356–357
    written statement regarding employment contract under, 335–336
  employment tribunal, 334–335
  EU law, labor law in context of, 332
  flexible working time, 370
  France, labor law compared, 333
  gender discrimination, 370
  Germany, labor law compared, 333
  harassment in workplace, 351–352
  holidays, 369
  hours of work, 367–368
  indirect discrimination, 373–374
  individual employment law, 334–359
    employment contracts (*See* employment contracts, above)
    employment tribunal, 334–335
    statutory employment law (*See* statutory employment law, below)
  individual redundancies, dismissal of employees for, 358–359
  Information and Consultation of Employees Regulations (ICE), 366–367
  labor and trade unions, 359–367
    bargaining units, 362
    Central Arbitration Committee (CAC), 361
    current state of, 361
    decline of, 360
    secret elections, 361–362
    statutory recognition, 361
    unfair practices, 362
    US, secret election system in compared, 363–364
    voluntary recognition, 361
      US compared, 363–364
  layoffs
    consultation regarding, 364–366
    Information and Consultation of Employees Regulations (ICE), 366–367
    notice requirement, 364
  maternity leave, 369
  minimum wage, 367
  mutual trust and confidence, duty of
    bullying in workplace and, 351–352
    constructive discharge, 350–351
    harassment and, 351–352
    intentional infliction of emotional distress in US compared, 352
    repudiation of contract, 350–351
    standard for determining breach, 355
    unfair dismissal distinguished, 340, 352–354
  mutual trust and confidence, implied term of, 340–355
  parental leave, 370
  paternity leave, 369
  personal data protection, 325
  political overview, 333
  privacy law, 392–393
    electronic monitoring of employees, 393
    EU law, in context of, 392
    personal data protection, 325
    piecemeal nature of, 392
    statutory authority, 392–393
    wearable computer technology, 393
  racial discrimination, 370
  sexual harassment, 371
  sexual orientation discrimination, 371–372
  sick leave, 369
  statutory employment law, 356–359
    authority, 356

United Kingdom *(cont.)*

    employment contracts compared, 334, 356

    employment tribunal, 334–335

    notice of dismissal, 359

    payment in lieu of notice (PILON), 359

    Polkey doctrine, 339

    redundancy as reason for dismissal, 358–359

    transfers of undertakings, 359

    unfair dismissal (*See* unfair dismissal, below)

    strikes

        decline in, 363

        historical development of right to strike, 362–363

        protection against dismissal during, 362

        restrictions on right to strike, 362

        unfair dismissal for participating in, 363

    Third Way, 333

    Trade Union and Labour Relations (Consolidation) Act 1992, 364–366

    transfers of undertakings

        consultation regarding, 366

        Information and Consultation of Employees Regulations (ICE), 366–367

        statutory requirements, 359

    unfair dismissal, 356–358

        antidiscrimination law and, 372

        breach of duty of mutual trust and confidence distinguished, 340, 352–354

        determination of unfairness, 356–357

        factually wrong valid reasons, assertion of, 358

        journalists, 358

        limitations period, 356

        noncompliance with dismissal or disciplinary procedures, 338–339

        noneconomic damages, 355

        reasonableness test, 357

        strikes, dismissal for participating in, 363

        teachers, 357

        wrongful dismissal distinguished, 339–340

    US, labor law compared, 332–333

    vacations, 369

    wages, hours and benefits, 367–370

        adoption leave, 370

        dependents, time off for, 370

        flexible working time, 370

        holidays, 369

        hours of work, 367–368

        maternity leave, 369

        minimum wage, 367

        parental leave, 370

        paternity leave, 369

        sick leave, 369

        vacations, 369

        Working Time Directive, opt-out provisions, 368–369

    wearable computer technology, 393

    Working Time Directive, opt-out provisions, 368–369

    Working Time Regulations 1998, 368–369

    wrongful dismissal, 339–340

United States

    action committees, 115–116

        Germany compared, 421–422

adversarial model of labor relations, 114

adverse action for union activity, 115

affirmative action

    beneficiaries, effects on, 128

    governmental employers, 127–128

    outcome versus neutrality, 128

    private employers, 128

    resentment toward, 128

Age Discrimination in Employment Act of 1967 (ADEA), 126, 607

Alien Tort Claims Act (*See* Alien Tort Claims Act)

Americans with Disabilities Act of 1990 (ADA), 92, 126, 134, 607

antidiscrimination law, 124–148

    ADA actions, 92, 126, 134, 607

    ADEA actions, 126, 607

    adverse effect discrimination in Canada compared, 196

    affirmative action (*See* affirmative action, above)

    bona fide occupational qualification defense, indispensable requirement defense in Germany compared, 423

    comparable worth, 316

    complex and subtle forms of discrimination, 135

    direct discrimination compared

        Canada, in, 196

        EU, in, 320–321

        UK, in, 372

    disparate impact discrimination, 129, 134

    disparate treatment discrimination, 129, 134

    federal law, 126–127

    France compared, 435, 455, 456–457, 458

    harassment, 144

    indirect discrimination in EU compared, 321

    innovator of law, US as, 127

    low level of ILO Convention ratification and, 127

    mixed motive cases, 143

    motivation, proving, 134, 143

    pretext, 143–144

    proof structure, UK compared, 391

    reasonable accommodations, 144

    reverse discrimination, 127

    sexual harassment (*See* sexual harassment, below)

    state law, 127

    UK compared, 370, 371

    uniform set of principles, problems with, 127

Bipartisan Trade Promotion Authority Act of 2002 (BTPAA), 275

Bureau of International Labor Affairs (ILAB), 69–70

CCAS tripartite consultation requirement and, 65–67

child labor in agricultural sector, 31–32

Civil Rights Act of 1964, 92, 126

Civil Rights Act of 1991, 92

codes of conduct, attempts to require, 605

collective employee rights, 110–122

    adverse action for union activity, 115

    concerted activity, protection of, 118

    EU compared, 301

    individual rights/discrimination paradigm and, 118

United States *(cont.)*
    low level of ILO Convention ratification, effect of,
        117
    plant closings and mass layoffs, requirements, 110
    protection of right of, 114
    sectoral bargaining, Germany compared, 408
    strikes (*See* strikes, below)
    unfair labor practice cases, 114
    worker representation in corporate governance in
        Germany compared, 421–422
    works councils in Germany compared, 419–420
  collective redundancies (*See* plant closings and mass
    layoffs, below)
  Commerce Department, safe harbor agreements and
    transfer of personal data from EU, 331
  common law actions in US courts, pursuing
    international labor standards through, 591–601
    (*See also* Common law actions in US courts)
  company unions, 115–116
  comparable worth, 316
  concerted activity, protection of, 118
  Consolidated Omnibus Budget Reconciliation Act,
    123, 124
  Constitution
    China compared, 468–469
    Japan compared, 525
    Mexican Constitution, as model for, 221
  Declaration on Fundamental Principles and Rights
    at Work, adoption of, 117, 122
  disability discrimination, 92, 126, 134, 607
  dismissal of employees, France compared, 439,
    444
  disparate impact discrimination, 129, 134
  disparate treatment discrimination, 129, 134
  dispute resolution systems
    Canada compared, 198–199
    Mexico compared, 235, 246
  domestic workers in, 16–17
  economic strikes, 121
  electronic monitoring of employees, 155–156
  Employee Retirement Income Security Act, 123, 124
  employee stock ownership plans, Germany
    compared, 421–422
  employer-dominated unions, 115–116
  employment at will doctrine, 93–105
    bad reasons for termination, exceptions carved out
      for, 102
    benefits of, 105
    bullying in workplace and, 105
    contract erosion of, 102–103
    Contrat Premiere Embauche (CPE) in France
      compared, 445
    defenses of, 101–102
    deference to, 100
    finality of termination decisions, importance of,
      101
    France compared, 433
    free market economy, importance to, 100–101
    historical trends in, 100
    intentional infliction of emotional distress and,
      103–104

    lack of understanding by employees, 102
    long-term employment system in Japan compared,
      527
    negotiation of employment contracts as alternative
      to, 101
    presumption of, 99–100
    public policy exceptions, 103
    sexual harassment and, 104–105
    state law, matter of, 100
    tort erosion of, 103
    uniqueness to US, 39
    wrongful discharge claims, 103
    wrongful termination in Japan compared, 533
  Equal Pay Act of 1963, 316
  extraterritorial application of statutes
    Age Discrimination in Employment Act of 1967,
      607
    Americans with Disabilities Act of 1990, 607
    Civil Rights Act of 1964, 607
    Congressional intent requirement, 607
  Fair Labor Standards Act, 92, 123
  Family Medical Leave Act, 92, 123
  fast track authority for negotiating free trade
    agreements
    BTPAA and, 275
    Free Trade Area of the Americas (FTAA), proposal
      for, 275
    OCRA and, 275
  Federal Trade Commission, safe harbor agreements
    and transfer of personal data from EU, 330
  foreign law, debate over use of, 32–37
    criticisms of, 37
    historical background, 32–33
    isolationist tendency of jurisprudence, 33
    recent trends, 33
  France, labor law compared, 435
  free trade agreements
    CAFTA–DR (*See* Central America–Dominican
      Republic Free Trade Agreement)
    fast track authority for negotiating
      BTPAA and, 275
      Free Trade Area of the Americas (FTAA),
        proposal for, 275
      OCRA and, 275
    Free Trade Area of the Americas (FTAA), proposal
      for, 275
    Jordan–US Free Trade Agreement (*See*
      Jordan–US Free Trade Agreement)
    NAALC, effect of, 273
    NAFTA (*See* North American Free Trade
      Agreement)
  freedom of association
    low level of ILO Convention ratification, effect of,
      117
    recognition of shortcomings, 117–118
  grievance procedures for sexual harassment, 148
  harassment, 144
  health insurance, relationship to labor law, 93
  historical background, 92–93
  hostile environment sexual harassment,
    147–148

United States (cont.)
  immigrant rights movement in, rise of, 28
  indemnities, payment for plant closings and mass
      layoffs, 110
  individual employment law, 93–110
    employment at will doctrine (See employment at
        will doctrine, above)
    plant closings and mass layoffs (See plant closings
        and mass layoffs, below)
  individual rights/discrimination paradigm, 92
    collective bargaining and, 118
    labor and trade unions and, 118
  intentional infliction of emotional distress
    breach of duty of mutual trust and confidence in
        UK compared, 352
    overview, 103–104
  isolationist tendency of jurisprudence, 33
  labor and trade unions, 110–122
    action committees, 115–116
    adverse action for union activity, 115
    company unions, 115–116
    decline of, 14, 118, 509
    employer-dominated unions, 115–116
    individual rights/discrimination paradigm and, 118
    majority support requirement, 115
    Mexico compared, 228
    minority representation, 115
    multi-location bargaining units, 115
    recognition upon showing of majority support,
        proposals to change law to require, 117
    representation cases, 114
    secret ballot elections, 116
    single-site bargaining units, 115
    strikes (See strikes, below)
    UK, voluntary recognition in compared, 363–364
    unfair labor practice cases, 114
    voluntary recognition, 116–117
    worker representation in corporate governance in
        Germany compared, 421–422
    works councils in Germany compared, 419–420
  layoffs (See plant closings and mass layoffs, below)
  Mexico, economic differences with, 209
  migrant workers in, 23
    Contrat Premiere Embauche (CPE) in France
        compared, 445–446
  multi-location bargaining units, 115
  NAALC
    New York State labor laws, submission regarding,
        271–272
  NAFTA
    economic impact of, 254
    Transitional Adjustment Assistance Program,
        255–256
  National Labor Relations Act, 27–28, 92, 110, 114
  National Labor Relations Board, 114–115
  New York State labor laws, NAALC submission
      regarding, 271–272
  Occupational Safety and Health Act, 123, 124
  Occupational Safety and Health Administration, 123
  Omnibus Trade and Competitiveness Act (OCRA),
      275

  organized labor/collective bargaining paradigm, 92
  parental leave, France compared, 455
  plant closings and mass layoffs, 105–110
    collective bargaining requirements, 110
    EU compared, 307
    federal and state law, interaction of, 110
    ILO Convention 158 and, 110
    indemnities, 110
    tax incentives, ability of governmental bodies to
        recover, 110
    WARN Act, notice requirements, 110
  polygraphs, 155
  privacy law, 149–156
    common law tort claims, 155
    electronic monitoring, 155–156
    federal Constitutional claims, 155
    federal statutory law, 155
    France compared, 458, 461
    interests protected, 155
    polygraphs, 155
    safe harbor agreements and transfer of personal
        data from EU, 330–331
    state action requirement, 155
    state Constitutional claims, 155
    state statutory law, 155
    wiretapping, 155
  Privileges and Immunities Clause to Constitution,
      free movement of workers in EU compared, 297
  quid pro quo sexual harassment, 147
  retirement plans. relationship to labor law, 93
  reverse discrimination, 127
  secret ballot elections for labor and trade unions, 116
  sexual harassment
    affirmative defenses, 148
    effect of law on workplace, 148
    employee training, 148
    employment at will doctrine and, 104–105
    grievance procedures, 148
    hostile environment, 147–148
    Japan compared, 541
    overview, 39, 144
    quid pro quo harassment, 147
    same-sex harassment, 147
  single-site bargaining units, 115
  statutory actions in US courts, pursuing international
      labor standards through, 607–618 (See also
      Statutory actions in US courts)
  strikes
    decline of, 121
    economic strikes, 121
    freedom of association and, 122
    recognition of unions, to force, 116–117
    replacement workers, hiring of, 121
    right to, protection of, 121
    unfair labor practice strikes, 121
  terminology, dichotomy of, 92–93
  transfer of enterprises, EU compared, 313–314
  Transportation Department, safe harbor agreements
      and transfer of personal data from EU, 330
  UK, labor law compared, 332–333
  unfair labor practice cases, 114

unfair labor practice strikes, 121
voluntary recognition of labor and trade unions,
    116–117
  UK compared, 363–364
Wage and Hour Division, 123
wages, hours and benefits, 122–124
  administration, 123
  enforcement, 123
  federal law, regulation by, 122, 123
  state law, regulation by, 122, 123
WARN Act, 110
wiretapping of employees, 155
wrongful discharge claims, 103
Unjust discharge
  Mexico, in, 247
US Council for International Business (USCIB)
  ILO delegation representative from, 59

Vacations
  Canada, in, 185
  France, in, 454
  Germany, in, 404
  Mexico, in, 224
Vietnam
  codes of conduct in, 603
Villa, Pancho, 211
Villepin, Dominique de, 434, 444
Voluntary recognition of labor and trade unions
  UK, in, 361
    US compared, 363–364
  US, in, 116–117
    UK compared, 363–364
Volunteer teachers, Article 24 representations
    regarding, 70–74

Wages, hours and benefits
  Canada, in, 186 (*See also* Canada)
  China, in, 470
  France, in, 455 (*See also* France)
  Germany, in, 403–404 (*See also* Germany)
  Mexico (*See* Mexico)
  UK, in, 367–370 (*See also* United Kingdom)
  US, in, 122–124 (*See also* United States)
Wal-Mart
  China, unionization in, 517
  codes of conduct, 601–602
    child labor, 602
    compensation, 601
    compliance with applicable laws and practice,
      601
    discrimination/human rights, 602
    employment conditions, 601–602
    factory inspections, 602
    forced/prison labor, 602

  freedom of association/collective bargaining, 602
  hours of labor, 601
  workplace environment, 602
  common law actions in US courts, vulnerability to,
      599–600
  domestic labor practices, 603
  economic might of, 600
  health care expenses of employees, 600
  impact on retail sector employment, 600–601
  low price/high volume business model, 600
  supply chain efficiencies, pursuit of, 600
  undercutting of worker compensation by, 600
Wiretapping of employees
  US, in, 155
Worker Rights Consortium (WRC), 604
Workers' compensation
  Canada, in, 185
  Japan, cases for stress and fatigue, 533
  Mexico, in, 224–225
Working Time Directive
  opt-out provisions, 368–369
Works agreements
  Germany, relationship with collective agreements in,
      418, 419, 420
Works Council Directive
  France, conformity with, 453
  UK, collective employee rights and, 361
Works councils
  EU, in (*See* European Union)
  France, in, 452–453
  Germany, in, 416–420 (*See also* Germany)
World Trade Organization (WTO)
  China, effect of WTO membership, 510–514
  Doha Ministerial Conference, 49
  greater involvement in enforcement of labor law,
      arguments for, 517
  ILO role in enforcing labor standards compared, 49
  Mexico, membership, 209
  public employment law and, 47–49
  Singapore Ministerial Declaration, 47–48, 49
WRAP Initiative, 603
Wrongful death
  ATCA, actions under, 614
  Japan, wrongful death from overwork, 529
Wrongful discharge
  Canada, in (*See* Canada)
  US, in, 103
Wrongful dismissal
  UK, in, 339–340
Wrongful termination
  Germany, in, 399–400
  Japan, in, 533–541 (*See also* Japan)

Zapata, Emiliano, 211